**Recommended by the Chartered Institute of Marketing**



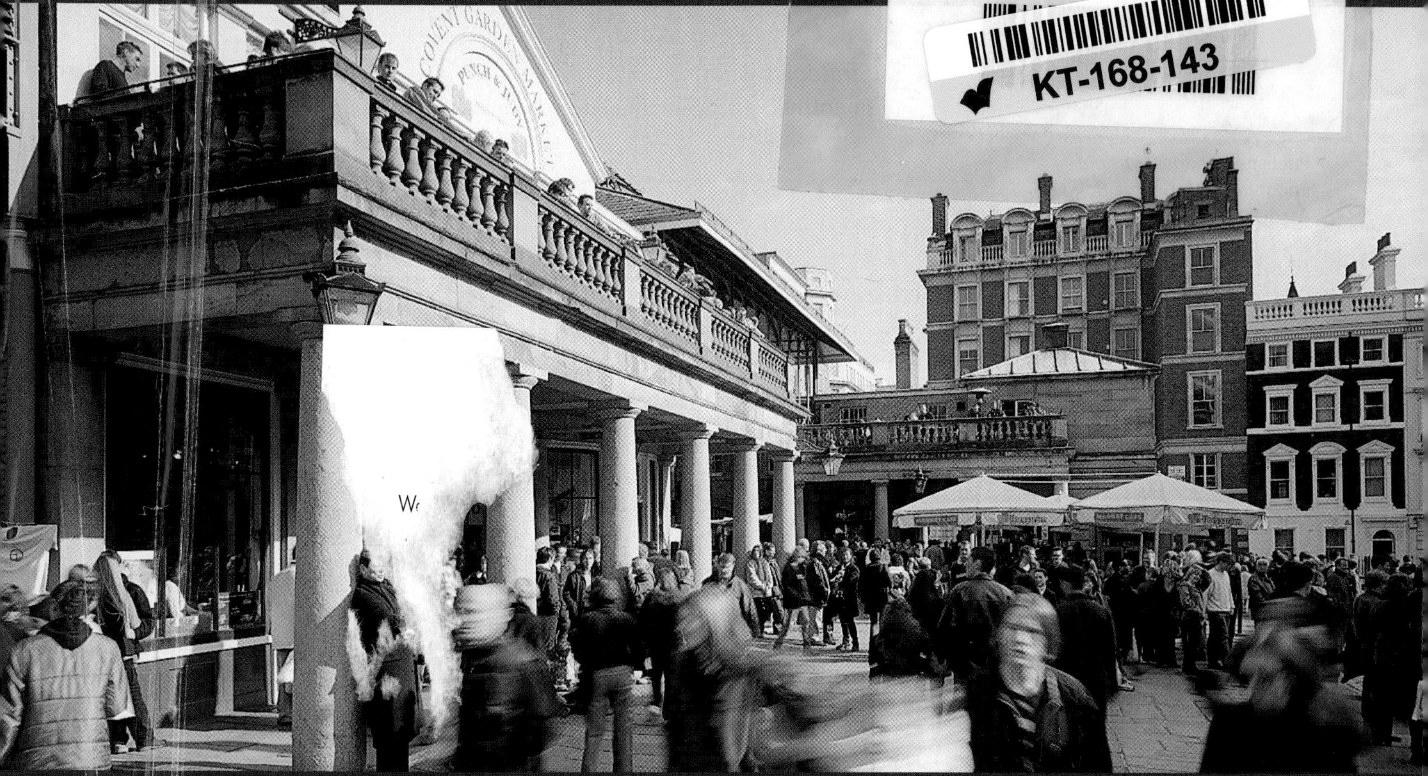


# Marketing

## Concepts and Strategies

**Fifth European Edition**

Sally Dibb University of Warwick

Lyndon Simkin University of Warwick

William M. Pride Texas A&M University

O.C. Ferrell Colorado State University

HOUGHTON MIFFLIN BOSTON NEW YORK ABINGDON

This edition of *Marketing: Concepts and Strategies* is for
Bex, James, Abby, Mae and 'Mamphy' (Samantha) – the 'Simkin clan'

Publisher: *Charles Hartford*
Editor-in-Chief: *George Hoffman*
Associate Sponsoring Editor: *Susan M. Kahn*
Project Editor: *Shelley Dickerson*
Manufacturing Manager: *Karen Banks*
Director of Sales and Marketing, International: *Andrew Neilson*
Marketing Manager, International: *Martin Crouch*

Cover design: *Andrew Oliver*
Cover image credits: *Left to right: Art Explosion, Nova Development; Art Explosion, Nova Development; david martyn hughes/Alamy; Comstock Images/Alamy*





Printed in the U.S.A.

ISBN: 0-618-53203-x

3456789-RRD-10 09 08 07

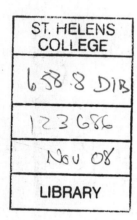

# Brief Contents


PART I
**Marketing Defined and Marketing in Context** 1

1 An Overview of the Marketing Concept 4
2 Marketing Strategy 35
3 The Marketing Environment 66
4 The Internet, Technology in Marketing and CRM 100
5 Marketing in International Markets 124

PART II
**Understanding and Targeting Customers** 158

6 Consumer Buying Behaviour 160
7 Business Markets and Business Buying Behaviour 189
8 Segmenting Markets, Targeting and Positioning 220
9 Marketing Research and Marketing Information Systems 257

PART III
**Product, Branding, Packaging and Service Decisions** 293

10 Product Decisions 295
11 Branding and Packaging 314
12 Developing Products and Managing Product Portfolios 344
13 The Marketing of Services 375

PART IV
**Place (Distribution and Marketing Channel) Decisions** 406

14 Marketing Channels 408
15 Wholesalers, Distributors and Physical Distribution 436
16 Retailing 471

PART V
**Promotion (Marketing Communications) Decisions** 507

17 An Overview of Marketing Communications 509
18 Advertising, Public Relations and Sponsorship 536
19 Sales Management, Sales Promotion, Direct Mail, the Internet and Direct Marketing 577

PART VI
**Pricing Decisions** 621

20 Pricing Concepts 623
21 Setting Prices 646

PART VII
**Manipulating the Marketing Mix** 677

22 Modifying the Marketing Mix for Business Markets, Services and in International Marketing 679

PART VIII
**Marketing Management** 713

23 Marketing Planning and Forecasting Sales Potential 715
24 Implementing Strategies, Internal Marketing Relationships and Measuring Performance 745
25 Social Responsibility and Marketing Ethics 785

PART IX
**Studying and Working in Marketing** 813

26 Case Study Analysis, Exam Revision Tips and Careers in Marketing 814

# Contents

Note: Each chapter contains a Summary, Key Links, a list of Important Terms, Discussion and Review Questions, Recommended Readings, an Internet Exercise and an Applied Mini-Case.

**PART I** Marketing Defined and Marketing in Context 1

1 **An Overview of the Marketing Concept** **4**
Marketing Explained and Defined 6
Marketing Orientation 6
Marketing Defined 7
The Definition Explored 9
Marketing Consists of Activities 9
Marketing is Performed by Individuals and Organisations 10
Marketing Facilitates Satisfying Exchange Relationships 11
Marketing Occurs in a Dynamic Environment 11
Marketing Involves Products, Distribution, Promotion, Pricing and People 12
Marketing Focuses on Goods, Services and Ideas 12
The Marketing Process 12
The Importance of Marketing 14
Marketing Activities are Used in Many Organisations 14
**Topical Insight Ireland: Marketing a Country** **15**
Marketing Activities are Important to Businesses and the Economy 15
Marketing Knowledge Enhances Consumer Awareness 16
Marketing Costs Consume a Sizeable Proportion of Buyers' Incomes 16
Business Performance 16
The Marketing Concept and its Evolution 16
The Evolution of the Marketing Concept 17
Implementing the Marketing Concept 18
The Essentials of Marketing 19
Marketing Analyses 19
Marketing Strategy 20
Marketing Opportunity Analysis 21
Internal Organisational Factors 21
Marketing Environment Forces 23
**Topical Insight The Marketing Environment Offers Threats and Opportunities: Miller Lite Versus Slimfast** **24**
Target Market Selection 25
Marketing Programmes 25
Marketing Mix Development 25
Marketing Management 28
The Organisation of This Book 29
What Does Each Part of This Book Cover? 29
Further Reading 30
*Case Study Sweden's IKEA Marches On* *33*

2 **Marketing Strategy** **35**
Marketing Strategy Defined 37
Organisational Mission, Goals and Corporate Strategy 41
Organisational Opportunities and Resources 43
Marketing Opportunities 43
Environmental Scanning 44
Capabilities and Assets 44
**Marketing Tools and Techniques Practitioners' Use of SWOT Analysis** **45**
Strategic Objectives and Strategic Focus 46
Intense Growth 47
Diversified Growth 47
Integrated Growth 48
Target Market Strategy and Brand Positioning 48
Competitive Advantage 49
Competitive Positions and Differential Advantage 50
Competitive Positions 51
**Marketing Tools and Techniques Practitioners' Use of Competitor Intelligence: the Dibb/Simkin Competitive Positions Proforma** **55**
Differential Advantage 56
Marketing Objectives 58
Marketing Mix Decisions 58
Implementation and Performance Monitoring 59
*Case Study St Andrew's Hospital: a Charity's Marketing Strategy* *64*

3 **The Marketing Environment** **66**
Examining and Responding to the Marketing Environment 68
Environmental Scanning and Analysis 69
**Marketing Tools and Techniques Practitioners' Assessment of the Macro Marketing Environment** **69**
Responding to Environmental Forces 71
Political Forces 72
Legal Forces 73
Procompetitive Legislation 73
Consumer Protection Legislation 74
Interpreting Laws 75
Regulatory Forces 75
Government 75
Local Authorities 76
Non-governmental Regulatory Forces 76
Deregulation 76
Societal/Green Forces 77
Living Standards and Quality of Life 77
Consumer Movement Forces 78
Technological Forces 78
**Marketing in Society Kraft and Nestlé Look to Fair Trade** **80**
The Impact of Technology 80
The Adoption and Use of Technology 81
Economic and Competitive Forces 82
General Economic Conditions 82
Consumer Demand and Spending Behaviour 85
Assessment of Competitive Forces 87
The Micro Marketing Environment 89
The Core Aspects of the Micro Marketing Environment 89
The Marketing Environment and Strategic Opportunities 92
Opening Strategic Windows 92
The Importance of Keeping a Lookout for the Strategic Window 93
*Case Study Social Awareness: BMW Recycling the Consumer* *98*

4 **The Internet, Technology in Marketing and CRM** **100**
Marketing on the Internet 102
The Basic Characteristics of Electronic Marketing 103
Addressability 103
Interactivity 104
Memory 105
Control 105
Accessibility 106
Digitalisation 107
E-marketing Strategies 107
Target Markets 107
Product Considerations 107
Distribution Considerations 109
Promotion Considerations 109
Pricing Considerations 110
Managing Customer Relationships 110
Customer Relationship Management (CRM) 111
Technology in Customer Relationship Management 111
**Building Customer Relationships Amazon's Marketers Depend on Technology to Serve their Customers** **112**
Stone's CRM requirements 113
CRM Systems 114
Technology Drives CRM 114
**Innovation and Change Fujitsu: Managing Customers** **115**
Customer Satisfaction is the End Result of CRM 116
Legal and Ethical Issues in E-marketing 117
*Case Study Customer Service Enhanced by E-commerce for Yellow Freight* *122*

5 **Marketing in International Markets** **124**
Involvement in International Marketing 126
Levels of International Involvement 126
Understanding Global Marketing 127
International Marketing Intelligence 129
Environmental Forces in International Markets 130
Cultural Forces 130
**Building Customer Relationships A Cross-cultural Comparison of Colour and International Branding** **132**
Social Forces 134
Economic Forces 135
Political, Regulatory and Legal Forces 135
Technological Forces 137
Regional Trade Alliances and Markets 137
The North American Free Trade Agreement (NAFTA) 137
The European Union (EU) 138
Pacific Rim Nations 139
Central and Eastern Europe (CEE) 140
General Agreement on Tariffs and Trade (GATT) and the World Trade Organization (WTO) 141
Alternative Market Entry Strategies 141
Exporting 141
Licensing 142

Franchising 142
Contract Manufacturing 142
Joint Ventures and Strategic Alliances 142
Trading Companies 143
**Topical Insight Airbus Vies with Boeing for Global Leadership 144**
Foreign Direct Investment 145
Customisation Versus the Globalisation of International Marketing Strategies 145
*Case Study Carrefour's International Strategy 151*
**Strategic Case**
**Avis Global Leadership 154**

**PART II** Understanding and Targeting Customers 158

**6 Consumer Buying Behaviour 160**
Types of Consumer Buying Behaviour 162
Routine Response Behaviour 162
Limited Decision-making 162
Extensive Decision-making 162
**Innovation and Change Impulse Shopping on the Increase 163**
Variations in Decision-making Behaviour 163
The Consumer Buying Decision Process 164
Stage 1: Problem Recognition 165
Stage 2: Information Search 166
Stage 3: Evaluation of Alternatives 167
Stage 4: Purchase 167
Stage 5: Post-purchase Evaluation 167
Personal Factors Influencing the Buying Decision Process 168
Demographic Factors 168
Situational Factors 169
Levels of Involvement 169
Psychological Factors Influencing the Buying Decision Process 171
Perception 171
Motives 173
Learning 174
Attitudes 177
Personality 178
Social Factors Influencing the Buying Decision Process 178
Roles and Family 178
Reference Groups 179
Social Classes 180
Culture and Sub-cultures 181
**Building Customer Relationships Marketing to Ethnic Consumers 182**
Understanding Consumer Behaviour 183
*Case Study IKEA: Stylish Furnishings at Affordable Prices 187*

**7 Business Markets and Business Buying Behaviour 189**
Types of Business Market 191
Producer Markets 191
Reseller Markets 191
Government and Public-sector Markets 193
Institutional Markets 194
Dimensions of Business Buying 194
Characteristics of Business Transactions 194
Attributes of Business Buyers 195
Primary Concerns of Business Buyers 195
Methods of Business Buying 198
Types of Business Purchase 198
Demand for Business Products 199
Business Buying Decisions 200
The Buying Centre 200
**Marketing Tools and Techniques Practitioners' Use of the Buying Behaviour Theory: the Dibb/Simkin Buying Proforma 201**
Relationship Marketing and Managing Exchange Relationships 203
Stages of the Business Buying Decision Process 204
Influences on Business Buying 207
Selection and Analysis of Business Markets 208
Identifying Potential Customers 208
**Topical Insight Unilever Targets Forecourts and Convenience Stores 209**
Marketing's Variations in Business Markets 212
*Case Study Nynas: in the Black and Leading 218*

**8 Segmenting Markets, Targeting and Positioning 220**
What are Markets? 222
Requirements for a Market 222
Types of Market 222
What is Market Segmentation? 222
Defining Market Segmentation 223
Reasons for Using Market Segmentation 224
Segmenting, Targeting and Positioning 225
Segmenting the Market 225
Targeting Strategy 226
Positioning the Product 226
Segmentation Variables 226

Selecting Appropriate Variables 227
Variables for Segmenting Consumer Markets 229
**Topical Insight Profiling and Targeting Customers with ACORN 235**
Variables for Segmenting Business Markets 238
Segmentation Effectiveness 240
Profiling Market Segments 241
Targeting Strategies 242
Undifferentiated Strategy 242
Concentrated Strategy 242
Differentiated Strategy 245
Factors Affecting Choice of Targeting Strategy 245
Positioning 247
Determining a Positioning 247
Steps in Determining a Positioning Plan 249
**Marketing Tools and Techniques Practitioners' Use of Brand Positioning Theory 249**
Evaluating Markets and Forecasting Sales 251
*Case Study Ethnic Marketing's Challenge to Mainstream Marketers 255*

**9 Marketing Research and Marketing Information Systems 257**
The Importance of Marketing Research 259
**Topical Insight The World's Largest Marketing Research Company 261**
The Marketing Research Process 262
Step 1: Locating and Defining Problems or Research Issues 263
Step 2: Designing the Research 264
Developing Research Objectives and Hypotheses 264
Types of Research 264
Research Reliability and Validity 265
Step 3: Collecting Data 265
Types of Data 265
Sources of Secondary Data 266
Primary Data Collection Methods 269
**Marketing Tools and Techniques 'Mystery Shopper' Research Programmes: Pros and Cons 276**
Step 4: Analysing and Interpreting Research Findings 278
Step 5: Reporting Research Findings 279
Using Technology to Improve Marketing Information Gathering and Analysis 279
Marketing Information Systems 279
Databases 280
Marketing Decision Support Systems 281
The Internet and On-line Information Services 281
The Importance of Ethical Marketing Research 281
*Case Study Focus Group Interviewing: In-depth Views from Group Discussions 287*
**Strategic Case**
**Reebok Reebok Races into the Urban Market 290**

**PART III Product, Branding, Packaging and Service Decisions 293**

**10 Product Decisions 295**
What is a Product? 297
Classifying Products 297
Consumer Products 297
Business or Industrial Products 299
The Three Levels of Product 301
Product Line and Product Mix 302
**Innovation and Change A New Generation of Nicotine Replacement Products 303**
Product Life Cycles 304
Introduction 305
Growth 306
Maturity 306
Decline 306
Why Some Products Fail and Others Succeed 307
Degrees of Product Failure 307
The Ingredients for Success 307
Tangible and Intangible Product Characteristics 307
**Topical Insight Old Brands Battle the Effects of Ageing 308**
Physical Characteristics and Product Quality 308
Supportive Product-related Services 309
*Case Study Heineken's Portfolio of Brands 312*

**11 Branding and Packaging 314**
Branding 316
Benefits of Branding 316
Brand Equity 319
Brand Personality, Values and Attributes 320
**Marketing Tools and Techniques Practitioners' Use of the Brand Development Theory: the Brand Personality Grid 320**
Types of Brand 322
Choosing a Brand Name 323
Protecting a Brand 324
**Marketing Tools and Techniques Who Thought of That Name?! 325**
Branding Policies 327

Brand Licensing 329
Managing Brands 330
Corporate Branding 331
Packaging and Labelling 331
Packaging Functions 332
Major Packaging Considerations 332
Packaging Development 334
Packaging and Marketing Strategy 335
Criticisms of Packaging 337
Labelling 337
*Case Study 3D and Environmentally Friendly Packaging Design* 342

**12 Developing Products and Managing Product Portfolios 344**
Organising to Manage Products 346
New Product Development 347
Line Extensions 352
Product Adoption Process 353
Product Life Cycle Management 354
Marketing Strategy in the Growth Stage 354
Marketing Strategy for Mature Products 355
**Innovation and Change E-banking, Telebanking, Text and TV Banking: What Next? 356**
Marketing Strategy for Declining Product 358
Deleting Products 358
Tools for Managing Product Portfolios 360
The Boston Consulting Group (BCG) Product Portfolio Analysis 360
Market Attractiveness–Business Position Model 361
**Marketing Tools and Techniques Practitioners' Use of the Directional Policy Matrix (DPM) 364**
Profit Impact on Marketing Strategy (PIMS) 365
The ABC Sales: Contribution Analysis 367
*Case Study Sellotape or Mustard? Increasing Market Penetration* 373

**13 The Marketing of Services 375**
The Nature and Importance of Services 377
Growth of Services 377
Characteristics of Services 378
**Building Customer Relationships Dutch Bankers Build Relationships – ABN AMRO Leads through Services 381**
Classification of Services 382
Developing Marketing Strategies for Services 384
Strategic Considerations 384
Creating a Differential Advantage in Services 385
The Extended Marketing Mix for Services 386
Service Quality 386
Customer Evaluation of Service Quality 387
Delivering Exceptional Service Quality 387
**Topical Insight Banks Remember Customer Service 388**
Non-profit Marketing 391
Why is Non-profit Marketing Different? 391
Non-profit Marketing Objectives 392
Developing Non-profit Marketing Strategies 393
Controlling Non-profit Marketing Activities 395
*Case Study Increasing Professionalism in Charity Marketing* 400
**Strategic Case**
**Aer Lingus Competing on Nationalistic Fervour: Irishness** 403

**PART IV Place (Distribution and Marketing Channel) Decisions 406**

**14 Marketing Channels 408**
The Nature of Marketing Channels and Supply Chain Management 410
Functions of Marketing Channels 412
Creating Utility 412
Facilitating Exchange Efficiencies 412
Alleviating Discrepancies 413
**Innovation and Change Tesco's Multi-channel Approach to Market Leadership 415**
Standardising Transactions 416
Providing Customer Service 416
Types of Channel 416
Channels for Consumer Products or Services 416
Channels for Industrial, Business-to-Business Products or Services 418
Multiple Marketing Channels 419
Channel Integration 419
Vertical Channel Integration 420
Horizontal Channel Integration 421
Different Levels of Market Coverage 422
Intensive Distribution 422
Selective Distribution 422
Exclusive Distribution 422
Choosing Distribution Channels 423
Organisational Objectives and Resources 423
**Building Customer Relationships Games Workshop: the Best Model Soldiers in the World! 424**
Market Characteristics 425
Buying Behaviour 426

Product Attributes 426
Environmental Forces 426
Behaviour of Channel Members 426
Channel Cooperation and Relationship Building 427
Channel Conflict 427
Channel Leadership 428
Legal Issues in Channel Management 429
Restricted Sales Territories 429
Tying Contract 430
Exclusive Dealing 430
Refusal to Deal 430
*Case Study First Direct's Innovative Banking Channels* 434

**15 Wholesalers, Distributors and Physical Distribution 436**
The Nature and Importance of Wholesaling 438
The Activities of Wholesalers 438
Services for Producers 438
Services for Retailers 440
Classifying Wholesalers 440
Merchant Wholesalers 440
Agents and Brokers 441
Manufacturers' Sales Branches and Offices 446
**Building Customer Relationships Daewoo's Innovative Distribution Appeals to Car Buyers 447**
Facilitating Agencies 448
Public Warehouses 448
Finance Companies 449
Transport Companies 449
Trade Shows and Trade Markets 450
Changing Patterns in Wholesaling 450
Wholesalers Consolidate Power 451
New Types of Wholesaler 451
The Importance of Physical Distribution 451
Physical Distribution Objectives 452
Customer Service 452
Total Distribution Costs 453
Cost Trade-offs 454
Order Processing 454
Materials Handling 455
Warehousing 455
Warehousing Functions 455
Types of Warehouse 456
Inventory Management 456
**Innovation and Change Benetton Benefits from Automated Distribution Systems 457**
Transportation 460
Transport Modes 460
Criteria for Selecting Transport 460
Coordinating Transport Services 463
Strategic Issues in Physical Distribution 464
*Case Study Today's Cash and Carry Mega-depots Depend on Effective Stockholding and Physical Distribution* 469

**16 Retailing 471**
The Nature of Retailing 473
Retail Locations 474
Central Business District 474
Suburban Centres 475
Edge-of-town Sites 475
Retail Parks 476
Major Store Types 476
Department and Variety Stores 476
Grocery Supermarkets, Superstores and Hypermarkets 478
Discount Sheds and 'Category Killers' 479
Warehouse Clubs 479
Speciality Shops 480
Convenience Stores 481
Mall Discounters 481
Factory Outlet Villages 481
Markets and Cash and Carry Warehouses 481
Catalogue Showrooms 482
Categories 482
Non-store Retailing 483
**Innovation and Change Upmarket Clothing Retailers Opt for Multi-channels 483**
In-home Retailing 484
Telemarketing 484
Automatic Vending 485
Mail-order Retailing 485
Franchising 487
Major Types of Retail Franchise 488
Advantages and Disadvantages of Franchising 488
Trends in Franchising 488
Strategic Issues and Trends Facing Retail Marketers 489
Location 489
Property Ownership 490
Product Assortment 490
Category Management 491
Retail Positioning 492
Atmospherics 492
Store Image 493
Scrambled Merchandising 493
Merchandising/Buying 494
The Wheel of Retailing 494

The Balance of Retailing Power 495
Technology 495
**Innovation and Change Current Developments in Retail Marketing 496**
*Case Study Dutch Retailer Ahold's Global Ambitions 501*
**Strategic Case**
**FedEx 40 Years of Growth, Innovation and Global Expansion 503**

**PART V Promotion (Marketing Communications) Decisions 507**

**17 An Overview of Marketing Communications 509**
The Role of Promotion 511
The Communication Process 512
Promotion and the Product Adoption Process 516
Product Adopter Categories 519
Aims of Promotion 519
The Promotional Mix 520
Promotional Mix Ingredients 521
**Innovation and Change Web Advertising Comes of Age 522**
**Topical Insight Microsoft's Image Builders: PR Deflects Regulators' Criticisms 524**
Integrated Marketing Communications (IMC) 526
Selecting Promotional Mix Ingredients 527
Push Policy versus Pull Policy 530
*Case Study Häagen-Dazs: Promoting an Adult Ice Cream 534*

**18 Advertising, Public Relations and Sponsorship 536**
The Nature of Advertising 538
**Innovation and Change First Ambient and Now 'Live' Advertising 538**
The Uses of Advertising 539
Promoting Products and Organisations 540
Stimulating Primary and Selective Demand 541
Off-setting Competitors' Advertising 544
Making Sales Personnel More Effective 544
Educating the Market 544
Increasing the Uses of a Product 545
Reminding and Reinforcing Customers 545
Reducing Sales Fluctuations 546
Developing an Advertising Campaign 546
Identifying and Analysing the Advertising Target 547
Defining the Advertising Objectives 547
Creating the Advertising Platform 548
Determining the Advertising Budget 549
Developing the Media Plan 550
Creating the Advertising Message 555
Executing the Campaign 558
Evaluating the Effectiveness of the Advertising 559
Who Develops the Advertising Campaign? 561
Publicity and Public Relations 562
Publicity and Advertising Compared 563
Kinds of Publicity 563
Uses of Publicity 565
The Requirements of a Publicity Programme 566
Dealing with Unfavourable Publicity 566
The Limitations of Using Publicity 567
Trends that Affect Advertising and Public Relations 567
**Innovation and Change Tesco TV 568**
Sponsorship 569
The Increasing Popularity of Sponsorship 569
Applications for Sponsorship 570
Reputable Partnerships 571
*Case Study 'Textbook PR': Public Relations and the Perrier Crisis 575*

**19 Sales Management, Sales Promotion, Direct Mail, the Internet and Direct Marketing 577**
The Nature of Personal Selling and Sales Management 579
**Building Customer Relationships IBM's Salesforce Expertise in Market Sectors 581**
Elements of the Personal Selling Process 581
Prospecting and Evaluating Opportunities 582
Preparing to Contact Prospects or Existing Customers 582
Approaching the Prospect or Existing Customer 583
Making the Presentation or Sales Pitch 583
Overcoming Objections and Reassuring the Prospect or Customer 583
Closing the Deal or Transaction 583
Following up to Ensure Customer Satisfaction and Enable Repeat Business 584
Types of Sales People 584
Order Getters 584
Order Takers 584
Support Personnel 585
Management of the Salesforce 585
Establishing Salesforce Objectives 586
Determining Salesforce Size 587
Recruiting and Selecting Sales Personnel 587
Training Sales Personnel 588

Compensating Sales Personnel 588
Motivating Sales People 590
Managing Sales Territories 592
Controlling and Evaluating Salesforce Performance 592
Internal Marketing 593
Sales Promotion 593
The Nature of Sales Promotion 593
Sales Promotion Opportunities and Limitations 594
Sales Promotion Methods 595
Consumer Sales Promotion Techniques 595
**Innovation and Change Tesco Moves Ahead with the Help of Clubcard 597**
Trade Sales Promotion Methods 600
Direct Mail 602
The Uses of Direct Mail 602
Attention-seeking Flashes 602
The Package 602
Mailing Lists 604
Copy Writing 604
The Strengths and Weaknesses of Direct Mail 604
The Internet 605
Direct Marketing 607
*Case Study Promoting Free Flights: How Hoover Came Unstuck 614*
**Strategic Case**
**Birmingham Women's Hospital Giving Birth: the Consumer's Choice! 617**

**PART VI** Pricing Decisions 621

**20 Pricing Concepts 623**
The Characteristics and Role of Price 625
Terms Used to Describe Price 625
The Importance of Price to Marketers 625
Price and Non-price Competition 626
Price Competition 627
Non-price Competition 628
**Building Customer Relationships Do Low Prices Build e-loyalty? 628**
Factors Affecting Pricing Decisions 630
Organisational and Marketing Objectives 630
Pricing Objectives 631
Costs 631
Other Marketing Mix Variables 631
Channel Member Expectations 634
Buyers' Perceptions 634
Competition 635
Legal and Regulatory Issues 636
Perceived Value 636
Pricing for Business Markets 636
Price Discounting 636
Geographic Pricing 638
Transfer Pricing 638
Price Discrimination 639
Economic Value to the Customer 639
**Marketing Tools and Techniques Business-to-Business Pricing using EVC Analysis 639**
*Case Study Perfume Discounting – Pricing Policies to Rattle the Leading Brands 644*

**21 Setting Prices 646**
Stages for Establishing Prices 648
Stage 1: Selection of Pricing Objectives 648
**Topical Insight ASDA's Permanently Low Prices 649**
Stage 2: Assessing the Target Market's Evaluation of Price and its Ability to Buy 649
Stage 3: Determining Demand 650
The Demand Curve 650
Demand Fluctuations 651
Gauging Price Elasticity of Demand 651
Stage 4: Analysis of Demand, Cost and Profit Relationships 652
Marginal Analysis 653
Break-even Analysis 655
Stage 5: Evaluation of Competitors' Prices 656
Stage 6: Selecting a Basis for Pricing 657
Cost-based Pricing 657
Cost Plus Pricing 657
Mark-up Pricing 657
Demand-based Pricing 658
Competition-based Pricing 658
Marketing-oriented Pricing 658
Stage 7: Selection of a Pricing Strategy 659
Differential Pricing 659
New Product Pricing 660
Product Line Pricing 661
Psychological Pricing 662
Professional Pricing 665
Promotional Pricing 665
Misleading Pricing 665
Stage 8: Determining a Specific Price 666
The 'Pricing Balance': the Need for Pragmatism 666
**Building Customer Relationships Keeping in Touch with the Affluent Consumers and their Spending Power 667**

*Case Study* *Buying Power Impacts on Toys 'Я' Us Pricing* *671*
Strategic Case
Napster Napster's Creation 673

**PART VII** Manipulating the Marketing Mix 677

**22 Modifying the Marketing Mix for Business Markets, Services and in International Marketing** **679**
Characteristics of Business Marketing Mixes 682
Product 681
**Topical Insight BUPA Targets Consumers and Business Customers** **682**
Place/Distribution 684
Promotion 686
Price 690
People 691
Amending the Marketing Mix for Services 692
Product 692
Promotion 694
Price 696
Place/Distribution 697
Process 697
Physical Evidence (Ambience) 698
People 698
Strategic Adaptation of Marketing Mixes for International Markets 699
Product and Promotion 699
Place/Distribution and Pricing 702
**Innovation and Change Pan-European Kraft Suchard Thinks Globally, Operates Locally** **703**
People 705
*Case Study* *Hewlett-Packard Targets the Developing Economies* *709*
Strategic Case
Colgate Globally Known Consumer Brands 710

**PART VIII** Marketing Management 713

**23 Marketing Planning and Forecasting Sales Potential** **715**
Marketing Planning 717
The Marketing Plan 721
Management or Executive Summary 722
Marketing Objectives 722
Product/Market Background 722
Marketing Analysis 722
Marketing Strategies 724
Expected Results 725
Marketing Programmes for Implementation 725
Controls and Evaluation 725
Financial Implications/Required Budgets 726
Operational Considerations 726
Appendices 726
Conducting Marketing Planning 726
**Marketing Tools and Techniques JCB's Adoption of Marketing Planning** **726**
Market and Sales Potential and Sales Forecasting 728
Market and Sales Potential 728
Developing Sales Forecasts 730
**Topical Insight Forecasting Sales at Nokia** **731**
Using Multiple Forecasting Methods 734
The Marketing Audit 736
*Case Study* *Binney & Smith Plans For Crayola Crayons* *743*

**24 Implementing Strategies, Internal Marketing Relationships and Measuring Performance** **745**
Organising Marketing Activities 747
The Place of Marketing in an Organisation 747
Centralisation versus Decentralisation 750
Major Alternatives for Organising the Marketing Unit 752
Marketing Implementation 754
Problems in Implementing Marketing Activities 756
Components of Marketing Implementation 757
Motivating Marketing Personnel 757
Communicating within the Marketing Unit 759
Coordinating Marketing Activities 759
**Marketing Tools and Techniques Practitioners' Implementation Management of Marketing Planning: The Dibb/Simkin Checklists** **759**
Concepts Related to Marketing Implementation 761
Relationship Marketing 762
Internal Marketing 762
Total Quality Management 765
Controlling Marketing Activities 766
Establishing Performance Standards 767
Evaluating Actual Performance 768
Taking Corrective Action 768
**Marketing Tools and Techniques The Dibb/Simkin Market Status Audit – As Applied to a B2B Company** **769**

Requirements for an Effective Control Process 771
Problems in Controlling Marketing Activities 771
Methods of Evaluating Performance 771
Sales Analysis 772
Marketing Cost Analysis 773
Marketing Shareholder Value Analysis 777
Performance Measures 777
*Case Study Timex Stands the Test of Time* 783

**25 Social Responsibility and Marketing Ethics 785**
Social Responsibility 787
The Nature of Social Responsibility 787
The Dimensions of Social Responsibility 787
Social Responsibility Issues 789
**Marketing in Society Customer Led, Ethically Guided ... the Co-operative Bank 790**
The Nature of Marketing Ethics 794
Ethical Issues in Marketing 795
**Topical Insight Is it Right to Market a No-smoking Vaccine? 796**
The Ethical Decision-making Process 797
Individual Factors 797
Organisational Factors 797
Opportunity 799
Improving Ethical Conduct in Marketing 799
Codes of Conduct 799
Ethics Officers 800
Implementing Ethics and Legal Compliance Programmes 801
Incorporating Social Responsibility and Ethics into Marketing Decisions 801
Being Socially Responsible and Ethical is Not Easy 802
Social Responsibility and Ethics Improve Marketing Performance 804
*Case Study Nestlé Faces Pressure Groups* 807
**Strategic Case**
**Mattel's Barbie Mattel Takes on the World 810**

**PART IX Studying and Working in Marketing 813**

**26 Case Study Analysis, Exam Revision Tips and Careers in Marketing 814**
The Use of Case Study Analysis 816
Situation Analysis 816
Company's Internal Position 816
Market Analysis 819
External Environment 819
Competition 819
The Case Study Process 820
Identify and Analyse Case Problem Areas 820
Derive Alternative Solutions 820
Analyse Alternative Solutions 821
Recommend the 'Best' Alternative 821
Implement the Chosen Solution 821
Presenting the Case Study Findings 821
Formal Presentations 822
Written Reports 822
**Marketing Tools and Techniques Writing an Effective Report 823**
Examination Revision Tips 823
The Examination Paper 823
Coping with Examination Conditions 823
Format of Answers 824
**Marketing Tools and Techniques Examination Techniques: Frequently Asked Questions 825**
Careers in Marketing 825
The Résumé or Curriculum Vitae 826
The Interview 827
Types of Marketing Career 827

# Preface

Marketing affects everyone: we are all consumers. Most businesses depend on marketing to provide an understanding of the marketplace, to identify opportunities, and to ensure that their products and services satisfy the needs of customers and that they are competing effectively. There is little doubt that marketing is an important part of today's society and commerce. In the majority of business schools and colleges in the UK, Eire, Benelux and Scandinavia, *Marketing: Concepts and Strategies* is used to introduce undergraduate and MBA students to the nature and scope of marketing.

The first edition of *Marketing: Concepts and Strategies* appeared in 1991. Since then, this text has become the leader in its market. Whether for undergraduates seeking a comprehensive introduction to marketing, MBAs requiring a grounding in marketing analysis or marketing management, or students in colleges wishing to pass degrees and diplomas, *Marketing: Concepts and Strategies* is used by lecturers and teaching staff to provide an accessible, topical and enlightening insight into the world of marketing. *Marketing: Concepts and Strategies* is also recommended by the Chartered Institute of Marketing.

This edition has been totally revised to reflect the current core themes of marketing in terms of academic content but also – given the authors' wide-ranging consultancy and research experience outside the lecture theatre – from a practitioner's perspective.

## The Authors

Sally Dibb and Lyndon Simkin have been at the leading UK university management centre, Warwick Business School, since the mid-1980s, teaching undergraduates, MBAs – full-time, part-time and distance learning – and executives the basics of marketing, advanced strategic marketing, marketing management, buyer behaviour, marketing communications and marketing research. Sally and Lyndon's research focuses on market segmentation, marketing planning, marketing communications, marketing strategy operationalisation and teaching methods, in which areas they have published extensively in the academic journals in the UK and USA.

In addition to being joint authors of *Marketing: Concepts and Strategies*, they produced the innovative *The Marketing Casebook: Cases and Concepts* (Thomson) in 1994 and 2001, mixing real-world cases with overviews of theory, and in 1996 and 1998 *The Market Segmentation Workbook* and *The Marketing Planning Workbook* (both published by Thomson), aimed at assisting marketing practitioners to reassess their target markets and understand the complexities of marketing planning. These workbooks were based on their consultancy experiences with organisations as diverse as Accenture, AstraZeneca, Calor, Conoco, DERA (MoD), Forte, Fujitsu, ICI, JCB, McDonald's, PowerGen, Raytheon, Standard Chartered and Tesco. Both *Workbooks* have recently been translated and published in China and Russia. In 2001, Sally and Lyndon published the revision aid, *Marketing Briefs* (Elsevier Butterworth – Heinemann), already revised and in its second edition in 2004. While primarily targeted at students preparing for examinations in marketing, *Marketing Briefs* is also ideal for providing time-pressured managers with concise and topical insights into the core concepts and tools of strategic marketing.

Bill Pride and O.C. Ferrell first teamed up to produce *Marketing* for Houghton Mifflin in 1977. Since then, the American sister of *Marketing: Concepts and Strategies*, now in its thirteenth edition, has been used by nearly two million students and has become one of the principal marketing texts in the USA. O.C. is Professor of Marketing in the College of Business at Colorado State University. Prior to his arrival at Colorado State, he was Distinguished Professor of Marketing and Business Ethics at the University of Memphis where he had also been Dean. He is a former President of the Academic Council for the prestigious American Marketing Association (AMA). He chaired committees that developed the AMA Code of Ethics and the AMA Code of Ethics for Marketing on the Internet. O.C. is the author of many texts, including *Marketing Strategy* (Dryden), *Business Ethics: Ethical Decision Making and Cases* (Houghton Mifflin) and *Business: A Changing World* (Irwin/McGraw-Hill). Bill Pride is Professor of Marketing at Texas A&M University where he specialises in marketing communications, strategic marketing planning and business marketing education. Like O.C., he has published a large number of journal papers and is widely recognised in the marketing field. Bill is also co-author of *Business* (Houghton Mifflin).

## Changes for the Fifth Edition

Marketing is a quickly evolving discipline in a rapidly changing world. The fifth edition of *Marketing: Concepts and Strategies* strives to explain the nature of marketing and the importance of understanding the complexities of the marketplace. In so doing, the intention as ever is for the text to be easy to read, informative, interesting and topical. To this end, there has been a major restructuring of the 26 chapters. Each Part has improved scene-setting openers and postscripts to explain the interrelationships of the many concepts and strategies introduced. Leading practitioners have contributed to these openers in order to emphasise the importance of strategic marketing. Each Part now concludes with a full-length strategic case study. The Parts follow a logical structure, which adheres to the premise that for effective marketing there must first be analysis of the marketplace, then the recommendation of a marketing strategy, and finally the production of marketing programmes with control processes to facilitate implementation of the desired strategy.

Every chapter has been updated in terms of the current research and thinking in the area, the latest statistics and industry figures where relevant, and to reflect the views of the leading academics and practitioners who have kindly reviewed the chapters, provided thought-provoking quotes and suggested the recommended readings in their area of expertise as additional references. Chapter openers have been redesigned and the concluding pages of each chapter now provide an Applied Mini-Case, a Case Study, an Internet Exercise, and Key Links to related chapters.

The principal aim of *Marketing: Concepts and Strategies* has always been to provide a book that students find easy to use and that reflects accurately the current thinking in the world of marketing. There have been extensive changes to the fifth edition – these have been made in order to reflect students' needs, suggestions by peers and the current developments in marketing as identified by practitioners, the journals and at conferences. There are new chapters addressing marketing strategy, e-marketing and studying marketing; more e-exercises; better cross-referencing between related concepts and chapters; and numerous practitioner insights and boxes describing marketing managers' real-world use of key concepts.

In summary, the improvements for the fifth edition include the following:

- Extensive coverage of currently in-vogue topics:
  - the role of the Internet and technology in marketing and e-marketing
  - relationship marketing and customer relationship management
  - internal marketing and implementation management
  - Green marketing and social awareness
  - direct marketing in channel selection and the promotional mix.
- Greater explanation of marketing strategy:
  - corporate strategy and mission enactment
  - marketing opportunity analysis
  - strategic focus and options
  - target marketing
  - competitive forces and positions.
- Significant attention to implementation issues:
  - marketing mix programmes
  - internal marketing
  - controls and managerial processes
  - performance measures and benchmarking
  - cultural and organisational operational barriers.
- Thorough explanation of the marketing process:
  - marketing analysis of customers, marketing environment forces, competitors and capabilities
  - marketing strategy development, opportunity identification and target marketing
  - marketing programme specification to enact the marketing strategy
  - marketing implementation and controls.
- A new final Part to offer applied help to students examining how to:
  - tackle case studies
  - write reports
  - make presentations
  - revise and prepare for examinations
  - handle job interviews
  - produce CVs.
- Full-length strategic case studies at the end of each Part to aid understanding of key concepts.
- More balanced coverage of the issues relating to marketing in consumer goods markets, services and business-to-business markets.
- Extensive cross-referencing between chapters, Parts and key concepts.
- The inclusion of the insights of leading marketing practitioners.
- The thoughts of the leading academic 'gurus', their recommended further readings and quotes.
- New chapter opening vignettes, boxes illustrating current developments, and end-of-chapter cases for discussion.
- The inclusion of applied cases and Internet exercises at the end of each chapter.
- Updated industry/market statistics, figures and examples for the EU and leading brands.
- Ancillaries for tutors including PowerPoint visual aids, testbank software, case answers and a student/tutor website.

- Website support for users of *Marketing: Concepts and Strategies*, as follows:
  - PowerPoint visual aids
  - student testbank
  - web links with case companies, brands and topics
  - extra cases
  - suggested examination formats and questions
  - selected course outlines and syllabus proposals
  - Q&A topics and solutions
  - financial analyses in marketing
  - full glossary of important terms
  - topical insights and evolving concepts.

www.dibbmarketing.com

As ever, *Marketing: Concepts and Strategies* is supported by comprehensive indexing, a full glossary of important terms appearing in the margins of the relevant chapters and cross-referenced in the subject index, questions for discussion and full listing of the key terms and jargon detailed chapter by chapter.

The views of student users and fellow academics have guided changes for this fifth edition, now produced entirely in the UK. These modifications have been made to improve *Marketing: Concepts and Strategies*, uprate its usability and to reflect how the discipline of marketing is evolving.

Current adopters of *Marketing: Concepts and Strategies* should find little difficulty in incorporating the new look in their teaching. New readers should find that *Marketing: Concepts and Strategies* is highly accessible and topical.

# The Running Order of Marketing: Concepts and Strategies, Fifth Edition

Part I: Marketing Defined and Marketing in Context – An introduction to the nature and scope of marketing and the marketing process, marketing strategy and competitive forces, the composition of the marketing environment, e-marketing and the importance of global marketing.

Part II: Understanding and Targeting Customers – Consumer and business-to-business buying behaviour, target marketing and brand positioning, marketing research and marketing information systems.

Part III: Product, Branding, Packaging and Service Decisions – The first ingredients of the marketing mix; product, service and people decisions.

Part IV: Place (Distribution and Marketing Channel) Decisions – The nature of marketing channels in the marketing mix and the key participating players.

Part V: Promotion (Marketing Communications) Decisions – The use of advertising, publicity and public relations, sponsorship, personal selling, sales promotion, direct mail, the Internet and direct marketing in marketing communications.

Part VI: Pricing Decisions – The concepts of price and value, setting price and determining pricing policies.

Part VII: Manipulating the Marketing Mix – Adapting the marketing mix for business-to-business, services and global markets.

Part VIII: Marketing Management – Marketing planning and sales forecasting; implementing strategies, internal marketing relationships and measuring performance; ethics and social responsibility in modern marketing.

Part IX: Studying and Working in Marketing – Case study analysis; examination revision; careers in marketing.

## Acknowledgements

This text would not have happened without the support and encouragement of American co-authors Bill Pride and O.C. Ferrell; Susan Kahn at Houghton Mifflin; the team in Cambridge (especially Karen Beaulah); the comments and enthusiasm from fellow marketing lecturers at Warwick and, above all, the feedback from our students past and present.

Specific Warwick colleagues whose comments, suggestions and ideas have helped shape this fifth edition include: David Arnott, Sue Bridgewater, Scott Dacko, Jonathan Freeman, T.C. Melewar, Phil Stern, Robin Wensley, Qing Wang and Claudia Simoes. So much of the essence of this book and our work in marketing are because of the insights, enthusiasm and abilities of former mentor – sadly departed – Peter Doyle.

Thanks are also due to the long-suffering and immensely helpful Janet Biddle and Sheila Frost in the Marketing office at Warwick Business School.

Specific thanks for stimulation, material and cooperation must go to:

Peter Jackson, *Adsearch,* Richmond-upon-Thames
John Wringe, *The Sandom Group,* Windsor
Ian Hunter, George Miller, David Olney, David Smith, Ken McIlwham, Alan Coulter and Peter Barrett, *Fujitsu Services*
Rohit Samani, *Tilda*
Jim Trail, Steve Glover, Neil McGovern, Andrew Watson, Paul Watson and Kevin Devaney, *Raytheon*
Alex Davis and Howard Kerr, *Calor*
James Watkins, *St Andrew's Group of Hospitals*
Tim Mason, *Tesco*
David Coupe, *Experian*

We also appreciate the help of these reviewers:

Professor Patrick De Pelsmacker, *University of Antwerp*
Aidan Daily, *National University of Ireland*, Galway
Ann Torres, *National University of Ireland*, Galway
John Gardener, *University of Central England*, Birmingham
Susan Scoffield, *Manchester Metropolitan University*

For much of the case research and sourcing of advertisements, we are indebted to Bex.

*Sally Dibb and Lyndon Simkin*
*Kenilworth*
*January 2005*

# I Marketing Defined and Marketing in Context

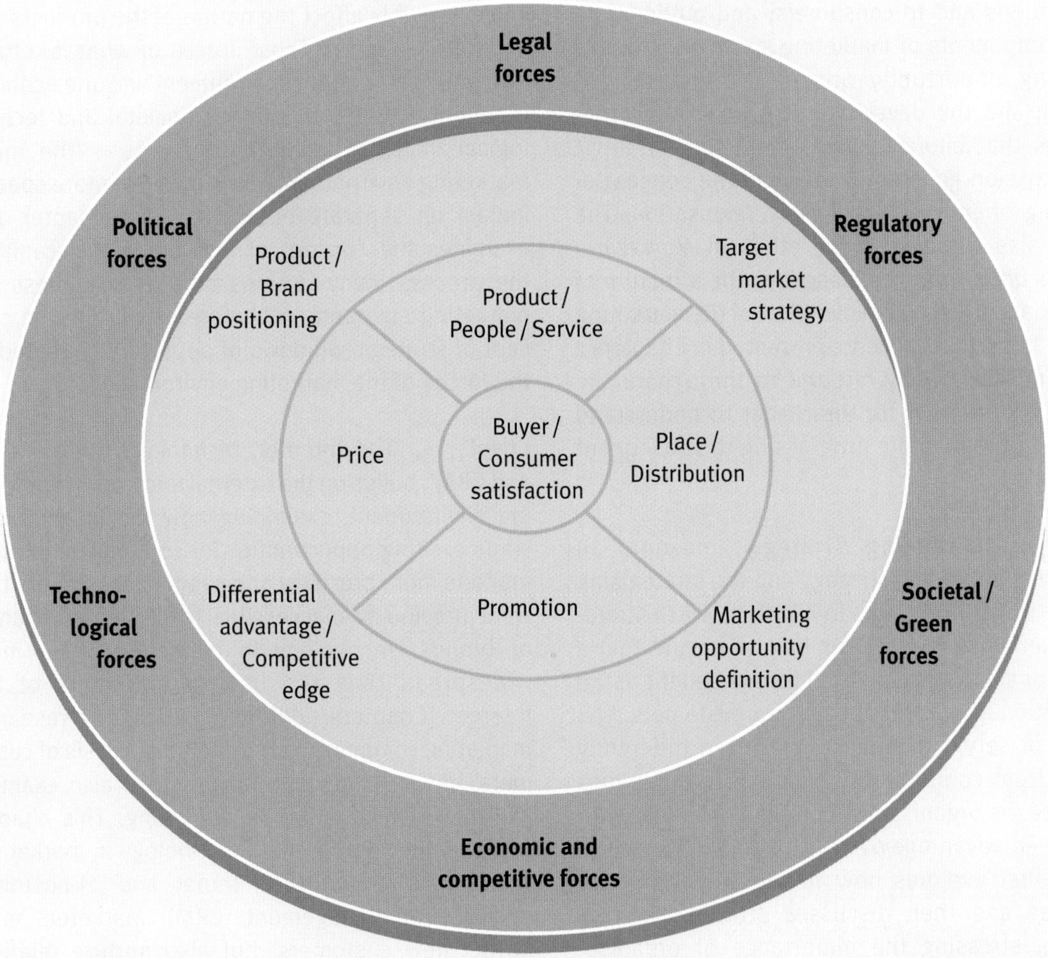


Marketing consists of individual and organisational activities that facilitate and expedite satisfying exchange relationships in a dynamic environment through the creation, distribution, promotion and pricing of goods, services and ideas. The simple premise of marketing is that, to be successful, any organisation must understand its customers' requirements and satisfy them in a manner that gives the organisation an edge over its competitors. This involves offering the 'right' mix of product, people, service, pricing, promotion and distribution channel. Marketing also depends on constant updating of ideas. Customers are often surprisingly fickle and modify their needs and wants, rivals alter their strategies, and forces in the marketplace change regularly.

**Part I of *Marketing: Concepts and Strategies*** introduces the concepts of marketing, marketing orientation, marketing strategy and the forces of the marketing environment, exploring their nature and scope.

**Chapter 1, 'An Overview of the Marketing Concept',** defines marketing; establishes its importance to organisations and to consumers; and outlines the major components of marketing strategy – notably marketing opportunity analysis, target market selection and the development of marketing programmes that implement the marketing strategy. The discussion goes on to examine the concept of marketing orientation within an organisation. The chapter also establishes the ethos of *Marketing: Concepts and Strategies*, describes the structure of the book and presents an overview of the marketing process. Important concepts presented in Chapters 1 and 2 are deliberately referred to throughout the book. It is important for the reader to understand and accept them before progressing to subsequent chapters.

**Chapter 2, 'Marketing Strategy'**, presents an overview of marketing strategy and the strategising process. This chapter aims to highlight which strategic marketing considerations help to ensure that a product or service is marketed for the benefit of the organisation as well as its targeted customers. The product or service should be marketed differently enough from competitors' marketing programmes to provide the organisation's product or service with a perceived advantage over those competitors. The chapter first explores how to develop marketing strategies and then discusses strategic market planning, stressing the importance of organisational mission, goals and corporate strategy. The discussion turns next to assessing organisational opportunities and resources, as well as identifying strategic objectives and strategic focus. The chapter addresses the all-important role of identifying market segments, targeting and brand positioning in marketing strategy: the development of clear target market priorities. The chapter then focuses on competitive strategies for marketing: the role of competition, its ramifications for strategy, competitive positions and warfare strategies. The link between marketing objectives and marketing-mix programmes is examined, along with implementation and performance monitoring.

**Chapter 3, 'The Marketing Environment'**, examines the many forces at work in a market over which consumers and businesses have little or no control but which tangibly affect the nature of the products and services marketed. These forces of what is termed 'the macro marketing environment' include economic, political, legal, regulatory, societal and technological impacts. Competitive forces – 'the micro marketing environment' – often have a more specific impact on separate businesses. The chapter also examines the concept of environmental scanning, the process many businesses use to address the marketing environment, before discussing the concept of strategic windows of opportunity created by the forces of the marketing environment.

**Chapter 4, 'The Internet, technology in Marketing and CRM'**, builds on the external forces of the marketing environment, examining how the Internet presents exciting opportunities for companies to target markets more precisely and even reach markets that were previously inaccessible to certain companies or brands. Technology in marketing is far more widespread than the use by marketers of the Internet. Chapters addressing marketing research, marketing communications and the analysis of customers' buying behaviour, for example, also examine the role of technology in marketing. This chapter explores two key facets of technology in marketing: (1) e-marketing and the Internet, and (2) customer relationship management (CRM). Marketers must attract new customers, but also nurture relationships with existing customers, extracting a greater share of their spending: CRM techniques, led by technology, facilitate this goal. Marketing practitioners increasingly devote significant resources to embracing technology via the Internet and CRM systems.

**Chapter 5, 'Marketing in International Markets'**, acknowledges that, today, many businesses operate across national borders and modify their marketing practices accordingly. The chapter defines the nature of marketing internationally, establishes why the concept is so important and explains the need for international marketing intelligence. The discussion then focuses on how forces of the marketing environment differ between territories and how regional trade alliances create the need to treat non-domestic markets differently. The chapter concludes with an examination of alternative market entry strategies for companies wishing to become involved in international marketing activities.

By the conclusion of Part I of *Marketing: Concepts and Strategies*, readers should understand what is meant by the terms *marketing, marketing orientation, marketing strategy* and the *marketing environment*. The essential themes in Part I are developed further as the book continues.

## Fujitsu

Marketing lies at the heart of business decision-making in driving profitable growth. There are three primary elements to this: go-to-market strategy, innovation and brand.

Go-to-market strategy: we help our business units prioritise who to talk to, about what and when; we provide them with the customer and competitor intelligence to engage with priority target customers in the most compelling manner; and we help them to powerfully position our business with this customer.

Innovation: we lead cross-functional teams from every part of our business in developing distinctive new-thinking that challenges the accepted norms; we package and communicate the new value propositions that emerge from this work; and we ensure that our sales and account teams understand and connect with it, so they can actively use these propositions to better engage with their customers.

Brand: we define our brand positioning, and how this positioning will develop over time; we make this positioning manifest in our internal and external communications; and we work with others across the business to ensure that the positioning translates into a coherent employee and customer experience.

Marketing strategy is critical to our business. Without it we are left behaving in an utterly responsive manner to the latest new business opportunity, whether or not it is well suited to our goals, talents and current market positioning. With it we can maximise the return from our marketing, sales and account management effort through targeting only those customers whose business we really want – and that we can realistically expect to win. Understanding the external trading environment is very important because this helps us to determine the nature and the scale of our resourcing requirements, and how we can best deploy these resources to generate the maximum business value.

**George Miller, group marketing director, Fujitsu Services**

Fujitsu is the world's third largest IT services group and works closely with large government and commercial organisations to help them seize the possibilities of effective, innovative IT.

# 1

# An Overview of the Marketing Concept

"**Marketing is concerned with the establishment and maintenance of mutually satisfying exchange relationships.**"

*Michael Baker, formerly of the University of Strathclyde*

## Objectives

- To understand the definition of marketing
- To appreciate the context of marketing and marketing orientation
- To explain the marketing process
- To understand the importance of marketing
- To gain insight into the basic elements of the marketing concept and its implementation
- To understand the major components of a marketing strategy and the marketing mix
- To gain a sense of general strategic marketing issues, such as market opportunity analysis, target market selection and marketing mix development
- To grasp the ethos and structure of this book

## Introduction

Marketing's aim is the identification of target markets and the satisfaction of these customers, now and in the future. In most organisations, marketing fulfils an analytical function, provides strategic direction and facilitates a set of tactical activities designed to attract the targeted customers to the organisation's products or services.

Organisations with a marketing orientation have more than a few staff engaged in marketing activities. Such organisations have a sound awareness of customers' needs and buying behaviour, of competitors' offerings and strategies, and of market trends. They take steps to ensure they know how these market conditions will evolve. In addition, they orientate their operational practices and coordinate their inter-functional thinking around these market conditions.

To be truly effective, marketing needs to be an analytical process combining marketing analysis, strategising, and the creation of marketing programmes designed to implement the designated marketing strategy. Marketing opportunity analysis is a pivotal part of marketing: the determination of emerging and existing market opportunities and the choice of which to address. At the heart of a marketing strategy is the formation of a target market strategy and a basis for competing in order to focus on the opportunities prioritised by the organisation.

Most members of the general public think of 'advertising', 'marketing research' or 'sales persuasion' when the term 'marketing' is mentioned. These brief introductory comments alone demonstrate that there is in fact much more to marketing. This first chapter of *Marketing: Concepts and Strategies* is designed to define marketing and explain its role.

## *Opener*

# Even Condoms Need Marketing

Not too long ago, no one would have seen advertisements for condoms. A mix of changing social attitudes, concerns about sexually transmitted diseases and campaigns to combat teenage pregnancies have led to a range of brands turning to mainstream TV and press advertising. This surge in marketing activity has not been without its critics, however.

Mates Condoms uses agency Real Adventure for its £2 million account. Mates, launched by Richard Branson in the 1980s, is now part of Ansell Healthcare and has made significant market share gains against long-standing market leader Durex. The latest ploy by Mates is to target women with a separate range of condoms, branded Pleasure. This new brand launch is to be placed next to cosmetics and haircare products in supermarkets and pharmacies, rather than among other condom lines. In targeting women, Mates is moving away from the traditional target audience, male purchasers. By persuading retailers to display the range among beauty products, the company is striving to achieve an edge over its competitors while demonstrating an affinity with the purchasing behaviour of its target customers. Mates' marketers are seeking to grow market share and to take advantage of changing attitudes to condoms.

A real storm was created when US brand Trojan broadcast TV advertisements for its Shared Pleasure brand, showing a couple having sex. The first adverts ran in the commercial breaks of TV reality show *Big Brother*, which attracted a viewing profile similar to the target market profile for the brand. Trojan attained approval from the UK's Broadcast Advertising Clearance Centre for a post-9.00 p.m. watershed showing of the 20-second adverts. Trojan claimed that this marked the first time an orgasm had been shown in a UK television advert. The advert, made by agency Media Therapy, apparently showed people captured at the height of pleasure, linking to the Shared Pleasure brand name. Building on the back of a poster campaign, this advertising was bound to court controversy, receiving complaints to the Advertising Standards Authority that the campaign was offensive, demeaning to women, pornographic and not suitable for television audiences. While the brand-building creativity may have been clever, Trojan's marketers nevertheless caused uproar in certain circles.

**Sources:** 'Trojan under fire for "her pleasure" ad', *Marketing Week*, 4 April 2004, p. 8; 'Trojan to screen first orgasm ad', *Marketing*, 26 April 2004, p. 6; 'Mates', *Marketing Week*, 3 June 2004, p. 10; 'Why is safe sex unpalatable?', *Marketing*, 8 April 2004, p. 15. Photo: Courtesy of Mates Healthcare

This chapter first overviews the concept of marketing orientation before developing a definition of marketing. The focus then moves on to some of the reasons people should study marketing and why marketing is important. The chapter proceeds to explore the marketing concept and examines several issues associated with successful implementation. The chapter explains the importance of an analytical process to effective marketing, from analysis to strategy formulation to the creation of marketing programmes. Mates – see 'Opener' box – analysed the purchasing behaviour of its targeted consumers before developing the marketing strategy for its new Pleasure range of condoms. The chapter concludes by discussing the organisation and running order of this book. The concepts and strategies discussed throughout this book are applicable to consumer goods and services, business-to-business products and services, as well as to not-for-profit and public-sector organisations.

Like all the chapters in *Marketing: Concepts and Strategies*, this one contains detailed topical illustrative examples in highlighted boxes, presents cases for discussion, suggests Internet exercises at its conclusion, lists at the end all the key terms presented in the chapter, provides discussion and review questions to emphasise the key themes and offers suggested further reading choices. In addition, as the principal definitions are introduced in the text, they are repeated in the margins for ease of understanding, glossary-style. If you have not yet done so, *before* tackling the chapters you should read the Preface to this book in order to understand the perspective, structure and chapter components of *Marketing: Concepts and Strategies.*

# Marketing Explained and Defined

## Marketing Orientation

**Marketing orientation**
A marketing-oriented organisation devotes resources to understanding the needs and buying behaviour of customers, competitors' activities and strategies, and of market trends and external forces – now and as they may shape up in the future; inter-functional coordination ensures that the organisation's activities and capabilities are aligned to this marketing intelligence

An organisation exhibiting a **marketing orientation** is said to have a sound understanding of customer needs, buying behaviour and the issues influencing the purchasing choices of customers. A marketing-oriented organisation also has a shrewd appreciation of competitors and external marketing environment forces and trends.[1] In addition to comprehending these customer, competitor and marketing environment issues, a marketing-oriented organisation ensures its operations, personnel and capabilities are aligned to reflect these external drivers. A truly marketing-oriented organisation understands these current issues, but is also focused on identifying how they will evolve, so ensuring that the organisation's strategy and capabilities are modified to reflect not just current market requirements but also future market conditions.

A marketing-oriented organisation, therefore, devotes resources to understanding the needs and buying behaviour of customers, competitors' activities and strategies, and market trends and external forces (now and as they may shape up in the future). Inter-functional coordination ensures that the organisation's activities and capabilities are aligned to this marketing intelligence.

Not all organisations can claim to have a marketing orientation. For example, some are purely sales led, concentrating on short-term sales targets, whereas other organisations are production oriented, choosing to emphasise product development and production efficiency in their business strategy. Few experts would argue against maximising sales or seeking leading-edge production practices, or indeed the adoption of best-practice financial and human resource approaches. Similarly, the adoption of a marketing orientation is also highly desirable. A marketing orientation is of significant benefit to an organisation, as it facilitates a better understanding of customers and helps a business to prepare for external market developments, threats and opportunities. It is difficult to contemplate a scenario where a marketing orientation would not be beneficial to an organisation.

An organisation practising the concepts explained in *Marketing: Concepts and Strategies* is well on the way to having a marketing orientation; but it is important that inter-functional coordination aligns the activities within the organisation to the marketplace, and specifically to customer buying behaviour, competitive pressures and marketing environment forces, and to the evolving nature of these market conditions. The use of some of marketing's concepts and an understanding of the role of marketing in attracting and satisfying customers, are not enough on their own to establish what is termed a *marketing orientation*. However, failure to comprehend the core concepts of marketing will make a marketing orientation impossible to achieve. The focus of this text, therefore, is on explaining the core concepts of marketing.

The theme of marketing orientation is revisited in Chapter 24. It is possible for an organisation lacking a full marketing orientation to nevertheless deploy aspects of the marketing toolkit as described in the following chapters. Indeed, it is common for a business to understand its customers adequately, but not its competitors' strategies or the external marketing environment forces. Obviously, it is better not to operate in ignorance of these external pressures, which may create threats or opportunities. The definition of marketing per se is not, therefore, the same as the definition of marketing orientation.

## Marketing Defined

Asking members of the public to define marketing is an illuminating experience. They will respond with a variety of descriptions, including 'advertising', 'selling', 'hype', 'conning people', 'targeting' and 'packaging'. In reality, marketing encompasses many more activities than most people realise and depends on a wealth of formal concepts, processes and models not implied by the soundbites just listed. Since it is practised and studied for many different reasons, marketing has been, and continues to be, defined in many different ways, whether for academic, research or applied business purposes. This chapter examines what is meant by the term **marketing**.

**Marketing**
Individual and organisational activities that facilitate and expedite satisfying exchange relationships in a dynamic environment through the creation, distribution, promotion and pricing of goods, services and ideas

> Marketing consists of individual and organisational activities that facilitate and expedite satisfying exchange relationships in a dynamic environment through the creation, distribution, promotion and pricing of goods, services and ideas.
>
> *Dibb, Simkin, Pride and Ferrell*

The basic rationale of marketing is that, to succeed, a business requires satisfied and happy customers who return to the business to provide additional custom. In exchange for something of value, typically payment or a donation, the customers receive a product or service that satisfies their needs. Such a product has an acceptable level of quality, reliability, customer service and support, is available at places convenient for the customer at the 'right' price and is promoted effectively by means of a clear message that is readily comprehended by the customers in question. For example, in return for quenching thirst at affordable prices with a reliable product that is widely available in easy-to-use containers, Coca-Cola receives a great deal of money from customers. Unfortunately for companies and their marketers, customers' requirements change as their needs alter, marketing messages infiltrate their thinking, friends and colleagues discuss purchases, and competing products are pushed by rival businesses. In the dynamic world of marketing, an effective solution to satisfying customer needs rarely has longevity. High-specification cassette decks no longer satisfy the majority of music lovers' needs: compact disc players and mp3 players, therefore, have taken over the dominant share of Sony's range. Marketers must constantly assess their customers' requirements and be prepared to modify their marketing activity accordingly. An assessment of marketing opportunities is an ever evolving process requiring regular revision and updating.

> Marketing is the management process responsible for identifying, anticipating and satisfying customer requirements profitably.
>
> *Chartered Institute of Marketing*

Understanding customers and anticipating their requirements is a core theme of effective marketing.[2] So, too, is understanding general market trends and developments that may affect both customers' views and the activities of businesses operating in a particular market.

**Marketing environment** External changing forces within the trading environment: laws, regulations, political activities, societal pressures, economic conditions and technological advances

These factors may include social trends, technological enhancements, economic patterns, and changes in the legal and regulatory arena, as well as political influences. These forces are often termed the **marketing environment**. Compared with five years ago, for example, look at how many companies now produce products in 'environmentally friendly' packaging in line with the social trend of the 'greening consumer'. A business does not have a marketplace to itself. There are direct competitors, new entrant rivals, substitute products with alternative solutions to a customer's specific need. Construction-equipment giant JCB markets trench-digging equipment to utilities and local authorities. The growth of subterranean tunnelling robotic 'moles' for pipe laying, requiring no trench digging, is a substitute for the traditional JCB backhoe loader and a major competitive threat. The competitive context is of fundamental importance to marketers of any good or service. So, too, are the internal resource base, and the strengths and weaknesses within the business that will determine which market opportunities are in fact viable for the business to pursue. Marketing, therefore, depends on the successful analysis of customers, the marketing environment, competition and internal capabilities.

> The aim of marketing is to make selling superfluous. The aim is to know and to understand the customer so well that the product or service fits him/her and sells itself!
>
> *US management guru Peter Drucker*

With an understanding of these aspects of the marketplace, a business must then develop a marketing strategy. Even the mighty global organisations such as GM/Vauxhall, DuPont or Unilever choose not to offer a product for every type of consumer or customer need. Instead, they attempt to identify groups of customers where each separate group, or 'market segment', has 'similar' needs. Each group of customers may then be offered a specifically tailored product or service proposition and a 'marketing mix' programme. The Ford Maverick off-roader appeals to a separate group of customers than does the Ford Focus town car, and it is marketed totally differently. In developing unique marketing programmes for individual market segments – groups of customers – a business must prioritise which particular groups of customers it has the ability to serve and which will provide satisfactory returns. Resources will not permit all segments in a market to be targeted. In deciding on which segments to target, a business must be clear about the message – or *positioning* – it intends to offer to each group of customers. The business should endeavour to serve those customers it targets in a manner that gives it an edge over its competitors. Knowing how to group customers sensibly into homogeneous market segments; determining which, ultimately, to target; selecting a suitable positioning platform; and seeking superiority over rivals, are some of the core elements of marketing strategy.

> The marketing concept holds that the key to achieving organisational goals lies in determining the needs and wants of target markets and delivering the desired satisfaction more efficiently and effectively than the competition.
>
> *US marketer Philip Kotler*

Once a company has devised a marketing strategy, its attention must switch to marketing mix programmes.[3] As consumers of food brands, audio products or banking services, all readers of this text will have experienced the marketing mix programmes of major companies such as Cadbury's, Sony or Lloyds TSB. These are the tactical actions of marketing departments, which are designed to implement the desired marketing strategy. The product or offer must be clearly defined in line with target customer needs; service levels and guarantees must be determined; pricing and payment issues decided; channels of distribution established to make the product or service available; and promotional strategies devised and executed to communicate with the targeted customers. These tactical aspects of marketing programmes – the marketing mix – must be supported with carefully managed controls in an organisation to ensure their effective execution and the monitoring of their effectiveness.

Marketers must understand their markets – customers, competitors, market trends – and their own capabilities before developing marketing programmes. A marketing strategy must be determined that reflects the analyses, before the marketing programmes required to action the recommended strategy are specified. **A**nalysis first, then **S**trategy decisions with, finally, the formulation of marketing **P**rogrammes: ASP. The focus must be on providing customer satisfaction, but in a manner that leads to the business's successful performance. For example, by addressing customers' needs and adopting a marketing culture incorporating clear controls, construction equipment manufacturer JCB has enjoyed the most successful financial returns in the company's history.

The intention of this introductory marketing text is to explore these facets of marketing comprehensively and thus provide a sound conceptual basis with which to understand the nature and activities of marketing. There are many definitions of marketing, since it is not a pure science. However, certain core ingredients of the various definitions collectively indicate the basic priorities of marketing:

- satisfying customers
- identifying/maximising marketing opportunities
- targeting the 'right' customers
- facilitating exchange relationships
- staying ahead in dynamic environments
- endeavouring to beat and pre-empt competitors
- utilising resources/assets effectively
- increasing market share
- enhancing profitability or income
- satisfying the organisation's stakeholders.

These aims form the objectives for many marketing directors and marketing departments. They are featured throughout this book, which adopts the following definition of marketing as developed by one of its authors for the American Marketing Association.

> Marketing consists of individual and organisational activities that facilitate and expedite satisfying exchange relationships in a dynamic environment through the creation, distribution, promotion and pricing of goods, services and ideas.

A definition of marketing must acknowledge that it relates to more than just tangible goods, that marketing activities occur in a dynamic environment and that such activities are performed by individuals as well as organisations.[4] The ultimate goal is to satisfy targeted customers, seeking their loyalty and consumption, in a way that adds value for the organisation and its stakeholders. This should be achieved in a manner that is differentiated in the view of customers vis-à-vis competitors' marketing mixes, that provides a company with a competitive edge over rivals and that is updated regularly to reflect market forces and developments.

These sentiments are echoed in the very latest American Marketing Association definition, hot off the presses.

> **Marketing.** Noun. An organisational function and a set of processes for creating, communicating and delivering value to customers and for managing customer relationships in ways that benefit the organisation and its stakeholders.

## The Definition Explored

### Marketing Consists of Activities

The marketing of products or services effectively requires many activities. Some are performed by producers; some are accomplished by intermediaries, who purchase products from producers or from other intermediaries and resell them; and some are even performed by purchasers. Marketing does not include all human and organisational activities, only those aimed at facilitating and expediting exchanges. Table 1.1 lists several major categories and examples of marketing activities, as ultimately encountered by the consumer or business customer, who remains at the 'sharp end' of such decisions and marketing programmes. Note that this list is not all-inclusive. Each activity could be sub-divided into more specific activities.

## Marketing is Performed by Individuals and Organisations

All organisations perform marketing activities to facilitate exchanges. Businesses as well as not-for-profit and public-sector organisations, such as colleges and universities, charitable organisations, community theatres and hospitals, perform marketing activities. For example, colleges and universities and their students engage in exchanges. To receive instruction, knowledge, entertainment, a degree, the use of facilities and sometimes room and board, students give up time, money and perhaps services in the form of labour; they may also give up opportunities to do other things! Many organisations engage in marketing activities. Various police forces have surveyed their communities in order to prioritise services and reassure the general public that people's concerns will be addressed. Politicians now conduct analyses before determining strategies; they think of target markets rather than just the electorate. Even the sole owner of and worker in a small corner shop decides which products will sell, arranges deliveries to the shop, prices and displays products, advertises and serves customers.

**Table 1.1 Possible Decisions and Activities associated with Marketing Mix Variables**

| Marketing Mix Variables | Possible Decisions and Activities |
|---|---|
| **Product** | Develop and test-market new products; modify existing products; eliminate products that do not satisfy customers' desires; formulate brand names and branding policies; create product guarantees and establish procedures for fulfilling guarantees; plan packages, including materials, sizes, shapes, colours and designs |
| **Place/distribution** | Analyse various types of distribution channels; design appropriate distribution channels; select appropriate channel members and partners; design an effective programme for dealer relations; establish distribution centres; formulate and implement procedures for efficient product handling; set up inventory controls; analyse transportation methods; minimise total distribution costs; analyse possible locations for plants and wholesale or retail outlets |
| **Promotion** | Set promotional objectives; determine major types of promotion to be used; select and schedule advertising media; develop advertising messages; measure the effectiveness of advertisements; recruit and train salespeople; formulate payment programmes for sales personnel; establish sales territories; plan and implement sales promotion efforts such as free samples, coupons, displays, competitions, sales contests and cooperative advertising programmes; prepare and disseminate publicity releases; evaluate sponsorships; provide direct mail; and establish websites or Internet facilities |
| **Price** | Analyse competitors' prices; formulate pricing policies; determine method(s) used to set prices; set prices; determine discounts for various types of buyer; establish conditions and terms of sales; determine credit and payment terms; understand the consumers' notion of value |
| **People** | Manipulate the marketing mix and establish service levels, guarantees, warranties, expertise, sales support, after sales back-up, customer handling requirements, personnel skills training and motivation (people as marketers); make products and services available (people as intermediaries); provide market for products (people as consumers) |

## Marketing Facilitates Satisfying Exchange Relationships

**Exchange**
The provision or transfer of goods, services and ideas in return for something of value

For an **exchange** to take place, four conditions must exist.

1. Two or more individuals, groups or organisations must participate.
2. Each party must possess something of value that the other party desires.
3. Each party must be willing to give up its 'something of value' to receive the 'something of value' held by the other party. The objective of a marketing exchange is to receive something that is desired more than that which is given up to get it – that is, a reward in excess of costs.
4. The parties to the exchange must be able to communicate with each other to make their 'something of value' available.[5]

Figure 1.1 illustrates the process of exchange. The arrows indicate that the parties communicate and that each has something of value available to exchange. Note, though, that an exchange will not necessarily take place just because these four conditions exist. Nevertheless, even if there is no exchange, marketing activities have still occurred. The 'somethings of value' held by the two parties are most often products and/or financial resources, such as money or credit. When an exchange occurs, products are traded for other products or for financial resources.

**Customer satisfaction**
A state that results when an exchange meets the needs and expectations of the buyer

An exchange should be *satisfying* to both the buyer and the seller. In fact, in a study of marketing managers, 32 per cent indicated that creating **customer satisfaction** was the most important concept in a definition of marketing.[6] Marketing activities should be oriented towards creating and maintaining satisfying exchange relationships. To maintain an exchange relationship, the buyer must be satisfied with the goods, service or idea obtained in the exchange; the seller must be satisfied with the financial reward or something else of value received in the exchange.

Maintaining a positive relationship with buyers is an important goal for a seller, regardless of whether the seller is marketing cereal, financial services or construction plant. Through buyer–seller interaction, the buyer develops expectations about the seller's future behaviour. To fulfil these expectations, the seller must deliver on promises made. Over time, a healthy buyer–seller relationship results in interdependencies between the two parties. The buyer depends on the seller to furnish information, parts and service; to be available; and to provide satisfying products in the future.

## Marketing Occurs in a Dynamic Environment

The marketing environment consists of many external changing forces within the trading environment: laws, regulations, political activities, societal pressures, changing economic conditions and technological advances. Each of these dynamic forces has an impact on how effectively marketing activities can facilitate and expedite exchanges. For example, the development and acceptance of the Internet in home PCs has given businesses another vehicle through which to promote their products. Another example is the impact EU regulations have had on reducing distribution headaches within much of Europe, along with recent strides towards economic monetary union and the launch of the euro.

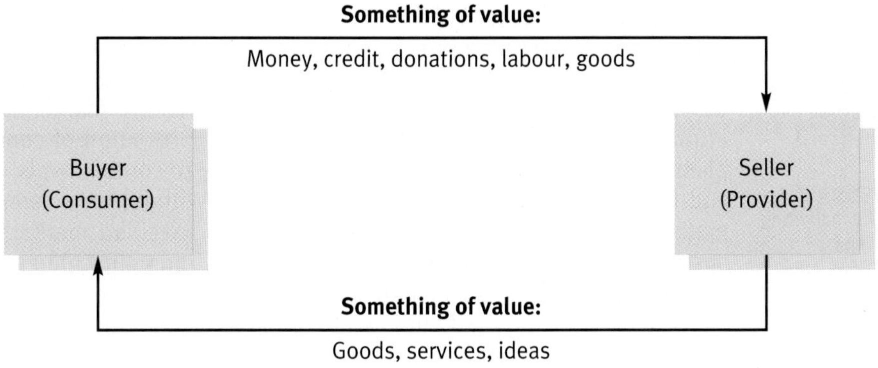


***Figure 1.1***
*Exchange between buyer and seller*

## Marketing Involves Products, Distribution, Promotion, Pricing and People

Marketing means more than simply advertising or selling a product; it involves developing and managing a product that will satisfy certain needs. It focuses on making the product available at the right place, at the right time, at a price that is acceptable to customers and with the right people and service support. It also requires transmitting the kind of promotional information that will help customers determine whether the product will in fact be able to satisfy their needs.

## Marketing Focuses on Goods, Services and Ideas

**Product**
A good, service or idea

**Good**
A physical entity that can be touched

**Service**
The application of human and mechanical efforts to people or objects in order to provide intangible benefits to customers

**Idea**
A concept, philosophy, image or issue

The word 'product' has been used a number of times in this chapter. For purposes of discussion in this text, a **product** is viewed as being a good, a service or an idea. A **good** is a physical entity that can be touched. A Ford Focus, a Sony compact disc player, Kellogg's Cornflakes, a bar of Lux soap and a kitten in a pet shop are examples of goods. A **service** is the application of human and mechanical efforts to people or objects in order to provide intangible benefits to customers. Services such as air travel, dry cleaning, hairdressing, banking, medical care and childcare are just as real as goods, but an individual cannot actually touch or stockpile them. Marketing is utilised for services but requires certain enhancements in order to be effective (see Part VII). **Ideas** include concepts, philosophies, images and issues. For instance, a marriage counsellor gives couples ideas and advice to help improve their relationships. Other marketers of ideas include political parties, charities, religious groups, schools and marketing lecturers.

# The Marketing Process

Marketers spend much of their time managing existing products, target markets and marketing programmes. Even with such so-called 'steady-state' operations, the dynamic nature of marketing leads to continual changes in the marketing environment, competitors and their activities, as well as in customers' needs, expectations, perceptions and buying behaviour. Without a sound understanding of these issues, marketing strategies and their associated marketing programmes cannot be truly effective. Marketers must, therefore, undertake analyses of these market conditions. As changes in the marketplace occur, marketers should revise their marketing strategies accordingly. Any strategy modifications will necessitate changes to the organisation's marketing programmes.

This analytical process of marketing analyses, strategy formulation and the creation or modification of marketing programmes is necessary for existing activities and target markets. This marketing process is also required when an organisation contemplates entering new markets, launching new or replacement products, modifying the brand strategy, changing customer service practices, rethinking advertising and promotional plans, altering pricing or evaluating distribution policies. Unexpected sales patterns also require such a process of understanding, thinking and action. This is the **marketing process**: analysis of market conditions, the creation of an appropriate marketing strategy, and the development of marketing programmes designed to action the agreed strategy, as depicted in Figure 1.2. Finally, as part of this process, the implementation of the marketing strategy and its associated marketing programmes must be managed and controlled.

**Marketing process**
Analysis of market conditions, the creation of an appropriate marketing strategy, the development of marketing programmes designed to action the agreed strategy and, finally, the implementation and control of the marketing strategy and its associated marketing programmes

With an understanding of customers' needs, buying behaviour, expectations and product or brand perceptions, marketers are able to create marketing programmes likely to attract, satisfy and retain customers. With an appreciation of competitors' activities and plans, the marketing programmes are more likely to combat rivals' marketing programmes and to differentiate an organisation's product. Without an awareness of changes in the marketing environment, it is unlikely that the specified marketing programme will be sustainable in the longer term. As trading environment changes occur, it is important that an organisation's capabilities are modified in order to reflect market conditions and likely demands. The marketing analysis stage of the marketing process is, therefore, of fundamental importance.

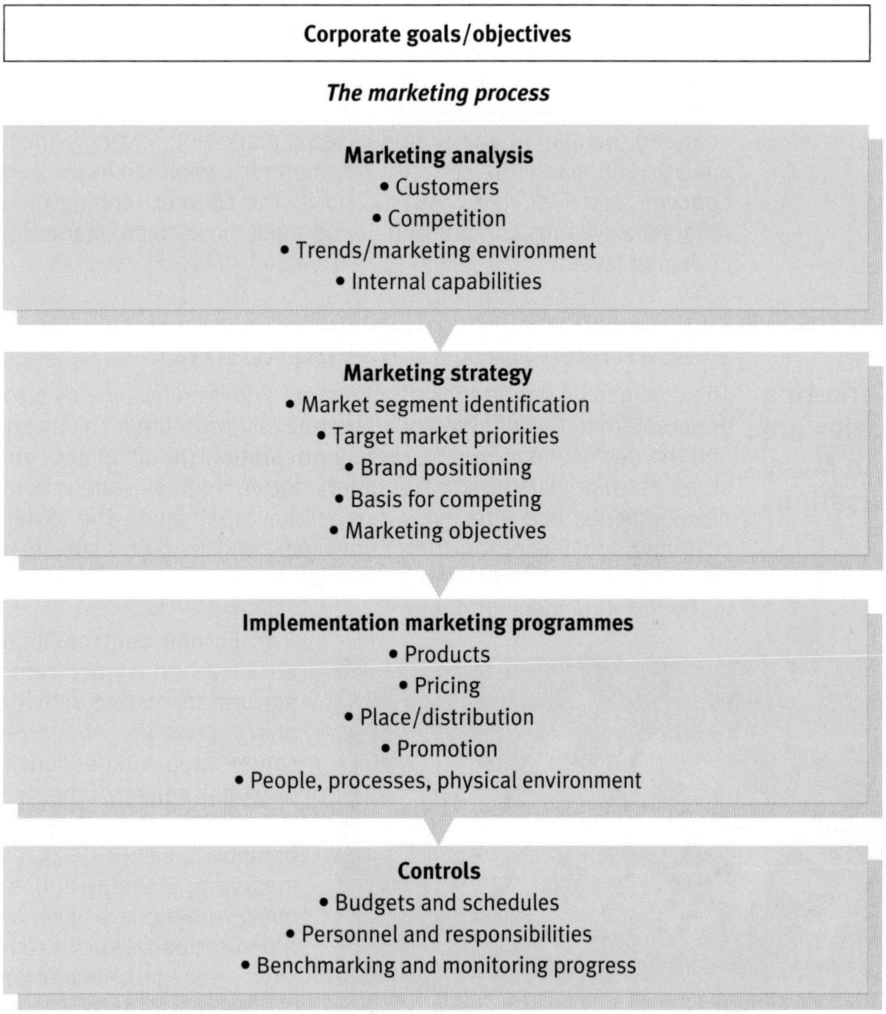


***Figure 1.2***
*The marketing process*
*Source: © Sally Dibb & Lyndon Simkin*

Equipped with an awareness of the marketplace made possible through marketing analyses, a marketing strategy may be derived. This involves selecting the opportunities to be pursued and devising an associated target market strategy. Few organisations have adequate financial, managerial and employee resources to address all of the possible marketing opportunities that exist: there must be some trade-offs. This generally involves selecting only some of the opportunities to pursue and focusing on specific target markets. Having made these decisions, marketers must ensure that they develop a compelling brand positioning and that they create a strong basis for competing versus their rivals, aimed specifically at attracting customers in the prioritised target markets. These strategic recommendations should then translate into specific marketing objectives, designed to hone the creation of marketing programmes.

In most organisations the majority of the budget, time and effort within the marketing function is devoted to creating and managing marketing programmes. These programmes revolve around specifying product, people, promotion, pricing and place (distribution channel) attributes and policies, designed to appeal to and serve those customers identified as being in the priority target market(s). In addition to these ingredients of the marketing mix, marketers of services include other ingredients, as detailed in Chapters 13 and 22. Finally, the marketing programmes must be rolled out and controlled.

Part VIII of *Marketing: Concepts and Strategies* addresses the final stage of this process, the implementation and controls phase. Parts III to VII examine extensively each of the ingredients of the marketing mix, which are the essentials for a marketing programme. However, the marketing programmes should not be created before marketers have fully analysed the market and then devised a marketing strategy. These aspects of marketing analysis and marketing strategy are, therefore, explored in the early stages of *Marketing: Concepts and Strategies*, Parts I and II. The chapter running order is also structured to reflect the syllabus content popular on most mainstream marketing modules and courses at degree level.

## The Importance of Marketing

**Marketing Activities are Used in Many Organisations**

The commercial importance of marketing and its relevance as a topic worth studying are apparent from the definition of marketing just presented. The use of marketing techniques and the development of a marketing orientation should enable an organisation to understand its customers and stakeholders better, address competitors' activities and market developments, and effectively harness its capabilities. The results should be enhanced customer satisfaction and retention, improved market share in key target markets and stronger financial performance. This section discusses several less obvious reasons why marketing should be studied.

In Europe and the United States between 25 per cent and 33 per cent of all civilian workers perform marketing activities. The marketing field offers a variety of interesting and challenging career opportunities, such as strategic planning, personal selling, advertising, packaging, transport, storage, marketing research, product development, creative design, wholesaling, retailing, marketing planning and consultancy. In addition, many individuals who work for not-for-profit organisations – such as charities or health agencies – engage in marketing activities. Marketing skills are used to promote political, cultural, religious, civic and charitable activities. The advertisement in Figure 1.3 encourages support of the British Heart Foundation, a non-profit organisation. Whether a person earns a living through marketing activities or performs them without compensation in non-business settings, marketing knowledge and skills are valuable assets. For both commercial and non-profit organisations there are needs to satisfy, exchanges to expedite, changing circumstances to monitor and decisions to make. Even a country benefits from marketing, as described in the Topical Insight box on page 15.

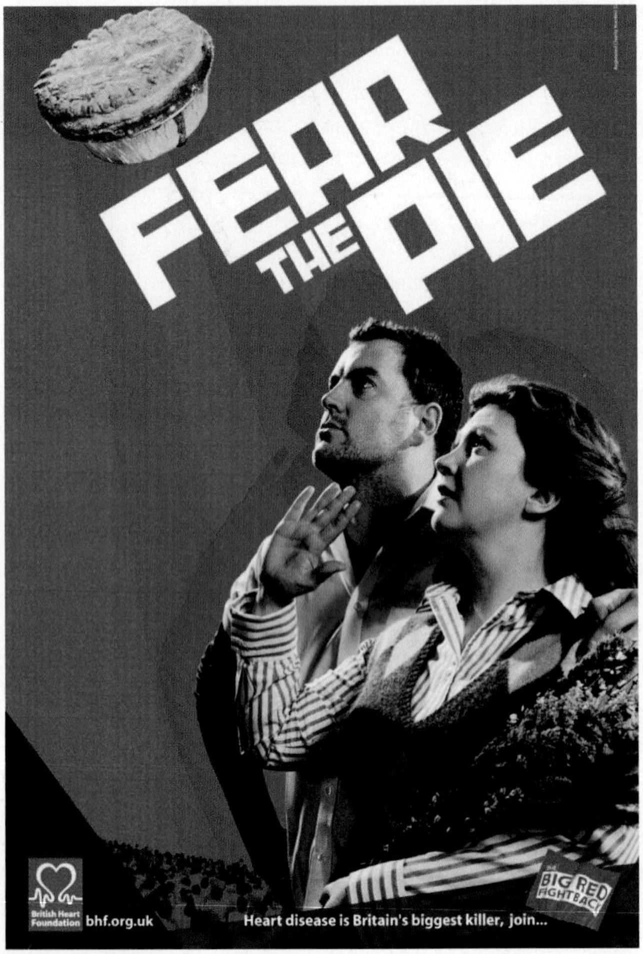


***Figure 1.3***
*Promotion of a non-profit organisation. The British Heart Foundation uses marketing to communicate its message*
*Source: Courtesy of the British Heart Foundation, Heart Week 2004 campaign*

## Topical Insight

### Ireland: Marketing a Country

How do you develop a marketing strategy for a country? This was a question faced by the Irish government during difficult times in the 1960s and 1970s. The challenge was to build the Irish economy to match the affluence enjoyed by some of its European neighbours. At the time, Ireland was viewed as being backward and unattractive for investment by international corporations. The Industrial Development Authority (IDA) played an important role in developing the country's economy, moving it away from its traditional overreliance on agriculture. Today, with well over a third of the country's GDP coming from industry, and services also accounting for approaching a third, agriculture's contribution has fallen to just 10 per cent.

Marketing and good promotion alone were not responsible for this turnaround. The Irish government realised that to attract investment from overseas it had to provide a stable economy, desirable residential suburbs, modern road and air infrastructure, state-of-the-art telecommunications and, crucially, a well-qualified, dynamic and motivated workforce. These improvements took some time to achieve, but today the companies located in Dublin and around Ireland's airports testify readily to the excellent infrastructure, communications, workforce and tax breaks. The Irish workforce is one of the best educated and most highly prized in Europe.

Having improved the amenities, infrastructure and the workforce, the perceptions of investors overseas had to be addressed. In order to instigate this change, the IDA established a clear strategy by pinpointing attractive sectors for growth and actively encouraging growth businesses in those areas. Consumer products, electronics, healthcare and financial services were some of the key targets. Once decisions about growth priorities had been made, the aim was to develop a marketing programme based around the particular assets that Ireland was able to offer. For example, promotional material focused on – among other things – the young, highly educated workforce, the low rates of corporate taxation, excellent digital and satellite telecommunications systems, and a stable currency with low inflation. The attractive countryside and vibrant cultural scene also featured prominently in the IDA's branding of Ireland.

Considerable care was taken to ensure that the propositions developed matched the requirements of the businesses targeted. This provided many overseas businesses with substantial, tangible reasons for establishing a base in Ireland, bringing with it the investment the country so badly craved. Leading computer manufacturers, pharmaceutical businesses, financial corporations and telecommunications businesses are just some of those who have located facilities in the country: over 1,000 well-known organisations have chosen Ireland ahead of other locations for their European operations.

**Sources:** Irish Embassy, London; Industrial Development Authority (IDA); 'Facts about Ireland', IDA, 1995, 1996, 1999, 2003.

## Marketing Activities are Important to Businesses and the Economy

A business organisation must sell products in order to survive and grow. Directly or indirectly, marketing activities help sell an organisation's products. By doing so, they generate financial resources that can be used to develop innovative products. New products allow a company to satisfy customers' changing needs more efficiently, which in turn enables the company to generate more profits. Charities and other not-for-profit organisations use marketing to generate revenues and funds.

Europe's highly complex economy depends heavily on marketing activities. These help produce the profits that are essential not only to the survival of individual businesses but also to the health and ultimate survival of the economy as a whole. Profits are essential to economic growth because without them businesses find it difficult, if not impossible, to buy more raw materials, recruit more employees, attract more capital and create the additional products that in turn lead to more profits.

**Marketing Knowledge Enhances Consumer Awareness**

Besides contributing to a country's economic well-being, marketing activities permeate everyone's lives. In fact, they help to improve quality of life. Studying marketing activities enables the costs, benefits and flaws of marketing to be evaluated. The need for improvement and ways to accomplish changes can be determined. For example, an unsatisfactory experience with a guarantee may lead consumers to demand that laws be enforced more strictly to make sellers fulfil their promises. Similarly, there may be the desire for more information about a product – or more accurate information – before purchase. Understanding marketing leads to the evaluation of the corrective measures – such as laws, regulations and industry guidelines – that may be required to stop unfair, misleading or unethical marketing practices. The results of the survey presented in Table 1.2 indicate that there is a considerable lack of knowledge about marketing activities, as reflected by the sizeable proportion of respondents who agree with the myths in the table.

**Marketing Costs Consume a Sizeable Proportion of Buyers' Incomes**

The study of the marketing discipline emphasises that many marketing activities are necessary to provide people with satisfying goods and services. Obviously, these marketing activities cost money. A family with a monthly income of £1000, of which £300 goes towards taxes and savings, spends about £700 on goods and services. Of this amount, typically £350 goes towards marketing activities. Clearly, if marketing expenses consume that much income, it is necessary to know how this money is used.

**Business Performance**

Marketing puts an emphasis on satisfying customers. Marketing analyses should lead a business to develop a marketing strategy that takes account of market trends, aims to satisfy customers, is aware of competitive activity and targets the right customers with a clear positioning message. In so doing, a business should benefit from customer loyalty and advantages over its rivals, while making the most efficient use of resources to effectively address the specific requirements of those markets it chooses to target. Hence, marketing should provide both a financial benefit and a greater sense of well-being for the organisation.

## The Marketing Concept and its Evolution

Some organisations have tried to be successful by buying land, building a factory, equipping it with people and machines, and then making a product that they believe consumers need. However, these organisations frequently fail to attract buyers with what they have to offer because they defined their business as 'making a product' rather than as 'helping potential customers satisfy their needs and wants'. Such organisations have failed to implement

**TABLE 1.2 POPULAR MARKETING MYTHS**

| Myths | Strongly Agree | Somewhat Agree | Neither Agree nor Disagree | Somewhat Disagree | Strongly Disagree |
|---|---|---|---|---|---|
| Marketing is selling | 14% | 34% | 26% | 18% | 8% |
| Marketers persuade | 21% | 25% | 20% | 11% | 23% |
| Dealers' profits significantly increase prices consumers pay | 21% | 32% | 12% | 8% | 27% |
| Marketing depends on advertising | 17% | 44% | 12% | 9% | 18% |
| Strategic planning has nothing to do with marketing | 19% | 19% | 21% | 17% | 24% |

**Sources:** Student surveys.

the marketing concept. It is not enough to be product-led, no matter how good the product. An organisation must be in tune with consumer or business customer requirements.

**Marketing concept**
The philosophy that an organisation should try to provide products that satisfy customers' needs through a coordinated set of activities that also allows the organisation to achieve its goals

According to the **marketing concept**, an organisation should try to provide products that satisfy customers' needs through a coordinated set of activities that also allows the organisation to achieve its goals. Customer satisfaction is the major aim of the marketing concept. First, an organisation must find out what will satisfy customers. With this information, it then attempts to create satisfying products. But the process does not end there. The organisation must continue to alter, adapt and develop products to keep pace with customers' changing desires and preferences. The marketing concept stresses the importance of customers, and emphasises that marketing activities begin and end with them.[7]

In attempting to satisfy customers, businesses must consider not only short-term, immediate needs but also broad, long-term desires. Trying to satisfy customers' current needs by sacrificing their long-term desires will only create future dissatisfaction. For instance, people want efficient, low-cost energy to power their homes and cars, yet they react adversely to energy producers that pollute the air and water, kill wildlife, or cause disease or birth defects. To meet these short- and long-term needs and desires, a company must coordinate all its activities. Production, finance, accounting, personnel and marketing departments must work together.

The marketing concept is not a second definition of marketing. It is a way of thinking: a management philosophy guiding an organisation's overall activities. This philosophy affects all the efforts of the organisation, not just marketing activities, and is strongly linked to the notion of marketing orientation. However, the marketing concept is by no means a philanthropic philosophy aimed at helping customers at the expense of the organisation. A company that adopts the marketing concept must not only satisfy its customers' objectives but also achieve its own goals, or it will not stay in business long. The overall goals of a business may be directed towards increasing profits, market share, sales or a combination of all three. The marketing concept stresses that an organisation can best achieve its goals by providing customer satisfaction. Thus, implementing the marketing concept should benefit the organisation as well as its customers.

## The Evolution of the Marketing Concept

**Production era**
The period of mass production following industrialisation

**Sales era**
The period from the mid-1920s to the early 1950s when competitive forces and the desire for high sales volume led a business to emphasise selling and the sales person in its business strategy

The marketing concept may seem an obvious and sensible approach to running a business. However, business people have not always believed that the best way to make sales and profits is to satisfy customers. A famous example is the marketing philosophy for cars widely attributed to Henry Ford in the early 1900s: 'The customers can have any colour car they want as long as it's black.' The philosophy of the marketing concept emerged in the third major era in the history of business, preceded by the **production era** and the **sales era**. Surprisingly, it took nearly 40 years after the **marketing era** began before many businesses started to adopt the marketing concept. The more advanced marketing-led companies have now entered a spin-off from the marketing era: the **relationship marketing era**.

**The Production Era** During the second half of the nineteenth century, the Industrial Revolution was in full swing in Europe and the United States. Electricity, railways, the division of labour, the assembly line and mass production made it possible to manufacture products more efficiently. With new technology and new ways of using labour, products poured into the marketplace, where consumer demand for manufactured goods was strong. This production orientation continued into the early part of the last century, encouraged by the scientific management movement that championed rigidly structured jobs and pay based on output.

**The Sales Era** In the 1920s, the strong consumer demand for products subsided. Businesses realised that products, which by this time could be made quite efficiently,

**Marketing era**
The period in which product and aggressive selling were no longer seen to suffice if customers either did not desire a product or preferred a rival brand, and in which customer needs were identified and satisfied

**Relationship marketing era**
The current period, in which the focus is not only on expediting the single transaction but on developing ongoing relationships with customers

would have to be 'sold' to consumers. From the mid-1920s to the early 1950s, businesses viewed sales as the major means of increasing profits. As a result, this period came to have a sales orientation. Business people believed that the most important marketing activities were personal selling and advertising.

**The Marketing Era** By the early 1950s, some business people began to recognise that efficient production and extensive promotion of products did not guarantee that customers would buy them. Businesses found that they first had to determine what customers wanted and then produce it, rather than simply making products first and then trying to change customers' needs to correspond to what was being produced. As organisations realised the importance of knowing customers' needs, businesses entered into the marketing era – the era of customer orientation.[8]

**The Relationship Marketing Era** By the 1990s, many organisations had grasped the basics of the marketing concept and had created marketing functions. However, their view of marketing was often largely transaction based. The priority for marketing was to identify customer needs, determine priority target markets and achieve sales through marketing programmes. The focus was on the individual transaction or exchange. It should be recognised that long-term success and market share gains depend on such transactions, but also on maintaining a customer's loyalty and on repeatedly gaining sales from existing customers. This requires ongoing, committed, reassuring and tailored relationship-building marketing programmes.

Relationship marketing refers to 'long-term, mutually beneficial arrangements in which both the buyer and seller focus on value enhancement through the creation of more satisfying exchanges'.[9] Relationship marketing continually deepens the buyer's trust in the company and, as the customer's confidence grows, this in turn increases the company's understanding of the customer's needs. Successful marketers respond to customers' needs and strive to increase value to buyers over time. Eventually this interaction becomes a solid relationship that allows for cooperation and mutual dependency.

As the era of relationship orientation has developed, it has been suggested that it is not only relationships with customers that are important. Suppliers, agents, distributors, recruiters, referral bodies (such as independent financial advisers recommending financial services companies' products), influencers (such as government departments, national banks or the EU), all should be 'marketed to' in order to ensure their support, understanding and resources. The internal workforce must be motivated and provided with a clear understanding of a company's target market strategy, marketing mix activities and, indeed, of the corporate strategy and planned direction. Hence, the current era is moving away from transaction-based marketing and towards relationship marketing.[10]

## Implementing the Marketing Concept

A philosophy may sound reasonable and look good on paper, but that does not mean it can be put into practice easily. The marketing concept is a case in point. To implement it, an organisation must focus on some general conditions and recognise several problems. Because of these conditions and problems, the marketing concept has yet to be fully accepted by some businesses.

Because the marketing concept affects all types of business activities, not just marketing activities, the top management of an organisation must adopt it wholeheartedly. High-level executives must incorporate the marketing concept into their philosophies of business management so completely that it becomes the basis for all the goals and decisions that they set for their companies. They should also convince other members of the organisation to accept the changes in policies and operations that flow from their acceptance of the marketing concept. Costs and budgetary controls are important, products and manufacturing essential, and personnel management necessary; but all are to no avail if the organisation's products or services are not desired by the targeted customers.

As a first step, management must establish an information system that enables it to discover customers' real needs and to use the information to create satisfying products. Because such a system is usually expensive, management must be willing to commit money and time for development and maintenance. Without an adequate information system, an organisation cannot be customer oriented.

Management's second major task is to restructure the organisation. If a company is to satisfy its customers' objectives as well as its own, it must coordinate all its activities. To achieve this, the internal operations and the overall objectives of one or more departments may need restructuring. If the head of the marketing unit is not a member of the organisation's top-level management, he or she should be. Some departments may have to be abolished and new ones created. Implementing the marketing concept demands the support not only of top management but also of managers and staff at all levels within the organisation.

Even when the basic conditions of establishing an information system and reorganising the company are met, the business's new marketing approach may not work perfectly, for the following reasons.

- There is a limit to a company's ability to satisfy customers' needs for a particular product. In a mass-production economy, most business organisations cannot tailor products to fit the exact needs of each customer.
- Although a company may attempt to learn what customers want, it may be unable to do so, and when the organisation does identify customers' needs correctly, it often has a difficult time developing a product that satisfies those needs. Many companies spend considerable time and money researching customers' needs and yet still create some products that do not sell well.
- By striving to satisfy one particular segment of society, a company sometimes dissatisfies other segments. Certainly, government and non-business organisations also experience this problem.
- A business organisation may have difficulty maintaining employee morale during any restructuring needed to coordinate the activities of various departments. Management must clearly explain the reasons for the various changes and communicate its own enthusiasm for the marketing concept.

Adoption of the marketing philosophy takes time, resources, endurance and commitment.

# The Essentials of Marketing

**Marketing Analyses**

Already, from these brief introductory comments, it should be evident that marketing can enhance an organisation's understanding of its customers, competitors, market trends, threats and opportunities. Marketing should, therefore, be able to direct an organisation's target market strategy, product development and communication to its distribution channels and customers. However, in order to contribute in these ways, marketing personnel must have marketing intelligence about these issues, which inevitably leads to marketing analysis.

The core aspects of marketing analysis should be:

- customers
- competitors
- marketing environment forces
- the organisation's capabilities and marketing assets.

As will be seen later in this book, there are many additional marketing analyses, but these are the essential building blocks for the development of marketing strategies and the creation of marketing programmes. The majority of the chapters in Parts I and II of

*Marketing: Concepts and Strategies* address these marketing analyses, which are the foundation of the marketing process.

# Marketing Strategy

To achieve the broad goal of expediting desirable exchanges, an organisation's marketing managers are responsible for developing and managing marketing strategies. Specifically, a **marketing strategy** encompasses selecting opportunities to pursue, analysing a target market (the group of people the organisation wants to reach), and creating and maintaining an appropriate **marketing mix** (the tactical 'toolkit' of product, place [distribution], promotion, price and people) that will satisfy those customers in the target market. A marketing strategy articulates a plan for the best use of the organisation's resources and directs the required tactics to meet its objectives.

**Marketing strategy**
The selection of which marketing opportunities to pursue, analysis of target market(s), and the creation and maintenance of an appropriate marketing mix that will satisfy those people in the target market(s)

**Marketing mix**
The tactical 'toolkit' of the marketing programme; product, place/distribution, promotion, price and people variables that an organisation can control in order to appeal to the target market and facilitate satisfying exchange

When marketing managers attempt to develop and manage marketing activities, they must deal with three broad sets of variables:

1 those relating to the marketing mix
2 those inherent in the accompanying target market strategy
3 those that make up the marketing environment.

The marketing mix decision variables – product, place/distribution, promotion, price and people – and the target market strategy variables are factors over which an organisation has control. As Figure 1.4 shows, these variables are constructed around the buyer or consumer. The marketing environment variables are political, legal, regulatory, societal/green, technological, and economic and competitive forces. These factors are subject

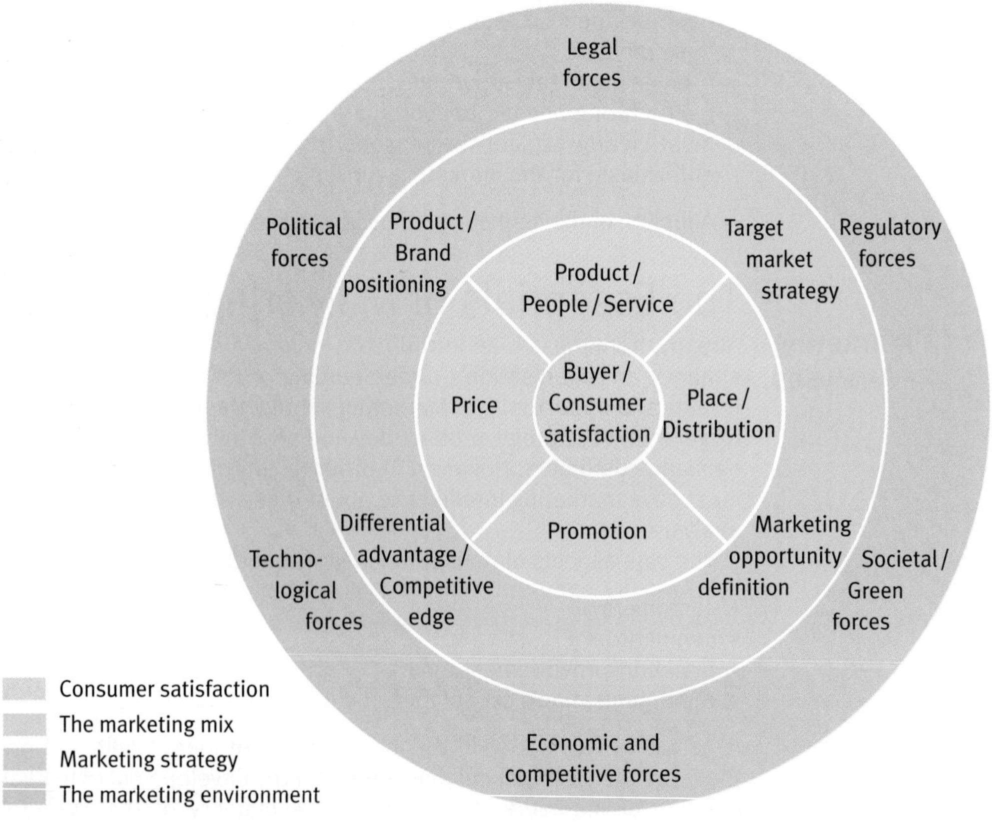


***Figure 1.4***
*The marketing environment, marketing strategy, the marketing mix and customer satisfaction; consumers and businesses are affected by the forces of the marketing environment; businesses must determine a marketing strategy, implemented through the ingredients of the marketing mix, which aims to satisfy targeted customers*

to less control by an organisation, but they affect buyers' needs as well as marketing managers' decisions regarding marketing mix variables.

To develop and manage marketing strategies, marketers must focus on several marketing tasks: marketing opportunity analysis and marketing analyses, the determination of a marketing strategy and target market selection, marketing mix development and management of the programmes that facilitate implementation of the marketing strategy. Figure 1.5 lists these tasks, along with the chapters of this book in which they are discussed.

## Marketing Opportunity Analysis

**Marketing opportunity**
One that exists when circumstances allow an organisation to take action towards reaching a particular group of consumer or business customers

A **marketing opportunity** exists when circumstances allow an organisation to take action towards reaching a particular group of customers. An opportunity provides a favourable chance or opening for a company to generate sales from identifiable markets for specific products or services. For example, during a heatwave, marketers of electric fans have a marketing opportunity – an opportunity to reach customers who need electric fans. Various 'no frills' airlines have entered the rapidly growing market for low-priced scheduled air travel, as consumers have demonstrated their liking for this alternative to high-priced full-service airlines or charters. Bluetooth connectivity is creating numerous opportunities for computer manufacturers and on-line service providers, as wireless access to the Internet offers users greater flexibility. Most new products or services reflect the identification by marketers of a marketing opportunity.

Marketers should be capable of recognising and analysing marketing opportunities. An organisation's long-term survival depends on developing products that satisfy its customers. Few organisations can assume that products popular today will interest buyers ten years from now. A marketing-led organisation can choose among several alternatives for continued product development through which it can achieve its objectives and satisfy buyers. It can modify existing products (for example, by reducing salt content and additives in foods to address increasing health consciousness among customers), introduce new products (such as Windows XP, pay-as-you-talk mobile phone packages or Hitachi digital flat-screen TVs) and delete some that customers no longer want (such as disc cameras or cassette decks). A company may also try to market its products to a greater number of customers, persuade current customers to use more of a product, or perhaps expand marketing activities into additional countries. Diversification into new product offerings through internal efforts or through acquisitions of other organisations may be viable options for a company. For example, Sony has established itself as a major supplier of business laptop and desktop computers, diversifying from its base of consumer home entertainment products; while Virgin has entered financial services. An organisation's ability to pursue any of these alternatives success-fully depends on its internal characteristics and the forces within the marketing environment. These strategic options are discussed further in Chapter 2.

## Internal Organisational Factors

The primary factors inside an organisation that should be considered when analysing marketing opportunities and devising target market strategies are organisational objectives, financial resources, managerial skills, organisational strengths and weaknesses, and cost structures. Most organisations have overall organisational objectives. Some marketing opportunities may be consistent with these objectives; others may not, and to pursue them is hazardous. Frequently, the pursuit of such opportunities ends in failure, or forces the company to alter its long-term objectives. The links with corporate strategy and an organisation's mission are discussed in Chapter 2.

Obviously, a business's financial resources constrain the type of marketing opportunities it can pursue. Typically, an organisation does not develop projects that can bring economic catastrophe. In some situations, however, a company must invest in a high-risk opportunity, because the costs of not pursuing the project are so great. Thus, despite an economic recession and reduced house and road building, construction equipment manufacturer JCB continued to launch new ranges and enter new markets. It developed and

*Figure 1.5* Marketing tasks: analysis, strategy and programmes for implementation and control

| Marketing Opportunity Analysis | Chapters |
|---|---|
| • Marketing strategy | 2 |
| • The marketing environment | 3, 4 |
| • Marketing in international markets | 5 |
| • Consumer buying behaviour | 6 |
| • Organisational markets and business-to-business buying behaviour | 7 |
| • Marketing research and information systems | 9 |

↓

| Target Market Strategy | Chapters |
|---|---|
| • Marketing strategy | 2 |
| • Market segmentation and prioritisation | 8 |
| • Product and brand positioning | 8 |
| • Competitive advantage | 2, 8 |

↓

| Marketing Mix Development | Chapters |
|---|---|
| • Product, branding, packaging and service decisions | 10–13 |
| • Place (distribution and marketing channel) decisions | 14–16 |
| • Promotion (marketing communications) decisions | 17–19 |
| • Pricing decisions | 20, 21 |
| • Manipulating the marketing mix | 22 |

↓

| Marketing Management | Chapters |
|---|---|
| • Marketing planning and forecasting sales potential | 23 |
| • Implementing strategies, internal marketing relationships and measuring performance | 24 |
| • Marketing ethics and social responsibility | 25 |

launched its Compact Division, emphasising mini excavators, at a cost of millions, to respond to changing market requirements. As the market for construction equipment became more buoyant JCB, with its new ranges, was well placed to take advantage of this.

The skills and experience of management also limit the types of opportunity that an organisation can pursue. A company must be particularly cautious when exploring the possibility of entering unfamiliar markets with new products. If it lacks appropriate managerial skills and experience, the business can sometimes acquire them by recruiting additional managerial personnel. Most organisations at some time are limited in their growth plans by a lack of sufficient managers with suitable skills and market insights.

Like people, most organisations have strengths and weaknesses. Because of the types of operation in which a company is engaged, it will normally have employees with specialist skills and technological information. Such characteristics are a strength when launching marketing strategies that require them. However, they may be a weakness if the company tries to compete in new, unrelated product areas. A major IT services business altered its strategy to focus on winning more business for IT infrastructure management from existing clients rather than from attracting new clients. This required a different set of selling skills, and managers with the ability to nurture relationships and exploit emerging sales opportunities within a client company. The revised target market strategy resulted in redundancies among the existing salesforce, and the recruitment of account managers with the requisite skills and interpersonal abilities.

An organisation's cost structure may be an advantage if the company pursues certain marketing opportunities, and a disadvantage if it pursues others. Such factors as geographic location, employee skills, access to raw materials, and type of equipment and facilities can all affect cost structure. Previous investment levels and priorities will have ramifications for the current cost structure. As discussed in Chapter 2, the cost structure of an organisation may provide a competitive advantage over rivals, or may place a business at a competitive disadvantage.

## Marketing Environment Forces

The marketing environment, which consists of political, legal, regulatory, societal/Green, technological, and economic and competitive forces, surrounds the buyer (consumer) and the marketing mix (see Figure 1.4). Each major environmental force is explored in considerable depth in Chapter 3. Marketers know that they cannot predict changes in the marketing environment with certainty. Even so, over the years marketers have become more systematic in taking these forces into account when planning their competitive actions.[11] A business that fails to monitor the forces of the marketing environment is likely to miss out on emerging opportunities at the expense of rivals with the foresight to examine these market drivers.

Marketing environment forces affect a marketer's ability to facilitate and expedite exchanges, in four general ways.

1. They influence customers by affecting their lifestyles, standards of living, preferences and needs for products. Because a marketing manager tries to develop and adjust the marketing mix to satisfy consumers or business customers, the effects of environmental forces on customers also have an indirect impact on the marketing mix components.
2. Marketing environment forces help determine whether and how a marketing manager can perform certain marketing activities. They may force marketers to cease certain practices or to adopt new strategies.
3. Environmental forces may affect a marketing manager's decisions and actions by influencing buyers' reactions to the company's marketing mix.
4. Marketing environment forces may provide an organisation with a window of opportunity over rivals that fail to notice the market development or that take no action themselves. Equally, market drivers may provide competitors with such an opportunity ahead of a marketer's own organisation.

Although forces in the marketing environment are sometimes viewed as 'uncontrollables', a marketing manager may be able to influence one or more of them. However, marketing environment forces fluctuate quickly and dramatically, which is one reason marketing is so interesting and challenging. Because these forces are highly interrelated, a change in one may cause others to change. For example, from Freons in fridges to additives in foods, most consumers have become increasingly aware of health and environmental issues. Manufacturers have altered product specifications and production methods. Legislators and regulatory bodies have also responded to expert and consumer opinions with new regulations and informal agreements, forcing companies to rethink their manufacturing and marketing policies.

Even though changes in the marketing environment produce uncertainty for marketers and at times impede marketing efforts, they can also create opportunities. After the 1989 oil spills, for example, more companies began developing and marketing products designed to contain or dissipate spilled oil. The BSE beef crisis gave producers of other meats significant opportunities. Environmental concerns have encouraged car manufacturers to develop emission-free engines. The growth in mobile phone use and improvements to network technology have enabled various information providers to tailor services to sports fans or stock-market investors. Thus a marketer must be aware of changes in environmental forces not only to adjust to and influence them but also to capitalise on the opportunities they provide. The marketing environment is discussed more fully in Chapters 2 and 3. The Topical Insight box below illustrates the impact of the marketing environment, in this case upon food products.

## Topical Insight

### The Marketing Environment Offers Threats and Opportunities: Miller Lite Versus Slimfast

During the early part of the decade, the Atkins diet hit the bookshelves, colour supplements and couches of day-time television. Thousands of consumers opted to try this new approach to losing weight and feeling healthier. While some experts are concerned about the longer-term impact of such an approach to dieting, other reports seem to support the loss of weight from cutting the intake of carbohydrates. Manufacturers have been quick to capitalise on this trend, with low-carb beers, breads and other foods quickly appearing on supermarket shelves. This diet has grown in popularity at a time when there is growing concern among policy-makers and health workers, widely publicised by the media, into childhood and adult obesity, increasing diabetes and heart disease, and the likely implications for the future provision of healthcare.

While certain fast-food chains and food brands have reacted by launching healthier menus or bringing out low-carb versions of popular brands, for other companies commercial prospects are not looking good. McDonald's has reduced the size of its portions, added fruit and salads and even Quorn burgers. Coca-Cola has launched a low-carb cola called C2 and Nestlé has created low-carb Rolos and Kit-Kats. For Krispy Kreme, however, there was a profits warning to investors as a result of consumers avoiding the carbohydrates in its doughnuts. By contrast, at Tiffin Bites, the Indian fast-food chain, its low-carb meal has become a best-seller, generating gratefully received positive publicity for the company. The Miller beer brand has been rejuvenated thanks to the low-carb content of Miller Lite, leading to significant increases in profitability.

Atkins is a health-driven diet phenomenon, so perhaps one of its biggest victims may come as something of a surprise. A leading brand for dieters for many years has been Slimfast, with its range of slimming food aids and supplements. Slimfast had become one of Unilever's leading brands. Sales of Slimfast plummeted as slimmers viewed the benefits of Atkins with glee. For Slimfast's marketers the social and regulatory trends had been very supportive, and the growth prospects for the brand appeared to be strongly encouraged by the forces of the marketing environment. The popularity of an alternative way of thinking for dieters offered by Atkins led to social and competitive marketing environment forces that seriously damaged the Slimfast brand and its market potential.

**Sources:** Unilever plc, 2004; Boots, 2004; 'Nestlé gambles on low-carb craze', *Marketing*, 3 June 2004, p. 16; Emily Rogers in *Marketing*, 8 January 2004, p. 4; Ben Bold in *Marketing*, 11 December 2003, p. 8.

### Target Market Selection

**Target market**
A group of people for whom a company creates and maintains a marketing mix that specifically fits the needs and preferences of that group

A **target market** is a group of people for whom a company creates and maintains a marketing mix that specifically fits the needs and preferences of that group.[12] When choosing a target market, marketing managers try to evaluate possible markets to see how entering them would affect the company's sales, costs and profits. Marketers also attempt to determine whether the organisation has the resources to produce a marketing mix that meets the needs of a particular target market, and whether satisfying those needs is consistent with the company's overall objectives and mission. The size and number of competitors already marketing products in possible target markets are also of concern.

Marketing managers may define a target market as a vast number of people or as a relatively small group. For example, Ford produces cars suitable for much of the population – although specific models are quite narrowly targeted, such as the family runaround Focus or the executive Mondeo. Porsche focuses its marketing effort on a small proportion of the population, believing that it can compete more effectively by concentrating on an affluent target market desiring sports coupés. Although a business may concentrate its efforts on one target market through a single marketing mix, organisations often focus on several target markets by developing and deploying multiple marketing mixes. Reebok, for example, markets different types of shoes to meet the specific needs of joggers, walkers, aerobics enthusiasts and other groups.

Target market selection is crucial to generating productive marketing efforts. At times, products and organisations fail because marketers do not identify the appropriate customer groups at which to aim their efforts. Organisations that try to be all things to all people typically end up not satisfying the needs of any customer group very well. It is important for an organisation's management to designate which customer groups the company is trying to serve and to have adequate information about these customers. The identification and analysis of a target market provide a foundation on which a marketing mix can be developed.

## Marketing Programmes

In order to make the devised marketing strategy a reality, marketers must specify a set of marketing mix ingredients that, collectively, become the marketing programme designed to implement the agreed marketing strategy. These marketing mix decisions occupy the majority of marketing personnel for most of their time, and account for most of a marketing department's budget. However, as previously explained, before the marketing mix is specified, marketers should undertake sufficient marketing analyses and reflect the findings of these analyses in their marketing strategy.

### Marketing Mix Development

Traditionally, the marketing mix was deemed to consist of four major components: product, place (distribution), promotion and price. Increasingly, a fifth component is viewed as 'people', who provide customer service and interact with customers and organisations within the supply chain. These components are called 'marketing mix decision variables' because a marketing manager decides which type of each component to use and in what amounts. A primary goal of a marketing manager is to create and maintain a marketing mix that satisfies consumers' needs for a general product type. Note that in Figure 1.4, the marketing mix is built around the buyer – as is stressed by the marketing concept and definition of marketing. Bear in mind, too, that the forces of the marketing environment affect the marketing mix variables in many ways.

Marketing mix variables are often viewed as controllable variables because they can be changed. However, there are limits to how much these variables can be altered. For example, because of economic conditions or government regulations, a manager may not be free to adjust prices daily. Changes in sizes, colours, shapes and designs of most tangible goods are expensive; therefore such product features cannot be altered very often. In addition, promotional campaigns and the methods used to distribute products ordinarily cannot be changed overnight. People, too, require training and motivating, and cannot be recruited or sacked overnight.

Marketing managers must develop a marketing mix that precisely matches the needs of the people – or organisations in business-to-business marketing – in the target market. Before they can do so, they have to collect in-depth, up-to-date information about those needs. The information might include data about the age, income, ethnic origin, sex and educational level of people in the target market; their preferences for product features; their attitudes towards competitors' products; and the frequency and intensity with which they use the product. Armed with these kinds of data, marketing managers are better able to develop a product, service package, distribution system, promotion programme and price that will satisfy the people in the target market.

This section looks more closely at the decisions and activities related to each marketing mix variable (product, place/distribution, promotion, price and people – the '5Ps' of the marketing mix). Table 1.1 contains a list of the decisions and activities associated with each marketing mix variable.

**Product variable**
The aspect of the marketing mix that deals with researching consumers' product wants and designing a product with the desired characteristics

**The Product Variable** A product can be a good, a service or an idea. The **product variable** is the aspect of the marketing mix that deals with researching consumers' product wants and designing a product with the desired characteristics. It also involves the creation or alteration of packaging and brand names, and may include decisions about guarantees, repair services and customer support. The actual manufacturing of products is not a marketing activity, but marketing-oriented businesses look to marketers to specify product development requirements that reflect customer needs and evolving expectations.

Product-variable decisions and related activities are important because they directly involve creating products and services that satisfy consumers' needs and wants. To maintain a satisfying set of products that will help an organisation achieve its goals, a marketer must be able to develop new products, modify existing ones and eliminate those that no longer satisfy buyers or yield acceptable profits. For example, after realising that competitors were capturing large shares of the low-calorie market, Heinz introduced new product items under its Weight Watchers name. To reflect greater use of microwave ovens, rice company Tilda introduced its Rizazz range of quick-cook microwavable sachets.

**Place/distribution variable**
The aspect of the marketing mix that deals with making products available in the quantities desired to as many customers as possible and keeping the total inventory, transport and storage costs as low as possible

**The Place/Distribution Variable** To satisfy consumers, products must be available at the right time and in a convenient location. In dealing with the **place/distribution variable,** a marketing manager seeks to make products available in the quantities desired to as many customers as possible, and to keep the total inventory, transport and storage costs as low as possible. A marketing manager may become involved in selecting and motivating intermediaries (wholesalers, retailers and dealers), establishing and maintaining inventory control procedures, and developing and managing transport and storage systems.

**Promotion variable**
The aspect of the marketing mix that relates to activities used to inform one or more groups of people about an organisation and its products

**The Promotion Variable** The **promotion variable** relates to communication activities that are used to inform one or more groups of people about an organisation and its products. Promotion can be aimed at increasing public awareness of an organisation and of new or existing products. In addition, promotion can serve to educate consumers about product features or to urge people to take a particular stance on a political or social issue. It may also be used to keep interest strong in an established product that has been available for decades. The advertisement in Figure 1.6 is an example. Marketers increasingly refer to the promotion variable in the marketing mix as 'marketing communications'.

**Price variable**
The aspect of the marketing mix that relates to activities associated with establishing pricing policies and determining product prices

**The Price Variable** The **price variable** relates to activities associated with establishing pricing policies and determining product prices. Price is a critical component of the marketing mix because consumers and business customers are concerned about the value

***Figure 1.6***
*Promoting an established brand. Champagne house Moët & Chandon uses its heritage in its advertising to reinforce its brand appeal*
*Source: Courtesy of Moët Hennessy UK Ltd*

obtained in an exchange. Price is often used as a competitive tool; in fact, extremely intense price competition sometimes leads to price wars. For example, airlines like Aer Lingus, British Airways and Virgin Atlantic are engaged in ruthless price cutting in the battle for transatlantic routes. Price can also help to establish a product's image. For instance, if Chanel tried to sell Chanel No. 5 in a two-litre bottle for £3 or €4, consumers would probably not buy it because the low price would destroy the prestigious image of this deluxe brand.

**People variable**
The aspect of the marketing mix that reflects the level of customer service, advice, sales support and after-sales back-up required, involving recruitment policies, training, retention and motivation of key personnel

**The People Variable** Product, place/distribution, promotion and price are traditionally the principal elements of the marketing mix: the '4Ps'. Marketers of services include *people* as a core element, along with other ingredients (see Chapters 13 and 22). Whether part of the product element or a separate element of the marketing mix, there is no doubt that people are important. As marketers, they manipulate the rest of the marketing mix. As intermediaries in the marketing channel, they help make products and services available to the marketplace. As consumers or business purchasers, they create the need for the field of marketing. In the marketing mix, the **people variable** reflects the level of customer service, advice, sales support and after-sales back-up required, involving recruitment policies, training, retention and motivation of key personnel. For many products and most services, personnel interface directly with the intended purchaser and are often perceived by such consumers as being part and parcel of the product offering.

Developing and maintaining an effective marketing mix is a major requirement for a strong marketing strategy. Thus, as indicated in Figure 1.5, a large proportion of this book

(Chapters 10–22) focuses on the concepts, decisions and activities associated with the components of the marketing mix. It is the marketing mix that readers, as consumers, will most frequently have experienced for products and services purchased. It is important to remember, however, that analysis must precede the development of a marketing strategy, which in turn must be formulated before the marketing mix is determined for a product or a service.

## Marketing Management

**Marketing management**
A process of planning, organising, implementing and controlling marketing activities to facilitate and expedite exchanges effectively and efficiently

**Marketing management** is the process of planning, organising, implementing and controlling marketing activities to facilitate and expedite exchanges effectively and efficiently. Effectiveness and efficiency are important dimensions of this definition. *Effectiveness* is the degree to which an exchange helps achieve an organisation's objectives. *Efficiency* is the minimisation of resources an organisation must spend to achieve a specific level of desired exchanges. Thus the overall goal of marketing management is to facilitate highly desirable exchanges and to minimise as much as possible the costs of doing so.

Marketing planning is a systematic process of assessing opportunities and resources, determining marketing objectives, developing a marketing strategy and developing plans for implementation and control. Planning determines when and how marketing activities will be performed and who is to perform them. It forces marketing managers to think ahead, to establish objectives and to consider future marketing activities. Effective marketing planning also reduces or eliminates daily crises.

Organising marketing activities refers to developing the internal structure of the marketing unit. The structure is the key to directing marketing activities. The marketing unit can be organised by function, product, region, type of customer or a combination of all four.

Proper implementation of marketing plans hinges on coordination of marketing activities, motivation of marketing personnel and effective communication within the unit. Marketing managers must motivate marketing personnel, coordinate their activities and integrate their activities, both with those in other areas of the company and with the marketing efforts of personnel in external organisations, such as advertising agencies and marketing research businesses. An organisation's communication system must allow the marketing manager to stay in contact with high-level management, with managers of other functional areas within the company and with personnel involved in marketing activities both inside and outside the organisation.

The marketing control process consists of establishing performance standards, evaluating actual performance by comparing it with established standards, and reducing the difference between desired and actual performance. An effective control process has the following four requirements.

1 The control process should ensure a rate of information flow that allows the marketing manager to quickly detect differences between actual and planned levels of performance.
2 The control process must accurately monitor different kinds of activities and be flexible enough to accommodate changes.
3 The control process must be economical so that its costs are low relative to the costs that would arise if there were no controls.
4 Finally, the control process should be designed so that both managers and subordinates can understand it. To maintain effective marketing control, an organisation needs to develop a comprehensive control process that evaluates marketing operations at regular intervals. Chapters 23 and 24 examine the planning, organisation, implementation and control of marketing activities in greater detail.

## The Organisation of This Book

The structure of this book adheres to the principle that it is important to analyse markets and marketing opportunities, then develop marketing strategies and construct marketing programmes that implement the desired marketing strategy, before ensuring suitable controls are in place to manage the roll-out of the strategy and programmes: the marketing process. Marketing analyses develop a thorough understanding of the marketplace – particularly customers, competitors and market trends. This knowledge of the marketplace provides a sound basis from which to devise marketing strategies. These strategies should determine marketing opportunities to pursue, identify attractive target markets, and develop a clear brand positioning and basis for competing. In order to implement the recommended target market strategy, marketing programmes must be designed with marketing mix combinations and control processes to ensure effective implementation. This marketing process, as presented in Figure 1.2, is fundamental to sound marketing practice.

### What Does Each Part of This Book Cover?

The first two parts of *Marketing: Concepts and Strategies*, therefore, address the essential marketing analyses, marketing opportunity analysis and target market selection:

- Part I – Marketing Defined and Marketing in Context
- Part II – Understanding and Targeting Customers.

The next five parts examine in detail the core ingredients of the marketing mix. These are the tactical marketing activities at the heart of marketing programmes that take a product or service to the targeted customers:

- Part III – Product, Branding, Packaging and Service Decisions
- Part IV – Place (Distribution and Marketing Channel) Decisions
- Part V – Promotion (Marketing Communications) Decisions
- Part VI – Pricing Decisions
- Part VII – Manipulating the Marketing Mix.

The implementation issues of effective marketing management are discussed in the penultimate part of the book. This set of chapters returns to the core issues of implementing a marketing strategy, and discusses marketing planning, implementing strategies, and the important consideration of ethical and social responsibility concerns in marketing:

- Part VIII – Marketing Management.

The final part of *Marketing: Concepts and Strategies* includes material designed to help students to tackle case studies as part of their studies, prepare for examinations and seek careers in marketing:

- Part IX – Studying and Working in Marketing.

*Marketing: Concepts and Strategies* also offers:

- an indexed margin/glossary of key terms
- full subject and name indexing
- extended cases to enhance readers' understanding of key topics
- detailed illustrative examples in every chapter
- up-to-date statistics for the marketing industry
- support material on its own website: www.dibbmarketing.com

## Further Reading

Readers may find the following books useful.

*Marketing Briefs: a Study and Revision Guide,* Sally Dibb and Lyndon Simkin (Oxford: Elsevier Butterworth-Heinemann), 2004.
As implied in the title, this is a revision aid, complete with brief overviews of concepts, illustrative examples and cases, trial questions and revision guidance.

*The Marketing Casebook*, Sally Dibb and Lyndon Simkin (London: Thomson), 2001.
For readers requiring concise summaries of essential concepts and explanatory applied cases.

*The Marketing Planning Workbook*, Sally Dibb, Lyndon Simkin and John Bradley (London: Thomson), 2001.
Aimed at marketing practitioners and offering a step-by-step guide to undertaking marketing planning.

*The Market Segmentation Workbook*, Sally Dibb and Lyndon Simkin (London: Thomson), 2001.
Aimed at marketing practitioners undertaking market segmentation and devising a target market strategy.

# Summary

Organisations that practise marketing do not necessarily have a *marketing orientation*. Organisations with a marketing orientation have a sound awareness of customers' needs and buying behaviour, of competitors' offerings and strategies, and of market trends. They also take steps to ensure they know how these market conditions will evolve. In addition, they orientate their operational practices and coordinate their inter-functional thinking around these market conditions. In order to have a marketing orientation, it is necessary to adopt the concepts and techniques described in *Marketing: Concepts and Strategies*. To practise marketing and to benefit from the activities of marketing, however, it is not necessary for an organisation to have a fully developed marketing orientation. A few managers, whether or not in an organisation's marketing function, utilising the concepts described in this book, will make a significant contribution to the organisation's fortunes and its understanding of its marketplace.

- *Marketing* consists of individual and organisational activities that facilitate and expedite satisfying exchange relationships in a dynamic environment through the creation, distribution, promotion and pricing of goods, services and ideas.

- Marketing opportunity analysis involves reviewing both internal factors (organisational objectives and mission, financial resources, managerial skills, organisational strengths, organisational weaknesses and cost structures) and external ones in the *marketing environment* (the political, legal, regulatory, societal/Green, technological, and economic and competitive forces).

- An *exchange* is the provision or transfer of goods, services and ideas in return for something of value. Four conditions must exist for an exchange to occur: (1) two or more individuals, groups or organisations must participate; (2) each party must have something of value desired by the other; (3) each party must be willing to give up what it has in order to receive the value held by the other; and (4) the parties to the exchange must be able to communicate with each other to make their 'somethings of value' available. In an exchange, products are traded either for other products or for financial resources, such as cash or credit. Through the exchange, the recipient (the customer) and the provider (the business) must be satisfied (leading to *customer satisfaction*). *Products* can be *goods, services or ideas.*

- The *marketing process* is the analysis of market conditions, the creation of an appropriate marketing strategy, the development of marketing programmes designed to action the agreed strategy and, finally, the implementation and control of the marketing strategy and its associated marketing programme(s). Organisations contemplating entering new markets or territories, launching new products or brands, modifying their strategies or manipulating their marketing programmes, should use this sequential analytical process. Even steady-state markets and products encounter changing market conditions, and marketers should continually analyse and then modify their marketing strategies and marketing programmes accordingly.

» It is important to study marketing because it permeates society. Marketing activities are performed in both business and non-business organisations. Moreover, marketing activities help business organisations generate profits and income, the life-blood of an economy. The study of marketing enhances consumer awareness. Marketing costs absorb about half of what the consumer spends. Marketing, practised well, improves business performance.

» The *marketing concept* is a management philosophy that prompts a business organisation to try to satisfy customers' needs through a coordinated set of activities that also allows the organisation to achieve its goals. Customer satisfaction is the major objective of the marketing concept. The philosophy of the marketing concept emerged during the 1950s, as the *marketing era* succeeded the *production era* and the *sales era*. As the 1990s progressed into the *relationship marketing era*, a focus on transaction-based marketing was replaced by relationship marketing. To make the marketing concept work, top management must accept it as an overall management philosophy. Implementing the marketing concept requires an efficient information system and sometimes the restructuring of the organisation.

» The essentials of marketing are that there are marketing analyses, a marketing strategy, marketing programmes centred around well-specified marketing mixes, plus marketing management controls and implementation practices. *Marketing strategy* involves selecting which marketing opportunities to pursue and analysing a target market (the group of people the organisation wants to reach), and creating and maintaining an appropriate *marketing mix* (product, place/distribution, promotion, price and people) to satisfy this target market. Effective marketing requires that managers focus on four tasks to achieve set objectives:
(1) marketing opportunity analysis, (2) target market selection, (3) marketing mix development, and (4) marketing management.

» Marketers should be able to recognise and analyse *marketing opportunities*, which are circumstances that allow an organisation to take action towards reaching a particular group of customers.

» A *target market* is a group of people for whom a company creates and maintains a marketing mix that specifically fits the needs and preferences of that group. It is important for an organisation's management to designate which customer groups the company is trying to serve and to have some information about these customers. The identification and analysis of a target market provide a foundation on which a marketing mix can be developed.

» The five principal variables that make up the marketing mix are product, place/distribution, promotion, price and people: the '5Ps'. The *product variable* is the aspect of the marketing mix that deals with researching consumers' wants and designing a product with the desired characteristics. A marketing manager tries to make products available in the quantities desired to as many customers as possible, and to keep the total inventory, transport and storage costs as low as possible – the *place/distribution variable*. The *promotion variable* relates to activities used to inform one or more groups of people about an organisation and its products. The *price variable* refers to establishing pricing policies and determining product prices. The *people variable* controls the marketing mix; provides customer service and often the interface with customers, facilitates the product's distribution, sale and service; and – as consumers or buyers – gives marketing its rationale. Marketing exists to encourage consumer satisfaction.

*Marketing management* is a process of planning, organising, implementing and controlling marketing activities to facilitate and expedite exchanges effectively and efficiently. Marketing planning is a systematic process of assessing opportunities and resources, determining marketing objectives, developing a marketing strategy, and developing plans for implementation and control. Organising marketing activities refers to developing the internal structure of the marketing unit. Properly implementing marketing plans depends on coordinating marketing activities, motivating marketing personnel and communicating effectively within the unit. The marketing control process consists of establishing performance standards, evaluating actual performance by comparing it with established standards, and reducing the difference between desired and actual performance.

## *Key Links*

At the end of each chapter summary, a 'Key Links' box will steer readers to any chapters that are directly related.

- Obviously, given that this is an introductory chapter, the other chapters of *Marketing: Concepts and Strategies* are all relevant links.
- Specifically, Chapters 2 and 3 are required associated reading.

## Important Terms

Marketing orientation
Marketing
Marketing environment
Exchange
Customer satisfaction
Product
Good
Service
Idea
Marketing process
Marketing concept
Production era
Sales era
Marketing era
Relationship marketing era
Marketing strategy
Marketing mix
Marketing opportunity
Target market
Product variable
Place/distribution variable
Promotion variable
Price variable
People variable
Marketing management

## Discussion and Review Questions

1. What is meant by market orientation?
2. What is marketing? How did you define marketing before you read this chapter?
3. Why should someone study marketing?
4. What is the marketing process? Why should the process be so sequenced?
5. Discuss the basic elements of the marketing concept. Which businesses use this concept? Have these organisations adopted the marketing concept? Explain your views.
6. Identify several organisations that obviously have not adopted the marketing concept. What characteristics of these organisations indicate non-acceptance of the marketing concept?
7. Describe the major components of a marketing strategy. How are these major components related?
8. Identify the tasks involved in developing a marketing strategy.
9. What are the primary issues that marketing managers consider when conducting a market opportunity analysis?
10. What are the variables in the marketing environment? How much control does a marketing manager have over environmental variables?
11. Why is the selection of a target market such an important issue?
12. Why are the elements of the marketing mix known as variables? What are these variables?
13. What type of management activities are involved in marketing management?
14. Why is it important to adhere to the principle of analyses first, then marketing strategy development, followed ultimately by programmes for implementing the recommended marketing strategy?

## Recommended Readings

- Baker, M., 'What is Marketing?', in M. Baker (ed.), *The Marketing Book* (Oxford: Butterworth-Heinemann, 2002).
- Day, G.S., *The Market Driven Organization: Attracting and Keeping Valuable Customers* (New York: Free Press, 1999).
- Hart, S., *Marketing Changes* (London: Thomson Learning, 2003).
- Kotler, P., *Marketing Insights from A to Z: 80 Concepts Every Manager Needs to Know* (Hoboken, NJ: Wiley, 2003).

## Internet Exercise

Seat cars used to be cheap and cheerful. Under VW's ownership the marque has been repositioned as sporty but good value. The range of cars is well specified, produced to VW's high standards, reasonably quick, but keenly priced. Take a look at Seat's website at:
www.seat.co.uk or www.seat.com

1 How user-friendly is the site?
2 To what extent does the site provide the information required by someone seeking additional product information in order to construct a shortlist of possible models to purchase?
3 Consider the decision-making process of a car buyer: to what extent is this website reflecting the issues considered by car buyers?

## *Applied Mini-Case*

The market for crisps (potato chips) is dominated by global giants such as P&G and PepsiCo. Brands including Pringles, Walkers and KP are household names. So what of Salty Dog? Never heard of these hand-cooked crisps? They are produced by a very small-scale operation, run from a barn deep in the Chiltern hills in the UK. Since their launch in 2002, sales have been way ahead of forecasts and exports are heading to France, Germany, Norway, Belgium and even China. So far so good, but in order to grow, the company has to attract major retailers and pub/bar chains, and broaden the brand's appeal among consumers – not easy tasks. Worse, the company is now attracting the attention of the major players in this market, which are unlikely to stand back and permit Salty Dog to steal their market shares.

### *Question*

As a newly recruited marketing manager for Salty Dog, what would be your priorities? How would you explain these to the owners of Salty Dog?

## *Case Study*

### Sweden's IKEA Marches On

When Swedish home furnishings retailer IKEA opened its first store in the UK, a retail shed near the M6 at Warrington, curious shoppers found queues jamming nearby roads, parking spaces at a premium and retailing analysts by the score. With just one store, IKEA had the UK furniture industry on its toes: large retail groups and manufacturers alike feared large market share losses. With its acquisition of the UK's Habitat and the opening of a national network of 13 stores, IKEA has conquered yet another territory. Such an impact is not confined to the UK market. The leading five countries for IKEA are Germany, the UK, the USA, France and Sweden.

IKEA has grown from one store in 1958 to 186 stores in 31 countries; 76,000 employees in 43 countries (retailing, distribution and manufacturing); and sales of over £5 billion. Close to 80 per cent of sales are from within Europe, but expansion in North America, South-east Asia and Australasia is now increasing sales in the rest of the world – despite some initial franchising difficulties in certain territories. IKEA's distinctive catalogue is produced in-house and now printed in 45 languages. IKEA is perhaps one of the world's most successful retailers, with a brand name that is known, recognised and discussed; a retail concept that stands for value, style and quality; everything for the home under one roof, with easy parking, children's play areas and cafés – in fact, 'a day out'!

As the company succinctly states in its advertising:

> IKEA: the furnishings store from Sweden
> More for your money
> IKEA is more than just furnishing ideas. It's a day out for all the family.
> Most of the time, beautifully designed home furnishings are created for a small part of the population – the few who can afford them. From the beginning, IKEA has taken a different path. We have decided to side with the many.
> That means responding to the home furnishing needs of people throughout the world. People with many different needs, tastes, dreams, aspirations ... and wallets. People who want to improve their home and create a better everyday life.
> For IKEA, helping create a better everyday life means offering a wide range of home furnishings in IKEA stores. Home furnishings that combine good design, good function and good quality with prices so low that as many people as possible can afford them.
>
> **Source:** IKEA

IKEA's huge volumes – 10,000 articles in a typical store – cheap out-of-town sites and dedication to keeping costs low through self-assembly packs mean that, unlike many competitors, the company can cope with any troughs in consumer spending. Low prices have been the key to IKEA's success, but price alone cannot create an international long-term marketing success story. Products are updated consistently to match consumers' expectations and lifestyles. In-store service and staff training are integral to the IKEA shopping experience. Sites are chosen to maximise catchment areas, to make access easy for shoppers and to bring the brand name to the attention of the whole community. Logistics give IKEA an edge, with carefully managed ordering and delivery reducing both stock holdings and stock-outs. Promotion emphasises the 'style without expense' philosophy and the IKEA name. The result has been a country-by-country revolution as staid furniture markets have been rejuvenated with the entry of IKEA. Shoppers intending to buy just a sofa return home with a sofa, a chair, some lamps and a general excitement about a new store where they can buy home furnishings at unbelievable prices. The IKEA vision is simple: 'Good design and function at low prices.'

The latest strategic developments for IKEA include entering eastern European markets, developing a new IKEA format and expanding its mail-order/electronic ordering. Eastern Europe has been a recent target for expansion, with IKEA stores opening in Poland, the Czech Republic and Hungary. The company is also sourcing furniture from eastern European manufacturers, which now supply 15 per cent of its range. The standard 'big box' IKEA concept was brought to a smaller stage with the New York opening in Manhattan of the first IKEA Marketing Outpost, a 720-square-metre (7500-square-foot) 'boutique', significantly smaller than the normal 19,000-square-metre (200,000-square-foot) IKEA superstore. Even more unusual was the decision to offer only a selected, themed, reduced range at any point in time. For example, IKEA Cook showcases the company's kitchen-related merchandise. Every 8 to 12 weeks the store closes completely to re-open with a new look, different merchandise, signage, lighting and staff uniforms. IKEA is also recognising the growing use of the Internet and is developing sales tools to utilise this new technology.

IKEA has its ideals and operating philosophies: standards matter. IKEA has a forceful, well-directed marketing strategy actioned – ignoring the trial of the Marketing Outpost in the USA – primarily through one tightly developed marketing mix for the core superstore operation. The result is a successful, expanding company, satisfied target customers and unhappy competitors.

**Sources:** www.ikea.co.uk, 2004; Helen Jones, 'IKEA's global strategy is a winning formula', *Marketing Week*, 15 March 1996, p. 22; Jennifer Pellet, 'IKEA takes Manhattan!', *Discount Merchandiser*, October 1995, pp. 22–3; 'IKEA', *Retail Business*, March 1995, pp. 78–81; Jonathan Pell, 'IKEA successfully penetrates east European consumer markets', *Central European*, June 1994, pp. 13–14; *IKEA Facts*, 1990 and 1992; B. Solomon, 'A Swedish company corners the business: worldwide', *Management Review*, 80 (4), 1991, pp. 10–13; IKEA HQ, 1998; www.ikea.com, 2004.

## Questions for Discussion

1. Explain why IKEA is successful.
2. To whom does the Marketing Outpost concept appeal? Why has IKEA developed this novel format?
3. In what ways does IKEA deploy the marketing concept?

# 2
# Marketing Strategy

**"A proper analysis of the strategic aspects of any competitive marketplace may not result in certain success, but it almost always helps to avoid failures."**

*Robin Wensley, Warwick Business School*

## Objectives

- To define marketing strategy and explore the relationship with a company's organisational mission, goals and corporate strategy
- To assess organisational opportunities, capabilities and the SWOT analysis
- To consider strategic objectives
- To appreciate the role of target market strategy and brand positioning in marketing strategy
- To examine competitive advantage, competitive positions and differential advantage
- To explore marketing objectives and marketing mix programmes in marketing strategy
- To understand the importance of implementation and performance monitoring in marketing strategy

## Introduction

Marketing strategy involves planning and decision-making over the longer term, with the aim of effectively selecting and pursuing marketing opportunities and establishing a competitive advantage. This requires an awareness of the external trading environment and market trends, an appreciation of the organisation's capabilities and resource base, and the ability to develop appropriate target market strategies. Marketing mix programmes must be developed to reflect these market conditions, organisational characteristics and target market strategies.

Marketing-oriented organisations have a marketing strategy that clearly articulates the opportunities the organisation has decided to address, and focuses the organisation on a specific set of target markets. These decisions will have been made with the knowledge of market drivers and marketing environment forces; an understanding of customer needs, expectations and buying behaviour; and with full knowledge of competitors' activities and their likely impact in target markets. The strategy will reflect, too, the marketing assets and capabilities of the organisation. This mix of external and internal awareness is pivotal to effective marketing strategy development. An organisation's marketing plan will then specify marketing programmes designed to achieve this marketing strategy.

*Opener*

# Diversification of a Brand: Coca-Cola's Move into Clothing

Leading on-line retailer of designer men's clothing and shoes, Otoko, states:

> Probably the best-known individual brand in the world today, Coca-Cola is also much more than a soft drink. Coca-Cola Ware is produced in Italy, under licence from Coca-Cola, using the same fabrics and design processes as its sister company Replay.
> Building on the heritage of the label, and using designs from the original bottle labels, Coca-Cola Ware is one of the most up-and-coming clothing labels ...

This is an impressive endorsement from a fashion retailer stocking brands such as 4:45, Armand Basi, Buckler, DiSanto, Junk de Luxe, Klaus Samsoe, Legless Horse, Marshall Artist, Moschino, Pepé and Ra:Re.

So why has Coca-Cola extended the well-known brand for soft drinks into new territory? In general, Coca-Cola has enjoyed the effects of massive growth in global soft drinks sales. However, towards the end of 1998, for the first time in many years, the company failed to hit its expected 7–8 per cent volume growth. Following this disappointing performance, senior managers were quick to deny that the core soft drinks business had reached maturity, blaming economic problems in key markets for the difficulties. The launch of Coca-Cola Ware was not, they stated, because of difficulties with the core business. Instead, the company sees the clothing as a promotional activity, an extension of Coca-Cola's licensing programme, which raises the profile of the brand around the world and is a core ingredient of the brand's strategy. The new clothing range certainly added an extra dimension to the company's existing licensing activities. With 250 licensees offering some 10,000 different items in 40 different countries, the precedent for such an arrangement was well established.

The clothing range, which comprises casual clothing and accessories, was test marketed prior to being launched globally. The target market for the jeans, woven clothing and knitwear is teenagers and young adults, but in future may include other age groups. According to US spokeswoman Susan McDermott, 'This is an integrated approach to create a fashion line with a cohesive feel and a sense of lifestyle.' Coca-Cola Ware is sold through department stores, fashion boutiques and specialist 'active' wear shops. The company has been quick to stress that the range is used to support and communicate Coca-Cola brand values, rather than to detract from the company's core products of soft drinks. This is a similar brand-building approach to that adopted by construction equipment giants CAT and JCB, whose footwear and clothing ranges have done much to raise the profile of their brands. However, some industry experts warn about the dangers of devaluing the core brand, suggesting that the fashion market is notoriously difficult to enter.

Jaguar also entered the fray, with a range of men's clothing competing with the likes of Boss and Armani. The appearance of Jaguar suits, shirts, ties, shorts and sweaters coincided with the launch of the Jaguar S-Type car. The clothing is sold through department stores and is supported by an advertising campaign. The rationale for the move was linked to the company's desire to target its cars at younger consumers. The Jaguar S-Type was the first of a series of models that Jaguar intended to appeal to the younger market, and the company believes that this appeal may be reflected in a desire to purchase fashion items carrying the same brand.

The extension of familiar brands into clothing is not a new trend. However, in a highly competitive market already saturated with well-known fashion house labels, success is difficult to achieve. One brand extension expert believes that brands seeking such a move must exhibit three crucial strengths: expertise, image and reputation. Few would deny that the classic and timeless brand of Coca-Cola possesses these qualities. Certainly Otoko's endorsement implies that Coca-Cola Ware is already creating the right impression. All marketers strive to promote their brands. Coca-Cola's marketers hope Coca-Cola Ware will lead to thousands of walking 'adverts', raising the profile of this already ubiquitous and successful brand. Nevertheless, the move into clothing was a significant diversification from the company's soft drinks business.

**Sources:** www.Coca-Cola.com, 2004; Amanda Wilkinson, 'Is Coke hip?', *Marketing Week*, 28 January 1999, pp. 26–9; Julia Day, 'Coke plans global clothing brands', *Marketing Week*, 21 January 1999, pp. 37–42; 'Jaguar drives in UK men's clothing market', *Marketing Week*, 18 March 1999, p. 7.

This chapter aims to highlight which strategic marketing considerations help to ensure that a product or service is marketed for the benefit of the organisation as well as its targeted customers. The product or service should be marketed differently enough from competitors' marketing programmes to provide the organisation's product or service with a perceived advantage over these competitors. These core components of marketing strategy are illustrated in Figure 2.1 and are clearly of great concern to the business described in this chapter's opener, Coca-Cola, as it chose to diversify into clothing.

The chapter first explores how to develop marketing strategies and then discusses strategic market planning, stressing the importance of organisational mission, goals and corporate strategy. The discussion next turns to assessing organisational opportunities and resources, as well as identifying strategic objectives and strategic focus. The chapter addresses the all-important role of identifying market segments, targeting and brand positioning in marketing strategy: the development of clear target market priorities. The chapter then focuses on competitive strategies for marketing: the role of competition, its ramifications for strategy, competitive positions and warfare strategies. The link between marketing objectives and marketing mix programmes is examined, along with implementation and performance monitoring.

## Marketing Strategy Defined

**Marketing strategy** A strategy indicating the opportunities to pursue, specific target markets to address, and the types of competitive advantages that are to be developed and exploited

**Strategic market plan** An outline of the methods and resources required to achieve an organisation's goals within a specific target market

**Strategic business unit (SBU)** A division, product line or other profit centre within a parent company

**Marketing strategy** articulates the best uses of a business's resources and tactics to achieve its marketing objectives. It states which opportunities are to be pursued by an organisation, indicates the specific markets towards which activities are to be targeted, and identifies the types of competitive advantage that are to be developed and exploited.[1] Implicitly, as described in Figure 2.1, the strategy requires clear objectives and a focus in line with an organisation's corporate goals; the 'right' customers must be targeted more effectively than they are by competitors, and associated marketing mixes should be developed as marketing programmes to implement the marketing strategy successfully.[2]

A **strategic market plan** is an outline of the methods and resources required to achieve an organisation's goals within a specific target market. It takes into account not only marketing but also all the functional aspects that must be coordinated, such as production, IT, logistics, finance and personnel. Environmental issues are an important consideration too. The concept of the strategic business unit is used to define areas for consideration in a specific strategic market plan. Each **strategic business unit (SBU)** is a division, product line or other profit centre within a parent company. Each sells a distinct set of products to an identifiable group of customers, and each competes with a well-defined set of competitors. Each SBU's revenues, costs, investments and strategic plans can be separated from those of the parent company and evaluated. SBUs operate in a variety of markets, which have differing growth rates, opportunities, degrees of competition and profit-making potential. Construction giant JCB, for example, includes the Compact Division for smaller machines, which is a strategic

*Figure 2.1*
*The components of marketing strategy*

**Organisational mission, goals and corporate strategy**

**Organisational opportunities and capabilities**
- Environmental scanning
- Customer and competitor analysis
- Marketing opportunities
- Capabilities and resources

**Strategic objectives**
- Intense growth
- Diversified growth
- Integrated growth
- Maintenance

**Target market strategy and brand positioning**
- Market segmentation
- Priority target markets
- Brand positioning
- Differential advantage

**Marketing objectives**

**Marketing programmes for implementation**
- Marketing mix tactics
- Operational controls

**Performance assessment and benchmarking**

**Strategic market planning**
A process that yields a marketing strategy that is the framework for a marketing plan

**Marketing plan**
The written document or blueprint for specifying, implementing and controlling an organisation's marketing activities and marketing mixes

business unit. Figure 2.2 illustrates one of Magnet's SBUs. Strategic planners, therefore, must recognise the different performance capabilities of each SBU and allocate resources carefully. They must also ensure that the SBUs complement each other for the greater good of the overall business.

The process of **strategic market planning** yields a marketing strategy that is the framework for a marketing plan. The planning process should be guided by a marketing-oriented culture and processes in the organisation.[3] A **marketing plan**, as described in Chapter 23, includes the framework and entire set of marketing activities to be performed; it is the written document or blueprint for specifying, implementing and controlling an organisation's marketing activities and marketing mixes. Thus a strategic market plan is not the same as a marketing plan – it is

TIKO
it's gorgeous on the inside, too
When we design a kitchen for you at Magnet, it goes without saying that it will be drop-dead-gorgeous to look at. But any kitchen worth its salt has to be practical, too. That's why we've introduced something called Smart Space Solutions. A range of innovative storage options that can significantly increase the internal space of your kitchen, from plate and pan drawers that extend fully so you can access every single millimetre of space to wine racks that pull out of base units. Ask your designer for details, who will happily recommend a variety of solutions designed around you and your needs. And pretty soon you'll find yourself getting just as excited about the inside of your new kitchen as the outside.
Magnet
designed around you
SERVICE
call 0845 123 6789 for details of your nearest showroom, quoting HB56 or visit www.magnet.co.uk


***Figure 2.2***
*Magnet's kitchen business unit strives to market the appeal of its range and services*
*Source: Courtesy of Magnet Kitchens*

a plan of all aspects of an organisation's strategy in the marketplace.[4] A marketing plan, in contrast, deals primarily with implementing the marketing strategy as it relates to target markets and marketing programmes.[5] The marketing plan states which are priority target markets and details the marketing programmes, specifying also timeframes, budgets and responsibilities.

Figure 2.3 shows the components of strategic market planning. The process is based on the establishment of an organisation's overall goals, and it must stay within the bounds of the organisation's opportunities and resources. When the business has determined its overall goals and identified its resources, it can then assess its opportunities and develop a corporate strategy. Marketing objectives must be designed so that their achievement will contribute to the overall corporate strategy and so that they can be accomplished through efficient use of the company's resources. For example, IT service company Fujitsu wants to be the dominant provider of IT solutions and outsourcing to government and the public sector, along with certain commercial sectors such as financial services. The marketing

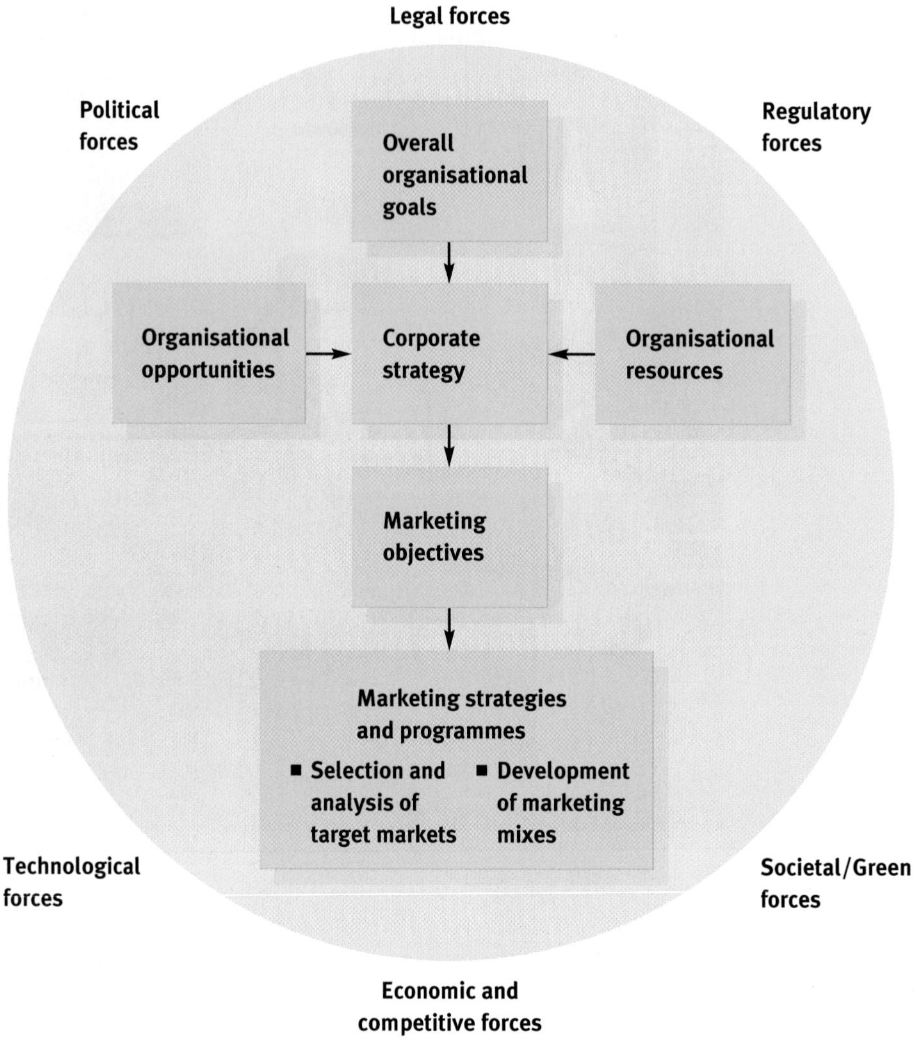


***Figure 2.3***
*The components of strategic market planning*

function in Fujitsu must identify opportunities to pursue in these sectors, specifying target market prospects, developing appropriate services and marketing messages, engaging with potential clients, and helping to win individual pieces of business within the organisation's priority sectors. In some organisations, marketers steer the development of the strategic market plan because they are the holders of market knowledge. In other organisations, the board of directors develops the strategic market plan and marketers focus on devising marketing strategies capable of achieving the aims of the top-line strategic market plan.

To achieve its marketing objectives, an organisation must develop a marketing strategy, or a set of marketing strategies, as shown in Figure 2.3. To operationalise a marketing strategy, a marketing mix must be developed. Most marketers refer to their marketing strategy and associated marketing mix activities as their **marketing programme**. Marketing programmes centre around a detailed marketing mix specification and include internal controls and procedures to ensure that they are implemented effectively. Through the process of strategic market planning, an organisation can develop marketing strategies that, when properly implemented and controlled, will contribute to the achievement of its marketing objectives and its overall goals. To formulate a marketing strategy, the marketer identifies and analyses the target market and develops a marketing mix to satisfy individuals in that

**Marketing programme**
A marketer's marketing mix activities and implementation processes designed to operationalise the marketing strategy

market. Marketing strategy is best formulated when it reflects the overall direction of the organisation and is coordinated with all the company's functional areas.

As indicated in Figure 2.3, the strategic market planning process is based on an analysis of the broader marketing environment. As detailed in Chapter 3, marketing environment forces can place constraints on an organisation and possibly influence its overall goals; they also affect the amount and type of resources that a business can acquire. However, these forces can create favourable opportunities as well – opportunities that can be translated into overall organisational goals and marketing objectives. For example, when oil prices declined during the second half of the 1980s, consumers viewed cars with high petrol consumption more favourably. This situation created an opportunity for manufacturers of large vehicles, such as BMW and Volvo. Political uncertainty in the Middle East is now resulting in higher fuel prices, creating opportunities for alternative energies and vehicle manufacturers with capabilities in these areas.

Marketers differ in their viewpoints concerning the effect of marketing environment variables on planning and strategy development. Some take a deterministic perspective, believing that companies must react to external conditions and tailor their strategies and organisational structures to deal with these conditions. According to others, however, companies can influence their environments by choosing in which markets to compete, lobbying regulators and politicians, striving to modify social views, joining forces with trade bodies for campaigning purposes, and so forth. They can also change the structures of their industries, engaging in activities such as mergers and acquisitions, demand creation or technological innovation.[6]

Regardless of which viewpoint is adopted, marketing environment variables play a part in the creation of a marketing strategy. When environment variables affect an organisation's overall goals, resources, opportunities or marketing objectives, they also affect its marketing strategies, which are based on these factors. Marketing environment forces more directly influence the development of a marketing strategy through their impact on consumers' needs and desires, as well as their effect on competitors' plans. In addition, these forces have a bearing on marketing mix decisions. For instance, competition strongly influences marketing mix decisions. The organisation must diagnose the marketing mix activities it performs, taking into account competitors' marketing mix decisions, and develop a differential advantage to support a strategy. Thus as Honda and Toyota entered the luxury car market with the Acura and Lexus models, European car makers BMW, Mercedes and Jaguar had to change their marketing strategies to maintain their market shares. They did so by lowering prices, introducing new models and creating brand-building marketing communications campaigns to compete with the new Japanese models.

## Organisational Mission, Goals and Corporate Strategy

**Mission**
The broad, long-term tasks that the organisation wants to accomplish

Central to the strategic market plan is a clear view of the organisational mission, goals and corporate strategy. A company's organisational goals should be derived from its **mission** – the broad, long-term tasks that the organisation wants to accomplish. IBM, for example, has stated that its mission is helping business people make decisions in a connected world on demand. When a company decides on its mission, it really answers two questions.

1 What is the company's core business/area of activity?
2 What should this be?[7]

Although these questions seem very simple, they are in fact two of the hardest, yet most important, for any business to answer.

Creating or revising a mission statement is very difficult because of the many complex variables that must be examined. However, having a mission statement can greatly benefit the organisation in at least five ways.[8] A mission statement:

1 gives the organisation a clear purpose and direction, keeping it on track and preventing it from drifting
2 describes the unique aim of the organisation that helps to differentiate it from similar competing organisations
3 keeps the organisation focused on customer needs rather than its own abilities. This ensures that the organisation remains externally rather than internally focused
4 provides specific direction and guidelines to top managers for selecting alternative courses of action. It helps them decide which business opportunities to pursue, as well as which opportunities not to pursue
5 offers guidance to all employees and managers of an organisation, even if they work in different parts of the world. As a result, the mission statement acts like 'glue' to hold the organisation together.

A company's mission and overall organisational goals should guide all its planning efforts. Its goals should specify the ends, or results, that are sought. Examples of organisational goals include profit, return on investment, an increase in market share, an increase/decrease in the number of active markets, the desire to enter specific market sectors, to develop a particular reputation and track record. Organisations can also have short-term and long-term goals. Companies experiencing financial difficulty may be forced to focus solely on the short-term results necessary to stay in business, such as increasing cash flow by lowering prices or selling off parts of the business. Other organisations may have more optimistic long-term goals. In many cases, companies that pursue long-term goals have to sacrifice short-term results to achieve them. Businesses that are successful over time tend to have a longer-term, market share-driven strategy, rather than a short-term, 'profits only' sales-led emphasis.

A business in serious financial trouble may be concerned solely with short-run results needed for remaining viable and fending off creditors. There is usually, for example, an airline or major retailer being forced by cash shortages to take drastic action to stay in business. Lowndes Queensway, once the UK's largest retailer of carpets and furniture, had to renegotiate its financing several times with city institutions, alter payment and credit lines and terms with its suppliers, and ultimately identify which of its 500 superstores should be closed to save costs. The company went into receivership despite all its efforts. BA had to cut costs drastically in order to return to profitability and regain the faith of investors. Sainsbury's and Marks & Spencer are still trying to find strategies that appease the financial analysts and journalists. On the other hand, some companies have more optimistic goals. Often manufacturers, such as General Motors, have goals that relate to return on investment. A successful company, however, may want to sacrifice the current year's profits for the long run and at the same time pursue other goals, such as increasing market share.

**Corporate strategy**
A strategy that determines how resources are to be used to meet the organisation's goals in the areas of production, logistics, finance, research and development, human resources, IT and marketing

**Corporate strategy** determines the means for utilising resources in the areas of production, logistics, finance, research and development, human resources, IT and marketing to reach the organisation's goals. A corporate strategy determines not only the scope of the business but also its resource deployment, differential advantages and overall coordination of R&D, production, finance, distribution, sales, marketing and the other functional areas. The term 'corporate' in this context does not apply only to corporations: corporate strategy is used by all organisations, from the smallest sole proprietorship to the largest multinational corporation.

Corporate strategy planners are concerned with issues such as diversification, competition, differentiation, interrelationships among business units, and environmental issues. Strategic planners attempt to match the resources of the organisation with the various opportunities and risks in the external environment. Corporate strategy planners are also concerned with defining the scope and role of the strategic business units of the organisation so that they are coordinated to reach the ultimate goals desired.

While not the focus of *Marketing: Concepts and Strategies*, it is important to recognise that the marketing strategy, marketing plan and marketing mix programmes actioned by a business's marketers must reflect the aims and ethos of the overall corporate plan. Unfortunately, in some instances those empowered to deliver marketing programmes are unaware of or are unconcerned about the nuances of the organisation's overall corporate plan, and may even be pursuing a course of action that is at odds with the Board's sense of purpose. In some businesses, this reflects the paucity of analysis behind corporate planning, and the failure to involve senior marketers in such strategy development. In most businesses, the forces of the external marketing environment, competitors' strategies and evolving customer expectations are poorly assessed. In other cases, only a business's marketers are aware of these issues and have the relevant marketing intelligence to be able to suggest likely scenarios. It is therefore essential that those responsible for establishing corporate plans tap into this expertise and knowledge within the marketing function, just as it is essential for marketers to devise target market strategies and marketing programmes that properly reflect the direction desired by the corporate strategy.

# Organisational Opportunities and Resources

There are three major considerations in assessing opportunities and resources:

1 evaluating marketing opportunities
2 environmental scanning (discussed in Chapter 3)
3 understanding the business's capabilities and assets.

An appreciation of these elements is essential if an organisation is to build up a sustainable differential advantage or competitive edge.

## Marketing Opportunities

**Marketing opportunity**
Circumstances and timing that allow an organisation to take action towards reaching a target market

**Strategic window**
A temporary period of optimum fit between the key requirements of a market and the particular capabilities of a company competing in that market

A **marketing opportunity** arises when the right combination of circumstances occurs at the right time to allow an organisation to take action towards reaching a target market. Government concerns about energy supplies have provided the turbine makers for wind farms with an opportunity that a few years ago did not exist. An opportunity provides a favourable chance or opening for an organisation to generate sales from identifiable markets. For example, in reaction to the overwhelming growth in cereals and other foods containing oat bran – which some researchers believe helps lower cholesterol levels – the Quaker Oats Company developed an advertising campaign to remind consumers that Quaker porridge oats have always contained oat bran. The advertisements told consumers that eating porridge is 'the right thing to do' and helped boost sales of Quaker Oats dramatically.[9] Increasing concerns about cancer and heart disease gave Quaker a marketing opportunity to reach consumers who are especially health-conscious by touting the health benefits of its oats. Kellogg's also took advantage of the popularity of oat bran by creating its Common Sense™ Oat Bran cereal. Interestingly, in 1990 a study published in a leading medical journal questioned the effectiveness of oat bran in lowering cholesterol, concluding that it was the elimination of high cholesterol animal products that really lowered cholesterol. Therefore, some of the oat bran mystique vanished overnight. The term **strategic window** has been used to describe what are often temporary periods of optimum fit between the key requirements of a market and the particular capabilities of a company competing in that market.[10]

The attractiveness of marketing opportunities is determined by market factors such as size and growth rate; by political, legal, regulatory, societal/Green, economic and competitive, and technological marketing environment forces; and by internal capital, plant, and human and financial resources.[11] Because each industry and each product is somewhat different, the factors that determine attractiveness tend to vary. Chapter 12 explains further some of the variables and techniques used to evaluate attractive opportunities.

**Market requirements**
Requirements that relate to customers' needs or desired benefits

**Market requirements** relate to customers' needs or desired benefits. Market requirements are satisfied by components of the marketing mix that provide buyers with these benefits. Of course, buyers' perceptions of what requirements fulfil their needs and provide the desired benefits determine the success of any marketing effort. Marketers must devise strategies to out-perform competitors by finding out what product attributes buyers use to select products. An attribute must be important and differentiating if it is to be useful in strategy development. As discussed in Chapters 6 and 7, when marketers fail to understand buyers' perceptions and market requirements, the result may be failure. Toyota had failed to attract prestige-led car purchasers, even though it produced well-specified executive cars. The brand image was not attractive enough to these target customers. As a result, Toyota created its highly successful Lexus marque, focusing on the brand values desired by these customers.

## Environmental Scanning

**Environmental scanning**
The process of collecting information about the marketing environment to help marketers identify opportunities and threats, and assist in planning

**Environmental scanning** is the process of collecting information about the marketing environment to help marketers identify opportunities, prepare for impending threats, and assist in planning. Some companies have derived substantial benefits from establishing an 'environmental scanning (or monitoring) unit' within the strategic planning group, as part of their marketing planning activity, or by including line management in teams or committees to conduct environmental analysis. This approach engages management in the process of environmental forecasting and enhances the likelihood of successfully integrating forecasting efforts into strategic market planning.[12] Results of forecasting research show that even simple quantitative forecasting techniques out-perform the unstructured intuitive assessments of experts.[13]

Environmental scanning to detect changes in the environment is extremely important if an organisation is to avoid crisis management. A change in the external marketing environment can suddenly alter an organisation's opportunities or resources. Reformulated strategies may then be needed to guide marketing efforts. For example, after the UK government legislated against heavy emissions from cars and gave unleaded fuel tax advantages, petrol suppliers and vehicle manufacturers had to reformulate their strategies and marketing programmes.[14] Because car manufacturers had engaged in environmental scanning and were aware that such legislation might indeed be enacted because of social and political concerns, most had already begun developing plans for cars powered by clean fuel. Environmental scanning should identify new developments and determine the nature and rate of change.

## Capabilities and Assets

**Capabilities**
A company's distinctive competencies to do something well and efficiently

**Marketing assets**
Customer, distribution and internal capabilities that managers and the marketplace view as beneficially strong

A company's **capabilities** relate to *distinctive competencies* that it has developed to do something well and efficiently. A company is likely to enjoy a differential advantage over its rivals in an area where its competencies out-do those of its potential competitors.[15] Often a company may possess manufacturing or technical skills that are valuable in areas outside its traditional industry. For example, BASF, known for the manufacture and development of audio and video tapes, produced a new type of lightweight plastic that has uses in other industries. Capabilities can be classified in terms of **marketing assets**, highlighting capabilities that managers and the marketplace view as beneficially strong. These capabilities can then be stressed to the company's advantage. Marketing assets are commonly classified as either customer based, distribution based or internal. *Customer-based assets* include capabilities that are customer-facing, such as brand image and reputation, product quality and customer service expertise; *distribution-based assets* relate to marketing channel issues and may involve density of dealers and geographic coverage, the responsiveness of distributors, after-sales support and logistical capabilities; *internal marketing assets* are operational, process and resource capabilities, including skills, experience, economies of scale, technology, working practices and people resources.[16] It is essential for a business to take time to assess its capabilities and assets, and to map these alongside identified opportunities. Research findings suggest that the mix of these capabilities and assets affects the types of strategy that should be pursued.[17]

**SWOT analysis**
The examination of an organisation's strengths and weaknesses, opportunities and threats, usually depicted on a four-cell chart

**SWOT Analysis** **SWOT analysis** (strengths, weaknesses, opportunities, threats) is one of the most simplistic used by marketers; fundamentally it is little more than a set of checklists. However, it cannot be ignored in a book such as this owing to its popularity and widespread use. The strengths it refers to relate to those internal operational, managerial, resource and marketing factors that managers believe provide a strong foundation for their organisation's activities and for their ability to compete effectively in the marketplace. Many marketers treat the notion of marketing assets as a means for classifying strengths. Weaknesses are again those aspects of the organisation, its products and activities in the marketplace that place the organisation at a disadvantage vis-à-vis competitors and in the view of targeted customers. Best practice indicates that an organisation should strive to remedy such faults, particularly those that may be exploited by rivals. An analysis of strengths and weaknesses is a fundamental aspect for developing a marketing strategy as an organisation must have an awareness of its capabilities and how these map out against competitors' strengths and weaknesses.

The other elements of the SWOT analysis are opportunities and threats, which are external-facing issues of the trading environment. As explained in Chapter 1, at the forefront of the marketing concept is marketing opportunity analysis. A sound appreciation of marketing environment forces and evolving market trends is essential for a marketing-oriented organisation. It is difficult to contemplate a scenario in which an organisation lacking such an external awareness is able to develop a truly meaningful marketing strategy. As described above, marketing environmental scanning identifies numerous issues that marketers must consider when developing marketing strategies. These market developments may offer opportunities for marketers to exploit or they may be the cause of threats to the fortunes of an organisation. As explained in more detail in the next chapter, an awareness of the marketing environment may lead to strategic windows of opportunity. The SWOT analysis, in its simplistic way, has the benefit of placing an organisation's strengths and weaknesses in the context of the identified opportunities and threats, so implying the extent to which an organisation is capable of leveraging an opportunity or fending off an apparent threat. The SWOT analysis can be an effective scene-setting tool, but *only* if the guidelines detailed in the Marketing Tools and Techniques box below are followed.

**Ansoff matrix**
Ansoff's product–market matrix for determining competitive strategies: market penetration, market development, product development or diversification

## Marketing Tools and Techniques

### Practitioners' Use of SWOT Analysis

The SWOT analysis is a very simplistic tool, yet it appears in most marketing plans and is popular with boards of directors because it conveys so much information: strengths (S) on which to build, weaknesses (W) to rectify, opportunities (O) to consider and threats (T) to address.

The SWOT depicted (top of page 46) is typical. This was produced by a brainstorming workshop involving 25 sales and marketing personnel. Workshops are often used to generate SWOTs; alternatively, individual managers may spend a few minutes producing them – while killing time at an airport, say. The problems in the example (top of page 46) are that:

- the lists were not ranked in order of importance, only listed in the order they were suggested
- many of the bulleted points are vague or ambiguous
- there is no validation or evidence to support these points being included, only the personal judgement of the managers present at the meeting
- the implications are not detailed
- there are far too many non-prioritised points listed to act upon.

| Strengths | Weaknesses |
|---|---|
| • Experience & quality of people<br>• Safety/environmental standards<br>• Brand heritage – low price perception<br>• Co-op mode of operation<br>• Teamwork/alignment<br>• New concept<br>• Merchandising<br>• Category management structure<br>• Store locations<br>• Streamlined organisation<br>• Fully integrated company<br>• Ability to change quickly<br>• Dealer Loyalty | • Multiple image<br>• Inconsistent site presentation<br>• Brand equity value<br>• Inflexible logistics<br>• Lack of maintaining business investment<br>• High break-even cost<br>• Lack of flexible resources<br>• Inflexible technology<br>• Inconsistent focus on retailing/lack of selling structure<br>• Staff turnover<br>• Quality of data and analysis<br>• Inadequate benchmarking<br>• Consumer research<br>• Reactive rather than proactive<br>• Communication – quality/mode<br>• Poor succession planning<br>• Cost control<br>• Total overheads too high<br>• Too many non-performing sites |
| **Opportunities**<br>• Dealer buying group<br>• Customer loyalty promotion<br>• Optimising distribution e.g. push/pull<br>• Market growth of forecourt convenience<br>• Synergies for services with other brands<br>• Green products<br>• European purchasing agreements<br>• Joint venture on payment card<br>• Detailed economical analysis for sites<br>• Concessions/cebranding<br>• Alcohol/fast food/bakeries<br>• Technology<br>• Small profitable dealers (brand standards)<br>• Cost effective store and design<br>• More and better use of consumer/customer research industry data<br>• Active selling by sales attendants<br>• Optimisation of site opening hours<br>• Promoting underperforming sites/micro marketing<br>• Margin enhancement through loyalty scheme<br>• Alliance with shop retailers<br>• Market attrition<br>• Linking site to local community<br>• Co-op portfolio management<br>• Differentiation through customer service excellence<br>• Closer supplier relations<br>• Telesales | **Threats**<br>• Industry restructuring<br>– by store categories<br>– by supplier/retailer alliances/JVs<br>• Lack of loyalty programme<br>• Government transport policy<br>• Lack of shop image and investment<br>• Majors targeting smaller dealers<br>• Cost of environmental legislation<br>• Control of costs<br>• Continued low margins<br>• Failure to capture convenience market growth |

By contrast, the following SWOT grid for a major insurance company has a more manageable set of issues, although the points are still ambiguous.

**SWOT Grid for an Insurance Business**

| | STRENGTHS | WEAKNESSES |
|---|---|---|
| Internal issues | Brand recognition<br>Expertise in underwriting<br>Network<br>British, leading UK market<br>Wide product range | Share price<br>Press reports ⟶ Media targeting<br>Uncertainty re. direction/market segments<br>Poor product differentiation<br>Cost base<br>Wide network |
| External issues | Profitable markets still far from mature<br>Broker loyalty<br>Business unit focus strategy<br>Technology<br>Joint ventures with 3rd parties, such as major retailers entering fin/servs | Regulation<br>Solvency<br>Share price & ownership<br>Negative press<br>Losing customers<br>Competitors – many mergers taking place<br>Our markets are desirable to Euro-rivals<br>Changing weather patterns |
| | OPPORTUNITIES | THREATS |

More importantly, this business has abided by the following essential guidelines.

- Be as focused as possible – no huge lists.
- Use teamwork to generate a range of opinions, then verify with external stakeholders (e.g. channel members, suppliers, customers) and benchmark against any available marketing research or customer satisfaction audit data.
- Concentrate on a customer orientation in allocating priorities: deal first with issues of importance to customers, particularly weaknesses that rivals could exploit.
- Strengths and weaknesses are more revealing when benchmarked against key rivals.
- Use an analysis of the macro marketing environment (see Chapter 3) as input to the opportunities and threats.
- Rank the points listed in order of importance: senior managers assume lists presented to them to be prioritised.
- Have supporting evidence, otherwise exclude the issue from the list.
- Be honest! Bad news, too.

Having produced the top-line SWOT depicted above left, the insurance company team then debated in detail each point in order to clarify the issues, verify their importance and discuss the implication of each issue to the business. This discussion led to a prioritisation of tasks to action. This phase is crucial if the SWOT is to help direct a business's thinking.

By following these guidelines, this insurance business produced a meaningful, objective SWOT that led to specific action programmes, notably to address the stated weaknesses and steer the board's thinking about possible opportunities to consider.

**Source:** © Dibb/Simkin.

**Note:** a more extensive explanation of this technique is offered in either *The Market Segmentation Workbook* (Dibb and Simkin) or *The Marketing Planning Workbook* (Dibb, Simkin and Bradley), both originally published in 1996 by Thomson (London).

## Strategic Objectives and Strategic Focus

**Strategic objectives**
Include intense growth, diversified growth or integrated growth

Having evaluated the overall corporate vision, those responsible for devising the marketing strategy must build on their analysis of opportunities and internal capabilities by analytically assessing the most promising directions for their business and marketing activity. Ansoff developed a well-known tool, the market-product matrix, popularly known as the **Ansoff matrix**, to assist in this decision-making, as depicted in Figure 2.4. A business may choose one or more competitive strategies as the basis for its **strategic objectives**,

*Figure 2.4*
*Ansoff's competitive strategies*
*Source: H.I. Ansoff,* The New Corporate Strategy *(New York, NY: John Wiley & Sons, 1988), p. 83. Reproduced by permission of the author*

| Market \ Product | Present | New |
|---|---|---|
| Present | Market penetration | Product development |
| New | Market development | Diversification |

**Intense growth**
Growth that occurs when current products and current markets have the potential for increasing sales

including intense growth, diversified growth and integrated growth. This matrix can help in determining growth that can be implemented through marketing strategies.

## Intense Growth

**Intense growth** can take place when current products and current markets have the potential for increasing sales. There are three main strategies for intense growth – market penetration, market development and product development.

**Market penetration**
A strategy of increasing sales of current products in current markets

**Market Penetration** **Market penetration** is a strategy of increasing sales in current markets with current products. For example, Coca-Cola and PepsiCo try to achieve increased market share through aggressive advertising.

**Market development**
A strategy of increasing sales of current products in new markets

**Market Development** **Market development** is a strategy of increasing sales of current products in new markets. For example, a European aircraft manufacturer was able to enter the US market by offering Eastern Airlines financing that Boeing could not match. Evian devised a new use for its mineral water by developing its Brumisateur, an atomiser spray for the skin.

**Product development**
A strategy of increasing sales by improving present products or developing new products for current markets

**Product Development** **Product development** is a strategy of increasing sales by improving present products or developing new products for current markets. PepsiCo and Coca-Cola both have new container sizes, low-calorie/low-sugar/low-carb versions and vending machine services.

## Diversified Growth

**Diversified growth**
Growth that occurs when new products are developed to be sold in new markets

**Diversified growth** occurs when new products are developed to be sold in new markets. Companies have become increasingly diversified since the 1960s. Diversification offers some advantages over single-business companies, because it allows businesses to spread their risk across a number of markets. More important, it allows them to make better and wider use of their management, technical and financial resources. For example, marketing expertise can be used across businesses, which may also share advertising themes, distribution channels, warehouse facilities or even salesforces.[18] The three forms of diversification are horizontal, concentric and conglomerate.

**Horizontal diversification**
A process that occurs when new products not technologically related to current products are introduced into current markets

**Horizontal Diversification** **Horizontal diversification** results when new products that are not technologically related to current products are introduced to current markets. Sony, for example, diversified from electronics to movie production through its purchase of Columbia Pictures. The purchase gave Sony a library of 2700 films, including *Ghostbusters 2* and *When Harry Met Sally*, as well as 23,000 television episodes, which it has used to establish its line of video tapes and DVDs.[19]

**Concentric Diversification** In **concentric diversification**, the marketing and technology of new products are related to current products, but the new ones are introduced into

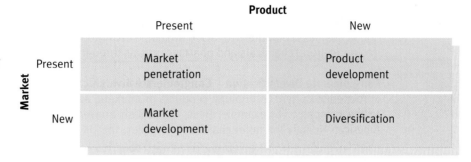

**Concentric diversification**
A process that occurs when new products related to current products are introduced into new markets

new markets. For instance, Sony developed business PCs and laptops based on its consumer flatscreen and electronics products, and then successfully used its established position in business computers to tackle the home computing market. Dow Chemical diversified into agricultural chemicals and pharmaceuticals through joint ventures in those industries.

**Conglomerate Diversification** **Conglomerate diversification** occurs when new products are unrelated to current technology, products or markets, and are introduced into markets new to the company. For example, Bass, the British brewer and pubs business, acquired the American Holiday Inn hotel chain. Laura Ashley, the UK clothing and furnishings company, moved into the fragrance market with Laura Ashley No. 1. Samsung diversified into everything from air conditioning and construction equipment to shipbuilding, home entertainment centres and mobile phones.

### Integrated Growth

**Integrated growth** can occur in the same industry that the company is in and in three possible directions: forwards, backwards or horizontally.

**Conglomerate diversification**
A process that occurs when new products unrelated to current technology, products or markets are introduced into new markets

**Integrated growth**
Growth that occurs in three possible directions: forwards, backwards or horizontally

1. A company growing through forward integration takes ownership or increased control of its distribution system. For example, a shoe manufacturer might start selling its products through wholly owned retail outlets.
2. In backward integration, a company takes ownership or increased control of its supply systems. A newspaper company that buys a paper mill is integrating backwards.
3. Horizontal integration occurs when a company takes ownership or control of some of its competitors, such as BMW's acquisition of Mini, or Ford's purchases of Land Rover, Jaguar, Volvo and Aston Martin.

In developing strategies, an organisation must consider the competitive positions in the marketplace and formulate marketing strategies and tactics accordingly. Some authors have adopted warfare analogies to describe the strategic options for competing in a market.[20] This chapter later examines the concept of competitive positions.

## Target Market Strategy and Brand Positioning

Central to achieving a company's corporate vision is the need to build up a loyal customer base of satisfied customers. Tesco did not overtake Sainsbury's by chance – it developed a clear marketing strategy based on a desire to fully satisfy a carefully targeted set of market segments. Tesco is continuously upgrading its stores, adding new services and product lines, and innovating with channels of distribution through Tesco Metro and Tesco Direct, with the aim of addressing its targeted-segment customer needs. Market segmentation is at the core of robust marketing strategy development. As explained in Chapter 8, this involves identifying customer needs, expectations, perceptions and buying behaviour, so as to group those customers who will be satisfied and marketed to in a similar manner into homogeneous groups or segments. One segment will differ from another in terms of customer profile and buying behaviour, and also with regard to the sales and marketing activity likely to satisfy these customers; but within a segment customers will share similar needs, buying behaviour and expectations. Without a thorough understanding of customers, therefore, it is difficult to produce a marketing strategy. Developing an understanding of customers is explored in Chapters 6 and 7.

Taking the time to objectively and sensibly group a market's customers into meaningful market segments is a discipline many businesses are only now discovering, particularly in business-to-business markets. Most of the fast movers, market leaders and successful brands in a marketplace base their marketing strategies on carefully honed market segmentation analyses. It is important to remember that the process of market segmentation involves more than simply grouping customers into segments. Shrewd targeting of certain

**Brand positioning**
The creation of a desirable, distinctive and plausible image for a brand in the minds of targeted customers

**Target market strategy**
The choice of for which market segment(s) an organisation decides to develop marketing programmes

segments and the development of a clear brand positioning are part of the market segmentation process. **Brand positioning** is the creation of a desirable, distinctive and plausible image for a brand that will have strong appeal for the customers in a target market segment. The basis of Chapter 8's coverage – identifying segments, deciding which to target and developing desirable positionings – is one of the foundations of a marketing strategy.

A **target market strategy** is the choice of which market segment(s) an organisation decides to prioritise and for which to develop marketing programmes. Organisations must identify priority target markets that are worthwhile targeting with bespoke marketing mix programmes: product, price, place (distribution), promotion and people. Even the mighty Ford or General Motors has to decide which segments in the car and van market to pursue, opting not to have models aimed at all buyers in the market. It is important to balance current core target markets with those offering future viability. Once determined, in each target market an organisation must strive to emphasise to those targeted customers the relevance and applicability of its product and marketing mix proposition. This is achieved through all ingredients of the marketing mix, but specifically through developing a distinctive, plausible and memorable brand positioning, such as BMW's 'The Ultimate Driving Machine'. This positioning imagery is communicated to targeted customers primarily through the promotional mix, packaging and design, but product attributes, pricing, choice of distribution and customer service provision must also support the positioning strategy. An upmarket restaurant, for example, requires a suitably lavish ambience, slick service, quality food, appropriate location and a suitable price to match its branding and promotional campaigns. It is important to agree on the target market strategy and required brand positioning before developing the marketing programmes destined to implement this strategy. These marketing mix activities must reflect the marketing analyses and target market strategy requirements rather than being merely a continuation of previous marketing mix activities.

## Competitive Advantage

**Competitors**
Organisations viewed as marketing products similar to, or substitutable for, a company's products, when targeted at the same customers

**Competitive advantage**
The achievement of superior performance vis-à-vis rivals, through differentiation to create distinctive product appeal or brand identity; through providing customer value and achieving the lowest delivered cost; or by focusing on narrowly scoped product categories or market niches so as to be viewed as a leading specialist

The competition is generally viewed by an organisation as those businesses marketing products similar to, or substitutable for, its products when targeted at the same customers. In order to persuade customers to purchase an organisation's products in preference to those products marketed by its **competitors**, leading strategists argue that it is necessary to develop a **competitive advantage**. Competitive advantage is the achievement of superior performance vis-à-vis rivals, through differentiation, to create distinctive product appeal or brand identity; through offering customer value and achieving the lowest delivered cost; or by focusing on narrowly scoped product categories or market niches so as to be viewed as a leading specialist. The creation of a competitive advantage is a core component of the development of a marketing strategy.

Marketing strategist Michael Porter identified the so-called **generic routes to competitive advantage**, claiming them to result in success for companies competing for position in any particular market. As depicted in Figure 2.5, these three generic strategies are as follows.

1 *Cost leadership*. This involves developing a low cost base, often through economies of scale associated with high market share and economies of experience, to give high contribution. This high financial contribution can then be used to further develop the low cost base. Very tight cost controls are essential to the success of this strategy. Generally, within a single market, only one competitor is secure in adopting this strategy for creating a competitive advantage: the organisation with the lowest cost base.
2 *Differentiation*. Companies adopting a differentiation strategy strive to offer product and marketing programmes that have a distinct advantage or are different to those offered by competitors. Differentiation can be achieved on a number of fronts, including creative and innovative product or brand designs, or novel distribution channel,

*Figure 2.5*
*Porter's generic routes to competitive advantage*

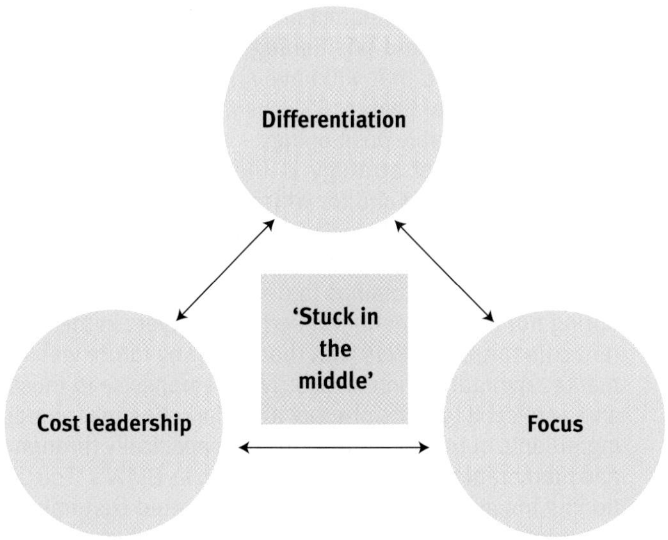


**Generic routes to competitive advantage**
Cost leadership, differentiation and focus; not mutually exclusive

pricing and customer service policies. This theme is taken further when marketers seek a *differential advantage*, as discussed later in this chapter.

3 *Focus*. Companies must maintain close links with the market so that product and marketing effort are designed with a particular target group in mind. Typically of small size, unable to achieve cost leadership or maintain significant differentiation, such companies succeed by effectively meeting customer needs that may be being missed by larger players in the market and by gaining a reputation for being experts or specialists in their narrowly defined area of activity.

Failure to achieve any of these strategies can result in companies becoming 'stuck in the middle', with no real competitive advantage. It is not usually possible to simultaneously follow all three generic strategies for competitive advantage, but it is common for businesses to gain cost leadership while also differentiating their proposition, and also for organisations to seek both a focused and a differentiated approach. Discounter Aldi adopts a cost leadership and a differentiated approach for developing a competitive advantage, as does no-frills airline easyJet. Sports coupé manufacturer Porsche adopts a focused and differentiated approach to defining a competitive advantage. It is sometimes more difficult to create a focused and cost leadership approach, as niche players rarely have the necessary scale economies, but it is not impossible.

# Competitive Positions and Differential Advantage

**Competitive set**
All competing organisations and brands, irrespective of size and history, including substitutable solutions to customers' needs, as defined by the target market customers

In order to compete effectively, marketers should seek to develop a differential advantage. In order to ensure this will be effective, marketers must understand the nature of the **competitive set** and also identify those rivals with which to do battle. The competitive set includes all competing organisations and brands, irrespective of size and history, including substitutable solutions to customers' needs, as defined by target market customers. Leading marketing strategists David Aaker and Michael Porter both argue that the scoping of the competitive set in many organisations is too limited. Ask most management teams who are their competitors and they will simply name the leading few organisations and brands in the market, ignoring smaller fast-moving rivals, probable new entrants to the market or substitutable solutions to their customers' needs offered by dissimilar organisations. It is often the case that when a company's customers are asked to name the

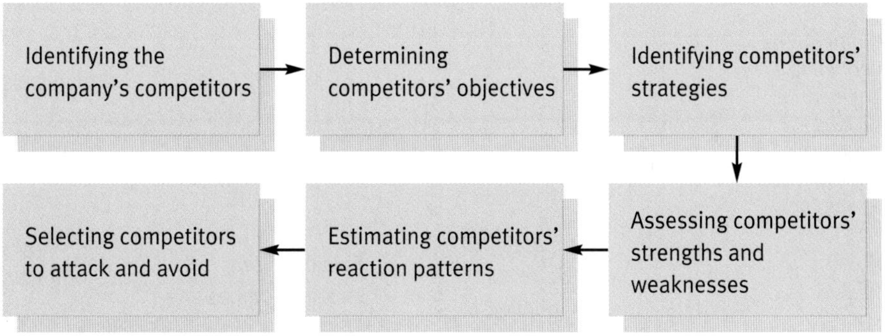


***Figure 2.6***
*Steps in analysing competitors*
*Source: Veronica Wong, FT MBA course notes, Warwick Business School, 1996*

competing companies or brands, they list a few names not routinely considered by the company's marketers. The customer's view of his or her options is of paramount importance and marketers should ensure that their interpretation of the competitive set is shared by their target market customers.

The scoping of the competitive arena and the identification of the competitive set are important marketing analysis tasks. Competitors are outside the control of an organisation, so the forces of competition are generally included within the forces of the *marketing environment*, as part of what is termed the 'micro marketing environment'. This concept is described in Chapter 3, which discusses further the forces of the competitive environment.

For the identified competitive set, marketers should assess the objectives and strategies of these rivals, their strengths and weaknesses, and determine how competitors are likely to react to their own marketing strategy and programmes. In effect, this leads to a decision about which competitors to 'fight', which to avoid antagonising and which to treat as unimportant. Veronica Wong suggests that competitor-aware marketers should be able to answer six key questions, as described in Figure 2.6.

Before examining the concept of differential advantage, this chapter looks at the increasingly popular use of warfare analogies in identifying the relative threat posed by the competitors in a market. While this book is not intended to be a marketing strategy text, analysis of the competition is a core principle for effective marketing and, as explained in Chapter 1, without a thorough appreciation of the competitive arena an organisation cannot have a marketing orientation.

## Competitive Positions

Evidently it is important to understand the nature of competition. This involves more than a cursory examination of like-for-like major rivals. Most organisations consider only similar companies or brands to be their competitors. As shown in Figure 2.7, there are other facets of competition that must be evaluated. What of the smaller players that may one day emerge as dominant in a market or specific segment? Why not pre-empt such an outcome by developing a strategy to destroy them while still only a small rival? What about the new entrant into the marketplace? Could its appearance have been foreseen? What actions are required to minimise its threat? How did Rover and Citroën fend off the entry of Daewoo in the small-car sector? Did they even anticipate Daewoo's entry? What of innovative solutions to customers' problems?

JCB produces construction equipment that digs trenches for pipes and cables. Microbore tunnelling moles lay pipes without the need for a trench. Not manufactured by the construction equipment companies, such moles – substitute competition – could be missed by JCB's marketers as a competitive threat without a rigorous analysis of the forces of the competitive environment.

The power of suppliers and of consumers can also vary per company and act as a competitive force, particularly if one business encounters greater supply problems or more severe customer bargaining than its rivals face from their suppliers and customers. These

*Figure 2.7*
*The five competitive forces determining industry competition*
*Source: Michael E. Porter,* Competitive Advantage *(New York: Free Press, 1985)*

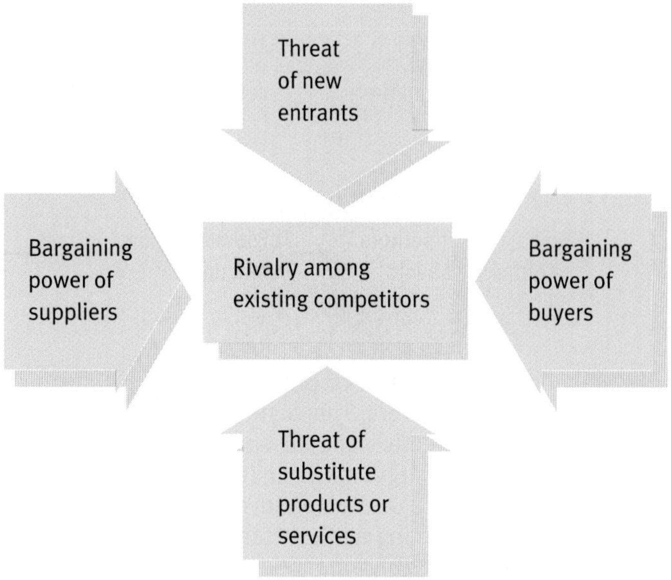


competitor categories are in addition to the like-for-like rivals considered by most businesses to be their competitors.

Michael Porter's view of defining the nature of the competitive arena, as illustrated in Figure 2.7, is particularly useful for scoping the nature of a market place. Porter defined **five competitive forces** that together determine competition in an industry or market:

**Five competitive forces** Together these determine competition in an industry or market: rivalry amongst existing like-for-like players; the threat of new entrants; the threat of substitute solutions; the bargaining power of buyers; and the bargaining power of suppliers

1 rivalry among existing like-for-like players
2 the threat of new entrants
3 the threat of substitute products or services as a solution to customers' problems or needs
4 the bargaining power of buyers
5 the bargaining power of suppliers.

Many marketing directors find this framework ideal for persuading their colleagues to consider competitive threats from more than just like-for-like rivals. Similarly, most marketing dissertations use Porter's framework in order to provide the perspective for describing the competitive pressures prevalent in a particular market.

In addition to realising the importance of examining all categories of competitors, it is necessary to understand what must be known. Most companies can describe their competitors: who, where, with what and at what price. Few businesses genuinely understand their rivals' strategies or endeavour to predict their rivals' reaction to moves they themselves may make. Very few companies attempt to identify those individual competitors it is sensible to avoid in a head-to-head marketing campaign or those most likely to be vulnerable to attack at low risk to the company's resource base. It is prudent to avoid head-to-head conflict with a similarly sized and resourced adversary. It is more desirable to identify the weaknesses of more vulnerable competitors and address these through the business's proposed marketing mix programmes. No marketing strategy should be formulated without a shrewd analysis of competitors. For some companies, carrying out this kind of analysis has recently been made more complex by the fact that they operate in both the physical and electronic marketplace.[21]

Many marketers view their marketplace as a battlefield, opting to compete on only certain fronts, engaging with carefully selected opponents, where there is a perceived differential advantage over the enemy. This warfare analogy has become increasingly popular and hinges on identifying the competitive positions of the various businesses competing in

**Competitive positions**
Competitors' roles in the marketplace, which influence their marketing strategies and programmes

**Market leader**
The single player enjoying the largest individual share in the market

a market segment.[22] The categories of **competitive positions** – competitors' roles in the marketplace that influence their marketing strategies and programmes – include the market leader, market challengers, fast movers, market followers and market nichers. These should be identified within each target market segment: a market challenger in one market segment may be a follower or even absent in a second market segment.

In the world of market shares, there has to be one, and only one, **market leader**: the player enjoying individually the largest slice of the market. In some business-to-business markets, a market leader can have a majority of industry sales, particularly when patent protection or technical innovation gives it an advantage over competitors. In most markets, however, the market leader may have only 10 to 20 per cent of the market's sales. The market leader has the highest market share and retains its competitive position by expanding the total market or expanding market share at the expense of its rivals, while protecting or defending current market share by retaining its customer base. In this context, the market leader, although successful, perhaps has the most difficult task: it must find strategies to increase market size and market share, as well as maintaining strategies to defend its current share. The marketing programmes necessary for maintaining ongoing relationships with existing customers are quite different to the marketing programmes used to attract and entice potential customers.

**Market challengers**
Non-market leaders that aggressively try to capture market share from their rivals

**Fast movers**
Smaller rival companies not yet destined to be major challengers, but growing rapidly on a smaller scale

Behind the market leader are competing companies, which are market challengers, fast movers, market followers or market nichers. **Market challengers** are non-market leaders that aggressively attack rivals, including the market leader, to take more market share. In most instances, these players are number two, three and perhaps four in a market, aspiring to market leadership. When Virgin entered the transatlantic air traffic market, its intention was to steal BA's market leadership. It is important to remember that to qualify as challengers these companies must be proactive and aggressive in their sales and marketing rather than passively reinforcing the existing hierarchy. **Fast movers** are smaller rival companies not yet destined to be major challengers, but growing rapidly on a smaller scale. A new entrant may have only 2 per cent of the market – but what is to stop it from increasing its share to 8 per cent within two years? A business may only have 4 per cent of the market, but three years ago it only had 1 per cent. What is to prevent it from having 8 per cent or 19 per cent in three years' time? The market leader and key challengers should take steps to prevent such continued growth.

**Market followers**
Low-share competitors without the resources, market position, research and development, or the commitment to challenge for extra sales and market share

**Market nichers**
Companies that specialise by focusing on only a very narrow range of products or on a select band of consumers

**Market followers** are low-share competitors without the resources, market position, research and development, or commitment to challenge for extra sales and market share. These companies tend to be the 'me-too, also-rans' in a market, whose raison d'être is to do as before and simply survive. In boom times these players can latch on to the success of their larger rivals, but in recession – or when faced with larger rivals' product innovations – they often struggle to achieve sales. Most markets also contain **market nichers**: companies that specialise by focusing on only a very narrow range of products such as Sock Shop or Saab, or on a select band of consumers, such as Body Shop or Porsche. Nichers survive by finding a safe, small, profitable market segment – often apparently too small to attract the market leaders and challengers. Nichers specialise and can genuinely prepare a marketing mix that exactly matches their target customers' needs. They are vulnerable to market downturns, the entry of rival nichers and the sudden attention of the major players in the marketplace, as happened to Porsche when the North American target market hit a recession and Japanese rivals appeared with cheaper, fast, two-seat sports coupés.

**Defensive warfare**
A policy of striking a balance between waiting for market developments or competitor activity and proactively parrying competitors' actions

A market leader must defend its position, while simultaneously seeking more market share. Only a market leader should consider **defensive warfare** as a strategic foundation. Strong defence involves striking a balance between waiting for market developments or competitor activity and proactively parrying competitors' actions. As market leader, the company must remember that a false sense of security and passive inactivity lead to disaster: the best defensive strategy is the courage to attack; and strong moves by competitors should always be blocked, never ignored. To defend its market share, a market leader must treat existing customers well and attentively, and never take them for granted. The marketing mix must be updated continually and target customers' needs must regularly be considered. New markets, products and opportunities should always be sought and evaluated. Occasionally, if faced by a strong challenger in a small or declining market, a market leader should consider divesting and concentrating resources in its other markets. Others may have to turn to defensive warfare when attacked by the market leader or challengers, but only the market leader should build a strategy around the desire to defend its current position.

A challenger has to attack for market share, but on what basis? The leader, and perhaps other challengers, will be strong and rich in resources. A challenger's attack must be well thought out and not suicidal in terms of the company's medium-term future. Few observers could accept the logic in Sainsbury's attacking market leader Tesco on the basis of price. Price anyway was not the core facet of Sainsbury's service-led culture, nor was Tesco the weakest of rivals to choose to fight. In **offensive warfare**, the main consideration is the market leader's strength: where are there any chinks in the leader's armour? A challenger seeking market share must identify a weakness in the leader's marketing mix and in other challengers' marketing programmes, and develop a genuine corresponding strength. With such a differential advantage or competitive edge, the challenger's resources may well be sufficient to steal ground successfully from the leader and the other challengers. Any attack, however, should be on a narrow front, where the challenger is perceived by the target customers to have an advantage and where resources can be focused. If no real weakness in the market leader exists, a challenger may attack head-on. Such an attack can be successful only if there are numerous, very weak market followers, if the leader is slow to react and if a price-cutting war does not result. In the last situation, the leader's resource base may fend off the challenger's attack.

**Offensive warfare**
A policy whereby challengers aggressively seek market share by identifying any weakness in the leader's and other challengers' marketing mixes and developing a genuine corresponding strength

Followers are vulnerable, but careful monitoring of market segments, marketing environment forces and competitive trends can help ensure their survival. They must serve exactly only a few market segments, specialising rather than diversifying in terms of products and markets, and making prudent use of what research and development resources are available. Nichers must watch for signs of competitor threats and possible changes in target segment customers' needs, and they may need to consider product development and, ultimately, diversification. Their marketing mixes must be tailored exactly to meet the expectations of their target segment.

All organisations should know, for all their markets and target segments, which companies occupy these competitive positions. They must alter their strategies and marketing programmes accordingly. Organisations should also review their rivals' marketing strategies and marketing programmes: many companies are surprisingly predictable. Response to rivals' pricing policies, frequency of new product launches, entry into new markets and timing of promotional campaigns, for example, can often be accurately anticipated. In this way, thorough **competitor scanning** – the monitoring of competitive positions and competitors' strategies – helps to establish more realistic marketing goals, develop successful strategies and programmes, and pre-empt nasty shocks caused by competitors' actions.[23] The leading marketing strategists agree that it is essential to understand competitors' strategies, their strengths and weaknesses in satisfying customers, and any differential advantages they hold that must be combated.[24] The **competitive positions proforma** has been developed by the authors of *Marketing: Concepts and Strategies*, in conjunction with many organisations, as a way of scoping the competitive set, helping a company in understanding the competitive positions in its target markets and diagnosing the effectiveness of a marketing strategy. This particular tool for practitioners is described in the Marketing Tools and Techniques box on page 55.

**Competitor scanning**
The monitoring of competitive positions and competitors' strategies

**Competitive positions proforma**
A tool for scoping the competitive set, helping a company to understand the competitive positions in its target markets and diagnosing the effectiveness of a marketing strategy

## Marketing Tools and Techniques

### Practitioners' Use of Competitor Intelligence: the Dibb/Simkin Competitive Positions Proforma

The understanding of competition is not generally strong in most organisations. Managers may be able to name their rivals, and these businesses' products, price points and outline promotional activity, but rarely are managers able to suggest rivals' next moves or to identify an individual competitor's strengths or weaknesses. Therefore, managers cannot be taking into account the capabilities and market standing of such rivals when they construct their own target market strategies. The result could be a significant waste, as a company's marketing programme may fail to enable the business to set itself apart from its principal rivals. Worse, the business may be incapable of combating their rivals' marketing strategies.

The ultimate goal in marketing is to produce a differential advantage: something desired by targeted customers and only offered by a single supplier. Failure to analyse rivals means that the creation of a differential advantage is going to occur only by chance, rather than due to knowledge of competitors' strengths and weaknesses.

The strategists also point to the need to address an organisation's own weaknesses. In particular, a management team should be aware of which rivals are best placed to exploit any weaknesses in the organisation or in its marketing mix. Over time, the competitive set will change, as new entrants and substitution solutions to customers' requirements emerge. The relative strengths and weaknesses of competitors will alter, too, often rapidly. The competitive set must be monitored closely and not just occasionally.

Chapter 9 identifies methods for collecting competitor intelligence. Once the competitive set has been defined – through the customer's eyes – and some knowledge has been built up about these brands, a useful tool to deploy is the competitive positions proforma.

This technique is based on warfare analogies and assumes that the analysis is replicated for each individual target market segment. Within each segment, it is necessary to allocate the competitive set – which may include substitutes and possible new entrants – into the following categories.

- *Market Leader.* Only ever one in a segment: the player or brand with the biggest market share. The market leader should (1) expand the total market, (2) expand its own market share, and (3) protect existing market share. The market leader has to defend and attack.
- *Market Challenger*(s). Non-market leaders that want to be the leader! Aggressively attacking for market share gains by investing in new product devel-opment, establishing distribution, promotional activity, field force increases or price incentives.
- *Market Follower*(s). Low-share rivals without resources, market position, R&D or commitment to challenge. The 'me-too' smaller players in a market segment.
- *Market Nicher*(s). Companies that specialise in terms of market/product/customers, by finding a safe, profitable niche or narrowly defined segment.
- *Market Fast Mover*(s). Smaller players with intentions to be much bigger. A rival not yet large enough to be classed as a Challenger, but one worth watching or 'knocking out' before it is too late.

One column of the proforma is completed for each market segment. A business should include itself within the columns. In this way, a management team may assess the business's relative performance across market segments and identify rivals making gains in more than one segment. In this context, the technique is of great value to the Board of a company and not only to marketing managers.

Marketing-oriented businesses repeat this analysis every few months, in order to reveal movements within the columns and to identify fast movers, new entrants or emerging substitute competition. The changing strengths and weaknesses of rivals also become apparent. If a business is not moving up the column – or 'league table' – it is likely that its marketing strategy and/or marketing programme are inappropriately specified. Remedial action should be taken.

**The Competitive Positions**

For reasons of commercial confidentiality, the identities of the cited retailers have been disguised.

**The Dibb/Simkin Competitive Positions Proforma**

| | | Grocery Superstores (out-of-town) | Supermarkets (town centres) |
|---|---|---|---|
| **Market Leader** | ID:<br>Market Share:<br>KCVs:<br>Weaknesses:<br>Differential Adv: | Doing Well plc<br>28%++ (growing)<br>Range, fresh produce, store amenities, deals<br>Board's focus overseas, Comp Commission<br>Loyalty card scheme | Still Trying plc<br>24% +/– (static)<br>Locations, fresh produce<br>No compelling wow factor, poor PR<br>– |
| **Challenger 1** | ID:<br>Market Share:<br>KCVs:<br>Weaknesses:<br>Differential Adv: | Going For It Ltd<br>21%+ (growing)<br>Range, non-food mix, clothing, amenities, value<br>Some tired stores, no town centre stores<br>US owner = greater resources, buying power | Doing Well plc<br>16++ (growing)<br>Brand reputation, e-service, fresh produce<br>Pulled out, now re-establishing<br>– |
| **Challenger 2** | ID:<br>Market Share:<br>KCVs:<br>Weaknesses:<br>Differential Adv: | Still Trying plc<br>19% – (declining)<br>Store ambiance, range, reputation, amenities<br>Poor analysis & PR, limited non-food<br>– | New Kid on the Block (Merger)<br>9%++ (growing)<br>Many good locations, fresh produce, value<br>Had lost its way, now catching up<br>– |
| **Challenger 3** | ID:<br>Market Share:<br>KCVs:<br>Weaknesses:<br>Differential Adv: | New Kid on the Block (Merger)<br>18%++ (growing)<br>Value, fresh produce<br>In-store amenities, no national coverage<br>– | Still Just About Here plc<br>9%+ (growing)<br>Value-for-money, brands stocked<br>Poor brand reputation, few strengths<br>– |
| **Follower 'Me Too'** | ID:<br>Market Share:<br>KCVs:<br>Weaknesses:<br>Differential Adv: | Still Just About Here plc<br>5% – (declining)<br>Store ambience<br>No brand strengths, no buying power<br>– | Also Just Surviving Ltd<br>7% +/– (static)<br>–<br>Mix of merchandise<br>– |
| **Fast Mover** | ID:<br>Market Share:<br>KCVs:<br>Weaknesses:<br>Differential Adv: | | SavaLot Ltd<br>6%++ (rapid expansion)<br>Value-for-money, merchandise mix<br>Low brand awareness, poor buying power |
| **Nicher** | ID:<br>Market Share:<br>KCVs:<br>Weaknesses:<br>Differential Adv: | HyperLand plc (JV)<br>3%<br>Range, value, store amenities, one-stop<br>Few outlets, few scale benefits<br>– | Deluxe Deli Ltd<br>2%+ (growing, SE only)<br>Service, staff attitude, opening hours, locations<br>Poor buying power, limited network, branding<br>Upscale appeal and target marketing |

The competitive positions proforma identifies:

- the key players and their relative positions
- current successes and probable reasons
- the KCVs (key customer values or needs) each rival is good at serving – rivals' customer-facing strengths that must be addressed
- any differential advantages (DAs) to fear – these must be combated
- the business's own standing, which should improve over time
- emerging and fast-moving rivals, including substitute solutions to customers' needs
- the evolving competitive set with which to do battle, and how!

The proforma, therefore, is a 'call to action' to a company's marketers. In addition, the technique acts as a diagnostic over time of a business's successes or failures in terms of its marketing strategy and programmes.

**Note:** The Dibb/Simkin Competitive Positions Proforma is copyright Sally Dibb and Lyndon Simkin. A more extensive explanation of this technique is offered in *The Market Segmentation Workbook* (Dibb and Simkin) and *The Marketing Planning Workbook* (Dibb, Simkin and Bradley), both originally published in 1996 by Thomson (London).

## Differential Advantage

**Differential advantage**
An attribute of a brand, product, service or marketing mix that is desired by the targeted customer and provided by only one supplier

If a marketing mix is developed that matches target market needs and expectations and is superior to those offered by competitors, there is a real – or perceived – differential advantage. A **differential advantage** is an attribute of a brand, product, service or marketing mix that is desired by the targeted customer and provided by only one supplier: it is a unique edge over rivals in satisfying this customer. If successful in developing a differential advantage, an organisation is likely to have its differential advantage copied by rivals. Direct Line innovated in selling car insurance over the telephone, cutting out the broker. This more convenient and cheaper service was very popular with customers, gaining market leadership for Direct Line. Very high profits followed. Rivals caught up, offering their own telephone-based direct selling of car insurance. Nevertheless, Direct Line developed a sizeable and successful customer base, which is still proving difficult for competitors to win back.

Achieving a differential advantage – or competitive edge – requires an organisation to make the most of its opportunities and resources while offering customers a satisfactory mix of tangible and intangible benefits.[25] When striking a balance between customer requirements on the one hand and company resources on the other, competitor activity must also be monitored. For example, there is little sense in promoting speedy distribution to customers if several large competing organisations offer a faster service. An understanding of competitors and customers' perceptions of companies' propositions is an essential part of identifying a differential advantage. Once determined, it is sensible to maximise the use of any differential advantage in the marketing mix, particularly in the promotional mix.

There are many different sources of differential advantage that companies can pursue. It is important to ensure that the promoted differential advantage is:

- unique to the one organisation, otherwise it is not a differential advantage only a strength or capability
- desirable to the targeted customer
- not simply the expected marketing mix taken for granted by the target market
- not simply an internal perception by a team of marketers.

For example, a new range may be superior to its predecessor, but compared to competitors' products may offer few benefits to the customer. The marketers could be guilty of identifying the new range's advantages over the former range, wrongly, as offering a differential advantage.

Low price should also be avoided as a differential advantage at the centre of a marketing programme unless a company genuinely has the scale economies to maintain a low cost base and offer cost leadership. Only one company in any market can occupy this platform, as explained by Porter's generic routes to achieving a competitive advantage. Others are vulnerable to being undercut and losing their apparent differential advantage. Jet's lowest price proposition was undermined by Esso's highly effective Tigerwatch lowest price guarantee. Low price can be utilised as a short-term tactic – to off-load excessive stocks, for example – but should not form a differential advantage unless it can be defended against all challenges.

**Basis for competing**
A business's combined strengths as identified in a SWOT analysis and any differential advantage, which should form the leading edge of the business's marketing strategy

If there is no observable differential advantage, a business must look to its strengths over its rivals. While not unique, these will still form the foundation for its ability to compete effectively. The SWOT analysis assists marketers in identifying their strengths and capabilities. The composite of any differential advantage with any strengths is a company's **basis for competing**, which should form the leading edge of the organisation's marketing strategy. For some companies, such as 3M, innovativeness is the basis for competing, while for others, like Vidal Sassoon hair salons, image plays an important part. The Body Shop concentrates on environmentally friendly cosmetics, whereas for multiplex cinemas the basis for competing is the choice of multiple screens at one location. Some of these ways of gaining an edge are easier to sustain than others. For example, many UK companies that have traditionally focused on low price have found this advantage difficult to maintain in the long term.[26] The airline industry is just one to be plagued by periodic price wars, with many companies turning instead to flexibility and customer service as the basis for competing, while others have adopted a value-based strategy.

**Identifying Differential Advantage** There is a straightforward sequence that marketers follow when attempting to identify a differential advantage.

1. Identify the market's segments.
2. Establish what product and service attributes are desired and demanded by customers in each segment.
3. Decide which of these attributes the company in question offers.
4. Determine which attributes the company's competitors offer.
5. Consider what the marketplace perceives the competitors' genuine strengths to be.
6. Identify whether any gaps exist between customer expectations of the product/ service on offer and perceptions of the competitors' marketing programmes.
7. Consider whether any gaps identified in step 6 are matched by the company and its own offerings. If the company is able to match one or more of these gaps, the potential exists for a differential advantage to be developed.

8 Question whether any of these potential advantages for the business can be emphasised through sales and marketing programmes.
9 Consider the sustainability of these advantages for the company. How easily and quickly can competitors catch up? Is it possible for the company to defend these advantages?
10 If there are no current advantages for the company, given the gaps identified between competitors' propositions and customer expectations, consider which areas offer potential for developing a future differential advantage.
11 In order to maximise any existing or potential differential advantages, detail the changes the company must make to its research and development, engineering, sales and marketing activities.

It is important to remember that companies frequently examine their relative strengths and weaknesses in relation to their rivals. A strength is not the same as a differential advantage. For example, many rivals may also have strong brand awareness, products that perform well, loyal distributors or high profitability. A differential advantage is something that targeted customers want and value, and that only one supplier is able to provide.

## Marketing Objectives

Once an organisation has agreed which marketing opportunities are worth pursuing and on which target markets to focus marketing and sales activities, the organisation must ensure that its marketing strategy specifies its core marketing objectives. These marketing objectives are typically defined in terms of which are the most desirable market segments to target and, for each of these priority market segments, what market share is being sought and thereby what sales volumes or levels are expected to be achieved.

Marketers must specify a raft of performance metrics, including customer satisfaction or brand awareness measures, profitability and financial contribution – or in retailing, sales per square metre of selling space. Marketing objectives may include various product and market developments that marketers expect to achieve. These developments may include new product launches, new territory or market segment entry, the creation of innovative distribution channels or partnerships with marketing channel members. Without specification of these expectations it is difficult to ensure a fit with the organisation's overall corporate strategy. It is impossible, too, to monitor ongoing performance or benchmark the effectiveness of the recommended marketing strategy against competitors' strategies. This very important theme of marketing performance is explored further in Chapter 24.

## Marketing Mix Decisions

As mentioned in Chapter 1, marketers must decide which products or services to offer to selected target markets, the attributes, specifications, performance characteristics and designs of these products, and the levels of customer service required to support them and to encourage customer satisfaction. In addition, prices must be set, payment terms and mechanisms agreed; distribution channels have to be chosen and distribution channel members orchestrated, in order to ensure product availability at places appropriate for the targeted customers. These customers must be made aware of the product through promotional activity – marketing communications – and their interest in the product maintained through promotional campaigns. These product, people, price, place and promotion decisions are what are termed the marketing mix decisions. They occupy the majority of marketers' time and account for most of a marketing department's budget.

Parts III to VII of this book explore in detail the ingredients of the marketing mix, and the tactical toolkit utilised by marketers in developing marketing programmes designed to implement their recommended marketing strategy and target market strategy.

These product, people, price, place/distribution and promotion issues should be determined only after the marketing strategy has been agreed. The marketing strategy itself should be developed only after the core marketing analyses have been undertaken on: market trends, marketing environment forces, customer buying behaviour, competition, opportunities and capabilities. The marketing process outlined in Chapter 1 requires analysis, strategy formulation and then the specification of a marketing mix to facilitate the implementation of the desired target market strategy. Nevertheless, marketing programmes created from the ingredients of the marketing mix are part of the creation of an effective marketing strategy. Without the specification of marketing mixes, marketing strategies will not be effectively operationalised.

## Implementation and Performance Monitoring

Marketing programmes depend on a detailed marketing mix specification: product, place/distribution, promotion, price and people issues. In addition, marketing programmes require the specification of budgets for actioning the desired marketing mix recommendations. These budgets must reflect the anticipated sales from the sales forecast – see Chapter 23 – and the trends inherent in the targeted market segments. Sales and marketing personnel must know of their responsibilities in implementing the recommended marketing programmes. There may be a requirement on colleagues outside the sales and marketing functions or on senior executives. Schedules must be determined so that it is clear when specific marketing mix activities are expected to occur.

It is essential that the implementation of a marketing strategy be facilitated. This involves specifying by whom, when, how and at what cost the desired marketing mix programmes will be actioned. There may be internal marketing issues to address, such as those connected with the sharing of marketing intelligence and strategies; communication channels within the business; hierarchical support and resources. Finally, marketing must demonstrate its worth. Marketing programmes should be evaluated against predetermined performance measures to ensure their effective implementation and success in terms of the desired marketing objectives detailed within the marketing strategy. These themes are explored in Chapter 24.

# Summary

*Marketing strategy* identifies which opportunities are to be pursued, indicates the specific markets towards which activities are to be targeted and defines the types of competitive advantage that are to be developed and exploited. A marketing strategy aims to target customer segments of most benefit to an organisation in a manner that best utilises the organisation's capabilities, provides a differential advantage over competitors and matches the organisation's corporate goals.

» A *strategic market plan* is an outline of the methods and resources required to achieve an organisation's goals within specific target markets; it takes into account all the functional areas of a business unit that must be coordinated. A *strategic business unit (SBU)* is a division, product line or other profit centre within a parent company, and is used to define areas for consideration in a specific strategic market plan. The process of *strategic market planning* yields a marketing strategy that is the framework for a marketing plan. A *marketing plan* includes the framework and entire set of activities to be performed; it is the written document or blueprint for specifying, implementing and controlling an organisation's marketing activities and marketing mixes.

» Through the process of strategic market planning, an organisation can develop marketing strategies that, when properly implemented and controlled, will contribute to achieving the organisation's overall goals. The marketing mix and associated implementation processes designed to operationalise the marketing strategy are the organisation's *marketing programme*. Most marketing programmes centre around a detailed marketing mix specification and include internal controls and procedures to ensure that they are implemented effectively. Marketing environment forces are important in – and profoundly affect – the strategic market planning process. These forces imply opportunities and threats that influence an organisation's overall goals.

» Central to the marketing strategy is a clear view of the corporate mission and goals. These may well be developed separately to the marketing strategy but the marketing strategy must aim to reflect the overall corporate vision. A company's organisational goals should be derived from its *mission* – that is, the broad, long-term tasks that the organisation wants to achieve. These goals should guide planning efforts and specify the ends, or results, that are sought. *Corporate strategy* determines the means for utilising resources in the areas of production, logistics, finance, research and development, human resources, IT and marketing to reach the organisation's goals.

» There are three major considerations in assessing opportunities and resources:
(1) evaluating marketing opportunities, (2) environmental scanning, and (3) understanding the company's capabilities and assets. A *marketing opportunity* arises when the right combination of circumstances occurs at the correct time, allowing an organisation to take action towards reaching a target market. An opportunity offers a favourable chance for the company to generate sales from identifiable markets. A *strategic window* is a temporary period of optimum fit between the key requirements of a market and the particular capabilities of a company competing in that market. *Market requirements* relate to customers' needs or desired benefits. Market requirements are satisfied by components of the marketing mix that provide buyers with these benefits. *Environmental scanning* is the process of collecting information about the marketing environment to help marketers identify opportunities and threats, and assist in planning. A company's *capabilities* relate to distinctive competencies that it has developed to do something well and efficiently. A company is likely to enjoy a differential advantage in an area in which its competencies and *marketing assets* out-do those of its potential competition. Marketing assets are a categorisation of an organisation's strengths or capabilities in terms of customer-facing assets; distribution-based assets; and internal, operational or resource assets.

» The *SWOT analysis* is little more than a set of checklists, but it is a popular tool for analysing the capabilities of an organisation in terms of strengths and weaknesses, and for linking identified opportunities and threats to these capabilities. So long as the analysis identifies the most important issues – supported with validation – and managers consider appropriate actions to address the emerging priorities, the SWOT analysis is useful for identifying necessary actions. It is important that any weaknesses that could be leveraged by competitors are rectified, and that managers strive to pre-empt any threats identified.

» Having evaluated the overall corporate vision, those responsible for devising the marketing strategy must build on their analysis of opportunities and internal capabilities by analytically assessing the most promising directions for their business and its marketing activity. *Ansoff's matrix* for determining competitive strategies is a suitable tool, offering four options: market penetration, market development, product development or diversification. *Strategic objectives* that can be implemented through marketing include intense growth, diversified growth and integrated growth. *Intense growth* includes *market penetration*, *market development* or *product development*. *Diversified growth* includes *horizontal*, *concentric* and *conglomerate diversification*. *Integrated growth* includes forwards, backwards and horizontal integration.

» Integral to achieving a company's corporate vision is the need to develop a loyal customer base of satisfied customers. It is essential to continuously improve the company's marketing programmes so as to address evolving target market customer needs and expectations. The market segmentation process of segmentation, targeting and positioning is a core element of a recommended marketing strategy. *Brand positioning* is the creation of a desirable, distinctive and plausible image for a brand that will have strong appeal for the customers in a target market segment. A *target market strategy* is the choice of which market segment(s) an organisation decides to prioritise and for which to develop marketing programmes.

» The *competition* is those organisations viewed as marketing products similar to, or substitutable for, a company's products, when targeted at the same customers. Strategists argue that organisations should work to attain a *competitive advantage*. While not always possible to achieve, success without a competitive advantage is unlikely in most markets. Competitive advantage is the achievement of superior performance vis-à-vis rivals: through differentiation to create distinctive product appeal or brand identity; through providing customer value and achieving the lowest delivered cost; or by focusing on narrowly scoped product categories or market niches so as to be viewed as a leading specialist. The so-called *generic routes to competitive advantage* are cost leadership, differentiation and focus, and are not mutually exclusive: while it is not possible to pursue all three routes to creating a competitive advantage, many businesses successfully pursue two of these routes.

» It is important to understand the nature of competition and to utilise this knowledge in determining a marketing strategy. Aspects of the marketing strategy should be purposively designed to maximise any weaknesses in competitors' activities and pre-empt any impending moves from rivals. As defined by Porter's *five competitive forces*, competitors should not be viewed only as like-for-like rivals: new entrants, substitute products or services, and the bargaining power of suppliers and of buyers can all form competitive threats or opportunities. The competitive set must be defined by marketers, ensuring it reflects customers' views of direct alternatives and substitute options.

» In developing strategies, an organisation should consider the *competitive positions* in the marketplace. The *market leader* must both defend its position and seek new sales opportunities. Attack may prove the best form of defence. *Market challengers* must aggressively seek market share gains but carefully select the basis on which to attack: a chink in the leader's armour, for example, or a quick response to changing consumer needs. *Fast movers* may be small but they have the potential to win market share from rivals and should be combated. *Market followers* are the 'me-too, also-rans', prone to be squeezed in times of recession or in response to challengers' aggression. *Market nichers* specialise in terms of product and customer segment: they can very successfully tailor their marketing to their customers' needs but are vulnerable to competitors' entry into their target segments. To compete successfully, any organisation needs to consider the principles of *defensive* and *offensive warfare* and to understand its competitors' strategies through *competitor scanning*. The competitive positions proforma is an increasingly popular tool for evaluating competition across a company's segments or markets.

» An organisation should strive for a *differential advantage* or competitive edge in its markets. A differential advantage is an attribute of a brand, product, service or marketing mix that is desirable to targeted customers and provided by only one supplier. Marketers should emphasise the desirable attributes of a company's marketing mix that their target customers consider unmatched by competitors. The combined strengths, as identified in a SWOT analysis, and any differential advantages make up the *basis for competing*, which should form the leading edge of a company's marketing strategy.

» A marketing strategy must specify its core marketing objectives, typically defined in terms of market segments to address, desired market shares, customer satisfaction or brand awareness measures, profitability and financial contribution, plus any planned product and market developments. Without specification of objectives it is difficult to assess the performance of the marketing strategy or to ensure its fit with the overall corporate strategy.

» The ingredients of the marketing mix – product, place/distribution, promotion, price and people issues – should be determined only after a marketing strategy has been specified. The marketing strategy must be decided only after the essential analyses of marketing – market trends, the marketing environment forces, customer buying behaviour, competition, opportunities and capabilities – have been undertaken. Analysis should come first, then strategic thinking and, finally, determination of implementation programmes, as explained in Chapter 1's examination of the marketing process.

» Marketing programmes depend on detailed marketing mix specifications, but also on the determination of budgets for implementing these marketing mix requirements. These budgets must reflect the sales forecast and trends in the targeted market segments. Sales and marketing personnel should take responsibility for implementing the marketing plan's recommendations, and schedules for marketing mix activity must be established. Implementation of a marketing strategy has to be facilitated, which involves specifying by whom, when, how and at what cost the desired marketing programmes will be implemented. These programmes must be evaluated against predetermined performance measures.

## » *Key Links*

This chapter, examining marketing strategy, must be read after having understood the scope of marketing and the marketing process as outlined in Chapter 1. Other links include:

- Chapter 3's explanation of the forces of the macro and micro marketing environment, and the importance of environmental scanning
- Chapter 8's discussion of the market segmentation process, central to developing a target market strategy
- Chapter 23's review of the marketing planning process and the production of a marketing plan
- Chapter 24's examination of marketing performance measurement and marketing strategy implementation processes.

## Important Terms

Marketing strategy
Strategic market plan
Strategic business unit (SBU)
Strategic market planning
Marketing plan
Marketing programme
Mission
Corporate strategy
Marketing opportunity
Strategic window
Market requirements
Environmental scanning
Capabilities
Marketing assets
SWOT analysis
Ansoff matrix
Strategic objectives
Intense growth
Market penetration
Market development
Product development
Diversified growth
Horizontal diversification
Concentric diversification
Conglomerate diversification
Integrated growth
Brand positioning
Target market strategy
Competitors
Competitive advantage
Generic routes to competitive advantage
Competitive set
Five competitive forces
Competitive positions
Market leader
Market challengers
Fast movers
Market followers
Market nichers
Defensive warfare
Offensive warfare
Competitor scanning
Competitive positions proforma
Differential advantage
Basis for competing

## Discussion and Review Questions

1 Why should an organisation develop a marketing strategy? What is the difference between strategic market planning and the strategy itself?
2 Identify the major components of strategic market planning and explain how they are interrelated.
3 In what ways do marketing environment forces affect strategic market planning? Give some specific examples.
4 What is a mission statement? Why must marketing strategists understand their business's corporate strategy?
5 What are some of the issues that must be considered in analysing a business's opportunities and resources? How do these issues affect marketing objectives and marketing strategy?
6 Why is marketing opportunity analysis necessary? What are the determinants of marketing opportunity?
7 What are the components of a SWOT analysis?
8 In relation to resource constraints, how can environmental scanning affect a company's long-term strategic market planning? Consider product costs and benefits affected by the environment.
9 What is the difference between market penetration, market development and product development?
10 Why do you think more companies are diversifying? Give some examples of diversified businesses.
11 Target marketing – the market segmentation process – is at the heart of a marketing strategy. Why must this be so?
12 What is competitive advantage?
13 Why should companies attempt to understand the strategies of their competitors? Explain your views.
14 How can a market leader best defend its competitive position?
15 What are the strengths of a market nicher? In what way is a nicher vulnerable?
16 What is meant by the term differential advantage? How does this relate to the concept of competitive advantage?
17 Why must a marketing strategy include detailed marketing objectives?
18 In what ways should implementation of a marketing strategy be facilitated?

## Recommended Readings

- Aaker, D., *Strategic Marketing Management* (New York: Wiley, 2001).
- Adcock, D., *Marketing Strategies for Competitive Advantage* (Chichester: Wiley, 2000).
- Baker, M., *Marketing Strategy and Management* (Basingstoke: Palgrave Macmillan, 2000).
- Cravens, D. and Piercy, N., *Strategic Marketing* (London: McGraw-Hill, 2002).
- Littler, D. and Wilson, D., *Marketing Strategy* (Oxford: Butterworth-Heinemann, 1995).
- Porter, M.E., *Competitive Strategy: Techniques for Analysing Industries and Competitors* (New York: Free Press, 1980).

## Internet Exercise

Consider a large, well-known company with which you have regular dealings, such as a major retailer, financial institution or hotel group. Or select a manufacturer whose products you purchase frequently, such as Nestlé, Sony or Vodafone. Log on to the selected organisation's website.

Ignore the investors' pages, corporate information pages, PR releases, and so forth. Look at the site from the perspective of a customer and access only the customer-relevant pages (those to do with products, services, offers, customer services, stockist location, and so on).

1 What customer-relevant information is offered by the website you have chosen?
2 In what ways is the website striving to make the organisation appear 'special' or particularly good?
3 Given the website material, how would you interpret the selected strategy for this organisation? What is its apparent sense of purpose and what seem to be its leading priorities?

# *Applied Mini-Case*

A decade ago, Korean car manufacturer Daewoo entered the European market with wacky advertising, innovative dealer arrangements and value-for-money cars. While based on dated car designs, the company nevertheless made reasonable inroads into the small and medium-sized car sectors. As part of Korea's well-publicised economic woes, conglomerate Daewoo headed for bankruptcy. The car business was acquired by strategic partner General Motors of the USA in 2002. A new corporate identity for Daewoo followed, as well as a relaunch for the brand in 2003.

General Motors, known for Vauxhall and Opel in Europe, owns the Chevrolet marque in the States, which is the company's value-based range and marque. General Motors is considering how to roll out its Chevrolet marque in Europe. Should it try to sell existing Chevrolet models in Europe, or develop more European-looking models for European consumers? Should Chevrolet establish a new dealer network in Europe, be sold alongside the Vauxhall and Opel ranges in existing GM dealers, or be retailed by third parties or through the Internet? Or should the Daewoo range of cars and dealers in Europe be rebadged as Chevrolet? These questions are not easy to answer and General Motor's senior managers have been agonising for some time to determine their strategy.

### Question

**As the senior marketer tasked to assess the market's probable response to these options, what steps would you take?**

## Case Study

## St Andrew's Hospital: a Charity's Marketing Strategy

St Andrew's Hospital in Northampton is the market leader in many types of mental health care in the UK. In addition to its large site in Northampton, St Andrew's has created satellite facilities in the south-east of England. As a leading specialist provider, the organisation's patients are referred to the hospital from throughout the UK and beyond.

As a charity, its focus is not on helping mental health sufferers in the community, or charity shop-style fundraising, or increasing the general public's awareness of mental health issues – other charities and bodies address these important tasks. St Andrew's Hospital is a fully specified hospital with leading experts, state-of-the-art care pathways and an eminent reputation within the mental health care profession. St Andrew's divisions address everything from adolescent learning difficulties through to major behavioural problems, with patients requiring secure accommodation and lengthy treatment programmes. It has a specialist unit dealing with brain injuries and, through an on-site partner, also offers clinic facilities for patients needing to 'dry out'. Its staff are recognised as being leading-edge thinkers.

The St Andrew's brand reputation is based on the quality of its care, its multiple care pathways and its ability to relate to patients, their families, and to the medical staff or personnel in social services who refer patients to the hospital. St Andrew's has charitable status, but strives to set its fees sufficiently high to permit it to provide the high-quality care that is at the core of its ethos, and to continually reinvest in its facilities and treatment programmes.

Despite its success, its diversity of operations places significant demands on its capital spending: wards and facilities require modernising, newly devised care programmes may require remodelled facilities, the expansion of demand led by reduced state provision of mental health facilities pressurises the organisation's caring professionals to provide expanded facilities. Private-sector commercial businesses have entered the more financially lucrative parts of the market. St Andrew's must defend its position in these segments, as fee income from these activities is required to support the hospital as a whole and to cross-subsidise other segments of the market deemed less financially attractive by new-entrant competitors. In order to defend its market share in these segments, the hospital has to develop marketing strategies and devote resources to marketing programmes designed to maintain the loyalty of referring GPs, medical consultants and social workers.

The requirement is growing to tailor marketing messages to a growing mix of audiences. Commercially minded competitors are developing 'glitzy' marketing programmes and St Andrew's has to maintain its visibility to key stakeholders in this quickly evolving marketplace.

While some patients deal directly with the charity, the vast majority are referred from the National Health Service (NHS). St Andrew's has a reputation for being able to deal with difficult patients suffering from complex problems. However, the NHS is increasingly moving towards centralised buying, with numerous NHS Trusts joining forces in order to be able to purchase services – such as those offered by St Andrew's – at lower rates. In addition to the medical staff diagnosing the patients' problems and recommending appropriate courses of treatment, the NHS has risk assessors, financial managers and professional purchasing executives, who all are involved in the decisions concerning which treatment programme to purchase and from which provider. For St Andrew's and other suppliers to the NHS, such formalised purchasing and group decision-making complicate the marketing activity and the engagement programmes the charity runs with its 'customers'. For the patient, to his/her family, to the referring medical staff and the numerous administrators involved, St Andrew's must develop bespoke messages, marketing communications and client-handling programmes. This complex buying centre must be addressed for St Andrew's to operate with full bed occupancy, in order to fulfil its mission to truly help those suffering with mental health problems.

The organisation has responded to these market forces by developing a corporate strategy and a marketing strategy, by allocating resources to producing and implementing marketing programmes, and by recruiting a set of marketing managers to support the various divisions' marketing activities.

**Sources:** St Andrew's Hospital, 2004; James Watkins, director of marketing and strategy, St Andrew's Hospital, 2003; *Marketing Briefs*, Sally Dibb and Lyndon Simkin (Oxford: Elsevier Butterworth-Heinemann), 2004.

## Questions for Discussion

1 For a non-profit organisation such as St Andrew's Hospital, what aspects of a marketing strategy will be the most important?
2 Why are organisations such as St Andrew's Hospital turning to marketing and the development of marketing strategies?
3 In what ways would a strategic market plan benefit St Andrew's Hospital?

# 3 The Marketing Environment

**"All businesses operate within an environment, which directly or indirectly affects the way in which they function, just as we as consumers live within a cultural and social environment which to a greater or lesser degree determines the way in which we behave as individuals."**

*Elaine O'Brien, University of Strathclyde*

## Objectives

- **To understand the concept of the marketing environment and the importance of environmental scanning and analysis**
- **To explore the broad forces of the macro marketing environment: political forces relevant to marketers, the influence of laws on marketing practices, the impact of government regulations and self-regulatory agencies, societal issues important to marketers, the effects of new technology on society and marketing activities, economic and competitive factors and their impact on organisations and customers' willingness and ability to buy**
- **To examine the company-specific micro marketing environment forces: the organisation, suppliers, marketing intermediaries, buyers, competitors and other publics**
- **To understand the role of the marketing environment in marketing opportunity analysis and the importance of strategic windows**

## Introduction

This chapter explores the external forces that impact on an organisation's trading and ability to satisfy its customers. These forces, over which organisations rarely have any direct control, are termed the *marketing environment* and fall into two categories: the macro and the micro forces of the marketing environment.

The very broad forces are the *macro marketing environment*: the political, legal, regulatory, societal, technological, and economic/competitive forces that impact on all organisations operating in a market and on their ability to carry out their affairs. Authors have increasingly distinguished these broad forces from an additional set of more company-specific external forces termed the *micro marketing environment* forces. These micro marketing environment forces are mostly aspects of the competitive arena.

After defining the marketing environment and considering why it is necessary for marketers to *scan* and analyse these forces, each of these macro and micro forces is discussed. Awareness of these issues and trends may create *strategic windows* of opportunity. Ignorance of such forces jeopardises an organisation's ability to perform well and may leave the organisation more vulnerable to the actions of more aware competitors.

*Opener*

# Regulatory Influence: the EU Single Market

In 1947 the launching of the Marshall Plan presented a blueprint for the economic reconstruction of a Europe devastated by the Second World War. This led in 1948 to the creation of the Organisation for European Economic Co-operation (OEEC), the precursor of today's economic union. In March 1957 the Treaty of Rome was signed to establish the European Economic Community (EEC). By 1973, with the arrival of Denmark, Ireland and the UK, the EEC had grown to nine member states. Greece joined in 1981 and Portugal and Spain in 1986 to create the 'Euro 12'. The momentous signing of the Maastricht Treaty in 1992 established the European Union (EU) and by 1 January 1993 the European single market was at last a reality. The single market is defined by the EU as 'an economic area within which persons, goods, services and capital have unrestricted freedom of movement, which entails not only the elimination of customs barriers, but also of technical, tax and legislative obstacles'. By 2004, membership had swelled to 25 countries, including many eastern European countries, such as the Czech Republic, Estonia, Hungary, Latvia, Lithuania, Poland, Slovakia and Slovenia, plus Mediterranean countries Cyprus, Greece and Malta. Applicant countries include Bulgaria, Romania and Turkey, leaving only Norway and Russia as major countries not seeking membership.

The single market has had a significant impact on the populations of member and non-member trading states, as well as on marketers representing their companies. With the removal of so many bureaucratic barriers on 1 January 1993, professionally qualified personnel could seek employment without retraining in other member states; companies could tender for government contracts throughout the EU; imports and exports became subject to far fewer restrictions, less 'red tape', reduced customs controls and much freer movement within and between EU states. Immigration and travel have become much quicker and simpler than before. Health and safety working regulations have been harmonised, as have air travel regulations and even standards for mobile phone networks and VAT collection. The creation of the euro – the currency to which many member states are now signed up – further simplified cross-border business transactions and travel arrangements.

The EU has many critics, not least due to its Common Agricultural Policy (CAP), which takes more than half of the entire EU budget, is a significant drain on the resources of the richer member states and is currently being renegotiated. There are moans about the often top-heavy bureaucracy of European government in Brussels; and the inevitable formalisation of a great number of working practices when so many countries' rules and regulations are combined to form a single, cohesive approach. The financial conditions that must be met in order to participate in the euro, and the apparent flouting of these conditions by certain 'major league' member states, have added to the criticisms. The inclusion of seemingly 'weaker' eastern European economies has concerned people in the western European economies, which may well cross-subsidise these new member economies. However, there are few marketers who would claim that in the years since the harmonisation of Europe in 1993, doing business across Europe has not been simplified, opening up significant marketing opportunities for many businesses and presenting new competitive threats. The recent expansion of EU membership – doubling the number of consumers inside the single market – is of great interest to marketers. The EU continues to present new challenges and a reason to rethink marketing strategies. There is little doubt that the EU is an external factor in the marketing environment of most businesses and consumers that cannot be ignored.

**Sources:** EU policy documents, 1990–2004; *Europe in Figures*, Eurostat, Luxembourg, 1995; *Europe on the Move, From Single Market to European Union, Internal Market* – all EU, Brussels, publications. Photo: Courtesy of Alain Dixon.

The EU has a tremendous impact on the decisions and activities of marketers. The regulations and legal directives produced by the EU, plus the financial implications of many of its policies – such as the CAP and the criteria for participating in the euro – are aspects of the macro marketing environment. This chapter discusses both macro and micro forces, commencing with the broader macro issues. It includes a discussion of why and how marketers scan the forces of the marketing environment. The chapter concludes with an examination of how an understanding of these marketing environment forces assists a company in identifying strategic windows and maximising marketing opportunities.

## Examining and Responding to the Marketing Environment

**Marketing environment** The external forces that directly or indirectly influence an organisation's acquisition of inputs and generation of outputs, comprising six categories of forces: political, legal, regulatory, societal/Green, technological, and economic/competitive

The **marketing environment** consists of external forces that directly or indirectly influence an organisation's acquisition of inputs and generation of outputs. Inputs might include personnel, financial resources, raw materials and information. Outputs could be information such as advertisements, packages, goods, services or ideas. As indicated in Chapter 1 and as shown in Figure 1.4, the broad marketing environment consists of six categories of forces: political, legal, regulatory, societal/Green, technological and economic/competitive. Although there are numerous environmental factors, most fall into one of these six categories. These are termed the 'macro forces' of the marketing environment as they affect all organisations operating in a particular market. In addition, many authors have identified a set of issues termed the 'micro forces' of the marketing environment. These micro forces are more situation- and company-specific, including the business's internal environment, suppliers, marketing intermediaries, buyers, competitors and the company's publics.

Whether they fluctuate rapidly or slowly, environmental forces are always dynamic. Changes in the marketing environment can create uncertainty, threats and opportunities for marketers. Although the future is not very predictable, marketers can estimate what will happen, although some fail to do so, thus negatively affecting the performance of their businesses. Astute marketers continually modify their marketing strategies in response to the dynamic environment. Marketing managers who fail to recognise changes in environmental forces leave their companies unprepared to capitalise on marketing opportunities or to cope with threats created by changes in the environment.

Organisations that cannot deal with an unfavourable environment are at risk of going under.[1] For example, during the OPEC-led recession of the mid-1970s many manufacturers cut back on their workforces, causing unemployment rates of over 40 per cent in many suburbs. Many local retailers and small shopkeepers, restaurants, take-aways and garages had anticipated neither the extent of the unemployment nor its effect on their businesses. Dozens of small, local businesses closed down. The 1990 Persian Gulf Crisis caused huge increases in the price of petrol, repeated in 2004 following the start of the latest Gulf War. In the 1990s, the car-buying public became even more concerned about fuel consumption, with a resultant decline in the sales of high-performance sports cars and executive saloons, causing problems for manufacturers such as Porsche and Jaguar. The Gulf Crisis also hit business travel and tourism, affecting the fortunes of many airlines and hotel operators. Civil war in the former Yugoslavia had tragic implications for the peoples of that region and an economic impact on the tour operators who specialised in holidays to the Yugoslav coast. The BSE beef crisis affected farmers, meat producers and supermarkets. Genetically modified (GM) foods caused a more recent storm with implications for food manufacturers and supermarkets. The activities of terrorists have had a significant impact on companies and the general public in many countries, with tourism and airline operators being particularly badly affected. Monitoring the marketing environment is crucial to an organisation's survival and to the long-term achievement of its goals.

## Environmental Scanning and Analysis

**Environmental scanning**
The process of collecting information about the forces in the marketing environment

**Environmental analysis**
The process of assessing and interpreting the information gathered through environmental scanning

To monitor changes in the marketing environment effectively, marketers must engage in environmental scanning and analysis. **Environmental scanning** is the process of collecting information about the forces in the marketing environment. Scanning involves: observation; keeping 'an ear to the ground'; perusal of secondary sources, such as the web, business, trade, government and general interest publications; and marketing research. However, managers must be careful not to gather so much information that sheer volume makes analysis impossible. **Environmental analysis** is the process of assessing and interpreting the information gathered through environmental scanning. A manager evaluates the information for accuracy, tries to resolve inconsistencies in the data and, if warranted, assigns significance to the findings. Through analysis, a marketing manager seeks to describe current environmental changes and to predict future changes. By evaluating these changes, the manager should be able to determine possible threats and opportunities linked to environmental fluctuations. Understanding the current state of the marketing environment and recognising the threats and opportunities arising from changes within it, help marketing managers assess the performance of current marketing efforts and develop marketing strategies for the future. The Marketing Tools and Techniques box below describes how organisations often conduct an analysis of the marketing environment.

## Marketing Tools and Techniques

### Practitioners' Assessment of the Macro Marketing Environment

The marketing environment forces are not obviously part of an individual's routine job specification, particularly within the marketing function. However, businesses must monitor these forces through environmental scanning in order to pre-empt possible problems caused by unfavourable market developments, but also in order to leverage any emerging opportunities ahead of competitors. The identification of strategic windows and the chance to take first mover advantage are desires among senior managers and marketers.

The forces of the micro marketing environment and competitive pressures are usually evaluated within a marketing team's analysis of competition (see Chapter 2). Companies must examine the macro forces, too, however. While research indicates that many fail to do so, 'best practice' companies typically adopt one of two approaches to assessing their marketing environments.

1 Individual managers or small work groups are allocated to each of the macro forces: social, economic, legal, regulatory, political, technological. As 'champions' for their allocated topic, such managers collate intelligence from stakeholders, employees and external sources in order to build up a picture of the key trends and developments. These managers either suggest the emerging implications for their business and make recommendations, or they present their findings at a sales and marketing meeting or to senior managers for their debate and consideration. The development of company intranets has significantly assisted the networking so important for the collation of topical and relevant information.

2 An organisation may intermittently stage workshops to which cross-functional and multi-hierarchical personnel are invited. For example, R&D personnel may be aware of technological trends, the company secretary of legal or regulatory issues, the salesforce of economic or social forces, and so on. Typically, each of the macro marketing environment forces is discussed in turn, in a 'brainstorming' exercise. Certain themes or 'hot topics' then emerge to be debated further within the workshop. The company then allocates an individual manager or creates a small taskforce to examine a particular issue in more detail, in order to subsequently develop an action plan based on more information.

Some companies invite external experts, suppliers, partners or even customers to such a workshop. If these external opinions are not sought as part of the workshop, any planned activity by the business resulting from this workshop-based analysis must await some external validation after the workshop.

Such sessions are an excellent way in which a business can harness the expertise across its functions and within its marketing channel in order to prioritise actions that should minimise the impact of a negative external development or maximise an emerging opportunity.

In this type of forum, the senior management team – supported by functional experts and channel partner personnel – brainstormed the key issues from the macro marketing environment for a leading insurance business. The priorities emerged as shown in the list (right).

While some of these forces, such as the weather, were outside the influence of the business, many of them could be addressed. Indeed, while the weather could not be altered, the company did decide to re-examine its exposure to flood plain customers and modified its policy cover accordingly.

Within each of these rather broad-brush summary bullets lay much detail to explore and to discuss. An example of a resulting action was to more closely manage the activities of the field salesforce, harnessing the latest mobile office technology solutions and customer relationship management field systems (see Chapter 4). As a result, the already low level of client complaints for inappropriate selling approaches virtually disappeared, and the highly ethical stance in controlling the salesforce bolstered the company's brand reputation and thereby its ability to recruit high-calibre personnel. This strategy also reflected the growing litigious culture among consumers and thereby addressed another of the trends identified during the workshop.

It is important to have a good mix of inputs – market information and personnel – to any assessment of the macro forces of the marketing environment, and to solicit the views of stakeholders other than those participating in the session. For example, partners, channel members, market analysts, industry experts or consultants, and even customers, are all useful sources both for marketing intelligence and for checking out suggested action plans.

Having identified the key issues – the macro marketing environment forces – currently of relevance, the business must consider the implications. The 'So what does this mean to us and to our business?' question has to be answered. Is the issue a threat or an opportunity? What resulting actions must be taken? Certain trends and developments may pose a threat, while other forces may be creating an opportunity. Sometimes, the same issue is both an opportunity and a threat. In the above example, had this company failed to implement changes to its field force's working practices, it would not have bolstered its reputation or improved the completion rate of its sales representatives. Worse, rivals may have been able to steal a march and measures designed to minimise the likelihood of client litigation would not now be in place.



**Note:** a more extensive explanation of this technique is offered in either *The Market Segmentation Workbook* (Dibb and Simkin) or *The Marketing Planning Workbook* (Dibb, Simkin and Bradley), both originally published in 1996 by Thomson, London.

**The Macro Marketing Environment for a Leading Insurance Company**

- Stock market (worthless investments, own share price/company value)
- New/more regulations (FSA, Gov, EU, within client sectors, accountancy)
- Over/under capacity in the industry/key sectors
- Many mergers and changes to the competitive set
- Structural changes in the sector and for clients
- Emerging compensation culture amongst clients and brokers
- Customers' expectation of better advice
- Greater role for technology (CRM, on-line quotes/claims, e-business)
- Distribution channel developments (role of brokers, e-commerce, tele-business, retailer new entrants)
- Recruitment problems/inability to make the sector attractive
- Global warming/changes to weather–greater claims

JCB, the construction equipment producer, allocated to individual managers the task of monitoring aspects of the macro marketing environment: political, legal, regulatory, societal (particularly the Green movement), technological, economic and competitive. A small committee met to prepare short papers and presentations to interested colleagues. When the laws relating to roadworks were amended, making contractors responsible for the safety of their sites and the long-term quality of the re-laid road surface, JCB recognised that many of its customers would have to alter their working practices as a result. So the company produced guides to assist these contractors in responding to the new legislation. In so doing, JCB was able to enhance its image and reputation as a leading player in the industry, and at the same time promote its products.

## Responding to Environmental Forces

In responding to environmental forces, marketing managers can take two general approaches: accept environmental forces as uncontrollable or confront and mould them. If environmental forces are viewed as uncontrollable, the organisation remains passive and reactive towards the environment. Instead of trying to influence forces in the environment, its marketing managers tend to adjust current marketing strategies to environmental changes. They approach marketing opportunities discovered through environmental scanning and analysis with caution. On the other hand, marketing managers who believe that environmental forces can be shaped adopt a proactive approach. For example, if a market is blocked by traditional environmental constraints, marketing

*Figure 3.1*
*The growing social awareness of healthy eating and the problems of obesity have created opportunities for many products, including Sunsweet's prunes*
*Source: Courtesy of Sunsweet*

managers may apply economic, psychological, political and promotional skills to gain access to it or operate within it. Once they identify what blocks a marketing opportunity, marketers can assess the power of the various parties involved and develop strategies to try to overcome environmental forces.[2]

In trying to influence environmental forces, marketers may seek to either create new marketing opportunities or extract greater benefits relative to costs from existing marketing opportunities. For instance, a company losing sales to competitors with lower-priced products may strive to develop technology that would make its production processes more efficient; greater efficiency would allow it to lower the prices of its own products. Political action is another way of affecting environmental forces. UK retailers, for example, successfully lobbied government to permit longer Sunday trading and legal opening of retail outlets all day. Airlines such as bmi lobbied government ministers to persuade the EU to enact its 'open skies' policy, providing more routes and landing slots for its planes. A proactive approach can be constructive and bring desired results. However, managers must recognise that there are limits on how much an environmental force can be shaped and that these limits vary across environmental forces. Although an organisation may be able to influence the enactment of laws through lobbying, it is unlikely that a single organisation can significantly increase the national birth rate or move the economy from recession to prosperity!

Generalisations are not possible. It cannot be stated that either of these approaches to environmental response is better than the other. For some organisations, the passive, reactive approach is more appropriate, but for other companies, the aggressive approach leads to better performance. What is certain is that ignorance of the forces of the marketing environment leads to problems and creates opportunities for rivals. The selection of a particular approach depends on an organisation's managerial philosophies, objectives, financial resources, customers and human skills, and on the specific composition of the set of environmental forces within which the organisation operates.

The rest of this chapter explores in detail the macro and micro marketing environment forces, and then examines the link between an understanding of these issues and marketing opportunity analysis.

## Political Forces

The political, legal and regulatory forces of the marketing environment are closely interrelated. Legislation is enacted, legal decisions are interpreted by the courts, and regulatory agencies are created and operated, for the most part, by people elected or appointed to political offices or by civil servants. Legislation and regulations (or the lack of them) reflect the current political outlook. Consequently, the political force of the marketing environment has the potential to influence marketing decisions and strategies.

Marketers need to maintain good relations with elected political officials for several reasons. When political officials are well disposed towards particular companies or industries, they are less likely to create or enforce laws and regulations unfavourable to these companies. For example, political officials who believe that oil companies are making honest efforts to control pollution are unlikely to create and enforce highly restrictive pollution control laws. In addition, governments are big buyers, and political officials can influence how much a government agency purchases and from whom. The UK government's liking of public–private partnerships for financing capital projects such as schools and hospitals has created significant opportunities for construction companies Amey and Jarvis or outsourcing specialists such as Capita and Fujitsu. Finally, political officials can play key roles in helping organisations secure foreign markets.

Many marketers view political forces as beyond their control; they simply try to adjust to conditions that arise from those forces. Some businesses, however, seek to influence political events by helping to elect to political office individuals who regard them positively. Much of this help is in the form of contributions to political parties. A sizeable contribution to a campaign fund may carry with it an implicit understanding that the party, if elected, will perform political favours for the contributing company. There are, though, strict laws governing donations and lobbying in most countries and, increasingly, ethical considerations for donor marketers (see Chapter 25).

# Legal Forces

A number of laws influence marketing decisions and activities. This discussion focuses on procompetitive and consumer protection laws and their interpretation.

## Procompetitive Legislation

**Procompetitive legislation**
Laws enacted to preserve competition and to end various practices deemed unacceptable by society

**Office of Fair Trading**
UK government office set up to oversee the trading practices of organisations and individuals in the UK

**Competition Commission**
An independent body in the UK that investigates monopolies to determine whether they operate against the public interest

**Procompetitive legislation** is enacted to preserve competition and to end various practices deemed unacceptable by society – for example, monopolies and mergers. In the UK, the president of the Board of Trade and the director general of the **Office of Fair Trading** can refer monopolies for investigation by the **Competition Commission**, an independent body whose members are drawn from a variety of backgrounds, including lawyers, economists, industrialists and trades unionists. The legislation defines a monopoly as a situation in which at least a quarter of a particular kind of good or service is supplied by a single person or a group of connected companies, or by two or more people acting in a way that prevents, restricts or distorts competition. Local monopolies can also be referred to the Commission. If the Commission finds that a monopoly operates against the public interest, the president of the Board of Trade has power to take action to remedy or prevent the harm that the Commission considers may exist. Alternatively, the director general of the Office of Fair Trading may be asked to negotiate undertakings to remedy the adverse effects identified by the Commission. The government believes that the market is a better judge than itself of the advantages and disadvantages of mergers, so most take-overs and proposed mergers are allowed to be decided by the companies' shareholders. However, when too much power would be placed in the hands of one organisation, company or person, the government will insist on a Monopolies and Mergers Commission appraisal. If the Commission believes it is against the public interest for a take-over or merger to proceed, then it will prohibit or limit any agreement between the companies or organisations involved. For example, when Morrisons acquired rival supermarket chain Safeway, the deal was permitted only on the basis that a number of Safeway stores were sold to a third party, ultimately Waitrose. The EU has a commissioner responsible for competition. In recent years, the commissioner has ruled on anti-competitive practices in many industries, from airlines to financial services, forcing companies to alter their trading practices and encouraging competition from a broader base of organisations.

Under the Financial Services Act of 1986, the director general of the Office of Fair Trading is required to consider the implications for competition of rules, regulations, guidance and other arrangements and practices of the regulatory bodies, investment exchanges and clearing houses. The director general must report to the president of the Board of Trade whenever a significant or potentially significant effect on competition has been identified. This legislation is for the protection of investors, and the secretary of state may refuse or revoke recognition of the organisation or require it to make alterations to its activities.

Under anti-competitive practices legislation, the director general of the Office of Fair Trading can investigate any business practice, whether in the public or private sector, that may restrict, distort or prevent competition in the production, supply or acquisition of goods or services. The Secretary of State has power to take remedial action. With the introduction of the Restrictive Trade Practices Act 1976, if two or more people who are party to the supply of goods or services accept some limitation on their freedom to make their own decisions about matters such as prices or conditions of sale, the Office of Fair Trading must be notified and such an agreement must be registered. Once an agreement has been registered, the director general is under a general duty to refer it to the Restrictive Practices Court, and the court must declare the restrictions in it contrary to the public interest unless the parties can satisfy the court that the public interest is not an issue. The vast majority of agreements never reach the court because parties elect to give up the restrictions rather than go through such a procedure.

Within the European Union, the objective of the competition policy is to ensure that there is free and fair competition in trade among member states and that the government trade barriers, which the Treaty of Rome seeks to dismantle, are not replaced by private barriers that fragment the Common Market. The EU has powers to investigate and terminate alleged infringements and to impose fines. The Treaty of Rome prohibits agreements or concertive practices that may affect trade among member states, and aims to prevent restriction or distortion of competition within the Common Market.[3] Most countries have similar procompetitive legislation. For example, in the United States the Sherman Anti-Trust Act prevents monopolistic situations, the Clayton Antitrust Act specifically prohibits price discrimination, and the Federal Trade Commission Act broadly prohibits unfair methods and empowers the Federal Trade Commission to work with the Department of Justice to enforce the provisions of the Clayton Antitrust Act. The Wheeler–Lea Act essentially makes unfair and deceptive acts or practices unlawful, regardless of whether they incur competition. The Robinson–Patman Act deals with discriminatory price differentials.[4]

## Consumer Protection Legislation

The second category of regulatory laws – consumer protection legislation – is not a recent development. However, consumer protection laws mushroomed in the mid-1960s and early 1970s. A number of them deal with consumer safety, while others relate to the sale of various hazardous products such as flammable fabrics and toys that might injure children. In the UK, the Fair Trading Act 1973 provides a mechanism – headed by the director general of the Office of Fair Trading – for the continuous review of consumer affairs, for actions dealing with trading practices that unfairly affect consumers' interests, for action against persistent offenders under existing law and for the negotiation of self-regulatory codes of practice to raise trading standards. Consumers' interests with regard to the purity of food, the description and performance of goods and services, and pricing information are safeguarded by the Food Act 1984, the Medicines Act 1968, the Misrepresentations Act 1967, the Trade Descriptions Act 1968, the Prices Act 1974, the Unfair Contract Terms Act 1977, the Sale of Goods Act 1979 and the Supply of Goods and Services Act 1982. The marking and accuracy of quantities are regulated by the Weights and Measures Act 1985. The Consumer Credit Act 1974 provides comprehensive protection for consumers who enter into credit or hire transactions. The Consumer Protection Act 1987 implements a harmonised European Union code of civil law covering product liability, creates a general criminal offence of supplying unsafe consumer goods, makes it an offence to give any misleading price indication and consolidates the powers provided under safety-related acts. The Financial Services Act 1986 offers greater protection to investors by establishing a new regulatory framework for the industry. Currently, legislation is pending concerning the production, packaging, supply and use of food.

In addition, consumer advice and information are provided to the general public at the local level by the Citizens Advice Bureau, and the Trading Standards or Consumer Protection departments of local authorities, and in some areas by specialist consumer advice centres. The independent, non-statutory National Consumer Council, which receives government finance, ensures that consumers' views are made known to those in government and industry. Nationalised industries and utilities have consumer councils whose members investigate questions of concern to the consumer, and many trade associations in industry and commerce have established codes of practice. In addition, several private organisations work to further consumer interests, the largest of which is the **Consumers' Association**, funded by the subscriptions of its membership of over one million people. The

**Consumers' Association** A private organisation, funded by members' subscriptions, that works to further consumer interests

association conducts an extensive programme of comparative testing of goods and investigation of services; its views and test reports are published in its monthly magazine *Which?*, and other publications.

**Interpreting Laws** Laws certainly have the potential to influence marketing activities, but the actual effects of the laws are determined by how marketers and the courts interpret them. Laws seem to be quite specific because they contain many complex clauses and sub-clauses. In reality, however, many laws and regulations are stated in vague terms that force marketers to rely on legal advice rather than their own understanding and common sense. Because of this vagueness, some organisations attempt to gauge the limits of certain laws by operating in a legally questionable way to see how far they can go with certain practices before being prosecuted. Other marketers, however, interpret regulations and statutes very conservatively and strictly to avoid violating a vague law. Although court rulings directly affect businesses accused of specific violations, they also have a broader, less direct impact on other businesses. When marketers try to interpret laws in relation to specific marketing practices, they often analyse recent court decisions, both to understand better what the law is intended to do and to gain a clearer sense of how the courts are likely to interpret it in the future.

## Regulatory Forces

Interpretation alone does not determine the effectiveness of laws and regulations; the level of enforcement by regulatory agencies is also significant. Some regulatory agencies are created and administered by government units; others are sponsored by non-governmental sources.

**Government** In the UK, the Department for Environment, Food and Rural Affairs (DEFRA) develops and controls policies for agriculture, horticulture, fisheries and food; it also has responsibilities for environmental and rural issues and food policies. The Department of Employment and Learning controls the Employment Service, employment policy and legislation, training policy and legislation, health and safety at work, industrial relations, wages councils, equal opportunities, small businesses and tourism, statistics on labour and industrial matters for the UK, the Careers Service, and international representation on employment matters and educational policy. DEFRA controls policies for planning and regional development, local government, new towns, housing, construction, inner-city matters, environmental protection, water, the countryside, sports and recreation, conservation, historic buildings and ancient monuments. The Export Credit Guarantee Department is responsible for the provision of insurance for exporters against the risk of not being paid for goods and services, access to bank finance for exports, and insurance cover for new investment overseas.

The Central Statistical Office prepares and interprets statistics needed for central economic and social policies and management; it coordinates the statistical work of other departments. The Department for Trade and Industry/Board of Trade controls industrial and commercial policy, promotion of enterprise and competition in the UK and abroad, and investor and consumer protection. Specific responsibilities include industrial innovation policy, regional industrial policy, business development, management development and business/education links, international trade policy, commercial relations and export promotions, competition policy, company law, insolvency, consumer protection and safety, radio regulations, and intellectual property. The Department of Transport is responsible for:- land, sea and air transport; rail network regulation; domestic and international civil aviation; international transport agreements; shipping and ports industries; navigation issues, HM Coastguard and marine pollution; motorways and trunk roads; road safety; and overseeing local authority transport.

These examples of British government departments are not unusual. Similar administrative bodies exist in most countries. Increasingly in the EU, political, legal and regulatory forces are being harmonised to reflect common standards and enforcement.

### Local Authorities

The functions of UK local authorities are far-reaching; some are primary duties, whereas others are purely discretionary. Broadly speaking, functions are divided between county and district councils on the basis that the county council is responsible for matters requiring planning and administration over wide areas or requiring the support of substantial resources, whereas district councils on the whole administer functions of a more local significance. English county councils are generally responsible for strategic planning, transport planning, highways, traffic regulations, local education, consumer protection, refuse disposal, police, the fire service, libraries and personal social services. District councils are responsible for environmental health, housing decisions, most planning applications and refuse collection. They may also provide some museums, art galleries and parks. At both county and district council level, arrangements depend on local agreements.

Most countries in Europe have a similar structure: resource-hungry issues with wide-ranging social and political consequences are controlled centrally. Planning and service provision within the community are viewed as being better controlled at the local level by the actual communities that will experience the advantages or problems resulting from such decision-making. The European Union aims to establish commonly accepted parameters for planning, service provision and regulation, and a framework to assist in inter- and intra-country disputes.

### Non-governmental Regulatory Forces

In the absence of governmental regulatory forces and in an attempt to prevent government intervention, some businesses try to regulate themselves. For example, many newspapers have voluntarily banned advertisements for telephone chat services used for undesirable activities, even though such services are technically not illegal. Trade associations in a number of industries have developed self-regulatory programmes. Even though these programmes are not a direct outcome of laws, many were established to stop or stall the development of laws and governmental regulatory groups that would regulate the associations' marketing practices. Sometimes trade associations establish codes of ethics by which their members must abide, or risk censure by other members or even exclusion from the programme. For example, many cigarette manufacturers have agreed, through a code of ethics, not to advertise their products to children and teenagers. The Ofcom Code of Advertising Standards and Practice aims to keep broadcast advertising 'legal, decent, honest and truthful'.[5]

Self-regulatory programmes have several advantages over governmental laws and regulatory agencies. They are usually less expensive to establish and implement, and their guidelines are generally more realistic and operational. In addition, effective industry self-regulatory programmes reduce the need to expand government bureaucracy. However, these programmes also have several limitations. When a trade association creates a set of industry guidelines for its members, non-member organisations do not have to abide by them. In addition, many self-regulatory programmes lack the tools or the authority to enforce guidelines. Finally, guidelines in self-regulatory programmes are often less strict than those established by government agencies.

### Deregulation

Governments can drastically alter the environment for businesses. In the UK, the privatisation of the public utilities created new terms and conditions for their suppliers and subcontractors. The state's sales of Jaguar and Rover in the car industry and of British Airways created commercially lean companies that suddenly had new impetus to become major competitors in their industries. In the European Union, deregulation has created opportunities across borders and also new threats. Car manufacturers were previously able to restrict certain models to specific countries. They placed rigorous controls on their dealers, forbidding them to retail cars produced by rival manufacturers in the same showroom or on the same site. Many of these controls have since been swept aside.

## Societal/Green Forces

**Societal/Green forces** Individuals and groups, and the issues engaging them, that pressure marketers to provide high living standards and enjoyable lifestyles through socially responsible decisions and activities

**Societal/Green forces** comprise the structure and dynamics of individuals and groups and the issues that engage them. Society becomes concerned about marketers' activities when those activities have questionable or negative consequences. For example, in recent times, well-publicised incidents of unethical behaviour by marketers and others have perturbed and even angered consumers. Chapter 25 takes a detailed look at marketing ethics and social responsibility. When marketers do a good job of satisfying society, praise or positive evaluation rarely follows. Society expects marketers to provide a high standard of living and to protect the general quality of life. This section examines some of society's expectations, the means used to express those expectations, and the problems and opportunities that marketers experience as they try to deal with society's often contradictory wishes.

### Living Standards and Quality of Life

Most people want more than just the bare necessities; they want to achieve the highest standard of living possible. For example, there is a desire for homes that offer not only protection from the elements but also comfort and a satisfactory lifestyle. People want many varieties of safe and readily available food that is also easily prepared. Clothing protects bodies, but many consumers want a variety of clothing for adornment and to project a certain image to others. Consumers want vehicles that provide rapid, safe and efficient travel. They want communications systems that give information from around the globe – a desire apparent in the popularity of products such as PDAs, mobile phones, fax machines and the 24-hour news coverage provided by cable and satellite television networks and by the Internet. In addition, there is a demand for sophisticated medical services that prolong life expectancy and improve physical appearance. Education is expected to help consumers acquire and enjoy a higher standard of living.

Society's high material standard of living is often not enough. Many desire a high degree of quality in their lives. People do not want to spend all their waking hours working: they seek leisure time for hobbies, voluntary work, recreation and relaxation. Quality of life is enhanced by leisure time, clean air and water, unlittered beaches, conservation of wildlife and natural resources, and security from radiation and poisonous substances. A number of companies are expressing concerns about quality of life. Consumers, too, are expressing concern over 'Green' issues such as pollution, waste disposal and the so-called greenhouse effect. Society's concerns have created both threats and opportunities for marketers. For example, one of society's biggest environmental problems is lack of space for refuse disposal, especially of plastic materials such as disposable nappies and Styrofoam packaging, which are not biodegradable. In the United States, several cities have passed laws banning the use of all plastic packaging in stores and restaurants, and governments around the world are considering similar legislation. This trend has created problems for McDonald's and other fast-food restaurants, which have now developed packaging alternatives. Other companies, however, see such environmental problems as opportunities. Procter & Gamble, for example, markets cleaners in bottles made of recycled plastic.[6] Environmentally responsible, or Green, marketing is increasingly extensive. For example, the German companies Audi, Volkswagen and BMW are manufacturing 'cleaner' cars that do not pollute the atmosphere as much as traditional ones. BP launched a 'Green' diesel fuel with hardly any noxious emissions. Italian chemical companies are investing billions to reduce toxic wastes from their plants, and British industry is investing equally large sums to scrub acid emissions from power stations and to treat sewage more effectively.[7]

**Green movement**
The trend arising from society's concern about pollution, waste disposal, manufacturing processes and the greenhouse effect

The **Green movement** is concerned about these environmental issues. Several years ago few consumers were concerned about the well-being of their natural environment – their planet. Resources were not seen as scarce, pollution was barely acknowledged and people had a short-term, perhaps selfish, perspective. Now there is a growing awareness that is affecting everyone: consumers, manufacturers and legislators. Supermarket shelves are rapidly filling with packaging that can be recycled or reused, and products for which manufacturing processes have altered. Children are now taught in the classroom to 're-educate' their parents to take a more responsible view of the earth's environment. The changes are not just in the supermarkets and schools, with ever more households sorting their rubbish into various containers for collection by local authorities striving to recycle growing amounts of trash.

The rising importance and role of the Green aspect of the societal forces must not be underestimated. Changes in the forces of the marketing environment require careful monitoring, and often demand a clear and effective response. Since marketing activities are a vital part of the total business structure, marketers have a responsibility to help provide what members of society want and to minimise what they do not want.

### Consumer Movement Forces

**Consumer movement**
A diverse collection of independent individuals, groups and organisations seeking to protect the rights of consumers

The **consumer movement** is a diverse collection of independent individuals, groups and organisations seeking to protect the rights of consumers. The main issues pursued by the consumer movement fall into three categories: environmental protection, product performance and safety, and information disclosure. The movement's major forces are individual consumer advocates, consumer organisations and other interest groups, consumer education and consumer laws.

Consumer advocates take it upon themselves to protect the rights of consumers. They band together into consumer organisations, either voluntarily or under government sponsorship. Some organisations, such as the Consumers' Association, operate nationally, whereas others are active at local levels. They inform and organise other consumers, raise issues, help businesses develop consumer-oriented programmes and pressure legislators to enact consumer protection laws. Some consumer advocates and organisations encourage consumers to boycott products and businesses to which they have objections. For marketers, it is better to work with such activists than to incur their displeasure.

Educating consumers to make wiser purchasing decisions is perhaps one of the most far-reaching aspects of the consumer movement, which is now impacting on a growing number of businesses (see Figure 3.2). This is a motive of the Fairtrade Organisation, as detailed in the Marketing in Society box (see page 80). Increasingly, consumer education is becoming a part of school curricula and adult education courses. These courses cover many topics – for instance, what major factors should be considered when buying specific products, such as insurance, housing, cars, appliances and furniture, clothes and food. The courses also cover the provisions of certain consumer protection laws and provide the sources of information that can help individuals become knowledgeable consumers.

## Technological Forces

**Technology**
The application of knowledge and tools to solve problems and perform tasks more efficiently

The word technology brings to mind creations of progress such as cellphones, computers, the web, superconductors, lasers, GM foods, wind farms, cloning and organ transplants. Even though such items are outgrowths of technology, none of them is technology. **Technology** has been defined as the application of knowledge and tools to solve problems and perform tasks more efficiently.[8] Often this knowledge comes from scientific research. The effects of technology are broad in scope and today exert a tremendous influence on everyone's lives. Technology grows out of research performed by businesses, universities and not-for-profit organisations. Much of this research is paid for by governments, which support investigations in a variety of areas, including health, defence, agriculture, energy and pollution. Because much centrally funded research requires the use of specialised

***Figure 3.2***
*Envirowise's business-to-business proposition capitalises on a growth in concern for natural resources and technological advancements in manufacturing processes*
*Source: Courtesy of Envirowise*

machinery, personnel and facilities, a sizeable proportion of this research is conducted by large business organisations or research institutions that already possess the necessary specialised equipment and people.

The rapid technological growth of recent decades is expected to continue. Areas that hold great technological promise include digital electronics, artificial intelligence, superconductors, materials research and biotechnology. Current research is investigating new forms of memory chips and computers that will think for themselves or be more responsive to their specific users' characteristics. Because these and other technological developments will clearly have an impact on buyers' and marketers' decisions, it is important to discuss here the effects of technology on society and marketers, and to consider several factors that influence the adoption and use of technology. Chapter 4 examines the role of technology in marketing in more detail.

## Marketing in Society

### Kraft and Nestlé Look to Fair Trade

Fairtrade labelling was created in the Netherlands in the 1980s, with coffee from Mexico being the first recipient of the eco-label. Fairtrade exists to guarantee that the suppliers of products consumed in the developed world, based in the developing regions, benefit from a fair price. By negotiating better deals, improving the negotiating power and marketing expertise of farmers and producers, and seeking a greater proportion of the retail price, the movement helps sustain development and is largely welcomed by the leading development agencies. A core aim is to minimise dramatically fluctuating prices that, when low, force farmers into crippling debt or out of production.

Now there are 18 organisations around the world, including the Fairtrade Foundation, overseeing the labelling of Fairtrade products. Over 360 Fairtrade-certified producer groups in 40 countries have helped many impoverished and vulnerable regions. In order to achieve this, the movement must lobby retailers, the media and consumers to purchase or support Fairtrade products. In the UK there are over 250 Fairtrade retail products, from tea to fruit, roses to footballs, snacks to wines. One key product receiving such high-profile attention is coffee.

Leading coffee houses Costa Coffee, Prêt à Manger and Starbucks have retailed Fairtrade coffees for a while, but now it is the turn of the major manufacturers. Until relatively recently, most Fairtrade products were niche brands produced by marginal manufacturers. Now, even the giants of the global food industry have embraced the movement, reflecting the growing interest in ethical trading by consumers and major retail chains.

First, Nestlé announced plans for a Fairtrade addition to its Nescafé brand. Before its launch, however, rival Kraft stole a march by introducing a Fairtrade coffee range under its well-known Kenco brand. Kenco Sustainable Development comprises two lines: a filter pack and an espresso bean pack. First available to consumers in restaurants, hotels, coffee shops and vending machines, if successful there will also be products offered through supermarkets. Both Kenco lines carry an eco-label from sustainable agriculture organisation the Rainforest Alliance, which guarantees that the beans are from certified farms. Kraft also reformulated its flagship brands Maxwell House and Kenco Really Smooth so that they contain at least 5 per cent certified beans, but they do not carry the eco-label.

Did growing consumer interest in Fairtrade encourage these manufacturers to launch the new lines? Were moves by socially aware retailers responsible? Had lobbying by organisations such as the Rainforest Alliance or Fairtrade Foundation created the necessary swell of positive public opinion? Were Kraft and Nestlé simply reaping the rewards of their environmental scanning of market trends? In reality, a mix of these drivers combined to create the impetus for these products.

**Sources:** Kraft, 2004; www.fairtrade.org.uk, 2004; Mark Sweeney, 'Kraft beats Nestlé to launch of fair trade coffee', *Marketing*, 7 July 2004, p. 1.

## The Impact of Technology

Marketers must be aware of new developments in technology and their possible effects because technology does affect marketing activities in many different ways. Consumers' technological knowledge influences their desire for goods and services. To provide marketing mixes that satisfy consumers, marketers must be aware of these influences. The various ways in which technology affects marketing activities fall into two broad categories:

1 effects on consumers and society in general
2 influences on what, how, when and where products are marketed.

**Effects of Technology on Society** Technology determines how consumers as members of society satisfy their physiological needs. In various ways and to varying degrees, eating and drinking habits, sleeping patterns, sexual activities and healthcare are all influenced both by existing technology and by changes in technology. Technological developments have improved standards of living, thus creating more leisure time; they have also enhanced information, entertainment and education. Nevertheless, technology can detract from the quality of life through undesirable side-effects, such as unemployment, polluted air and water, and other health hazards. Some people believe that further applications of technology can soften or eliminate these undesirable side-effects. Others argue, however, that the best way to improve the quality of our lives is to decrease the use of technology.

**Effects of Technology on Marketing** Technology also affects the types of product that marketers can offer. The introduction and general acceptance of cassette tapes and compact discs drove most manufacturers of vinyl long-playing (LP) albums out of business or forced them to invest in new technology. Yet this technology provided new marketing opportunities for recording artists and producers, record companies, retailers and those in related industries. More recently, music downloads from the web have created a new set of opportunities and challenges for marketers in the music industry. The following items are just a few of the many thousands of existing products that were not available to consumers 20 years ago: webcams, digital cameras, cellphones, ultra-light laptop computers, high-resolution televisions, hand-held video cameras and the Internet. All of these are products that have transformed lifestyles and people's access to information.

Computer technology helps make warehouse storage and keeping track of stored products more efficient and, therefore, less expensive. Often, these savings can be passed on to consumers in the form of lower prices. Because of technological changes in communications, marketers can now use a variety of media to reach large masses of people more efficiently. The development and widespread use of fax, e-mail and text messaging, for example, allow marketers to send their advertisements or sales specifications directly to selected groups of customers who want their products. In recent years the Internet has permeated the lives of many, bringing a world of information into the home and allowing consumers to shop for products on-line. Technological advances in transport enable consumers to travel further and more often to shop at a larger number of stores. Changes in transport have also affected producers' ability to get products to retailers and wholesalers. The ability of present-day manufacturers of relatively lightweight products to reach any of their dealers within hours via express-delivery services would astound their counterparts of 50 years ago.

## The Adoption and Use of Technology

**Technology assessment**
A procedure by which managers try to foresee the effects of new products and processes on their company's operation, on other business organisations and on society in general

Through a procedure known as **technology assessment**, some managers try to foresee the effects of new products and processes on their company's operation, on other business organisations and on society in general. With the information gained through a technology assessment, management tries to estimate whether the benefits of using a specific kind of technology outweigh the costs to the business and to society at large. The degree to which a business is technologically based will also influence how its management responds to technology. Companies whose products and product changes grow out of recent technology strive to gather and use technological information. Although available technology could radically improve their products or other parts of the marketing mix, some companies may put off applying this technology as long as their competitors do not try to use it. The extent to which a business can protect inventions stemming from research also influences its use of technology. The extent to which a product is secure from imitation depends on how easily others can copy it without violating its patent. If new products and processes cannot be protected through patents, a company is less likely to market them and make the benefits of its research available to competitors. How a company uses – or does not use – technology is important for its long-term survival. A business that makes the wrong decisions may well lose out to the competition. Poor decisions may also affect its profits by requiring expensive corrective action. Poor decisions about technological forces may even drive a company out of business.

# Economic and Competitive Forces

The **economic and competitive forces** in the marketing environment influence both marketers' and customers' decisions and activities. This section first examines the effects of general economic conditions, also focusing on buying power, willingness to spend and spending patterns. Then the discussion moves to the broad competitive forces, including types of competitive structure, competitive tools and some methods for monitoring competitive behaviour. The strategic importance of understanding and evaluating the competitive arena has been discussed in Chapter 2.

## General Economic Conditions

**Economic and competitive forces**
Factors in the marketing environment—such as the effects of general economic conditions; buying power; willingness to spend; spending patterns; types of competitive structure, competitive tools and competitive behaviour—that influence both marketers' and consumers' decisions and activities

**Business cycle**
Fluctuations in the economy that follow the general pattern of prosperity, recession, depression and recovery

**Prosperity**
A period during which unemployment is low and total income is relatively high

**Recession**
A period during which unemployment rises and total buying power declines

**Depression**
A period during which unemployment is extremely high, wages are very low, total disposable income is at a minimum and consumers lack confidence in the economy

The overall state of the economy fluctuates in all countries. Table 3.1 presents some economic measures of performance for Europe. These changes in general economic conditions affect – and are affected by – the forces of supply and demand, buying power, willingness to spend, consumer expenditure levels and the intensity of competitive behaviour. Therefore, current economic conditions and changes in the economy have a broad impact on the success of organisations' marketing strategies.

Fluctuations in the economy follow a general pattern often referred to as the **business cycle**. In the traditional view, the business cycle consists of four stages: prosperity, recession, depression and recovery.

**Prosperity** During **prosperity**, unemployment is low and total income is relatively high. Assuming a low inflation rate, this combination causes buying power to be high. To the extent that the economic outlook remains prosperous, consumers are generally willing to buy. In the prosperity stage, marketers often expand their marketing mixes (product, place/distribution, promotion, price and people) to take advantage of the increased buying power. They sometimes capture a larger market share by intensifying distribution and promotion efforts.

**Recession** Unemployment rises during a **recession**, so total buying power declines. The pessimism that accompanies a recession often stifles both consumer and business spending. As buying power decreases, many consumers become more price- and value-conscious; they look for products that are basic and functional. For instance, people ordinarily reduce their consumption of more expensive convenience foods and strive to save money by growing and preparing more of their own food. Individuals buy fewer durable goods and more repair and do-it-yourself products. During a recession, some companies make the mistake of drastically reducing their marketing efforts and thus damage their ability to survive. Obviously, marketers should consider some revision of their marketing activities during a recessionary period. Because consumers are more concerned about the functional value of products, a company must focus its marketing research on determining what product functions buyers want and then make sure that these functions become part of its products. Promotional efforts should emphasise value and utility.

**Depression** A **depression** is a period in which unemployment is extremely high, wages are very low, total disposable income is at a minimum and consumers lack confidence in the economy. Governments have used both monetary and fiscal policies to off-set the effects of recession and depression. Monetary policies are employed to control the money supply, which in turn affects spending, saving and investment by both individuals and businesses. Through the establishment of fiscal policies, the government is able to influence the amount of saving and expenditure by adjusting the tax structure and by changing the levels of government spending. Some economic experts believe that the effective use of monetary and fiscal policies can completely eliminate depressions from the business cycle.

## Table 3.1 Some Economic Measures of Performance for Europe

### Data on Western European Countries[1]

| | | | Austria | Belgium | Denmark | France | Germany | Ireland | Italy | Netherlands | Norway | Spain | Sweden | Switzerland | UK |
|---|---|---|---|---|---|---|---|---|---|---|---|---|---|---|---|
| A | Total population, 2001 | millions | 8.13 | 10.29 | 5.36 | 59.19 | 82.33 | 3.84 | 57.95 | 16.04 | 4.51 | 41.12 | 8.89 | 7.23 | 58.80 |
| A | Population growth at annual rates | | | | | | | | | | | | | | |
| | 2000/2001 | % | 0.2 | 0.4 | 0.4 | 0.5 | 0.1 | 1.3 | 0.5 | 0.8 | 0.4 | 1.5 | 0.2 | 0.7 | 0.1 |
| | 1991/2001 | % | 3.8 | 2.9 | 4.1 | 3.9 | 2.9 | 8.8 | 2.1 | 6.4 | 5.9 | 5.7 | 3.1 | 6.3 | 1.8 |
| A | Population by sex and age, 2001 | | | | | | | | | | | | | | |
| | Male | % | 48.6 | 49.1 | 49.5 | 48.6 | 49.1 | 49.5 | 48.5 | 49.5 | 49.6 | 48.9 | 49.6 | 49.6 | 49.1 |
| | Female | % | 51.4 | 50.9 | 50.6 | 51.4 | 50.9 | 50.5 | 51.5 | 50.5 | 50.5 | 51.1 | 50.4 | 50.4 | 50.9 |
| | Under 15 | % | 16.4 | 17.2 | 18.4 | 18.7 | 15.3 | 21.5 | 14.1 | 18.4 | 20.0 | 14.9 | 17.9 | 16.7 | 18.6 |
| | 15–64 | % | 67.7 | 66.1 | 66.6 | 65.1 | 68.2 | 67.1 | 67.0 | 67.8 | 65.0 | 67.4 | 64.5 | 67.4 | 65.3 |
| | 65+ | % | 15.6 | 16.6 | 14.9 | 16.1 | 16.4 | 11.2 | 18.3 | 13.7 | 15.1 | 16.7 | 17.5 | 15.3 | 16.1 |
| A | Births, 2001 | per '000 | 9.3 | 11.1 | 12.3 | 13.1 | 9.0 | 15.1 | 9.0 | 12.6 | 12.6 | 10.1 | 10.4 | 10.1 | 11.1 |
| B | Marriages, 2001[2] | per '000 | 4.2 | 4.1 | 6.6 | 5.1 | 4.7 | 5.0 | 4.9 | 5.1 | 5.6 | 5.2 | 4.0 | 5.0 | 5.1 |
| C | Inhabitants per sq km 2002[3] | no. | 103 | 336 | 125 | 109 | 230 | 56 | 192 | 475 | 15 | 80 | 22 | 176 | 242 |
| C | Number of households, 2002[3] | '000s | 3,320 | 4,278 | 2,456 | 26,735 | 38,456 | 1,291 | 22,226 | 6,941 | 1,954 | 13,461 | 4,363 | 3,006 | 24,600 |
| | Persons per household[3] | no. | 2.5 | 2.4 | 2.2 | 2.2 | 2.1 | 3.0 | 2.6 | 2.3 | 2.3 | 3.0 | 2.0 | 2.4 | 2.4 |
| D | Commonly used unemployment rate, 2001 | | | | | | | | | | | | | | |
| | Proportion of labour force[4] | % | 4.3 | 7.3 | 4.5 | 8.7 | 8.6 | 4.4 | 9.0 | 2.8 | 3.9 | 11.3 | 4.9 | 2.5 | 5.1 |
| E | Civilian employment by main sectors | | | | | | | | | | | | | | |
| | Agriculture | % | 5.7 | 2.2 | 3.2 | 3.6 | 2.5 | 6.9 | 5.1 | 3.0 | 3.8 | 5.9 | 2.1 | 4.1 | 1.4 |
| | Industry | % | 29.7 | 24.0 | 24.5 | 23.5 | 32.5 | 27.8 | 32.1 | 20.3 | 21.8 | 31.3 | 23.1 | 25.1 | 24.1 |
| | Services | % | 64.7 | 73.8 | 72.3 | 72.8 | 65.0 | 65.3 | 62.9 | 76.6 | 74.4 | 62.7 | 74.7 | 70.8 | 74.5 |
| F | Strikes, 1999[5] | | | | | | | | | | | | | | |
| | Working days lost per 1000 employees | no. | — | 47 | 24 | 83 | 1 | 82 | 66 | 6 | — | 152 | 3 | 6 | 20 |
| D | Gross Domestic Product[6] | | | | | | | | | | | | | | |
| | Total, 2001 | $ billion | 204.1 | 247.8 | 172.2 | 1,417.7 | 1,984.1 | 116.8 | 1,184.3 | 419.7 | 193.0 | 643.7 | 240.3 | 271.3 | 1,555.7 |
| | Per capita, 2001 | $ '000s | 25.1 | 24.1 | 32.1 | 24.0 | 24.1 | 30.4 | 2.4 | 26.2 | 42.8 | 15.7 | 27.0 | 37.5 | 26.5 |
| G | Gross fixed capital formation, 2002 | | | | | | | | | | | | | | |
| | Proportion of GDP | % | 21.7 | 19.5 | 19.5 | 19.7 | 18.4 | 22.0 | 19.7 | 21.0 | 17.0 | 25.4 | 17.1 | 18.2 | 15.8 |

**Notes:** [1] **Where data for the reference period were not available, the most recent were used.**
[2] Data for Italy, Norway and the UK are for 2000.
[3] Data for France, Germany, Italy, Netherlands, Spain, Sweden, Switzerland and the UK refer to 2001.
[4] Data for Switzerland refer to 2001.
[5] In all industries and services.
[6] All current prices and exchange rates.

**Sources:**
A World Bank Development Indicators, 2003.
B Eurostat: Yearbook, 2003.
C European Marketing Pocket Book, 2003, WARC.
D OECD Main Economic Indicators, June 2003.
E OECD Labour Force Statistics, 1982–2002.
F Labour Market Trends, April 2003, published by Office for National Statistics, quoting International Labour Office (ILO).
G International Financial Statistics, July 2003.

## Table 3.1 Some Economic Measures of Performance for Europe

**DATA ON WESTERN EUROPEAN COUNTRIES (continued)**

| | | Austria | Belgium | Denmark | France | Germany | Ireland | Italy | Netherlands | Norway | Spain | Sweden | Switzerland | UK |
|---|---|---|---|---|---|---|---|---|---|---|---|---|---|---|
| **Consumption per head per year, 2001** | | | | | | | | | | | | | | |
| A Beer | litres | 106.9 | 98.0 | 98.6 | 35.9 | 123.1 | 150.8 | 28.9 | 80.5 | 50.8 | 75.0 | 55.3 | 57.1 | 97.1 |
| Wine | litres | 31.0 | 18.7 | 31.2 | 56.9 | 23.9 | 11.8 | 50.0 | 18.9 | 11.0 | 36.2 | 15.5 | 43.1 | 17.5 |
| Spirits | 100% alc., litres | 1.4 | 1.2 | 1.1 | 2.4 | 1.9 | 2.4 | 0.4 | 1.7 | 0.8 | 2.4 | 1.0 | 1.6 | 1.5 |
| B Chocolate confectionery | kg | 9.6 | 5.3 | 8.4 | 4.9 | 8.2 | 8.8 | 3.1 | 4.7 | 8.6 | 1.6 | 6.4 | 10.6 | 7.8 |
| Sugar confectionery | kg | 3.2 | 4.8 | 6.0 | 3.6 | 5.5 | 5.7 | 2.2 | 6.4 | 4.8 | 3.0 | 11.6 | 3.1 | 5.4 |
| Biscuits and like | kg | 5.9 | 12.9 | 7.4 | 9.2 | 7.2 | 12.1 | 8.0 | 14.2 | — | 7.2 | 1.0 | 7.5 | 11.4 |
| **C Media and telecommunications** | | | | | | | | | | | | | | |
| Daily newspapers, 2000[1] | per '000 popn. | 296 | 160 | 283 | 201 | 305 | 150 | 104 | 306 | 569 | 100 | 410 | 373 | 329 |
| Mobile telephones, 2001 | per '000 popn. | 807 | 746 | 738 | 605 | 682 | 729 | 839 | 767 | 825 | 655 | 790 | 731 | 770 |
| Radios, 2001[2] | per '000 popn. | 753 | 793 | 1,400 | 950 | 570 | 695 | 878 | 980 | 3,324 | 330 | 2,811 | 1,002 | 1,446 |
| Telephone mainlines, 2001 | per '000 popn. | 468 | 498 | 719 | 573 | 634 | 485 | 471 | 621 | 720 | 431 | 739 | 746 | 588 |
| TVs, 2001 | per '000 popn. | 542 | 543 | 857 | 632 | 586 | 399 | 494 | 553 | 883 | 598 | 965 | 554 | 950 |
| Personal computers, 2001 | per '000 popn. | 335 | 233 | 540 | 337 | 382 | 391 | 195 | 428 | 508 | 168 | 561 | 540 | 366 |
| Internet users, 2001 | millions | 2.60 | 3.20 | 2.90 | 15.65 | 30.80 | 0.90 | 16.40 | 7.90 | 2.70 | 7.39 | 4.60 | 2.22 | 24.00 |
| **C Indicators of living standards** | | | | | | | | | | | | | | |
| Physicians, 2000[3] | per '000 popn. | 3.1 | 3.9 | 3.4 | 3.0 | 3.6 | 2.3 | 6.0 | 3.2 | 2.9 | 3.3 | 2.9 | 3.5 | 1.8 |
| Life expectancy at birth, 2000 | years | 78.5 | 78.3 | 76.5 | 79.2 | 77.6 | 76.6 | 78.5 | 77.9 | 78.7 | 78.2 | 79.8 | 79.8 | 77.4 |
| Infant mortality, 2001 | per '000 live births | 5.0 | 5.0 | 4.0 | 4.0 | 4.0 | 6.0 | 4.0 | 5.0 | 4.0 | 4.0 | 3.0 | 5.0 | 6.0 |
| Health expenditure, 2000 | % of GDP | 8.0 | 8.7 | 8.3 | 9.5 | 10.6 | 6.7 | 8.1 | 8.1 | 7.8 | 7.7 | 8.4 | 10.7 | 7.3 |
| Public spending on education, 2000[4] | % of GDP | 5.8 | 5.9 | 8.2 | 5.8 | 4.6 | 4.4 | 4.6 | 4.8 | 6.9 | 4.5 | 7.8 | 5.5 | 4.5 |
| **D Vehicles** | | | | | | | | | | | | | | |
| Share of foreign cars, 2001 | % | 100.0 | 100.0 | 100.0 | 39.6 | 33.3 | 100.0 | 65.3 | 98.7 | 100.0 | 100.0 | 70.2 | 100.0 | 75.8 |
| Vehicles, 1999 | per '000 popn. | 536.1 | 496.6 | 410.9 | 564.5 | 529.2 | 305.3 | 591.0 | 426.8 | 505.3 | 471.8 | 478.2 | 526.5 | 418.5 |
| **E The retail grocery trade, 2000** | | | | | | | | | | | | | | |
| Grocery store numbers | | — | — | 3,161 | 37,637 | 64,200 | 9,118 | 116,150 | 5,583 | 1,564 | 62,590 | 5,140 | 6,366 | 33,348 |
| Market share by store type: | | | | | | | | | | | | | | |
| Hypermarkets | % | — | — | 19 | 52 | 26 | 19 | 17 | 5 | 4 | 34 | 16 | 19 | 53 |
| Large supermarkets | % | — | — | 25 | 25 | 17 | 35 | 17 | 36 | 18 | 15 | 37 | 32 | 24 |
| Small supermarkets | % | — | — | 37 | 11 | 37 | 11 | 21 | 28 | 47 | 18 | 30 | 25 | 12 |
| Superettes | % | — | — | 18 | 5 | 15 | 34 | 19 | 21 | 28 | 19 | 14 | 19 | 11 |
| Small shops | % | — | — | 2 | — | 5 | — | — | 10 | 2 | — | — | — | — |
| **C International tourism, 1999/2001** | | | | | | | | | | | | | | |
| Arrivals, 2001 | % of popn. | 223.6 | 62.7 | 37.8 | 129.3 | 21.7 | 168.0 | 67.4 | 59.2 | 94.0 | 120.4 | 32.5 | 148.0 | 38.8 |
| Departures, 1999 | % of popn. | 48.9 | 76.0 | 91.0 | 28.5 | 89.4 | 95.3 | 32.9 | 89.7 | 16.9 | 12.2 | 118.5 | 168.2 | 90.6 |

**Note:** **In each category, where data for the reference point were not available, the most recent ones have been used.**

[1] Data for Austria, Belgium, Ireland, Italy, Netherlands are for 1996. Data for France are for 1997. Data for Germany are for 1998. Data for Switzerland are for 1999.

[2] Data for Austria, Belgium, France, Ireland, Italy, Netherlands, Spain, Switzerland, UK are for 1997.

[3] Graduates of any faculty or school of medicine who are working in the country and in any medical field. Data for France are for 1998. Data for Denmark, Ireland, Sweden are for 1999.

[4] Data for Belgium, Germany, Ireland, Italy, Netherlands, Spain, Sweden, Switzerland, UK are for 1999.

**Source:**
A World Drink Trends 2002, WARC: Productschap voor Gedistilleerde Dranken/WARC.
B The Biscuit, Cake, Chocolate & Confectionery Alliance (BCCCA); CAOBISCO.
C World Bank World Development Indicators 2002.
D The Society of Motor Manufacturers & Traders Limited.
E ACNielson.

**Sources:** *The Marketing Pocket Book*, published by the World Advertising Research Center, Henley-on-Thames, 2004.

**Recovery**
The stage of the business cycle in which the economy moves from depression or recession to prosperity

**Recovery** **Recovery** is the stage of the business cycle in which the economy moves from depression or recession to prosperity. During this period, the high unemployment rate begins to decline, total disposable income increases and the economic gloom that lessened consumers' willingness to buy subsides. Both the ability and the willingness to buy rise. Marketers face some problems during recovery – for example, the difficulty of ascertaining how quickly prosperity will return and of forecasting the level of prosperity that will be attained. During this stage, marketers should maintain as much flexibility in their marketing strategies as possible to be able to make the required adjustments as the economy moves from recession to prosperity. Fluctuations in economic conditions have a significant impact on marketers' activities and fortunes.

## Consumer Demand and Spending Behaviour

Marketers must understand the factors that determine whether, what, where and when people buy. Chapters 6 and 8 look at the behavioural factors underlying these choices, but here the focus is on the economic components: buying power, willingness to purchase and spending patterns.

**Buying power**
Resources such as goods, services and financial holdings that can be traded in an exchange situation

**Income**
The amount of money received through wages, rents, investments, pensions and subsidy payments for a given period

**Disposable income**
After-tax income, which is used for spending or saving

**Discretionary income**
Disposable income that is available for spending and saving after an individual has purchased the basic necessities of food, clothing and shelter

**Buying Power** The strength of a person's **buying power** depends on the size of the resources that enable the individual to purchase, as well as on the state of the economy. The resources that make up buying power are goods, services and financial holdings. Fluctuations of the business cycle affect buying power because they influence price levels and interest rates. For example, during inflationary periods, when prices are rising, buying power decreases because more pounds or euros are required to buy products. The major financial sources of buying power are income, credit and wealth. From an individual's viewpoint, **income** is the amount of money received through wages, rents, investments, pensions and subsidy payments for a given period, such as a month or a year. Normally, this money is allocated among taxes, spending for goods and services, and savings. However, because of the differences in people's educational levels, abilities, occupations and wealth, income is not distributed equally in any country.

Marketers are most interested in the amount of money that is left after payment of taxes. After-tax income is called **disposable income** and is used for spending or saving. Because disposable income is a ready source of buying power, the total amount available in a nation is important to marketers. Several factors affect the size of total disposable income. One, of course, is the total amount of income. Total national income is affected by wage levels, rate of unemployment, interest rates and dividend rates. These factors in turn affect the size of disposable income. Because disposable income is the income left after taxes are paid, the number of taxes and their amount directly affect the size of total disposable income. When taxes rise, disposable income declines; when taxes fall, disposable income increases. Disposable income that is available for spending and saving after an individual has purchased the basic necessities of food, clothing and shelter is called **discretionary income.** People use discretionary income to purchase entertainment, holidays, cars, education, pets and pet supplies, furniture, appliances, and so on. Changes in total discretionary income affect the sales of these products – especially cars, furniture, large appliances and other costly durable goods. The marketers of such products must monitor factors likely to alter their target customers' discretionary income.

Credit enables people to spend future income now or in the near future. However, credit increases current buying power at the expense of future buying power. Several factors determine whether consumers use or forgo credit. First, credit must be available to them. Interest rates, too, affect consumers' decisions to use credit, especially for expensive purchases such as homes, appliances and cars. When credit charges are high, consumers are more likely to delay buying expensive items. Use of credit is also affected by credit terms, such as the size of the down payment and the amount and number of monthly payments. Many marketers offer 'interest-free credit' or low interest rates as part of the marketing proposition for their products.

**Wealth**
The accumulation of past income, natural resources and financial resources

A person can have a high income and very little wealth. It is also possible, but not likely, for a person to have great wealth but not much income. **Wealth** is the accumulation of past income, natural resources and financial resources. It may exist in many forms, including cash, securities, savings accounts, jewellery, antiques and property. Like income, wealth is distributed unevenly. The significance of wealth to marketers is that as people become wealthier they gain buying power in three ways: they can use their wealth to make current purchases, to generate income and to acquire large amounts of credit. Buying power information is available from government sources, trade associations and research agencies. One of the most current and comprehensive sources of buying power data is the Central Statistical Office's *National Income and Expenditure Survey*. The EU's *Eurostat* provides similar data. Income, wealth and credit equip consumers to purchase goods and services. Marketing managers should be aware of current levels and expected changes in buying power in their own markets because buying power directly affects the types and quantities of goods and services that consumers purchase, as explained later in the discussion of spending patterns. Just because consumers have buying power, however, does not necessarily mean that they will buy. Consumers must also be willing to use their buying power. Marketers must encourage them to do so.

**Willingness to spend**
A disposition towards using buying power, influenced by the ability to buy, expected satisfaction from a product and numerous psychological and social forces

**Consumers' Willingness to Spend** People's **willingness to spend** is, to some degree, related to their ability to buy – that is, people are sometimes more willing to buy if they have the buying power. However, a number of other elements also influence willingness to spend. Some elements affect specific products; others influence spending in general. A product's absolute price and its price relative to the price of substitute products influence almost everyone. The amount of satisfaction currently received or expected in the future from a product already owned may also influence consumers' desire to buy other products. Satisfaction depends not only on the quality of the functional performance of the currently owned product, but also on numerous psychological and social forces.

Factors that affect consumers' general willingness to spend are expectations about future employment, income levels, prices, family size and general economic conditions. If people are unsure whether or how long they will be employed, willingness to buy ordinarily declines. Willingness to spend may increase if people are reasonably certain of higher incomes in the future. Expectations of rising prices in the near future may also increase willingness to spend in the present. For a given level of buying power, the larger the family, the greater the willingness to buy. One of the reasons for this relationship is that as the size of a family increases, a larger amount of money must be spent to provide the basic necessities of life to sustain the family members. Finally, perceptions of future economic conditions influence willingness to buy. For example, rising short-term interest rates cool consumers' willingness to spend.

**Consumer spending patterns**
Information indicating the relative proportions of annual family expenditures or the actual amount of money spent on certain kinds of goods and services

**Comprehensive spending patterns**
The percentages of family income allotted to annual expenditures for general classes of goods and services

**Product-specific spending patterns**
The annual monetary amounts families spend for specific products within a general product class

**Consumer Spending Patterns** Marketers must be aware of the factors that influence consumers' ability and willingness to spend, but they should also analyse how consumers actually spend their disposable incomes. Marketers obtain this information by studying consumer spending patterns. **Consumer spending patterns** indicate the relative proportions of annual family expenditures or the actual amount of money spent on certain kinds of goods and services. Families are usually categorised by one of several characteristics, including family income, age of the head of household, geographic area and family life cycle. There are two types of spending pattern: comprehensive and product-specific.

The percentages of family income allotted to annual expenditures for general classes of goods and services constitute **comprehensive spending patterns**. Comprehensive spending patterns or the data to develop them are available in government publications and in reports produced by the major marketing research companies and by trade associations. **Product-specific spending patterns** indicate the annual monetary amounts families spend for specific products within a general product class. Information sources used to construct product-specific spending patterns include government publications, trade publications and consumer surveys. A marketer uses spending patterns to analyse general trends in the ways that families spend their incomes for various kinds of product. Analyses of spending patterns yield information that a marketer can use to gain perspective and background for decision-making. However, spending patterns reflect only general trends and thus should not be used as the sole basis for making specific decisions.

## Assessment of Competitive Forces

**Competition**
Those companies marketing products that are similar to, or can be substituted for, a given business's products in the same geographic area

**Monopoly**
A market structure that exists when a company turns out a product that has no close substitutes

Few organisations, if any, operate free of competition. Broadly speaking, all companies compete with each other for consumers' money. From a more practical viewpoint, however, a business generally defines **competition** as those organisations marketing products that are similar to, or can be substituted for, its own products in the same geographic area. For example, a local Tesco or Aldi supermarket manager views all grocery stores in a town as competitors, but almost never thinks of other types of local or out-of-town stores (DIY or electrical, for example) as competitors. This section considers the types of competitive structure and the importance of monitoring competitors.

**Types of Competitive Structure** The number of businesses that control the supply of a product may affect the strength of competition. When only one or a few companies control supply, competitive factors will exert a different sort of influence on marketing activities than when there are many competitors. Table 3.2 presents four general types of competitive structure: monopoly, oligopoly, monopolistic competition and perfect competition.

A **monopoly** exists when a company turns out a product that has no close substitutes. Because the organisation has no competitors, it completely controls the supply of the

**Table 3.2 Selected Characteristics of Competitive Structures**

| Type of Structure | Number of Competitors | Ease of Entry into Market | Product | Knowledge of Market | Examples |
|---|---|---|---|---|---|
| Monopoly | One | Many barriers | Almost no substitutes | Perfect | Non-privatised railways, many government departments |
| Oligopoly | Few | Some barriers | Homogeneous or differentiated (real or perceived differences) | Imperfect | Airlines, petroleum retailers, some utility providers |
| Monopolistic competition | Many | Few barriers | Product differentiation with many substitutes | More knowledge than oligopoly; less than monopoly | Jeans, fast food, audio-visual |
| Perfect competition | Unlimited | No barriers | Homogeneous products | Perfect | The London commodity markets, vegetable farms |

product and, as a single seller, can erect barriers to potential competitors. In reality, the monopolies that survive today are some utilities, such as telephone, electricity and some railways (in many countries), and cable companies, which are heavily regulated. These monopolies are tolerated because of the tremendous financial resources needed to develop and operate them; few organisations can obtain the resources to mount any competition against a local electricity producer, for example. An **oligopoly** exists when a few sellers control the supply of a large proportion of a product. In this case, each seller must consider the reactions of other sellers to changes in marketing activities. Products facing oligopolistic competition may be homogeneous, such as aluminium, or differentiated, such as cigarettes and cars. Usually, barriers of some sort make it difficult to enter the market and compete with oligopolies. For example, because of the enormous financial outlay required, few companies or individuals could afford to enter the oil-refining or steel-producing industries. Moreover, some industries demand special technical or marketing skills that block the entry of many potential competitors.

**Oligopoly**
A market structure that exists when a few sellers control the supply of a large proportion of a product

**Monopolistic competition** exists when a business with many potential competitors attempts to develop a differential marketing strategy to establish its own market share. For example, Levi's has established a differential advantage for its blue jeans through a well-known trademark, design, advertising and a quality image. Although many competing brands of blue jeans are available, this company has carved out its market share through use of a differential marketing strategy. **Perfect competition**, if it existed at all, would entail a large number of sellers, not one of which could significantly influence price or supply. Products would be homogeneous, and there would be full knowledge of the market and easy entry. The closest thing to an example of perfect competition would be an unregulated agricultural market. Few, if any, marketers operate in a structure of perfect competition. Perfect competition is an ideal at one end of the continuum, with monopoly at the other end. Most marketers function in a competitive environment that falls somewhere between these two extremes.

**Monopolistic competition**
A market structure that exists when a business with many potential competitors attempts to develop a differential marketing strategy to establish its own market share

**Perfect competition**
A market structure that entails a large number of sellers, not one of which could significantly influence price or supply

**Competitive Tools** Another set of factors that influences the level of competition is the number and types of competitive tools used by competitors. To survive, a business uses one or several available competitive tools to deal with competitive economic forces. Once a company has analysed its particular competitive environment and decided which factors in that environment it can or must adapt to or influence, it can choose among the variables that it can control to strengthen its competitive position in the overall marketplace. Probably the competitive tool that most organisations grasp is price. Bic, for example, markets disposable pens and lighters that are similar to competing products but less expensive. However, there is one major problem with using price as a competitive tool: competitors will often match or beat the price. This threat is one of the primary reasons for employing non-price competitive tools that are based on the differentiation of market segments, product offering, service, promotion, distribution or enterprise.[9] By focusing on a specific market segment, a marketer sometimes gains a competitive advantage. For instance, Saab cars and Porsche sports coupés are narrowly targeted at specific groups of consumers. Most manufacturers try to gain a competitive edge by incorporating product features that make their brands distinctive to some extent. Companies use distinguishing promotional methods to compete, such as advertising and personal selling. Competing producers sometimes use different distribution channels to prevail over one another. Retailers may compete by placing their outlets in locations that are convenient for a large number of shoppers. Dealers and distributors offer wide ranges, advice and service.

**Monitoring Competition** Marketers in an organisation need to be aware of the actions of major competitors. They should monitor what competitors are currently doing and assess the changes occurring in the competitive environment, as explained in Chapter 2. **Competitor monitoring** allows businesses to determine what specific strategies competitors are following and how those strategies affect their own. It can also guide marketers as they try to develop competitive advantages and can aid them in adjusting current marketing strategies, as well as in planning new ones. Information may come from direct observation or from sources such as the web, sales people, customers, trade publications, syndicated marketing research services, distributors and marketing studies. An organisation needs information about competitors that will allow its marketing managers to assess the performance of its own marketing efforts. Comparing their company's performance with that of competitors helps marketing managers recognise strengths and weaknesses in their own marketing strategies. Data about market shares, product movement, sales volume and expenditure levels can be useful. However, accurate information on these matters is often difficult to obtain.

**Competitor monitoring** The process by which a company studies the actions of its major competitors in order to determine what specific strategies they are following and how those strategies affect its own; also used by marketers as they try to develop competitive advantages, adjust current marketing strategies and plan new ones

Competition exists in most markets and situations. Even charities compete with one another and with manufacturers for consumers' attention and financial commitment. Marketing places an emphasis on meeting consumers' needs and offering satisfaction. To be successful, however, competing organisations need to identify unique marketing mixes; otherwise all rival products and services will merely replicate each other. The search for a competitive edge over competitors is central to effective marketing strategy. As well as monitoring direct competitors, marketers should be aware of new entrants coming into a market with competing propositions, and of the danger of substitute products or services being developed. Marketers' strategic understanding of competition is addressed in Chapter 2.

**Macro marketing environment** The broader forces affecting all organisations in a market: political, legal, regulatory, societal/Green, technological and economic/competitive

**Micro marketing environment** The more company-specific forces reflecting the nature of the business, its suppliers, marketing intermediaries, buyers, all types of competitors—direct, substitute and new entrant—and its publics

# The Micro Marketing Environment

Many authors, notably Michael Porter,[10] have made a distinction between the very broad forces of the **macro marketing environment** discussed up to now in this chapter – political, legal, regulatory, societal/Green, technological, economic/ competitive – and a set of more company-specific forces often termed the **micro marketing environment** forces. The distinction, put simply, is that the broad macro forces have an impact on every organisation operating in a particular market, from manufacturers to distributors to customers, and such an impact is largely universally felt by such organisations. The micro forces, on the other hand, often have an organisation-specific impact subject to the characteristics and status of the individual business.

## The Core Aspects of the Micro Marketing Environment

Although categorisations vary among authors, the core aspects of the micro marketing environment worthy of note include the business, suppliers, marketing intermediaries, buyers, competitors and publics (see Figure 3.3).

**The Business** It is necessary when creating and implementing marketing strategies and marketing mix programmes to consider the reaction, attitudes and abilities of the internal environment: top management, finance, research and development, purchasing, manufacturing, sales and marketing, and logistics. The marketing function's recommendations must be consistent with senior management's corporate goals; be conveyed to other functions within the business; and reflect colleagues' views, input, concerns and abilities to implement the desired marketing plan. Marketers must be aware of these organisational factors, monitor them, and modify their actions accordingly to ensure internal take-up of their ideas and plans.

*Figure 3.3*
*The forces of the marketing environment: macro and micro*

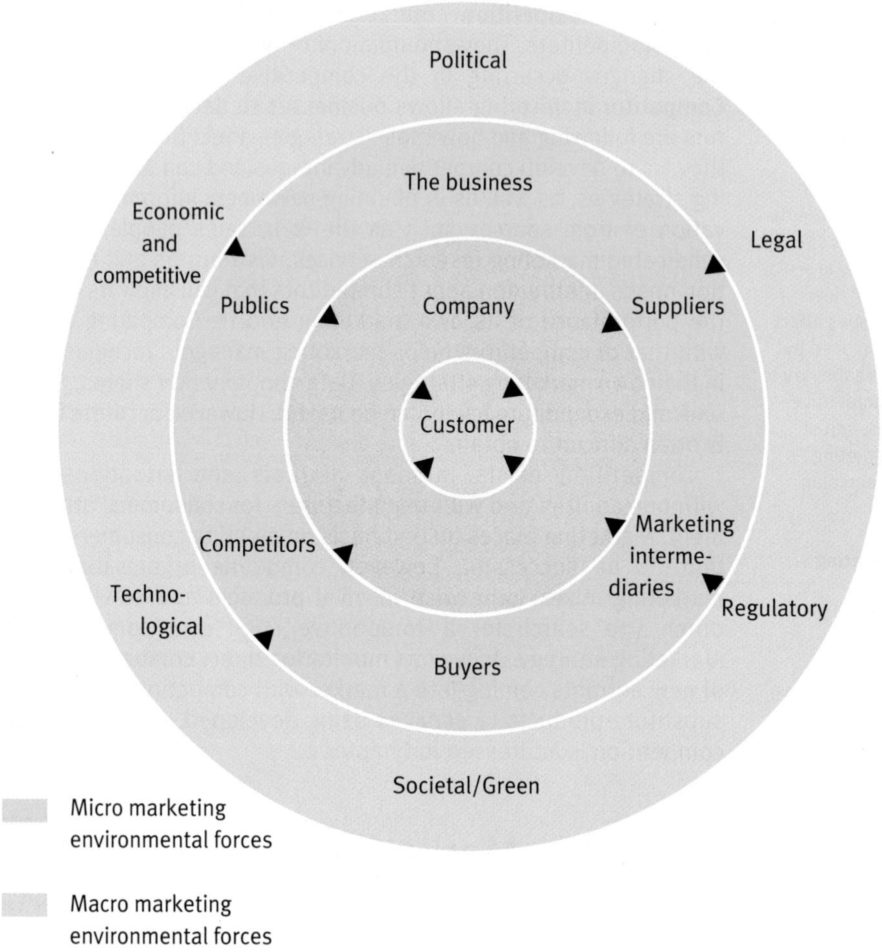


**Suppliers** Most organisations source raw materials, components or supplies from third parties. Without the understanding and cooperation of these other organisations, a business would fail to deliver a quality product or service that satisfies its customers' needs. Marketers must be aware of aspects of supply that might affect the way in which their business functions in satisfying its customers. These forces could include supplier innovations; deals with rivals; supply shortages, delays or quality concerns; strikes or recruitment difficulties; legal actions or warranty disputes; supply costs and price trends; new entrants into the supply chain; or anything prone to altering the business's receipt of its required supplies.

**Marketing Intermediaries** Some businesses sell directly to their targeted customers. Most, though, utilise the skills, network and resources of intermediaries to make their products available to the end-user customer. Intermediaries are discussed later (see Part IV) and include resellers such as retailers, wholesalers, agents, brokers, dealers; as well as physical distribution companies responsible for logistical needs; providers of marketing services such as advertising agencies or packaging design consultancies; and financial facilitators of credit lines and export guarantees. Without the smooth cooperation of such intermediaries, a business is unlikely to be able to deliver its products as required by its customers. For example, the collapse of a credit company or bank severely reduces the ability of a client business to fund its activities. A striking workforce in a business's preferred road haulage company will lead to the urgent need to negotiate alternative logistical support with a new haulier, requiring time and perhaps legal intervention given existing contractual arrangements. An advertising agent's new account win might be that of a direct rival to an existing client. The existing client business might sensibly choose to find a different advertising agency, but this move will have a penalty in terms of management time and perhaps the timely execution of a planned advertising campaign.

In each of these examples, shrewd awareness of developments by an organisation's marketers would have reduced the likelihood of any impediment to its own activities and ability to serve its own customers. Failure to pick up on any of these events would have resulted in a loss of business as the marketers and colleagues in other business functions sought alternative lines of credit, haulage agreements or advertising expertise.

**Buyers** Customers are central to the marketing concept. They are often fickle and have ever changing requirements, needs and perceptions, which marketers must understand, anticipate and satisfy. As Chapters 6 and 7 describe, consumers and business customers should be analysed, and the marketing mix developed by a set of marketers must be designed to satisfy these customers' requirements. Each individual business will have a unique set of resources, skills, marketing programmes and products to offer its customers. Therefore, as customers' needs evolve, separate businesses will find that their required response is different. As the consumer has come to demand more customer service from supermarket retailers, Tesco and Sainsbury's have been better placed to upgrade their service-oriented propositions than, say, Somerfield or Iceland. This micro environmental force has had a variable impact on these retailers' strategies.

**Competitors** Marketers must strive to satisfy their target customers but in a manner that differentiates their product, brand and overall proposition from competing companies' marketing mixes. In order to achieve this, marketers require an in-depth understanding of their competitive arena, as explained in Chapter 2. There are two important considerations in this analysis. First, competition stems not only from like-for-like or direct rivals. There are substitute solutions to monitor and new entrants to anticipate. For example, construction equipment manufacturer JCB competes with a plethora of similar businesses such as Caterpillar or Case. Iseki manufactures none of the same equipment, but it produces a micro-bore tunnelling 'mole' that lays pipes without the need to dig trenches, thus rendering the need for a JCB backhoe loader digger redundant. Such substitute competition can seriously erode a business's market position if not observed and combated. New entrant car producer Daewoo made significant sales inroads in the European small and medium car market. Certain car manufacturing rivals had anticipated Daewoo's arrival with pre-emptive product launches and marketing campaigns. Other rivals had no contingency plans and saw their market share seriously eroded.

The second consideration is the business's own position: resources, market standing, capabilities, strengths and any competitive edge held over rivals. These characteristics are different for each organisation, so the impact of any competitive activity will vary between businesses. Marketers must be aware of direct, substitute and new entrant competitor activity but should also gauge the likely impact of competition on their own business in the context of a sound understanding of their capabilities and standing as explained in Chapter 2.

**Publics** The micro marketing environment also includes any group – public – that does or could impact on a business's ability to satisfy its target customers and achieve its corporate objectives.[11] These include: financial bodies such as banks, investment houses, financial analysts or shareholders; newspaper, magazine, radio, television, or Internet media that carry features about a business, its products and activities; government bodies that may intervene over operating or consumer issues; consumer and pressure groups; neighbourhood publics such as residents adjacent to a large manufacturing plant; the general public, whose view of a business must be assessed and taken into account when developing marketing programmes; and internal publics such as the workforce. Most businesses are increasingly recognising the importance of communicating effectively with these sets of people. The notion of relationship marketing outlined in Chapter 1 is designed to emphasise the need to address more publics than solely customers through marketing programmes and communications (see also Chapter 24). In order to achieve this effectively, however, it is necessary for an organisation to understand these micro marketing environment forces.

## The Marketing Environment and Strategic Opportunities

**Strategic windows**
Major developments or opportunities triggered by changes in the marketing environment

When changes occur in the marketing environment they can trigger major developments. If large enough, such changes are called **strategic windows** or paradigm shifts.[12] If market leaders have failed to spot the underlying development or evolutionary change, rivals may have an opportunity to gain an advantage over established companies and brands by 'stepping through the open window'. The established company must strive to 'close the window' with its own proposition speedily enough to pre-empt competitors' inroads. Failure to monitor the marketing environment and take appropriate action invariably results in an organisation being unable to react to the change quickly enough to keep out competitors.

### Opening Strategic Windows

Marketing strategists believe there are six broad causes of strategic windows opening, as described below.[13]

**New Technology** Duracell overtook market leader EverReady because it took advantage of new lithium technology before EverReady modified its product range. Direct Line gained leadership in the car insurance market because it turned to direct selling via telephone call centres before any of the major insurance companies recognised this evolving use of technology.

**New Markets** Security services and logistics company Securicor was quick to spot the likely take-off of the mobile phone market, taking the majority share in the then leading network provider Cellnet (O2). This awareness of new markets enabled Securicor to firmly establish itself as a multi-faceted communications business.

**New Distribution Channels** Telecommunications provider Vodafone was quick to recognise that some customers were reluctant to venture into specialist mobile phone shops, feeling they would be confused by the sales person's fast patter. Vodafone created point-of-sale displays with self-service selection for mainstream retailers such as Woolworths and Halfords. This self-selection appealed to a segment of the market and this innovative channel of distribution – cutting out mobile phone shops and specialists – helped to expand Vodafone's market share.

**Market Redefinition** NCR – National Cash Registers – used to dominate the market for providing electronic cash tills in retailers' stores. As retailers discovered the convenience of stock management through barcodes and EPoS systems, they turned to more sophisticated systems. Retail management's desire to monitor and record detailed sales data altered the buyer's requirement for in-store technology. ICL and Nixdorf were quick to spot this change and build on their computer industry resources to develop all-in retail systems that incorporated the cash till with much more. This redefinition of the market eroded NCR's once dominant position while giving rivals a marketing opportunity.

**New Legislation and Regulation** Laws, regulations and international agreements create strategic windows. The 'open skies' policy of the EU has created route opportunities for smaller airlines once precluded from hubs by state-protected national airlines. Privatisation of the UK rail network enabled Stagecoach and Virgin to diversify their businesses into rail services.

**Financial and Political 'Shocks'** Sudden changes in currency prices, interest rates, trade agreements, inflation, unemployment levels, protectionist policies or political leadership can have a major impact on business. A new government might decide to privatise state-owned assets or regulate an industry's activities more tightly. A trade war between states will impact on businesses operating in such markets.

## The Importance of Keeping a Lookout for the Strategic Window

Often managers only notice sales dips months after a marketing environment force has created a problem. In the meantime, this has created a window for competitors to enter. While there are many psychological factors that can hinder managerial activity, such as a preference for retrenchment and an aversion to change,[14] a common problem is simply the failure to formally and routinely monitor the forces of the marketing environment through environmental scanning – the process of collecting and analysing information about the forces of the marketing environment. A business must determine which aspects of the marketing environment – macro and micro – to monitor and how. Strategists believe a regular and routinised system enables identification of strongly signalled issues, which senior management or a marketing function can then prioritise for more detailed investigation. Clearly, given the vast array of issues examined in this chapter, it is not feasible or desirable for a set of managers to address every conceivably pertinent facet of the trading environment. However, failure to examine the marketing environment is a major problem for many poorly run organisations lacking a marketing orientation.

As described, companies opt for different solutions.[15] Some require line managers to undertake environmental scanning in addition to their other responsibilities. Occasionally, a strategic planner undertakes such monitoring, although this head office position is often too divorced from the business's operations to identify which crucial core forces to investigate. A few large companies have created a bespoke marketing environment unit of cross-functional managers responsible for researching, analysing, disseminating and recommending. This ensures scanning occurs but is costly and, again, can be too removed from a company's operations. More frequently, marketing planning identifies core trends and evolving forces to monitor.[16]

Marketing planning is practised in most medium-sized and large companies, and part of the cross-functional, multi-hierarchical team's remit is to report annually on marketing environment forces likely to have implications for the business (see Chapter 23). Some companies have no more than a box in the centre of an open-plan office in which any manager can deposit marketing environment information stemming from press comments, customer feedback, dealer observations, trade show intelligence, analysts' reports or any other inputs. This material is sifted regularly, summarised and circulated, with individual issues followed up as determined necessary by managerial judgement. Other businesses have formalised this approach using e-mail newsletters and intranet boards to personnel and sites within the organisation, often globally, with interactive dialogue aiding the understanding of the environmental forces noted.

**PEST analysis**
A popular name for an evaluation of the marketing environment, looking at political—including legal and regulatory issues—economic, social and technological developments, and assessing the implications of such issues

No matter how it is orchestrated, it is essential that the marketing environment is monitored thoroughly and regularly.[17] This must translate into managerial recommendations when necessary, with target market strategies and marketing programmes reflecting the issues identified. Such an analysis is often termed a **PEST analysis**, looking at political (P) – including legal and regulatory issues – economic (E), social (S) and technological (T) developments, and assessing the implications of such issues. An understanding of the marketing environment – macro and micro forces – is essential for a rigorous and meaningful assessment of marketing opportunities. Without such an analysis, any recommended marketing strategy is unlikely to take account of newly opening strategic windows. Competitors may be offered the chance to make inroads and the business may fail to benefit from potential marketing opportunities.

# Summary

The *marketing environment* consists of external forces that directly or indirectly influence an organisation's acquisition of inputs (personnel, financial resources, raw materials, information) and generation of outputs (information, packages, goods, services, ideas). Generally, the forces of the marketing environment are divided into two categories: macro and micro. The macro marketing environment comprises political, legal and regulatory forces, societal forces, including Green concerns for the earth's natural environment, and technological forces. Along with economic forces and trends, these macro, broader, aspects of the marketing environment have an impact on manufacturers and their customers. The forces of the micro marketing environment are more company-specific and include the business's internal environment, suppliers, marketing intermediaries, buyers, competitors and publics.

» To monitor changes in these forces, marketers should practise environmental scanning and analysis. *Environmental scanning* is the process of collecting information about the forces in the marketing environment; *environmental analysis* is the process of assessing and interpreting the information obtained in scanning. This information helps marketing managers predict opportunities and threats associated with environmental fluctuation. Marketing management may assume either a passive, reactive approach or an active, aggressive approach in responding to these environmental fluctuations. The choice depends on an organisation's structure and needs, and on the composition of the environmental forces.

» The political, legal and regulatory forces of the marketing environment are closely interrelated. The current political outlook is reflected in legislation and regulations, or the lack of them. The political environment may determine what laws and regulations affecting specific marketers are enacted, and how much the government purchases and from which suppliers; it can also be important in helping organisations secure foreign markets.

» Legislation affecting marketing activities can be divided into *procompetitive legislation* – laws designed to preserve competition and to end various practices deemed unacceptable by society – and consumer protection laws. In the UK, the Restrictive Trade Practices Act and the Competition Act sought to prevent monopolies and activities that limit competition; while legislation such as the Financial Services Act, the Sale of Goods Act and the Consumer Credit Act was directed towards more specific practices. Consumer protection laws generally relate to product safety and information disclosure. The actual effects of legislation are determined by how marketers and the courts interpret the laws.

» Regulatory agencies influence most marketing activities. For example, in the UK the *Competition Commission* and the *Office of Fair Trading* usually have the power to enforce specific laws and some discretion in establishing operating rules and drawing up regulations to guide certain types of industry practice. Self-regulation by industry represents another regulatory force; marketers are more in favour of this type of regulation than government action, because they have more opportunity to take part in creating the guidelines. Self-regulation may be less expensive than government regulation, and its guidelines are often more realistic. However, such regulation generally cannot assure compliance as effectively as government agencies.

» *Societal/Green forces* refer to the structure and dynamics of individuals and groups, and the issues that concern them. Many members of society want a high standard of living and a high quality of life, and they expect business to help them achieve these goals. Of growing concern is the well-being of the earth, its resources, climate and peoples. The *Green movement* is increasing general awareness of the natural environment and is altering product design, manufacture, packaging and use. The *consumer movement* is a diverse collection of independent individuals, groups and organisations that attempt to protect the rights of consumers. The major issues taken up by the consumer movement fall into three categories: environmental protection, product performance and safety, and information disclosure. Consumer rights organisations inform and organise other consumers, raise issues, help businesses develop consumer-oriented programmes and pressure legislators to enact consumer protection laws. Some are quite formally organised, such as the *Consumers' Association*.

» *Technology* is the knowledge of how to accomplish tasks and goals. Product development, packaging, promotion, prices and distribution systems are all influenced directly by technology. Several factors determine how much and in what way a particular business will make use of technology. These factors include the company's ability to use technology; consumers' ability and willingness to buy technologically improved products; the business's perception of the long-term effects of applying technology; the extent to which the company is technologically based; the degree to which technology is used as a competitive tool; and the extent to which the business can protect technological applications through patents. Many businesses conduct a *technology assessment*.

» The *economic forces* that can strongly influence marketing decisions and activities are general economic conditions, buying power, willingness to spend, spending patterns and *competitive forces*. The overall state of the economy fluctuates in a general pattern known as the *business cycle*. The stages of the business cycle are *prosperity*, *recession*, *depression* and *recovery*.

» Consumers' goods, services and financial holdings make up their *buying power*—their ability to purchase. The financial sources of buying power are *income*, credit and wealth. After-tax income used for spending or saving is called *disposable income*. Disposable income left after an individual has purchased the basic necessities of food, clothing and shelter is called *discretionary income*. It is important to identify levels of *wealth*. Two measures of buying power are: effective buying income (which includes salaries, wages, dividends, interest, profits and rents, less taxes); and the buying power index (a weighted index consisting of population, effective buying income and retail sales data). The factors that affect consumers' *willingness to spend* are product price, the level of satisfaction obtained from currently used products, and expectations about future employment, family size, income, prices and general economic conditions. *Consumer spending patterns* indicate the relative proportions of annual family expenditures, or the actual amount of money spent, on certain kinds of goods and services. *Comprehensive spending patterns* specify the percentages of family income allotted to annual expenditures for general classes of goods and services. *Product-specific spending patterns* indicate the annual amounts families spend for specific products within a general product class.

» *Competition* is a fundamental concern for all marketers. Although all businesses compete for consumers' spending, a company's direct competitors are usually the businesses in its geographic area marketing products that resemble its own or which can be substituted for them. The number of businesses that control the supply of a product may affect the strength of competition. There are four general types of competitive structure: *monopoly*, *oligopoly*, *monopolistic competition* and *perfect competition*. Marketers use *competitor monitoring* to determine what competitors are currently doing and to assess the changes occurring in the competitive environment.

» Increasingly, marketers make a distinction between the broader trading *macro marketing environment* forces – political, legal, regulatory, societal/Green, technological, economic/competitive – and the more company-specific forces of the *micro marketing environment*. Micro forces include the business in question, its suppliers, marketing intermediaries, buyers, business-specific competition – direct, substitute and new entrant rivals – and the various publics of an organisation: financial bodies, media, government, consumer and pressure groups, neighbours, the general public and the internal workforce.

Changes in the marketing environment often create *strategic windows* that, if they are not quickly identified, can enable rivals to gain an edge. There are six key causes of the creation of strategic windows, all aspects of the macro or micro marketing environment: new technology, new markets, new distribution channels, market redefinition, new legislation and regulation, plus financial and political 'shocks'. Often, managers fail to notice sales dips until months after the impact of an aspect of the marketing environment. This may be because they are averse to change and prefer retrenchment, but often it stems from a lack of environmental scanning. Strategists believe a regular and routinised assessment of the marketing environment is essential prior to the formulation of any target market strategies or marketing mix programmes. Practitioners often name such an assessment a *PEST analysis*. Companies adopt different solutions to monitoring the marketing environment, it can be carried out by: line managers, strategic planners, bespoke units or be incorporated as an integral part of the annual marketing planning process. It is essential that the marketing environment – macro and micro forces – is monitored continually in order to maximise marketing opportunities and fend off competitors' actions.

## *Key Links*

Marketers must analyse the marketing environment in order to identify opportunities and minimise threats. This chapter should be read in conjunction with:

- Chapter 1, which examines marketing opportunity analysis
- Chapter 2, which offers an overview of marketing strategy development
- Chapter 4, which focuses on the growing role of technology in marketing
- Chapter 5, which stresses the importance of understanding the forces of the marketing environment in international marketing.

## Important Terms

Marketing environment
Environmental scanning
Environmental analysis
Procompetitive legislation
Office of Fair Trading
Competition Commission
Consumers' Association
Societal/Green forces
Green movement
Consumer movement
Technology
Technology assessment
Economic and competitive forces
Business cycle
Prosperity
Recession
Depression
Recovery
Buying power
Income
Disposable income
Discretionary income
Wealth
Willingness to spend
Consumer spending patterns
Comprehensive spending patterns
Product-specific spending patterns
Competition
Monopoly
Oligopoly
Monopolistic competition
Perfect competition
Competitor monitoring
Macro marketing environment
Micro marketing environment
Strategic windows
PEST analysis

## Discussion and Review Questions

1. Why are environmental scanning and analysis so important?
2. How are political forces related to legal and regulatory forces?
3. Describe marketers' attempts to influence political forces.

4 What types of procompetitive legislation directly affect marketing practices?
5 What is the major objective of most procompetitive laws? Do the laws generally accomplish this objective? Why or why not?
6 What types of problem do marketers experience as they interpret legislation?
7 What are the goals of the Competition Commission? How does the Commission affect marketing activities?
8 Name several non-governmental regulatory forces. Do you believe that self-regulation is more or less effective than governmental regulatory agencies? Why?
9 How is the so-called 'Green movement' altering the shape of business?
10 Describe the consumer movement. Analyse some active consumer forces in your area.
11 What does the term 'technology' mean to you?
12 How does technology affect you as a member of society? Do the benefits of technology outweigh its costs and dangers?
13 Discuss the impact of technology on marketing activities.
14 What factors determine whether a business organisation adopts and uses technology?
15 In what ways can each of the business cycle stages affect consumers' reactions to marketing strategies?
16 What is the current business cycle stage? How is this stage affecting businesses in your area?
17 Define income, disposable income and discretionary income. How does each type of income affect consumer buying power?
18 How is consumer buying power affected by wealth and consumer credit?
19 How is buying power measured? Why should it be evaluated?
20 What factors influence a consumer's willingness to spend?
21 What are the principal types of competition?
22 What differentiates the forces of the micro marketing environment from those of the macro marketing environment?
23 Why must marketers monitor changes in supplier and marketing intermediary practices?
24 Why should marketers not only track direct, like-for-like competitors? What other types of competitor are there?
25 Why should marketers be aware of their organisation's publics?
26 How does an assessment of marketing environment forces assist in marketing opportunity analysis?
27 What are the main causes of the opening of strategic windows?
28 How can a business instigate environmental scanning?

## Recommended Readings


- Dibb, S., Simkin, L. and Bradley, J., *The Marketing Planning Workbook* (London: Thomson, 1998).
- Drucker, P., *Management in Turbulent Times* (London: Butterworth-Heinemann/Pan, 1993).
- Jain, S.C., *Marketing Planning & Strategy* (Cincinnati, OH: South Western, 1999).
- Leeflang, P.S.H. and van Raaij, W.F., 'The changing consumer in the European Union: a meta-analysis', *International Journal of Research in Marketing*, 1995, 12 (5), pp. 373–87.
- Palmer, A. and Hartley, B., *The Business and Marketing Environment* (Maidenhead: McGraw-Hill, 1996).
- Peattie, K., *Environmental Marketing Management* (London: Pitman, 1995).
- Porter, M.E., 'How competitive forces shape strategy', *Harvard Business Review*, March–April 1979, pp. 137–45.


## Internet Exercise

Choose the websites of key government departments, EU departments or of leading regulatory bodies and learn more about the ways in which their activities and powers impact on marketers and consumers. For example, log on to the websites for the Competition Commission and the Office of Fair Trading at:
www.comp-comm.org.uk and www.oft.gov.uk

1 What are the implications of these organisations' powers and recommendations for marketers?
2 In what ways do the activities of these bodies impact on consumers?

## Applied Mini-Case

Until recently, excepting the low-sugar variants, few observers would have included the producers of the leading colas as aiding healthy diets or encouraging greater awareness of obesity issues. First, the leading suppliers launched low-carb versions, and now they are proactively striving to educate consumers. Coca-Cola, for example, launched a major initiative to encourage people to exercise more. Coke launched an anti-obesity campaign under the title 'Active Lifestyle', engaging with young people through a variety of media. The initiative aims to promote the route to a healthy lifestyle through a combination of effective hydration, a balanced diet and physical activity.

**Sources:** Coca-Cola, 2004; Ben Bold, 'Coca-Cola debuts healthy living initiative in UK', *Marketing*, 1 July 2004, p. 1.

### Question

**As Coca-Cola's marketing manager, how would an understanding of the marketing environment have led to the Active Lifestyle initiative? How might the company have monitored the forces of its marketing environment?**

## Case Study

### Social Awareness: BMW Recycling the Consumer

The creation of the European Recovery and Recycling Association (ERRA) is indicative of growing concern for the environment and consumer awareness of this social issue. With members including Cadbury Schweppes, Coca-Cola, Heineken, Nestlé, L'Oréal, and Tetra Pak, the Brussels-based ERRA has developed a recycling scheme that could lead to the regular collection of discarded packaging – containers and bottles from housing estates, factories, schools, offices and shops – and their sorting and reuse. The scheme in many countries is far from becoming reality, requiring the significant commitment of government, local authorities and, of course, consumers. However, ERRA exists, supported by an extensive array of manufacturers and environmental pressure groups. The public's interest in the environment and in safeguarding the planet and its resources for generations to come has led companies to pay real attention to the Green lobby.

BMW, the German deluxe car maker, has been stressing the 'recyclability' of its vehicles in its television and press advertising for its 3 Series range. These cars are produced using more environmentally friendly production processes, with a greater proportion of components suitable for reworking. BMW's commitment to the future, however, goes further. In Landshut, Germany, it has a recycling factory. Two workers can strip all the reusable parts from a 1970s car in under 45 minutes, including the careful draining of all fluids, at a cost of about £90.

Landshut's role is as a huge scrap merchant, but one that adheres to the strictest code of ethical working practices and the latest understanding of how to dispose of redundant vehicles with the least harm to the environment. BMW executives support the notion of a Europe-wide initiative, requiring an authorised recycler to issue a disposal certificate for every car at the end of its life. Until such a certificate is issued, the last registered owner would continue to be liable to pay road taxes. This initiative would eventually require legislation and the support of governments. Meanwhile, several leading car manufacturers have joined forces, adopting standardised colour coding for all reusable parts.

The investment for BMW is significant, but anticipating eventual EU legislation to enforce recycling, the German manufacturer believes it is thinking strategically and is working towards maintaining its position as a major producer of vehicles. BMW has many partner recycling plants worldwide, with its first UK site in Sussex. Simultaneously, BMW is striving to make more of its cars reclaimable: 50 per cent of the current 3 Series can be stripped down and reused. BMW is clear: 'we feel socially, politically and ecologically responsible for everything we do', leading to the creation of the 'Sustainability. It can be done' forum for addressing manufacturing issues of concern to the wider community.

It is not only companies such as BMW that have responded to increasing social awareness of environmental and Green issues. Bottle banks, which exist in most towns at multiple locations, have been joined by collection containers for waste paper, food and drink cans, and even discarded clothes. The charity Oxfam has provided clothing collection banks in many car parks nationwide. Local councils collect householders' waste paper separately from their refuse for recycling. School children are taught to care for their environment and to encourage their parents to use bottle banks and waste paper collections. Societal pressure has created a new way of thinking that marketers must reflect.

**Sources:** www.bmwgroup.com/e, 2004; 'The can and bottle story: environment', Coca-Cola & Schweppes Beverages Ltd, 1993; 'Helping to solve the waste management puzzle', ERRA, Brussels, 1991; John Eisenhammer, 'Where cars will go when they die', *Independent on Sunday*, 21 February 1993, pp. 24–5; 'Helping the earth begins at home', Central Office of Information, Department of the Environment, HMSO, 1992; BMW 3 Series promotional material, 1995–2004; Warwickshire County Council, 1999; Oxfam, Kenilworth, 1999, 2004; Warwickshire County Council, 2004.

## Questions for Discussion

1. What has persuaded BMW to launch such initiatives as its recycling plants and the 'Sustainability. It can be done' forum?
2. In what ways are local authorities encouraging recycling?
3. What are the implications of the growing consumer interest in recycling for manufacturers of consumer goods?

# 4 The Internet, Technology in Marketing and CRM

"Throughout the '80s and '90s, technology has been as much a hindrance as a help for marketers. That time has passed. Customer data driven marketing is an idea whose time has finally come."

*Alan Tapp, Bristol Business School*

## Objectives

- To define electronic marketing and electronic commerce, and recognise their increasing importance in marketing strategy
- To understand the characteristics of electronic marketing: addressability, interactivity, memory, control, accessibility and digitalisation – and how they differentiate electronic marketing from traditional marketing activities
- To comprehend the role of customer relationship management in modern-day marketing
- To understand how electronic marketing and information technology can facilitate customer relationship management
- To identify the legal and ethical considerations in electronic marketing

## Introduction

The previous chapter examined the forces of the marketing environment as they apply to marketers endeavouring to operate in their respective markets. The forces of the marketing environment have recently impacted significantly on the actual toolkit utilised by marketers, notably in the context of technological changes. Electronic commerce (e-commerce) refers to sharing business information, maintaining business relationships, and conducting business transactions by means of telecommunications networks. Electronic marketing (e-marketing) is the strategic process of creating, distributing, promoting and pricing products for targeted customers in the virtual environment of the Internet. The Internet has changed the way marketers communicate and develop relationships with their customers, employees and suppliers.

Customer relationship management (CRM) uses technology-enhanced customer interaction to shape appropriate marketing offers – designed to nurture ongoing relationships with individual customers – within an organisation's target markets. CRM has adopted recent advances in database management and customer communications to develop ongoing dialogues tailored to nurture one-to-one relationships with specific customers, to claim a greater share of an individual customer's purchases, or 'share of wallet'.

*Opener*

# Google finds Success with Technology and Positive Relationships

Google has become the most popular web search engine, from being a rank outsider six years ago. Revenue is now estimated at over US$1 billion per annum, most of which comes from the advertisements that run alongside its searches. Its database of six billion pages is searched over 200 million times each day! Even the mighty Microsoft admits that Google is number one in terms of web searches. How did it achieve this?

By providing a search engine with an uncanny knack for generating relevant results. The company derived its name from the term 'googol' – which refers to the number represented by 1 followed by 100 zeros – to reflect its mission to organise the seemingly infinite amount of information available on the World Wide Web. Founded by two Stanford University drop-outs, Sergey Brin and Larry Page, in 1998, the company has succeeded where so many other dotcoms have failed by following a conservative strategy; providing a simple, easy-to-use website; and developing effective relationships with advertisers.

From the beginning, the company has refused to follow the pack of free-spending Internet start-ups and has instead focused on what it does best: providing the most efficient access to information on the Internet. The company can search more than six billion documents and return results in less than half a second. Although most search engines generate results based on the number of times the search criteria appears in a website's content, Google looks for hyperlinks pointing to a web page from other websites to create a more reliable search result.

Google does not permit banner and pop-up ads, which many Internet users find annoying, or accept payment for giving advertisers better placement in the search result. Instead, Google's advertising clients benefit from web surfers' appreciation of the company's ability to generate relevant results as well as an advertisement click-through rate that is five times as fast as the industry standard. The company continually collects and analyses data to identify popular search topics and phrases, and then solicits advertisers in relevant industries. Google emphasises the importance of establishing strong advertising client relationships and works to find beneficial matches with each client.

In addition to providing an award-winning search engine for web surfers, Google has agreements to provide search services for more than 300 corporate websites, including Sony and Cingular Wireless. The company plans to expand this and related search services to more corporate clients around the globe. It is also considering offering a new service that will permit Internet users to browse on-line through printed catalogues scanned in to Google's servers. By maintaining a conservative strategy, Google has become the most popular web search engine, and the world's fifth most popular website.

**Sources:** 'Google history', Google, www.google.com/corporate/history.html; Liane Gouthro, 'Going ga-ga for Google', *CNN*, 24 April 2000, www.cnn.com; Kara Swisher, 'Lifting Google's dot-com shell reveals serious Internet player', *Wall Street Journal*, 21 January 2002, http://on-line.wsj.com; Celia Walden, 'The hit factory', Night & Day, pp. 14–17, *Mail on Sunday*, 4 April 2004. Photo: Courtesy of Google

The phenomenal growth of the Internet presents exciting opportunities for companies such as Google to forge interactive relationships with consumers and business customers. The interactive nature of the Internet, particularly the World Wide Web, has made it possible to target markets more precisely and even reach markets that were previously inaccessible to certain companies or brands. The Internet also facilitates customer relationship management (CRM), allowing companies to network with manufacturers, wholesalers, retailers, suppliers and outsource organisations to serve customers more efficiently. Owing to its ability to enhance the exchange of information between customer and marketer, the Internet has become an important component of many organisations' marketing strategies.

Technology in marketing is far more widespread than the use by marketers of the Internet. Chapters addressing marketing research, marketing communications and the analysis of customers' buying behaviour, for example, also examine the role of technology in marketing. This chapter explores two key facets of technology in marketing:

1 e-marketing and the Internet
2 customer relationship management.

Marketing practitioners increasingly devote significant resources to embracing technology via the Internet and CRM systems.

## Marketing on the Internet

**Electronic commerce (e-commerce)**
Sharing business information, maintaining business relationships and conducting business transactions by means of telecommunications networks

**Electronic marketing (e-marketing)**
The strategic process of creating, distributing, promoting and pricing products for targeted customers in the virtual environment of the Internet

A number of terms have been coined to describe marketing activities and commercial transactions on the Internet. One of the most popular is **electronic commerce (e-commerce)**, which has been defined as 'the sharing of business information, maintaining business relationships, and conducting business transactions by means of telecommunications networks'.[1] In this chapter, the focus is on how the Internet, especially the World Wide Web, relates to all aspects of marketing, including strategic planning. Thus, the term **electronic marketing (e-marketing)** has been adopted to refer to the strategic process of creating, distributing, promoting and pricing products for targeted customers in the virtual environment of the Internet.

One of the most important benefits of e-marketing is the ability of marketers and customers to share information. Through company websites, consumers can learn about a business's products, including features, specifications and even prices. Many websites also provide feedback mechanisms through which customers can ask questions, voice complaints, indicate preferences, and otherwise communicate about their needs and desires. The Internet has changed the way marketers communicate and develop relationships not only with their customers but also with their employees and suppliers. Many companies use e-mail, groupware – software that allows people in different locations to access and work on the same file or document over the Internet – and videoconferencing to coordinate activities and communicate with employees. Because such technology facilitates and lowers the cost of communications, the Internet can contribute significantly to any industry or activity that depends on the flow of information, such as entertainment, healthcare, government services, education, travel services and software.[2]

Telecommunications technology offers additional benefits to marketers, including rapid response, expanded customer service capability (e.g. 24 hours a day, 7 days a week, or 24/7), decreased operating costs and reduced geographic barriers. Data networks have decreased cycle and decision times, and permitted companies to treat customers more efficiently.[3] In today's fast-paced world, the ability to shop for books, clothes and other merchandise at midnight, when conventional stores are usually closed, is a benefit for both some buyers and sellers. The Internet allows even small businesses to reduce the impact of geography on their operations. For example, relatively small businesses, lacking sales teams or advertising budgets, can cater for client requirements over a very large geographic area.

Despite these benefits, many companies that chose to make the Internet the core of their marketing strategies – often referred to as 'dotcoms' – failed to earn profits or acquire sufficient resources to remain in business. Many dotcoms failed because they thought the only thing that mattered was brand awareness. In reality, however, Internet markets are more similar to traditional markets than they are different: successful e-marketing strategies, like traditional marketing ones, depend on creating, distributing, promoting and pricing products that customers need or want, not merely developing a brand name or reducing the costs associated with on-line transactions.[4] In fact, traditional retailers continue to do quite well in some areas that many people, just a few years ago, thought the Internet would dominate. For example, although many marketers believed there would be a shift to buying cars on-line, experts predict that just 4 per cent of all new cars will be sold through the Internet in 2010. Research suggests that on-line shoppers are very concerned about price, and a company's profits can vanish quickly as competition drives prices down. Few consumers are willing to spend £25,000 on-line to purchase a new car. However, consumers are increasingly making car-buying decisions on the basis of information found on-line.[5]

Indeed, e-marketing has not changed all industries, although it has had more of an impact in some industries in which the costs of business and customer transactions are very high. For example, trading stocks/shares has become significantly easier and less expensive for customers who can go on-line and execute their own orders. Companies such as E*Trade and Charles Schwab have been innovators in this area, and traditional brokerage businesses such as Merrill Lynch have had to introduce on-line trading for their customers in order to remain competitive. In many other industries, however, the impact of e-marketing may be incremental.

## The Basic Characteristics of Electronic Marketing

Although e-marketing is similar to traditional marketing, it is helpful to understand the basic characteristics that distinguish this environment from the traditional marketing environment. These characteristics include addressability, interactivity, memory, control, accessibility and digitalisation.

### Addressability

The technology of the Internet makes it possible for visitors to a website to identify themselves and provide information about their product needs and wants *before* making a purchase. The ability of a marketer to identify customers before they make a purchase is called **addressability**.

**Addressability**
A marketer's ability to identify customers before they make a purchase

Many websites encourage visitors to register in order to maximise their use of the site or to gain access to premium areas; some even require it. Registration forms or questionnaires typically ask for basic information, such as name, e-mail address, age and occupation, from which marketers can build user profiles to enhance their marketing efforts. CDNow, for example, asks music lovers to supply information about their listening tastes so the company can recommend new releases. Some websites even offer contests and prizes to encourage users to register. Marketers can also conduct surveys to learn more about the people who access their websites, perhaps offering prizes as motivation for participation.

Addressability represents the ultimate expression of the marketing concept. With the knowledge about individual customers garnered through the web, marketers can tailor marketing mixes more precisely to target customers with narrow interests, such as recorded blues music or golf. Addressability also facilitates tracking website visits and on-line buying activity, which makes it easier for marketers to accumulate data about individual customers in order to enhance future marketing efforts. Amazon.co.uk, for example, stores data about customers' purchases and uses that information to make recommendations the next time they visit the site.

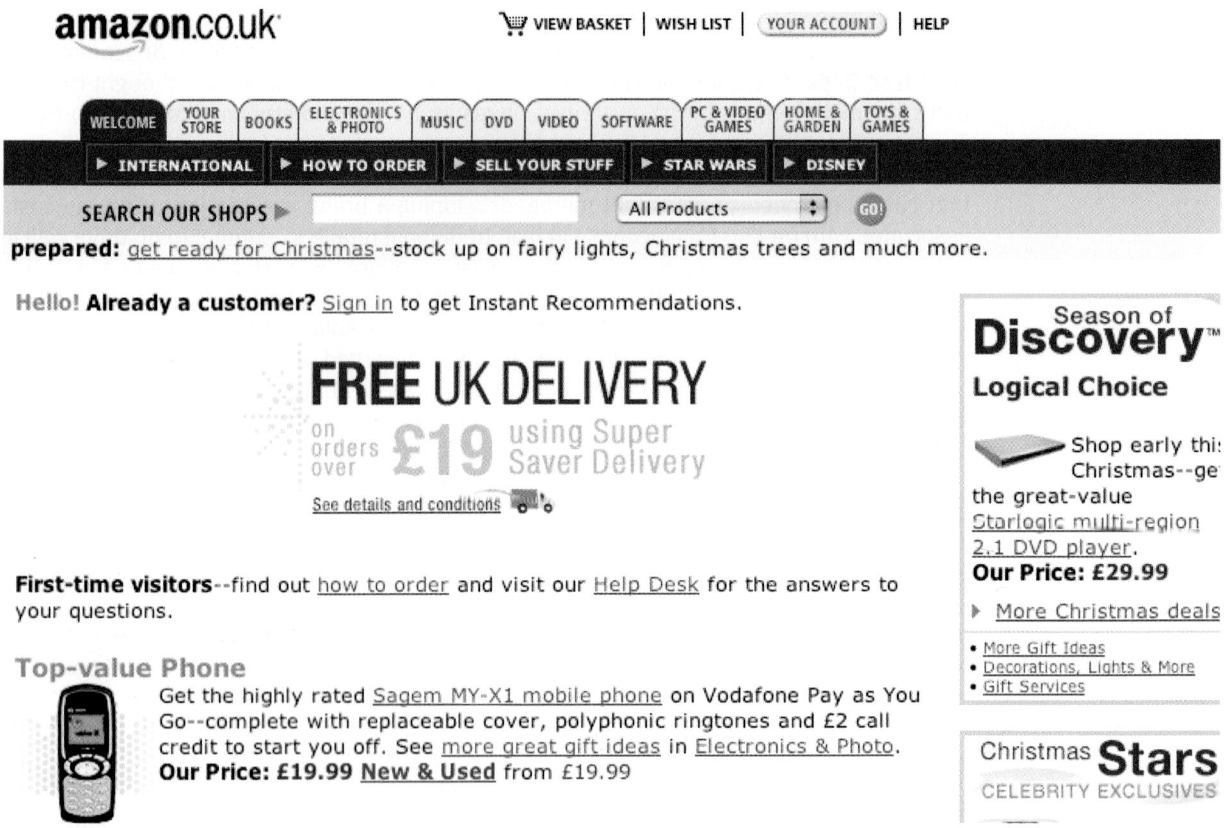


***Figure 4.1***
*Amazon's interactivity enables customers to create tailored wish lists and find out more information about products and ordering*
*Screen capture: Courtesy of Amazon.co.uk*

**Cookie**
An identifying string of text stored on a website visitor's computer

**Interactivity**
The ability to allow customers to express their needs and wants directly to the business in response to the company's marketing communications

Some website software can store a **cookie** – an identifying string of text – on a visitor's computer. Marketers use cookies to track how often a particular user visits the website, what he or she may look at while there, and in what sequence. Cookies also permit website visitors to customise services, such as virtual shopping trolleys, as well as the particular content they see when they log on to a web page. The BBC, CNN or Sky News, for example, allow visitors to their websites to create a customised or personalised news page tailored to their particular interests. The use of cookies to store customer information can be an ethical issue, however, depending on how the data are used. If a website owner can use cookies to link a visitor's interests to a name and address, that information could be sold to advertisers and other parties without the visitor's consent or even knowledge. The potential for the misuse of cookies has made many consumers wary of this technology. Because technology allows access to large quantities of data about customers' use of websites, companies must consider carefully how the use of such information affects the individual's privacy.

## Interactivity

Another distinguishing characteristic of e-marketing is **interactivity**, which allows customers to express their needs and wants directly to a company in response to its marketing communications. This means that marketers can interact with prospective customers in real time, or at least a close approximation of it. Of course, sales people have always been able to do this, but at a much greater cost. The web provides the advantages of a virtual sales representative, with broader market coverage and at lower cost.

One implication of interactivity is that a company's customers can also communicate with other customers and non-customers. For this reason, differences in the amount and type of information possessed by marketers and their customers are not as pronounced as in the past. One result is that the new and used car businesses have become considerably more competitive because buyers are coming into dealerships armed with more complete product and cost information obtained through comparison shopping on-line. By providing information, ideas and a context for interacting with other customers, e-marketers can enhance customers' interest and involvement with their products.

**Community**
A sense of group membership or feeling of belonging

Interactivity enables marketers to capitalise on the concept of community to help customers derive value from the company's products and website. **Community** refers to a sense of group membership or feeling of belonging by individual members of a group.[6] One such community is Tripod, a website where users can create their own web pages and chat or exchange messages on bulletin boards about topics ranging from cars and computers to health and careers. Much of the site's content has been developed by members of the Tripod community. Like many on-line communities, Tripod is free but requires members to register in order to access the site.[7] The success of websites like Tripod corroborates an analysis by *Business Week* suggesting that the most successful on-line marketers do not just duplicate existing businesses on-line but fully exploit the interactivity of the World Wide Web for the benefit of their customers. The most successful websites become 'virtual communities' where 'like-minded cybernauts congregate, swap information, buy something, and come back week after week'.[8] They encourage visitors to 'hang out' and contribute to the community – and see the website's advertising – instead of clicking elsewhere. Because such communities have well-defined demographics and common interests, they represent a valuable audience for advertisers, which typically generate the funds to maintain such sites.[9]

**Database**
A collection of information arranged for easy access and retrieval

## Memory

**Memory**
The ability to access databases or data warehouses containing individual customer profiles and past purchase histories, and to use these data in real time to customise a marketing offer

**Memory** refers to a company's ability to access databases or data warehouses containing individual customer profiles and past purchase histories, and use these data in real time to customise its marketing offer to a specific customer. A **database** is a collection of information arranged for easy access and retrieval. Although companies have had database systems for many years, the information these systems contain did not become available on a real-time basis until fairly recently. Current software technology allows a marketer to identify a specific visitor to its website instantaneously, locate that customer's profile in its database, and then display the customer's past purchases or suggest new products based on past purchases while he or she is still visiting the site. Applying memory to large numbers of customers represents a significant advantage when a company uses it to learn more about individual customers each time they visit the website.

## Control

**Control**
Customers' ability to regulate the information they view, and the rate and sequence of their exposure to that information

In the context of e-marketing, **control** refers to customers' ability to regulate the information they view, as well as the rate and sequence of their exposure to that information. The web is sometimes referred to as a *pull* medium because users determine what they view at websites; website operators' ability to control the content that users look at and in what sequence is limited. In contrast, television can be characterised as a *push* medium because the broadcaster determines what the viewer sees once he or she has selected a particular channel. Both television and radio provide 'limited exposure control': the recipient sees or hears whatever is broadcast until he or she changes the station.

For e-marketers, the primary implication of control is that attracting – and retaining – customers' attention is more difficult. Marketers have to work harder and more creatively to communicate the value of their websites clearly and quickly, or the viewer will lose interest and click to another site. With literally hundreds of millions of unique pages of content available to any web surfer, simply putting a website on the Internet does not guarantee anyone will visit it or make a purchase. Publicising the website may require innovative promotional activities. For this reason, many companies pay millions to advertise their products or websites on high-traffic sites such as AOL. Because of AOL's growing status as a **portal** – a multi-service website that serves as a gateway to other websites – companies are eager to link to it and other such sites to help draw attention to their own sites. Indeed, consumers spend most of their time on-line on portal sites such as MSN and Yahoo!, checking e-mail, tracking stocks, and perusing news, sports reports and weather forecasts.

**Portal**
A multi-service website that serves as a gateway to other websites

## Accessibility

**Accessibility**
The ability to obtain information available on the Internet

An extraordinary amount of information is available on the Internet. The ability to obtain it is referred to as **accessibility**. Because customers can access in-depth information about competing products, prices, reviews, and so forth, they are much better informed about a company's products and their relative value than before. Someone looking to buy a new truck, for example, can go to the websites of Ford, Mercedes Benz or Volvo to compare the features of the models available. The truck purchaser can also access on-line magazines and pricing guides to obtain more specific information about product features, performance and prices.

Accessibility also dramatically increases the competition for Internet users' attention. Without significant promotion, such as advertising on portals like AOL, MSN, Yahoo!, and other high-traffic sites, it is becoming increasingly difficult to attract a visitor's attention to a particular website. Consequently, e-marketers are having to become more creative and innovative in order to attract visitors to their sites.

**Uniform resource locator (URL)**
A website address

A related consideration is the recognition value of a business's **uniform resource locator (URL)**, or website address. The first organisation to register a particular URL gains the exclusive right to use that URL as its website address. Imagine the difficulty of promoting a website for Coca-Cola and being unable to use www.coke.com as a URL. As the number

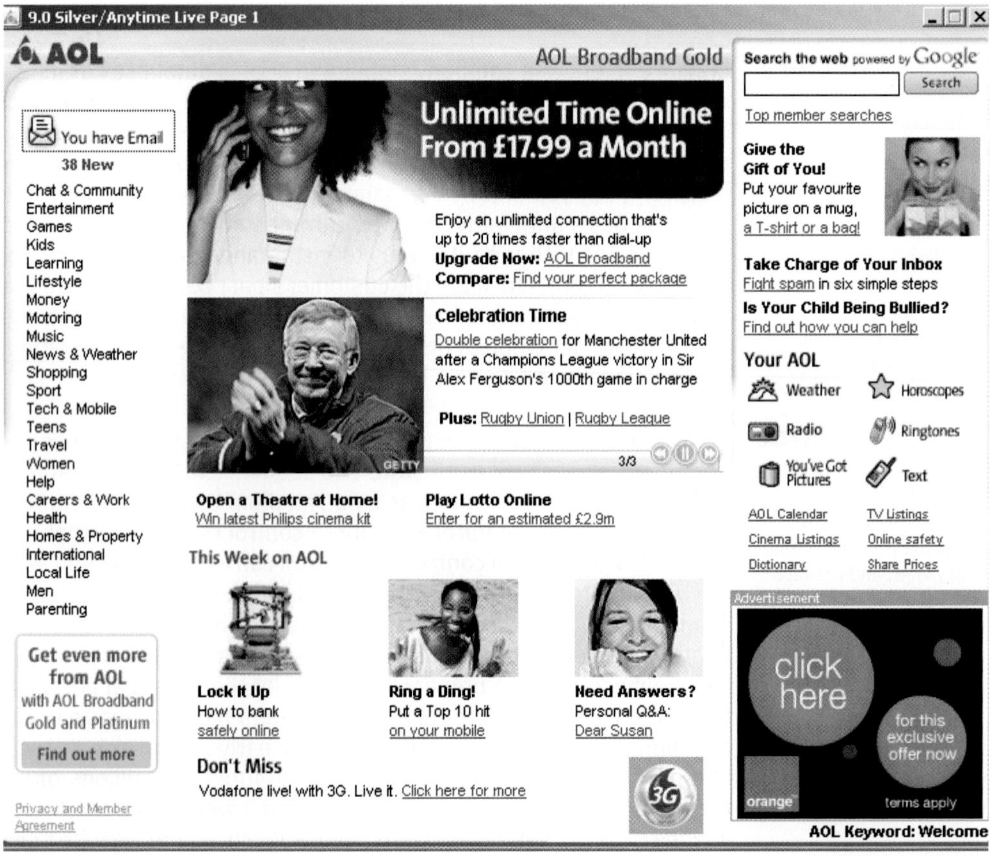


*Figure 4.2*
*AOL's broadband services have taken AOL to the top of the league for Internet portals, enabling it to attract many advertisers such as Orange*
*Source: Courtesy of AOL (UK) Ltd*

of websites proliferates, web surfers will find it increasingly difficult to learn or remember the URLs for various companies and products. A URL that does not match the brand or company name can represent a serious obstacle to new or first-time visitors looking for a particular product on the web.

### Digitalisation

**Digitalisation**
The ability to represent a product, or at least some of its benefits, as digital bits of information

**Digitalisation** is the ability to represent a product, or at least some of its benefits, as digital bits of information. Digitalisation allows marketers to use the Internet to distribute, promote and sell those features apart from the physical item itself. Federal Express, TNT and Securicor, for example, have developed web-based software that allows consumers and business customers to track their own packages from starting point to destination. Distributed over the web at very low cost, the on-line tracking system adds value to these delivery services. Digitalisation can be enhanced for users who have broadband access to the Internet, because broadband's faster connections allow streaming audio and video, and other new technologies.

In addition to providing distribution efficiencies, digitising part of a product's features allows new combinations of features and services to be created quickly and inexpensively. For example, a car service department that keeps a customer's history of oil changes in a database can e-mail that customer when the next oil change is due and at the same time suggest other types of preventative maintenance, such as tyre balancing or a tune-up. Digital features are easy to mix and match to meet the demands of individual customers.

## E-marketing Strategies

Having examined some distinguishing characteristics of doing business on the Internet, it is time to consider how these characteristics affect marketing strategy. Marketing strategy involves identifying and analysing a target market and creating a marketing mix to satisfy individuals in that market, regardless of whether those individuals are accessible on-line or through more traditional avenues. However, in the electronic environment of the web, there are significant differences in how the marketing mix components are developed and combined into a marketing strategy. Keep in mind that the Internet is a very dynamic environment, meaning that e-marketing strategies may need to be modified frequently to keep pace.

### Target Markets

As overviewed in Chapter 1, marketing strategy involves identifying an opportunity, analysing a target market and creating a marketing mix to satisfy individuals in that market. With over a third of European households on-line and the proportion growing rapidly (see Table 4.1), the Internet has become an important medium for reaching consumers. Although Internet access outside Europe and the United States has lagged behind, people around the world are now rapidly discovering the web's potential for communication and e-marketing.

Over 13 million males and 11 million females are regular users of the Internet in the UK. One in ten UK consumers has purchased on-line and 50 per cent of UK households surf the web regularly. Two in ten UK businesses trade on-line, while six out of ten business customers (B2B) value the role of the web in sourcing suppliers or customers; 92 per cent of CEOs claim their companies are endorsing the web as a channel to market and for communication with key stakeholders.

### Product Considerations

The issues for marketers of introducing successful products and managing product portfolios are discussed in Part III. The growth of the Internet and the World Wide Web presents exciting opportunities for marketing products both to consumers and business customers. Computers and computer peripherals, industrial supplies, and packaged software are the leading business purchases on-line. According to International Data Corp (IDC), the total value of goods and services purchased by businesses worldwide through e-commerce will climb from US$282 billion in 2000 to US$4.3 trillion by 2005, an annual rate of 73 per cent.[10] Consumer products

**TABLE 4.1 INTERNET ACCESS AND GROWTH IN EUROPE**

| | Internet Access in European Households[1] (%) | Internet % Growth[2] |
|---|---|---|
| Iceland | 67 | N/A |
| UK | 66 | 123 |
| Sweden | 62 | 66 |
| Belgium | 58 | 89 |
| Denmark | 58 | 73 |
| Finland | 56 | 38 |
| Ireland | 54 | 68 |
| Germany | 38 | 84 |
| Italy | 31 | 46 |
| Austria | 31 | 59 |
| France | 27 | 159 |
| Spain | 24 | 160 |
| Portugal | 23 | 48 |
| Greece | 14 | 100 |
| European average | 35 | 94 |

[1]**Source:** Eurobarometer.
[2]**Sources:** IWS; *The European Marketing Pocket Book*, published by the World Advertising Research Center, Henley-on-Thames, 2004.

account for a small but rapidly growing percentage of Internet transactions, with financial services products, securities trading, travel/tourism, tickets for sporting and cultural events, and books, music CDs and videos/DVDs among the most frequent consumer purchases.

Through e-marketing, companies can provide products – including goods, services and ideas – that offer unique benefits and improve customer satisfaction. The on-line marketing of goods such as computer hardware and software, books, videos, DVDs, CDs, toys, cars and groceries is accelerating rapidly. Dell Computer was one of the first tangible goods manufacturers to embrace e-commerce, and sold close to $35 billion worth of computers and related software and hardware last year, about half of that amount through its website.[11] Insurance and banking have seen huge growth on-line in the past 18 months. Services may have the greatest potential for on-line marketing success. Many websites offer, or enhance, services ranging from home- and car-buying assistance to travel reservations and stock trading.

The proliferation of information on the World Wide Web has itself spawned new services. Web search engines and directories such as Yahoo!, Google, Excite, Lycos, and Alta Vista are among the most heavily accessed sites on the Internet. Without these services, which track and index the vast quantity of information available on the web, the task of finding something of interest would be tantamount to searching for the proverbial needle in a haystack. Many of these services, most notably Yahoo!, have evolved into portals by offering additional services, including news, weather, chat rooms, free e-mail accounts and shopping.

Even ideas have potential for success on the Internet. Web-based distance learning and educational programmes are becoming increasingly popular. Corporate employee training is a growing industry, and on-line training modules are growing rapidly. Additional ideas being marketed on-line include marriage and personal counselling, medical, tax and legal advice, and even psychic services.

Anything associated with the Internet seems to move at the speed of light; thus, statistics on Internet access and usage are obsolete almost as soon as they appear in print. One valuable source of up-to-date statistics for marketers is CyberAtlas (http://cyberatlas.Internet.com/), which provides an easily accessible clearing house of Internet data from leading research businesses such as Forrester Research, Jupiter Research, Gartner Dataquest and Nielsen/NetRatings. The award-winning site offers the latest demographic and geographic, usage and traffic statistics, as well as articles about Internet advertising, business-to-business markets, retailing and more.

### Distribution Considerations

The role of distribution is to make products available at the right time at the right place in the right quantities (see Part IV). The Internet can be viewed as a new distribution channel. Physical distribution is especially compatible with e-marketing. The ability to process orders electronically and increase the speed of communications via the Internet reduces inefficiencies, costs and redundancies throughout the marketing channel.

More companies are exploiting advances in information technology to synchronise the relationships between their manufacturing or product assembly and their customer contact operations. This increase in information-sharing among various operations of a business makes product customisation easier to accomplish. Marketers can use their websites to ask customers about their needs and then manufacture products that fit those needs exactly. Gateway and Dell, for example, help their customers build their own computers by asking them to specify what components to include; these computer manufacturers then assemble and ship the customised product direct to the customer in a few days.

One of the most visible members of any marketing channel is the retailer, and the Internet is increasingly becoming a retail venue. Although just 1 per cent of all retail purchases occur on-line, it is predicted that the percentage of the European population shopping on-line will grow to 66 per cent by 2006. The Internet provides an opportunity for marketers, of everything from computers to travel reservations, to encourage exchanges. Amazon.com's success at marketing books on-line has been so phenomenal that many imitators have adopted its retailing model for everything from CDs to toys. Another retailing venture is on-line auctioneers, such as eBay and Haggle On-line, which auction everything from fine wines and golf clubs to computer goods and electronics.

### Promotion Considerations

The Internet is an interactive medium that can be used to inform, entertain and persuade target markets to accept an organisation's products. In fact, gathering information about goods and services is one of the main reasons people use the Internet. The accessibility and interactivity of the Internet allow marketers to complement their traditional media usage for promotional efforts. As is explained in Part V, many marketers have embraced the Internet within their promotional mix activity. The control characteristic of e-marketing means that customers who visit a company's website are there because they choose to be, which implies that they are interested in the company's products and, therefore, can be at least somewhat involved in the message and dialogue provided by the company. For these reasons, the Internet represents a highly cost-effective communication tool for small businesses.

Many companies augment their TV and print advertising campaigns with web-based promotions. Both Kraft and Ragu, for example, have created websites with recipes and entertaining tips to help consumers get the most out of their products. Many movie studios have set up websites at which visitors can view clips of their latest releases, and television advertisements for new movies often encourage viewers to visit these sites. In addition, many companies choose to advertise their goods, services, and ideas on portals, search engines and even other companies' websites. Table 4.2 describes the most common types of advertisement found on websites.

Many marketers are also offering buying incentives and adding value to their products on-line through the use of sales promotions, especially coupons. The characteristics of e-marketing make promotional efforts on the Internet significantly different from those using more traditional media. First, because Internet users can control what they see, customers

**TABLE 4.2 TYPES OF ADVERTISING ON WEBSITES**

| | |
|---|---|
| Banner ads | Small, rectangular, static or animated advertisements that typically appear at the top of a web page |
| Keyword ads | Adverts that relate to text or subject matter specified in a web search |
| Button ads | Small, square or rectangular adverts bearing a corporate or brand name or logo, and usually appearing at the bottom or side of a web page |
| Pop-up ads | Large adverts that open in a separate web browser window on top of the website being viewed |
| Pop-under ads | Large adverts that open in a new browser window underneath the website being viewed |
| Sponsorship ads | Adverts that integrate companies' brands and products with the editorial content of certain websites |

who visit a company's website are there because they choose to be, which implies that they are interested in the company's products. Second, the interactivity characteristic allows marketers to enter into dialogue with customers to learn more about their interests and needs. This information can then be used to tailor promotional messages to the individual customer. Finally, addressability can make marketing efforts directed at specific customers more effective. Indeed, direct marketing (see Chapter 19) combined with effective analysis of customer databases may become one of e-marketing's most valuable promotional tools.

### Pricing Considerations

Pricing relates to perceptions of value and is the most flexible element of the marketing mix (see Part VI). E-marketing facilitates both price and non-price competition, because the accessibility characteristic of e-marketing gives consumers access to more information about the cost and price of products than has ever been available to them before. For example, car shoppers can access manufacturers' web pages, configure an ideal vehicle, and get instant feedback on its cost. Try looking at the websites for Smart or Mini, for example.

The creation of effective websites and their use by marketers in marketing communications and for direct marketing are discussed extensively in Chapter 19.

## Managing Customer Relationships

Much marketing activity is targeted at attracting new customers. This transaction-led approach has been criticised by some experts, who argue that while it is obviously important to attract new customers, it is also important to maintain relationships with 'hooked' customers. To rectify this suggested shortcoming in marketing, the concept of relationship marketing has emerged, which – as suggested by the term and explained in Chapter 1 – focuses on winning the customer's business but then maintaining an ongoing, mutually beneficial relationship with the customer. Related to relationship marketing are the concepts of customer relationship management and one-to-one marketing, both of which often depend heavily on the increasing availability of customer database and customer contact IT systems. **Customer relationship management (CRM)** uses technology-enhanced customer interaction to shape appropriate marketing offers designed to nurture ongoing relationships with individual customers within an organisation's target markets. **One-to-one marketing** is the 'segment of one': bespoke marketing messages and propositions targeted at individual customers. More is said about one-to-one marketing in Chapter 8, which examines the concept of market segmentation.

**Customer relationship management (CRM)** Uses technology-enhanced customer interaction to shape appropriate marketing offers designed to nurture ongoing relationships with individual customers within an organisation's target markets

**One-to-one marketing** The 'segment of one': bespoke marketing messages and propositions targeted at individual customers

The emphasis of relationship marketing (see Chapter 1) is on the share of the individual's purchasing rather than the share of the overall market, with concentration on customer retention and repeat buying through an ongoing and responsive dialogue. The focus is on extracting more sales from existing customers through marketing activity, rather than marketing programmes designed to attract new customers. Marketers develop a more detailed, ongoing understanding of the customer, engaging in a dialogue that aims to enhance the buyer–seller relationship, and to continually offer product and customer service in an attractive proposition that is updated regularly. Customer relationship management (CRM), supported significantly these days by IT-based systems, is linked closely to the concept of relationship marketing. The aim of CRM is to gain from individual customers a greater 'share of wallet' over a prolonged period of time.

# Customer Relationship Management (CRM)

The processes inherent in managing ongoing customer relationships – particularly those involving database, technology and communications tools – have led to a growth in marketing of customer relationship management (CRM). Database advances and direct marketing, in particular, have led to:

- a focus on customer retention
- improvements in the share of the customer's purchasing
- the database being used as a device for managing direct communication
- integrated use of marketing channels.

The development of customer databases, the decreasing costs of collecting, storing and using information; better information systems technology; as well as the desire to build ongoing relationships with existing customers, have led to the growth of interest in customer relationship management. Database advances have enabled marketers to identify which customers they particularly want to keep and with whom to nurture ongoing loyalty. The quality of captured information in many businesses permits bespoke product and marketing communications packages to be specified to appeal to individual customers or narrowly defined groups of customers.

As illustrated in the Building Customer Relationships box on page 112, leading e-retailer Amazon has harnessed the latest technology in order to tailor messages to its customers. Promotional mix developments – particularly the growth of direct marketing techniques and web-based communication – have facilitated the more accurate and timely delivery of the customised message to these customers.

## Technology in Customer Relationship Management

One characteristic of companies engaged in e-marketing is a renewed focus on relationship marketing by building customer loyalty and retaining customers – in other words, on customer relationship management (CRM). CRM focuses on using information about customers to create marketing strategies that develop and sustain desirable long-term customer relationships. A focus on customer relationship management is possible in e-marketing because of marketers' ability to target individual customers. This effort is enhanced over time as customers invest time and effort into 'teaching' the company what they want. This investment in the company also increases the costs that a customer would incur by switching to another company. Once a customer has learned to trade stocks and shares on-line through Charles Schwab, for example, there is a cost associated with leaving to find a new brokerage business: another company may offer a lesser service, and it may take time to find a new company and learn a new system. If a marketer can learn more about its customers to strengthen the match between its marketing mix and target customers' desires and preferences, it increases the perceived costs of switching to another business.

E-marketing permits companies to target customers more precisely and accurately than ever before. The addressability, interactivity and memory characteristics of e-marketing allow marketers to identify specific customers, establish interactive dialogue with them to learn about their needs, and combine this information with their purchase histories to

## Building Customer Relationships

### Amazon's Marketers Depend on Technology to Serve their Customers

Amazon, the on-line provider of books, music and other products, works hard to retain its customers. Without a network of stores, the e-shopping experience is at the core of Amazon's marketing activity, and the company has embraced the latest CRM approaches. The company offers an extremely wide product range at competitive prices through a seamless and responsive shopping experience. Amazon records each customer's purchases. Its sophisticated databases then identify other currently top-selling titles of a similar type.

By updating and responding to customer purchase information, Amazon is able to recommend other products customers might like to buy. In the case of books, for example, this is achieved by matching titles purchased by an individual with the buying patterns of other customers who bought the same title. Thus a customer who purchases a celebrity chef cook book might on a subsequent visit to the site be offered an alternative cooking title that proved popular with other customers buying the celebrity chef cook book.

In the words of the company's chief executive, Amazon 'is a place where [customers] can buy anything they might want to buy on-line. This notion is that you take customers and put them at the centre of their own universe.' Amazon's use of technology cleverly customises the messages an individual customer receives, subject to that customer's previous purchasing and product tastes. The customer is not faced with the endless 'wallpaper' of seemingly irrelevant or uninteresting purchase suggestions evident in non-personalised e-selling.

If customers do not frequently access the Amazon site, e-mails notify them of new titles or current leading sellers that match their apparent purchasing interests. Without the IT capability to track an individual's purchases, such 'one-to-one' marketing would not be possible.

**Sources:** Amazon.co.uk, 2004; distance learning MBA notes, Sally Dibb and Lyndon Simkin, Warwick Business School, summer 2004.

customise products to meet those needs. Amazon.co.uk/Amazon.com, for example, stores and analyses purchase data to understand each customer's interests. This information helps the on-line retailer improve its ability to satisfy individual customers and thereby increase sales of books, music, movies and other products to each customer. The ability to identify individual customers allows marketers to shift their focus from targeting groups of similar customers to increasing their share of an individual customer's purchases. Thus, the emphasis shifts from *share of market* to *share of customer*. In moving to a share-of-customer perspective, however, a company should ensure that individual target customers have sufficient potential to justify such specialised efforts. Indeed, one benefit arising from the addressability characteristic of e-marketing is that companies can track and analyse individual customers' purchases, and identify the most profitable and loyal customers.

Focusing on *share of customer* requires recognising that all customers have different needs and that all customers do not have equal value to a business. The most basic application of this idea is the 80/20 rule: 80 per cent of business profits come from 20 per cent of customers. Although this idea is not new, advances in technology and data collection techniques now permit businesses to profile customers in real time. The goal is to assess the worth of individual customers and thus estimate their lifetime value (LTV) to the business. Some customers – those that require considerable hand-holding or who return products frequently – may simply be too expensive to retain given the low level of profits they generate. Companies can discourage these unprofitable customers by requiring them to pay higher fees for additional services. For example, many banks and brokers charge hefty maintenance fees on small accounts. Such practices allow companies to focus their resources on developing and managing long-term relationships with more profitable customers.

## Stone's CRM requirements

The effective implementation of CRM has attracted much attention in the marketing literature. Much of this debate centres around the practices adopted by companies engaged in CRM activities. Leading exponent Merlin Stone argues that robust CRM involves:[12]

(i) Analysis of the behaviour and value of different customers or customer groups and the development of an appreciation of what really are the customers' experiences of dealing with the company.

(ii) Planning activity and interactions with the customer in order to maximise the value of the customer base, focusing on retention, efficiency, acquisition and penetration of the customer.

(iii) Proposition development to ensure the customer's needs are met and new customers attracted.

(iv) The use of information and technology to store customer information, facilitate customer engagement and enable CRM practices to flourish.

(v) The recruitment, development, motivation and deployment of bespoke customer management personnel, not just in the company but also amongst suppliers and channel members.

(vi) Process management to ensure customer management personnel are operating effectively and are harnessed by the rest of the business.

(vii) Customer management activity, including targeting, enquiry management, welcoming of new or upgrading customers, understanding customer characteristics and issues, the development of customers so that customers who require it receive a higher or different level of service, the managing of problems customers may have with the business, win-back activity to redress problems with lost customers.

(viii) Measurement of the value of the CRM function and personnel. All of the CRM activity should be benchmarked against customer expectations, competitors' standards and industry best practice.

Stone explains that an organisation must take the time to appreciate the nature of the interactions customers have with it, the customer's perception of these experiences, and the extent to which the reality of this set of experiences fits with a customer's expectations. A customer's needs often evolve, so Stone points out that an organisation must modify its way of dealing with an individual customer over time. CRM is not only concerned with extracting more business from a customer through additional interactions, it is also about rectifying problems with existing points of interaction with customers.

Key requirements for effective CRM are rooted in the marketing concept per se. CRM relies on the ability to understand and anticipate customers' requirements. Assuming that an organisation has been able to develop the necessary understanding of its customers' needs and expectations, the emphasis of CRM then moves to the internal operating systems, personnel and processes for handling customer interactions. Stone's message is that if an organisation does not develop well-specified propositions and then procedures for interfacing with customers in an appropriate and timely manner, there will be no mutually beneficial, ongoing relationship.

One of the key objectives of customer relationship management (CRM) is to use the principles of a learning relationship to develop a deep understanding of the customer. The banking sector has, for example, been attracted by the benefits of CRM. In this sector, any implementation of CRM is dependent upon the ability to record details of customer contacts. This can be achieved by dealing in person with the customer, over the telephone, by mail or via the Internet. Thus when Prudential launched its banking service, Egg, the interaction with customers was seen to be vital. According to Egg's website, 'every conversation and interaction with a customer needs to set up the opportunity for the next – this creates the opportunity for the relationship to develop as the customers' financial and lifestyle needs change, ie: when moving house, having children or retiring'.

At a time when rapid developments in information technology (IT) are providing better access to usable customer data than ever before, further developments in target marketing have been possible in certain markets and product categories. Better customer information and the IT systems to capture, analyse and utilise this information, have led to what has been termed one-to-one marketing or the 'segment of one'. One-to-one marketing is the use of advances in marketing databases and technology to strive to build relationships with individual customers within target market segments. As with relationship marketing, an aim is to capture a greater proportion of an individual customer's purchasing by better understanding his or her evolving needs, purchasing patterns and buying behaviour, and by tailoring marketing communications to the individual.

In many businesses, database improvements are allowing access to a wider range of segmentation or customer classification variables. In particular, the popularity of demographics and other consumer-related variables is being replaced with more sophisticated schemes built upon behavioural characteristics. Many marketing practitioners, who see these behavioural variables as a better basis for building lasting customer relationships, have traditionally favoured such schemes. Improvements in data management technology are increasing the opportunities for segmentation based on product-related factors, such as benefits and product usage patterns. In turn, this enables marketers to hone their marketing propositions and tailor their marketing communications more accurately. The concept of market segmentation is explored in Chapter 8.

## CRM Systems

CRM hinges on: the effective identification of customer-based marketing intelligence; the collection, analysis, storage and dissemination of customer data; and the facilitation of rapid, accurate and relevant customer–supplier interactions. The role of IT systems cannot be underestimated. CRM for marketing practitioners ranks alongside the Internet as a key application of technology in marketing.

As an example of the challenge for CRM and thereby marketers, the following illustration from retail banking is useful.

Most retail banks have separate business units with bespoke personnel, handling customers' day-to-day banking requirements, mortgages, insurance, savings and investments, pension schemes, and other products. However, the typical time-pressured customer who visits a branch is not prepared for queries concerning different services to be handed between separate staff. Equally, customers become frustrated if the member of staff dealing with their query cannot readily access information about their various accounts or the bank's different products. Increasingly, customers expect a single point of contact in terms of a member of staff who is properly informed both about the bank's various products and about a customer's existing pieces of business with the bank. This applies to in-branch, telephone or e-banking. To manage this challenge is no easy task, but in many banks it is being achieved through the increasing sophistication of CRM systems.

The benefits to the bank from addressing this challenge are increased customer satisfaction – or decreased customer dissatisfaction! – and also an enhanced likelihood that customers will purchase a greater selection of products. This is known as the cross-selling opportunity: persuading the same customer to purchase products from different product groups or business units within the same supplier. When this occurs, revenues will increase and, possibly, profitability will improve. There is also greater likelihood of maintaining customer loyalty and minimising the propensity for brand switching.

In the Innovation and Change box on page 115, a leading provider of IT-based customer management solutions, Fujitsu, explains the relevance of CRM system solutions to its prospective business clients.

## Technology Drives CRM

Customer relationship management (CRM), therefore, focuses on building satisfying exchange relationships between buyers and sellers by gathering useful data at all customer-contact points – telephone, fax, on-line, and personal/face-to-face – and analysing those data to better understand customers' needs and desires. As the Fujitsu example

## Innovation and Change

### Fujitsu: Managing Customers

**Business Need**

Our clients [other businesses] seek a single, integrated view of their customers. *Single* in the sense that customer interaction can be personalised effectively, regardless of communication media. *Integrated* in the sense that all relevant customer data can be used to shape customer interaction, for example for cross-selling purposes. They also want to *simplify* and *automate* the processing of customer queries and cases, to *improve customer perception of service* and to *reduce operational costs.*

**The Solution**

Fujitsu can help to profitably retain customers and to sell more products to those customers. Our engagement model utilises some specific tools to ensure a rapid return on investment:

- The Macroscope® framework for the definition and articulation of the business drivers for the solution and for managing the implementation phase of the project.
- A structure for the definition, capture and automation of specific process-orientated engagements; for example, delivering customer advice or processing a mortgage application.

**Business Benefits**

1 Increased customer uptake of products: Fujitsu helped a major UK bank increase its product-per customer measure from 1.1 to 2.4; the highest in the industry.
2 Increased customer satisfaction: another UK bank was able to reduce its personal loan application process from 2 weeks to 30 minutes.
3 Increased staff satisfaction: a call-centre operator implementing a Fujitsu solution was able to reduce staff turnover by 40 per cent.
4 Achievement of regulatory and governmental targets: such as e-Government targets for citizen access to local authority data, and regulatory compliance for financial services customers.

**Our Approach**

A typical project of this type would take the form of:

- Discovery phase – a limited-duration 'Insight Service' would rapidly quantify and solve a specific client problem relating to customer management. The experienced multi-skilled team of a business consultant, subject-matter expert and project manager works to solve the problem.
- Where relevant, follow-up activities may include the illustration of specific business outcomes for additional projects, geared to achieving business plans.

**Partners and Skills**

- Fujitsu works with industry-leading CRM system vendors.
- Call-centre-based and IT-based CRM solutions.
- Dramatically speeding up and simplifying the application process for complex products such as mortgages and other financial products.
- Re-focusing ongoing CRM integration projects onto specific quick-wins, to enhance investor confidence and gain management commitment.
- Undertaking data source analysis and data cleansing services in order to feed CRM systems with consistent, integrated customer data.

**Source:** Courtesy of Fujitsu Services

demonstrates, companies are increasingly automating and managing customer relationships through technology. Indeed, one fast-growing area of CRM is customer support and call centre software, which helps companies capture information about all interactions with customers and provides a profile of the most important aspects of the customer experience on the web and on the phone. Using technology, marketers can analyse interactions with customers to identify performance issues and even build a library of 'best practices' for customer interaction. Customer support and call centre software can focus on those aspects of customer interaction that are most relevant to performance, such as how long customers have to wait on the phone to ask a question of a service representative or how long they must wait to receive a response from an on-line request. This technology can also help marketers determine whether call centre personnel are missing opportunities to promote additional products or to provide better service. For example, after buying a new Saab car, the customer is supposed to meet a member of staff who can answer any technical questions about the new car during the first service visit. Saab follows up this visit with a telephone survey to determine whether the new car buyer met the Saab member of staff and to learn about the buyer's experience with the first service call.

Sales automation software can link a company's sales force to e-marketing applications that facilitate selling and providing service to customers. Often these applications enable customers to assist themselves instead of using traditional sales and service organisations. At Cisco, for example, 80 per cent of all customer support questions can be answered on-line through the company's website, eliminating 75,000 phone calls a month. In addition, CRM systems can provide sales managers with information that helps provide the best product solution for customers and thus maximise service. Dell, for example, employs CRM data to identify those customers with the greatest needs for computer hardware and then provides these select customers with additional value in the form of free, secure, customised websites. These 'premier pages' allow customers – typically large companies – to check their order status, arrange deliveries and troubleshoot problems. Although Dell collects considerable data about its customers from its on-line sales transactions, the company avoids selling customer lists to outside vendors. CRM applications like that used by Dell include software for marketing automation, sales automation, customer support and call centres.

## Customer Satisfaction is the End Result of CRM

Although technology drives CRM and can help companies build relationships with desirable customers, it is used too often as a cost-reduction tactic or a tool for selling, with little thought given to developing and sustaining long-term relationships. Some companies spend millions to develop CRM systems yet fail to achieve the associated benefits. These companies often see themselves as sophisticated users of technology to manage customers, but they do not view customers as 'assets'. Customer relationship management cannot be effective, however, unless it is developed as a relationship-building tool. CRM is a process of reaching out to customers and building trust, not a technology solution for customer sales.

Perhaps because of the software and information technology associated with collecting information from consumers and responding to their desires, some critics view CRM as a form of manipulation. It is possible to use information about customers at their expense to obtain quick results – for example, charging higher prices whenever possible and using available data to maximise profits. However, using CRM to foster customer loyalty does not require collecting every conceivable piece of data from consumers or trying to sell customers products they do not want. Marketers should not try to control customers; they should try to develop relationships that derive from the trust gained over many transactions and are sustained by customers' belief that the company genuinely desires their continued patronage. Trust reduces the costs associated with worrying about whether expectations will be honoured and simplifies the customers' buying efforts in the future.

With CRM technology, marketers are able to identify their most valuable customers so that they can make an investment in building long-term relationships with those key customers. To be effective, marketers must measure the effectiveness of CRM systems in terms of their progress towards developing satisfactory customer relationships. Fewer than 20 per cent of companies track customer retention, but developing and assessing customer loyalty is important in managing long-term customer relationships.

The most important component of customer relationship management is remembering that it is not about technology but about relationships with customers. CRM systems should ensure that marketers listen to customers and then respond to their needs and concerns, and thereby build long-term relationships. The Internet can provide a valuable listening post and serve as a medium to manage customer relationships.

## Legal and Ethical Issues in E-marketing

How marketers use technology to gather information – both on- and off-line – to foster long-term relationships with customers has raised numerous legal and ethical issues. The popularity and widespread use of the Internet grew so quickly that global legal systems have not been able to keep pace with advances in the technology. Among the issues of concern are personal privacy, unsolicited e-mail, and the misappropriation of copyrighted intellectual property.

One of the most significant privacy issues involves the personal information companies collect from website visitors. A survey by the Progress and Freedom Foundation in the USA found that 96 per cent of popular commercial websites collect personally identifying information from visitors.[13] Several companies have been criticised for the improper use of personal data, both on-line and off-line.[14] Cookies are the most common means of obtaining such information. Some people fear that the collection of personal information from website users may violate users' privacy, especially if done without their knowledge.

In response to privacy concerns, some companies are cutting back on the amount of information they collect. The 96 per cent of websites identified by the Progress and Freedom Foundation survey as collectors of personal information was down from 99 per cent two years before, and 84 per cent of the surveyed sites indicated that they are collecting less data than before.[15] Public concerns about on-line privacy remain, however, and many in the industry are urging self-policing on this issue to head off potential regulation. Few laws specifically address personal privacy in the context of e-marketing, but the standards for acceptable marketing conduct implicit in other laws and regulations can generally be applied to e-marketing. With few regulations on how businesses use information, companies can legally buy and sell information about customers in order to gain competitive advantage. Some have suggested that if personal data were treated as property, customers would have greater control over their use.

The most serious strides towards regulating privacy issues associated with e-marketing are emerging in Europe. The 1998 European Union Directive on Data Protection specifically requires companies that want to collect personal information to explain how the information will be used and to obtain the individual's permission. Companies must make customer data files available on request. The law also bars website operators from selling e-mail addresses and using cookies to track visitors' movements and preferences without first obtaining permission. Because of this legislation, no company may deliver personal information about EU citizens to countries whose privacy laws do not meet EU standards.[16] The directive may ultimately establish a precedent for Internet privacy that other nations emulate.

**Spam**
Unsolicited commercial e-mail

**Spam**, or unsolicited commercial e-mail (UCE), is likely to be the next target of government regulation. This has already happened in North America. Many Internet users believe spam violates their privacy and steals their resources. Spam has been likened to receiving a direct mail promotional item with postage still due. Some angry recipients of spam have even organised boycotts against companies that advertise in this manner. Other recipients, however, appreciate the opportunity to learn about new products. Most commercial on-line services, such as AOL, offer their subscribers the option to filter out e-mail from certain Internet addresses that generate a large volume of spam. Many reputable companies are cutting back on unsolicited bulk e-mailings designed to acquire new customers, in favour of more targeted e-mail campaigns designed to retain customers who have indicated their willingness to receive such mailings. Nevertheless, the debate over spam is far from over, and legislation to regulate it is being considered in many countries. Whatever the outcome, it will certainly affect the ability to use e-mail for marketing purposes.

The Internet has also created issues associated with intellectual property, the copyrighted or trademarked ideas and creative materials developed to solve problems, carry out applications, and educate and entertain others. Intellectual property losses in the

United States total more than US$11 billion a year in lost revenue from the illegal copying of computer programs, movies, compact discs and books. This issue has become a global concern because of disparities in the enforcement of laws throughout the world. The software industry estimates that worldwide piracy costs its companies roughly US$12 billion every year.[17] Protecting trademarks can also be problematic. For example, some companies have discovered that another company has registered a URL that duplicates or is very similar to their own trademarks. The 'cyber-squatter' then attempts to sell the right to use the URL to the legal trademark owner. Companies such as KFC have paid thousands of dollars to gain control of domain names that match or parallel their company trademarks.[18]

As the Internet continues to evolve, more legal and ethical issues will certainly arise. Recognising this, the American Marketing Association has developed a Code of Ethics for Marketing on the Internet (see Table 4.3). Such self-regulatory policies may help head off government regulation of electronic marketing and commerce. Marketers and all other users of the Internet should make an effort to learn and abide by basic 'netiquette' (Internet etiquette) to ensure they get the most out of the resources available on this growing medium. Fortunately, most marketers recognise the need for mutual respect and trust

| TABLE 4.3 THE AMERICAN MARKETING ASSOCIATION CODE OF ETHICS FOR MARKETING ON THE INTERNET |
|---|
| The Internet, including on-line computer communications, has become increasingly important to marketers' activities, as they provide exchanges and access to markets worldwide. The ability to interact with stakeholders has created new marketing opportunities and risks that are not currently specifically addressed in the American Marketing Association Code of Ethics. The American Marketing Association Code of Ethics for Internet marketing provides additional guidance and direction for ethical responsibility in this dynamic area of marketing. The American Marketing Association is committed to ethical professional conduct and has adopted these principles for using the Internet, including on-line marketing activities utilising network computers. |
| **General responsibilities**<br>Internet marketers must assess the risks and take responsibility for the consequences of their activities. Internet marketers' professional conduct must be guided by:<br>1 support of professional ethics to avoid harm by protecting the rights of privacy, ownership and access<br>2 adherence to all applicable laws and regulations with no use of Internet marketing that would be illegal, if conducted by mail, telephone, fax or other media<br>3 awareness of changes in regulations related to Internet marketing<br>4 effective communication to organisational members on risks and policies related to Internet marketing, when appropriate<br>5 organisational commitment to ethical Internet practices communicated to employees, customers and relevant stakeholders. |
| **Privacy**<br>Information collected from customers should be confidential and used only for expressed purposes. All data, especially confidential customer data, should be safeguarded against unauthorised access. The expressed wishes of others should be respected with regard to the receipt of unsolicited e-mail messages. |
| **Ownership**<br>Information obtained from Internet sources should be properly authorised and documented. Information ownership should be safeguarded and respected. Marketers should respect the integrity and ownership of computer and network systems. |
| **Access**<br>Marketers should treat access to accounts, passwords and other information as confidential, and only examine or disclose content when authorised by a responsible party. The integrity of the information systems of others should be respected with regard to the placement of information, advertising or messages. |
| **Source:** American Marketing Association, www.marketingpower.com |

when communicating in any public medium. They know that doing so will allow them to maximise the tremendous opportunities the Internet offers to foster long-term relationships with customers.

# Summary

*Electronic commerce (e-commerce)* refers to sharing business information, maintaining business relationships and conducting business transactions by means of telecommunications networks. *Electronic marketing (e-marketing)* is the strategic process of creating, distributing, promoting and pricing products for targeted customers in the virtual environment of the Internet. The Internet has changed the way marketers communicate and develop relationships with their customers, employees and suppliers. Telecommunications technology offers marketers potential advantages, including rapid response, expanded customer service capability, reduced costs of operation and reduced geographic barriers. Despite these benefits, many dotcom companies failed because they did not realise that Internet markets are more similar to traditional markets than they are different and thus require the same marketing principles.

- A marketer's ability to identify customers before they make a purchase is called *addressability*. One way websites achieve addressability is through the use of *cookies*: strings of text placed on a visitor's computer. *Interactivity* allows customers to express their needs and wants directly to a company in response to its marketing communications. Interactivity also enables marketers to capitalise on the concept of *community*; and customers to derive value from the use of the company's products and websites. *Memory* refers to a company's ability to access collections of information in *databases* or data warehouses containing individual customer profiles and past purchase histories. Companies can then use these data in real time to customise their marketing offer to a specific customer.

- *Control* refers to customers' ability to regulate the information they view as well as the rate and sequence of their exposure to that information. A *portal* is a multiservice website serving as a gateway to other websites. *Accessibility* refers to customers' ability to obtain the vast amount of information available on the Internet. This is enhanced by the recognition value of a company's *uniform resource locator* (*URL*) or website address. *Digitalisation* is the representation of a product, or at least some of its benefits, as digital bits of information.

- The addressability, interactivity and memory characteristics of e-marketing enable marketers to identify specific customers, establish interactive dialogues with them to learn their needs, and combine this information with their purchase histories to customise products to meet their needs. E-marketers can thus focus on building customer loyalty and retaining customers.

- The growth of the Internet and the World Wide Web presents opportunities for marketing products (goods, services and ideas) to both consumers and organisations. The Internet can also be viewed as a new distribution channel. The ability to process orders electronically and to increase the speed of communications via the Internet reduces inefficiencies, costs and redundancies throughout the marketing channel. The Internet is an interactive medium that can be used to inform, entertain and persuade target markets to accept an organisation's products. The accessibility of the Internet presents marketers with an opportunity to expand and complement their traditional media promotional efforts. The Internet gives consumers access to more information than ever about the cost and price of products.

- *Customer relationship management (CRM)* has adopted recent advances in database management and customer communications to develop ongoing dialogues tailored to nurture one-to-one relationships with specific customers. CRM utilises improved customer data and marketing information systems (MISs) to focus on customer retention – claiming a greater share of an individual customer's purchases – as well as using the database as a device for managing direct communications, and integrated use of channels. CRM is part of the relationship marketing toolkit.

Database analysis has led marketers to identify the individual existing customers worth keeping and nurturing. Specific programmes of communication and bespoke marketing programmes can be developed for these customers in order to manage these ongoing relationships. The necessary customer management activities include: targeting, enquiry management, welcoming of new or upgrading customers, understanding customer characteristics and issues, focusing on customer development so that customers requiring higher or different levels of service are so served, the managing of problems that customers may have with the business, and win-back activity to redress problems with lost customers.

Different authors have adopted various terms to describe *one-to-one marketing*, notably the 'segment of one' or 'customer-centric marketing'. The underlying rationale stems from the basis of relationship marketing and customer relationship management (CRM), popularised during the 1990s. For certain products and customers, owing to IT advances, it is now possible to tailor one-to-one marketing propositions, communications and customer interactions. Technology is often the facilitator and the enabler.

A characteristic of companies engaged in e-marketing is a focus on customer relationship management (CRM), employing information about customers to create marketing strategies that develop and sustain desirable long-term customer relationships. The addressability, interactivity and memory characteristics of e-marketing allow marketers to identify specific customers, establish interactive dialogues with them to learn about their needs, and combine this information with customers' purchase histories to tailor products that meet those needs. It also permits marketers to shift their focus from share of market to share of customer. Although technology drives CRM and can help companies build relationships with desirable customers, customer relationship management cannot be effective unless it is developed as a relationship-building tool.

One of the most controversial issues is personal privacy – especially the personal information that companies collect from website visitors, often through the use of cookies. Additional issues relate to *spam*, or unsolicited commercial e-mail (UCE), and the misappropriation of copyrighted or trademarked intellectual property. More issues are likely to emerge as the Internet and e-marketing continue to evolve rapidly.

## *Key Links*

This chapter has examined an evolving aspect of the marketing environment as it applies directly to today's marketers: technology. This chapter should be read in conjunction with Chapter 3. In addition, there are links with:

- the nature of relationship marketing and its link with CRM, as featured in Chapter 1
- the role of the web in marketing communications and direct marketing, as explained in Chapter 19, which also examines the requisites for building effective websites
- segmentation and the role of one-to-one marketing, facilitated increasingly by marketers' use of technology, as detailed in Chapter 8.

## Important Terms

Electronic commerce (e-commerce)
Electronic marketing (e-marketing)
Addressability
Cookie
Interactivity
Community
Memory
Database
Control
Portal
Accessibility
Uniform resource locator (URL)
Digitalisation
Customer relationship management (CRM)
One-to-one marketing
Spam

## Discussion and Review Questions

1. What is the difference between e-marketing and e-commerce?
2. How does addressability differentiate e-marketing from the traditional marketing environment? How do marketers use cookies to achieve addressability?
3. Define interactivity and explain its significance. How can marketers exploit this characteristic to improve relationships with customers?
4. Memory gives marketers quick access to customers' purchase histories. How can a company use this capability to customise its product offerings?
5. Explain the distinction between *push* and *pull* media. What is the significance of control in terms of using websites to market products?
6. What is the significance of digitalisation?
7. How can marketers exploit the characteristics of the Internet to improve the product element of the marketing mix?
8. How do the characteristics of e-marketing affect the promotion element of the marketing mix?
9. What is the ethos of customer relationship management?
10. How does e-marketing facilitate customer relationship management?
11. How can technology help marketers improve their relationships with customers?
12. Electronic marketing has raised several ethical questions related to consumer privacy. How can cookies be misused? Should the government regulate the use of cookies by marketers?

## Recommended Readings


- Adams, N.R., Dogramaci, O., Gangopadhyay, A. and Yesha, Y., *Electronic Commerce: Technical, Business and Legal Issues* (New Jersey: Pearson, 1999).
- Chaffey, D., Mayer, R., Johnston, K. and Ellis-Chadwick, F., Internet Marketing (Harlow: Pearson/FT, 2002).
- Cram, T., *The Power of Relationship Marketing: Keeping Customers for Life* (Harlow: Pearson/FT, 1994).
- Peppers, D. and Rogers, M., *The One-to-One Manager* (New York: Currency Doubleday, 1999).
- Rouilly, J, *E-business: Principles and Practice* (Basingstoke: Palgrave Macmillan, 2002).
- Stone, M. and Foss, B., *Successful Customer Relationship Marketing: New Thinking, New Strategies, New Tools for Getting Closer to Your Customers* (London: Kogan Page, 2001).
- Tapp, A., *Principles of Direct and Database Marketing* (Harlow: Pearson/FT, 2000).
- Zikmund, W., *Customer Relationship Management* (Chichester: Wiley, 2003).
- Zikmund, W. and d'Amico, M., *Marketing: Creating and Keeping Customers in an E-Commerce World* (Cincinnati, OH: South Western, 2001).


## Internet Exercise

John Lewis is a typical upmarket department store retailer. Stores feature furniture, electrical goods, children's toys, nursery equipment, fabrics and soft furnishings, lighting, perfumery, china and glass tableware, giftware and shoes, along with men's, ladies' and children's clothing, supported by many in-store amenities, such as restaurants, parent and baby rooms, personal shopping and merchandise collection points. The company's extensive on-line retailing operation offers much of the same merchandise but not the same extensive in-store ranges of clothing lines.

Visit its website at:
www.johnlewis.com

1. Why does the John Lewis on-line service offer only a limited amount of fashion clothing lines?
2. How does the site present the store's many product lines in customer-relevant themes?
3. What approaches to offering customer-enticing promotions does the on-line service provide?

## Applied Mini-Case

Egg was originally created by leading financial services group Prudential as one of the pioneer on-line banking companies, with no branch network. All of Egg's transactions and interactions with its clients are handled through technology. According to Egg's website, 'every conversation and interaction with a customer needs to set up the opportunity for the next – this creates the opportunity for the relationship to develop as the customers' financial and lifestyle needs change, ie: when moving house, having children or retiring'. The notion is that as clients' purchasing activity changes, and as they evolve to different lifestyle stages, Egg can offer products and customer service directly relevant to an individual client, whether it is an overdraft facility, mortgage, investment opportunity, savings scheme, insurance cover or any of a growing range of financial services products.

**Source**: Egg.

### Question

How does an ongoing dialogue with clients enable Egg and similar financial services players to tailor products and service propositions to an individual client's evolving needs?

## Case Study

# Customer Service Enhanced by E-commerce for Yellow Freight

Shipping costs are a major expense in the physical distribution process, and companies around the world are always looking for the most efficient, reliable and convenient means of moving supplies and products in order to satisfy their own customers. To help marketers fulfil these objectives, Yellow Freight, a global transportation company and market leader in North America, has introduced new high-tech services, including electronic data interchange, E-Tools, Yellow Live/Voice, and Yellow Freight's E-Channels.

Electronic data interchange (EDI) allows Yellow Freight and its customers to share documents over the Internet. This service can be useful for transferring invoices, bills of loading, shipment tracking and other data files. The use of EDI almost eliminates the need for paper communications, and establishes a new medium for communication between Yellow Freight and its customers. Most logistics companies now use EDI for communicating with regular clients. However, a look at www.myyellow.com reveals the extent to which Yellow Freight has harnessed technology in its dealings with clients.

My Yellow E-Tools is a system designed to simplify business interactions by allowing customers to use the Internet to create bills of loading, schedule collections, track shipments, view account information and invoices, and, if necessary, dispute invoices. Through E-Tools, customers can obtain instant quotes, and then complete bills of loading and schedule collections if the quoted rates are satisfactory. Registered customers of Yellow Freight's E-Tools can also grant designated partners access to their application information. The customer chooses what information to share, and to whom it can be provided. For example, a PC manufacturer may opt to permit customers to track the progress of their order. The web service offers a simple three-stage service to clients:

**1** quote
**2** book
**3** track.

With Yellow Live/Voice, Yellow Freight became the first transportation company to offer live voice capability through its website. This service allows customers to have real-time audio conversations with customer-service representatives by downloading voice-enabling software. Customers who use a computer equipped with a microphone and speakers can engage in two-way audio communication, while those whose computers lack a microphone can type text questions and then listen to audio feedback from customer service.

E-Channels, which includes Yellow Live/Voice, helps customers stay connected to Yellow Freight via the Internet. This service allows customers to track shipments sent through Yellow Freight from any mobile phone that has wireless Internet capabilities. Customers can also track shipments using a palmtop organiser. These features grant customers greater options and control over how, when, from where and how often they access information about their shipments.

Yellow Freight's e-commerce services provide customers with greater control over their accounts and efficiency in shipping. The entire shipping process, from price quotes to collection to tracking, can now be accomplished on-line. By expanding the options available to customers who need to track their shipments, Yellow Freight has gained a competitive advantage in the global shipping industry.

**Sources:** 'E-channels', Yellow Freight, www.yellowfreight.com/ecommerce/echannels/, accessed 17 January 2002; 'The first Internet-based live voice ecommerce service in the transportation industry', Yellow Freight, press release, 18 September 2000, www.yellowfreight.com/aboutyellow/newsroom/pressreleases/pr_archive/pr_091800.html; the Yellow Freight website, www.yellowfreight.com, accessed 17 January 2002; www.myyellow.com, accessed 19 April 2004.

## Questions for Discussion

1 Why has Yellow Freight turned to technology to this extent?
2 For a company manufacturing PCs, retailed directly to customers over the Internet, why might services such as those offered by Yellow Freight be attractive?
3 Why is www.myyellow.com presented in simple staged instructions, such as quote, order, track?

# 5 Marketing in International Markets

"An international perspective on marketing management is critical in the contemporary era of global competition."

*Colin Egan, Leicester De Montfort University*

## Objectives

- To define international marketing and understand the nature of international involvement
- To understand the importance of international marketing intelligence
- To recognise the impact of environmental forces on international marketing efforts
- To become aware of regional trade alliances and markets
- To look at alternative market entry strategies for becoming involved in international marketing activities
- To appreciate that international marketing strategies fall along a continuum from customisation to globalisation

## Introduction

International marketing generally refers to marketing activities performed across national boundaries.[1] Many products and brands are marketed in national markets or even restricted to regions of a country. Others, however, are marketed across international borders and are familiar to consumers in many countries. Not only consumer goods such as those produced by Pepsi, Nike and Sony involve marketing in many parts of the world. Services, from healthcare to education, banking to management consultancy, theme parks to real estate, are marketed internationally, as are industrial products in many business markets.

The fundamental concepts and practices of marketing apply whether the product is a consumer good, service or business product, in local, national or international markets. Nevertheless, the marketer involved with international markets has a more complex task than colleagues only responsible for national markets. Market knowledge outside the domestic market may be less robust and complete; understanding of the forces of the marketing environment is essential for all marketers but is a more complex undertaking when scanning numerous countries; there are market entry strategies to consider; and the operationalisation of marketing programmes is far more challenging to control. Assuming that the marketing concept and marketing process are similar to the marketing activities described so far in *Marketing: Concepts and Strategies*, this chapter examines the nuances of international marketing, building on the exploration of the marketing environment presented in the previous two chapters.

*Opener*

# Global Expansion ... at 200 mph

For many decades, independently owned Aston Martin produced the luxury sports coupés of James Bond fame. Despite the reputation and mystique of the marque, the company's cars were not marketed across the globe. Now part of the Ford empire, with a new design and manufacturing base located close to two of Ford's other prestige brands, Land Rover and Jaguar, the strategy is to build on the enviable heritage by increasing models in the Aston Martin range and making these premium-priced high-performance monsters available in many more countries.

The Vanquish S, capable of over 200 mph, has been joined by the DB9 (replacing the DB7). The V8 Vantage will start rolling out of the rural headquarters in Warwickshire in mid-2005. To support these product developments, sales must increase. To achieve this growth, Aston Martin plans to extend its dealership network, notably by entering countries previously unserved or under-represented. The company's marketers have analysed the market dynamics, trends in the marketing environment, competitive arena and, crucially, purchasing patterns in many countries, identifying a target market strategy that will enable growth targets to be achieved in territories whose affluent consumers fit the desired customer profile.

Purchasing an Aston Martin is no 'normal' car-buying experience; the company's waiting list is currently running at 6–12 months. Aston Martin's marketers have a different set of issues to address than their colleagues in a typical mass producer. Marketing a consumer product that costs as much as a medium-sized house or child's complete education presents unique challenges. The competitive arena includes luxury items as diverse as diamond jewellery, motor yachts, jet-set travel, property and investment opportunities. The Aston Martin purchaser is acquiring a lifestyle statement, not merely a mode of transport. The number of prospective customers is relatively small and these 'high rollers' may be prone to stock market fluctuations, investment decisions and global lifestyle changes not prevalent in more mundane markets.

The assessment of target market opportunities requires a more rigorous and inclusive analysis than is undertaken in most markets. Include the global aspirations of the marque and the international lifestyles of the intended targeted customers, and the marketing remit becomes far more complex.

By the end of 2004, the dealer network had been increased to 125 dealers globally, with most newly appointed franchises in North America, Japan and other emerging markets in Asia. Currently 30 per cent of sales are in the UK, 30 per cent in other European markets, and 30 per cent in North America. The new production facility has a capacity of 5000 cars per annum, many of which are now destined for Asia and the 40 dealers in North America. 'If we are to increase our visibility and provide the levels of customer care which our owners deserve, it is essential we increase our worldwide representation,' states Dr Ulrich Bez, the company's CEO. This expansion strategy hinges on the shrewd identification of priority target market countries and consumers within each, which places significant importance on Aston Martin's analyses of the marketing environment forces and consumer spending behaviour in each country with potential for expansion.

**Sources:** Aston Martin, 2004; Stewart Smith, 'New models take lead in growth', *Coventry Evening Telegraph*, 6 August 2004, p. 73; www.astonmartin.com, August 2004. Photo: Reproduced with permission of Aston Martin

This chapter looks closely at the unique features of international marketing. It begins by examining companies' level of commitment to and degree of involvement in international marketing, and then considers the importance of international marketing intelligence when a company is moving beyond its domestic market. Next the chapter focuses on the need to understand various environmental forces in international markets and discusses several regional trade alliances and markets. The concluding section describes alternative market entry strategies for becoming involved in international marketing.

**Export marketing** Marketing activities through which a business takes advantage of opportunities outside its home market but continues production in the home country

# Involvement in International Marketing

In order to practise international marketing, companies with the necessary resources and skills have to develop an interest in expanding their businesses beyond national boundaries. Once interested, marketers engage in international marketing activities at several levels of involvement. Regardless of the level of involvement, however, they must decide on the degree to which it is possible to standardise their marketing strategies for different markets.

## Levels of International Involvement

**Domestic marketing** Marketing activities directed exclusively in a business's home market

The level of involvement in international marketing covers a wide spectrum, as shown in Figure 5.1. A business that undertakes marketing activities exclusively in its home market is involved in **domestic marketing**. Such organisations may have deliberately chosen to restrict their business to domestic customers or may simply not have considered the possibility of international marketing. **Export marketing** takes place when a business takes advantage of opportunities outside its home market. In some cases, exporting activity begins almost by accident. For example, the products of a small medical supplies manufacturer may occasionally be purchased by hospitals or clinics in nearby countries, or its

| Domestic marketing | Export marketing | International marketing | Multinational marketing | Global marketing |
|---|---|---|---|---|
| Home market involvement only. | This is an attempt to create sales without significant changes in the company's products and overall operations. An active effort to find foreign markets for existing products is most typical. | Greater commitment to international markets. International marketing activities are seen as part of overall planning. Direct investment in non-domestic markets is likely and products may also be sourced away from the home market. | Further steps are taken to adapt to local tastes. Modifications may be made to aspects of the marketing mix to make them more appealing to local markets. | Total commitment to international marketing which involves applying the organisation's assets, experience and products to develop and maintain marketing strategies on a global scale. Although a single global marketing strategy is required, some adaptation to local needs is still needed. |

**Domestic orientation** ⟷ **Global orientation**

*Figure 5.1*
*Levels of involvement in international marketing*

**International marketing** Marketing activities in which a business reduces reliance on intermediaries and establishes direct involvement in the countries in which trade takes place

**Multinational marketing** Adaptation of some of a company's marketing activities to appeal to local culture and differences in taste

products may be purchased by other countries through an export agent. Whatever the reasons behind the initial export activity, production in the home country will be used to supply these new markets; for most companies the domestic market will remain the key area of business. Companies that go beyond simple exporting become involved in **international marketing**, reducing their reliance on intermediaries and establishing direct links in the countries in which trading takes place. At this stage a foreign subsidiary may be set up, and products may be sourced away from the domestic market.

**Multinational marketing** takes marketing for non-domestic markets one step further by adapting some of the company's marketing activities, such as marketing communications, to appeal to local culture and differences in tastes. **Multinational companies** are those that behave in their foreign markets as if they were local companies. Full-scale **global marketing** requires total commitment to international marketing and involves applying the organisation's assets, experience and products to develop and maintain marketing strategies on a global scale. **Globalised marketing** occurs when marketing strategies are developed for major regions or the entire world to enable organisations to compete globally.

## Understanding Global Marketing

**Multinational companies** Companies that behave in their foreign markets as if they were local companies

**Global marketing** A total commitment to international marketing, in which a company applies its assets, experience and products to develop and maintain marketing strategies on a global scale

**Globalised marketing** Marketing strategies are developed for major regions or the entire world to enable organisations to compete globally

Global marketing is the most extreme case of international involvement, representing the full integration of international marketing into strategic planning.[2] The underlying principle is to identify products or services for which similarities across many markets allow a single global strategy to be pursued. This approach is attractive to managers because one marketing strategy can be used across a number of markets; a business can spread the costs of its research and development, technology and distribution, taking advantage of economies of scale in the process.

Despite the fact that global marketing strives for a single over-arching global strategy,[3] it is a mistake to assume that local differences can be ignored. During the 1980s, marketers sought to globalise the marketing mix as much as possible by employing standardised products, promotion campaigns, prices and distribution channels for all markets. The potential economic and competitive pay-offs for such an approach were certainly great. More recently, marketers have realised that, while it may be feasible to standardise a company's offerings in different markets, a degree of adaptation to local differences is also required. While brand name, product characteristics, packaging and labelling may be relatively straightforward to standardise, media allocation, retail outlets and price may be more difficult. For example, a supplier of animal feeds may decide to send promotional material about a new product range to farmers and producers in a variety of different markets. Although the business may have decided on a suitable platform for the promotion, help may be needed from each country's marketing team to devise an appropriate mailing list. In many business markets, interaction between customer personnel and an organisation's own staff is integral to the marketing and sales processes: cultural differences vary significantly between countries, and a standardised marketing approach is unlikely to succeed. This is particularly so in global banking, management consultancy and corporate legal affairs, where marketers must take account of local practices, cultures and behaviours.

Some companies have moved from customising or standardising products for a particular region of the world to offering globally standardised products that are advanced, functional, reliable and low in price.[4] Reebok, for example, provides a standardised product worldwide. Examples of globalised products are electrical equipment, DVDs, films, soft drinks, rock music, cosmetics and toothpaste. Sony televisions, Levi's jeans and UK confectionery brands seem to make annual gains in the world market. Even McDonald's restaurants seem to be widely accepted in markets throughout the world. Yet, even here, there is some adaptation to local tastes, with small variations in McDonald's menus in certain countries. For example, in Portugal there is more emphasis on ice creams and in Switzerland more on beer and wine than in the UK. Some products that are regarded by many as globally standard, such as Coca-Cola, are in fact adapted

***Figure 5.2***
*Reebok practices global marketing*
*Photo © Michael S. Yamashita/CORBIS*

for certain markets. Coke's flavouring, packaging, promotion and range are often modified between countries.

Debate about the feasibility of globalised marketing strategies has continued for nearly 40 years. Questions about standardised advertising have been a primary concern. The debate about customisation versus globalisation will doubtless continue, although neither is implemented in its pure form.[5] In the end, the feasibility of globalisation is determined by the degree of similarity between the various environmental and market conditions. For some products – such as sports footwear – a global marketing strategy, including advertising, seems to work well; while for other products – such as beer – strategies must make considerable concessions to accommodate local, regional and national differences.[6] Some marketers now believe that some of the best global opportunities are presented by 'global market segments', so long as similar product needs, buying behaviour and brand perceptions are evident across national borders. Even if such global market segments are identified – and there is no doubt they exist for many consumer goods, services and business products – the marketing programmes may require modification to reflect local market conditions and customer purchasing. Marketers must understand the detail of the markets being considered, and this requires international marketing intelligence.

## International Marketing Intelligence

Despite the ongoing debate over globalisation, most businesses perceive international markets as differing in some ways from domestic markets, which is often true. Analyses of international markets and possible marketing efforts can be based on many dimensions. Table 5.1 lists the types of information that international marketers need. Chapter 9 contains a more detailed discussion of marketing research and data collection.[7]

**TABLE 5.1 INFORMATION NEEDED FOR INTERNATIONAL MARKETING ANALYSES**

| Preliminary Screening | Analysis of Industry Market Potential | Analysis of Company Sales Potential |
|---|---|---|
| *Demographic/Physical Environment*<br>Population size, growth, density<br>Urban and rural distribution<br>Climate and weather variations<br>Shipping distance<br>Product-significant demographics<br>Physical distribution and communications network<br>Natural resources<br><br>*Political Environment*<br>System of government<br>Political stability and continuity<br>Ideological orientation<br>Government in business<br>Government in communications<br>Attitudes towards foreign business (trade restrictions, tariffs, non-tariff barriers, bi-lateral trade agreements)<br>National economic and developmental priorities<br><br>*Economic Environment*<br>Overall level of development<br>Economic growth: GNP, industrial sector<br>Role of foreign trade in economy<br>Currency, inflation rate, availability, controls, stability of exchange rate<br>Balance of payments<br>Per capita income and distribution<br>Disposable income and expenditure patterns<br><br>*Social/Cultural Environment*<br>Literacy rate, educational level<br>Existence of middle class<br>Similarities and differences in relation to home market<br>Language and other cultural considerations | *Market Access*<br>Limitations on trade: tariff levels, quotas<br>Documentation and import regulations<br>Local standards, practices, other non-tariff barriers<br>Patents and trademarks<br>Preferential treaties<br>Legal considerations: investment, taxation, repatriation, employment, code of laws<br><br>*Product Potential*<br>Customer needs and desires<br>Local production, imports, consumption<br>Exposure to and acceptance of product<br>Availability of linking products<br>Industry-specific key indicators of demand<br>Attitudes towards products of foreign origin<br>Competitive offerings<br>Availability of intermediaries<br>Regional and local transport facilities<br>Availability of manpower<br>Conditions for local manufacture | *Sales Volume Forecasting*<br>Size and concentration of customer segments<br>Projected consumption statistics<br>Competitive pressures<br>Expectations of local distributors/agents<br><br>*Landed Cost*<br>Costing method for exports<br>Domestic distribution costs<br>International freight insurance<br>Cost of product modification<br><br>*Cost of Internal Distribution*<br>Tariffs and duties<br>Value added tax<br>Local packaging and assembly<br>Margins/commission allowed for the trade<br>Local distribution and inventory costs<br>Promotional expenditures<br><br>*Other Determinants of Profitability*<br>Going price levels<br>Competitive strengths and weaknesses<br>Credit practices<br>Current and projected exchange rates |

**Source:** Adapted from S. Tamer Cavusgil, 'Guidelines for export market research', *Business Horizons*, November–December 1985, pp. 30–31. Used by permission.

Gathering secondary data (see Chapter 9) should be the first step in analysing a foreign market. Sources of information include government publications, financial services companies, international organisations such as the United Nations, foreign governments and international trade organisations. UK companies seeking to market their products in Russia, for example, can obtain information about Russian markets and regulations from the Department of Trade and Industry (DTI), the Russian Chamber of Commerce and Industry, the Russian trade organisation Amtorg and numerous other organisations. Marketers must, however, be vigilant in assuring the reliability, validity and comparability of data, as information from some sources may be misleading.

In some circumstances, marketers may need primary data to understand consumers' buying behaviour in the country under investigation. Buying behaviour is discussed in detail in Chapters 6 and 7. Marketers may have to adjust their techniques of collecting primary data for foreign markets. Attitudes towards privacy, unwillingness to be interviewed, language differences and low literacy rates can be serious research obstacles. In a bi-cultural country such as Canada, a uniform national questionnaire cannot be used because of the cultural and language differences. In China, restrictions on free speech mean that many businesses are reluctant to respond to questionnaires.

Primary research should uncover significant cultural characteristics before a product is launched so that the marketing strategy is appropriate for the target market. It may be necessary to investigate basic patterns of social behaviour, values and attitudes to plan a final marketing strategy. Overall, the cost of obtaining such information may be higher than the cost of domestic research; the reasons include the large number of foreign markets to be investigated, the distance between the marketer and the foreign market, unfamiliar cultural and marketing practices, language differences, and the scarcity or unreliability of published statistics.[8]

After analysing secondary and primary data, marketers should plan a marketing strategy, as explained in Chapter 2. An organisation must be clear about which consumers or business customers are being targeted, with what proposition, through which marketing programme, against which rivals, and with the involvement of which partners and marketing channel members. A full appreciation of the forces of the marketing environment (as described in Chapter 3) is critical to ensuring markets with growing potential are prioritised as part of the marketing strategy. A full assessment of the market situation will enable decisions to be made about whether to withdraw from the foreign market, to continue to expand operations or to consider additional foreign markets. Marketers must ensure they acquire the necessary marketing intelligence in order to provide a full understanding of trading conditions in all of the non-domestic markets.

## Environmental Forces in International Markets

A detailed analysis of the marketing environment is essential for any business considering entry into a foreign market. If a marketing strategy is to be effective across national borders, the complexities of all the environments involved must be understood. This section examines how the cultural/social, economic, political, legal and technological forces of the marketing environment in different countries vary. The process for examining the forces of the marketing environment as described in Chapter 3 also apply in this context.

### Cultural Forces

Culture can be defined as the concepts, values and tangible items (such as tools, buildings and foods) that make up a particular society. Culture is passed on from one generation to another and is a kind of blueprint for acceptable behaviour in a particular society. When products are introduced into one nation from another, acceptance is far more likely if there are similarities between the two cultures.

The connotations associated with body motions, greetings, colours, numbers, and shapes, sizes and symbols vary considerably across cultures. For example, as shown in Table 5.2, the

**TABLE 5.2 SAMPLING OF CULTURAL VARIATIONS**

| Country/ Region | Body Motions | Greetings | Colours | Numbers | Shapes, Sizes, Symbols |
|---|---|---|---|---|---|
| Japan | Pointing to one's own chest with a forefinger indicates one wants a bath.<br>A forefinger to the nose indicates 'me'. | Bowing is the traditional form of greeting. | Positive colours are in muted shades.<br>Combinations of black, dark grey, and white have negative overtones. | Positive numbers are 1, 3, 5, 8.<br>Negative numbers are 4, 9. | Pine, bamboo or plum patterns are positive.<br>Cultural shapes such as Buddha shaped jars should be avoided. |
| India | Kissing is considered offensive and is not usually seen on television, in films or in public places. | The palms of the hands touch and the head is nodded for greeting.<br>It is considered rude to touch or shake hands with a woman. | Positive colours are bold such as green, red, yellow or orange.<br>Negative colours are black and white if they appear in relation to weddings. | To create brand awareness, numbers are often used as a brand name. | Animals such as parrots, elephants, tigers or cheetahs are often used as brand names or on packaging.<br>Sexually explicit symbols are avoided. |
| Europe | When counting on one's fingers, the number 1 is often indicated by thumb, 2 by thumb and forefinger. | It is acceptable to send flowers in thanks for a dinner invitation, but not roses (for sweethearts) or chrysanthemums (for funerals). | Generally, white and blue are considered positive.<br>Black often has negative overtones. | The numbers 3 or 7 are usually positive; 13 is a negative number. | Circles are symbols of perfection.<br>Hearts are considered favourably at Christmas time. |
| Latin America | General arm gestures are used for emphasis. | The traditional greeting is a hearty embrace and slap on the back. | Popular colours are generally bright or bold yellow, red, blue or green. | Generally, 7 is a positive number.<br>Negative numbers are 13, 14. | Respect religious symbols.<br>Avoid national symbols such as flag colours. |
| Middle East | The raised eyebrow facial expression indicates 'yes'. | The word 'no' must be mentioned three times before it is accepted. | Positive colours are brown, black, dark blues and reds.<br>Pink, violets and yellows are not favoured. | Positive numbers are 3, 5, 7, 9; 13, 15 are negative. | Round or square shapes are acceptable.<br>Symbols of six-pointed star, raised thumb or Koranic sayings are avoided. |

**Sources:** James C. Simmons, 'A matter of interpretation', *American Way*, April 1983, pp. 106–111; 'Adapting export packaging to cultural differences', *Business America*, 3 December 1979, pp. 3–7.

use of colour has different connotations in different cultures. In many parts of Europe black has negative overtones, whereas in the Middle East it has positive connotations.

The Building Customer Relationships box on page 132 details more examples of the role of colour in marketing. Yet even here it is important to watch out for more subtle cultural differences. For example, Table 5.2 treats the whole of Europe as if it were one nation, although in practice it is very difficult to generalise for the region as a whole. This is important because multinational marketers know that cultural differences have implications for product development, personal selling, advertising, packaging and pricing. For example, the illustration of feet is regarded as despicable in Thailand. An international marketer

## Building Customer Relationships

### A Cross-cultural Comparison of Colour and International Branding

Anthony Grimes and Isobel Doole explored the relationship between colour and international branding. Their cross-cultural comparison, which focused on consumers in the UK and Taiwan, used a series of semi-structured focus groups to examine perceptions of colour and international branding. The findings of their research appear to suggest that associations of colour are surprisingly similar across national boundaries, and apparently support the notion that standardisation of brand colours across international markets may be possible. However, the research also highlights that colour is only one aspect of the make-up of an international brand and, as such, may have a relatively small role to play in developing brand image. This is demonstrated clearly by the fact that while perceptions of colour across cultures may fluctuate relatively little, impressions of international brands may vary widely.

**COLOUR ASSOCIATION IN THE UK AND TAIWAN**

| Colour | UK associations | Taiwan associations |
|---|---|---|
| Green | Inexpensive, reliable, light and good-tasting<br>Old, quiet, traditional, trustworthy and safe<br>Life, calm, tenderness, health and happiness<br>Environment, natural, pure and fresh<br>Ireland, and Italy to some extent | Inexpensive, reliable, light and good-tasting<br>Quiet, calm, male and old<br>Safe, trustworthy, unadventurous and stable<br>Environment, life, tender, pure, fresh, natural<br>Ireland, and to some extent UK |
| Red | Expensive, premium, high quality and good-tasting<br>Young, warm, fun, loud, playful and happy<br>Dangerous, adventurous, luxurious and exciting<br>Life, love, passion, power and aggression<br>China, and the US to some extent | High quality, expensive and good-tasting<br>Warm, female, loud, playful and adventurous<br>Love, passion, danger and aggression<br>Life, excitement and happiness<br>US, and to some extent Italy |
| Blue | Heavy, reliable, high quality and expensive<br>Male, mature, quiet, subdued, calm and thoughtful<br>Serious, trustworthy, dependable, dignified and sad<br>US and UK to a limited extent | Heavy, reliable, high quality and expensive<br>Male, old, quiet, serious<br>Calm, dignified, trustworthy<br>Sadness, depression and to some extent power |
| Black | Expensive, high quality, high tech and premium products<br>Old, heavy and reliable objects<br>Male, old, quiet and serious<br>Mysterious, luxurious, sophisticated and dangerous<br>Death, dignity, power and aggression | High quality, high tech, premium and expensive<br>Old, male, quiet and heavy<br>Mysterious, sophisticated and serious<br>Death, sadness, depression, power, fear and aggression<br>Strongly associated with China |
| Yellow | High quality, expensive, reliable, light and good-tasting<br>Pert, fresh and playful<br>Luxury, sophistication and to some extent safety<br>Life, happiness, tenderness and warmth | New, expensive, light and good-tasting<br>Young, warm, loud, playful and adventurous<br>Life, love, happiness and power<br>Strongly associated with China |
| Purple | Expensive, luxurious and good-tasting<br>Warm, and to some extent female<br>Sophisticated and mysterious<br>Death, dignity, passion and power<br>France, and to some extent Japan | High quality, premium and expensive<br>Warm, female, old and quiet<br>Love, passion, luxury, sophisticated and mystery<br>Serious, sadness, dignity, power and aggression<br>France, and to some extent Japan |

**Perceptions of key brands in the UK and Taiwan**

| Brand | UK | Taiwan |
|---|---|---|
| Pepsi | Male, muscular, young, sexy and energetic<br>Wild, fun and sporty<br>Associated with beach settings<br>Not very healthy – sugar and caffeine<br>Challenger to Coca-Cola and the status quo | Male, muscular, young, energetic, sporty and attractive<br>Fun, sexy, loud, wild and a little crazy<br>Associated with the beach, the sun and the Spice Girls<br>Good tasting and refreshing<br>Intensely competitive with regard to Coca-Cola |
| Marlboro | Original brand is masculine, American and red<br>Cool, sexy, wild, adventurous and strong<br>Rough but with a lot of style<br>Associated with cowboys, the desert and music<br>Unhealthy and anti-social – cancer, smoke and smells<br>Marlboro Lights are less damaging and more popular<br>Associated with pubs, music, youth and the colour gold | Masculine, American and red<br>Cool, strong, young, adventurous and exciting<br>Powerful and stylish<br>Associated with cowboys, the desert and music |
| Kodak | Masculine, mature, intelligent, creative and well-respected<br>Warm, friendly and colourful<br>High quality, high technology and very professional<br>Associated with happy times, sunshine, happiness, fun, colourfulness and the colour yellow<br>Safe, reliable, trustworthy, affordable and popular | Masculine, intelligent, innovative and creative<br>High quality, expensive and professional<br>Modern, colourful and hugely popular<br>Associated with high technology |
| Cadbury's | Feminine, smooth, silky, sexy and sultry<br>Beautiful, luxurious, stylish and expensive<br>High in quality, reliability and class<br>Associated with velvet, satin and silk<br>Old, friendly, aristocratic and eccentric<br>Very young, sweet and cute | Masculine, old, friendly, warm, loving but poor brand<br>Feminine, young, sweet, sensual and cute<br>Overall: low quality, cheap, no class and largely unpopular<br>A sticky, sickly, lazy brand, predominantly for children |
| BP | Masculine, big, old, greedy, rich, powerful and British<br>Grey, faceless, boring, uncaring, mysterious, even sinister and arrogant to some extent<br>Associated with intelligence, power, wealth, technology, heavy production and pollution | Masculine, rich, powerful, distinguished and serious<br>High in class and style, intelligent and authoritative – a leader |
| Guinness | Masculine, modern, young, cool, streetwise, sociable, attractive, quiet, secretive and mysterious<br>Old, traditional, simple and genuine<br>Associated with goodness, honesty and hard work<br>Overall: smooth, creamy, bitter, heavy and good quality | Male, powerful, intelligent, attractive and mysterious<br>Calm, quiet and distant on the surface, but crazy inside<br>Independent, unique, stylish and dangerous |

**Source:** reprinted with permission from the *Journal of Marketing Management*, 15 (6), pp. 449–62.


must also know a country's customs regarding male–female social interaction. In Italy it is unacceptable for a salesman to call on a woman if her husband is not at home.

It is also important for marketers to tune in to changes in culture. For example, in Japan, the government has expressed concern about its citizens' emphasis on work and has declared that people should start enjoying life. With an official reduction of the working week to 40 hours, many new leisure industry opportunities are being created. In one year alone, 200 companies applied for permits to develop new theme parks. Meanwhile, to help people deal with these new leisure opportunities, the National Recreation Association is offering a one-year course on how to enjoy life.[9]

Product adoption and use are also influenced by consumers' perceptions of other countries.[10] When consumers are generally unfamiliar with products from another country, their perceptions of the country itself affect their attitude towards and adoption of its products.

If a country has a reputation for producing quality products, marketers will want to make the country of origin well known. For example, a generally positive image of western computer technology has fuelled sales of HP and IBM personal computers and Microsoft software in Japan.[11] Consumers' perceptions of a country are influenced by more than its products, however. Recently, President Bush's 'war on terrorism' created a problem for the marketers of many US companies, as consumers in parts of the world and particularly those adhering to specific religions boycotted US brands. Even US pop and rock stars found it difficult to tour in parts of the world previously visited routinely.

Culture may also affect the marketing negotiations and decision-making behaviour of marketers, business buyers and other executives. Research has shown that when marketers use a problem-solving approach – that is, gain information about a particular client's needs and tailor products or services to meet those needs – it leads to increased customer satisfaction in marketing negotiations in France, Germany, the United Kingdom and the United States. Furthermore, the role and status of the seller are particularly important in both the UK and France.[12] However, the attractiveness of the sales person and his or her similarity to the customer increase the levels of satisfaction only for Americans.

## Social Forces

Marketing activities are primarily social in purpose; therefore, they are structured by the institutions of family, religion, education, health and recreation (see Figure 5.3). For example,

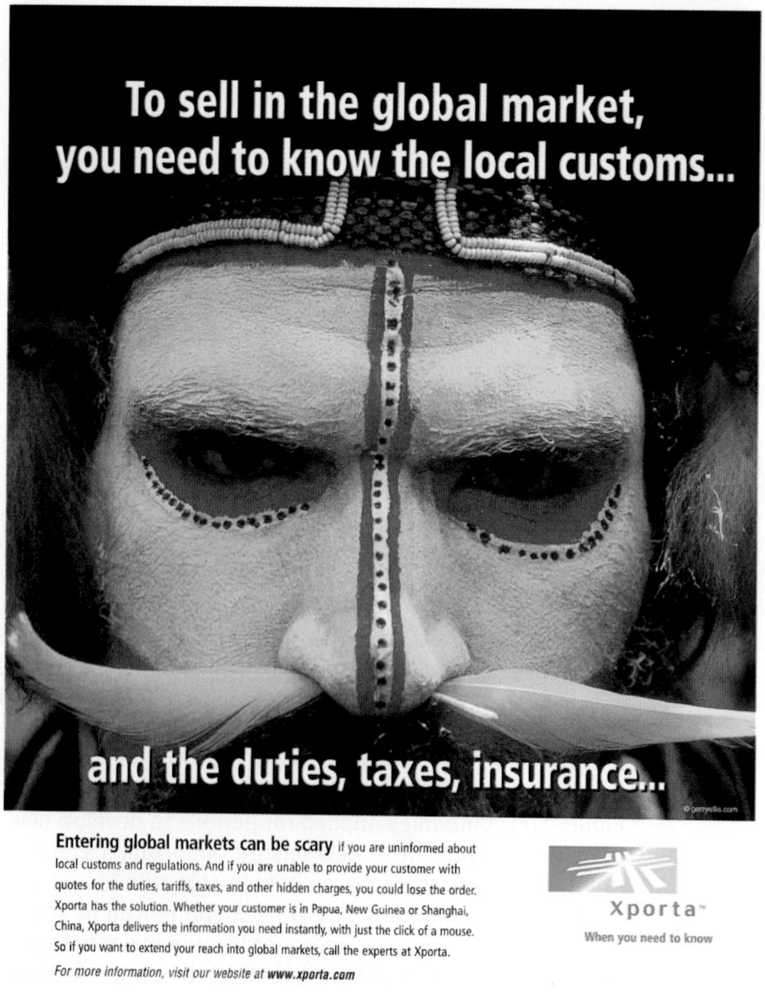


***Figure 5.3***
*Xporta assists in determining the customs of international trade*
*Source: Courtesy of XPORTA*

in the UK, where listening to music on hi-fi systems or personal stereos is a common form of relaxation, Japanese products have a large target market. In all countries, these social institutions can be identified. By finding major deviations in institutions among countries, marketers can gain insights into the adaptation of a marketing strategy. Although American football is a popular sport in the United States and a major opportunity for many television advertisers, football is the most popular television sport in Europe. Yet football hooliganism caused major advertisers in the United Kingdom to have second thoughts about supporting such events with vast sums spent on advertising.[13] The role of children in the family and a society's overall view of children also influence marketing activities. For example, in the Netherlands, children are banned from appearing in advertisements for sweets, and confectionery manufacturers are required to place a little toothbrush symbol at the end of each confectionery advertisement.[14]

## Economic Forces

Economic differences dictate many of the adjustments that must be made in marketing abroad. The most prominent adjustments are caused by differences in standards of living, availability of credit, discretionary buying power, income distribution, national resources and conditions that affect transport. Exchange rate fluctuations and differences in interest rates can also have a major impact. The strength of a country's currency and high interest rates may make it difficult for companies to succeed in exporting their goods and services.

**Gross domestic product (GDP)**
The total value of all goods and services produced by a country in one year

**Gross domestic product (GDP)** is the total value of all goods and services produced by a country in one year. A comparison of GDP for Europe, the USA and Japan shows that the United States has the largest gross domestic product in the world. By dividing this figure by the size of the population, an understanding of the standard of living can be achieved. In this way it is possible to gain insight into the level of discretionary income or buying power of individual consumers. Knowledge about aggregate GDP, credit and the distribution of income provides general insights into market potential.

Opportunities for international marketers are certainly not limited to those countries with the highest incomes. Indeed, as recent events in the Asia Pacific region have shown, high income is no guarantee of an attractive market. Some countries are progressing faster than they were even a few years ago; and these countries – especially in eastern Europe, Latin America, Africa and parts of the Middle East – have great market potential for specific products. However, marketers must first understand the political and legal environment before they can convert buying power into actual demand for specific products.

## Political, Regulatory and Legal Forces

**Tariffs**
Taxes that affect the movement of goods across economic or political boundaries, and that can also affect imports, exports or goods in transit

**Quotas**
Physical restrictions on the amount of goods that can be imported into a particular country or region

A country's political system, national laws, regulatory bodies, national pressure groups and courts each have a great impact on global marketing. A government's policies towards public and private enterprise, consumers and foreign companies, influence marketing across national boundaries. The types of measure a government can take to govern cross-border trade include the use of tariffs, quotas and non-tariff barriers. For example, the Japanese have established many barriers to imports into their country. Even though they are reducing the tariffs on certain items, many non-tariff barriers still make it difficult for other companies to export their products to Japan.[15] **Tariffs** are taxes that affect the movement of goods across economic or political boundaries, and can affect imports, exports or goods in transit.[16] These taxes provide government with revenue and can give domestic companies an important advantage. For example, import tariffs in the form of import duties effectively increase the price of imported products, giving local companies an automatic advantage. **Quotas** involve physical restrictions on the amount of goods that can be imported into a particular country or region. The imposition of quotas is not always in the best interest of consumers, as choice is limited and allocations tend to be used up on imports of goods carrying the greatest profit margin. **Non-tariff barriers** are much more difficult to define: they include a wide range of rules, regulations and taxes that have an impact on trade. As shown in Table 5.3, these barriers can include anything from port and

**TABLE 5.3 NON-TARIFF TRADE BARRIERS**

| Formal Trade Restrictions | Administrative Trade Restrictions |
|---|---|
| **A. Non-tariff Import Restrictions (Price-related Measures)**<br>Surcharges at border<br>Port and statistical taxes<br>Non-discriminatory excise taxes and registration charges<br>Discriminatory excise taxes, government insurance requirements<br>Non-discriminatory turnover taxes<br>Discriminatory turnover taxes<br>Import deposit<br>Variable levies<br>Consular fees<br>Stamp taxes<br>Various special taxes and surcharges | **D. State Participation in Trade**<br>Subsidies and other government support<br>Government trade, government monopolies, and granting of concessions or licences<br>Laws and ordinances discouraging imports<br>Problems relating to general government policy<br>Government procurement<br>Tax relief, granting of credit and guarantees<br>Boycott |
| **B. Quantitative Restrictions and Similar Specific Trade Limitations (Quantity-related Measures)**<br>Licensing regulations<br>Ceilings and quotas<br>Embargoes<br>Export restrictions and prohibitions<br>Foreign exchange and other monetary or financial controls<br>Government price setting and surveillance<br>Purchase and performance requirements<br>Restrictive business conditions<br>Discriminatory bi-lateral arrangements<br>Discriminatory regulations regarding countries of origin<br>International cartels<br>Orderly marketing agreements<br>Various related regulations | **E. Technical Norms, Standards, and Consumer Protection Regulations**<br>Health and safety regulations<br>Pharmaceutical control regulations<br>Product design regulations<br>Industrial standards<br>Size and weight regulations<br>Packing and labelling regulations<br>Package marking regulations<br>Regulations pertaining to use<br>Regulations for the protection of intellectual property<br>Trademark regulations |
| **C. Discriminatory Freight Rates (Flag Protectionism)** | **F. Customs Processing and Other Administrative Regulations**<br>Anti-dumping policy<br>Customs calculation bases<br>Formalities required by consular officials<br>Certification regulations<br>Administrative obstacles<br>Merchandise classification<br>Regulations regarding sample shipment, return shipments and re-exports<br>Countervailing duties and taxes<br>Appeal law<br>Emergency law |

**Source:** Beatrice Bondy, *Protectionism: Challenge of the Eighties* (Zurich: Union Bank of Switzerland Economic Research Department, 1983), p. 19. Reprinted by permission.

**Non-tariff barriers** A wide range of rules, regulations and taxes that have an impact on trade

border taxes to trademark and health and safety regulations. For example, just a few years ago, companies exporting electronic equipment to Japan had to wait for the Japanese government to inspect each item. A government's attitude towards cooperation with importers has a direct impact on the economic feasibility of their exporting to that country. As barriers to trade decline, opportunities are presented. Attempts to bring trade barriers down and improve the flow of goods between countries have come to the forefront in recent decades, notably in the practices adopted between 'partner' countries within the EU. The rules and frameworks for world trade are partly determined by the General Agreement on Tariffs and Trade (GATT). From a marketing standpoint, principles such as those defended by GATT increase competition.

Differences in political and government ethical standards are enormous. The use of pay-offs and bribes is deeply entrenched in many governments and trade authorities, while in others such involvement is prohibited. European companies that do not engage in such practices may have a hard time competing with foreign businesses that do. Some businesses that refuse to make pay-offs are forced to hire local consultants, public relations businesses or advertising agencies – resulting in indirect pay-offs. The ultimate decision about whether to give small tips or gifts where they are customary must be based on a company's code of ethics. It is a difficult challenge in many markets for international marketers striving to compete effectively in a country exhibiting markedly different – 'worse' – ethics than in the domestic market, while adhering to the laws governing the company's head office and the codes stipulated by the company's domestic stakeholders.

### Technological Forces

Much of the marketing technology used in Europe and other industrialised regions of the world may be inappropriate for developing countries. For example, promoting products via the Internet will be difficult in countries where computer ownership is low. None the less, many countries – particularly China, South Korea, Mexico and the countries of the former Soviet Union – want to engage in international trade, often through partnerships with American, European and Japanese businesses, so that they can gain valuable industrial and agricultural technology. However, there may be export restrictions that limit trade in certain goods. For example, the export of defence equipment is tightly controlled by many European governments. Distribution channels, logistics, the tracking of goods in transit, automatic reordering using IT, CRM systems, customer interaction and internal company communications, may be severely impeded in certain countries owing to their infancy in terms of the life cycles of technology used routinely in North America, the EU or Asia Pacific to manage such marketing activities. Tesco's Clubcard is soon to appear in its stores in Asia, becoming the first loyalty card to embrace the opportunities provided by current CRM technology in those markets. In other instances, the non-domestic market may be more advanced than the domestic market, providing marketers with a different set of challenges.

## Regional Trade Alliances and Markets

While some businesses are beginning to view the world as one huge marketplace, opportunities for companies are affected by a range of regional trade alliances. This section examines several regional trade alliances and changing markets, including NAFTA, the European Union, the Pacific Rim markets, changing conditions in central and eastern Europe, GATT and the World Trade Organization.

### The North American Free Trade Agreement (NAFTA)

The **North American Free Trade Agreement (NAFTA)**, implemented in 1994, effectively merged Canada, Mexico and the United States into one market of more than 400 million consumers. NAFTA will eliminate virtually all tariffs on goods produced and traded between Canada, Mexico and the United States to create a free trade area by 2009. The estimated annual output for this trade alliance is US$6 trillion.

NAFTA makes it easier for businesses to invest in the participating countries; provides protection for intellectual property – of special interest to high-tech and entertainment industries; expands trade by requiring equal treatment of companies in all countries; and simplifies country-of-origin rules, hindering Japan's use of Mexico as a staging ground for further penetration into US markets. Although most tariffs on products coming to the United States will be lifted, duties on more sensitive products, such as household glassware, footwear and some fruits and vegetables, will be phased out over a 15-year period.

**North American Free Trade Agreement (NAFTA)** Implemented in 1994, and designed to eliminate all tariffs on goods produced and traded between Canada, Mexico and the United States, providing for a totally free trade area by 2009

NAFTA also links the United States with other Latin American countries, providing additional opportunities to integrate trade among all the nations in the western hemisphere. Chile, for example, is expected to become the fourth member of NAFTA, but political forces may delay its entry into the agreement for several years.

Although NAFTA has been controversial, it has become a positive factor for US companies wishing to engage in international marketing. Because licensing requirements have been relaxed under the pact, smaller businesses that previously could not afford to invest in Mexico and Canada will be able to do business in those markets without having to locate there. NAFTA's long phase-in period provides ample time for adjustment by those companies affected by reduced tariffs on imports. Increased competition should lead to a more efficient market.

## The European Union (EU)

**European Union (EU)** The major grouping in western Europe, the EU has 25 members: Austria, Belgium, Denmark, Finland, France, Germany, Greece, Ireland, Italy, Luxembourg, the Netherlands, Portugal, Spain, Sweden and the United Kingdom have been joined by the Czech Republic, Cyprus, Estonia, Hungary, Latvia, Lithuania, Malta, Poland, Slovenia and Slovakia

**Maastricht Treaty** The treaty, signed in 1992, that established the European Union

The **European Union (EU)** is one of three major market groups in western Europe.[17] Formed by the Treaty of European Union, the EU has its origins in the European Common Market, set up in 1958, which later became known as the European Community (EC). Following the signing of the **Maastricht Treaty** in 1992 and the creation of the single European market in 1993, the group became known as the European Union. Today the EU has 25 members: Austria, Belgium, Denmark, Finland, France, Germany, Greece, Ireland, Italy, Luxembourg, the Netherlands, Portugal, Spain, Sweden and the United Kingdom have been joined by the Czech Republic, Cyprus, Estonia, Hungary, Latvia, Lithuania, Malta, Poland, Slovenia and Slovakia. The objectives of the Union are set out in the following extract from Article B of the Treaty on European Union.[18]

- to promote economic and social progress which is balanced and sustainable, in particular through the creation of an area without internal frontiers, through the strengthening of economic and social cohesion and through the establishment of economic and monetary union, ultimately including a single currency in accordance with the provisions of this Treaty;
- to assert its identity on the international scene, in particular through the implementation of a common foreign and security policy including the eventual framing of a common defence policy, which might in time lead to a common defence;
- to strengthen the protection of the rights and interests of the nationals of its Member States through the introduction of a citizenship of the Union;
- to develop close co-operation on justice and home affairs.

On 1 January 1999 the European Union moved closer to economic and monetary union with the launch of the euro, the unit of European currency;[19] 11 of the then 15 European Union members became committed to the new currency. Only Sweden, Denmark and Britain postponed participation in the single currency, while Greece failed to meet the economic criteria.

Although the 25 countries of the EU essentially function as one large market, and consumers in the EU are likely to become more homogeneous in their needs and wants, marketers know that cultural and social differences among the member states will require modifications in the marketing mix for consumers in many countries. Some researchers believe that eventually it will be possible to segment the European Union into six markets on the basis of cultural, geographic, demographic and economic variables. For example, the United Kingdom and Ireland would form one market, while Greece and southern Italy would form another.[20] Differences in taste and preferences among these markets are significant for international marketers. For example, the British consume far more instant coffee than their European neighbours. Consumers in Spain eat far more poultry products than Germans do.[21] In some geographic regions, preferences even vary within the same country. Thus international marketing intelligence efforts remain very important in determining European consumers' needs and in developing marketing strategies that will satisfy those needs. It is also clear that EU organisations will have to face up to considerable changes in the way they operate and, for some, such as pharmaceutical companies, the prospects include harmonisation of prices and formulations and likely job losses.

## Pacific Rim Nations

Countries in the Pacific Rim represent an enormous part of the world market, with 60 per cent of the world's population living there. Although the region is characterised by considerable diversity, in general companies of the Pacific Rim nations – Japan, China, South Korea, Taiwan, Singapore, Hong Kong, the Philippines, Malaysia, Indonesia, Australia and Indochina – have become increasingly competitive and sophisticated in their marketing efforts in the last three decades. Throughout the early to mid-1990s the performances of Japan and the four so-called Tiger economies of the region – South Korea, Singapore, Taiwan and Hong Kong – were particularly impressive.[22] The Japanese, in particular, made considerable inroads into the world consumer markets for cars, motorcycles, watches, cameras and audio-visual equipment. Products made by Sony, Sanyo, Toyota, Honda, Canon, Suzuki and others are sold all over the world and have set quality standards by which other products are often judged. Through direct investment in Europe, the Japanese built strong distribution and developed a keen understanding of the market. However, Japan's marketing muscle attracted criticism in certain quarters, fuelled partly by fears that Japanese products might swamp the market. These concerns are compounded by Japan's reluctance to accept imports from other countries.[23] In practice, the sale of Japan's products in Europe is limited by the existence of quotas, but many of these quotas are nearing their end.

South Korea also became very successful in world markets with familiar brands such as Samsung, Daewoo and Hyundai. South Korean companies even took market share away from Japanese companies in the world markets for VCRs, colour televisions and computers, despite the fact that the South Korean market for these products is limited. In Canada, the Hyundai Excel overtook Japan's Honda in just 18 months.[24] Towards the end of the 1990s many Far Eastern markets were substantially affected by economic recession. Currency markets in Japan, South Korea and Hong Kong were badly hit, affecting the economic strength of the Pacific Rim region. While the immense success of the 1980s and early 1990s may be difficult to replicate, many major Asia-Pacific corporations have divested unprofitable operations and are again performing successfully.

Less visible Pacific Rim regions, such as Singapore, Taiwan and Hong Kong, are major manufacturing and financial centres. Singapore also has large world markets for pharmaceutical and rubber goods. Hong Kong continues to face an uncertain future following its move in 1997 from British control to control by the People's Republic of China. Taiwan may have the most promising future of all the Pacific Rim nations. It has a strong local economy and has lowered many import barriers, sending imports up. Taiwan has privatised state-run banks and is also opening its markets to foreign businesses. Some analysts believe that it may replace Hong Kong as a regional financial power centre.[25]

Much attention is now being given to the four Pacific Rim nations that have reached the point of massive industrial growth. Thailand, Malaysia, Indonesia and China all offer considerable marketing potential.[26] For example, the People's Republic of China has great market potential and opportunities for joint venture projects. Analysts are keeping a close watch on how these countries are affected by economic uncertainty in the region. In the case of China, an important consideration is the risk associated with doing business there. Political and economic instability have the potential to spoil the chances of businesses seeking a stake in this growing market.[27] The emergence of China, however, presents marketers with considerable opportunities for exporting via joint ventures or trading alliances aided by China's 'open door' policy. There is also a threat to western companies, as Chinese enterprises strive to emulate Japan and enter global markets with their own products and services.

**Association of South East Asian Nations (ASEAN)**
Formed in 1967 with the intention of building trade and other links among its six members: Brunei, Indonesia, Malaysia, the Philippines, Singapore and Thailand

In general, attempts to form groups promoting trade and other links between Pacific Rim countries have not been particularly successful. Perhaps the best known is the **Association of South East Asian Nations (ASEAN)**, formed in 1967, which aims to build trade and other links between its six members: Brunei, Indonesia, Malaysia, the Philippines, Singapore and Thailand. With 340 million consumers in the group and a combined GNP of some £350 billion, in practice the progress towards the trading links that the organisation sought has been hampered by the inability of member states to agree on key issues.[28] At the moment it seems that the future of ASEAN is in the balance, with an economic treaty being discussed that aims to set up a free trade area by 2008.[29] More recently, the **Asia Pacific Economic Co-operative (APEC)** has been set up to include the six ASEAN members, the United States, Australia, Canada, New Zealand, Japan, China, South Korea, Hong Kong and Taiwan.[30] Currently APEC is little more than a weakly joined group of countries aiming to promote trade, and what the future holds is unclear.

**Asia Pacific Economic Co-operative (APEC)**
Aims to promote trade between its members: the six ASEAN members plus the United States, Australia, Canada, New Zealand, Japan, China, South Korea, Hong Kong and Taiwan

## Central and Eastern Europe (CEE)

**Central and Eastern Europe (CEE)** encompasses the Commonwealth of Independent States (CIS, formerly the Soviet Union), the Czech and Slovak Republics, Hungary, Poland, Slovenia, Croatia, Bosnia and Herzegovina, Serbia and Montenegro, Bulgaria, FYR Macedonia and Albania. The decline of communism in central and eastern Europe, the fall of the Berlin Wall in 1989 and the break-up of the former Soviet Union in 1990 resulted in a host of new marketing opportunities in the region.

**Central and Eastern Europe (CEE)**
Encompasses the Commonwealth of Independent States (formerly the Soviet Union), the Czech and Slovak Republics, Hungary, Poland, Slovenia, Croatia, Bosnia and Herzegovina, Serbia and Montenegro, Bulgaria, FYR Macedonia and Albania

Following a policy of *perestroika*, encompassing considerable political and economic change, the CEE countries replaced the Communist Party's centrally planned economies with marketing-oriented democratic institutions. This process of market reforms, designed to lead to greater imports and exports, has not been without difficulty. The challenge for many of the eastern European countries has been to move forward from the inefficiencies of state-owned industry and to develop the marketing expertise, business culture, infrastructures and legal frameworks required to trade with capitalist countries.[31] If the CEE countries wish to compete effectively with nations from other parts of the world, these changes are essential. For example, the poorly developed distribution infrastructure in many parts of central and eastern Europe currently restricts the outlets where western products can be sold and limits the opportunities domestic companies can pursue.[32] However, the move towards market change has resulted in considerable social upheaval and, in some cases, unrest in countries going through it. For example, in Russia, annual inflation rates of up to 900 per cent have dampened the people's enthusiasm for reform.

The **Commonwealth of Independent States (CIS)** emerged in 1996 as a loosely connected group of former Soviet Union states. The CIS unites Azerbaijan, Armenia, Belarus, Georgia, Kazakhstan, Kyrgyzstan, Moldova, Russia, Tajikistan, Turkmenistan, Ukraine and Uzbekistan.[33] Reviewing key economic data for the CIS and comparing them with those for EU countries provides a stark reminder of the difficult position in which many eastern European nations find themselves. The highest GNP per capita figure for the CIS, £1940, is found in Belarus, while the lowest for the region, £320, is in Tajikistan. These figures compare with an EU high of £23,507 in Luxembourg and a low of £4787 in Greece.[34]

**Commonwealth of Independent States (CIS)**
The CIS unites Azerbaijan, Armenia, Belarus, Georgia, Kazakhstan, Kyrgyzstan, Moldova, Russia, Tajikistan, Turkmenistan, Ukraine and Uzbekistan in a trading bloc

Although after it was set up there were potential opportunities for the CIS to trade as a market group, in practice this idea has been severely restricted by the lack of cooperation between member states and, in particular, by the continuing economic and political problems in Russia.[35] The importance of Russia – the largest market, with 150 million consumers – cannot be overlooked in the region's development.[36] For western companies, the potential is considerable. Hewlett-Packard enjoyed a fourfold increase in sales in one year alone, and others – such as Coca-Cola and McDonald's – have also taken advantage of the new opportunities.

The reformers of the CEE economies want to reduce trade restrictions on imports and offer incentives to encourage exports to, and investment in, their countries.[37] One such move involved seven UK companies, which formed a consortium to look at opportunities in the personal care and food and drink areas of the Russian market. So far, the initiative has led to a number of developments, including joint venture agreements between Tambrands and the

Ukrainian ministry of public health to sell tampons to a market of 70 million women.[38] Because of these economic and political reforms, productivity in central and eastern Europe is expected to increase as workers are given more incentives and control. Some eastern European nations have sought to join the European Union, allowing freer trade across all European borders.[39] In free elections, East Germany voted in 1990 to reunify with West Germany. Although there were initial teething problems and some social unrest, the unification of Germany also had a great impact on the European Union and world economy. Exactly how the changing face of the CEE in general will affect world trade remains to be seen. However, because of the swift and uncontrolled nature of the changes taking place in eastern Europe and the former Soviet Union, businesses considering marketing their products in these countries must monitor events carefully and proceed with caution, particularly in safeguarding payments for products and services from trading partners and government departments in these countries.

### General Agreement on Tariffs and Trade (GATT) and the World Trade Organization (WTO)

**General Agreement on Tariffs and Trade (GATT)**
An agreement between countries to reduce worldwide tariffs and increase international trade

**Dumping**
Selling products at unfairly low prices outside domestic markets

**World Trade Organization (WTO)**
An entity that promotes and facilitates free trade between member states

Like NAFTA and the EU, the **General Agreement on Tariffs and Trade (GATT)** is based on negotiations among member countries to reduce worldwide tariffs and increase international trade. Originally signed by 23 countries in 1947, GATT provides a forum for tariff negotiations, and a place where international trade problems can be discussed and resolved. GATT negotiations currently involve some 124 countries and have had far-reaching ramifications for the international marketing strategies of many companies.

GATT sponsors rounds of negotiations aimed at reducing trade restrictions. Seven rounds of GATT negotiations have reduced the average worldwide tariffs on manufactured goods from 45 per cent to 5 per cent, and negotiators have been able to eliminate or ease non-tariff trade restrictions such as import quotas, 'red tape' in customs procedures, and 'buy national' agreements. The Uruguay Round further reduced trade barriers for most products and provided new rules to prevent **dumping** – the selling of products at unfairly low prices.

The most significant outcome of the Uruguay Round was the establishment of the **World Trade Organization (WTO)** to promote free trade among member countries. Fulfilling this purpose requires eliminating trade barriers; educating individuals, companies and governments about trade rules around the world; and assuring global markets that no sudden changes of policy will occur. The WTO also serves as a forum for trade negotiations and dispute resolution. At the heart of the WTO are agreements that provide legal ground rules for international commerce and trade policy.

## Alternative Market Entry Strategies

The level of commitment to international marketing is a major variable in deciding what kind of involvement is appropriate. A company's market entry options range from occasional exporting to expanding overall operations (production and marketing) into other countries. This section examines exporting, licensing, franchising, contract manufacturing, joint ventures, trading companies, foreign direct investment and other approaches to international involvement.[40]

### Exporting

**Exporting**
Use of an intermediary that performs most marketing functions associated with selling to other countries; entails the minimum effort, cost and risk involved in international marketing

**Exporting** is the lowest and most flexible level of commitment to international marketing. A business may find an exporting intermediary that can perform most marketing functions associated with selling to other countries. This approach entails minimum effort and cost. Modifications in packaging, labelling, style or colour may be the major expenses in adapting a product. There is limited risk in using export agents and merchants because there is no direct investment in the foreign country.

Export agents bring together buyers and sellers from different countries; they collect a commission for arranging sales. Export houses and export merchants purchase products from different companies and then sell them to foreign countries. They specialise in understanding customers' needs in foreign countries.

Foreign buyers from companies and governments provide a direct method of exporting and eliminate the need for an intermediary. Foreign buyers encourage international exchange by contacting domestic businesses about their needs and the opportunities available in exporting. Domestic companies that want to export with a minimum of effort and investment seek out foreign importers and buyers.

## Licensing

**Licensing**
System in which a licensee pays commissions or royalties on sales or supplies used in manufacturing

When potential markets are found across national boundaries – and when production, technical assistance or marketing know-how is required – **licensing** is an alternative to direct investment. The licensee (the owner of the foreign operation) pays commissions or royalties on sales or supplies used in manufacturing. An initial fee may be charged when the licensing agreement is signed. Exchanges of management techniques or technical assistance are primary reasons for licensing agreements. Yoplait is a French yoghurt that is licensed for production in the United States and numerous other countries; but the Yoplait brand tries to maintain a French image.

Licensing is an attractive alternative to direct investment when the political stability of a foreign country is in doubt or when resources are unavailable for direct investment. This approach is especially advantageous for small manufacturers wanting to launch a well-known brand internationally. For example, Pierre Cardin has issued 500 licences and Yves St Laurent 200 to make their products.[41] Löwenbrau has used licensing agreements to increase sales worldwide without committing capital to build breweries.

## Franchising

**Franchising**
A form of licensing granting the right to use certain intellectual property rights, such as trade names, brand names, designs, patents and copyrights

Another alternative to direct investment in non-domestic markets is **franchising**. This form of licensing, which grants the right to use certain intellectual property rights, such as trade names, brand names, designs, patents and copyrights, is becoming increasingly popular in Europe.[42] Under this arrangement the franchiser grants a licence to the franchisee, who pays to be allowed to carry out business under the name owned by the franchiser. The franchiser retains control over the manner in which the business is conducted and assists the franchisee in running the business. The franchisee retains ownership of his or her own business, which remains separate from that of the franchiser.[43]

Franchising has recently experienced a period of rapid growth. Companies such as Benetton, Burger King, Holiday Inn and IKEA are particularly well known for their commitment to growing global business in this way. There are various reasons why the popularity of franchising has increased so rapidly.[44] First, the general world decline in manufacturing and shift to service industries has increased the relevance of franchising. This is significant, because franchising is a very common internationalisation process for service organisations. Second, franchising has been relatively free of restrictions from legislation, especially in the EU. Third, an increase in self-employment has provided a pool of individuals willing to become involved in franchising, and this activity has generally been supported by the major clearing banks. Franchising is discussed further in Chapter 16.

**Contract manufacturing**
The practice of hiring a foreign company to produce a designated volume of product to a set specification

## Contract Manufacturing

**Contract manufacturing** is the practice of hiring a foreign company to produce a designated volume of the domestic company's product to a set specification. The final product carries the domestic company's name. Gap, for example, relies on contract manufacturing for some of its clothing, and Reebok uses Korean contract manufacturers to produce many of its sports shoes. Marketing activity may be handled by the contract manufacturer or by the contracting company.

## Joint Ventures and Strategic Alliances

In international marketing, a **joint venture** is a partnership between a domestic company and a foreign company or government. Joint ventures are especially popular in industries that call for large investments, such as natural resources extraction or car manufacturing. Control of the joint venture can be split equally or can be retained by one party. Joint ventures are often a political necessity because of nationalism and governmental restrictions on

**Joint venture**
A partnership between a domestic company and a foreign company or government

foreign ownership. They also provide legitimacy in the eyes of the host country's people. Local partners have first-hand knowledge of the economic and socio-political environment, access to distribution networks or privileged access to local resources (raw material, labour management, contacts, and so on). Moreover, entrepreneurs in many less developed countries actively seek associations with an overseas partner as a ready means of implementing their own corporate strategy.[45]

Joint ventures are assuming greater global importance because of cost advantages and the number of inexperienced businesses entering foreign markets. They may be the result of a trade-off between a company's desire for completely unambiguous control of an enterprise and its quest for additional resources. They may occur when internal development or acquisition is not feasible or unavailable, or when the risks and constraints leave no other alternative. As project sizes increase in the face of global competition, and businesses attempt to spread the huge costs of technological innovation, there is increased impetus to form joint ventures.[46] Several European truck makers used mergers and joint ventures with other European companies to consolidate their power after the unification of the EU in 1992 and the deregulation of the European haulage industry in 1993. Volvo and Renault developed such a partnership.[47] Of course, joint ventures are also possible between partners from different continents. LDV, a European van manufacturer, joined forces with Korean company Daewoo to develop a new range of vans, to be produced by both companies but marketed in Europe by LDV and in the Asia Pacific region by Daewoo. The leading IT consultancies frequently form joint ventures or alliances with partners in order to exploit domestic and non-domestic opportunities.

Joint ventures are sometimes criticised as being inherently unstable,[48] or because they might result in a take-over attempt. For businesses trying to build longer-term joint ventures, there is also the danger that the relationship stifles flexibility. Of course, for many companies that become involved in joint ventures this may be their only feasible mode of entry at the time and may in any case be regarded purely as a transitional arrangement.[49] For example, European construction companies bidding for business in Saudi Arabia have found that joint ventures with Arab construction companies gain local support among the handful of people who make the contracting decisions.

**Strategic alliances**
Partnerships formed to create a competitive advantage on a worldwide basis

**Strategic alliances**, the newest form of international business structure, are partnerships formed to create a competitive advantage on a worldwide basis. They are very similar to joint ventures. Strategic alliances have been defined as 'cooperation between two or more industrial corporations, belonging to different countries, whereby each partner seeks to add to its competencies by combining its resources with those of its partner'.[50] The number of strategic alliances is growing at an estimated rate of about 20 per cent per year.[51] In fact, in some industries, such as cars and high technology, strategic alliances are becoming the predominant means of competing. International competition is so fierce and the costs of competing globally so high that few businesses have the required individual resources, and it makes sense to collaborate with other companies.[52]

The partners forming international strategic alliances share common goals, yet often retain their distinct identities, each bringing a distinctive competence to the union. What distinguishes international strategic alliances from other business structures is that member companies in the alliance may have been traditional rivals competing for market share in the same product class.[53] This situation is common in the aerospace industry. Raytheon may partner certain companies in bidding for work from Boeing, while competing with the same suppliers when seeking work with Lockheed or Airbus. The Topical Insight box on page 144 explains how knowledge of international marketing opportunities has enabled Europe's Airbus to overtake long-term market leader Boeing.

## Trading Companies

A **trading company** provides a link between buyers and sellers in different countries. As its name implies, a trading company is not involved in manufacturing or owning assets related to manufacturing. The trading company buys in one country at the lowest price consistent

# Topical Insight

## Airbus Vies with Boeing for Global Leadership

There can be few other markets as 'international' as the highly competitive market for commercial aircraft. While a plethora of companies compete for executive jet sales, cargo planes and short-haul aircraft, the market for large passenger aircraft is now dominated by two major players: Airbus from Europe and America's Boeing.

In the next 20 years, it is predicted by Boeing that over 25,000 passenger jets will be purchased at a value of £2 trillion. The industry is highly volatile and the forces of the marketing environment play a significant role in the fortunes of these manufacturers. The aftermath of the 'Twin Towers' terrorist atrocity in 2001 led to cancelled orders as airlines struggled to entice enough passengers to fly on their existing fleets. Oil price increases, following instability in the Middle East in 2003 and in Russian oil production in 2004, led to Boeing shelving plans for a super-sized airliner. However, the rapid growth in low-fare airlines targeting business travellers flying between European destinations led to an increase in demand for aircraft carrying 70 to 140 passengers.

In all industries, it is important to understand the forces of the marketing environment and to analyse the buying behaviour of prospective customers. In the marketplace for aircraft, it impossible to succeed without understanding these market dynamics. An order for US$2 billion worth of aircraft will not be made in a few minutes by only one or two managers. The buying process will be very formal and drawn out, and will involve numerous decision-makers within the buying centre. Each manager or government official within the buying centre will require bespoke marketing messages and careful handling by potential aircraft suppliers.

To further complicate the situation, there are at any one time only a handful of customers actively seeking to purchase new aircraft. Some of these customers may be financially successful, while others require extensive credit lines and may prove to be incapable of completing the purchase. Some airlines are still state-owned, involving an extra layer of bureaucracy in the buying process and adding to the customer needs that must be fulfilled in order to win an order or achieve customer satisfaction. Each major airline tends to represent a geographic territory: the cultural buying issues and management styles vary significantly from country-to-country and between regions of the world.

For many decades, Boeing dominated the global market for wide-bodied passenger aircraft. By 2004, Airbus had overtaken Boeing's sales. In the first six months of 2004, major orders included those listed in the table below.

In July 2004 Airbus announced both a huge order from rapidly growing Etihad Airways based in Abu Dhabi and plans to increase its annual production by 50 per cent, whereas Boeing's production projections are static. Etihad had discussed its expansion plans with both Boeing and Airbus. The latter won the contract owing to its appreciation of the fledging airline's requirements, which included training and maintenance, in addition to the aircraft. An industry insider stated that Airbus was, 'more "tuned in" to the evolving market conditions and the decision-making criteria within Etihad'. This sentiment was echoed by Virgin Atlantic, which in August 2004 announced its single biggest ever order, for 25 new aircraft from Airbus. It would seem Airbus has practised international marketing to good effect, understanding well the nuances of its global target markets.

**Sources:** Airbus PR; 'Current market outlook', *Boeing*, 2004; Angela Jameson, 'Airbus wins $7bn Abu Dhabi order', *The Times*, 21 July 2004, pp. 36–7.

| **Airbus** | | **Boeing** | |
|---|---|---|---|
| US$905 m | Independence Air | US$564 m | Unidentified |
| US$196 m | Tarom | US$287.5 m | Qantas |
| US$949 m | Spirit Airlines | US$862.5 m | GOL Airlines |
| US$1.29 bn | China Southern Airlines | US$375 m | China Airlines |
| US$1.89 bn | JetBlue Airways | US$287.5 m | US Navy |
| Total orders: US$7.1 bn | | Total orders: US$5.3 bn | |
| Back orders: US$175 bn | | Back orders: US$155 bn | |

**Trading company**
A company that provides a link between buyers and sellers in different countries

with quality and sells to buyers in another country. An important function of trading companies is taking title to products and undertaking all the activities necessary to move the products from the domestic country to a foreign country. Large, grain trading companies, for example, control a major portion of the world's trade in basic food commodities. These trading companies sell agricultural commodities that are homogeneous, and can be stored and moved rapidly in response to market conditions.

Trading companies reduce risk for companies interested in becoming involved in international marketing, assisting producers with information about products that meet quality and price expectations in domestic or international markets. Additional services a trading company may provide include consulting, marketing research, advertising, insurance, research and development, legal assistance, warehousing and foreign exchange.

## Foreign Direct Investment

**Foreign direct investment (FDI)**
A long-term commitment to marketing in a foreign nation through direct ownership of a foreign subsidiary or division

**Multinational enterprise**
A company with operations or subsidiaries in many countries

Once a company makes a long-term commitment to foreign marketing, direct ownership of a foreign subsidiary or division is a possibility. **Foreign direct investment (FDI)** involves making a long-term commitment to marketing in a foreign nation through direct ownership of a foreign subsidiary or division. The expense of developing a separate foreign distribution system, in particular, can be tremendous. For example, as French hypermarket chain Carrefour discovered, the opening of retail stores in neighbouring countries can require a large financial investment in facilities, research and management.

The term **multinational enterprise** refers to companies that have operations or subsidiaries located in many countries. Often the parent company is based in one country and cultivates production, management and marketing activities in other countries. The company's subsidiaries may be quite autonomous in order to respond to the needs of individual international markets. Companies such as ICI, Unilever and General Motors are multinational companies with worldwide operations. Table 5.4 lists the top 50 European companies, ranked by market capitalisation. Most of these companies are active in different countries and across several continents.

A wholly owned foreign subsidiary may be allowed to operate independently of the parent company so that its management can have more freedom to adjust to the local environment. Cooperative arrangements are developed to assist in marketing efforts, production and management. A wholly owned foreign subsidiary may export products to the home country. Some car manufacturers, such as Ford and General Motors, for example, import cars built by their foreign subsidiaries. A foreign subsidiary offers important tax, tariff and other operating advantages. The greatest advantages of direct foreign investment are greater strategy control and enhanced market capacity. To maximise these, a subsidiary may operate under foreign management, so that a genuinely local identity can be developed. A company's success in achieving these advantages will tend to depend on whether the business has a competitive advantage allowing it to recover the costs of its investment.

# Customisation Versus the Globalisation of International Marketing Strategies

As for domestic marketers, international marketers develop marketing strategies to serve specific target markets. Traditionally, international marketing strategies have customised marketing mixes according to cultural, regional and national differences. Detergent producers such as Procter & Gamble or Lever Brothers customise their products to local water conditions, weather, equipment and washing habits. Colgate-Palmolive even developed a cheap hand-powered washing machine for households lacking electricity in developing regions. Such customisation of the product or service, to reflect local nuances, attitudes and behaviours, can bring significant rewards to marketers. Failure to reflect such localised market conditions may leave marketers with an unattractive customer-facing proposition.

**TABLE 5.4 TOP 50 EUROPEAN COMPANIES BY REVENUE 2003**

| Rank | Company | Country | Sector | Revenue US$m |
|---|---|---|---|---|
| 1 | Royal Dutch/Shell Group | Netherlands/UK | Oil & gas | 179,431 |
| 2 | BP | UK | Oil & gas | 178,721 |
| 3 | DaimlerChrysler | Germany | Automobile | 140,777 |
| 4 | Allianz Worldwide | Germany | Insurance | 101,466 |
| 5 | Total | France | Oil & gas | 96,504 |
| 6 | ING Group | Netherlands | Diversified finance | 87,754 |
| 7 | Volkswagen Group | Germany | Automobile | 84,707 |
| 8 | Siemens Group | Germany | Multi-industry | 77,013 |
| 9 | Carrefour Group | France | Food & drug retail | 64,683 |
| 10 | AXA Group | France | Insurance | 61,768 |
| 11 | Ahold | Netherlands | Food & drug retail | 59,184 |
| 12 | Nestlé | Switzerland | Food | 57,204 |
| 13 | Credit Suisse Group | Switzerland | Diversified finance | 53,649 |
| 14 | Deutsche Bank Group | Germany | Diversified finance | 52,731 |
| 15 | Fiat Group | Italy | Automobile | 52,164 |
| 16 | Peugeot Group | France | Automobile | 51,231 |
| 17 | BNP Paribas | France | Banking | 50,881 |
| 18 | Deutsche Telecom | Germany | Telecom services | 50,528 |
| 19 | Metro | Germany | Food & drug retail | 48,493 |
| 20 | Aviva | UK | Insurance | 48,441 |
| 21 | Generall Group | Italy | Insurance | 48,052 |
| 22 | Vodafone | UK | Telecom services | 46,947 |
| 23 | ENI | Italy | Oil & gas | 46,117 |
| 24 | Unilever | Netherlands/UK | Food products | 45,428 |
| 25 | Fortis | Netherlands | Diversified finance | 44,174 |
| 26 | France Telecom | France | Telecom services | 43,885 |
| 27 | Suez Group | France | Diversified utility | 43,377 |
| 28 | UBS | Switzerland | Diversified finance | 43,371 |
| 29 | Credit Agricole | France | Banking | 42,817 |
| 30 | HSBC Group | UK | Banking | 41,151 |
| 31 | RWE Group | Germany | Diversified utility | 40,927 |
| 32 | Munich Re | Germany | Insurance | 40,708 |
| 33 | Zurich Financial | Switzerland | Insurance | 40,448 |
| 34 | Tesco | UK | Food & drug retail | 40,353 |
| 35 | BMW-Bayerische Group | Germany | Automobile | 39,793 |
| 36 | Deutsche Post | Germany | Air freight & couriers | 36,944 |
| 37 | Bayer HypoVereinsbank | Germany | Banking | 36,190 |
| 38 | ABN-Amro Holding | Netherlands | Banking | 35,737 |
| 39 | Prudential | UK | Insurance | 35,635 |
| 40 | Royal Bank of Scotland | UK | Banking | 35,267 |
| 41 | Legal & General Group | UK | Insurance | 35,131 |
| 42 | Renault Group | France | Automobile | 34,197 |
| 43 | E.on | Germany | Electricity | 33,999 |
| 44 | ThyssenKrupp Group | Germany | Metals & mining | 33,639 |
| 45 | GlaxoSmithKline | UK | Pharmaceuticals | 31,845 |
| 46 | Societé Generale Group | France | Banking | 31,827 |
| 47 | Statoil Group | Norway | Oil & gas | 30,334 |
| 48 | BASF Group | Germany | Chemicals | 30,319 |
| 49 | HBOS | UK | Banking | 30,234 |
| 50 | Philips Group | Netherlands | Multi-industry | 29,947 |

**Source:** Forbes International 500, July 21, 2003 Forbes, reprinted with permission; *The European Marketing Pocket Book*, published by the World Advertising Research Center, Henley-on-Thames, 2004.

**Globalisation**
The development of marketing strategies that treat the entire world, or its major regions, as a single entity

Along the continuum, away from customisation, is the globalisation of marketing. **Globalisation** involves developing marketing strategies as though the world's consumers or business customers share homogeneous product needs and purchasing behaviour. Nike and Adidas footwear, for example, are standardised globally and the same advertising campaigns are run across the globe. Mobile phones, televisions, clothing, movies, soft drinks, cosmetics, toothpaste, batteries and cigarette brands are examples of globalised products: the same product attributes and specifications are marketed around the world.

Throughout the 1980s and 1990s, the trend was for large corporations to globalise their products and, wherever possible, the remaining ingredients of their marketing programmes, notably marketing communications, pricing and distribution channels. The goals were to reduce costs – by harmonising product mixes, branding, packaging and labelling – and to create a more cohesive and recognisable brand identity. The choice of marketing channels, media options for advertising, pricing and particularly customer service often proved more challenging to harmonise: different practices and cultures from region to region or country to country proved difficult to address through a single marketing mix.

Over time, the champions of globalised marketing recognised that a 'think globally, act locally' compromise was sensible. Economies of effort and scale in a single product and brand identity were worthwhile, but the route to market, the way in which the brand and product were communicated to the intended target audiences, the pricing and service required, often had to be manipulated at a local level to reflect the pertinent localised market conditions. Even such ubiquitous brands as McDonald's and Coca-Cola modify their marketing mixes to reflect local tastes, customs, buying behaviour and social values. This requirement by international marketers to manipulate the ingredients of the marketing mix in order to reflect local needs is developed further in Chapter 22.

International marketing requires strategic planning, if a company is to incorporate non-domestic sales into its overall marketing strategy. International marketing activities often require customised marketing mixes to achieve an organisation's goals. Globalisation requires a total commitment to the world, regions or multinational areas as an integral part of the company's markets. Regardless of the extent to which a company chooses to globalise its marketing strategy, extensive analysis of the marketing environment, marketing intelligence and often marketing research, are required in order to understand the needs and desires of the target market(s) and to implement the selected marketing strategy successfully. While a global presence does not guarantee a global competitive advantage (see Chapter 2) a global presence does generate five opportunities for creating value:

1 to adapt to local market differences
2 to exploit economies of global scale
3 to exploit economies of global scope
4 to mine optimal locations for activities and resources
5 to maximise the transfer of knowledge across locations.

However, without a sound appreciation of the forces of the marketing environment internationally, an organisation's ability to seek suitable opportunities will be limited. A marketing strategy, as described in Chapter 2, must be developed in order to specify the opportunities to be pursued internationally, select an appropriate target market strategy and basis for competing, and specify applicable marketing programmes to operationalise the agreed international marketing strategy. This use of the marketing process may suggest customisation, full globalisation or some hybrid part-way between these two extremes.

# Summary

Marketing activities performed across national boundaries are usually significantly different from domestic marketing activities. International marketers must have a profound awareness of the foreign environment. The marketing strategy is ordinarily adjusted to meet the needs and desires of markets across national boundaries.

» The level of involvement in international marketing covers a wide spectrum from *domestic marketing* to *export marketing*, *international marketing*, *multinational marketing* and *global marketing*. Although all companies involved in international marketing must make some modifications to their marketing activities, full-scale global marketing requires total commitment to international marketing and involves applying the company's assets, experience and products to develop and maintain marketing strategies on a global scale. *Globalised marketing* occurs when marketing strategies are developed for major regions or the entire world to enable organisations to compete globally. *Multinational companies* are those that operate in overseas markets as if they were local companies.

» Marketers must rely on international marketing intelligence to understand the complexities of the international marketing environment before they can formulate a marketing strategy and develop a marketing mix. That is why they collect and analyse secondary data and primary data about international markets.

» Environmental aspects of special importance include cultural, social, economic, political, regulatory, legal and technological forces. Cultural aspects of the environment that are most important to international marketers include customs, concepts, values, attitudes, morals and knowledge. Marketing activities are primarily social in purpose; they are structured by the institutions of family, religion, education, health and recreation. The most prominent economic forces that affect international marketing are those that can be measured by income and resources. *Gross domestic product (GDP)* is the total value of all goods and services produced by a country in a year. Credit, buying power and income distribution are aggregate measures of market potential. Political and legal forces include the political system, national laws, regulatory bodies, national pressure groups and courts.

» Measures that governments can take to govern cross-border trade include the use of tariffs, quotas and non-tariff barriers. *Tariffs* are taxes that affect the movement of goods across economic or political boundaries. *Quotas* involve physical restrictions on the amount of goods that can be imported. *Non-tariff barriers* include a wide range of rules, regulations and taxes that have an impact on trade. The foreign policies of all nations involved in trade determine how marketing can be conducted. The level of technology helps define economic development within a nation and indicates the existence of methods to facilitate marketing.

» Various regional trade alliances and specific markets are creating both difficulties and opportunities for organisations. The *North American Free Trade Agreement (NAFTA)*, set up in 1994, aims to eliminate all tariffs on goods produced and traded between Canada, Mexico and the USA, and to provide for a totally free trade area by 2009. The creation of the single European market in 1993, following the signing of the *Maastricht Treaty* in 1992, led to the formation of the *European Union (EU)*, which was enlarged in 2004 to include 25 member states: Austria, Belgium, Denmark, Finland, France, Germany, Greece, Ireland, Italy, Luxembourg, the Netherlands, Portugal, Spain, Sweden and the United Kingdom have been joined by the Czech Republic, Cyprus, Estonia, Hungary, Latvia, Lithuania, Malta, Poland, Slovenia and Slovakia. The best-known trading group in the Pacific Rim is the *Association of South East Asian Nations (ASEAN)*, which was formed in 1967. More recently, the *Asia Pacific Economic Co-operative (APEC)* has been set up to promote trade in the region. The group includes the USA, Australia, Canada, New Zealand, Japan, China, South Korea, Hong Kong, Taiwan and

ASEAN members. Trade in the Asia Pacific region has been substantially affected by economic recession, but many of the leading corporations are recovering well. *Central and Eastern Europe (CEE)* encompasses the *Commonwealth of Independent States (CIS)*, the Czech and Slovak Republics, Hungary, Poland, Slovenia, Croatia, Bosnia and Herzegovina, Serbia and Montenegro, Bulgaria, FYR Macedonia and Albania. The CIS unites Azerbaijan, Armenia, Belarus, Georgia, Kazakhstan, Kyrgyzstan, Moldova, Russia, Tajikistan, Turkmenistan, Ukraine and Uzbekistan. The *General Agreement on Tariffs and Trade*, known as GATT, is an agreement between countries to reduce worldwide tariffs and increase international trade. There is a particular focus on preventing *dumping* – the selling of products at unfairly low prices outside domestic markets. An important development from GATT has been the *World Trade Organization (WTO)*, an entity that promotes and facilitates free trade between member states.

There are several ways of becoming involved in international marketing. *Exporting* is the easiest and most flexible method. *Licensing* is an alternative to direct investment; it may be necessitated by political and economic conditions. *Franchising* is a form of licensing granting the right to use certain intellectual property rights such as trade names, brand names, designs, patents and copyrights. *Contract manufacturing* is the practice of hiring a foreign company to produce a designated volume of product to a specification. *Joint ventures* and *strategic alliances* are often appropriate when outside resources are needed, when there are governmental restrictions on foreign ownership or when changes in global markets encourage competitive consolidation. *Trading companies* are experts at buying products in the domestic market and selling to foreign markets, thereby taking most of the risk in international involvement. *Foreign direct investment (FDI)* in divisions or subsidiaries is the strongest commitment to international marketing and involves the greatest risk. When a company has operations or subsidiaries located in many countries, it is termed a *multinational enterprise*.

Most organisations adjust their marketing programmes to reflect differences in target markets and marketing environments. Some companies, however, standardise their marketing activity worldwide. Traditionally, international marketing has involved customising products according to cultural, regional or national differences. *Globalisation*, on the other hand, involves developing marketing strategies for the whole world, or major regions, ignoring localised market dynamics. A globalised company standardises products in the same way, everywhere.

International marketing demands strategic planning, the assessment of the international marketing environment and the development of a marketing strategy in order to specify the opportunities to be pursued internationally, select an appropriate target market strategy and basis for competing, and specify applicable marketing programmes to operationalise the agreed international marketing strategy. This use of the marketing process may suggest customisation, full globalisation, or some hybrid part-way between these two extremes.

## *Key Links*

This chapter should be read in conjunction with:

- Chapter 2's explanation of marketing strategy
- Chapter 3's examination of the forces of the marketing environment and environmental scanning
- Chapter 22's exploration of the manipulation of the marketing mix to reflect localised market conditions.

## Important Terms

Domestic marketing
Export marketing
International marketing
Multinational marketing
Multinational companies
Global marketing
Globalised marketing
Gross domestic product (GDP)
Tariffs
Quotas

Non-tariff barriers
North American Free Trade Agreement (NAFTA)
European Union (EU)
Maastricht Treaty
Association of South East Asian Nations (ASEAN)
Asia Pacific Economic Co-operative (APEC)
Central and Eastern Europe (CEE)
Commonwealth of Independent States (CIS)
General Agreement on Tariffs and Trade (GATT)
Dumping
World Trade Organization (WTO)
Exporting
Licensing
Franchising
Contract manufacturing
Joint venture
Strategic alliances
Trading company
Foreign direct investment (FDI)
Multinational enterprise
Globalisation

## Discussion and Review Questions

1 How does international marketing differ from domestic marketing?
2 What must marketers consider before deciding whether to become involved in international marketing?
3 Are the largest industrial companies in Europe committed to international marketing? Why or why not?
4 Why do you think so much of this chapter is devoted to an analysis of the international marketing environment?
5 A manufacturer recently exported peanut butter with a green label to a nation in the Far East. The product failed because it was associated with jungle sickness. How could this mistake have been avoided?
6 How do religious systems influence marketing activities in foreign countries?
7 Recent recession in the Asia Pacific region has affected trade opportunities for many European businesses. How could such businesses minimise the impact of such problems?
8 If you were asked to provide a small tip or bribe to have a document approved in a foreign nation where this practice was customary, what would you do?
9 What should marketers consider as they decide whether to license or to enter into a joint venture in a foreign nation?
10 Discuss the impact of strategic alliances on marketing strategies.
11 What is meant by globalisation?
12 What are the differences between customisation and globalisation?

## Recommended Readings

- Bradley, F., *International Marketing Strategy* (London: FT Prentice Hall, 2002).
- Bridgewater, S. and Egan, C., *International Marketing Relationships* (Basingstoke: Palgrave Macmillan, 2002).
- Jeannet, J.-P. and Hennessey, H.D., *Global Marketing Strategies* (Boston: Houghton Mifflin, 2001).
- Paliwoda, S. and Thomas, M.J., *International Marketing* (Oxford: Butterworth-Heinemann, 1998).
- Terpstra, V. and Sarathy, R., *International Marketing* (Cincinnati, OH: South Western, 2000).

## Internet Exercise

There are many organisations with global aspirations. Examine a selection by logging on to the following websites:

www.jcb.com
www.ikea.com
www.sony.com
www.ford.com
www.carrefour.com

1 To what extent have these organisations tailored their messages to specific geographic regions?
2 To what extent are these organisations practising globalised marketing?
3 To what extent do these organisations' websites infer a knowledge of their international marketing environments?

## *Applied Mini-Case*

What is your favourite flavour of lollipop? Cherry? Root beer? Blue raspberry? These are options in the USA, but the choice may have been liquorice in the Netherlands, lychee nut in China or tarte-tatin in France. Barcelona-based Chupa Chups produces over four billion lollipops each year, distributed to more than 270 countries. The sixth largest seller of hard candy in the world now achieves more than 90 per cent of sales from outside Spain. The lollies distributed across the globe vary in flavour from country to country. Chupa Chups has opted to tailor its products to suit tastes in specific target market territories.

**Source:** Chupa Chups, 2004.

## Question

As the marketing director of Chupa Chups, when considering an additional country in which to operate, what information about the territory would be required before the country in question received Chupa Chups lollipops?

## Case Study

# Carrefour's International Strategy

Carrefour has been in the business of managing hypermarkets for more than 35 years. The original business idea was generated in the early 1960s, when Marcel Fournier and Denis and Jacques Defforey visited a retailing conference in the United States. The hypermarket concept they developed is based on choice, low prices, self-service and free car parking, allowing consumers to do all of their shopping under one roof. The first outlets were opened in the Paris suburbs, followed in 1966 by Europe's largest self-service hypermarket outside Lyon.

The main features of the Carrefour concept are:

- large, spacious stores with wide aisles and free car parks
- store size of around 10,000 square metres, serving three million shoppers each year
- flexibility in product and service offerings to reflect local tastes
- food representing about 45 per cent of sales, gross margins of about 18 per cent
- narrow profit margins and high-volume purchases, allowing discount prices to be offered on a daily basis
- a choice of branded, private and generic labels, usually arranged on the shelves vertically in that order.

An early foray into international expansion, with new stores in Belgium, Italy, Switzerland and the United Kingdom, was not particularly successful and the group quickly abandoned this activity to concentrate on its home operations. However, in the mid-1970s a period of organic growth began, with new openings in France, Spain and Brazil. This continued until the early 1980s, with Carrefour opening its first Argentinian and Taiwanese outlets. During this same time period, Carrefour France concentrated on developing new retail concepts and formats that might be adopted in overseas markets. Once such initiative was the change of name in Spain from Carrefour to Pryca.

At the beginning of the 1990s, Carrefour decided to concentrate on growth by acquisition, buying the French chains Montlaur and Euromarché. But Carrefour was not confining its growth to the hypermarket sector. By acquiring Picard Sugelés, a French frozen-food business, Carrefour was signalling its expansion into other retail sectors, such as eyewear, frozen food, discounting, cash and carry, and office supply stores in 15 different countries.

Carrefour's commitment to an international strategy was initially encouraged by problems in developing its domestic business. These difficulties were caused partly by government regulations designed to protect small retailers. For example, tight controls were imposed on the opening of new stores and, in some cases, on the increase of selling space in existing outlets. For Carrefour, this restricted new domestic opportunities to those that could be gleaned through the acquisition of existing businesses. Once these opportunities had been exploited, the only other growth option for Carrefour was to expand overseas.

The international success the business has enjoyed can be attributed to a number of factors. First, the business has been a fast mover in many of the countries in which it has expanded. By carefully choosing the right time to enter new countries, Carrefour has been able to make the most of appropriate retail conditions. Second, Carrefour has consistently applied its proven and well-developed hypermarket concept. In many cases, by maintaining the same basic operational and marketing characteristics, the business has been able simply to transplant its operation to a new market. However, Carrefour has also shown the flexibility to make appropriate modifications to local taste where required. Finally, the business has a deep-seated commitment to its international expansion strategy.

In the words of company Chairman Daniel Bernard:

> internationalisation is a difficult learning curve which is expensive at the outset. After setting up the basics, it becomes necessary to be patient enough to fine-tune the concept and to await profitability, which may be quite distant. Internationalisation represents long-term investment.

In recent years, attempts to improve profit margins have focused on supply chain management. In 1993, Carrefour teamed up with food suppliers to develop 'controlled supply chains', making use of the latest developments in EDI and ECR. The aim was to offer consumers healthy, good-quality products at margins that are attractive to the business and its suppliers. Using new technology allowed Carrefour to achieve this by providing suppliers with information on store product sales, allowing for better stock level control.

By 2005, leading-edge systems and logistics have enabled Carrefour to develop a network of close to 11,000 stores. The 1999 acquisition of Promodes created the world's second largest retail group behind only Wal-Mart of the USA. Current successes lie primarily outside France, where the domestic supermarket chain is having to stage something of a recovery. There has been significant success for Carrefour in Poland and Greece, Argentina, Brazil, Mexico and Colombia, Korea and Taiwan, and now China.

The Carrefour commitment to expansion means that the business has often been prepared to forgo short-term profits in the interests of longer-term competitive advantage. However, as retail globalisation continues, Carrefour will have to continue reacting with speed and flexibility if it is to maintain its position. In particular, as the growing use of the Internet and home shopping begin to alter buying behaviour, the company must address whether or not the hypermarket concept will be able to adapt to changing consumer needs and profiles.

**Sources:** www.carrefour.com, 2004; M. Rocha, 'The globalisation of supermarkets: a case study approach', MBA project, Warwick Business School, 1998; Carrefour, *Annual Report*, Paris, 1997; Carrefour, *Annual Report*, Paris, 1998; P. Damour, 'Carrefour keeps its customers loyal', *International Journal of Retail and Distribution Management*, 23 (2), 1995; R. Redman, 'Carrefour details its international expansion plans', *Supermarket News*, 7 October 1996, pp. 41, 46; D. Merrerfield, 'Carrefour: exporting formats risky', *Supermarket News*, 7 June 1993, pp. 23, 43; D. Merrerfield and M. Tosh, 'Carrefour's crossroad', *Supermarket News*, 6 June 1992, pp. 1, 42; K. Morris, 'Carrefour: hyper-extension', *Financial World*, 26 May 1992, pp. 11, 161; J. Veenker, 'European food retail: industry report', *Meespierson*, 14 May 1997; J.L. Johnson, 'Carrefour revisited', *Discount Merchandiser*, August 1990; Daniel Bernard, Carrefour, 2004.

## Questions for Discussion

1. What drove Carrefour to expand its businesses internationally?
2. What new international opportunities might be open to Carrefour?
3. To what extent has Carrefour adopted a strategy of globalisation?

# Postscript

Effective marketing hinges on satisfying customers and establishing relationships. There are many forces at work, however, which affect how organisations endeavour to achieve these goals. Part I of *Marketing: Concepts and Strategies* has explored the nature and scope of the concepts of marketing, marketing orientation and marketing strategy, and gone on to describe the forces of the macro and micro marketing environment and the essential requirements for marketing in global markets.

The focus of *Marketing: Concepts and Strategies* now turns to the customer and the identification of target markets. As outlined in Figure 1.4, the customer must be at the centre of the marketing process. Organisations must target specific groups of customers, understand their needs and endeavour – through their marketing activities – to satisfy those needs. It is essential, though, to recognise that a business does not deal with its customers in a vacuum: there are many marketing environment forces at work, affecting the behaviour of customers and those organisations attempting to market to them. The role of technology, in particular, has created many opportunities for marketers to communicate with customers and build relationships. For businesses operating across national borders, involved with marketing in global markets, the impact of these forces and the trading decisions required are even more complex. These are the issues that have been examined in Part I.

Before progressing, readers should be confident that they are now able to do the following.

## Define and explain the marketing concept

- What is marketing?
- What is a marketing orientation?
- What is the marketing process?
- Why is marketing important?
- What are the basic elements of the marketing concept and its implementation?
- How has marketing evolved?
- What are the core stages of marketing strategy?
- What are the general strategic marketing issues?

## Define and explain the nature of marketing strategy

- What is marketing strategy?
- What is the relationship with a company's organisational mission, goals and corporate strategy?
- What is the role in marketing strategy of assessing organisational opportunities, capabilities and the SWOT analysis?
- What are strategic objectives?
- What is the role of target market strategy and brand positioning in marketing strategy?
- Why must marketers consider competitive advantage, competitive positions and differential advantage?
- Why must marketers include marketing objectives and marketing programmes in creating a marketing strategy?
- What is the importance of implementation and performance monitoring in marketing strategy?

## Outline the forces at work in the marketing environment

- What is environmental scanning?
- Why are the forces of the marketing environment important considerations for marketers?
- What are the macro and micro marketing environment forces?
- What are strategic windows?

## Understand the role of the Internet and technology in marketing

- What are electronic marketing and electronic commerce?
- In what ways are they growing in importance in strategic planning?
- What are the characteristics of electronic marketing and how do they differentiate electronic marketing from traditional marketing activities?
- How do the characteristics of electronic marketing affect marketing strategy?
- What is the role of customer relationship management in modern-day marketing?
- How do electronic marketing and information technology facilitate customer relationship management?
- What are the core requisites for effective customer relationship management systems?
- What are the legal and ethical considerations in electronic marketing?

**Describe the additional complexities facing marketers engaged in international markets**

- What is the nature of marketing in international markets?
- Why is marketing intelligence so important?
- Why are the forces of the marketing environment integral to international marketing?
- Why are regional trade alliances important considerations?
- What market entry strategies can businesses use to become involved in international marketing activities?

## *Strategic Case*

# Avis
# Global Leadership

Avis is one of the largest and best-known car rental brands, but the brand is controlled by different companies in various parts of the world. Avis is active in 107 countries with over 3100 locations; there are 14 corporate countries and licence arrangements in 93 others. Avis acquired Budget in 2003 and now Budget has 900 locations in 62 countries, mainly franchised businesses, and corporate operations in Austria and Switzerland. Avis Europe has close ties with US-based Cendant Corporation, which owns the global rights to the Avis and Budget brands. Avis Europe separated from its former US owner in 1986 and now operates in Europe, Africa, the Middle East and Asia under an exclusive licence via the globally recognised Avis and Budget brands. Cendant Corporation and Avis Europe share technology developments, buying policies, marketing initiatives, strategic alliances with other travel and leisure operators, and marketing information. The companies act together to provide customers with seamless services from country to country.

Recent expansion for Avis Europe has been in Japan, India, China, Tanzania, Mali and Budapest. In Europe, Avis and Europcar are head to head, each with 18 per cent market share and both are growing rapidly year on year. Hertz has 13 per cent, National 11 per cent, Sixt 8 per cent and Budget 6 per cent market share. Avis and Budget together control around a quarter of the European vehicle rental market.

### Avis Europe's Values

Avis Europe has a clearly stated mission:

> Our aim is to be the most valued and successful vehicle rental company in our markets, for our customers, our employees and our shareholders and to this end Avis is a dynamic global organization perpetually trying harder and committed to delivering the very highest levels of service through continuous investment in our six strategic priorities:
>
> Customer satisfaction / Cost efficiency
> Brand leadership / Employee satisfaction
> Profitable growth / People development

www.avis-europe.com/immediacy-7, August 2004.

The following statements encapsulate our beliefs and values and our approach to doing business throughout our operating territories.

**Business Ethics**
We believe it is in the interest of our shareholders, our customers and our employees that we maintain a highly acceptable public image supporting a progressively profitable company. Honesty, integrity and fairness are an integral basis of our total philosophy.

**Customers**
We believe in providing consistently high standards of integrity, service, quality and value in satisfying customer needs. This operating ethos maintains our industry leadership and retains the loyalty and respect of our customers.

**Employees**
We aim to stimulate duty, mutual loyalty and a sense of pride in working for Avis through employee involvement at all levels, continuous updating of knowledge and skills and attractive and competitive recognition and reward systems. We believe that employees should be actively encouraged to grow and develop their careers with Avis and we always seek first to appoint candidates from within the Company to fill positions at every level – both nationally and internationally. To this end, we will provide the environment to help employees improve and develop themselves.

**Management and leadership**
Our management philosophy is one of decentralisation and local autonomy, underpinned by strong support services and leadership provided from Group Headquarters, an approach which stimulates entrepreneurialism whilst promoting consistency of image, service levels and operational efficiency.

**Avis 'We Try Harder.' ethos**
We believe that sustainable competitive advantage comes from out innovating the competition continuously. In achieving this we look for continuous improvement, no matter how small, in everything we do and at the same time quantum improvement in the way we do business. We will never hesitate to adapt to new and more profitable ways of working provided that the integrity and honesty we apply to our business is not compromised. We actively encourage a 'try harder' and 'can do' mentality and operate a climate of TRUST at all levels. The only mistake is not to try something.

**Community**
We operate as responsible members of the community and within the laws of the countries within which we do business. We recognise and respect the attitudes, characteristics and customs of local populations.

**Environment**
We recognise our corporate responsibility to the community at large for public health and safety and environmental protection. We fully comply with all legislation in this respect and actively pursue environmental and safety initiatives on a local, industry wide and global basis.

**Suppliers**
We ensure integrity and professionalism in all dealings with suppliers and expect the same in return. We seek economic quality and efficiency of service in all supplier relationships and, where possible, 'added value' to the mutual benefit of both. We continuously foster strategic alliances and partnerships with major travel industry organisations who share a mutual respect of the customer, a commitment to quality and a desire to maximise and enhance the reputation and value of the brand.

**Costs**
We regard efficiency as central to our whole business philosophy and we continuously search for means to reduce the cost of delivering a better product for the customer.

## Avis's Buying Power

Avis's size plays an important role in the company's success. In particular, its position as the largest company in its sector buys a strong bargaining position with the car manufacturers. Avis UK, for example, has a fleet of around 20,000 cars. By changing these vehicles two or three times a year, the company may buy up to 60,000 cars per annum, which is a large slice of the total annual sales of new cars in the UK. In order to maintain its power in relationships and ensure competitiveness from its suppliers, Avis will sometimes switch to different manufacturers. Avis is able to use the power it has built up to negotiate good buying terms, sometimes up to 50 per cent off list prices. In addition, the company often negotiates generous 'sell-back' terms when the vehicles are replaced. This arrangement is also in the interests of the car manufacturers, who wish to maintain a degree of control over the sale of 'nearly new' vehicles and enjoy the benefits of market share publicity. The scale economies Avis is able to achieve as a result of its size further enable the company to secure attractive credit terms from financial institutions. These benefits of scale also impact on technology: the company invests significant sums in managing its databases, providing customers and agents with the latest e-commerce solutions, updating and harmonising its global websites, and creating effective CRM systems.

## The Car Rental Business

The companies operating in the car rental business can be divided into four groups:

1 companies such as Avis, Budget and Hertz, which operate internationally under a strong global brand
2 operators using a national or international brand name such as Europcar or United Kenning, including some manufacturers' dealers such as Ford Rent-A-Car and Vauxhall Rental, which hire out 'nearly new' fleet cars
3 local chains and franchises, such as Salford Van Hire
4 hundreds of independent operators, typically targeting more price-sensitive customers, and trading from one or two outlets.

Rivalry among competing car rental companies is intense. Perhaps the major difficulty operators face is that, to many renters, one car is much like another. Once rental companies have attempted to differentiate themselves on the basis of car age and make, which may be unimportant to the renter in any case, there are few tools left to use in the battle for customers. Not surprisingly, many operators are also reluctant to engage in a price war, despite the price sensitivity of renters – although the entry by easyJet offering cheap car rental added a new dimension to this sector. The fact that the largest operators are close together in terms of market share should come as no surprise.

## Avis's Market Segments

Avis's stated strategy is to achieve balanced geographic growth and a broad range of customers. The company believes such a situation provides the basis for sustainable market share gains. The four main customer segments are leisure (36 per cent of revenue), corporate (22 per cent), replacement (23 per cent) and premium (19 per cent).

- *Leisure*: travel companies, tour operators and consumers booking directly with Avis. Avis Europe has trading relationships with over 80 airlines, many railway networks and most leading travel companies.
- *Corporate*: large global corporations through to local small to medium-sized businesses. Avis is a dominant player in the provision of contracted vehicle rental programmes with larger businesses. Such customers demand a competitive product, speed and quality of service, and availability of management information and geographical coverage.
- *Replacement*: business in this segment stems from corporate long-term rental contracts, insurance and leasing companies.
- *Premium*: rentals with travel partnerships and customers who do not pre-reserve their rental.

A total of 61 per cent of Avis Europe's revenue is derived from domestic customers, 26 per cent from intra-Europe travellers and 13 per cent from long-haul travellers. Within Europe, France accounts for 20 per cent of Avis's revenue, Spain 17 per cent, Germany 15 per cent, Italy 14 per cent and the UK 14 per cent. These five countries' vehicle rentals add up to approximately €7 billion each year.

## Developing a Competitive Advantage

Developing a competitive advantage in this market is difficult. Even company size is no guarantee that Avis will be able to sustain its current position. While the company is among the world's largest car rental companies, leading rivals are never far behind. The largest car rental chains all renew their cars every four to six months, so it is not possible for Avis to differentiate its offering on the basis of the age or make of its vehicles. The company, like many others in the industry, is also reluctant to use price as a potential differentiator. Not surprisingly, in what is essentially a service business, Avis devotes considerable resources to providing efficient and friendly customer service.

Avis's emphasis on computer technology is an area in which the business has developed considerable strength and is now an important factor in its success. Increasing computer technology is seen as a way of reducing operating costs and generating increases in volume. The Avis IT system directly links nearly 15,000 terminals around the world, as well as interfacing with the airlines' computerised reservation systems. These links allow easier booking: customers can reserve a vehicle anywhere in the world from any one of the terminals available. In addition, the system offers more efficient check-in and check-out, easier tracking of vehicles and better price management. Avis's website permits customers to connect directly into its booking system, downloading price comparisons or vehicle availability information and making on-line bookings within seconds.

In addition to its strengths in computer technology, the company has a number of other important strengths that play a role in establishing its positioning in the market, including:

- the Avis global brand name, which offers the company a high level of buying power in its relationships with suppliers
- an extensive worldwide network of outlets, which allows customers easy access and makes it easier to build customer loyalty
- a high proportion of company owned – rather than franchised – outlets, which gives Avis a high level of control over operating and service standards.

**Note:** This case study was not prepared in conjunction with Avis and may not reflect the views of Avis.

## Questions for Discussion

1 What are Avis Europe's strengths? How does the company exploit these strengths to develop a competitive advantage?
2 How is the car rental market segmented and in what ways do the customers' needs differ in the key segments of leisure and corporate?
3 To what extent do the company's mission statement and values reflect a customer-facing ethos?

# II Understanding and Targeting Customers

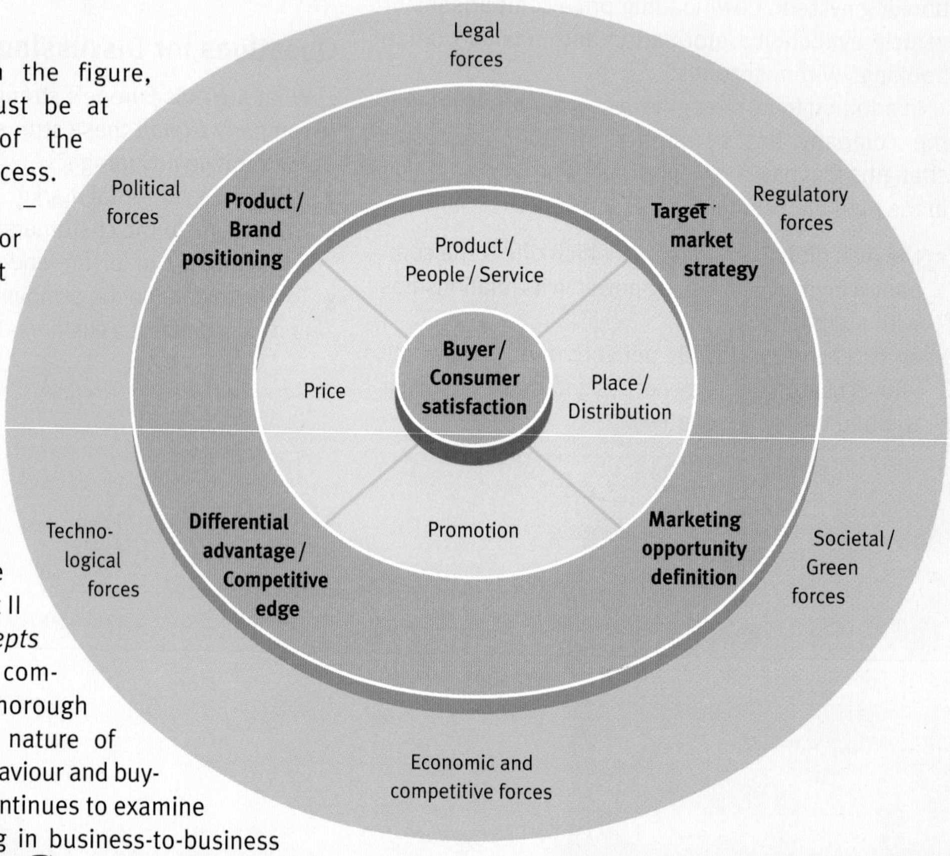


As outlined in the figure, customers must be at the centre of the marketing process. Organisations – whether for-profit or not-for-profit – must target specific groups of customers or stakeholders, understand their needs and endeavour through their marketing activities to satisfy these customer needs. Part II of *Marketing: Concepts and Strategies* commences with a thorough examination of the nature of consumer buying behaviour and buying processes, and continues to examine the nature of buying in business-to-business or organisational markets. Having developed an understanding of a marketplace and particularly the customers within it, marketers must then develop a marketing strategy. This should identify which customers they wish to target, what positioning they intend to use and which approach will provide an advantage over competitors. Part II includes, therefore, an examination of target market strategy selection and the all-important concept of market segmentation. There are times when managers' existing knowledge of their customers is sufficient for marketing decision-making, or when they are content to trust their intuition. On many occasions, however, marketers may not feel confident with the level of marketing intelligence available and will instigate research into the market in order to fill any gaps in their understanding of customers, competitors or market trends. The nature, uses and types of marketing research are introduced in the final chapter of Part II of *Marketing: Concepts and Strategies*.

**Part II of *Marketing: Concepts and Strategies*** examines buying behaviour for consumers and organisations, the issues concerned with target market strategy selection, and the nature and tools of marketing research.

**Chapter 6, 'Consumer Buying Behaviour'**, describes the different types of consumer buying behaviour, the stages of consumer buying decision-making and the different categories of buying decision. The chapter examines how personal, psychological and social factors influence the consumer buying decision process. Finally, Chapter 6 explains why marketers must understand consumer buying behaviour and use their understanding to determine marketing strategy. Having an understanding of customers' buying is fundamental to the marketing concept and to developing a marketing orientation.

**Chapter 7, 'Business Markets and Business Buying Behaviour'**, familiarises readers with the various types of business market, identifies the major characteristics of business-to-business buyers and transactions, outlines the attributes of business-to-business demand and presents the concept of the buying centre. The chapter emphasises the notion of relationship marketing and exchanges between business buyers and sellers. The focus then shifts to the stages of the business-to-business buying process and the factors that influence it. The chapter concludes by examining how to select and analyse business-to-business target markets. Marketers in business-to-business markets modify the marketing toolkit differently to marketers interacting with consumers: this theme is introduced in this chapter, but is explored more comprehensively in Part VII of *Marketing: Concepts and Strategies*.

**Chapter 8, 'Segmenting Markets, Targeting and Positioning'**, explains the core aspect of developing a marketing strategy: the process of target market strategy selection. The chapter commences by defining the concept of a market and outlining the various types of market. The focus then shifts to how organisations segment markets, how they make targeting decisions and prioritise target markets, and how they determine a brand or product positioning strategy for each segment selected as a target market. The chapter also highlights how important it is for an organisation to attempt to develop an edge over its competitors in the market(s) it has chosen to target, as explained in Chapter 2.

**Chapter 9, 'Marketing Research and Marketing Information Systems'**, explains the importance of research and information systems in marketing decision-making, distinguishes between research and intuition in solving marketing problems, and outlines the five basic steps for conducting formal marketing research. The fundamental methods of gathering data for marketing research are examined. The chapter then introduces the wide variety of marketing research tools available and explains their relative pros and cons.

By the conclusion of Part II of *Marketing: Concepts and Strategies*, readers should understand the concepts of buying behaviour in consumer and business-to-business markets, the fundamentals of target market strategy selection, and the nature and

## Tesco

Marketing – it's fundamental. But our definition of marketing is perhaps different to many other companies. First and foremost we think of marketing as looking after our customers. Our core purpose is to create value for customers to earn their lifetime loyalty. We do this by responding to the different and constantly changing needs of all of our customers to deliver what they want, when they want it. Marketing sets the customer priorities for the business and keeps us on track to deliver. It also guides our entry into new product areas and markets. From simplifying phone tariffs to opening convenience shops in Japan, we always start with understanding the customer.

The marketing discipline is absolutely vital to implementing and executing effective marketing strategies. Because the customer leads our business, marketing has to provide the insight and independence to help make the right decisions for them. In the last year alone, we have held over 200 'Customer Question Time' sessions in our stores, helping us to learn and understand what is important for customers. We would like all our customers to say that they feel welcome at Tesco, that they trust us and that we give them the best all-round shopping trip of all our competitors.

**Tim Mason, marketing director, Tesco**

Tesco is the market-leader supermarket retailer in the UK, with a significant presence in eastern Europe and South-east Asia.

# 6 Consumer Buying Behaviour

**"Anticipating consumer behaviour is not an option for marketing managers: it is their job description."**

*Gordon Foxall, Cardiff Business School, University of Wales*

## Objectives

- To understand the different types of consumer buying behaviour
- To recognise the stages of the consumer buying decision process and understand how this process relates to different types of buying decisions
- To explore how personal factors may affect the consumer buying decision process
- To learn about the psychological factors that may affect the consumer buying decision process
- To examine the social factors that influence the consumer buying decision process
- To understand why it is important for marketers to attempt to understand consumer buying behaviour and the role of this behaviour in marketing strategy

**Buying behaviour**
The decision processes and actions of people involved in buying and using products

**Consumer buying behaviour**
The buying behaviour of ultimate consumers – those who purchase products for personal or household use

## Introduction

The decision processes and actions of people involved in buying and using products are termed their **buying behaviour.**[1] **Consumer buying behaviour** is the buying behaviour of ultimate consumers – those who purchase products for personal or household use. Consumer buying behaviour is not concerned with the purchase of items for business use.

There are important reasons for marketers to analyse consumer buying behaviour. The success of a company's marketing strategy will depend on how buyers react to it. As Chapter 1 indicates, the marketing concept requires companies to develop a marketing mix that meets customers' needs. To find out what satisfies customers, marketers must examine the main influences on what, where, when and how consumers buy. Having a good understanding of these consumer buying behaviour factors enables marketers to satisfy customers better because they are able to develop more suitable marketing strategies. Ultimately, this information helps companies compete more effectively in the marketplace.

Although marketers try to understand and influence consumer buying behaviour, they cannot control it. Some critics credit them with the ability to manipulate buyers, but marketers have neither the power nor the knowledge to do so. Their knowledge of behaviour comes from what psychologists, social psychologists and sociologists know about human behaviour in general.

*Opener*

# Pester Power Hits Parents Everywhere

Pressure exerted by children on their parents while shopping has become widely known as 'pester power'. Certain products, such as snacks, training shoes, video games and leisure activities, are known to be particularly susceptible to this form of persuasion. How often when shopping in the supermarket have you heard a small child plaintively asking their parents to purchase a particular brand of breakfast cereal? In many cases the request may simply reflect the taste preferences of the child. However, research also suggests that these incidents are often triggered by an advertisement the child has seen on the television, or by a promotion the manufacturer is currently running.

Pester power was first mentioned back in 1979. Today it is widely recognised by many parents, even having its own definition: 'The ability children have to nag their parents into purchasing items they would otherwise not buy or performing actions they would otherwise not do' (www.wordspy.com). The fact that children influence the purchase decisions made by their parents is well established. In fact, this is just one of many influences on the buying decision processes of these individuals. A typical incidence of pester power starts when a child expresses interest in or requests the purchase of a product. This may take place at home, perhaps triggered by the viewing of a television or print advertisement. Perhaps it follows a discussion among classmates at school earlier in the day. In other cases the pestering starts in-store when a favoured brand is spotted on the supermarket shelves or in a shop window. Often a period of negotiation between the child and parent will follow. During this time the views of both parties will be discussed to a greater or lesser extent. This discussion may or may not result in a purchase being made.

Recently, pester power has attracted bad publicity due to increasing problems with childhood obesity. As snack foods are a key target for this kind of pestering, some health experts have criticised the marketing and advertising of unhealthy foodstuffs aimed at children. They point out that, in some countries, advertising aimed at children is banned. As a result of these emerging concerns many marketing practitioners are looking carefully at how their companies' products are marketed to youngsters. For example, Coca-Cola is carrying out its promise to stop advertising to those under the age of 12. As part of this initiative, the company has removed advertising images from vending machines in schools. At this time, a key challenge for marketers is the need to balance the desire to target children using certain kinds of marketing message with not antagonising their parents. Of course, pester power is not limited to foodstuffs. Children are increasingly playing a role in the decisions their families make about larger purchases such as holidays, the family car and even housing. Whatever the result of current initiatives to curtail some of the marketing activities aimed at kids, it seems that their influence in many buying decisions will remain.

**Sources:** David Murphy, 'Pester-free POP', *Marketing*, 11 March 2004, pp. 27–8; John Roedder, 'Consumer socialization of children: 25 years of research', Journal of Consumer Research, 1999, 26 (3), www.wordspy.com; www.foe.co.uk; James McNeal, *Kids as Customers*, 1992, Lexington Books. Photo: Courtesy of Art Explosion, Nova Development

Throughout their lives consumers purchase numerous products of different kinds. In most families, children play an important role in a wide range of these purchase decisions. Given their role it is not surprising that manufacturers and retailers go to such trouble in their marketing efforts to influence these young consumers. However, the views of the kids are just one of many influences that shape the consumer buying process. These influences on what and how consumers buy are considered in more detail later in this chapter.

This chapter begins by examining the types of decision-making in which consumers engage. It then analyses the major stages of the consumer buying decision process and the personal, psychological and social factors that influence it. The chapter concludes by examining why marketers must develop a good understanding of consumer buying behaviour. The buying behaviour of organisations – business-to-business buying – is discussed in the following chapter.

**Routine response behaviour** Behaviour that occurs when buying frequently purchased, low-cost, low-risk items that need little search and decision effort

**Limited decision-making** Behaviour that occurs when buying products purchased only occasionally, for which a moderate amount of information gathering and deliberation is needed

## Types of Consumer Buying Behaviour

Different consumers have a varied and wide range of needs and wants. The acquisition of products and services helps these consumers to satisfy their current and future needs. To achieve this objective, consumers make many purchasing decisions. For example, people make many decisions daily regarding food, clothing, shelter, medical care, education, recreation or transport. When making these decisions, they engage in decision-making behaviour. The amount of time and effort, both mental and physical, that buyers expend in decision-making varies considerably from situation to situation – and from consumer to consumer. Consumer decisions can thus be classified into one of three broad categories: routine response behaviour, limited decision-making and extensive decision-making.[2]

### Routine Response Behaviour

A consumer practises **routine response behaviour** when buying frequently purchased, low-cost, low-risk items that need very little search and decision effort. When buying such items, a consumer may prefer a particular brand, but will probably be familiar with several brands in the product class and view more than one as acceptable. The products a consumer buys through routine response behaviour are purchased almost automatically. For most buyers, the time and effort involved in selecting a bag of sugar or a bar of soap is minimal. If the supermarket has run out of the preferred brand, the buyers will probably choose an alternative brand instead.

### Limited Decision-making

Buyers engage in **limited decision-making** when they buy products occasionally and when they need to obtain information about an unfamiliar brand in a familiar product category. This type of decision-making requires a moderate amount of time for information gathering and deliberation. For example, if Nintendo launches a new computer game aimed at teenagers, buyers may seek additional information about the new product, perhaps by asking a friend who has tested the game or seen it reviewed. Similarly, if a well-known brand appears in a new form, the consumer will take extra time.

### Extensive Decision-making

The most complex decision-making behaviour, **extensive decision-making**, comes into play when a purchase involves unfamiliar, expensive, high-risk or infrequently bought products – for instance, cars, homes, holidays or personal pensions. The buyer uses many criteria to evaluate alternative brands or choices, and takes time seeking information and comparing alternative brands before making the purchase decision.

**Impulse buying** Behaviour that involves no conscious planning but results from a powerful, persistent urge to buy something immediately

**Impulse Buying** By contrast, **impulse buying** involves no conscious planning but a powerful, persistent urge to buy something immediately. Self-control failure is one factor that appears to affect whether or not consumers indulge in this kind of buying.[3] As the Innovation and Change box on page 163 explains, research suggests that consumers are increasingly engaging in

## Innovation and Change

### Impulse Shopping on the Increase

How often have you come back from a shopping expedition with more items than you planned to buy? If the answer is 'usually', then you are not alone! Consumers are apparently becoming increasingly impulsive in their shopping behaviour. People are now more likely than ever to buy items on impulse when they go out shopping. The trend is away from the carefully planned shopping trips and routine saving of spare income of the past. Recent research highlights that over the last 20 years consumer attitudes toward impulse buying have shifted. Figures for the purchase of clothing, food, toiletries, mobile phones and home electronics all suggest increasing levels of buying on impulse. However, the extent of impulse shopping in these categories varies, with consumers being much more likely to buy clothing or food on impulse than mobile phones or other electrical goods. This apparently relates to the level of pre-planning involved in different kinds of purchases. Thus shoppers are more likely to impulse buy less complex or routinely purchased products. Ready meals, snacks, cosmetics and magazines are just a few of the typical purchases.

Different consumers vary in their levels of impulse buying. Research suggests that the impulse buying trait is particularly marked among young consumers and those in the 55–64 age range. One of the reasons for the trend might be rising disposable income, as these groups are known to have relatively high levels of spare income once day-to-day expenses have been met. Experts suggest that other influential factors are the ready availability of credit, increasingly well-designed and tempting retail environments, and a greater emphasis on shopping as a leisure activity. The ease with which consumers can acquire store payment cards and the widespread promotion of personal loans mean that even those with restricted incomes can indulge in such impromptu buying behaviour. Enticing retail design and greater variety on the high street contribute to the notion of shopping as a leisure activity. Many consumers enjoy the opportunity to meet up with friends or family, and spend time perusing the products and brands in their local shopping centres. Some are prepared to travel further afield to larger towns or shopping villages to maximise the leisure experience. Recent research highlights the connection between this kind of enjoyment and the propensity to impulse buy, showing that consumers are more likely to make unplanned purchases when they have enjoyed the shopping experience.

The implications of these trends for marketing practitioners and retailers are far-reaching. If consumers are devoting less attention to advance planning in favour of more impulse buying, the retail environment will become more important than ever in shaping the buying decisions that are made. One outcome might be that balance of marketing spend will shift away from traditional media and towards in-store promotions. For example, recent initiatives to introduce in-store television and radio into supermarkets and department stores typify some of the possible developments in this area. Part of the rationale is that consumers walking into the likes of Tesco, Sainsbury's and Carrefour are already in shopping mode and are therefore likely to be receptive to these kinds of media. Retail experts believe that one of the keys to success will be to design content that dovetails with the shopping experience in which the consumer is engaged. Thus short, snappy commercials will be favoured over longer 30-second formats.

**Sources:** Caroline Parry, 'Enthusiastic for listless shopping', *Marketing Week*, 4 March 2004, pp. 30–1; Amanda Wilkinson, 'Box on shelf on box on ...', *Marketing Week*, 26 February 2004, pp. 24–7.

impulse buying. For some individuals, impulse buying may be the dominant buying behaviour. Impulse buying, however, often provokes emotional conflict. For example, a young woman buying a new outfit for clubbing, may later regret the expense because a friend has purchased the same item. Marketers often capitalise on the tendency towards impulse buying – for example, by placing magazines and confectionery next to supermarket checkout counters.

## Variations in Decision-making Behaviour

The purchase of a particular product does not always elicit the same type of decision-making behaviour.[4] In some instances, buyers engage in extensive decision-making the first time they purchase a certain kind of product but find that limited decision-making suffices when they

**Extensive decision-making**
Behaviour that occurs when a purchase involves unfamiliar, expensive, high-risk or infrequently bought products for which the buyer spends much time seeking information and comparing brands before deciding on the purchase

**Consumer buying decision process**
A five-stage process that includes problem recognition, information search, evaluation of alternatives, purchase and post-purchase evaluation

buy the product again. If a routinely purchased brand no longer pleases the consumer, either limited or extensive decision processes may be used to switch to a new brand. For example, if the video tapes a family usually buys are too easily damaged, a better-quality brand may be sought in the future.

## The Consumer Buying Decision Process

A major part of buying behaviour is the decision process used in making purchases. The **consumer buying decision process**, shown in Figure 6.1, includes five stages:

1 problem recognition
2 information search
3 evaluation of alternatives
4 purchase
5 post-purchase evaluation.

Although a detailed understanding of these stages is needed, a number of general observations are also pertinent. First, the actual act of purchasing is only one stage in the process; the process begins several stages before the purchase itself. Second, not all decision processes lead to a purchase, even though the diagrammatical process implies that they do. A consumer may stop the process at any time. It is also possible that a different sequence of stages will be followed, with buyers revisiting certain stages. Finally, consumer decisions do not always include all five stages. People engaged in extensive decision-making usually go through all stages of this decision process, whereas those engaged in limited decision-making and routine response behaviour may omit certain parts.

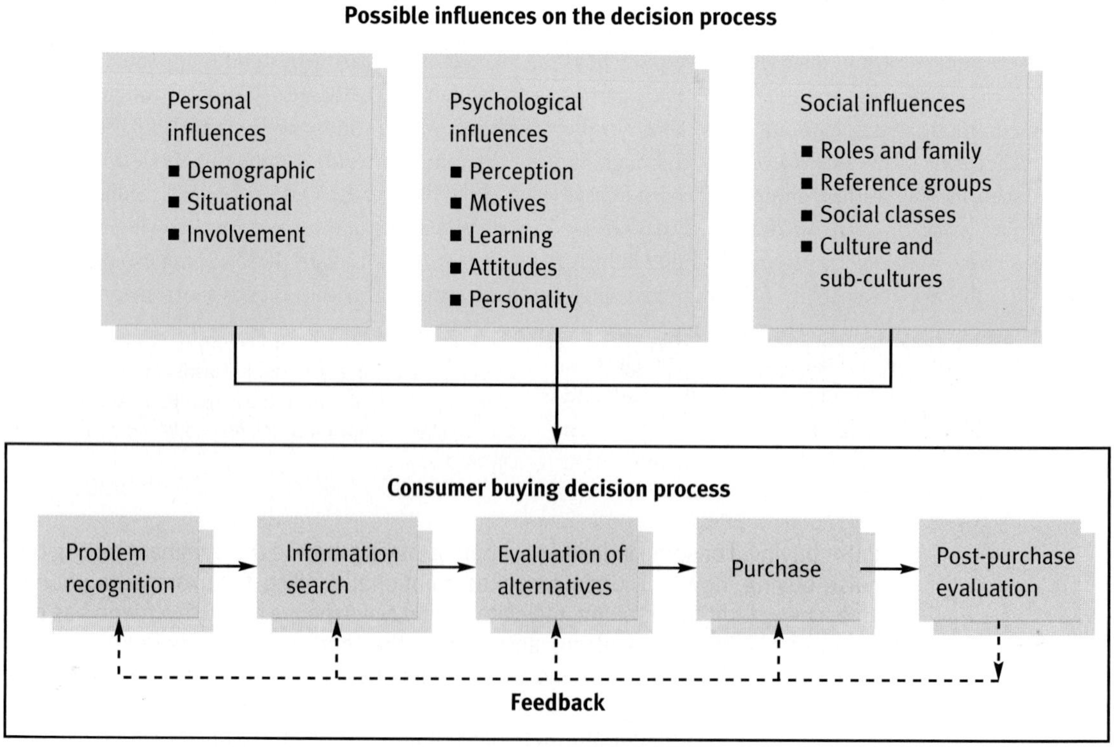


***Figure 6.1***
*The consumer buying decision process and possible influences on the process*

**Stage 1: Problem Recognition**

Problem recognition occurs when a buyer becomes aware that there is a difference between a desired state and an actual condition. For example, consider a sales manager who needs to keep a record of appointments. When, at the end of the year, her old diary is finished, she recognises that a difference exists between the desired state (a current diary) and the actual condition (an out-of-date one). She therefore makes the decision to buy a new diary.

Sometimes a person has a problem or need but is unaware of it. Some consumers may be concerned about their weight but may not be aware that Hellmann's has introduced a low-calorie mayonnaise. Marketers use sales staff, advertising, sales promotion and packaging to help trigger such need recognition. For example, travel agents may advertise package holidays immediately after the Christmas and New Year holidays. People who see the advertisements may realise that now is a good time to plan their summer holidays. The speed of consumer problem recognition can be either slow or rapid, depending on the individual concerned and the way in which need recognition was triggered.

***Figure 6.2***
*Along with the web, travel agents provide a valuable source of information for consumers selecting a holiday*
*Photo © Royalty-Free/CORBIS*

## Stage 2: Information Search

After recognising the problem or need, the buyer (if continuing the decision process) searches for information about products that will resolve the problem or satisfy the need. For example, after people have recognised the need to plan their holiday, they may search for information about different tour operators, travel options and possible locations. Information is acquired over time from the consumer's surroundings and, ever more frequently, on the Internet. The impact the information has will depend on how the consumer interprets it.

**Internal search**
One in which the buyer searches his or her memory for information about products

**External search**
One that focuses on information not available from the consumer's memory

There are two aspects to information search. In the **internal search**, buyers search their memory for information about products that might solve the problem. If they cannot retrieve enough information from their memory to make a decision, they seek additional information in an **external search**. The external search may involve communicating with friends and colleagues, comparing available brands and prices, or reviewing television or press advertisements, and public sources including the Internet. An individual's personal contacts – friends, relatives, associates – are often viewed as credible sources of information because the consumer trusts and respects them. A consumer study has shown that word-of-mouth communication often impacts more strongly on consumer judgements of products than printed communications. Using marketer-dominated information sources, such as sales staff, advertising, packaging, in-store demonstrations and displays, typically does not require much effort on the consumer's part. Buyers can also obtain information from public sources – for instance, government reports, news stories, the Internet, consumer publications and reports from product testing organisations. Many companies use public relations to try to capitalise on these sources because consumers often perceive them as factual and unbiased. The external search is also characterised by the extensiveness, manner and order in which brands, stores, attributes and sources are considered. For example, a man buying a new suit for work may look at or try on several styles at a number of clothing outlets before reaching a final decision.

Consumer groups are increasingly demanding access to greater quantities of relevant product information. However, research shows that buyers make poorer choices if overloaded with too much information.[5] Improving the quality of information and stressing features important to buyers in the decision process may help buyers make better purchase decisions.

How consumers use and process the information obtained in their search depends on features of the information itself, namely availability, quantity, quality, repetition and format. If all the necessary information for a decision is available in the store, consumers may have no need to conduct an internal information search and the decision process may be easier.[6] However, adequate information may not always be available, and consumers may have to make do with whatever data are to hand. For example, a motorist replacing a broken windscreen following a road accident may not have enough time to review all relevant sources of information because the car is needed again urgently.

**Repetition** Repetition, a technique well known to advertisers, increases consumer learning of information. When seeing or hearing an advertisement for the first time, the recipient may not grasp all its important details but learns more as the message is repeated. Nevertheless, even when commercials are initially effective, repetition eventually causes 'wear-out': consumers pay less attention and respond less favourably to the advertisement than they did at first.[7] Consumers are more likely to be receptive to repetition when making a low-involvement purchase. **Involvement** refers to the level of interest, emotion and activity the consumer is prepared to expend on a particular purchase. For example, a consumer who buys a box of light bulbs may have very low interest in the product itself but may elect to buy the particular brand because it has been discounted.

**Involvement**
The level of interest, emotion and activity the consumer is prepared to expend on a particular purchase

**Format** The format in which information is transmitted to the buyer may also determine its effectiveness. Information can be presented verbally, numerically or visually. Consumers often remember pictures better than words, and the combination of pictures and words further enhances learning.[8] Consequently, marketers pay great attention to the visual components of their advertising materials.

**Evoked set**
The group of products that a buyer views as possible alternatives after conducting an information search

A successful information search yields a group of possible brand alternatives. This group of products is sometimes called the buyer's **evoked set**. For example, an evoked set of compact disc players might be those manufactured by Sony, Aiwa, JVC and Philips.

## Stage 3: Evaluation of Alternatives

When evaluating the products in the evoked set, a buyer establishes criteria for comparing the products. These criteria are the characteristics or features that the buyer wants (or does not want). For example, one buyer may favour a mobile phone with blue-tooth technology, whereas another may require a model with a flap, but be unwilling to pay a premium for blue tooth. The buyer also assigns a certain **salience**, or level of importance, to each criterion; some features carry more weight than others. The salience of criteria varies from buyer to buyer. For example, when choosing a newspaper one buyer may consider the political stance of the editorial to be crucial, while another may place greater importance on the quality and coverage of sports. The criteria and their salience are used by the buyer to rank the brands in the evoked set. This involves comparing the brands with each other as well as with the criteria. If the evaluation stage does not yield a brand that the buyer wishes to buy, further information search may be necessary.

**Salience**
The level of importance a buyer assigns to each criterion for comparing products

Marketers can influence consumers' evaluation by *framing* the alternatives – that is, by the manner in which the alternative and its attributes are described. Framing can make a characteristic seem more important and can facilitate its recall from memory. For example, by emphasising whitening ingredients in toothpaste, manufacturers can encourage the consumer to consider this particular aspect to be important. Framing affects the decision processes of inexperienced buyers more than those of experienced ones. If the evaluation of alternatives yields one or more brands that the consumer is willing to buy, the consumer is ready to move on to the next stage of the decision process: the purchase.

## Stage 4: Purchase

The purchase stage, when the consumer chooses which product or brand to buy, is mainly the outcome of the consumer's evaluation of alternatives, but other factors have an impact, too. The closeness of alternative stores and product availability can both influence which brand is purchased. For example, if the brand the buyer ranked highest is not available locally, an alternative may be selected.

During this stage, the buyer also picks the seller from whom the product will be purchased and finalises the terms of the sale. Other issues such as price, delivery, guarantees, service agreements, installation and credit arrangements are discussed and settled. Finally, provided the consumer does not terminate the buying decision process before then, the purchase is made.

## Stage 5: Post-purchase Evaluation

After the purchase has taken place, the buyer begins evaluating the product to check whether its actual performance meets expected levels. Many of the criteria used in evaluating alternatives are revisited during this stage. The outcome will determine whether the consumer is satisfied or dissatisfied, and will influence future behaviour. The level of satisfaction a consumer experiences will determine whether they make a complaint, communicate with other possible buyers or purchase the product again.[9] The extent to which consumers are angered by the outcome of a purchase also influences how they will behave in the future.[10] Figure 6.3 illustrates the types of action that dissatisfied consumers may take. The likelihood that consumers will stop buying a particular product will depend on a range of factors, including how much knowledge they have about alternatives.[11] Some marketing experts believe that increasing consumer assertiveness is a positive move, which illustrates industry's willingness to respond to feedback about products and services.[12] The impact of post-purchase evaluation is illustrated by the feedback loop in Figure 6.1.

*Figure 6.3*
*The nature of customer complaints*
*Source: Neill Denny, 'Why complaining is our new hobby', from* Marketing Magazine, *26 November 1998, p. 16. Reprinted with permission*

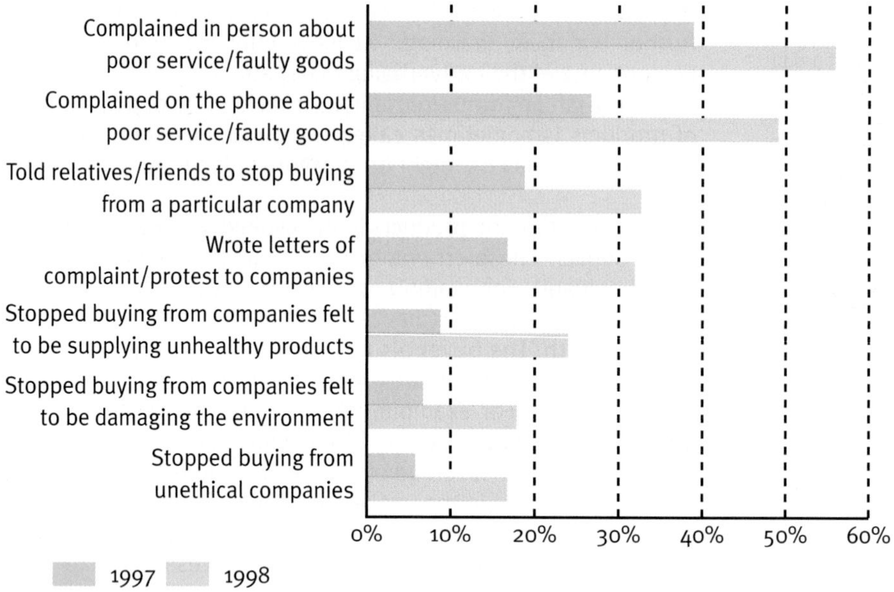


**Cognitive dissonance** Doubts that occur as the buyer questions whether he or she made the right decision in purchasing the product

The evaluation that follows the purchase of some products, particularly expensive or important items, may result in **cognitive dissonance** – doubts that occur because the buyer questions whether the best purchase decision was made. For example, after buying a new personal computer, an accountant may feel anxious about whether the brand will be reliable or if the warranty is adequate. A buyer who experiences cognitive dissonance may attempt to return the product or may seek positive information about it to justify the choice. For example, motoring journalists often note with amusement that car shows and exhibitions are frequented by consumers who have recently purchased a new car.

As shown in Figure 6.1, three major categories of influence are believed to affect the consumer buying decision process: personal, psychological and social factors. These factors determine which particular instant coffee, shampoo, washing powder, DVD player, holiday, car or house a particular consumer will buy. Understanding these aspects helps marketers gain valuable insights into their customer base and can help ensure that a more suitable marketing mix is developed. The remainder of this chapter focuses on these factors. Although each major factor is discussed separately, it is a combination of their effects that influences the consumer buying decision process.

# Personal Factors Influencing the Buying Decision Process

**Personal influencing factors** Factors unique to a particular individual

**Personal influencing factors** are unique to a particular person. Many different personal factors can influence purchasing decisions. In this section, three types are considered: demographic factors, situational factors and level of involvement.

## Demographic Factors

**Demographic factors** are individual characteristics such as age, sex, race, ethnic origin, income, family life cycle and occupation. (These and other characteristics are discussed in Chapter 8 as possible segmentation variables.) Given the potential impact of such features on buying requirements and behaviour, marketing professionals must develop a clear understanding of such characteristics.

Demographic factors have a bearing on who is involved in family decision-making. For example, it is estimated that in the next few years the UK, Germany and Turkey will have

**Demographic factors** Individual characteristics such as age, sex, race, ethnic origin, income, family life cycle and occupation

the largest market for children's toys and clothes in the EU, based on the number of children in the population. Children aged 6 to 17 are known to have growing influence in the buying decision process for breakfast cereals, ice cream, soft drinks, holidays and even the family car.[13] This influence is increasingly reflected in the way such products are designed and marketed. For example, holiday brochures now contain pictures and information designed to appeal to children and teenagers. Demographic factors may also shape behaviour during a specific stage of the decision process. For example, during information search, a young person may consult a greater number of information sources than an older, more experienced adult.

Demographic factors also affect the manner in which products in a specific product category are used. While consumers aged 18 to 30 may spend a lot of their disposable income on necessities for establishing their households, such as furniture, appliances and DIY products, those aged 45 to 54 whose children have left home spend more on luxury and leisure items.[14] Brand preferences, store choice and timing of purchases are also affected by demographic factors. Consider, for example, how differences in occupation result in variations in product needs. A car mechanic and a nanny may earn similar incomes, yet spend their earnings entirely differently. While both require work clothes to carry out their jobs, the mechanic will buy heavy-duty boots and overalls, while the nanny opts for a smart, more formal uniform. Their choice of vehicle will also be quite different. While the mechanic selects a basic but robust van, the nanny buys a small four-door hatchback with room for her charges and a pushchair. Thus occupation clearly affects consumer buying behaviour.

## Situational Factors

**Situational factors** External circumstances or conditions that exist when a consumer is making a purchase decision

**Situational factors** are the external circumstances or conditions that exist when a consumer is making a purchase decision. These factors can influence the buyer at any stage of the consumer buying decision process and may cause the individual to shorten, lengthen or terminate the process. For example, a school teacher who usually commutes to work by car may be forced to travel by train while her car is being serviced. Similarly, a family holiday may have to be postponed if the children fall ill with chickenpox.

The effects of situational factors can be felt throughout the buying decision process. Uncertainty about employment may sway a consumer against making a purchase. On the other hand, a conviction that the supply of a particular product is sharply limited may impel an individual to buy it. For example, consumers have purchased and hoarded petrol, food products and even toilet tissue when these products were believed to be in short supply. These and other situational factors can change rapidly; their influence on purchase decisions is generally as sudden as it is short-lived.

The amount of time a consumer has available to make a decision strongly influences buying decisions. If there is little time for selecting and purchasing a product, an individual may quickly decide to buy a readily available brand. The time available also affects the way consumers process the information contained in advertisements[15] and the length of the stages within the decision process. For example, if a family is planning to redecorate their house, everyone may get together to collect and review a wide range of information from a variety of sources. They may read home and garden magazines, visit DIY outlets to collect paint charts and wallpaper samples, talk to friends and decorators, look at a number of advertisements and spend time comparing special offers in a number of stores. However, if the family is hit by a house fire that destroys the existing decorations in the house, the extent of the information search, the number of alternatives considered and the amount of comparative shopping may be much more restricted.

## Levels of Involvement

Many aspects of consumer buying decisions are affected by the individual's **level of involvement**. This term refers to the level of interest, emotional commitment and time spent searching for a product in a particular situation. The level of involvement determines the extent to which a buyer is motivated to spend time seeking information about a particular product or brand. The extensiveness of the buying decision process therefore varies

**Level of involvement** The level of interest, emotional commitment and time spent searching for a product in a particular situation

greatly with the consumer's level of involvement. The sequence of the steps in the process may also be altered. Low-involvement buyers may form an attitude towards a product – perhaps as a result of an advertising campaign – and evaluate its features after purchasing it rather than before.[16] Conversely, high-involvement buyers often spend a great deal of time and effort researching their purchase beforehand. For example, the purchase of a car is a high-involvement decision.

The level of consumer involvement is linked to a number of factors. Consumers tend to be more involved in the purchase of high-priced goods and products that are visible to others, such as clothing, white goods or cars. As levels of perceived risk increase, involvement levels are likely to rise.

**Enduring Involvement** Sometimes individuals experience enduring involvement with a product class. Enduring involvement is an ongoing interest in a product class because of personal relevance. For example, people often have enduring involvement with products

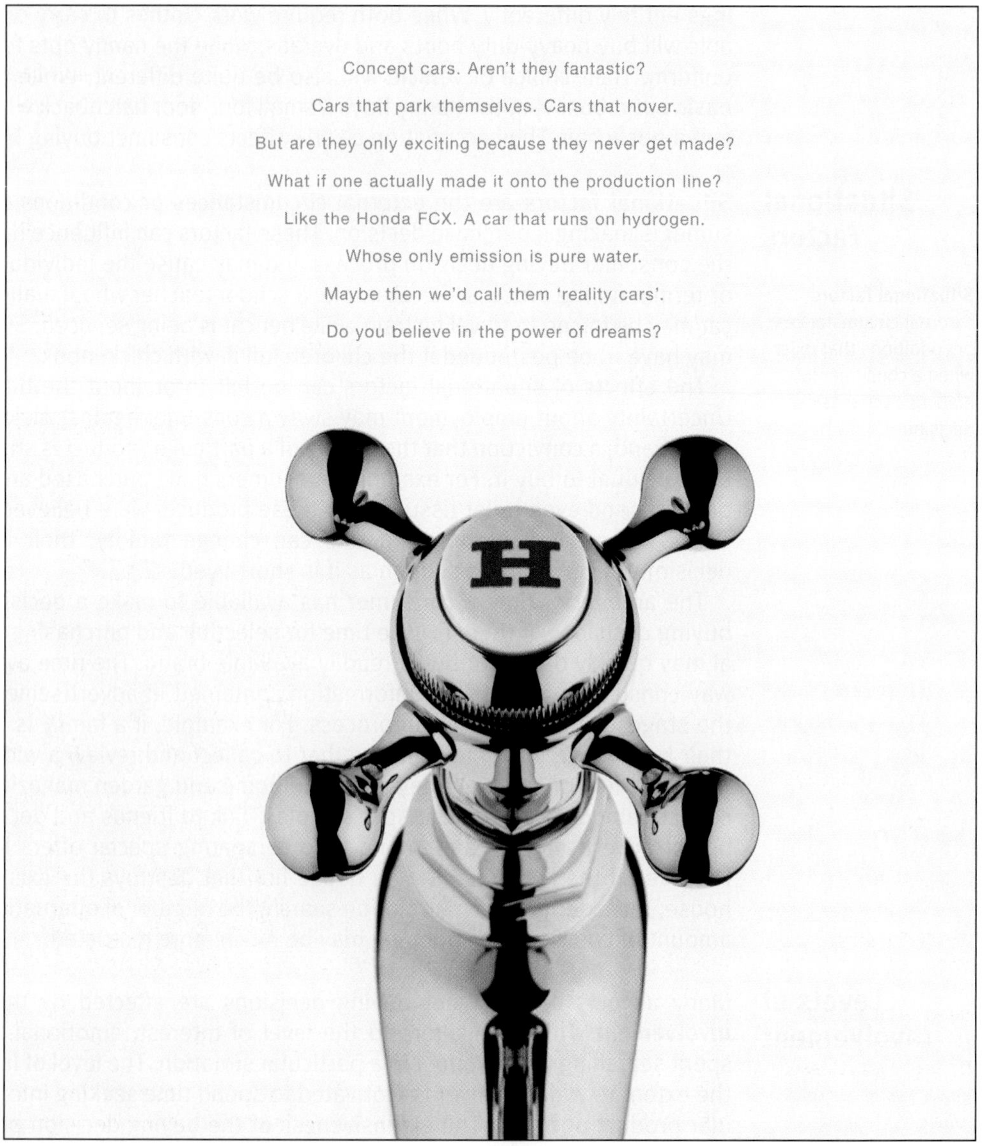


*Figure 6.4*
*The purchase of a car is high involvement, particularly for those utilising unfamiliar and innovative energy solutions*
*Source: Courtesy of Wieden & Kennedy*

associated with their leisure activities. These individuals engage in ongoing search and information gathering for these products over extensive periods of time, irrespective of whether or not a purchase is imminent. Football fans often watch the sport on television, attend their local club's games, read the football pages of the newspaper and may even buy their favourite team's football strip.

**Situational Involvement** Situational involvement is experienced by buyers as a result of the particular circumstance or environment in which they find themselves. This type of involvement, sometimes also called pre-purchase involvement, is temporary because the conditions that triggered this high involvement may change.[17] A man searching for an engagement ring for his prospective fiancée, for example, will probably experience a high level of involvement in the purchase decision. His information search and evaluation of alternatives may be lengthy. However, once the choice is made, an engagement ring is probably no longer personally relevant.

**Low Consumer Involvement** Many purchase decisions do not generate much consumer involvement. When the involvement level is low, as with routine response purchases, the buying is almost automatic, and the information search and evaluation of alternatives are extremely limited. Thus the purchase of floor cleaner is low involvement for many consumers; the product is chosen out of habit and with minimal effort.

## Psychological Factors Influencing the Buying Decision Process

**Psychological factors**
Factors that influence consumer behaviour, including perception, motives, learning, attitudes and personality

**Psychological factors** operating within individuals partly determine people's general behaviour and thus influence their behaviour as consumers. The primary psychological influences on consumer behaviour are:

- perception
- motives
- learning
- attitudes
- personality.

Even though these psychological factors operate internally, it will become apparent later in this chapter that they are highly affected by social forces external to the individual.

*Figure 6.5*
*Fish or birds? Do you see the fish changing into birds or the birds changing into fish?*
*Source: M.C. Escher's "Fish and Birds" © 2004 The M.C. Escher Company – Baarn – Holland. All rights reserved.*

### Perception

**Perception**
The process of selecting, organising and interpreting information inputs to produce meaning

**Information inputs**
The sensations received through sight, taste, hearing, smell and touch

In Figure 6.5, are the fish changing into birds or is it the other way round? It could be either depending on how you perceive it. People's perception of the same thing varies. Similarly, the same individual at different times may perceive the same item in a number of ways. **Perception** involves a three-step process of selecting, organising and interpreting information inputs to produce meaning. **Information inputs** are the sensations received through sight, taste, hearing, smell and touch. Each time we see an advertisement, go on-line, visit shops or use a product, we receive information inputs.

The first step of the perceptual process is the selection of information. Individuals receive numerous pieces of information all the time, yet only a few of these reach awareness. Certain inputs are selected while others are ignored. **Selective exposure** occurs because consumers cannot be conscious of all inputs at the same time, and involves the selection of inputs that are to be exposed to awareness. A student word-processing a report may be unaware that the light is on, that the computer is making a humming sound, that there is background noise in the room or that other students are working at the same table. All of these inputs are being received, but the student will ignore them unless their attention is specifically drawn to them.

**Selective exposure**
The selection of inputs that people expose to their awareness

An input is more likely to reach awareness if it relates to an anticipated event or relates to current needs. If a violent storm has damaged the roof of a couple's house, they are much more likely to notice a local newspaper advertisement promoting a building and repairs service. Similarly, hungry people are more likely to notice a KFC sign than are those who are not. Finally, an input is more likely to be noticed if its intensity changes significantly. Consumers are much more likely to notice if a furniture store cuts its prices by half than if the same store offers a much smaller reduction.

The selective nature of perception leads to two other conditions: selective distortion and selective retention. **Selective distortion** is the changing or twisting of currently received information. This sometimes happens when someone receives information that is inconsistent with personal feelings or beliefs. For example, an individual who reads some favourable publicity about a company he or she dislikes is likely to distort the information to make it more consistent with personally held views. The publicity may therefore have greater impact on another consumer who views the same brand more positively. **Selective retention** means that an individual remembers information inputs that support personal feelings and beliefs, and forgets inputs that do not. After hearing a sales presentation and leaving the shop, a customer may forget many of the selling points if they contradict pre-existing beliefs.

**Selective distortion**
The changing or twisting of currently received information

**Selective retention**
The process of remembering information inputs that support personal feelings and beliefs, and of forgetting those that do not

The information inputs that do reach awareness are not received in an organised form. For them to be meaningful, an individual must enter the second step of the perceptual process – organising and integrating the new information with that already stored in the memory. Although this step is usually carried out quickly, it may take longer when the individual is considering an unfamiliar product area.

Interpretation – the third step in the perceptual process – is the assignment of meaning to what has been organised. All consumers base their interpretation on what is familiar, on knowledge already stored in memory. For this reason, a company that changes a package design or logo faces a major problem. Since people look for the product in the old, familiar package, they may not recognise it in the new one. Unless a package or logo change is accompanied by a promotional programme making people aware of the change, a company may lose sales. Even when such a programme is conducted, positive reaction from the consumer cannot be guaranteed. For example, when British Airways changed its corporate identity and redesigned its aeroplane tail fins to reflect themes from around the world, consumer reaction to the reduction in the company's overt Britishness was mixed. Companies often try to get around this difficulty by making only small changes to their logo or brand identity.

Although marketers cannot control people's perceptions, they often try to influence them. This may be difficult to achieve for a number of reasons. First, a consumer's perceptual process may prevent the information from being received. Second, a buyer may receive the information but perceive it differently from the way that was intended. For example, when an anti-wrinkle face cream manufacturer advertises that '80 per cent of consumers using this product notice a reduction in wrinkles', a customer might infer that 20 per cent of the people who use the product have more wrinkles. Third, buyers who perceive information inputs to be inconsistent with their personally held beliefs tend to forget the information quickly. Sometimes consumers can be overwhelmed by the large number of information inputs they encounter, making it difficult to interpret the information.[18] For example, a student travelling by bus to college may pass more than 30 different advertising hoardings, but notice only one or two.

**Self-concept**
A person's perception of himself or herself; self-image

In addition to perceptions about packages, products, brands and organisations, individuals also have self-perceptions. These perceptions are known as the **self-concept** or self-image. It seems likely that a person's self-concept affects purchase decisions and consumption behaviour. The results of some studies suggest that buyers purchase products that reflect and enhance their self-concepts. For instance, one man might buy a Boss suit to project a sophisticated and businesslike image, while another might buy an outfit from Gap to enhance acceptability within their peer group.

## Motives

**Motive**
An internal, energy-giving force that directs a person's activities towards satisfying a need or achieving a goal

A **motive** is an internal, energy-giving force that directs an individual's activities towards satisfying a need or achieving a goal. Motivation is the set of mechanisms for controlling movement towards goals.[19] At any time a buyer's actions are affected by a set of motives rather than by just one. These motives are unique to the individual and to the situation. At any point in time some motives in the set will have priority. For example, someone's motives for taking a shower are particularly strong after a trip to the gym. Motivation affects the direction and intensity of behaviour, as individuals must choose which goals to pursue at a particular time.

**Patronage motives**
Those motives that influence where a person purchases products on a regular basis

Motives influencing where a person regularly purchases products are called patronage motives. A buyer may use a particular shop because of **patronage motives** such as price, service, location, honesty, product variety or friendliness of sales staff. Marketers seeking to capitalise on these motives should determine why regular customers patronise a store and then emphasise these characteristics in the store's marketing mix.

Motivation research can be used to analyse the major motives that influence whether consumers buy particular products. However, some of these motives are subconscious and people are therefore unaware of them. As a consequence, marketers cannot always elicit these motives through direct questioning. Most motivation research therefore relies on interviews or projective techniques.

**In-depth interview**
The collection of data from an individual by interview

**Focus group**
A semi-structured discussion involving six to twelve people, led by a moderator

Researchers using interviews to study motives may use individual **in-depth interviews**, focus groups or a combination of the two. In an in-depth interview, the researcher encourages the subject to talk freely about general topics before focusing the discussion on the areas of interest. In a process that may last for several hours, the interviewer can then probe the subject's answers for clarification. In a **focus group**, the moderator – through leadership that appears to be not highly structured – tries to generate discussion about one or several topics in a group of six to twelve people. Through what is said in the discussion, the moderator attempts to discover people's motives relating to some issue such as the use of a product. The researcher usually cannot probe as far in a focus group as in an in-depth interview, and some products may not be suitable for such group discussion. To determine successfully the subconscious motives reflected in the interviews, motivation researchers must have certain qualities: they must be perceived as non-threatening by members of the group, must be able to adopt a demeanour appropriate to the characteristics of those in the group and must be well trained in clinical psychology. The use of sound and video recordings can simplify the process of analysis. Both in-depth and focus-group techniques can yield a variety of information. For example, they may help marketers discover why customers continue to buy and smoke cigarettes despite being aware of the profound health risks.

**Projective techniques**
Tests in which subjects are asked to perform specific tasks for particular reasons, while actually being evaluated for other purposes

**Projective techniques** are tests in which subjects are asked to perform specific tasks for particular reasons, while actually being evaluated for other purposes. Such tests are based on the assumption that subjects will unconsciously 'project' their motives through the tasks they perform. Researchers trained in projective techniques can analyse the results and make predictions about the subject's subconscious motives. Common types

***Figure 6.6***
*Discussing customers' buying decision-making, perceptions and attitudes is an important aspect of the marketer's role*
*Photo © Helen King/CORBIS*

of projective technique include word association tests, sentence completion tests and bubble drawings. These are illustrated in Figure 6.7. Such tests can be useful to marketers in a number of ways, such as helping to make advertising more effective.[20]

The complexity of motivation research means that marketers wishing to research people's motives should employ the services of professional psychologists with specific skills in the area.[21]

## Learning

**Learning**
Changes in a person's behaviour caused by information and experience

**Learning** refers to changes in behaviour caused by information and experience. The consequences of behaviour strongly influence the learning process. Thus behaviour resulting in satisfying consequences tends to be repeated. For example, if a consumer buys a hair gel that he believes makes him appear more fashionable, he is more likely to buy the same brand next time. In fact, he may continue to purchase the brand until he is no longer satisfied with it. If the consumer's hair subsequently starts to look out of condition, he may switch allegiance to an alternative brand.

***Figure 6.7***
*Common types of projective technique*

**Word association tests**

Subjects are asked to say what words come into their minds when a particular topic/product is mentioned.

| Fresh foods are . . . | Frozen foods are . . . |
|---|---|
| Natural | Processed |
| Fresh | Quick |
| Healthy | Simple |
| Expensive | Convenient |
| Good for you | Preservatives |
| Real | Manufactured |

**Sentence completion tests**

Subjects are asked to complete the sentences.

'People who use recycled toilet tissue . . .'
'People who look for the ingredients on packets before they buy them are . . .'
'People who buy Swatch watches . . .'

**Bubble drawings**

Subjects are asked to say what the man is thinking.

The ability of buyers to process information when making purchasing decisions varies. For example, when purchasing a computer, a well-educated potential buyer who has experience with computers may be able to read, comprehend and synthesise the considerable quantities of information found in the technical brochures for competing brands. On the other hand, a buyer with more limited abilities may be incapable of performing this task and will have to rely instead on information obtained from advertisements or from sales representatives.

**Knowledge**
Familiarity with the product and expertise – the ability to apply the product

A critical aspect of an individual's ability to process information is knowledge. **Knowledge**, in this context, has two components: familiarity with the product, and expertise or the ability to apply the product.[22] The duration and intensity of the buying decision process depends on the buyer's familiarity with or prior experience in purchasing and using the product. The individual's knowledge influences his or her search for, recall and use of information.[23]

Inexperienced buyers may use different types of information from more experienced shoppers when making purchasing decisions. Inexperienced buyers use price as an indicator of quality more frequently than buyers who are knowledgeable about a particular product category.[24] Thus two potential buyers of a pedigree dog may use quite different types of information in making their purchase decision. The more experienced buyer, wishing to take the animal to dog shows, may seek detailed information about the dog's pedigree; the less experienced buyer, looking for a loyal family pet, may judge the animal by how approachable and friendly it appears.

Consumers who lack expertise are more likely to seek advice from others when making a purchase. More experienced buyers have greater confidence; they also have more knowledge about the product or service, and can tell which features are reliable indicators of product quality. For example, consider two families choosing a long-haul holiday. Members of one family are unused to overseas travel, are unsure of the suitability of locations offered in travel brochures, and do not understand how to investigate flight options or medical and insurance requirements. Members of the other family have holidayed abroad on a regular basis. Although on this occasion they intend to visit a country that is new to them, they are sufficiently conversant with this type of travel to make their purchase without assistance and with confidence.

***Figure 6.8***
*These advertisements for 'posh' crisps evidently play on consumers' aspirations to portray a certain image through the brands and products they select*
*Source: Courtesy of Kate Plumb, Abbot Mead Vickers. BBDO*

Marketers sometimes help customers to learn about and gain experience of their products. Free samples encourage consumer trial and reduce purchase risk. In-store demonstrations help people acquire knowledge of product uses. DIY retailer B&Q has, over several years, run a series of extended television advertisements offering detailed guidance on home improvements and decorating. Each advertisement featured step-by-step instructions towards the completion of a particular project. This helps consumers to learn and can create a more favourable attitude towards the company's products. Consumers also learn when they experience products indirectly through information received from sales people, friends and relatives.

Influencing what consumers learn is difficult to achieve. Marketers encounter problems in attracting and holding consumers' attention, providing the kinds of information that are important for making purchase decisions, and convincing consumers to try the product. These attempts are most likely to be successful when designed to appeal to a well-defined target market.

## Attitudes

**Attitude**
An individual's enduring evaluation, feelings and behavioural tendencies towards an object or activity

An **attitude** is an individual's enduring evaluation, feelings and behavioural tendencies towards an object or activity. These objects or activities may be tangible or intangible, living or non-living. Some attitudes relate to things that have a major impact on our lives, while others are less important. For example, we have attitudes towards relationships, culture and politics, just as we do towards rock music, skiing and pizza.

An individual learns attitudes through experience and interaction with others. Just as attitudes are learned, they can also be changed. Nevertheless, an individual's attitudes are generally quite stable and do not change from moment to moment. Likewise, at a particular point in time, some attitudes may be stronger than others. For example, a consumer who recently became the victim of credit card fraud after shopping on the Internet, may have strong views about the need for consumer protection legislation in this area.

An attitude consists of three major components: cognitive, affective and behavioural. The cognitive (or thinking) component is a person's knowledge and information about the object or idea, whereas the affective (or feeling) component comprises feelings and emotions towards the object or idea. The behavioural (or action) component consists of the action tendencies exhibited towards the object or idea. Changes in one of these components may or may not alter the other components. Thus consumers may become more knowledgeable about a specific brand without changing the affective or behavioural components of their attitude towards that brand.

Consumer attitudes towards a company and its products greatly influence the products individuals will buy, and therefore impact on the success or failure of the company's marketing strategy. When consumers are strongly negative towards aspects of a business's marketing practices, they may stop using the business's product, and may urge relatives and friends to do the same. For example, following the execution of human rights activists in Nigeria, some motorists chose to boycott Shell petrol because of allegations about Shell's activities in Nigeria.

Since attitudes can play such an important part in determining consumer behaviour, marketers should measure consumer attitudes towards prices, package designs, company logos and brand names, advertisements, warranties, store design and location, features of existing or proposed products, and social responsibility issues. Marketers can use a range of techniques to gauge these attitudes. One of the simplest ways is to question people directly. A marketing research agency carrying out attitude research for Rayban, for example, might question consumers about their opinions on the latest trends in eye wear. Sometimes marketers evaluate attitudes through attitude scales. An **attitude scale** usually consists of a series of adjectives, phrases or sentences about an object. Subjects are asked to indicate the intensity of their feelings towards the object by reacting to the adjectives, phrases or sentences in a certain way. For example, attitudes towards flexible mortgages might be measured by asking respondents to state the degree to which they agree or disagree with a

**Attitude scale**
A series of adjectives, phrases or sentences about an object used by a subject to indicate his or her feelings towards that object

number of statements, such as 'When I have spare money I would like the opportunity to pay more than my usual monthly repayment amount.'

If marketers identify particularly negative attitudes towards an aspect of a marketing mix, they may try to make consumer attitudes more favourable. This task is generally long, expensive, difficult and may require extensive promotional efforts. For example, in the UK, Post Office Counters has been advertising to draw customers' attention to the fact that local post offices offer a wide range of services. This publicity is attempting to alter customers' perceptions away from the traditional view that the Post Office exists purely for mailing letters and parcels.

### Personality

**Personality**
All the internal traits and behaviours that make a person unique

**Personality** includes all the internal traits and behaviours that make a person unique. Each person's unique personality is both inherited and the result of personal experiences. Personalities are typically described as having one or more characteristics, such as compulsiveness, ambitiousness, gregariousness, dogmatism, authoritarianism, introversion, extroversion, aggressiveness and competitiveness. Many marketers believe that a consumer's personality does influence the types and brands of products purchased, and there has been a drive to increase research in this area.[25] For example, the type of make-up or clothing that people buy, as well as the social activities in which they engage, may reflect one or more personality characteristics. Perhaps surprisingly, marketing researchers who have tried to find relationships among such characteristics and buying behaviour have reported inconclusive results. However, some of these researchers see this apparently weak association between personality and buying behaviour as due to unreliable measures rather than because no such relationship exists.[26]

At times, marketers aim advertising campaigns at general types of personality. In doing so, they use positively valued personality characteristics, such as gregariousness, independence or competitiveness. Products promoted in this way include drinks, cars, cigarettes, clothing and computer games. For example, television advertising promoting the alcoholic beverage Lambrini are designed to appeal to young, outgoing consumers.

## Social Factors Influencing the Buying Decision Process

**Social factors**
The forces other people exert on buying behaviour

The forces that other people exert on buying behaviour are called **social factors**. As shown in Figure 6.1, they can be grouped into four major areas:

1 roles and family
2 reference groups
3 social classes
4 culture and sub-cultures.

### Roles and Family

**Role**
A set of actions and activities that a person in a particular position is supposed to perform, based on the expectations of both the individual and surrounding people

All of us occupy positions within our family, social setting, organisations and institutions. Associated with each position is a **role** – a set of actions and activities that a person is supposed to perform, based on their own expectations and those of others around them. Because people occupy numerous positions, they also have many roles. For example, one woman may perform the roles of mother, wife, grandmother, daughter, sister, teacher, part-time youth club organiser and member of the local music society. Thus there are several sets of expectations for each person's behaviour.

An individual's roles influence both general behaviour and buying behaviour. The demands of different roles may be inconsistent and confusing. For example, assume that a man is thinking about buying a boat. While he wants a boat for fishing, his children want one suitable for water skiing. His wife wants him to delay the boat purchase until next year. A colleague at work insists that he should buy a particular brand, known for high performance. Thus an individual's buying behaviour may be partially affected by the opinions of family and friends.

Family roles relate directly to purchase decisions. The male head of household is likely to be involved heavily in the purchase of products such as household insurance and alcohol. Although female roles have changed, women still make buying decisions related to many household items, including healthcare products, washing products, household cleaners and food. Husbands and wives are often jointly involved in buying many durable goods, such as a washing machine or television set. As this chapter's 'Opener' explained, children are increasingly involved in household purchase decisions that were traditionally made only by husbands and wives. Some buying decisions, such as the purchase of a family holiday, are made by the whole family, with different family members playing different roles in the process. When two or more individuals participate in a purchase, their roles may dictate that each is responsible for performing certain tasks: initiating the idea, gathering information, deciding whether to buy the product or selecting the specific brand. The particular tasks performed depend on the types of product being considered.

Marketers need to be aware of how roles affect buying behaviour. To develop a marketing mix that precisely meets the target market's needs, marketers must know not only who does the actual buying but also what other roles influence the purchase.

## Reference Groups

**Reference group**
A group with which an individual identifies so much that he or she takes on many of the values, attitudes or behaviour of group members

A group is referred to as a **reference group** when an individual identifies with it so much that he or she takes on many of the values, attitudes or behaviour of group members. Most people have several reference groups, such as families, friends, work colleagues, and social, religious and professional organisations.

A group can be a negative reference group for an individual. Someone may have been a part of a specific group at one time but later have rejected its values and members, even taking specific action to avoid it.[27] However, in this discussion reference groups mean those that the individual involved views positively.

An individual may use a reference group as a point of comparison and a source of information. Sometimes individuals may change their behaviour to be more in line with other group members. For example, a student may stop visiting a particular nightclub on the advice of a close friend. An individual may seek information from a reference group about the best brand to buy or about other purchase factors, such as where to buy a certain product. The degree to which a reference group will affect a purchase decision depends on an individual's susceptibility to its influence, and the strength of his or her involvement with the group. Young people are often especially susceptible to this kind of influence. In general, the more conspicuous a product, the more likely the brand decision will be influenced by reference groups.

A marketer sometimes tries to use reference group influence in advertisements by suggesting that people in a specific group buy and are highly satisfied with a product. The advertiser is hoping that people will accept the suggested group as a reference group and buy (or react more favourably to) the product as a result. Whether this kind of advertising succeeds depends on three factors:

1. how effectively the advertisement communicates the message
2. the type of product
3. the individual's susceptibility to reference group influence.

**Opinion leader**
The member of a reference group who provides information about a specific sphere of interest to reference group participants seeking information

In most reference groups, one or more members stand out as opinion leaders. An **opinion leader** provides information about a specific sphere of interest to reference group participants who seek such information. Opinion leaders are viewed by other group members as being well informed about a particular area, and easily accessible. Such individuals often feel a responsibility to remain informed about the sphere of interest, and thus seek out advertisements, manufacturers' brochures, sales people, websites and other sources of information.

## Social Classes

**Social class**
An open group of individuals who have similar social rank

Within all societies, people rank others into higher or lower positions of respect. This ranking results in social classes. A **social class** is an open group of individuals who have similar social rank. A class is referred to as 'open' because people can move into and out of it. The criteria for grouping people into classes vary from one society to another. In the UK, as in other western countries, many factors are taken into account, including occupation, education, income, wealth, race, ethnic group and possessions. In the former Soviet Union, wealth and income are less important in determining social class than education and occupation: although Russian doctors and scientists do not make a great deal of money, they are highly valued in Russian society. A person who is ranking someone does not necessarily apply all of a society's criteria. The number and importance of the factors chosen depend on the characteristics of the individual being ranked and the values of the person who is doing the ranking. For example, one individual may particularly respect status within a church or religious sect, while another may regard it as having little relevance.

To some degree, people within social classes develop and assume common patterns of behaviour. They may have similar attitudes, values, language patterns and possessions. Social class influences many aspects of people's lives. For example, it affects whom they marry, their likelihood of having children and the children's chances of surviving infancy. It influences childhood training, choice of religion, selection of occupation and the way in which people spend their time. Because social class has a bearing on so many aspects of a person's life, it also affects buying decisions. For example, upmarket fashion labels Donna Karan and Versace are popular among upper-class Europeans because they believe these brands symbolise their status, income and aspirations.

Social class affects the type, quality and quantity of products that a person buys and uses. Social class also affects an individual's shopping patterns and the types of store patronised. Advertisements are sometimes based on an appeal to a specific social class. Different countries often collate data about their populations based on social or socio-economic factors. For example, for many years the UK, like some other countries, used a relatively simple classification based on social status and occupation (see Table 6.1). However, in 2001, the UK's Office for National Statistics introduced a modified system known as NS SEC (National Statistics Socio-Economic Status). This approach is still based on occupation, but

**TABLE 6.1 SOCIO-ECONOMIC CLASSIFICATION**

| Social grade | Social status | Head of household's occupation |
|---|---|---|
| A | Upper middle class | Higher managerial, professional or administrative positions; often living in expensive accommodation in the best residential areas |
| B | Middle class | Middle managerial, professional or administrative jobs; good living standards, usually in good accommodation in reasonable areas |
| C1 | Lower middle class | Junior managerial, professional or administrative, supervisory or clerical jobs; sometimes referred to as 'white collar' workers |
| C2 | Skilled working class | Skilled manual workers, perhaps who have served some kind of apprenticeship to train |
| D | Manual workers | Semi-skilled and unskilled manual workers |
| E | Those at lowest levels of subsistence | Old age pensioners, widows, casual workers, the unemployed or those who are dependent on social security or have little in the way of independent means |

See www.medialive.ie for more details of socio-economic groups.

aims to more closely reflect consumers' purchasing power on the basis of their position in the labour market.[28] Table 6.2 describes the new NS SEC social class categories.

## Culture and Sub-cultures

**Culture**
All the things around us that are made by human beings: tangible items, such as food, furniture, buildings, clothing and tools; and intangible concepts, such as education, the legal system, healthcare and religion; plus values and behaviours

**Culture** consists of everything in our surroundings that is made by human beings. It includes tangible items, such as food, furniture, buildings, clothing and tools, and intangible concepts, such as education, the legal system, healthcare and religion. Culture also includes the values and wide range of behaviours that are acceptable within a specific society. The concepts, values and behaviours that make up a culture are learned and passed on from one generation to the next.

Culture influences buying behaviour, determining what people wear and eat, how they socialise, where they live and travel. Society's interest in the health-giving aspects of food has affected companies' approaches to developing and promoting their products. Recent concern about increasing levels of obesity and its impact on health has caused the food industry to question how it markets high-fat and high-sugar products.[29] Culture also influences how consumers buy and use products, and the satisfaction gained from them. For example, the consumption of packaged goods, and the usage and ownership of durable goods varies across cultures.[30] In many western cultures, shortage of time is a growing problem because of the increasing number of women who work and the current emphasis placed on physical and mental self-development. Many people buy convenience and labour-saving products to cope with this problem.[31]

Because culture partly determines how products are purchased and used, it also affects the development, promotion, distribution and pricing of products. Food marketers have needed to radically overhaul their marketing efforts to reflect day-to-day changes in how consumers live their lives. Some 30 years ago, most families ate at least two meals a day together, and the mother devoted four to six hours a day to preparing those meals. Today, more than

**TABLE 6.2 NS SEC EIGHT-CLASS SOCIO-ECONOMIC CLASSIFICATION**

| Class | Occupation groups |
|---|---|
| 1 | *Higher managerial and professional occupations* (ABs):<br>e.g. business executives, doctors, vets, teachers |
| 2 | *Lower managerial and professional occupations* (C1s):<br>e.g. nurses, police sergeants and constables, market researchers, junior managers |
| 3 | *Intermediate occupations* (C2s):<br>e.g. secretaries, clerical staff, technicians and telephone engineers |
| 4 | *Small employers and own-account workers*:<br>e.g. the self-employed and those employing fewer than 25 people |
| 5 | *Lower supervisory and technical occupations*:<br>e.g. supervisors in factories |
| 6 | *Semi-routine occupations*:<br>e.g. drivers, assembly-line workers, shop staff |
| 7 | *Routine occupations*: e.g. porters, labourers, domestic staff |
| 8 | *Never worked or long-term unemployed* |

**Source:** adapted from Angela Donkin, Yuan Huang Lee and Barbara Toson, 'Implications of change in the UK social and occupational classifications in 2001 for vital statistics', *Population Trends*, 107, *National Statistics*, Spring 2002, pp. 23–9.

60 per cent of women aged 25 to 54 are employed outside the home, and average family incomes have risen considerably. These shifts, along with lack of time, have resulted in dramatic increases in per capita consumption of shelf-stable foods like Pot Rice and Pot Noodle, frozen meals and take-away foods.[32] As a result of increasing demands from those wishing to 'eat on the move', petrol stations now stock a variety of prepared sandwiches and snacks.

An increase in ethnic diversity in many societies has important implications for the way in which new products and services are developed and marketed. A key part of this process is

## Building Customer Relationships

### Marketing to Ethnic consumers

The 2001 census revealed the true multicultural character of the UK population. Approaching 8 per cent of those living in the UK belong to an ethnic minority, an increase of more than 50 per cent over a 10-year period. The commercial implications of these changes are huge, with professional marketers facing increasing pressure to cater more effectively for the needs and buying requirements of these groups. Studies on culture illustrate the diversity of attitudes and behaviour across ethnic groups, showing that these differences are also reflected in product preferences and consumer buying behaviour. Yet recent research findings suggest that not enough is being done to reflect these characteristics in product design and marketing.

For example, despite a recent rise in Bollywood-style advertisements, such as those for Peugeot and Walkers Crisps, the advertising industry has been accused of tokenism and ethnic stereotyping. Even though an analysis of television advertising reveals 13 per cent of actors used are non-white, a more systematic review shows that the vast majority of these are included in minor roles. According to a report by Mediaedge:cia, a large global player in media communications and part of the WPP Group, current advertising campaigns are still failing to reflect the cultural characteristics of Asian, African-Caribbean and other ethnic minorities.

So what needs to be done to ensure that cultural variety is better reflected in marketing practice? Industry experts suggest that the first challenge is to develop a fuller picture of ethnic diversity by collecting appropriate research data across the different communities. This raises challenges of its own, as agencies must equip themselves to overcome the cultural and religious barriers sometimes associated with such data-collection exercises. For example, some experts highlight the importance of including community leaders in the process; others suggest that researchers from the same ethnic groups as respondents must be used and that appropriate settings for the research must be chosen. Not surprisingly, the number of marketing research agencies specialising in researching ethnic minorities is on the increase and various initiatives have been established to improve the availability and quality of work in this area. For example, the Market Research Society recently established the Ethnic Research Network. This body provides a forum for those with interests in ethnic research, aiming to share knowledge and drive forward best practice in the area.

The potential benefits of such research are readily apparent. When broadcaster Sky researched the viewing behaviour of the UK's South Asian population, it identified the importance this group attaches to Asian TV channels such as Zee TV and StarTV. According to the findings, 96 per cent of respondents from this group regarded these kinds of channel as essential. Yet only 54 per cent had the same view about ITV1. The analysis also revealed the level of Internet access among South Asians to be much higher than the UK norm. The implications for advertisers and marketers seeking to target these individuals are readily apparent. Yet, even here, care is needed. The research also showed striking viewership patterns across the South Asian community, illustrating the danger of developing ethnic stereotypes. In the words of Saber Khan, the research director of Ethnic Focus (the specialist research company conducting the study):

> These channels reflect the heterogeneity of the Asian community. Marketers have had the will to reach communities. But what they sometimes need assistance with is to capture the diversity. It's more than just Bollywood or Caribbean – it's capturing the fusion.

**Sources:** Robert Gray, 'Ethnic insight', *Marketing*, 4 March 2004, pp. 25–6; 'Ethnic marketing: "a double edged sword"', www.redhotcurry.com, 3 March 2003; www.mediaedge.com; www.mrw.org.uk.

ensuring the availability of good-quality data, so that the attitudes and behaviour of minority groups are properly understood. The Building Customer Relationships box below shows how the need to better understand cultural diversity among ethnic minorities and its impact on consumer behaviour is spawning initiatives to drive forward best practice in marketing research.

When marketers sell products overseas, they often see the tremendous impact that culture has on the purchase and use of products. International marketers find that people in other regions of the world have different attitudes, values and needs, which call for different methods of doing business. Some international marketers fail because they do not adjust to cultural differences. The effect of culture on international marketing programmes is discussed in greater detail in Chapter 5.

**Sub-cultures**
Sub-divisions of culture according to geographic regions or human characteristics, such as age or ethnic background

A culture can be divided into **sub-cultures** according to geographic regions or human characteristics, such as age or ethnic background. In any country, there are a number of different sub-cultures. Within these, there are even greater similarities in people's attitudes, values and actions than within the broader culture, resulting in stronger preferences for specific types of clothing, furniture or leisure activity. For example, the wearing of kilts tends to be confined to Scotland rather than England or Wales. Marketers must recognise that, even though their operations are confined to one country, state or city, sub-cultural differences may dictate considerable variations in what products people buy and how they make their purchases. To deal effectively with these differences, marketers may have to alter their product, promotion, distribution systems, price or people to satisfy members of particular sub-cultures.

# Understanding Consumer Behaviour

Marketers try to understand consumer buying behaviour so that they can satisfy consumers more effectively. For example, consumer concerns about the exploitation of workers in less developed countries have encouraged supermarkets to stock more ethical products. An appreciation of how and why individuals buy products and services helps marketers design more appropriate and relevant marketing programmes.[33] For example, by understanding the readership habits of prospective digital camera buyers, companies such as Pentax and Nikon are able to make more informed decisions about where to place print advertisements for their products.

At a time when consumer expectations of products and services are rising, it is more important than ever to keep abreast of trends in consumer behaviour. If marketers are to keep consumers satisfied, they must focus carefully on the marketing concept and on being consumer oriented. In particular, they must be equipped with a clear understanding of the process and motivations of consumer buying.

The fact that it may be difficult to analyse consumer behaviour precisely, does not detract from the importance of doing so. Even though research on consumer buying behaviour has not supplied all the knowledge that marketers need, considerable progress has been made in recent years. Advances in technology and changing shopping habits are increasing the opportunities for capturing and managing information about consumers. For example, the increasing use of on-line banking has been made possible by the development of computer systems that can handle the full range of banking transactions in which consumers wish to engage. The same systems are enabling providers such as First Direct and ing.com to store and analyse a huge variety of information about customers' spending and savings patterns. When analysed, this information provides vital insights into the needs and wants of different customer types. These insights can be used to develop and market new products and services. At a time when an increasingly competitive business environment is making it more difficult to develop an edge over rival businesses, the demands for such information are only likely to grow.

# Summary

*Buying behaviour* comprises the decision processes and actions of people involved in buying and using products. *Consumer buying behaviour* refers to the buying behaviour of ultimate consumers – those who purchase products for personal or household use, not for business purposes. Analysing consumer buying behaviour helps marketers to determine what satisfies customers, so that they can implement the marketing concept and better predict how consumers will respond to different marketing programmes.

» Consumer decisions can be classified into three categories: routine response behaviour, limited decision-making and extensive decision-making. A consumer uses *routine response behaviour* when buying frequently purchased, low-cost, low-risk items that require very little search and decision effort. *Limited decision-making* is used for products purchased occasionally or when a buyer needs to acquire information about an unfamiliar brand in a familiar product category. *Extensive decision-making* is used when purchasing an unfamiliar, expensive, high-risk or infrequently bought product. *Impulse buying* is an unplanned buying behaviour involving a powerful, persistent urge to buy something immediately. The purchase of a certain product does not always elicit the same type of decision-making behaviour. Individuals differ in their response to purchase situations. Even the same individual may make a different decision in other circumstances.

» The *consumer buying decision process* comprises five stages: problem recognition, information search, evaluation of alternatives, purchase and post-purchase evaluation. Decision processes do not always culminate in a purchase, and not all consumer decisions include all five stages. Problem recognition occurs when a buyer becomes aware that there is a difference between a desired state and an actual condition. After recognising the problem, the buyer searches for product information that will help resolve the problem or satisfy the need. *Internal search* involves buyers searching their memory for information about products that might solve the problem. If insufficient information is retrieved in this way, additional information is sought through *external search*. A successful information search will yield a group of brands, called an *evoked set*, that are viewed as possible alternatives. The level of involvement, which is the amount of interest, emotion and activity expended on a purchase, affects the degree of the external search. To evaluate the products in the evoked set, a buyer establishes certain criteria and assigns each a certain *salience* – or level of importance – by which to compare, rate and rank the different products. During purchase, the consumer selects the product or brand on the basis of results from the evaluation stage and on other factors. The buyer also chooses the seller from whom to buy the product. After the purchase, the buyer evaluates the product's actual performance. Shortly after the purchase of an expensive product the post-purchase evaluation may provoke *cognitive dissonance* – dissatisfaction brought on by the consumer's doubts as to whether he or she should have bought the product in the first place. The results of the post-purchase evaluation will affect future buying behaviour.

» Three major categories of influences are believed to affect the consumer buying decision process: personal, psychological and social factors. A *personal factor* is one that is unique to a particular person. Personal factors include demographic factors, situational factors and level of involvement. *Demographic factors* are individual characteristics such as age, sex, race, ethnic origin, income, family life cycle and occupation. *Situational factors* are the external circumstances or conditions that exist when a consumer is making a purchase decision, such as the time available. An individual's *level of involvement* – the level of interest, emotional commitment and time spent searching for a product in a particular situation – also affects the buying decision process. Enduring involvement is an ongoing interest in a product class because of personal relevance. Situational involvement is a temporary interest resulting from the particular circumstance or environment in which buyers find themselves.

- *Psychological factors* partly determine people's general behaviour and thus influence their behaviour as consumers. The primary psychological influences on consumer behaviour are perception, motives, learning, attitudes and personality. *Perception* is the process of selecting, organising and interpreting *information inputs* (the sensations received through sight, taste, hearing, smell and touch) to produce meaning. The first step in the perceptual process is the selection of information. *Selective exposure* is the phenomenon of people selecting the inputs that are to be exposed to their awareness; *selective distortion* is the changing or twisting of currently received information. *Selective retention* involves remembering information inputs that support personal feelings and beliefs, and forgetting those that do not. The second step of the perceptual process requires organising and integrating the new information with that already stored in memory. Interpretation – the third step in the perceptual process – is the assignment of meaning to what has been organised. In addition to perceptions of packages, products, brands and organisations, individuals also have a *self-concept*, or self-image.

- A *motive* is an internal, energy-giving force directing a person's activities towards satisfying a need or achieving a goal. *Patronage motives* influence where a person purchases products on a regular basis. To analyse the major motives that influence consumers to buy or not buy products, marketers conduct motivation research, using *in-depth interviews, focus groups* or *projective techniques*. Common types of projective technique include word association tests, bubble drawings and sentence completion tests.

- *Learning* refers to changes in a person's behaviour caused by information and experience. *Knowledge*, in this context, has two components: familiarity with the product, and expertise – the ability to apply the product.

- *Attitude* refers to an individual's enduring evaluation, feelings and behavioural tendencies towards an object or activity. Consumer attitudes towards a company and its products greatly influence the success or failure of its marketing strategy. Marketers measure consumers' attitudes using *attitude scales*.

- *Personality* comprises all the internal traits and behaviours that make a person unique. Though the results of many studies have been inconclusive, some marketers believe that personality does influence the types and brands of products purchased.

- *Social factors* are the forces that other people exert on buying behaviour. They include the influence of roles and family, reference groups, social classes, and culture and sub-cultures. We all occupy positions within groups, organisations and institutions. Each position has a *role* – a set of actions and activities that a person in a particular position is supposed to perform. A group is a *reference group* when an individual identifies with the group so much that he or she takes on many of the values, attitudes or behaviours of group members. In most reference groups, one or more members stand out as *opinion leaders*. A *social class* is an open group of individuals who have similar social rank. *Culture* is everything in our surroundings that is made by human beings. A culture can be divided into *sub-cultures* on the basis of geographic regions or human characteristics, such as age or ethnic background.

- Marketers try to understand consumer buying behaviour so that they can offer consumers greater satisfaction. Improvements in technology and refinements in research methods are increasing opportunities to capture and manage data about consumers and their behaviour. The combination of the pressure of rising consumer expectations, combined with an increasingly competitive business environment, will spur marketers to seek a fuller understanding of consumer decision processes.

## Key Links

This chapter, about consumer buying behaviour, should be read in conjunction with Chapter 7, which examines buying behaviour in business markets.

- Without an understanding of customers' buying behaviour, it is difficult for marketers to develop effective marketing programmes, as discussed in Parts III–VI.
- An understanding of customer buying behaviour is also essential for two core facets of marketing strategy: developing target market strategies (see Chapter 8); creating powerful brand propositions (see Chapter 11).

## Important Terms

Buying behaviour
Consumer buying behaviour
Routine response behaviour
Limited decision-making
Extensive decision-making
Impulse buying
Consumer buying decision process
Internal search
External search
Involvement
Evoked set
Salience
Cognitive dissonance
Personal influencing factors
Demographic factors
Situational factors
Level of involvement
Psychological factors
Perception
Information inputs
Selective exposure
Selective distortion
Selective retention
Self-concept
Motive
Patronage motives
In-depth interview
Focus group
Projective techniques
Learning
Knowledge
Attitude
Attitude scale
Personality
Social factors
Role
Reference group
Opinion leader
Social class
Culture
Sub-cultures

## Discussion and Review Questions

1 Name the types of buying behaviour consumers use. List some products that you have bought using each type of behaviour. In what circumstances have you bought a product on impulse?
2 What are the five stages in the consumer buying decision process? Are all these stages used in all consumer purchase decisions?
3 What are the personal factors that affect the consumer buying decision process? How do they affect the process?
4 How does a consumer's level of involvement affect his or her purchase behaviour?
5 What is the function of time in a consumer's buying decision process?
6 What is selective exposure and what effect does it have on consumer buying?
7 How do marketers attempt to shape consumers' learning?
8 Why are marketers concerned about consumer attitudes?
9 Describe reference groups. How do they influence buying behaviour? Name some of your own reference groups.
10 In what ways does social class affect a person's purchase decisions?
11 What is culture? How does it affect a person's buying behaviour?
12 Describe the sub-cultures to which you belong. Identify buying behaviour that is unique to your sub-culture.
13 What is the impact of post-purchase evaluation on future buying decisions?
14 If consumers are dissatisfied with a particular purchase, what actions are open to them? What can marketers do to respond to these actions?

## Recommended Readings


- Engel, J.F., Blackwell, R.D. and Miniard, P.W., *Consumer Behaviour* (Fort Worth: West, 2001).
- Foxall, G.R., Goldsmith, R.E and Brown, S., *Consumer Psychology for Marketing* (London: Thomson Learning, 1998).
- Lamkin, M., Foxall, G., Van Raaij, F. and Heilbrunn, B., *European Perspectives on Consumer Behaviour*, (Harlow: Pearson/FT, 1998).
- Solomon, M., Bamossy, G. and Askegaard, S., *Consumer Behaviour* (Harlow: Pearson/FT, 2001).

## Internet Exercise

Some mass-market e-commerce sites, such as Amazon.co.uk, have extended the concept of customisation to their customer base. Amazon has analysed its customer data, then used its understanding of certain users' likes and dislikes to make recommendations to other users. Take a look at this on-line retailer at:
www.amazon.co.uk or www.amazon.com

1 What might motivate some consumers to read a 'best-selling' list?
2 Is the consumer's level of involvement with on-line book purchase likely to be high or low?
3 Discuss the consumer buying decision process as it relates to a decision to purchase from Amazon.co.uk.

## *Applied Mini-Case*

Whitbread Hotels, one of Europe's largest leisure businesses, has a portfolio that includes a range of four-star deluxe establishments, an extensive network of motel-style budget-priced Travel Inns, health and fitness centres, pub and pizza restaurants, and coffee shops. The luxury Marriott hotels brand is franchised in the UK from Marriott International. With 62 UK outlets trading under the Marriott, Renaissance and Courtyard by Marriott brands, Whitbread is targeting a mix of different customers. During the week business people using the hotels' conference accommodation are an important visitor group. At the weekends private consumers seeking luxury breaks or attending family celebrations hosted by the hotels make up much of the trade.

**Sources:** Sally Dibb and Lyndon Simkin, *Marketing Briefs: A Revision and Study Guide*, 2004, Oxford: Butterworth Heinemann; www.whitbread.co.uk; Whitbread hotels marketing materials.

### *Question*

**A large hotel group such as Whitbread is interested in finding out more about the factors that influence people buying hotel weekend breaks. Relating your answer to this example, review the different personal, psychological and social influences that might impact on someone seeking to make this kind of purchase.**

## *Case Study*

### IKEA: Stylish Furnishings at Affordable Prices

Swedish company IKEA is a mass-market producer of cheap and stylish home furnishings that appear to transcend national boundaries. The company was founded in 1943 by Ingvar Kamprad, a small-town handyman from southern Sweden, who devised the company name by combining his initials with the first initials of his farm (Elmtaryd) and the parish (Agunnaryd) where he was raised. Today, IKEA's business mission is clear. In the words of the company's founder, 'We shall offer a wide range of furnishing items of good design and function, at prices so low that the majority of people can afford to buy them.'

Since expanding internationally in 1973, IKEA's incremental growth approach to spreading into overseas markets has continued. Today the company is one of the world's largest retailers. Now located in more than 32 countries, with over 200 outlets, the company almost tripled its turnover worldwide between 1984 and 1990. In 2004, turnover reached an awesome 13 billion euros. Offering affordable and varied furniture is central to IKEA's strategy. The company maintains its cost advantages by doing what it does best, and concentrates on its core business and on the adoption of a long-term strategy.

IKEA's ability to maintain its success across so many markets is impressive. Some studies suggest that one possible reason for this success is that when prices are very competitive, cultural barriers become smaller and it becomes easier to reach a larger percentage of the total furniture-buying population. To maintain its low cost base, the company needs to shift volume, which it does by selling broadly the same range of stylish, flat-packed Swedish products in all of its stores worldwide.

Price is not the only reason for IKEA's success. In the design of its stores and products, it has done much to appeal to consumers' underlying reasons for buying. The company understands that shopping is a purposeful activity: people buy in order to make their lives richer. In IKEA's case, the challenge has been to make the apparent essence of a Swedish lifestyle – beautiful homes and high-quality living – available at affordable prices. IKEA has also used the opportunity to innovate where it can. For example, the retailer opened its first New York outlet, a 7400-square-foot scaled-down version of its usual 200,000-square-foot stores. The 'boutique style' outlet is essentially a marketing vehicle for the company. Known as the Marketing Outpost, the shop aims to concentrate on only one product at a time. Every eight to twelve weeks IKEA will close the store for a complete refit and transformation.

Consumer interest in IKEA has revived the flagging fortunes of furniture retailers. In areas where new IKEA stores have opened, the company's lively approach has led to an increase in the time spent shopping for home-related products. Research also suggests that the proportion of their income that consumers are prepared to spend on these products is increasing. IKEA therefore believes it is competing with purchases of new cars and holidays – anything that claims the disposable income in the consumers' pocket – not just with other furniture retailers.

Although the company does not deliberately use demographic and psychographic variables to segment its customer base, IKEA products seem to appeal particularly to people in their twenties and thirties. In order to expand the product line further into other life cycle stages, the company is trying to grow with its customers by adopting a policy of offering products that cater for families with teenage children and those whose children have left home.

While IKEA recognises that consumers shop to improve their lives, the company also acknowledges their practical needs. People are much more likely to visit retail outlets that are conveniently located and where the shopping experience is fun. IKEA meets these important needs by locating its stores close to motorways and major trunk roads, and by offering extensive parking, childcare, toilet and restaurant facilities. A full range of furnishings is presented in real room settings that combine expensive, high-risk purchases such as living room suites and carpets with cheaper, lower-involvement items such as pictures, ornaments and lampshades.

**Sources**: www.ikea.co.uk, 2004; Jennifer Pellet, 'IKEA takes Manhattan!', *Discount Merchandiser*, October 1995; 'IKEA', *Retail Business – Retail Trade Reviews*, 33, March 1995; Peter Wingard, 'A study of six Swedish firms' approach to marketing', Warwick Business School MBA Programme, 1991; S. Redmond, 'Home truths', *Marketing*, 7 April 1988; J. Bamford and A. Dunlap Smith, 'Why competitors shop for ideas at IKEA', *Business Week*, 9 October 1989; P. Corwin, 'The Vikings are back – with furniture', *Discount Merchandiser*, 27 (4), April 1987; B. Saporito, 'IKEA's got 'em lining up', *Fortune*, 123 (5), 11 March 1991; J. Reynolds, 'IKEA: a competitive company with style', *Retail and Distribution Management*, 16 (3), 1988; 'Report on the UK furniture market', Key Note, 1989; www.ikea.com, 2004.

## Questions for Discussion

1. How do families go about purchasing a new item of furniture? Who influences and who is involved in the buying decision process?
2. What factors influence the way in which a newly married couple buy furniture?
3. How important is price to IKEA because of its position as a retailer of home furnishings?

# 7 Business Markets and Business Buying Behaviour

**"Business marketing is not simply about making sales. It's the task of establishing, developing and managing a portfolio of customer relationships."**

*David Ford, University of Bath*

## Objectives

- To become familiar with the various types of business market
- To identify the major characteristics of business buyers and transactions
- To understand several attributes of business demand
- To become familiar with the major components of a buying centre
- To understand relationship marketing and exchanges between industrial buyers and sellers
- To understand the stages of the business buying decision process and the factors that affect this process
- To learn how to select and analyse business target markets
- To appreciate some of the nuances of marketing business products

## Introduction

Most readers of this book will have related the material in the previous chapter to their own purchasing experiences as consumers. Many marketers, though, do not address consumers. Instead, their target customers are other businesses or organisations. This chapter addresses the nature of business-to-business marketing, known here as business marketing.

A **business market** is one in which the customer is not a consumer – a private individual or household. In business markets, the target customers are other businesses and organisations that purchase a specific type of product or service for resale, for use in making other products or for use in their daily operations. In older books, this used to be known as **industrial** or **organisational marketing**. More recently, the term **business-to-business marketing** has become popular. Now, this has been abbreviated to 'business marketing'. Whether known as industrial, organisational, business-to-business or simply business marketing, the emphasis is on other businesses and organisations as customers, rather than end-user consumers.

*Opener*

# Sara Lee Courtaulds: Consumer Brands but Mainly Business Customers

Sara Lee Courtaulds is a large international producer of fabrics to garment makers and ready-made garments to retailers including Marks & Spencer, Victoria's Secret and other leading retailers. With production facilities across the globe, the company has significant design and manufacturing interests in the UK and France. The business is divided into two units: fabrics and garments.

The fabric marketers are constantly innovating in terms of fabrics, designs and seaming techniques. Some of the latest products are fabrics that, when warm, release smells such as citrus odours – very useful in sports and swimwear. Only a few of the fabric brands are known to consumers (Calais-produced Desseilles lace, for example, is world renowned). On the whole, however, the various fabric brands are familiar only to Sara Lee Courtaulds' immediate business customers, the garment makers and retailer merchandisers.

For the garment-producing side of Sara Lee Courtaulds, most of the clothing produced is retailer own-label branded goods, purchased by consumers as St Michael (Marks & Spencer), Bhs or Tesco own-label branded merchandise. In addition, Sara Lee Courtaulds' garment division produces brands that are promoted directly to the consumer under the very familiar lingerie, clothing and household textiles names of Well, Aristoc, Berlei, Gossard, Georges Rech, Zorbit and Christy towels.

Although Berlei and Gossard underwear are advertised in consumer magazines, and Aristoc lingerie appears on billboards, the vast majority of the company's marketing activity is targeted at companies retailing or manufacturing clothing: business marketing.

For Sara Lee Courtaulds' businesses supplying the large retail chains, retail merchandisers expect them to provide all the packaging, design, labelling and photography, but to the retailers' own specifications. Sara Lee Courtaulds must do much more than simply produce a satisfactory product for a customer such as Marks & Spencer (M&S). Subsidiary Meridian, for example, pays for photography, packaging, hangers, ticketing and displays for Bhs and Tesco. The retailers only have to find space for the display stand and manage inventory levels.

For garments, each season for a design eventually included in the ranges sold in M&S or Bhs stores, between 25 and 35 new products are offered by Sara Lee Courtaulds. There is a lead time of three seasons to enable the design, selection, manufacturing and promotion of the new ranges. First, there are fabric searches, then design searches. The garment makers and, separately, the retailer merchandisers travel the world for ideas: fabrics, seaming methods and designs. Retailers give some guidelines to their garment makers. Then the garment makers produce prototypes in the right colours and fabrics in order to pitch their wares to M&S or Bhs. There is a round of selection meetings in which buyers turn down most prototypes and then make the final choice. A supplier is almost assured that if the garment maker supplied three items in this season's M&S range, it will receive three slots in next season's range. The difficulty is in seeking the fourth item, particularly as the overall range will not grow – any additional item will be at the expense of a competitor garment maker. To win an additional inclusion requires innovation in design, method, fabric or price – a new look alone will not suffice.

The fact is that, before a new line in lingerie, nightwear or clothing is even stocked in a retailer's stores – let alone before a member of the public has made any purchase – the fabric and made-up garment have both been marketed to Sara Lee Courtaulds' customers: the retailers. This is business marketing.

**Sources:** Well; Sara Lee Courtaulds, Courtaulds Textiles; Desseilles Textiles, France and UK.
Photo © Royalty-Free/CORBIS

**Business market**
The customers are not consumers, private individuals or households: instead the target customers are other businesses and organisations that purchase a specific type of product or service for resale, for use in making other products or for use in their daily operations

**Industrial, organisational** or **business-to-business marketing**
See *business market*

Sara Lee Courtaulds has some consumer brands such as Gossard or Aristoc, but mainly it markets products to garment manufacturers and retailers – other businesses. This chapter explores what is meant by business marketing, before examining the characteristics of business buying and the nature of demand for business products. The chapter's focus is on the buying centre and the buying decision process as applied to business-to-business marketing. The chapter concludes by examining how marketers select and analyse business markets, and the ways in which marketers in business markets modify their use of the marketing toolkit. For example, in terms of branding, addressing customer needs, determining market segments, understanding competitive forces, undertaking marketing research and in constructing marketing programmes.

# Types of Business Market

There are four kinds of business markets: producers, resellers, public sector and governments, plus institutions (see also Chapter 8). This section describes the characteristics of the customers that make up these markets.

## Producer Markets

**Producer markets**
Buyers of raw materials and semi-finished and finished items used to produce other products or in their own operations

**Reseller markets**
Intermediaries, such as wholesalers and retailers, who buy finished goods and resell them to make a profit

Individuals and business organisations that purchase products to make a profit by using them to produce other products or by using them in their own operations are classified as **producer markets**. Producer markets include buyers of raw materials and semi-finished and finished items used to produce other products. For example, a manufacturer buys raw materials and component parts to use directly in the production of its products. Grocers and supermarkets are producer markets for numerous support products, such as paper and plastic bags, displays, scanners and floorcare products. Hotels are producer markets for food, cleaning equipment, laundry services and furniture. Producer markets cover a broad array of industries, ranging from agriculture, forestry, fisheries and mining, to construction, transport, communications and public utilities.

Manufacturers tend to be geographically concentrated. This concentration occurs in Europe too, with heavy industry centred on the Ruhr valley in Germany, and on the Midlands and the north-west in the UK. Sometimes an industrial marketer may be able to serve customers more efficiently as a result. Within certain areas, production in just a few industries may account for a sizeable proportion of total industrial output.

## Reseller Markets

**Reseller markets** consist of intermediaries, such as wholesalers and retailers, who buy finished goods and resell them to make a profit. These intermediaries are discussed in Chapters 15 and 16. Other than making minor alterations, resellers do not change the physical characteristics of the products they handle. With the exception of items that producers sell directly to consumers, all products sold to consumer markets are first sold to reseller markets.

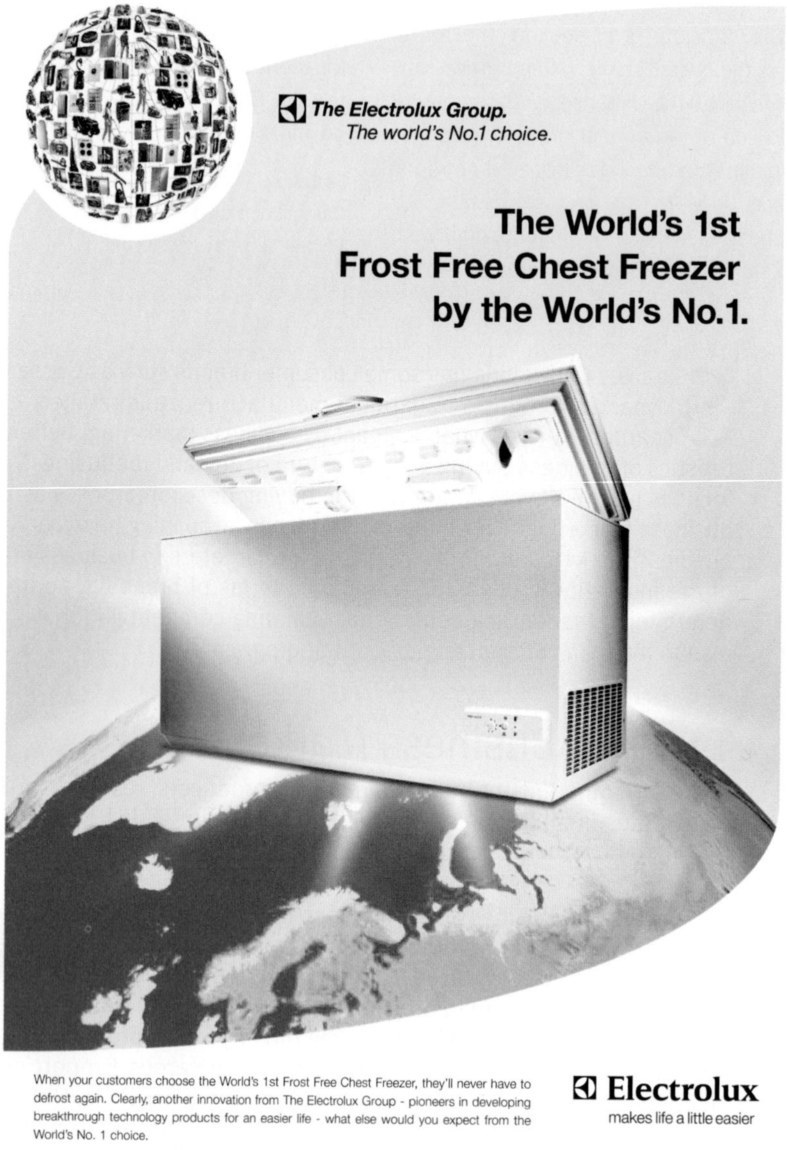

The Electrolux Group.
The world's No.1 choice.
The World's 1st
Frost Free Chest Freezer
by the World's No.1.
When your customers choose the World's 1st Frost Free Chest Freezer, they'll never have to defrost again. Clearly, another innovation from The Electrolux Group - pioneers in developing breakthrough technology products for an easier life - what else would you expect from the World's No. 1 choice.
Electrolux
makes life a little easier


*Figure 7.1*
*This Electrolux advertisement targets retailers stocking the manufacturer's range of freezers*
*Source: Courtesy of Electrolux Home Products*

**Wholesalers**
Intermediaries who purchase products for resale to retailers, other wholesalers and producers, governments and institutions

**Retailers**
Intermediaries that purchase products and resell them to final consumers

**Wholesalers** **Wholesalers** purchase products for resale to retailers, other wholesalers and producers, governments and institutions. Although some highly technical products are sold directly to end users, many products are sold through wholesalers, who in turn sell products to other companies in the distribution system. Thus wholesalers are very important in helping to get a producer's product to customers. Wholesalers often carry many products, perhaps as many as 250,000 items. From the reseller's point of view, having access to such an array of products from a single source makes it much simpler to buy a variety of items. When inventories are vast, the reordering of products is normally automated and the wholesaler's initial purchase decisions are made by professional buyers and buying committees.

**Retailers** **Retailers** purchase products and resell them to final consumers. Some retailers carry a large number of items. Chemists, for example, may stock up to 12,000 items, and some supermarkets may handle in excess of 20,000 different products. In small, family-owned retail stores, the owner frequently makes purchasing decisions. Large department stores or supermarket retailers have one or more employees in each department who are responsible for buying products for that department. As for chain stores, a buyer or buying committee in the central office frequently decides whether a product will be made available for selection by store managers. For many products, however, local store managers make the actual buying decisions for a particular store.

**Factors Considered by Resellers** When making purchase decisions, resellers consider several factors. They evaluate the level of demand for a product to determine in what quantity and at what prices it can be resold. They assess the amount of space required to handle a product relative to its potential profit. Sometimes resellers will put a product on trial for a fixed period, allowing them to judge customers' reactions and to make better-informed decisions about shelf space and positions as a result. Retailers, for example, sometimes evaluate products on the basis of sales per square metre of selling area. Since customers often depend on a reseller to have a product when they need it, a reseller typically evaluates a supplier's ability to provide adequate quantities when and where wanted. Resellers also take into account the ease of placing orders, and the availability of technical assistance and training programmes from the producer.

More broadly, when resellers consider buying a product not previously carried, they try to determine whether the product competes with or complements the products the company is currently handling. These types of concern distinguish reseller markets from other markets. Sometimes resellers will start stocking a new line of products in response to specific requests from customers. Marketers dealing with reseller markets must recognise these needs and be able to serve them.

## Government and Public-sector Markets

**Government markets**
Departments that buy goods and services to support their internal operations, and to provide the public with education, water, energy, national defence, road systems and healthcare

**Public-sector markets**
Government and institutional not-for-profit customers and stakeholder groups

National and local governments make up **government markets** and contribute to **public-sector markets**. They spend huge amounts annually for a variety of goods and services to support their internal operations and to provide the public with education, utilities, national defence, road systems and healthcare. In Europe, the amount spent by local governments varies from country to country, depending on the level and cost of services provided. As a result of the European single market, the services provided by different governments may eventually become standardised.

The types and quantities of products bought by government markets reflect social demands on various government agencies. As the public's needs for government services change, so do the government markets' demands for products.

Because government agencies spend public funds to buy the products they need to provide services, they are accountable to the public. This accountability is responsible for a relatively complex set of buying procedures. Some businesses, unwilling to deal with so much red tape, do not even try to sell to government buyers, while others have learned to deal efficiently with government procedures. For certain companies, such as BAe, and for certain products, such as defence-related items, the government may be one of only a few customers.

Governments usually make their purchases through bids or negotiated contracts. To make a sale under the bid system, a company must apply and receive approval to be placed on a list of qualified bidders. When a government unit wants to buy, it sends out a detailed description of the products to these qualified bidders. Businesses that wish to sell such products then submit bids. The government unit is usually required to accept the lowest bid. When buying non-standard or highly complex products, a government unit often uses a negotiated contract. Under this procedure, the government unit selects only a few companies, negotiates specifications and terms, and eventually awards the contract to one of the negotiating companies. Most large defence contracts held by such companies as BAe or Raytheon are reached through negotiated contracts.

Although government markets have complicated requirements, they can also be very lucrative. When government departments or healthcare providers modernise obsolete computer systems, for example, successful bidders can make high sales with attractive margins during the life of a contract, which may last for five years or more. Some companies have established separate departments to facilitate marketing to government units, while others specialise entirely in this area. The buying behaviour of governments is complex, though. A business such as Fujitsu sells IT services to banks, retailers, manufacturers and utility companies. Fujitsu is a leading supplier of IT services to central and local government and the health service: it has specialist management teams and sales and marketing specialists who focus purely on these public-sector clients owing to the specialised nature of their buying.

### Institutional Markets

**Institutional markets** Organisations with charitable, educational, community or other non-business goals

Organisations with charitable, educational, community or other non-business goals constitute **institutional markets**. Members of institutional markets include libraries, museums, universities, charitable organisations, and some churches and hospitals. Some of these are also public-sector bodies, such as libraries and museums. Increasingly, government and institutional markets are being grouped together and referred to as public-sector markets. Institutions also purchase large amounts of products annually to provide goods, services and ideas to members, congregations, students and other stakeholder groups. For example, a library must buy new books for its readers; pay rent, fuel and water bills; fund the staffing and cleaning of its buildings; invest in IT facilities; and pay to produce publicity material about its services. Because such institutions often have different goals and fewer resources than other types of organisation, marketers may use special marketing activities to serve these markets. Public-sector markets consist of government and institutional not-for-profit customers and stakeholder groups: public-sector marketing is a significant growth area within the marketing discipline.

## Dimensions of Business Buying

Having clarified the different types of business customer, the next step is to consider the dimensions of business-to-business buying. After first examining several characteristics of business transactions, this section then discusses various attributes of business buyers and some of their primary concerns when making purchase decisions. Next it looks at methods of business buying and the major types of purchase that organisations make. The section concludes with a discussion of how the demand for business products and services differs from the demand for consumer products and services.

### Characteristics of Business Transactions

Although the marketing concept is equally applicable to business and consumer markets, there are several fundamental differences between the transactions that occur in each. Business buyers tend to order in much larger quantities than do individual consumers. Suppliers must often sell their products in large quantities to make profits; consequently, they prefer not to sell to customers who place small orders.

Generally, business purchases are negotiated less frequently than consumer sales. Some purchases involve expensive items, such as machinery or office equipment, that are used for a number of years. Other products, such as raw materials and component items, are used continuously in production and may have to be supplied frequently. However, the contract regarding the terms of sale of these items is likely to be a long-term agreement, requiring periodic negotiations.

Negotiations in business sales may take much longer than those for consumer sales. Most consumers do not negotiate on prices paid, whereas many business customers never pay the list price. Purchasing decisions are often made by a committee; orders are frequently large, expensive and complex; and products may be custom built. There is a good chance that several people or departments in the purchasing organisation will be involved.

One department might express a need for a product; a second department might develop its specifications; a third might stipulate the maximum amount to be spent; and a fourth might actually place the order. This approach allows individuals with relevant expertise to be incorporated into the process when required. Sales personnel play an important role in negotiations with customers. The quality of the relationship that develops has been shown to impact on the outcome of such negotiations.

**Reciprocity**
An arrangement unique to business-to-business marketing in which two organisations agree to buy from each other

One practice unique to business-to-business sales is **reciprocity**, an arrangement in which two organisations agree to buy from each other. In some countries, reciprocal agreements that threaten competition are illegal, and action may be taken to stop anti-competitive reciprocal practices. None the less, a certain amount of reciprocal dealing occurs among small businesses and, to a lesser extent, among larger companies as well. Such companies often find that developing long-term relationships of this kind can be an effective competitive tool.[1] Reciprocity can create a problem because coercive measures may be used to enforce it or because reciprocity influences purchasing agents to deal only with certain suppliers.

## Attributes of Business Buyers

Business buyers are usually thought of as being different from consumer buyers in their purchasing behaviour because they are better informed about the products they purchase. The viability of their employer's business and thereby their own careers may well depend on their purchasing decisions, so they must be well informed. To make purchasing decisions that fulfil an organisation's needs, business buyers demand detailed information about a product's functional features and technical specifications.

Business buyers, however, also have personal goals that may influence their buying behaviour. Most buyers seek the psychological satisfaction that comes with promotion and financial rewards. In general, agents are most likely to achieve these personal goals when they consistently exhibit rational buying behaviour and perform their jobs in ways that help their companies achieve their organisational objectives. Suppose, though, that a business buyer develops a close friendship with a certain supplier. If the buyer values the friendship more than organisational promotion or financial rewards, he or she may behave irrationally from the company's point of view. Dealing exclusively with that supplier regardless of better prices, quality or service from competitors may indicate an unhealthy or unethical alliance between the buyer and seller. Companies have different ways of dealing with such problems. Some require more than one person to be involved in buying products, while others periodically review their use of suppliers.

## Primary Concerns of Business Buyers

When they make purchasing decisions, business customers take into account a variety of factors. For example, the business advertisement in Figure 7.2 offers retailers an exciting selection of easy-to-display pack options for Winalot. Among their chief considerations are quality, delivery, service and price. Product range, innovation, reliability and logistical support may also be significant considerations. Increasingly, business buyers are concerned with service support levels and ongoing commitment from their selected suppliers. There is a growing view, too, that a supplier's personnel in terms of knowledge, motivation, attitude and passion for assisting the customer, are an integral part of the product proposition being 'consumed' by the business customer (see Chapter 10).

Most business customers try to achieve and maintain a specific level of quality in the products they offer to their target markets. To accomplish this goal, they often buy their products on the basis of a set of expressed characteristics, commonly called specifications. These allow a business buyer to evaluate the quality of the products being considered according to particular features and thus to determine whether or not they meet the organisation's needs.

Meeting specifications is extremely important to business customers. If a product fails to meet specifications and malfunctions for the ultimate consumer, that product's supplier may be dropped and an alternative sought. On the other hand, a business buyer is usually

*Figure 7.2*
*This business-to-business advertisement for pet food Winalot promotes the wide selection of pack options offered to retail stockists*
*Source: All work created by Star Chamber*

cautious about buying products that exceed specifications, because such products often cost more and thus increase production costs. Suppliers, therefore, need to design their products carefully to come as close as possible to their customers' specifications without incurring any unnecessary extras.

Business buyers also value service. The services offered by suppliers directly and indirectly influence their customers' costs, sales and profits. When tangible goods are the same or quite similar – as with most raw materials – they may have the same specifications and be sold at the same price in the same kind of containers. Under such conditions, the mix of services a business marketer provides to its customers represents its greatest opportunity to gain a competitive advantage. For example, bitumen supplier Nynas has a reputation for technical expertise, technical assistance and flexible logistics. Competitors may be able to offer a similar bitumen product, but few can emulate Nynas's ability to look after customers.

Among the most commonly expected services are market information, inventory maintenance, on-time delivery, flexible ordering and logistical support, technical assistance, warranty back-up, repair services and credit facilities. Specific services vary in importance, however, and the mix of services that companies need is also affected by environmental conditions.

**Market Information** Business buyers in general are likely to need technical product information, data regarding demand, information about general economic conditions or supply and delivery information. For example, when technology is changing rapidly, forcing companies to change their production machinery, the demand for consultancy support services and warranty assurances will be especially high.

**Inventory Maintenance** It is critical for suppliers to maintain an adequate inventory in order to keep products accessible for when a business buyer needs them and to reduce the buyer's inventory requirements and costs.

**On-time Delivery** Reliable, on-time delivery by suppliers also enables business customers to carry less inventory.

**Warranty Back-up** Purchasers of machinery are especially concerned about adequate warranties. They are also keen to obtain repair services and replacement parts quickly, because equipment that cannot be used is costly.

**Credit Facilities** Suppliers can also give extra value to business buyers by offering credit. Credit helps to improve a business customer's cash flow, reduces the peaks and troughs of capital requirements and thus lowers the company's cost of capital. Although no single supplier can provide every possible service to its customers, a marketing-oriented supplier will try to create a service mix that satisfies the target market.

**The Importance of Service Quality** Service quality has become a critical issue because customer expectations of service have broadened. Marketers also need to strive for uniformity of service, simplicity, truthfulness and accuracy; to develop customer service objectives; and to monitor or audit their customer service programmes. Companies can monitor the quality of their service by formally surveying customers or calling on them informally to ask questions about the service they have received. Marketers with a strong customer service programme reap a reward: their customers keep coming back long after the first sale.[2] With customer expectations increasing, it is becoming more difficult for companies to achieve a differential advantage in these areas, and companies must take care to ensure that complaints are handled properly.[3] This reduces the likelihood that dissatisfied customers will give negative feedback to others in the marketplace.[4] One study found that boosting customer retention by 5 per cent could double a small company's profitability.[5]

**The Importance of Price** Price matters greatly to a business customer because it influences operating costs and costs of goods sold, and these costs affect the customer's selling price and profit margin. When purchasing major equipment, an industrial buyer views the price as the amount of investment necessary to obtain a certain level of return or savings. Such a purchaser is likely to compare the price of a machine with the value of the benefits that the machine will yield. Caterpillar lost market share to foreign competitors because its prices were too high. A business buyer does not compare alternative products by price alone, though; other factors, such as product quality and supplier services, are also major elements in the purchase decision. For example, one study found that in the buying decision process for mainframe computer software operating systems, intangible attributes, such as the seller's credibility and understanding of the buyer's needs, were very important in the buyer's decision process.[6]

## Methods of Business Buying

Although no two business buyers go about their jobs in the same way, most use one or more of the following purchase methods: description, inspection, sampling and negotiation.

**Description** When products being purchased are commonly standardised according to certain characteristics – such as size, shape, weight and colour – and graded using such standards, a business buyer may be able to purchase simply by describing or specifying quantity, grade and other attributes. Agricultural produce often falls into this category. In some cases a buyer may specify a particular brand or its equivalent when describing the desired product. Purchases on the basis of description are especially common between a buyer and seller who have established an ongoing relationship built on trust.

**Inspection** Certain products, such as large industrial machinery, used vehicles and buildings, have unique characteristics and are likely to vary in condition. For example, a transport depot may need its parking area to be resurfaced. Consequently, buyers and sellers of such products must base their purchase decisions on inspection.

**Sampling** In buying based on sampling, a sample of the product is taken from the lot and evaluated. It is assumed that the characteristics of this sample represent the entire lot. This method is appropriate when the product is homogeneous – for instance, grain – and examination of the entire lot is not physically or economically feasible.

**Negotiation** Some business purchasing relies on negotiated contracts. In certain instances, a business buyer describes exactly what is needed and then asks sellers to submit bids. The buyer may take the most attractive bids and negotiate with those suppliers. In other cases, the buyer may not be able to identify specifically what is to be purchased but can provide only a general description – as might be the case for a special piece of custom-made equipment. A buyer and seller may negotiate a contract that specifies a base price and contains provisions for the payment of additional costs and fees. These contracts are most likely to be used for one-off projects, such as buildings and capital equipment. For example, the prices that Orbital Sciences Corporation charges its customers for launching and placing satellites in orbit are determined through negotiated contracts.

## Types of Business Purchase

Most business purchases are one of three types: new task purchase, modified rebuy purchase or straight rebuy purchase. The type of purchase affects the number of individuals involved and the length of the buying process.

**New task purchase**
An organisation's initial purchase of an item to be used to perform a new job or to solve a new problem

**New Task Purchase** In a **new task purchase**, an organisation makes an initial purchase of an item to be used to perform a new job or to solve a new problem. This may take a long time because it might require the development of product specifications, supplier specifications and procedures for future purchases. To make the initial purchase, the business buyer usually needs a good deal of information and may formally review a set of possible suppliers. A new task purchase is important to the supplier because it may lead to the sale of large quantities of the product over a period of years.

**Modified rebuy purchase**
A new task purchase that is changed when it is reordered or when the requirements associated with a straight rebuy purchase are modified

**Modified Rebuy Purchase** In a **modified rebuy purchase**, a new task purchase is changed the second or third time it is ordered, or the requirements associated with a straight rebuy purchase are modified. For example, an organisation might seek faster delivery, lower prices or a different quality of product specifications. When modified rebuying occurs, regular suppliers may become more competitive to keep the account. Competing suppliers may have the opportunity to obtain the business.

**Straight Rebuy Purchase** A **straight rebuy purchase** occurs when a buyer repurchases the same products routinely under approximately the same terms of sale. For example,

**Straight rebuy purchase**
A routine repurchase of the same products under approximately the same terms of sale

when reordering photocopying paper, a buyer requires little additional information and can usually place the order relatively quickly, often using familiar suppliers that have provided satisfactory service and products in the past. These suppliers try to set up automatic reordering systems to make reordering easy and convenient for business buyers, and may even monitor the organisation's inventory to indicate to the buyer what needs to be ordered.

## Demand for Business Products

Products sold to business customers are called business products and, consequently, the demand for these products is called business demand. Unlike consumer demand, business demand – formerly known as industrial demand – is:

- derived
- inelastic
- joint, and
- more fluctuating.

**Derived demand**
Demand for business products that arises from the demand for consumer products

**Derived Demand** As business customers, especially producers, buy products to be used directly or indirectly in the production of goods and services to satisfy consumers' needs, the demand for business products arises from the demand for consumer products; it is, therefore, called **derived demand**. In fact, all business demand can in some way be traced to consumer demand. This occurs at a number of levels, with business sellers being affected in various ways. For instance, consumers today are more concerned with good health and nutrition than ever before, and as a result are purchasing food products containing less cholesterol, saturated fat, sugar and salt. When some consumers stopped buying high-cholesterol cooking fats and margarine, the demand for equipment used in manufacturing these products also dropped. Thus factors influencing consumer buying of various food products have ultimately affected food processors, equipment manufacturers, suppliers of raw materials and even fast-food restaurants, which have had to switch to lower-cholesterol oils for frying. Changes in derived demand result from a chain reaction. When consumer demand for a product changes, a wave is set in motion that affects demand for all of the items involved in the production of that consumer product.

**Inelastic demand**
Demand that is not significantly affected by a price increase or decrease

**Inelastic Demand** The demand for many business products at the industry level is **inelastic demand** – that is, a price increase or decrease will not significantly alter demand for the item. The concept of price elasticity of demand is discussed further in Chapters 20 and 21. Because many business products contain a number of parts, price increases that affect only one or two parts of the product may yield only a slightly higher per-unit production cost. Of course, when a sizeable price increase for a component represents a large proportion of the total product's cost, demand may become more elastic, because the component price increase will cause the price at the consumer level to rise sharply. For example, if manufacturers of aircraft engines substantially increase the price of these engines, forcing Boeing in turn to raise the prices of its aircraft, the demand for aircraft may become more elastic as airlines reconsider whether they can afford them. An increase in the price of windscreens, however, is unlikely to affect greatly the price of the aircraft or the demand for them.

The characteristic of inelasticity applies only to industry demand for the business product, not to the demand curve faced by an individual company. For example, suppose that a car component company increases the price of rubber seals sold to car manufacturers, while its competitors retain their lower prices. The car component company would probably experience reduced unit sales because most of its customers would switch to the lower-priced brands. A specific organisation is vulnerable to elastic demand, even though industry demand for a particular product is inelastic.

**Joint demand**
Demand that occurs when two or more products are used in combination to produce another product

**Joint Demand** The demand for certain business products, especially raw materials and components, is subject to joint demand. **Joint demand** occurs when two or more items are used in combination to produce a product. For example, a company that manufactures cork noticeboards for schools and colleges needs supplies of cork and wood to produce the item; these two products are demanded jointly. A shortage of cork will cause a drop in the production of wooden surrounds for noticeboards.

Marketers selling many jointly demanded items must realise that when a customer begins purchasing one of the jointly demanded items, a good opportunity exists for selling related products. Similarly, when customers purchase a number of jointly demanded products, the producer must take care to avoid shortages of any one of them, because such shortages jeopardise sales of all the jointly demanded products. The susceptibility of producers to the shortage of a particular item is illustrated clearly when industrial action at companies producing microchips results in a halt in production at manufacturers of computers and related goods.

**Fluctuating Demand** Because the demand for business products fluctuates according to consumer demand, when particular consumer products are in high demand, their producers buy large quantities of raw materials and components to ensure that they can meet long-run production requirements. Such producers may also expand their production capacity, which entails the acquisition of new equipment and machinery, more workers, a greater need for business services, and more raw materials and component parts.

Conversely, a decline in the demand for certain consumer goods significantly reduces the demand for business products used to produce those goods. When consumer demand is low, business customers cut their purchases of raw materials and components, and stop buying equipment and machinery, even for replacement purposes. This trend is especially pronounced during periods of recession.

A marketer of business products may notice changes in demand when its customers change their inventory policies, perhaps because of expectations about future demand. For example, if several dishwasher manufacturers who buy timers from one producer increase their inventory of timers from a two-week to a one-month supply, the timer producer will experience a significant immediate increase in demand.

Sometimes price changes can lead to surprising temporary changes in demand. A price increase for a business item may initially cause business customers to buy more of the item because they expect the price to rise further. Similarly, demand for a business product may be significantly lower following a price cut as buyers wait for further price reductions. Such behaviour is often observed in companies purchasing information technology. Fluctuations in demand can be significant in industries in which price changes occur frequently.

## Business Buying Decisions

**Business (or business-to-business) buying behaviour**
The purchase behaviour of producers, resellers, the public sector, government units and institutions

**Business (or business-to-business) buying behaviour** refers to the purchase behaviour of producers, resellers, the public sector, government units and institutions. Although several of the same factors that affect consumer buying behaviour (discussed in Chapter 6) also influence business buying behaviour, a number of factors are unique to the latter. This section first analyses the buying centre to learn who participates in making business purchase decisions and then focuses on the stages of the buying decision process and the factors that affect this process.

### The Buying Centre

Most business-to-business purchase decisions are made by more than one person. The group of people within an organisation who are involved in making business purchase decisions are usually referred to as the **buying centre**. These individuals include users, influencers, buyers, deciders and gatekeepers, although one person may perform several

**Buying centre** The group of people within an organisation who are involved in making business-to-business purchase decisions

of these roles.[7] Participants in the buying process share the goals and risks associated with their decisions. Effective marketers strive to understand the constituents of risk, as perceived by their target customer personnel, so that they may tailor their messages and marketing propositions to reassure members of the buying centre. In this way, marketers hope to gain an advantage over those rivals that fail to understand these customer concerns and issues.

Users are those in the business who actually use the product being acquired. They frequently initiate the purchase process and/or generate the specifications for the purchase. After the purchase, they also evaluate the product's performance relative to the specifications. Although users do not ordinarily have sufficient power to make the final decision to buy, it is important that their views be considered. A user who is unhappy with a piece of equipment may not work efficiently. Influencers are often technical personnel, such as engineers, who help develop the specifications and evaluate alternative products. Technical personnel are especially important influencers when the products being considered involve new, advanced technology. For example, a chemicals manufacturer seeking to install new processing equipment may take advice from a wide range of technical experts.

Buyers are responsible for selecting suppliers and actually negotiating the terms of purchase. They may also become involved in developing specifications. Buyers are sometimes called purchasing agents or purchasing managers and in retailers, merchandisers. Their choices of suppliers and products, especially for new task purchases, are heavily influenced by individuals occupying other roles in the buying centre. For straight rebuy purchases, the buyer plays a major role in the selection of suppliers and in negotiations with them. Deciders actually choose the products and suppliers. Although buyers may be the deciders, it is not unusual for different people to occupy these roles. For routinely purchased items, buyers are commonly the deciders. However, a buyer may not be authorised to make purchases that exceed a certain monetary value, in which case higher-level management personnel are the deciders. Gatekeepers, such as secretaries and technical personnel, control the flow of information to and among others in the buying centre. The flow of information from supplier sales representatives to users and influencers is often controlled by buyers or other personnel in the purchasing department. Unfortunately, relations between members of the buying centre can become strained at times.

## Marketing Tools and Techniques

### Practitioners' Use of the Buying Behaviour Theory: the Dibb/Simkin Buying Proforma

Most practitioners do not want to read an 800-page text book about understanding customers, but equally they recognise that in order to fully appreciate a business customer's requirements or consumers' buying behaviour, they must be able to:

- profile the targeted customers/consumers – be them!
- understand the composition of the buying centre
- identify their key customer values (KCVs) – customer/consumer needs and expectations
- determine how the customers/consumers buy – their buying process
- understand the influences at work on this process.

In order to devise effective marketing strategies and programmes, marketers must be able to answer three key questions.

1 What needs must be satisfied and for whom?
2 Where should marketers be active in the customer/consumer buying process?
3 Which influencing factors can they in turn influence?

There are many approaches to addressing such an understanding of business customers or consumers, but one proposed by Dibb and Simkin has been widely adopted across consumer, business and service markets. Two examples are presented here in order to illustrate this approach.

A leading supplier of herbicides, pesticides and seeds segmented the farmers – the customers – in Latin America, identifying 22 market segments (see Chapter 8). As an example, one segment is profiled below, illustrating the types of farmer in this segment, the nature of the buying centre and the very specific, ego-led customer needs. In order to operate successfully in this market segment, a supplier has to satisfy these needs but also tailor marketing campaigns to the characteristics of these farmers and the varied mix of professionals within this buying centre. In developing a better understanding of the buying process, this agrochemicals business realised there were important influencing factors impacting on customer choice that it had previously ignored. Contact was made with organisers of the technical seminars and the trade association in order to gain an advantage over rivals.

In common with most banks and building societies, the bank that conducted this research marketed its products directly to the targeted consumers: first-time house buyers. Marketing research (see Chapter 9) identified the important influencing role played by the parents of these potential customers, and of independent financial advisers, estate agents and the bank's own staff involved in daily routine banking activities with such customers. Different marketing messages and campaigns were produced to appeal to these various target audiences. The real added value came from targeting information about its mortgage products to the parents of young adults aged in their 20s. It was quite straightforward for this bank to trawl through its customer database in order to identify customers with children in such an age range. Market share in this mortgage segment duly quadrupled in less than a year. This bank undertook a similar analysis across all of its segments in both consumer markets – as illustrated below – and in its business markets.

The Dibb/Simkin Buying Proforma:

- forces managers to 'think customer'!
- provides much more than just a description of 'who to sell to'
- identifies exactly what a company must provide/offer
- reveals the influences the company in turn must strive to influence
- provides a framework against which to compare competitors' moves and marketing programmes.

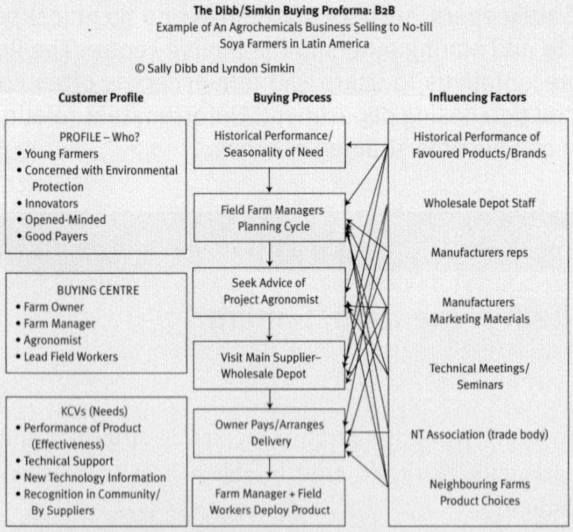


The Dibb/Simkin Buying Proforma is copyright Sally Dibb and Lyndon Simkin. A more extensive explanation of this technique is offered in either *The Market Segmentation Workbook* (Dibb and Simkin) or *The Marketing Planning Workbook* (Dibb, Simkin and Bradley), both originally published in 1996 by Thomson, London.

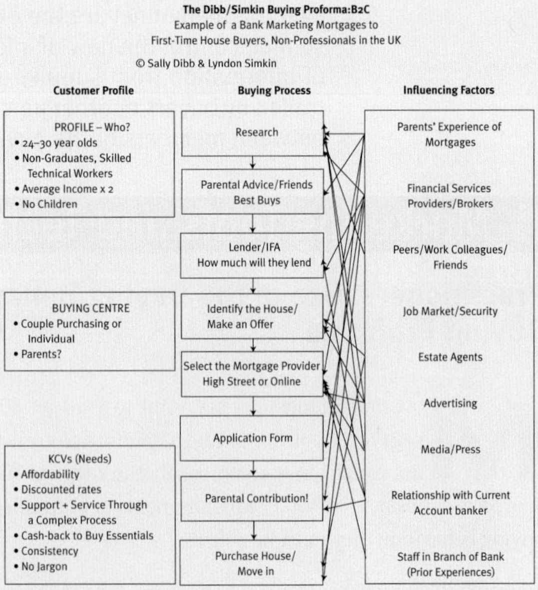


The size and characteristics of an organisation's buying centre are affected by the number of its employees and its market position, the volume and types of products being purchased and the company's overall managerial philosophy regarding exactly who should be involved in purchase decisions. A marketer attempting to sell to a business customer needs to know who is in the buying centre, the types of decisions each individual makes and which individuals are the most influential in the decision process. The marketer should also strive to understand the respective needs of these members and how each perceives risk in terms of the proposed purchase: the marketer should then tailor messages to reassure the various members of the buying centre. Then the marketer will be in a position to contact those in the buying centre who have the most influence. Such an approach is detailed in the Marketing Tools and Techniques box on pages 201–202, which also explains how many businesses deploy the buying behaviour concepts presented in this chapter as they build up an understanding of their customers.

## Relationship Marketing and Managing Exchange Relationships

**Relationship marketing**
All of the activities an organisation uses to build, maintain and develop customer relations

The relationship that exists between a supplying organisation and its customers is an important aspect of the buying process that deserves special consideration. In fact, marketing experts have recently become much more interested in marketing relationships in general.[8] The term **relationship marketing** has been used to express this particular development as explained in Chapter 1. Instead of being concerned about individual transactions between suppliers and buyers, the relationship marketing approach emphasises the importance of the whole relationship between the parties. Relationship marketing can, therefore, be regarded as all of the activities an organisation uses to build, maintain and develop ongoing customer relations.[9] The intention is to nurture a mutually beneficial sustainable relationship and to maximise the 'share of wallet' from the customer over a period of time.

Put simply, relationship marketing is concerned with getting and keeping customers by ensuring that an appropriate combination of marketing, customer service and quality is provided.[10] Underlying the relationship marketing concept is the idea that the relationship between a supplying organisation and its buyers is essentially similar to the relationship between two individuals. For example, bitumen company Nynas, featured in the Case Study at the end of this chapter, has achieved market leadership through building ongoing relationships with a diversity of customers 24 hours a day, 365 days a year. Such relationships are conducted over a period of time through a series of meetings, which allow each party to get to know the other, to share information, to adapt to each other, and generally to build trust and cooperation.[11]

As explained in Chapter 1, the concept of relationship marketing is changing the way in which marketers are looking at marketing. However, it is also particularly pertinent to this chapter's discussion of the exchange relationships that develop between buyers and sellers.[12] When a company buys a product or service from another company, both organisations become involved in an exchange process. During the transaction, both buyer and seller will exchange items of value in return for something else. For example, when a software company provides a printer with a desktop publishing package, it will provide the buyer with a package of benefits that include the software disks, detailed users' guide, warranty details, a variety of payment options and the opportunity to attend a training course. In exchange, the printer will agree to pay the price negotiated with the manufacturer. Figure 7.3 shows the range of factors that can be exchanged during the purchase process.

**Relationship management**
The process of encouraging a match between the seller's competitive advantage and the buyer's requirements over an item's life cycle

It is often in the interests of both parties to develop long-term relationships. If buying and selling companies are used to dealing with each other, they are more likely to be able to adapt to each other's needs and to reach an agreement quickly and easily. Some research suggests that adaptation by suppliers happens more often than adaptation by buyers. However, long-term relationships are often attractive to both companies because they reduce the level of risk – financial and practical – associated with the purchase. The trend towards long-term relationships has resulted in the development of what is called **relationship management**.[13] This process encourages a match between the seller's competitive advantage and the buyer's requirements over the life cycle of the item being purchased.

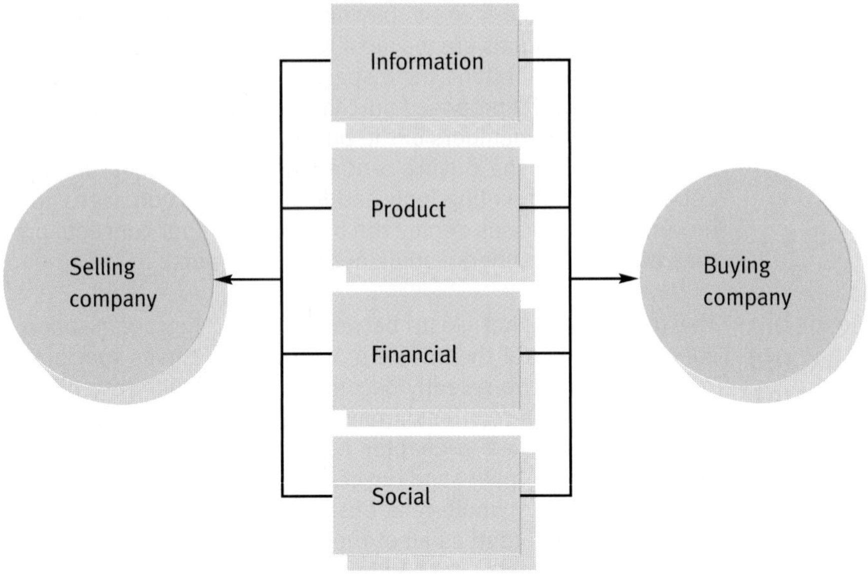


*Figure 7.3*
*The exchange process in business buying*

## Stages of the Business Buying Decision Process

Like consumers, businesses follow a buying decision process. This process is summarised on the right-hand side of Figure 7.4.

**Stage 1** In the first stage, one or more individuals recognise that a problem or need exists. Problem recognition may arise under a variety of circumstances, either from inside or outside the company. For example, a machine might reach the end of its working life and need to be replaced, or changes in fire regulations might dictate the need for a new approach to manufacturing. Often, the problem recognised is simply the need to replenish stocks of raw materials or components. Individuals in the buying centre, such as users, influencers or buyers, may be involved in problem recognition, but this may be stimulated by external sources, such as sales representatives or customers.

**Stage 2** The second stage of the process – development of product specifications – requires those involved to assess the problem or need, and to determine what is necessary to resolve or satisfy it. During this stage, users and influencers, such as technical personnel, production managers and engineers, often provide information and advice for developing product specifications. By assessing and describing needs, the organisation should be able to establish product specifications.

**Stage 3** Searching for possible products to solve the problem and then locating suitable suppliers is the third stage in the decision process. Search activities may involve surfing the Internet, looking in company files and trade directories, contacting suppliers for information, visiting trade shows, identifying suppliers used by rivals, soliciting proposals from known suppliers, and examining catalogues and trade publications. Suppliers may be viewed as unacceptable because they are too small to supply the quantities needed, or because they do not have the necessary information technology systems to keep appropriate delivery records. In some instances, the product may not be available from any existing supplier and the buyer must then find an innovative company, such as 3M, that can design and build the product. During this search stage, some businesses engage in **value analysis**, which is an evaluation of each component of a potential purchase. Value analysis examines quality, designs, materials, and possibly item reduction or deletion to acquire the product in the most cost-effective way. Usually suppliers are judged against several criteria

**Value analysis**
An evaluation of each component of a potential purchase

*Figure 7.4*
*The business buying decision process and factors that may influence it*
*Source: adapted from Frederick E. Webster, Jr, and Yoram Wind,* Organisational Buying Behaviour *(Englewood Cliffs, NJ: Prentice-Hall, 1972), pp. 33–7 Adapted by permission*

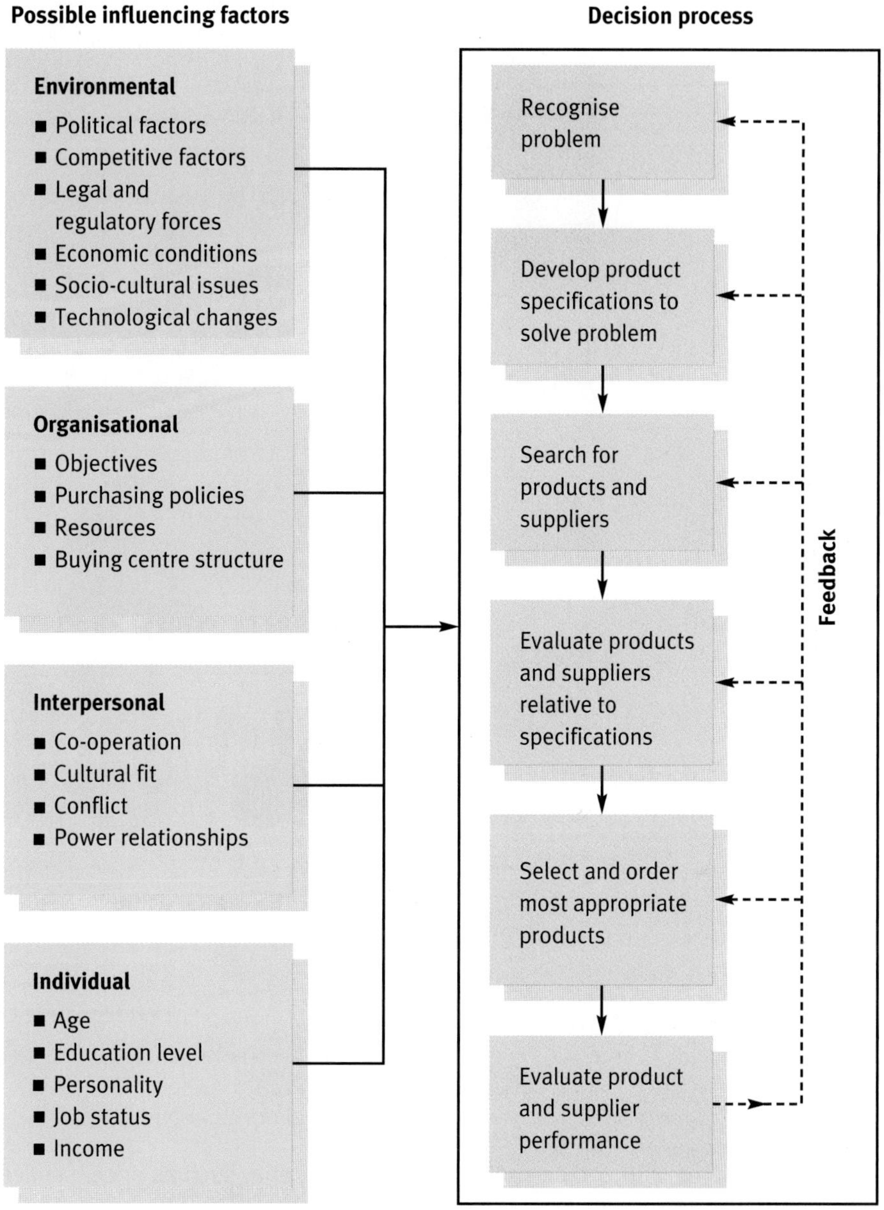


**Supplier analysis**
A formal and systematic evaluation of current and potential suppliers

and some will be ruled unsuitable. Some businesses practice **supplier analysis**, a formal and systematic appraisal of current and potential suppliers or vendors, focusing on factors such as price, product quality, delivery service, product availability, reliability, reputation, client profile and customer service.

If all goes well, the search stage will result in a list of several alternative products and suppliers.

**Stage 4** The fourth stage is evaluating the products on the list to determine which options (if any) meet the product specifications developed in the second stage. The advertisement in Figure 7.5 stresses the particular product quality attributes that may help customers evaluate whether a particular offering meets their requirements. At this point, too, various suppliers

*Figure 7.5*
*Dalgety promotes the quality and reliability of its seeds, targeted at the farming community*
*Source: Courtesy of Dalgety – a division of MASSTOCK ARABLE (UK) LTD*

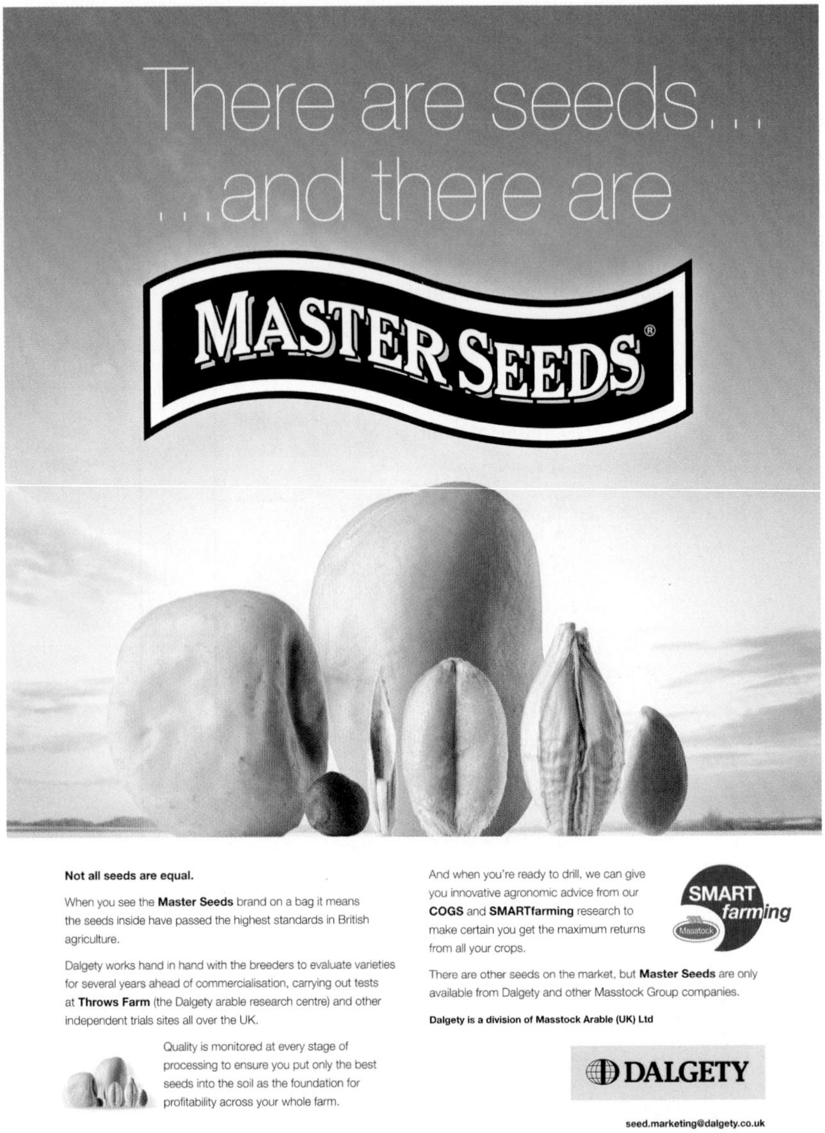


are evaluated according to multiple criteria, such as price, service, technical support and ability to deliver.

There are seeds...
...and there are
MASTER SEEDS®
Not all seeds are equal.
When you see the Master Seeds brand on a bag it means the seeds inside have passed the highest standards in British agriculture.
Dalgety works hand in hand with the breeders to evaluate varieties for several years ahead of commercialisation, carrying out tests at Throws Farm (the Dalgety arable research centre) and other independent trials sites all over the UK.
Quality is monitored at every stage of processing to ensure you put only the best seeds into the soil as the foundation for profitability across your whole farm.
And when you're ready to drill, we can give you innovative agronomic advice from our COGS and SMARTfarming research to make certain you get the maximum returns from all your crops.
SMART farming
Masstock
There are other seeds on the market, but Master Seeds are only available from Dalgety and other Masstock Group companies.
Dalgety is a division of Masstock Arable (UK) Ltd
DALGETY
seed.marketing@dalgety.co.uk

**Sole sourcing**
A buying process that involves the selection of only one supplier

**Multiple sourcing**
A business's decision to use several suppliers

**Stage 5** The results of the deliberations and assessments in the fourth stage are used during the fifth stage to select the most appropriate product and supplier. In some cases the buyer may decide on several suppliers. In others, only one supplier is selected – a situation known as **sole sourcing**. Sole sourcing has traditionally been discouraged except when a product is available from only one company. In recent times sole sourcing has become more popular, partly because such an arrangement means better communications between buyer and supplier, stability and higher profits for the supplier and, often, lower prices for the buyer. The popular manufacturing approach of just-in-time often requires sole sourcing, in order to facilitate the logistical arrangements between buyer and supplier. However, many organisations prefer to purchase goods and services from several suppliers – **multiple sourcing** – to reduce the possibility of disruption caused by strikes, shortages, quality problems, delivery glitches or bankruptcy. The actual product is ordered in this fifth stage and specific details regarding terms, credit arrangements, delivery dates and methods, and technical assistance are worked out.

**Stage 6** During the sixth stage, the product's performance is evaluated by comparing it with specifications and customer expectations of the relationship. Sometimes, even though the product meets the specifications, its performance does not adequately solve the problem or satisfy the need recognised in the first stage. In such cases, the product specifications must be adjusted. The supplier's performance is also evaluated during this stage, and if it is found wanting, the buyer seeks corrective action from the supplier or searches for a new supplier. Buyers are increasingly concerned with obtaining high-quality service from suppliers and may formally set performance targets for them. The results of such performance evaluations become feedback for the other stages and influence future purchase decisions. In many business relationships, particularly long-term relationships, suppliers formally audit their customers' satisfaction levels in order to minimise any problems that may eventually lose a customer to a competitor.

**Uses of the Business Buying Decision Process** This business buying decision process is used in its entirety primarily for new task purchases. Several of the stages, but not necessarily all, are used for modified rebuying and straight rebuying, and fewer individuals are likely to be involved in these decisions. If a buyer–supplier relationship is working well, there may be no consideration of alternative suppliers, for example. Indeed, customers may work with such well-regarded suppliers when specifying their next product or purchasing needs. There is a desire in many business markets, particularly in supplier–manufacturer relationships, to create mutually beneficial ongoing partnerships, with customers and suppliers openly sharing market data, knowledge of product or competitor developments, and future plans.

## Influences on Business Buying

Figure 7.4 also lists the four major categories of factors that influence business buying decisions: environmental, organisational, interpersonal and individual.

**Environmental factors** Uncontrollable forces such as politics, competitive and economic factors, legal and regulatory issues, technological changes and socio-cultural issues

**Environmental Factors** Chapter 3 explained that **environmental factors** are uncontrollable forces such as politics, laws, regulations and regulatory agencies, activities of interest groups, changes in the economy, competitors' actions and technological changes. These forces generate a considerable amount of uncertainty for an organisation, which can make individuals in the buying centre apprehensive about certain types of purchase. Changes in one or more environmental forces can create new purchasing opportunities. For example, changes in competition and technology can make buying decisions difficult in the case of products such as computers, a field in which competition is increasingly affected by new cooperative strategies between companies. Compaq Computers, for instance, grew into a billion-dollar company by competing only against IBM and developing cooperative relationships with all other potential competitors, ultimately tying up with HP.[14]

**Organisational factors** Include the buyer's objectives, purchasing policies and resources, as well as the size and composition of its buying centre

**Organisational Factors** **Organisational factors** influencing the buying decision process include the buyer's objectives, purchasing policies and resources, as well as the size and composition of its buying centre. An organisation may have certain buying policies to which buying centre participants must conform. For instance, a company's policies may require long-term contracts, perhaps longer than most sellers desire. The nature of an organisation's financial resources may require special credit arrangements. Any of these conditions could affect purchase decision processes.

**Interpersonal factors** The relationships among the people in the buying centre

**Interpersonal Factors** **Interpersonal factors** are the relationships among the people in the buying centre, where the use of power and the level of conflict significantly influence organisational buying decisions. Certain managers in the buying centre may be better communicators than others and thus more persuasive. Often these interpersonal dynamics are hidden, making them difficult for marketers to appraise. There are also interpersonal factors to consider between supplier and customer personnel. While a customer may be purchasing a particular product, the supplier's personnel involved with placing the order, offering technical assistance or customer service, and in logistical arrangements, become a very important concern for the customer's managers. No matter how good the product may be, if the supplier's personnel are not regarded in a good light by the customer's managers, there is unlikely to be a high level of customer satisfaction. Suppliers must select, train, motivate and reward, control and orient their customer-facing personnel very carefully. The individual factors pertinent to particular managers are, therefore, important.

**Individual factors**
The personal characteristics of individuals in the buying centre, such as age, education, personality, position in the organisation and income level

**Individual Factors** **Individual factors** are the personal characteristics of individuals in the buying centre, such as age, education, personality, position in the organisation and income level. For example, a 60-year-old manager who left school at 16 and has been with the organisation ever since may affect the decisions of the buying centre differently from a 30 year old with a two-year employment history, who left university with a business studies degree and an MBA. How influential these factors will be depends on the buying situation, the type of product being purchased and whether the purchase is new task, modified rebuy or straight rebuy. The negotiating styles of individuals will undoubtedly vary within an organisation and from one organisation to another. To be effective, a marketer needs to know customers well enough to be aware of these individual factors and the effects they may have on purchase decisions.

# Selection and Analysis of Business Markets

**Business marketing**
Activities directed towards facilitating and expediting exchanges between business markets and business producers

Marketing research is becoming more important in business markets. Most of the marketing research techniques discussed in Chapter 9 can be applied to **business marketing**. This section focuses on important and unique approaches to selecting and analysing business markets.

Many business marketers have easy access to a considerable amount of information about potential customers, particularly in industrial or manufacturing markets, for much of this information appears in government and industry publications. However, comparable data about ultimate consumers are not available. Even though marketers may use different procedures to isolate and analyse target markets, most follow a similar pattern:

1 determining who potential customers are and how many there are
2 locating where they are
3 estimating their purchase potential.

The forecasting techniques described in Chapter 23 are particularly relevant to business marketers when estimating market potential and likely sales.

## Identifying Potential Customers

All marketers must determine who are potential customers. In the Topical Insight box (see page 209), for example, food giant Unilever has decided to market its new-look ice cream units to convenience stores and forecourt outlets, rather than to the supermarkets.

**The Standard Industrial Classification System** Much information about business customers is based on the **Standard Industrial Classification (SIC) system**, which provides information on different industries and products, and was developed to classify selected economic characteristics of industrial, commercial, financial and service organisations. In the UK, this system is administered by the Central Statistical Office. Table 7.1 shows how the SIC system can be used to categorise products.

## Topical Insight

### Unilever Targets Forecourts and Convenience Stores

In the battle for market share in the ice cream market, it has long been the practice of the major manufacturers to make branded freezer units available to retailers. The hope is that prominently branded units will both encourage consumers to purchase ice cream lines but also persuade retailers to maintain stocks of a particular manufacturer's ice cream brands. Until recently, the freezer units were chests with sliding tops: there was no access from the front or sides. There was only limited display potential, as consumers could only see inside through the top by leaning over the units.

In the summer of 2004, Wall's owner Unilever launched eye-catching three-tier units that displayed the contents at three tilted levels. The new units also made the merchandise easier to access. In test market trials, the Maxivision freezer increased forecourt sales by 29 per cent. In addition to being more eye-catching and easier to access, the unit holds much more than its predecessor and reduces running costs by around 15 per cent. However, the improved freezer was more expensive. The older unit cost retailers around £600, whereas the new unit costs over £900. These prices to retail customers include £300 worth of Wall's stock vouchers.

For Unilever's marketers, the challenge had been to increase consumer sales by providing the company's retail customers with a better display and storage solution. The new unit had to encourage more consumer demand, help maximise floor space utilisation and minimise operating costs. The older storage units were cumbersome, often unsightly and, out of season, occupied a disproportionate amount of space relative to winter sales levels. The test market revealed that retailers appreciated the better space utilisation as much as the improved appeal to their shoppers.

Unilever decided not to prioritise the major supermarket chains as sales targets for these freezer units. These retailers tend to have their own freezer units designed to display and store many lines from a variety of manufacturers. Unilever's marketers instead determined that garage forecourts and convenience stores were far better sales prospects. Even within these target categories, the national chains were targeted as priority sales prospects, ahead of the independently owned one-off retailers and small regional chains. The units were made available to all retailers, but promotional activity and the salesforce were tasked to initially focus on convenience stores and forecourt chains.

**Sources:** *The Grocer*, 8 May 2004, p. 64; One Stop Stores; Unilever Wall's.

**Standard Industrial Classification (SIC) system**
A system that provides information on different industries and products, and classifies economic characteristics of industrial, commercial, financial and service organisations

The most recent SIC manual contains 10 broad divisions, each denoted by a single digit from 0 to 9. These are sub-divided into classes (each denoted by the addition of a second digit), the classes are divided into groups (three digits) and the groups into activity headings (four more digits). There are 10 divisions, 60 classes, 222 groups and 334 activity headings. For example, Division 4 (see Table 7.1), 'Other manufacturing industries', has 8 classes, 50 groups and 91 activity headings. The numbering system follows that of NACE (Nomenclature Générale des Activités Économiques dans les Communautés Européennes) as far as possible.[15] To categorise manufacturers in more detail, the *Census of Distribution* further sub-divides manufacturers.

Data are available for each SIC category through various government publications and departments. Table 7.2 shows the types of information that can be obtained from government sources. Some data are available by town, county and metropolitan area. Business market data also appear in such non-government sources as Dun & Bradstreet's *Market Identifiers*.

The SIC system is a ready-made tool that allows business marketers to divide industrial organisations into market segments based mainly on the type of product manufactured or handled. Although the SIC system is a vehicle for segmentation– identifying groupings of customers (see Chapter 8) – it must be used in conjunction with other types of data to enable a business marketer to determine exactly which customers he or she can reach and

**TABLE 7.1 THE STANDARD INDUSTRIAL CLASSIFICATION (SIC) SYSTEM FOR CATEGORISING INDUSTRIAL CONSUMERS**

| | |
|---|---|
| 0 | Agriculture, forestry and fishing |
| 1 | Energy and water supply industries |
| 2 | Extraction of minerals and ores other than fuels; manufacture of metals, mineral products and chemicals |
| 3 | Metal goods, engineering and vehicles |
| 4 | Other manufacturing industries |
| 5 | Construction |
| 6 | Distribution, hotels and catering; repairs |
| 7 | Transport and communication |
| 8 | Banking, finance, insurance, business services and leasing |
| 9 | Other services |

**TABLE 7.2 TYPES OF GOVERNMENT INFORMATION AVAILABLE ABOUT INDUSTRIAL MARKETS (BASED ON SIC CATEGORIES)**

| |
|---|
| Value of industry shipments |
| Number of establishments |
| Number of employees |
| Exports as a percentage of shipments |
| Imports as a percentage of apparent consumption |
| Compound annual average rate of growth |
| Major producing areas |

how many of them can be targeted. The SIC system is a convenient grouping categorisation, but it does not negate the need to fully explore customer buying behaviour, as depicted in the Marketing Tools and Techniques box on pages 201–202, in order to properly consider target market priorities.

**Input–Output Analysis** Input–output analysis works well in conjunction with the SIC system. This type of analysis is based on the assumption that the output or sales of one industry are the input or purchases of other industries. For example, component manufacturers provide products that form an input for manufacturers of white goods such as washing machines, dishwashers and fridges. **Input–output data** tell what types of industries purchase the products of a particular industry.

**Input–output data** Information on what types of industries purchase the products of a particular industry

After discovering which industries purchase the major portion of an industry's output, the next step is to find the SIC numbers for those industries. Because businesses are grouped differently in the input–output tables and the SIC system, ascertaining SIC numbers can be difficult. However, the Central Statistical Office does provide some limited conversion tables with the input–output data. These tables can assist business marketers in assigning SIC numbers to the industry categories used in the input–output analysis. Having determined the SIC numbers of the industries that buy the company's output, a business marketer is in a position to ascertain the number of establishments that are potential buyers nationally, by town and by county. Government publications report the number of establishments within SIC classifications, along with other types of data, such as those shown in Table 7.2.

**Identifying and Locating Potential Customers** Once business marketers have achieved this level of information, they can identify and locate potential customers using the Internet or business directories such as *Kompass* and *Kelly's*. These sources contain information about a company such as its name, SIC number, address, phone number and annual sales, allowing organisations to develop lists of potential customers by area.

A second approach, which is more expedient but also more expensive, is to use one of the many marketing services businesses. For example, Market Locations and Experian are able to provide lists of organisations that fall into particular SIC groups. Information can include name, location, sales volume, number of employees, types of product handled and names of chief executives. Business marketers can then decide which companies on the list to pursue (see Figure 7.6). This will usually involve an assessment of attractiveness and purchase potential. As described in Chapter 12, there are also many techniques that assist marketers in assessing the relative attractiveness of customers and market segments, such as the directional policy matrix and 'ABC sales: contribution' analysis.

In business marketing, situation-specific variables may be more relevant in segmenting markets than general customer characteristics. Business customers concentrate on benefits

***Figure 7.6***
*Networking, discussing and engaging with prospective business customers is an important part of identifying likely sales leads and honing an appropriate marketing proposition*
*Photo © Royalty-Free/CORBIS*

sought; therefore, understanding the end use of the product is more important than the psychology of decisions or socio-economic characteristics. Segmenting by benefits rather than by customer characteristics can provide insight into the structure of the market and opportunities for new customers.[16]

To estimate the purchase potential of business customers or groups of customers, a marketer must find a relationship between the size of potential customers' purchases and a variable available in SIC data, such as the number of employees. For example, a fabric manufacturer might attempt to determine the average number of metres of different materials purchased by a specific type of potential clothing manufacturer relative to the number of people employed. If the marketer has no previous experience in this market segment, it will probably be necessary to survey a random sample of potential customers in order to establish a relationship between purchase sizes and numbers of people employed. Once this relationship has been established, it can be applied to potential customer segments to estimate their purchases. After deriving these estimates, the marketer selects the customers to be included in the target market.

More and more businesses are adopting segmentation schemes that are based on the needs, buying behaviour and characteristics of their customers, rather than on simple trade categories or SIC codes. Such segmentation demands a thorough understanding of the nature of purchasing, the buying decision-making process and influencing factors, as described in this chapter. The next chapter explores the ways in which business marketers derive market segments and establish target market strategies.

## Marketing's Variations in Business Markets

Business marketers often have to address the needs of business customers within a marketing channel and the needs of their intended business customers. Some business marketers must also serve the needs of consumers. Marketers of consumer goods often manage many products and deal with perhaps thousands of customers. Mostly, although not always, such consumer products pass through a marketing channel so that a manufacturer's marketing managers deal primarily with channel member business customers. So for example, the marketers handling Snickers or Mars bars are concerned with understanding and satisfying their retail customers, such as the large cash-and-carry groups and the supermarkets. However, these marketers are also developing the marketing programmes targeting the end user consumers – Mars' marketers also handle the company's marketing activity aimed at the individual consumer. While a manufacturer's marketers often have to address dual audiences – channel member customers and consumers – it is more likely that their focus will be on the business customer.

Many business marketers handle a relatively small number of clients and the need to tailor marketing propositions to these customers' wishes is arguably more important than in consumer markets. While all marketers must properly understand buying behaviour and purchasers' characteristics, it is absolutely crucial in business marketing for marketers to develop such an understanding. Sales staff play a central role in building this understanding. Their relationships with customers can be leveraged to gain a particularly in-depth appreciation of customers' needs. Not surprisingly, the sales and marketing personnel in many business-to-business companies work together very closely.

There are other nuances, too, that it is worth mentioning. Most advertisements shown on television over the course of an evening are for consumer goods and services: they are eye-catching, emotive and highly persuasive. This style of advertising reflects the emotive brand positionings developed for many consumer goods, such as Nike or Guinness. While business marketers also strive to create strong brands (see Chapter 11) that are distinctive and attractive, much business branding lacks the emotion of consumer branding and suffers from a relative paucity of investment in supportive marketing communications activity and spending. Business branding tends to be more simplistic, focusing on identification and product differentiation. There are, of course, exceptions, with some business-to-business brands such as IBM or JCB being just as powerful as consumer brands.

The role of competition is different, too. It is unlikely that arch-rivals Tesco, Sainsbury's and ASDA would ever cooperate and work together. Similarly, why would KP and Walkers ever unite? Many brands between which a consumer may choose are unlikely ever to cooperate and work in harmony with each other. Indeed, the Competition Commission and EU regulators would probably be unimpressed if they did. In many business situations, though, individual companies pool their expertise and resources in order to win contracts with customers. For example, to offer retailers a viable chip-and-pin payment service, IT services company Fujitsu joined forces with Barclaycard Merchant Services (payment transactions), Box (hardware) and Cybertill (installation and maintenance) as a partnership. However, partners in one market segment may in fact be arch-rivals in another. Fujitsu may compete with KPMG, BT or IBM in one segment, but partner such companies in order to serve the needs of business customers in another. The implication is that the understanding of competitive forces is often more complex and intriguing in many business markets and rivals cannot always be treated as the enemy!

Target market strategies are important to all marketers. In order to develop a target market strategy, marketers must be able to allocate a market's customers into groups or market segments. The consumer marketer may use lifestyles, socio-economic information or consumers' perceived benefits to create market segments or groups of like-minded consumers. The business marketer, however, may fall back on more simple criteria, such as SIC codes or the trade sectors of their customers, in order to determine market segments. This very important aspect of marketing strategy is explored in Chapter 8. Until an understanding of business customers' buying behaviour has been developed, as described in this chapter, it is not possible to produce a market segmentation scheme.

If consumer marketers feel they have an inadequate appreciation of consumers' issues and buying behaviour, it is relatively straightforward to embark on suitable marketing research activities in order to rectify this deficiency. As described in Chapter 9, undertaking observations or surveys of consumers is fairly routine. However, busy executives and decision-makers inside business customers rarely offer to attend focus groups, they discard questionnaires and are not easy to access for interviews. Apart from access problems, business customers may well use any surveying to lobby. For example, they may feedback to the supplier's marketers behind the survey, the apparent importance of a better pricing option or improved customer service systems, rather than objectively and openly engage in the marketing research activity. Consumer products are readily visible on retailers' shelves; their prices, marketing communications campaigns, product features or attributes, and their channels to market are there to be seen by competitors' marketers. In most business markets, it is not easy to gain access to rivals' products or services, and the marketing programmes are not so readily visible.

The marketing mix is the set of tactical ingredients manipulated by marketers in marketing programmes designed to implement a target market strategy. As described in Parts III to VI of this book, all marketers manipulate the marketing mix in order to reflect the nature of their market, customer buying behaviour, the activities of competitors, organisational capabilities and corporate objectives. Compared with consumer marketers, those tasked with marketing business products have to make certain adjustments to their marketing mix programmes. These specific nuances are discussed in Part VII.

The overall implication is that business marketers must modify their use of the marketing toolkit to reflect the nature of their markets and the characteristics of their business customers. The overall marketing process and the toolkit apply irrespective of the marketplace, but it is evident that business marketers, consumer goods marketers and the marketers of services need to make certain modifications. These themes are discussed in more detail in Chapters 13 and 22.

Business marketers often have to address the needs of customers within a marketing channel as well as the needs of their intended customers. Some business marketers must also serve the needs of consumers. Many business marketers handle a relatively small number of customers and must tailor marketing propositions to these customers' specific wishes. The sales and marketing personnel in many business-to-business companies work together very closely.

# Summary

*Business marketing* used to be known as *organisational, industrial* or *business-to-business marketing*. Business markets consist of individuals or groups that purchase a specific kind of product for resale, for direct use in producing other products, or for use in their day-to-day operations. *Producer markets* include those individuals and business organisations that purchase products for the purpose of making a profit by using them either to produce other products or in their own operations. Classified as *reseller markets* are intermediaries, such as *wholesalers* and *retailers*, who buy finished products and resell them for the purpose of making a profit. *Government markets* consist of national and local governments, which spend huge amounts annually on goods and services to support their internal operations and provide citizens with needed services. Many businesses refer to government, local government and institutions collectively as the public sector, and the *public-sector market* is a growing area of activity within the marketing discipline. Organisations that seek to achieve charitable, educational, community or other non-business goals constitute *institutional markets*.

» Business-to-business transactions differ from consumer transactions in several ways. The transactions tend to be larger, and negotiations occur less frequently, though they are often lengthy. Business transactions sometimes involve more than one person or one department in the purchasing organisation. They may also involve *reciprocity*, an arrangement in which two organisations agree to buy from each other, although some countries have strict rules governing such agreements. Business customers are usually viewed as more rational and more likely to seek information about a product's features and technical specifications than are ultimate consumers.

» When purchasing products, business customers must be particularly concerned about quality, delivery, service and price. Quality is important because it directly affects the quality of the organisational buyer's ultimate product. To achieve an exact standard, organisations often buy their products on the basis of a set of expressed characteristics, called specifications. Reliable and fast delivery is crucial to many organisations, whose production lines must be fed with a continuous supply of component parts and raw materials. Because services can have a direct influence on a company's costs, sales and profits, such matters as market information, on-time delivery and availability of parts can be crucial to a business buyer. Although a business customer does not decide which products to purchase solely by their price, cost is of prime concern because it directly influences a company's profitability. Product range, innovation, reliability and logistical support may also be significant considerations. Increasingly, business buyers are concerned with service support levels and the ongoing commitment from their selected suppliers. There is a view that a supplier's personnel in terms of knowledge, motivation, attitude and passion for assisting the customer, are an integral part of the product proposition being 'consumed' by the business customer.

» Business buyers use several purchasing methods, including description, inspection, sampling and negotiation. Most business purchases are new task, modified rebuy or straight rebuy. In a *new task purchase*, an organisation makes an initial purchase of an item to be used to perform a new job or to solve a new problem. In a *modified rebuy purchase*, a new task purchase is changed the second or third time it is ordered, or the requirements associated with a straight rebuy purchase are modified. A *straight rebuy purchase* occurs when a buyer repurchases the same products routinely under approximately the same terms of sale.

» Business demand differs from consumer demand along several dimensions. *Derived demand* is the demand for business products that arises from the demand for consumer products. At the industry level, *inelastic demand* is a demand that is not significantly affected by a price increase or decrease. If the price of an industrial item changes, demand for the product will not change proportionally. Some business products are subject to *joint demand*, which occurs when two or more items are used in combination to make a product. Finally, because business demand ultimately derives from consumer demand, the demand for business products can fluctuate widely.

» *Business (or business-to-business) buying behaviour* refers to the purchase behaviour of producers, resellers, government units and institutions. Business purchase decisions are made through a *buying centre* – the group of people who are involved in making organisational purchase decisions. Users are those in the organisation that actually use the product. Influencers help develop the specifications and evaluate alternative products for possible use. Buyers are responsible for selecting the suppliers and negotiating the terms of the purchases. Deciders choose the products and suppliers. Gatekeepers control the flow of information to and among people who occupy the other roles in the buying centre.

» When a company buys a product or service from another company, both organisations enter into a process during which items of value are exchanged in return for something else. This exchange process may lead to a long-term relationship between buyer and seller. *Relationship marketing* is the term used to explain the special attention being given to this area and is defined as the activities an organisation uses to build, maintain and develop customer relations. The trend toward long-term relationships has resulted in *relationship management*, increased *value analysis* and the more systematic evaluation of suppliers in *supplier analysis*.

» The stages of the business buying decision process are (1) problem recognition, (2) development of product specifications to solve the problem, (3) search for products and suppliers, (4) evaluation of products relative to specifications, (5) selection and ordering of the most appropriate product, and (6) evaluation of the product's and the supplier's performance. The evaluation of product and suppliers will directly affect future purchasing decisions. *Sole sourcing*, the process of selecting only one supplier, is becoming more popular, particularly where manufacturers are practising just-in-time production. Many organisations still opt to practise *multiple sourcing*.

» Four categories of factors influence business buying decisions: environmental, organisational, interpersonal and individual. *Environmental factors* include politics, laws and regulations, economic conditions, competitive forces and technological changes. *Organisational factors* include the buyer's objectives, purchasing policies and resources, as well as the size and composition of its buying centre. *Interpersonal factors* refer to the relationships among the people in the buying centre, and relationships between supplier and customer personnel. *Individual factors* refer to the personal characteristics of individuals in the buying centre, such as age, education, personality, position in the organisation, and income.

» *Business marketing* is a set of activities directed at facilitating and expediting exchanges involving business products and customers in business markets.

» Business marketers have a considerable amount of information available to them for use in planning their marketing strategies and for identifying sales potential. Much of this information is based on the *Standard Industrial Classification (SIC) system*, which classifies businesses into major industry divisions, classes, groups and activities. The SIC system provides business marketers with information needed to identify market segments. It can best be used for this purpose in conjunction with other information, such as *input–output data*. After identifying target industries, the marketer can locate potential customers by using the Internet or directories, or by employing a marketing services business. The marketer must then estimate the potential purchases of business customers by finding a relationship between a potential customer's purchases and a variable available (information which is available in published sources).

» Business-to-business branding tends to be more simplistic than is the case with consumer brands, focusing on identification and product differentiation. In many business situations, individual companies pool their expertise and resources in order to win contracts with customers. However, partners in one market segment may in fact be arch-rivals in another. The implication is that the understanding of competitive forces is often more complex and intriguing in business markets and rivals cannot always be treated as 'the enemy'.

» Although SIC codes and industry trade categories are often used by business marketers, increasingly the approaches deployed by consumer marketers in creating market segments are being deployed in business markets. The next chapter explores market segmentation and target marketing in more detail. Undertaking marketing research in business markets is quite different from researching consumers. Compared with consumer markets, those tasked with marketing business products have to reflect certain market nuances when developing their marketing mix programmes, as discussed in Part VII.

## Key Links

This chapter must be read in conjunction with Chapter 6, which details the buying behaviour of consumers.

- A popular examination question is to compare and contrast the buying behaviour models in consumer and business markets.
- In strategic marketing, a key use of an understanding of customer behaviour is the construction of market segments, as discussed in Chapter 8.
- The marketing mix should reflect the nuances of the market in question, as described in Chapters 13 and 22.

## Important Terms

Business market
Industrial, organisational or business-to-business market
Producer markets
Reseller markets
Wholesalers
Retailers
Government markets
Public-sector markets
Institutional markets
Reciprocity
New task purchase
Modified rebuy purchase
Straight rebuy purchase
Derived demand
Inelastic demand
Joint demand
Business (or business-to-business) buying behaviour
Buying centre
Relationship marketing
Relationship management
Value analysis
Supplier analysis
Sole sourcing
Multiple sourcing
Environmental factors
Organisational factors
Interpersonal factors
Individual factors
Business marketing
Standard Industrial Classification (SIC) system
Input–output data

## Discussion and Review Questions

1. Identify, describe and give examples of four major types of business market.
2. Why are business buyers generally considered more rational in regard to their purchasing behaviour than ultimate consumers?
3. What are the primary concerns of business customers?
4. List several characteristics that differentiate business transactions from consumer ones.

5 What are the commonly used methods of business buying?
6 Why do buyers involved in a straight rebuy purchase require less information than those making a new task purchase?
7 How does industrial/business demand differ from consumer demand?
8 What are the major components of a buying centre?
9 What elements may be exchanged by a buyer and seller when a purchase transaction takes place?
10 Why has relationship management attracted so much interest in business markets?
11 Identify the stages of the business buying decision process. How is this decision process used when making straight rebuys?
12 What impact does the evaluation of a particular purchase have on future buying decisions?
13 How do environmental, organisational, interpersonal and individual factors affect business purchases?
14 What function does the SIC system help business marketers perform?
15 List some sources that a business marketer can use to determine the names and addresses of potential customers.
16 In what ways do business marketers have to reflect the nuances of business markets when deploying the marketing toolkit?

## Recommended Readings


- Chisnall, P., *Strategic Business Marketing* (Harlow: Pearson, 1995).
- Ford, D., *Understanding Business Markets and Purchasing* (London: Thomson Learning, 2001).
- Ford, D., Gadde, L.-E., Hakansson, H. and Snehota, I., *Managing Business Relationships* (Chichester: Wiley, 2003).
- Hutt, M.D. and Speh, T.W., *Business Marketing Management: Strategic View of Industrial and Organisational Markets* (Cincinnati, OH: South Western, 2003).
- Naude, P., Michel, D., Salle, R. and Valla, J.-P., *Business to Business Marketing* (Basingstoke: Palgrave Macmillan, 2003).
- Webster, F.E., *Industrial Marketing Strategy* (New York: Wiley, 1995).


### Internet Exercise

Log on to Sony's website.
www.sony.com
Ignore the sections aimed at consumers. Instead, go to 'Solutions for Business'. This section details Sony's business-to-business products, services and upcoming events such as trade shows. There are sections offering solutions to Healthcare, Media and Retail target markets. Specifically, look at the section detailing 'Professional Services Support'.

1 In what ways do Sony's 'Solutions for Business' web pages reflect the requirements of business customers?
2 How have the messages in the 'Professional Services Support' pages been tailored to reflect the buying behaviour of Sony's business customers?

## *Applied Mini-Case*

St Andrew's Hospital in Northampton is the market leader in mental health hospital care in the UK. Its divisions address everything from adolescent learning difficulties through to major behavioural problems with patients requiring secure accommodation and lengthy treatment programmes. St Andrew's – a charity – has a specialist unit dealing with brain injuries and, through an on-site partner, also offers clinic facilities for patients needing to 'dry out'. Its staff are recognised as being leading-edge thinkers. St Andrew's brand reputation is based on the quality of its care, its multiple care pathways and its ability to relate to patients, their families and to the medical staff or personnel in social services who refer patients to the hospital.

While some patients deal directly with St Andrew's Hospital, the vast majority of patients are referred from the National Health Service (NHS). St Andrew's has a reputation for being able to deal with difficult patients suffering from complex problems. However, the NHS is increasingly moving towards centralised buying, with numerous Trusts joining forces in order to be able to purchase services – such as those offered by St Andrew's – at lower rates. In addition to the medical staff who diagnose the patients' problems and recommend appropriate courses of treatment, the NHS has risk assessors, financial managers and professional purchasing executives, who are all involved in the decision concerning which treatment programme to purchase from which provider. For St Andrew's and other suppliers to the NHS, such formalised purchasing and group decision-making complicate the marketing activity and the engagement programmes the charity runs with its customers. For the patient, for his/her family, for the referring medical staff and the numerous administrators involved, St Andrew's must develop bespoke messages, marketing communications and client-handling programmes. This complex buying centre must be addressed in order for St Andrew's to operate with full bed occupancy, and to fulfil its mission to truly help those suffering with mental health problems.

**Sources:** St Andrew's Hospital, 2004; James Watkins, director of marketing and strategy, St Andrew's Hospital, 2003; Sally Dibb and Lyndon Simkin, *Marketing Briefs*, Oxford: Butterworth-Heinemann, 2004.

### *Question*

As the marketing director of such an organisation, what aspects of customer buying behaviour would you identify as priorities to understand?

## *Case Study*

# Nynas: in the Black and Leading

For most people, oil is evident as a fuel for cars, heating and the generation of electricity, or as the basis for the plastics industry. What about the black surfaces of pavements, roads, driveways, car parks and school playgrounds? Bitumen is an oil-based product most of us take for granted, but it is a major part of the revenue for companies such as Shell, BP, Esso, Total, Colas or Lanfina. The leading bitumen player in the UK, Scandinavia and much of western Europe is Stockholm-based Nynas. In the UK, this relatively small player in the petrochemicals industry has overall market leadership in the bitumen market and is renowned for its innovative product development with polymer formulations.

Bitumen is one of the most ubiquitous materials made by industry, underfoot almost everywhere as a core ingredient of the macadams and asphalts in roads and pavements. There are numerous specialist applications too, such as the backing for carpet tiles, roofing felts, sealants for mighty dams and waterproofing for bridge decks. Inevitably this results in a diverse customer base for an organisation such as Nynas. In a market with competitors as large as Esso or Shell, Nynas's leadership has not occurred by accident. Nynas has established its enviable position by astutely utilising the resources required to develop innovative products, customer service schemes and flexible delivery capabilities in order to ensure customer satisfaction. At the heart of its business strategy is a desire to innovate, listen to customers and develop services that genuinely enable customers to be served properly.

Nynas believes it has several important edges over its rivals, as described below.

### Customer Dialogue

As a major producer with significant R&D technical support, Nynas's laboratories can determine a product formulation for most bitumen-based applications. Whether the customer is a local authority requiring a cost-effective thin surfacing for a housing estate's ageing pavements; a contractor such as Tarmac requiring 24-hour supply of high-quality, state-of-the-art bitumen for the construction of a new motorway; or a builder buying polymer-enhanced mastic asphalts to act as a waterproofing membrane for regency mews properties, Nynas can develop a quality bitumen-based product.

### Consistent Quality and Innovative Product Development

Refineries in Belgium, Sweden and the UK, supported by a network of terminals and research laboratories across Europe, enable Nynas to continually improve its products and their performance. Customers do not want to have to resurface major roads or busy shopping centre pavements on a frequent basis. Specialist applications such as waterproofing dams or houses are time consuming, costly and inconvenient remedial activities that clients do not want to repeat in a hurry. Nynas has access to high-grade Venezuelan bitumen, not readily available to its major competitors, which gives it added flexibility in producing high-quality bitumen grades for specific applications. Whether it is for a routine commodity bulk job such as a school playground surface or an unusual requirement for waterproofing a royal building, Nynas has developed a reputation as being a leading supplier.

**Logistical Support**

Users of bitumen often require deliveries at very short notice, in specific quantities and to guaranteed quality levels. These deliveries may be anywhere at any time. A contractor repairing a busy commuter route out of daylight hours needs on-time delivery of ready-to-use bitumen products. Repairs to a remote bridge still require guaranteed on-time delivery. Nynas's depots operate around the clock despatching computer monitored deliveries by tanker to clients as and when the customer has specified. Twenty-four hours a day, 365 days a year, Nynas prides itself on its high levels of responsiveness and reliability of delivery.

Nynas's composition of customers is varied. A major new road-building scheme will involve formal tendering and guarantees with penalties for inferior product or missed deliveries. The buying process of such customers will be highly formal, involving numerous managers, and functions as diverse as purchasing, technical support, construction, finance and logistical support. On both sides – customer and Nynas – cross-functional teams of scientists, engineers, managers and the field force will spend many months agreeing on the product requirements, contractual obligations, delivery requirements and application techniques. For other customers, the purchase is perhaps more of a routine rebuy, with only limited interaction and discussion between Nynas and the customer. On other occasions, the Nynas helpline may receive a midnight telephone call from a highways agency surveyor who has just discovered cracks in the surface of a major road and requires immediate assistance in both identifying the cause of the problem and rectifying the situation before commuters awake the next morning.

For a rather bland-looking substance such as bitumen, the market is diverse and challenging. Nynas has established its successful position in the European market for bitumen-based products by practising the best principles of marketing. The company strives to understand its customers' needs and to offer reliable products supported with effective customer service, round the clock. Product innovation is at the forefront of the company's strategy and, coupled with constantly improving ways of offering peace of mind to customers, provides an edge over rivals. Shrewd marketing analysis constantly monitors product changes, customers' expectations, competitors' activities and those aspects of the marketing environment – notably technological and regulatory forces – that will impact on the business's fortunes. Resources are allocated to match this thorough assessment of market opportunities and marketing requirements.

**Sources:** Siobhan McKelvey and Willie Hunter, Nynas UK; *Network* magazine; the Nynas Annual Review.

## Questions for Discussion

1. Who are Nynas's customers?
2. What types of business markets – as classified in this chapter – purchase the products made by Nynas?
3. Would most purchases of Nynas's products be new task, modified rebuy or straight rebuy?

# 8

# Segmenting Markets, Targeting and Positioning

> **"The essence of successful segmentation lies not in fragmentation but in building an excellent understanding of the marketplace."**
>
> *Sally Dibb, Warwick Business School*

## Objectives

- To understand the definition of a market
- To recognise different types of market
- To learn how companies segment markets
- To understand targeting decisions
- To discover how marketers prioritise target markets
- To learn about strategies for positioning

## Introduction

As explained in Chapter 2, marketing strategy revolves around the choice of which opportunities should be pursued and the specification of an appropriate target market strategy. Market segmentation is a fundamental part of marketing strategy, assisting organisations to deal with the fact that not all consumers or business customers share identical needs, buying behaviour or product requirements. Limited resources generally result in organisations being unable to serve all of the needs in the market, and marketers must make trade-off choices based on the relative merits of different market segments in determining which groups to prioritise. The consumers or business customers in those market segments deemed to be priorities for a company must be communicated with in a manner that emphasises their importance to the company: this is the positioning task. The market segmentation process, therefore, has a number of stages: segmenting, targeting and positioning. Many marketers believe these aspects of marketing are the most important decisions made by marketers.[1]

## Opener

## Targeting Students and the Over-50s

*Marketing* magazine targets marketing practitioners such as brand managers, marketing managers, marketing directors and those working in agencies supplying advertising or marketing research to the marketing community. Recently, a flyer inserted in the weekly magazine promoted a conference that specifically aimed to address the marketing of products and services to students.

The accompanying text explained that students in the UK spend more than £13 billion per annum. With over two million UK students, more and more brands are targeting marketing programmes at these consumers. Such consumers are very aware of current forms of communication, possibly more so than the older marketers attempting to entice them with marketing communications. Texting, e-mail, the Internet, posters, stunts aimed at students, sponsoring student events and advertising on campus radio stations are important forms of communicating with students, often requiring a separate campaign from many brands' more mainstream marketing communications. It is not only marketing communications that must be modified. Peer group influences are important among students, buying processes are very specific in nature and purchasing is driven by a mix of value for money, brand image and utility drivers.

Another *Marketing*-sponsored conference was entitled 'Older Richer Wiser? Challenge your perceptions of the over-50s market'. This conference targeted clients and agency personnel currently targeting, or who should be targeting, the over-50s age group. The text explained:

> Fifty somethings lived through the sixties, seventies, eighties and nineties. They know more about music; more about money and business; more about freedom and creativity. They understand what is good value. They have more money than any other sector of the population.
>
> They have 80% of the country's personal wealth and account for 40% of consumer spending. They've seen it all, heard it all and experienced a lot of it. And now you've got to find a way to catch their hearts, imaginations and wallets.

Speakers examined how to advertise to a 'disenfranchised generation'; how to harness the Internet, cinema and other marketing communications; the importance of creating propositions directly relevant to these consumers; and the role of understanding their buying behaviour. Keynote speakers represented Saga FM, Help the Aged, health and fitness clubs, the travel industry, pensions and investments.

*Marketing* magazine is itself targeted at a narrowly defined market segment: marketing professionals. The two conferences were designed to help marketers address students and the over-50s, with the belief that these two demographic groups exhibit different buying behaviour and have needs that are different to those of the rest of the population. Such sub-division of the overall population into homogeneous groups of consumers for marketing purposes is the aim of market segmentation.

**Sources:** *Marketing* magazine, 2004/5; *Marketing to Students, Marketing* and Campus Vision, London, 29 June 2004; 'Older Richer Wiser?', *Marketing*, 7 July 2004. Photo © Ariel Skelley/CORBIS

This chapter begins by considering the nature of markets, first defining the term and then describing the different types. The market segmentation concept is then explained and the rationale for its use explored. Not only conferences aimed at attracting students or the over-50s apply the concept of market segmentation. Management consultancies, manufacturers, healthcare providers, leisure operators and universities all practise market segmentation. The segmenting, targeting and positioning stages of the segmentation process are explored in turn. The explanation of segmenting focuses on the variables used to segment consumer and business markets. An understanding of customer needs and buying behaviour, as described in Chapters 6 and 7, is essential for developing market segments. The review of targeting considers the strategies used to select and prioritise target markets. Approaches for developing a positioning are examined. The chapter concludes by emphasising the importance of assessing the sales potential in the market segments deemed to be the focus of the organisation's target market strategy.

# What are Markets?

The word 'market' has various meanings. It used to refer primarily to the place where goods were bought and sold. It can also refer to a large geographic area. In some cases, the word is used to describe the relationship between the demand and supply of a specific product. For instance, 'What is the state of the market for copper?' Sometimes, 'market' is used to mean the act of selling something. The dictionary defines 'market' as an occasion on which goods are publicly exposed for sale, a place in which goods are exposed for sale, or to offer for sale. In marketing terms, a market is defined in terms of customers, their need for a product, and their ability to purchase or consume.

**Market**
An aggregate of people who, as individuals or within organisations, have a need for certain products and the ability, willingness and authority to purchase such products

In this book a **market** is defined as a group of people who, as consumers or as part of organisations, need and have the ability, willingness and authority to purchase products in a product class. In general use, the term 'market' sometimes refers to the total population, or mass market, that buys products. However, the definition used here is more specific, referring to individuals seeking products in a specific product category. For example, students are part of the market for textbooks, as well as being markets for calculators, pens and pencils, paper, food, music and other products. Obviously, there are many different markets in any economy. In this section, the requirements for markets are considered in conjunction with these different types.

## Requirements for a Market

For a group of people to be a market, the members of the group must meet the following four requirements.

1 They must need or want a particular product or service.
2 They must have the ability to purchase the product or service. Ability to purchase is related to buying power, which consists of resources such as money, goods and services that can be traded in an exchange situation.
3 They must be willing to use their buying power.
4 They must have the authority to buy the specific products or services.

**Business market**
Individuals or groups that purchase a specific kind of product to resell, use directly in producing other products or use in general daily operations

Individuals sometimes have the desire, the buying power and the willingness to purchase certain products but may not be authorised to do so. For example, secondary school students may want, have the money for and be willing to buy alcoholic drinks, but a brewer does not consider them a market until they are legally old enough to buy alcohol. An aggregate of people that lacks any one of the four requirements thus does not constitute a market.

## Types of Market

Markets can be divided into two categories: consumer markets and business markets. A **consumer market** consists of purchasers and/or individuals in their households who personally consume or benefit from the purchased products and who do not buy products primarily to make a profit. Each of us belongs to numerous consumer markets for such products as housing, cars, appliances, furniture, clothing, food, financial services and leisure activities. Consumer markets are discussed in more detail in Chapter 6.

**Consumer market**
Purchasers or individuals in their households who personally consume or benefit from the purchased products and do not buy products primarily to make a profit

A **business market** – also referred to as an *organisational* or *business-to-business market* – consists of individuals or groups that purchase a specific kind of product for one of three purposes: resale, direct use in producing other products or use in general daily operations. The four categories of business market – producer, reseller, government and institutional – are discussed in Chapters 7 and 22.

# What is Market Segmentation?

Chapter 1 explained that at the heart of marketing strategy are the decisions about which opportunities to pursue and which market segments to target. As will be explained later in this chapter, businesses sometimes decide to target the total market, using an **undifferentiated (or total market) approach**. However, it is much more usual for a differentiated approach using market segmentation to be followed.

## Defining Market Segmentation

**Heterogeneous markets**
Markets in which all customers have different requirements

**Market segmentation**
The process of grouping customers in markets with some heterogeneity into smaller, more similar or homogeneous segments. The identification of target customer groups in which customers are aggregated into groups with similar requirements and buying characteristics

**Market segment**
A group of individuals, groups or organisations sharing one or more similar characteristics that cause them to have relatively similar product needs and buying characteristics

**Undifferentiated (or total market) approach**
An approach which assumes that all customers have similar needs and wants, and can be served with a single marketing mix

The varying characteristics, needs, wants and interests of customers mean that there are few markets where a single product or service is satisfactory for all. The extensive array of goods on supermarket shelves reflects basic differences in customers' requirements. The trend, it seems, is away from a mass-marketing approach. Even markets that were traditionally undifferentiated have undergone change, with an ever increasing number of products on offer. For instance, the market for food seasoning used to be dominated by salt. Now, low-sodium substitutes are being offered as alternatives for the increasingly health-conscious consumer.

Markets in which all customers have different requirements are termed **heterogeneous markets**. For example, the market for wrist watches is quite diverse. Swatch designs relatively low-priced watches for the fashion-conscious customer; Rotary markets much more conservative and expensive designs for an older customer group. In completely heterogeneous markets the only way to satisfy everyone is by offering tailor-made or bespoke products. This situation is more prevalent in business-to-business markets, where, for example, plant machinery is designed for a specific task and situation. However, while it may not be feasible to offer every customer a tailor-made product, it is often possible to aggregate customers into groups with similar product needs and wants.

**Market segmentation** is the process by which customers in markets with some heterogeneity can be grouped into smaller, more similar or homogeneous segments. A **market segment** is therefore a group of individuals, groups or organisations sharing one or more similar characteristics that cause them to have relatively similar product needs and buying characteristics. Market segmentation involves identifying such groups, so that marketers are better able to develop product or service benefits that are appropriate for them (see Figure 8.1). They do this by designing products and brands to appeal to particular target segments and to be supported by an appropriate promotional campaign, relevant customer service, and suitable pricing and place/distribution strategies. For example, clothing sold through Top Shop or New Look is manufactured for youthful female consumers; this is reflected in both the product styling and the promotional campaign.

Once market segments have been identified, marketers decide which, if any, they intend to enter. A marketing programme covering all elements of the marketing mix can then be designed to suit the particular requirements of the segments targeted. German-owned BMW previously concentrated on selling premium-priced luxury vehicles aimed at the luxury and executive segments of the car market. In order to appeal to a younger age group, during the 1990s BMW introduced the Compact version of its popular 3 Series. This had the desired effect of attracting buyers who previously could not afford this aspirational marque. Now BMW has gone further, with the launch of the 1 Series, aiming to further broaden the appeal of its brand – to young professionals.

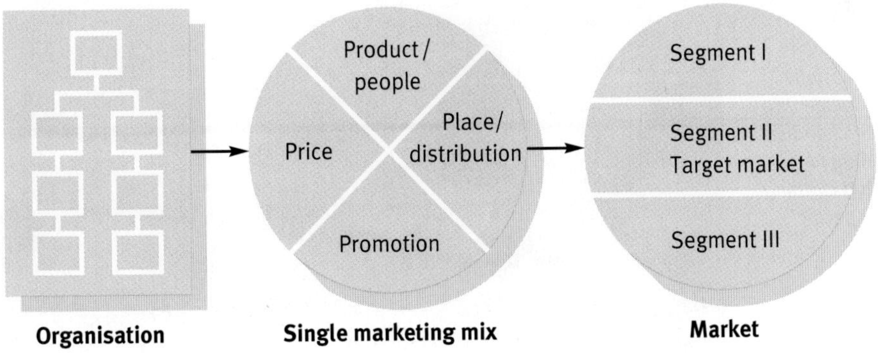


*Figure 8.1*
*Market segmentation approach*

## Reasons for Using Market Segmentation

Companies have turned to market segmentation with good reason.[2] Whitbread, Diner's Club and Bird's Eye Walls have all demonstrated that success can follow the effective implementation of market segmentation strategies. For example, the variety of offerings in the market for frozen, ready-to-eat meals illustrates the spread of customer needs: healthy options, quick snacks, gourmet selections. Careful segmentation, and the customer understanding underlying it, can make it easier for companies to identify and exploit different market opportunities. For example, segmentation can help minor players in the market achieve a foothold in a particular niche, perhaps by identifying an opportunity not directly exploited by market leaders. Figure 8.2 relates to construction equipment manufacturer Caterpillar's entry into footwear and clothing.

Segmentation is seen to offer businesses a number of advantages that make it easier to develop and capitalise on opportunities available to them. These advantages can be considered at the customer level, in relation to the competition or in terms of the effectiveness of resource allocation and strategic planning.[3]

***Figure 8.2***
*Appreciation for Caterpillar Inc. products goes far beyond the people who work with the machines and engines daily. Licencing the image and lifestyle of Caterpillar, the company has been able to successfully transfer its image into licenced merchandise including rugged footwear and clothing ranges for specific target market segments*
*Source: Courtesy of Caterpillar Inc.*

**Customer Analysis** Segmenting markets facilitates a better understanding of customers' needs, wants and other characteristics. The sharper focus that segmentation offers, allows those personal, situational and behavioural factors that characterise customers in a particular segment to be considered. In short, questions about how, why and what customers buy can be addressed. By being closely in touch with segments, marketers can respond quickly to even slight changes in what target customers want. For example, by monitoring the trends towards healthier eating and lifestyles, McDonald's was able to respond by introducing a wider range of salads and healthy eating options – including grilled chicken, fruit and yoghurt – on to its menus.

**Competitor Analysis** Most markets are characterised by intense competition. Within this environment, companies need to understand the nature of the competition they face. Who are their main competitors? At which segments are they targeting their products? Answering these questions allows marketers to make decisions about the most appropriate segments to target and the kind of competitive advantage to seek. For example, before opening a new café outlet, Costa needs to build a picture of the existing café, restaurant and other outlets offering a comparable service in the location. The company must also appraise the extent to which the needs of the consumers it aims to target are already served by what is currently available. Companies that do not understand their competitive environment risk encountering competition they had not envisaged or putting resources into unattractive areas of the market.

**Effective Resource Allocation** All companies have limited resources. To target the whole of the market is usually unrealistic. The effectiveness of personnel and material resources can be greatly improved when they are more narrowly focused on a particular segment of customers. With limited resources, Saab and Porsche target only a few market segments compared with Ford or GM. Segmentation enables Saab and Porsche to identify homogeneous groups of customers at whom the Saab 95 or Porsche 911 models can be targeted. This maximises these companies' use of resources and marketing mix activities.

**Strategic Marketing Planning** Companies operating in a number of segments are unlikely to follow the same strategic plans in them all. Dividing up markets allows marketers to develop plans that give special consideration to the particular needs and requirements of customers in different segments. The timescale covered by the strategic plan can also be structured accordingly, because some segments change more rapidly than others. The market for recorded music is a typical example. While tastes in classical music remain fairly steady, tastes in pop music change very rapidly. Companies like EMI and Sony clearly need to consider this factor when developing corporate plans.

## Segmenting, Targeting and Positioning

There are three stages to carrying out market segmentation: segmentation, targeting and positioning. Figure 8.3 gives an overview of these stages.

### Segmenting the Market

There are many ways in which customers can be grouped and markets segmented. In different markets, the variables that are appropriate change. The key is to understand which are the most suitable for distinguishing between different product requirements. Understanding as much as possible about the customers in the segments is also important, as marketers who 'know' their targets are more likely to design an appropriate marketing mix for them. For example, the Post Office has reintroduced savings stamps after an absence of 40 years to help people who struggle to balance their finances. They are aimed at people who have regular outgoings such as household bills; in particular, they are targeted at the five million people in the UK who do not have any kind of bank account.

### Targeting Strategy

Once segments have been identified, decisions about which and how many customer groups to target can be made. There are several options:

- adopt an undifferentiated approach, focusing on the total market
- concentrate on a single segment with one product and marketing programme
- offer one product and marketing programme to a number of segments
- target a different product and marketing programme at each of a number of segments.

These options are explored in more detail later in this chapter. The choices companies make should take resource implications into consideration.

### Positioning the Product

Companies must decide precisely how and where within the targeted segments to aim a product or products, brand or brands. The needs and wants of targeted customers must be translated into a tangible mix of product/service, personnel, price, promotion and place/distribution. The consumers' view of the product and where it is positioned relative to the competition is particularly critical. After all, the paying public does not always perceive a product or brand in the way the manufacturer would like. For example, to the dismay of those who developed it, the Sinclair C5 electric trike was perceived as an object of ridicule.

Each of the three market segmentation stages will now be considered.

**Segmentation variables** or **bases**
The dimensions or characteristics of individuals, groups or businesses that are used for dividing a total market into segments

## Segmentation Variables

**Segmentation variables** or **bases** are the dimensions or characteristics of individuals, groups or businesses that are used for dividing a total market into segments.[4] There is rarely one best way to segment a market. Companies must make choices about the most appropriate variables to use but they must consider the needs and buying behaviour of their intended customers, as discussed in Chapters 6 and 7. In consumer markets, background characteristics

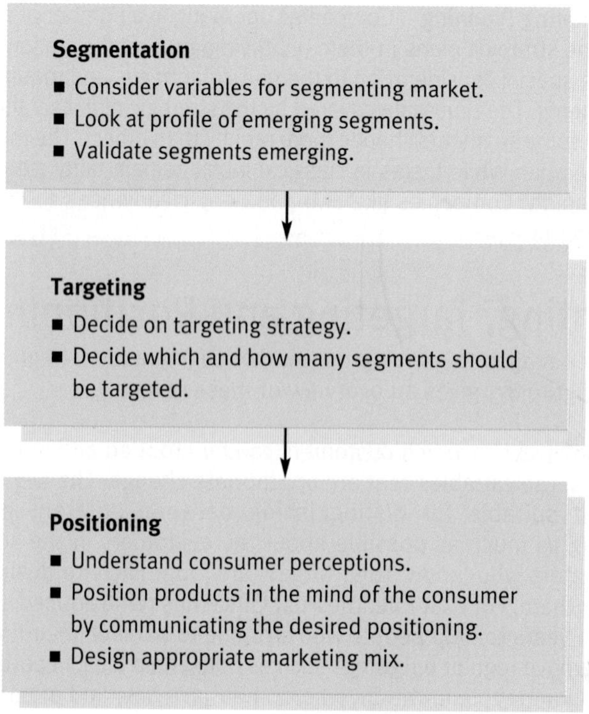

Segmentation
■ Consider variables for segmenting market.
■ Look at profile of emerging segments.
■ Validate segments emerging.
Targeting
■ Decide on targeting strategy.
■ Decide which and how many segments should be targeted.
Positioning
■ Understand consumer perceptions.
■ Position products in the mind of the consumer by communicating the desired positioning.
■ Design appropriate marketing mix.


*Figure 8.3*
*Basic elements of segmentation*

like age, sex and occupation are widely used. In business-to-business markets, customer size, location and product use are often the focus.

The choice of segmentation variables is based on several factors. The variables chosen should relate to customers' needs for, uses of or behaviour towards the product or service. The selected bases should be usable and easy to measure. Laptop computer manufacturers might segment the market on the basis of income and age, but not on the basis of religion, because one person's usage of computer equipment does not differ from those of people of other religions. Furthermore, if individuals or businesses in a total market are to be classified accurately, the segmentation variable must be measurable. For example, segmenting a market on the basis of intelligence or moral standards would be quite difficult because these attributes are hard to measure accurately.

Creativity is also a factor; sometimes businesses benefit from moving away from a traditionally popular segmentation approach. For example, First Direct led the way in telephone banking, by responding to the fact that some customers' needs were not being met by existing banking operations. By developing a better understanding of the demographics, lifestyle and needs of these customers, the bank was able to develop a new kind of service. Later in this chapter there is a more detailed review of segmentation effectiveness, which focuses on some of these issues.

## Selecting Appropriate Variables

Selecting appropriate variables for market segmentation is an important marketing management decision, because the variable is the primary factor in defining the target market.[5] In some cases, segmentation is based on more than one variable. Decisions about the number of segmentation variables used are partly based on a company's resources and capabilities. The type of product and degree of variation in customers' needs also dictate the number and size of segments targeted.

In general, as developments in information technology make it easier to capture and manage customer information, the move is towards more complex segmentation schemes. Many businesses now have databases providing a wider range of segmentation variables than was previously possible.[6] One outcome is that there is, increasingly, a tendency to use multivariable segmentation rather than single-variable segmentation.[7] Indeed, technological advance means that it is now technically feasible to capture information about and respond to the needs and wants of smaller and smaller segments.[8] Taken to its extreme, this means that instead of dealing at the mass-market or segment level, it is even possible to develop relationships with *individual* customers. This principle has been variously referred to as 'customer-centric marketing'[9] or 'one-to-one marketing'.[10] **One-to-one marketing** involves developing long-term relationships with individual customers in order to understand and satisfy their needs.[11] However, despite the attention these new ideas have attracted, it is widely recognised that one-to-one segmentation involves a substantial injection of resources, raising concerns about whether the returns are sufficiently high to justify the required investment.

**One-to-one marketing**
Involves developing long-term relationships with individual customers in order to understand and satisfy their needs

**Single Variable Segmentation** **Single variable segmentation**, which is the simplest to perform, is achieved by using only one variable – for example, country. However, the sales of one product in different countries will differ and the numbers of relevant consumers in each country will vary. A single characteristic gives marketers only moderate precision in designing a marketing mix to satisfy individuals in a specific segment.

**Single variable segmentation**
Segmentation achieved by using only one variable, the simplest type of segmentation to perform

**Multivariable Segmentation** To achieve **multivariable segmentation**, more than one characteristic is used to divide a total market (see Figure 8.4). Notice in the figure that the market is segmented by three variables: annual income, population density and volume usage. The people in the highlighted segment earn more than £40,000, are urban dwellers and heavy users. Multivariable segmentation provides more information about the individuals in each

**Multivariable segmentation**
Segmentation using more than one characteristic to divide a total market

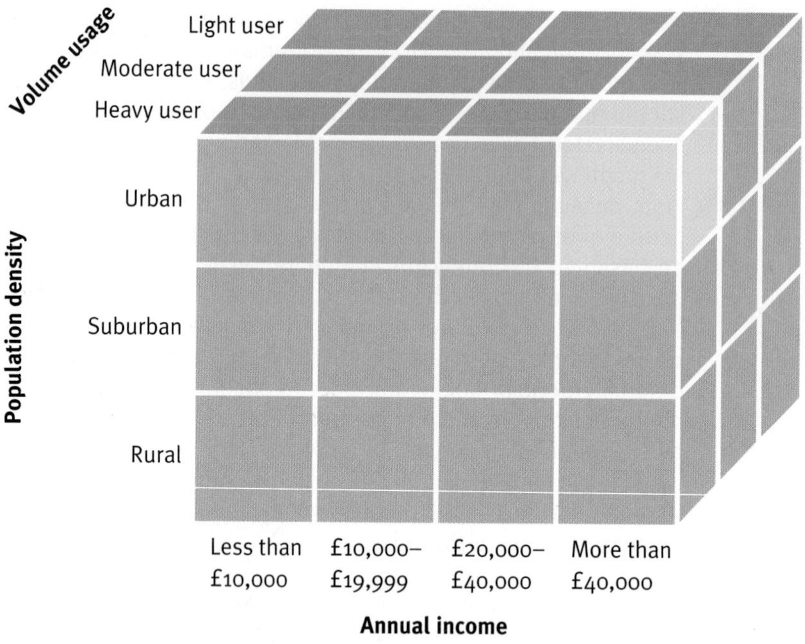


*Figure 8.4* *Multivariable segmentation*

segment, which may enable a company to develop a marketing mix that will satisfy customers in a given segment more precisely.

The major disadvantage of multivariable segmentation is that the more variables used, the greater the number of segments likely to be identified. This proliferation reduces the sales potential of many of the segments. It may also be more complicated to resource and manage the proliferation of segments that result. A marketing manager must therefore consider whether additional variables will actually help improve the company's marketing mix. Where many variables are deployed, it may be prudent to utilise multivariate statistical techniques – such as cluster analysis[12] – to assist in the grouping of customers into market segments.

**Demographic variables**
- Age
- Gender
- Race
- Ethnicity
- Income
- Education
- Occupation
- Family size
- Family life cycle
- Religion
- Social class

**Geographic variables**
- Population
- Region
- Urban, suburban, rural
- City size
- Market density
- Climate

**Psychographic variables**
- Personality attributes
- Motives
- Lifestyles

**Behaviouristic variables**
- Volume usage
- End use
- Benefit expectations
- Brand loyalty
- Price sensitivity

*Figure 8.5* *Segmentation variables for consumer markets*

## Variables for Segmenting Consumer Markets

Companies developing their strategy for segmentation can choose one or several variables or bases from a wide range of choices. As Figure 8.5 shows, segmentation variables can be grouped into four categories: demographic, geographic, psychographic and behaviouristic.

**Demographic Variables** Demographers study aggregate population characteristics such as the distribution of age and gender, fertility rates, migration patterns and mortality rates. Demographic characteristics that marketers commonly use in segmenting markets include age, gender, race, ethnicity, income, education, occupation, family size, family life cycle, religion and social class. Marketers rely on these demographic characteristics because they are often closely linked to customers' needs and purchasing behaviour, and can readily be measured. Manufacturers of tea bags, such as PG and Twinings, offer their products in packages of different sizes to satisfy the needs of consumers ranging from singles to large families.

Financial institutions such as banks and building societies attempt to interest children in their products by offering free gifts such as book vouchers. Meanwhile, retired customers

***Figure 8.6***
*Many brands develop specific marketing programmes targeting children*
*Photo © Royalty-Free/ CORBIS*

are targeted with products designed for a leisure-oriented lifestyle. The emphasis is on tailoring the service package to suit particular needs.

Age is a commonly used segmentation variable. Population statistics help marketers to understand and keep track of changing age profiles (see Table 8.1 and Figure 8.7). As the population of western Europe continues to increase, the numbers in the 0- to 19-year-old age band is falling, while the number of those over 60 continues to rise. This has ramifications for marketers, who must increasingly cater for an ageing population. Given the relative affluence of this particular group, many companies (particularly those in leisure and service industries) have benefited from this demographic change. Marketers are also recognising the purchasing influence of children and are targeting their marketing efforts at them. Numerous products are aimed specifically at children: toys, clothing, food, drinks, video games and entertainment. In addition, children profoundly influence certain purchasing decisions made by their parents.[13] For example, in households with only one parent or in which both parents work, children often take on additional responsibilities such as cooking, cleaning and food shopping, and thus influence the products and brands that are purchased.

Gender is another demographic variable commonly used to segment markets, including the markets for clothing, alcoholic drinks, books, magazines, non-prescription drugs and even cigarettes. EU statistics show that women and girls outnumber men and boys by just over 1 per cent in the population.

The confectionery market did not traditionally segment its market on the basis of gender. Chocolate manufacturers, including Cadbury's, tried to change this by developing assortments

**TABLE 8.1 POPULATION STATISTICS, EUROPE**

**POPULATION FORECASTS (in thousands)**

| | 2005 | 2010 | 2015 | 2020 | 2025 | 2030 | 2040 | 2050 |
|---|---|---|---|---|---|---|---|---|
| Austria | 8,183 | 8,231 | 8,279 | 8,323 | 8,368 | – | – | 8,206 |
| Belgium | 10,426 | 10,530 | 10,625 | 10,724 | 10,818 | 10,894 | 10,965 | 10,953 |
| Denmark | – | 5,421 | – | 5,431 | – | 5,428 | 5,358 | 5,261 |
| Finland | – | 5,268 | – | 5,317 | – | 5,291 | – | – |
| France | – | 61,061 | 61,975 | 62,734 | – | 63,927 | – | 64,032 |
| Germany | – | 81,422 | 80,909 | 80,152 | – | 77,672 | 74,155 | 69,940 |
| Greece | 10,627 | 10,653 | 10,626 | 10,555 | – | – | – | – |
| Ireland[1] | 3,938 | 4,014 | 4,040 | 4,039 | 4,009 | 3,955 | – | – |
| Italy[2] | 58,409 | 58,587 | – | 57,936 | – | 56,807 | 54,778 | 51,890 |
| Luxembourg | 399 | 403 | 406 | 410 | – | – | – | – |
| Netherlands[1] | – | 16,938 | – | 17,545 | – | 17,947 | – | – |
| Norway | – | 4,692 | – | – | – | 5,085 | – | 5,220 |
| Poland | 38,634 | 38,788 | 39,005 | 39,003 | 38,657 | 38,025 | – | – |
| Portugal | 10,562 | 10,626 | 10,587 | 10,489 | 10,356 | – | – | – |
| Slovenia | 1,988[1] | 2,012[2] | 2,020[1] | 2,019 | – | – | – | – |
| Sweden | 9,013[1] | 9,308[1] | – | 9,765 | – | 10,130 | – | – |
| Switzerland | 7,274 | 7,332 | – | 7,389 | – | – | – | – |
| Turkey | 70,225 | – | – | – | – | – | – | – |
| Ukraine | – | 50,040 | – | 49,936 | – | 49,831 | – | – |
| UK | – – | 61,956 | – | 64,105 | – | 65,568 | 65,822 | – |

**Notes:** [1] Add 1 year to date(s) shown. [2] Add 2 years to date(s) shown.
**Sources:** National statistical offices.

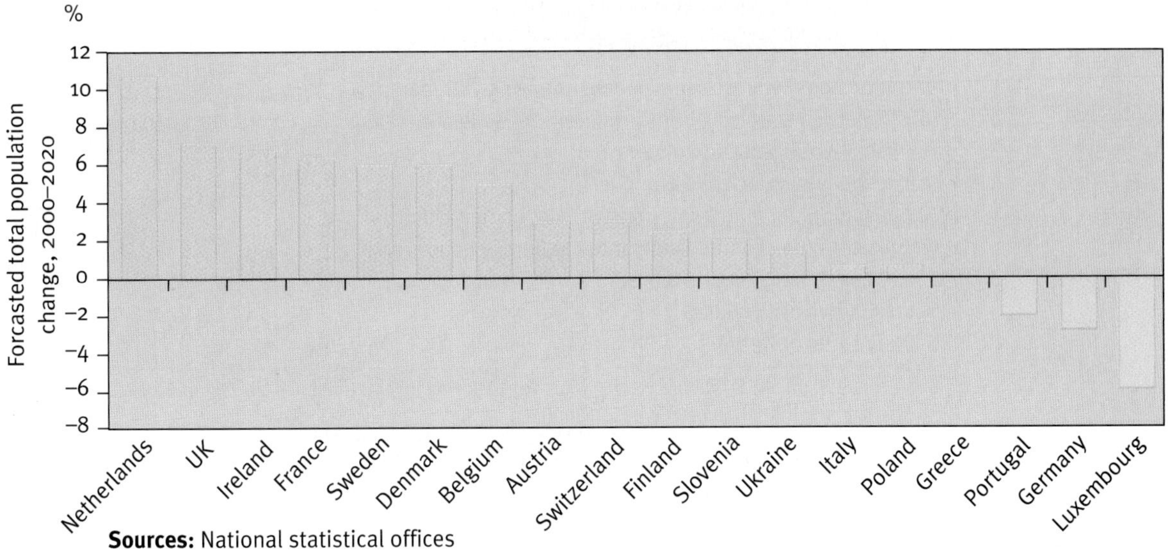


***Figure 8.7***
*Forecasted total population change 2000–2020*
*Source:* The European Marketing Pocket Book, *published by the World Advertising Research Center, Henley-on-Thames, 2004*

aimed primarily at men. In general, despite the care taken in each product's design, packaging and promotion, these were not successful. However, efforts by manufacturers of skincare products to develop lines specifically aimed at men have been more successful.

The way in which marketers treat ethnicity varies in different parts of the world. For instance, in the USA, where a quarter of the population is made up of ethnic minorities, ethnicity is widely used as a means of segmenting markets for goods and services of all kinds. The US Hispanic population, comprising people of Mexican, Cuban, Puerto Rican, and Central and South American heritage, is growing five times faster than the general population. Consequently, it is being targeted by more and more companies, including Campbell Soup Co., Nabisco and Procter & Gamble. However, targeting Hispanic customers is not an easy task. For example, although marketers have long believed that Hispanic consumers are exceptionally brand loyal and prefer Spanish-language media, research does not support these assumptions. Not only do advertisers disagree about the merits of using Spanish-language media, they also question whether it is appropriate to advertise to Mexicans, Puerto Ricans and Cubans using a common Spanish language.[14] In other areas the proportion of ethnic minorities is much lower than in the USA, affecting the level of marketing attention they receive. In the UK, the percentage of the population from ethnic minorities increased from 3.9 per cent in 1980 to 7.4 per cent in 2001. As the Case Study at the end of this chapter (pages 255–256) explains, marketers are now looking for new ways to connect with the needs of these particular groups.

Product and service needs also vary according to marital status, and the number and age of children. These factors are collectively taken into consideration by the 'family life cycle' concept. Some of the more obvious markets in which the impact of different life cycles is seen are tourism, housing and financial services. The family life cycle has been broken down in several different ways. Table 8.2 illustrates one such scheme.

The scheme presented in Table 8.2 assumes that individuals at different life cycle stages have varying product needs. Marketers can respond to this by targeting such groups with marketing mixes designed to capitalise on these differences. For example, parents whose children have grown up and left home ('empty nesters') tend to have more disposable income than those with young children, and tend to spend more on the home, holidays and new cars.

**TABLE 8.2 THE WELLS AND GUBAR LIFE CYCLE STAGES**

| |
|---|
| Bachelor stage (young single people not living with parents) |
| Newly married couples without children |
| Full nest I (youngest child under 6) |
| Full nest II (youngest child 6 or over) |
| Full nest III (older married couple with dependent children) |
| Empty nest I (no children living at home, family head working) |
| Empty nest II (family head retired) |
| Solitary survivor (working) |
| Solitary survivor (retired) |

**Source:** Copyright © ESOMAR® 2000. Permission for using this material has been granted by ESOMAR®, Amsterdam, the Netherlands (www.esomar.nl).

Banks and financial institutions in particular are getting better at gearing their marketing efforts to life cycle changes. Critics of the life cycle concept point out that it can be difficult to decide to which categories families belong. Some households, such as single-parent families and older married couples who have never had children, do not appear to fit in at all.

Obviously, this discussion of demographic variables is not exhaustive. However, the variables described above probably represent the most widely used demographics. Other examples of the use of demographics include segmenting the cosmetic and haircare markets on the basis of race and directing certain types of food and clothing towards people of specific religious sects.

Socio-economic variables include income, occupation, education and social class. Some marketing academics and practitioners include certain of these variables under the 'demographics' label. Income can be a very useful way of dividing markets because it strongly influences people's product needs. It affects their ability to buy (as discussed in Chapter 2) and their aspirations for a certain style of living. Obvious products in this category include housing, furniture, clothing, cars, food, certain kinds of sporting goods, and leisure activities.

The occupations of the members of the household are known to have an impact on the types of products and services that are purchased. The type of housing individuals and families own or rent is strongly linked to this variable. It is obvious, for example, that sales of products for refurbishment and decoration, such as paints, fabrics and wallpapers, will occur predominantly among those professions that have owner-occupier status. Occupation is also known to affect the types of sporting and leisure activities people prefer. For example, professionals may be active with walking, swimming, cycling and jogging, but not so involved with darts or football. Intermediate managers enjoy walking, swimming and keep fit/yoga. Unskilled manual workers are not particularly active in sports and physical activities.[15]

Other socio-economic variables that may be used to segment markets include education level and social class.

**Geographic Variables** The needs of consumers in different geographic locations may be affected by their local climate, terrain, natural resources and population density. Markets may be divided into regions because one or more geographic variables may cause customers' needs to differ from one region to another. A company that sells products throughout the EU will, for example, need to take the different languages spoken into account when labelling its goods.

City size can be an important segmentation variable. For example, one franchised restaurant organisation will not locate in cities of fewer than 100,000 people because experience shows that a smaller population base could make the operation unprofitable. The same company may add a second, or even a third, restaurant once the city reaches a certain size. Other businesses, however, seek out opportunities in smaller towns. The major petroleum retailers, such as Esso and Shell, have traffic density thresholds, below which they perceive a local market as unviable. It is, therefore, quite common – particularly in villages and small towns in rural areas – for petroleum retailing to be dominated by independent garage owners and the smaller petroleum companies.

**Market density**
The number of potential customers within a unit of land area

**Market density** refers to the number of potential customers within a unit of land area, such as a square kilometre. Although market density is generally related to population density, the correlation is not exact. For example, in two different geographic markets of approximately equal size and population, the market density for office supplies might be much higher in the first than in the second if the first contains a significantly greater proportion of business customers. Market density may be a useful segmentation variable because low-density markets often require different sales, advertising and distribution activities from high-density markets.

In Europe, climate can be used as a geographic segmentation variable. Companies entering new markets in Europe increasingly need to consider the impact of climate on their customer base. For example, washing machines sold in Italy do not require such fast spin speeds as those sold in Germany because the Italian climate is much sunnier. Other markets affected by climate include air conditioning and heating equipment, clothing, gardening equipment, recreational products and building materials.

**Geodemographic segmentation**
Clustering people according to postcode areas and census data

Marketers are increasingly using geodemographic segmentation. **Geodemographic segmentation** clusters people according to postcode areas. For example, ACORN (A Classification Of Residential Neighbourhoods) uses information taken from census data and allows people to be grouped according to a number of factors, including geography, socio-economics, culture and lifestyle. All 1.9 million UK postcodes have been described using over 125 demographic statistics and 287 lifestyle variables. The underlying concept is that customers living in different residential neighbourhoods have different profiles in respect of these variables. Their product needs in terms of styling and features, therefore, also vary. Consumers can be classified under ACORN on the basis of the postcode of their home address and then allocated to one of the groups in Table 8.3. These categories further sub-divide to give a total of 17 groups and 56 neighbourhood types. For example, *Wealthy Achievers* includes several groups, such as *Wealthy Executives, Affluent Greys* and *Flourishing Families*. The *Wealthy*

**TABLE 8.3 THE ACORN CATEGORISATION OF UK CONSUMERS**

| Category | Group | Type |
|---|---|---|
| Wealthy Achievers | Wealthy Executives | 01 Affluent mature professionals, large houses<br>02 Affluent working families with mortgages<br>03 Villages with wealthy commuters<br>04 Well-off managers, larger houses |
| | Affluent Greys | 05 Older affluent professionals<br>06 Farming communities<br>07 Old people, detached houses<br>08 Mature couples, smaller detached houses |
| | Flourishing Families | 09 Larger families, prosperous suburbs<br>10 Well-off working families with mortgages<br>11 Well-off managers, detached houses<br>12 Large families & houses in rural areas |

*(Continued...)*

**Table 8.3 The Acorn Categorisation of UK Consumers (continued)**

| Category | Group | Type |
|---|---|---|
| Urban Prosperity | Prosperous Professionals | 13 Well-off professionals, larger houses and converted flats<br>14 Older professionals in detached houses and apartments |
| | Educated Urbanites | 15 Affluent urban professionals, flats<br>16 Prosperous young professionals, flats<br>17 Young educated workers, flats<br>18 Multi-ethnic young, converted flats<br>19 Suburban privately renting professionals |
| | Aspiring Singles | 20 Student flats and cosmopolitan sharers<br>21 Singles & sharers, multi-ethnic areas<br>22 Low-income singles, small rented flats<br>23 Student terraces |
| Comfortably Off | Starting Out | 24 Young couples, flats and terraces<br>25 White collar singles/sharers, terraces |
| | Secure Families | 26 Younger white-collar couples with mortgages<br>27 Middle income, home-owning areas<br>28 Working families with mortgages<br>29 Mature families in suburban semis<br>30 Established home-owning workers<br>31 Home-owning Asian family areas |
| | Settled Suburbia | 32 Retired home owners<br>33 Middle income, older couples<br>34 Lower income people, semis |
| | Prudent Pensioners | 35 Elderly singles, purpose-built flats<br>36 Older people, flats |
| Moderate Means | Asian Communities | 37 Crowded Asian terraces<br>38 Low-income Asian families |
| | Post-industrial Families | 39 Skilled older family terraces<br>40 Young family workers |
| | Blue-collar Roots | 41 Skilled workers, semis and terraces<br>42 Home-owning, terraces<br>43 Older rented terraces |
| Hard-pressed | Struggling Families | 44 Low-income larger families, semis<br>45 Older people, low income, small semis<br>46 Low income, routine jobs, unemployment<br>47 Low-rise terraced estates of poorly-off workers<br>48 Low incomes, high unemployment, single parents<br>49 Large families, many children, poorly educated |
| | Burdened Singles | 50 Council flats, single elderly people<br>51 Council terraces, unemployment, many singles<br>52 Council flats, single parents, unemployment *(Continued...)* |

**Table 8.3 The Acorn Categorisation of UK Consumers (continued)**

| Category | Group | Type |
|---|---|---|
| Hard-pressed (continued) | High-rise Hardship | 53 Old people in high rise flats<br>54 Singles & single parents, high rise estates |
| | Inner-city Adversity | 55 Multi-ethnic purpose-built estates<br>56 Multi-ethnic, crowded flats |

**Source:** ACORN categories by CACI.

## Topical Insight

### Profiling and Targeting Customers with ACORN

Along with Experian's Mosaic system, ACORN from CACI is a leading geodemographic tool used by marketing practitioners to identify and understand the UK population and the demand for products and services. Clients of CACI use this information to improve their understanding of customers and target markets, and to determine where to locate operations. The geodemographic and lifestyle data provided by ACORN's detailed analysis of the official census statistics, supplemented with financial, purchasing and behaviour information, are an invaluable input to the market segmentation analyses of many consumer marketers.

As CACI explains, informed decisions can be made on where direct marketing and advertising campaigns will be most effective; where branches should be opened or closed; or where sites are located, including retail outlets, leisure facilities and public services.

ACORN categorises all 1.9 million UK postcodes, which have been described using over 125 demographic statistics within England, Scotland, Wales and Northern Ireland, and 287 lifestyle variables, making it a most powerful discriminator, which offers a clearer understanding of clients and prospects. The basic principle is that people in similar areas – postcode zones – have the same needs and lifestyles.

With the 2001 government census of the entire population fully analysed, CACI had to update its ACORN profiles, as detailed in Table 8.3. The associated analysis revealed some interesting shifts since the last full census. Consumer habits and behaviour have changed over the past decade, and the new ACORN takes into account these key shifts.

Here are some examples.

- As the wealth of the nation increases and borrowing becomes easier, car ownership has risen and more people commute by car.
- More consumers are asset-rich, with a growth of 20 per cent of home owners having paid off their mortgages.
- Conversely, there is much less unemployment.
- New building has increased, with more detached and semi-detached properties. There are now different types of people living in traditional housing.
- The workplace is now more flexible, illustrated by an increase in people working from home.
- The population is becoming more educated and the number of students has nearly doubled.
- Family structure is changing, with significant growth in the number of single parents. Despite an increase in the number of grown-up children remaining in the family home, there are more 'empty nester' consumers than ever before as older couples become free of the financial responsibility of schoolchildren.
- There is a significant growth of the very elderly: the population is becoming older.

Such changes present both opportunities and threats for the marketers of a large selection of products and services.

CACI claims the new ACORN is more accurate for targeting than previous versions, across all sectors – for example, finance, automotive, e-commerce, holidays, food shopping and brown goods. As detailed on CACI's website, just some of the consumer profiling and targeting information available includes:

- mortgages
- winter snow holidays
- time left on mortgage
- weekend breaks
- company medical insurance
- classical music/opera
- private pension
- weekly food spend
- car insurance
- eating out
- child savings plan
- family income
- guaranteed income bonds
- house price
- National Savings
- 'new player' credit cards
- stocks and shares
- own a DVD player
- unit trusts
- have cable TV/phone
- buy new car
- have satellite TV
- buy car over £20,000
- own a laptop computer
- can choose company car
- use PC for finance
- car kept in garage
- use PC for education
- European holidays
- use e-mail
- USA holidays.

Marketers may purchase reports about specific products or concerning ACORN's consumer classifications. A popular application is to capture the postcodes of customers of a company, so as to analyse the ACORN profile of these customers. Armed with such a profile, the client company's marketers are able to locate similar consumers to target with their marketing communications.

**Source:** CACI, 2004.

*Executives* group then sub-divides into several types, such as *Affluent Working Families with Mortgages*, *Villages with Wealthy Commuters*, or *Well-off Managers in Larger Houses*. The Topical Insight box above describes ACORN in more detail.

**Psychographic Variables** Marketers sometimes use psychographic variables such as personality characteristics, motives and lifestyles to segment markets. A psychographic dimension can be used by itself or combined with other types of segmentation variable.

Personality characteristics are useful when a product is similar to many competing products and when consumers' needs are not significantly affected by other segmentation variables. However, segmenting a market according to personality characteristics can be problematic. Although marketing practitioners have long believed that consumer choice and product use should vary with personality and lifestyle, marketing research has shown only weak relationships. However, the weakness of such relationships may be due to the difficulty of accurately measuring personality traits, because most existing personality tests were developed for clinical use, not for segmentation purposes. As the reliability of more recent measurement instruments increases, a greater association between personality and consumer behaviour has been demonstrated.[16] For example, it has been shown that personality sometimes influences the clothes, make-up and hairstyles that individuals adopt.

When motives are used to segment a market, it is divided on the basis of consumers' reasons for making a purchase. Product durability, value for money, concern for the environment, convenience and status are all motives affecting the types of product purchased and the choice of stores in which they are bought. For example, one consumer may be motivated to purchase recycled kitchen paper out of concern for the environment. Another may travel to a large supermarket in order to buy the most absorbent, high-quality brand of kitchen towel.

Individuals are grouped by lifestyle segmentation according to how they live and spend their time, the importance of items in their surroundings (their homes or their jobs, for example), their beliefs about themselves and broad issues, and some socio-economic

characteristics, such as income and education.[17] Lifestyle analysis provides a broad view of buyers because it encompasses numerous characteristics related to people's activities, interests and opinions (see Table 8.4). It can be thought of as going beyond a simple understanding of personality.

The use of lifestyle as a segmentation variable is problematic, because it is so difficult to measure accurately compared with other types of segmentation variable. In addition, the relationships between psychographic variables and consumers' needs are sometimes obscure and unproven, and the segments that result from psychographic segmentation may not be reachable.[18] For example, a marketer may determine that highly compulsive individuals want a certain type of clothing. However, no specific stores or particular media – such as television or radio programmes, newspapers or magazines – appeal precisely to this group and this group alone. Psychographic variables can sometimes offer a more useful way of understanding segments that have been defined using other base variables.

One of the more popular programmes studying lifestyles is conducted by the Stanford Research Institute's Value and Lifestyle Programme (VALS). This programme surveys consumers to select groups with identifiable values and lifestyles. Initially, VALS identified three broad consumer groups: Outer-directed, Inner-directed, and Need-driven consumers. The current VALS classification categorises consumers into eight basic lifestyle groups: Innovators, Thinkers, Achievers, Experiencers, Believers, Strivers, Makers and Survivors. The VALS studies have been used to create products as well as to segment markets.

**Behaviouristic Variables** Marketers can also segment markets on the basis of an aspect of consumers' behaviour towards the product. This might relate to the way the particular product is used or purchased, or perhaps to the benefits consumers require from it.

Purchase behaviour can be a useful way of distinguishing between groups of customers, giving marketers insight into the most appropriate marketing mix. For example, brand-loyal customers may require a different kind of treatment from those who switch between brands. On-pack sales promotions are often geared towards building loyalty in brand switchers.

The occasion on which customers buy a particular product may impact upon product choice because in different sets of circumstances different product selection criteria may be applied. For instance, a customer who replaces a car tyre in an emergency will probably be less concerned about price than one who is routinely maintaining his or her car.

**Benefit segmentation**
The division of a market according to the benefits consumers want from the product

**Benefit segmentation** is the division of a market according to the benefits consumers want from the product.[19] Although most types of market segmentation are based on the

**TABLE 8.4 CHARACTERISTICS RELATED TO ACTIVITIES, INTERESTS AND OPINIONS**

| Activities | Interests | Opinions |
|---|---|---|
| Work | Family | Themselves |
| Hobbies | Home | Social issues |
| Social events | Job | Politics |
| Holidays | Community | Business |
| Entertainment | Recreation | Economics |
| Club membership | Fashion | Education |
| Community | Food | Products |
| Shopping | Media | Future |
| Sports | Achievements | Culture |

**Source:** Reprinted, adapted from Joseph Plummer, 'The concept and application of life style segmentation', *Journal of Marketing*, January 1974, p. 34. Reprinted by permission of the American Marketing Association.

assumption that there is a relationship between the variable and customers' needs, benefit segmentation is different in that the benefits the customers seek are their product needs. By determining the benefits desired, marketers may be able to divide people into groups seeking certain sets of benefits.

The effectiveness of benefit segmentation depends on several conditions. First, the benefits people seek must be identifiable. Second, using these benefits, marketers must be able to divide people into recognisable segments. Finally, one or more of the resulting segments must be accessible to the companies' marketing efforts.

Product usage is another method marketers sometimes use to segment their customers. Individuals can be divided into users and non-users of a particular product. Users can then be classified further as heavy, moderate or light. To satisfy a specific user group, marketers sometimes create a distinctive product, set special prices or initiate special promotion and distribution activities. Thus airlines such as British Airways and KLM offer frequent-flier programmes to reward their regular customers with free trips and discounts for car hire and hotel accommodation. Light users or non-users of products often receive little attention from companies. There is a tendency sometimes to dismiss these groups when developing a marketing programme. For example, research in the holiday industry tends to focus on feedback from current customers, often forgetting to question why non-users failed to buy.

How customers apply the product may also determine segmentation. To satisfy customers who use a product in a certain way, some feature – say, packaging, size, texture or colour – may have to be designed with special care to make the product easier to use, more convenient or more environmentally friendly. For instance, Lever Brothers and Procter & Gamble are focusing more and more on the development of refill packs of detergents and other household products, to cater for increasing consumer concerns about the environment.

The varying attitude of customers towards products constitutes another set of variables that can be used to segment markets. Clothing retailers like River Island and Benetton are particularly conscious of this. While one customer seeks outfits that are practical and comfortable, another is concerned with achieving a highly fashionable image.

As this brief discussion shows, consumer markets can be divided according to numerous characteristics. Ultimately, the choices marketers make will depend on a host of market and company factors.

## Variables for Segmenting Business Markets

Like consumer markets, business (organisational) markets are often segmented. Here the marketer's aim is to satisfy the needs of businesses for products. Marketers may segment business markets according to company demographics, operating variables, purchasing approach, situational factors or the personal characteristics of buyers.

Marketers attempting to segment business markets may face various problems.[20] The particular characteristics of the market or the distribution structure in place may restrict the types of segment bases that can be used. For example, many European car manufacturers are dependent upon the fleet car market. This market tends to be structured on the basis of car engine and vehicle size, with companies providing their more senior managers with more powerful, larger and expensive vehicles. It is likely that customers would resist a move away from this accepted structure by the car manufacturers, who are therefore not in a position to use possibly contradictory segmentation approaches. Various segmentation approaches have been developed to try to make it easier for companies to deal with these kinds of constraints.[21]

Whatever the approach adopted, just as in consumer markets, some segment bases are easier to measure and apply than others.[22] For example, it is much more straightforward to segment on the basis of company size, which is a measurable and visible characteristic, than on the basis of buying centre structure (see Chapter 7), which may be much more difficult to appraise. Table 8.5 provides an overview of the variables for segmenting business markets, and illustrates the relative ease with which they can be measured. Variables at the base of the table are easier to measure and more objective than those at the top.

**Table 8.5 Variables for Segmenting Business Markets**

**Personal Characteristics of Buyers**
Just as in consumer markets, the demographics, personality and lifestyle of those individuals in the buying centre impact upon purchasing decisions, practices, attitudes towards risk and loyalty to suppliers.

**Situational Factors**
The urgency of purchase, size of order or product application can play an important role in the choices that are made.

**Purchasing Approach**
Buying centre structure (centralised/decentralised), buying policies (sealed bidding, service contracts, leasing), nature of existing relationships (focus on new or existing customers), balance of power among decision-makers and buying criteria (quality, delivery, service, price, product range, innovation) may shape an organisation's purchase decisions.

**Operating Variables**
The technologies applied by an organisation, the manner in which products are used or customer capabilities can fundamentally affect purchase choice.

**Demographics**
Company age, location, industry (SIC code) and size are likely to alter product requirements.

**Company Demographics** Variables relating to the type of business or industry, geographic location, company age and size are probably the most widely used segmentation variables in business markets.

A company sometimes segments a market by the types of business within that market, perhaps on the basis of industry area or SIC code (see Chapter 7). Different types of organisation often require different product features, distribution systems, price structures and selling strategies. Given these variables, a company may either concentrate on a single segment with one marketing mix (concentration strategy) or focus on several groups with multiple mixes (multi-segment strategy). A paint manufacturer could segment customers into several groups, such as paint wholesalers, do-it-yourself retail outlets, vehicle manufacturers, decorators and housing developers.

The demand for some consumer products can vary considerably by geographic area because of differences in climate, terrain, customer preference or similar factors. Demand for business-to-business products also varies according to geographic location. For example, the producers of certain types of timber divide their markets geographically because their customers' needs vary regionally. Geographic segmentation may be especially appropriate for reaching industries that are concentrated in certain locations, for example, textiles in West Yorkshire, information technology (IT) along the M4 corridor in England or financial services in London. Examples of such concentration in Europe include heavy industry around Lille or in the Ruhr Valley, and banking in Zurich.

**Operating Variables** Customer requirements can be affected in a range of ways by different operating variables such as the technology applied by the buying organisation or the product types used. Certain products, especially raw materials such as steel, petrol, plastics and timber, are used in numerous ways. Sometimes the technology used by a company will play an important role. How a company uses products affects the types and amounts it purchases, as well as the method of making the purchase.[23] For example, computers are used for engineering purposes, basic scientific research, business operations such as word processing and bookkeeping, as well as Internet access and games in the home. A computer manufacturer may segment the computer market by types of use because organisations' needs for computer hardware and software depend on the purpose for which the products are purchased.

**Purchasing Approach** Although it may be difficult for a company to appraise the buying approach of its customers, this is none the less sometimes an appropriate way for business markets to be segmented. The characteristics of the buying centre, including its structure (where the balance of buying power lies), and the nature of any buying policies can all affect the product requirements of customers. For example, suppliers of building materials must organise their sales efforts to satisfy a wide array of customer types who organise their buying activities in vastly different ways. While dealing with large buyers, such as Wimpey or Tarmac, will require an understanding of a relatively complex buying structure, small local builders may be perfectly satisfied with a much simpler supply arrangement.

**Situational Factors** Sometimes it is appropriate to segment a business market on the basis of situational factors such as the urgency or size of an order. How urgently the order is required may have an impact on the importance a customer attaches to particular product features. For example, if a robot on a car production line has broken down, bringing the entire production process to a standstill, the price of replacement parts to fix it may be less important than their availability. However, if the same part is being replaced as part of a routine service, price may be the most important factor. The size and frequency of different orders can be effective segmentation variables because they have ramifications concerning the way the customer relationship is handled. For example, a university that regularly orders vast amounts of stationery would expect a different level of service to that of a small business that only infrequently buys small quantities of paper and envelopes.

**Personal Characteristics** Although individuals involved in business buying may not have as much control over the products and services selected as when they are making purchases for personal or family use, their individual characteristics still play a role in the preferences they demonstrate. For this reason it is sometimes appropriate to segment business markets on the basis of the characteristics of individuals within the buying centre. For example, the demographics, personality and lifestyle of managers tasked with buying a selection of new office furniture will influence the preferred designs. If power in the buying centre rests with one senior manager who strongly dislikes modern designs, say, this will influence the final selection of products.

# Segmentation Effectiveness

As Table 8.6 illustrates, segmentation analysis invariably involves several stages. Marketers must be aware that whatever the approach followed and whichever base variables are used, haphazard implementation can lead to ineffective market segmentation, missed opportunities and inappropriate investment. To avoid such difficulties marketers should take note of the following criteria. The first is that there must be real differences in the needs of consumers for the product or service. There is no value in segmenting a homogeneous market. Equally, dissimilar consumers in terms of their needs and purchasing behaviour must not be grouped together in the same market segment. In addition, the segments revealed must be:

- *measurable* – easy to identify and measure; some basis must be found for effectively separating individuals into groups or segments with relatively homogeneous product or service needs
- *substantial* – large enough to be sufficiently profitable to justify developing and maintaining a specific marketing mix
- *accessible* – easy to reach with the marketing mix developed – for example, the promotional effort should target the relevant consumers

**TABLE 8.6 STAGES IN SEGMENTATION ANALYSIS**

**Objectives**
Marketers must know the purpose of the exercise and have clear objectives.

**Data**
Required information must be specified and collected. This may encompass a qualitative phase to develop a robust view of consumer attitudes, motives, behaviour and perceptions, and a quantitative phase involving larger samples and statistical analysis of questionnaire responses (see Chapter 9).

**Analysis**
Various statistical packages, such as SPSS, can be used. Factor analysis, conjoint analysis and cluster analysis are commonly used techniques for analysing the collected data. Multidimensional scaling (MDS) is widely used in product positioning studies. Such techniques should not be applied by those without the necessary statistical skills, if inappropriate solutions are to be avoided.[24]

**Interpretation**
Marketers must interpret the proposed solutions to ensure any adopted segmentation scheme is statistically valid (complies with the relevant statistical significance tests) and managerially or intuitively valid, and that it presents market segments that are effective. Ultimately, the analysis should comply with statistical validity tests. Any recommendations must also be sensible in the view of managers.[25]

**Recommendation**
The final proposed solution must first be presented internally to senior and line managers expected to approve the segments, and then actioned for the external audience of distributors and customers.

**Sources**[26, 27, 28]

- *stable* – the question of segment stability over time is not often addressed; if companies are to make strategic decisions on the basis of revealed segments, they need to be reasonably certain that those segments will be around long enough for action to be taken
- *useful* – the selected segments must be meaningful to the managers tasked with operationalising them and be likely to enable the company to better satisfy its target market.

Using market segmentation also requires a good deal of common sense. It is often difficult for companies to implement totally new segmentation schemes because they would be at odds with the existing marketing structures and ways of doing things. In such cases companies sometimes choose to make minor changes to what is already in place.

# Profiling Market Segments

Whatever the variable, or combination of variables, used to group customers, a more comprehensive understanding of the characteristics of individuals is likely to be required. For example, a company that segments the market for energy drinks on the basis of age, focusing on customers in their late teens, would do well to understand as much as possible about its particular target group in other respects. What reference groups influence them? Where do they live? Where and when do they socialise? What social background are they from? What motivates them? The more comprehensive the image developed, the better the opportunity to develop an effective marketing mix with maximum appeal.

**Profiling**
The task of building up a fuller picture of the target segments

**Descriptors**
Variables used to profile or build a fuller picture of target segments

**Profiling** is the task of building up a fuller picture of target segments, and the variables being used in the description are termed **descriptors**. The types of descriptors available to marketers are broadly the same as the variables used to segment markets in the first place – that is, demographics, socio-economics, and so on. This is sometimes a cause of confusion for students, who struggle to remember whether they are dealing with base or descriptor variables. It helps to note that while base variables should discriminate between customer needs, descriptors are simply used to enrich the picture, to help summarise what else can be gleaned about the customers in a particular segment. This gives added inspiration to the creative team developing the product and promotional material, and helps to fine-tune decisions on price and distribution. Overall, profiling segments in this way ensures that the impact of the marketing mix on the customer is maximised. If segments are not properly profiled, it is unlikely sales personnel, advertising agency staff or senior managers will fully comprehend the proposed segmentation scheme. Therefore its effective implementation may be jeopardised.

## Targeting Strategies

**Targeting**
The decision about which market segment(s) a business decides to prioritise for its sales and marketing efforts

**Targeting** involves marketers in decisions about which market segment(s) a business should prioritise for its sales and marketing efforts. As Figure 8.8 shows the three basic targeting strategies are: undifferentiated, concentrated and differentiated. The decision made on the targeting strategy to follow must be based on a clear understanding of company capabilities and resources, the nature of the competition and the characteristics of the product markets in question.

### Undifferentiated Strategy

An organisation sometimes defines an entire market for a particular product as its target market. When a company designs a single marketing mix and directs it at the entire market for a particular product, it is using an undifferentiated targeting strategy. This is a strategy in which an organisation defines an entire market for a particular product as its target market, designs a single marketing mix, and directs it at that market. The strategy assumes that all customers in the target market for a specific kind of product have similar needs, and thus the organisation can satisfy most customers with a single marketing mix. This mix consists of one type of product with little or no variation, one price, one promotional programme aimed at everybody, and one distribution system to reach most customers in the total market. Products marketed successfully through the undifferentiated strategy include staple food items, such as sugar and salt, and certain kinds of farm produce.

The undifferentiated targeting strategy is effective under two conditions. First, a large proportion of customers in a total market must have similar needs for the product, a situation termed a 'homogeneous market'. A marketer using a single marketing mix for a total market of customers with a variety of needs would find that the marketing mix satisfies very few people. A 'universal car' meant to satisfy everyone would satisfy very few customers' needs for cars because it would not provide the specific attributes a particular person wants. Second, the organisation must be able to develop and maintain a single marketing mix that satisfies customers' needs. The company must be able to identify a set of needs common to most customers in a total market and have the resources and managerial skills to reach a sizeable portion of that market.

**Concentration strategy**
A process by which a business directs its marketing effort towards a single market segment through one marketing mix

Although customers may have similar needs for a few products, for most products their needs are quite different. In such instances, a company should use a concentrated or a differentiated strategy.

### Concentrated Strategy

When a business directs its marketing efforts towards a single market segment by creating and maintaining one marketing mix, it is employing a **concentration strategy**. The fashion house Chanel targets the exclusive fashion segment, directing its marketing effort towards high-income customers who want to own the most chic apparel. Cross Pen Company aims its products at the upmarket gift segment of the pen market and does not compete with Bic, which focuses on the inexpensive, disposable pen segment.

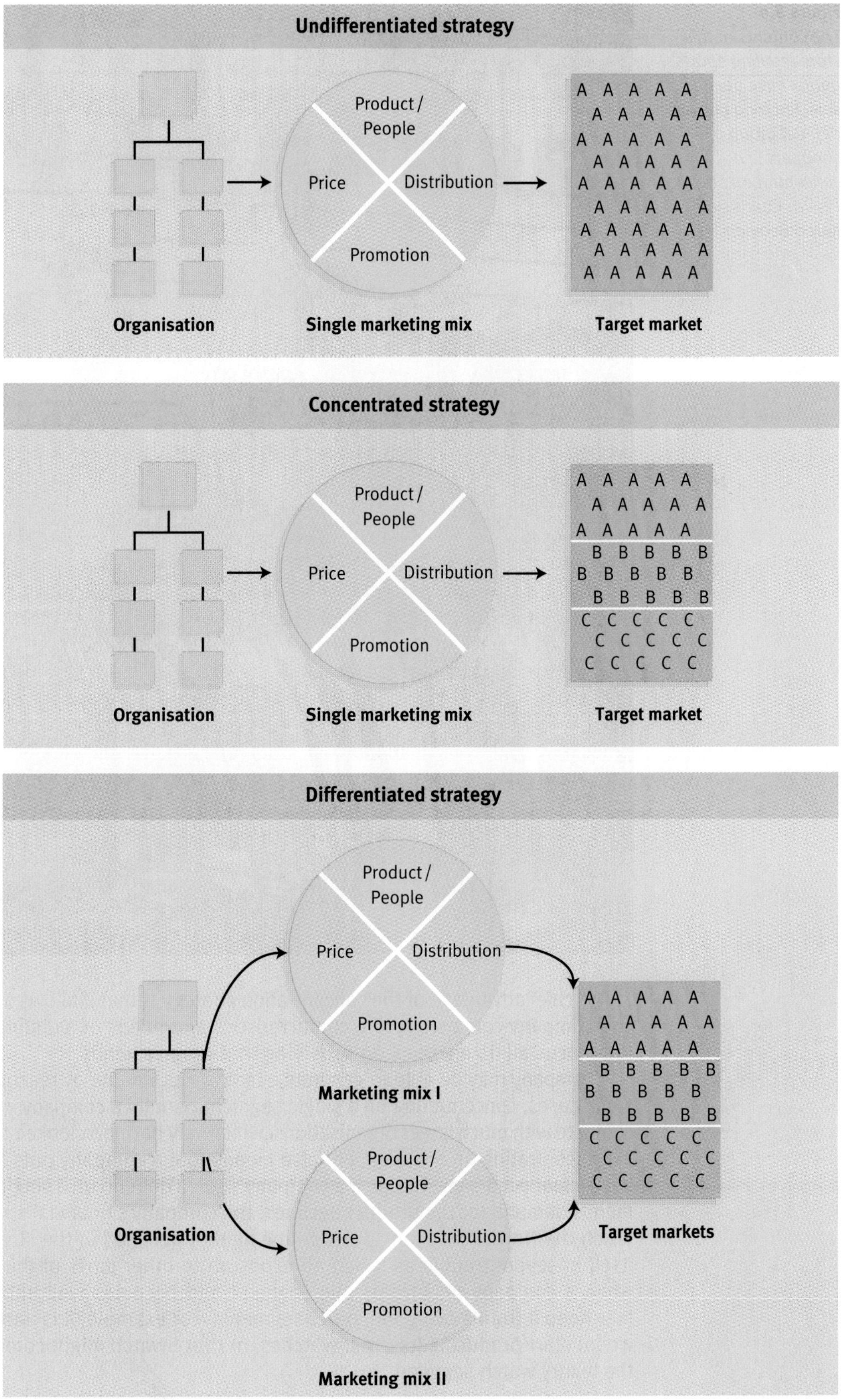


***Figure 8.8***
*Targeting Strategies. The letters in each target market represent potential customers. Customers with the same letters have similar characteristics and similar product needs*

***Figure 8.9***
*The contents of this store retailing sports goods have been selected for a narrowly defined group of shoppers in a concentration strategy*
*Photo: Courtesy of Karen Beaulah*

The chief advantage of the concentration strategy is that it allows a company to specialise. The company can analyse the characteristics and needs of a distinct customer group and then focus all its energies on satisfying that group's needs.

A company may be able to generate a large sales volume by reaching a single segment. In some cases, concentrating on a single segment permits a company with limited resources to compete with much larger organisations, which may have overlooked some smaller segments.

Concentrating on one segment also means that a company puts 'all its eggs in one basket' – clearly a disadvantage. If a company's sales depend on a single segment and the segment's demand for the product declines, the company's financial strength declines as well. When the North American sports coupé market declined in the late 1980s, Porsche found itself in severe trouble as it had no exposure to other parts of the car market. Moreover, when a company penetrates one segment and becomes well entrenched, its popularity may keep it from moving into other segments. For example, it is hard to imagine that Rolex would start producing low-cost watches, or that Swatch might compete at the high end of the luxury watch segment.

## Differentiated Strategy

**Differentiated strategy**
A strategy by which a business directs its marketing efforts towards two or more market segments by developing a marketing mix for each

With a **differentiated strategy** (see Figure 8.8), a business directs its marketing efforts at two or more market segments by developing a marketing mix for each segment selected. Sometimes this is a natural progression from the successful application of a concentration strategy in one market segment. For example, Jockey underwear has traditionally been aimed at one segment: men. However, the company has expanded its efforts and now markets underwear for women and children as well. The marketing mixes used for a differentiated strategy may vary as to product/service differences, place/distribution methods, promotion methods and prices. The majority of users of Gatwick Airport near London are packaged holiday travellers. A significant minority, however, are business users.

A business can usually increase its sales in the aggregate market through a differentiated strategy because its marketing mixes are aimed at more people. For example, Gap, which established its retail clothes reputation by targeting people under 25, now targets several age groups, from infants to people over 60. A company with excess production capacity may find a differentiated strategy advantageous because the sale of products to additional segments may absorb this excess capacity. On the other hand, a differentiated strategy often demands a greater number of production processes, materials and people. Thus production costs may be higher than with a concentration strategy.

## Factors Affecting Choice of Targeting Strategy

Irrespective of the type of targeting strategy a business chooses to adopt, when faced with the decision about whether or not to enter a new segment, it must consider a number of issues. These issues include:

1 the nature of the needs and wants of end users
2 the size, structure and future potential of the segment
3 the availability of company resources
4 the intensity of the competition
5 the size of the company's existing market share, and
6 the possibility of any production/marketing scale economies.

Figure 8.10 sums up the core factors affecting the choice of targeting strategy. A company may recognise that a fit between its products or capabilities and target customer needs is

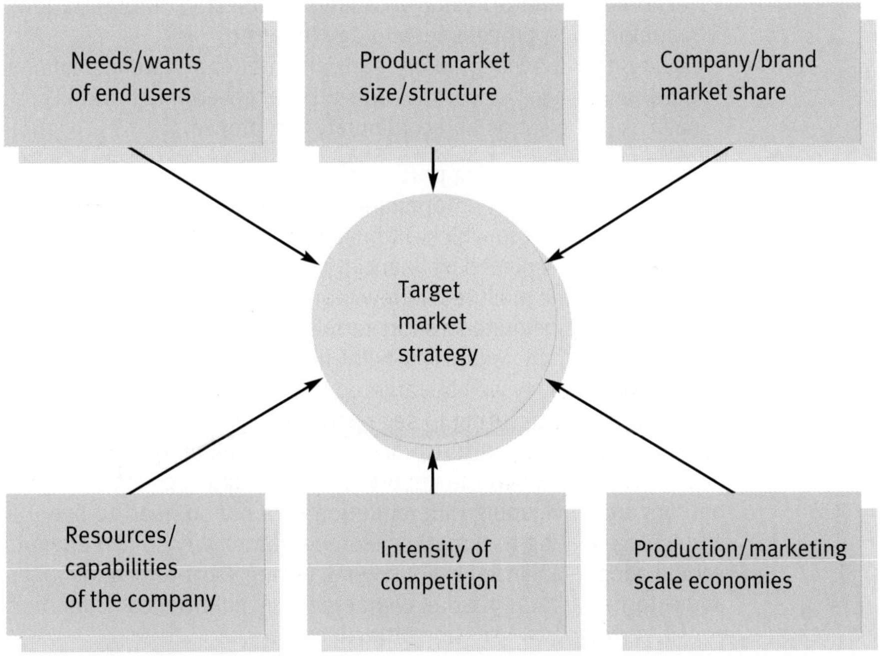


***Figure 8.10***
*Factors affecting choice of target market strategy*
*Source: data from D. Cravens,* Strategic Marketing *(Homewood, Ill.: Irwin, 1982)*

stronger and more 'marketable' in one market segment than in another. In some cases a decision may be made to expand into a new area, market or territory where the fit between customer needs and the product and marketing proposition is poor, with the intention of rectifying such shortcomings. Certain markets' size or value makes them attractive, as does a company's existing or potential sizeable market share. There may be economies of scale available in targeting a particular market segment alongside related ones, so that certain aspects of the production, sales and marketing activity may be shared. Of course, if truly homogeneous market segments have been identified, then each segment will require certain unique aspects of sales and marketing activity. If two segments really can be treated identically in terms of tactical marketing mix programmes, then they are probably one segment. Highly intensive and well-established competition may to some companies be something of a 'turn-off', whereas others may take such competitor activity to be indicative of extensive market growth and business opportunity. Finally, even a company the size of Ford or GM does not have the time, people or financial resources to develop a marketing mix for every single segment in the vehicle market. Available resources play a significant role in management's target market decisions.

There are many factors considered by companies determining which markets to target and which target market strategy to deploy. Figure 8.10 is nevertheless a useful summary of the core factors. Marketing planning (see Chapter 23) expert Malcolm McDonald suggests[29] a variety of issues to consider when determining which and how many target market segments to prioritise. These include market, competition, financial and economic, technological, socio-political and regulatory factors – the forces of the marketing environment (see Chapter 3) and core market trends, as outlined below.

- *Market factors* – size (money, units or both); growth rate per annum; diversity of the market; sensitivity to price, service features and external factors; cyclicality; seasonality; bargaining power of upstream and downstream suppliers.
- *Competition* – types of competitor; degree of concentration; changes in type and mix; entries and exits; changes in market share; substitution by new technology; degrees and types of integration.
- *Financial and economic* – contribution margins; leveraging factors such as economies of scale and experience; barriers to entry or exit; capacity utilisation.
- *Technology* – maturity and volatility; complexity; differentiation; patents and copyrights; manufacturing process technology required.
- *Socio-political and regulatory* – social attitudes and trends; influence with pressure groups, government and regulatory bodies; laws, government and EU regulations; human factors such as unionisation and community acceptance.

A survey[30] of marketing practices in the largest UK companies revealed an interesting set of variables utilised in determining target market attractiveness (see Table 8.7). This study revealed the extent to which UK businesses are overly restricted by the City's short-termism, and the emphasis placed by financial journalists and pundits on performance only in terms of profitability in the most recent few months. US, German and South-east Asian financial markets tend not to be quite so short-termist in their thinking.[31] Outside the UK, businesses worry about market share and profitability, not just for today and tomorrow, but for a few years to come. A market may well be targeted because of its future potential, not just because of current sales. It is reassuring to see customer satisfaction, sustainable differential/competitive advantage and likely product differentiation well up the list of factors considered in the UK, as Chapter 1 explained the importance in marketing of satisfying customers, outpacing competitors and developing differentiation. It is not so good to see the marketing environment and issues relating to non-direct competitor activity so low down the list. Businesses really should adopt a balanced list of criteria, mixing short-term and longer-term issues and internal and external factors – market characteristics, financial considerations and trends. Chapter 12 considers tools for assessing attractiveness.

**TABLE 8.7 MARKET ATTRACTIVENESS FACTORS ADOPTED BY UK COMPANIES**

| Companies' Market Attractiveness Criteria | |
|---|---|
| **First Tier:**<br>• Profitability<br>**Second Tier:**<br>• Market growth<br>• Market size<br>• Likely customer satisfaction<br>• Sales volume<br>**Third Tier:**<br>• Likelihood of a sustainable differential advantage over rivals<br>• Ease of access for the business<br>• Opportunities in the industry<br>• Product differentiation<br>• Competitive rivalry | • Market share<br>• Relative strength/key functions<br>• Customers' price sensitivity<br>• Customer image of company<br>**Fourth Tier:**<br>• Technological factors<br>• Fit with business strategy<br>• Stability of market<br>• Environmental factors<br>• Threat of substitutes<br>• Barriers to entry<br>• Negotiating power of buyers<br>• Ease of profiling customers<br>• Supplier power |

**Source:** Reprinted with permission from S. Dibb and L. Simkin, 'Marketing planning: still barriers to overcome', European Marketing Academy Conference Proceedings, Warwick Business School, University of Warwick, UK.

# Positioning

Figure 8.3 illustrated the link between market segmentation, targeting and positioning. Having identified the segments in a market and decided on which segment (or segments) to target, a company must position its product, service or idea. A product's positioning has been described as the place occupied in a particular market, as perceived by the customer segment at which that product is targeted.[32] Another definition suggests that the positioning of a product is

> the sum of those attributes normally ascribed to it by the consumers – its standing, its quality, the type of people who use it, its strengths, its weaknesses, any other unusual or memorable characteristics it may possess, its price and the value it represents.[33]

**Positioning**
The process of creating an image for a product in the minds of target customers

Positioning starts with a product, a piece of merchandise, a service, a company, an institution or even a person. **Positioning** is not what is done to the product, it is what is created in the minds of the target customers. The product is positioned in the minds of these customers and is given an image.[34] There may be a few cosmetic changes to the product, to its name, price, packaging, styling or channel of distribution, but these are to facilitate the successful promotion of the image desired by the target customers. Target customers must perceive the product to have a distinct image and positioning vis-à-vis its competitors. Product differentiation is widely viewed as the key to successful marketing; the product must stand out and have a clearly defined positioning.

## Determining a Positioning

Positioning is based on customers' perceptions and is therefore only partly within the control of marketers. Positionings are essentially selected by customers, based on variables and within parameters that are important to them. Price may be the key in grocery shopping, service level in selecting a bank, quality and reliability in buying computer hardware, value for money in choosing which theme park to visit. In-depth marketing research (commonly using depth interviews or focus group discussions) is required if customer motivations and expectations in a particular market are to be fully understood. Management's intuition is not always sufficient. For example, research revealed that consumers often have to decide between replacement living room or dining room furniture and a family package holiday abroad. Managers at most leading furniture retailers perceived other furniture retailers to be their competitors, when in reality they were competing for consumer's disposable income against other product areas. In the budget-conscious sector of the furniture buying market, retailers believed only price to be important. In-depth research proved that value for money, a concept that includes product quality and durability in addition to price, was perceived to be the main purchase consideration.

Consumers generally assign positionings to a company or a product that is the market leader – and probably has the highest profile – and the limited number of competitors they can recollect are oriented to this market leader. For example, in the market for tomato ketchup, perceptions of brands are oriented towards market leader Heinz. Occasionally the brand consumers regard as the market leader may not be the genuine market leader in terms of market share, but simply the one most visible at that time, possibly because of heavy promotional exposure. Customers respond to the attributes of a product and to its promotional imagery, but the product's positioning as perceived by its target customers is affected by the reputation and image of the company, coupled with its other products, and by the activities of its competitors. For example, bad publicity, such as that experienced by British Airways following allegations of dirty tricks against Virgin Atlantic, can negatively affect a brand's positioning.

**Perceptual mapping**
A tool used by marketers and marketing researchers to visually depict consumer perceptions and prioritising of brands and their perceived attributes

In-depth marketing research leads to an understanding of how consumers perceive different brands and companies, which marketing variables they believe to be most important and by what magnitude. **Perceptual mapping** is a tool commonly adopted by marketers and marketing researchers to visually depict such consumer perceptions and prioritising of brands and their perceived attributes. Figure 8.11 illustrates a hypothetical example in which consumers thought product range width and price – the two axes – were the key characteristics of the market. A cross marks the ideal positioning, with high product range width and above average price (typical of high-quality shopping goods such as cameras or

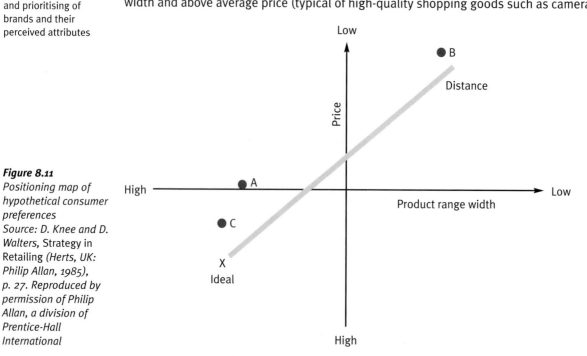

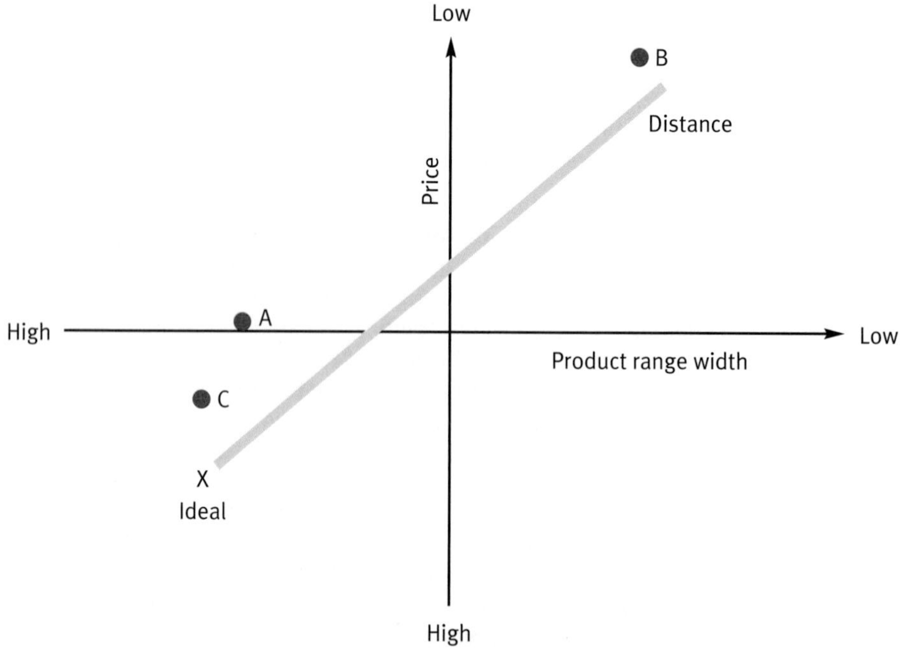


***Figure 8.11***
*Positioning map of hypothetical consumer preferences*
*Source: D. Knee and D. Walters,* Strategy in Retailing *(Herts, UK: Philip Allan, 1985), p. 27. Reproduced by permission of Philip Allan, a division of Prentice-Hall International*

hi-fi systems). Brands (or companies) A and C are perceived as being relatively close to the ideal – their pricing policy does not fully match the image required – but brand (or company) B is viewed as being too cheap, with inadequate product range width.

## Steps in Determining a Positioning Plan

Although customers' perceptions play an important role in positioning, the role of marketers is also crucial. A simple step-by-step approach can be used for establishing a clear positioning plan for a product. This process commences with the identification of target market priorities, as outlined below.

1 Define the segments in a particular market.
2 Decide which segment(s) to target.
3 Understand what the target consumers expect and believe to be the most important considerations when deciding on the purchase.
4 Develop a product or products catering specifically for these needs and expectations.
5 Evaluate the positioning and images, as perceived by the target customers, of competing products in the selected market segment or segments.
6 Select an image that sets the product or products apart from the competing products, thus ensuring that the chosen image matches the aspirations of the target customers. The selected positioning and imagery must be credible: consumers would not believe Kia or Skoda if they promoted their cars in the same manner as Porsche or Aston Martin.
7 Inform target consumers about the product. Although this is primarily a promotional task, it is also vital that the product is made readily available at the right price, through the development of the full marketing mix.

The Marketing Tools and Techniques box on page 250 illustrates how Ford developed the positioning of the Focus to broaden its appeal to female drivers.

## Marketing Tools and Techniques

### Practitioners' Use of Brand Positioning Theory

There are five essential stages in developing a brand positioning.

1 Identify the positionings of the competitive set.
2 Determine the desired positioning for the brand in question.
3 Develop a set of actions in order to achieve the desired positioning – it will not happen by itself!
4 Decide on an appropriate brand positioning statement to communicate the positioning.
5 Produce a marketing communications plan to promote the brand positioning to the target audience: the target market segment and key stakeholders inside the business and within the marketing channel.

Ford benchmarks itself against many competitors, but particularly VW. The Ford Focus is either market leader in its category or a leading challenger in most countries. In order to build on this success, the company had to attract greater numbers of customers, but also to stretch the brand so that not only middle-aged males purchased the Focus. A few years ago, the company wanted to attract more female purchasers, to emulate VW's Golf customer profile. This resulted from production of a perceptual map of the competing brands, featuring the age and sex of the drivers.

'Life's Better When You Take Control' was one of several working brand positioning statements developed, aimed to appeal to younger, aspirational female car buyers.

The action plan included:

- no TV campaign targeted at independent, confident females; the company could not confuse the marketplace and risk alienating the existing customer base
- special edition models of the Focus; research identified the required product features and colours

- direct mail dialogue campaign, with 48-hour test drive on offer
- brand liaison with relevant magazines, such as *Elle*; led to the Ford Focus Elle special edition
- targeted interactive promotional campaign, such as at Handbag.com or TotallyJewish.com
- interactive micro sites, such as public relations at the *Elle* Style Awards and associated branding, including key rings.

Subscribers to *Elle* magazine received bespoke brochures, linking Ford, *Elle* magazine and the Ford Focus Elle special edition:

*Ford Focus Elle*
*The place to be seen this season*

In colours such as Ebony, Moondust Silver and Chic, this model offered a 1.6i three-door Zetec, with alloy wheels, chrome tailpipe, remote-control CD/radio, air conditioning, ABS, side airbags and leather trim. The brochures featured a fashion shoot and the Focus Elle car, with captions such as:

*Pink sheer 'Butterfly' dress, Rodeo Drive*
*Two-tone V-neck contoured vest, Milan*
*Ford Focus, the perfect accessory*

Visitors to *Elle*'s website were greeted with information about the Focus Elle, plus a pop-up link directly into Ford's website. If they wanted further information or to arrange a test drive, the Ford system dealt with such requests, not *Elle*'s.

This strategy proved to be highly effective for Ford. Every two months, a new special edition was offered, in limited numbers to maintain exclusivity. All editions sold out quickly. This success for Ford resulted from researching the target market's requirements, thinking carefully about the required brand positioning, and being smart in terms of executing the associated promotional activity.

At the heart of this marketing activity was the use of the brand positioning perceptual map, the development of a brand positioning statement deemed relevant by the target audience – aspirational young female drivers – and the specification of a detailed action plan. Note, though, that without the clearly thought through action plan, the desired brand positioning would never have been achieved. Marketers must plan their brand positioning strategy but then manage its implementation and roll-out.



**Sources:** Ford; *Elle* magazine; 'Ford Focus Elle – the place to be seen this season' (brochure), Ford GB, August 2002; automotive sources.

**Note:** the information above, and the interpretation placed upon it, is not the official Ford view and is based on a variety of industry sources. A more extensive explanation of these brand positioning techniques is offered in either *The Market Segmentation Workbook* (Dibb and Simkin) or *The Marketing Planning Workbook* (Dibb, Simkin and Bradley), both originally published in 1996 by Thomson, London.

There are various options when determining a positioning:

1. The approach most plausible in terms of the consumer and the most defensible against competitors' marketing ploys is to identify product attributes or features that are superior, desirable and matched by few or no rivals. This is at the heart of the positioning deployed by Bang & Olufsen, BMW and Bosch.
2. The next best option is to identify key benefits encountered as a result of consumption, as illustrated by Anadin's painkiller advertising or Andrew's Salts saving the day from *that* hangover.

If a product has no such distinctions or is lagging behind major rivals, there are other approaches, such as:

3. emphasising specific usage occasions, such as Campbell's soups as a cooking ingredient
4. depicting user groups, as with the Pepsi Generation
5. deliberately adopting a head-to-head positioning against a rival – 'Avis is No. 2, but we try harder' ran for over two decades.

Or, if all else fails:

6. dissociating from direct rivals in order to develop a clear image and differentiation – Dr Pepper and 7 Up both try to persuade the marketplace they are fizzy and refreshing drinks, but not sickly brown colas.

**Positioning statement** A plausible, memorable image-enhancing written summation of a product's or brand's desired stature

The final stage in developing a positioning in many instances is the determination of a suitable **positioning statement**, a plausible, memorable image-enhancing written summation of a product's or brand's desired stature. This should strike a chord with the targeted consumers; reflect the nature of the product, its branding and attributes; plus demonstrate to targeted consumers the company's understanding of customer needs – similar to a strapline in advertising. Everest double glazing's positioning statement is decades old, yet instantly recognisable: 'Fit the best, fit Everest'. 'The ultimate driving machine' can only be BMW; 'Because I'm worth it' is L'Oréal; and 'We try harder' is still used by car rental company Avis, as mentioned above. Ultimately, a product or brand positioning must be memorable, plausible and relevant to the target market's perceptions. The intention is to develop a distinctive image for the product or service and, through a well-honed positioning statement, to establish a platform for its effective communication.

## Evaluating Markets and Forecasting Sales

Whatever segmentation choices organisations make, measuring the sales potential of the chosen target market or markets is crucial. Moreover, a marketing manager must determine the portion or share of the selected market that the company can capture relative to its objectives, resources and managerial skills, as well as to those of its competitors. Developing and maintaining a marketing mix consumes a considerable amount of a company's resources. Thus the target market or markets selected must have enough sales potential to justify the costs of developing and maintaining one or more marketing mixes.

The potential for sales can be measured along several dimensions, including product, geographic area, time and level of competition.[35] With respect to product, potential sales can be estimated for a specific product item (for example, Diet Coke) or an entire product line (for example, Coca-Cola, Coca-Cola Classic, Diet Coke, Diet Caffeine-Free Coke and Cherry Coca-Cola are one product line). A manager must also determine the geographic area to be included in the estimate. In relation to time, sales potential estimates can be: short range, one year or under; medium range, one to five years; or long range, longer than five years. The competitive level specifies whether sales are being estimated for a single company or for an entire industry. Marketers measure sales potential both for the entire market and for their own companies, and then develop a sales forecast. A detailed discussion of market potential, sales potential and sales forecasting is given in Chapter 23. A target market strategy is incomplete without an appraisal of the likely sales potential and expected levels of sales within the prioritised target market segments.

# Summary

A *market* is defined as a group of people who, as consumers or as part of organisations, need and have the ability, willingness and authority to purchase products in a product class. A *consumer market* consists of purchasers and/or those in their households who intend to consume or benefit from the purchased products and who do not buy products for the main purpose of making a profit. A *business market* consists of people and groups who purchase a product for resale, direct use in producing other products or for general day-to-day operations. Because products are classified according to use, the same product may be classified as both a consumer product and an industrial product.

» At the heart of marketing strategy are the decisions about which opportunities to pursue and which market segments to target. The varying characteristics, needs, wants and interests of customers mean that there are few markets where a single product or service is satisfactory for all.

» Markets made up of individuals with different needs are called *heterogeneous markets*. The *market segmentation* approach divides the total market into smaller groups of customers who have similar product needs and buying characteristics. A *market segment* is a group of individuals, groups or organisations sharing one or more similar characteristics that cause them to have relatively similar product needs.

» Segmentation and the customer understanding underlying it can make it easier for companies to identify and exploit different market opportunities. The approach offers businesses a number of advantages at the customer level, in relation to the competition or in terms of the effectiveness of resource allocation and strategic planning.

» There are three stages to carrying out market segmentation: segmentation, targeting and positioning. Segmentation uses one or more base variables to group similar customers into segments. *Targeting* involves decisions about which and how many customer groups to target. *Positioning* involves deciding precisely how and where within the targeted segments to aim a product or products, brand or brands.

» Marketers must decide how many segmentation variables to use. *Single variable segmentation* involves only one variable, but in *multivariable segmentation*, more than one characteristic is used to divide a total market. The latter is often more meaningful. *One-to-one marketing* involves developing long-term relationships with individual customers in order to understand and satisfy their needs. Although technological advances are making it easier for companies to achieve this goal, this approach involves considerable investment.

» *Segmentation variables or bases* are the dimensions or characteristics of individuals, groups or businesses that are used for dividing a total market into segments. The segmentation variable should be related to customers' needs for, uses of or behaviour towards the product. Consumer segmentation variables can be grouped into four categories: demographics (age, gender, race, ethnicity, income, education, occupation, family size, family life cycle, religion and social class), geographic (population, *market density*, climate), psychographic (personality traits, motives, lifestyles) and behaviouristic (volume usage, end use, expected benefits, brand loyalty, price sensitivity). *Geodemographic segmentation*, which combines geographic and demographic factors, involves clustering people according to postcode areas. Variables for segmenting business markets include demographic factors, operating variables, purchasing approach, situational factors and the personal characteristics of buyers. *Benefit segmentation* is the division of a market according to the benefits consumers want from the product.

» Certain conditions must exist for market segmentation to be effective. First, consumers' needs for the product should be heterogeneous. Second, the segments of the market should be measurable so that the segments can be compared with respect to estimated sales potential, costs and profits. Third, at least one segment must be substantial enough to have the profit potential to justify developing and maintaining a special marketing mix for that segment. Fourth, the company must be able to access the chosen segment with a particular marketing mix. Fifth, the segment should be reasonably stable over time. Sixth, the resulting segmentation scheme must be managerially useful. Customers with dissimilar needs and buying behaviour must not be grouped together in the same market segment.

» *Profiling* segments using *descriptor* variables can help the marketer build up a fuller picture and design a marketing mix (or mixes) that more precisely matches the needs of people in a selected market segment (or segments).

» *Targeting* is the task of prioritising which market segment(s) to address. When a company designs a single marketing mix and directs it at the entire market for a particular product, it is using an *undifferentiated (or total market) approach* as its targeting strategy. Although customers may have similar needs for a few products, for most products their needs are very different. In such instances, a company should use a concentrated or a differentiated strategy. In the *concentration strategy*, a business directs its marketing efforts towards a single market segment through one marketing mix. In the *differentiated strategy*, a business develops different marketing mixes for two or more market segments. The decisions about which segment or segments to enter are linked to considerations about company resources, expertise and the nature of customers and competitors.

Having decided which segment or segments to target, the marketer must position the product in order to create a clearly defined image in the minds of its target consumers. The product's positioning must be perceived by its consumers to be different from the positionings of competing products.

*Perceptual maps* assist marketers in graphically depicting the relative positionings of the products in a particular market. Although a product's attributes and styling, along with its pricing, service levels and channel of distribution, contribute to how consumers perceive the product, a marketer uses mainly promotion to establish a product's positioning. The final stage in developing a positioning is the *positioning statement*, a plausible and memorable written summation of a product's or brand's desired stature.

Measuring the sales potential of the chosen target market or markets is crucial, as a target market strategy is incomplete without an appraisal of the likely sales potential and expected levels of sales within the prioritised target market segments. This can be measured along several dimensions, including product, geographic area, time and level of competition.

## *Key Links*

This chapter has explained a core aspect of marketing strategy: target market selection. It should be read in conjunction with:

- Chapter 2's overview of marketing strategy
- The requirement to understand consumers and business customers, as described in Chapters 6 and 7
- Chapter 11's explanation of effective branding
- The analytical tools – notably the directional policy matrix – used for choosing priority target markets, as presented in Chapter 12
- The role of implementation, as explored in Chapter 24.

## Important Terms

Market
Consumer market
Business market
Undifferentiated or total market approach
Heterogeneous markets
Market segmentation
Market segment
Segmentation variables or bases
One-to-one marketing
Single variable segmentation
Multivariable segmentation
Market density
Geodemographic segmentation
Benefit segmentation
Profiling
Descriptors
Targeting
Concentration strategy
Differentiated strategy
Positioning
Perceptual mapping
Positioning statement

## Discussion and Review Questions

1 What is a market? What are the requirements for a market?
2 In the area where you live, is there a group of people with unsatisfied product needs who represent a market? Could this market be reached by a business organisation? Why or why not?
3 Identify and describe the two major types of market. Give examples of each.
4 What is the total market approach? Under what conditions is it most useful? Describe a current situation in which a company is using a total market approach. Is the business successful? Why or why not?
5 What is the market segmentation approach? Describe the basic conditions required for effective segmentation. Identify several companies that use the segmentation approach.

6 List the differences between concentration and differentiated strategies. Describe the advantages and disadvantages of each strategy.
7 Identify and describe four major categories of base variables that can be used to segment consumer markets. Give examples of product markets that are segmented by variables in each category.
8 What dimensions are used to segment business markets?
9 How do marketers decide whether to use single variable or multivariable segmentation? Give examples of product markets that are divided using multivariable segmentation.
10 Choose a product and discuss how it could best be positioned in the market. Determine a suitable positioning statement.
11 What are the essential stages in developing a positioning?
12 Why must marketers evaluate the sales potential of possible priority target market segments?

## Recommended Readings


- Dibb, S. and Simkin, L., 'Market segmentation: diagnosing and overcoming the segmentation barriers', *Industrial Marketing Management*, 30, 2001, pp. 609–25.
- Dibb, S. and Simkin, L., *The Market Segmentation Workbook* (London: Thomson, 1996).
- Dibb, S. and Wensley, R., 'Segmentation analysis for industrial marketing: problems of integrating customer requirements into operations strategy', *European Journal of Marketing*, 36 (1/2), 2002, pp. 231–51.
- Hooley, G., Saunders, J. and Piercy, N.F., *Marketing Strategy and Competitive Positioning* (Harlow: Pearson/FT, 2004).
- Hutt, M.D. and Speh, T.W., *Business Marketing Management: A Strategic View of Industrial and Organizational Markets* (Cincinnati, OH: South Western, 2003).
- Keller, K.L., *Building, Measuring and Managing Brand Equity* (Englewood Cliffs, NJ: Pearson, 2003).
- McDonald, M. and Dunbar, I., *Market Segmentation* (London: Palgrave Macmillan, 1998).
- McDonald, M. and Dunbar, I., *Market Segmentation: how to do it, how to profit from it* (Oxford: Elsevier Butterworth-Heinemann, 2004).
- Ries, A. and Trout, J., *Positioning: The Battle for Your Mind* (New York: McGraw-Hill, 2000).
- Stone, M. and Foss, B., *Successful Customer Relationship Marketing: New Thinking, New Strategies, New Tools for Getting Closer to Your Customers* (London: Kogan Page, 2001).
- Webber, H., *Divide and Conquer: Target your Customer through Market Segmentation* (Hoboken, NJ: Wiley, 1998).
- Weinstein, A., *Handbook of Market Segmentation: Strategic Targeting for Business and Technology Firms* (New York: Haworth Press, 2004).


## Internet Exercise

Voyage is an Internet company that offers a variety of travel and adventure products. Learn more about its goods, services and travel advice through its website at: www.voyageconcepts.co.uk

1 Based on the information provided at the website, what are some of Voyage's basic products?
2 What market segments does Voyage appear to be targeting with its website?
3 What segmentation variables is the company using to segment these markets?

## *Applied Mini-Case*

Banking is not generally perceived as innovative or creative. HSBC's telephone and on-line bank, First Direct, broke the mould when it was launched in the 1980s, and it still strives to be different, as explained on its website:

> The real difference about First Direct is simple. Most banks are about money. First Direct is about people. Simple but revolutionary.
>
> We believe banking should fit around you. It's your money. You come first. The way we respond to you is what matters. That's why our people have personality and attitude. We are keen to learn.
>
> Quick and efficient, yes, but with a touch of what we call 'magical rapport'. Wit, intelligence, common sense. It's what separates us from the others, why we're the most recommended bank with the most satisfied customers.

Respect for the individual is our philosophy. It's how we treat each other and how we treat you.

So whether it's your day-to-day banking, agreeing a loan or arranging an offset mortgage, it's just the same. You come first.

**Sources:** First Direct, April 2004; www.firstdirect.com/whyus/whyus.shtml, May 2004.

### *Question*

**What is the brand positioning proposition at the heart of First Direct's marketing strategy? To what extent does this differentiate First Direct from the other principal banking groups?**

## *Case Study*

# Ethnic Marketing's Challenge to Mainstream Marketers

Mediaedge:cia is a global media communications specialist, part of the WPP group, with billings of over US$15 billion in 80 countries. The company produced a report in 2003 in conjunction with the UK's Channel 4 television, News International and the Broadcasting Standards Commission, examining how mainstream marketers could better reach the larger ethnic groups – notably Asians and African-Caribbeans – through gaining a deeper insight into the cultural differences that impact on their acceptance of marketing communications.

An important finding from the study was that many advertisers fail to connect with ethnic audiences through perceived stereotyping and tokenism. Too many mainstream brand managers have created an ethnic market segment to sit alongside their core mainstream target markets. Such 'we have an interest in ethnic markets' tokenism fails to reflect that, as in the so-called 'mainstream market', the ethnic market is in fact sub-divided into many groups. This sub-division represents generation, age, language, location, country of origin, and acculturation (the process by which minority groups adapt to the culture of the majority or the mainstream market).

The use of ethnic actors, settings and experiences in advertising is seen as desirable, but not if the advertisement simply draws attention to perhaps false stereotyping, and ultimately fails to strike a chord with either the intended ethnic target audience or the mainstream market also addressed by a particular brand.

The research revealed some interesting challenges for marketers, as described below.

- Asians were typically more up-front in their response to advertising, seeking an instant answer to the questions 'What is being offered?' and 'What is the relevance to me?'
- The impact of mainstream culture varied, too. The family home provides a 'cultural earthing point', either rejecting mainstream culture or deliberately embracing aspects of it, and amalgamating such practices and values with the ethnic group's own culture. Clearly, marketers must understand the extent to which a group of consumers has embraced mainstream values and buying characteristics.
- Some households are a hybrid of media behaviour, viewing mainstream and traditional ethnic broadcast media, while others have either turned their backs on their heritage or have refused to allow mainstream media to enter their households.
- Children tend to be more influenced by mainstream culture and marketing programmes than their parents.
- More so than in many mainstream households, a great deal of consumer decision-making is made at a family level, and there are interesting dynamics between male and female family members.

These variations in attitudes, behaviour and perceptions of mainstream values have important implications for marketers seeking to attract these consumers, make them aware of their products and influence their buying behaviour.

At a time when 'ethnic marketing' is seen as increasingly important by a large number of mainstream brands and retailers, the Mediaedge:cia study also identified a significant gap in the understanding of minority ethnic groups by these marketers and their advertising agency colleagues. There is no doubt that ethnic marketing will be embraced by ever more mainstream brands, but in so doing, their marketers must properly understand the buying behaviour and decision-making of these important consumers.

**Sources:** *Ethnic Marketing: 'A Double Edged Sword?'*, Mediaedge:cia, London, March 2003; www.redhotcurry.com/news/ethnic_marketing.htm, March 2004.

## Questions for Discussion

1. Why are mainstream marketers increasingly interested in targeting ethnic markets?
2. Are certain mainstream brands or products more likely to be marketed along these lines? If so, which and why?
3. For a product as ubiquitous as Coca-Cola, does the notion of ethnic marketing present any benefits or potential? Why or why not?

# 9 Marketing Research and Marketing Information Systems

**"The researcher's challenge is not just generating data, but in creating a vision from that data."**

*Dave Birks, University of Bath*

## Objectives

- To understand the importance of marketing research in marketing decision-making
- To distinguish between research and intuition in solving marketing problems
- To learn the five basic steps of the marketing research process
- To understand the fundamental methods of gathering data for marketing research
- To gain a sense of the relative advantages and disadvantages of marketing research tools
- To understand how tools such as databases, decision support systems and the Internet facilitate marketing research
- To identify key ethical considerations in marketing research

**Marketing research**
The process of gathering, interpreting and reporting information to help marketers solve specific marketing problems or take advantage of marketing opportunities

## Introduction

As the preceding chapters have explained, effective marketing is contingent upon marketers having a clear understanding of customers, competitors, market trends and aspects of the marketing environment. **Marketing research** is the systematic design, collection, interpretation and reporting of information to help marketers solve particular problems or take advantage of marketing opportunities. As the word 'research' implies, it is the process of gathering information not currently available to decision-makers. The purpose of marketing research is to inform a business about customers' needs and desires, marketing opportunities for particular goods and services, and changing attitudes and purchase patterns. Detecting shifts in buyers' behaviour and attitudes helps companies stay in touch with the ever-changing marketplace.

*Opener*

# P&G and Reactivity

Imagine waking up in the morning, stumbling to the bathroom wash basin, putting Crest toothpaste on your toothbrush and looking up to see the fuzzy reflection of a video camera in the mirror. Maybe you think that you might have signed up for a reality TV show? No, it's just the Procter & Gamble (P&G) research crew you allowed into your home to observe how you perform your daily activities. Although marketing research has traditionally focused on problems that consumers generally recognise, P&G researchers hope this direct observation approach will help them identify and address problems that consumers do not even know they have.

Globally, around one-third of consumers buys products made by US-based P&G. With sales growth of just a few per cent each year, the company hopes to boost its revenues by capitalising on growth opportunities in its overseas markets. To achieve this goal, much of P&G's marketing research effort is now targeted in international markets such as the UK, Italy, Germany and China.

Compared with other research methods, direct observation of consumers provides several benefits. Video clips can be placed on a secure website for viewing by 150 P&G employees. A bigger audience gives the company greater potential for valuable feedback. More problems can be identified and solutions found to address those issues. Direct observation can also generate information that participants might normally forget or choose not to disclose when being interviewed or surveyed. For example, many people say they brush their teeth twice a day because they believe this is the correct and expected response. But the reality is that many people do not brush twice daily. Direct observation of consumers can uncover such information. Another advantage of this approach is that it contributes to the insights gained through the coordinated and integrated research studies it conducts annually or to its existing database of 50,000 studies. Finally, P&G gets global perspectives on the wants and needs of its target market.

This new form of research also has some drawbacks, however – especially in terms of concerns about privacy. Although participants in these studies willingly allow themselves to be videotaped, the company must be careful about what it records, inform any unsuspecting visitors about the recording, and guarantee the videos will only be viewed internally for research purposes. Another issue is reactivity, which occurs when participants modify normal behaviours because they know they are being watched. For example, a participant might increase his or her daily intake of vegetables during the observation period to appear more in line with social norms or expectations. Another drawback is that it is not practical to pore through hours of videotape for just a few clues about human behaviour. Although the information gained may be interesting, not all of it will be relevant. Finally, such research does not guarantee than any product innovation or improved marketing programme will result.

**Photo:** Courtesy of Karen Beaulah

The marketing research conducted by P&G illustrates that to implement marketing concepts, marketers need information about the characteristics, needs and desires of target market customers. When used effectively, such information facilitates the relationship with the customers, by helping businesses focus their efforts on meeting, and even anticipating, the needs of their customers.

This chapter begins by defining marketing research and examining its importance. It then analyses the five basic steps of the marketing research process, including various methods of collecting data. This is followed by a review of how technology aids in collecting, organising and interpreting marketing research data. Finally, the ethical aspects of marketing research are considered.

## The Importance of Marketing Research

Building an understanding of customers, competitors, market trends and the marketing environment requires that marketers have access to information and marketing intelligence.[1] Sometimes the available information will be judged inadequate to tackle a specific decision or marketing task, in which case marketing research may provide the additional insights required. Such research is generally conducted on a project-by-project basis, with research methods being adapted to the context and problems being studied.

The Market Research Society defines marketing research in the following way:

> The collection and analysis of data from a sample of individuals or organisations relating to their characteristics, behaviour, attitudes, opinions or possessions. It includes all forms of marketing and social research such as consumer and industrial surveys, psychological investigations, observational and panel studies.[2]

The purpose of marketing research is to provide information about customers' needs and desires, marketing opportunities for particular goods and services, and the changing attitudes and purchase patterns of customers. Marketing planning requires marketing research to facilitate the process of assessing opportunities and threats. Marketing research can help a company better understand market opportunities, ascertain the potential for success of new products, and determine the feasibility of a particular marketing strategy. Pizza Hut, for example, conducted research to learn more about its most profitable group of customers: school and college students. The research involved asking a carefully chosen group of 350 students to refrain from eating pizza products for 30 days and record their cravings for pizza and feelings about 'going without' during the study period. One objective was to help better understand the effects of 'pizza deprivation', food cravings and food desires among this attractive market, which may lead to modifications in its marketing strategy.[3]

**Marketing intelligence** The composite of all data and ideas available within an organisation, which assists in decision-making

**Quantitative research** Research aimed at producing data that can be statistically analysed and whose results can be expressed numerically

**Qualitative research** Research that deals with information too difficult or expensive to quantify, such as subjective opinions and value judgements, typically unearthed during interviews or discussion groups

All organisations have some marketing intelligence. **Marketing intelligence** is the composite of all data and ideas available within an organisation – for example, a company or a marketing department that assists in decision-making. Often the available information is deemed inadequate, which may lead to the commissioning of marketing research. There are, broadly, two types of marketing research: quantitative and qualitative.[4] In **quantitative research**, techniques and sample sizes lead to the collection of data that can be statistically analysed and whose results can be expressed numerically. These data tend to come from large surveys, sales data or market forecasts (see Figure 9.1). **Qualitative research** deals with information that is too difficult or expensive to quantify: subjective opinions and value judgements that are not amenable to statistical analysis and quantification,[5] typically unearthed during in-depth interviews or discussion groups.

While some businesses continue to handle their own information needs, others buy in help from outside agencies that specialise in market research. The global marketing and opinion

**ABOUT THE PRODUCTS YOU OWN AND USE**

Q27    Please indicate which, if any, of the following items you or other members of your household (a) currently own or (b) are likely to buy in the next 12 months?

Digital ca
Home
s

TV wo
DVD

Q28    How many cars o
(including those c

Nc
C

*Please answer the*
*and*

Q29a    Was the vehicle n

Q29b    If the vehicle is a
and model?

Q29c    What was the pri

**PETS CONT'D**

Which of the following cat foods do you feed your cat?

| | Bought less often | Our main brand | | Bought less often | Our main brand |
|---|---|---|---|---|---|
| **DRY** | | | **TINNED** | | |
| Hi Life | ☐ | ☐ | | | |
| Felix | ☐ | ☐ | | | |
| Whiskas | ☐ | ☐ | | | |
| Friskies | ☐ | ☐ | | | |
| Hills | ☐ | ☐ | | | |
| Iams | ☐ | ☐ | | | |
| Go Cat | ☐ | ☐ | | | |
| Vital Balance | ☐ | ☐ | | | |
| Supermarket/Other | ☐ | ☐ | | | |
| **TRAYS/POUCH** | | | | | |
| Sheba | ☐ | ☐ | | | |
| Whiskas Singles | ☐ | ☐ | | | |
| Arthurs | ☐ | ☐ | | | |
| Friskies | ☐ | ☐ | | | |

Which of the following dog foo

| | Bought less often | Our main bran |
|---|---|---|
| **TINNED/TRAYS** | | |

**ABOUT YOU**

Q33    Which, if any, of the following activities have you undertaken in the past 12 months?

Been interviewed on TV, radio or by the press ☐ 1

shed an article, paper or book ☐ 2

professional conference as an official speaker ☐ 3

official spokesperson for your npany/profession to the public ☐ 4

dustry/professional committee ☐ 5

l members of the Government (national or local) ☐ 6

**CUSTOMER SURVEY**                    J00M0501

*If you could spare a few minutes of your time, we would very much appreciate it if you would complete and send us this sho: questionnaire. Unless you indicate otherwise, this will ensure you are on our mailing list, and help us to match our service t your needs.*

Title
First Name
Surname
Address

Town

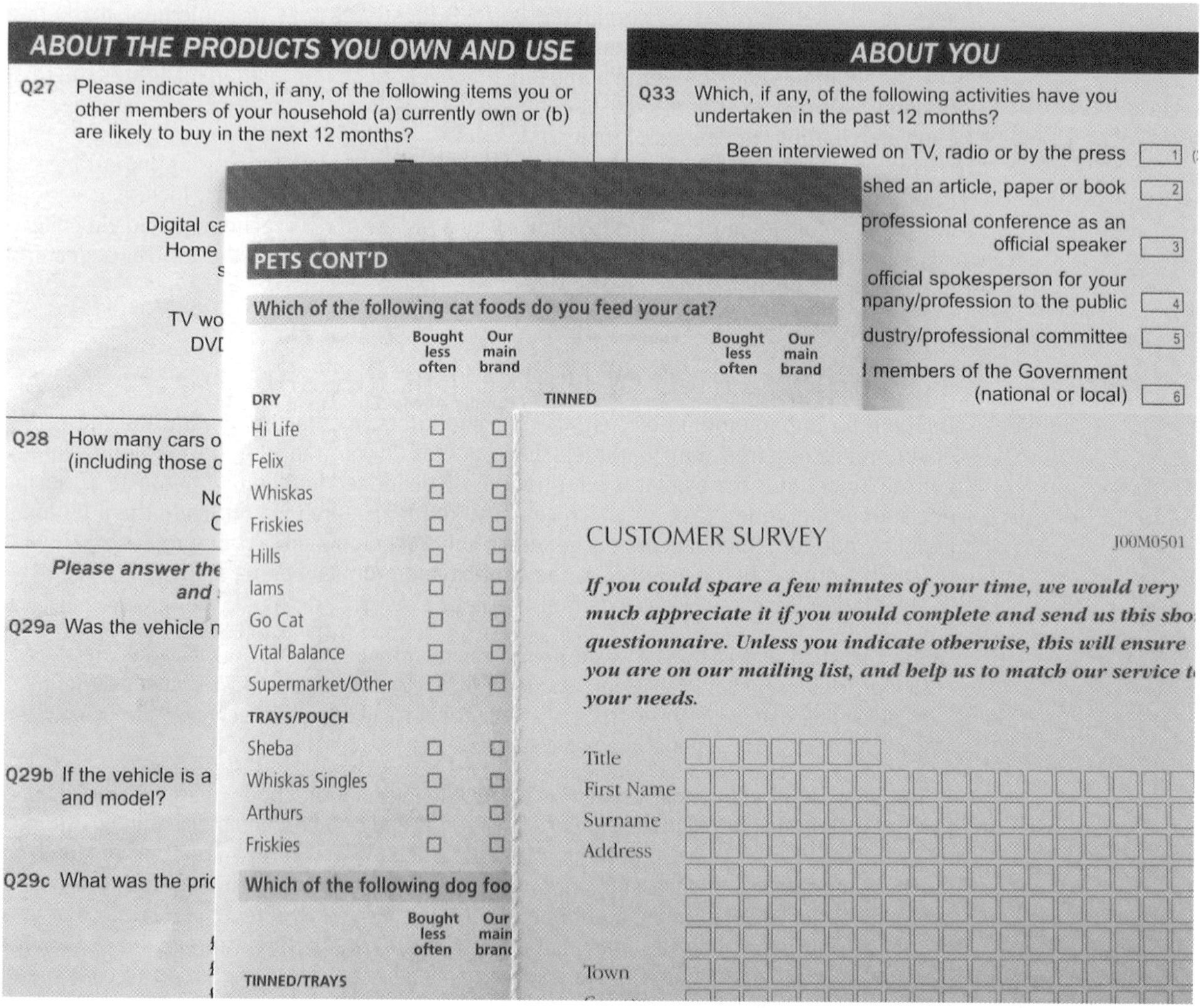

**Figure 9.1**

*Questionnaires are an integral part of marketing research, often but not exclusively for quantitative studies*
Photo: Courtesy of Karen Beaulah

research industry is huge, accounting for over £10 billion (more than €15 billion) and employing more than 650,000 people. With ten countries accounting for more than 80 per cent of the turnover globally, it is also highly competitive and increasingly dominated by international research agencies.[6] Recent growth in the industry highlights marketing research's status as a management tool. Some experts suggest that this is also because the marketing research agencies have worked hard to quantify the effects of their work on business performance.[7]

The Topical Insight box on page 261 describes the kinds of activities undertaken by VNU, the world's largest marketing research company.

All kinds of businesses use marketing research to help them develop marketing programmes that match the needs of customers. The CEO of a large marketing research business recently generalised the categories in which his company received requests for research help. For quantitative studies, these included customer satisfaction surveys, advertising tracking analyses, evaluations of new or modified products, brand awareness studies and customer attitude surveys. For qualitative research, the main categories were customer attitude and

## Topical Insight

### The World's Largest Marketing Research Company

Publishing company VNU Inc., founded in the Netherlands in 1964, became the largest marketing research business after acquiring ACNielsen and Nielsen Media in 2001. Originally called Verenigde Nederlandse Uitgeversbedrijven (United Dutch Publishers), the company now serves clients in more than 100 countries, answering questions such as 'What is happening in the marketplace?', 'Why is it happening?', 'What will happen next?' and 'What is the best way to grow my business?'

Through the ACNielsen group, VNU provides retail measurement information on competitive sales volume, market share, distribution, pricing, merchandising and promotional activities to manufacturers and retailers of fast-moving consumer goods. Its consumer panel services provide marketers with insights based on actual consumer purchase information for more than 155,000 households in 22 countries. To provide customised research services in more than 60 countries, VNU conducts hundreds of thousands of customer surveys, interviews and focus groups every year in order to offer its clients greater understanding of consumer attitudes and purchase behaviour. The company's modelling and analytical services integrate and analyse information from a variety of sources to improve marketing decisions on pricing, promotion, product, and media use and placement.

Although most marketing businesses rely on outside sources such as VNU to gain insight into key marketing questions, it is crucial that marketing managers know what questions to ask and are able to recognise effective marketing research and information system development. It is important that companies acquire the data that provides them with the insights necessary to develop effective marketing strategies. The marketing research conducted by VNU enables marketers to implement the marketing concept by helping them acquire information about the characteristics, needs and desires of target market customers. When used effectively, such information facilitates relationship marketing by helping marketers focus their efforts on meeting, and even anticipating, the needs of their customers.

**Sources:** 'VNU Inc.', *Marketing News*, 9 June 2003, pp. H6–H8; 'Insights into today's global customers', VNU, www.vnu.com/vnu/page.jsp?id=104 (accessed 20 December 2003); 'A leading information and media company', VNU, www.vnu.com/vnu/page.jsp?id=84 (accessed 20 December 2003).

satisfaction studies, followed by concept testing (new products or new brand identities). After these came the testing of advertisements, packaging concepts and promotional offers.

As managers recognise the benefits of marketing research, they assign it a much greater role in decision-making. For example, Japanese managers, who put much more faith in information they get directly from wholesalers and retailers, are beginning to grasp the importance of consumer surveys and scientific methods of marketing research as they seek ways to diversify their companies.[8]

**Intuition**
The personal knowledge and past experience on which marketing managers may base decisions

**Scientific decision-making**
An orderly and logical approach to gathering information

The increase in marketing research activities represents a transition from intuitive to scientific problem-solving. In relying on **intuition**, marketing managers base decisions on personal knowledge and past experience. However, in **scientific decision-making**, managers take an orderly and logical approach to gathering information. They seek facts on a systematic basis, and they apply methods other than trial and error or generalisation from experience. This does not mean that intuition has no value in marketing decision-making; successful decisions blend both research and intuition. Consider an extreme example. A marketing research study conducted for Xerox Corporation in the late 1950s indicated a very limited market for an automatic photocopier. Xerox management judged that the researchers had drawn the wrong conclusions from the study, and they decided to launch the product anyway. That product, the Xerox 914 copier, was an instant success. An immediate backlog of orders developed, and the rest is history. Although the Xerox example is certainly an extreme one, by and large a proper blend of research and intuition offers the best formula for a correct decision. Table 9.1 distinguishes between the roles of research and intuition in decision-making.

| TABLE 9.1 DISTINCTIONS BETWEEN RESEARCH AND INTUITION IN MARKETING DECISION-MAKING | | |
|---|---|---|
| | **Research** | **Intuition** |
| **Nature** | Formal planning, predicting based on a scientific approach | Preference based on personal feelings or 'gut instinct' |
| **Methods** | Logic, systematic methods, statistical inference | Experience and demonstration |
| **Contributions** | General hypotheses for making predictions, classifying relevant variables, carrying out systematic description and classification | Minor problems solved quickly through consideration of experience, practical consequences |
| **Situation** | High risk decision-making involving high costs, investment, strategic change or long-term effects | Low-risk problem solving and decision-making |

Despite the obvious value of formal research, marketing decisions are often made without it. Certainly, minor, low-risk problems that must be dealt with at once can and should be handled on the basis of personal judgement and common sense. If good decisions can be made with the help of currently available information, costly formal research may be superfluous. However, as the financial, social or ethical risks increase or the possible courses of action multiply, full-scale research as a prerequisite for marketing decision-making becomes both desirable and rewarding.

Marketing research improves a marketer's ability to make decisions. Marketers should treat information in the same manner as other resources utilised by the company, and they must weigh the costs of obtaining information against the benefits derived. Information is worthwhile if it results in marketing activities that better satisfy the needs of the company's target markets, leads to increased sales and profits, or helps the company achieve some other goal.

# The Marketing Research Process

To maintain the control needed for obtaining accurate information, marketers approach marketing research in logical steps, as follows (see Figure 9.2):

1 locating and defining problems or research issues
2 designing the research
3 collecting data
4 analysing and interpreting research findings
5 reporting research findings.

These five steps should be viewed as an overall approach to conducting research rather than a rigid set of rules to be followed in each project. In planning research projects, marketers must think about each of the steps and how they can best be adjusted for each particular problem.

***Figure 9.2***
*The five steps of the marketing research process*

## Step 1: Locating and Defining Problems or Research Issues

**Problem definition** The process of uncovering the nature and boundaries of a situation or question

The first step in launching a research study is **problem definition**, which focuses on uncovering the nature and boundaries of a situation or question related to marketing strategy or implementation. The first sign of a problem is usually a departure from some normal function, such as failures to attain objectives. If a company's objective is a 12 per cent return on investment and the current return is 6 per cent, this discrepancy should be analysed to help guide future marketing strategies. Decreasing sales, increasing expenses or decreasing profits also signal problems. Conversely, when an organisation experiences a dramatic rise in sales, or some other positive event, it may conduct marketing research to discover the reasons and maximise the opportunities stemming from them.

To pin down the specific boundaries of a problem or an issue through research, marketers must define the nature and scope of the problem in a way that requires probing beneath

Top brands are switching over to jra
jra
research
PROVEN RESULTS
Whatever your research brief, you can rely on jra for dazzling results everytime. Tried and tested by 100's of top UK brands.
Call Paul Summers on
0115 9551133
or email paul@jraresearch.com
Victoria Court
Kent Street
Nottingham NG1 3LZ
Tel: 01159551133
Fax: 01159537077
www.jraresearch.com
jra
RESEARCH


*Figure 9.3*
*Many marketing research agencies, data analysis houses and marketing services businesses support marketers*
*Source: Courtesy of jra research*

the superficial symptoms. The interaction between the marketing manager and the marketing researcher should yield a clear definition of the problem. Researchers and decision-makers should remain in the problem definition stage until they have determined precisely what they want from the research and how they will use it. Deciding how to refine a broad, indefinite problem into a clearly defined and researchable statement is a prerequisite for the next step in planning the research: the design phase.

## Step 2: Designing the Research

**Research design**
An overall plan for obtaining the information needed to address a research problem or issue

Once the problem or issue has been defined, the next step is **research design**, an overall plan for obtaining the information needed to address it. This step requires detailed research objectives or hypotheses to be formulated, and the most appropriate type of research to be designed to ensure that the results are reliable and valid.

### Developing Research Objectives and Hypotheses

**Research objective**
The desired outcome from the marketing research project being undertaken

**Hypothesis**
An informed guess or assumption about a certain problem or set of circumstances

A clear statement of research objectives plays an important part in guiding a research project. A **research objective** is the desired outcome from the marketing research project being undertaken. Sometimes researchers develop hypotheses that may be drawn both from previous research and expected research findings. A **hypothesis** is an informed guess or assumption about a certain problem or set of circumstances. It is based on all the insight and knowledge available about the problem from previous research studies and other sources. As information is gathered, a researcher can test the hypothesis. For example, a food manufacturer such as Kellogg's might propose the hypothesis that children today have more influence than those of previous generations on their families' buying decisions with regard to breakfast cereals and other grocery products. A marketing researcher would then gather data, perhaps through surveys of children and their parents, and draw conclusions as to whether or not the hypothesis was correct.

Supermarkets worried about shoplifting would be interested in the findings of research showing that 40 per cent of supermarket managers surveyed reported cigarettes and alcohol as their most frequently shoplifted items. If a supermarket manager had hypothesised that other products, such as confectionery, were more susceptible to shoplifting, the research would lead this individual to reject that hypothesis. Sometimes several hypotheses are developed during the actual study; the hypotheses that are accepted or rejected become the study's chief conclusions.

### Types of Research

**Exploratory research**
Deliberately flexible data gathering used to discover the general nature of a problem and the factors that relate to it

The research objectives and any hypotheses being tested determine the approach to be used for gathering data. When marketers need more information about a problem or want to make a tentative hypothesis more specific, they may conduct **exploratory research**. Exploratory studies discover the general nature of a problem and the factors that relate to it. The design is deliberately flexible.[9] For instance, this kind of research may involve reviewing the information in the company's own records or examining publicly available data. Questioning knowledgeable people inside and outside the organisation may also yield new insights into the problem. Information available on the Internet about industry trends or demographics may also be an excellent source for exploratory research. For example, information on the buying power of different ethnic groups is readily available through this source.

**Descriptive research**
Data collection that focuses on providing an accurate description of the variables in a situation

If marketers need to understand the characteristics of certain phenomena to solve a particular problem, **descriptive research** can aid them. Descriptive studies focus on providing an accurate description of the variables in a situation. Such studies may range from general surveys of consumers' education, occupation or age to specifics on how many pairs of sports shoes individuals purchase each year. For example, if Nike and Reebok wanted to target more young women, they might ask 15–34-year-old females how often they work out, how often they buy sports footwear and whether they wear them for casual use.

Descriptive studies generally demand much prior knowledge and assume that the problem is clearly defined. The marketers' major task is to choose adequate methods of collecting and measuring data.

**Causal research**
Data collection that assumes that a particular variable *X* causes a variable *Y*

Hypotheses about causal relationships call for a more complex approach than a descriptive study. In **causal research**, it is assumed that a particular variable *X* causes a variable *Y*. Marketers must plan the research so that the data collected prove or disprove that *X* causes *Y*. To do so, marketers must try to hold constant all variables except *X* and *Y*. For example, to find out whether new carpeting, curtains and ceiling fans increase the leasing rate in a block of flats, marketers need to keep all variables constant except the new furnishings and the leasing rate. Table 9.2 compares the features of these types of research study.

### Research Reliability and Validity

**Reliability**
The quality of producing almost identical results in successive repeated trials

**Validity**
A condition that exists when an instrument measures what it is supposed to measure

In designing research, marketing researchers must ensure that their research techniques are both reliable and valid. A research technique has **reliability** if it produces almost identical results in successive repeated trials. But a reliable technique is not necessarily valid. To have **validity**, the method must measure what it is supposed to measure, not something else. A valid research method provides data that can be used to test the hypothesis being investigated. For example, although a group of customers may express the same level of satisfaction based on a rating scale, the individuals may not exhibit the same repurchase behaviour because of different personal characteristics. This result might cause the researcher to question the validity of the satisfaction scale if the purpose of rating satisfaction was to estimate repurchase behaviour.[10]

## Step 3: Collecting Data

The next step in the marketing research process is collecting data to satisfy research objectives and to help prove (or disprove) research hypotheses. The research design must specify what types of data to collect and how they will be collected.

### Types of Data

**Primary data**
Information gathered by observing phenomena or surveying respondents

**Secondary data**
Information compiled inside or outside the organisation for some purpose other than the current investigation

Marketing researchers have two types of data at their disposal. **Primary data** are observed and recorded or collected directly from respondents. This type of data must be gathered by observing phenomena or surveying respondents. **Secondary data** are compiled inside or outside the organisation for some purpose other than the current investigation. Secondary data include general reports supplied to an enterprise by various data services. Such reports might concern market share, retail inventory levels and consumer buying

**Table 9.2 Comparison of Data-Gathering Approaches**

| Project Component | Exploratory Studies | Descriptive or Causal Studies |
|---|---|---|
| Purpose | Provide general insights | Confirm insights, Verify hypotheses |
| Data sources | Ill-defined | Well defined |
| Collection form | Open-ended | Structured |
| Sample | Small | Large |
| Collection procedure | Flexible | Rigid |
| Data analysis | Informal | Formal |
| Recommendations | Tentative | Conclusive |

**Source:** A. Parasuraman, *Marketing Research*, p. 122, © 1986. Reprinted by permission.

behaviour. Figure 9.4 illustrates how primary and secondary sources differ. Secondary data are generally already available in private or public reports, or have been collected and stored by the organisation itself. Because secondary data are already available – 'second hand' – to save time and money they should be examined prior to the collection of any primary data. Clearly, primary data collection is bespoke and therefore both time-consuming and costly. For relatively straightforward problems, secondary data may prove adequate. More complex or risky situations may require specific primary data collection. Figure 9.5 reveals how Wegener promotes its data analysis services.

## Sources of Secondary Data

Marketers often begin the marketing research process by gathering secondary data. They may use available reports and other information from both internal and external sources to study a marketing problem.

Internal sources of secondary data can contribute tremendously to research. An organisation's own databases may contain information about past marketing activities, such as sales records and research reports, that can be used to test hypotheses and pinpoint problems. From sales reports, for example, a company may be able to determine not only which product sold best at certain times of the year, but also which colours and sizes were preferred. Such information may have been gathered for management or financial purposes.[11] Table 9.3 reveals some commonly available internal company information that may be useful for marketing research purposes.

An organisation's accounting records and feedback available from any service function are excellent sources of data that are often overlooked. This is partly because the volumes

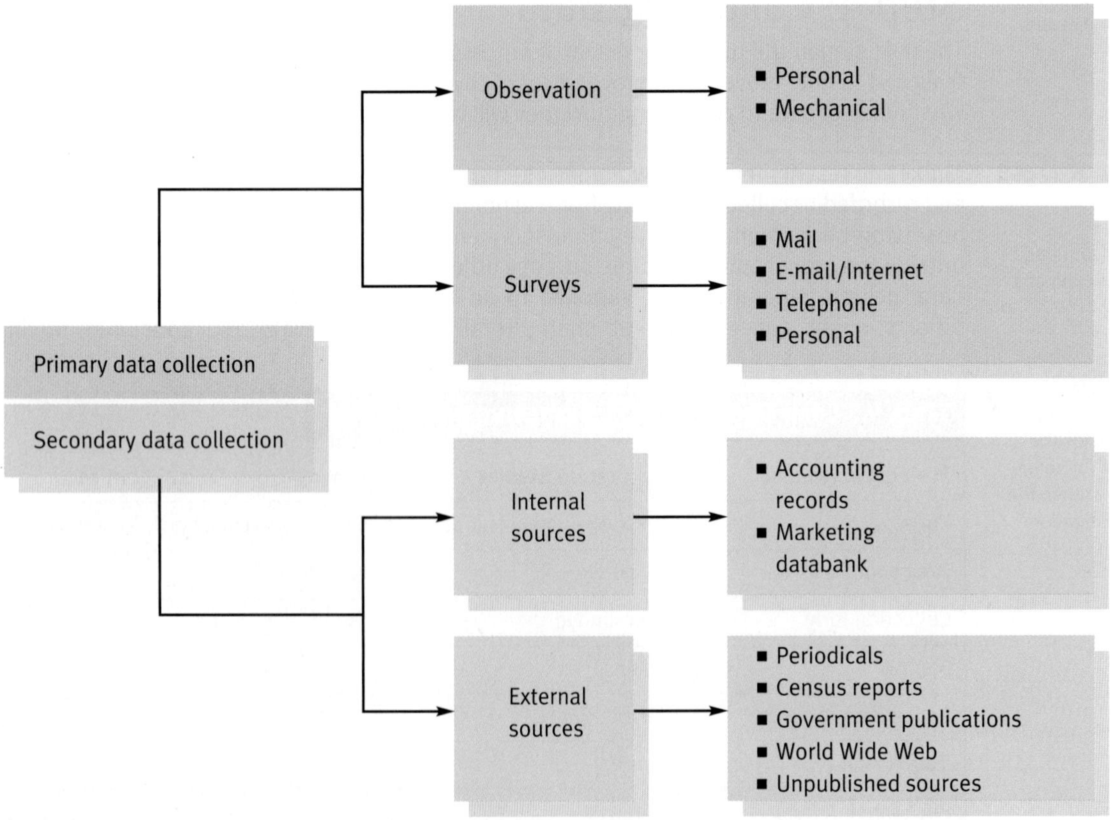


***Figure 9.4***
*Approaches to collecting data*

***Figure 9.5***
*A business-to-business advertisement for Wegener's data collection, data analysis and data modelling services*
*Source: Courtesy of Wegener DM*

**Table 9.3 Internal Sources of Secondary Data**

| | |
|---|---|
| Sales data taken from periodic sales reports | The frequency with which this information is updated will vary for different businesses and industry sectors. However, the increasing use of technology to monitor sales is leading to improvements in the quality and availabiliy of such data. |
| Customer feedback gathered by the salesforce or services functions | In addition to sales information, the salesforce is in a position to provide other data on customer views and preferences. The service functions of many businesses also have access to a range of customer feedback. Organisations with systems in place for capturing and managing these data are more likely to be able to take advantage of such insights. |
| Accounting information | This can include detailed data on sales, expenses and profit levels in different product categories. |
| Competitive information collected by the salesforce | Through contact with customers and by attending sales-related events, such as trade shows, the salesforce is often in a position to accumulate information about competitors, their product portfolios and strategies. |

of data that these departments collect may not automatically flow to the marketing area. As a result, detailed information about costs, sales, customer accounts or profits by product category may not be part of the marketing information system (MIS) (see page 279). This situation occurs particularly in organisations that do not store marketing information on a systematic basis.

External sources of secondary data include periodicals, census reports, government publications, the Internet and unpublished sources. Periodicals such as *Investors' Chronicle*, *Marketing*, *Campaign*, *Marketing Week*, *Wall Street Journal* and *Fortune* print general information that is helpful for defining problems and developing hypotheses. Business Monitor contains sales data for major industries. Mintel publishes sector reports. The World Advertising Research Center's *Marketing Pocket Books* are an excellent source of consumer, market, media and product information for national and international marketing. Table 9.4 summarises the major external sources of secondary data, excluding syndicated services.

**Syndicated data services**
Organisations that collect general information and sell it to clients

**Syndicated data services** periodically collect general information, which they sell to clients. BARB, for example, supplies television stations and media buyers with estimates of

**TABLE 9.4 GUIDE TO EXTERNAL SOURCES OF SECONDARY DATA**

| | |
|---|---|
| **Trade Journals** | Virtually every industry or type of business has a trade journal. These journals give a feel for the industry – its size, degree of competition, range of companies involved and problems. To find trade journals in the field of interest, check *The Source Book*, a reference book that lists periodicals by subject. |
| **Trade Associations** | Almost every industry, product category and profession has its own association. Depending on the strength of each group, they often conduct research, publish journals, conduct training sessions and hold conferences. A telephone call or a letter to the association may yield information not available in published sources. |
| **International Sources** | Periodical indices, such as *Anbar*, are particularly useful for overseas product or company information. More general sources include the *United Nations Statistical Yearbook* and the *International Labour Organisation's Yearbook of Labour Statistics*. |
| **Commercial Sources** | Market survey/report organisations produce many sector reports and analyses of companies or brands, for example, *Verdict, Mintel, Kompass, The Times 1000, Key British Enterprises*. |
| **Governments** | Governments, through their various departments and agencies, collect, analyse and publish statistics on practically everything. Government documents also have their own set of indices. A useful index for government generated information in the UK is the government's weekly *British Business*. |
| ***Books in Print (BIP)*** | *BIP* is a several volume reference book found in most libraries. All books issued by publishers and currently in print are listed by subject, title and author. |
| **Periodical Indices** | Library reference sections contain indices on virtually every discipline. *ABI Inform* (*Pro-Quest*), for example, indexes each article in all major periodicals. |
| **Computerised Literature Retrieval Databases** | Literature retrieval databases are periodical indices stored on computer disks. Books and dissertations are also included. Key words (such as the name of a subject) are used to search a database and generate references. Examples include *Textline*, *Harvest* and *Pro-Quest*. |
| **WWW pages** | Many companies have established 'home pages' on the Internet's World Wide Web for disseminating information on their products and activities. |

the number of viewers at specific times. SAMI furnishes monthly information that describes market shares for specific types of manufacturer. ACNielsen provides retail tracking and other data. This information includes total sales in a product category, sales of clients' own brands and sales of important competing brands.

Another type of secondary data, which is available for a fee, is demographic analysis. Companies, such as CACI or Experian (formerly CCN), that specialise in demographic databanks have special knowledge and sophisticated computer systems to work with the very complex census databanks. These were explored in Chapter 8. As a result, they are able to respond to specialised requests. Such information may be valuable in tracking demographic changes that have implications for consumer behaviour and the targeting of products.[12]

## Primary Data Collection Methods

The collection of primary data is a more lengthy, expensive and complex process than the collection of secondary data. To gather primary data, researchers use sampling procedures, survey methods, observation and experimentation. These efforts can be handled in-house by the company's own research personnel or contracted out to private research businesses such as Taylor Nelson Sofres, Millward Brown UK or Research International.

**Population**
All elements, units or individuals that are of interest to researchers for a specific study

**Sample**
A limited number of units chosen to represent the characteristics of a total population

**Sampling**
The selection of representative units from a total population

**Probability sampling**
Every element in the population has a known chance of being selected for study

**Random sampling**
A sampling method in which all the units in a population have an equal chance of appearing in the sample

**Stratified sampling**
A sampling method in which the population of interest is divided according to a common characteristic or attribute; a probability sampling is then conducted within each group

**Sampling** Because the time and resources available for research are limited, it is almost impossible to investigate all the members of a target market or other population. A **population**, or 'universe', comprises all elements, units or individuals that are of interest to researchers for a specific study. A **sample** is a limited number of units chosen to represent the characteristics of a total population. For example, if a Gallup poll is designed to predict the results of an election, all the registered voters in the country would constitute the population. A representative national sample of several thousand registered voters would be selected in the Gallup poll to project the probable voting outcome. The projection would be based on the assumption that no major political events would occur before the election. The objective of **sampling** in marketing research, therefore, is to select representative units from a total population. Sampling procedures allow marketers to predict buyer behaviour fairly accurately on the basis of responses from the representative portion of the population of interest. Most types of marketing research employ sampling techniques.

There are two basic types of sampling: probability sampling and non-probability sampling. With **probability sampling**, every element in the population being studied has a known chance of being selected for study. Random sampling is basic probability sampling. When marketers employ **random sampling**, all the units in a population have an equal chance of appearing in the sample. The various events that can occur have an equal or known chance of taking place. For example, a specific playing card in a pack has a 1/52 probability of being drawn at any one time. Sample units are ordinarily chosen by selecting from a table of random numbers which have been statistically generated so that each digit, from zero to nine, will have an equal probability of occurring in each position in the sequence. The sequentially numbered elements of a population are sampled randomly by selecting the units whose numbers appear in the table of random numbers.

Another kind of probability sampling is **stratified sampling**, in which the population of interest is divided into groups according to a common characteristic or attribute, and a probability sampling is then conducted within each group. Employing a stratified sample may reduce some of the error that could occur as a result of using a simple random sample. By ensuring that each major group or segment of the population receives its proportionate share of sample units, investigators avoid including too many or too few sample units from each stratum. Usually, samples are stratified when researchers believe that there may be variations among different types of respondent. For example, many political opinion surveys are stratified by sex, race and age.

**Area sampling**
A sampling method that involves selecting a probability sample of geographic areas and selecting units or individuals within the selected areas for the sample

**Area sampling**, a variation of stratified sampling, involves two stages:

1 selecting a probability sample of geographic areas, such as streets, census tracts or census enumeration districts
2 selecting units or individuals within the selected geographic areas for the sample.

To select the units or individuals within the geographic areas, researchers may choose every *n*th house or unit, or they may adopt random selection procedures to pick out a given number of units or individuals from a total listing within the selected geographic areas. Area sampling may be used when a complete list of the population is not available.

**Quota sampling**
A sampling method in which the final choice of respondents is left to the interviewers, who base their choices on two or three variables (such as age, sex and education)

In **quota sampling**, researchers divide the population into groups and then arbitrarily choose participants from each group. A study of consumers who wear glasses, for example, may be conducted by interviewing any person who wears glasses. In quota sampling, there are some controls—usually limited to two or three variables such as age, sex and education – over the selection of respondents. The controls attempt to ensure that representative categories of respondents are interviewed. Because quota samples are not probability samples, not everyone has an equal chance of being selected and sampling error therefore cannot be measured statistically. Quota samples are used most often in exploratory studies, in which hypotheses are being developed. Often a small quota sample will not be projected to the total population, although the findings may provide valuable insights into a problem. A probability sample used to study people allergic to cats would be highly inefficient.

**Survey methods**
Interviews by mail, telephone, web and personal interviews

**Survey Methods** Marketing researchers often employ sampling to collect primary data through mail, telephone, on-line or personal interview surveys. Selection of a **survey method** depends on the nature of the problem, the data needed to satisfy the research objectives and any hypotheses, and the resources, such as funding and personnel, that are available to the researcher. Table 9.5 illustrates the current breakdown of research budgets across the different techniques in Great Britain.

Gathering information through surveys is increasingly difficult because respondent rates are declining. Many people believe that responding to surveys takes too long and have become fatigued by the frequency with which they are asked to become involved in such studies. The unethical use of 'sugging' ('selling under the guise of marketing research', i.e. sales techniques disguised as market surveys) has also contributed to decreased respondent cooperation, while Internet surveys have been affected by concerns about spam (junk e-mails).

**Mail surveys**
Questionnaires sent by mail to respondents, who are encouraged to complete and return them

In a **mail survey**, questionnaires are sent by mail to respondents, who are encouraged to complete and return them. Mail surveys are used most often when the individuals chosen for questioning are spread over a wide area and funds for the survey are limited. A mail survey is the least expensive survey method as long as the response rate is high enough to produce reliable results. The main disadvantages of mail surveys are the possibility of a low response rate or of misleading results, if respondents are significantly different from the population being sampled.

Researchers can boost response rates in mail surveys by offering respondents an incentive to return the questionnaire. Incentives and follow-ups have consistently been found to increase response rates. On the other hand, promises of anonymity, special appeals for cooperation and questionnaire length have no apparent impact on the response rate. Other techniques for increasing the response rate, such as advance notification, personalisation of survey materials, type of postage, corporate or university sponsorship, or foot-in-the-door techniques, have had mixed results, varying according to the population surveyed.[13] Although such techniques may help increase the response rates, they can introduce sample composition bias, or non-response bias, which results when those responding to a survey differ in some important respect from those not responding to the survey. In other words, response-enhancing techniques may alienate some people in the sample and appeal

**TABLE 9.5 BREAKDOWN OF RESEARCH BUDGETS ACROSS THE DIFFERENT TECHNIQUES IN THE UK**

**Expenditure on Marketing Research**

**Value of GB commissioned marketing research**

| | 1996 | 1997 | 1998 | 1999 | 2000 | 2001 | 2002 |
|---|---|---|---|---|---|---|---|
| Members' turnover, £m | 446 | 502 | 720 | 714 | 819 | 814 | 835 |

**Notes:** The AMSO merged with the ABMRC in 1998 to form the BMRA (British Market Research Association). Data for 1998 onwards refer to sales turnover of all 220 BMRA members. Data prior to 1998 refer to sales turnover of AMSO members. The BMRA estimate for total industry turnover in 2002 is approximately £1,147m.

**Source of Income by Client's Business, 2002**

| | % of total | %[1] | | % of total | %[1] |
|---|---|---|---|---|---|
| Food | 9.6 | 10.4 | Professional services | 1.3 | 5.9 |
| Financial | 8.0 | −4.0 | Media & marketing | 3.6 | 2.8 |
| Non-OTC pharmaceutical | 14.9 | 16.3 | Household durables | 0.7 | 47.4 |
| Media (broadcasting) | 6.5 | −17.6 | Printing & publishing | 1.5 | 6.8 |
| Health & beauty | 5.6 | −7.9 | Leisure & tourism | 1.4 | 1.8 |
| Government | 4.9 | 8.4 | Business/industrial | 0.1 | – |
| Public services | 4.0 | 8.4 | Soft drinks | 0.7 | 40.0 |
| Vehicle manufacturers | 5.9 | −7.2 | Tobacco | 0.7 | −12.1 |
| Retailers | 6.0 | 1.2 | IT | 1.5 | −3.0 |
| Telecommunications | 4.1 | 43.0 | Oil companies | 0.9 | −26.9 |
| Alcoholic drinks | 1.7 | −2.7 | Clothing (incl. footwear) & textiles | 0.3 | 8.3 |
| Advertising agencies | 1.1 | 9.3 | Education | 0.4 | – |
| Household products | 2.7 | 44.3 | Other | 9.9 | −13.7 |
| Travel & trans. companies | 2.0 | 7.7 | | | |

**Nature of Fieldwork**

| | Percentage of total 2001 | Percentage of total 2002 | | Percentage of total 2001 | Percentage of total 2002 |
|---|---|---|---|---|---|
| Personal interview | 24 | 27 | Depth interview | 4 | 3 |
| Telephone interview | 22 | 22 | Street interview | 3 | 2 |
| Audit/panel | 15 | 11 | Mystery shopping | 3 | 3 |
| Discussion group | 10 | 10 | Web/Internet interview | 0.5 | 0.5 |
| Hall test | 8 | 8 | Other | 5 | 6 |
| Self-completion/post | 7 | 7 | | | |

**Notes:** [1]2001–2002 percentage change. Percentages are based on returns by BMRA members accounting for c. half the Association's total sales turnover, representing c. one third of estimated UK industry turnover.
**Sources:** British Market Research Association, 2003; *The European Marketing Pocket Book*, published by the World Advertising Research Center, Henley-on-Thames, 2004.

to others, making the results non-representative of the population of interest. Businesses devote relatively little funding to mail surveys.

**Mail panels**
Groups of consumers selected to represent a market or market segment, who agree to be interviewed regularly by mail

Premiums or incentives encouraging respondents to return questionnaires have been effective in developing panels of respondents who are interviewed by mail on a regular basis. **Mail panels** of consumers selected to represent a market or market segment are especially useful for evaluating new products, providing general information about consumers and providing records of consumers' purchases. Many companies use consumer mail panels; others use **consumer purchase diaries**. These surveys are similar to mail panels, but consumers keep track of purchases only. Consumer mail panels and

**Consumer purchase diaries**
A marketing research tool in which consumers record their purchases

consumer purchase diaries are much more widely used than mail surveys, but they do have shortcomings. Research indicates that the people who take the time to fill out a consumer purchase diary have a higher income and are better educated than the general population. If researchers include less well-educated consumers in the panel, they must risk poorer response rates.[14]

**Telephone surveys**
Surveys in which respondents' answers to a questionnaire are recorded by interviewers on the phone

**Telephone surveys**, where respondents' answers to a questionnaire are recorded by interviewers on the phone, are widely used by businesses. A telephone survey has some advantages over a mail survey. The rate of response is higher because it takes less effort to answer the telephone and talk than to fill out a questionnaire and return it. If there are enough interviewers, telephone surveys can be conducted very quickly. Thus they can be used by political candidates or organisations seeking an immediate reaction to an event. In addition, this survey technique permits interviewers to develop a rapport with respondents and ask some probing questions.

Telephone interviews also have drawbacks, especially as a large proportion of the population is becoming increasingly unwilling to become involved. Furthermore, these interviews are limited to oral communication; visual aids or observation cannot be included. Interpreters of results must make adjustments for subjects who are not at home or who do not have telephones. Many households are excluded from the telephone directory. Others use answering machines, voicemail or caller ID to screen or block calls. Researchers seeking business respondents can also face non-response problems, particularly as secretaries frequently 'gatekeep' calls, preventing researchers from talking to their targets.

Telephone surveys, like mail and personal interview surveys, are sometimes used to develop panels of respondents who can be interviewed repeatedly to measure changes in attitudes or behaviour. Reliance on such panels is increasing.

**Computer-assisted telephone interviewing**
A survey method that integrates questionnaire, data collection and tabulations, and provides data to aid decision-makers in the shortest time possible

**Computer-assisted telephone interviewing** integrates questionnaire, data collection and tabulations, and provides data to aid decision-makers in the shortest time possible. Questionnaire responses are entered on a terminal keyboard, or the interviewer can use a light-pen (a pen-shaped torch) to record a response on a light-sensitive screen. On the most advanced devices, the interviewer merely points to the appropriate response on a touch-sensitive screen with his or her finger. Open-ended responses can be typed on the keyboard or recorded with paper and pencil. This kind of interviewing saves time and facilitates monitoring the progress of interviews. Because data are available as soon as they are entered into the system, interim results can be retrieved quickly. With some systems, a laptop computer may be taken to off-site locations for use in data analysis. Some researchers believe that computer-assisted telephone interviewing is less expensive than conventional paper and pencil methods.[15]

**On-line survey**
Questionnaires that are sent to an individual's e-mail account or that are available over the Internet or via a website

On-line surveys have evolved as an alternative to telephone surveys. In an **on-line survey** questionnaires can be transmitted to respondents who have agreed to be contacted and have provided their e-mail addresses. Because e-mail is semi-interactive, recipients can ask for clarification of specific questions or pose questions of their own. The fact that the data are instantly available in electronic format also eases the process of data entry. The potential advantages of e-mail surveys are quick response and lower costs than traditional mail and telephone surveys. However, these advantages cannot yet be fully realised because of limited access to some respondents. In general, though, the opportunities for using e-mail and the Internet to collect data are increasing. Organisations are now pooling their e-mail address lists and, increasingly, some are selling these lists to third parties wishing to conduct research.

**Personal interview survey**
Face-to-face situation in which the researcher meets the consumer and questions him or her about a specific topic

In a **personal interview survey**, participants respond to questions face to face.[16] Various audio-visual aids – pictures, products, diagrams or pre-recorded advertising copy – can be incorporated into a personal interview. Rapport gained through direct interaction usually permits more in-depth interviewing, including probes, follow-up questions or psychological tests. In addition, because personal interviews can be longer, they can yield more information.

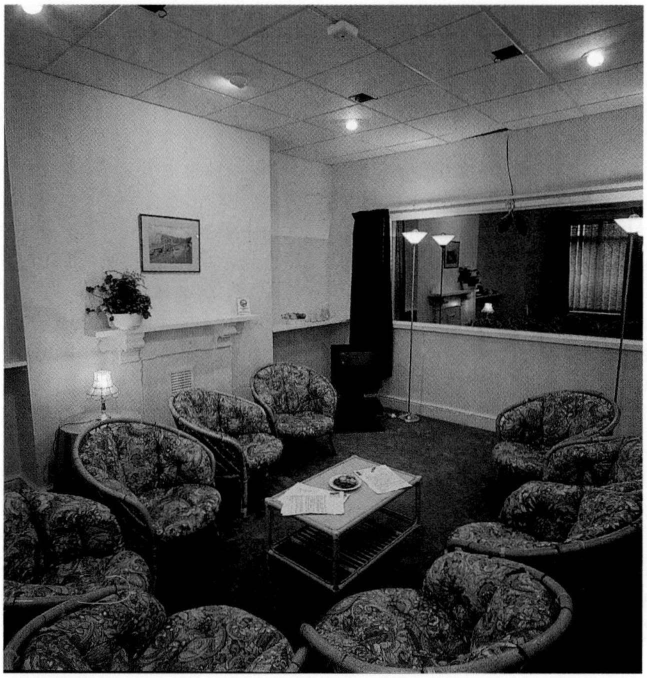

***Figure 9.6***
*Primary data collection. Viewing facilities are often used for experiments or for conducting focus group interviews*
*Photo: Courtesy of West Midlands Viewing Facility*

Finally, respondents can be selected more carefully, and reasons for non-response can be explored. A **depth interview** is a lengthy, one-to-one structured interview examining a consumer's views about a product in detail.

The object of a **focus group interview** is to observe group interaction when members are exposed to an idea or concept. Focus groups are frequently held in viewing facilities, as illustrated in Figure 9.6. Often these interviews are conducted informally, without a structured questionnaire, in small groups of 8 to 12 people. Consumer attitudes, behaviour, lifestyles, needs and desires can be explored in a flexible and creative manner through this widely used technique (see Chapter 8). Questions are open-ended and stimulate consumers to answer in their own words. Researchers can ask probing questions to clarify something they do not fully understand, or something unexpected and interesting that may help to explain consumer behaviour.

When Cadbury's used information obtained from focus groups to change its advertising and to test product concepts, the new advertisements and product launches pushed up sales.[17] The Case Study at the end of this chapter describes the future of this marketing research technique. Focus group interviews usually start with a general discussion, which will be led by a researcher or moderator. The conversation is then narrowed during the course of the session, enabling the moderator to home in on a specific brand, product or advertisement – hence the term 'focus' group.

**Depth interview** A lengthy, one-to-one structured interview, examining in detail a consumer's views about a product

**Focus group interview** A survey method that aims to observe group interaction when members are exposed to an idea or concept

**Quali-depth interviews** 25- to 30-minute intercept interviews that incorporate some of the in-depth advantages of focus group interviews with the speed and flexibility of shopping mall/pavement intercept interviews

**Quali-depth interviews** are 25- to 30-minute intercept interviews that incorporate some of the in-depth advantages of focus group interviews with the speed and flexibility of shopping mall/pavement intercept interviews (see below). Typically, intercepted consumers are taken to a nearby hall or café and asked more probing and searching questions than is possible in a three- to four-minute shopping mall/pavement intercept interview. They can also be shown a greater variety of stimulus material. This is a useful approach for sensitive issues that people might not wish to discuss in a group – gambling and drugs, for example.

Another research technique is the **in-home interview**. Because it may be desirable to eliminate group influence, the in-home interview offers a clear advantage when thoroughness of self-disclosure is important. In an in-depth interview of 45 to 90 minutes, respondents can be probed to reveal their real motivations, feelings, behaviours and aspirations. In-depth interviews permit the discovery of emotional 'hot buttons' that provide psychological insights.[18] Door-to-door interviews last only a few minutes and are similar to pavement intercepts.

The nature of personal interviews has changed. In the past, most personal interviews, which were based on random sampling or pre-arranged appointments, were conducted in the respondent's home. Today, most personal interviews are conducted in shopping centres or malls, or on pavements. **Shopping mall/pavement intercept interviews** involve interviewing a percentage of people who pass by certain 'intercept' points in a shopping centre or pavement. Like any face-to-face interviewing method, shopping mall/pavement intercept interviewing has many advantages. The interviewer is in a position to recognise and react to respondents' non-verbal indications of confusion. Respondents can be shown product prototypes, videotapes of advertisements and the like, and reactions can be

**In-home interview**
45- to 90-minute interview in which the researcher visits the respondent in his or her home

**Shopping mall/ pavement intercept interviews**
Personal interviewing of a percentage of individuals who pass by certain 'intercept' points in a shopping centre or on a pavement

**On-site computer interviewing**
A survey method that requires respondents to complete a self-administered questionnaire displayed on a computer monitor

**Questionnaire**
Base document for research purposes, providing the questions and structure for an interview or self-completion, and providing space for respondents' answers

sought. The environment lets the researcher deal with complex situations. For example, in taste tests, researchers know that all the respondents are reacting to the same product, which can be prepared and monitored from the shopping centre's test kitchen or some other facility. In addition, lower cost, greater control and the ability to conduct tests requiring bulky equipment make shopping mall/pavement intercept interviews popular.

Research indicates that given a comparable sample of respondents, shopping mall/pavement intercept interviewing is a suitable substitute for telephone interviewing.[19] In addition, there seem to be no significant differences in the completeness of consumer responses between telephone interviewing and shopping mall/pavement intercept interviewing. In fact, for questions dealing with socially desirable behaviour, shopping mall/ pavement intercept respondents appear to be more honest about their past behaviour.[20]

In **on-site computer interviewing**, a variation of the shopping mall/pavement intercept interview, respondents complete a self-administered questionnaire displayed on a computer monitor. A computer software package can be used to conduct such interviews in shopping centres. After a brief lesson on how to operate the software, respondents can go through the survey at their own pace. Questionnaires can be adapted so that respondents see only those items that may provide useful information about their attitudes.[21]

**Questionnaire Construction** A carefully constructed questionnaire is essential to the success of any survey. A **questionnaire** is a base document for research purposes that provides the questions and the structure for an interview or self-completion, and has provision for respondents' answers.[22] Questions must be designed to elicit information that meets the study's data requirements. These questions must be clear, easy to understand and directed towards a specific objective. Researchers need to define the objective before trying to develop a questionnaire because the objective determines the substance of the questions and the amount of detail. A common mistake in constructing questionnaires is to ask questions that interest the researchers but do not yield information useful in deciding whether to accept or reject a hypothesis. Finally, the most important rule in composing questions is to maintain impartiality.

The questions are usually of four kinds:

1 open-ended
2 dichotomous
3 multiple choice
4 Likert scale.

Here are some examples.

1. OPEN-ENDED QUESTION
What is your general opinion of broadband Internet access for your computer?
________________________________________
________________________________________
________________________________________

2. DICHOTOMOUS QUESTION
Do you presently have broadband access at home, work, school or college?
Yes ____ Provider's identity ____
No ____

3. MULTIPLE-CHOICE QUESTION
What age group are you in?
Under 20 ____
20–29 ____
30–39 ____

40–49 ____
50–59 ____
60 and over ____

4. LIKERT SCALE QUESTION
To what extent do you expect to use the Internet for buying travel products (flights, hotel accommodation) in the future?

| Not at all | 1 | 2 | 3 | 4 | 5 | A great deal |
|---|---|---|---|---|---|---|

The design of questionnaires is extremely important because it affects the validity and usefulness of the results. Testing a questionnaire on a few respondents before conducting a full survey helps to eliminate such difficulties. There are also certain guidelines that should be followed when undertaking questionnaire design. The questions must relate to the research objectives. The layout of the questionnaire must not be off-putting to respondents or to the researchers conducting the work. This is particularly pertinent given that technological advances mean that carefully laid-out questionnaires can be read (scanned) and analysed by computers. This can save researchers a great deal of time. Question type is also an important factor. Open-ended questions can be the most revealing, but are time-consuming – and therefore off-putting – for respondents, as well as difficult to analyse. Dichotomous questions are straightforward but not very revealing. Multiple-choice questions are popular, but care must be exercised in the choice of categories. Likert scale questions are very popular and can enable batches or strings of questions to be listed together in a space-saving style that can be time-saving for the respondent. They allow respondents to express degrees of a positive or negative response, rather than give an absolute yes or no. There is also the option to give a 'neutral' ('3') answer. Most questionnaires include a mix of question styles.

Sometimes respondent fatigue can affect the quality of questionnaire responses. This may result in answers being rushed, or the questionnaire being abandoned altogether. For example, sometimes when faced with a long list of Likert scale questions, respondents move through the questions ticking the same point in the scale, rather than taking time to reflect on their answers. The wording of questions is also critical. Researchers must ensure that personal questions, such as those about income or educational attainment, are worded in as inoffensive a manner as possible. These types of question are often placed towards the end of the questionnaire, because it is believed that they are more likely to be answered once the respondent has invested time in the research instrument.

**Observation methods** Methods by which researchers record respondents' overt behaviour and take note of physical conditions and events

**Observation Methods** In using **observation methods**, researchers record respondents' overt behaviour, taking note of physical conditions and events. Direct contact with respondents is avoided; instead, their actions are examined and noted systematically. For example, researchers might use observation methods to answer the question, 'How long does the average McDonald's restaurant customer have to wait in line before being served?'. As the 'Opener' box at the beginning of this chapter demonstrates, observation may include the use of ethnographic techniques, such as watching customers interact with a product in a real-world environment. Ethnography is increasingly being used by many marketing research agencies to gain greater insights into consumer lifestyles. Indeed, in a recent survey of the marketing research industry, 27 per cent of respondents giving an opinion about the most exciting developments mentioned ethnographic research.[23]

Observation may also be combined with interviews. For example, during a personal interview, the condition of a respondent's home or other possessions may be observed and recorded, and demographic information such as ethnic origin, approximate age and sex can be confirmed. Observation is not confined to consumers; shops and service establishments can also be observed, through 'mystery shopper' research, as the Marketing Tools and Techniques box below explains.

## Marketing Tools and Techniques

### 'Mystery Shopper' Research Programmes: Pros and Cons

Retailers and providers of services depend increasingly not only on the products they sell or deliver but also on the ability, attitude and quality of their personnel and the internal environment of their branch outlets. The regional directors and head office managers who check such standards all too often enter through the staff door at the rear of the branch, focusing primarily on operations and not on customer concerns. The branch's customers enter from the front, having first seen the exterior of the branch. They deal with all levels of personnel, not just the manager or manageress to whom the visiting director talks. These customers are not wrapped up in the company's products and operations; they seek help and advice. They expect courtesy and professionalism.

Customers buy a company's products; quite often the company's management never does, instead requesting items direct from storage at staff discount rates without ever visiting shops or showrooms. Car manufacturers give their senior management vehicles and offer all employees highly attractive deals. The result is that few senior managers ever visit a showroom or dealer – even their servicing is taken care of – so they never see the 'sharp end', their dealers, as customers do.

MG Rover instigated a programme of 'mystery shopper' surveys. This programme involved visits by bogus potential car buyers to dealers to rate the upkeep and appearance of showrooms, technical knowledge and attitude of personnel, quality of displays, negotiating criteria and adherence to company policies. Dealers did not know who the bogus buyers were, nor when they were to visit. Service reception staff were similarly targeted. A favourite ploy by the researchers was to book a car service by telephone and then phone again to cancel, judging the receptionist's response to the lost business. As a result of these frequent – always anonymous – visits, Rover was able to improve the standards of its dealers, the attitude of its personnel and ultimately the quality of its service and customer satisfaction.

This form of marketing research – 'mystery shopper' – is one of the fastest-growing areas in the industry. The largest research company in the UK, BEM, has 3000 mystery shoppers on its books, many working part-time, and its annual sales exceed £5 million – £3.5 million from mystery shopper surveys. BEM's employees are trained to evaluate how customers are greeted, how the store looks and whether shop assistants understand the products on sale. They are expected to blend in inconspicuously while assessing branches; they are not loud customers visibly asking awkward questions. For many businesses, mystery shopper researchers are evaluating standards and service quality, and supplying management with measures of performance and benchmarks against which improvements can be made.

The European Society for Opinion and Marketing Research (ESOMAR) is attempting to clamp down on the use of mystery shopper research, arguing that it is laudable for organisations to wish to improve the appearance of their facilities and the capabilities of their personnel, but not by tricking employees into handling awkward customers in an off-hand or aggressive manner. ESOMAR is concerned that the staff member does not have the up-front opportunity to withdraw from the interview – something respondents can do in other forms of research surveys – and that the process of dealing with the mystery shopper takes up valuable staff time, which may put pressure on the member of staff when dealing with the next customer.

Another concern is that in most forms of ethical marketing research, the respondent is guaranteed anonymity, but if mystery shopper research is deployed to check up on staff or to develop 'league tables' of branch performance, it is difficult for the research findings not to identify the personnel in question. ESOMAR's recommendations are that mystery shopper research must not waste informants' time and should permit anonymity, or that staff should be told beforehand of the impending research and the ultimate uses for the findings. A study intended to form a supervisory procedure for checking individuals' performance is not permitted under ESOMAR's code: the purpose of any mystery shopper research should be solely to boost consumer demand.

**Sources:** *Marketing Guides: Market Research*, 13 June 1996; Customer Concern and BEM promotional literature; Rover Cars; Peter Jackson, *Adsearch*, 1999; ESOMAR, Amsterdam, 1998.

Data gathered through observation can sometimes be biased if the respondent is aware of the observation process. An observer can be placed in a natural market environment, such as a grocery store, without biasing or influencing shoppers' actions. However, if the presence of a human observer is likely to bias the outcome or if human sensory abilities are inadequate, mechanical means may be used to record behaviour. **Mechanical observation devices** include cameras, recorders, counting machines and other equipment that records physiological changes in individuals. For instance, a special camera can be used to record the eye movements of respondents looking at an advertisement, and to detect the sequence of reading and the parts of the advertisement that receive greatest attention. Electronic scanners in supermarkets can provide accurate data on sales and consumers' purchase patterns, and marketing researchers may buy such data from the supermarket.

**Mechanical observation devices** Cameras, recorders, counting machines and other equipment that records physiological changes in individuals

Observation is straightforward and avoids a central problem of survey methods: motivating respondents to state their true feelings or opinions. However, observation tends to be descriptive. When it is the only method of data collection, it may not provide insights into causal relationships. Another drawback is that analyses based on observation are subject to the biases of the observer or the limitations of the mechanical device.

**Experimentation** Data collection that involves maintaining certain variables as constant so that the effects of the experimental variables can be measured

**Experimentation** **Experimentation** can be used to determine which variable or variables caused an event to occur. It involves keeping certain variables constant so that the effects of the experimental variables can be measured. For instance, if an on-line fashion vendor wishes to examine the effect of a price reduction on sales, all other marketing variables should be held constant except the change in price.

**Independent variable** A variable not influenced by or dependent on other variables in experiments

**Dependent variable** A variable that is contingent on, or restricted to, one value or a set of values assumed by the independent variable

In experimentation, an **independent variable** (a variable not influenced by or dependent on other variables) is manipulated and the resulting changes measured in a **dependent variable** (a variable contingent on, or restricted to, one value or a set of values assumed by the independent variable). Figure 9.7 illustrates the relationship between these variables. For example, when Houghton Mifflin Company introduces a new edition of its *American Heritage Dictionary*, it may want to estimate the number of dictionaries that could be sold at various levels of advertising expenditure and price. The dependent variable would be sales, the independent variables would be advertising expenditure and price. Researchers would design the experiment to control other independent variables that might influence sales, such as distribution and variations of the product.

**Laboratory settings** Central locations at which participants or respondents are invited to react or respond to experimental stimuli

Experiments may be conducted in the laboratory or in the field; each research setting has advantages and disadvantages. In **laboratory settings**, participants or respondents are invited to a central location to react or respond to experimental stimuli. In such an isolated setting it is possible to control independent variables that might influence the outcome of an experiment. The features of laboratory settings might include a taste kitchen, video equipment, slide projectors, tape recorders, Internet hook-ups, one-way mirrors, central telephone banks and interview rooms. In an experiment to determine the influence of price (independent

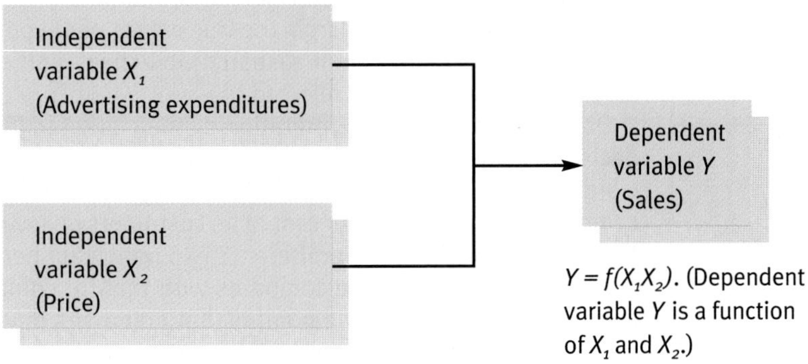


*Figure 9.7* *Relationship between independent and dependent variables*

variable) on sales of a new canned soup (dependent variable), respondents would be invited to a laboratory – a room with table, chairs and sample soups – before the soup was available in stores. The soup would be placed on a table with competitors' soups. Analysts would then question respondents about their reactions to the soup at various prices. One problem with a laboratory setting is its isolation from the real world, making it difficult, or impossible, to duplicate all the conditions that affect choices in the marketplace.

**Field settings**
'Real world' environments in which experiments take place

**Home placements**
Experiments in which a product is used in a home setting

**Diary tests**
Experiments in which households log their weekly purchases and consumption patterns

The experimental approach can also be used in **field settings**, which are 'real world' environments. A taste test of regional cheeses conducted in a supermarket is one example of an experiment in a field setting. Field settings can allow a more direct test of marketing decisions than laboratory settings. However, these experiments also have their drawbacks. It may be difficult to encourage respondents to cooperate with the experiment, or the findings may be influenced or biased by unexpected events, such as the weather or major economic news. Sometimes the experiment itself can cause bias. For example, in **home placements** (when a product is used in the home in a real setting) or **diary tests** (when households log their weekly purchases and consumption patterns), people may become artificially involved with the product. They might sniff items they would not normally sniff, or ask for their children's opinions about a food item when, normally, they would just give their children the meal and expect them to eat it.[24]

## Step 4: Analysing and Interpreting Research Findings

After collecting data to test their hypotheses, marketers analyse and interpret the research findings. Interpretation is easier if marketers plan their data analysis methods carefully and early in the research process. All too often, when data collection has been completed, it is discovered that different wording of questions or ordering of the sections in a questionnaire could have simplified the analysis. Marketers should also allow for continual evaluation of the data during the entire collection period. They can then gain valuable insight into areas that ought to be probed during the formal interpretation.

The first step in drawing conclusions from most research is displaying the data in table format. If marketers intend to apply the results to individual categories of the things or people being studied, cross-tabulation may be quite useful, especially in tabulating joint occurrences. For example, a cross-tabulation of data using the two variables 'gender' and 'purchase rates of car tyres' would show differences in how men and women purchase this product.

**Statistical interpretation**
An analysis of data that focuses on what is typical or what deviates from the average

After the data are tabulated, they must be analysed. **Statistical interpretation** focuses on what is typical or what deviates from the average. It indicates how widely responses vary and how they are distributed in relation to the variable being measured. This interpretation is another facet of marketing research that relies on marketers' judgement or intuition. Moreover, when they interpret statistics, marketers must take into account estimates of expected error or deviation from the true values of the population. The analysis of data helps researchers to achieve their research objectives and may lead to the hypothesis being studied being accepted or rejected.[25]

Data require careful interpretation by the marketer. If the results of a study are valid, the decision-maker should take action; however, if it is discovered that a question has been worded incorrectly, the results should be ignored. For example, if a study by an electricity company reveals that 50 per cent of its customers believe that meter readers are 'friendly', is that finding good, bad or indifferent? Two important benchmarks help interpret the result: how the 50 per cent figure compares with that for competitors and how it compares with a previous time period. The point is that managers must understand the research results and relate them to a context that permits effective decision-making.[26]

## Step 5: Reporting Research Findings

The final step in the marketing research process is reporting the research findings. Before preparing the report, the marketer must take a clear, objective look at the findings to see how well the gathered facts answer the research question, or support or negate the hypotheses posed in the beginning. In most cases, it is extremely doubtful that the study can provide everything needed to answer the research question. Thus the report must highlight the deficiencies and the reasons for them, perhaps suggesting areas that require further investigation.

The report presenting the results is usually a formal, written document. Researchers must allow time for the writing task when they plan and schedule the project. Since the report is a means of communicating with the decision-makers who will use the research findings, researchers need to determine beforehand how much detail and supporting data to include. They should keep in mind that corporate executives prefer reports that are short, clear and simply expressed. Often researchers will give their summary and recommendations first, especially if decision-makers do not have time to study how the results were obtained. Such summary findings tend to be presented via an audio-visual presentation. A technical report allows its users to analyse data and interpret recommendations because it describes the research methods/procedures and the most important data gathered. Thus researchers must recognise the needs and expectations of the report user and adapt to them.

When marketing decision-makers have a firm grasp of research methods and procedures, they are better able to integrate reported findings and personal experience. If marketers can spot limitations in research from reading a report, their personal experience assumes additional importance in the decision-making process. Marketers who cannot understand basic statistical assumptions and data gathering procedures may misuse research findings. Consequently, report writers should be aware of the backgrounds and research abilities of those who will rely on the report in making decisions. Clear explanations presented in plain language make it easier for decision-makers to apply the findings and less likely that a report will be misused or ignored. Talking to potential research users before writing a report can help researchers supply information that will improve decision-making.

Care must be taken when writing the report to avoid bias and distortion. Marketing researchers want to find out about behaviour and opinions, and they need accurate data for making decisions. Reliable marketing research and marketing information systems provide a clearer understanding of dynamics in the marketplace and are more likely to be used by managers in decision-making.

# Using Technology to Improve Marketing Information Gathering and Analysis

## Marketing Information Systems

**Marketing information system (MIS)**
The framework for the day-to-day management and structuring of information gathered from sources both inside and outside an organisation

A **marketing information system (MIS)** is a framework for the day-to-day management and structuring of information gathered regularly from sources both inside and outside an organisation. As such, an MIS provides a continuous flow of information about prices, advertising expenditure, sales, competition and distribution expenses.[27] Kraft General Foods, for example, operates one of the largest marketing information systems in the food industry, maintaining, using and sharing information with others to increase the value of what the company offers customers. Kraft seeks to develop a dialogue with customers by providing Freefone numbers. It receives hundreds of thousands of calls annually from customers asking questions and providing product feedback.

The main focus of the marketing information system is on data storage and retrieval. Regular reports of sales by product or market category, data on inventory levels and records of sales people's activities are all examples of information that is useful in making marketing decisions. In the MIS, the means of gathering data receive less attention than do the procedures for expediting the flow of information. Figure 9.8 illustrates the chief components of an MIS. The inputs into a marketing information system include the information sources inside and outside the organisation assumed to be useful for future decision-making.

An effective marketing information system starts by determining the objective of the information – that is, by identifying decision needs that require certain information. The business can then specify an information system for continuous monitoring to provide regular, pertinent information on both the external and internal environment. FedEx, for example, has developed interactive marketing systems to provide instantaneous communication between the company and its customers. Through the telephone and the Internet, customers can track packages and receive immediate feedback concerning delivery. The company's website provides valuable information about customer usage, and it allows customers to express directly what they think about company services. The evolving telecommunications and computer technology is allowing marketing information systems to cultivate one-to-one relationships with customers.

## Databases

Most marketing information systems include internal databases. A database is a collection of information arranged for easy access and retrieval. Databases allow marketers to tap into an abundance of information useful in making marketing decisions: internal sales reports, newspaper articles, company press releases, government economic reports, bibliographies and more, often accessed through a computer system. Information technology has made it possible to develop databases to guide strategic planning and help improve customer services. Wal-Mart, for example, maintains one of the largest company databases, with data on sales and inventory levels, as well as data mined from customer receipts in its stores. These data help Wal-Mart pinpoint purchasing patterns, which helps the business manage inventory levels and determine effective product placement. Many commercial websites require consumers to register and provide personal information in order to access the site or make a purchase. Frequent-flier programmes permit airlines to ask loyal customers to participate in surveys about their needs and desires, allowing the airlines to track their best customers' flight patterns by time of day, week, month and year. Supermarkets, such as Tesco and Sainsbury's, gain a substantial amount of data through checkout scanners tied to loyalty cards.

Marketing researchers can also use commercial databases developed by information research businesses to obtain useful information for marketing decisions. Many of these commercial databases are accessible on-line for a fee. In most commercial databases, the user typically does a computer search by key word, topic or company, and the database service generates abstracts, articles or reports that can be printed out. Accessing multiple reports or a complete article may cost extra. Information provided by a single company – for example, on household demographics, purchases, television viewing behaviour, and responses to promotions such as coupons or loyalty schemes, is called **single-source data.**[28]

**Single-source data**
Information provided by a single marketing research company

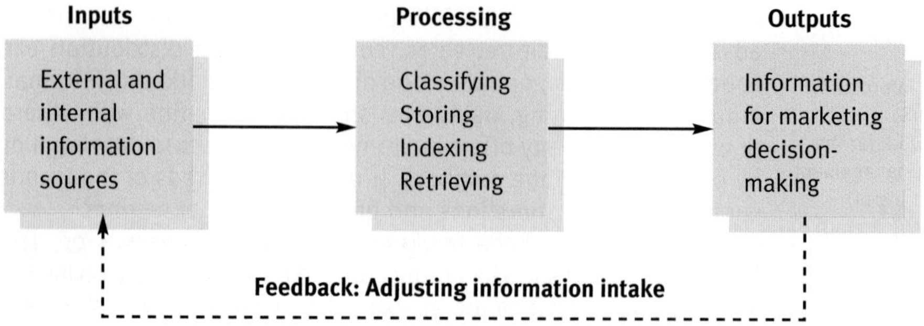


***Figure 9.8***
*An organisation's marketing information system*

For example, CACI provides demographic and lifestyle information on people living in different UK neighbourhoods.

### Marketing Decision Support Systems

**Marketing decision support system (MDSS)** Customised computer software that aids marketing managers in decision-making

A **marketing decision support system (MDSS)** is customised computer software that aids marketing managers in decision-making by helping them anticipate the effects of certain decisions. Some decision support systems have a broader range and offer greater computational and modelling capabilities than spreadsheets; they let managers explore a greater number of alternatives. For example, a decision support system can determine how sales and profits might be affected by higher or lower interest rates or how sales forecasts, advertising expenditures, production levels and the like might affect overall profits. For this reason, decision support system software is often a major component of a company's marketing information system. For example, both Oracle and Ford Motor Company use a software product called NeuroServer that acts as a customer interface to solve problems and answer questions for customers. Based on customised parameters, it allows marketers to acquire specific information on customers, which then goes into the decision support system.[29] Some decision support systems incorporate artificial intelligence and other advanced computer technologies.

### The Internet and On-line Information Services

The Internet has evolved as a powerful communication medium, linking customers and companies around the world via computer networks with e-mail, forums, web pages and more. Growth of the Internet, and especially the World Wide Web, has launched an entire industry that is working to make market information easily accessible both to marketing businesses and customers.

Companies can also mine their own websites for useful information. Amazon, for example, has built a relationship with its customers by tracking the types of books and music they purchase. Each time a customer logs on to its website, Amazon can offer recommendations based on the customer's previous purchases. Such a marketing system helps the company track the changing desires and buying habits of its most valued customers.

Marketing researchers can also subscribe to on-line services such as CompuServe and MSN. These services typically offer their subscribers such specialised services as databases, news services and forums, as well as access to the Internet itself. Marketers can subscribe to 'mailing lists' that periodically deliver electronic newsletters to their computer screens and they can participate in on-screen discussions with thousands of network users. This enhanced communication with a business's customers, suppliers and employees provides a high-speed link that boosts the capabilities of the business's marketing information system.

While most web pages are open to anyone with Internet access, big organisations like Cisco Systems also maintain internal web pages, called 'intranets', that allow employees to access such internal data as customer profiles and product inventory – information once hidden in databases only technicians could unlock. Such sensitive company information can be protected from outside users of the World Wide Web by special security software called firewalls. Marketers who get into the habit of accessing their companies' internal web pages often move on to seek information externally as well, via the rest of the World Wide Web.

## The Importance of Ethical Marketing Research

Marketing managers and other professionals are relying more and more on marketing research, marketing information systems and new technologies to make better decisions. It is therefore essential that professional standards are established by which to judge the reliability of such research. Such standards are necessary because of the ethical and legal issues that develop in gathering marketing research data. In addition, the relationships between research suppliers, such as marketing research agencies, and the marketing managers who make strategy decisions require ethical behaviour. Without such clear standards, ethical conflict can lead to mistrust and questionable research results.[30] Attempts to stamp out shoddy practices and establish generally accepted procedures for conducting research are important developments in marketing research. Other issues of great concern relate to researchers' honesty, manipulation of research techniques, data manipulation, invasion of privacy, and failure to disclose the purpose or sponsorship of a study in some situations. Too often, respondents are unfairly manipulated and research clients are not told about flaws in data. For example, one dubious practice that damages the image of marketing research is 'sugging', as mentioned earlier in the chapter. More recently, direct marketers have disguised their selling mailings with questionnaires, adding to respondents' confusion and dislike of honest marketing research.[31] Organisations like ESOMAR and the Market Research Society have developed codes of conduct and guidelines to promote ethical marketing research.[32] To be effective, such guidelines must instruct those who participate in marketing research on how to avoid misconduct. Table 9.6, which illustrates part of the ICC/ESOMAR International Code of Marketing and Social Research Practice, details the information to which any research client is entitled.

Marketing research is essential in planning and developing marketing strategies. Information about target markets provides vital input in planning the marketing mix and in controlling marketing activities. It is no secret that companies can use information technology as a key to gaining an advantage over the competition.[33] In short, the marketing concept – the marketing philosophy of customer orientation – can be implemented better when adequate information about customers, competition and trends is available.

**TABLE 9.6 INFORMATION ABOUT MARKETING RESEARCH PROJECTS TO WHICH RESEARCH CLIENTS ARE ENTITLED**

1 **Background**
For whom the study was conducted
The purpose of the study
Names of subcontractors and consultants performing any substantial part of the work

2 **Sample**
- (a) A description of the intended and actual universe covered
- (b) The size, nature and geographical distribution of the sample (both planned and achieved); and, where relevant, the extent to which any of the data collected were obtained from only part of the sample
- (c) Details of the sampling method and any weighting methods used
- (d) When technically relevant, a statement of response rates and a discussion of any possible bias due to non-response

3 **Data collection**
- (a) A description of the method by which the information was collected
- (b) A description of the field staff, briefing and field quality control methods used
- (c) The method of recruiting respondents, and the general nature of any incentives offered to secure their cooperation
- (d) When the fieldwork was carried out
- (e) In the case of 'desk research', a clear statement of the sources of the information and their likely reliability

4 **Presentation of results**
- (a) The relevant factual findings obtained
- (b) Bases of percentages (both weighted and unweighted)
- (c) General indicators of the probable statistical margins of error to be attached to the main findings, and of the levels of statistical significance of differences between key figures
- (d) The questionnaire and other relevant documents and materials used (or, in the case of a shared project, that portion relating to the matter reported on)

**Source:** Rule 25, http://www.esomar.org/print.php?a=2&p=75 © Copyright 2004 by ESOMAR® – The World Association of Research Professionals. This article first appeared in ICC/ESOMAR International Code of Marketing and Social Research Practice, published by ESOMAR.

# Summary

Effective marketing is contingent on marketers having information about the characteristics, needs and wants of their target markets. Marketing research and information systems that furnish practical, unbiased information help businesses avoid the assumptions and misunderstandings that could lead to poor marketing performance.

- *Marketing research* is the systematic design, collection, interpretation and reporting of information to help marketers solve specific marketing problems or take advantage of marketing opportunities. Marketing research projects are adapted to the context and problems under study.

- All organisations have some *marketing intelligence*, which is the composite of all data and ideas available within the organisation. Often the information is inadequate, leading to the commissioning of marketing research.

- *Quantitative marketing research* leads to findings that can be quantified and statistically analysed. *Qualitative research* examines subjective opinions and value judgements.

- The increase in marketing research activities represents a transition from intuitive to scientific problem-solving. Intuitive decisions are made on the basis of personal knowledge and past experience. *Scientific decision-making* is an orderly, logical and systematic approach to gathering information. Minor, non-recurring low-risk problems can be handled successfully by *intuition*. As the amount of risk and alternative solutions increases, the use of research becomes more desirable and rewarding.

- The five basic steps of planning marketing research are: (1) locating and defining problems or research issues; (2) designing the research; (3) collecting data; (4) analysing and interpreting research findings; (5) reporting research findings.

- The first step towards finding a solution or launching a research study means uncovering the nature and boundaries of a negative, or positive, situation or question. Researchers and decision-makers should remain in the *problem definition* stage until they have determined precisely what they want from the research and how they will use it.

- Careful *research design* is of vital importance as a clear statement of research objectives guides a research project. Sometimes hypotheses – or informed guesses or assumptions about a certain problem or set of circumstances – are formulated. The *research objectives* and any *hypotheses* determine the approach for gathering data: *exploratory research*, *descriptive research* or *causal research*. Researchers need to be concerned about issues of reliability and validity: techniques are *reliable* if they produce almost identical results in successive repeated trials; they have *validity* if they measure what they are supposed to measure and not something else.

- Collecting data is the third step of the research process. *Secondary data* are compiled inside or outside the organisation for some purpose other than the current investigation. Secondary data may be collected from an organisation's databank and other internal sources; from periodicals, census reports, government publications, the World Wide Web and unpublished sources; and from *syndicated data services*, which collect general information and sell it to clients. Secondary data 'pre-exists' and should be examined prior to the collection of any primary data.

- To gather *primary data*, researchers use sampling procedures, survey methods, observation and experimentation. *Sampling* involves selecting a limited number of representative units, or a *sample*, from a total *population*. There are two basic types of sampling: probability and non-probability. In *probability sampling*, every element of the population has a known chance of being selected. In *random sampling*, all the units in a population have an equal chance of appearing in the sample. In *stratified sampling*, the population of interest is divided into groups according to a common characteristic or attribute, and then a probability sampling is conducted within each group. *Area sampling* involves selecting a probability sample of geographic areas such as streets, census tracts or census enumeration districts, and selecting units or individuals within the selected geographic areas for the sample. *Quota sampling* differs from other forms of sampling in that it is judgemental (or non-probability).

- *Survey methods* include *mail surveys* and *mail panels*, e-mail and Internet surveys (*on-line surveys*), *consumer purchase diaries, telephone surveys, computer assisted telephone interviewing* and *personal interview surveys*, such as *depth interviews, shopping mall/pavement intercept interviews, on-site computer interviewing, focus group interviews, quali-depth interviews* and *in-home interviews. Questionnaires* are instruments used to obtain information from respondents and to record observations; they should be unbiased and objective. *Observation methods* including ethnographic techniques that involve researchers recording respondents' overt behaviour and taking note of physical conditions and events. Observation may be facilitated by *mechanical observation devices*.

- *Experimentation* involves maintaining as constants those factors that are related to or may affect the variables under investigation, so that the effects of the experimental variables can be measured. Marketing experimentation is a set of rules and procedures according to which the task of data gathering is organised so as to expedite analysis and interpretation. In experimentation, an *independent variable* is manipulated and the resulting changes are measured in a *dependent variable*.

- Experiments may take place in *laboratory settings*, which provide maximum control over influential factors, or in *field settings*, which are preferred when marketers want experimentation to take place in 'real world' environments, such as with *home placements* and *diary tests*.

- To apply research findings to decision-making, marketers must tabulate, analyse and interpret their findings properly. *Statistical interpretation* is analysis of data that focuses on what is typical or what deviates from the average. After interpreting their research findings, researchers must prepare a report of the findings that the decision-makers can use and understand. Information provided by a single firm is called *single-source data*.

- The *marketing information system (MIS)* is a framework for the day-to-day managing and structuring of information regularly gathered from sources both inside and outside an organisation. The inputs into a marketing information system include the information sources inside and outside the organisation considered useful for future decision-making. They may include internal databases. Processing information involves classifying it and developing categories for meaningful storage and retrieval. Marketing decision-makers then determine which information – the output – is useful for making marketing decisions. Feedback enables those who are responsible for gathering internal and external data to adjust the information inputs systematically.

- A *marketing decision support system (MDSS)* is customised computer software that aids marketing managers in decision-making. Some decision support systems have a broader range and offer greater computational and modelling capabilities than spreadsheets, allowing managers to explore a greater number of alternatives.

- Growth of the Internet, and especially the World Wide Web, has launched an entire industry that is working to make market information easily accessible to both marketing businesses and customers. Companies can also mine their own websites for useful information, subscribe to on-line services, and join 'mailing lists' that periodically deliver electronic newsletters to their computer screens so that they can participate in on-screen discussions with thousands of network users.

» Marketing managers and other professionals are relying more and more on marketing research, marketing information systems and new technologies to make better decisions. Professional standards are needed to judge the reliability of such research. These enable ethical and legal issues associated with data gathering to be handled.

## *Key Links*

This chapter has concentrated on the marketing research tools available to capture information about markets and customers. It should be read in conjunction with:

- Chapter 2's examination of the nature of opportunity analysis and the importance of analysing competitors
- Chapters 6 and 7, reviewing the required insights into buying behaviour
- Chapter 8's discussion of how to create market segments from an understanding of customers, and how best to develop a brand positioning strategy.

## Important Terms

Marketing research
Marketing intelligence
Quantitative research
Qualitative research
Intuition
Scientific decision-making
Problem definition
Research design
Research objective
Hypothesis
Exploratory research
Descriptive research
Causal research
Reliability
Validity
Primary data
Secondary data
Syndicated data services
Population
Sample
Sampling
Probability sampling
Random sampling
Stratified sampling
Area sampling
Quota sampling
Survey methods
Mail surveys
Mail panels
Consumer purchase diaries
Telephone surveys
Computer-assisted telephone interviewing
On-line survey
Personal interview survey
Depth interview
Focus group interview
Quali-depth interviews
In-home interview
Shopping mall/pavement intercept interviews
On-site computer interviewing
Questionnaire
Observation methods
Mechanical observation devices
Experimentation
Independent variable
Dependent variable
Laboratory settings
Field settings
Home placements
Diary tests
Statistical interpretation
Marketing information system (MIS)
Single-source data
Marketing decision support system (MDSS)

## Discussion and Review Questions

1. What is the MIS of a small organisation likely to include?
2. What is the difference between marketing research and marketing information systems? In what ways do marketing research and the MIS overlap?
3. What are the differences between quantitative and qualitative marketing research?
4. How do the benefits of decisions guided by marketing research compare with those of intuitive decision-making? How do marketing decision-makers know when it will be worthwhile to conduct research?
5. Give specific examples of situations in which intuitive decision-making would probably be more appropriate than marketing research.
6. What are the differences between exploratory, descriptive and causal research?
7. What are the major limitations of using secondary data to solve marketing problems?
8. List some of the problems of conducting a laboratory experiment on respondents' reactions to the taste of different brands of beer. How would these problems differ from those of a field study of beer taste preferences?

9 In what situation would it be best to use random sampling? Quota sampling? Stratified or area sampling?
10 Suggest some ways to encourage respondents to cooperate in mail surveys.
11 What are the benefits of the focus group technique?
12 Give some examples of marketing problems that could be solved through information gained from observation.
13 Why is questionnaire design important? Why should questionnaires be tested?
14 What is 'sugging'? Why is it damaging to the marketing research industry?

## Recommended Readings


- Birn, R., *The Effective Use of Market Research* (London: Kogan Page, 1999).
- Chisnall, P.M., *Marketing Research* (Maidenhead: McGraw-Hill, 2001).
- McQuarrie, E.F., *The Market Research Toolbox: A Concise Guide for Beginners* (London: Sage, 1996).
- Malhotra, N.K. and Birks, D.F., *Marketing Research: An Applied Approach* (Harlow: FT Prentice Hall, 2002).
- Tull, D.S. and Hawkins, D.I., *Marketing Research* (New York: Macmillan, 1993).


## Internet Exercise

The World Association of Opinion and Marketing Research Professionals (ESOMAR, founded as the European Society for Opinion and Marketing Research in 1948) is a non-profit association for marketing research professionals. ESOMAR promotes the use of opinion and marketing research to improve marketing decisions in companies worldwide and works to protect personal privacy in the research process. Visit the association's website at:
www.esomar.nl/

1 How can ESOMAR help marketing professionals conduct research to guide marketing strategy?
2 How can ESOMAR help marketers protect the privacy of research subjects when conducting marketing research in other countries?
3 ESOMAR introduced the first professional code of conduct for marketing research professionals in 1948. The association continues to update this document to address new technology and other changes in the marketing environment. According to ESOMAR's code, what are the specific professional responsibilities of marketing researchers?

## *Applied Mini-Case*

Advances in information technology, especially in terms of data storage and processing capacity, have made available an ever-growing quantity of data about customer buying behaviour. To extract from this mound of data potentially useful information to guide marketing decisions, marketers are developing methods of mining data. Data mining refers to the discovery of patterns hidden in databases that have the potential to contribute to marketers' understanding of customers and their needs. Data mining employs computer technology to extract data from internal and external sources; translate and format the data; analyse, substantiate, and assign meaning to data; organise databases; and build and implement decisions support systems to make data mining results accessible to decision-makers.

### *Question*

Adopt the role of a retail analyst who is helping a large retail group to organise its databases. You have been asked to help guide the process by providing a list of the kind of information that is helpful to a business when making decisions about marketing strategy.

## Case Study

# Focus Group Interviewing: In-depth Views from Group Discussions

Focus group interviews, which are generally informal group discussions about marketing ideas or concepts conducted by a marketer or marketing research business, are used by most major organisations in developing marketing or business plans. In the 1980s, focus group interviewing became one of the most widely practised types of marketing research, expanding from the packaged goods industry into financial services and industrial applications.

However, the function of focus group interviewing is expected to change. Traditionally, companies have relied on focus group interviews to define the input going into quantitative studies, but a new trend is to conduct focus group interviews after tabulating research results, to provide insight into why the results were achieved. The trend is also towards higher costs (the average today is £1400 for 90 minutes and £1900 for an extended, video-recorded group lasting two and a half hours).

Other changes pertain to moderator guides and their reports. The moderator guides will be expected to involve clients in the development process. Their reports will concentrate on providing conclusions that interpret the findings and on making recommendations for action by the client. The reports will also contain fewer actual quotations from individual focus group participants. The post-focus group debriefing techniques are also being altered. The shift is towards disciplined debriefing that asks participants their reactions to the group session. Such debriefing can provide the link between concept development and application, and can serve as a rough check on validity and reliability.

Another new development in focus group interviewing is the use of electronics to offer three-way capabilities. Computerised decision-making software can supplement research findings and consolidate opinions from three different audiences. For example, in healthcare research in a hospital setting, the three audiences would be former patients, medics and employees. The advantages of using electronics include easier scheduling of participating groups and more interaction among the three audiences.

A major UK service retailer was faced with declining sales and two new competitors. In order to re-establish itself as the dominant force in its market, it decided to undertake some in-depth qualitative marketing research using focus groups. The retailer's new competitors were opening stores at the rate of six per month, and the company realised it had to act quickly to defend its position. However, it had conducted no consumer research for many years and was uncertain why its customers preferred its stores, how competitors were perceived and what types of people constituted its customer profile. Before modifying its marketing mix and launching an advertising campaign to combat its new competitors, the company had to gain a better understanding of its target market. For approximately £14,000 (1989), using a specialist consumer qualitative agency, in just three weeks the company managed to get a good 'feel' for its standing in its core trading area, as perceived by customers. The table shows that the information resulted from a fairly 'standard' programme of focus groups.

Each group had eight consumers, four of whom were shoppers in the retailer's stores and four of whom shopped in competitors' stores. Each group

| Group Composition | Social Class | Location |
|---|---|---|
| 1 Male 25–39, white-collar commuters† | A, B | Eastcheap |
| 2 Male 40–55, white-collar commuters | A, B | Hitchin |
| 3 Female 25–44, executives/PAs | A, B, C1 | Bristol |
| 4 Female 25–44, semi-skilled | C2 | Woking |
| 5 Female 35–40 'housewives'† | A, B | Leamington |
| 6 Female 25–34, 'housewives' | C1, C2 | Sheffield |
| 7 Male 18–29, young earners† | C1, C2 | Ealing |
| 8 Female 18–29, young earners | C1, C2 | Telford |

†Held in branches after hours

session lasted three hours, and a free merchandise voucher and buffet meal were provided for participants. The same moderator ran all eight groups to maintain consistency. Each session was tape recorded, the tapes being transcribed later into a report and presentation to the retailer's board of directors. Two sessions were video recorded, and several were 'secretly viewed' by the company's marketing executives.

**Sources:** Lynne Cunningham, 'Electronic focus groups offer 3-way capability', *Marketing News*, 8 January 1990, pp. 22, 39; Thomas L. Greenbaum, 'Focus group spurt predicted for the '90s', *Marketing News*, 8 January 1990, pp. 21, 22; Nino DeNicola, 'Debriefing sessions: the missing link in focus groups', *Marketing News*, 8 January 1990, pp. 20, 22; Peter Jackson, *Adsearch*, Richmond, 1989 and 2004.

## Questions for Discussion

1. What are the strengths and benefits of focus group marketing research?
2. This retailer chose to commission a programme of focus groups. Given the aims of the company's research, what other research tools might the company have used? Explain your selection.

# Postscript

Academics and practitioners define marketing as involving the understanding and satisfying of customers. It is not possible to accomplish these requirements without a sound understanding of buying behaviour, the processes involved and the associated influencing factors. Accordingly, Part II of *Marketing: Concepts and Strategies* has presented a comprehensive examination of the nature of consumer buying behaviour and then business-to-business buying behaviour.

Part II built on understanding customers' buying behaviour by examining one of the principal elements of marketing strategy: target market selection. The concept of market segmentation is of paramount importance to effective marketing. Over time, marketers develop knowledge of their markets. Many marketing decisions are based on this experience and on the intuition of the managers concerned. Frequently, though, marketers recognise that they do not fully understand their customers, competitors or aspects of the marketing environment forces. In such instances, they conduct marketing research. The nature and use of marketing research have also been discussed in Part II of *Marketing: Concepts and Strategies*.

Before progressing, readers should be confident that they are now able to do the following.

## Describe consumer buying behaviour

- What are the types of consumer buying behaviour?
- What are the stages of consumer buying decision-making?
- How do personal, psychological and social factors influence this decision-making?
- Why should marketers understand consumer buying behaviour?

## Describe business-to-business buying behaviour

- What are the types of organisational markets?
- What are the characteristics of business-to-business buyers and transactions?
- What are the attributes of business-to-business demand?
- What is the buying centre?
- Why are relationships so important in business markets?
- What are the stages of the business buying decision process?
- How can business-to-business markets be selected and analysed?
- What are the nuances of business products?

## Explain the process of target market selection

- Why is target market selection so important?
- What is the definition of a market?
- What types of market are there?
- How do marketers determine market segments?
- How do companies choose which market segments to target?
- What is the role of positioning in the target market process?

## Outline the core aspects of marketing research and marketing information systems

- What is the importance of research and information systems in marketing?
- What distinguishes intuition from marketing research?
- What are the five steps of the marketing research process?
- What are the main methods for gathering data for marketing research?
- What are the relative merits of these various tools and techniques?
- To understand how tools such as databases, decision support systems and the Internet facilitate marketing research
- To identify key ethical considerations in marketing research

Strategic Case

# Reebok
# Reebok Races into the Urban Market

Reebok's UK founder produced some of the first ever running shoes with spikes, as athletes in the late 1890s wanted to run even faster. In 1924, J.W. Forster & Sons was making by hand the running shoes used in the 1924 Summer Games, as depicted in the hit film *Chariots of Fire*. In 1958, two of the founder's grandsons started a sister company called Reebok, named after a type of African gazelle. By 1979, three running shoe styles were introduced to the USA: at US$60 per pair, they were the most expensive on the market. In 1982, Reebok caught the market unawares with the launch of Freestyle, the first ever athletic shoe designed specifically for women. By the 1980s, Reebok was a publicly quoted company active in more than 170 countries. Continual product innovation and customer research gave the company leadership in most of its key target markets.

Step Reebok followed in 1989, a totally revolutionary workout programme that led to millions of users across the globe. By 1992 the company was broadening its ranges to include footwear and clothing products linked to many sports. These moves were supported with major sponsorship deals linked with leading sports stars, teams and sporting events. Venus Williams is one of the latest Reebok stars.

Recently, Reebok has again transformed the way in which people train, with the creation of Core Training, based on a board that tilts, twists, torques and recoils with the body's movements. In 2002, Reebok launched the Rbk brand for street-inspired clothing and footwear, aimed at young men and women who expect the style of their gear to reflect the attitude of their lives – cool, edgy, authentic and aspirational.

Reebok wants to give front-runner Nike a run for its money in the race for market share in athletic footwear, clothing and equipment. Reebok, now based in Massachusetts, USA, gained speed from the 1980s into the early 1990s by marketing special aerobics shoes for women, before Nike pulled ahead with new clothing and equipment endorsed by high-profile athletes such as Michael Jordan and Tiger Woods. Nike has remained the market leader, completely outdistancing all competitors to dominate the industry with a 35 per cent share of the market. In contrast, Reebok's market share is about half that of Nike's; and Reebok's US$3.5 billion in annual sales are about a third of the figure for Nike. Now Reebok is seeking to close the gap by changing its selection of target markets. In the process, Reebok is aiming to change consumers' perceptions of and attitudes towards its brand and its products, with the objective of boosting both sales and profits.

## Breaking Tradition with Hip-hop

Traditionally, manufacturers of athletic shoes have captured market attention by signing successful or up-and-coming sports stars to promote their shoes. Reebok still likes to link its brand to popular sports and individual champions. The fierce rivalry with Nike continues on the playing field: Reebok has lucrative contracts to make branded hats for the US National Basketball Association (NBA) and to supply the US National Football League (NFL) with uniforms and equipment, while Nike has an exclusive contract to provide performance wear to all 30 Major League Baseball teams. Many other sports around the world are similarly supported by Reebok and Nike, including stadia, teams and individual players.

Looking beyond sports, Reebok's marketers investigated the urban market, where fashion, rather than performance, is the deciding factor in buying decisions. Urban teens tend to be extremely style-conscious, buying as many as ten pairs of athletic shoes a year so they can be seen in the very latest thing. In the States, many are also fans of hip-hop music and buy clothing designed by hip-hop celebrities such as Jay-Z, Sean 'P. Diddy' Combs and Russell Simmons. Reebok's marketing research confirmed this market's considerable buying power and the influence of hip-hop artists. To reach this market effectively, Reebok needed a new brand, new products and new promotional efforts: the Reebok brand did not have a suitably desirable image with this youth market in any of the company's principle countries of operation. First, the company took the focus off its mainstream Reebok brand by creating Rbk as a new brand specifically for the urban market. Next, it partnered with hip-hop artists such as Jay-Z and 50 Cent to develop special footwear collections, backed by targeted promotional efforts emphasising style with attitude.

## New Street Credibility

Reebok found it was tapping into a significant marketing opportunity. Soon after it introduced its soft leather, flat-soled S. Carter shoes – after Jay-Z's original name, Shawn Carter – the line sold out. Demand for the US$100 shoes quickly peaked, leading to eager buyers bidding up to US$250 for one pair on the eBay auction website. Within eight months, the company had shipped 500,000 pairs to retailers around the USA and was preparing to launch a second S. Carter shoe.

On the back of this success, Reebok introduced G-Unit footwear, named after a hit song by rapper 50 Cent, who says that 'Reebok's Rbk Collection is the real thing when it comes to connecting with the street and hip-hop culture.' Hip-hop's Eve was also asked to design a shoe. 'She is one of the first artists in the campaign who has male and female appeal, urban and suburban,' observed Reebok's director of global advertising; 'she is as much a fashion icon as a music icon'.

The company also found a way to bring sports and hip-hop together by launching the 13 Collection line of shoes by basketball star Allen Iverson. Iverson promoted the line by appearing in a series of fast-paced adverts filmed in rap video style. Although he was shown playing basketball for a second or two, the adverts focused more on his off-court style than his on-court technique.

Despite the added credibility that such celebrities bring to the Rbk brand, the strategy entails some risks. Fads in street fashion and music can come and go at a dizzying pace, which means a shoe that is 'red hot' on one day may be 'ice cold' the next. Reebok could also suffer from negative repercussions if one of its celebrities runs into trouble. Still, the company's chief marketing executive is committed to the strategy. 'With athletes, they wear the shoes for the length of a basketball season,' he comments. 'With hip-hop, the publicity is intense but short, just like movies.' The advantage, in his view, is that, 'you'll know very quickly whether you hit or miss'.

## Targeting Urban Markets in China

In pursuit of growth, Reebok is also targeting promising global markets, with China high on its list of priorities. Interest in sports is skyrocketing in China, thanks in part to Chinese basketball star Yao Ming's move to the NBA. According to the company's research, 93 per cent of Chinese males aged 13–25, a prime market for athletic shoes, watch NBA broadcasts on a regular basis. Reebok's Asia Pacific general manager cites one projection showing 50 per cent annual growth in footwear sales, stating that, 'it's hard to say what the [actual sales] numbers are going to be, but they are going to be huge'. China's successes at the 2004 Olympics in Athens merely fuelled market growth.

To make the most of this opportunity, Reebok has set up 'Yao's House' basketball courts around central Shanghai. Each features the Reebok trademark and a giant *Sports Illustrated* cover showing the basketball star. By giving teens and young adults a place to hone their slam-dunks, Reebok hopes to shape their attitudes towards its products. 'The trends [in China] are made in the urban areas and on street basketball courts, just like in the United States,' says one Reebok executive. Reebok is not the only athletic shoe manufacturer entering this market. Nike sponsors a basketball court in Beijing, New Balance is building awareness of its shoes, and Pony is selling sneakers in Beijing, Shanghai and Guandong. With the Summer Olympics coming to Beijing in 2008, sports fever is likely to spread throughout the major cities.

## Reebok's New 'Vector'

Nike has one of the most recognised trademarks in the world and now Reebok has its Vector, a streamlined trademark designed to communicate the brand's attributes in a fast and fun way. The idea is to make the Vector synonymous with Reebok, just as the Swoosh is synonymous with Nike. 'Our research suggests that consumers react better to logos than words, and it's a very effective marketing tool,' stresses Reebok's head of marketing.

In addition, the company is giving its brand a touch of glamour with 'showcase stores' in major cities. In New York City, for example, Reebok opened a new men's store right next to its women's store. Both feature footwear, clothing and accessories, and both share the building with the Reebok Sport Club/NY. The displays are as stylish as the products, showing a mix of cashmere sweaters, jackets, wristwatches and sunglasses along with shoes. 'We want people to say, "I didn't know Reebok made that",' notes Reebok's director of retailing. CEO Paul Fireman sums things up by saying, 'The ultimate thing we are striving for is not brand recognition, but how people perceive us'.

## Questions for Discussion

1. What segmentation variables is Reebok using for its products? Why are these variables appropriate?
2. Which of the three targeting strategies is Reebok applying? Explain.
3. What influences on the consumer buying decision process appear to have the most impact on Reebok's customers' purchase decisions?
4. In terms of segmentation and buying behaviour, explain the meaning of this statement by a Reebok executive: 'The trends are made in the urban areas and on street basketball courts, just like in the United States.'

# III Product, Branding, Packaging and Service Decisions

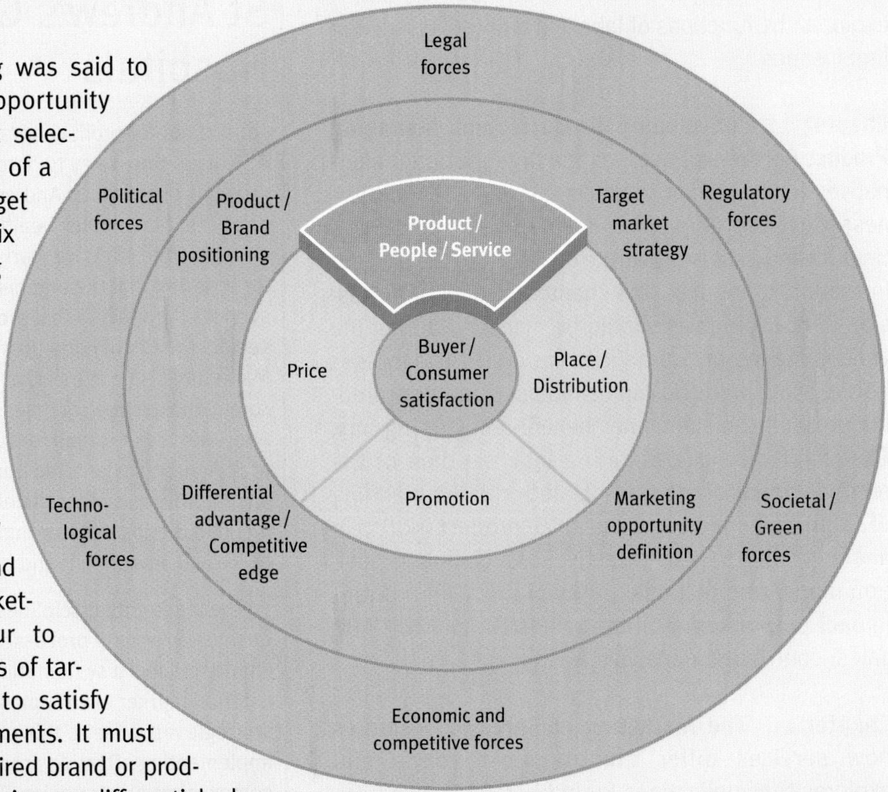


In Chapter 1, marketing was said to involve marketing opportunity analysis, target market selection and the development of a marketing mix for each target market. The marketing mix is the set of marketing programme activities deployed by marketing managers in order to implement a company's agreed marketing strategy. The marketing mix centres on the '5Ps' of product, people, place/distribution, promotion and pricing decisions. The marketing mix must endeavour to match the identified needs of target customers in order to satisfy these customers' requirements. It must also communicate the desired brand or product positioning and emphasise any differential advantage held by a business and its products over its rivals. As explained in Chapters 1 and 2, marketers should first analyse the forces of the marketing environment, customer buying behaviour, competitors' strategies and their own organisational capabilities before developing their marketing strategies. The marketing mix for a specific target market segment should only be specified once the marketing strategy has been formulated and agreed by senior management.

**Part III of *Marketing: Concepts and Strategies*** examines the product and people ingredients of the marketing mix, the integral issues of branding, packaging and customer service, as well as the important concepts of the product life cycle and the management of product portfolios.

**Chapter 10, 'Product Decisions'**, introduces the concepts of how marketers define and classify products; examines the differences between product item, product line and product mix; and explores the important concept of the product life cycle. The chapter then discusses organisational structures available to manage products, and concludes by examining the importance of the levels of a product in determining a competitive edge over rivals' products.

**Chapter 11, 'Branding and Packaging'**, recognises the fundamental importance of brands and brand equity in marketing, and looks at different types of brand, their benefits, selection, naming, protection and licensing. In most organisations, marketers are the champions of the brand; the chapter presents the key concepts for creating strong and effective brands. The chapter goes on to discuss the functions of packaging, design considerations and the role of packaging in marketing strategy. Finally, it explores the functions of labelling and the associated legal issues.

**Chapter 12, 'Developing Products and Managing Product Portfolios'**, outlines the organisational alternatives for managing products, explains how a business develops a product idea into a commercial product and analyses the role of product development in the marketing mix. The chapter includes a discussion of how products should be managed during the various stages of a product's life cycle. It discusses how existing products can be modified and how product deletion can sometimes benefit a marketing mix. The chapter concludes with a look at some of the related analytical tools associated with the planning of a product portfolio: the BCG product portfolio analysis, the market attractiveness–business position model or directional policy matrix (DPM), Profit Impact on Marketing Strategy (PIMS), and the ABC sales: contribution analysis.

**Chapter 13, 'The Marketing of Services'**, explores how services differ from tangible goods and explores the implications for marketers. The chapter begins by explaining the nature and characteristics of services, classifying services and the development of marketing strategies for services. It goes on to discuss the significant problems encountered in developing a differential advantage for a service and also addresses the crucial concept of service quality. The chapter then explores the concept of marketing in non-business situations, the development of marketing strategies in non-business organisations and methods for controlling non-business marketing activities. The ways in which marketers handling services manipulate the ingredients of the marketing mix are explored further in Part VII.

By the conclusion of Part III of *Marketing: Concepts and Strategies*, readers should understand the core product decisions that must be made in determining a marketing mix, including branding, packaging, people and service issues, as well as the management of product life cycles and portfolios of products.

## St Andrew's Group of Hospitals

As a not-for-profit charitable healthcare provider, marketing is key to determining the charity's strategic direction. St Andrew's Group of Hospitals operates in a complex healthcare market environment and therefore effective marketing planning is essential for ensuring that the organisation delivers clinical services ('products') that are required by the healthcare sectors the Charity operates in, at affordable prices. Marketing also ensures that St Andrew's effectively communicates the core messages about what the St Andrew's brand stands for to its key stakeholders. Part of St Andrew's charitable purpose is to develop new and improved services. An effective analysis of their markets is critical to making sure that the charity makes successful investment and new service decisions.

The marketing discipline drives St Andrew's business planning processes by ensuring that the charity follows a systematic approach to analysing its external market environment; determining a sensible strategic response to this environment; and implementing effective promotional and communication strategies. The marketing planning approach provides a common framework and language, for both clinical and commercial staff, to review the Hospital's clinical services and make well-informed decisions about where the charity should be investing in future services in order to best meet its charitable objectives.

**James Watkins, group director of strategic development and marketing, St Andrew's Group of Hospitals**

St Andrew's Group of Hospitals is the UK's leading charitable provider of specialist mental health, learning disabilities and acquired brain injury services, working in partnership with the NHS in serving these patient groups.

# 10
# Product Decisions

**"Developing great new products is not just about great ideas. It's about transforming them into products and services that customers want, that competitors have difficulty in copying and that exploit the strengths of the company."**

*Susan Hart, University of Strathclyde*

## Objectives

- To learn how marketers define products
- To define product levels
- To understand how to classify products
- To become familiar with the concepts of product item, product line and product mix
- To understand the concept of product life cycle
- To understand the types of organisational structure used to manage products
- To grasp the importance of the levels of a product in determining a competitive edge

## Introduction

The product is defined as everything that is received in an exchange, whether favourable or unfavourable. It is a complexity of tangible and intangible attributes, including functional, social and psychological utilities or benefits.[1] A product can be a physical good, a service, an idea, or any combination of these three. This definition also covers supporting services that go with goods, such as installation, guarantees, product information and promises of repair or maintenance.

The product is a key element of the marketing mix and is central to a company's marketing proposition. Without the 'right' product it is unlikely that marketers will be able to satisfy their customers and persuade them to become repeat buyers. As will be explored in this chapter, there is much more to the product component of the marketing mix than the actual tangible product or the service supplied to a customer.

A successful product will not remain so indefinitely. Marketers must judge when to modify their products, launch new ones and delete existing – perhaps once highly successful – products.

*Opener*

# Smelly Fabrics!

Ambrosia, Apple, Bouquet, Coffee, Cola, Eau de Cologne, Fiji, Forest, Lavender, Lemon, Lime, Orange, Peppermint, Pineapple, Pizza, Rose, Strawberry, Tropical Paradise, Vanilla, Wild Flowers, Floral Bouquet, Jasmine and Banana.

What is the connection between these exotic-sounding names? Foods? Paint colours? Brand names? No, the connection is that they are all odours! Courtaulds Textiles, part of Sara Lee, has developed an innovative range of Fragrance Fabrics. The 'micro-encapsulated' scent is 'glued' to the fabric via an acrylic polymer and applied in solution to the fabric during its final production process (known as the 'stenter run'). When the fabric is rubbed, the scent 'capsules' are broken, releasing the fragrance. Staggeringly, after over 30 washes at 40°C, the fragrance is still evident.

The Japanese producers of the micro-capsules have carried out extensive skin-sensitivity tests at the Japanese Laboratory for Cutaneous (Skin) Health. Courtaulds Jersey Underwear Ltd has found ways of 'sticking' the fragrance to 150g cotton single jersey and to 150g cotton/Lycra fabrics. The following are the core fragrances in demand.

- *Lemon* – a refreshing scent, with characteristic uplifting properties, associated with cleansing and the ability to revive the skin.
- *Orange* – a slightly sweet scent, known for its calming qualities.
- *Rose* – the 'queen' of essential oils, associated with beauty, femininity and purity, as well as a relaxed state of mind.
- *Vanilla* – commonly linked with taste, a distinctive smell that is obtained from the pods of a beautiful tropical orchid.
- *Lavender* – a beautiful scent with endearing qualities, encourages restful sleep and has balancing properties; widely used in perfumery and with an oil base to ease muscular aches and pains.
- *Apple and strawberry* – fresh and fruity fragrances that are the essence of a sunny summer.
- *Forest and wild flowers* – mirroring the scents of woodland, two fragrances that combine tranquillity and freshness.

So why the excitement? Well, in fabric development, innovations tend to be based around texture and durability – for example, the stretchy Lycra phenomenon. New product development has rarely been so innovative in this market, and for Sara Lee Courtaulds the result has been a competitive edge over rivals. The main target market is currently users of sportswear: using this new technology, such clothing emits a pleasant odour when the wearer gets hot and sweaty on the squash court or in the gym. However, it's not only overheated sports enthusiasts for whom this new product technology has appeal – it can also be used in the creation of 'intelligent' fabrics, which can detect, for example, when a women is menstruating, and will then release soothing lavender or rose fragrances.

It is likely that, in the next few years, many clothing applications will make use of these micro-encapsulated scents. The task for fabric manufacturers' marketers will be to promote these attributes to the garment makers, whose marketers will need to entice retailers to stock these new lines and consumers to trial these fragrant products.

**Sources:** *Fragrance Fabrics* and *Essential Oils and Their 'Well Being' Qualities*, Courtaulds Jersey Underwear; Courtaulds Textiles, Nottingham.
Photo: Courtesy of Karen Beaulah

**Product**
Everything, both favourable and unfavourable, tangible and intangible, received in an exchange of an idea, service or good

Products such as the Fragrance Fabrics devised by Sara Lee Courtaulds, are among a company's most crucial and visible contacts with buyers. If a company's products do not meet its customers' desires and needs, the company will have to adjust its offering in order to survive. Developing a successful **product** requires knowledge of fundamental marketing and product concepts. Courtaulds' range of Fragrance Fabrics will need to appeal both to garment makers and consumers if it is to achieve long-term success. This chapter starts by introducing and defining the concepts that help clarify what a product is, and looks at how buyers view products. The next section examines the concepts of product mix and product line as an introduction to product planning. The chapter then explores the stages of the product life cycle. Each life-cycle stage generally requires a specific marketing strategy, operates within a certain competitive environment and has its own sales and profit pattern. The final section discusses the elements that make up a product.

# What is a Product?

**Good**
A tangible physical entity

**Service**
The application of human and mechanical efforts to people or objects in order to provide intangible benefits to customers

**Ideas**
Concepts, philosophies, images or issues that provide the psychological stimulus to solve problems or adjust to the environment

A **good** is a tangible physical entity, such as a bottle of Pantene shampoo, a loaf of Hovis bread or a Busted CD. A **service**, by contrast, is intangible; it is the result of the application of human and mechanical efforts to people or objects. Examples of services include hairdressing, tennis tuition and medical treatment. (Chapter 13 provides a detailed discussion of services marketing.) **Ideas** are concepts, philosophies, images or issues. They provide the psychological stimulus to solve problems. For example, Oxfam provides famine relief and attempts to improve the long-term prospects of people in hunger-stricken countries.

When buyers purchase a product, they are really buying the benefits and satisfaction they think the product will provide. A pair of Predator football boots, for example, is purchased for status and image, not just to protect the feet. Services, in particular, are bought on the basis of promises of satisfaction. Promises, with the images and appearances of symbols, help consumers make judgements about tangible and intangible products.[2] Symbols and cues are often used to make intangible products more tangible to the consumer. MasterCard, for example, uses globes to symbolise the company's financial power and worldwide coverage.

# Classifying Products

**Consumer products**
Items purchased to satisfy personal or family needs

**Industrial** or **business products**
Items bought for use in a company's operations or to make other products

Products fall into one of two general categories. **Consumer products** are purchased to satisfy personal and family needs. **Industrial** or **business products** are bought for use in a company's operations or to make other products. The same item can be both a consumer product and an industrial product. For example, when consumers purchase light bulbs for their homes, they are classified as consumer products. However, when a large company purchases light bulbs to provide lighting in a factory or office the same goods are considered industrial products. Thus the buyer's intent, or the ultimate use of the product, determines whether an item is classified as a consumer or an industrial product. It is common for more people to be involved in buying an industrial product than in a consumer purchase. Chapters 6 and 7 explain the differences in buying and decision-making for consumer and business-to-business products.

It is important to know about product classifications because different classes of product are aimed at particular target markets, and classification affects distribution, promotion and pricing decisions. Furthermore, the types of marketing activity and effort needed – in short, the entire marketing mix – differ according to how a product is classified. This section examines the characteristics of consumer and industrial products and explores the marketing activities associated with some of them.

## Consumer Products

The most widely accepted approach to classifying consumer products relies on the common characteristics of consumer buying behaviour. It divides products into four categories:

convenience, shopping, speciality and unsought products. However, not all buyers behave in the same way when purchasing a specific type of product. Thus a single product can fit into more than one category. To minimise this problem, marketers think in terms of how buyers *generally* behave when purchasing a specific item. In addition, they recognise that the 'correct' classification can be determined only by considering a particular company's intended target market.

**Convenience products** Inexpensive, frequently purchased and rapidly consumed items that demand only minimal purchasing effort

**Convenience Products** Relatively inexpensive, frequently purchased and rapidly consumed items on which buyers exert only minimal purchasing effort are called **convenience products**. They range from chocolate, magazines and chewing gum to petrol and soft drinks. The buyer spends little time planning the purchase or comparing available brands or sellers. Even a buyer who prefers a specific brand will readily choose a substitute if the preferred brand is not conveniently available.

Classifying a product as a convenience product has several implications for a company's marketing strategy. A convenience product is normally marketed through many retail outlets. Because sellers experience high inventory turnover, the per unit gross margins can be relatively low. Producers of convenience products such as PG Tips tea and Domestos bleach expect little promotional effort at the retail level and so must provide their own through advertising, sales promotion and the item's packaging. The package may have an especially important role to play, because many convenience items are available only on a self-service basis at the retail level. The use of on-pack sales promotion and point-of-sale displays are ways to maximise the impact of the package.

**Shopping products** Items chosen more carefully than convenience products; consumers will expend effort in planning and purchasing these items

**Shopping Products** Items that are chosen more carefully than convenience products are called **shopping products**. They are purchased infrequently and are expected to last a long time. Buyers are willing to expend effort in planning and purchasing these items. They allocate time for comparing stores and brands with respect to prices, credit, product features, qualities, services and perhaps guarantees. Appliances, furniture, bicycles, stereos, jewellery and cameras are examples of shopping products. Even though shopping products are more expensive than convenience products, few buyers of shopping products are particularly brand loyal. If they were, they would be unwilling to shop and compare brands.

Marketers seeking to market shopping products effectively must consider that they require fewer retail outlets than convenience products. Because they are purchased less frequently, inventory (stock) turnover is lower and middlemen (retailers) expect to receive higher gross margins. Although large sums of money may be required to advertise shopping products, an even larger proportion of resources is likely to be used for personal selling. Indeed, the quality of the service may be a factor in the consumer's choice of outlet. Thus a couple that buys a new dishwasher might expect sales personnel in the chosen retail outlet to explain the advantages and features of competing brands. In many cases, the producer and the middlemen also expect some cooperation from one another with respect to providing parts and repair services, and performing promotional activities.

**Speciality products** Items that possess one or more unique characteristic; consumers of speciality products plan their purchases and will expend considerable effort to obtain them

**Speciality Products** Products that possess one or more unique characteristic and which a significant group of buyers is willing to expend considerable effort to obtain are called **speciality products**. Buyers plan the purchase of a speciality product carefully; they know exactly what they want and will not accept a substitute. An example of a speciality product is a painting by L.S. Lowry or a Cartier watch. When searching for speciality products, buyers do not compare alternatives; they are concerned primarily with finding an outlet that has a preselected product available.

The marketing of a speciality product is very distinctive. The exclusivity of the product is accentuated by the fact that speciality products are often distributed through a limited number of retail outlets. Some companies go to considerable lengths to control this aspect

*Figure 10.1*
*Confectionary brands are convenience products*
*Photo © Ashley Cooper/CORBIS*

of their distribution. Like shopping goods, speciality products are purchased infrequently, causing lower inventory turnover and thus requiring relatively high gross margins.

**Unsought products**
Items that are purchased when a sudden problem arises or when aggressive selling is used to obtain a sale that would not otherwise take place

**Unsought Products** Products that are purchased when a sudden problem arises or when aggressive selling obtains a sale that otherwise would not take place are called **unsought products**. The consumer does not usually expect to buy these products regularly. Emergency windscreen replacement services and headstones are examples of unsought products. Life insurance is an example of an unsought product that often needs aggressive personal selling.

## Business or Industrial Products

Business products are usually purchased on the basis of a company's goals and objectives. The functional aspects of these products are usually more important than the psychological rewards sometimes associated with consumer products. Business products can be classified into seven categories according to their characteristics and intended uses:

1 raw materials
2 major equipment
3 accessory equipment
4 component parts
5 process materials
6 consumable supplies
7 industrial/business services.[3]

**Raw materials**
The basic materials that become part of physical products

**Raw Materials** The basic materials that become part of physical products are **raw materials**. These include minerals, chemicals, agricultural products, and materials from forests and oceans. They are usually bought and sold in relatively large quantities according to grades and specifications.

**Major equipment**
Large tools and machines used for production purposes

**Major Equipment** Large tools and machines used for production purposes, such as cranes and spray painting machinery, are types of **major equipment**. Major equipment is often expensive, may be used in a production process for a considerable length of time and is often custom-made to perform specific functions. For example, Alsthom manufactures purpose-built large gears and turbines. Other items are more standardised, performing similar tasks for many types of company. Because major equipment is so expensive, purchase decisions are often long and complex, and may be made by senior management. Marketers of major equipment are frequently called upon to provide a variety of services, including installation, training, repair, maintenance assistance and financing. This may lead to long-term relationships being developed between suppliers of major equipment and their customers.

**Accessory equipment**
Tools and equipment used in production or office activities that do not become part of the final physical product

**Accessory Equipment** Equipment that does not become a part of the final physical product, but is used in production or office activities is referred to as **accessory equipment**. Examples include telephone systems, stationery supplies, fractional horsepower motors, and tools. Compared with major equipment, accessory items are usually much cheaper, are purchased routinely with less negotiation and are treated as expenditure items rather than capital items because they are not expected to last long. More outlets are required for distributing accessory equipment than for major equipment, but sellers do not have to provide the multitude of services expected of major equipment marketers.

**Component parts**
Parts that become a part of the physical product and are either finished items ready for assembly or products that need little processing before assembly

**Component Parts** Parts that become part of the physical product and are either finished items ready for assembly or products that need little processing before assembly are called **component parts**. Although they become part of a larger product, component parts can often be easily identified and distinguished. Tyres, spark plugs, gears, lighting units, screws and wires are all component parts of a delivery van. Buyers purchase such items according to their own specifications or industry standards. They expect the parts to be of specified quality and delivered on time so that production is not slowed or stopped. Producers that are primarily assemblers, such as most washing machine or lawnmower manufacturers, depend heavily on suppliers of component parts.

**Process materials**
Materials used directly in the production of other products, but not readily identifiable

**Process Materials** Materials that are used directly in the production of other products are called process materials. Unlike component parts, however, **process materials** are not readily identifiable. For example, Reichhold Chemicals markets a treated fibre product: a phenolicresin, sheet-moulding compound used in the production of flight deck instrument panels and aircraft cabin interiors. Although the material is not identifiable in the finished aircraft, it retards burning, smoke and formation of toxic gas when subjected to fire or high temperatures.

**Consumable supplies**
Supplies that facilitate production and operations but do not become part of the finished product

**Consumable Supplies** Supplies that facilitate production and operations but do not become part of the finished product are referred to as **consumable supplies**. Paper, pencils, oils,

**MRO items**
Consumable supplies in the subcategories of maintenance, repair and operating (or overhaul) supplies

**Industrial/business services**
The intangible products that many businesses use in their operations, including financial, legal, marketing research, computer programming and operation, caretaking and printing services

**Core product**
The level of a product that provides the perceived or real core benefit or service

**Actual product**
A composite of the features and capabilities offered in a product, quality and durability, design and product styling, packaging and brand name

**Augmented product**
Support aspects of a product, including customer service, warranty, delivery and credit, personnel, installation and after-sales support

cleaning agents and paints are in this category. They are purchased by many different types of business. Consumable supplies are purchased routinely and sold through numerous outlets. To ensure that supplies are available when needed, buyers often deal with more than one seller. Consumable supplies can be divided into three subcategories – maintenance, repair and operating (or overhaul) supplies – and are sometimes called **MRO items**.

**Industrial/Business Services** **Industrial/Business Services** are the intangible products that many businesses use in their operations. They include financial, legal, marketing research, computer programming and operation, caretaking and printing services for business. Some companies decide to provide their own services internally, while others outsource them. This decision depends largely on the costs associated with each alternative and the frequency with which the services are needed.

# The Three Levels of Product

The product may appear obvious – a carton of fresh orange juice or a designer handbag – but generally the purchaser is buying much more than a drink or a means of carrying personal items. To be motivated to make the purchase, the product must have a perceived or real core benefit or service. This level of product, termed the **core product**, is illustrated in Figure 10.2. The **actual product** is a composite of several factors: the features and capabilities offered, quality and durability, design and product styling, packaging and, often of great importance, the brand name.

In order to make the purchase, the consumer often needs the assistance of sales personnel; there may be delivery and payment credit requirements and, for bulky or very technical products, advice regarding installation. The level of warranty back-up and after-sales support, particularly for innovative, highly technical or high value goods, will be of concern to most consumers. Increasingly, the overall level of customer service constitutes part of the purchase criteria, and in many markets it is deemed integral to the product on offer. These 'support' issues form what is termed the **augmented product** (see Figure 10.2).

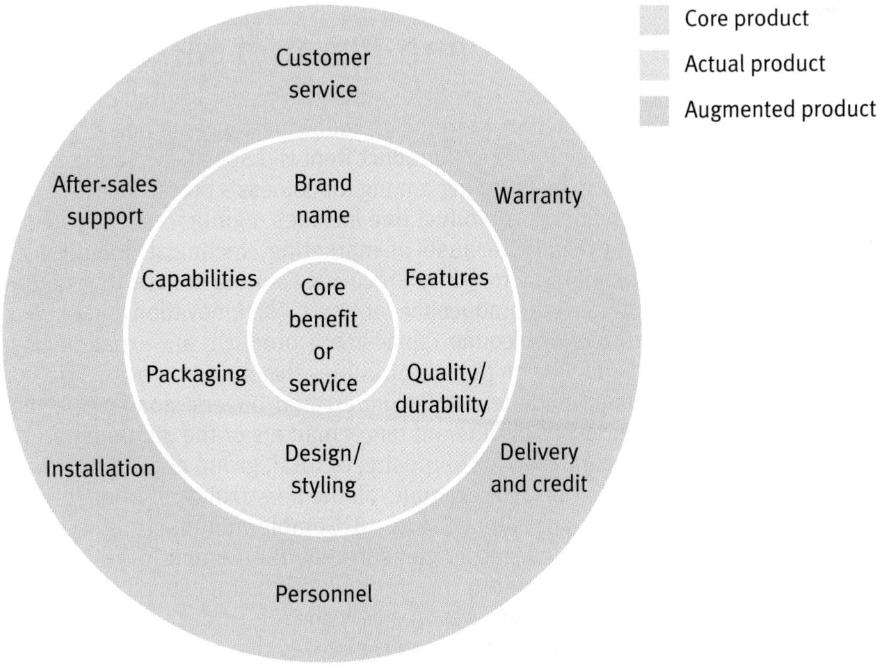


*Figure 10.2*
*The three levels of product: core, actual and augmented*

When a £25,000 BMW 3 Series executive car is purchased, the vehicle's performance specification and design may have encouraged the sale. Speed of delivery and credit payment terms may have been essential to the conclusion of the deal. The brand's image, particularly in the case of a car costing £25,000, will also have influenced the sale. Once behind the wheel of the BMW, its new owner will expect reliability and efficient, friendly, convenient service in the course of maintenance being required. The purchase might have been lost at the outset had the salesperson mishandled the initial enquiry. Repeat servicing business and the subsequent sale of another new car may be ruled out if the owner encounters incompetent, unhelpful service engineers. The core benefit may have been a car to facilitate journeys to work, transport for the family or the acquisition of a recognised status symbol. Customer satisfaction will depend on the product's actual performance and also on service aspects of the augmented product. This example is not unusual. For most consumer or business products and services, the consumer is influenced by the three levels of the product: core, actual and augmented. Marketers need to take this into consideration when developing product offers. Careful consideration of all levels of the product can provide the basis for a competitive edge. Several years ago BP launched an environmentally friendly diesel fuel with 90 per cent reduced emissions. This coincided with increasing environmental awareness among customers and provided a benefit at the augmented product level. Soon all rivals were offering similar clean diesels. This illustrates how businesses must increasingly strive to consider all product levels when developing their offerings.[4]

Many marketers now recognise the important role that personnel play in product exchanges. People are responsible for the design, production, marketing, sale and distribution of products. As will be explained in Chapter 13, personnel are especially important in the sale and delivery of services. Thus, a financial services adviser must have considerable expertise in the sector to give good advice. Similarly, a good-quality haircut can only be delivered by a skilled hairdresser. As consumers, people make decisions and ultimately adopt products for use and consumption. When deciding which products to adopt and use, people now pay considerable attention to the skills, attitudes and motivations of personnel involved in the marketing channel. As explained in Chapter 1, personnel also constitute an essential ingredient of the marketing mix for consumer and business goods.

**Product item**
A specific version of a product that can be designated as a distinct offering among a business's products

**Product line**
A group of closely related product items that are considered a unit because of marketing, technical or end-use considerations

**Product mix**
The composite group of products that a company makes available to customers

**Depth** (of product mix)
The number of different products offered in each product line

**Width** (of product mix)
The number of product lines a company offers

## Product Line and Product Mix

Marketers must understand the relationships between all their business's products if they are to coordinate their marketing. The following concepts describe the relationships between an organisation's products. A **product item** is a specific version of a product that can be designated as a distinct offering among a business's products – for example, Procter & Gamble's Pantene shampoo. A **product line** includes a group of closely related product items that are considered a unit because of marketing, technical or end-use considerations. All the shampoos manufactured by Procter & Gamble constitute one of its product lines. Figure 10.3 illustrates the product line for Hovis. The Innovation and Change box below explains how manufacturers of nicotine replacement products are expanding their product line to allow them to capitalise on the opportunities this market provides. To come up with the optimum product line, marketers must understand buyers' goals.[5] Specific items in a product line reflect the desires of different target markets or the different needs of consumers.

A **product mix** is the composite, or total, group of products that a company makes available to customers. For example, all the personal care products, laundry detergent products and other products that Procter & Gamble manufactures constitute its product mix. The **depth** of a product mix is measured by the number of different products offered in each product line. The **width** of a product mix is measured by the number of product lines a company offers. Figure 10.4 shows the width of the product mix and the depth of each product line for selected Procter & Gamble products in the USA. Procter & Gamble is

# Innovation and Change

## A New Generation of Nicotine Replacement Products

Nicotine replacement therapy (NRT) fights nicotine dependence and relieves the symptoms of withdrawal in smokers who are trying to give up. Leading brands include Nicotinell, NiQuitin CQ and Nicorette. Novartis, the company behind Nicotinell nicotine replacement gum and patches, also launched food products designed to help smokers quit the habit. Many consumers are already familiar with the Nicotinell brand. As smoking becomes increasingly socially unacceptable, the company now believes that there are a variety of new product development opportunities for its brand. Novartis launched a nicotine replacement lozenge that, when sucked, provides a continual, low-level boost of nicotine for relatively light smokers. Other initiatives include the possible development of nicotine-enhanced food and a detoxification programme for ex-smokers. Supportive counselling services are viewed as a key part of the therapy, and most of the leading players have examined how to offer such services alongside their patches, gums, pills and lozenges.

It is not difficult to understand the attractions of the nicotine replacement therapy market and to appreciate why Novartis is seeking to extend its product offerings. As millions seek to leave their smoking habit behind, the market for nicotine replacement products is growing rapidly. Indications also show that 1 in 20 of those attempting to 'kick the habit' will use some form of nicotine replacement therapy. Not surprisingly, Novartis is not alone in seeking to develop its product range. Since NRT products were first launched in the UK a decade ago, several companies have dominated the market: Novartis, with its Nicotinell patch and gum; Pharmacia & Upjohn (P&U), with its Nicorette gum, inhalator and patches; and Boots, with its own-label patches and gum. Recent developments include Boots' inhalator and competing brand Nicorette's launch of its micro-tab, a kind of nicotine pill that, when placed under the tongue, takes half an hour to dissolve.

Perhaps the most aggressive challenge to the market has come from pharmaceutical giant SmithKline Beecham (SKB), which spent £12 million on the UK launch of NiQuitin CQ (CQ stands for 'committed quitters'). SKB claimed this to have been the largest ever over-the-counter launch in the UK. Clearly the company expected the brand, already the best-seller in the USA, to claim a large slice of the UK market. Company representatives suggested that this was achieved by the unique 'personalised literature pack' included with the NiQuitin CQ product. This pack includes a questionnaire for smokers to fill in, detailing the circumstances in which they are most vulnerable to lighting up. Advice is then offered that is tailored to match the answers provided in the questionnaire. According to Elaine MacFarlane, SKB's director of consumer healthcare communications, this represented a unique approach in the NRT market. She explains, 'When these products first launched, they were positioned as a magic bullet – "take this and you won't want to smoke". Now with all the noise from the political, health and economic perspectives, you know it doesn't make sense to smoke any more, and we felt the time was right for a more mature consideration of people's motivation'.

In such a volatile market, future trends are difficult to predict. When NRT products were first launched in the UK in 1993, they were met with considerable consumer excitement. However, following an initial growth in sales, consumer confidence in the capabilities of the products declined. Today, with the products widely available in supermarkets as well as pharmacies, and governments throughout the EU considering bans on smoking in public places and other anti-smoking measures, the key players are looking for innovative ways to ensure that their products play a major role in the continued fight against smoking. New product development is likely to be just part of the solution, with manufacturers also seeking a fresh and more realistic promotional stance. For Novartis, with the slogan 'Helps you stop smoking', this involves repositioning the brand to stress its role in harm reduction and Nicotinell's role in supporting the quitter's willpower and resolve to stop smoking. With smokers over 35 years old as the key target, and the biggest increase in new smokers among those in their early teens and twenties, the market potential is considerable. Time will tell whether Novartis and the other players continue to meet the challenge.

**Sources:** Novartis Consumer Healthcare, 2004; Neil Denny, 'Smokers may be offered nicotine food to help quit', *Marketing*, 28 January 1999, p. 1; Sue Beenstock, 'Queuing up to quit', *Marketing*, 28 January 1999, p. 1; www.Nicotinell.com, June 2004; www.mypharmacy.co.uk/medicines/topics/n/nicotine_replacement_therapy, June 2004.

*Figure 10.3*
*This advertisement for leading bread brand Hovis makes clear that the Hovis line includes more than the familiar Hovis brown loaf*
*Source: All work created by Star Chamber*

known for using distinctive technology, branding, packaging and consumer advertising to promote individual items in its detergent product line. Tide, Bold and Cheer – all Procter & Gamble detergents – share similar distribution channels and manufacturing facilities. Yet due to variations in product formula and attributes, each is promoted as distinct, adding depth to the product line.

**Product life cycle**
The four major stages through which products move: introduction, growth, maturity and decline

## Product Life Cycles

Just as biological cycles progress through growth and decline, so too do **product life cycles**. A new product is introduced into the marketplace; it grows; it matures; and when it loses appeal and sales decline, it is terminated.[6] As explained in Chapter 12, different marketing

Product line depth (vertical axis) / Product mix width (horizontal axis)

| Laundry detergents | Toothpastes | Bar soaps | Deodorants | Shampoos | Tissue/towel |
|---|---|---|---|---|---|
| Ivory Snow 1930 | Gleem 1952 | Ivory 1879 | Old Spice 1948 | Head & Shoulders 1961 | Charmin 1928 |
| Dreft 1933 | Crest 1955 | Camay 1926 | Secret 1956 | Pantene Pro 1965 | Puffs 1960 |
| Tide 1946 | | Zest 1952 | Sure 1972 | Vidal Sassoon 1974 | Bounty 1965 |
| Cheer 1950 | | Safeguard 1963 | | Pert Plus 1979 | Royale 1996 |
| Bold 1965 | | Olay 1993 | | Ivory 1983 | |
| Gain 1966 | | | | | |
| Era 1972 | | | | | |

*Figure 10.4*
*The concepts of width of product mix and depth of product line applied to selected Procter & Gamble products*
*Source: information provided and reprinted by permission of the Procter & Gamble Company, Public Affairs Division, 1 Procter & Gamble Plaza, Cincinnati, OH 45202-3315*

strategies are appropriate at different stages in the product life cycle. Thus packaging, branding and labelling techniques can be used to help create or modify products that have reached different points in their life.

As Figure 10.5 shows, a product life cycle has four major stages:

1 introduction
2 growth
3 maturity
4 decline.

When a product moves through its cycle, the strategies relating to competition, promotion, place/distribution, pricing and market information must be evaluated periodically and possibly changed. Astute marketing managers use the life-cycle concept to make sure that the introduction, alteration and termination of a product are timed and executed properly. By understanding the typical life-cycle pattern, marketers are better able to maintain profitable products and drop unprofitable ones.

## Introduction

**Introduction stage**
A product's first appearance in the marketplace, before any sales or profits have been made

The **introduction stage** of the life cycle begins at a product's first appearance in the marketplace, when sales are zero and profits are negative. Profits are below zero because a new product incurs development costs, initial revenues are low, and at the same time a company must generally incur the significant expenses incurred during promotion and distribution. As time passes, sales should move upwards from zero and profits should build up from the negative position (see Figure 10.5).[7]

Because of cost, very few product introductions represent major inventions. Developing and introducing a new product can mean an outlay of many millions of pounds. The failure rate for new products is quite high, ranging from 60 to 90 per cent depending on the industry and on how product failure is defined. For example, in the food and drinks industry, 80 per cent of all new products fail. Typically, however, product introductions involve a new deodorant, a new type of vacuum cleaner or a new leisure concept rather than a major product innovation. In general, the more marketing-oriented the company, the more likely it will be to launch innovative products that are new to the market.[8]

New product ideas are more likely to be successful when senior management is involved in product development and launch. In addition, research shows that a clear, stable vision, flexibility and improvisation, information exchange and collaboration are also key ingredients in new product success.[9]

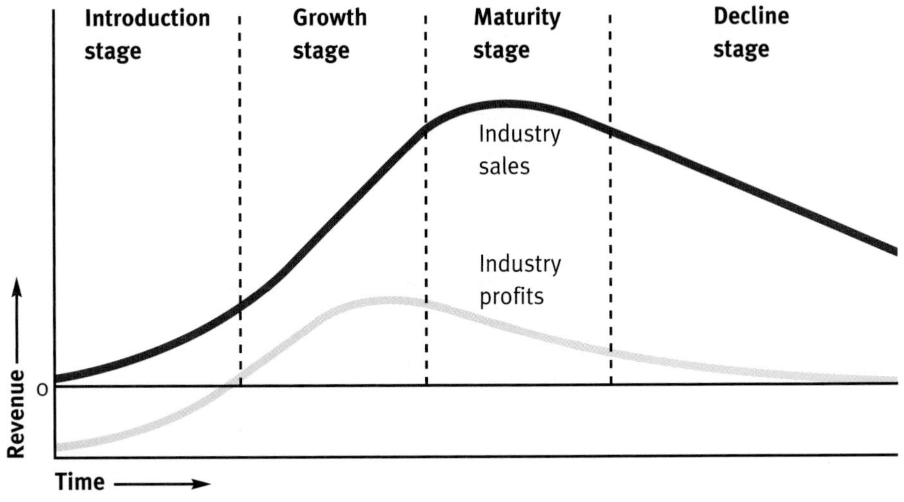


*Figure 10.5*
*The four stages of the product life cycle*

Potential buyers must be made aware of the new product's features, uses and advantages. Two difficulties may arise at this point. Only a few sellers may have the resources, technological knowledge and marketing know-how to launch the product successfully; and the initial product price may have to be high in order to recoup expensive marketing research or development costs. Given these difficulties, it is not surprising that many products never get beyond the introduction stage; indeed many are never launched commercially at all.

## Growth

**Growth stage**
The stage at which a product's sales rise rapidly and profits reach a peak, before levelling off into maturity

During the **growth stage**, sales rise rapidly, and profits reach a peak and then start to decline (see Figure 10.5). The growth stage is critical to a product's survival because competitive reactions to its success during this period will affect the product's life expectancy. For example, Mars successfully launched Ice Cream Mars, the first ice-cream version of an established confectionery product. Today the product competes with more than a dozen other brands. Some of the competing brands failed quickly and others followed. Profits decline late in the growth stage as more competitors enter the market, driving prices down and creating the need for heavy promotional expenses. At this point a typical marketing strategy encourages strong brand loyalty, perhaps using sales promotion, and competes with aggressive emulators of the product. During the growth stage, a company tries to strengthen its market share and develop a competitive position by emphasising the product's benefits.

Aggressive promotional pricing, including price cuts, is typical during the growth stage. The Internet industry is now well into its growth stage, and many competitors have entered the market. Companies like AOL must battle hard to maintain their existing positions in this competitive arena.

## Maturity

**Maturity stage**
The stage during which a product's sales curve peaks and starts to decline, and profits continue to decline

During the **maturity stage**, the sales curve peaks and starts to decline, and profits continue to decline (see Figure 10.5). This stage is characterised by severe competition, with many brands in the market. Competitors emphasise improvements and differences in their versions of the product. Inevitably, during the maturity stage, some weaker competitors are squeezed out or switch their attention to other products. For example, some brands of DVD player are perishing now that the product is reaching the maturity stage.

During the maturity stage, the producers who remain in the market must make fresh promotional and distribution efforts. These efforts must focus on dealers as much as on consumers to ensure that brand visibility is maintained at the point of sale. Advertising and dealer-oriented promotions are typical during this stage of the product life cycle. The promoters must also take into account the fact that, as the product reaches maturity, buyers' knowledge of it attains a high level. Consumers of the product are no longer inexperienced generalists, but rather experienced specialists.

## Decline

**Decline stage**
The last stage of a product's life cycle, during which sales fall rapidly

During the **decline stage**, sales fall rapidly (see Figure 10.5). New technology or a new social trend may cause product sales to take a sharp downturn. When this happens, the marketer must consider pruning items from the product line to eliminate those not earning a profit. Sony recently surprised the market by announcing it would be pulling out of selling PDAs. The decision came because Sony believes that technology changes are signalling a move away from handheld organisers towards multifunctional mobile phones.[10] At this time, too, the marketer may cut promotion efforts, eliminate marginal distributors and, finally, plan to phase out the product.

Because most businesses have a product mix consisting of multiple products, a company's destiny is rarely tied to one product. A composite of life-cycle patterns is formed when various products in the mix are at different stages in the cycle. As one product is declining, other products are in the introduction, growth or maturity stage. Marketers must deal with the dual problems of prolonging the life of existing products and introducing new products to

meet sales goals. More details of this kind of portfolio management activity are given in Chapter 12, which also explores the development of new products and considers how they can be managed in their various life-cycle stages.

## Why Some Products Fail and Others Succeed

Thousand of new products are introduced each year and many of them fail. Some estimates put the product failure rate as high as 60 to 90 per cent. Failure and success rates vary in different industries and from company to company. Figures suggest that consumer products are more likely to fail than those directed at business markets. Being one of the first brands launched in a product category is no guarantee of success. One study found that in 50 product categories, only half of the pioneers survived.[11]

Products fail for many reasons. One of the most common is the company's failure to match product offerings to customer needs. When products do not offer value and lack the feature customers want, they fail in the marketplace. Ineffective or inconsistent branding has also been blamed for product failures. Other reasons often given for new product failure include technical or design problems, poor timing, overestimation of market size, ineffective promotion and inefficient distribution. The problems leading to the downfall of Coca-Cola's UK launch of bottled water Dasani were widely debated in the press. Technical difficulties led to bromide contamination at the company's plant. At a time when consumers were already concerned about the purity of tap water, the withdrawal of the product was inevitable.[12] For Cadbury Trebor Bassett's 24-7 chewing gum, failure was blamed on distribution problems and lack of in-store support.[13]

### Degrees of Product Failure

It is important to distinguish between degrees of product failure. Absolute failure occurs when a company loses money on a new product because it is unable to recover development, production and marketing costs. Such a product is usually deleted from the product mix. Relative product failure occurs when a product returns a profit but does not meet a company's profit or market share objectives. If a relative product failure is repositioned or improved, it may become a successful member of the product line. Some products experience relative product failure after years of success. Drinks business Diageo recently stepped in to stem declining sales of Guinness stout. Part of this effort involved reformulating the canned version of the drink, to make its taste closer to that of draught Guinness. The cans were also redesigned to appeal to a younger segment of drinkers. As the Topical Insight box on page 308 explains, Guinness has been looking at various ways to reinvigorate its brand.

## The Ingredients for Success

Despite this gloomy picture of product failure, some new products are very successful. Perhaps the most important ingredient for success is the product's ability to provide a significant and perceivable benefit to a sizeable number of customers. New products with an observable advantage over similar available products – such as more features, ease of operation or improved technology – have a greater chance of success.

## Tangible and Intangible Product Characteristics

When developing products, marketers make many decisions. Some of these involve the tangible, or physical, characteristics of the product; others focus on less tangible support services that are very much a part of the total product.

## Topical Insight

### Old Brands Battle the Effects of Ageing

Guinness and Kit-Kat have something in common. They are both well-established brands that have attracted considerable customer support over the lengthy relationship they have enjoyed with different generations of consumers. Yet these well-loved brands are also facing crisis. Diageo's Guinness has seen UK sales decline by 3 per cent, with a net fall in sales of 1 per cent in the second half of December 2003. In Ireland, the brand's domestic market, the sales fall reached 7 per cent during the same period. Meanwhile Nestlé's Kit-Kat is also struggling, with UK sales declining by 5.4 per cent in just 12 months.

So what are the reasons for this malaise? According to the former executive chairman of The Henley Centre, 'The trouble with most mature brands is that they are being marketed to a population that is changing rapidly.' The challenge for both brands is to continue to communicate strongly with their loyal customer base, while doing more to reflect the needs of potential new customers.

For Guinness, there is a positive side to figures for the brand: the stout's global fortunes appear to be on the ascendant, with a 3 per cent increase in volume. So what has gone wrong in the UK and Ireland? Some believe that the brand's marketing may be partly to blame for the decline. During its 75 years of advertising, Guinness developed a reputation for innovative campaigns, many of which achieved iconic status. This started in 1929, with the now famous 'Guinness is good for you' strapline. Soon afterwards, in 1935, the toucan was featured for the first time on advertising posters. Initially the plan had been to use a pelican. The idea was to run a 'Guinness-a-day' theme (building on the 'Guinness is good for you' concept). The plan was to feature an image of a pelican with seven pints positioned along its beak. In the event, a toucan was substituted and an appropriate verse was written to accompany the advertising:

'If he can say as you can  
Guinness is good for you  
How grand to be a toucan  
Just think what toucan do'

The toucan was finally retired in 1982. Other high-profile campaigns, such as the 'Pure Genius' advertising, followed. However, recent advertising executions, including the 'moth' advertisement, which features young people leaving a car in a dark forest to follow a cloud of moths towards the light coming from a Guinness bar, have been criticised as uninspiring. Other industry experts suggest that the Guinness brand has been diluted by confusing innovations. Product extension Guinness Extra Cold, which some argue flies in the face of the warmth associated with traditional Guinness, has been pinpointed as one culprit. Now Diageo wants to battle the effects of the mature stage of Guinness's life cycle, by focusing on its heritage as a status brand, and is backing up this strategy with a range of new advertising initiatives.

**Sources:** 'Guinness in facelift as volume dips', *Marketing Week*, 20 May 2004, p. 8; Sonoo Singh, 'Struggling to keep up', *Marketing Week*, 20 May 2004, pp. 24–7; www.thetoucan.co.uk.

## Physical Characteristics and Product Quality

**Quality**
The core product's ability to achieve the basic functional requirements expected of it

The question of how much **quality** to build into the product is crucial for marketers. In the core product, quality constitutes the product's ability to achieve the basic functional requirements expected of it. A major dimension of quality is durability. Higher quality often demands better materials and more expensive processing, which increases production costs and, ultimately, the product's price. How much the target market is prepared to pay will affect the level of quality specified. The concepts of quality and value are related. A consumer may be happy to pay a premium for a hard-wearing paint, because they perceive it as better value than competing offerings. In general, a company should set consistent quality levels for all products with a similar brand. The quality of competing brands is also an important consideration. As explained in Chapter 9, marketing research plays an important role in determining the optimum physical features – such as quality – of a product.

## Supportive Product-related Services

All products possess intangible features. When prospective customers are unable to experience the product in advance, they are making decisions based on promises of satisfaction.[14] A woman buying lingerie over the Internet hopes that when the garments she ordered arrive, they will meet her expectations of quality, look and fit. Should she be disappointed, she will expect to be able to return the items. Arrangements for product returns are just one of many product-related services. Others include product guarantees, credit and repair facilities. Although these product features may be less tangible than the product itself, they are often a strong influence on the choices that customers make. Can you imagine buying a watch with no guarantee, or a television that cannot be repaired?

**Guarantee**
An agreement specifying what the producer or supplier will do if the product malfunctions

The type of guarantee a company provides can be critical for buyers, especially when expensive, technically complex goods such as appliances are involved. A **guarantee** specifies what the producer or supplier will do if the product malfunctions. Photographic processors such as SupaSnaps offer free processing on prints not ready within 24 hours. Guarantors are legally required to state more simply and specifically the terms and conditions under which the company will take action. For example, changes in EU law now require electrical items to carry a two-year guarantee. Marketers are now using guarantees more aggressively as tools to give their brands a competitive advantage.

An effective guarantee should be unconditional, easy to understand and communicate, meaningful, easy to invoke, and quick and easy to act on. The customer should be able to return a product and get a replacement, a refund or a credit for the returned item. Such guarantees are beneficial because they generate feedback from customers and help build customer loyalty and sales.[15] Although it is more difficult to provide guarantees for services than for goods, some service marketers do guarantee customer satisfaction. For example, some photo labs that offer a one-hour photograph development service do not charge customers who have to wait longer than this time.

Establishing a system to provide replacement parts and repair services is an essential support service for complex and expensive consumer or business products. For example, builders expect construction machinery manufacturers like Caterpillar to be able to provide replacement parts quickly and without fuss. Sometimes these services are provided directly to buyers, in other cases regional service centres or middlemen are used.

Finally, a company must sometimes provide credit services to customers. Even though credit services place a financial burden on a business, they can be beneficial. For instance, a company may acquire and maintain a stable market share. Many major oil companies, for example, have competed effectively against petrol discounters by providing credit services. For marketers of relatively expensive items, such as cars or soft furnishings, offering credit services enables a larger number of people to buy the product, thus enlarging the market for the item.

# Summary

A *product* is everything, both favourable and unfavourable, that is received in an exchange. It is a complex set of tangible and intangible attributes, including functional, social and psychological utilities or benefits. A product can be a *good*, a *service*, an *idea* or any combination of these three. Consumers buy the benefits and satisfaction they think the product will provide.

» Products can be classified on the basis of the buyer's intentions. *Consumer products* are purchased to satisfy personal and family needs. *Industrial* or *business products* are purchased for use in a company's operations or to make other products. The same product may be classified as both a consumer product and a business product. Consumer products can be subdivided into *convenience*, *shopping*, *speciality* and *unsought products*. Business products can be divided into *raw materials, major equipment*, *accessory equipment*, *component parts, process materials, consumable supplies (MRO items)* and *business services*.

» It is important to remember that a product has three levels: core, actual and augmented. The purchaser buys a core benefit or service (the *core product*) in addition to the product's brand name, features, capabilities, quality, packaging and design (the *actual product*). Increasingly, aspects of the *augmented product* are important considerations for purchasers of consumer goods, services and business goods. Warranties, delivery and credit, personnel, installation, after-sales support and customer service are integral to the actual product's appeal and perceived benefits. The role of personnel in particular is of fundamental concern to marketers; people and customer service now form a central part of the marketing mix.

» A *product item* is a specific version of a product that can be designated as a distinct offering among a business's products. A *product line* is a group of closely related product items that are a unit because of marketing, technical or end-use considerations. A company's total group of products is called the *product mix*. The *depth* of a product mix is measured by the number of different products offered in each product line. The *width* of the product mix is measured by the number of product lines a company offers.

» The *product life cycle* describes how product items in an industry move through four major stages: (1) *introduction stage*, (2) *growth stage*, (3) *maturity stage* and (4) *decline stage*. The life-cycle concept is used to make sure that the introduction, alteration and termination of a product are timed and executed properly. The sales curve is at zero on introduction, rises at an increasing rate during growth, peaks at maturity and then declines. Profits peak towards the end of the growth stage of the product life cycle. The life expectancy of a product is based on buyers' wants, the availability of competing products and other environmental conditions. Most businesses have a composite of life-cycle patterns for various products. It is important to manage existing products and develop new ones to keep the overall sales performance at the desired level.

» Thousands of new products are introduced each year and many of them fail. Some estimates put the product failure rate as high as 60 to 90 per cent. Failure and success rates vary in different industries and from company to company. Products fail for many reasons: because of a failure to match product offerings to customer needs, ineffective or inconsistent branding, technical or design problems, poor timing, over-estimation of market size, ineffective promotion and inefficient distribution.

» It is important to distinguish between degrees of product failure. Absolute failure occurs when a company loses money on a new product because it is unable to recover development, production and marketing costs. Relative product failure occurs when a product returns a profit but does not meet a company's profit or market share objectives.

» Despite this gloomy picture of new product failure, some new products are very successful. Perhaps the most important ingredient for success is the product's ability to provide a significant and perceivable benefit to a sizeable number of customers.

» When creating products, marketers must take into account other product-related considerations, such as physical characteristics and less tangible support services. Specific physical product characteristics that require attention are the level of quality and product features, such as textures, colours and sizes. Support services that may be viewed as part of the total product include guarantees, repairs/replacements and credit.

## Key Links

This chapter has given an overview of the product element of the marketing mix.

- It must be read in conjunction with Chapter 12, which examines how marketers manage portfolios of products.
- For those involved in marketing services, there are additional considerations, as discussed in Chapters 13 and 22.
- Marketers, in certain circumstances, have to manipulate their marketing mixes, including the product element, as explored in Chapter 22.

## Important Terms

Product
Good
Service
Ideas
Consumer products
Industrial or business products
Convenience products
Shopping products
Speciality products
Unsought products
Raw materials
Major equipment
Accessory equipment
Component parts
Process materials
Consumable supplies
MRO items
Industrial/business services
Core product
Actual product
Augmented product
Product item
Product line
Product mix
Depth
Width
Product life cycle
Introduction stage
Growth stage
Maturity stage
Decline stage
Quality
Guarantee

## Discussion and Review Questions

1. List the tangible and intangible attributes of a spiral notebook. Compare the benefits of the spiral notebook with those of an intangible product such as life insurance.
2. A product has been referred to as a 'psychological bundle of satisfaction'. Is this a good definition of a product?
3. Is a roll of carpet in a shop a consumer product or a business product? Defend your answer.
4. How do convenience products and shopping products differ? What are the distinguishing characteristics of each type of product?
5. Would a music system that sells for £500 be a convenience, shopping or speciality product?
6. In the category of business products, how do component parts differ from process materials?
7. How does a company's product mix relate to its development of a product line? When should a company add depth to its product lines rather than width to its product mix?
8. How do industry profits change as a product moves through the four stages of its life cycle?
9. What is the relationship between the concepts of product mix and product life cycle?
10. What factors must marketers consider when deciding what quality level to build in to a product? What support services can be offered to back up product quality?
11. What are aspects of the augmented product for a new car?
12. Why is the augmented product increasingly important when determining a differential advantage?

## Recommended Readings


- M. Baker and S. Hart, *Product Strategy and Management* (Harlow: Pearson/FT, 1998).
- A. Craig and S. Hart, 'Where to now in new product development research?', *European Journal of Marketing*, vol. 26, no. 11, 1992, pp. 1–49.
- D. Lehmann, and R. Winer, *Product Management* (Boston, Mass.: McGraw-Hill, 2001).
- G. Rifkin, 'Product development: the myth of short life cycles', *Harvard Business Review*, vol. 72, no. 4, 1994, p. 11.
- P. Trott, *Innovation Management and New Product Development* (Harlow: Pearson/FT, 2002).
- Y.J. Wind, *Product Policy: Concepts, Methods and Strategy* (Reading, Mass.: Addison-Wesley, 1982).

## Internet Exercise

**Goodyear Tyres**

In addition to providing information about the company's products, Goodyear's website helps customers find the exact products they want and will even direct them to the nearest Goodyear retailer. Visit the Goodyear site at: www.goodyear.com

1 How does Goodyear use its website to communicate information about the quality of its tyres?
2 How does Goodyear's website demonstrate product design and features?
3 Based on what you learned at the website, describe what Goodyear has done to position its tyres.

## *Applied Mini-Case*

The Volkswagen Golf has hit 30! Now VW is celebrating the launch of the fifth generation of the model, which seems to have defied middle age and maintained its status as a trendy brand. An advertising campaign accompanying the launch charts the development of the Golf through its three decades of life. The creative work highlights the changing design and features of the car over time. This illustrates VW's decision to continually upgrade the Golf, rather than replace it with a different model.

**Source:** Samuel Solley, 'VW plays on Golf's heritage with evolutionary approach', *Marketing*, 25 March 2004, p. 9.

### *Question*

Several years from now you have secured a job as brand manager for the Golf. Assume that VW is about to make a decision about whether to launch a new generation of the Golf or replace it with a new model with a new name. Prepare a report arguing in support of one of these options. You should explore the arguments for and against each option.

## *Case Study*

# Heineken's Portfolio of Brands

Heineken is Europe's largest brewer. While around half of its sales are European, worldwide Heineken is second only to US-based Anheuser-Busch. Heineken beer is recognised around the globe. With a presence in more than 175 countries and more than 80 per cent of sales originating outside the domestic Dutch market, Heineken has been described as the most international beer brand. However, there is more to the company than the single Heineken brand. While some rivals have tackled the global market with a strategy of focusing only on international premium beer brands, Heineken has adopted a tiered approach, with strong international premium brands such as Amstel and Heineken; dominant national brands rarely seen outside their respective countries; plus a raft of speciality beers.

Despite its activities in the USA, Latin America, Africa, South-east Asia and Asia, Heineken recognises the significance of its strength in Europe – a particularly important market, which accounts for over 40 per cent of world beer sales. Here, despite the mass appeal of the Heineken brand, to stay ahead of the competition the company has to adjust its product mix to suit the needs of different countries, fitting in with local cultures and tastes. In general, Heineken achieves this goal by offering a portfolio of three core brands in each European country:

1 a local brand, aimed at the standard and largest market segment. In Italy this is Dreher, in France '33' and in Spain Aguila Pilsener
2 a brand targeted at the 'upper' end of the market; sometimes this is a locally produced brand, such as the Spanish Aguila Master, in other cases a newer Heineken brand, Amstel, is preferred
3 the Heineken brand itself, aimed at the premium market segment; the beer offered may be manufactured locally or it may be exported from the Netherlands; either way, the Dutch head office works hard to maintain product quality and brand image.

Chairman Thony Ruys believes that it is the proven combination of the Heineken brand with local mainstream brands that creates the successful level of distribution in the market and adequate economies of scale in production. Heineken has a share in over 60 brewing companies around the globe to help facilitate this strategy. The company also keeps up with trends, including Murphy's, iced beers and non-alcoholic brews such as Buckler.

Branding policy in the UK differs slightly from that implemented in other parts of Europe. The standard Heineken brand in the UK is a lower-strength version of the beer offered in Europe. The lower-strength lager first became popular in pubs across the UK in the 1960s. With the increasing sophistication of the UK beer drinker, the company introduced the Heineken Export Strength brand – more closely related to the 'standard' Heineken offered throughout Europe.

Currently, significant growth is evident in the company's sales in Italy, Poland, Spain, France and the Far East. Sales of Heineken in the premium segment are rising at around 6 per cent per annum, while Amstel's sales are rising at close to 2 per cent per annum. Sales of Amstel Light are more sluggish. No brewer has secured strong market positions in as many countries, Heineken is proud to state, and no individual beer brand is as successful in as many countries as the Heineken brand. Heineken is market leader in Austria, Romania, Hungary, Poland, Slovakia, Bulgaria and Macedonia, illustrating the company's identification some time ago of the growing commercial opportunities in eastern Europe. The new additions to the EU, and Russia, are currently priority targets. Outside Europe, the focus for growth is on the east coast of North America, North Africa, China, Vietnam, Chile and Argentina.

**Sources:** www.Heineken.com, 2004; Caroline Farquhar, Warwick MBA, 1991–92; 'The Netherlands trade review – the beverage market', Economic Intelligence Unit, *Marketing in Europe*, no. 347, October 1991, p. 36; Heineken annual report and accounts, 1991, 1994 and 1996; David Benardy, 'Heineken Euro '96 plot', *Marketing Week*, 23 February 1996, p. 7; Nina Munk, 'Make mine Hoegaarden', *Forbes*, 18 December 1995, pp. 124–6; Havis Dawson, 'Brand brewing', *Beverage World*, October 1995, pp. 50–60; 'Heineken stresses sponsorship in marketing non-alcoholic beer', *Crossborder Monitor*, 11 January 1995, p. 9; Thony Ruys, Heineken, 2003.

### Questions for Discussion

1 Why was the UK's version of Heineken lager weaker than its counterpart in the rest of Europe? What problems has this product variation caused Heineken?
2 Why does Heineken opt for a mix of internationally known brands marketed alongside local beers?
3 In what ways is Heineken continuously updating its product portfolio and its marketing mix?

# 11

# Branding and Packaging

"**Brands are at the very heart of marketing. When a company creates a strong brand it attracts customer preference and builds a defensive wall against competition.**"

*Peter Doyle, formerly of Warwick Business School*

## Objectives

- **To recognise the importance of brands and brand equity**
- **To understand the types and benefits of brands and how to select, name, protect and license them**
- **To appreciate the best practice guidelines for creating strong brands**
- **To examine the roles of brand attributes, brand values and brand personality in brand development**
- **To understand the role of branding at the corporate level**
- **To become aware of the major packaging functions and packaging design considerations**
- **To consider the ways in which packaging is used in marketing strategies**
- **To examine the functions of labelling and the legal issues associated with labelling**

## Introduction

Effective marketing requires product or service differentiation. Differentiation entails product design, features and attributes, customer service, branding and the other ingredients of the marketing mix. Branding is seen as a core activity of a company's marketing function.

Brands enable customers to readily identify their favoured products and marketers to more easily communicate their advantages. Marketers invest vast sums in persuading targeted customers to prefer their products over and above those supplied by competitors, as they strive to create brand loyalty. Effectively creating a well-differentiated and memorable image for the brand is a core requirement for a marketing-oriented organisation.

Brand equity is increasingly important in many boardrooms and results from the financial and marketing value that can be placed on a brand owing to its market position and standing. Brand awareness, brand loyalty, perceived brand quality and brand associations create brand equity. An effective brand has what is termed 'brand strength', and generally marketers will have defined brand attributes, values and personality.

Packaging and labelling are also part of the marketing process. Packaging includes the immediate container (the primary packaging) and the shipping packaging (the secondary packaging). Both need to exhibit functionality in order to protect and convey the product inside, and facilitate its easy use and storage. Additionally, packaging should support the product's branding and differentiation.

Labelling is integral to packaging, but must increasingly conform to regulations and ethical controls. Labelling should be informative, truthful and – to assist in product differentiation – distinctive.

*Opener*

# Polos: No Longer Just in a Tube

At a factory in York, each day a mountain of thumbnail-sized tyre-shaped white mints is deemed slightly imperfect: chipped, broken or improperly moulded. The sight is awe-inspiring, but gives a clue as to the volume of perfectly formed Polo mints manufactured: millions are produced, packaged and shipped daily; 147 Polos are consumed every second, with more than 100 million polo mints eaten every week in the UK alone. Nestlé's take-over of Rowntree assured the world domination of Polo, 'the mint with the hole'.

Polo is the UK's top-selling mint, with sales of £35 million per annum, and has established leadership in many other countries, too. It was not too long before trial flavours and strengths were tested by product developers at Nestlé. However, the end of 1998 saw one of the most successful spin-offs from the original Polo concept: the sugar-free Polo Supermint, for 'instant refreshment'. This was not only a masterful brand extension of the Polo name but also proved to be an inspired packaging execution.

The Polo Supermint from Nestlé has even been awarded 'Millennium Products' status by the Design Council, an accolade reserved for just a few new designs. The new mini-mints 'with the hole' weigh only a tenth of the original, yet contain four times the amount of peppermint oil in relation to their size. This super-strength mint has not only appealed to traditional Polo mint buyers, but has also enabled the brand to compete head to head with the plethora of extra-strong mints produced by rival manufacturers such as Trebor.

The new size and extra-strong Polo would inevitably have caught the eye of confectionery buyers on the back of the Polo heritage and the extensive distribution network established by the mighty Nestlé. Marketers at Nestlé wanted to ensure a successful launch and were determined to make the new item distinctive and appealing in its own right. The innovative packaging design and eye-catching styling of the new item made an immediate impact in a rather crowded marketplace. The Supermints are packed in plastic dispensers, developed by RPC Market Rasen, which are themselves shaped as giant versions of the original and very familiar Polo mint. The pack houses a pop-up hatch that enables it to dispense individual mini-Polos and to be resealed easily. The regular user soon develops the ability to dispense one-handed and in suitable quantities to appease friends also requiring a refreshing treat. The plastic dispenser is itself packaged in a cool blue, square container with eye-catching graphics, permitting easy stocking and shelf displays.

Nestlé says that while the mini-Polos were launched to celebrate the Polo brand's 50th birthday, the new item has emerged as one of the company's greatest successes ever. Nestlé believes this demonstrates that it is possible to innovate with a 50-year-old brand. The new item, though, matched the brand values and positioning of the original Polo mint: an effective brand extension must have an affinity with existing brand values. This, and other related Polo product developments, reflected competitor moves and responded to consumer tastes. With the Polo Supermint, the combination of astute branding and clever packaging has certainly created a very successful product for Nestlé and a welcome alternative for Polo fans. More importantly, the successful brand extension demonstrates that Nestlé's marketers are, rightly, seeking to leverage further sales from this long-term brand, first launched in 1948.

**Sources:** Nestlé Rowntree, York, 1999; One Stop, 2004; *Marketing*, 4 February 1999, p. 22; www.nestle.co.uk, May 2004. Photo © Niall MacLeod/ CORBIS

Brands and packages are part of a product's tangible features, the verbal and physical cues that help customers identify the products they want and influence their purchase choices. For Nestlé's Polo Supermints, branding and packaging have been central to the product's success. A good brand is distinctive and memorable; without one, companies could not differentiate their products and shoppers' choices may, essentially, be arbitrary. A good package design is cost effective, safe, environmentally responsible and valuable as a promotional tool.

This chapter first defines branding and explains its benefits to customers and sellers; it then examines the importance of brand equity, brand attributes, values and personality, strong brands and the various types of brand. The next section explores how companies choose brands, how they protect them, the various branding policies that companies employ, and brand licensing. The chapter goes on to discuss how businesses manage brands and how they ensure that they contribute effectively to a company's fortunes. Packaging is then the focus, as part of the product and how it is marketed: the functions of packaging, issues to consider in packaging design, packaging development and how the package can be a major element in marketing strategy. After considering criticisms of packaging, the chapter concludes with a brief discussion of labelling.

## Branding

Most marketers believe a key focus for their activity is the differentiation of their product proposition vis-à-vis competing products and services. For many consumer, service or business products, such differentiation entails a mix of product design, features and attributes with the creation of a distinctive image. This generally involves creating a brand and brand identity for products or services. Indeed, without distinctive branding, many service products in particular would struggle to differentiate themselves against rivals (see Chapter 13).

In addition to making decisions about actual products, as described in Chapter 10, marketers must make many decisions associated with branding, such as brands, brand names, brand marks, trademarks and trade names. A **brand** is a name, term, design, symbol or any other feature that identifies one seller's good or service as distinct from those of other sellers. A brand may identify one item, a family of items or all items of that seller.[1] A **brand name** is that part of a brand that can be spoken – including letters, words and numbers – such as Coca-Cola. A brand name is often a product's only distinguishing characteristic. Without the brand name, a company could not identify its products. To consumers, brand names are as fundamental as the product itself. Brand names simplify shopping, guarantee a specific level of quality and allow self-expression. Table 11.1 details the world's most valuable brands. For many marketers, establishing a distinctive brand, which is easily remembered and recognised by targeted customers, is one of the primary activities of effective marketing management.

The element of a brand that is not made up of words but is often a symbol or design is called a **brand mark**. One example is the symbol of a baby on Procter & Gamble's Fairy Liquid detergent. Occasionally, brand marks are modified for local markets. For example, Microsoft tops its brand name with a butterfly in France, a fish in Portugal and a sun in Spain. A **trademark** is a legal designation indicating that the owner has exclusive use of a brand or a part of a brand, and that others are prohibited by law from using it. To protect a brand name or brand mark a company must register it as a trademark with the appropriate patenting office. Finally, a **trade name** is the full and legal name of an organisation, such as Ford Motor Company, rather than the name of a specific product.

**Brand**
A name, term, design, symbol or any other feature that identifies one seller's good or service as distinct from those of other sellers

**Brand name**
That part of a brand that can be spoken, including letters, words and numbers

**Brand mark**
The element of a brand that cannot be spoken – often a symbol or design

**Trademark**
Legal designation indicating that the owner has exclusive use of a brand

**Trade name**
The full and legal name of an organisation

### Benefits of Branding

Branding provides benefits for both buyers and sellers.[2] Brands help buyers identify specific products that they do and do not like, a process that in turn facilitates the purchase of

**TABLE 11.1 WORLD'S MOST VALUABLE BRANDS**

| Rank | Brand | Value (US$ bn) | Country of origin |
|---|---|---|---|
| 1 | Coca-Cola | 70,453 | USA |
| 2 | Microsoft | 65,174 | USA |
| 3 | IBM | 51,767 | USA |
| 4 | GE | 42,430 | USA |
| 5 | Intel | 31,112 | USA |
| 6 | Nokia | 29,440 | Finland |
| 7 | Disney | 28,036 | USA |
| 8 | McDonald's | 24,699 | USA |
| 9 | Marlboro | 22,183 | USA |
| 10 | Mercedes | 21,371 | Germany |
| 11 | Toyota | 20,784 | Japan |
| 12 | Hewlett-Packard | 19,860 | USA |
| 13 | Citibank | 18,571 | USA |
| 14 | Ford | 17,066 | USA |
| 15 | American Express | 16,833 | USA |
| 16 | Gillette | 15,978 | USA |
| 17 | Cisco | 15,789 | USA |
| 18 | Honda | 15,625 | Japan |
| 19 | BMW | 15,106 | Germany |
| 20 | Sony | 13,153 | Japan |
| 21 | Nescafé | 12,336 | Switzerland |
| 22 | Budweiser | 11,894 | USA |
| 23 | Pepsi | 11,777 | USA |
| 24 | Oracle | 11,263 | USA |
| 25 | Samsung Electronics | 10,846 | South Korea |
| 26 | Morgan Stanley | 10,691 | USA |
| 27 | Merrill Lynch | 10,521 | USA |
| 28 | Pfizer | 10,455 | USA |
| 29 | Dell | 10,367 | USA |
| 30 | Merck | 9,407 | USA |

**Sources:** Interbrand; JP Morgan Chase; Citigroup; Morgan Stanley; *The Marketing Pocket Book*, 2004.

items that satisfy their needs and reduces the time required to purchase the product. Without brands, product selection would be quite random, because buyers could have no assurance that they were purchasing what they preferred. Imagine the chaos in a supermarket if every shopper entered not knowing which products and brands to purchase! Research indicates, however, that the bulk of supermarket shoppers are highly brand loyal. So much so, that in-store redesigns and new shelf-space allocations cause significant distress and generate high levels of customer complaints.

A brand also helps buyers evaluate the quality of a product, especially when they are unable to judge its characteristics. In other words, a purchaser for whom a brand symbolises a certain quality level will transfer that perception of quality to the unknown item. A brand thus helps to reduce a buyer's perceived risk of purchase. In addition, it may offer the psychological reward that comes from owning a brand that symbolises status. Certain brands of watches (Rolex) and cars (Rolls-Royce) fall into this category.[3]

Sellers benefit from branding because each company's brands identify its products, which makes repeat purchasing easier for consumers. Branding helps a company introduce a new product that carries the name of one or more of its existing products, because buyers are already familiar with the company's existing brands. For example, Heinz regularly introduces new tinned products. Because consumers are used to buying the brand and have a high regard for its quality, they are likely to try the new offerings. Branding also facilitates promotional efforts because the promotion of each branded product indirectly promotes all other products that are similarly branded.

**Brand loyalty**
A strongly motivated and long-standing decision to purchase a particular product or service

Branding also helps sellers by fostering brand loyalty. **Brand loyalty** is a strongly motivated and long-standing decision to purchase a particular product or service. To the extent that buyers become loyal to a specific brand, the company's market share for that product achieves a certain level of stability, allowing the company to use its resources more efficiently.[4] Loyal customers are highly desirable and much marketing activity is aimed at reassuring existing customers and canvassing their ongoing support and interest. When a company succeeds in fostering some degree of customer loyalty to a brand, it can charge a premium price for the product. For example, brand loyal buyers of Anadin aspirin are willing to pay two or three times more for Anadin than for a generic brand of aspirin with the same amount of pain-relieving agent.

However, brand loyalty is declining, partly because of marketers' increased reliance on discounted sales, coupons and other short-term promotions, and partly because of the sometimes overwhelming array of similar new products from which consumers can choose. In the brand-dominated US, a *Wall Street Journal* survey found that 12 per cent of consumers are not loyal to any brand, whereas 47 per cent are brand loyal for one to five product types. Only 2 per cent of the respondents were brand loyal for more than 16 product types. To stimulate loyalty to their brands, some marketers are stressing image advertising, mailing personalised catalogues and magazines to regular users, and creating membership clubs for brand users, for example, Tesco's ClubCard or Sainsbury's Nectar points. Sometimes consumers make repeat purchases of products for reasons other than brand loyalty. Spurious loyalty is not stable and may result from non-availability of alternative brands or the way in which products are displayed in retail outlets.

There are three degrees of brand loyalty: recognition, preference and insistence.

**Brand recognition**
A customer's awareness that a brand exists and is an alternative to purchase

**Brand Recognition** **Brand recognition** exists when a customer is aware that a brand exists and views it as an alternative to purchase if the preferred brand is unavailable or if the other available brands are unfamiliar to the customer. This is the mildest form of brand loyalty. The word loyalty is clearly being used very loosely here. One of the initial objectives of a marketer introducing a new brand is to create widespread awareness of the brand in order to generate brand recognition. This theme is reconsidered in Part V, on promotion decisions.

**Brand preference**
The degree of brand loyalty in which a customer prefers one brand over competitive offerings

**Brand Preference** **Brand preference** is a stronger degree of brand loyalty in which a customer definitely prefers one brand over competitive offerings and will purchase this brand if it is available. However, if the brand is not available, the customer will accept a substitute brand rather than expend additional effort finding and purchasing the preferred brand. A marketer is likely to be able to compete effectively in a market when a number of customers have developed brand preference for its specific brand.

**Brand insistence**
The degree of brand loyalty in which a customer strongly prefers a specific brand and will accept no substitute

**Brand Insistence** **Brand insistence** is the degree of brand loyalty in which a customer strongly prefers a specific brand, will accept no substitute and is willing to spend a great deal of time and effort to acquire that brand. If a brand-insistent customer goes to a store and finds the brand unavailable, rather than purchasing a substitute brand, he or she will seek the brand elsewhere. Brand insistence is the strongest degree of brand loyalty. It is a marketer's dream. However, it is the least common type of brand loyalty. Customers vary considerably regarding the product categories for which they may be brand insistent.

## Brand Equity

**Brand equity**
The marketing and financial value associated with a brand's strength in a market

A well-managed brand is an asset to an organisation. The value of this asset is often referred to as brand equity. **Brand equity** is the marketing and financial value associated with a brand's strength in a market. Besides the actual proprietary brand assets, such as patents and trademarks, four major elements underlie brand equity. These components are brand name awareness, brand loyalty, perceived brand quality and brand associations, as shown in Figure 11.1.[5]

Being aware of a brand leads to brand familiarity, which in turn results in a level of comfort with the brand. A familiar brand is more likely to be selected than an unfamiliar brand because often the familiar brand is viewed as reliable and of acceptable quality compared to the unknown brand. The familiar brand is likely to be in a customer's evoked set (see Chapter 6), whereas the unfamiliar brand is not.

Brand loyalty is a valued component of brand equity because it reduces a brand's vulnerability to competitors' actions. Brand loyalty allows an organisation to keep its existing customers and avoid having to spend enormous amounts of resources gaining new ones. Loyal customers provide brand visibility and reassurance to potential new customers. And because customers expect their brand to be available when and where they shop, retailers strive to carry the brands known for their strong customer following.

Customers associate a certain level of perceived overall quality with a brand. A brand name itself actually stands for a certain level of quality in a customer's mind and is used as a substitute for actual judgement of quality. In many cases, customers cannot actually judge the quality of the product for themselves and instead must rely on the brand as a quality indicator. Perceived high brand quality helps to support a premium price, allowing a marketer to avoid severe price competition. Also, favourable perceived brand quality can ease the introduction of brand extensions, as the high regard for the brand is likely to translate into high regard for the related products.

The set of associations linked to a brand is another key component of brand equity. At times a marketer works to connect a lifestyle, or in some instances a certain personality type, with a particular brand. For example, customers associate Volvo cars with protecting family members; a De Beers diamond with a loving, long-lasting relationship (a diamond is for ever); and Drambuie liqueur with a unique taste. These types of brand association contribute significantly to the brand's equity.

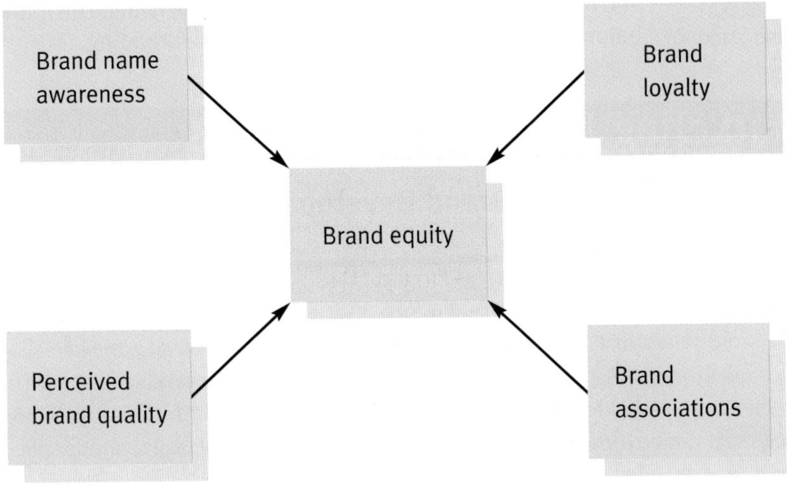


*Figure 11.1*
*Major elements of brand equity*
*Source: Adapted with the permission of The Free Press, a division of Simon & Schuster, Inc., from* Managing Brand Equity: Capitalizing on the Value of a Brand Name *by David A. Aaker. Copyright © 1991 by David A. Aaker*

Although difficult to measure, brand equity represents the value of a brand to an organisation. An organisation may buy a brand from another company at a premium price because outright brand purchase may be less expensive and less risky than creating and developing a brand from scratch – for example, IKEA's purchase of Habitat. Brand equity helps to give a brand the power to capture and maintain a consistent market share, which provides stability to an organisation's sales volume. The top brands with the highest economic value are shown in Table 11.1. Any company that owns a brand listed in Table 11.1, such as Nestlé with Nescafé, would agree that the economic value of that brand is likely to be the greatest single asset in the organisation's possession. A brand's overall economic value rises and falls with the brand's profitability, brand awareness, brand loyalty, perceived brand quality and strength of positive brand associations.

## Brand Personality, Values and Attributes

**Brand attributes**
The bullet-point specific benefits to the consumer from purchasing or using the brand

**Brand values**
The emotional benefits and less tangible identifiers attached to the brand, providing reassurance and credibility for targeted consumers, supplementing the specific brand attributes in making the brand attractive

**Brand personality**
The psychological cues and less tangible desirable facets of a well-presented brand

Most companies have identified specific attributes that may be linked to their brands. **Brand attributes** are the bullet-point features listed in brochures or in an advertisement: the specific benefits to the consumer from purchasing or using the brand. A decade or so ago, it became fashionable to also identify brand values to help differentiate a brand and build its appeal to target audiences. **Brand values** are the emotional benefits and less tangible identifiers attached to the brand, providing reassurance and credibility for targeted consumers, supplementing the specific brand attributes in making the brand attractive to current or potential purchasers. For example, IT services company Fujitsu has many brand attributes, including its ability to manage business clients' IT infrastructure, offer the latest technology and thinking, and be cost effective and reliable. Its brand values are defined as offering knowledge, dependability, technical excellence, reassurance and passion. These values are far more emotional than the brand attributes. Together, the brand values and brand attributes constitute a more compelling proposition in the marketplace.

Many branding experts argue that in addition to brand attributes and brand values, an effective brand strategy should identify brand personality variables in order to facilitate greater differentiation in relation to competitors' products and to form a stronger affinity with customers. **Brand personality** traits are the psychological cues and less tangible desirable facets of a well-presented brand. In Fujitsu's case, the brand personality variables include having friendly, customer-focused personnel who are confident, technically savvy and passionate about assisting clients to improve their businesses. In the market for IT services to large corporations, these are desirable traits. Many companies readily identify the brand attributes and, after a little deliberation, they are able to scope out a few brand values. However, the identification of an attractive set of brand personality traits is often more difficult, yet once developed, such emotive sentiments often 'bring the brand to life' and help to establish differentiation vis-à-vis rivals. The Marketing Tools and Techniques box below illustrates this approach to effective branding.

## Marketing Tools and Techniques

### Practitioners' Use of the Brand Development Theory: the Brand Personality Grid

Leading branding exponents, such as Prophet (David Aaker) and Interbrand, suggest that businesses identify core values that are reflected in their business capabilities and their brands' positionings, and in the perceptions of their target stakeholders. In addition, specific features or attributes that can be construed as brand benefits should be defined. In order to truly make a brand 'come alive' and be distinctive in the marketplace, leading branding experts argue that a *brand personality* should be specified and communicated to stakeholders. Such personality traits are the emotive characteristics of the brand, whereas the brand benefits are more tangible and specific attributes, as outlined opposite.

1 *Personality*
   What sets the company apart/describes its character and personality
2 *Values*
   The heart of the emotive market-facing proposition
3 *Brand benefits/attributes*
   Detailed/specific features of benefit to the customer

Fujitsu's evolving branding is a good example of this.

Japanese-based Fujitsu is one of the world's biggest businesses, focusing mainly on electronics and IT services. The company had traded under different names across the world and in the UK was familiar to business clients as ICL. Fujitsu decided to maximise its global standing under the Fujitsu name and looked to create a leading brand. Globally, Fujitsu is the world's number three IT services company, is growing and is increasingly successful. In the UK, Fujitsu handles IT outsourcing and management for major banks and retailers, central and local government, the Post Office and many manufacturers.

The old brand in the UK was somewhat staid: hardware-led, overly 'techy', 'grey' and stood for ICL's old values from when the business focused on producing mainframe computers rather than offering innovative IT solutions and management options to leading-edge businesses. The new-look Fujitsu is a dynamic, progressive, forward-thinking business, partnering other leading-edge suppliers to address clients' fast-changing IT requirements and to help clients to transform their business practices.

There are many providers of IT support and many may be able to offer the brand benefits stated above, in the right-hand column. However, fewer B2B companies could claim to have a reputation for being caring, passionate, likeable, dependable and knowledgeable about clients' business issues. In IT services, interpersonal relationships between the supplier and the client are of paramount importance. Clients also perceive high risks in handing over their IT – on which the success of their operations may depend – to a third party. The brand values and brand personality suggested in this analysis would be highly attractive to many senior executives in current or potential business clients.

Having developed a brand proposition – personality, values and attributes – as hypothesised in the example above, the marketing challenges are then to ensure that both:

- all promotional activity reflects this overall message
- any interface with clients and suppliers or partners conveys these sentiments, whether in print format, e-communications, broadcast media or even with any personnel meeting and working with clients.

In addition to developing suitable marketing communications materials, therefore, there is a core requirement to ensure that a company's workforce understands and utilises the brand proposition developed, not only a company's marketers. There is a requirement for internal marketing.

The brand personality grid for Fujitsu could easily look like this:*

**Fujitsu**
***The Possibilities are Infinite***

| Brand Personality | Brand Values | Brand Benefits |
|---|---|---|
| **Friendly People**<br>**Customer-focused**<br>**Confident**<br>**Dynamic**<br>**Future-focused**<br>**Passionate**<br>**Likeable Staff**<br>**Global** | **Knowledge**<br>Customers business<br>Across sectors<br>**Dependability**<br>Trusted to deliver<br>30/40 year track record<br>**Technical Excellence**<br>At forefront of change<br>Tap into Fujitsu's huge R&D<br>**Passion**<br>Staff are passionate<br>Deliver for customers<br>**Collaboration**<br>Working together<br>Networking with partners | **Infrastructure Management**<br>**Free-up Resources**<br>**Operational Efficiency**<br>**Customers Enabled to Focus on *Their* Business Imperatives**<br>**Latest Technology**<br>**Total Solutions**<br>**Leading-edge Partnerships**<br>**Reliable**<br>**Cost Effective** |



* The suggested brand personality grid for Fujitsu is an external observer's view and does not necessarily reflect the company's own analyses or intended brand strategy.

Implicit in this discussion is the need to determine a strong and relevant brand image that is managed effectively. As explained in Chapter 8's examination of brand positioning, a management team must determine the desired brand proposition and manage its portfolio of brands in order to ensure that the target market recognises the specified brand attributes, values and personality. Targeted customers should never be left to deduce for themselves a brand's proposition and messages.

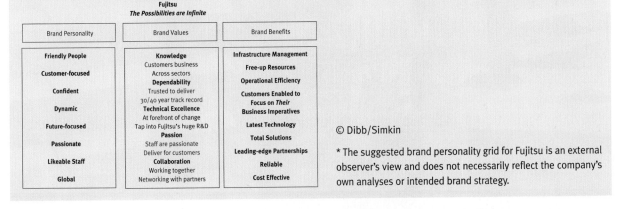

## Types of Brand

There are three categories of brand: manufacturer brands, own-label brands (also called private brands, store brands or dealer brands) and generic brands.

**Manufacturer brands**
Brands initiated by producers to ensure that they are identified with their products at the point of purchase

**Manufacturer Brands** **Manufacturer brands** are initiated by producers and ensure that they are identified with their products at the point of purchase – for example, Green Giant, Apple Computer and Wall's ice cream. A manufacturer brand usually requires a producer to become involved in distribution, promotion and, to some extent, pricing decisions. Brand loyalty is encouraged by promotion, quality control and guarantees; it is a valuable asset to a manufacturer. The producer tries to stimulate demand for the product, which tends to encourage middlemen to make the product available.

***Figure 11.2***
*There are many examples of retailer own-label brands, but Boots deliberately created a stand-alone brand for its own, highly popular, range of No. 7 cosmetics, emulating the major manufacturer brands*
*Photo: Courtesy of Karen Beaulah*

**Own-label brands**
Brands initiated and owned by resellers – wholesalers or retailers

**Own-label Brands** **Own-label brands** are initiated and owned by resellers (wholesalers or retailers). The major characteristic of own-label brands is that the manufacturers are not identified on the products. Retailers and wholesalers use these brands to develop more efficient promotion, to generate higher gross margins and to improve store images. Own-label brands give retailers or wholesalers freedom to purchase products of a specified quality at the lowest cost without disclosing the identity of the manufacturer. Wholesale brands include Roca, Family Choice, Happy Shopper and Lifestyle. Familiar retailer brand names include St Michael (Marks & Spencer), Yessica (C&A) and George (ASDA). Many successful own-label brands are distributed nationally. Matsui domestic appliances (Currys) are as well known as most name brands. Sometimes retailers with successful distributor brands start manufacturing their own products to gain more control over product costs, quality and design in the hope of increasing profits. While one might think that store brands appeal most strongly to lower-income shoppers or to upmarket shoppers who compare labels, studies indicate that buyers of own-label brands have characteristics that match those of the overall population.[6] One reason for the growth of store brands is that retailers advertise the manufacturer brands, which brings customers to their stores, but sell the store brands, especially to price-sensitive customers.[7] Another reason is that retailers with store labels negotiate better prices from producers of manufacturer brands.[8]

**Generic brand**
A brand that indicates only the product category and does not include the company name or other identifying terms

**Generic Brands** Some marketers of products that have traditionally been branded have embarked on a policy of not branding, often called generic branding. A **generic brand** indicates only the product category – such as aluminium foil – and does not include the company name or other identifying terms. Usually generic brands are sold at prices lower than those of comparable branded items. Although at one time generic brands may have represented as much as 10 per cent of all retail grocery sales, today they account for less than 1 per cent.[9] They are popular for pharmaceuticals and in some discount grocery stores.

**The Battle of the Brands** Competition between manufacturer brands and own-label brands – sometimes called 'the battle of the brands' – is intensifying in several major product categories, particularly tinned foods, breakfast cereal, sugar and soft drinks. Own-label brands now account for around 40 per cent of all supermarket sales.[10] Both men and women are quite favourable towards own-label brands of food products, with women – still the major grocery purchasers – even more favourable than men. For manufacturers, developing multiple manufacturer brands and distribution systems has been an effective means of combating increased competition from own-label brands. By developing a new brand name, a producer can adjust various elements of a marketing mix to appeal to a different target market. For example, Scott Paper has developed lower-priced brands of paper towels; it has tailored its new products to a target market that tends to purchase own-label brands.

Manufacturers find it hard to ignore the marketing opportunities that come from producing own-label brands for resellers. If a manufacturer refuses to produce an own-label brand for a reseller, a competing manufacturer will. Moreover, the production of own-label brands allows the manufacturer to use excess capacity during periods when its own brands are at non-peak production. The ultimate decision whether to produce an own-label or a manufacturer brand depends on a company's resources, production capabilities and goals.

## Choosing a Brand Name

Marketers should consider a number of factors when they choose a brand name. The name should be easy for customers – including foreign buyers, if the company intends to market its products in other countries – to say, spell and recall. Short, one-syllable names such as

Mars or Tide satisfy this requirement. The brand name should indicate the product's major benefits and, if possible, should suggest in a positive way the product's uses and special characteristics: negative or offensive references should be avoided. For example, a deodorant should be branded with a name that signals freshness, dryness or long-lasting protection, as do Sure, Right Guard and Arrid Extra Dry. The brand should be distinctive, to set it apart from competing brands. If a marketer intends to use a brand for a product line, it must be compatible with all products in the line. Finally, a brand should be designed so that it can be used and recognised in all of the various types of media.

Finding the right brand name has become a challenging task, because many obvious product names have already been used. The Marketing Tools and Techniques box opposite outlines the role played by brand name consultancies in the naming process.

How are brand names derived? Brand names can be created from single or multiple words – for example, Bic or Findus Lean Cuisine. Initials, numbers or sometimes combinations of these are used to create brands such as IBM PC. At times, words, numbers and initials are combined to yield brand names such as Mazda MX5 or Mitsubishi 3000GT. To avoid terms that have negative connotations, marketers sometimes use fabricated words that have absolutely no meaning at the time they are created – for example, Kodak and Esso. Occasionally, a brand is simply brought out of storage and used as it is or modified. Companies often maintain banks of registered brands, some of which may have been used in the past. Cadillac, for example, has a bank of approximately 360 registered trademarks. The LaSalle brand, used in the 1920s and 1930s, may be called up for a new Cadillac model soon to be introduced. Possible brand names are sometimes tested in focus groups or in other settings to assess customers' reactions.

Who actually creates brand names? Brand names can be created internally by the organisation. Sometimes a name is suggested by individuals who are close to the development of the product. Some organisations have committees that participate in brand name creation and approval. Large companies that introduce numerous new products annually are likely to have a department that develops brand names. Increasingly, outside consultants are used in the process of developing brand names. An organisation may also hire a company that specialises in brand name development.

Even though most of the important branding considerations apply to both goods and services, services branding has some additional dimensions. The brand of the service is usually the same as the company name. For example, American Express, Vidal Sassoon, ProntoPrint, and Sheraton are names of companies and the services that they provide. Whereas companies that produce tangible goods (such as Procter & Gamble) can use separate brand names for separate products (such as Daz, Head & Shoulders, Flash and Camay), service providers (such as British Airways) are perceived by customers as having one brand name, even though they offer multiple products (first class, business class and economy). Because the service brand name and company name are so closely interrelated, a service brand name must be flexible enough to encompass a variety of current services, as well as new ones that the company may offer in the future. For example, British Airways (BA) has Club World or Eurotraveller (economy) services, each separately branded, but both strongly branded as BA. Geographical references like 'western' and descriptive terms like 'trucking' limit the scope of associations that can be made with the brand name. Northwest Airlines becomes less of a good name as the company begins to fly south and east more regularly.[11] Frequently, a service marketer will employ a symbol along with its brand name to make the brand distinctive and to communicate a certain image.

## Protecting a Brand

Marketers need to design brands that can be protected easily through registration. Among the most difficult to protect are generic words, such as aluminium foil, surnames, and descriptive geographic or functional names.[12] Research shows that, overall, consumers prefer descriptive and suggestive brand names, and find them easier to recall than fanciful and arbitrary

## Marketing Tools and Techniques

### Who Thought of That Name?!

Burger King, Coca-Cola, JCB, Nike, Sony or Virgin – no matter what the brand, someone, somewhere, sometime created the names now recognised instantly by millions of loyal customers. David Rivett of Design Bridge, responsible for many new product development projects and the creation of brand names, believes that all too often clients focus on the physical properties of their new products – features, size, colours, quality, operation – at the expense of name consideration, which is 'tacked on' to the new product development process just prior to launch. Branding consultancies believe that creating the right atmosphere and having a very clear understanding of both client culture and target market characteristics are fundamental to the creation of a suitable brand name. Very often a creative workshop is used by the consultancy to probe the minds of the client personnel in order to establish buzzwords or emotive trigger descriptions for the new product that may be incorporated into the brand name. The name for Anchor's So Soft new spreadable butter was created in this way.

The real difficulty comes not from creating a suitable name, but in registering the preferred choice. Intellectual property lawyers now specialise in trademark registration and searching. Qualitative research, such as focus groups, often throws up many brand names consumers believe might be appropriate. Marketing strategy workshops amongst managers in a company frequently do the same. The result is that some organisations compile extensive lists of names with potential for their types of product, which are then registered, even though at the time there is no expectation of using these names. Companies such as Cadbury's and Ford have large lists of already registered brand names which at some time they may use but that are no longer available to any other company. This is not 'sharp practice', merely a logical extension of marketers hearing good suggestions from colleagues, distributors and consumers and marking them down for possible future use.

Another consideration for branding consultancies is how the new product's name will work alongside the client's umbrella brand. For example, Novon is given independence from owner Sainsbury's, and Cap Colombie from Nescafé; whereas the Focus, Mondeo and Fiesta names are very much tied to the Ford umbrella brand. There is no right or wrong in this dilemma. Some companies, such as Sainsbury's with Novon, want to create sub-brands that, in the eyes of target consumers, are apparently free-standing. For Ford, the logic of cross-promotion and economies of scale in creating brand awareness have persuaded senior marketers to always utilise the Ford brand alongside the individual model name.

Most brand names are, at some point in the creation process, tested out on consumers, but according to leading branding consultancy Interbrand Newell & Sorrell, such tests have to be carefully constrained so as not to allow consumer suggestions to set the process back to square one. The research, argues Interbrand, should identify profoundly incorrect name suggestions, rather than present consumers with a blank sheet of paper for totally new suggestions. Interbrand's Nometrics testing methodology is well respected in the branding fraternity. First, names are tested in isolation of any product or service. Consumers are invited to nominate likely products to be associated with the suggested names. In the second stage of the Nometrics process, names are linked overtly to specific products, and the research gauges the views of consumers and the likelihood that they will purchase products that are so named. Ultimately, a good name cannot overcome product deficiencies, poor distribution, ineffectual promotion, incorrect pricing or inferior customer service, nor can it combat the superiority of a competitor's marketing strategy. A poor, inappropriate, confusing, unmemorable or misleading name can, though, do much harm to an otherwise good product offering.

**Sources:** Peter Doyle, 2001; Tom Blackett, Interbrand Newell & Sorrell; Deborah Carter, Dragon; David Rivett, Design Bridge; Colin Mechan, FLB; Paul Gander, 'Generation game', *Marketing Week*, 22 October 1998, pp. 45–8; Prophet, 2004; Interbrand, 2004.

names.[13] Because of their designs, some brands can be legally infringed upon more easily than others. Although registration provides trademark protection, a company should develop a system for ensuring that its trademarks will be renewed as needed. To protect its exclusive rights to a brand, the company must make certain that the selected brand is not likely to be considered an infringement on any existing brand already registered with the relevant patent office. This task may be complex because infringement is determined by the courts, which base their decisions on whether a brand causes consumers to be confused, mistaken or deceived about the source of the product. McDonald's is one company that aggressively protects its trademarks against infringement; it has brought charges against a number of companies with 'Mc' names because it fears that the use of the 'Mc' will give consumers the impression that these companies are associated with or owned by McDonald's.

If possible, marketers must guard against allowing a brand name to become a generic term used to refer to a general product category.[14] Generic terms cannot be protected as exclusive brand names. For example, names such as aspirin, escalator and shredded wheat – all brand names at one time – were eventually declared generic terms that refer to product classes; thus they could no longer be protected. To keep a brand name from becoming a generic term, the business should spell the name with a capital letter and use it as an adjective to modify the name of the general product class, as in Kellogg's Rice Krispies.[15] Including the word 'brand' just after the brand name is also helpful. An organisation can deal with this problem directly by advertising that its brand is a trademark and should not be used generically. The company can also indicate that the brand is a registered trademark by using the symbol ®.

Companies that try to protect a brand in a foreign country frequently encounter problems. In many countries, brand registration is not possible; the first company to use a

***Figure 11.3***
*Unilever opts to develop individual brands, in this case for its range of Sure deodorants*
*Source: SURE is a registered trade mark of Unilever*

brand in such a country has the rights to it. In some instances, a company has actually had to buy its own brand rights from a company in a foreign country because the foreign company was the first user in that country.

Marketers trying to protect their brands must also contend with brand counterfeiting. In many countries, for instance, it is possible to buy fake General Motors parts, fake Rolex watches, fake Chanel perfume, fake Microsoft software, fake Walt Disney character dolls and a host of other products illegally marketed by manufacturers that do not own the brands. Many counterfeit products are manufactured overseas – in South Korea, Italy, Taiwan and China, for example – but some are counterfeited in the countries in which they are sold. The International Anti-Counterfeiting Coalition estimates that roughly $70 billion in annual world trade involves counterfeit merchandise. The sale of this merchandise obviously reduces the brand owners' revenues from marketing their own legitimate products.

Brand counterfeiting is particularly harmful because the usually inferior counterfeit product undermines consumers' confidence in the brand and their loyalty to it. After unknowingly purchasing a counterfeit product, the buyer may blame the legitimate manufacturer if the product is of low quality or – even worse – if its use results in damage or injury. Since counterfeiting has become such a serious problem, many companies are taking legal action against counterfeiters. Others have adopted such measures as modifying the product or the packaging to make counterfeit items easier to detect, conducting public awareness campaigns, and monitoring distributors to ensure that they stock only legitimate brands.

## Branding Policies

Before it establishes branding policies, a company must first decide whether to brand its products at all. If a company's product is homogeneous and similar to competitors' products, it may be difficult to brand. Raw materials – such as coal, salt, sand and milk – are hard to brand because of the homogeneity of such products and their physical characteristics. Marketers must also consider the degree to which consumers differentiate among brands of a product. For example, while brand may be an important factor in the purchase of coffee, snacks and frozen foods, it is not usually so important a consideration in buying light bulbs, cheese and cling film.

If a company chooses to brand its products, it may opt for one or more of the following branding policies: individual, overall family, line family and brand extension branding.

**Individual branding**
A policy of naming each product differently

### Individual Branding

**Individual branding** is a policy of naming each product differently. Procter & Gamble relies on an individual branding policy for its line of fabric washing products, which includes Tide, Bold, Daz and Dreft. In Table 11.2, there are two Unilever brands in the UK's top 20 biggest consumer brands: Persil and Flora.

A major advantage of individual branding is that if an organisation introduces a poor product, the negative images associated with it will not contaminate the company's other products. An individual branding policy may also facilitate market segmentation when a company wishes to enter many segments of the same market. Separate, unrelated names can be used, and each brand can be aimed at a specific segment.

**Overall family branding**
A policy of branding all of a company's products with the same name, or at least part of the name

### Overall Family Branding

In **overall family branding**, all of a company's products are branded with the same name, or at least part of the name, such as Kraft, Heinz, Microsoft or Ford. In some cases, a company's name is combined with other words to brand items. Heinz uses its name on its products along with a generic description of the item, such as Heinz Salad Cream, Heinz Baked Beans, Heinz Spaghetti and Heinz Tomato Soup. The quality image of its products increases consumer confidence in what they are buying. This brand consistency is stressed in Heinz advertisements (see Figure 11.4). Unlike individual branding, overall family branding means that the promotion of one item with the family brand promotes the company's other products.

**Table 11.2 The UK's Biggest Retail Consumer Brands**

| Rank | Brand | Manufacturer | Sales value (£ million) |
|---|---|---|---|
| 1 | Coca-Cola | Coca-Cola | 520–525 |
| 2 | Walkers | PepsiCo | 440–445 |
| 3 | Muller | Muller | 335–340 |
| 4 | Nescafé | Nestlé | 285–290 |
| 5 | Stella Artois | Interbrew | 255–260 |
| 6 | Andrex | Kimberly-Clark | 240–245 |
| 7 | Persil | Lever Brothers | 235–240 |
| 8 | Hovis | British Bakeries | 220–225 |
| 9 | Robinsons | Britvic | 200–205 |
| 10 | Warburtons | Warburtons | 200–205 |
| 11 | Kingsmill | Allied Bakeries | 200–205 |
| 12 | Bernard Matthews | Bernard Matthews | 185–190 |
| 13 | Whiskas | Pedigree | 175–180 |
| 14 | Ariel | Masterfoods | 165–170 |
| 15 | Pampers | Procter & Gamble | 160–165 |
| 16 | Carling | Coors | 150–155 |
| 17 | McCain Chips | McCain Foods | 150–155 |
| 18 | Kit-Kat | Nestlé Rowntree | 140–145 |
| 19 | Flora | Unilever Bestfoods | 135–140 |
| 20 | Bird's Eye frozen poultry | Bird's Eye | 135–140 |

**Source:** *The Marketing Pocket Book*, published by the World Advertising Research Center, Henley-on-Thames, 2004.

**Line family branding**
A policy of using family branding only for products within a single line

**Line Family Branding** Sometimes an organisation uses family branding only for products within a single line. This policy is called **line family branding**. Colgate-Palmolive, for example, produces a line of cleaning products that includes a cleanser, a powdered detergent and a liquid cleaner, all with the name Ajax. Colgate also produces several brands of toothpaste, none of which carries the Ajax brand name.

**Brand extension branding**
A company's use of one of its existing brand names as part of an improved or new product, usually in the same product category as the existing brand

**Brand Extension Branding** **Brand extension branding** occurs when a company uses one of its existing brand names as part of a brand for an improved or new product that is usually in the same product category as the existing brand. The makers of Timotei shampoo extended the name to hair conditioner and skincare products. There is one major difference between line family branding and brand extension branding. With line family branding, all products in the line carry the same name, but with brand extension branding this is not the case. The producer of Arrid deodorant, for example, also makes other brands of deodorant. Waterford, an upmarket Irish brand of crystal, extended its name to writing instruments when seeking sales growth beyond closely related product categories, such as china, cutlery and table linens.[16]

**Choice of Branding Policy** An organisation is not limited to a single branding policy. Instead, branding policy is influenced by the:

- number of products and product lines the company produces
- characteristics of its target markets

***Figure 11.4***
*Overall family branding. Heinz uses its name on its products, along with a generic description of the item*
*Photos: Courtesy of Heinz*

- number and type of competing products available
- size of its resources.

Anheuser-Busch, for example, uses both individual and brand extension branding. Most of the brands are individual brands; however, the Michelob Light brand is an extension of the Michelob brand. Sometimes companies must update brands so that they remain fresh and interesting.

## Brand Licensing

A recent trend in branding strategies involves the licensing of trademarks. By means of a licensing agreement, a company may permit approved manufacturers to use its trademark on other products for a licensing fee. Royalties may be as low as 2 per cent of wholesale revenues or higher than 10 per cent. The licensee is responsible for all manufacturing, selling and advertising functions, and bears the costs if the licensed product fails. Not long ago, only a few companies licensed their corporate trademarks but today the licensing business is worth billions of pounds and is growing. Harley-Davidson, for example, has authorised the use of its name on non-motorcycle products such as cologne, wine coolers, gold rings and shirts. Disney also licenses its brand for use on a range of products. JCB and Coca-Cola both now license ranges of clothing sold in high-street stores.

The advantages of licensing range from extra revenues and low cost to free publicity, new images and trademark protection. For example, Coca-Cola has licensed its trademark for use on glassware, radios, trucks and clothing in the hope of protecting its trademark. Similarly, Jaguar has licensed a range of leisure wear. However, brand licensing is not without its drawbacks. The major disadvantages are a lack of manufacturing control, which could hurt the company's name, and the undesirability of bombarding consumers with too many unrelated products bearing the same name. Licensing arrangements can also fail because of poor timing, inappropriate distribution channels or mismatching of product and name.

## Managing Brands

With the need for brands to create product differentiation, assist in establishing a competitive edge and encourage product awareness, marketers must manage their brands with care.[17] As explained in detail in the next chapter, this involves understanding when a brand requires repositioning, modifying, deleting or simply being left alone. Most companies operate with a portfolio of separate brands and products, and must make difficult decisions in terms of which are to receive support and the bulk of a business's marketing resource, and which are to be killed off or given only minimal support. Chapter 12 explores these strategic choices.

As explained in Chapter 6's discussion of consumer buying behaviour, without an understanding of brand loyalty and brand switching, it is difficult to manage a business's brands effectively. It is essential, therefore, for companies to make an effort to research brand loyalty and brand perceptions to help them make sensible decisions that accurately reflect consumers' views.

**Successful brands**
Brands for which a company must prioritise quality, offer superior service, get there first, differentiate brands, develop a unique positioning concept, have a strong communications programme, and be consistent and reliable

Research shows that to create **successful brands**, a company must:

- prioritise quality – the top brands are all high quality in their product fields
- offer superior service – less easily copied by competitors than pure product attributes
- get there first – not necessarily technologically but, in the minds of targeted customers, by
  - exploiting new technology (Rank Xerox, Sony)
  - new positioning concepts (Body Shop, First Direct)
  - new distribution channels (Argos, Direct Line)
  - new market segments (Orange, Ocado)
  - using gaps resulting from environmental change (Ecover, Daz Ultra)
- differentiate its brands – so that consumers perceive the brands on offer as being different
- develop a unique positioning concept – making the brand and its differentiating characteristics stand out with a clear image and positioning message against rival brands
- support the brand and its positioning with a strong communications programme – so that target consumers are aware of the brand and its positioning proposition
- deliver consistency and reliability over time – keeping the brand's values trustworthy as perceived by target consumers.

**Brand strength**
A function of the product's attributes and functionality, its differentiation, plus any demonstrable added value to the purchaser or user

Branding expert Peter Doyle[18] stated that, to build effective brands, it is essential for a business to understand that there is more to a brand than simply a catchy name and visible logo. Doyle argued that **brand strength** is a function of the product's attributes and functionality, its differentiation, plus any demonstrable added value to the purchaser or user. For example, Nike sports shoes are designed for serious running and are fit for this core purpose, but Nike has a reputation for innovation and progression, so the brand is perceived as a 'first mover', providing differentiation versus rival brands. For the purchaser, the reputation of the brand for being state-of-the-art and highly desirable, provides 'street cred', which is the added value to the consumer.

**Levels of brands**
The tangible product, the 'basic' brand, the 'augmented' brand and the 'potential' of the brand

There are, in fact, four **levels of brands**: the tangible product, the 'basic' brand, the 'augmented' brand and the 'potential' of the brand. Level 1, the tangible product, is the degree of quality, performance, features and actual attributes. Level 2, the 'basic' brand, is the identity, differentiation and positioning. Level 3, the 'augmented' brand, is the aggregated impact from including supplementary products and service support. Level 4, the 'potential' of the brand, is reached when customers will not willingly accept substitutes and are unhappy to switch to rival brands; psychological benefits and barriers in the minds of target customers are important determinants of brand potential.

There are three essential acid tests for determining whether a brand is successful. Although most companies consider only the overall profit contribution to the end-of-year financial annual report and accounts, when determining a brand's success they should ask the following three fundamental questions:

1 Has the brand captured the leading share in its market segment or distribution channel?
2 Does the brand command prices sufficiently high enough to produce a high profit margin?
3 Will the brand sustain its strong share of profits when rival and generic versions of the product enter the market?

Using these core criteria, many brands are relatively unsuccessful. For marketers, managing brands must include knowing when a brand is succeeding, when it is faltering but may be saved, and when a brand is a lost cause and should be deleted from the company's range of brands. Chapter 12 examines this difficult issue in more detail.

## Corporate Branding

**Corporate branding**
The application of product branding at the corporate level, reflected visibly through the company name, logo and visual presentation, and in the business's underlying values

**Corporate image**
Reflects the perceptions that external audiences hold about an organisation

**Corporate identity**
Overlapping with the corporate branding concept: branding at the corporate level

**Corporate branding** involves applying the principles of product branding at the corporate level. Corporate branding is reflected in visible manifestations such as the company name, logo and visual presentation, and also in the business's underlying and guiding values. Thus British Airways, McDonald's, Wal-Mart and Manchester United Football Club each has a corporate brand that is based around the organisation itself. Sometimes the terms **corporate image** and **corporate identity** are also used in relation to corporate branding. The concepts of corporate identity and corporate branding overlap: both referring to what the company transmits about itself.[19] Corporate image reflects the perceptions that external audiences hold about the organisation.[20]

Corporate branding plays a role in guiding all of a company's marketing activities. The corporate brand is transmitted through tangible and intangible features. The tangible dimensions include visual features of the corporate brand, such as corporate logo and symbols, typography, colour, buildings, staff uniforms, vehicles and stationery. For example, Unilever has recently overhauled its corporate identity to fit with the company's mission: 'to add vitality to life'. The corporate brand will be reflected in a new logo featuring flowers, animals and stars, which will be carried by the business's products.[21] Less tangible features include how the corporate brand is portrayed through what people inside and outside the business believe and say about it.

To be effective, the corporate brand should be embedded in all company actions. This means that all aspects of the company's communication, including internal communication with employees and external marketing activities ranging from the annual report through to its advertising and PR, must convey a consistent message about the corporate brand. Corporate branding is particularly important for services businesses, because customers look for help in understanding and visualising the services product. A strong corporate brand can therefore help buyers to overcome the intangibility of some of these products. For example, First Direct bank has worked hard to build a corporate image based on service quality, which reflects the company's reliability and flexible approach to meeting customer needs. This has helped to build a corporate image based around the notion of good service. The fact that this image is also reflected in research examining service in the financial services sector adds credibility to the bank's offering.

# Packaging and Labelling

Packaging and labelling are also part of the marketing process. They impact upon the image of the product, its functionality and, ultimately, upon the customer's perception of satisfaction. At times, they create differentiation vis-à-vis rival products. For example, Coca-Cola introduced limited-edition packaging for its iconic glass bottle to appeal to upmarket consumers. Working with fashion designer Matthew Williamson, the designer bottle was available in three wrap-around prints, each taken from Williamson's summer clothing collection. The bottles were retailed only through selected style bars and restaurants.[22]

**Packaging**
The development of a product's container and label, complete with graphic design

**Packaging** involves the development of a container and label, complete with graphic design for a product. A package can be a vital part of a product, making it more versatile, safer or easier to use. Like a brand name, a package can influence customers' attitudes towards a product and thus affect their purchase decisions. For example, several producers of sauces, salad dressings and ketchups have packaged their products in squeezable containers to make use and storage more convenient. Package characteristics help shape buyers' impressions of a product at the time of purchase or during use. This section examines the main functions of packaging and considers several major packaging decisions. The role of the package in marketing strategy is also analysed.

## Packaging Functions

Effective packaging means more than simply putting products into containers and covering them with wrappers. First of all, packaging materials serve the basic purpose of protecting the product and maintaining its functional form. Fluids such as milk, orange juice and hairspray need packages that preserve and protect them; the packaging should prevent damage that could affect the product's usefulness and increase costs. Since product tampering has become a problem for marketers of many types of goods, several packaging techniques have been developed to counter this danger. Some packages are also designed to foil shoplifters.

Another function of packaging is to offer convenience for consumers. For example, small, sealed packages – individual sized boxes or plastic bags that contain liquids and do not require refrigeration – appeal strongly to children and young adults with active lifestyles. The size or shape of a package may relate to the product's storage, convenience of use or replacement rate. Small, single-serving tins of fruit, such as Del Monte's Fruitinni, may prevent waste and make storage easier. Low, regular-shaped packets may be easier to stack and use cupboard space more efficiently. A third function of packaging is to promote a product by communicating its features, uses, benefits and image. At times, a reusable package is developed to make a product more desirable. For example, some ice-cream containers can be used again as food storage containers.

## Major Packaging Considerations

Packaging must support a product's brand image and positioning, helping develop differentiation vis-à-vis rival products. When developing packages, marketers must take many factors into account. Some of these factors relate to consumers' needs; others relate to the requirements of resellers. Retailers, wholesalers and distributors will be required to handle and stock the products, and in many instances to display and deliver them. Packaging solutions must reflect the needs of these channel members in addition to the requirements of end-user customers. Obviously, one major consideration is cost. Although a variety of packaging materials, processes and designs are available, some are rather expensive. In recent years buyers have shown a willingness to pay more for improved packaging, but there are limits. Marketers should try to determine, through research, just how much customers are willing to pay for packages.

Developing tamper-resistant packaging is very important. Although no package is totally tamper-proof, marketers can develop packages that are difficult to tamper with and that also make any tampering evident to resellers and consumers. Because new, safer packaging technologies are being explored, marketers should be aware of changes in packaging technology and legislation, and prepared to make modifications that will ensure consumer safety. One packaging innovation includes an inner pouch that displays the word 'open' when air has entered the pouch after opening. Marketers now also have an obligation to inform consumers of the possibilities and risks of product tampering by educating them to recognise possible tampering and by placing warnings on packaging.[23] For example, the tops of many sauce and condiment bottles now have plastic seals around them, so that consumers can be confident they have not been opened. Baby food manufacturers, such as Cow & Gate and Heinz, have taken this protection method one step further by using special metal jar tops with pop-up discs showing when a jar has been opened. This move followed cases of tampering in which foreign bodies were introduced into baby foods. Now the special tops expressly warn consumers to watch out for tampering. Although effective tamper-resistant packaging may be expensive to develop, when balanced against the costs of lost sales, loss of consumer confidence and a company's reputation, and potentially expensive product liability lawsuits, the costs of ensuring consumer safety are minimal.[24]

Marketers should consider how much consistency is desirable in a company's package designs. The best policy may be not to attempt consistency, especially if a company's products are unrelated or aimed at vastly different target markets. To promote an overall company image, a company may decide that all packages are to be similar or include one major element of the design. This approach is called **family packaging**. Sometimes it is used only for lines of products, as with Campbell's soups, Weight Watchers foods and Planters nuts.

**Family packaging**
An approach in which all of a company's packages are similar or include one major element of the design

A package's promotional role is an important consideration. Through verbal and non-verbal symbols, the package can inform potential buyers about the product's content, features, uses, advantages and hazards. A company can create desirable images and associations by its choice of colour, design, shape and texture. Many cosmetics manufacturers, for example, design their packages to create impressions of richness, luxury and exclusiveness. A package performs a promotional function when it is designed to be safer or more convenient to use, if such characteristics help stimulate demand.

To develop a package that has a definite promotional value, a designer must consider size, shape, texture, colour and graphics.[25] Beyond the obvious limitation that the package must be large enough to hold the product, a package can be designed to appear taller or shorter. For instance, thin vertical lines make a package look taller; wide horizontal stripes make it look shorter. A marketer may want a package to appear taller because many people perceive something that is taller as being larger.

Colours on packages are often chosen to attract attention. People associate specific colours with certain feelings and experiences, as outlined below.

Blue is soothing, it is also associated with wealth, trust and security.
Grey is associated with strength, exclusivity and success.
Orange can stand for low cost.
Red has connotations of excitement, stimulation and danger.
Yellow is associated with cheerfulness and joy.
Purple is linked with dignity and stateliness.
Black is associated with being strong and masterful.[26]

When selecting packaging colours, marketers must decide whether a particular colour will evoke positive or negative feelings when it is linked to a specific product. Rarely, for example, do processors package meat or bread in green materials, because customers may associate green with mould. However, recent concern about the state of the environment has, in general, led to an increase in the use of green-coloured packaging. Marketers must also decide whether a specific target market will respond favourably or unfavourably to a particular colour. Cosmetics for women are more likely to be sold in pastel-coloured packaging than are personal care products for men. Packages designed to appeal to children often use primary colours and bold designs.

Packaging must also meet the needs of resellers. Wholesalers and retailers consider whether a package facilitates transportation, storage and handling. Packages must allow these resellers to make maximum use of storage space, both in transit and in the shops. Products should be packed so that sales staff can transfer them to the shelves with ease. The shape and weight of packaging are also important. Resellers may refuse to carry certain products if their packages are cumbersome. Figure 11.5 shows how these factors have been taken into consideration in developing Cuprinol's Castlepak woodcare varnish container.

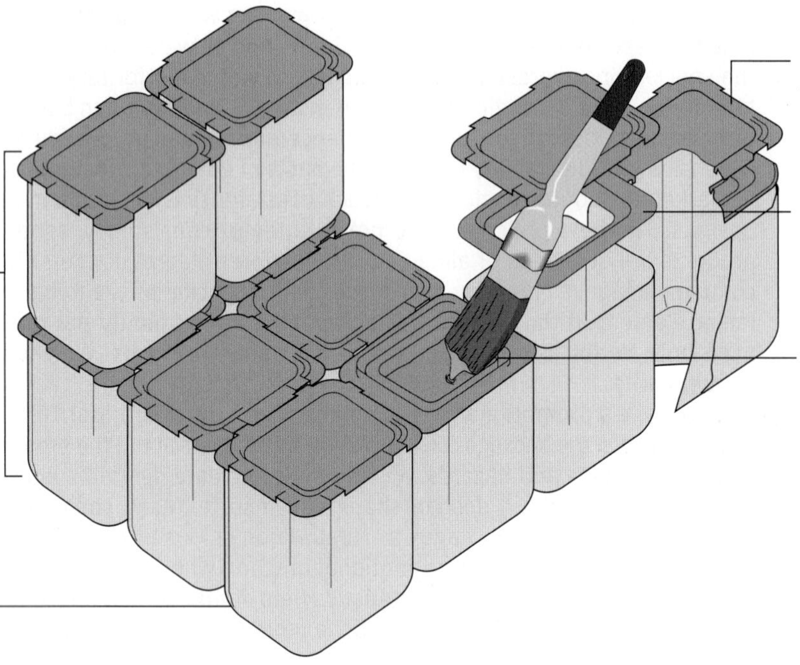


***Figure 11.5***
*Cuprinol's Castlepak™ woodcare varnish container highlights how environmental consumer usage and operation needs can be incorporated into a single packaging solution*
*Source: Courtesy of* Marketing Magazine, *London*

A final consideration is whether to develop packages that are environmentally responsible. A Cable News Network (CNN) report on the growing refuse disposal problem in the USA stated that nearly 50 per cent of all rubbish consists of discarded plastic packaging, such as polystyrene containers, plastic soft drink bottles, carrier bags and other packaging items. Plastic packaging material does not biodegrade, and using paper requires the destruction of valuable forest lands. Consequently, a number of companies are recycling more materials and exploring packaging alternatives, helped by packaging experts such as Tetra Pak. Heinz, for example, is looking for alternatives to its plastic squeezable ketchup bottles.

Companies that decide to develop environmentally responsible packaging have not always received a positive response. For example, customers' responses to US burger chain Wendy's paper plates and coffee cups have been mixed; some customers prefer the old non-biodegradable foam packaging. Other companies searching for alternatives to environmentally harmful packaging have experienced similar problems. Thus marketers must carefully balance society's desires to preserve the environment against consumers' desires for convenience.

**Packaging development**
A mix of aesthetic considerations and structural necessities to guarantee the functionality of the design

## Packaging Development

**Packaging development** requires a mix of aesthetic considerations and structural necessities to guarantee the functionality of the design. There are cartons, bottles, tubes, cans, tubs and jars, multipacks, clamshells and blister packs, CD boxes, gift packs, plus many innovative formats for storing, displaying and dispensing products in a manner that is ahead of the competition. Material selection is an important stage in the design process, as are the specification and application of surface graphics and typography. Decisions must be made concerning information layout and the hierarchy of messages, front-of-pack versus back-of-pack detailing, choice of language and jargon, the photography and images to be selected, illustrations and use of colour, deployment of symbols and icons, final finishes and effects. There are often practical requirements to consider, such as weights, measures, ingredients, nutritional information and barcoding to display.

## Packaging and Marketing Strategy

Packaging can be a major component of a marketing strategy. A new cap or closure, a better box or wrapping, or a more convenient container may give a product a competitive edge. The right type of package for a new product can help it gain market recognition very quickly. In the case of existing brands, marketers should periodically re-evaluate packages. Particularly in the case of consumer convenience products, marketers should view packaging as a major strategic tool. This section examines ways in which packaging can be used strategically.

**Altering the Package** At times, a marketer changes a package because the existing design is no longer in style, especially when compared with competitive products. Smith & Nephew redesigned its Simple range of toiletries to show that the products have evolved with the times. A package may also be redesigned because new product features need to be highlighted on the package, or because new packaging materials have become available. A company may decide to change a product's packaging to make the product more convenient or safer to use, or to reposition the product. A major redesign of a simple package costs about £25,000, and the redesign of a line of products may cost up to £300,000. Choosing the right packaging material is an important consideration when redesigning. Different materials vary in popularity at different times. For example, glass is becoming more popular as views on the environment and the need for recyclability come to the fore.

**Secondary use package**
A package that can be reused for purposes other than its initial use

**Secondary Use Packaging** A **secondary use package** is one that can be reused for purposes other than its initial one. For example, a margarine container can be reused to store left-overs, a jam jar can be used as a drinking glass, and shortbread tins can be reused for storing cakes and biscuits. Secondary use packages can be viewed by customers as adding value to products. If customers value this type of packaging, then its use should stimulate unit sales.

**Category-consistent packaging**
The packaging of a product according to the packaging practices associated with a particular product category

**Category-consistent packaging** **Category-consistent packaging** means that the product is packaged in line with the packaging practices associated with a particular product category. Some product categories – for example, mayonnaise, mustard, ketchup and jam – have traditional package shapes. Other product categories are characterised by recognisable colour combinations – red and white for soup; red and yellow for tea; red, white and blue for Ritz-type crackers. When a company introduces a brand in one of these product categories, marketers will often use traditional package shapes and colour combinations to ensure that customers will recognise the new product as being in that specific product category.

**Innovative Packaging** Sometimes, a marketer will employ a unique cap, design, applicator or other feature to make the product competitively distinctive, as illustrated in Figure 11.6. Such packaging can be effective when the innovation makes the product safer or easier to use, or when the unique package provides better protection for the product. In some instances, marketers use innovative or unique packages that are inconsistent with traditional packaging practices, to make the brand stand out relative to its competitors. Procter & Gamble, for example, used an innovative, crush-proof cylinder to package its Pringles potato crisps. Innovative packaging generally requires considerable resources, not only for the package design itself but also to make customers aware of the unique package and its benefit. Sometimes, innovative packaging can change the way in which consumers use a product. The introduction of cardboard-boxed, single-serving soft drinks made it easier for consumers to have a drink while travelling by car, train and plane. Even cyclists can drink with ease while on the move.

***Figure 11.6***
*Leading packaging supplier Tetrapak promotes the functionality and applicability of its cartons*
*Source: Courtesy of Ian Bilbey/CIA, Abbott Mead Vickers. BBDO*

**Multiple packaging**
Packaging that includes more than one unit of a product, such as twin packs, tri-packs and six-packs

**Multiple Packaging** Rather than packaging a single unit of a product, marketers sometimes use twin packs, tri-packs, six-packs or other forms of **multiple packaging**. For certain types of product, multiple packaging is used to increase demand because it increases the amount of the product available at the point of consumption – in consumers' houses, for example. However, multiple packaging does not work for all types of product. Consumers would not use additional table salt simply because an extra box was in the cupboard. Multiple packaging can make products easier to handle and store, as in the case of six-packs for soft drinks; it can also facilitate special price offers, such as two-for-one sales. In addition, multiple packaging may increase consumer acceptance of the product by encouraging the buyer to try the product several times.

**Handling Improved Packaging** Packaging of a product may be changed to make it easier to handle in the distribution channel – for example, changing the outer carton, special bundling, shrink wrapping or palletising. In some cases the shape of the package may need to be changed. For example, an ice cream producer may switch from a cylindrical package to a rectangular one to facilitate handling. In addition, at the retail level, the ice cream producer may be able to get more shelf facings with a rectangular package as opposed to a round one. Outer containers for products are sometimes changed so that they will proceed more easily through automated warehousing systems.

As package designs improve, it becomes harder for any one product to dominate because of packaging. However, marketers still attempt to gain a competitive edge through packaging.

Skilled artists and package designers who have experience in marketing research, test out packaging to see what sells well, not just what is aesthetically appealing. Since the typical large store stocks 15,000 items or more, products that stand out are more likely to be bought.

## Criticisms of Packaging

The last few decades have seen a number of improvements in packaging. However, some packaging problems still need to be resolved. Some packages simply do not work well. The packaging for flour and sugar is, at best, often not much better than poor. Both grocers and consumers are very much aware that these packages leak and are easily torn. Can anyone open and close a bag of flour without spilling at least a little bit? Certain packages, such as biscuit tins, milk cartons with fold-out spouts and potato crisp bags, are frequently difficult to open. The traditional shapes of packages for products such as ketchup and salad dressing make the products inconvenient to use. Have you ever questioned, when slapping a ketchup bottle, why the producer did not put the ketchup in a mayonnaise jar?

Certain types of packaging are being questioned with regard to their recyclability and biodegradability. For example, throw-away bottles take considerably more resources to produce than do reusable glass bottles.

Although many steps have been taken to make packaging safer, critics still focus on health and safety issues. Containers with sharp edges and easily broken glass bottles are sometimes viewed as a threat to safety. Certain types of plastic packaging and aerosol containers represent possible health hazards.

At times, packaging is viewed as being deceptive. Package shape, graphic design and certain colours may be used to make a product appear larger than it actually is. The inconsistent use of certain size designations – such as 'giant', 'economy', 'family', 'king' and 'super' – can certainly lead to customer confusion. Although customers have traditionally liked attractive, effective, convenient packaging, the cost of such packaging is high. For some products, such as cosmetics, the cost of the package is higher than the cost of the product itself.

## Labelling

**Labelling**
Packaging information that can be used for a variety of promotional, informational and legal purposes

**Labelling** is very closely related to packaging and can be used for a variety of promotional, informational and legal purposes. The label can be used to facilitate the identification of a product by presenting the brand and a unique graphic design. For example, Heinz's ketchup is easy to identify on a supermarket shelf because the brand name is easy to read and is coupled with a distinctive, crown-like graphic design. Labels have a descriptive function. For certain types of product, the label indicates the grade of the product, especially for tinned fruit. Labels can describe the source of the product, its contents and major features, how to use the product, how to care for the product, nutritional information, type and style of the product, and size and number of servings. The label can play a promotional function through the use of graphics that attract attention. The food and drug administrations and consumer protection agencies in different countries have varying requirements concerning warnings, instructions, certifications and manufacturers' identifications. Increasingly, however, the EU is demanding similar standards in all member countries. Despite the fact that consumers have responded favourably to the inclusion of this type of information on labels, evidence as to whether they actually use it has been mixed. Several studies indicate that consumers do not use nutritional information, whereas other studies indicate that the information is considered useful. Labels can also promote a manufacturer's other products or encourage proper use of products, resulting in greater customer satisfaction with them.

**Universal product code (UPC) or barcode**
A series of thick and thin lines that identifies the product, and provides inventory and pricing information readable by an electronic scanner

The label for many products includes a **universal product code (UPC) or barcode** – a series of thick and thin lines that identifies the product, and provides inventory and pricing information that can be read by an electronic scanner. The UPC is read electronically at the retail checkout counter. This information is used by retailers and producers for price and inventory control purposes.

Colour and eye-catching graphics on labels overcome the jumble of words – known to designers as 'mouse print' – that have been added to satisfy government regulations.

Because so many similar products are available, an attention-getting device or 'silent salesperson' is needed to attract interest. As one of the most visible parts of a product, the label is an important element in a marketing mix.

Labelling is an integral part of packaging that can be used effectively to convey product information and benefits to customers, and to promote a brand's positioning image. There are increasing legal considerations that marketers must address, such as EU regulations in terms of food sourcing, ingredient content, weights and measures, as well as cooking or application instructions. Ethical marketing requires that consumers are not misled or 'oversold' owing to the information provided on labels. In 2004, Coca-Cola had to withdraw its 'pure still water' Dasani after a batch was contaminated with an excess of the cancer-causing mineral, bromate. Just before Dasani's withdrawal from the market, the Food Standards Agency in the UK had been examining the manufacturer's claim that the product – heavily filtered tap water – was 'pure'. Partly in response, the members of the Natural Mineral Water Association, including Danone Waters, Nestlé Waters, Spadel and Highland Spring, launched an over-arching symbol to appear on the packing of their respective brands, indicating their products as pure, natural mineral water: 'Natural Mineral Water Certified'. This 'purity' symbol is intended to signify which brands are unadulterated pure mineral water, in a highly competitive and fast-evolving market, with a plethora of flavoured and modified waters now widely available.[27]

# Summary

A *brand* is a name, term, design, symbol or any other feature that identifies one seller's good or service as distinct from those of other sellers. A *brand name* is that part of a brand that can be spoken, including letters, words and numbers; the element that cannot be spoken – often a symbol or design – is called a *brand mark*. A *trademark* is a legal designation indicating that the owner has exclusive use of a brand or part of a brand, and that others are prohibited by law from using it. A *trade name* is the legal name of an organisation.

» Branding helps buyers identify and evaluate products, helps sellers facilitate repeat purchasing and product introduction, and fosters *brand loyalty* – a customer's strongly motivated and long-standing decision to purchase a particular product or service. The three degrees of brand loyalty are recognition, preference and insistence. *Brand recognition* exists when a customer is aware that a brand exists and views it as an alternative to purchase if the preferred brand is unavailable. *Brand preference* is the degree of brand loyalty in which a customer prefers one brand over competing brands and will purchase it if it is available. *Brand insistence* is the degree of brand loyalty in which a customer will accept no substitute. *Brand equity* is the marketing and financial value associated with a brand's strength in a market. It represents the value of a brand to an organisation. The four major elements underlying brand equity are brand name awareness, brand loyalty, perceived brand quality and brand associations.

» Branding experts believe that well-managed, strong and desirable brands should identify a set of specific tangible benefits to attach to the brand, known as *brand attributes*, a set of reassuring and more emotive *brand values*, plus a set of appealing and desirable *brand personality* traits. Implicit in this view is the importance of effectively creating a well-differentiated and memorable image for the brand that is carefully controlled.

» A *manufacturer brand*, initiated by the producer, makes it possible to associate the company more easily with its products at the point of purchase. An *own-label brand* is initiated and owned by a reseller, such as a retailer. A *generic brand* indicates only the product category and does not include the company name or other identifying terms. Manufacturers combat the growing competition from own-label brands by developing multiple brands.

» When selecting a brand name, a marketer should choose one that is easy to say, spell and recall, and that alludes to the product's uses, benefits or special characteristics. Brand names are created inside an organisation by individuals, committees or branding departments, or by outside consultants. Brand names can be devised from words, initials, numbers, nonsense words or a combination of these. Services as well as products are branded, often with the company name and an accompanying symbol that makes the brand distinctive or conveys a desired image.

» Producers protect ownership of their brands through patent and trademark offices. Marketers at a company must make certain that their selected brand name does not infringe on an already-registered brand by confusing or deceiving consumers about the source of the product. In many countries, brand registration is on a first-come, first-served basis, making protection more difficult. Brand counterfeiting, increasingly common, has potential for undermining consumer confidence in, and loyalty to, a brand.

» Companies brand their products in several ways. *Individual branding* designates a unique name for each of a company's products; *overall family branding* identifies all of a company's products with the same name; *line family branding* assigns all products within a single line the same name; and *brand extension branding* applies an existing name to a new or improved product. Trademark licensing enables producers to earn extra revenue, receive low-cost or free publicity, and protect their trademarks. Through a licensing agreement, and for a licensing fee, a company may permit approved manufacturers to use its trademark on other products.

» *Successful brands* tend to prioritise quality, offer superior service, get to market or the targeted segment first, be clearly differentiated from rival brands, have a unique positioning concept supported by a strong communications programme and be consistent over time. *Brand strength* is a function of the product's attributes and functionality, its differentiation, plus any demonstrable added value to the purchaser or user. Strong brands usually create product differentiation, help establish a competitive edge, encourage product awareness and demand a significant amount of management and control. Four *levels of brands* need to be addressed: the tangible product, the 'basic' brand, the 'augmented' brand and the 'potential' of the brand. To be successful, a brand should capture the leading share in its market segment or distribution channel, command prices sufficiently high to offer high profit margins and be likely to maintain its profit position after more brands and generic versions enter the market. Many companies should be more effective in managing their brands, many of which do not live up to these success criteria.

» *Corporate branding* involves applying the principles of product branding at the corporate level. Corporate branding is reflected in visible manifestations such as the company name, logo and visual presentation, and also in the business's underlying and guiding values. Sometimes the terms *corporate image* and *corporate identity* are also used in relation to corporate branding. Corporate branding plays a role in guiding all of a company's marketing activities. Corporate branding is transmitted through tangible and intangible features and, to be effective, should be embedded in all company actions.

» *Packaging* involves the development of a container and label, complete with graphic design for a product. Effective packaging offers protection, economy, safety and convenience. It can influence the customer's purchase decision by promoting a product's features, uses, benefits and image. When developing a package, marketers must consider costs relative to how much the target market is willing to pay. Other considerations include how to make the package tamper-resistant; whether to use *family packaging, secondary use packaging, category-consistent packaging* or *multiple packaging*; how to design the package as an effective promotional tool; how best to accommodate resellers; and whether to develop environmentally responsible packaging.

*Packaging development* involves aesthetic and structural choices. Other considerations include: material selection, surface graphics, typography, information layout and hierarchies, front-of-pack versus back-of-pack detailing, language and jargon, photography and illustrations, use of colour, symbols and icons, final finishes and effects, labelling practicalities and barcoding/tracking. There are numerous primary packaging options: cartons, bottles, tubes, cans, tubs and jars, multipacks, clamshells, blister packs, CD boxes, gift packs and a host of innovative solutions for storing, displaying and dispensing products.

Packaging can be a major component of a marketing strategy. Companies choose particular colours, designs, shapes and textures to create desirable images and associations. Producers alter packages to convey new features or to make them safer or more convenient. If a package has a secondary use, the product's value to the consumer may be increased. Category-consistent packaging makes products more easily recognised by consumers, and innovative packaging enhances a product's distinctiveness. Consumers may criticise packaging that doesn't work well, is not biodegradable or recyclable, poses health or safety problems, or is deceptive in some way.

*Labelling* is an important aspect of packaging that can be used for promotional, informational and legal purposes. Because labels are attention-getting devices, they are significant features in the marketing mix. Various regulatory agencies can require that products be labelled or marked with warnings, instructions, certifications, nutritional information and the manufacturer's identification. Increasingly, most products – even cars – have a *universal product code (UPC) or barcode*. There are ethical considerations for marketers as customers should not be misled or mis-sold owing to the information conveyed on a product's packaging.

## *Key Links*

- This chapter, about effective branding, should be read in conjunction with the section of Chapter 8 that addresses the linked concept of brand positioning.
- The branding strategy must reflect the characteristics of the product too, as explored in Chapter 10.
- Many companies operate a portfolio of brands and often must select some for priority investment and marketing spend, as described in Chapter 12.

## Important Terms

Brand
Brand name
Brand mark
Trademark
Trade name
Brand loyalty
Brand recognition
Brand preference
Brand insistence
Brand equity
Brand attributes
Brand values
Brand personality
Manufacturer brands
Own-label brands
Generic brand
Individual branding
Overall family branding
Line family branding
Brand extension branding
Successful brands
Brand strength
Levels of brands
Corporate branding
Corporate image
Corporate identity
Packaging
Family packaging
Packaging development
Secondary use packaging
Category-consistent packaging
Multiple packaging
Labelling
Universal product code (UPC) or barcode

## Discussion and Review Questions

1 What is the difference between a brand and a brand name? Compare and contrast the terms brand mark and trademark.

2 How does branding benefit customers and organisations?
3 What are the advantages associated with brand loyalty?
4 What are the distinguishing characteristics of own-label brands?
5 Given the competition between own-label brands and manufacturer brands, should manufacturers be concerned about the popularity of own-label brands? How should manufacturers fight back in the brand battle?
6 Identify and explain the major considerations consumers take into account when selecting a brand.
7 The brand name Xerox is sometimes used generically to refer to photocopying machines. How can Xerox Corporation protect this brand name?
8 Identify and explain the four major branding policies and give examples of each. Can a company use more than one policy at a time? Explain your answer.
9 What are the major advantages and disadvantages of licensing?
10 Why is there more to a brand than its name? Explain your response.
11 What are the most commonly found foundations for successful brands? Illustrate your response with brand examples.
12 What constitutes brand strength?
13 What are the differences between brand attributes, brand values and brand personality?
14 What is brand equity and why is this notion increasingly important?
15 What are the three core criteria for assessing the success of a brand?
16 Describe the functions that a package can perform. Which function is most important? Why?
17 When developing a package, what are the major issues that a marketer should consider?
18 In what ways can packaging be used as a strategic tool?
19 What are the major criticisms of packaging?
20 What are the major functions of labelling?

## Recommended Readings


- Aaker, D., *Building Strong Brands* (New York: Free Press, 2002).
- Aaker, D.A. and Joachimsthaler, E., *Brand Leadership* (New York: Free Press, 2002).
- Calver, G., *What is Packaging Design?* (Mies, Switzerland: RotoVision SA, 2004).
- De Chernatony, L. and McDonald, M., *Creating Powerful Brands* (Oxford: Butterworth-Heinemann, 2004).
- Doyle, P., *Marketing Management and Strategy* (Harlow: Pearson/FT, 2002).
- Keller, K.L., *Building, Measuring and Managing Brand Equity* (Englewood Cliffs, NJ: Pearson, 2003).
- Lehmann, D. and Winer, R., *Product Management* (Boston, Mass: McGraw-Hill, 2001).
- Macrae, C., *The Brand Chartering Handbook* (London: Thomson, 1999).
- Ries, A. and Ries, L., *The 22 Immutable Laws of Branding: How to Build any Product or Line into a World Class Brand* (London: HarperCollins, 2002).
- Rosenau, M.D., Griffin, A., Castellion, G. and Anschuetz, N., eds, *The PDMA Handbook of New Product Development* (New York: John Wiley, 1996).
- Trott, P., *Innovation Management and New Product Development* (Harlow: Pearson/FT, 2002).


## Internet Exercise

Packaging has to reflect manufacturers' requirements and also evolving consumer issues. Log on to: www.tetrapak.com

Consider the information on this leading packaging company's website, notably the information offered about the company, its ethos, One Step Ahead programme, innovation and new product development.

1 To what extent and in what ways is Tetra Pak addressing changing and evolving manufacturer and consumer issues?
2 What innovative packaging solutions is Tetra Pak currently developing?

# *Applied Mini-Case*

In the 1980s, one of Europe's retailing success stories was the creation by George Davies of fashion chain Next. Leading out-of-town grocery retailer ASDA persuaded Davies to rekindle the fortunes of its clothing range. The result was the George range of men's, women's and children's clothing, positioned as a low-price, high-style fashion brand. 'Styles straight off the catwalk' at affordable prices, targeted at ASDA's value-conscious shoppers, proved incredibly successful. In the highly competitive clothing market, in 2004 the George range in ASDA grocery superstores overtook Debenhams to become the UK's third-biggest retailer of clothing. A few years ago, George Davies moved on and, to the surprise of many onlookers, was approached by erstwhile arch-rival Marks & Spencer to help improve the former market leader's fortunes. The result for Marks & Spencer was the recently launched highly successful range of stylish fashion, branded Per Una.

Both ASDA, with George, and Marks & Spencer, with Per Una, decided to utilise newly created brands for their new clothing ranges. In the case of Marks & Spencer, this was even more remarkable, as previously all of its merchandise retailed under the St Michael retailer own-label brand, familiar to generations of shoppers. It is believed that without brand identities so deliberately far removed from the host retailers' own brands, neither George nor Per Una would have been so successful. Both brands have themselves enabled their owners to extend their operations: George is available by catalogue, and both George and Per Una have now been given fashion-only high-street branches.

**Sources:** George/ASDA, 2004; Marks & Spencer stores, 2003/2004; Rachel Barnes, 'ASDA to highlight style in George repositioning', *Marketing*, 25 March 2004, p. 4.

### *Question*

**Why did ASDA and Marks & Spencer both opt to launch clothing ranges with new brand identities that were different to the host retailers' brands?**

## *Case Study*

# 3D and Environmentally Friendly Packaging Design

Three-dimensional packaging does much more than protect products and make them easy to distribute, handle and use. For marketers, 3D packaging can help differentiate a brand, add value or simply aid consumer recognition. The distinctive shape of the Coca-Cola bottle, recognised worldwide, is synonymous with the brand. The importance of creative packaging design is well established. Maximising packaging design benefits requires an integrated approach that considers financial, manufacturing, distribution and marketing requirements. In some companies this total business approach is achieved by forming staff teams with representatives from all business areas. The teams will consider all aspects of packaging design: materials, size and shape, opening and closure features, material conversion efficiency, retail storage and display, transportability, disposability, filling speed and costs.

Research shows that for some products, innovative packaging is seen to add value in the eyes of target consumers. There is the sensual pleasure of handling the product, a perception of creativity and added prestige from the purchase, as well as the implication that the manufacturer 'cares' about the consumer.

Growing consumer concern about the environment and government targets for recycling are putting new pressures on packaging design and development, in addition to all the other marketing and operational requirements of the process. As they look for ways to increase the environment-friendliness of their packaging, companies need to ask a series of questions.

- Can the amount of material in the package be reduced?
- Can the size of the package be reduced?
- Is recyclable material a possibility?
- Are the necessary recycling processes available?
- Are the raw materials used easy to replenish?

Environmental concerns are causing companies to reconsider the appropriateness of traditional packaging materials. For example, glass is coming back to supermarket shelves, while new developments in the use of plastics and paper/board are leading to improvements in recyclability. Even when companies are able to move towards more ecologically sympathetic packaging, there may be hidden problems. For example, the process of recycling itself may waste energy and create pollution. To ensure that the disadvantages of changing packaging design do not outweigh the benefits, a company should undertake a 'cradle to grave' analysis of the proposed packaging, looking at all aspects of its manufacture, distribution, use and disposal.

In the rush to meet consumer demands and regulatory requirements, companies are in danger of introducing ineffective packaging solutions. For example, manufacturers have recently introduced flexible refill pouches as a replacement for plastic bottles. To the consumer, who sees rigid plastic bottles as bulky and difficult to dispose of, this seems to be a positive step. The lightweight alternative may look better but in practice is awkward to distribute, problematic to stock, hard to open and difficult to recycle. Packaging must be sensible and capable of adding to the brand's image.

These concerns led to Lever Brothers adopting a novel packaging solution for its best-selling Comfort fabric conditioner. In 1998 it launched crushable refill containers, which are easier to stock, display and keep at home than refill pouches. On-pack instructions explain to consumers that the concentrated liquid and thinner packaging save 60 per cent of packaging material versus regular fabric conditioner bottles, and that this bottle 'is crushable and can be recycled'.

With BMW setting up plants to recycle and dispose of old BMW cars, PC World retailing reused inkjet cartridges and Sainsbury's encouraging the reuse of carrier bags, Lever Brothers is not alone in seeking and promoting environmental solutions. Packaging is increasingly a concern, though, for 'Green' consumers. For Lever Brothers, it does appear that the crushable container has overcome consumer aversion to the flimsy refill pouches tried out in the mid-1990s.

As ever, packaging is an evolutionary process and no doubt by the time this book hits the bookshops, a more innovative technique will have been deployed.

**Sources:** Sainsbury's, May 2004; Lever Brothers, 1999; CGM, *Marketing Guide 14: 3D Packaging Design*, Haymarket Publishing Services Ltd, 1992; John S. Blyth, 'Packaging for competitive advantage', *Management Review*, May 1990, p. 64; Dagmar Mussey and Juliana Kanteng, 'Packaging strict Green rules', *Advertising Age*, 2 December 1991, p. S-10; Katrina Carl, 'Good package design helps increase consumer loyalty', *Marketing News*, 19 June 1995, p. 4; Andy Gilgrist, 'The shape of things to come', *Marketing Week*, 16 September 1994, pp. 43–7; DTI, 1999; www.tetra.pak.com, May 2004.

## Questions for Discussion

1 What are the functions and benefits of 3D packaging?
2 How does innovative packaging add value to products?
3 In what ways are companies such as Lever Brothers addressing environmental concerns regarding packaging materials?

# 12

# Developing Products and Managing Product Portfolios

**"In the globally competitive world, product and brand management represents the most important resource responsibility in the portfolio of the marketing manager's job."**

*Michael J. Thomas, University of Strathclyde*

## Objectives

- **To become aware of organisational alternatives for managing products**
- **To understand how businesses develop a product idea into a commercial product**
- **To understand the importance and role of product development in the marketing mix**
- **To acquire knowledge of the management of products during the various stages of a product's life cycle**
- **To become aware of how existing products can be modified**
- **To learn how product deletion can be used to improve product mixes**
- **To examine tools for the strategic planning of product or market portfolios**

## Introduction

Companies have to create new ideas for products and turn some of these into marketable product or service propositions. Such a process is far from easy, with more new product launches failing than succeeding.

As additional products are included in a company's portfolio, it becomes increasingly difficult to identify on which of them investment and sales/marketing resources should be focused. A range of tools, known as product portfolio techniques, exists to assist marketers in such decision-making.

A related and important concept is that of product life cycle management: the logic being that products are launched and – if successful – they grow, then mature, before going into decline. Marketers must be aware of the relative standings of their respective products and brands.

## Opener

# Virgin Money: is Innovation Enough?

Richard Branson's Virgin brand is known to consumers across a range of products and services, from airlines to entertainment to mobile phones. In 1995, Virgin launched its financial services arm with Virgin Direct. At a time when major retailers such as Marks & Spencer and Tesco were entering many sectors of financial services, from banking to insurance, the entry of Virgin Direct made many of the traditional businesses in the financial services sector very anxious. Branson's reputation among consumers for 'taking on faceless corporations' gave Virgin Direct a head start.

Virgin Direct, replicating the activities of Virgin in other sectors, intended to be seen as an innovator that always strives to offer a value-for-money proposition that strongly benefits the consumer. Virgin launched a tracker fund that tracked shares across the entire stock market rather than across only a limited selection. This innovation was subsequently copied by many rivals. Then Virgin lobbied the government to launch stakeholder pensions. Although successful, it is widely accepted that the eventual appearance of stakeholder pensions has been far from a success story for the industry. Virgin also led the way with off-set mortgages, with the Virgin One account. Virgin found this complex proposition difficult to market to consumers, without face-to-face contact via branches. In 2001, the One Account was handed over to Royal Bank of Scotland, which did have a suitable branch network and has been able to sell this mortgage product to consumers.

Despite such teething problems, Virgin Money – as the business is now known – is profitable and thanks largely to its tie-up with card provider MBNA, has a growing credit card business, too. The philosophy is simple: Virgin Money intends to introduce more interesting propositions, rather than simply churning out new products. The company has a focus on being customer-led, rather than product-led. The Virgin-branded financial services products are always innovative and place an emphasis on addressing consumer needs and consumer concerns about the sprawling global financial services corporations. However, innovation alone is not always enough to guarantee success, particularly in a traditional sector and with products with which consumers may not wish to gamble. Nevertheless, the Virgin approach is clear: the aim is to develop products with clear consumer benefits that avoid simply replicating the existing array of financial services provided by the large financial services corporations.

**Sources:** Virgin Money; David Benady, 'Virgin Money pushes for its renaissance', *Marketing Week*, 6 May 2004, pp. 20–1.
Logo: Courtesy of Virgin Money

To compete effectively and achieve their goals, companies must develop products that reflect consumer needs and preferences, while seeking to be different from competitors. This is certainly the approach adopted by Virgin Money. A company often has to modify existing products, introduce new products or eliminate products that were successful perhaps only a few years ago. Sometimes, product alterations are required to keep pace with changing consumer demographics and new technologies. Whatever the reasons for altering products, the product mix must be managed and kept fresh, reflecting customer expectations, changing market trends and competitors' products. It may be appropriate to expand a company's product mix to take advantage of excess marketing and production capacity.

The product portfolio approach tries to create specific marketing strategies to achieve a balanced mix of products that will maximise a company's longer-term profits. This chapter begins by considering how businesses are organised to develop and manage products. Next, several ways to improve a company's product mix, including new product development from idea generation to commercialisation, are reviewed. The chapter then considers issues and decisions associated with managing a product through the growth, maturity and declining stages of its life cycle. Different types of product modification are also examined. The deletion of weak products from the product mix, often one of the hardest decisions for a marketer, is examined. The chapter concludes with a look at some of the related analytical tools associated with the planning of product portfolio: the BCG product portfolio analysis, the market attractiveness–business position model or directional policy matrix (DPM), Profit Impact on Marketing Strategy (PIMS), and the ABC sales: contribution analysis.

## Organising to Manage Products

A company must often manage a complex set of products, markets or both. Often, too, it finds that the traditional functional form of organisation – in which managers specialise in business functions such as advertising, sales and distribution – does not fit its needs. Consequently, management must find an organisational approach that accomplishes the tasks necessary to develop and manage products. Alternatives to functional organisation include the product or brand manager approach, the marketing manager approach, and the venture or project team approach.

**Product manager**
The person responsible for a product, a product line or several distinct products that make up an interrelated group within a multiproduct organisation

**Brand manager**
The person responsible for a single brand

**The Product or Brand Manager Approach** A **product manager** is responsible for a product, a product line or several distinct products that make up an interrelated group within a multiproduct organisation. A **brand manager**, on the other hand, is responsible for a single brand – for example, Lipton's Yellow Label tea or Virgin Cola. A product or brand manager operates cross-functionally to coordinate the activities, information and strategies involved in marketing an assigned product. Product managers and brand managers plan marketing activities to achieve objectives by coordinating a mix of place/distribution, promotion – especially sales promotion and advertising – and price. They must consider packaging and branding decisions, and work closely with research and development, engineering and production departments. The product manager or brand manager approach is used by many large, multiproduct companies in the consumer goods business. Increasingly it is a popular approach adopted by marketers responsible for services brands and business-to-business markets.

**Marketing manager**
The person responsible for managing the marketing activities that serve a particular group or class of customers

**The Marketing Manager Approach** A **marketing manager** is responsible for managing the marketing activities that serve a particular group or class of customers. This organisational approach is particularly effective when a company engages in different types of marketing activity to provide products to diverse customer groups. For example, a company may have one marketing manager for business markets and another for consumer markets. These broad market categories may be broken down into more limited market responsibilities.

IT services company Fujitsu has identified core target market sectors, such as government customers, retail, financial services, utilities, and so forth – there is a separate marketing manager responsible for each sector, all reporting to the central marketing director. Each Fujitsu marketing manager handles the implementation of marketing programmes bespoke to his or her clients, but is also tasked with developing new products or services relevant to their category of clients.

**Venture** or **project team** The group that creates entirely new products, perhaps aimed at new markets, and is responsible for all aspects of the products' development

**The Venture or Project Team Approach** A **venture** or **project team** is designed to create entirely new products that may be aimed at new markets. Unlike a product or marketing manager, a venture team is responsible for all aspects of a product's development: research and development, production and engineering, finance and accounting, and marketing. Venture teams work outside established divisions to create inventive approaches to new products and markets. As a result of this flexibility, new products can be developed to take advantage of opportunities in highly segmented markets. Fujitsu has a separate team of marketers and new product development specialists working outside any specific client sectors, who are also striving to develop the next generation of attractive IT services but are not focused on a particular client sector, which is the role of the marketing managers.

The members of a venture team come from different functional areas of an organisation. Companies are increasingly using such cross-functional teams for product development in an effort to boost product quality. Quality may be positively related to information integration within the team, customers' influence on the product development process, and a quality orientation within the business.[1] When the commercial potential of a new product has been demonstrated, the members may return to their functional areas, or they may join a new or existing division to manage the product. The new product may be turned over to an existing division, a marketing manager or a product manager. Innovative organisational forms such as venture teams are especially important for well-established companies operating in mature markets. These companies must take a dual approach to marketing organisation. They must accommodate the management of mature products and also encourage the development of new ones.[2]

## New Product Development

Developing and introducing new products is frequently expensive and risky. The development of Gillette's Sensor razor took over eight years and resulted in a £150 million investment.[3] Thousands of new consumer products are introduced annually, and, as indicated in Chapter 10, anywhere from 60 to 90 per cent of them fail. Lack of research, technical problems in design or production, and errors in timing the product's introduction are all causes of failure. Although developing new products is risky, so is failing to introduce new products. For example, the makers of Timex watches gained a large share of the watch market through effective marketing strategies during the 1960s and early 1970s. By 1983, Timex's market share had slipped considerably, in part because the company had failed to introduce new products. Timex has since regained market share by introducing a number of new products, but in the meantime competitors such as Swatch established their brands and stole significant market share from Timex.

The term 'new product' can have more than one meaning. It may refer to a genuinely new product – such as digital cameras – offering innovative benefits. But products that are merely different and distinctly better are also often viewed as new, such as lighter-weight wireless laptops. The following items, listed in no particular order, are product innovations of the last 30 or 40 years: Post-it notes, birth-control pills, personal computers, felt-tip pens, anti-ulcer drugs, Viagra, VCRs, DVDs, deep-fat fryers, compact disc players, mobile phones, e-mail, soft contact lenses and telephone banking. Thus, a new product can be an innovative variation of an existing product, as in the example shown in Figure 12.1.

A radically new product involves a complex development process, including an extensive business analysis to determine the possibility of success.[4] It can also be a product that a

***Figure 12.1***
*Building on the popularity of crisps and cheesy snacks, Quaker launched rice and corn-based Snack-a-Jacks, promoting the product's low fat content*
*Source: All work created by Star Chamber*

**New product development**
The process a product goes through before introduction, involving seven phases: idea generation, screening ideas, concept testing, business analysis, product development, test marketing and commercialisation

given company has not marketed previously, although similar products may be available from other companies. The first company to introduce a video cassette recorder was clearly launching a new product, yet if Boeing introduced its own brand of video cassette recorder, this would also be viewed as a new product for Boeing, because it has not previously marketed such products. Managers in companies trying something new are often highly excited by sales prospects, yet the targeted consumers have probably been able to purchase similar products from a variety of other suppliers for some time; so, to be successful, the new entrant must have a visible and desirable competitive edge.

Before a product is introduced, it goes through the seven phases of **new product development** shown in Figure 12.2:

1 idea generation
2 screening ideas
3 concept testing
4 business analysis
5 product development
6 test marketing
7 commercialisation.

A product may be dropped, and many are, at any of these stages of development. This section examines the process through which products are developed from the inception of an idea to a product offered for sale. Table 12.1 shows how companies can improve their new product success rate.

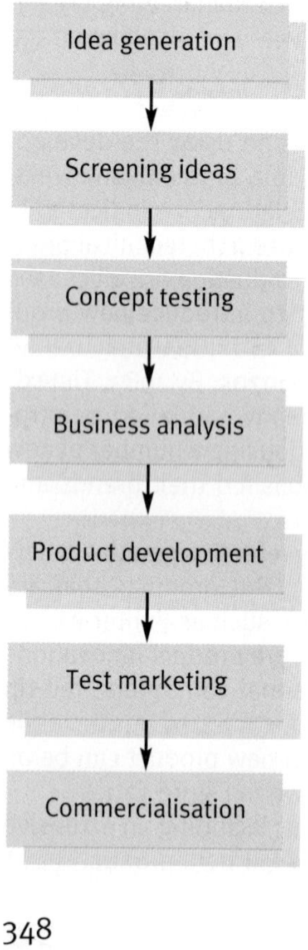


***Figure 12.2***
*Phases of new product development*

**Table 12.1 How to Improve New Product Success**

| | |
|---|---|
| 1 | Talk with consumers; don't introduce a product just because you have the technology to make it. |
| 2 | Set realistic sales goals. Unrealistic goals can result in potentially successful products being terminated. |
| 3 | Make all parts of the company (research, manufacturing, marketing and distribution) work together for customer orientation. |
| 4 | At each stage of development, the product should have consumer acceptance, the ability to be manufactured at an acceptable cost and sales support. |
| 5 | Test market a product long enough to get an accurate assessment. Some products fail because consumers buy them early as a novelty only. |
| 6 | Carefully evaluate all product failures to provide information for future product introductions. |
| 7 | Monitor competitor developments – a new product must not merely replicate a rival. |
| 8 | Keep internal colleagues up-to-date and explain new developments to them. |

**Source:** Christopher P. Power, Kathleen Kerwin, Ronald Grover, Keith Alexander and Robert D. Hof, 'Flops: too many new products fail. Here's why – and how to do better', from *Business Week*, 16 August 1993, pp. 78–9.

**Idea generation**
The process by which businesses and other organisations seek product ideas that will help them achieve their objectives

**Idea Generation** **Idea generation** involves businesses and other organisations seeking product ideas that will help them achieve their objectives. This task is difficult because only a few ideas are good enough to be commercially successful. Although some organisations get their ideas almost by chance, companies trying to manage their product mixes effectively usually develop systematic approaches for generating new product ideas. Indeed, there is a relationship between the amount of market information gathered and the number of ideas generated by work groups in organisations.[5] At the heart of innovation is a purposeful, focused effort to identify new ways to serve a market. Unexpected occurrences, incongruities, new needs, industry and market changes, and demographic changes may all indicate new opportunities.[6] The forces of the marketing environment (see Chapter 3) often create new opportunities – as well as threats to combat.

New product ideas can come from several sources. They may come from internal sources: marketing managers, researchers, sales personnel, engineers or other organisational personnel. Brainstorming and incentives or rewards for good ideas are typical intra-organisation devices for stimulating the development of ideas. The company 3M is well known for encouraging the generation of new ideas. The idea for 3M's Post-it adhesive-backed yellow notes came from an employee. As a church choir member, he used slips of paper for marking songs in his hymn book. Because the pieces of paper fell out, he suggested developing an adhesive-backed note. Hewlett-Packard keeps its labs open to engineers 24 hours a day to help generate ideas; it also encourages its researchers to devote 10 per cent of company time to exploring their own ideas for new products.[7] Company suggestion boxes for employees' ideas provide many of the stimuli for BMW's automotive innovations.

New product ideas may also arise from sources outside the company – for example, customers, competitors, advertising agencies, management consultants and private research organisations. Johnson & Johnson, for example, acquired the technology for its new, clear orthodontic braces through a joint venture with Saphikon, the developer of the technology behind the braces. Developing new product alliances with other businesses has also been found to enhance the acquisition and use of information helpful for creating new product ideas.[8] Sometimes ideas come from potential buyers of a product. Asking weekend fishermen what they wanted in a sonar fish finder led Techsonic to develop its LCR (liquid crystal recorder) fish finder. The practice of asking customers what they want from its products has helped Techsonic maintain its leadership in the industry.[9] For example, Chapter 3 outlined how companies such as Fujitsu discuss with clients their marketing environment drivers so that they can develop new products and services that reflect these client issues. In some markets, it is particularly important for new ideas to stem from customers. For example, many defence programmes take ten years to instigate, and the big defence equipment manufacturers are led by the stated buying plans and budgets of government defence departments.

**Screening ideas**
The process by which a company assesses whether product ideas match its organisational objectives and resources

**Screening Ideas** **Screening ideas** involves first assessing whether they match organisational objectives and resources, and then choosing the best ideas for further review. Next, the company's overall ability to produce and market the product is analysed. Other aspects of an idea that should be weighed are the nature and wants of buyers, and possible marketing environment changes. More new product ideas are rejected during the idea-screening phase than during any other phase.

Sometimes a checklist of new product requirements is used to ensure that the screening process is as systematic as possible. If a critical factor on the checklist remains unclear, the type of formal marketing research described in Chapter 9 may be needed. To screen ideas properly, it may be necessary to test product concepts; a product concept and its benefits can be described or shown to consumers. Several product concepts may be tested to discover which might appeal most to a particular target market.

**Concept testing**
Seeking potential buyers' responses to a product idea

**Concept Testing** **Concept testing** is a phase in which a small sample of potential buyers is presented with a product idea, often in focus groups, through a written or oral description – and perhaps a few drawings – to determine their attitudes and initial buying intentions regarding the product. For a single product idea, an organisation can test one or several concepts of the same product. Concept testing is a low-cost procedure that lets a company determine customers' initial reactions to a product idea before it invests considerable resources in research and development. The results of concept testing can be used by product development personnel to better understand which product attributes and benefits are most important to potential customers.

**Business analysis**
A company's evaluation of a product idea to determine its potential contribution to the company's sales, costs and profits

**Business Analysis** During the **business analysis** phase, the product idea is evaluated to determine its potential contribution to the company's sales, costs and profits. In the course of a business analysis, evaluators ask a variety of questions.

- Does the product fit in with the company's existing product mix? Does the company have the right expertise to develop the new product?
- Is demand strong enough to justify entering the market and will the demand endure?
- What types of environmental and competitive changes can be expected, and how will these changes affect the product's future sales, costs and profits?
- Are the organisation's research, development, engineering and production capabilities adequate?
- If new facilities must be constructed, how quickly can they be built and how much will they cost?
- Is the necessary financing for development and commercialisation on hand or obtainable at terms consistent with a favourable return on investment?
- Will the new product or idea benefit the company's existing portfolio of products?
- Is there any danger that existing products or services will be cannibalised?

In the business analysis stage, companies seek market information. The results of consumer surveys, along with secondary data, supply the specifics needed for estimating potential sales, costs and profits. At this point, a research budget should explore the financial objectives and related considerations for the new product.

**Product development**
The phase in which the organisation determines if it is technically and financially feasible to produce a new product

**Product Development** **Product development** is the phase in which the organisation determines if it is technically feasible to produce the product and if it can be produced at costs low enough to make the final price reasonable. To test its acceptability, the idea or concept is converted into a prototype, or working model. Concept cars are used in the development of new vehicles. The prototype should reveal tangible and intangible attributes associated with the product in consumers' minds. The product's design, mechanical features and intangible aspects must be linked to wants in the marketplace. This includes the service aspects of the product, which are a vital component of many products. Failure to determine how consumers feel about the product and how they would use it may lead to the product's failure. For example, the Sinclair C5 electric buggy was developed as a serious on-road, single-seater car for city or country use. However, drivers felt unsafe in the buggy, and campus students ended up using the remaining stocks as on-pavement runabouts.

The development phase of a new product is frequently lengthy and expensive; thus a relatively small number of product ideas are put into development. If the product appears sufficiently successful during this phase to merit testing, then during the latter part of the development phase marketers begin to make decisions regarding branding, packaging, labelling, pricing and promotion for use in the test marketing phase.[10]

**Test marketing**
The limited introduction of a product in geographic areas chosen to represent the intended market

**Test Marketing** The limited introduction of a product in geographic areas chosen to represent the intended market is called **test marketing**. Its aim is to determine the reactions of probable buyers. For example, after McDonald's developed fried chicken products for its fast-food menu, it test marketed the idea in certain McDonald's restaurants to find out how those customers felt about eating chicken at McDonald's. The company followed a similar strategy for test marketing its range of salads and pizza. Test marketing is not an extension of the development phase – it is a sample launching of the entire marketing mix, and should be conducted only after the product has gone through development and after initial plans regarding the other marketing mix variables have been made.

Companies of all sizes use test marketing to reduce the risk of product failure. The dangers of introducing an untested product include undercutting already profitable products and, should the new product fail, loss of credibility with distributors and customers. When Lever Brothers launched Wisk – previously only a washing powder – in liquid form in 1986, the company had misjudged consumer usage. Many blocked washing machines later, P&G offered liquid Ariel with Arielettes, containers to be placed inside the machines together with the clothes. Costly reformulations overcame such problems.

Test marketing provides several benefits. It lets marketers expose a product to a natural marketing environment to gauge its sales performance. While the product is being marketed in a limited area, the company can seek to identify weaknesses in the product or in other parts of the marketing mix. Corrections can be made more cheaply than if the product had already been introduced nationwide. Test marketing also allows marketers to experiment with variations in advertising, price and packaging in different test areas and to measure the extent of brand awareness, brand switching and repeat purchases that result from alterations in the marketing mix.

The accuracy of test marketing results often hinges on where the tests are conducted. The selection of appropriate test areas is very important. The validity of test marketing results depends heavily on selecting test sites that provide an accurate representation of the intended target market. The criteria used for choosing test cities or television regions depend on the product's characteristics, the target market's characteristics, and the company's objectives and resources.

Test marketing can be risky because it is expensive and a company's competitors may try to interfere. This is common in the confectionery market. A competitor may invalidate test results in an attempt to 'jam' the test programme by increasing advertising or promotions, lowering prices or offering special incentives – all to combat the recognition and purchase of a new brand. Sometimes, too, competitors copy the product in the testing stage and rush to introduce a similar product. It is therefore desirable to move quickly and commercialise as soon as possible after testing. When the product introduction is delayed to the point where the public begins to doubt its existence, such products may become known as 'vapourware', particularly in the computer software industry.[11]

To avoid these risks, companies may use alternative methods to gauge consumer preferences. One such method is simulated test marketing. Typically, consumers at shopping centres are asked to view an advertisement for a new product and are given a free sample to take home. These consumers are subsequently interviewed over the phone and asked to rate the product. The major advantages of simulated test marketing are lower costs, tighter security and, consequently, a reduction in the flow of information to competitors, and the elimination of jamming. Scanner-based test marketing is another, more sophisticated version of the traditional test marketing method. Some marketing research companies, such as ACNielsen, offer test marketing services to help provide independent assessment of products.

**Commercialisation**
The process of refining and settling plans for full-scale manufacturing and marketing

**Commercialisation** During the **commercialisation** phase, plans for full-scale manufacturing and marketing must be refined and settled, and budgets for the project must be prepared. Early in the commercialisation phase, marketing management analyses the results of test marketing to find out what changes in the marketing mix are needed before the product is introduced. For example, the results of test marketing may tell the marketers to change one or more of the product's physical attributes, modify the distribution plans to include more retail outlets, alter promotional efforts or change the product's price. During this phase, the company also has to gear up for production and may therefore face sizeable capital expenditure and personnel costs.

The product enters the market during the commercialisation phase. One study indicates that only 8 per cent of new product projects started by major companies reach this stage.[12] When introducing a product, marketers often spend enormous sums of money on advertising, personal selling and other types of promotion. These expenses, together with capital outlays, can make commercialisation extremely costly; such expenditures may not be recovered for several years. For example, when Ford introduced its new Focus model, the company spent millions of pounds on advertising to communicate the new car's attributes. Commercialisation is easier when customers accept the product rapidly, which they are more likely to do if marketers can make them aware of its benefits.

## Line Extensions

**Line extension**
A product that is closely related to existing products in the line, but meets different customer needs

A **line extension** is the development of a product that is closely related to one or more products in the existing product line but is designed specifically to meet the somewhat different needs of customers. For example, Fairy Liquid washing-up detergent was used as a springboard for various detergent-based Fairy products including washing powder for automatic washing machines. Many of the so-called new products introduced each year by organisations are in fact line extensions. Line extensions are more common than new products because they are a less expensive, lower-risk alternative for increasing sales. A line extension may focus on a different market segment or may be an attempt to increase sales within the same market segment by more precisely satisfying the needs of people in that segment. For example, Nestlé launched an extra-strong variant of its Polo mints, Supermints, aimed at lovers of strong peppermints. However, one side-effect of employing a line extension is that it may result in a more negative evaluation of the core product.[13] It has been suggested that the success of line extensions is partly affected by consumer perceptions of how well the extension fits with the core brand.[14]

# Product Adoption Process

**Product adoption process**
The stages buyers go through in accepting a product: awareness, interest, evaluation, trial, and adoption

The following stages of the **product adoption process** are generally recognised as those that buyers go through in accepting a product, from gaining awareness of it to buying the product.

1 *Awareness* – the buyer becomes aware of the product.
2 *Interest* – the buyer seeks information and is generally receptive to learning about the product.
3 *Evaluation* – the buyer considers the product's benefits and determines whether to try it.
4 *Trial* – the buyer examines, tests or tries the product to determine its usefulness relative to his or her needs.
5 *Adoption* – the buyer purchases the product and can be expected to use it when the need for this general type of product arises again.[15]

In the first stage, when individuals become aware that the product exists, they have little information about the product and are not concerned about obtaining more. Consumers enter the interest stage when they are motivated to attain information about the product's features, uses, advantages, disadvantages, price or location. During the evaluation stage, individuals consider whether the product will satisfy certain criteria that are crucial for meeting their specific needs. In the trial stage, they use or experience the product for the first time, possibly by purchasing a small quantity, by taking advantage of a free sample or demonstration, or by borrowing the product from someone. Supermarkets, for instance, frequently offer special promotions to encourage consumers to taste products. During this stage, potential adopters determine the usefulness of the product under the specific conditions for which they need it.

Individuals move into the adoption stage by choosing the specific product when they need a product of that general type. However, the fact that a person enters the adoption process does not mean that she or he will eventually adopt the new product. Rejection may occur at any stage, including adoption. Both product adoption and product rejection can be temporary or permanent. Just because a consumer or business customer adopts a particular product once, does not guarantee future loyalty to the product or brand. As described in Chapters 4 and 11, marketers must work hard to achieve a customer's ongoing loyalty.

This adoption process model has several implications for the commercialisation phase. First, the company must promote the product to create widespread awareness of its existence and its benefits. Samples or simulated trials should be arranged to help buyers make initial purchase decisions. Marketers should also emphasise quality control and provide solid guarantees to reinforce buyer opinion during the evaluation stage. Finally, production and physical distribution must be linked to patterns of adoption and repeat purchase. The product adoption process is also discussed in Chapter 17, as marketing communications are not only important for achieving awareness, but also for informing and persuading customers right through the product adoption process. When launching a new product, companies must realise that buyers differ in the speed with which they adopt a product. Identifying buyers who are most open to new products can help expedite this process.

Consumers do not always pass through all the stages of the product adoption process as formally as this overview may have implied. A minor upgrade to a familiar brand may not cause consumers much concern, whereas an innovative product launched by an unknown supplier will give rise to much more extensive consumer decision-making. Business customers making routine rebuys or consumers making routine response purchases – see Chapters 6 and 7 – already have awareness of a particular product and are interested in it. Previously, they have tried and adopted the product, so their limited decision-making does not require them to pass through this product adoption process in this manner. On the whole, though, marketers would do well to remember the importance of all five stages in this important concept. Consumers and business-to-business customers must be aware of, have interest in, and be prepared to evaluate and try out a product or service if they are to adopt it: that is, to buy and consume it. The marketing task does not end with first-time adoption, however. The ongoing requirement for marketers is to ensure customer loyalty and repeat purchase, as discussed in Chapters 4 and 11.

Products are not usually launched nationwide overnight but are introduced through a process called a roll-out. In a roll-out, a product is introduced in stages, starting in a set of geographic areas and gradually expanding into adjacent areas. Thus, Cadbury's Wispa bar appeared initially in the north-east of England. It may take several years to market a product nationally. Sometimes the test cities are used as initial marketing areas, and the introduction becomes a natural extension of test marketing. Gradual product introduction reduces the risks of introducing a new product. If the product fails, the company will experience smaller losses. Furthermore, it may take some time for a company to develop a suitable distribution network. Also, the number of units needed to satisfy the national demand for a successful product can be enormous, and a company cannot usually produce the required quantities in a short time.

Despite the good reasons for introducing a product gradually, marketers realise that this approach creates some competitive problems. A gradual introduction allows competitors to observe what a company is doing and to monitor results, just as the company's own marketers are doing. If competitors see that the newly introduced product is successful, they may enter the same target market quickly with similar products. Avoiding competition is critical when a company introduces a brand into a market in which it already has one or more brands. Marketers usually want to avoid cannibalising sales of their existing brands, unless the new brand generates substantially larger profits. When Coca-Cola reintroduced Tab, it attempted to position the cola so as to minimise the adverse effects on Diet Coke sales. Similarly, when KP introduces a new snack brand, it must take care to ensure that sales of other KP brands do not suffer.

If a product has been planned properly, its attributes and brand image will give it the distinctive appeal needed. Style, shape, construction, quality of work and colour help create the image and the appeal. Of course buyers are more likely to purchase the product if they can easily identify the benefits. When the new product does not offer some preferred attributes, there is room for another new product or for repositioning of an existing product.[16] Methods of positioning are discussed in the final part of Chapter 8.

# Product Life Cycle Management

Most new products start off slowly and seldom generate enough sales to produce profits immediately. As buyers learn about the new product, marketers should be looking out for any weaknesses and be ready to make corrections quickly, in order to prevent the product's early demise. Computer software companies expect to modify 'bugs' when launching new software products. Consumers must be informed quickly and efficiently of any difficulties if damage to the brand image is to be avoided. Marketing strategy should be designed to attract the segment that is most interested in, and has the fewest objections to, the product. If any of these factors need adjustment, this action, too, must be taken quickly to sustain demand. As the sales curve moves upwards and the break-even point is reached, the growth stage begins. See Figure 10.5 in Chapter 10 for an explanation of the product life cycle concept, which assumes a path from introduction to growth, into maturity and then decline.

## Marketing Strategy in the Growth Stage

As sales increase, management must support the momentum by adjusting the marketing strategy. The goal is to establish the product's position and to fortify it by encouraging brand loyalty. As profits increase, the company must brace itself for the entrance of aggressive competitors, who may make specialised appeals to selected market segments.

During the growth stage, product offerings may have to be expanded. To achieve greater penetration of an overall market, segmentation may have to be used more intensely. That would require developing product variations to satisfy the needs of customers in several different market segments. Marketers should analyse the product position regarding competing products, and correct weak or omitted attributes. Further quality, functional or style modifications may be required.

Gaps in the marketing channels should be filled during the growth period. Once a product has won acceptance, new distribution outlets may be easier to obtain. Sometimes marketers tend to move from **exclusive distribution** or **selective distribution** to a more **intensive distribution** of dealers to achieve greater market penetration. Marketers must also make sure that the physical distribution system is running efficiently and delivering supplies to distributors before their inventories are exhausted. Because competition increases during the growth period, good service and an effective mechanism for handling complaints are important.

**Exclusive distribution** Market coverage in which only one outlet is used in a geographic area

**Selective distribution** Market coverage in which only some available outlets in an area are chosen to distribute a product

**Intensive distribution** Market coverage in which all available outlets are used for distributing a product

Advertising expenditure may be lowered slightly from the high level of the introductory stage but still needs to be quite substantial. As sales increase, promotion costs should drop as a percentage of total sales. A falling ratio between promotion expenditure and sales should contribute significantly to increased profits. The advertising messages should aim to stress brand benefits and emphasise the product's positioning. Coupons and samples may be used to increase market share.

After recovering development costs, a business may be able to lower prices. As sales volume increases, efficiencies in production can result in lower costs. These savings may be passed on to buyers. If demand remains strong and there are few competitive threats, prices tend to remain stable. If price cuts are feasible, they can improve price competition and discourage new competitors from entering the market. For example, when compact disc players were introduced in the early 1980s, they carried an £800 price tag. Primarily because of the price, the product was positioned as a 'toy for audiophiles' – a very small market segment. To generate mass-market demand, compact disc player manufacturers dropped their prices to around £150, and the cost of discs also dropped. The price is now at a point where the margin is low but the turnover is high, and more homes are now investing in compact disc players. A similar pattern has emerged in the sale of mobile phones and home PCs. Widescreen home entertainment systems and DVD players will follow this pattern, over the next few years.

## Marketing Strategy for Mature Products

As many products are in the maturity stage of their life cycles, marketers must always be ready to improve the product and marketing mix. During maturity, the competitive situation stabilises and some of the weaker competitors drop out. It has been suggested that as a product matures, its customers become more experienced and their requirements more diverse, so that market segmentation opportunities increase. As customers' needs change, new marketing strategies for mature products may be called for.[17] For example, in the wake of competition from Eurotunnel, car ferry operators now stress excellent on-board shopping, catering facilities and spacious accommodation in their advertising. Marketers may also need to modify the product. Symptoms of a mature product include price cutting, increased competitive action and shifting from a product orientation to a non-product orientation (price, promotion and place/distribution adaptation); in addition, market growth slows.[18]

**Product modification** The alteration of one or more characteristics of a company's product

**Product modification** means changing one or more characteristics of a company's product. This strategy is most likely to be used in the maturity stage of the product life cycle to give a company's existing brand a competitive edge. Even well-established brands such as Sellotape must be modified from time to time, with innovative dispensers or versions with 'Happy Birthday' or suchlike printed along the tape. Altering a product mix in this way entails less risk than developing a new product because the product is already established in the market. For example, publishers may launch new editions of popular reference books updated with the latest information.

If certain conditions are met, product modification can improve a company's product mix. First, the product must be modifiable. Second, existing customers must be able to perceive that a modification has been made, assuming that the modified item is still aimed at them. Third, the modification should make the product more consistent with customers' desires so that it provides greater satisfaction. If these conditions are not met, it is unlikely that the product modification, however innovative, will be successful. The Innovation and Change box below describes several successful modifications to personal banking that have been developed due to emerging technology. Product modifications fall into three major categories: quality, functional and style modifications.

**Quality modifications** Changes that affect a product's dependability and durability

**Quality Modifications** Changes concerning a product's dependability and durability are called **quality modifications**. Usually, they are executed by altering the materials or the production process. Reducing a product's quality may allow a company to lower its price and direct the item at a larger target market.

## Innovation and Change

### E-banking, Telebanking, Text and TV Banking: What Next?

Marketers must constantly look at ways to keep their products 'fresh' and up to date, modifying existing products as appropriate or bringing out new ones. Personal banking has gone through many phases. Many readers will remember the days when high-street banks were open only until mid-afternoon Monday to Friday, and there were no ATMs for easy cash withdrawals. Queuing at ageing tills in austere branches was the primary means of operating current bank accounts. Direct debits and standing orders helped, but the real revolution came in the late 1970s with the growth of ATMs – cash dispensers – and then in the early 1990s as most leading banks extended their opening hours and range of services aimed at private customers. Technology has emerged as a driving force for change via other banking services in addition to ATMs. HSBC's First Direct broke ranks by launching as a telephone-only, 365-days-a-year, 24-hour full-service personal banking provider. The rapid take-off of First Direct encouraged its traditional high-street competitors to offer their own 24-hour telephone banking services – such as Barclays' BarclayCall – based on heavy investment in call centres.

Internet banking is changing the way in which many customers interact with their banks. Barclays initially launched a limited service owing to security fears. The company held back on a full-service launch until its systems could offer greater security to users and until customer concerns about hackers were allayed. The Royal Bank of Scotland, Lloyds TSB and Nationwide led the way in launching Internet banking to their customers. It is not only the major high-street banking giants that have turned to technology. The Prudential also turned to e-banking with its Egg brand of e-commerce financial services; 65,000 people enquired about this intriguing product departure in the first five days after its launch, more than double the number anticipated by the Prudential. Now many customers prefer e-banking.

Another departure from the traditional high-street bank branch is the launch of TV banking. NatWest joined with Microsoft to provide an interactive banking service on Microsoft's WebTV network. The service included information about mortgages, travel insurance, currency rates, plus standard current account banking, based on NatWest's PC banking package already established on-line. NatWest has its own On-Line division, which has focused on high-security access for its PC-based customers using only a direct dial service rather than any Internet server or third-party host. This is in response to customer fears about hackers being able to access their financial dealings via Internet links. Telephones, Internet-hooked home PCs, even TVs with set-top boxes are all emerging as means by which personal bankers can avoid traipsing into their local branch in order to execute financial transactions and manage their accounts. First Direct offers mobile phone users texting access to their banking details. No doubt other technological solutions will emerge. To banking customers, such product developments are revolutionising their banking habits.

**Sources:** NatWest, First Direct and Barclays websites, 2000–04.

By contrast, increasing the quality of a product may give a company an advantage over competing brands. During the last 25 years, marketers have been forced by increased global competition, technological change and more demanding customers to improve product integrity.[19] Higher quality may enable a company to charge a higher price by creating customer loyalty and by lowering customer sensitivity to price. However, higher quality may require the use of more expensive components, less standardised production processes, and other manufacturing and management techniques that force a company to charge higher prices.[20] At the beginning of the 1990s, concern for quality increased significantly, with many companies, such as Tesco, Volvo and Caterpillar, finding ways both to increase quality and reduce costs.

**Functional modifications**
Changes that affect a product's versatility, effectiveness, convenience or safety

**Functional Modifications** Changes that affect a product's versatility, effectiveness, convenience or safety are called **functional modifications**; they usually require the product to be redesigned. Typical product categories that have undergone considerable functional modifications include home computers, audio equipment and cleaning products. Functional modifications can make a product useful to more people, thus enlarging its market, or improve the product's competitive position by providing benefits that competing items do not offer. Functional modifications can also help a company achieve and maintain a progressive image. For example, washing machine manufacturers such as Whirlpool or AEG have developed appliances that use less heat and water. In Figure 12.3, well-known detergent brand Surf has opted to promote stain removal and freshness. At times, too, functional modifications are made to reduce the possibility of product liability claims.

**Style modifications**
Changes that alter a product's sensory appeal – taste, texture, sound, smell or visual characteristics

**Style Modifications** **Style modifications** change the sensory appeal of a product by altering its taste, texture, sound, smell or visual characteristics. Such modifications can be important, because when making a purchase decision, a buyer is swayed by how a product looks, smells, tastes, feels or sounds.

Although style modifications can be used by a company to differentiate its product from competing brands, their major drawback is that their value is highly subjective. A company may strive to improve the product's style, but customers may actually find the modified product less appealing. Some companies try to minimise these problems by altering product style in subtle ways. For example, Mattel's Barbie doll has gradually changed over the years to reflect changing fashions.

During the maturity stage of the cycle, marketers actively encourage dealers to support the product, perhaps by offering promotional assistance or help in lowering their inventory costs. In general, marketers go to great lengths to serve dealers and to provide incentives for selling the manufacturer's brand, partly because own-label or retailer brands are a

*Figure 12.3*
*Surf's functional modification focused on stain removal and laundry freshness*
*Source: All work created by Star Chamber*

threat at this time. As discussed in Chapter 11, own-label brands are both an opportunity and a threat to manufacturers, who may be able to sell their products through recognised own-label or retailer brand names as well as their own. However, own-label or retailer brands frequently undermine manufacturers' brands.

Maintaining market share during the maturity stage requires moderate and sometimes heavy advertising expenditure. Advertising messages focus on differentiating a brand from numerous competitors, and sales promotion efforts are aimed at both consumers and resellers.

A greater mixture of pricing strategies is used during the maturity stage. In some cases, strong price competition occurs and price wars may break out. Sometimes marketers develop price flexibility to differentiate offerings in product lines. Mark-downs and price incentives are more common, but prices may rise if distribution and production costs increase. Marketers of mature products also often alter packaging and even positioning strategies. For example, in the USA, Heinz repackaged and repositioned its vinegar as an all-natural cleaning product.

## Marketing Strategy for Declining Product

As a product's sales curve turns downwards, industry profits continue to fall. A business can justify maintaining a product as long as it contributes to profits or enhances the overall effectiveness of a product mix. In this stage of the product life cycle, marketers must determine whether to eliminate the product or seek to reposition it in an attempt to extend its life. Usually, a declining product has lost its distinctiveness because similar competing products have been introduced. Competition engenders increased substitution and brand switching as buyers become insensitive to minor product differences. For these reasons, marketers do little to change a product's style, design or other attributes during its decline. New technology, product substitutes or environmental considerations may also indicate that the time has come to delete a product. For example, the ill-fated Betamax video cassette technology was quickly pushed out by the VHS format, which in turn is threatened by DVDs.

During a product's decline, outlets with strong sales volumes are maintained and unprofitable outlets are weeded out. An entire marketing channel may be eliminated if it does not contribute adequately to profits. Sometimes a new marketing channel, such as a factory outlet, will be used to liquidate remaining inventory of an obsolete product. Advertising expenditure is at a minimum. Advertising or special offers may slow the rate of decline. Sales promotions, such as coupons and premiums, may temporarily regain buyers' attention. As the product continues to decline, the sales staff shifts its emphasis to more profitable products.

To have a product return a profit may be more important to a company than to maintain a certain market share. To squeeze out all possible remaining profits, marketers may maintain the price despite declining sales and competitive pressures. Prices may even be increased as costs rise if a loyal core market still wants the product, such as those consumers preferring turntables to CD players. In other situations, the price may be cut to reduce existing inventory so that the product can be deleted. Severe price reductions may be required if a new product is making an existing product obsolete.

## Deleting Products

**Product deletion**
The process of eliminating a product that no longer satisfies a sufficient number of customers

**Product deletion** is the process of eliminating a product that no longer satisfies a sufficient number of customers. Products cannot usually contribute to an organisation's goals indefinitely, and a declining product reduces a company's profitability, draining resources that could be used to modify other products or develop new ones. A marginal product may require shorter production runs, which can increase per unit production costs. Finally, when a dying product completely loses favour with customers, the negative feelings may transfer to some of the company's other products.

Most companies find it difficult to delete a product. It was probably a hard decision for IPC to drop magazine Options and admit that it was a failure. A decision to drop a product may be opposed by management and other employees who feel that the product is necessary in the product mix, or by sales people who still have some loyal customers. Considerable resources and effort are sometimes spent in trying to improve the product's marketing mix enough to increase sales and thus avoid having to delete it.

Some companies delete products only after they have become heavy financial burdens. Robert Maxwell's London newspaper the *Daily News* closed after only a few weeks, having lost £25 million. A better approach is to institute some form of systematic review to evaluate each product and monitor its impact on the overall effectiveness of the company's product mix. Such a review should analyse a product's contribution to the company's sales for a given period and should include estimates of future sales, costs and profits associated with the product. It should also gauge the value of making changes in the marketing strategy to improve the product's performance. A systematic review allows a company to improve product performance and to ascertain when to delete products. Although many companies do systematically review their product mixes, one research study found that few companies have formal, written policies concerning the process of deleting products. The study also found that most companies base their decisions to delete weak products on poor sales and profit potential, low compatibility with the company's business strategies, unfavourable market outlook and historical declines in profitability.[21]

Basically, there are three ways to delete a product, either:

**Phase out**
An approach that lets the product decline without a change in marketing strategy

**Run out**
A policy that exploits any strengths left in the product

**Immediate drop**
An option that drops an unprofitable product immediately

1. phase it out
2. run it out
3. drop it immediately (see Figure 12.4).

A **phase out** approach lets the product decline without a change in the marketing strategy. No attempt is made to give the product new life. A **run out** policy exploits any strengths left in the product. Intensifying marketing efforts in core markets or eliminating some marketing expenditures, such as advertising, may cause a sudden profit increase. This approach is commonly taken for technologically obsolete products, such as older models of camcorders or computers, and is often accompanied by a price reduction. Some car manufacturers use a run out approach to dispose of certain models just before a new launch. The third option, an **immediate drop** of an unprofitable product, is the best strategy when losses are too great to prolong the product's life.

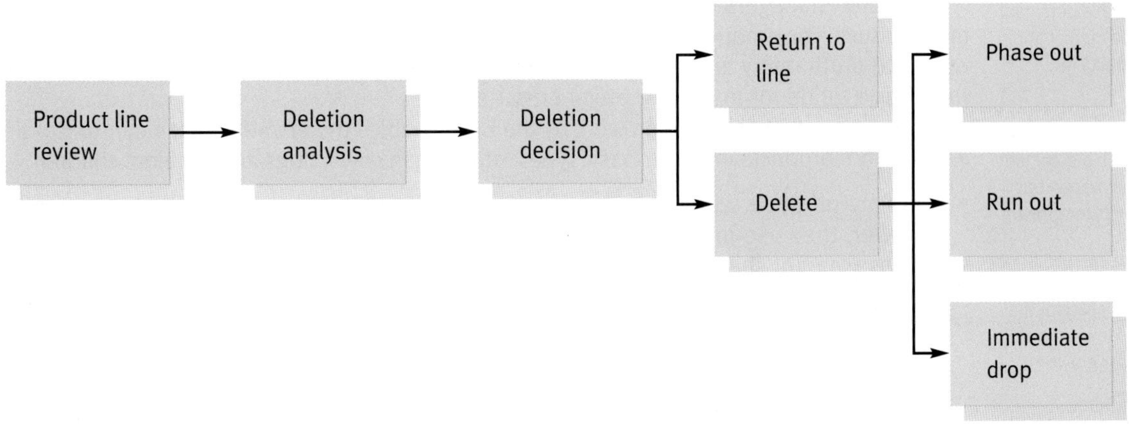


***Figure 12.4***
*Product deletion process*
*Source: Martin L. Bell,* Marketing: Concepts and Strategies, *3rd edn, p. 267; copyright © 1979, Houghton Mifflin Company. Reproduced by permission of Mrs Martin L. Bell*

# Tools for Managing Product Portfolios

A number of tools have been developed to aid marketing managers in their planning efforts. Based on ideas used in the management of financial portfolios, several models that classify an organisation's product portfolio have been proposed. These models allow strategic business units (SBUs) or products to be classified and visually displayed both according to the attractiveness of various markets and a business's relative market share within those markets. Four of these tools are the Boston Consulting Group (BCG) product portfolio analysis, the market attractiveness – business position model, the Profit Impact on Marketing Strategy (PIMS) and the ABC sales: contribution analysis. In addition, the product life cycle concept explored in Chapter 10 is an important tool often utilised in determining future strategies for brands and products. This assessment – based on the notion of the introduction, growth, maturity and decline stages in the life of a product or market – is useful in recommending marketing strategy. As described above, the options are quite different for marketers facing growth or mature stages, and markedly so for the introduction versus the decline stages. The Boston Consulting Group matrix, described next, builds on this suggestion.

## The Boston Consulting Group (BCG) Product Portfolio Analysis

**Product portfolio analysis**
A strategic planning tool that takes a product's market growth rate and its relative market share into consideration in determining a marketing strategy

**Stars**
Products with a dominant share of the market and good prospects for growth

**Cash cows**
Products with a dominant share of the market but low prospects for growth

**Dogs**
Products that have a subordinate share of the market and low prospects for growth

**Problem children**
Products that have a small share of a growing market, generally requiring a large amount of cash to build share

Just as financial investors have different investments with varying risks and rates of return, businesses have a portfolio of products characterised by different market growth rates and relative market shares. **Product portfolio analysis**, the Boston Consulting Group approach, is based on the philosophy that a product's market growth rate and its relative market share are important considerations in determining its marketing strategy. All the company's products should be integrated into a single, overall matrix and evaluated to determine appropriate strategies for individual SBUs and the overall portfolio strategies. However, a balanced product portfolio matrix is the end result of a number of actions, not just the analysis alone. Portfolio models can be created on the basis of present and projected market growth rates and proposed market share strategies. These strategies include four options:

1 build share
2 maintain share
3 harvest share
4 divest business.

Managers can use these models to determine and classify each product's expected future cash contributions and future cash requirements.

Generally, managers who use a portfolio model must examine the competitive position of a product – or product line – and the opportunities for improving that product's contribution to profitability and cash flow.[22] The BCG analytical approach is more of a diagnostic tool than a guide for making strategy prescriptions.

Figure 12.5, which is based on work by the BCG, enables the marketing manager to classify a company's products into four basic types: stars, cash cows, dogs and problem children.[23]

- **Stars** are products with a dominant share of the market and good prospects for growth. However, they use more cash than they generate to finance growth, add capacity and increase market share.
- **Cash cows** have a dominant share of the market but low prospects for growth. Typically, they generate more cash than is required to maintain market share. Cash cows generate much needed funds to support the stars and problem children.
- **Dogs** have a subordinate share of the market and low prospects for growth. These are struggling products. They are frequently found in mature markets and often should be phased out or withdrawn immediately.
- **Problem children**, sometimes called 'question marks', have a small share of a growing market and generally require a large amount of cash to build share. The question is, are they capable of becoming star products or are they destined to be dogs?

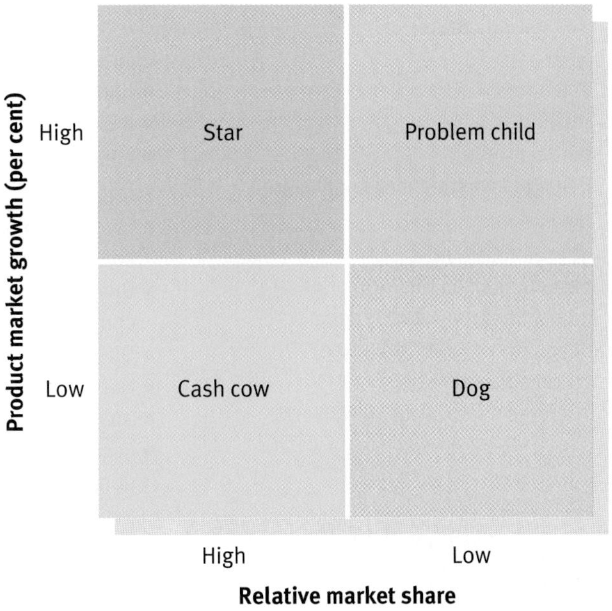


***Figure 12.5*** *Illustrative growth-share matrix developed by the Boston Consulting Group*
*Source:* Perspectives, *66, 'The product portfolio'. Reprinted by permission from the Boston Consulting Group, Inc., Boston, MA. Copyright © 1970*

The product portfolio growth-share matrix in Figure 12.5 can be expanded to show a company's whole portfolio by providing for each product:

- its cash sales volume, illustrated by the size of a circle on the matrix
- its market share *relative* to competition, represented by the horizontal position of the product on the matrix
- the growth rate of the market, indicated by the position of the product in the vertical direction.

It should be noted that relative market share is a company's own market share relative to the biggest competitor's. Figure 12.6 suggests marketing strategies appropriate for cash cows, stars, dogs and problem children. By following these guiding philosophies, a business can make strategic decisions based on the diagnosis of the BCG product portfolio growth-share matrix.

The long-term health of an organisation depends on having some products that generate cash and provide acceptable profits, plus others that use cash to support growth. Among the indicators of overall health are the size and vulnerability of the cash cows, the prospects for the stars, if any, and the number of problem children and dogs. Particular attention must be paid to those products with large cash appetites. Unless the company has an abundant cash flow, it cannot afford to sponsor many such products at one time. If resources, including debt capacity, are spread too thinly, the company will end up with too many marginal products and will be unable to finance promising new product entries or acquisitions in the future.

**Market attractiveness – business position model**
A two-dimensional matrix that helps determine which SBUs have an opportunity to grow and which should be divested

Although a popular tool in the 1980s, the BCG growth-share matrix is not commonly deployed these days. Many marketers believe that market attractiveness equates to more than simply the growth rate of a market and a product's – or brand's – respective market share. As marketers have sought more complex approaches, utilising many variables, the market attractiveness – business position model has grown in popularity.

## Market Attractiveness–Business Position Model

The **market attractiveness–business position model**, illustrated in Figure 12.7, is another two-dimensional matrix, often known as the directional policy matrix or DPM. However, rather than using single measures to define the vertical and horizontal dimensions of the matrix, the model employs multiple measurements and observations. It is an increasingly popular tool, particularly in businesses producing detailed annual marketing plans. The

| Product market growth (per cent) | Relative market share: High | Relative market share: Low |
|---|---|---|
| High | **Stars**<br>Characteristics<br>■ Market leaders<br>■ Fast growing<br>■ Substantial profits<br>■ Require large investment to finance growth<br>Strategies<br>■ Protect existing share<br>■ Re-invest earnings in the form of price reductions, product improvements, providing better market coverage, production efficiency and so on<br>■ Obtain a large share of the new users | **Problem children**<br>Characteristics<br>■ Rapid growth areas<br>■ Poor profit margins<br>■ Enormous demand for cash<br>Strategies<br>■ Invest heavily to get a disproportionate share of new sales<br>■ Buy existing market shares by acquiring competitors<br>■ Divestment (see Dogs)<br>■ Harvesting (see Dogs)<br>■ Abandonment (see Dogs)<br>■ Focus on a definable niche where dominance can be achieved |
| Low | **Cash cows**<br>Characteristics<br>■ Profitable products<br>■ Generate more cash than needed to maintain market share<br>Strategies<br>■ Maintain market dominance<br>■ Invest in process improvements and technological leadership<br>■ Maintain price leadership<br>■ Use excess cash to suppport research and growth elsewhere in the company | **Dogs**<br>Characteristics<br>■ Greatest number of products fall in this category<br>■ Operate at a cost disadvantage<br>■ Few opportunities for growth at a reasonable cost<br>■ Markets are not growing; therefore, little new business<br>Strategies<br>■ Focus on a specialised segment of the market that can be dominated and protected from competitive inroads<br>■ Harvesting—cut back all support costs to a minimum level; support cash flow over the product's remaining life<br>■ Divestment—sale of a growing concern<br>■ Abandonment—deletion from the product line |

**Figure 12.6**
*Characteristics and strategies for the four basic product types in the growth-share matrix*
*Source: concepts in this figure adapted from George S. Day, 'Diagnosing the product portfolio',* Journal of Marketing, *April 1977, pp. 30–1. Reprinted by permission of the American Marketing Association*

vertical dimension – market attractiveness – includes all the strengths and resources that relate to the market. For example, seasonality, economies of scale, competitive intensity, industry sales, and the overall cost and feasibility of entering the market. The horizontal axis – business position – is a composite of factors – for example, sales, relative market share, research and development, price competitiveness, product quality and market knowledge. These are only examples, because each set of marketers will select variables as they relate

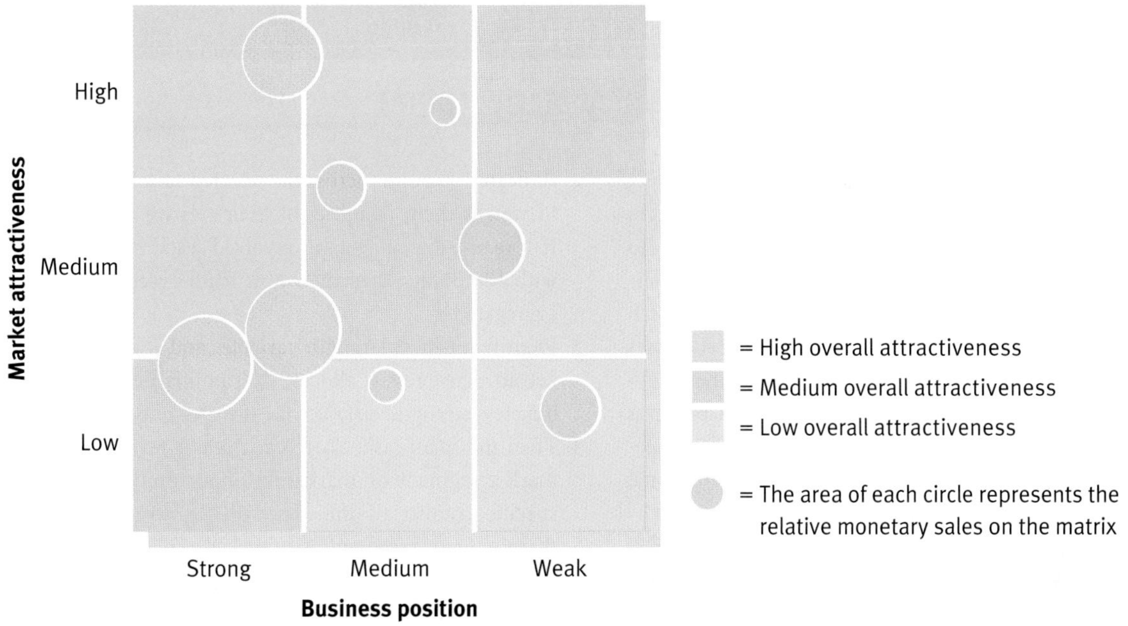


***Figure 12.7***
*Market attractiveness – business position model*
*Source: adapted from Derek F. Abell and John S. Hammond,* Strategic Market Planning: Problems and Analytical Approaches *(Englewood Cliffs, NJ: Prentice-Hall, 1979), p. 213. Used by permission*

to the product and particular market. Each company deploying this tool selects its own criteria, but uses these same ones over time to analyse changes. A slight variation of this matrix is called General Electric's Strategic Business Planning Grid because General Electric is credited with extending the product portfolio planning tool to examine market attractiveness and business strength.

The best situation for a company is to have a strong business position in an attractive market. The upper-left area in Figure 12.7 represents the opportunity for an invest/grow strategy, but the matrix does not indicate how to implement this strategy. The purpose of the model is to serve as a diagnostic tool to highlight SBUs that have an opportunity to grow or that should be divested or approached selectively.[24] SBUs that occupy the invest/grow position can lose their position through faulty marketing strategies.

Decisions on allocating resources to SBUs of medium overall attractiveness should be arrived at on a basis relative to other SBUs that are either more or less attractive. The lower-right area of the matrix is a low-growth harvest/divest area. Harvesting is a gradual withdrawal of marketing resources on the assumption that sales will decline at a slow rate but profits will still be significant at a lower sales volume. Harvesting and divesting – even abandonment, or deletion from the product line – may be appropriate strategies for SBUs characterised by low overall attractiveness.

Marketers proficient in this technique often use the agreed variables and weightings to evaluate market segments in order to determine investment priorities: certain segments will be more attractive than others, while the organisation's strengths will vary between segments (see Chapter 8).

**Directional policy matrix (DPM)**
A more commonly used name for the market attractiveness – business position model

The Marketing Tools and Techniques box on page 364 offers a step-by-step example of one company's use of the **directional policy matrix (DPM)**, in this instance examining the relative performance of different market segments. The same approach could be deployed to examine SBUs' products, rather than market segments.

## Marketing Tools and Techniques

### Practitioners' Use of the Directional Policy Matrix (DPM)

Most businesses have more than one product and operate in several markets. This results in the need to prioritise in which markets to focus resources, particularly in terms of sales and marketing activities. Often the 'who shouts the loudest' approach to management meetings wins, or else historical successes with specific clients, products or markets colour the judgement of decision-makers irrespective of current business performance. One effective approach to ensuring that objectivity has an input into such prioritisation is the directional policy matrix (DPM) or GE grid.

Along with the PEST analysis described in Chapter 3, the directional policy matrix is a pivotal tool in strategic business planning. The DPM is useful to marketers as a means for identifying the relative merits of apparently attractive opportunities. Suggested worthwhile opportunities may be benchmarked against a company's existing activities to judge the value of supporting the new ideas. The tool can be used to evaluate the relative merits of individual products or product groups.

The DPM is useful, too, in selecting between market segments (see Chapter 8). The market attractiveness criteria identified for the DPM can easily be utilised to assess the relative merits of market segments.

So, how is a DPM produced? Occasionally, a strategic planner or marketing director may produce such an analysis, but often the variables to be used in order to construct the DPM are selected and weighted by a team of senior decision-makers, often the board of directors, supplemented by marketing managers and analysts who understand the trends and dynamics of individual markets. The steps are as follows.

1. Identify a set of opportunity or market attractiveness criteria. These should be a mix of short-term variables (e.g. sales volumes and current profitability) and longer-term variables (e.g. market growth prospects or ability to sustain a differential advantage). In addition, some variables should be internal-facing (e.g. profitability) and some variables must be market-facing (e.g. customer satisfaction or intensity of competition). The aim is to have a balanced set of criteria.
2. Allocate 100 points across the selected variables in order to weight them in terms of their relative importance. If a team of managers is involved, each should 'vote' with 100 points, then the whole team's votes should be aggregated.
3. Identify business strength variables and – as with market attractiveness – allocate 100 points between these business strength variables for their weighting.
4. Then the main task. Score each major product group, market segment or marketing opportunity (given the specific context of the analysis). To score, a simple three-category scoring system is usually adequate: $n \times 1$ = strong/ good; $n \times 0.5$ = 'so-so'/average; $n \times 0$ = low/ weak/poor (where $n$ = the selected variable). When scoring, business strength variables are usually taken as being relative to the dominant player(s) in the market, while market attractiveness scoring is usually one market segment versus 'the others' in the company's portfolio.
5. Weight × score = total to be plotted. Each product group, segment or opportunity is, therefore, allocated a value between 0 and 100 for market attractiveness and for business strength, so its position may be plotted on the DPM grid. The Y axis represents market attractiveness (0–100), while the X axis represents business strength (0–100).

In the real B2B example depicted on page 365, the company identified 11 market attractiveness criteria and 10 business strength criteria. Each market segment was in turn judged against all 21 variables, warranting 1, 0.5 or 0. For example, market segment 'A' scored 0.5 for 'long-term prospects with the client' ($14 \times 0.5 = 7$) and 0.5 for 'current presence in the client' ($8 \times 0.5 = 4$), and so forth. However, segment 'B' scored 1 for the first variable ($14 \times 1 = 14$). The result is depicted in the DPM chart on page 365.

Having assessed each of its many market segments, this business plotted them on a DPM. In addition, the management team predicted where the segments would head over the following three years. The circle size represents the proportionate income to the company from each market segment.

| Marketing Attractiveness | *weighting* | Business Strengths | *weighting* |
|---|---|---|---|
| Long-term prospects with the client | 14 | Clarity and cohesion of message | 19 |
| Profitability | 14 | Thought leadership | 16 |
| Strategic fit | 12 | Easy to do business with/flexibility | 15 |
| Size of the opportunity | 12 | Right people/right support/right milieu | 14 |
| (Right) relationship | 9 | Perceived quality of delivery | 12 |
| Ability to deliver the necessary solution | 9 | Understanding of the market sector | 10 |
| How well the opportunity can be defined/realised | 8 | Referenceability | 7 |
| Current presence in the client | 8 | Price competitive | 3.6 |
| Nature of competition | 6 | Winning business/closure mindset | 5 |
| Risk | 5 | Breadth and depth | 2.4 |
| Whether the task can be replicated or referenced | 3 | | |

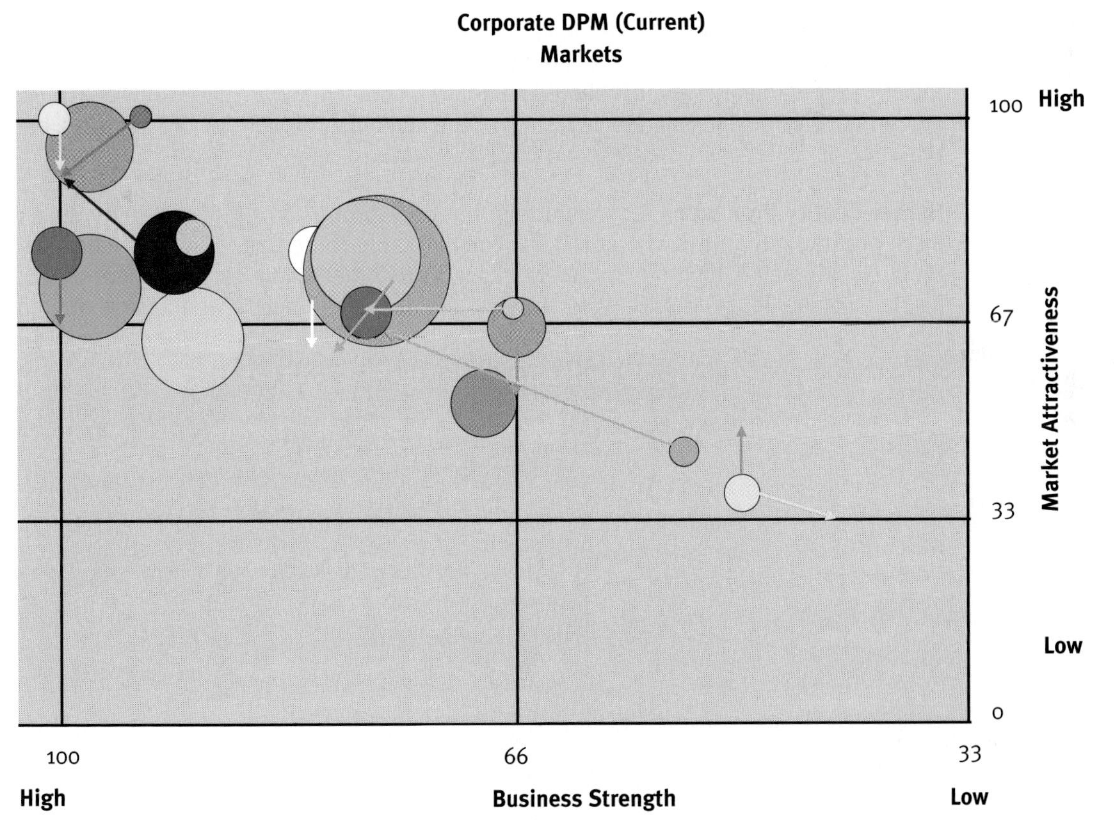


## Profit Impact on Marketing Strategy (PIMS)

The US Strategic Planning Institute (SPI) developed a databank of information on 3000 strategic business units of 200 different businesses during the period 1970 to 1983 for the **Profit Impact on Marketing Strategy (PIMS)** research programme.[25] The sample is somewhat biased because it is composed primarily of large, profitable manufacturing companies marketing mature products; service organisations and distribution companies are

**Profit Impact on Marketing Strategy (PIMS)**
A research programme that compiled a databank of information on 3000 strategic business units of 200 different businesses in order to assist in analysing marketing performance and formulating marketing strategies

under-represented. However, 19 per cent of the sample is composed of international businesses.[26] The member organisations of the Institute provided confidential information on successes, failures and marginal products. The data have been analysed to provide members with information about how similar organisations performed under a given set of circumstances and about the factors that contributed to success or failure in given market conditions.

The unit of observation in PIMS is the SBU. Table 12.2 shows the types of information provided on each business in the PIMS database. The PIMS database includes both diagnostic and prescriptive information to assist in analysing marketing performance and formulating marketing strategies. The analysis focuses on options, problems, resources and opportunities. The PIMS project has identified more than 30 factors that affect the performance of businesses. These factors can be grouped into three sets of variables:

1 those relating to the structure of the marketplace in which the company competes
2 those that describe the company's competitive position within that market
3 those that relate to the strategy chosen by the company.[27]

These factors may interact, as well as directly affect performance and profitability. Some of the main findings of the PIMS project are as follows.

**Strong Market Position**    Market position refers to the relative market share that a company holds in relation to its competition. Companies that have a large share of a market tend to be the most profitable. However, it should be noted that market share does not necessarily create profitability. Business strategies, such as the marketing of high-quality products, and the provision of good service result in profitability.

**Higher-quality Products**    Organisations that offer products of higher quality tend to be more profitable than their competitors. They are able to demand higher prices for those products. Moreover, high-quality offerings instil customer loyalty, foster repeat purchases, insulate companies from price wars and help build market share, as in the case of premium

---

### TABLE 12.2 TYPES OF INFORMATION PROVIDED ON EACH BUSINESS IN THE PIMS DATABASE

**Characteristics of the Business Environment**
  Long run growth rate of the market
  Short run growth rate of the market
  Rate of inflation of selling price levels
  Number and size of customers
  Purchase frequency and magnitude

**Competitive Position of the Business**
  Share of the served market
  Share relative to largest competitors
  Product quality relative to competitors
  Prices relative to competitors
  Pay scales relative to competitors
  Marketing efforts relative to competitors
  Pattern of market segmentation
  Rate of new product introductions

**Structure of the Production Process**
  Capital intensity (degree of automation, etc.)
  Degree of vertical integration
  Capacity utilisation
  Productivity of capital equipment
  Productivity of people
  Inventory levels

**Discretionary Budget Allocations**
  Research and development budgets
  Advertising and promotion budgets
  Salesforce expenditures

**Strategic Moves**
  Patterns of change in the controllable elements above

**Operating Results**
  Profitability results
  Cash flow results
  Growth results

**Source:** Reproduced by permission of the Strategic Planning Institute [PIMS programme], Cambridge, Mass.

***Figure 12.8***
*Waitrose has a reputation for retailing superior products, a theme emphasised in this advertisement for its honey*
*Source: Courtesy of Waitrose*

supermarket chain Waitrose (see Figure 12.8). It appears impossible for companies to overcome inferior offerings with high levels of marketing expenditures. Advertising is no substitute for product quality.

**Lower Costs** Companies achieve lower costs through economies of scale, ability to bargain with suppliers or backward integration. Low costs heighten profitability levels.

**Investment and Capital Intensity** The higher the investment required to compete in an industry, the more pressure there is on a company to use its production capacity fully. Moreover, these factors tend to have a negative impact on profitability.

In practice, few businesses these days deploy PIMS-style analysis, but in many respects the principal findings still direct companies' strategic thinking.

## The ABC Sales: Contribution Analysis

The **ABC sales: contribution analysis** can be conducted at product group or product line level; for the total market, territories or sub-markets; for customer groups/market segments; or for individual customer accounts. In other words, whatever the unit of analysis, the ABC sales: contribution analysis is revealing. In the context of this chapter, individual products or product groups may be plotted. Sales managers focusing on key accounts may plot individual key customer accounts, instead of products (see Chapter 21), while marketers developing target market strategies may well plot different market segments in order to understand their relative performance better (see Chapter 8).

**ABC sales: contribution analysis**
An approach that examines the financial worth to a company of its products, product groups or customers

The aim of this analysis is to show both the amount of sales and the financial contribution from these sales – that is, the financial worth – to the company's fortunes. Financial success, after all, is not confined to sales volume figures; a business must have an adequate level of contribution – sales revenue minus all variable costs – from its sales. This analysis helps companies to identify the relative value of different products, markets or even individual customer accounts, assisting with the allocation of resources.

An example of an ABC sales: contribution analysis chart is shown in Figure 12.9. The 45-degree diagonal line from bottom left to top right is the optimum. It is a straightforward rule, not a regression line. Ideally, the dots plotted on the chart would be located on the line – having both good sales and contribution – and be at the top right of the graph, with high sales and high contribution. These 'sell a lot, make a lot' plots to the top right, are the 'A' class. Typically, however, this is not the case: often the majority of products, customers or markets – depending on the selected unit of analysis – fall to the bottom left of the graph. Here, they are low sales and low contribution (the 'C' class) or they have average sales and average contribution (the 'B' class).

Three important conclusions can be drawn from an ABC analysis.

1 The analysis can identify highly attractive customers, markets or products (depending on the chosen unit of analysis) in terms of the associated contributions, but where sales are relatively low. For such accounts, an increase in sales, no matter how slight, with associated high prices and good financial returns, will be highly rewarding.
2 The analysis can determine accounts with high sales figures but low or pitiful contributions. Cash flow may be good, but the company's profitability is not helped. Even a slight increase in contribution is most desirable and will greatly assist the company's overall fortunes.
3 The analysis can challenge the historical perspective that often clouds judgement as to what constitutes a good product, market or customer. Every business has its historically

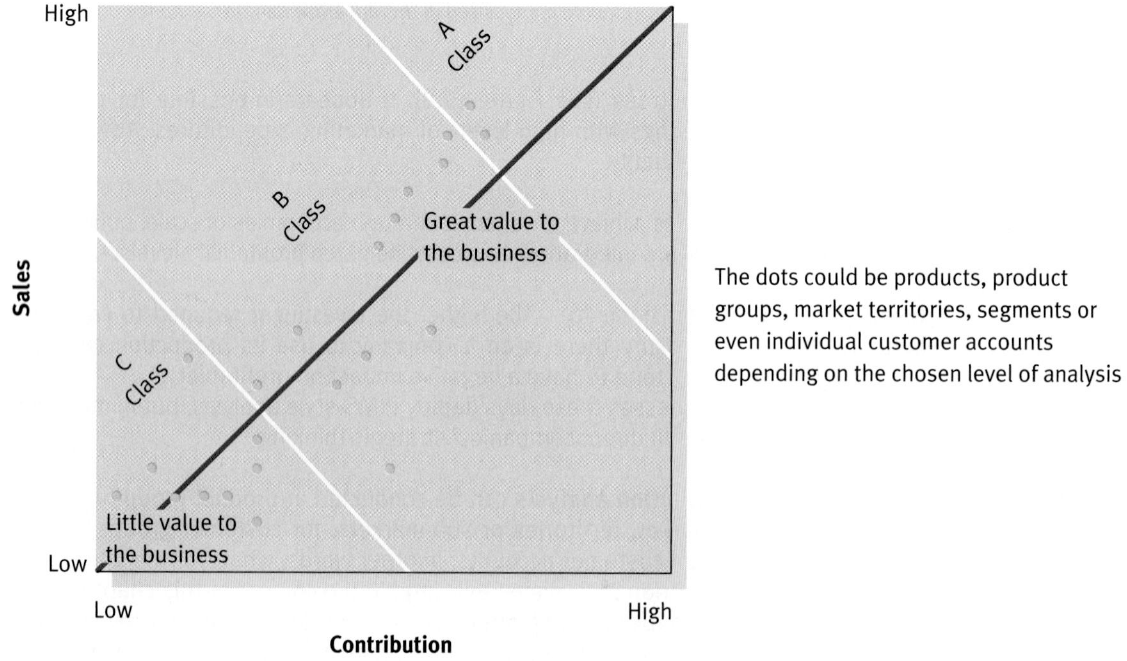


*Figure 12.9*
*Example of an ABC sales: contribution chart*

most rewarding customers and products that in reality are no longer performing in terms of sales, contribution or both. Often, managers still believe the historical rhetoric rather than recognise that the situation has moved on; new priorities must benefit from the available resources and marketing effort. The ABC analysis generally unearths a few such instances and identifies the rump of unrewarding accounts or customers that are not worth pursuing.

The approaches presented here provide an overview of the most popular analytical methods used in strategic market planning. This chapter has focused on the management of product portfolios, but as has been explained, techniques such as the directional policy matrix (DPM) and the ABC sales: contribution analysis are extremely helpful in evaluating the relative merits of market segments or even individual customer accounts.

The Boston Consulting Group's portfolio analysis, the market attractiveness – business position model, the Profit Impact on Marketing Strategy research programme, the ABC sales: contribution analysis and the product life cycle concept are used not only to diagnose problem areas or to recognise opportunities but also to facilitate the allocation of resources among business units. They are not intended to serve as formulae for success or prescriptive guides, which lay out specific strategic action plans.[28] These approaches are supplements to, not substitutes for, the marketing manager's own judgement. The real test of each approach, or any integrated approach, is how well it helps management diagnose the company's strengths and weaknesses and prescribe strategic actions for maintaining or improving performance. The emphasis should be on making sound decisions with the aid of these analytical tools.[29]

# Summary

To maximise the effectiveness of a product mix, a company usually has to alter its mix through the modification of existing products, deletion of a product or new product development. Developing and managing products is critical to a company's survival and growth. The various approaches available for organising product management share common activities, functions and decisions necessary to guide a product through its life cycle. A *product manager* is responsible for a product, a product line or several distinct products that make up an interrelated group within a multiproduct organisation. A *brand manager* is responsible for a single brand. *Marketing managers* are responsible for managing the marketing activities that serve a particular group or class of customers. A *venture or project team* is sometimes used to create and develop entirely new products that may be aimed at new markets.

» A new product may be an innovation that has never been sold by any organisation; or it can be a product that a given company has not marketed previously, although similar products have been available from other organisations. Before a product is introduced, it goes through the seven phases of *new product development*. (1) In the *idea generation* phase, new product ideas may come from internal or external sources. (2) In the process of *screening ideas*, those with the greatest potential are selected for further review. (3) *Concept testing* presents a small number of potential buyers with the concept idea in order to ascertain early approval indicators. (4) During the *business analysis* stage, the product idea is evaluated to determine its potential contribution to the company's sales, costs and profits. (5) *Product development* is the phase in which the organisation determines if it is technically feasible to produce the product and if it can be produced at costs low enough for the final price to be reasonable. (6) *Test marketing* is a limited introduction of a product in geographic areas chosen to represent the intended market. (7) The decision to enter the *commercialisation* phase means that full-scale production of the product begins and a complete marketing strategy is developed.

- Not all 'new' products are genuinely new! Many product introductions are in fact a *line extension* – the development of a product that is closely related to products in the existing product line, but designed to meet different customer needs. The *product adoption process* that buyers go through in accepting a product includes awareness, interest, evaluation, trial and adoption.

- As a product moves through its life cycle, marketing strategies will require continual adaptation. In the growth stage, it is important to develop brand loyalty and a market position. Marketers may move from an *exclusive distribution* or *selective distribution* to a more *intensive distribution* of dealers. In the maturity stage, a product may be modified or new market segments may be developed to rejuvenate its sales.

- *Product modification* involves changing one or more characteristics of a company's product. This approach to altering a product mix can be effective when the product is modifiable, when customers can perceive the change and when customers want the modification. *Quality modifications* are changes that relate to a product's dependability and durability. Changes that affect a product's versatility, effectiveness, convenience or safety are called *functional modifications*. *Style modifications* change the sensory appeal of a product.

- A product that is declining may be maintained as long as it makes a contribution to profits or enhances the product mix. Marketers must determine whether to eliminate the declining product or to reposition it to extend its life.

- *Product deletion* is the process of eliminating a product that is unprofitable, consumes too many resources and no longer satisfies a sufficient number of customers. *Phase out*, *run out* and *immediate drop* are three ways to delete a product. A product mix should be systematically reviewed to determine when to delete products.

- A number of tools have been developed to aid marketing managers in their portfolio planning efforts; these include the Boston Consulting Group (BCG) *product portfolio analysis*, the market attractiveness–business position model, the Profit Impact on Marketing Strategy (PIMS) and the ABC sales: contribution analysis. The product life cycle concept is also important in determining marketing strategies. The BCG approach is based on the philosophy that a product's market growth rate and its relative market share are key factors influencing marketing strategy. All the company's products are integrated into a single, overall matrix – including *stars*, *cash cows*, *dogs* and *problem children* – and are evaluated to determine appropriate strategies for individual SBUs and the overall portfolio strategies.

- The *market attractiveness – business position model* is a two-dimensional matrix, often known as the *directional policy matrix (DPM)*. The market attractiveness dimension includes variables that relate to the attractiveness of the market or product opportunity, such as seasonality, economies of scale, competitive intensity, industry sales and the cost of competing. The business position axis measures variables that relate to a business's strengths and capabilities, such as sales levels, relative market share, research and development expertise, and other factors that support building market share for a product. Each set of marketers will select variables pertinent to the respective company and industry.

- The *Profit Impact on Marketing Strategy (PIMS)* research programme of the US Strategic Planning Institute developed a databank of confidential information on the successes, failures and marginal products of more than 3000 strategic business units of 200 different businesses. The unit of observation in PIMS is an SBU. The results of PIMS include both diagnostic and prescriptive information to assist in analysing marketing performance and formulating marketing strategies. The analysis focuses on options, problems, resources and opportunities.

- The *ABC sales: contribution analysis* examines the financial worth to a company of its products, product groups or customers. The analysis highlights areas in which to avoid or limit further investment and sales and marketing activity. It also reveals specific targets for financial contribution improvement or sales volume improvement.

Tools for portfolio planning are used only to diagnose problem areas or recognise opportunities. They are supplements to, not substitutes for, the marketing manager's own judgement. The real test of each approach, or any integrated approach, is how well it helps management diagnose the company's strengths and weaknesses, and prescribe strategic actions for maintaining or improving performance.

The portfolio planning approaches presented here provide an overview of the most popular analytical methods used in strategic market planning. This chapter has focused on the management of product portfolios, but techniques such as the market attractiveness–business position model – more commonly now known as the directional policy matrix (DPM) – and the ABC sales: contribution analysis are extremely helpful in evaluating the relative merits of market segments or even individual customer accounts.

## *Key Links*

- This chapter has examined the development of products and the first part should be read in conjunction with Chapter 10, on product decisions.
- The management of products should be considered in harmony with the material presented in Chapter 11, on branding.
- The product portfolio techniques explained in this chapter, particularly the directional policy matrix and ABC sales: contribution analysis, are often deployed by marketers making trade-off decisions between emerging opportunities or various market segments. These techniques are useful when reading about targeting in Chapter 8's discussion of market segmentation.

## Important Terms

Product manager
Brand manager
Marketing manager
Venture or project team
New product development
Idea generation
Screening ideas
Concept testing
Business analysis
Product development
Test marketing
Commercialisation
Line extension
Product adoption process
Exclusive distribution
Selective distribution
Intensive distribution
Product modification
Quality modifications
Functional modifications
Style modifications
Product deletion
Phase out
Run out
Immediate drop
Product portfolio analysis
Stars
Cash cows
Dogs
Problem children
Market attractiveness–business position model
Directional policy matrix (DPM)
Profit Impact on Marketing Strategy (PIMS)
ABC sales: contribution analysis

## Discussion and Review Questions

1 What organisational alternatives are available to a company with two product lines, each consisting of four product items?
2 When is it more appropriate to use a product manager than a marketing manager?
3 What type of company might use a venture team to develop new products? What are the advantages and disadvantages of such a team?
4 Do small companies that manufacture one or two products need to be concerned about developing and managing products? Why or why not?
5 Why is product development a cross-functional activity within an organisation? That is, why must finance, engineering, manufacturing and other functional areas be involved?
6 Develop a list of information sources for new product ideas for the car industry.

7 What are the advantages and disadvantages of test marketing?
8 Compare and contrast three ways of modifying a product.
9 What are the stages of the product adoption process, and how do they affect the commercialisation phase?
10 Detail the key stages of the product life cycle.
11 How can a company prolong the life of a mature product? What actions should be taken to try to stem the product's decline?
12 Give several reasons why a company might be unable to eliminate an unprofitable product.
13 In what ways do the stages of the product life cycle impact on a company's management of its product portfolio?
14 What are the major considerations in developing the BCG product portfolio matrix? Define and explain the four basic types of product suggested by the Boston Consulting Group.
15 When should marketers consider using PIMS for strategic market planning?
16 What are the advantages of the directional policy matrix (DPM) over the BCG product portfolio matrix?
17 What are the diagnostic capabilities of the ABC sales: contribution analysis?

## Recommended Readings


- Baker, M. and Hart, S., *Product Strategy and Management* (Harlow: Pearson/FT, 1998).
- Day, G.S., *Analysis for Strategic Marketing Decisions* (St Paul, Minnesota: West, 1986).
- Doyle, P., *Marketing Management and Strategy* (Harlow: Pearson/FT, 2002).
- Lehmann, D. and Winer, R., *Product Management* (Boston, Mass: McGraw-Hill, 2001).
- Trott, P., *Innovation Management and New Product Development* (Harlow: Pearson/FT, 2002).
- Wind, Y.J., *Product Policy: Concepts, Methods and Strategy* (Reading, MA: Addison-Wesley, 1982).


## Internet Exercise

The success of BMW's Mini has been phenomenal. Despite a limited range of cars, each one on the road appears unique, and research reveals that Mini owners feel they have the power to tailor their car to suit their specific tastes and driving styles. BMW and Mini have incorporated this individualisation, of what in reality is far from a bespoke one-to-one product,
in their product development process and in their commercialisation of this product. Take a look at either:
www.mini.co.uk or www.mini.com
and in particular the section detailing accessories.

1 What product features and characteristics are portrayed on the Mini website?
2 To what extent does Mini's commercialisation enable customers to individualise or personalise their cars?

## *Applied Mini-Case*

People visit cinemas to watch a film for many reasons: to catch the latest release, because friends are going, to be entertained, to go on a date, to occupy the children, to escape from the children, to be with people, to have an emotional experience, to kill time, to have a rest, or 'just because it's somewhere to go'. The choice of which film to see may often be the first decision, but these days, with the growth of multiplexes and record cinema attendances, the choice may be which multiplex: Odeon, MGM, UCI or Showcase? For rival operators, the 'augmented' product is becoming increasingly important as they seek to develop a competitive edge and to encourage customer loyalty. For example, Showcase strongly emphasises many once secondary or minor features in an attempt to add to the appeal of its cinemas:

- state-of-the-art film projection
- acres of free, illuminated car parking
- best seats in town – exclusive rocking loungers
- bargain matinees daily
- freshly popped popcorn
- cinema hire and special group rates
- on main coach/bus routes
- Dolby stereo-equipped auditoria
- air conditioning
- excellent facilities for the disabled
- late-night shows every Friday and Saturday
- efficient, courteous service
- gift certificates always available
- art gallery with prints for sale.

For many companies, not only Showcase, the augmented product is an increasingly important element in the marketing strategy and the search for customer satisfaction. The new product development process increasingly includes the required customer service attributes desired by targeted customers to accompany the purchased product.

**Source:** Showcase Cinema, Coventry.

### *Question*

As a marketing manager, to what extent does inclusion of the augmented product simplify or complicate the new product development process?

## *Case Study*

# Sellotape or Mustard? Increasing Market Penetration

Just as JCB is a generic term for backhoe diggers in the construction industry, Hoover for vacuum cleaners, Post-it for those useful sticky stationery tags, and Bic for disposable pens, for many decades Sellotape has been the term applied to sticky transparent tape. Over the years, however, many other brands and suppliers have entered the market and eaten away Sellotape's once dominant market share. So where next for Sellotape?

At the end of 1995, following nearly two years of research and planning, Sellotape enjoyed a £2 million relaunch. This represented the 'most significant change in the brand's 60 year history', according to Neil Ashley, executive director of the company, renamed the Sellotape Company. The name Sellotape has been the company's core marketing asset for many decades, with nine out of ten consumers familiar with the brand. However, the company has for some time sold a wider range of products than its sticky tape association implies. Michael Peters of the branding specialist Identica, responsible for the Sellotape rethink, was more fervent in his view: 'while it is a very famous trademark, it's a grey one'. Qualitative marketing research revealed that, although well known, hardly any consumer asked for Sellotape by name. Worse, they readily accepted other brands because they could see no obvious product or brand features that gave Sellotape a competitive edge or differentiation over rival products.

The relaunch aimed to address the inherent weakness in becoming a generic name for a product by re-establishing a new brand identity alongside existing core brand values. Rival products not using cellulose are cheaper, so alongside its traditional tape, the Sellotape Company now offers a range of tape made from other source materials. Elephant Tape, for example, is a heavy-duty fabric tape that is targeted at the do-it-yourself (DIY) market.

Under the sub-brand Sellotape Office, a range of products aimed at office use has been launched. Ranges have also been targeted at the children's market and the home security market. The view that there are, in effect, three distinct markets – retail, DIY and office – has led to the development of novel product applications and totally separate ranges.

The key problem to overcome has been 'the Colman's mustard dilemma'. Colman's, the market leader, had tremendously high brand awareness, and consumers perceived its mustards to be of high quality. Unfortunately, these consumers usually bought only one type of mustard, English; and that one jar lasted for years! Colman's had to increase usage. It achieved this by both:

**1** demonstrating in advertisements and cookery supplements that mustard could be used in a variety of ways, particularly as an additional ingredient in many sauces, just like a herb or spice

**2** bringing out a range of different mustards, each with unique strengths, flavours and applications – French, Italian and American mustards, along with the traditional English.

Consumers were encouraged to have several jars in their cupboards and to consume greater quantities.

For Sellotape, research showed that most customers bought only one roll of sticky tape each year, often around Christmas. The launch of ranges designed for different target audiences – retail, DIY and office – and for various applications – children's activities and home security uses – emulated the brand extension principles so well deployed by Colman's.

Sellotape's strong brand awareness and identity meant that the company did not need to advertise heavily. Instead, the Sellotape Company relied on direct marketing and point-of-sale promotion to create awareness of its new sub-brands and their applications. A core task for the company has been to break down the traditional views of the product and its customers held by employees, and to establish additional channels of distribution through toy shops and garden centres to reflect the extended and additional product ranges. It is away from the once core stationery retailers that the Sellotape Company expects to see the strongest growth, particularly in the DIY sector. There, pan-European sales are rising by around 8 per cent each year and now amount to over £70 million.

If the Sellotape Company can, like Colman's, encourage its customers to buy two products annually instead of just one and to look for its branded products by name, the heritage of the brand and the reorganisation of the company will have reaped significant rewards.

**Sources:** 'Sellotape acts to avoid getting stuck in a rut', *Independent on Sunday*, 26 November, 1995, IB8; the Sellotape Company, 1996; B&Q, 1996; Sainsbury's Homebase, 1996, 2004.

With grateful thanks to Meg Carter.

## Questions for Discussion

1 At what stages in their product life cycle are the different Sellotape products, and what are the management implications?
2 Why was it necessary for the Sellotape Company to relaunch its Sellotape range?
3 How might new lines help Sellotape develop its competitive position in this market?

# 13
# The Marketing of Services

"Delivering services is people's business: only great customers and great employees can guarantee great service quality."

*Hans Kasper, Rijksuniversiteit Limburg, Maastricht*

## Objectives

- To understand the nature and characteristics of services
- To classify services
- To understand the development of marketing strategies for services
- To understand the problems involved in developing a differential advantage in services
- To examine the crucial concept of service quality
- To explore the concept of marketing in non-profit situations
- To understand the development of marketing strategies in non-profit organisations
- To describe methods for controlling non-profit marketing activities

**Service**
An intangible product involving a deed, a performance or an effort that cannot physically be possessed

## Introduction

As discussed in Chapter 10, all products – goods, services and ideas – possess a certain amount of intangibility. A **service** is an intangible product involving a deed, a performance or an effort that cannot physically be possessed.[1] This chapter presents concepts that apply specifically to the marketing of services. Services marketing involves marketing in non-profit organisations such as education, healthcare, charities and government, as well as for profit-making areas such as entertainment, tourism, finance, personal services and professional services.

## Opener

# Keeping TV Sets and Wallets Tuned to Nickelodeon

The cable television network Nickelodeon – Nick for short – has to satisfy a number of tough audiences. Toddlers want fun, engaging programmes such as *Blue's Clues* and *Dora the Explorer*. School-age viewers enjoy slightly wacky cartoons such as *SpongeBob SquarePants*. Younger teens tune in for programmes like *All That* while older teens watch the celebrity specials. And parents want to be sure that Nick's programmes entertain without violence or sex when a child is holding the remote control. Nick delivers for all these audiences, with ratings that top the list of basic cable networks and annual revenues exceeding US$1 billion. Nick airs a range of different channels, such as Nickelodeon, Nicktoonstv, Nick Replay and, for toddlers, the award-winning Nick Jr.

Every programme presents new opportunities to give viewers a good experience and encourage them to tune in again and again. Nick is known for its in-depth marketing research, and its careful control of animation and production. Because no one can predict precisely which characters and shows will resonate with viewers, the network has had both tremendous successes and big disappointments. Management was surprised by the immediate and immense popularity of *SpongeBob SquarePants*. *SpongeBob* first aired as a weekend series then, as the audience grew, it became a regular part of the Saturday-morning schedule and the prime-time weekday schedule. However, children did not take to either the *Animorphs* series or the *Noah Knows Best* series. One Nick executive says these programmes were 'too talky and a little too old'.

With millions of children tuning in every week, Nick has been able to profit from selling advertising time and from licensing its brand for an ever wider mix of goods and services. Retail sales of its branded products total US$3 billion annually. Seeing the problems that Warner Brothers and Walt Disney have had in operating their own retail chains, Nick instead licensed its brand for sale in department stores.

One of its newest licensing ventures involves a theme resort in Florida called the Nickelodeon Family Suites by Holiday Inn. In addition to waterslides, pools and games rooms, the hotel will be decorated with Nick-character furnishings, offer breakfast with Nick characters and stage live shows starring Nick characters. This deal will present entirely different service challenges to those of Nick's television business. Still, Nick believes that viewers who enjoy Nick characters will look forward to staying at a Nick-themed hotel – and they are working with Holiday Inn to open several more resorts soon. Can the resort deliver the kind of service that is consistent with the Nick brand? Stay tuned.

**Sources:** based on information from Karyn Strauss, 'Move over Disney', *Hotels*, January 2004, p. 13; 'He lives in a pineapple under the sea', *Hotel & Motel Management*, 3 November 2003, p. 126; Joe Flint, 'Testing limits of licensing', *Wall Street Journal*, 9 October 2003, p. B1; Diane Brady and Gerry Khermouch, 'How to tickle a child', *Business Week*, 7 July 2003, pp. 48–50.
Logo: Courtesy of Nickelodeon UK

The entertainment and leisure products offered by Nickelodeon are services rather than tangible goods: they are experiential. This chapter presents concepts that apply specifically to products that are services. The organisations that market service products include: for-profit businesses, such as those offering financial, personal and professional services; and non-profit organisations, such as educational institutions, religious groups, charities and governments.

The chapter begins by considering the contribution of service industries to the economy. It then addresses the unique characteristics of services and the problems they present to marketers: these traits often form the basis for examination questions and they explain why marketers of services have to manipulate an extended marketing mix, devote extensive resources to branding and often struggle to create a differential advantage over rivals. Next, the chapter presents various classification schemes that can help services marketers develop marketing strategies. Then a variety of marketing mix considerations are discussed, along with the associated problems of creating and sustaining a differential advantage. The important concept of service quality is then explored. Finally, the chapter defines non-profit marketing and examines the development of non-profit marketing strategies and the control of non-profit marketing activities.

# The Nature and Importance of Services

Few products can be classified as a pure good or a pure service. Consider, for example, the purchase of a laptop computer. When consumers buy a laptop, they take ownership of a physical item which they might use at work and at home, but the maintenance contract linked with the purchase is a service. Similarly, a helpline facility offering software support is providing a service. Most products, such as computers and other brown goods, contain both tangible and intangible components. One component, however, will dominate, and it is this dominant component that leads to the classification of goods, services and ideas.

Figure 13.1 illustrates the tangibility concept by placing a variety of 'products' on a continuum of tangibility and intangibility. Tangible dominant products are typically classified as goods, and intangible dominant products are typically considered services. A restaurant meal or taxi cab may be tangible and physical, but the restaurant or taxi operator is providing a service: refreshment or transportation. Thus, as defined in Chapter 10, services are intangible dominant products that involve the application of human and mechanical efforts to people or objects.

## Growth of Services

In Europe, as in the United States, the importance of services in the economy is increasing, with nearly two-thirds of the EU workforce employed in the sector. Service industries encompass trade, communications, transport, leisure, food and accommodation, financial and medical services, education, government and technical services. There are services intended for consumers – **consumer services** – and those designed to satisfy businesses – **business services**.

Economic prosperity has been a major catalyst for consumer services growth, leading to an increase in financial services, travel, entertainment and personal care. Lifestyle changes

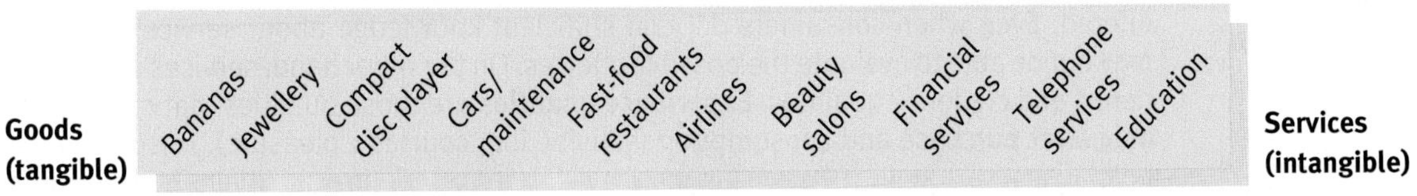


***Figure 13.1***
*A continuum of product tangibility and intangibility*

**Consumer services**
Services such as education, healthcare, leisure, catering, tourism, financial, entertainment, home maintenance and other services to help consumers

**Business services**
Services such as repairs and maintenance, consulting and professional advice, installation, equipment leasing, marketing research, advertising, temporary office personnel and caretaking services

have also encouraged expansion of the service sector. Smaller families result in more free time and relatively higher disposable income. Consumers are keener than ever to 'buy in' outside services. With the number of women in the workforce more than doubling in the last 50 years, consumers want to avoid tasks such as meal preparation, house cleaning, home maintenance and preparation of tax returns. Furthermore, Europeans have become more fitness and recreation oriented and, with greater leisure time, the demand for fitness and recreational facilities has escalated. In terms of demographics, the population is growing older, and this change has promoted tremendous expansion of healthcare services. Finally, the number and complexity of goods needing servicing have spurred demand for repair services.

Not only have consumer services grown in the economy, business services have prospered as well. Business or industrial services include repairs and maintenance, consulting and professional advice, installation, equipment leasing, marketing research, advertising, temporary office personnel and caretaking services. Expenditures for business and industrial services have risen even faster than expenditures for consumer services. This growth has been attributed to the increasingly complex, specialised and competitive business environment.[2]

There are three key reasons behind the growth of business-to-business services.

1 Specialisation – the delegation of non-care tasks, such as advertising, executive recruitment and car fleet management.
2 Technology – the increase in sophistication leading to the 'buying in' of expert knowledge and skills, such as IT computing consultants.
3 Flexibility – the need in many organisations to avoid fixed overhead costs; for example, marketing research, maintenance and cleaning are frequently brought in only on an ad hoc basis.

## Characteristics of Services

**Intangibility**
An inherent quality of services that are performed and therefore cannot be tasted, touched, seen, smelled or possessed

**Search qualities**
Tangible attributes of a service that can be viewed prior to purchase

**Experience qualities**
Attributes that can be assessed only after purchase and consumption, including satisfaction and courtesy

**Credence qualities**
Attributes that cannot be assessed even after purchase and consumption

The marketing of services is distinct from goods marketing.[3] To understand the nature of services marketing, it is necessary to appreciate the particular characteristics of services. Services have four key basic characteristics:

1 intangibility
2 inseparability of production and consumption
3 perishability
4 heterogeneity.[4]

Table 13.1 summarises these characteristics and the resulting marketing challenges.

**Intangibility** The characteristic of **intangibility** stems from the fact that services are performances. They cannot be seen, touched, tasted or smelled, nor can they be possessed. Intangibility also relates to the difficulty that consumers may have in understanding service offerings.[5] Services have a few tangible attributes, called **search qualities**, that can be viewed prior to purchase, such as the décor in a restaurant or the array of tools in a car mechanic's shop. Business-to-business design specialists JKR offer clients a packaging design service, and use existing clients' executions to entice new clients (see Figure 13.2). When consumers cannot examine a service product in advance, they may not understand exactly what is being offered. Even when consumers do gain sufficient knowledge about service offerings, they may not be able to evaluate the possible choices. On the other hand, services are rich in experience and credence qualities. **Experience qualities** are those qualities that can be assessed only after purchase and consumption (satisfaction, courtesy, pleasure). Leisure centres and holidays are examples of services that are high in experience qualities. **Credence qualities** are those qualities that cannot be assessed even after purchase and consumption.[6] An appendix operation, car repairs, consulting and legal representation are examples of services

**Table 13.1 Service Marketing Challenges**

| Service characteristics | Resulting marketing challenges |
|---|---|
| Intangibility | Difficult for customer to evaluate<br>Customer does not take physical possession<br>Difficult to advertise and display<br>Difficult to set and justify prices<br>Service process is not usually protectable by patents |
| Inseparability of production and consumption | Service provider cannot mass-produce services<br>Customer must participate in production<br>Other consumers affect service outcomes<br>Services are difficult to distribute |
| Perishability | Services cannot be stored<br>Very difficult to balance supply and demand<br>Unused capacity is lost forever<br>Demand may be very time-sensitive |
| Heterogeneity | Service quality is difficult to control<br>Difficult to standardise service delivery |
| Client-based relationships | Success depends on satisfying and keeping customers over the long term<br>Generating repeat business is challenging<br>Relationship marketing becomes critical |
| Customer contact | Service providers are critical to delivery<br>Requires high levels of service employee training and motivation<br>Changing a high-contact service into a low-contact service to achieve lower costs without reducing customer satisfaction |

**Sources:** K. Douglas Hoffman and John E.G. Bateson, *Essentials of Services Marketing* (Fort Worth, TX: Dryden Press, 1997), pp. 25–38; Valarie A. Zeithaml, A. Parasuraman and Leonard L. Berry, *Delivering Quality Service: Balancing Customer Perceptions and Expectations* (New York: Free Press, 1990); Leonard L. Berry and A. Parasuraman, *Marketing Services: Competing through Quality* (New York Free Press, 1991), p. 5.

high in credence qualities. How many consumers are knowledgeable enough to assess the quality of an appendectomy, even after the surgery has been performed?

A Renault car can be test-driven before being purchased. It can be viewed in the dealer's showroom and on the streets. It can, to an extent, be consumed prior to purchase. The same is not true of a beauty treatment or an opera seat. The beauty treatment and the opera may fail to live up to expectations, but by the time this disappointment is recognised it is too late – the service has been partially consumed and paid for.

**Inseparability**
In relation to production and consumption, a characteristic of services that means they are produced at the same time as they are consumed

**Inseparability** Related to intangibility, therefore, is **inseparability** of production and consumption. Services are normally produced at the same time as they are consumed. A medical examination is an example of simultaneous production and consumption. In fact, the doctor cannot possibly perform the service without the patient's presence, and the consumer is actually involved in the production process. With other services, such as taking tennis lessons, consumers are simultaneously involved in production. Because of high consumer involvement in most services, standardisation and control are difficult to maintain. The Building Customer Relationships box on page 381 illustrates how Dutch banking giant ABN AMRO addresses this difficulty.

***Figure 13.2***
*Many services are targeted at business customers. Here packaging design experts jkr attempt to entice new clients for its services*
*Source: Courtesy of jones knowles ritchie*

**Perishability**
A characteristic of services whereby unused capacity on one occasion cannot be stockpiled or inventoried for future occasions

**Perishability** As production and consumption are simultaneous, services are also characterised by **perishability**. The consumer of a service generally has to be present and directly involved in the consumption of the service at the time of its production. This means that unused capacity in one time period cannot be stockpiled or inventoried for future time periods. This is a problem that airline operators face every day. Each operator engages in an ongoing struggle to maintain seat occupancy levels. Empty seats mean lost business. Many operators offer 'last-minute' cut-price deals to reduce the numbers of empty seats. In many cases it is not possible to change the flight on which the seat is booked and monies paid are generally not refunded in the event of cancellation. This example illustrates how service perishability presents problems very different from the supply and demand problems encountered in the marketing of goods.[7] While an empty airline seat on a flight is a sale lost for ever, cans of soup remaining on the supermarket shelf at the close of business will be available for sale the following day.

**Heterogeneity**
Variability in the quality of service because services are provided by people, and people perform inconsistently

**Heterogeneity** As most services are labour intensive, they are susceptible to **heterogeneity**. For the service to be provided and consumed, the client generally meets and deals directly with the service provider's personnel. Direct contact and interaction are distinguishing features of services. However, the people delivering services do not always perform consistently. There may be variation from one service to another within the same organisation or variation in the service that a single individual provides from day to day and from customer to customer. A good branch manager is crucial for a restaurant chain such

## Building Customer Relationships

### Dutch Bankers Build Relationships – ABN AMRO Leads through Services

The 1991 merger between Algemene Bank Nederland and Amsterdam-Rotterdam Bank to create Dutch-based ABN AMRO Bank produced the dominant financial institution in the Netherlands, the 11th-ranked bank in Europe and 23rd in the world, based on tier 1 capital. With branches throughout the Netherlands and Benelux, and over 3000 branches in more than 60 other countries, ABN AMRO deals daily with thousands of customers face to face or through telecommunications. There are 110,000 full-time equivalent staff and the company has assets of €640 billion.

The company's policy is to buy relatively small banking operations around the globe and integrate them fully within its existing business. It does not seek mega-mergers with other large international banks. ABN AMRO North America agreed to buy Chicago Corp, which merged with ABN AMRO Securities, Inc., resulting in the addition of 20,000 staff outside the Netherlands and a significant New York-based operation destined for rapid growth. Hoare Govett has already been so integrated, creating the 17th largest insurance broker in the world. Nordic Alfred Berg is now also part of the network. Significant alliances have been established in South-east Asia, with China now seen to be an important market. The strategy is recognised as successful well beyond the banking fraternity; ABN has received many prestigious awards for the competitive success of its global operation.

To facilitate this growth, the bank is one of the world's leading spenders on information systems, maintaining that today's technology helps it to offer an efficient and reliable service to its most valuable asset – its customer base. Customers are kept to the fore through the company's policy of relationship management, a core strategy since 1980. The bank targets only a small number of clients, who are subsequently handled by a large team of relationship managers.

Many consumers find banks' history and formal procedures intimidating, and view them as powerful institutions with which they can enjoy little personal interaction. ABN AMRO has tackled this perception head on recognising that, as fundamentally a service provider dealing with people, its success depends on the attitude and ability of its own personnel. In this respect, ABN AMRO realises it must behave as a service provider and adopt the practices of services marketing.

The company states that it is an ambitious institution, committed to continuous improvement. 'Our success depends on excellent performance and a solid reputation. Transparency and dialogue are of crucial importance in all our relationships if we are to maintain our reputation as a respectable and reliable institution. We strive to provide excellent service.' The bank publicises its corporate values as: integrity, teamwork, respect and professionalism, and says, 'We are determined to deliver outstanding quality so that our relationships with our clients will be long-lasting and close'.

ABN AMRO places significant emphasis on its employees, who are integral to its products, marketing and the services it provides. The bank's internal marketing focuses on training and motivating its staff worldwide to deliver a consistent, friendly, proficient and superior service to ABN AMRO's many customers. ABN AMRO acknowledges that it is only as good as its personnel – those people who, to many customers, epitomise the bank's products and services. The company's human resources and marketing executives highlight these employees' skills in handling customer contact and delivering the bank's services.

**Sources:** ABN AMRO, 2004; 'European 100', *Information Week*, 11 December 1995, pp. 32–41; Yvette Kantrow, 'ABN AMRO/Chicago Corp will expand "significantly" in NY', *Investment Dealers' Digest*, 2 October 1995, pp. 8–9; 'Jan Kalff, chairman, ABN AMRO', *Euromoney*, September 1995, p. 64; John Anderson et al., 'The 1995 industry all stars', *Independent Energy*, September 1995, pp. 24–30; Matthew Ball, 'ABN AMRO aims for 380 of the best', *Corporate Finance*, July 1995, p. 40; 'Berg sale raises broking stakes', *Euroweek*, June 1995, p. 45; Caroline Farquhar; ABN AMRO annual report and accounts; Barclays de Zoete Wedd Securities; Credit Suisse First Boston; Financial Times Analysis; 'Banking industry report', Salomon Brothers, April 1992; ABN AMRO Utrecht, 1999; www.abnamro.com, June 2004.

as Pizza Express or a coffee shop like Starbucks. Poor customer reaction and branch performance can often be traced back to a poor branch manager.[8] Waiting times in either outlet can vary greatly, often due to teamwork, speed and efficiency variations between branches.

This may result in varying levels of customer satisfaction – for example, between one Starbucks and another. Thus standardisation and quality are extremely difficult to control. However, it is also true that the characteristics of services themselves may make it possible for marketers to customise their offerings to consumers. In such cases, services marketers often face a dilemma: how to provide efficient, standardised service at an acceptable level of quality, while simultaneously treating each customer as a unique person.

**Client-based relationships**
Interactions that result in satisfied customers who use a service repeatedly over time

**Client-based Relationships** The success of many services depends on creating and maintaining **client-based relationships**, interactions with customers that result in satisfied customers who use a service repeatedly over time.[9] In fact, some service providers, such as solicitors, accountants and financial advisers, call their customers 'clients' and often develop and maintain close, long-term relationships with them. Customers are generally more satisfied in relational exchanges than they are with exchanges based on single transactions. Indeed, research suggests that customer loyalty and re-patronage behaviour can be encouraged through this approach.[10] The building of such relationships has also been shown to be important in non-profit contexts.[11] It seems that services businesses are successful only to the degree to which they can maintain a group of clients who use their services on an ongoing basis. For example, a dentist may serve a family for many years. If the family members are confident in the dentist and think he or she offers a good service, they are likely to recommend the dentist to friends. If this positive word-of-mouth communication continues, the dentist may acquire a large number of clients through this route. To ensure that client-based relationships are created and maintained, a service provider must take action to build trust, demonstrate customer commitment, and satisfy customers so well that they become very loyal to the provider and unlikely to switch to competitors.

**Customer contact**
The level of interaction between the provider and customer needed to deliver the service

**Customer Contact** Not all services require a high degree of **customer contact**, but many do. Customer contact refers to the level of interaction between the service provider and the customer that is necessary to deliver the service. High-contact services include healthcare, real estate, and hair and beauty services. Examples of low-contact services are car repairs and dry cleaning. As the following section explains, the level of customer contact is sometimes used as the basis for classifying services.

# Classification of Services

Services are a very diverse group of products, and an organisation may provide more than one kind. Examples of services include car hire, maintenance services, healthcare, hairdressing, health centres, childcare, domestic services, legal advice, banking, insurance, air travel, education, entertainment, catering, business consulting, dry cleaning and accounting. Nevertheless, services can be meaningfully analysed using a **five-category classification** scheme:

**Five-category classification**
A method of analysing services according to five criteria: type of market, degree of labour intensiveness, degree of customer contact, skill of the service provider and goal of the service provider

1 type of market
2 degree of labour intensiveness
3 degree of customer contact
4 skill of the service provider, and
5 goal of the service provider.

Table 13.2 summarises this scheme.

**Type of Market** Services can be viewed in terms of the market or type of customer they serve – consumer or business.[12] The implications of this distinction are very similar to those for all products and do not require detailed discussion here. Figure 13.2 illustrates two kinds of marketing services, which brand design company jkr offers to its clients.

**Table 13.2 Classification of Services**

| Category | Examples |
| --- | --- |
| **Type of market** | |
| Consumer | Childcare, legal advice, entertainment |
| Business | Consulting, caretaking services, installation |
| **Degree of labour intensiveness** | |
| Labour based | Education, haircuts, dentistry |
| Equipment based | Telecommunications, fitness centres, public transport |
| **Degree of customer contact** | |
| High | Healthcare, hotels, air travel |
| Low | Home deliveries, postal service |
| **Skill of the service provider** | |
| Professional | Legal advice, healthcare, accountancy |
| Non-professional | Domestic services, dry cleaning, public transport |
| **Goal of the service provider** | |
| Profit | Financial services, insurance, tourism |
| Non-profit | Healthcare, education, government |

**Degree of Labour Intensiveness** A second way to classify services is by degree of labour intensiveness. Many services – such as domestic cleaning, education and medical care – rely heavily on human labour. Other services – such as telecommunications, fitness centres and public transport – are more equipment intensive.

Labour-based (that is, people-based) services are more susceptible to heterogeneity than most equipment-based services. Marketers of people-based services must recognise that the service providers are often viewed as the service itself. Therefore, strategies relating to selecting, training, motivating and controlling employees are crucial to the success of most service businesses. A bad attitude from Ryanair's ground staff would colour the customer's view not just of the employee concerned but also of the company and all of its service products. A customer who has flown quite happily with Ryanair for many years may, so prompted, consider taking his or her business to a rival company.

**Degree of Customer Contact** The third way in which services can be classified is by degree of customer contact. High-contact services include healthcare, hotels, property agents and restaurants; low contact services include home deliveries, theatres, dry cleaning and spectator sports.[13] High contact services generally involve actions that are directed towards individuals. Because these services are directed at people, the consumer must be present during production. Sometimes – for example, in the case of a car valeting service – it is possible for the service provider to go to the consumer. However, high-contact services typically require that the consumer goes to the production facility. Consequently, the physical appearance and ambience of the facility may be a major component of the consumer's overall evaluation of the service. The enjoyment of a visit to a health spa stems not just from the quality of the beauty treatments, or the suitability of the dietary or fitness programmes on offer, but also from the décor and furnishings, general ambience, and the abilities and attitude of the staff. Because the consumer must be present during production of a high-contact service, the process of production may be just as important as its final outcome. For example, open-plan banks, quick queue systems and ATM facilities aim to improve the transaction process and make the service more enjoyable for the consumer.

Low-contact service, in contrast, commonly involves actions directed at things. Although consumers may not need to be present during service delivery, their presence may be required to initiate or terminate the service. The Post Office maintains a network of branches, sorting offices and vehicles. The process of sending a parcel from Edinburgh to Cardiff or Lille is lengthy. Yet consumers only need to be present to initiate the service. The appearance of the production facilities and the interpersonal skills of actual service providers are thus not as critical in low-contact services as they are in high-contact services.[14]

**Skill of the Service Provider** Skill of the service provider is a fourth way to classify services. Professional services tend to be more complex and more highly regulated than non-professional services. In the case of legal advice, for example, the final product is situation specific. As a result, consumers often do not know what the actual service will involve or how much it will cost until the service is completed.

**Goal of the Service Provider** Finally, services can be classified according to whether they are profit or non-profit. The second half of this chapter examines non-profit (not-for-profit) marketing, such as that present in the public sector and charities. Most non-profit organisations provide services rather than goods.

## Developing Marketing Strategies for Services

### Strategic Considerations

In developing marketing strategies, the marketer must first understand what benefits the customer wants, how the company's service offer and brand are perceived relative to the competition and what services consumers buy.[15] In other words, the marketer must develop the right service for the right people at the right price, in the right place with the right positioning and image. The marketer must then communicate with consumers so that they are aware of the need-satisfying services available to them. The key aspects of effective target marketing – as explained in Chapter 8 – and of managing the implementation of the determined marketing strategy – as detailed in Chapters 23 and 24 – apply strongly to the marketing of services.[16]

One of the unique challenges service marketers face is matching supply and demand. Price can be used to help smooth out demand for a service. There are also other ways in which marketers can alter the marketing mix to deal with the problem of fluctuating demand. Through price incentives, advertising and other promotional efforts, marketers can remind consumers of busy times and encourage them to come for service during slack periods. Additionally, the product itself can be altered to cope with fluctuating demand. Restaurants, for example, may change their menus, vary their lighting and décor, open or close the bar, and change the entertainment on offer. A historical tourist destination may stage theatrical events and firework displays to attract customers out of season. Finally, distribution can be modified to reflect changes in demand. For example, some libraries have mobile units that travel to different locations during slack periods.[17]

The strategies that services marketers implement are contingent upon a good understanding of the pattern and determinants of demand. Does the level of demand follow a cycle? What are the causes of this cycle? Are the changes random?[18] An attempt to use price decreases to shift demand for public transport to off-peak periods would achieve only limited success because of the cause of the cyclical demand for public transport. Employees have little control over their working hours and are therefore unable to take advantage of pricing incentives.

Table 13.3 summarises a range of marketing and non-marketing strategies that service businesses may use to deal with fluctuating demand. Non-marketing strategies essentially involve internal, employee-related actions.[19] They may be the only choices available when

**Table 13.3 Strategies for Coping with Fluctuations in Demand for Services**

| Marketing strategies | Non-marketing strategies |
|---|---|
| Use different pricing | Hire extra staff/lay off employees |
| Alter product | Work employees overtime/part time |
| Change place/distribution | Cross-train employees |
| Use promotional efforts | Use employees to perform non-vital tasks during slack times |
| Modify customer service levels | Subcontract work/seek subcontract work |
| Alter branding and positioning | Slow the pace of work |
| | Turn away business |

fluctuations in demand are random. For example, a strike or natural disaster may cause fluctuations in consumer demand for public transport.

## Creating a Differential Advantage in Services

**Differential advantage**
Something desired by the customer that only one company – not its rivals – can offer

The aim of marketing is to satisfy customers, achieving product or brand differentiation with an advantage over competitors' products. This **differential advantage**, sometimes termed a 'competitive edge', is determined by customers' perceptions. A differential advantage is something desired by the customer that only one company can offer, as explained in Chapter 2. If the targeted customers do not perceive an advantage, in marketing terms the product offers no benefit over rival products.

For any product, achieving and sustaining a differential advantage is difficult, but for services the challenge is even greater. The intangibility of the service product and the central role of people in its delivery are the prime causes of this difficulty, but, as Table 13.4 shows, there are others, such as difficulties ensuring consistent service quality and the fact that the interface with the customer may be difficult to control.

The difficulty encountered in creating a differential advantage in services makes it even more important that marketing activities are carried out in a systematic and appropriate manner. Thus services marketers must ensure that the needs of targeted markets are well understood in order to bring service products and the marketing mix into line with customers' exact requirements. There must be a clear appreciation of competitors' service offerings and marketing programmes, and regular efforts are needed to research customers' satisfaction levels. Branding, supported with well-constructed promotional campaigns, is even more central to the reinforcement and communication of any differential advantage for services.

**Table 13.4 Difficulties in Creating a Differential Advantage in Services**

| Intangibility minimises product differentiation |
|---|
| No – or little – patent protection exists |
| Few barriers to entry enable competitors to set up and copy successful initiatives |
| The interface with customers is difficult to control |
| Growth is hard to achieve, particularly since key personnel can only be spread so far |
| Service quality is irregular |
| It is difficult to improve productivity and lower the cost to the consumer |
| Innovation leads to imitation |
| Restrictive regulations abound, particularly in the professions |

## The Extended Marketing Mix for Services

The standard marketing mix comprises the '4Ps':

- product
- promotion
- price
- place/distribution.

**Extended marketing mix for services**
In addition to the standard '4Ps' marketing mix – product, promotion, price and place/distribution – there are 3Ps: process, physical evidence (ambience) and people

The discussion about the classification of services has emphasised the importance of three additional elements:

- process
- physical evidence (ambience)
- people.

Collectively, these seven elements, which are sometimes called the '7Ps', form what is termed the **extended marketing mix for services** (see Figure 13.3), which is discussed in detail in Chapter 22. It is essential for services marketers to recognise the importance of these additional '3Ps'.

# Service Quality

**Service quality**
Customers' perception of how well a service meets or exceeds their expectations

The delivery of high-quality services is one of the most important and difficult tasks that any service organisation faces. Because of their unique characteristics, services are very difficult to evaluate. Hence customers must look closely at service quality when comparing services. **Service quality** is defined as customers' perception of how well a service meets or exceeds their expectations.[20] Service quality is judged by customers, not the organisation. This distinction is critical because it forces services marketers to examine their quality from the customer's viewpoint. For example, a dental surgery may view service quality as having friendly and knowledgeable employees. However, the customers may be more concerned with waiting time, cleanliness and the effectiveness of patient pain relief. Thus it is important for service organisations to determine what customers expect and then develop service products that meet or exceed those expectations.

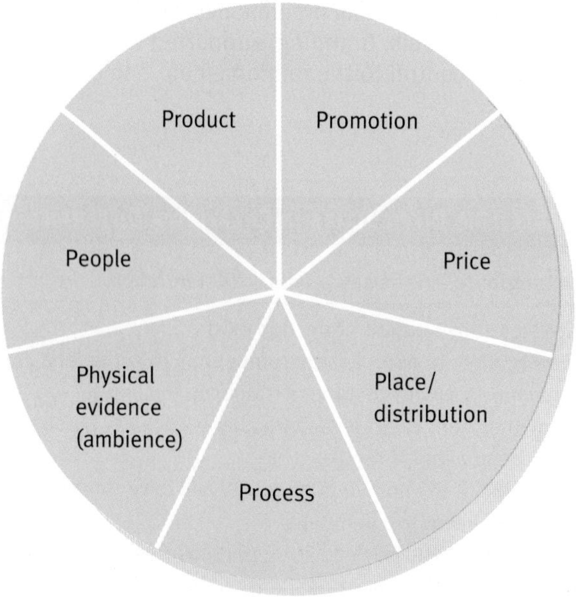


*Figure 13.3*
*The extended marketing mix for services*

## Customer Evaluation of Service Quality

The biggest obstacle for customers in evaluating service quality is the intangible nature of the service. How can customers evaluate something they cannot see, feel, taste, smell or hear? The evaluation of a good is much easier because all goods possess 'search qualities' in the form of tangible attributes, such as colour, style, size, feel or fit, that can be evaluated prior to purchase. Trying on a new coat and taking a car for a test drive are examples of how customers evaluate search qualities. Services, on the other hand, have very few search qualities; instead, they abound in experience and credence qualities. Experience qualities, such as taste, satisfaction or pleasure, are attributes that can be assessed only during the purchase and consumption of a service. Restaurants and holidays are examples of services high in experience qualities. Credence qualities are attributes that customers may be unable to evaluate even after the purchase and consumption of the service. Examples of services high in credence qualities are surgical operations, vehicle repairs, consulting, and legal representation. Most consumers lack the knowledge or skills to evaluate the quality of these types of service. Consequently they must place a great deal of faith in the integrity and competence of the service provider.

Despite the difficulties in evaluating quality, service quality may be the only way customers can choose one service over another. For this reason, service marketers live or die by understanding how consumers judge service quality. This is one reason behind many retail banks now returning staff to their branches and refocusing on their branches as a key part of their customer relationship building, as described in the Topical Insight box on page 388. Table 13.5 defines five dimensions consumers use when evaluating service quality:

1 tangibles
2 reliability
3 responsiveness
4 assurance
5 empathy.

Note that all of these dimensions have links to employee performance. Of the five, reliability is the most important in determining customer evaluations of service quality.[21]

Services marketers pay a great deal of attention to the tangibles dimension of service quality. Tangible attributes, or search qualities, such as the appearance of facilities and employees, are often the only aspects of a service that can be viewed before purchases and consumption. Therefore, services marketers must ensure that these tangible elements are consistent with the overall image of the service product.

Except for the tangibles dimension, the criteria that customers use to judge service quality are intangible. For instance, how does a customer judge reliability? Since dimensions such as reliability cannot be examined with the senses, consumers must rely on other ways of judging service criteria. One of the most important factors in customer judgements of service quality is **service expectations**. These are influenced by past experiences with the service, word-of-mouth communication from other customers and the service company's own advertising. For example, customers are usually eager to try a new restaurant, especially when friends recommend it. These same customers may also have seen advertisements placed by the restaurant. As a result, these customers have an idea of what to expect when they visit the restaurant for the first time. When they finally dine at the restaurant, the quality they experience will change the expectations they have for their next visit and affect their own comments to friends. That is why providing consistently high service quality is important. If the quality of a restaurant, or any services marketer, begins to deteriorate, customers will alter their own expectations and word-of-mouth communication to others accordingly.

**Service expectations**
A factor used in judging service quality involving impressions from past experiences, word-of-mouth communication and the company's advertising

## Delivering Exceptional Service Quality

Providing high-quality service on a consistent basis is very difficult. All consumers have experienced examples of poor service: long queues at retail checkouts, trains and buses that are late, or rude cinema employees. Obviously, it is impossible for a service organisation to

## Topical Insight

### Banks Remember Customer Service

A trend for close to 20 years has been for banks to close rural branches and reduce the number of town-centre branches. Many Victorian banks, with their large chambers, grand facades and prime locations, have been turned into bars or restaurants. TV viewers in the UK will have seen a well-known retail bank advertising the last of its branches being turned into wine bars: instead it was decided that branches were to be kept open. A separate advertisement revealed that customers would once again be able to talk directly to staff in their local branch, rather than only to anonymous personnel in a far-flung faceless call centre. So, why the about-turn in these policies?

For some time pundits had forecast the demise of the bank branch, as first telephone banking and then the Internet enabled customers to conduct their transactions and make enquiries via telecommunications. The era of the call centre permitted banks to make further cost savings by directing apparently local calls to regional call centres rather than into branches. This also reduced the number of personnel in branches and often removed mortgage, investment and insurance specialists altogether. In effect, for many customers, this had the impact of further reducing or downgrading the appeal of visiting branches. Mergers and acquisitions in the banking sector have also encouraged a reduction in branch numbers, as newly merged chains close and relocate branches in order to reduce duplication and operating costs. In the five years up to 2003, estimates were that over 1700 UK bank branches closed.

There is little doubt that telephone and e-banking have become increasingly popular. Despite their detractors, call centres have reduced operating costs. Mergers are continuing and banks' boards also routinely seek to reduce operating costs. Nevertheless, there recently has been talk of an end to the culling of bank branches. This is because marketing research reveals that not all customers wish to deal with call centres or to conduct their business via a PC or laptop. Many customers find face-to-face contact reassuring, and only the bank branch environment provides this direct interaction.

The role of the branch may be rejuvenated even further, however. Leading consultants Booz Allen Hamilton produced a report pointedly entitled Implementing the Customer-centric Bank – the Rebirth of the Forgotten Branch. The report concluded that 90 per cent of customer relationships are made – and lost – in branches. Even customers utilising e-banking often need to visit branches, and the vast majority of customers still believe that complex enquiries or topics perceived as risky by the consumer are better handled face to face, inside a bank branch. Unfortunately, the removal of specialist staff from many branches and the downgrading of the majority of branches to simple transaction-processing points, have led to a growing level of customer dissatisfaction with bank branches.

Now, in a strategy shift, the leading high-street banking brands are acknowledging that they must reinvest in their bank branches: more and better trained staff, improved IT enabling speedy processing of enquiries and creating more opportunities for the cross-selling of products, plus enhanced interior designs. As part of this shift in emphasis, different staff – with a greater customer orientation – are required. NatWest announced that it planned to invest in 1000 additional members of branch staff. Barclays, Abbey and the other leading brands quickly followed suit. As Alliance & Leicester head Richard Pym stated, 'We want staff who can relate to customers, understand their needs and get something into a computer accurately. That's someone with interpersonal skills, not banking skills.' In order to achieve this, Abbey instigated an additional 60,000 training days for its customer-facing personnel.

While efficiency and reducing operating costs are still important to the boards of these companies, there is an acceptance that customers expect improved service and that many prefer the bank branch as the setting for interactions with, it is hoped, more customer-oriented personnel.

**Sources:** NatWest 2003; Barclays, 2004: 'Back to the branch', *Marketing*, 26 May 2004, pp. 30–2; Fujitsu Services, 2003.

ensure exceptional service quality 100 per cent of the time. However, there are many steps that can be taken to increase the likelihood of providing high-quality service. First, though, the service company must understand the four **service quality factors**. These are:

**Table 13.5 Dimensions of Service Quality**

| Dimension | Evaluation criteria | Examples |
|---|---|---|
| **Tangibles**<br>Physical evidence of the service | Appearance of physical facilities<br>Appearance of service personnel<br>Tools or equipment used to provide the service | A clean and professional-looking doctor's office<br>A clean and neatly dressed repair person<br>The appearance of food in a restaurant<br>The equipment used in a medical examination |
| **Reliability**<br>Consistency and dependability in performing the service | Accuracy of billing or recordkeeping<br>Performing services when promised | An accurate bank statement<br>A confirmed hotel reservation<br>An airline flight departing and arriving on time |
| **Responsiveness**<br>Willingness or readiness of employees to provide the service | Returning customer phone calls<br>Providing prompt service<br>Handling urgent requests | A server refilling a customer's cup of tea without being asked<br>An ambulance arriving within three three minutes |
| **Assurance**<br>Knowledge/competence of employees and ability to convey trust and confidence | Knowledge and skills of employees<br>Company name and reputation<br>Personal characteristics of employees | A highly trained financial adviser<br>A known and respected service provider<br>A doctor's bedside manner |
| **Empathy**<br>Caring and individual attention provided by employees | Listening to customer needs<br>Caring about customers' interests<br>Providing personalised attention attention | A store employee listening to and trying to understand a customer's complaint<br>A nurse counselling a heart patient |

**Sources:** Adapted from Leonard L. Berry and A. Parasuraman, *Marketing Services: Competing through Quality* (New York: Free Press, 1991); Valarie A. Zeithaml, A. Parasuraman and Leonard L. Berry, *Delivering Quality Service: Balancing Customer Perceptions and Expectations* (New York: Free Press, 1990); A. Parasuraman, Leonard L. Berry and Valarie A. Zeithaml, 'An empirical examination of relationships in an extended service quality model', *Marketing Science Institute Working Paper Series*, report no. 90–112 (Cambridge, MA: Marketing Science Institute, 1990), p. 29.

**Service quality factors** Factors that increase the likelihood of providing high-quality service: understanding customer expectations, service quality specifications, employee performance, managing service expectations

1 analysis of customer expectations
2 service quality specifications
3 employee performance
4 managing service expectations.[22]

**Analysis of Customer Expectations** Providers need to understand customer expectations when designing a service to meet or exceed those expectations. Only then can they deliver good service. Customers usually have two levels of expectations: desired and acceptable. The desired level of expectations is what the customer really wants. If this level of expectations is provided, the customer would be very satisfied. The acceptable level is viewed as a reasonable level of performance that the customer considers as being adequate. The difference between these two levels of expectations is called the **customer's zone of tolerance.**[23]

Service marketers sometimes use marketing research, such as surveys and focus groups, as a means of discovering customer needs and expectations. Other services

**Customer's zone of tolerance**
The difference between the customer's desired level of expectations and the customer's acceptable level of expectations

companies, such as hotel chains, seek customer feedback using comment cards. Another approach is to ask employees. Because customer-contact employees interact daily with customers, they often know what customers want from the company. Service managers should interact regularly with their employees to ensure that they remain in touch with this useful source of information.

**Service Quality Specifications** Once an organisation understands its customers' needs, it must establish goals to help ensure good service delivery. These goals, or service specifications, are typically set in terms of employee or machine performance. For example, a bank may require its employees to conform to a dress code. The same bank may insist that all incoming phone calls are answered by the third ring. Specifications like these can be very important in providing quality service as long as they are linked to customer needs.

Service managers who are visibly committed to service quality become role models for all employees in the organisation.[24] Such commitment motivates personnel at all levels in the business, from customer-contact employees through to senior managers, to comply with service specifications.

**Employee Performance** Once an organisation sets service quality standards and managers are committed to them, the organisation must find ways to ensure that customer contact employees perform their jobs well. Contact employees in many service industries – bank tellers, flight cabin crew, waiters, sales assistants – are often the least trained and lowest-paid members of the organisation. Yet these individuals represent the most important link to the customer, and thus their performance is critical to customer perceptions of service quality.[25] Well-managed recruitment and training are essential if employees are to understand properly how to do their jobs. Providing information about customers, service specifications and the organisation itself during the training promotes this understanding.[26]

The use of evaluation and remuneration systems plays a part in employee performance. Many service employees are evaluated and rewarded on the basis of output measures such as sales volume for car salespeople, or lack of errors during work for data-input clerks. Such systems may overlook certain key aspects of job performance: friendliness, teamwork, effort and customer satisfaction. As the importance of customer relationship building comes more to the fore, companies are increasingly considering that customer-oriented measures of performance may be a better basis for evaluation and reward. For example, Dun & Bradstreet has tied employee commissions to customer satisfaction surveys rather than sales volume.[27] This type of system stimulates employees to take care of customer needs rather than focus solely on sales or profits.

**Managing Service Expectations** Because expectations are so significant in customer evaluations of service quality, service companies recognise that they must set realistic expectations about the service they can provide. These expectations can be set through advertising and good internal communication. In their advertisements, service companies make promises about the kind of service they will deliver. In fact, a service company is forced to make promises since the intangibility of services prevents it from showing them in the advertisement. However, the advertiser should not promise more than it can deliver; doing otherwise may mean disappointed customers.

To deliver on promises made, a company needs to have good internal communication among its departments – especially management, advertising and operations. Assume, for example, that a supermarket's advertising guarantees that shoppers will not have to queue at the checkout for more than 10 minutes. In order to meet this promise, the retailer will need to ensure that its operations and staff levels can support such a guarantee. Failure to do so may result in customers' service expectations not being met, with a consequent loss of credibility for the company.

Word-of-mouth communication from other customers also shapes customer expectations. However, service companies cannot manage this 'advertising' directly. The best way to ensure positive word-of-mouth communication is to provide exceptional service quality. It has been estimated that customers tell four times as many people about bad service as they do about good service. Consequently, services marketers must provide four good service experiences for every bad experience just to break even.

# Non-profit Marketing

Marketing was broadly defined earlier as a set of individual and organisational activities aimed at facilitating and expediting satisfying exchanges in a dynamic environment through the creation, distribution, promotion and pricing of goods, services and ideas. Most of the concepts and approaches to managing marketing activities discussed above also apply to non-profit situations such as the public sector and charities. Of special relevance is the material offered in the first half of this chapter, because many non-profit organisations provide services. As a discipline, marketing is becoming increasingly important in the non-profit sector. The Case Study at the end of this chapter focuses on the changing role of marketing in charities.

**Non-profit marketing**
Activities conducted by individuals and organisations to achieve some goal other than the ordinary business goals of profit, market share or return on investment

**Cause-related marketing**
The linking of an organisation's products to a particular social cause on a short-term or ongoing basis

**Negotiation**
Mutual discussion or communication of terms and methods in an exchange situation

**Persuasion**
The act of prevailing upon someone by argument to facilitate an exchange

**Non-profit marketing** includes marketing activities conducted by individuals and organisations to achieve some goal other than the ordinary business goals of profit, market share or return on investment. However, although a non-profit organisation has primary goals that are non-economic, it may be required to become involved in 'profit making' in order to achieve those goals.[28] Thus a charity, such as the Red Cross, must raise funds to support its charitable work. Non-profit marketing can be divided into two categories: non-profit organisation marketing and social marketing. Non-profit organisation marketing is the application of marketing concepts and techniques to organisations such as hospitals and colleges. Social marketing is the development of programmes designed to influence the acceptability of social ideas, such as getting people to recycle more newspapers, plastics and aluminium, or promoting the regeneration of a deprived inner-city area.[29] **Cause-related marketing** is the linking of an organisation's products to a particular social cause, Body Shop-style, on an ongoing or short term basis.

As discussed in Chapter 1, an exchange situation exists when individuals, groups or organisations possess something that they are willing to give up in an exchange. In non-profit marketing, the objects of the exchange may not be specified in financial terms. Usually, such exchanges are facilitated through **negotiation** – mutual discussion or communication of terms and methods – and **persuasion** – convincing and prevailing upon by argument. Often, negotiation and persuasion are conducted without reference to, or awareness of, marketing's role in transactions. The discussion here concerns the non-profit performance of marketing activities, whether exchange takes place or not.

The rest of this chapter first examines the concept of non-profit marketing to determine how it differs from marketing activities in business organisations. Next it explores the overall objectives of non-profit organisations, their marketing objectives and the development of their marketing strategies. The discussion closes by illustrating how a marketing audit can control marketing activities and promote marketing awareness in a non-profit organisation.

## Why is Non-profit Marketing Different?

Traditionally and mistakenly, people have not thought of non-profit exchange activities as marketing; but consider the following example. Warwick Business School used to promote its degree courses solely through the University of Warwick's prospectuses. In the early 1980s, its main programmes received small advertising budgets. As courses were improved, the wider use of advertising increased awareness of the school and its programmes. The school is not commercially driven in the context of seeking profits for stakeholders: any income from fees, training and consultancy is reinvested into its degree programmes and facilities. A new corporate identity was developed by Coley Porter Bell of

London, and each degree programme, led by the MBA, developed its own full marketing mix and more extensive promotional strategy – all in line with the school's new mission statement. Even when, in the 1990s, the corporate identity was updated, the school continued to ensure a good fit between the marketing mixes for its different programmes and its overall strategy. As the school moved into the twenty-first century, it became a budget holder within the university and managed its own budgets. This move facilitated the appointment of a marketing director, public relations manager and external affairs manager. These personnel developed target market strategies, updated the school's marketing programmes, and monitored the performance of these marketing activities, just as marketers in a for-profit business would do. Many university departments and state-maintained schools are now engaging in developing a marketing strategy and associated marketing programmes.

Many non-profit organisations strive for effective marketing activities. Charitable organisations and supporters of social causes are major non-profit marketers. Political parties, unions, religious groups and student organisations also perform marketing activities, yet they are not considered businesses. Whereas the chief beneficiary of a business enterprise is whoever owns or holds shares in it, the main beneficiaries of a non-profit organisation are its clients, its members or the public at large.

Non-profit companies have a greater opportunity for creativity than most business organisations, but trustees or board members of these companies may find it harder to evaluate the performance of doctors, lecturers or social workers than it is for sales managers to evaluate the performance of salespeople in a for-profit organisation.

Another way in which non-profit marketing differs from for-profit marketing is that non-profit organisations are sometimes quite controversial. Amnesty International, the RSPCA and Greenpeace spend lavishly on lobbying efforts to persuade government and even the courts to support their interests, in part because acceptance of their aims is not always guaranteed. Although marketing aims to provide a body of knowledge to further an organisation's goals, it does not attempt to judge their appropriateness. It is for individuals to decide whether they approve of an organisation's goal orientation. Most marketers would agree that profit and consumer satisfaction are appropriate goals for business enterprises, but there may be considerable disagreement about the goals of a controversial non-profit organisation.

## Non-profit Marketing Objectives

The basic aim of non-profit organisations is to obtain a desired response from a target market. The response could be a change in values, a financial contribution, the donation of services or some other type of exchange. Non-profit marketing objectives are shaped by the nature of the exchange and the goals of the organisation. BBC-sponsored Children in Need and Comic Relief telethons have raised millions of pounds. Telethons have three specific marketing objectives:

1. to raise funds to support programmes
2. to plead a case on behalf of disadvantaged groups
3. to inform the public about the organisation's programmes and services.

Tactically, telethons have received support by choosing good causes; generating extensive grass-roots support; portraying disadvantaged people in a positive and dignified way; developing national, regional and local support; and providing quality entertainment.[30] Figure 13.4 illustrates how the exchanges and the purpose of the organisation can influence marketing objectives. These objectives are used as examples and may or may not apply to specific organisations.

Non-profit marketing objectives should state the rationale for an organisation's existence. An organisation that defines its marketing objective merely in terms of providing a product can be left without a purpose if the product becomes obsolete. However, serving

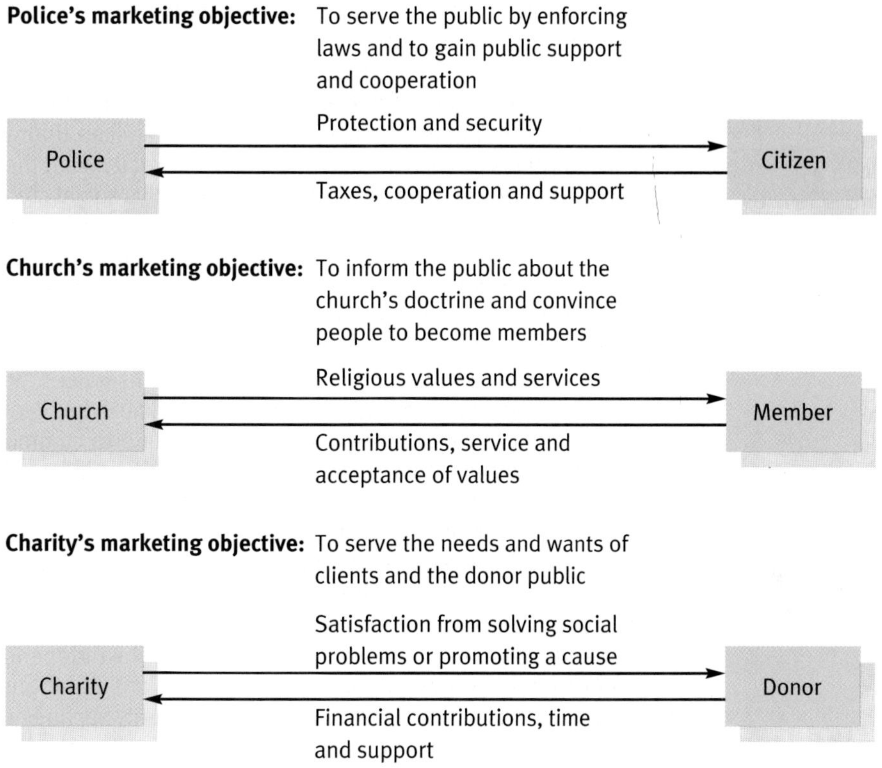
**Police's marketing objective:**
To serve the public by enforcing laws and to gain public support and cooperation
Protection and security
Police
Citizen
Taxes, cooperation and support
**Church's marketing objective:**
To inform the public about the church's doctrine and convince people to become members
Religious values and services
Church
Member
Contributions, service and acceptance of values
**Charity's marketing objective:**
To serve the needs and wants of clients and the donor public
Satisfaction from solving social problems or promoting a cause
Charity
Donor
Financial contributions, time and support

***Figure 13.4***
*Examples of marketing objectives for different types of exchange*
*Source: Philip Kotler,* Marketing for Non-profit Organisations, *2nd edn, © 1982, p. 38. Adapted by permission of Prentice-Hall, Inc., Englewood Cliffs, NJ*

and adapting to the perceived needs and wants of a target public or market, enhances an organisation's chances of surviving and achieving its goals.

## Developing Non-profit Marketing Strategies

Non-profit organisations must also develop marketing strategies by defining and analysing a target market, and creating and maintaining a marketing mix that appeals to that market.

**Target public**
A collective of individuals who have an interest in or concern about an organisation, a product or a social cause

**Client publics**
In non-profit organisations, direct consumers of a product

**General publics**
In non-profit organisations, indirect consumers of a product

**Target Markets** The concept of target markets needs to be revised slightly to apply to non-profit organisations. Whereas a business is supposed to have target groups that are potential purchasers of its product, a non-profit organisation may attempt to serve many diverse groups. A **target public** is broadly defined as a collective of individuals who have an interest in or concern about an organisation, a product or a social cause. The terms target market and target public are difficult to distinguish for many non-profit organisations. The target public for campaigns promoting healthy eating is adults and teenagers of all ages. However, the target market for many of the advertisements may be individuals currently suffering from a weight problem. When an organisation is concerned about changing values or obtaining a response from the public, it views the public as a market.[31]

In non-profit organisations, direct consumers of a product are called **client publics** and indirect consumers are called **general publics**.[32] For example, the client public for a university is its student body, and its general public includes parents, graduates, employers and the university senate. The client public usually receives most of the attention when an organisation develops a marketing strategy. The techniques and approaches to segmenting and defining target markets discussed in Chapter 8 also apply to non-profit target markets.

**Developing a Marketing Mix** A marketing mix strategy limits choices and directs marketing activities towards achieving organisational goals. The strategy should outline or develop a blueprint for making decisions about product, place/distribution, promotion, price and personnel. These decision variables should be blended to serve the target market as specified in the marketing strategy.

When considering the product variable, it is important to recognise that non-profit organisations deal more often with ideas and services than with goods. This means it is crucial for organisations to have clearly defined exactly what they are providing. For example, what products do the Women's Institute or a work's social club provide? They offer a forum for social gatherings, courses, outings and a sense of cooperation. Their products are more difficult to define than the average business product. As indicated in the first part of this chapter, the intangibility of services means that the marketing of ideas and concepts is more abstract than the marketing of tangibles, and it requires considerable effort to present benefits.

Because most non-profit products are ideas and services, distribution decisions relate to how these ideas and services will be made available to clients. If the product is an idea, selecting the right media (the promotional strategy) to communicate the idea will facilitate distribution. The availability of services is closely related to product decisions. By nature, services consist of assistance, convenience and availability. Availability is part of the total service. For example, making a product such as health services available on the high street calls for knowledge of such retailing concepts as site location analysis and logistics management.

Developing a channel of distribution to coordinate and facilitate the flow of non-profit products to clients is a necessary task, but in a non-profit setting the traditional concept of the marketing channel may need to be reviewed. The independent wholesalers available to a business enterprise do not exist in most non-profit situations. Instead, a very short channel – non-profit organisation to client – is prevalent, because production and consumption of ideas and services are often simultaneous. For example, local government departments often deal directly with householders. Charities generally pitch their fundraising activities directly to their target customers/householders/donors.

Making promotional decisions may be the first sign that non-profit organisations are performing marketing activities. Non-profit organisations use advertising and publicity to communicate with clients and the public. As the Case Study at the end of this chapter explains, direct mail remains the primary means of fundraising for services such as those provided by Christian Aid and UNICEF. In addition to direct mail, organisations such as these use press advertising, public relations and sponsorship. Many non-profit organisations now have websites to promote their causes. Face-to-face selling is also used by non-profit organisations, although it may be called something else. Churches and charities rely on personal selling when they send volunteers to recruit new members or request donations. The armed forces use personal selling when recruiting officers and when attempting to persuade men and women to enlist. Special events to obtain funds, communicate ideas or provide services are sales promotion activities. Contests, entertainment and prizes offered to attract donations resemble the sales promotion activities of business enterprises. Amnesty International, for example, has held worldwide concert tours, featuring artists such as Sting and Phil Collins, to raise funds and increase public awareness of political prisoners around the world.

The number of advertising agencies that are donating their time for public service announcements (PSAs) or public information films is increasing, and the quality of print PSAs is improving. Not-for-profit groups are becoming more interested in the impact of advertising on their organisations, and they realise that second-rate PSAs can cause a credibility loss.[33] For example, each year the UK government's 'Don't drink and drive' campaign, usually timed to coincide with the Christmas and New Year period, is a high-spending, hard-hitting programme of advertisements designed to attract as much attention as possible.

Although product and promotion techniques may require only slight modification when applied to non-profit organisations, the pricing structure is generally quite different and the decision-making more complex. The different pricing concepts that the non-profit organisation faces include pricing in user and donor markets. There are two types of monetary pricing: fixed and variable. Membership fees, such as the amount paid to become a member of an amateur operatic society, represent a fixed approach to pricing, whereas fundraising activities that lead to donations that help with the society's running costs represent a variable pricing structure.[34]

The broadest definition of price (valuation) must be used when considering non-profit products or services. Financial price, an exact monetary value, may or may not be charged for a non-profit product. Economists recognise the giving up of alternatives as a cost. **Opportunity cost** is the value of the benefit that is given up by selecting one alternative rather than another. This traditional economic view of price means that if a non-profit organisation can persuade someone to donate time to a cause, or to change his or her behaviour, the alternatives given up are a cost to – or a price paid by – the individual. Volunteers who answer phones for a university counselling service or suicide hotline, for example, give up the time they could have spent studying or doing other things, as well as the income they might have earned from working in a business organisation.

**Opportunity cost**
The value of the benefit that is given up by selecting one alternative instead of another

For other non-profit organisations, financial price is an important part of the marketing mix. Non-profit organisations today are raising money by increasing the prices of their services or starting to charge for services if they have not done so before. For example, many museums and art galleries, which traditionally allowed free entry to their exhibits, are now charging nominal entrance fees. Organisations like these often use marketing research to determine for what kinds of product people will pay.[35] The pricing strategies of non-profit organisations often stress public and client welfare over equalisation of costs and revenues. If additional funds are needed to cover costs, then donations, contributions or grants may be solicited.

The additional elements of the marketing mix for services are also important in non-profit marketing. The physical environment quite often poses problems: subscribers and donors want an organisation with the appearance of businesslike efficiency without any extravagance. It is important that funds do not appear to have been wasted on luxuries. The process for transactions is increasingly important: regular donors are offered direct debits, automatic payment methods, and regular information packs or leaflets detailing the recipient organisation's activities, expenditures and plans. People, too, are important: capable administrators, sympathetic helpers, trustworthy fundraisers – they, too, must project a caring yet efficient image to the client and general publics.

## Controlling Non-profit Marketing Activities

To control marketing activities in non-profit organisations, managers use information obtained in the marketing audit to make sure that goals are achieved. The marketing audit, controls and measuring performance of marketing activities are discussed in Chapter 24. Table 13.6 lists several summary statistics that are useful for both planning and control. Control is designed to check that the activities outlined in the marketing strategy have taken place and to take corrective action where any deviations are found. The purpose of control is not only to point out errors but to revise organisational goals and marketing objectives as necessary. One way to measure the impact of an advertisement is to audit the number of requests for information or applications, such as those received by Amnesty International, the Army or the WWF. Hits on an organisation's website via leading search engines are also counted (see Figure 13.5).

Many potential contributors decide which charities to support based on the amount of money actually used for charitable purposes. Charities are more aggressively examining their own performance and effectiveness. For example, compared with other charities, the Salvation Army contributes the majority of every pound (£) it receives to the needy; its employees are largely volunteers, who work for almost nothing. Charities are making internal changes to increase their effectiveness, and many are hiring professional managers and fundraisers to help

**TABLE 13.6 EXAMPLES OF DATA USEFUL IN CONTROLLING NON-BUSINESS MARKETING ACTIVITIES**

1 **Product mix offerings**
- A Types of product or services
- B Number of organisations offering the product or service

2 **Financial resources**
- A Types of funding used
  - 1 Local government grants
  - 2 Government grants
  - 3 Foundations
  - 4 Public appeals
  - 5 Fees/charges
- B Number using each type of funding
- C Number using combinations of funding sources

3 **Size**
- A Budget (cash flows)
- B Number of employees
  - 1 By organisation
  - 2 Total industry wide
- C Number of volunteers
  - 1 By organisation
  - 2 Total industry wide
- D Number of customers serviced
  - 1 By type of service
  - 2 By organisation
  - 3 Total industry wide

4 **Facilities**
- A Number and type
  - 1 By organisation
  - 2 Total industry wide
- B Location
  - 1 By address
  - 2 By postcode

**Source:** Adapted from Philip D. Cooper and George E. McIlvain, 'Factors influencing marketing's ability to assist non-profit organizations', John H. Summey and Ronald D. Taylor, eds, *Evolving Marketing Thought* for 1980, *Proceedings of the Southern Marketing Association* (19–22 November 1980), p. 315. Used by permission.

with strategic planning in developing short-term and long-range goals, marketing strategies and promotional plans.

To control non-profit marketing activities, managers must make a proper inventory of activities performed, and be prepared to adjust or correct deviations from standards. Knowing where and how to look for deviations and knowing what types of deviation to expect are especially important in non-profit situations. Because non-profit marketing activities may not be perceived as marketing, managers must define clearly what activity is being examined and how it should function.

It may be difficult to control non-profit marketing activities, because it is often hard to determine whether goals are being achieved. A support group for victims of childhood abuse that wants to inform community members of its services may not be able to find out whether it is communicating with those people who need assistance. Surveying to discover the percentage of the population that is aware of the assistance the group offers can show whether the awareness objective has been achieved, but it fails to indicate what percentage of victims of abuse has been assisted. The detection and correction of deviations from standards are certainly major purposes of control, but standards must support the organisation's overall goals. Managers can refine goals by examining the results that are being achieved and analysing the ramifications of those results.

Techniques for controlling overall marketing performance must be compatible with the nature of an organisation's operations. Obviously, it is necessary to control the marketing budget in most non-profit organisations, but budgetary control is not tied to standards of profit and loss; responsible management of funds is the objective. Central control responsibility can facilitate orderly, efficient administration and planning. For example, most universities evaluate graduating students' progress to control and improve the quality of education provided. The audit phase typically relies on questionnaires sent to students and eventual employers. The employer completes a questionnaire to indicate the former student's progress; the graduate completes a questionnaire to indicate what additional

***Figure 13.5***
*Many non-business organisations judge the effectiveness of their marketing in terms of hits on their websites and requests for information*
*Source: Courtesy of Google*

concepts or skills were needed to perform duties. In addition, a number of faculty members may interview certain employers and former students to obtain information for control purposes. Results of the audit are used to develop corrective action if university standards have not been met. Corrective action could include an evaluation of the deficiency and a revision of the curriculum.

These aspects of marketing – managing services and non-profit – are discussed further in Chapter 22.

# Summary

*Services* are intangible, dominant products that cannot physically be possessed, the result of applying human or mechanical efforts to people or objects. The importance of services in the economy is increasing. There are *consumer services* and *business services*.

» Services have a number of distinguishing characteristics: *intangibility*, *inseparability* of production and consumption, *perishability*, *heterogeneity*, *client-based relationships* and *customer contact*. Intangibility places greater importance on *search*, *experience* and *credence qualities*. Services can be viewed in terms of a *five-category classification*: type of market, degree of labour intensiveness, degree of customer contact, skill of the service provider and goal of the service provider.

» Fluctuating demand is a major problem for most service organisations. Marketing strategies and the marketing mix as well as non-marketing strategies and primarily internal, employee-based actions can be used to deal with the problem. Before attempting to undertake any such strategies, however, services marketers must understand the patterns and determinants of demand. The intangibility of the service product, together with the importance of the people component of the extended marketing mix for services, leads to significant difficulties in creating and sustaining a *differential advantage*.

» The basic marketing mix is augmented for services through the addition of people, physical evidence (ambience) and the process of transaction in order to produce the '7Ps' or the *extended marketing mix for services*.

» *Service quality* is the perception of how well a service meets or exceeds customers' *service expectations*. The intangibility of services makes service quality very difficult for customers to evaluate. When competing services are very similar, service quality may be the only way for customers to distinguish between them. It is crucial for marketers to comprehend the four *service quality factors*: (1) understanding customer expectations, (2) service quality specifications, (3) employee performance, and (4) managing service expectations. To achieve customer satisfaction, a service must fall within the *customer's zone of tolerance*.

» *Non-profit marketing* includes marketing activities conducted by individuals and organisations to achieve goals other than normal business goals. The chief beneficiary of a business enterprise is whoever owns or holds shares in the business, but the beneficiary of a non-profit enterprise should be its clients, its members or its public at large. The goals of a non-profit organisation reflect its unique philosophy or mission. Some non-profit organisations have very controversial goals, but many organisations exist to further generally accepted social causes.

» The marketing objective of non-profit organisations is to obtain a desired response from a target market, often through *negotiation* or *persuasion*. Developing a non-profit marketing strategy consists of defining and analysing a target market, and creating and maintaining a marketing mix. *Target*, *client* and *general publics* must all be identified. In non-profit marketing, the product is usually an idea or service. Distribution is involved not so much with the movement of goods as with the communication of ideas and the delivery of services, which results in a very short marketing channel. Promotion is very important in non-profit marketing; personal selling, sales promotion, advertising and publicity are all used to communicate ideas and inform people about services. Price is more difficult to define in non-profit marketing because of *opportunity costs* and the difficulty of quantifying the values exchanged.

» It is important to control marketing strategies in non-profit situations. Control is designed to identify what activities have occurred in conformity with marketing strategy and to take corrective action where deviations are found. The standards against which performance is measured must support the non-profit organisation's overall goals.

## » *Key Links*

This chapter about marketing services should be read in conjunction with:

- Chapter 22, which discusses in more detail the extended marketing mix for services
- Chapter 10, the overview of the product ingredient of the marketing mix.

## Important Terms

Service
Consumer services
Business services
Intangibility
Search qualities
Experience qualities
Credence qualities
Inseparability

Perishability
Heterogeneity
Client-based relationships
Customer contact
Five-category classification
Differential advantage
Extended marketing mix for services
Service quality
Service expectations
Service quality factors
Customer's zone of tolerance
Non-profit marketing
Cause-related marketing
Negotiation
Persuasion
Target public
Client publics
General publics
Opportunity cost

## Discussion and Review Questions

1. Identify and discuss the distinguishing characteristics of services. What problems do these characteristics present to marketers?
2. What is the significance of 'tangibles' in service industries?
3. Use the five-category classification scheme to analyse a car valeting service, and discuss the implications for marketing mix development.
4. How do search, experience and credence qualities affect the way consumers view and evaluate services?
5. What additional elements must be included in the marketing mix for services? Why?
6. Why is it difficult to create and maintain a differential advantage in many service businesses?
7. Analyse the demand for the hire of sunbeds and discuss ways to cope with fluctuating demand.
8. What is the most important dimension in determining customer evaluation of service quality?
9. Compare and contrast the controversial aspects of non-profit versus business marketing.
10. Relate the concepts of product, place/distribution, promotion and price to a marketing strategy aimed at preventing drug abuse.
11. What are the differences between clients, publics and consumers? What is the difference between a target public and a target market?
12. Discuss the development of a marketing strategy for a university. What marketing decisions should be made in developing this strategy?

## Recommended Readings


- L. Berry, *On Great Service* (New York: Free Press, 1995).
- B. Edvardsson, B. Thomasson and J. Ovretveit, *Quality of Service, Making It Really Work* (London: McGraw-Hill, 1994).
- A. Gilmore, *Services Marketing and Management* (London: Sage, 2003).
- C. Grönroos, *Service Management and Marketing* (Chichester: Wiley, 2000).
- H. Kasper, P. van Helsdingen and W. de Vries Jr, *Services Marketing Management: An International Perspective* (Chichester: Wiley, 1999).
- C.H. Lovelock, *Principles of Services Marketing and Management* (Englewood Cliffs, NJ: Prentice-Hall, 2001).
- A. Palmer, *Principles of Services Marketing* (Maidenhead: McGraw-Hill, 2000).


### Internet Exercise

As Internet usage rises, the number of people using this method to communicate with friends, family and colleagues is also increasing. The founders of the Friends Reunited website spotted an opportunity to provide a service that helped people to get back in touch with friends and acquaintances. Take a look at this online organisation at:
www.friendsreunited.com

1. Classify Friends Reunited's product in terms of its position on the service continuum.
2. How does Friends Reunited enhance customer service and foster its relationship with customers through its Internet marketing efforts?
3. Discuss the degree to which experience and credence qualities exist in the services offered by Friends Reunited.

## Applied Mini-Case

Express carriers such as TNT, UPS and Federal Express do much more than provide a swift delivery service for letters and packages. As the sector has become more competitive, the expectations of clients have also risen. Inventory handling, assistance with customs clearance, barcoded tracking that can be monitored over the Internet, and the provision of a responsive customer services function, are just some of the extra services that are now expected as part of the product offering. Some clients even require their carriers to play a role in the packing process in their pursuit of a delivery solution that eases the movement of packages from the point of dispatch to the point of receipt.

**Sources:** 'Value-added takes on a new meaning', *Purchasing, no.* 120, 15 February 1996, pp. 68 – 9; Sally Dibb and Lyndon Simkin, *Marketing Briefs*, 2004, Oxford: Butterworth Heinemann.

### Question

**Assume the role of a management consultant who has been retained by one of the express carriers to undertake an analysis of service quality. Prepare a report that outlines the key dimensions of service quality.**

## Case Study

### Increasing Professionalism in Charity Marketing

Marketing is not an activity that consumers automatically associate with charities. Instead they link advertising and sales promotion with big brands such as Coca-Cola, McDonald's and Virgin. In reality, while commercial organisations such as these seek high returns and profits, charities must find ways to increase their revenues to fund their good causes. In recent years, the fundraising activities of charities have become characterised by an increasing professionalism, often involving the appointment of marketing managers, strategists and public relations executives. This has resulted in a greater variety of fundraising methods than ever before, including the use of viral campaigns, creative affinity tie-ups, e-marketing and Internet-based approaches. For example, the Multiple Sclerosis Trust and the Multiple Sclerosis Society are backing a joint fundraising initiative with shoe retailers. Known as MyShoes, the innovative scheme involves a partnership with footwear retailers, who donate a fixed amount to the MS charities for every pair of shoes they sell. MyShoes provides participating retailers with point-of-sales material that educates shoppers about MS (there are 85,000 MS sufferers in the UK). Such innovative fundraising is critical in a climate in which all forms of charity participation are thriving but the public's preferences for methods of collecting are changing.

Recent research shows that nearly 90 per cent of UK adults have participated in charitable activities in the past 12 months. Most are involved in giving money, but a third of these have taken part in a special charity activity or event. Others have been involved in organising events or have worked for a charity. Face-to-face fundraising remains the most popular way to give, with 67 per cent of all those donating using this approach. There has, however, been a trend away from traditional tin-rattling and towards the use of 'chugging' or face-to-face recruitment, designed to encourage would-be donors to agree to regular direct debit or covenant arrangements. More than ever, charities are recognising that fundraising activities should be targeted particularly at those in the population who are prepared to become committed donors. In some cases this means attracting a new generation of people prepared to donate regularly. A recent NOP survey suggested that just 15 per cent of fundraising revenue is accrued from long-term donors, with human rights charities the biggest winners, and good causes supporting the young or elderly gaining least from this means.

Even though many consumers dislike the use of direct marketing methods such as direct mail and telephone calls to solicit funds, the second most important channel for donations is by post. This approach has proved particularly popular with human rights and wildlife causes. However, relatively few supporters of children's charities and those supporting the elderly choose this method. Indeed, it seems that traditional personal approaches to collecting funds, such as the use of collecting tins in shopping malls and high streets, are declining in effectiveness. Instead, the public's imagination has been captured by a host of media-based activities. For example, specially organised events, and television appeals and programmes have been shown to be particularly effective ways of attracting funds. The use of high-profile individuals in such appeals, such as royalty, television personalities, and well-known actors or sports stars, is particularly popular. In a recent survey, 80 per cent of consumers questioned also supported the use of commercial and promotional schemes, such as the sale of products through gift shops and catalogues. A similar percentage stated that they like to buy products that involve the manufacturer making a contribution to charity.

Evidence of increasing professionalism in fundraising is readily apparent across the charity sector. Cancer Research has recently overhauled its marketing strategy to focus afresh on fundraising. This follows a period when the charity concentrated on brand building, following its creation out of the merger of Imperial Cancer Research and the Cancer Research Campaign. With plans for a £10m (€15m) spend on advertising and direct marketing, the organisation has engaged two advertising agencies to develop activities in these areas. This comes after the charity's recent highly successful 'All Clear' television advertising campaign.

The promise of the Internet as a medium for generating donations has frequently been suggested, but is yet to develop fully. Relatively few charities have evolved effective means of raising funds online. So far, human rights charities have been among the more successful but, even for this group, online donations represent only 2.9 per cent of the total. However, fundraising using the Internet could soon increase, with a range of innovative campaigns being created. For example, the World Society for the Protection of Animals (WSPA) has developed a joint initiative with Orange, to offer consumers a range of animal ringtones for their mobile phones. Consumers can purchase the ringtones, including everything from an African elephant to a coyote or a Siberian tiger, from the Orange website, and 10 per cent of the royalties for downloading the tones will be donated to the charity. Meanwhile, children's charity Barnardo's has signalled its intention to increase its emphasis on the Internet as a means of recruiting and communicating with its younger donors. In the age of television, the Internet and the mobile phone, it seems that charities such as these must be ready, willing and able to use the full range of media-based approaches available.

**Sources:** Emily Rogers, 'MS charity initiative to roll out brand identity', *Marketing*, 1 April 2004, p. 10; Ben Bold, 'Cancer Research £10m work goes to Ogilvy Group', *Marketing*, 8 April 2004, p. 3; Caroline Parry, 'Factfile: it's a matter of give and take', *Marketing Week*, 19 February 2004, pp. 36–7; Mark Sweney, 'Barnardo's focuses fundraising on web', *Marketing*, 1 April 2004, p. 8; 'Charities unite in donor appeal', *Marketing*, 14 January 1999, p. 4; 'Spotlight: charity', *Marketing Week*, 17 December 1998, pp. 28–9; Tony Lees, NOP Research Group; www.wspa.org.uk.

## Questions for Discussion

1 Why are charities such as Barnardo's and Cancer Research UK turning more to the marketing tactics deployed by consumer goods companies?

2 To what kinds of donor must charities appeal? How might collection methods vary for these different groups?

3 How might the marketing strategy vary according to whether a charity is targeting consumers or corporate donors?

# Postscript

Having identified marketing opportunities to pursue, a business should recommend a marketing strategy that involves selecting the target market, determining the required positioning and developing a competitive advantage. For the recommended target market strategy to be implemented, a marketing mix must be developed. The marketing mix centres on the '5Ps' of product, people, place/distribution, promotion and pricing decisions.

Part III of *Marketing: Concepts and Strategies* has addressed the product ingredient of the marketing mix and its integral component, the people ingredient. This part has also examined the associated aspects of customer service, branding, packaging, labelling and services, as well as exploring the important concepts of product life cycles and portfolio management. Special consideration has been given to the role of marketing in non-business or not-for-profit organisations.

Before progressing, readers should be confident that they are now able to do the following.

## Describe the basic product decisions

- What are the definitions and classifications of products adopted by marketers?
- What are the levels of a product?
- What distinguishes product items, product lines and product mixes?
- Why is the product life cycle so important?
- Why are the different levels of a product so important in determining a competitive edge over rivals' products?

## Explain the importance of branding and packaging

- Why are brands and brand equity important?
- What are the types of brand, their benefits and the ways in which they can be selected, named, protected and licensed?
- What are the best practice guidelines for creating strong brands?
- What are the roles of brand attributes, brand values and brand personality in brand development?
- What are the functions and design considerations of packaging?
- What is the role of packaging in marketing strategy?
- What are the functions of labelling and the associated legal issues?

## Outline the requirements for developing products and managing product portfolios

- What alternatives are there for managing products?
- How does a business develop a product idea into a commercial product?
- What is the role of product development in the marketing mix?
- Why must products be managed differently in the various stages of the product life cycle?
- How can product modification or product deletion benefit the marketing mix?
- What are the key tools for the strategic planning of product or market portfolios?

## Understand the special requirements for the marketing of services

- What are the nature and characteristics of services?
- How can services be classified?
- How can marketing strategies be developed for services?
- What are the '7Ps' of services marketing?
- Why are there difficulties in creating a differential advantage for services?
- Why is the concept of service quality crucial?
- Why is marketing in non-business situations unique?
- How can marketing strategies be developed and marketing activities be controlled for non-business organisations?

*Strategic Case*

# Aer Lingus
## Competing on Nationalistic Fervour: Irishness

The airline industry is unusual: its strategic importance, and exacting safety and technical requirements make it highly regulated. People skills, whether those of pilots, ground crew or cabin staff, are specialised and expensive. The cost of leasing or buying aircraft is very high. Routes are highly sought after, particularly into the major international hubs such as London, Amsterdam and Paris. The much-vaunted EU 'freedom of the skies' policy, central to the harmonisation of European deregulation and the creation of the European Union, has yet to materialise fully, with major carriers still defending near-monopoly conditions on certain routes. Few airlines are profitable, yet many governments still strive to have a 'national' carrier of which the population can be proud.

Most states in the EU have a host of smaller airlines attempting to emulate Air France, British Airways, KLM and Lufthansa. A significant development has been the emergence of low-price, no-frills operators such as pioneer easyJet, Ryanair, Go and Virgin Express. Few industries are as prone to the impact of the macro marketing environment. Oil price rises lead to surcharged passengers, the terror threat has added security costs and reduced passenger numbers on certain routes, industrial relations problems with baggage handlers or air traffic controllers frequently blight travellers' plans, and attempts by airlines to create scale economies through mergers and acquisitions are often blocked by regulators.

### Ireland's Growth

The situation in Ireland is no different, except that the country has recently enjoyed tremendous success in economic growth and in attracting investment from an impressive and diverse list of international corporations that includes Dell, IBM, Siemens, CIGNA, McGraw-Hill, ABN AMRO, Chase Manhattan, Deutsche Bank, General Electric, Diageo, Sumitomo, Ericsson, Hitachi, Sandoz, Schering-Plough, Fruit of the Loom, Glen Dimplex, Krups, Heineken, Nestlé and the ubiquitous Coca-Cola. As a result of this influx – Ireland's economic growth outstripped that of most of Europe for over a decade – good communications are crucial. For the government and people of Ireland, as well as the expanding international business community, air travel has increasingly become a necessity. The Shannon duty-free zone and continued prosperity of Dublin have added to the volume of freight traffic heading to Ireland. For the quasi state airline Aer Lingus, these growing demands provided a welcome boost to business; they are also the reason more and more rival airlines are seeking slots for flights into Dublin. Fellow Irish airline Ryanair has also been quick to benefit from these trends.

### Complex Competitive Situation

The highly competitive airline industry is characterised by four strategic groups:

1. global carriers with truly global networks, such as American Airlines, British Airways, KLM, Qantas and United
2. medium-sized international carriers, with significant international routes but less global reach, such as Cathay Pacific, SAS and Virgin
3. regional carriers focused on regional networks and destinations, such as bmi, Iberia and Swiss
4. local carriers serving domestic short-hop, intercity destinations, such as flybe, Ryanair and TAT.

In addition, there are numerous charter operators, such as TUI's various airlines and First Choice Airways, plus businesses dealing only with air freight and couriers. Aer Lingus is a regional carrier with a few key international routes emanating from Dublin, an impressive network with most major British regional airports and a growing selection of European destinations. As such, the company competes with rivals in all four strategic groups, contending with the Club branding and high service levels offered by British Airways, the cut-price deals of Ryanair and the high promotional spends of most major European airlines. In addition, Ireland's proximity to the Welsh coast forces Aer Lingus to consider the ferry operators as competitors for much business to and from the UK.

## High Expectations

A lot is expected of Aer Lingus, until quite recently Ireland's official national carrier. In terms of sales, it is one of Ireland's largest companies, and by number of employees (12,000) it is ranked third. Now standing on its own commercial platform, the company has a monumental mission. According to a former marketing director, it is tough for the airline because:

> we have to compete with several of the really big players on the transatlantic routes, the large airlines in the European Union as well as the smaller, 'no frills' operators within certain UK and Irish domestic routes. So while we have to be commercially competitive with other major carriers in different segments of the free market, back home in Ireland and as a major employer, people expect us to take an accommodating attitude to labour relations, work practices and to provide long-term employment.

The official mission statement is equally stretching:

> The Aer Lingus mission is to be a strong niche airline, primarily carrying passengers and freight into and out of Ireland, capable of sustained profitability through commercially viable products and practices and a keen customer focus, delivered by committed and well-motivated staff. It will strive to attain a position in which its subsidiaries are profitable and viable within themselves, are strategic to the core airline business, and the ownership of which enhances the achievability of the airline's objectives.

For the core airline business, there is stiff and varied competition. On its transatlantic routes, American Airlines, British Airways, Delta, KLM, Northwest and Singapore offer premium service competition, while Virgin and Air India provide value-for-money rivalry. Principal competition on its European routes stems from the trimmer regional carriers such as bmi and a host of medium-sized European airlines. On the London and UK provincial routes, BA provides competition, while Air France's Dublin-based CityJet and its major challenger Ryanair provide significant competition. Nevertheless, Aer Lingus believes it holds a successful operating niche, helped by its distinct national identity, which appeals strongly to the Irish both at home and abroad. By the late 1990s, Aer Lingus had created an enviable reputation for customer service, punctuality and empathy with travellers. Before labour relations problems and then the horrific 2001 Twin Towers terrorist attack, Aer Lingus had become, financially, one of the best-performing airlines in the world, and its ability to meet the demands of customers was desired by most of its competitors. Despite the woes faced by all airlines in the past few years, Aer Lingus is once again profitable – most are not.

## Irish Nationalism

The essence of the successful niche central to Aer Lingus's marketing was Irish nationalism. Its transatlantic routes, where it has no other Irish-based rivals, are its most profitable. To feed these routes, Aer Lingus operates Dublin as a hub for all of its domestic, London, other UK and European flights. These flights operate on coordinated timetables with the US flights to offer passengers 'seamless' travel. There are believed to be over 44 million Americans of Irish ancestry. Henry Ford, John Paul Getty, Gene Kelly, Gregory Peck, the Kennedys, Ronald Reagan and Bill Clinton are just some of the more famous examples. Accordingly, there are US Immigration and Naturalisation Service clearing facilities in Dublin and Shannon airports, offering users of the Aer Lingus Dublin hub destined for Boston and New York significant time savings.

Its transatlantic routes are at the forefront of Aer Lingus's development programme and marketing initiatives. The highly profitable business class offers complimentary chauffeur-driven service, has 52-inch-pitch sleeperettes instead of the standard 42-inch-pitch business-class seats found in most airlines; multi-channel personal entertainment systems, loyalty programmes for frequent fliers and luxury lounges at airports; these have given Aer Lingus an edge over rivals on its transatlantic lifeline. Because business-class passengers generate up to five times as much profit as tourist-class passengers, Premier-class accommodation was expanded from 24 to 36 seats on many flights. In the economy cabin section, price competition with rivals has reached a peak, but by removing in-flight entertainment and reducing refreshments, Aer Lingus Ireland Vacations has been able to undercut rivals' discount deals. Regular fliers, chambers of commerce and Ireland's Air Transport Users' Committee have welcomed the attention being devoted to the Premier class: 'best executive class on transatlantic routes', 'best transatlantic airline', 'best Ireland/UK airline', 'best Ireland/Europe airline' are just some of the accolades. High take-up of the 'no frills' economy service and Aer Lingus Ireland Vacations indicates that those passengers, too, are satisfied with Aer Lingus's efforts.

While pricing is often critical in the airline wars, operators such as British Airways and Singapore Airlines are perpetually seeking to create a competitive advantage through improvements in customer service and customer handling: larger and more comfortable seats, better-trained cabin crew, superior entertainment and food, faster check-ins, in-flight fax, e-mail and phone facilities, limousine pick-up and delivery, smart airport lounges, exercise facilities and more pleasant staff. The challenge has not gone unnoticed by Aer Lingus.

## A Future for Customer Service?

The future seems far from clear for Aer Lingus and its product specification. Should the focus be to enhance customer service levels, particularly in Aer Lingus's premium class? Or should Aer Lingus emulate Irish rival Ryanair, by offering a price-based proposition with 'no frills'? Should the product specified for long-haul travellers be markedly different to the product offered on short-haul routes? Originally, the airline's existing standing and service culture prompted management to adhere to a full-service proposition, focusing in particular on premium passengers desiring extensive customer service. Now there is an attempt by the airline to cut operating costs in order to reduce fares. While this may attract value-led travellers, it has to be at the expense of the full-service approach previously offered. In mid-2004, Aer Lingus opted for the 'no frills' approach on its short-haul routes, jettisoning its award-winning full-service products. This change risks alienating existing customers and it is possible that other rivals already have both the reputation for low price and a low-cost operating structure ahead of Aer Lingus.

Certain observers believe that Aer Lingus now risks being 'stuck in the middle'. Perhaps there is a middle-ground option that builds on the airline's heritage of service and reflects the market's trend towards discounted prices? Some industry experts believe it is possible to reduce costs, to offer lower fares to travellers still prepared to pay a moderate price premium over the truly no frills operators – such as easyJet – in order to benefit from some customer service. This is the marketing approach now being adopted by BA on its short-haul routes and it is possible Aer Lingus could have modified its product offering to emulate BA's approach. On BA's short-haul routes, passengers now pay considerably less than they did two years ago, yet still receive allocated seats (important for time-pressured business travellers wishing to disembark quickly), generous baggage allowances including two items in the cabin (aimed at business users carrying laptops), bar service and food. For now, the message from Aer Lingus is clear: 'aerlingus.com. Low fares. Way better.' How low these prices go, the impact on customer service and the resulting degree of acceptance by passengers, remain to be seen.

## Questions for Discussion

1 Why is Aer Lingus's complex competitive situation a problem for its economy-class business? Discuss the implications of this situation.
2 Discuss the importance of customer service in the original product proposition for Aer Lingus. What is the implication for Aer Lingus's competitive advantage?
3 Should Aer Lingus be a full-service airline or focus on the value-led segment? Why? What are the implications for the airline's product specification?

# IV Place (Distribution and Marketing Channel)

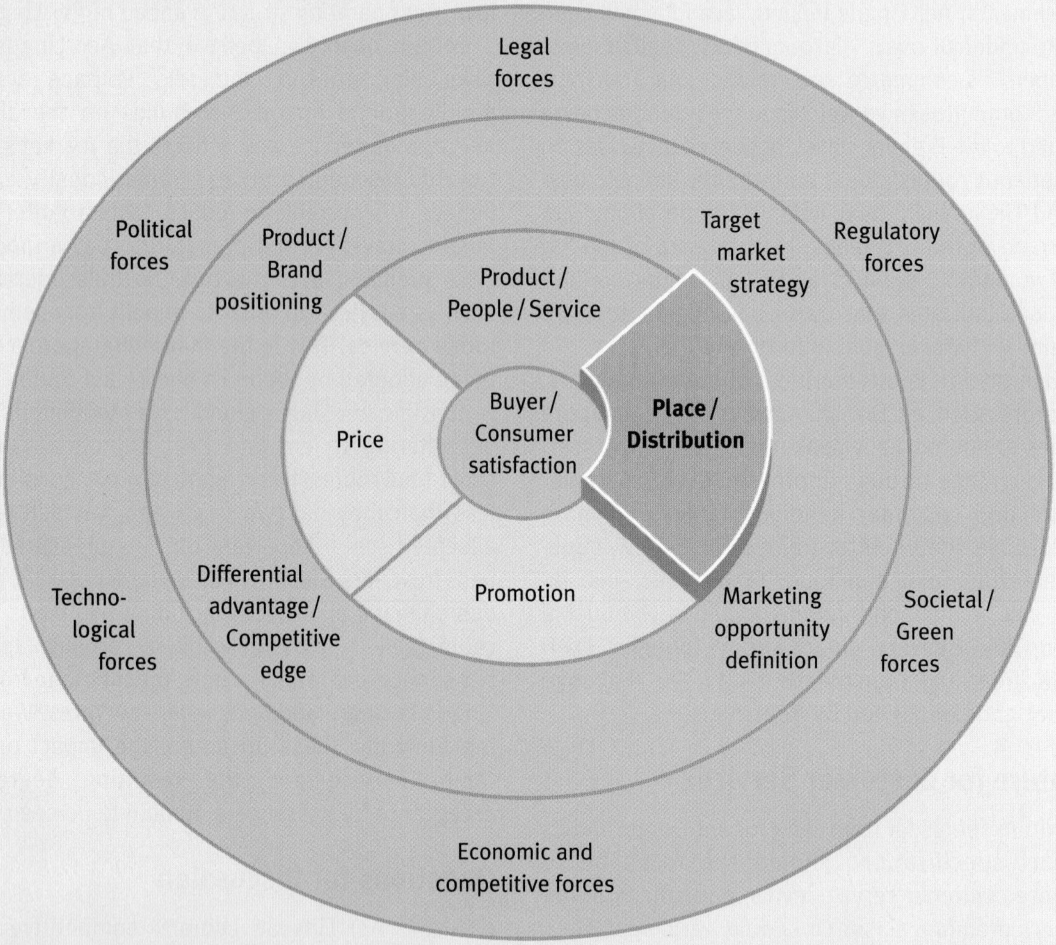


Having identified a marketing opportunity and selected a target market, the marketer must design a product and service package that will satisfy the consumers or business customers targeted, while maximising the marketing opportunity for the business in question. The product may be exactly what the targeted customers desire, but if it is not made available to them, they will not be able to adopt the product. The place ingredient of the marketing mix addresses the distribution and marketing channel decisions that are necessary to provide the target market with convenient and ready access to the product or service, but in a manner that is beneficial to the supplier of the product or service.

**Part IV of** *Marketing: Concepts and Strategies* examines the nature of marketing channels, wholesalers and distributors, the physical distribution of products and services, plus retail marketing.

**Chapter 14, 'Marketing Channels'**, explains the marketing channel concept, the role of supply chain management, the functions and different types of marketing channel. The chapter considers channel integration and the levels of market coverage, and then examines the selection of distribution channels, including the increasingly popular option of direct marketing. Behavioural aspects of channels, particularly the concepts of cooperation and relationship building, conflict and leadership, are then explored. The chapter concludes by examining legal issues in channel management.

**Chapter 15, 'Wholesalers, Distributors and Physical Distribution'**, presents a description of the nature of wholesaling in its broadest forms in the marketing channel, explains wholesalers' activities and their classification, examines agencies that facilitate wholesaling and explores some changing patterns in wholesaling and distribution. The chapter then moves on to discuss physical distribution management and objectives. It explains order processing, materials handling, and different types of warehousing and their objectives. The chapter then examines inventory management and concludes with an analysis of different methods of transportation.

**Chapter 16, 'Retailing'**, explains the purpose and function of retailing in the marketing channel, provides an overview of retail locations and major store types, and describes non-store retailing and franchising. The chapter highlights the many strategic issues concerning modern retailing and concludes with a look at current trends in retailing. A large proportion of products purchased by consumers pass through retail channels. Retail marketers have some additional concerns to add to their target market strategising and marketing mix specification.

By the conclusion of Part IV of *Marketing: Concepts and Strategies*, readers should understand the essential place that decisions concerning marketing channels and distribution require in the marketing mix.

## Calor

At Calor, marketing is the essential, dynamic process through which we maximise shareholder value, by profiling, identifying and locating individuals or companies, enabling us to establish intimate, relevant, long-term relationships that bring continuous mutual satisfaction and tangible financial benefit. Marketing has banished the historical darkness of prejudice, arrogance and self-interest, providing insight and enlightenment, which beams on the customer as our sole and ultimate focus.

Marketing strategy should not remain the property of the Marketing Department, but must be both 'understood' and 'owned' company-wide. At Calor, cross-functional business planning is directed by our marketing strategy and all action plans delivered 'in concert' with it. Successful deployment of actions arising from the marketing strategy requires 'buy-in' from all functional departments and reinforcement via unambiguous direction from the board room. Having said that, markets are dynamic, and therefore assumptions and strategies must be continually and constructively challenged, to ensure ongoing relevance and effectiveness in their deployment. Communication of marketing strategy must cascade down through the organisation and, within the boundaries of commercial sensitivity, future intentions must be shared across the spectrum of stakeholders, who individually impact directly on customer relationships.

### Alex Davis, sales and marketing director, Calor

Calor, part of the Dutch SHV Group, is the UK's leading supplier of LPG with over 65 years' experience in this flexible and environmentally sensitive energy market. Around 4 million homes and businesses rely on Calor for an enormous variety of applications. Calor's own depots deal directly with many of these customers, but dealers and agents are also important channel members for Calor.

# 14 Marketing Channels

"Effective management of manufacturer–dealer relationships is formidably problematic but strategically imperative."

*David Shipley, Trinity College, University of Dublin*

## Objectives

- To understand the marketing channel concept and the nature of marketing channels
- To discuss the functions of marketing channels
- To examine different types of channel
- To examine channel integration and levels of market coverage
- To consider the selection of distribution channels and the emergence of direct marketing
- To explore the behavioural aspects of channels, especially the concepts of cooperation, relationship building, conflict and leadership
- To examine legal issues in channel management

## Introduction

Distribution involves activities that make products available to customers when and where they want to purchase them. It is sometimes referred to as the 'place' element in the marketing mix of the 5Ps: product, place/distribution, promotion, price and people. Choosing which channels of distribution to use is a major decision in the development of marketing strategies. High customer service levels may require heavy investment in distribution and the shrewd identification of channel members with which to work. There has to be a compromise between adequate responsiveness to customers' needs and expectations in a cost-effective manner for the company.

This chapter focuses on the description and analysis of marketing channels, first discussing the nature of channels and their functions, and then explaining the main types of channel and their structures. These sections are followed by a review of several forms of channel integration. Consideration is given to how marketers determine the appropriate intensity of market coverage for a product and to the factors that are considered when selecting suitable channels of distribution. After examining behavioural patterns within marketing channels, and the relationships that develop between channel members, the chapter concludes by looking at several legal issues affecting channel management. Subsequent chapters in Part IV further explore the roles of channel members or intermediaries, and of physical distribution management.

# Opener

## BA's Focus on E-booking

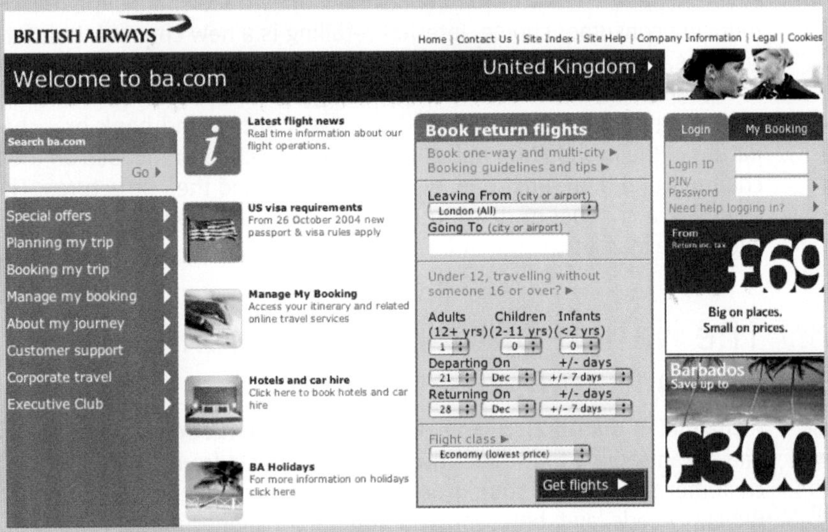


Not too many years ago, the bulk of BA flights were booked either via travel agents or over the telephone by passengers. BA introduced e-tickets, rather than sending out traditional books of travel coupon tickets, and passengers could print off their own documentation. Soon, even such behaviour was passé, as a simple booking reference sufficed and paperless travel had arrived. Passengers either insert their credit card into a ticket dispenser at the airport or tell a customer service agent their allocated booking reference code in order for the agent to allocate a seat and boarding pass. No paper is necessary.

In late 2003, BA made a radical decision. Its 24-hour telephone booking service ceased: night-time tele-booking or changes to travel itineraries became a thing of the past, too. Although partly driven by a cost-saving strategy, the reduction in call centres also reflected the growth in the airline's e-booking service. 'If you choose to complete your booking by phone, you will incur a £15 off-line service fee per passenger', greeted customers dialling 0870 8507850 intending to book seats by phone, as BA steered customers towards its web-based operation. While passengers wishing to book at night could no longer speak over the telephone to a BA customer service agent, they could go on-line 24 hours a day in order to make or change a booking.

The BA website reflects this shift in emphasis, suggesting special offers, linking to customer support and providing web users with corporate information, while also providing links to:

- Latest Flight News
- Why Fly BA?
- Manage My Booking
- Hotels/Cars/Holidays
- Executive Club.

The primary focus on the home page, though, is on a 'Book Return Flights' menu-driven system providing speedy access to BA's network and timetable. 'Book Return Flights' enables users to check for routes, suitable times, prices and seat availability in seconds, or to place a confirmed booking in under a minute.

The company launched a set of related mobile services in 2004, with timetables for PCs, pocket PCs, palmtops or as pdf downloads, and a booking/ timetable service on 'Vodafone Live!'. Regular users find the e-channel to market both faster and more convenient than call centres or accessing BA via a travel agent. BA still uses advertising, brochures and direct mail, plus travel agencies and telephone call centres to interface with its customers, but the airline has fully embraced e-commerce as a channel to market.

**Sources:** www.BA.com, May 2004; BA. Screen capture by kind permission of British Airways.

As in the example of BA's move to focus on e-commerce, changes in the manner in which products are distributed have a major impact on customers. For example, moves by food retailers to sell petrol from sites adjacent to their supermarkets have affected the UK petrol market in a number of important ways. Reducing petrol prices and increasing promotional activity are damaging margins to a point where profitability is severely threatened. In the long term this may force small suppliers out of business, thus reducing consumer choice. Internet retailing is a new channel that, for some products and services, increasingly cuts out the need for wholesalers and retail stores. It is forecast that, soon, the bulk of music sales and banking transactions will be via e-commerce. Such direct marketing negates the need for high-street shops and bank branches, and changes the nature of the proposition being marketed. This chapter focuses on the nature of marketing channels and their functions, types of channel and their structures. The factors relevant in selecting a channel of distribution are discussed, along with the nature of relationships within the marketing channel.

## The Nature of Marketing Channels and Supply Chain Management

**Channel of distribution (or marketing channel)** A group of individuals and organisations that direct the flow of products from producers to customers

A **channel of distribution** (sometimes called a **marketing channel**) is a group of individuals and organisations that direct the flow of products from producers to customers. Providing customer satisfaction should be the driving force behind all marketing channel activities. Buyers' needs and behaviour are, therefore, important concerns of channel members. Channels of distribution make products available at the right time, in the right place and in the right quantity by providing such product-enhancing functions as transport and storage.[1]

The basic premise is simple. A manufacturer of a particular product could sell directly to the intended ultimate consumers, or the manufacturer could utilise the services of wholesalers, retailers or other channel members, rather than bear the hassle and costs of dealing with many end-user consumers directly. Alternatively, the manufacturer could opt to use a mix of routes to convey its products to the ultimate consumers: some direct selling, links with wholesalers and retailers, and possibly alliances with the selling activities of other manufacturers. There has, though, to be a balance between optimising customer satisfaction and making an adequate return on investment. These are the challenges of channel management for marketers.

**Marketing intermediary** A middleman who links producers to other middlemen or to those who ultimately use the products

**Merchants** Intermediaries who take title to products and resell them

**Functional middlemen** Intermediaries who do not take title to products

Most, but not all, channels of distribution have marketing intermediaries, although there is currently a growth in direct marketing, with some suppliers interacting with consumers without the use of intermediaries (see Chapter 19). A **marketing intermediary**, or middleman, links producers to other middlemen or to those who ultimately use the products. Marketing intermediaries perform the activities described in Table 14.1. There are two major types of intermediary: merchants and functional middlemen – agents and brokers. **Merchants** take title to products and resell them, whereas **functional middlemen** do not take title to products. Both types facilitate the movement of goods and services from producers to consumers.

Both retailers and wholesalers are intermediaries. Retailers purchase products for the purpose of reselling them to users. Merchant wholesalers resell products to other wholesalers and to retailers. Functional wholesalers, such as agents and brokers, expedite exchanges among producers and resellers, and are compensated by fees or commissions. For purposes of discussion in this chapter, all wholesalers are considered merchant middlemen unless otherwise specified.

Channel members share certain significant characteristics. Each member has different responsibilities within the overall structure of the distribution system, but mutual profit and success can be attained only if channel members cooperate in delivering products to the market. The area of relationship management has recently received a great deal of

**Table 14.1 Marketing Channel Activities Performed by Intermediaries**

| Category of Marketing Activities | Possible Activities Required |
|---|---|
| Marketing information | Analyse information such as sales data; perform or commission marketing research studies |
| Marketing management | Establish objectives; plan activities; manage and co-ordinate financing, personnel and risk taking; evaluate and control channel activities |
| Facilitating exchange | Choose and stock product assortments that match the needs of buyers |
| Promotion | Set promotional objectives; co-ordinate advertising, personal selling, sales promotion, publicity, sponsorship, direct mail and packaging |
| Price | Establish pricing policies and terms of sales |
| Physical distribution | Manage transport, warehousing, materials handling, inventory control and communication |
| Customer service | Provide channels for advice, technical support, after sales back-up and warranty provision |
| Relationships | Facilitate communication, products and parts, financial support and credit, inventory levels, after market needs, on-time delivery and customer service to maintain relationships with other marketing intermediaries and between suppliers and their targeted customers |

attention in marketing circles. This is increasingly important in delivering adequate customer service to target market customers. A supplier desires an ongoing and lucrative relationship with its customers: it recognises the importance of the various channel members in maintaining this relationship and strives for mutually beneficial relationships with its channel intermediaries.

Although distribution decisions need not precede other marketing decisions, they do exercise a powerful influence on the rest of the marketing mix. Channel decisions are critical because they determine a product's market presence and buyers' accessibility to the product. They also affect customers' overall satisfaction with the product or service provider.[2] At a time when organisations increasingly offer their products through multiple channels, the challenge of maintaining quality of delivery irrespective of the channel used, is very much to the fore. The strategic significance of channel decisions is further heightened by the fact that they often entail long-term commitments. For example, it is much easier for a company to change prices or packaging than to change existing distribution systems.

It may be necessary for companies to use different distribution paths in different countries, for different target market segments or for the various products in its portfolio. The links in any channel, however, are the merchants – including producers – and agents who oversee the movement of products through that channel. Marketing channels are commonly classified into channels for consumer products/services or channels for industrial, business-to-business products/services.

**Supply chain management**
Long-term partnerships among marketing channel members that reduce inefficiencies, costs and redundancies in the marketing channel and develop innovative approaches to satisfying targeted customers

Increasingly, an important function of the marketing channel is the joint effort of all channel members to create a supply chain: a total distribution system that serves customers and creates a competitive advantage (see also Chapter 15). **Supply chain management** refers to long-term partnerships among marketing channel members that reduce inefficiencies, costs and redundancies in the marketing channel and develop innovative approaches to satisfying targeted customers. The goal is still to provide customers with the product or service demanded, in line with their expectations, but in a more coordinated way that builds on the combined strengths of the members of the distribution channel. Key tasks in supply chain management include: planning and coordination of marketing channel partnerships; sourcing necessary resources, goods and services to support the supply chain; facilitating delivery; and relationship building in order to nurture ongoing customer relationships.

## Functions of Marketing Channels

Marketing channels serve many functions. Although some of these functions may be performed by a single channel member, most are accomplished through both the independent and joint efforts of channel members. These functions include creating utility, facilitating exchange efficiencies, alleviating discrepancies, standardising transactions and providing customer service.

### Creating Utility

Marketing channels create four types of utility: time, place, possession and form.

1. Time utility is having products available when the customer wants them.
2. Place utility is created by making products available in locations where customers wish to purchase them.
3. Possession utility is created by giving the customer access to the product to use or to store for future use. Possession utility can occur through ownership or through arrangements such as lease or rental agreements that give the customer the right to use the product.
4. Channel members sometimes create form utility by assembling, preparing or otherwise refining the product to suit individual customer needs.

### Facilitating Exchange Efficiencies

Marketing intermediaries can reduce the costs of exchanges by performing certain services or functions efficiently. Even if producers and buyers are located in the same city, there are costs associated with exchanges. As Figure 14.1 shows, when four buyers seek products from four producers, sixteen transactions are possible. If one intermediary serves both producers and buyers, the number of transactions can be reduced to eight. Intermediaries are specialists in facilitating exchanges. They provide valuable assistance because of their access to, and control over, important resources used in the proper functioning of marketing channels.

Nevertheless, the press, consumers, public officials and other marketers freely criticise intermediaries, especially wholesalers – retail wholesalers, dealers, distributors. In a US survey of the general public, 74 per cent believed that 'wholesalers frequently make high profits, which significantly increase prices that consumers pay'.[3] Critics accuse wholesalers of being inefficient and parasitic. Consumers often wish to make the distribution channel as short as possible, assuming that the fewer the intermediaries, the lower the price. For example, Virgin's financial services operation aims to offer competitive prices by cutting out brokers. Because suggestions to eliminate them come from both ends of the marketing channel, wholesalers must be careful to perform only those marketing activities that are truly desired. To survive, they must be more efficient and more customer focused than alternative marketing institutions.

Critics who suggest that eliminating wholesalers would lower consumer prices do not recognise that doing so would not remove the need for services that wholesalers provide. Although wholesalers can be eliminated, in many markets the functions they perform cannot. Other channel members would have to perform those functions, and customers would still have to fund them. In addition, all producers would have to deal directly with retailers or consumers, so that every producer would have to keep voluminous records and hire enough personnel to deal with a multitude of customers. Customers might end up paying a great deal more for products because prices would reflect the costs of less efficient channel members.

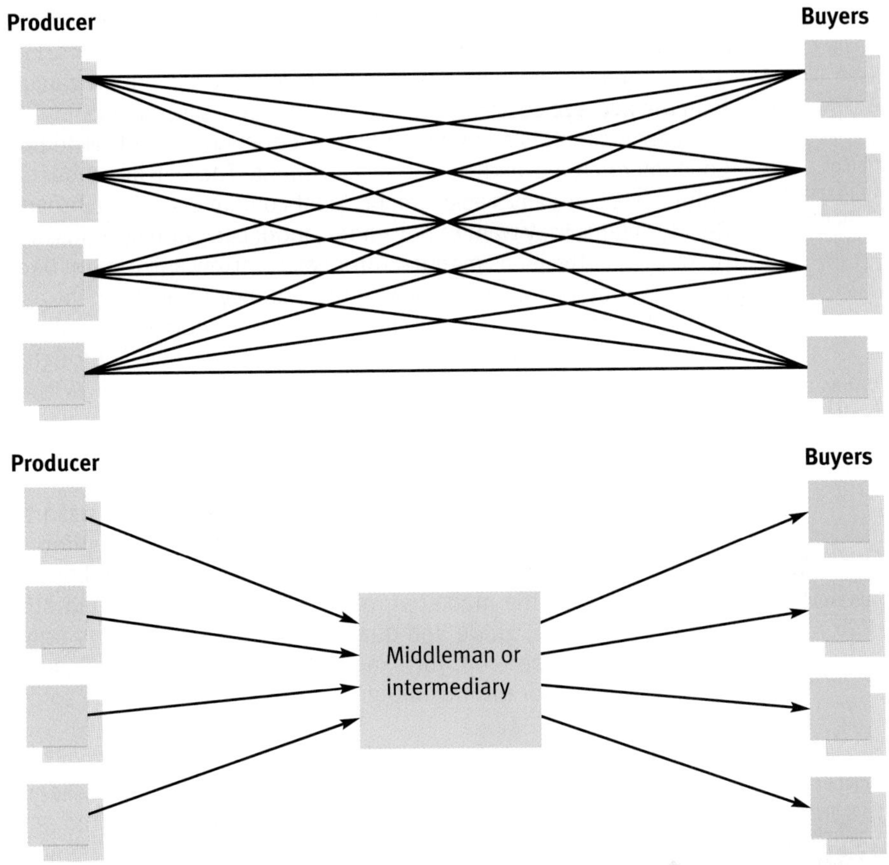


*Figure 14.1* *Efficiency in exchanges provided by an intermediary*

Direct customer–supplier marketing is possible in some markets. For instance, telesales-led Direct Line has a successful direct relationship with its insurance- and mortgage-buying customers. JCB, on the other hand, would find it difficult to sell directly and depends on its dealers for parts and maintenance provision to its construction equipment customers. Heinz, Kellogg's, Sony, Ford and BA all utilise channel members – retailers, dealers or travel agents – in order to sell their products and services. These companies may well use direct mail and the web to contact their existing or potential customers, but channel members play an important role in some of their marketing programmes.

To illustrate wholesalers' efficient services, assume that all wholesalers have been eliminated. Because there are more than 1.5 million retailers, a widely purchased consumer product – say, toilet paper – would require an extraordinary number of sales contacts, possibly more than a million, to maintain the current level of product exposure. For example, Scott would have to deliver its paper products, establish warehouses all over Europe and maintain fleets of trucks. Selling and distribution costs for Scott's products would rocket. Instead of a few contacts with food brokers, large retail businesses and merchant wholesalers, such manufacturers would face thousands of expensive contacts with, and shipments to, smaller retailers. Such an operation would be highly inefficient, and costs would be passed on to consumers. Wholesalers are often more efficient and less expensive.

## Alleviating Discrepancies

The functions performed within marketing channels help to overcome two major distribution problems: discrepancies in quantity and discrepancies in assortment. With respect to discrepancies in quantity, consider a company that manufactures jeans. The company specialises in the goods it can produce most efficiently: denim clothing. To make jeans most economically, the producer turns out 100,000 pairs of jeans each day. Few people, however, want to buy 100,000 pairs of jeans – they just want a few pairs. Retail customers may want a few hundred pairs. Thus the quantity of jeans the company can produce efficiently is more than the average customer wants. This is called 'discrepancy in quantity'.

**Assortment**
A combination of products put together to provide customer benefits

An **assortment** is a combination of products put together to provide customer benefits. Consumers create and hold an assortment. The set of products made available to customers is a company's assortment. Most consumers want a broad assortment of products. Besides jeans, they want to buy shoes, food, cars, hi-fi systems, soft drinks and many other products. Yet the jeans manufacturer has a narrow assortment because it only makes jeans and a few other denim clothes. A discrepancy in assortment exists because consumers want a broad assortment, but an individual manufacturer produces a narrow assortment.

**Sorting activities**
Functions that let channel members divide roles and separate tasks

Quantity and assortment discrepancies are resolved through the sorting activities of channel members. **Sorting activities** are functions that allow channel members to divide roles and to separate tasks; they include sorting out, accumulation, allocation and assorting of products (see Figure 14.2).[4]

**Sorting out**
Separating products into uniform, homogeneous groups

**Sorting Out** **Sorting out**, the first step in developing an assortment, is separating conglomerates of heterogeneous products into relatively uniform, homogeneous groups based on product characteristics such as size, shape, weight or colour. Sorting out is especially common in the marketing of agricultural products and other raw materials, which vary widely in size, grade and quality, and would be largely unusable in an undifferentiated mass. A grape crop, for example, must be sorted into grapes suitable for making wine, those best for turning into grape juice and those to be sold by food retailers.

**Accumulation**
The development of a bank of homogeneous products with similar production or demand requirements

**Accumulation** **Accumulation** is the development of a bank, or inventory, of homogeneous products with similar production or demand requirements. Farmers who grow relatively small quantities of grapes, for example, transport their sorted grapes to central collection points, where they are accumulated in large lots for movement into the next level of the channel. Accumulation lets producers continually use up stocks and replenish them, thus minimising losses from interruptions in the supply of materials.

**Allocation**
The breaking down of large homogeneous inventories into smaller lots

**Allocation** **Allocation** is the breaking down of large homogeneous inventories into smaller lots. This process, which addresses discrepancies in quantity, enables wholesalers to buy efficiently in lorry loads or railway car loads, and apportion products by cases to other members. A food wholesaler, for instance, serves as a depot, allocating products according to market demand. The wholesaler may divide a single lorry load of Del Monte canned tomatoes among several retail food stores.

**Assorting**
The grouping of products that buyers want to have available in one place

**Assorting** **Assorting** is the process of combining products into collections or assortments that buyers want to have available in one place. Assorting eliminates discrepancies in assortment by grouping products in ways that satisfy buyers. Assorting is especially

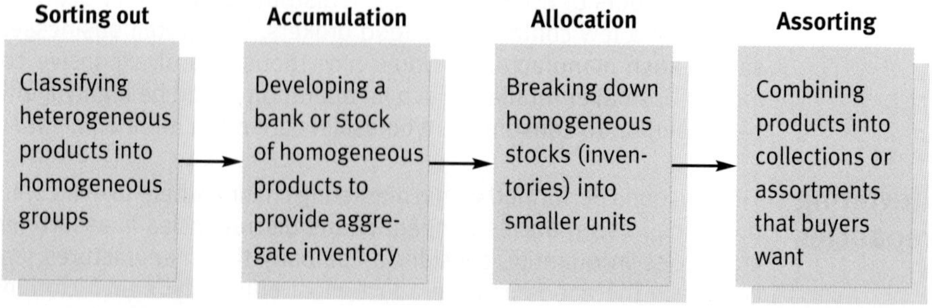


***Figure 14.2***
*Sorting activities conducted by channel members*

# Innovation and Change

## Tesco's Multi-channel Approach to Market Leadership

The Internet is changing the way in which consumers shop. In the past, those seeking to replenish their kitchen cupboards, fridges and freezers would usually visit their local supermarket or hypermarket. Now, these same consumers can visit the Internet and order their groceries for direct delivery to their homes. The concept is seen to be particularly attractive to professional, high-earning, ABC1 men and women who work long hours and have limited leisure time. The Tesco Direct concept is one service that allows customers to buy their groceries direct over the Internet. Consumers can access the Tesco website at Tesco.com and select their purchase items. Their orders are then compiled by a team of in-store sales assistants for delivery to consumers' homes at a time of their choosing.

Initially, the Tesco Direct concept was trialled in 11 stores in two major UK cities. The company's preliminary research showed that around 200,000 consumers were using the service offered by these 11 stores and that this was increasing by 10,000 every week. Before long, the obvious popularity of Internet shopping prompted Tesco to roll out Tesco Direct to other parts of the UK. By the end of the first year, the company offered the service from 100 Tesco stores. Careful consideration has been given to the marketing of the Internet shopping service. The sight of the Tesco Direct logo displayed by the company's delivery vans is already becoming familiar to those living in the areas where the service is offered. In addition, the retailer is using a combination of local poster and in-store advertising, direct mail and an Internet campaign to promote the Tesco Direct operation.

It seems as if the home shopping concept is enjoying a new wave of popularity among consumers. Major competitors ASDA and Sainsbury's have also launched Internet shopping facilities, while Somerfield is engaged in a national roll-out of its home shopping operation. Frozen food retailer Iceland already enjoyed considerable success with its service. Increasing familiarity with shopping on the Internet looks set to increase the demand for services like Tesco Direct, now Tesco.com. How substantial a part of Tesco's business the service will become remains to be seen. However, Tesco management clearly understands that retaining its market-leading position means being ready to respond to changing shopping needs. Even so, industry experts are warning that the new shopping trend could be harmful for supermarket giants, providing considerable opportunities for their smaller rivals. For such smaller businesses, the Internet could offer important additional sales. For example, Waitrose is offering e-sales in territories not serviced by its limited network of supermarkets. By contrast, for the likes of Tesco and Sainsbury's, the danger is that existing sales will be cannibalised. Furthermore, a substantial shift in grocery shopping from the supermarkets to the Internet could damage scale advantages and affect profitability. For Tesco, on-line retailing is supporting its portfolio of stores. Recently Tesco.com became the first fully profitable grocery on-line operation in the world (with profits of £12 million in 2004), making Tesco the largest e-retailer of groceries worldwide.

**Sources:** 'Tesco to roll out Internet shopping service', *Marketing Week*, 15 April 1999, p. 6; Alexandra Jardine, 'Tesco Direct rolls out to 100 outlets', *Marketing*, 15 April 1999, p. 1; Alan Mitchell, 'Home shopping boom a threat to market leaders', *Marketing Week*, 1 April 1999, pp. 26–7; Gordon Ellis-Brown, 'Inspiring new users is key to home shopping survival', *Marketing Week*, 25 March 1999, p. 14; Ben Rosier, 'Web TV ties with Tesco for interactive TV tests', *Marketing*, 1 April 1999, p. 15; Michael Kavanagh, 'Tangled in the net', *Marketing Week*, 28 January 1999, pp. 53–5; Lisa Campbell, 'Tesco in Excite tie-up', *Marketing*, 18 February 1999, p. 12; www.tesco.co.uk. Photo: Courtesy of Tesco Direct.

important to retailers, for they strive to create assortments matching the demands of consumers who patronise their stores. Although no single customer is likely to buy one of everything in the store, retailers must anticipate the probability of purchase and provide a satisfactory range of product choices. For example, the same food wholesaler that supplies supermarkets with Del Monte tomato products may also buy canned goods from competing food processors so that the grocery store can choose from a wide assortment of canned fruit and vegetables. The Innovation and Change box on page 415 outlines Tesco's multi-channel strategy and the importance of assorting.

### Standardising Transactions

Marketing channels help to standardise the transactions associated with numerous products. In many purchase situations, the price is not negotiable; it is predetermined. Although there may be some variation in units of measurement, package sizes, delivery schedules and location of the exchange, marketing channel members tend to limit customers' options with respect to these types of issue. When a customer goes to a supermarket to purchase a loaf of bread, it is unlikely that the individual will be able to buy half a loaf of bread, buy a loaf sliced lengthwise, negotiate the price, obtain a written warranty or return an unused portion of the loaf. Many of the details associated with the purchase of a loaf of bread are standardised.

### Providing Customer Service

Channel members participate in providing customer service. Retailers of durable goods are expected to provide in-store advice and demonstrations, technical know-how, delivery, installation, repair services, parts, and perhaps instruction or training. Channel members above the retailers are responsible for supporting retailers' efforts to provide end-user service and satisfaction, even though they may not come into direct contact with ultimate customers. To gain and maintain a differential advantage, channel members make decisions and take actions to provide excellent customer service and support.

In mature markets with relatively little product differentiation between rival brands – such as packaged holidays, audio/hi-fi systems, conference venues or replacement car exhausts/tyres – and in newly emerging markets with innovative products and inexperienced consumers, it is often the customer service provided through the distribution channel that provides marketers with an edge over their competitors. In many markets – from cars and financial services to grocery retailing and PCs – it is the service provided by channel members that maintains an ongoing, mutually satisfactory relationship between supplier and consumer, and that may be responsible for maintaining brand loyalty.

## Types of Channel

Because marketing channels appropriate for one product may be less suitable for others, many different distribution paths have been developed. The various marketing channels can be classified generally as channels for consumer products and services, or channels for industrial, business-to-business products and services.

### Channels for Consumer Products or Services

Figure 14.3 illustrates several channels used in the distribution of consumer products or services. Besides the channels listed, a manufacturer may use sales branches or sales offices.

**Channel A** Channel A describes the direct movement of goods from producer to consumers. Customers who pick their own fruit from commercial orchards or buy cosmetics from door-to-door sales people are acquiring products through a direct channel. A producer who sells goods directly from the factory to end users and ultimate consumers is using a direct marketing channel (for example, Direct Line's teleselling of car insurance). Although this channel is the simplest, it is not necessarily the cheapest or the most efficient

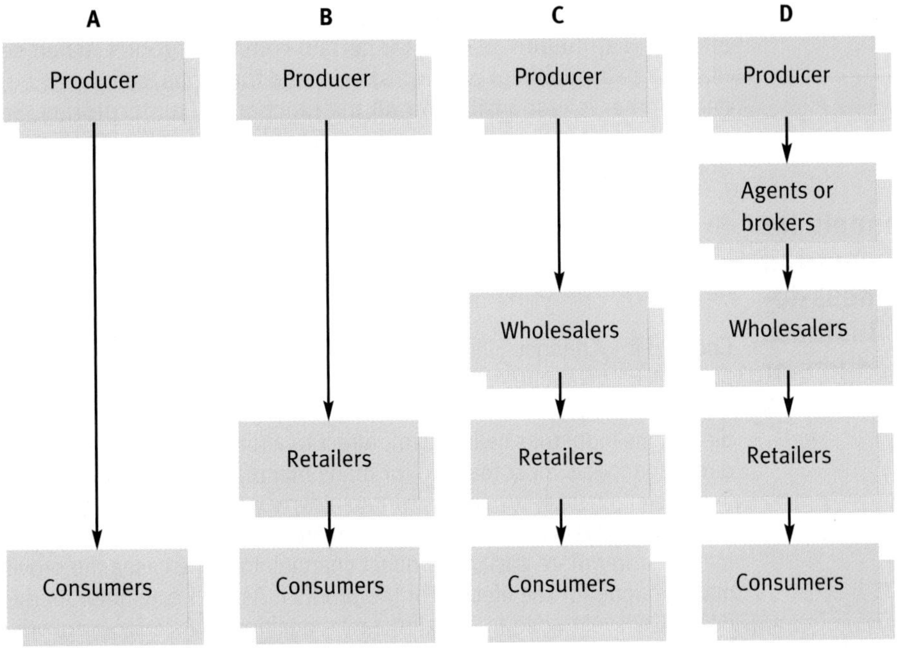


***Figure 14.3***
*Typical marketing channels for consumer products*

**E-commerce**
The use of the Internet for marketing communications, selling and purchasing

method of distribution. As explored in Chapter 19, **e-commerce** – the use of the Internet for marketing communications, selling and purchasing – has in recent years led to a growth in direct marketing for a variety of products, notably travel tickets, books, videos and CDs, financial services and merchandise retailed by the traditional mail-order catalogue operators. Channel A, the direct approach, is no longer the preserve of farm shops and factory outlets.

**Channel B** Channel B, which moves goods from producer to retailers and then to consumers, is often used by large retailers that can buy in quantity from a manufacturer. Such retailers as Marks & Spencer, Sainsbury's, Aldi and Carrefour, for example, sell clothing, food and many other items they have purchased directly from the producers. Cars are also commonly sold through this type of marketing channel.

**Channel C** A long-standing distribution channel, especially for consumer products, channel C takes goods from producer to wholesalers, then to retailers and finally to consumers. This option is very practical for a producer who sells to hundreds of thousands of consumers through thousands of retailers. A single producer finds it hard to do business directly with thousands of retailers. For example, consider the number of retailers that stock Coca-Cola. It would be extremely difficult, if not impossible, for Coca-Cola to deal directly with all the retailers that sell its brand of soft drink. Manufacturers of tobacco products, confectionery, some home appliances, hardware and many convenience goods sell their products to wholesalers, who then sell to retailers, who in turn do business with individual consumers.

**Channel D** Channel D – through which goods pass from producer to agents to wholesalers to retailers, and only then to consumers – is frequently used for products intended for mass distribution, such as processed food. For example, to place its biscuit line in specific retail outlets, a food processor may hire an agent (or a food broker) to sell the biscuits to wholesalers. The wholesalers then sell the biscuits to supermarkets, vending machine operators and other retail outlets.

**Benefits of a Long Channel** Contrary to popular opinion, a long channel may be the most efficient distribution channel for certain consumer goods. When several channel intermediaries are available to perform specialised functions, costs may be lower than if one channel member is responsible for all the functions in all territories. Some manufacturers opt for all or most of these four channels in order to cater for the needs and buying processes of the different customers that make up their various targeted market segments.

## Channels for Industrial, Business-to-Business Products or Services

Figure 14.4 shows four of the most common channels for industrial or business products and services. Like their consumer products counterparts, manufacturers of industrial or business products sometimes work with more than one level of wholesalers.

**Channel E** Channel E illustrates the direct channel for industrial or business products. In contrast with consumer goods, many business products – especially expensive equipment, such as steam generators, aircraft and mainframe computers – are sold directly to the buyers. For example, Airbus Industries sells aircraft direct to airlines such as British Airways and Air France. The direct channel is most feasible for many manufacturers of business goods because they have fewer customers, and those customers may be clustered geographically, as explained in Chapter 7. Buyers of complex industrial products can also receive technical assistance from the manufacturer more easily in a direct channel. In some cases the provision of such information may continue for the lifetime of the product. As with consumer markets, e-commerce and the desire to develop one-to-one direct relationships have led to a growth in the use of channel E.

**Industrial distributor**
An independent business that takes title to industrial products and carries inventories

**Channel F** If a particular line of business products is aimed at a larger number of customers, the manufacturer may use a marketing channel that includes **industrial distributors**, merchants who take title to products and carry inventory (channel F). Construction products made by Case or JCB, for example, are sold through industrial or business-to-business distributors as are building materials, operating supplies and air-conditioning equipment. Industrial distributors are carrying an increasing percentage of business products. Due to mergers and acquisitions, they have become larger and more powerful.[5] Industrial distributors can be most effectively used when a product has broad market appeal, is easily stocked and serviced, is sold in small quantities and is needed rapidly to avoid high losses.[6]

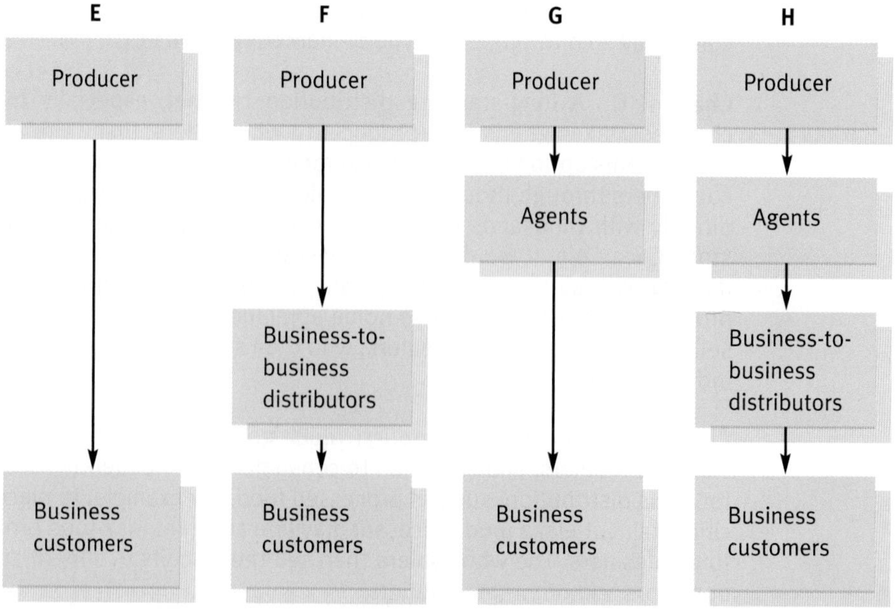


*Figure 14.4*
*Typical marketing channels for industrial, business-to-business products*

**Channel G** Channel G – from producer to agents to industrial or business buyers – may be chosen when a manufacturer without a marketing department needs market information, when a company is too small to field its own salesforce or when a company wants to introduce a new product or to enter a new market without using its own sales people. Thus a large soya bean producer might sell its product to animal food processors through an agent.

**Channel H** Channel H is a variation of channel G: goods move from producer to agents to industrial distributors and then to business customers. A manufacturer without a salesforce may rely on this channel if its business customers purchase products in small quantities or if they must be resupplied frequently and therefore need access to decentralised inventories. Japanese manufacturers of electronic components, for example, work through export agents who sell to industrial distributors serving small producers or dealers overseas.

## Multiple Marketing Channels

When aiming at diverse target markets, it may be appropriate for a manufacturer to use several marketing channels simultaneously, with each channel involving a different group of intermediaries. For example, a manufacturer turns to multiple channels when the same product is directed to both consumers and business customers. When Procter & Gamble sells cleaning products for household use, the products are sold to supermarkets through grocery wholesalers or, in some cases, directly to the larger retailers, whereas the cleaning products going to restaurants or institutions follow a different distribution channel. In some instances, a producer may prefer **dual distribution**: the use of two or more marketing channels for distributing the same products. Villeroy & Boch is a respected supplier of fine china and glassware to households across the world. The company also has ranges for the catering industry, sold and promoted through a separate marketing channel.

**Dual distribution**
A channel practice whereby a producer distributes the same products through two or more different channels

**Strategic channel alliance**
Arrangement for distributing the products of one organisation through the marketing channels of another

A **strategic channel alliance** exists when the products of one organisation are distributed through the marketing channels of another. The products are often similar with respect to target markets or product uses, but they are not direct competitors. For example, a brand of bottled water might be distributed through a marketing channel for soft drinks, or a US cereal producer could form a strategic channel alliance with a European food processor. Alliances can provide benefits both for the organisation that owns the marketing channel and for the company whose brand is being distributed through the channel. An example of this is the 'chip and pin' system, which is replacing signatures on credit card slips. Barclaycard Merchant Services provides the banking/payment service, while IT company Fujitsu supplies the technology. In a joint venture, each company markets the same service to its respective clients – in retailing, catering and entertainment establishments.

# Channel Integration

Channel functions may be transferred among intermediaries, to producers and even to customers. This section examines how channel members can either combine and control most activities or pass them on to another channel member. Remember, though, that the channel member cannot eliminate functions; unless buyers themselves perform the functions, they must pay for the labour and resources needed for the functions to be performed. The statement that, 'you can eliminate middlemen but you can't eliminate their functions', is an accepted principle of marketing.

Many marketing channels are determined by consensus. Producers and intermediaries coordinate their efforts for mutual benefit. Some marketing channels, however, are organised and controlled by a single leader, which can be a producer, a wholesaler or a retailer, depending on the industry. The channel leader may establish channel policies and coordinate the development of the marketing mix. Marks & Spencer and IKEA, for example, are channel leaders for several of the many products they sell, exerting significant pressure on suppliers to adhere to their production, delivery and pricing standards. The various links or stages of the channel may be combined under the management of a channel leader, either horizontally or vertically. Integration may stabilise supply, reduce costs and increase coordination of channel members.

## Vertical Channel Integration

**Vertical channel integration**
The combination of two or more stages of the channel under one management

Combining two or more stages of the channel under one management is **vertical channel integration**. One member of a marketing channel may purchase the operations of another member or simply perform the functions of the other member, eliminating the need for that intermediary as a separate entity. For example, changes in the regulations controlling the UK electricity industry have led to an increase in vertical channel integration, as some companies controlling the supply and distribution of electricity have merged. Total vertical integration encompasses all functions from production to ultimate buyer; it is exemplified by oil companies that own oil wells, pipelines, refineries, terminals and service station forecourts.

Whereas members of conventional channel systems work independently and seldom cooperate, participants in vertical channel integration coordinate their efforts to reach a desired target market.[7] This more progressive approach to distribution enables channel members to regard other members as extensions of their own operations. Vertically integrated channels are often more effective against competition because they result in increased bargaining power, the ability to inhibit competitors, and the sharing of information and responsibilities.[8] At one end of an integrated channel, for example, a manufacturer might provide advertising and training assistance, and the retailer at the other end would buy the manufacturer's products in quantity and actively promote them.

**Vertical marketing system (VMS)**
Marketing channel in which a single channel member coordinates or manages channel activities to achieve efficient, low-cost distribution aimed at satisfying target market customers

In the past, integration has been successfully institutionalised in marketing channels called vertical marketing systems. A **vertical marketing system (VMS)** is a marketing channel in which a single channel member coordinates or manages channel activities to achieve efficient, low-cost distribution aimed at satisfying target market customers. Because the efforts of individual channel members are combined in a VMS, marketing activities can be coordinated for maximum effectiveness and economy, without duplication of services. Vertical marketing systems are also competitive, accounting for a growing share of retail sales in consumer goods. Most vertical marketing systems today take one of three forms: corporate, administered or contractual.

**The Corporate VMS** The corporate VMS combines all stages of the marketing channel, from producers to consumers, under a single ownership. Supermarket chains that own food-processing plants, and large retailers that purchase wholesaling and production facilities, are examples of corporate VMSs. Figure 14.5 contrasts a conventional marketing channel with a VMS, which consolidates marketing functions and institutions.

**The Administered VMS** In an administered VMS, channel members are independent, but a high level of inter-organisational management is achieved by informal coordination. Members of an administered VMS may agree, for example, to adopt uniform accounting and ordering procedures, and to cooperate in promotional activities. Although individual channel members maintain their autonomy, as in conventional marketing channels, one channel member – such as the producer or a large retailer – dominates the administered VMS, so that distribution decisions take into account the system as a whole. Because of its size and power as a retailer, Marks & Spencer exercises a strong influence over the independent manufacturers in its marketing channels, as do Kellogg's (cereals) and BMW (cars).

**The Contractual VMS** Under a contractual VMS, the most popular type of vertical marketing system, inter-organisational relationships are formalised through contracts. Channel members are linked by legal agreements that spell out each member's rights and obligations. For instance, franchise organisations such as McDonald's and KFC are contractual VMSs. Other

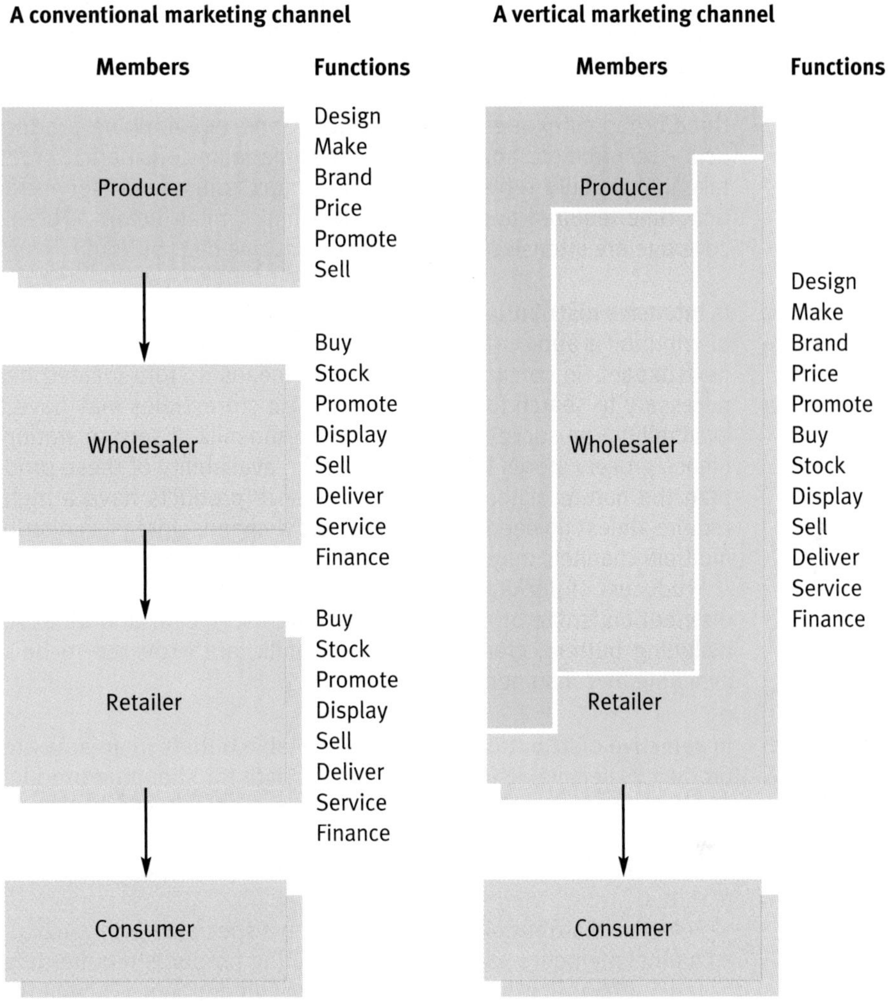


***Figure 14.5***
*Comparison of a conventional marketing channel and a vertical marketing system*
*Source: Adapted from* Strategic Marketing, *by D.J. Kollat et al. Copyright © 1972. Reprinted by permission*

contractual VMSs include wholesaler-sponsored groups such as SPAR, Mace or IGA (Independent Grocers' Alliance) stores, in which independent retailers band together under the contractual leadership of a wholesaler.

## Horizontal Channel Integration

**Horizontal channel integration**
The combination of institutions at the same level of channel operation under one management

Combining institutions at the same level of channel operation under one management constitutes **horizontal channel integration**. An organisation may integrate horizontally by merging with other organisations at the same level in a marketing channel. For example, the owner of a bistro chain may buy another bistro or a bar chain and then rebrand it in the same way as the existing business and merge the two chains' supply channels. Horizontal integration may enable a business to generate sufficient sales revenue to integrate vertically as well.

Although horizontal integration permits efficiencies and economies of scale in purchasing, marketing research, advertising and specialised personnel, it is not always the most effective method of improving distribution. The increase in size may result in decreased flexibility, difficulties in coordination, and the need for additional marketing research and large-scale planning. Unless distribution functions for the various units can be performed more efficiently under unified management than under the previously separate managements, horizontal integration will not reduce costs or improve the competitive position of the integrating company.

# Different Levels of Market Coverage

The kind of coverage that is appropriate for different products is determined by the characteristics and behaviour patterns of buyers. Chapter 10 divided consumer products into three broad categories – convenience products, shopping products and speciality products – according to how the purchase is made. In considering products to buy, consumers take into account replacement rate, product adjustment (services), duration of consumption, time required to find the product and similar factors.[9] Three major levels of market coverage are intensive, selective and exclusive distribution.

## Intensive Distribution

**Intensive distribution**
The use of all available outlets for distributing a product

In **intensive distribution**, all available outlets are used for distributing a product. Intensive distribution is appropriate for convenience products such as bread, chewing gum, beer and newspapers. To consumers, availability means a store located nearby and minimal time necessary to search for the product at the store. Sales may have a direct relationship to availability. The successful sale of bread and milk at service stations or of petrol at convenience grocery stores has shown that the availability of these products is more important than the nature of the outlet. Convenience products have a high replacement rate and require almost no service. To meet these demands, intensive distribution is necessary, and multiple channels may be used to sell through all possible outlets.

Producers of packaged consumer items rely on intensive distribution. In fact, intensive distribution is one of Anchor's key strengths: Anchor and other Arla Foods UK products, including butters, cream, cheese and milk, are expected to be readily and intensively available by consumers.

## Selective Distribution

**Selective distribution**
The use of only some available outlets in an area to distribute a product

In **selective distribution**, only some available outlets in an area are chosen to distribute a product. Selective distribution is appropriate for shopping products. Durable goods such as electrical appliances and exclusive fragrances usually fall into this category. Such products are more expensive than convenience goods. Consumers are willing to spend more time searching: visiting several retail outlets to compare prices, designs, styles and other features.

Selective distribution is desirable when a special effort – such as customer service from a channel member – is important. Shopping products require differentiation at the point of purchase. To motivate retailers to provide adequate pre-sale service, selective distribution and company-owned stores are often used. Many business products are sold on a selective basis to maintain a certain degree of control over the distribution process. For example, agricultural herbicides are distributed on a selective basis because dealers must offer services to buyers, such as instructions about how to apply the herbicides safely, or offer the option of having the dealer apply the herbicide.

## Exclusive Distribution

**Exclusive distribution**
The use of only one outlet in a relatively large geographic area to distribute a product

In **exclusive distribution**, only one outlet is used in a relatively large geographic area. Exclusive distribution is suitable for speciality products that are purchased rather infrequently, consumed over a long period of time, or require service or information to fit them to buyers' needs. Exclusive distribution is not appropriate for convenience products and many shopping products. It is often used as an incentive to sellers when only a limited market is available for products. For example, cars such as the Rolls-Royce are sold on an exclusive basis. Royal Copenhagen's premium china is retailed through carefully selected, exclusive retail outlets. A producer who uses exclusive distribution generally expects a dealer to be very cooperative with respect to carrying a complete inventory, sending personnel for sales and service training, participating in promotional programmes and providing excellent customer service. Exclusive distribution gives a company tighter image control because the types of distributors and retailers that distribute the product are monitored closely.[10]

*Figure 14.6*
*Anchor butter and other dairy lines are intensively distributed*
*Source: Courtesy of Staniforth/Arla Foods*

# Choosing Distribution Channels

Choosing the most appropriate distribution channels for a product can be a complex affair. The Building Customer Relationships box on page 424 outlines the channel strategy developed by Games Workshop. Producers must choose specific intermediaries carefully, evaluating their sales and profit levels, performance records, other products carried, clientele, availability, and so forth. In addition, producers must examine other factors that influence distribution channel selection, including organisational objectives and resources, market characteristics, buying behaviour, product attributes and environmental forces. In some markets, such as the distribution of insurance products, these factors may indicate that multiple channels should be used.[11]

## Organisational Objectives and Resources

Producers must consider carefully their objectives and the cost of achieving them in the marketplace. A company's objectives may be broad – such as higher profits, increased market share and greater responsiveness to customers – or narrow, such as replacing an intermediary that has left the channel. The organisation may possess sufficient financial and marketing clout to control its distribution channels – for example, by engaging in direct marketing or by operating its own fleet of lorries. On the other hand, an organisation may have no interest in performing distribution services or may be forced by lack of resources and experience to depend on middlemen.

# Building Customer Relationships

## Games Workshop: the Best Model Soldiers in the World!

As its name suggests, Games Workshop manufactures and sells games, but these are no ordinary games and this is no ordinary business. Games Workshop is 'the largest and most successful tabletop fantasy and futuristic battle-games company in the world'. With a turnover of over £100 million, this fast-growing company employs more than 2000 people and has over 350 retail outlets in Australia, Canada, France, Germany, Hong Kong, Spain, the USA and the UK, with the growing Italian market still being serviced from the UK. The fantasy games produced by Games Workshop take place in one of two settings:

1 a fantasy world filled with Dwarves, Elves, rat-like Scaven, green Orcs and Goblins
2 the future of a war-torn universe in the forty-first millennium – a setting occupied by the enigmatic Eldar, genetically enhanced Space Marines and an alien race called the Tyranids, who are all battling for survival.

Games Workshop enthusiasts can buy from a range of boxed games, containing the rule book, charts and templates, dice and miniature figures needed to begin their fantasy battle. The basics can then be added to from the extensive range of Games Workshop troops, special squads and war machines. As enthusiasts develop their armies and paint them in colours of their choice, they begin to build their own personalised version of their game of choice. The success of Peter Jackson's The Lord of the Rings films has added a new dimension, as Games Workshop holds a global licence for a game based on this award-winning trilogy.

For those unfamiliar with the fantasy game concept, the uncharted territory of the retail outlets can itself feel like alien territory. Wall space is stacked high with numerous games, figures, paints, magazines, books and T-shirts. In the centre is a gaming table, which is usually covered with the remains of an ongoing battle. At other times, the shops are full of teenagers and children, conducting a closely fought Warhammer contest. On some days the outlets resemble a crèche for big kids, with staff carefully orchestrating activities. The battles organised in-store are an important part of the weekly itinerary. The featured game varies on different days, so that enthusiasts of Warhammer, Warhammer 40,000, Necromunda and the other Games Workshop products can all get their turn. These games induct newcomers into the gaming experience, while for 'old hands' they showcase new product launches.

The shop staff, always Games Workshop enthusiasts, are vital to the success of the retail outlets. They must be able to maintain an enthusiasm for the brand, keeping up to date with all of the latest new product launches. The ability to handle customers of all ages and backgrounds – from the young teenagers who regularly hang out at the stores to the uninitiated visiting the outlets for the first time – is also essential. Nonplussed parents clutching 'Christmas lists' or birthday present suggestions experience a friendly welcome from staff, who will happily search among the reams of Games Workshop packaging to retrieve some bizarrely named item.

As well as its network of retail stores, Games Workshop has agencies – typically specialist modelling and hobbyist shops – distributing its figures and games, while even the likes of Toys 'Я' Us has been known to stock the popular gaming sets. In total, more than 3500 independent shops retail the company's ranges. In addition, there is a mail-order operation that can be accessed through the retail stores as well as directly by telephone or the Internet. The on-line operation has grown significantly recently. This £35 million mail-order operation has 40 staff and a database of 250,000 contacts. The aim is to provide a fast and efficient service, despatching all orders within 24 hours. This facility handles up to a thousand calls daily and can deal with enquiries in a range of languages. While the stores are an integral feature of the Games Workshop 'experience', the company has been quick to recognise the value of adopting a mix of distribution channels to support its rapid expansion plans: on-line sales and mail order contribute significantly to the company's sales. The company believes its destiny is in its own hands, saying, 'Games Workshop remains a vertically integrated company, retaining control over every aspect of design, manufacture, distribution, and retail of our models and rulebooks'.

**Sources:** Jervis Johnson and Chris Prentice of Games Workshop; Games Workshop website, www.games-workshop.co.uk; James Dibb-Simkin; Sally Dibb and Lyndon Simkin, *The Marketing Casebook*, 2nd edn (London: ITBP, 2001); www.games-workshop.com/aboutus.htm, May, 2004.

Companies must also consider how effective their past distribution relationships and methods have been, and question their appropriateness with regard to current objectives. One business might decide to maintain its basic channel structure but add members for increased coverage in new territories. Another company might alter its distribution channel so as to provide same-day delivery on all orders.

## Market Characteristics

Beyond the basic division between consumer markets and business markets, several market variables influence the design of distribution channels. Geography is one factor; in most cases, the greater the distance between the producer and its markets, the less expensive is distribution through intermediaries rather than through direct sales. Market density must also be considered; when customers tend to be clustered in several locations, the producer may be able to eliminate middlemen.

Transport, storage, communication and negotiation are specific functions performed more efficiently in high-density markets. Market size – measured by the number of potential customers in a consumer or business market – is yet another variable. Direct sales may be effective if a producer has relatively few buyers for a product, but for larger markets the services of middlemen may be required.[12] As explored in Chapter 19, e-commerce is encouraging many suppliers to deal directly with customers, even when they are geographically spread or diverse in nature. There is no doubt that the growing popularity of direct marketing and web-based marketing is forcing marketers to reappraise their market characteristics

***Figure 14.7***
*Department store retailer John Lewis now operates a successful on-line catalogue operation, requiring a fleet of home delivery vehicles for this quickly growing marketing channel*
*Photo: Courtesy of John Lewis*

and deployment of channel intermediaries. This results in direct customer–supplier relationships in those channels where wholesaler/retailer channel members once dominated, such as CDs, books, holidays, clothing and financial services.

**Buying Behaviour**

Buying behaviour is a crucial consideration in selecting distribution channels. To be able to match intermediaries with customers, the producer must have specific, current information about customers who are buying the product, and how, when and where they are buying it.[13] A manufacturer may find direct selling economically feasible for large-volume sales but inappropriate for small orders.

The producer must also understand how buyer specifications vary according to whether buyers perceive products as convenience, shopping or speciality items (see Chapter 10). Customers for magazines, for example, are likely to buy the product frequently – even impulsively – from a variety of outlets. Buyers of home computers, however, carefully evaluate product features, dealers, prices and after-sales services.

Buyers may be reached most effectively when producers are creative in opening up new distribution channels. In the UK, effective distribution, the essential tool in the highly competitive soft drinks sector, is forcing brand leaders Coca-Cola and Schweppes Beverages to find creative ways of extending distribution. Schweppes launched a company, Vendleader, to increase penetration of sales through vending machines.

**Product Attributes**

Another variable in the selection of distribution channels is the product itself. Because producers of complex industrial products must often provide technical services to buyers both before and after the sale, these products are usually shipped directly to buyers. Perishable or highly fashionable consumer products with short shelf lives are also marketed through short channels. In other cases, distribution patterns are influenced by the product's value; the lower the price per unit, the longer the distribution chain. Additional factors to consider are the weight, bulkiness and relative ease of handling the products. Producers may find wholesalers and retailers reluctant to carry items that create storage or display problems.[14] For example, manufacturers of breakfast cereals, such as Kellogg's, must use packaging that retailers find easy to handle and display.

**Environmental Forces**

Finally, producers making decisions about distribution channels must consider the broader forces in the total marketing environment – that is, the political, legal, regulatory, societal/Green, technological, economic and competitive forces. Technology, for example, has made possible electronic scanners, computerised inventory systems such as EPOS (electronic point-of-sale) and electronic shopping devices, all of which are altering present distribution systems and making it harder for technologically unsophisticated companies to remain competitive. Internet access has led to a growth in home shopping and direct marketing. Changing family patterns and the emergence of important minority consumer groups are driving producers to seek new distribution methods for reaching market segments. Interest rates, inflation and other economic variables affect members of distribution channels at every level. Environmental forces are numerous and complex, and must be taken into consideration if distribution efforts are to be appropriate, efficient and effective (see Chapter 3). For example, EU regulation changes have impacted on the retailing of cars, resulting in a power shift away from the car manufacturers to the independently owned showrooms, which can now source vehicles from a variety of manufacturers to sell at a single location.

## Behaviour of Channel Members

The marketing channel is a social system with its own conventions and behaviour patterns. Each channel member performs a different role in the system and agrees – implicitly or explicitly – to accept certain rights, responsibilities, rewards and sanctions for non-conformity.

Channel members have certain expectations of other channel members. Retailers, for instance, expect wholesalers and manufacturers to maintain adequate inventories and to deliver goods on time. For their part, wholesalers expect retailers to honour payment agreements and to keep them informed of inventory needs. This section discusses several issues related to channel member behaviour, including cooperation and relationship building, conflict and leadership. Marketers need to understand these behavioural issues in order to make effective channel decisions, and to maintain relationships with facilitating channel members and loyal customers.

## Channel Cooperation and Relationship Building

Channel cooperation is vital if each member is to gain something from other members.[15] Without cooperation, neither overall channel goals nor member goals can be realised. Policies must be developed that support all essential channel members, otherwise failure of one link in the chain could destroy the channel.

There are several ways to improve channel cooperation. A marketing channel should consider itself a unified system, competing with other systems. This way, individual members will be less likely to take actions that would create disadvantages for other members. Similarly, channel members should agree to direct their efforts towards a common target market so that channel roles can be structured for maximum marketing effectiveness, which in turn can help members achieve their individual objectives.

Heineken, for example, was having difficulty with its 450 distributors; at one point, the time between order and delivery stretched to 12 weeks. A cooperative system of supply chain management, with Internet-based communications, decreased the lead time from order to delivery to four weeks, and Heineken's sales increased 24 per cent.[16] It is crucial to define precisely the tasks that each member of the channel is to perform. This definition provides a basis for reviewing the intermediaries' performance and helps reduce conflicts because each channel member knows exactly what is expected of it. As explained in Chapter 5, it is often in the interests of channel members to build long-term relationships. These relationships can improve channel cooperation and help individual channel members adapt better to the needs of the others.[17]

## Channel Conflict

Although all channel members work towards the same general goal – distributing goods and services profitably and efficiently – members may sometimes disagree about the best methods for attaining this goal.[18] Each channel member wants to maximise its own profits while maintaining as much autonomy as possible.[19] However, if this self-interest leads to misunderstanding about role expectations, the end result is frustration and conflict for the whole channel. For individual organisations to function together in a single social system, each channel member must communicate clearly and understand role expectations, especially as channel conflict often arises when a channel member does not conduct itself in the manner expected by the other channel members. Communication difficulties are a particular form of channel conflict and can lead to frustration, misunderstandings and poorly coordinated strategies.

The increased use of multiple channels of distribution, driven partly by new technology, has increased the potential for conflict between manufacturers and intermediaries. For example, Hewlett-Packard makes products available directly to consumers through its website (www.hewlett.packard.com), thereby directly competing with existing distributors and retailers.[20]

Channel conflicts also arise when dealers overemphasise competing products or diversify into product lines traditionally handled by other, more specialised intermediaries. In some cases, conflict develops because producers strive to increase efficiency by circumventing intermediaries, as is happening in marketing channels for microcomputer software and video games. Many software-only stores are establishing direct relationships with software producers, bypassing wholesale distributors altogether. Some dishonest retailers also pirate software and make unauthorised copies, thus cheating other channel members of their due compensation. Consequently, suspicion and mistrust may heighten tensions in software marketing channels.

Although there is no single method for resolving conflict, an atmosphere of cooperation can be re-established if two conditions are met. First, the role of each channel member must be specified. To minimise misunderstanding, all members must be able to expect unambiguous, agreed-on levels of performance from one another. Second, channel members must institute certain measures of channel coordination, a task that requires leadership and the benevolent exercise of control.[21] To prevent channel conflict, producers or other channel members may provide competing resellers with different brands, allocate markets among resellers, define direct sales policies to clarify potential conflict over large accounts, negotiate territorial issues between regional distributors and provide recognition to certain resellers for the importance of their role in distributing to others. Hallmark, for example, distributes its Ambassador greetings card line in discount stores and its name brand Hallmark line in upmarket department and specialist card stores, thus limiting the amount of competition among retailers carrying its products.[22]

## Channel Leadership

**Channel power**
The ability to influence another channel member's goal achievement

The effectiveness of marketing channels hinges on channel leadership, which may be assumed by producers, retailers or wholesalers. To become a leader, a channel member must want to influence and direct overall channel performance. Furthermore, to attain desired objectives, the leader must possess **channel power**, which is the ability to influence another channel member's goal achievement. As Figure 14.8 shows, the channel leader derives power from seven sources, two of them economic and five non-economic.

The five non-economic sources of power – reward, expert, referent, legitimate and coercive – are crucial for establishing leadership.

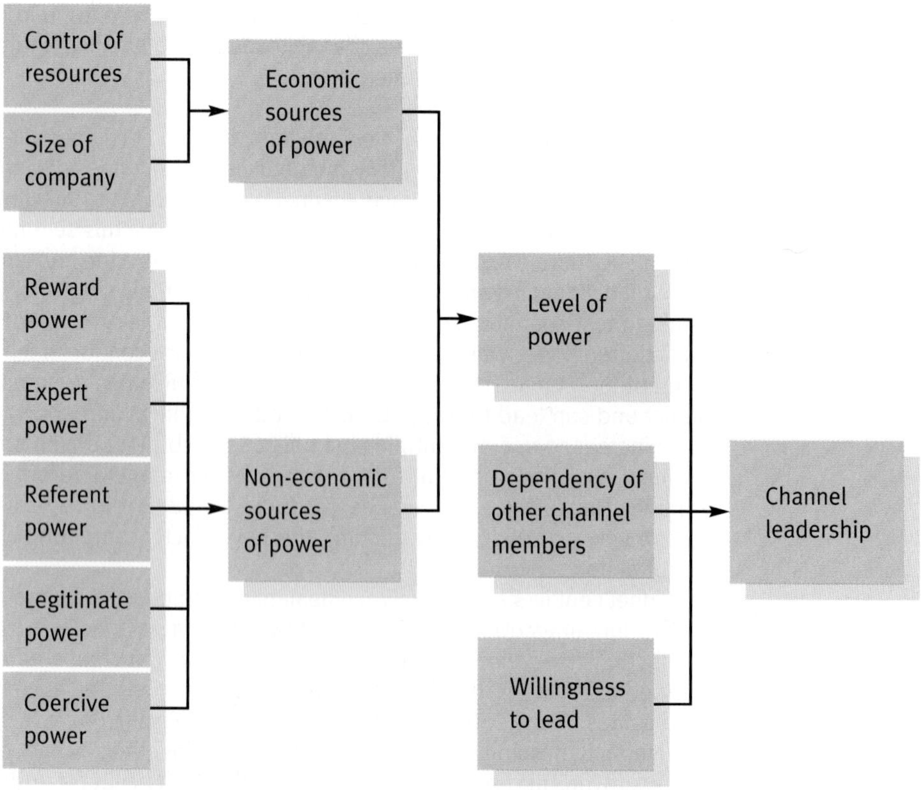


***Figure 14.8***
*Determinants of channel leadership*
*Source: R.D. Michman and S.D. Sibley,* Marketing Channels and Strategies, *2nd edn (Worthington, Ohio: Publishing Horizons, Inc., 1980), p. 413. Reproduced by permission*

1 A channel leader gains *reward* power by providing financial benefits.
2 *Expert* power exists when other channel members believe that the leader provides special expertise required for the channel to function properly.
3 *Referent* power emerges when other members identify strongly with and emulate the leader.
4 *Legitimate* power is based on a superior–subordinate relationship.
5 *Coercive* power is a function of the leader's ability to punish other channel members.[23]

In many countries, producers assume the leadership role in marketing channels. A manufacturer – whose large-scale production efficiency demands increasing sales volume – may exercise power by giving channel members financing, business advice, ordering assistance, advertising and support materials.[24] For example, BMW and Mercedes-Benz control their dealers totally, specifying showroom design and layout, discount levels and quotas of models. Coercion, though, causes dealer dissatisfaction that is stronger than any impact from rewards, so the use of coercive power can be a major cause of channel conflict.[25]

Retailers can also function as channel leaders, and with the domination of national chains and own-label merchandise they are increasingly doing so. For example, Sainsbury's challenged Coca-Cola with its own-label cola, whose packaging bore a strong resemblance to that of the market leader. Small retailers, too, may share in the leadership role when they command particular consumer respect and patronage in local or regional markets. Among large retailers, Carrefour, IKEA, Marks & Spencer and Tesco base their channel leadership on wide public exposure to their products. These retailers control many brands and sometimes replace uncooperative producers. IKEA exercises power by dictating manufacturing techniques, lead times, quality levels and product specifications.

Wholesalers assume channel leadership roles as well, although they were more powerful decades ago, when most manufacturers and retailers were small, under-financed and widely scattered. Today, wholesaler leaders may form voluntary chains with several retailers, which they supply with bulk buying or management services or which market their own brands. In return, the retailers shift most of their purchasing to the wholesaler leader. In Scandinavia, buying groups act as wholesalers, with bulk ordering price advantages, expert advertising and purchasing. Other wholesaler leaders, such as Intersport or SPAR, may also help retailers with store layouts, accounting and inventory control.

# Legal Issues in Channel Management

The multitude of laws governing channel management are based on the general principle that the public is best served when competition and free trade are protected. Under the authority of such national legislation as the UK's Competition Commission, Fair Trading Act, Prices Act, Trades Descriptions Act and Consumer Protection Act, or EU Competition Laws and dictates, the courts and regulatory agencies determine under what circumstances channel management practices violate this underlying principle and must be restricted, and when these practices may be permitted. Although channel managers are not expected to be legal experts, they should be aware that attempts to control distribution functions may have legal repercussions. The following practices are among those frequently subject to legal restraint.

**Restricted sales territories**
System by which a manufacturer tries to prohibit intermediaries from selling its products outside designated sales territories

## Restricted Sales Territories

To tighten its control over the distribution of its products, a manufacturer may try to prohibit intermediaries from selling its products outside designated sales territories, creating **restricted sales territories**. The intermediaries themselves often favour this practice, because it lets them avoid competition for the producer's brands within their own territories. Many companies have long followed the policy of restricting sales in this fashion. In recent years, the courts have adopted conflicting positions with regard to restricted sales

**Exclusive dealing** System by which a manufacturer forbids an intermediary to carry the products of competing manufacturers

territories. Although they have deemed restricted sales territories a restraint of trade among intermediaries handling the same brands – except for small or newly established companies – the courts have also held that exclusive territories can actually promote competition among dealers handling different brands. At present, the producer's intent in establishing restricted territories and the overall effect of doing so on the market must be evaluated for each individual case.

## Tying Contract

**Tying contract** Arrangement whereby a supplier (usually a manufacturer or franchiser) furnishes a product to a channel member with the stipulation that the channel member must purchase other products as well

When a supplier – usually a manufacturer or franchiser – furnishes a product to a channel member with the stipulation that the channel member must purchase other products as well, a **tying contract** exists.[26] Suppliers, for instance, may institute tying arrangements to move weaker products along with more popular items. To use another example, a franchiser may tie the purchase of equipment and supplies to the sale of franchises, justifying the policy as necessary for quality control and protection of the franchiser's reputation. A related practice is full-line forcing. In this situation, a supplier requires that channel members purchase the supplier's entire line to obtain any of the products. Manufacturers sometimes use full-line forcing to ensure that intermediaries accept new products and that a suitable range of products is available to customers. The courts accept tying contracts when the supplier alone can provide products of a certain quality, when the intermediary is free to carry competing products as well, and when a company has just entered the market. Most other tying contracts are considered illegal.

## Exclusive Dealing

When a manufacturer forbids an intermediary to carry the products of competing manufacturers, the arrangement is called **exclusive dealing**. A manufacturer receives considerable market protection in an exclusive dealing arrangement and may cut off shipments to an intermediary that violates such an agreement. An exclusive dealing contract is generally legally permitted if dealers and customers in a given market have access to similar products or if the exclusive dealing contract strengthens an otherwise weak competitor.

## Refusal to Deal

**Refusal to deal** Situation in which suppliers will not do business with wholesalers or dealers simply because these wholesalers or dealers have resisted policies that are anti-competitive or in restraint of trade

Producers have the right to choose the channel members with whom they will do business and the right not to choose others. Within existing distribution channels, however, suppliers may not refuse to deal with wholesalers or dealers just because these wholesalers or dealers have resisted policies that are anti-competitive or in restraint of trade. Suppliers are further prohibited from organising some channel members in **refusal to deal** actions against other members who choose not to comply with illegal policies.[27] Recently several supermarket chains, such as ASDA and Tesco, have sought designer clothing from manufacturers such as Levi's. Following the manufacturers' refusal to supply those retailers – as they expected them to discount their lines – the retailers instead acquired the branded leisure wear on the 'grey market', often in eastern Europe or South-east Asia. Several court cases have ensued, with the manufacturers arguing their case for being entitled to select which types of retailer to supply.

# Summary

Distribution refers to activities that make products available to customers when and where they want to purchase them. A *channel of distribution* (or *marketing channel*) is a group of individuals and organisations that direct the flow of products from producers to customers.

In most channels of distribution, producers and customers are linked by *marketing intermediaries* or middlemen, called *merchants* if they take title to products and *functional middlemen* if they do not take title. Channel structure reflects the division of responsibilities among members. Ongoing relationships with customers are seen as increasingly important via relationship marketing. Effective distribution channels and the deployment of channel intermediaries are central to the development of mutually satisfactory ongoing relationships between intermediaries, and between producers and their customers.

» *Supply chain management* is the creation of long-term partnerships among marketing channel members that reduce inefficiencies, costs and redundancies in the marketing channel and develop innovative approaches to satisfying targeted customers. The goal is still to provide customers with the product or service demanded, in line with their expectations, but in a more coordinated way that builds on the combined strengths of the members of the distribution channel. Key tasks in supply chain management include planning, sourcing, facilitating delivery and relationship building to nurture ongoing customer relationships.

» Marketing channels serve many functions that may be performed by a single channel member but are mostly accomplished through both the independent and joint efforts of channel members. These functions include creating utility, facilitating exchange efficiencies, alleviating discrepancies, standardising transactions and providing customer service. Although intermediaries can be eliminated, their functions are vital and cannot be dropped; these activities must be performed by someone in the marketing channel or passed on to customers. Because intermediaries serve both producers and buyers, they reduce the total number of transactions that would otherwise be needed to move products from producer to ultimate users. Intermediaries' specialised functions also help keep down costs.

» An *assortment* is a combination of products assembled to provide customer benefits. Intermediaries perform *sorting activities* essential to the development of product assortments. Sorting activities allow channel members to divide roles and separate tasks. Through the basic tasks of *sorting out*, *accumulation*, *allocation* and *assorting* products for buyers, intermediaries resolve discrepancies in quantity and assortment. The number and characteristics of intermediaries are determined by the assortments and the expertise needed to perform distribution activities.

» Direct marketing, aided by *e-commerce*, has recently encouraged many marketers to cut out channel intermediaries (see below) in both consumer and business-to-business transactions.

» Channels of distribution are broadly classified as channels for consumer products or channels for business products. Within these two broad categories, different marketing channels are used for different products. Although some consumer goods move directly from producer to consumers, consumer product channels that include wholesalers and retailers are usually more economical and efficient. Business goods move directly from producer to end users more frequently than do consumer goods. Channels for business products may also include agents, *industrial distributors* or both. Most producers use *dual distribution* or multiple channels so that the distribution system can be adjusted for various target markets. Sometimes *strategic channel alliances* are used so that the products of one organisation can be distributed through the marketing channels of another.

» Integration of marketing channels brings various activities under the management of one channel member. *Vertical channel integration* combines two or more stages of the channel under one management. In the *vertical marketing system (VMS)* a single channel member coordinates or manages channel activity for the mutual benefit of all channel members. Vertical marketing systems may be corporate, administered or contractual. *Horizontal channel integration* combines institutions at the same level of channel operation under a single management.

» A marketing channel is managed so that products receive appropriate market coverage. In *intensive distribution*, producers distribute a product using all available outlets. In *selective distribution*, outlets are screened to use those most qualified for exposing a product properly. *Exclusive distribution* usually uses one outlet to distribute a product in a large geographic area when there is a limited market for the product.

» When selecting distribution channels for products, manufacturers evaluate potential channel members carefully. Producers consider the organisation's objectives and available resources; the location, density and size of a market; buying behaviour in the target market; product attributes; and external forces in the marketing environment. Technology, notably e-commerce, has recently played a major role in certain markets in the selection of distribution channels.

» A marketing channel is a social system in which individuals and organisations are linked by a common goal: the profitable and efficient distribution of goods and services. The positions or roles of channel members are associated with rights, responsibilities and rewards, as well as sanctions for non-conformity. Channels function most efficiently when members cooperate; when they deviate from their roles, channel conflict can arise. Effective marketing channels are usually a result of channel leadership and of relationship building between channel members.

» Channel leaders can facilitate or hinder other channel members' goal achievement, deriving this *channel power* from seven sources, two of them economic and five non-economic. Producers are in an excellent position to structure channel policy and to use technical expertise and consumer acceptance to influence other channel members. Retailers gain channel control through consumer confidence, wide product mixes and intimate knowledge of consumers. Wholesalers and buying groups become channel leaders when they have expertise that other channel members value and when they can coordinate functions to match supply with demand.

» Channel management is governed by a variety of legal issues. These are based on the principle that the public is best served when competition and free trade are protected. Various practices may be subject to legal restraint. To tighten their distribution control, manufacturers may try to operate *restricted sales territories*, where intermediaries are barred from selling products outside designated areas. A *tying contract* occurs when a supplier stipulates that another channel member must purchase other products in addition to the one originally supplied. *Exclusive dealing* occurs when a manufacturer forbids an intermediary to carry the products of competing manufacturers. *Refusal to deal* means that a producer will not do business with a wholesaler or dealer that has resisted policies that are anti-competitive or in restraint of trade.

## Key Links

The choice of marketing channel is critical to the success of a marketing strategy, as explored in this chapter, and channel selection is very much a part of the marketing remit. If you only have time for limited reading as part of your course, this chapter is the key one to browse in Part IV of *Marketing: Concepts and Strategies*.

- Although wholesaling and logistical support are rarely controlled by the marketing function, they do impact on the customer's ability to attain a product, and on the customer's experience, buying behaviour and satisfaction.
- This chapter, therefore, should be read in conjunction with Chapter 15, which examines the nature of wholesaling and physical distribution.
- The specialist world of retail marketing is examined in greater detail in Chapter 16.

## Important Terms

Channel of distribution (or marketing channel)
Marketing intermediary
Merchants
Functional middlemen
Supply chain management
Assortment
Sorting activities
Sorting out
Accumulation
Allocation
Assorting

E-commerce
Industrial distributor
Dual distribution
Strategic channel alliance
Vertical channel integration
Vertical marketing system (VMS)
Horizontal channel integration
Intensive distribution
Selective distribution
Exclusive distribution
Channel power
Restricted sales territories
Exclusive dealing
Tying contract
Refusal to deal

## Discussion and Review Questions

1 Compare and contrast the four major types of marketing channel for consumer products. Through which type of channel is each of the following products most likely to be distributed: (a) new cars, (b) cheese biscuits, (c) cut-your-own Christmas trees, (d) new textbooks, (e) sofas, (f) soft drinks?
2 'Shorter channels are usually a more direct means of distribution and therefore are more efficient.' Comment on this statement.
3 Describe an industrial distributor. What types of product are marketed through industrial distributors?
4 Under what conditions is a producer most likely to use more than one marketing channel?
5 Why do consumers often blame intermediaries for distribution inefficiencies? List several reasons.
6 How do the major functions that intermediaries perform help resolve discrepancies in assortment and in quantity?
7 How does the number of intermediaries in the channel relate to the assortments retailers need?
8 Can one channel member perform all channel functions?
9 Identify and explain the major factors that influence decision-makers' selection of marketing channels.
10 Name and describe companies that use (a) vertical integration and (b) horizontal integration in their marketing channels.
11 Explain the major characteristics of each of the three types of vertical marketing system (VMS).
12 Explain the differences among intensive, selective and exclusive methods of distribution.
13 What impact has the growing popularity of e-commerce had on marketing channels?
14 'Channel cooperation requires that members support the overall channel goals to achieve individual goals.' Comment on this statement.
15 How do power bases within the channel influence the selection of the channel leader?

## Recommended Readings


- Christopher, M., *Marketing Logistics* (Oxford: Butterworth-Heinemann, 2003).
- Christopher, M., *Logistics and Supply Chain Management* (Harlow: Pearson/FT, 1999).
- Friedman, L. and Furey, T., *The Channel Advantage* (Oxford: Butterworth-Heinemann, 1999).
- Gattorna, J., ed., *Strategic Supply Chain Alignment: Best Practices in Supply Chain Management* (Aldershot: Gower, 1998).
- Hines, T., *Supply Chain Strategies* (Oxford: Butterworth-Heinemann, 2003).
- Lambert, D.M. and Stock, J.R., *Strategic Logistics Management* (Homewood, Ill.: Richard D. Irwin, 1993).
- Rosenbloom, B., *Marketing Channels: A Management View* (Cincinnati, OH: South Western, 2003).
- Waters, D., *Global Logistics and Distribution Planning: Strategies for Management* (London: Kogan Page, 2003).


## Internet Exercise

The fortunes of many manufacturers depend on their dealer network, particularly producers of construction equipment. Take a look at two such companies' websites, and examine what they say about their dealer network and parts/service support: www.caterpillar.com and www.jcb.com

1 In the context of these websites, how important to these businesses is the chosen route to market: the dealer network?
2 In terms of delivering customer service, what is the role in the marketing channel of these dealerships?

## Applied Mini-Case

Most recorded music used to be purchased by consumers from music stores or mail-order catalogues. First the Internet enabled e-selling from retailers' catalogues, but now it has permitted the instant downloading of a fan's favourite tracks. Not only are bands cutting out traditional distribution channels by offering new material directly to their fans via the web, but mainstream labels are also side-tracking the music store as a response to this growing trend.

It is not only artists and record labels that have embraced the Internet. Non-music brands wishing to appeal to youthful target markets have also sought to do so by making music available on-line to their customers. For example, Sony – wanting to sell more MPV players, Walkmans and hi-fi systems – has its Connect music download system; Coke launched mycokemusic.com; Starbucks has developed an in-store music service called Hear Music to let coffee drinkers download tracks; and T-Mobile has created a mobile phone-based music download service designed to appeal to its younger mobile phone users.

**Source:** Rachel Barnes, 'Retailers take on digital music', *Marketing*, 25 March 2004.

### Question

**How can music store operators such as HMV and Virgin strive to maintain a strong customer base in the face of such substitute competition from e-downloads and even non-music stores providing music downloads?**

## Case Study

# First Direct's Innovative Banking Channels

> First Direct is a refreshingly different bank.
> We like to keep things simple and easy. We put the customer first.
>
> - our services are designed around your day-to-day needs, not ours, so you can talk to a real person 24 hours a day, 365 days a year
> - you can call us any time, anywhere, to check a balance, arrange a bill payment or talk about extending your credit limit ...
> - and when you don't want to talk, you can view, analyse and manage your money on-line
> - you can even receive information by text message.
>
> Enjoy a little magical support.
> www.firstdirect.com/banking/banking.shtml, May 2004

Most consumers have a bank cheque account from which cash is drawn, bills are paid and cheques written, and into which salaries, pensions or grant cheques are paid. For many consumers, the bank is a high-street or shopping-centre office – imposing, formal and often intimidating. Whether it's NatWest, Barclays or Lloyds TSB in the UK, or ABN AMRO or Rabobank in the Netherlands, each high-street bank is fairly alike, with similar products and services, personnel, branch layouts, locations and opening hours. Differentiation has been difficult to achieve and generally impossible to maintain over any length of time as competitors have copied rivals' moves. Promotional strategy and brand image have been the focus for most banking organisations, supported with more minor tactical changes in, for example, opening hours or service charges. For the majority of bank account holders, however, the branch – with its restricted openings, formal ambience and congested town-centre location – is the only point of contact for the bulk of transactions.

First Direct, owned by HSBC but managed separately, broke the mould in 1989. Launched with a massive £6 million promotional campaign, First Direct bypassed the traditional marketing channel.

First Direct has no branches and no branch overhead and operating costs. It provides free banking, unlike its high-street competitors with their systems of bank charges combined with interest paid on positive balances. First Direct is a telephone and on-line banking service that offers full banking, mortgage, loan, investment/saving, insurance, foreign currency and credit card services, plus ATM 'hole in the wall' cash cards through HSBC's international service-till network.

HSBC has established a purpose-built administrative centre for First Direct in Leeds, UK, guaranteeing immediate, personal response to calls 24 hours a day. All normal banking transactions can be completed over the telephone.

Initial reactions were positive, with many non-HSBC account holders switching to the innovative new style of banking. The more traditional consumer – who equates the marbled halls of the Victorian branches with heritage, security and traditional values – has been less easily converted. For the targeted, more financially aware and independent income earner, First Direct is proving very popular. Research shows that First Direct is the most recommended bank with the most satisfied customers.

First Direct's services and products are not new, but the chosen marketing channels are innovative: no branches, only telephone call centres, on-line banking and texting. Customers no longer have to reach inaccessible, parked-up, town-centre branches with queues and restricted opening hours. First Direct has introduced a service, alien to some more traditional tastes perhaps, that is more readily available and with fewer costs. Hundreds of thousands of consumers have welcomed the launch of this new option, but millions have preferred to bank the traditional way. For HSBC, this is fine: its HSBC proposition caters for those consumers preferring the more traditional banking format, while First Direct caters for the new breed of telephone, on-line and texting customers.

**Sources:** 'Midland fails to bank on a third successive win', *Marketing*, 19 July 1990, p. 7; Mat Toor, 'Taxis fare well with First Direct', *Marketing*, 19 April 1990, p. 1; 'Banking industry report', Salomon Brothers, 1992; First Direct advertising, 1993; First Direct fact file, 1993; Beverly Crany, 'Reading your MIND', *Marketing*, 22 February 1996, pp. 33–4; HSBC, 1999; Fujitsu, 2003; HSBC, 2004; www.firstdirect.com, 2004.

## *Questions for Discussion*

1 Why is innovation in marketing channels generally difficult to achieve?
2 Why was First Direct different from its rivals? What gave it differentiation when it first launched?
3 Why might some potential customers of First Direct have reservations about the innovative nature of the service?

# 15 Wholesalers, Distributors and Physical Distribution

**"One of the most neglected, yet potentially most powerful, elements of the marketing mix is the way we reach and service the customer."**

*Martin Christopher, Cranfield University School of Management*

## Objectives

- **To understand the nature of wholesaling in its broadest forms in the marketing channel**
- **To learn about wholesalers' activities and how wholesalers are classified**
- **To examine agencies that facilitate wholesaling, and explore changing patterns in wholesaling**
- **To understand how physical distribution activities are integrated into marketing channels and overall marketing strategies, and to examine physical distribution objectives**
- **To learn about order processing, materials handling and different types of warehousing and their functions**
- **To appreciate the importance of inventory management and the development of adequate assortments of products for target markets**
- **To gain insight into different transportation methods and how they are selected and coordinated**

## Introduction

This chapter examines the roles of wholesaling and physical distribution management within the marketing channel.

Wholesaling includes all transactions in which the purchaser intends to use the product for resale, for making other products or for its general business operations. Wholesaling does not include exchanges with the ultimate consumers. Hence, the term wholesaling is used in its broadest sense: intermediaries' activity in the marketing channel between producers and business customers. Marketers, therefore, use wholesaling to mean much more than the function of retail wholesalers, as described in the next chapter. The focus is on:

- merchant wholesalers and distributors
- agents and brokers
- manufacturers' own branches and offices – the 'middlemen' in many marketing channels.

Physical distribution is a set of activities that moves products from producers to consumers or end users. These activities include order processing, materials handling, warehousing, inventory management and transportation. While none of these activities would normally be the responsibility of marketing managers, their smooth deployment impacts on customer service levels, customer satisfaction and also customers' perceptions of a brand or business.

The main objective of physical distribution is to decrease costs while increasing customer service. Order processing, the first stage in a physical distribution system, is the receipt and transmission of sales order information. Materials handling, or the physical handling of products, is an important element of physical distribution: packaging, loading, movement and labelling systems must be coordinated to maximise cost reduction and the meeting of customer requirements. Warehousing involves the design and operation of facilities for storing and moving goods. The objective of inventory management is to minimise inventory costs while maintaining a supply of goods adequate for customers' needs. Transportation adds time and place utility to a product by moving it from where it is made to where it is purchased and used. Physical distribution activities should be integrated with marketing channel decisions and adjusted to meet the unique needs of a channel member customer or facilitator.

*Opener*

## Warehousing: More than Stacks of Crates

Technological advances and faster, more reliable, transportation make it possible for companies to operate with much smaller inventories, and are transforming the nature of warehousing. To survive in today's competitive marketplace, traditional warehouses are making radical changes to become effective supply chain members.

For example, one significant trend is the increased use of cross-docking, an approach whereby products received at a warehouse are immediately shipped out without ever being put into storage. With computerised information systems, warehouses can pre-assign a shipping door for each in-bound carton. When the shipment arrives, a receiving dock employee can quickly apply a barcoded shipping label that includes destination data, and place the carton directly on an out-bound vehicle. Cross-docking greatly reduces the labour and time associated with handling materials. Cross-docking is even changing the configuration of the warehouse. Although traditional warehouses are square, with truck doors on one side and rail/truck doors on the other, combination storage/cross-dock warehouses look more like a modified 'U' with storage at either end and cross-docking areas in the centre. Goods are received through the cross-dock area and moved directly to shipping doors or, if necessary, to short-term storage, which minimises the distance goods have to travel within the warehouse.

Warehouses are also providing more value-added services, such as packaging, assembly, consolidation, end-aisle display creation, labelling, barcoding and automatic shipment notifications. Warehouses can often provide these services to manufacturers at a lower cost than the manufacturers could manage themselves. For many public warehouses, these services comprise as much as 50 per cent of their activities. Certain retailers even sort items linked to a category or theme within the warehouse so that, on delivery to the store, the collection of products – often sourced from various suppliers – can quickly be put on display or on to shelves.

With more and more companies eliminating inventory, warehouses are performing fewer storage functions. Instead, they are growing adept at keeping products moving quickly and accurately. This requires sophisticated computer information systems (and computer-literate warehouse employees) to minimise storage costs and time while maximising quality service to warehouse customers. The best warehouses are therefore reinventing their role as supply chain members by becoming expertly managed 'flow through' centres.

**Sources:** Lisa H. Harrington, 'Taking stock of warehousing', *Inbound Logistics*, July 1995, pp. 24–8; M6 corridor, 2004.
Photo: Courtesy of Art Explosion, Nova Development

Chapter 15 of *Marketing: Concepts and Strategies* addresses wholesalers' and distributors' activities within a marketing channel, plus the importance of physical distribution management. Wholesaling is viewed here as *all* exchanges among organisations and individuals in marketing channels, except transactions with ultimate consumers. After examining the role of wholesaling and the major types, the chapter then turns to physical distribution, its concepts, objectives and techniques: primarily order processing, materials handling, warehousing, inventory management and transportation. As explained in this chapter's 'Opener', technology plays an increasingly significant role in distribution, and today's warehouses often provide much more than a point for storage.

## The Nature and Importance of Wholesaling

Wholesaling comprises all transactions in which the purchaser intends to use the product for resale, for making other products or for general business operations. It does not include exchanges with ultimate consumers. Wholesaling establishments are engaged primarily in selling products directly to industrial, reseller (such as retailers), government and institutional users. This is a broader definition than that applied by the retail trade for cash-and-carry wholesale suppliers.

The term **wholesaling** is used in its broadest sense: intermediaries' activity in the marketing channel between producers and business customers to facilitate the exchange – buying and selling – of goods. A **wholesaler** is an individual or business engaged in facilitating and expediting exchanges that are primarily wholesale transactions. Only occasionally does a wholesaler engage in retail transactions, which are sales to ultimate consumers. A related topic is that of **supply chain management**, which is the orchestration of the channel of distribution – from sourcing supplies, manufacture to delivery to the customer – often with the intention of creating long-term mutually beneficial relationships. Although not part of marketing's remit, those responsible for a business's logistics often focus on the concept of supply chain management.

**Wholesaling**
Intermediaries' activity in the marketing channel between producers and business customers to facilitate the exchange—buying and selling—of goods

**Wholesaler**
An individual or business engaged in facilitating and expediting exchanges that are primarily wholesale transactions

**Supply chain management**
The orchestration of the channel of distribution from sourcing supplies, manufacture to delivery to the customer

## The Activities of Wholesalers

In the USA and in Europe more than 50 per cent of all products are exchanged, or their exchange is negotiated, through wholesaling institutions. Owing to the strength of large, national retailers in the UK, wholesaling is not as important in consumer markets. There are also far fewer wholesalers. For example, just 27 wholesale companies and buying groups account for 85 per cent of the grocery wholesale market. In Scandinavia, Iberia and much of eastern Europe, wholesaling companies (or buying groups) account for the bulk of exchanges. Of course, it is important to remember that the distribution of all goods requires wholesaling activities, whether or not a wholesaling institution is involved. Table 15.1 lists the major activities wholesalers perform. The activities are not mutually exclusive; individual wholesalers may perform more or fewer activities than Table 15.1 shows. Wholesalers provide marketing activities for organisations above and below them in the marketing channel.

### Services for Producers

Producers, above wholesalers in the marketing channel, have a distinct advantage when they use wholesalers. Wholesalers perform specialised accumulation and allocation functions for a number of products, thus allowing producers to concentrate on developing and manufacturing products that match business customers' or consumers' wants.

Wholesalers provide services to producers as well. By selling a manufacturer's products to retailers and other customers, and by initiating sales contacts with the manufacturer, wholesalers serve as an extension of the producer's salesforce. Wholesalers also provide four forms of financial assistance:

**Table 15.1 Major Wholesaling Activities**

| Activity | Description |
|---|---|
| Supply chain management | Creating long-term partnerships among channel members |
| Wholesale management | Planning, organising, staffing and controlling wholesaling operations |
| Negotiating with suppliers | Serving as the purchasing agent for customers by negotiating supplies |
| Promotion | Providing a salesforce, advertising, sales promotion, publicity and other promotional mix activity |
| Warehousing and product handling | Receiving, storing and stockkeeping, order processing, packaging, shipping outgoing orders and materials handling |
| Transport | Arranging and making local and long-distance shipments |
| Inventory control and data processing | Controlling physical inventory, bookkeeping, recording transactions, keeping records for financial analysis |
| Security | Safeguarding merchandise |
| Pricing | Developing prices and providing price quotations |
| Financing and budgeting | Extending credit, borrowing, making capital investments and forecasting cash flow |
| Management and marketing assistance to clients | Supplying information about markets and products and providing advisory services to assist customers in their sales efforts |

1 they often pay the costs of transporting goods
2 they reduce a producer's warehousing expenses and inventory investment by holding goods in inventory
3 they extend credit and assume the losses from buyers who turn out to be poor credit risks
4 when they buy a producer's entire output and pay promptly or in cash, they are a source of working capital.

In addition, wholesalers are conduits for information within the marketing channel, keeping manufacturers up to date on market developments and passing along the manufacturers' promotional plans to other middlemen in the channel.

Ideally, many producers would like more direct interaction with retailers, as close contact with major retail chains may lead to greater shelf-space allocation and higher margins for a producer's goods, there being no middlemen to take a cut. Wholesalers, however, often have close contact with retailers because of their strategic position in the marketing channel. Besides, even though a producer's own salesforce is probably more effective in its selling efforts, the costs of maintaining a salesforce and performing the activities normally carried out by wholesalers are usually higher than the benefits received from better selling. Wholesalers can also spread their costs over many more products than most producers, resulting in lower costs per product unit. For these reasons, many producers have chosen to control promotion and influence the pricing of products, and have shifted transport, warehousing and financing functions to wholesalers. It must be remembered that the close relationship in the UK, Benelux, France and Germany between manufacturers and the large retail groups is not typical of much of Europe, where wholesalers tend to act as the manufacturer–retailer interface, particularly in southern, central and eastern Europe.

### Services for Retailers

Wholesalers help their retailer customers select inventory (stock). In industries where obtaining supplies is important, skilled buying is essential. A wholesaler that buys is a specialist in understanding market conditions and an expert at negotiating final purchases. For example, based on its understanding of local customer needs and market conditions, a building supply wholesaler purchases inventory ahead of season so that it can provide its retail customers with the building supplies they want when they want them.[1] A retailer's buyer can thus avoid the responsibility of looking for and coordinating supply sources. Moreover, if the wholesaler makes purchases for several different buyers, expenses can be shared by all customers. A manufacturer's sales people can offer retailers only a few products at a time, but independent wholesalers – or dealers – have a wide range of products always available, often from a variety of producers.

By buying in large quantities and delivering to customers in smaller lots, a wholesaler can perform physical distribution activities – such as transport, materials handling, stock planning, communication and warehousing – more efficiently and can provide more service than a producer or retailer would be able to do with its own physical distribution system. Furthermore, wholesalers can provide quick and frequent delivery even when demand fluctuates. They are experienced in providing fast delivery at low cost, thus allowing the producer and the wholesalers' customers to avoid the risks associated with holding large product inventories.[2]

Because they carry products for many customers, wholesalers can maintain a wide product line at a relatively low cost. Often wholesalers can perform storage and warehousing activities more efficiently, permitting retailers to concentrate on other marketing activities. When wholesalers provide storage and warehousing, they generally take on the ownership function as well, an arrangement that frees retailers' and producers' capital for other purposes.

Wholesalers are very important in reaching global markets. Approximately 85 per cent of all prescription drugs sold in Europe go through wholesalers that are within national borders. In the future, it is anticipated that more wholesalers will operate across borders, particularly as changing EU regulations and the movement towards European monetary union reduce EU restrictions.[3]

## Classifying Wholesalers

Many types of wholesaler meet the different needs of producers and retailers. In addition, new institutions and establishments develop in response to producers and retail organisations that want to take over wholesaling functions. Wholesalers adjust their activities as the forces of the marketing environment change.

Wholesalers are classified along several dimensions. Whether a wholesaler is owned by the producer – often termed a company-owned dealership – influences how it is classified. Wholesalers are also grouped according to whether they take title to (actually own) the products they handle. The range of services provided is another criterion used for classification. Finally, wholesalers are classified according to the breadth and depth of their product lines. Using these dimensions, this section discusses three general categories, or types, of wholesaling establishment:

**Merchant wholesalers** Wholesalers that take title to goods and assume the risks associated with ownership

1 merchant wholesalers
2 agents and brokers
3 manufacturers' sales branches and offices.

Remember that the term 'wholesaling' is used here in its broader context: intermediaries' activity in the marketing channel between producers and business-to-business customers.

### Merchant Wholesalers

**Merchant wholesalers** (see Figure 15.1) take title to goods and assume the risks associated with ownership. They are independently owned businesses, buying and reselling products to business or retailer customers. Some are involved with packaging and developing their

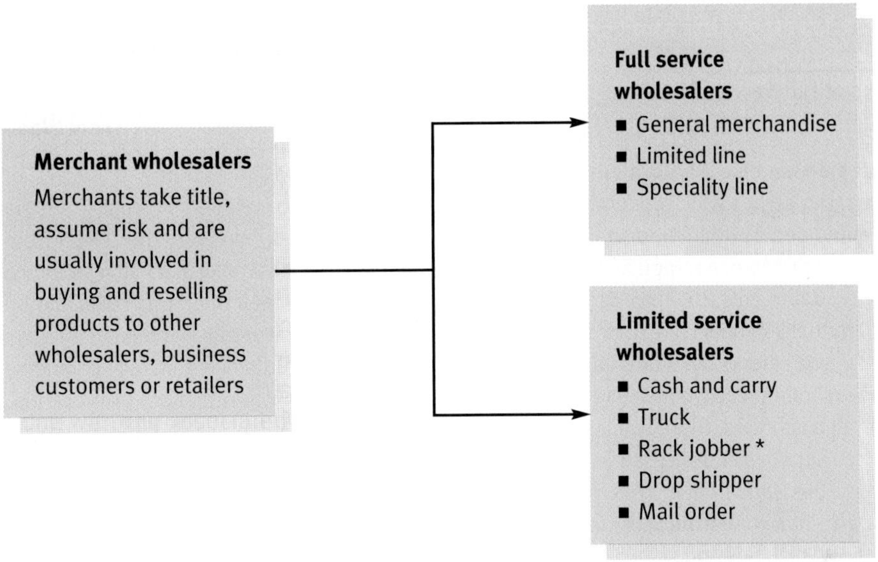


***Figure 15.1***
*Types of merchant wholesaler (*rack jobbers, in many cases, provide such a large number of services that they can be classified as full service, speciality line wholesalers)*

**Full service wholesalers**
Middlemen who offer the widest possible range of wholesaling functions

**Limited service wholesalers**
Middlemen who provide only some marketing services and specialise in a few functions

**General merchandise wholesalers**
Middlemen who carry a wide product mix but offer limited depth within the product lines

**Distributors**
Companies that buy and sell on their own account but tend to deal in the goods of only certain specified manufacturers

**Limited line wholesalers**
Wholesalers that carry only a few product lines but offer an extensive assortment of products within those lines

own-label brands for their retailer customers. Industrial product merchant wholesalers tend to be better established and earn higher profits than consumer goods wholesalers and are likely to have selective distribution arrangements with manufacturers. These wholesalers enable producers to service customers if they have inadequate resources to sell directly. Wholesalers provide the producer with market coverage, making sales contacts, storing stock, handling orders, collecting marketing intelligence and providing customer service.[4] Merchant wholesalers are referred to by various names: wholesaler, jobber, distributor, assembler, exporter and importer. They fall into two categories: full service or limited service.

**Full Service Merchant Wholesalers** **Full service wholesalers** are middlemen who offer the widest possible range of wholesaling functions. Their business customers rely on them for product availability, suitable assortments, bulk breaking of larger quantities into smaller orders, financial assistance and credit lines, technical advice and after-sales service. Full service wholesalers often provide their immediate customers with marketing support. Grocery wholesalers help smaller retailers with store design and layout, site selection, personnel training, financing, merchandising, advertising, coupon redemption and scanning. Gross margins are high, but so are operating expenses.

**Limited Service Merchant Wholesalers** **Limited service wholesalers** provide only some marketing services and specialise in few functions. The other functions are provided by producers, other middlemen or even by customers. Limited service merchant wholesalers take title to merchandise, but often do not deliver the merchandise, grant credit, provide marketing intelligence, carry stocks or plan ahead for customers' future needs. They earn smaller profit margins than full service merchant wholesalers. Relatively few in number, these wholesalers are important for speciality foods, perishable items, construction supplies and coal.

Table 15.2 summarises the different categories of full service and limited service merchant wholesalers: **general merchandise wholesalers**, including **distributors**, **limited line wholesalers**, **speciality line wholesalers**, plus: **rack jobbers**; **cash and carry wholesalers**; **truck wholesalers**; **drop shippers**; and **mail-order wholesalers**.

## Agents and Brokers

Agents and brokers (see Figure 15.2) negotiate purchases and expedite sales but do not take title to products. They are **functional middlemen**; intermediaries who perform a limited number of marketing activities in exchange for a commission, which is generally based on the products'

**TABLE 15.2 TYPES OF FULL AND LIMITED SERVICE MERCHANT WHOLESALERS**

| Categories of Full Service Merchant Wholesalers | Categories of Limited Service Merchant Wholesalers |
|---|---|
| **1 General Merchandise Wholesalers**<br>Middlemen who carry a wide product mix but offer limited depth within product lines. Medicines, hardware, non-perishable foods, cosmetics, detergents, tobacco. Develop strong, mutually beneficial relationships with local retail stores, who often buy all their needs from these wholesalers.<br>For industrial customers, these wholesalers provide all supplies and accessories and are often called *industrial distributors* or *mill supply houses.* **Distributors** are companies which buy and sell on their own account but tend to deal in the goods of only certain specified manufacturers. | **1 Cash and Carry Wholesalers**<br>Their customers are retailers or small industrial businesses who provide their own transport and collect from wholesale depots. Some full service wholesalers also set up cash and carry depots in order to reduce their operating costs and boost margins when supplying smaller retailer or business customers.<br>Cash and carry middlemen generally handle a limited line of products with a high turnover rate, such as groceries, building materials, electrical supplies, office supplies. For example, Booker has a network of cash and carry warehouse depots stocking fresh and frozen foods, cigarettes, wines and spirits, meats and provisions. Selling only to the trade, Booker offers bulk discounts to hotels, restaurants, the catering industry and local small shops.<br>Cash and carry operators have little or no expenditures for outside sales staff, marketing, research, promotion, credit or delivery. Their business customers benefit from lower prices and immediate access to products. |
| **2 Limited Line Wholesalers**<br>Wholesalers that carry only a few product lines, such as groceries, lighting fixtures, drilling equipment, construction equipment, but offer an extensive assortment of products within these lines. They provide similar services to general merchandise wholesalers.<br>In business markets, they serve large geographic areas and provide technical expertise. In consumer goods markets, they often supply single or limited line retailers. Some computer limited line wholesalers provide customers with the products of only four or five manufacturers, but for only a limited number of their lines. | **2 Truck Wholesalers**<br>These wholesalers, sometimes called *truck jobbers*, transport a limited line of products directly to customers for on-the-spot inspection and selection. Often small operators who own and drive their own trucks or vans, they tend to have regular routes, calling on retailers and businesses to determine their needs. They may carry items, such as perishables, which other wholesalers do not stock. Meat, service station supplies and tobacco lines are often carried by truck jobbers.<br>Truck jobbers sell, promote and transport goods, but tend to be classified as limited service merchant wholesalers because they do not provide credit lines. Low volume sales and relatively high levels of customer service result in high operating costs. In eastern and southern Europe, truck jobbers are common marketing channel intermediaries. |
| **3 Speciality Line Wholesalers**<br>These middlemen carry the narrowest range of products, often only a single product line or a few items within a product line. Shellfish, fruit or cheese wholesalers are speciality line wholesalers.<br>They understand the particular requirements of the ultimate buyer and offer their customers detailed product knowledge and depth of choice. To assist retailers, they may set up displays and arrange merchandise. | **3 Drop Shippers**<br>These intermediaries, also known as *desk jobbers*, take title to goods and negotiate sales, but never take actual possession of products. They forward orders from retailers, industrial buyers or other wholesalers to manufacturers and arrange for large shipments of items to be delivered directly from producers to customers. The drop shipper assumes responsibility for products during the entire transaction, including the costs of any unsold goods. |

**Table 15.2 Types of Full and Limited Service Merchant Wholesalers (continued)**

| Categories of Full Service Merchant Wholesalers | Categories of Limited Service Merchant Wholesalers |
|---|---|
| In industrial markets, they are often better placed than the manufacturer to offer customers technical advice and service.<br>*Rack jobbers* are speciality line wholesalers who own and maintain their display racks in supermarkets and pharmacies. They specialise in non-food items, notably branded, widely advertised products sold on a self-service basis, which retailers prefer not to order or stock themselves because of inconvenience or risk. Health and beauty aids, toys, books, magazines, videos and CDs, hardware, housewares and stationery are typical products handled by rack jobbers. They send out delivery personnel who set up displays, mark merchandise, stock shelves and keep billing records. The retailer customer only has to provide the space. Most rack jobbers operate on a pay and display basis, taking back any unsold stock from the retailer. | Drop shippers are involved most commonly in the large volume purchases of bulky goods such as coal, coke, oil, chemicals, timber and building materials. Normally sold in wagon loads, these products are expensive to handle and ship relative to their unit value, so it is sensible to minimise unloading. One facet of drop shipping is its use by the large supermarket retailers, direct from manufacturers to the larger supermarket stores. These large supermarkets can each sell an entire lorry load of certain produce.<br>Drop shippers incur no stockholding costs and provide only minimal customer assistance, leading to low operating costs which can be passed on to customers. They do provide planning, credit and personal selling services.<br>**4 Mail Order Wholesalers**<br>These wholesalers use catalogues instead of salesforces to sell to retail, institutional and industrial buyers. Customers use telecommunications, the Internet or post to send orders which are often despatched through courier companies or the postal service. This enables customers in remote, inaccessible areas to be serviced. As explained in Chapters 17 and 19, mail order in general is growing, and is particularly important for cosmetics, speciality foods, hardware, sporting goods, business and office supplies, car parts, clothing and music. Payment is usually expected up-front by cash or credit card, but discounts may be offered for bulk orders. Mail order wholesalers hold stocks but provide little other service. |

**Sources:** Louis W. Stern, Barton A. Weitz, 'The revolution in distribution: challenges and opportunities' (Special Issue: The Revolution in Retailing), *Long Range Planning*, December 1997, vol. 30, no. 6, p. 823(7); Leonard J. Kistner, C. Anthony Di Benedetto, Sriraman Bhoovaraghavan, 'An integrated approach to the development of channel strategy', *Industrial Marketing Management*, October 1994, vol. 23, no. 4, p. 315(8); Elizabeth Jane Moore, 'Grocery distribution in the UK: recent changes and future prospects', *International Journal of Retail & Distribution Management*, 19 July 1991, pp. 18–24; 'Drop-shipping grows to save depot costs', *Supermarket News*, 1 April 1985, pp. 1, 17.

**Speciality line wholesalers**
Middlemen who carry the narrowest range of products, usually a single product line or a few items within a product line

**Rack jobbers**
Speciality line wholesalers that own and maintain their own display racks in supermarkets and chemists

selling price. **Agents** are middlemen who represent buyers or sellers on a permanent basis. **Brokers** are usually middlemen whom either buyers or sellers employ temporarily.

Although agents and brokers perform even fewer functions than limited service wholesalers, they are usually specialists in particular products or types of customer, and can provide valuable sales expertise. They know their markets well and often form long-lasting associations with customers. Agents and brokers enable manufacturers to expand sales when resources are limited, to benefit from the services of a trained salesforce and to hold down personal selling costs. However, despite the advantages they offer, agents and brokers face increased competition from merchant wholesalers, manufacturers' sales branches and offices, and direct sales efforts, including the growing use of the Internet.

This section concentrates on three types of agent:

1. manufacturers' agents
2. selling agents
3. commission merchants

*Figure 15.2*
*Types of agent and broker*

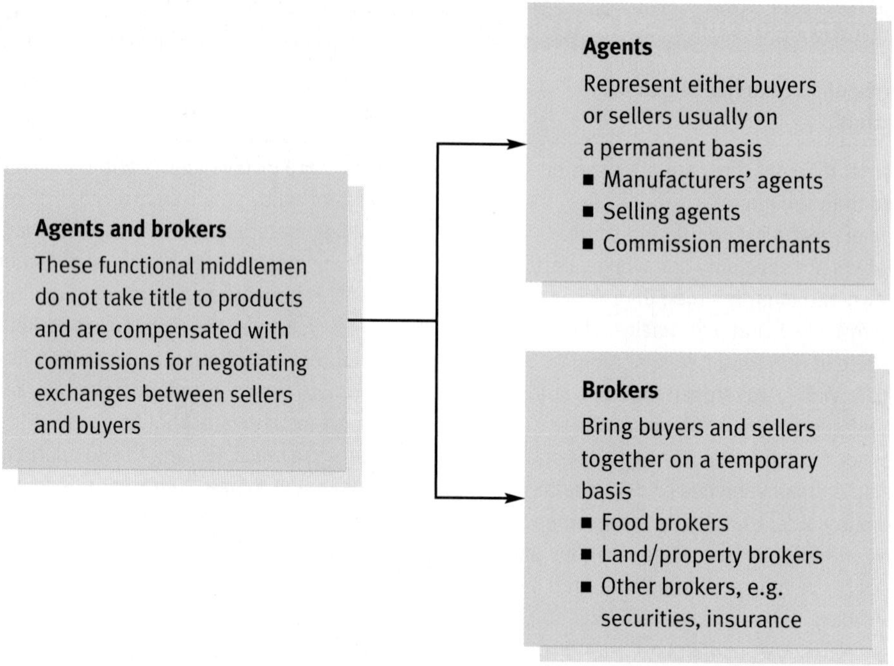

Agents and brokers
These functional middlemen do not take title to products and are compensated with commissions for negotiating exchanges between sellers and buyers
Agents
Represent either buyers or sellers usually on a permanent basis
■ Manufacturers' agents
■ Selling agents
■ Commission merchants
Brokers
Bring buyers and sellers together on a temporary basis
■ Food brokers
■ Land/property brokers
■ Other brokers, e.g. securities, insurance


**Cash and carry wholesalers**
Middlemen whose customers will pay cash and provide transport

**Truck wholesalers**
Limited service wholesalers that transport products direct to customers for inspection and selection

**Drop shippers**
Intermediaries who take title to goods and negotiate sales but never actually take possession of products

**Mail-order wholesalers**
Wholesalers that use catalogues instead of salesforces to sell products to retail, industrial and institutional buyers

**Functional middlemen**
Intermediaries who perform a limited number of marketing activities in exchange for commission

**Agents**
Middlemen who represent buyers or sellers on a permanent basis

**Brokers**
Middlemen employed temporarily by either buyers or sellers

as well as examining the brokers' role in bringing about exchanges between buyers and sellers. Table 15.3 summarises services provided by wholesalers including limited service merchant wholesalers, agents and brokers.

**Agents** **Manufacturers' agents** – who account for over half of all agent wholesalers – are independent middlemen or distributors who represent two or more sellers and usually offer customers complete product lines. They sell and take orders year round, much as a manufacturer's sales office does. Restricted to a particular territory, a manufacturer's agent handles non-competing and complementary products. The relationship between the agent and each manufacturer is governed by written agreements explicitly outlining territories, selling price, order handling and terms of sale relating to delivery, service and warranties. Manufacturers' agents are commonly used in the sale of clothing and accessories, machinery and equipment, iron, steel, furniture, automotive products, electrical goods and certain food items.

Although most manufacturers' agents run small enterprises, their employees are professional, highly skilled sales people. The agents' major advantages, in fact, are their wide range of contacts and strong customer relationships. These intermediaries help large producers minimise the costs of developing new sales territories and adjust sales strategies for different products in different locations. Agents are also useful to small producers who cannot afford outside salesforces of their own, because they incur no costs until the agents have actually sold something. By concentrating on a limited number of products, agents can mount an aggressive sales effort that would be impossible with any other distribution method except producer-owned sales branches and offices. In addition, agents are able to spread operating expenses among non-competing products and thus offer each manufacturer lower prices for services rendered.

The chief disadvantage of using agents is the higher commission rate (usually 10 to 15 per cent) they charge for new product sales. When sales of a new product begin to build, total selling costs go up, and producers sometimes transfer the selling function to in-house sales representatives. For this reason, agents try to avoid depending on a single product

**Table 15.3 Services Provided by Wholesalers**

| a Various services provided by limited service merchant wholesalers | Cash and Carry | Truck Wholesaler[a] | Drop Shipper[b] | Mail Order |
|---|---|---|---|---|
| Physical possession of merchandise | Yes | Yes | No | Yes |
| Personal sales calls on customers | No | Yes | No | No |
| Information about market conditions | No | Yes | Yes | Yes |
| Advice to customers | No | Yes | Yes | No |
| Stocking and maintenance of merchandise in customers' stores | No | Yes | No | No |
| Credit to customers | No | No | Yes | Some |
| Delivery of merchandise to customers | No | Yes | No | No |
| **b Various services agents and brokers provide** | **Brokers** | **Manufacturers' Agents** | **Selling Agents** | **Commission Merchants** |
| Physical possession of merchandise | No | Some | No | Yes |
| Long term relationship with buyers or sellers | No | Yes | Yes | Yes |
| Representation of competing product lines | Yes | No | No | Yes |
| Limited geographic territory | No | Yes | No | No |
| Credit to customers | No | No | Yes | Some |
| Delivery of merchandise to customers | No | Some | Yes | Yes |

[a]Also called truck jobber.
[b]Also called desk jobber.

**Manufacturers' agents**
Independent middlemen or distributors who represent two or more sellers, and usually offer customers complete product lines

**Selling agents**
Agents who market either all of a specified product line or a manufacturer's entire output

**Commission merchants**
Agents who receive goods on consignment from local sellers and negotiate sales in large central markets

line; most work for more than one manufacturer. Manufacturers' agents have little or no control over producers' pricing and marketing policies. They do occasionally store and transport products, assist with planning and provide promotional support. Some agents help retailers advertise and maintain a service support organisation. The more services offered, the higher an agent's commission.

**Selling agents** market either all of a specified product line or a manufacturer's entire output. They perform every wholesaling activity except taking title to products. Selling agents usually assume the sales function for several producers at a time and are often used in place of a marketing department. In contrast to other agent wholesalers, selling agents generally have no territorial limits, and have complete authority over prices, promotion and distribution. They play a key role in the advertising, marketing research and credit policies of the sellers they represent, at times even advising on product development and packaging.

Selling agents, who account for about 1 per cent of the wholesale trade, are used most often by small producers or by manufacturers who find it difficult to maintain a marketing department because of seasonal production or other factors. A producer having financial problems may also engage a selling agent. By so doing, the producer relinquishes some control of the business but may gain working capital by avoiding immediate marketing costs. To avoid conflicts of interest, selling agents represent non-competing product lines. The agents play an important part in the distribution of textiles, and they also sometimes handle canned foods, household furnishings, clothing, timber and metal products. In these industries, competitive pressures increase the importance of marketing relative to production, and the selling agent is a source of essential marketing and financial expertise.

**Commission merchants** are agents who receive goods on consignment from local sellers and negotiate sales in large central markets. Most often found in agricultural marketing, commission merchants take possession of commodities in lorry loads, arrange for any necessary grading or storage, and transport the commodities to auction or markets where they are sold. When sales have been completed, an agent deducts a commission plus the expense of making the sale and then turns over the profits to the producer.

Sometimes called factor merchants, these agents may have broad powers regarding prices and terms of sale, and they specialise in obtaining the best price possible under market conditions. Commission merchants offer planning assistance and sometimes extend credit, but they do not usually provide promotional support. Because commission merchants deal in large volumes, their per unit costs are usually low. Their services are most useful to small producers who must get products to buyers but choose not to field a salesforce or accompany the goods to market themselves. In addition to farm products, commission merchants may handle textiles, art, furniture or seafood products. Businesses – including farms – that use commission merchants have little control over pricing, although the seller can specify a minimum price. Generally, the seller is able to supervise the agent's actions through a check of the commodity prices published regularly in newspapers. Large producers, however, need to maintain closer contact with the market and so have limited need for commission merchants.

**Brokers** Brokers seek out buyers or sellers and help negotiate exchanges. In other words, brokers' primary purpose is to bring buyers and sellers together. Thus brokers perform fewer functions than other intermediaries. They are not involved in financing or physical possession, have no authority to set prices and assume almost no risks. Instead, they offer their customers specialised knowledge of a particular commodity and a network of established contacts.

**Food brokers**
Intermediaries who sell food and general merchandise items to retailer-owned and merchant wholesalers, grocery chains, industrial buyers and food processors.

**Sales branches**
Manufacturer-owned middlemen selling products and providing support services to the manufacturer's salesforce, especially in locations where large customers are concentrated and demand is high

Brokers are especially useful to sellers of certain types of product who market those products only occasionally. Sellers of used machinery, seasonal food products, financial securities and land/property may not know of potential buyers. A broker can furnish them with this information. The party who engages the broker's services – usually the seller – pays the broker's commission when the transaction is completed. Many consumers these days deal with insurance brokers when insuring a car or house contents, or with a mortgage broker when buying a house or moving.

**Food brokers** – the most common type of broker – are intermediaries who sell food and general merchandise items to retailer-owned and merchant wholesalers, grocery chains, industrial buyers and food processors. Food brokers enable buyers and sellers to adjust to fluctuating market conditions. They also aid in grading, negotiating and inspecting foods, and in some cases they store and deliver products. Because of the seasonal nature of food production, the association between broker and producer is temporary – though many mutually beneficial broker–producer relationships are resumed year after year. Because food brokers provide a range of services on a somewhat permanent basis and in specific geographic territories, they can more accurately be described as manufacturers' agents.

## Manufacturers' Sales Branches and Offices

Sometimes called manufacturers' wholesalers or dealerships, manufacturers' sales branches and offices resemble merchant wholesalers' operations. These producer-owned middlemen account for about 9 per cent of wholesale establishments and generate approximately a third (31 per cent) of all wholesale sales.[5]

**Sales branches** are manufacturer-owned middlemen selling products and providing support services to the manufacturer's salesforce, especially in locations where large customers are concentrated and demand is high. They offer credit, deliver goods, give promotional assistance and furnish other services. In many cases, they carry inventory, although this practice often duplicates the functions of other channel members and is now declining. Customers include retailers, business buyers and other wholesalers. Branch operations are common in the electrical supplies, plumbing, timber and car parts industries.

## Building Customer Relationships

### Daewoo's Innovative Distribution Appeals to Car Buyers

When Korean Daewoo entered the European car market, it was an unknown brand. The company made everything from forklift trucks to electrical appliances, aeroplanes to earthmovers, but it is perhaps now for its competitively priced family cars that Daewoo is best known. In its first six months of operation in the UK, Daewoo sold an incredible 14,000 cars. The company established sales operations in most of northern Europe, and bought into Austrian and Polish manufacturers in order to capitalise on market opportunities in eastern Europe. As the parent holding company imploded, like many of the so-called 'tiger economy' businesses at the turn of the century, US manufacturer GM stepped in to acquire the Daewoo car business.

Daewoo's launch marketing blitz had been innovative and inspired. The company's marketing research revealed all the aspects of car buying that consumers mistrust or despise: dealers on commission, hard-sell aggressive sales personnel, over-exaggerated promotional campaigns and poor after-sales service. The original launch promotional executions used the following themes to explain how Daewoo is different:

- good-value, reliable cars with ABS brakes
- door impact protection and power steering
- non-commission sales advisers
- three-year warranties
- courtesy cars or pick-up and collection for services
- AA road cover, no-fuss guarantees.

More important, in a market known for its hype, all these features have been shown to be true.

Daewoo also managed to differentiate itself and to be innovative in its choice of distribution. Most car manufacturers opt for a network of franchised dealerships (independent companies that operate a particular manufacturer's franchise). Such franchises are often notoriously over-hungry for business: sales staff, paid on commission, traditionally 'pounce' on customers as they enter showrooms, and they have a poor reputation for looking after customers who have their cars serviced there after making a purchase.

Daewoo avoided this traditional distribution channel. Instead it owns its own dealerships and sells direct. These are genuinely places for showing rather than selling cars. Personnel are sales advisers earning full salaries rather than commissions on hard-fought sales, and they are trained to respond to queries with helpful information rather than 'foot-in-the-door' sales tactics. Many showrooms have crèches and children's play areas, plus café facilities. The innovative choice of channel to market is intended to take the pressure off consumers as they make what is generally their hardest and most expensive purchasing decision after buying a house.

Under GM, the Daewoo proposition has continued, as explained on its website:

> We offer a hassle-free environment in which to purchase our cars and peace of mind in the form of:
>
> - 3 years/60,000 miles of free servicing
> - 3 years/60,000 miles' comprehensive warranty
> - 3 years' Total AA Roadside Cover
> - 6 years' anti-perforation corrosion warranty
> - An advanced driving course in association with the Institute of Advanced Motorists
>
> This pioneering approach to no hassle purchase and ownership ... offers tremendous reassurance for our customers and is still leading the industry today.
> (www.daewoo-cars.co.uk/info/customer_care/ index.htm)

**Sources:** *What Car?*, February 1996, p. 27; Andy Fry, 'Channels of communication', *Marketing*, 5 October 1995, pp. III–V; Tony Taylor, 'Campaign of the week: Daewoo', *Marketing*, 3 August 1995, p. 8; Michael Newman, 'Driving for exports', *Far Eastern Economic Review*, 158 (25), 1995, pp. 54–5; Neil Merrick, 'Putting pushy sales people out of commission', *People Management*, 1 (9) 1995, pp. 10–11, *What Car?*, March 1999; Daewoo, 1999; GM/Daewoo press releases, 2003; Daewoo website, May, 2004.

**Note:** In 2004, GM decided to re-brand its acquired European Daewoo business as Chevrolet.

**Sales offices**
Manufacturer-owned operations that provide support services normally associated with agents

**Sales offices** are manufacturer-owned operations that provide support services that are normally associated with agents. Like sales branches, they are located away from manufacturing plants, but unlike branches, they carry no inventory. A manufacturer's sales offices or branches may sell products that enhance the manufacturer's own product line. For example, Hiram Walker, a distiller, imports wine from Spain to increase the number of products its sales offices can offer wholesalers. Most large manufacturers have their own networks of sales branches and sales offices.

Manufacturers may set up sales branches or sales offices so that they can reach customers more effectively by performing wholesaling functions themselves. Daewoo opted for this approach as detailed in the Building Customer Relationships box on page 447. A manufacturer may also set up these branches or offices when the required specialist wholesaling services are not available through existing middlemen. In some situations, however, a manufacturer may bypass its wholesaling organisation entirely – for example, in the case of Daewoo's show-rooms or if the producer decides to serve large retailer customers directly. One major distiller bottles own-label spirits for a UK grocery chain and separates this operation completely from the company's sales office, which serves other retailers.

# Facilitating Agencies

**Facilitating agencies**
Organisations such as transport companies, insurance companies, advertising agencies, marketing research agencies and financial institutions that perform activities that enhance channel functions

The total marketing channel is more than a chain linking the producer, intermediary and buyer. **Facilitating agencies** – transport companies, insurance companies, advertising agencies, marketing research agencies and financial institutions – may perform activities that enhance channel functions. Note, however, that any of the functions these facilitating agencies perform may be taken over by the regular marketing intermediaries in the marketing channel.

The basic difference between channel members and facilitating agencies is that channel members perform the negotiating functions (buying, selling and taking title), whereas facilitating agencies do not: they perform only the various tasks that are detailed below.[6] In other words, facilitating agencies assist in the operation of the channel, but they do not sell products. The channel manager may view the facilitating agency as a sub-contractor to which various distribution tasks can be farmed out according to the principle of specialisation and division of labour.[7]

Channel members (producers, wholesalers, distributors or retailers) may rely on facilitating agencies because they believe that these independent businesses will perform various activities more efficiently and more effectively than they themselves could. Facilitating agencies are functional specialists that perform special tasks for channel members without getting involved in directing or controlling channel decisions. Public warehouses, finance companies, transport companies, and trade shows and trade markets are facilitating agencies that expedite the flow of products through marketing channels.

## Public Warehouses

**Public warehouses**
Storage facilities available for a fee

**Public warehouses** are storage facilities available for a fee. Producers, wholesalers and retailers may rent space in a warehouse instead of constructing their own facilities or using a merchant wholesaler's storage services. Many warehouses also order, deliver, collect accounts and maintain display rooms where potential buyers can inspect products.

To use goods as collateral for a loan, a channel member may place products in a bonded warehouse. If it is too impractical or expensive to transfer goods physically, the channel member may arrange for a public warehouser to verify that goods are in the channel member's own facilities and then issue receipts for lenders.[8] Under this arrangement, the channel member retains possession of the products but the warehouser has control. Many field public warehousers know where their clients can borrow working capital and are sometimes able to arrange low-cost loans.

**Finance Companies**

Wholesalers and retailers may be able to obtain financing by transferring ownership of products to a sales finance company or bank while retaining physical possession of the goods. Often called 'floor planning', this form of financing enables wholesalers and retailers – especially car and electrical appliance dealers – to offer a greater selection of products for customers and thus increase sales. Loans may be due immediately upon sale, so products financed this way are usually well known, sell relatively easily and present little risk.

Other financing functions are performed by factors – organisations that provide clients with working capital by buying their accounts receivable or by lending money, using the accounts receivable as collateral. Most factors minimise their own risks by specialising in particular industries, in order to better evaluate individual channel members within those industries. Factors usually lend money for a longer time than banks. They may help clients improve their credit and collection policies, and may also provide management expertise.

**Transport Companies**

Rail, road, air and other carriers are facilitating agencies that help manufacturers and retailers transport products. Each form of transport has its own advantages. Railways ship

*Figure 15.3*
*Many consumer durables and food lines depend on sea freight to reach their intended markets*
*Photo © Royalty-Free/ CORBIS*

large volumes of bulky goods at low cost; in fact, outside the UK, a 'unit train' is the cheapest form of overland transport for ore, grain or other commodities. Air transport is relatively expensive but is often preferred for shipping high-value or perishable goods. Trucks, which usually carry short-haul, high-value goods, now carry more and more products because factories are moving closer to their markets. As a result of technological advances, pipelines now transport powdered solids and fluidised solid materials, as well as petroleum and natural gas.

Transport companies sometimes take over the functions of other middlemen. Because of the ease and speed of using air transport for certain types of product, parcel express companies can eliminate the need for their clients to maintain large stocks and branch warehouses. In other cases, freight forwarders perform accumulation functions by combining less than full shipments into full loads and passing on the savings to customers – perhaps charging a wagon rate rather than a less-than-wagon rate.

### Trade Shows and Trade Markets

**Trade shows**
Industry exhibitions that offer both selling and non-selling benefits

Trade shows and trade markets enable manufacturers or wholesalers to exhibit products to potential buyers, and so help the selling and buying functions. **Trade shows** are industry exhibitions that offer both selling and non-selling benefits.[9] On the selling side, trade shows let vendors identify prospects; gain access to key decision-makers; disseminate facts about their products, services and personnel; and actually sell products and service current accounts through contacts at the show.[10] Trade shows also allow a company to reach potential buyers who have not been approached through regular selling efforts. In fact, many trade show visitors have not recently been contacted by a sales representative of any company within the past year. Many of these individuals are, therefore, willing to travel several hundred miles to attend trade shows to learn about new goods and services. The non-selling benefits include opportunities to maintain the company image with competitors, customers and the industry; gather information about competitors' products and prices; and identify potential channel members.[11] Trade shows have a positive influence on other important marketing variables, such as maintaining or enhancing company morale, product testing and product evaluation.

Trade shows can permit direct buyer–seller interaction and may eliminate the need for agents. Companies exhibit at trade shows because of the high concentration of prospective buyers for their products. Studies show that it takes, on average, 5.1 sales calls to close an industrial business-to-business sale but less than 1 sales call (0.8) to close a trade show lead. The explanation for the latter figure is that more than half of the customers who purchase a product based on information gained at a trade show order the product by mail or by phone after the show. When customers use these more impersonal methods to gather information, the need for major sales calls to provide such information can be eliminated. Most manufacturers have sales and technical personnel who attend relevant trade shows in key target market territories. Birmingham's National Exhibition Centre (NEC) offers a 240-hectare (600-acre) site, with open display areas, plus 125,000 square metres (156,000 square yards) of covered exhibition space, hotels, parking for thousands of cars, plus rail and air links. Each year there are toy, fashion, giftware and antique trade fairs at the NEC, when trade customers can select merchandise for their next sales seasons. **Trade markets** are relatively permanent facilities that businesses can rent to exhibit products year round. At these markets, such products as furniture, home decorating supplies, toys, clothing and gift items are sold to wholesalers and retailers.

**Trade markets**
Relatively permanent facilities that businesses can rent to exhibit products year round

## Changing Patterns in Wholesaling

The nature of the wholesaling industry is changing. The distinction between wholesaling activities that any business can perform and the traditional wholesaling establishment is becoming blurred. Changes in the nature of the marketing environment itself have transformed various aspects of the industry. For instance, they have brought about an increasing reliance on computer technology to expedite the ordering, delivery and handling of goods. The trend towards the globalisation of world markets has resulted in other changes to which astute wholesalers are responding. The predominant shifts in wholesaling today are:

- the consolidation of the wholesaling industry
- the development of new types of wholesaler.

### Wholesalers Consolidate Power

Like most major industries, the wholesale industry is experiencing a great number of mergers. Wholesaling businesses are acquiring or merging with other businesses primarily to achieve more efficiency in the face of declining profit margins.[12] Consolidation also gives larger wholesalers more pricing power over producers. Some analysts have expressed concern that wholesalers' increased price 'power' will increase the number of single-source supply deals, which may reduce competition among wholesalers as well as retailers and producers. Nevertheless, the trend towards consolidation of wholesaling businesses appears to be continuing. It is also crossing national borders, as many European companies take advantage of the EU's cross-border trade and regulatory improvements. One of the results of the current wave of consolidation in the wholesale industry is that more wholesalers are specialising. For example, McKesson once distributed chemicals, wines and spirits but now focuses only on medicines. The new larger wholesalers can also afford to purchase and use more modern technology to manage inventories physically, provide computerised ordering services and even help manage their retail customers' operations.[13]

### New Types of Wholesaler

The trend towards larger retailers (discussed in Chapter 16) will offer opportunities as well as dangers for wholesaling establishments. Opportunities will develop from the expanded product lines of these mass merchandisers. A merchant wholesaler of groceries, for instance, may want to add other low-cost, high-volume products sold in superstores. On the other hand, some limited-function merchant wholesalers may no longer have a role to play. For example, the volume of sales may eliminate the need for rack jobbers, who usually handle slow-moving products that are purchased in limited quantities. The future of independent wholesalers, agents and brokers depends on their ability to delineate markets and furnish the desired services. The trend is also towards large global groups such as Makro, now present throughout Latin America, Asia and the Pacific, as well as its European heartland.

## The Importance of Physical Distribution

**Physical distribution**
A set of activities – consisting of order processing, materials handling, warehousing, inventory management and transportation – used in the movement of products from producers to consumers or end users

Wholesalers, in their various guises, are essential 'players' in many businesses' marketing channels. Also important is the ability to physically deliver products to customers. **Physical distribution** is a set of activities – consisting of order processing, materials handling, warehousing, inventory management and transportation – used in the movement of products from producers to consumers, or end users. Planning an effective physical distribution system can be a significant decision in developing a marketing strategy. A company that has the right goods in the right place at the right time in the right quantity, and with the right support services is able to sell more than competing businesses that fail to accomplish these goals. Physical distribution is an important variable in a marketing strategy because it can decrease costs and increase customer satisfaction. In fact, speed of delivery, along with service and dependability, is often as important to buyers as cost. In some situations – for example, the emergency provision of a spare part for vital production-line machinery – it may even be the single most important factor. For most companies, physical distribution accounts for about a fifth of a product's retail price.

Physical distribution deals with physical movement and inventory holding – the storing and tracking of inventory or stock until it is needed – both within and among marketing channel members. Often, one channel member will arrange the movement of goods for all channel members involved in exchanges. For example, a packing company ships fresh salmon and champagne (often by air) to remote markets on a routine basis. Frequently, buyers are found while the goods are in transit.

The physical distribution system is often adjusted to meet the needs of a channel member. For example, an agricultural equipment dealer who keeps a low inventory of replacement parts requires the fastest and most dependable service when parts not in stock are needed. In this case, the distribution cost may be a minor consideration when compared with service, dependability and promptness. Grocery retailers such as Aldi and ASDA receive some deliveries to central and regional warehouses, whereas other deliveries from manufacturers such as Heinz or Kellogg's go directly to individual stores as required, and insisted upon, by the retail companies. Failure to deliver products to customers where, when and how they demand is likely to lose orders, diminish customer loyalty and provide opportunities for competing suppliers, and is not going to create a mutually satisfying relationship between supplier and customer.

## Physical Distribution Objectives

**Objective of physical distribution**
Decreasing costs while increasing customer service

For most companies, the main **objective of physical distribution** is to decrease costs while increasing customer service.[14] In the real world, however, few distribution systems manage to achieve these goals in equal measure. The large stock inventories and rapid transport, essential to facilitate high levels of customer service, drive up costs. On the other hand, reduced inventories and slower, cheaper shipping methods cause customer dissatisfaction because of stock-outs or late deliveries. Physical distribution managers strive for a reasonable balance of service, costs and resources. They determine what level of customer service is acceptable yet realistic, develop a 'system' outlook of calculating total distribution costs, and trade higher costs at one stage of distribution for savings in another. In this section these three performance objectives are examined more closely.

## Customer Service

**Customer service**
Customer satisfaction in terms of physical distribution, availability, promptness and quality

To varying degrees, all businesses attempt to satisfy customer needs and wants through a set of activities known collectively as **customer service**. Many companies claim that service to the customer is their top priority. These companies see service as being as important in attracting customers and building sales as the cost or quality of the companies' products.

Customers require a variety of services. At the most basic level, they need fair prices, acceptable product quality and dependable deliveries.[15] There are many facets of service, as described throughout this book, but in the physical distribution area, availability, promptness and quality are the most important dimensions of customer service. These are the main factors that determine how satisfied customers are likely to be with a supplier's physical distribution activities.[16] Customers seeking a higher level of customer service may also want sizeable inventories, efficient order processing, availability of emergency shipments, progress reports, post-sale services, prompt replacement of defective items and warranties. Customers' inventory requirements influence the level of physical distribution service they expect. For example, customers who want to minimise inventory storage and shipping costs may require that suppliers assume the cost of maintaining inventory in the marketing channel, or the cost of premium transport.[17] Because service needs vary from customer to customer, companies must analyse – and adapt to – customer preferences. Attention to customer needs and preferences is crucial to increasing sales and obtaining repeat sales. A company's failure to provide the desired level of service may mean the loss of customers. Without customers there can be no profit.

Companies must also examine the service levels offered by competitors and match those standards, at least when the costs of providing the services can be balanced by the sales generated. For example, companies may step up their efforts to identify the causes of customer complaints or institute corrective measures for billing and shipping errors. In extremely competitive businesses, such as the market for vehicle parts, businesses may concentrate on product availability. To compete effectively, manufacturers may strive for inventory levels and order processing speeds that are deemed unnecessary and too costly in other industries.[18]

Services are provided most effectively when service standards are developed and stated in terms that are specific, measurable and appropriate for the product – for example, 'Guaranteed delivery within 48 hours.' Standards should be communicated clearly both to customers and employees, and rigorously enforced. In many cases, it is necessary to maintain a policy of minimum order size to ensure that transactions are profitable: special service charges are added to orders smaller than a specified quantity. Many carrier or courier companies operate on this basis. Many service policies also spell out delivery times and provisions for back ordering, returning goods and obtaining emergency shipments. The overall objective of any service policy should be to improve customer service just to the point beyond which increased sales would be negated by increased distribution costs.

## Total Distribution Costs

Although physical distribution managers try to minimise the costs of each element in the system – transportation, warehousing, inventory carrying, order entry/customer service and administration – decreasing costs in one area often raises them in another. Figure 15.4 shows the percentage of total costs that physical distribution functions represent. By using a total cost approach to physical distribution, managers can view the distribution system as a whole, not as a collection of unrelated activities. The emphasis shifts from lowering the separate costs of individual functions to minimising the total cost of the entire distribution system.

**Total cost analysis**
Weighs inventory levels against warehousing expenses; and materials handling costs against various modes of transport; and all distribution costs against customer service standards

The total cost approach calls for analysing the costs of all possible distribution alternatives, even those considered too impractical or expensive. **Total cost analysis** weighs inventory levels against warehousing expenses; materials handling costs against various modes of transport; and all distribution costs against customer service standards. The costs of potential sales losses from lower performance levels are also considered. In many cases, accounting procedures and statistical methods can be used to calculate total costs. Where hundreds of combinations of distribution variables are possible, computer simulations may be helpful. In no case is a distribution system's lowest total cost the result of using a combination of the cheapest functions; instead, it is the lowest overall cost compatible with the company's stated service objectives.

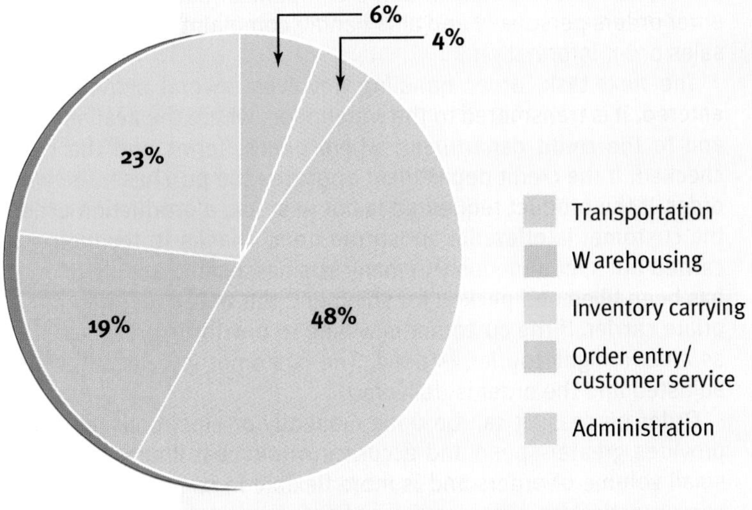


***Figure 15.4*** *Proportional cost of each physical distribution function as a percentage of total distribution costs Source: Establish, Inc./ Herbert W. Davis & Company, Ft. Lee. NJ.* Logistics Cost and Service, 2000, *www.establishinc.com. Reprinted by permission*

## Cost Trade-offs

**Cost trade-offs**
The off-setting of higher costs in one area of the distribution system by lower costs in another area, to keep the total system cost-effective

A distribution system that attempts to provide a specific level of customer service for the lowest possible total cost must use **cost trade-offs** to resolve conflicts about resource allocations. That is, higher costs in one area of the distribution system must be offset by lower costs in another area if the total system is to remain cost-effective.

Trade-offs are strategic decisions to combine and recombine resources for greatest cost-effectiveness. When distribution managers regard the system as a network of interlocking functions, trade-offs become useful tools in a unified distribution strategy. The furniture retailer IKEA uses a system of trade-offs. To ensure that each store carries enough inventory to satisfy customers in the area, IKEA groups its retail outlets into regions, each served by a separate distribution centre. In addition, each IKEA store carries a five-week back stock of inventory. Thus IKEA has chosen to trade higher inventory warehousing costs for improved customer service.[19]

The remainder of this chapter focuses on order processing, materials handling, warehousing, inventory management and transportation, all of which are essential physical distribution activities. While none of these activities would normally be the responsibility of marketing managers, their smooth deployment impacts on customer service levels, customer satisfaction and also customers' perceptions of a brand or business.

# Order Processing

**Order processing**
The receipt and transmission of sales order information

**Order processing** – the first stage in a physical distribution system – is the receipt and transmission of sales order information. Although management sometimes overlooks the importance of these activities, efficient order processing facilitates product flow. Computerised order processing, used now by many businesses, speeds the flow of information from customer to seller.[20] Indeed, in many industries key suppliers are linked 'live' to retailers' or distributors' tills and order books: they are then able to replenish or supply exactly in line with demand and actual sales. When carried out quickly and accurately, order processing contributes to customer satisfaction, repeat orders and increased profits.

Generally, there are three main tasks in order processing:

1. order entry
2. order handling
3. order delivery.[21]

Order entry begins when customers or sales people place purchase orders by mail, telephone, fax or computer. In some companies, sales service representatives receive and enter orders personally and also handle complaints, prepare progress reports and forward sales order information.[22]

The next task, order handling, involves several activities. Once an order has been entered, it is transmitted to the warehouse, where the availability of the product is verified; and to the credit department, where prices, terms and the customer's credit rating are checked. If the credit department approves the purchase, the warehouse begins to fill the order. If the product requested is not in stock, a production order is sent to the factory or the customer is offered a substitute item. Thanks to technology, these various tasks are carried out simultaneously in many businesses and in only a few seconds. When the order has been filled and packed for shipment, the warehouse schedules pick up with an appropriate carrier. If the customer is willing to pay for express service, priority transport, such as an overnight courier, is used. The customer is sent an invoice, inventory records are adjusted and the order is delivered.

Order processing can be done manually or electronically, depending on which method provides greater speed and accuracy within cost limits. Manual processing suffices for a small volume of orders and is more flexible in special situations; electronic processing is more practical for a large volume of orders and lets a company integrate order processing,

**Electronic data interchange (EDI)**
The use of IT to integrate order processing with production, inventory, accounting and transportation

production planning, inventory, accounting and transport planning into a total information system.[23] These days, most companies use **electronic data interchange (EDI)**, which uses IT to integrate order processing with production, inventory, accounting and transportation. Many leading retail groups, with products from groceries to electrical goods, have their stores networked to the head office. Suppliers are also linked electronically to the retailers' head offices, so that stock can be ordered electronically.

# Materials Handling

**Materials handling**
The physical handling of products

**Unit loading**
Grouping one or more boxes on a pallet or skid, permitting movement of efficient loads by mechanical means

**Containerisation**
The practice of consolidating many items into a single large container that is sealed at its point of origin and opened at its destination, greatly increasing efficiency and security in shipping

**Materials handling**, or the physical handling of products, is important for efficient warehouse operations, as well as in transport from points of production to points of consumption. The characteristics of the product itself often determine how it will be handled. For example, fresh dairy produce has unique characteristics that determine how it can be moved and stored. Materials handling procedures and techniques should increase the usable capacity of a warehouse, reduce the number of times a good is handled, improve service to customers and increase their satisfaction with the product. Packaging, loading, movement and labelling systems must be coordinated to maximise cost reduction and customer satisfaction.

In Chapter 11, it was noted that the protective functions of packaging are important considerations in product development. Appropriate decisions about packaging materials and methods allow for the most efficient physical handling; most companies employ packaging consultants or specialists to accomplish this important task. Materials handling equipment is used in the design of handling systems. **Unit loading** is grouping one or more boxes on a pallet or skid; it permits movement of efficient loads by mechanical means, such as forklifts, trucks or conveyor systems. **Containerisation** is the practice of consolidating many items into a single large container that is sealed at its point of origin and opened at its destination. The containers are usually 2.5 metres (8 feet) wide, 2.5 metres (8 feet) high, and 3, 6, 7.5 or 12 metres (10, 20, 25 or 40 feet) long. They can be conveniently stacked and sorted as units at the point of loading. Because individual items are not handled in transit, containerisation greatly increases efficiency and security in shipping.

# Warehousing

**Warehousing**
The design and operation of facilities for storing and moving goods

**Warehousing**, the design and operation of facilities for storing and moving goods, is an important physical distribution function. Warehousing provides time utility by enabling companies to compensate for dissimilar production and consumption rates. That is, when mass production creates a greater stock of goods than can be sold immediately, companies may warehouse the surplus goods until customers are ready to buy. Warehousing also helps stabilise the prices and availability of seasonal items. There follows a description of the basic functions of warehouses and the different types of warehouse available. Distribution centres, special warehouse operations designed so that goods can be moved rapidly, are also examined.

## Warehousing Functions

**Private warehouse**
A warehouse operated by a company for shipping and storing its own products

Warehousing is not limited simply to the storage of goods. When warehouses receive goods by wagon loads or lorry loads, they break the shipments down into smaller quantities for individual customers; when goods arrive in small lots, the warehouses assemble the lots into bulk loads that can be shipped out more economically.[24] Warehouses perform the following basic distribution functions.

1 *Receiving goods* – the merchandise is accepted, and the warehouse assumes responsibility for the goods.
2 *Identifying goods* – the appropriate stock-keeping units are recorded, along with the quantity of each item received; the item may be marked with a physical code, tag or

**Public warehouses** Warehouses that rent storage space and related physical distribution facilities to other companies and sometimes provide distribution services such as receiving and unloading products, inspecting, reshipping, filling orders, financing, displaying products and coordinating shipments

other label, or it may be identified by an item code (a code on the carrier or container) or by physical properties.

3 *Sorting goods* – the merchandise is sorted for storage in appropriate areas.
4 *Despatching goods to storage* – the merchandise is put away so that it can be retrieved when necessary.
5 *Holding goods* – the merchandise is kept in storage and properly protected until needed.
6 *Recalling and picking goods* – items customers have ordered are retrieved efficiently from storage and prepared for the next step.
7 *Marshalling the shipment* – the items making up a single shipment are brought together and checked for completeness or explainable omissions. Order records are prepared or modified as necessary.
8 *Despatching the shipment* – the consolidated order is packaged suitably and directed to the right transport vehicle; necessary shipping and accounting documents are prepared.[25]

## Types of Warehouse

**Field public warehouse** A warehouse established by a public warehouse at the owner's inventory location

**Bonded storage warehouse** A warehousing arrangement by which imported or taxable products are not released until the owners of the products have paid customs duties, taxes or other fees

**Distribution centre** A large, centralised warehouse that receives goods from factories and suppliers, regroups them into orders and ships them quickly to customers

A company's choice of warehouse facilities is an important strategic consideration. By using the right warehouse, a company may be able to reduce transportation and inventory costs or improve its service to customers; the wrong warehouse may drain company resources. For example, a company that produces processed foods must locate its warehousing close to main transport routes to facilitate delivery to supermarkets in different parts of the country. Besides deciding how many facilities to operate and where to locate them, a company must determine which type of warehouse will be most appropriate. Warehouses fall into two general categories: private and public. In many cases, a combination of private and public facilities provides the most flexible approach to warehousing. Table 15.4 summarises the basic types of warehouses: **private warehouse**; **public warehouses**, including **field public warehouse** and **bonded storage warehouse**; and **distribution centre**. Many companies operate their own warehousing, whereas others outsource this requirement to specialist inventory management and haulage companies.

# Inventory Management

**Inventory management** The development and maintenance of adequate assortments of products to meet customers' needs

**Stock-outs** Shortages of products resulting from a lack of products carried in inventory

**Inventory management** involves developing and maintaining adequate assortments of products to meet customers' needs. Because a company's investment in inventory usually represents 30 to 50 per cent of its total assets, inventory decisions have a significant impact on physical distribution costs and the level of customer service provided. When too few products are carried in inventory, the result is a **stock-out**, or shortage of products, which results in fewer sales and customers switching to alternative brands. But when too many products or too many slow-moving products are carried, costs increase, as do the risks of product obsolescence, pilferage and damage. The objective of inventory management, therefore, is to minimise inventory costs while maintaining an adequate supply of goods. The Innovation and Change box opposite shows how staff at Benetton use information and technology to ensure that the company's inventory is managed efficiently.

There are three types of inventory cost.

1 *Carrying costs* are holding costs; they include expenditures for storage space and materials handling, financing, insurance, taxes and losses from spoilage of goods.
2 *Replenishment costs* are related to the purchase of merchandise. The price of goods, handling charges and expenses for order processing contribute to replenishment costs.
3 *Stock-out costs* include sales lost when demand for goods exceeds supply, and the clerical and processing expenses of back ordering.

A company must control all the costs of obtaining and maintaining inventory in order to achieve its profit goals. Management must therefore have a clear idea of the level of each

## Innovation and Change

### Benetton Benefits from Automated Distribution Systems

How important can 24 people be to a multinational clothing manufacturer and retailer? To Benetton, the Italian casual wear company, the 24 people who run the warehouse that handles its distribution of 110 million pieces of clothing a year are extremely important. These 24 people are responsible for processing deliveries of clothing to serve over 5000 stores in 120 countries. Though sales in the garment industry have sagged recently, Benetton is still moving tremendous amounts of knit and cotton clothing. After its small clothing business expanded into an international fashion sensation, executives at Benetton realised that highly efficient physical distribution methods were essential.

Benetton has linked its sales agents, factory and warehouse together using an international electronic data interchange (EDI) system. Suppose a student in Maastricht wants to buy a Benetton sweater identical to his older brother's. He goes to a Benetton store and searches for it, only to be disappointed when he finds that the sweater is not there. The sales person assures him that the sweater will arrive in a month. The sales person then calls a Benetton sales agent, who places the sweater order on a personal computer. Several times a day, this information is collected and sent to the company's mainframe system in Italy, where the computer searches inventory data to find out if the requested item is in stock. If not, an order travels automatically to a machine that cuts the materials and immediately starts to knit the sweater. Workers put the finished sweater in a box with a barcoded label and send it to the warehouse. In the warehouse, a computer commands a robot to retrieve the sweater and any other merchandise that needs to be transported to the same store.

From its creation, Benetton opted to control its logistics and to invest heavily in state-of-the-art systems. Automated processes achieve integration within the production cycle, customer orders, packing and delivery. The automated shipping centre at Castrette has a capacity of 400,000 boxes and can handle 20,000 inward and 20,000 outgoing boxes daily. The automated sorting system is capable of assembling individual orders for Benetton shops worldwide. Flat and hanging garments are sorted automatically, packed into boxes and sent direct to the automated distribution system. This system covers an area of over 20,000 square metres, and automatically stocks, invoices, selects and ships garments direct to the 5000 stores.

In the mid-1990s, Benetton surprised the clothing industry by announcing that it was to launch a 'direct sell' operation – home shopping via catalogues and courier delivery businesses. Benetton in the UK was the first high street store-based retailer to opt for direct home shopping since Next launched its Next Directory in 1986. Effective stock control and distribution became even more important for Italy's Benetton.

Through efficient management of physical distribution activities and the use of technologically advanced equipment, Benetton ensures that its products are available to consumers when and where they want them. Close attention to physical distribution activities has helped the company achieve its objectives and become a major competitor in the fashion industry. With the addition of a home shopping operation, it is essential for Benetton's logistical support to be 'state of the art'.

**Sources:** Harriet Fox, 'Benetton opts for direct sell', *Marketing*, 16 March 1995, p. 5; Tom O'Sullivan and David Benady, 'Unravelling of Benetton?', *Marketing Week*, 3 February 1995, pp. 21–2; Fiorenza Belussi, 'The Italian job', *RDM*, Summer 1994, pp. ix–x; Benetton Stores UK, 2003; www.benetton.com/flash/home.html, May 2004.

type of cost incurred. Customers' expectations of product availability and tolerable delivery lead times will vary between target market segments.

Inventory managers deal with two issues of particular importance. They must know when to reorder and how much merchandise to order. For example, many high-street banks no longer require current account customers to order new cheque books. Once a certain cheque number is reached, a new book is automatically sent to the customer.

**Reorder point**
The inventory level that signals the need to order more inventory

In general, to determine when to order, a marketer calculates the **reorder point**, which is the inventory level that signals that more inventory should be ordered. Three factors determine the reorder point:

**TABLE 15.4 BASIC TYPES OF WAREHOUSE**

**Private Warehouses**

Are operated by a company for the purpose of storing and distributing its own products. Leased or purchased when a business builds up sales to warrant a long term physical presence in a territory, they are important for businesses requiring specialised storage and handling, such as JCB or Ford for after-market parts. The large retail chains such as Aldi, Carrefour and Marks & Spencer are the biggest users of private warehouses. Private warehouses face fixed costs such as land rents, insurance, taxes, maintenance and debt expense and should only be considered if sales levels are sufficient and stable over time. They also tie up capital and resources and require expert management. Private warehouses give companies more control over the distribution of their products and may offer secondary benefits such as property appreciation.

**Public Warehouses**

Rent storage space and related physical distribution facilities to other companies, sometimes providing distribution services such as receiving and unloading products, inspecting, re-shipping, filling orders, financing, displaying products and co-ordinating shipments. Public warehouses are very useful to businesses (a) experiencing seasonal demand for their products, (b) with low volume storage needs, (c) needing to maintain stocks at various locations, (d) testing new markets or operations, (e) with private warehouses needing additional storage space. There are no fixed costs to the user, who only rents space as and when required. There are two specialised types of public warehouses: field and bonded.

*Field Public Warehouse* A warehouse established by a public warehouser at the owner's inventory location. The warehouser becomes the custodian for the products and issues a receipt which can be used as collateral for a loan by the products' producer.

*Bonded Storage* A warehousing arrangement under which imported or taxable products are not released until the product owners have paid customs duties, taxes or other fees. Bonded warehouses are used by some businesses to defer tax payments until products are delivered to customers.

**The Distribution Centre**

Receives goods from factories and suppliers, re-groups them into orders and quickly ships them to customers. These large, centralised warehouses can be seen at many motorway intersections and are used by most large manufacturers. The focus is on rapid active movement rather than passive storage. One storey, large buildings adjacent to major transport arteries, they are highly automated with computer controlled robots, forklifts and hoists collecting and moving products to loading docks. Most distribution centres are privately owned. They serve customers in regional markets or supply the company's smaller branch warehouses. The core benefit is the enhancement of customer service by ensuring product availability, full product lines and quick turnaround, with reduced costs. Factories can ship large quantities at bulk load rates, reducing transport costs. Rapid turnaround reduces stock holding costs. Some distribution centres also facilitate production by receiving and consolidating raw materials and providing final assembly for some products.

**Sources:** James C. Johnson and Donald F. Wood, *Contemporary Physical Distribution & Logistics*, 2nd edn (Tulsa, Okla.: Penn Well Publishing Company, 1982), p. 356; Carl M. Guelzo, *Introduction to Logistics Management* (Englewood Cliffs, NJ: Prentice-Hall, 1986), p. 102.

**Order lead time**
The average time lapse between placing the order and receiving it

**Usage rate**
The rate at which a product's inventory is used or sold during a specific time period

1. the **order lead time**, which is the expected time between the date an order is placed and the date the goods are received and made ready for resale to customers
2. the **usage rate** or rate at which a product is sold or used up
3. the quantity of **safety stock** on hand, or inventory needed to prevent stock-outs.

The reorder point can be calculated using the following formula:

reorder point = (order lead time × usage rate) + safety stock

Thus, if order lead time is 10 days, usage rate is 3 units per day and safety stock is 20 units, the reorder point is 50 units.

**Safety stock**
Inventory needed to prevent stock-outs

The inventory manager faces several trade-offs when reordering merchandise. Large safety stocks ensure product availability and thus improve the level of customer service; they also lower order-processing costs because orders are placed less frequently. Small safety stocks, on the other hand, cause frequent reorders and high order-processing costs but reduce the overall cost of carrying inventory. Figure 15.5 illustrates two order systems involving different order quantities but the same level of safety stocks. Figure 15.5a shows inventory levels for a given demand of infrequent orders; Figure 15.5b illustrates the levels needed to fill frequent orders at the same demand.

**Economic order quantity (EOQ)**
The order size that minimises the total cost of ordering and carrying inventory

To quantify this trade-off between carrying costs and order-processing costs, a model for an **economic order quantity (EOQ)** has been developed (see Figure 15.6); it specifies the order size that minimises the total cost of ordering and carrying inventory.[26] The fundamental relationships underlying the widely accepted EOQ model are the basis of many inventory control systems. Remember, however, that the objective of minimum total inventory cost must be balanced against the customer service level necessary for maximum profits. Therefore, because increased costs of carrying inventory are usually associated with a higher level of customer service, the order quantity will often lie to the right of the optimal point in the figure, leading to a higher total cost for ordering and larger carrying inventory.

Fluctuations in demand – for example, in times of economic recession – mean that it is not always easy to predict changing inventory levels. When management miscalculates reorder points or order quantities, inventory problems develop. Warning signs include an inventory that grows at a faster rate than sales, surplus or obsolete inventory, customer deliveries that are consistently late or lead times that are too long, inventory that represents a growing percentage of assets, and large inventory adjustments or write-offs. However, there are several tools for improving inventory control.

From a technical standpoint, an inventory system can be planned so that the number of products sold and the number of products in stock are determined at certain checkpoints. The control may be as simple as tearing off a code number from each product sold so that the correct sizes, colours and models can be tabulated and reordered. Many bookshops insert reorder slips of paper into each item of stock, which can be removed at the checkout. A sizeable amount of technologically advanced electronic equipment is available to assist with inventory management. In many larger stores, such as Tesco and Toys 'Я' Us, checkout terminals connected to central computer systems instantaneously update inventory and sales records. For continuous, automatic updating of inventory records, some companies use pressure-sensitive circuits installed under ordinary industrial shelving to weigh inventory, convert the weight to units and display any inventory changes on a video screen or computer printout.

Various techniques have also been used successfully to improve inventory management. The just-in-time concept calls for companies to maintain low inventory levels and purchase products and materials in small quantities, just at the moment they are needed for production. Ford, for example, sometimes receives supply deliveries as often as every two hours.[27]

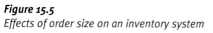

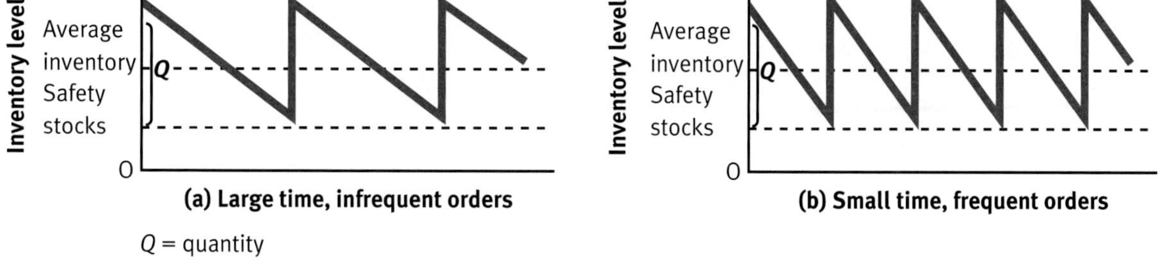


***Figure 15.5***
*Effects of order size on an inventory system*

*Figure 15.6*
*Economic order quantity (EOQ) model*

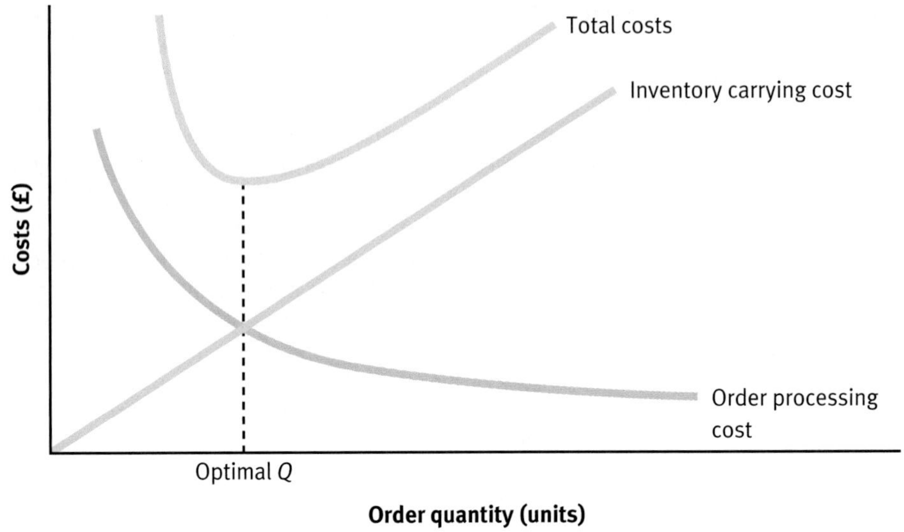


Just-in-time inventory management depends on a high level of coordination between producers and suppliers, but the technique enables companies to eliminate waste and reduce inventory costs significantly. When Polaroid implemented just-in-time techniques as part of its zero base pricing programme to reduce the overall cost of purchased materials, equipment and services, it saved an average of £15 million per year.[28]

Another inventory management technique, the 80/20 rule, holds that fast-moving products should generate a higher level of customer service than slow-moving products, on the theory that 20 per cent of the items account for 80 per cent of the sales. Thus an inventory manager attempts to keep an adequate supply of fast-selling items and a minimal supply of the slower-moving products. ABC sales: contribution analysis strives to maintain inventory levels while maximising financial returns to the business (see Figure 12.9).

**Transportation**
The process of moving a product from where it is made to where it is purchased and used

**Transport modes**
Methods of moving goods; these include railways, motor vehicles, inland waterways, airways and pipelines

# Transportation

**Transportation** adds time and place utility to a product by moving it from where it is made to where it is purchased and used.[29] Because product availability and timely deliveries are so dependent on transport functions, a company's choice of transport directly affects customer service and satisfaction. A business may even build its distribution and marketing strategy around a unique transport system if the system ensures on-time deliveries that will give the business a competitive edge. This section considers the principal modes of transport, the criteria companies use to select one mode over another, and several methods of coordinating transport services.

## Transport Modes

There are five major **transport modes**, or methods of moving goods: railways, motor vehicles, inland waterways, airways and pipelines. Each mode offers unique advantages; many companies have adopted physical handling procedures that facilitate the use of two or more modes in combination. Table 15.5 summarises the core transport modes.

## Criteria for Selecting Transport

Marketers select a transport mode on the basis of costs, transit time, reliability, capability, accessibility, security and traceability.[30] Table 15.6 summarises various cost and performance considerations that help determine the selection of transport modes. It is important to remember that these relationships are approximations and that the choice of a transport mode involves many trade-offs. These attributes all have a significant impact on a customer's perception of customer service levels.

## Table 15.5 Major Transport Modes

**Motor Vehicles**

Provide the most flexible schedules and routes of all transport modes because they can go almost anywhere. Uniquely can transport goods from factory or warehouse directly to customer. Other modes, such as rail or air freight, often depend on trucks and vans to complete the journey for goods being transported. More expensive than rail and prone to bad weather disruption. Restricted in terms of weight and size of loads. Often criticised for damage and pilferage of goods in transit. In response, new technology now tracks shipments and eases loading/handling. Computerised route planning is now the norm, with companies ensuring goods are delivered efficiently.

**Planning distribution routes**

Area routes connect customers in concentratred areas.

Arc (circumferential) routes link customers in arcs at different distances from the distribution centre.

Radial routes link customers in radial groups to and from the distribution centre.

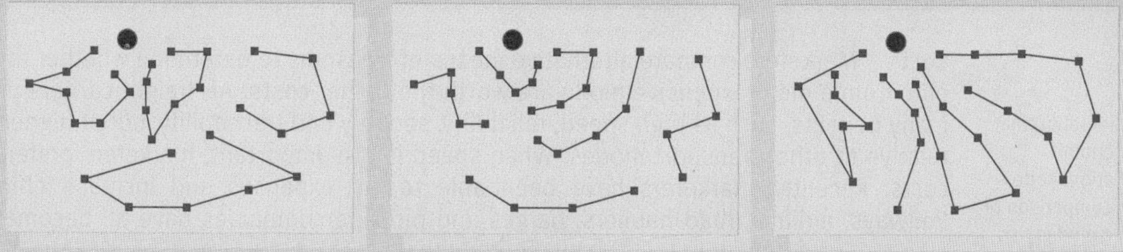

The figure above shows three types of routes which can be used, depending on vehicle capacity, order size, geographic characteristics and existence of suitable major routes. Road haulage dominates within Europe: quick, flexible and relatively cost efficient, it has overtaken rail.

**Rail**

Used for heavy, bulky freight that must be transported over land for long distances: minerals, sand, timber, pulp, chemicals, farm products, cars, low value manufactured goods. Efficient for transporting full wagon car loads with little handling, not for smaller quantities. Some factories and warehouses are purposively located adjacent to rail links. The opening of the Channel Tunnel has encouraged businesses to locate near the new Euro-hubs for cross-Channel rail freight. This trend may reverse the steady decline in rail freight tonnage. High fixed costs, shortages of wagons at peak times, poor track investment and increased competition from road and air hauliers have plagued European rail operators.

**Inland Waterways**

The cheapest method of shipping heavy, low value, non-perishable goods such as coal, grain, sand, petroleum. Considerable capacity: barges on inland rivers, canals and navigation systems can haul many times the weight of one railway wagon, but much more slowly. Require links with road and rail and can be hampered by harsh winters freezing waterways or summer droughts drying up channels. Although only of peripheral importance for freight in the UK, the inland waterways are very important in Germany and Benelux. Very fuel efficient haulage. Seen by many as an environmentally friendly transport solution. Observers believe tonnages will increase.

**Air Freight**

The fastest growing and most expensive form of shipping. Helped by the rapid growth in airport locations, flights and acceptance of this mode of transport. Generally deployed for perishable goods; high value, low bulk items; and products to be delivered long distances quickly, such as emergency products or replacement parts. Capacity is limited only by the size and number of aircraft. A medium-ranged jet carries about 18,000 kilos (40,000 pounds) of freight, but purpose built cargo planes can now carry up to 90,000 kilos (200,000 pounds). Most freight is carried on passenger aircraft, along with mail. Despite its expense, air freight reduces stockholding costs and in-transit losses from theft and damage. Ground transport for pick up and final delivery adds time and cost to the air freight bill.

*(continued...)*

**TABLE 15.5 MAJOR TRANSPORT MODES (CONTINUED)**

**Pipelines**

The most automated of transport modes, usually belong to the shipper and carry the shipper's products, typically petroleum or chemicals. The Trans-Alaska Pipeline, owned by a consortium of oil companies such as Exxon, Mobile and BP, transports crude oil from remote drilling sites to shipping terminals on the coast. Slurry pipelines have been developed to transport pulverised coal, grain or wood chips suspended in water. Pipelines move products slowly but continuously at relatively low cost. They are reliable and reduce damage to goods in transit and theft. However, their goods suffer from evaporation shrinkage, sometimes by up to 1 per cent, and minimum quantities of 25,000 barrels are required for efficient pipeline operation. North Sea oil and gas in Scandinavia, the Netherlands and the UK depend on pipelines. Installation leaks worry environmentalists, but oil tankers leak too.

**Sources:** Carl M. Guelzo, *Introduction to Logistics Management* (Englewood Cliffs, NJ: Prentice-Hall, 1986), pp. 50–52; John Gattorna, *Handbook of Physical Distribution Management* (Aldershot: Gower Publishing Co. Ltd, 1983), pp. 263–6; Charles A. Taff, *Management of Physical Distribution and Transportation* (Homewood, Ill.: Irwin, 1984), p. 126.

**Costs**
One consideration that helps determine transportation mode, involving comparison of alternative modes to determine whether the benefits of a more expensive mode are worth the higher costs

**Costs** Marketers compare alternative means of transport to determine whether the benefits from a more expensive mode are worth the higher **costs**. Air freight carriers provide many benefits, such as high speed, reliability, security and traceability, but at higher costs relative to other transport modes. When speed is less important, marketers prefer lower costs. Recently, marketers have been able to cut expenses and increase efficiency. Railways, airlines, road hauliers, barges and pipeline companies have all become more competitive and more responsive to customers' needs. Surveys reveal that in recent years transport costs per tonne and as a percentage of sales have declined, now averaging 7.5 per cent of sales. This figure varies by industry, of course: electrical machinery, textiles and instruments have transport costs of only 3 or 4 per cent of sales, whereas timber products, chemicals and food have transport costs close to 15 per cent of sales.

**Transit time**
The total time a carrier has possession of goods

**Transit Time** **Transit time** is the total time a carrier has possession of goods, including the time required for pick up and delivery, handling, and movement between the points of origin and destination. Closely related to transit time is frequency, or number of shipments per day. Transit time obviously affects a marketer's ability to provide service, but there are some less obvious implications as well. A shipper can take advantage of transit time to process orders for goods en route, a capability especially important for agricultural and raw materials shippers. Some railways also let shipments that are already in transit to be redirected, for maximum flexibility in selecting markets.

**Reliability**
The consistency of service provided

**Reliability** The total **reliability** of a transport mode is determined by the consistency of service provided. Marketers must be able to count on their carriers to deliver goods on time

**TABLE 15.6 RANKING OF TRANSPORT MODES BY SELECTING CRITERIA, HIGHEST TO LOWEST**

| | Costs | Transit time | Reliability | Capability | Accessibility | Security | Traceability |
|---|---|---|---|---|---|---|---|
| **Most** | Air | Water | Pipeline | Water | Road | Pipeline | Air |
| | Pipeline | Rail | Rail | Road | Rail | Water | Road |
| | Rail | Pipeline | Road | Rail | Air | Rail | Rail |
| | Road | Road | Air | Air | Water | Air | Water |
| **Least** | Water | Air | Water | Pipeline | Pipeline | Road | Pipeline |

**Source:** Selected information adapted from J. L. Heskett, Robert Ivie and J. Nicholas Glaskowsky, *Business Logistics* (New York: Ronald Press, 1973). Reprinted by permission of John Wiley & Sons, Inc.

and in an acceptable condition. Along with transit time, reliability affects a marketer's inventory costs, which include sales lost when merchandise is not available. Unreliable transport necessitates maintaining higher inventory levels to avoid stock-outs. Reliable delivery service, on the other hand, enables customers to save money by reducing inventories; for example, if pharmacists know that suppliers can deliver drugs within hours of ordering, they can carry a smaller inventory.

**Capability**
The ability of a transport mode to provide the appropriate equipment and conditions for moving specific kinds of goods

**Capability** **Capability** is the ability of a transport mode to provide the appropriate equipment and conditions for moving specific kinds of goods. For example, many products must be shipped under conditions of controlled temperature and humidity. Other products, such as liquids or gases, require special equipment or facilities for their shipment.

**Accessibility**
The ability to move goods over a specific route or network

**Accessibility** A carrier's **accessibility** refers to its ability to move goods over a specific route or network: flights, rail lines, waterways or roads.

**Security**
The measure of the physical condition of goods upon delivery

**Security** A transport mode's **security** is measured by the physical condition of goods on delivery. A business does not incur costs directly when goods are lost or damaged, because the carrier is usually held liable in these cases. Nevertheless, poor service and lack of security will lead indirectly to increased costs and lower profits for the company, since damaged or lost goods are not available for immediate sale or use. In some cases, companies find it necessary to transport products using courier companies such as UPS, TNT or Omega.

**Traceability**
The relative ease with which a shipment can be located and transferred

**Traceability** **Traceability** is the relative ease with which a shipment can be located and transferred – or found if it is lost. Quick traceability is a convenience that some businesses value highly. Shippers have learned that the ability to trace shipments, along with prompt invoicing and processing of claims, increases customer loyalty and improves a company's image in the marketplace.[31] Courier companies now offer clients Internet tracking of goods in transit.

## Coordinating Transport Services

**Inter-modal transport**
The combination and coordination of two or more modes of transport

To take advantage of the benefits various types of carrier offer, and to compensate for their deficiencies, marketers often must combine and coordinate two or more modes of transport. In recent years, **inter-modal transport**, as this integrated approach is sometimes called, has become easier because of new developments within the transport industry. Several kinds of inter-modal shipping are available, all combining the flexibility of road haulage with the low cost or speed of other forms of transport. Containerisation facilitates inter-modal transport by consolidating shipments into sealed containers for transport by piggyback (shipping that combines truck trailers and railway flatcars), fishyback (truck trailers and water carriers), and birdyback (truck trailers and air carriers). As transport costs increase, inter-modal services gain in popularity. Inter-modal services have been estimated to cost 25 to 40 per cent less than all-road transport in the USA, where they account for about 12 to 16 per cent of total transport business.[32]

**Freight forwarders**
Specialised agencies that coordinate and combine shipments from several businesses into efficient lot sizes

Specialised agencies, **freight forwarders**, provide other forms of transport coordination. These agencies combine shipments from several businesses into efficient lot sizes. Small loads – less than 225 kilos (500 pounds) – are much more expensive to ship than full lorry loads and frequently must be consolidated. The freight forwarder takes small loads from various shippers, buys transport space from carriers and arranges for the goods to be delivered to their respective buyers. The freight forwarder's profits come from the margin between the higher, less-than-full car load rates charged to each shipper and the lower car load rates the agency pays. Because large shipments require less handling, the use of a freight forwarder can speed transit time. Freight forwarders can also determine the most efficient carriers and routes, and are useful for shipping goods to foreign markets.

**Megacarriers**
Freight companies that provide several methods of shipment, such as rail, road and air service

One other transport innovation is the development of **megacarriers**, freight companies that provide several methods of shipment, such as rail, road and air service. Air carriers have increased their ground transport services. As they have expanded the range of transport alternatives, carriers have also placed greater emphasis on customer service.

## Strategic Issues in Physical Distribution

The physical distribution functions discussed in this chapter – order processing, materials handling, warehousing, inventory management and transportation – account for about a third of all marketing costs. Moreover, these functions have a significant impact on customer service and satisfaction, as well as people's perceptions of a brand's or business's image, which are of prime importance to marketers.[33] Effective marketers accept considerable responsibility for the design and control of the physical distribution system. They work to ensure that the business's overall marketing strategy is enhanced by physical distribution, with its dual objectives of decreasing costs while increasing customer service. Remember, to ensure that customers are satisfied, they must be able to obtain, within reason, the product or service when and where they want it and with a perception of 'no hassle'.

The strategic importance of physical distribution is evident in all elements of the marketing mix. Product design and packaging must allow for efficient stacking, storage and transport; decisions to differentiate products by size, colour and style must take into account the additional demands that will be placed on warehousing and shipping facilities. Competitive pricing may depend on a company's ability to provide reliable delivery or emergency shipments of replacement parts; a company trying to lower its inventory costs may offer quantity discounts to encourage large purchases. Promotional campaigns must be coordinated with distribution functions so that advertised products are available to buyers; order processing departments must be able to handle additional sales order information efficiently. Distribution planners must consider warehousing and transportation costs, which may influence, for example, the company's policy on stock-outs or its choice to centralise or decentralise its inventory.

No single distribution system is ideal for all situations, and any system must be evaluated continually and adapted as necessary. For instance, pressures to adjust service levels or reduce costs may lead to a total restructuring of the marketing channel relationships; changes in transportation, warehousing, materials handling and inventory may affect speed of delivery, reliability and economy of service. Marketing strategists must consider customers' changing needs and preferences, and recognise that changes in any one of the major distribution functions will necessarily affect all other functions. Consumer-oriented marketers will analyse the various characteristics of their target markets and *then* design distribution systems to provide products at acceptable costs. In many instances, external logistics specialists are subcontracted to handle inventory and physical distribution requirements. The use of third parties may in fact be fully outsourced: **outsourcing** is where a third party is empowered to manage and control a particular activity – such as catering, IT infrastructure management, fleet cars, human resources and recruitment or, as in this case, a company's logistics.

**Outsourcing**
Where a third-party organisation is empowered to manage and control a particular activity, such as logistics

# Summary

Wholesaling includes all transactions in which the purchaser intends to use the product for resale, for making other products or for general business operations. It does not include exchanges with the ultimate consumers. Hence, the term *wholesaling* is used in its broadest sense: intermediaries' activity in the marketing channel between producers and business-to-business customers to facilitate the exchange – buying and selling – of goods. Marketers use wholesaling to mean much more than the function of retail wholesalers, as described in the next chapter. *Wholesalers* are individuals or businesses that facilitate and expedite primarily wholesale transactions between producers and business-to-business customers. *Supply chain management* has become strategically important in recent years and, for marketers, this involves an improved appreciation of the role of wholesaling and marketing intermediaries.

- Except in many consumer markets, where large multiple retailers dominate, more than half of all goods are exchanged through wholesalers (middlemen in the distribution channel), although the distribution of any product requires that someone must perform wholesaling activities, whether or not a wholesaling institution is involved. For producers, wholesalers perform specialised accumulation and allocation functions for a number of products, letting the producers concentrate on developing and manufacturing the products. For retailers, wholesalers provide buying expertise, wide product lines, efficient distribution, and warehousing and storage services.

- Various types of wholesaler serve different market segments. How a wholesaler is classified depends on whether the wholesaler is owned by a producer, whether it takes title to products, the range of services it provides, and the breadth and depth of its product lines. The three general categories of wholesaler are (1) merchant wholesalers, (2) agents and brokers, and (3) manufacturers' sales branches and offices.

- *Merchant wholesalers* are independently owned businesses that take title to goods and assume risk; they account for over half of all wholesale revenues. They are either *full service wholesalers*, offering the widest possible range of wholesaling functions, or *limited service wholesalers*, providing only some marketing services and specialising in a few functions. Distributors buy and sell on their own account but tend to deal in the goods of only certain manufacturers. Full service wholesalers include: (1) *general merchandise wholesalers*, which offer a wide but relatively shallow product mix; (2) *limited line wholesalers*, which offer extensive assortments in a few product lines; and (3) *speciality line wholesalers*, which offer great depth in a single product line or in a few items within a line. *Rack jobbers* are speciality line wholesalers that own and service display racks in supermarkets and chemists. There are four types of limited service wholesalers. (1) *Cash-and-carry wholesalers* sell to small businesses, require payment in cash and do not deliver. (2) *Truck wholesalers* transport a limited line of products directly to customers for inspection and selection. (3) *Drop shippers* own goods and negotiate sales but never take possession of products. (4) *Mail-order wholesalers* sell to retail, industrial and institutional buyers through direct mail catalogues.

- Agents and brokers, sometimes called *functional middlemen*, negotiate purchases and expedite sales but do not take title to products. They are usually specialists and provide valuable sales expertise. *Agents* represent buyers or sellers on a permanent basis. *Manufacturers' agents* offer customers the complete product lines of two or more sellers; *selling agents* market a complete product line or a producer's entire output, and perform every wholesaling function except taking title to products; *commission merchants* receive goods on consignment from local sellers and negotiate sales in large central markets. *Brokers*, such as *food brokers*, negotiate exchanges between buyers and sellers on a temporary basis.

- Manufacturers' sales branches and offices are vertically integrated units owned by manufacturers. *Sales branches* sell products and provide support services for the manufacturer's salesforce in a given location. *Sales offices* carry no inventory, and function much as agents do.

- *Facilitating agencies* do not buy, sell or take title but perform certain activities that enhance channel functions. They include *public warehouses*, finance companies, transport companies, and *trade shows* and *trade markets*. In some instances, these organisations eliminate the need for a wholesaling establishment.

» The nature of the wholesaling and distribution industry is changing in response to changes in the marketing environment. The predominant changes are the increasing consolidation of the wholesaling industry and the growth of new types of wholesaler.

» *Physical distribution* is a set of activities that moves products from producers to consumers or end users. These activities include order processing, materials handling, warehousing, inventory management and transportation. While none of these activities would normally be the responsibility of marketing managers, their smooth deployment impacts on customer service levels, customer satisfaction and also customers' perceptions of a brand or business. An effective physical distribution system can be an important component of an overall marketing strategy, because it can decrease costs and lead to higher levels of customer satisfaction. Physical distribution activities should be integrated with marketing channel decisions and should be adjusted to meet the unique needs of a channel member. For most companies, physical distribution accounts for about a fifth of a product's retail price.

» The main *objective of physical distribution* is to decrease costs while increasing customer service. Physical distribution managers therefore try to balance service, distribution costs and resources. Companies must adapt to customers' needs and preferences, offer service comparable to – or better than – that of their competitors, and develop and communicate desirable *customer service* policies. The costs of providing service are minimised most effectively through the *total cost analysis* approach, which evaluates the costs of the system as a whole rather than as a collection of separate activities. *Cost trade-offs* must often be used to offset higher costs in one area of distribution against lower costs in another area.

» *Order processing*, the first stage in a physical distribution system, is the receipt and transmission of sales order information. Order processing consists of three main tasks: (1) order entry is the placement of purchase orders from customers or sales people by mail, telephone, fax or computer; (2) order handling involves checking customer credit, verifying product availability and preparing products for shipping; and (3) order delivery is provided by the carrier most suitable for a desired level of customer service. Order processing may be done manually or electronically, depending on which method gives greater speed and accuracy within cost limits. *Electronic data interchange (EDI)* helps facilitate order processing.

» *Materials handling*, or the physical handling of products, is an important element of physical distribution. Packaging, loading, movement and labelling systems must be coordinated to maximise cost reduction and customer requirements. Basic handling systems include *unit loading* on pallets or skids, permitting movement by mechanical devices, and *containerisation*, the practice of consolidating many items into a single large container.

» *Warehousing* involves the design and operation of facilities for storing and moving goods. It is important for companies to select suitable warehousing conveniently located close to main transport routes. *Private warehouses* are owned and operated by a company for the purpose of storing and distributing its own products. *Public warehouses* rent storage space and related physical distribution facilities to other companies. Public warehouses may furnish security for products that are being used as collateral for loans by establishing *field public warehouses*. They may also provide *bonded storage warehouses* for companies wishing to defer tax payments on imported or taxable products. *Distribution centres* are large, centralised warehouses specially designed to facilitate the rapid movement of goods to customers. In many cases, a combination of private and public facilities provides the most flexible approach to warehousing.

» The objective of *inventory management* is to minimise inventory costs while maintaining a supply of goods adequate for customers' needs. All inventory costs – carrying, replenishment and stock-out costs – must be controlled if profit goals are to be met. To avoid *stock-outs* without tying up too much capital in inventory, a business must have a systematic method of determining a *reorder point*, the inventory level at which more inventory is ordered. The *order lead time* is lapsed time between order placement and delivery. The *usage rate* is the rate at which inventory is used during a specific period of time. The trade-offs between the costs of carrying larger average *safety stocks* and the costs of frequent orders can be quantified using the *economic order quantity (EOQ)* model. Inventory problems may take the form of surplus inventory, late deliveries, write-offs and inventory that is too large in proportion to sales or assets. Methods for improving inventory management include systems that monitor stock levels continuously, and techniques such as just-in-time management and the 80/20 rule.

*Transportation* adds time and place utility to a product by moving it from where it is made to where it is purchased and used. The five major *transport modes* are motor vehicles, railways, inland waterways, airways and pipelines. Marketers evaluate transport modes with respect to *costs*, *transit time*, *reliability*, *capability*, *accessibility*, *security* and *traceability*; the final selection of a transport mode involves many trade-offs. *Inter-modal transport* allows marketers to combine the advantages of two or more modes of transport; this method is facilitated by containerisation, *freight forwarders* (who coordinate transport by combining small shipments from several businesses into efficient lot sizes) and *megacarriers* (freight companies that offer several methods of shipment).

Physical distribution affects every element of the marketing mix: product, price, promotion, place/distribution and personnel/customer service. To give customers products at acceptable prices, marketers consider consumers' changing needs and any shifts within the major distribution functions. They then adapt existing physical distribution systems for greater effectiveness. Physical distribution functions account for about a third of all marketing costs and have a significant impact on customer satisfaction. Therefore, effective marketers are actively involved in the design and control of physical distribution systems. Increasingly, many of the logistics activities described in this chapter are subject to *outsourcing*.

## Key Links

Although wholesaling and logistical support are rarely controlled by the marketing function, they do impact on the customer's ability to attain a product, and on the customer's experience, buying behaviour and satisfaction.

- This chapter should be read in conjunction with Chapter 14, which examines the nature of marketing channels and key participating channel members.

## Important Terms

Wholesaling
Wholesaler
Supply chain management
Merchant wholesalers
Full service wholesalers
Limited service wholesalers
General merchandise wholesalers
Distributors
Limited line wholesalers
Speciality line wholesalers
Rack jobbers
Cash and carry wholesalers
Truck wholesalers
Drop shippers
Mail-order wholesalers
Functional middlemen
Agents
Brokers
Manufacturers' agents
Selling agents
Commission merchants
Food brokers
Sales branches
Sales offices
Facilitating agencies
Public warehouses
Trade shows
Trade markets
Physical distribution
Objective of physical distribution
Customer service
Total cost analysis
Cost trade-offs
Order processing
Electronic data interchange (EDI)

Materials handling
Unit loading
Containerisation
Warehousing
Private warehouse
Public warehouses
Field public warehouse
Bonded storage warehouse
Distribution centre
Inventory management
Stock-outs
Reorder point
Order lead time
Usage rate
Safety stock
Economic order quantity (EOQ)
Transportation
Transport modes
Costs
Transit time
Reliability
Capability
Accessibility
Security
Traceability
Inter-modal transport
Freight forwarders
Megacarriers
Outsourcing

## Discussion and Review Questions

1 Is there a distinction between wholesalers and wholesaling? If so, what is it?
2 Generically, what services do wholesalers provide to producers and retailers?
3 Drop shippers take title to products but do not accept physical possession. Commission merchants take physical possession of products but do not accept title. Defend the logic of classifying drop shippers as wholesale merchants and agents as commission merchants.
4 What are the advantages of using agents to replace merchant wholesalers? What are the disadvantages?
5 Why are manufacturers' sales offices and branches classified as wholesalers? Which independent wholesalers are replaced by manufacturers' sales branches? Which independent wholesalers are replaced by manufacturers' sales offices?
6 Discuss the role of facilitating agencies. Identify three facilitating agencies and explain how each type performs this role.
7 Discuss the cost and service trade-offs involved in developing a physical distribution system.
8 What factors must physical distribution managers consider when developing a customer service mix?
9 What is the advantage of using a total cost approach to distribution?
10 What are the main tasks involved in order processing?
11 How does a product's package affect materials-handling procedures and techniques?
12 Explain the major differences between private and public warehouses. What is a field public warehouse?
13 Describe the costs associated with inventory management.
14 How can managers improve inventory control? Give specific examples of techniques.
15 Compare the five major transport modes in terms of costs, transit time, reliability, capability, accessibility, security and traceability.
16 Discuss how the elements of the marketing mix affect physical distribution strategy.

## Recommended Readings


- Christopher, M., *Marketing Logistics* (Oxford: Butterworth-Heinemann, 2003).
- Christopher, M., *Logistics and Supply Chain Management* (Harlow: Pearson/FT, 1999).
- Friedman, L. and Furey, T., *The Channel Advantage* (Oxford: Butterworth-Heinemann, 1999).
- Gattorna, J., ed., *Strategic Supply Chain Alignment: Best Practices in Supply Chain Management* (Aldershot: Gower, 1998).
- Hines, T., *Supply Chain Strategies* (Oxford: Butterworth-Heinemann, 2003).
- Lambert, D.M. and Stock, J.R., *Strategic Logistics Management* (Homewood, Ill.: Richard D. Irwin, 1993).
- Rosenbloom, B., *Marketing Channels: A Management View* (Cincinnati, OH: South Western, 2003).
- Waters, D., *Global Logistics and Distribution Planning: Strategies for Management* (London: Kogan Page, 2003).


## Internet Exercise

Look at the websites for leading haulage and freight-forwarding companies, such as Fritz, Stobbard or Excel.

1 What are the principal services offered by such businesses?
2 Why would such services be of concern to marketers in a client business of such logistics companies?

## Applied Mini-Case

FedEx Custom Critical is a service provided by the global delivery company that focuses on meeting critical delivery times. Weekdays and weekends, at any hour, in any weather, FedEx Custom Critical is ready to collect a shipment within 90 minutes of a customer's call. Once the company sets a delivery time, it guarantees to have the cargo at its destination within 15 minutes of that time. If the delivery is late, the customer receives a substantial refund or discount. FedEx rarely has to give discounts. However, the company has to make money on this service and depends on technology to operate it efficiently and reliably. Its vehicles are equipped with satellite dishes and computers to facilitate tracking and route planning. When required, trained operators can use special equipment for fragile, hazardous or precious loads. While not necessary for all loads, many manufacturers and suppliers may have use for such a 'time critical' service at some point in time.

### Question

How do FedEx Custom Critical and similar services relate to the issues of customer service and costs of physical distribution within the distribution channel?

## Case Study

### Today's Cash and Carry Mega-depots Depend on Effective Stockholding and Physical Distribution

The wholesale grocery trade is worth £16 billion in the UK, 42 per cent of which is delivered trade and 58 per cent cash and carry. Cash and carry businesses stock manufacturers' products and have as their customers other businesses, which select merchandise appropriate for their respective target consumers. In order to satisfy the demands of small retail businesses, for example, the leading grocery cash and carry operators have to stock extensive ranges, only a small part of which may be selected by an individual retailer client. Inventory control is particularly important to these cash and carry businesses, but so too are the logistical considerations of receiving deliveries from manufacturers and enabling customers to take out their orders. In the UK, Today's Supergroup operates 346 depots with an average size of 30,000 square feet, while Booker has 177 depots at an average of 80,000 square feet; Makro, however, has 30 depots at an average size of 150,000 square feet. For Makro, the task of replenishing such mighty cash-and-carry depots is a core part of its business proposition.

Although price remains a core trading proposition, service and brand image are increasingly important. Indeed, the cash and carry sector was shaken up by the entry of Holland's Makro, a self-service wholesaler. Makro is part of SHV Holdings, a large international distribution and energy company, and one of the largest companies in the Netherlands. Makro's depots have the latest computer systems, customer service points and in-store displays. Makro serves the trade as a cash and carry wholesaler of groceries, fresh foods, wines, spirits, beer and cigarettes, household goods, clothing, toys and sports equipment. The company retails a clutch of own-label brands in these categories, including Aro, Louis Chevalier and Roca.

In a relatively traditional sector dominated by several long-standing companies, Dutch Makro had a major impact in a short time. Its mix of merchandise is more comprehensive than that of its competitors, forcing several – such as Booker and Landmark – to rethink their merchandising strategies. Because depth and breadth of stock within individual product categories are not as extensive as those of UK rivals, the industry has been prompted to rethink, and most companies have reduced the number of lines stocked. Although not the first wholesaler with own-label products, Makro's promotion of its own ranges has encouraged its competitors to divert more attention to this area.

Perhaps Makro's biggest impact has been in the sales and marketing techniques it has brought to the UK. Cash and carry warehouses used to be dowdy depots that paid little attention to layout, upkeep, design or ambience, and demonstrated even less regard for customer service and satisfaction. Price was the name of the game: customers could buy in bulk at a discount but were offered few additional benefits. Makro's philosophy brings to the cash and carry sector the retailing techniques of the hypermarket: carefully controlled branch designs and layouts, high levels of staff training and a significant emphasis on building ongoing relationships with customers. An emphasis on managing its inventory and the associated need for effective physical distribution are pivotal to Makro's ability to serve its business customers in the retail and catering trades.

Makro's philosophy is encouraging other wholesalers to follow suit. Now customers are being offered better service, together with assistance in building their own company image through local press and television advertising. The leading cash and carry companies are offering marketing support to their key accounts not just to stimulate sales but also to build up those customers' loyalty to their nearby warehouse. Depots have been uprated by the leading groups, with new equipment, better stocking systems and improved physical distribution. They have also initiated sales promotions campaigns and incentive programmes. Computerisation has helped lower costs and improve efficiency. For example, with Germany's Siemens Nixdorf, Booker created MIDAS (management information depot application system), giving each of its depots a comprehensive invoicing, mailing, sales data, customer information and stock control system. This system improved Booker's ability to target customers and monitor stock needs. Systems such as MIDAS have enabled the leading companies to reduce their product lines without alienating customers. For example, Nurdin & Peacock used to carry 60,000 lines but reduced its coverage to 40,000 without losing customers. In most of the leading businesses, branches are being rationalised, both to respond to economic downturns, and to benefit from cost economies and enhanced computer systems. For example, companies are either consolidating three outdated neighbouring depots into one central, spacious, service-oriented depot, or they are closing a branch while extending and refurbishing a neighbouring one.

**Sources:** Nick Higham, 'Independent – at any price?', *Marketing Week*, 11 February 1994, p. 19; Makro Leicester; *Marketing Pocket Book* (WARC Publications, 2004); Charles Thurston, 'Testing Latin waters', *Global Finance*, June 1995, p. 25; Institute of Grocery Distribution – *Grocery Wholesaling* 2003; Today's Supergroup, 2004; Booker Cash & Carry, 2004; Makro, 2004.

## Questions for Discussion

1 How are the major cash and carry companies responding to changing customer needs?
2 In what ways are state-of-the-art inventory management and physical distribution systems important to companies such as Makro or Booker?

# 16 Retailing

**"The power, prestige and proactivity of major retailers now exceeds that of their manufacturer suppliers."**

*Peter J. McGoldrick, Manchester Business School*

## Objectives

- **To understand the purpose and function of retailing in the marketing channel**
- **To describe and distinguish retail locations and major store types**
- **To understand non-store retailing and franchising**
- **To learn about strategic issues addressed by retail marketers**
- **To appreciate the current trends in retailing**

## Introduction

Retailers are an important part of the marketing channel for many products. In addition to being part of the distribution channel for a host of products, the characteristics of retailing present retail marketers with many challenges.

Retailers are an influential link in the marketing channel because they are both marketers for, and customers of, producers and wholesalers. They perform many marketing activities, such as buying, selling, grading, risk-taking and developing information about consumers' requirements. Of all marketers, retailers are often the most visible to ultimate consumers. They are in a strategic position to gain feedback from consumers, and to relay ideas to producers and intermediaries in the marketing channel. Retailing is an extraordinarily dynamic area of marketing.

## Opener

## Makro's Retail Marketers Respond to Client Needs

Makro is a leading international cash and carry company targeting primarily catering and retail customers. Makro's marketers are not retailing to private consumers: the company's target markets are other businesses, such as cafés, restaurants, canteens, and retailers. Owned by Dutch holding company SHV, which also owns Calor Gas and NPM Capital, Makro truly is a global cash and carry retailer, with depots across the world, from Belgium, Brazil and Malaysia to South Africa. Forever at the forefront of retailing technologies and systems, Makro's marketers strive to reflect evolving customer requirements.

In Thailand, for example, Makro has just launched the Fresh Educational Programme, an intensive staff training course designed to support the company's new 'fresh' concept for fresh produce. Makro's business customers increasingly require greater variety and quantity of fresh foods as their own customers become more discerning and less tolerant of pre-prepared foods. The sales area inside Makro stores allocated to fresh produce has been trebled in size, responding to Makro's business clients in the sectors of catering and retailing placing greater emphasis on fresh produce. This 'fresh' concept has boosted Makro's sales, attracted more customers and, importantly, increased customer satisfaction: all goals at the very heart of the marketing principle.

Makro has always concentrated on meeting evolving customer requirements. Likewise, the catering and retail customers who shop there have to meet the requirements of their own customers. Makro has to ensure that trade customers can be guaranteed a good-quality product at prices that will enable caterers to hold firm their own menu prices. Inconsistent product quality and fluctuating prices would cause problems for clients wanting to offer a consistent menu to their customers at stable prices. If product availability, quality, delivery and pricing varied rapidly and significantly, many business customers might cease purchasing from Makro.

The retailing of fresh fish by Makro is a case in point. Clients must be reassured that if they require a particular quantity of a certain variety of fish, they will in fact find the right availability at a Makro depot. The fish must be fresh: employees are trained in checking freshness and in how to deal with any merchandise that falls below Makro's high standards. These procedures are replicated for all fresh products, vegetables, meat and poultry retailed by Makro. Attractive displays of such merchandise are integral to the marketing mix offered to customers, so staff are trained and dressed accordingly. Staff must be able to clean the fresh produce and offer advice to customers on how to handle the fresh produce, store and prepare it, and even how to cook it.

The Fresh Educational Programme is an intensive seven-day training event designed to address these requirements. Programme participants are Makro fresh produce buyers, coordinators, store managers, section heads and customer development managers. Operational procedures are part of the programme, as are the use of CRM systems and the importance of financial aspects. In addition to formal training sessions, the programme includes visits to catering and retail clients, cookery classes and market surveys. The intention is to create an enhanced appreciation of customers' needs by listening to them, seeing how they operate and observing them in order to learn from their purchasing practices. Not only is the 'fresh' initiative reflecting customers' expectations, but the associated training programme is enabling Makro employees to properly understand the buying requirements and product usage issues of customers.

**Sources:** Makro Thailand; *Sharing News*, 11, April 2004; SHV Holdings, Utrecht. Photo: Courtesy of Makro

In order to understand the issues faced by retail marketers, this chapter first examines the nature of retailing, before moving on to examine retail store locations, store types and the 'standard' categories of retailing activity, including cash and carry businesses such as Makro. Of course, not all retailing activity requires stores: with the growth of e-commerce and direct marketing – as described in Chapters 4 and 19 – non-store retailing is increasing. This chapter examines in-home retailing, telemarketing, automatic vending, mail order and catalogue retailing. The use of franchising in retailing is also discussed. The chapter then addresses strategic issues in retailing, including location decisions, property ownership, product assortment, retail positioning, atmospherics, store image, scrambled merchandising, the role of merchandising or professional buying, the wheel of retailing, the balance of retailing power and technology. Finally, there is an overview of recent research examining current trends, focusing on developments in company ownership and competitive strategy, consumer trends impacting on retailers' strategies, branding, information and technology impact on retail strategy, the use of multiple retail formats within certain retailers' portfolios, and micro (localised) marketing mix manipulation by national retail chains.

## The Nature of Retailing

**Retailing**
All transactions in which the buyer intends to consume the product through personal, family or household use

**Retailer**
A business that purchases products for the purpose of reselling them to ultimate consumers – the general public – often from a shop or store

**Retailing** includes all transactions in which the buyer intends to consume the product through personal, family or household use. The buyers in retail transactions are the ultimate consumers. A **retailer**, then, is a business that purchases products for the purpose of reselling them to the ultimate consumers, the general public, often from a shop or store. As the link between producers and consumers, retailers occupy an important and highly demanding position in the marketing channel. It is complicated, too: retailers sell other companies' products, yet have to devise their own product/service mixes. They devise their own target market strategies and conduct analyses of marketing opportunities. The merchandise they sell derives from producers that have undertaken their own analysis of marketing opportunities and developed their own target market strategies and brand positionings. These strategies – producers' and retailers' – have, to a degree, to mesh in order for all channel members to make adequate financial returns, while ultimately striving to give satisfaction to the consumer. The growth of retail own-label brands has added to the complexity, with retailers now creating their own brands, products and designs of merchandise, often retailed alongside the proprietary brands of manufacturers. Although most retailers' sales are to consumers, non-retail transactions occasionally occur when retailers sell products to other businesses. Retailing activities usually take place in a store or in a service establishment, but exchanges through telephone selling, vending machines, mail-order retailing and the Internet occur outside stores. Such non-store sales are increasing owing largely to the growth of e-commerce and direct marketing. On-line retailing and e-commerce are explored further in Chapter 4. Indeed, new store formats and advances in information technology are making the retail store environment highly dynamic and competitive. For example, instant messaging technology is helping on-line retailers converse with customers so they don't click away to another site. Rather than e-mail a retail site and wait for a response, shoppers on Lands' End's website simply click to communicate directly with a customer service representative about size, colour or other product details.[1]

It is common knowledge that retailing is important to the economy, being a large employer and major service sector component. Table 16.1, for example, shows the level of retail sales in the UK. Also, most disposable personal income is spent in retail stores. There are 188,700 VAT-registered retail businesses in the UK, trading from 310,000 stores. In 2003, retail sales were £235.6 billion and accounted for 5.6 per cent of Gross Value Added. According to the British Retail Consortium, over a third of consumer spending goes through shops, and the retail industry employs over 2.7 million people or 11 per cent of the UK workforce.[2]

By providing assortments of products to match consumers' requirements, retailers create place, time, possession and form utilities:

- *Place utility* means moving products from wholesalers or producers to a location where consumers want to buy them.
- *Time utility* involves maintaining specific business hours to make products available when consumers want them.
- *Possession utility* means facilitating the transfer of ownership or use of a product to consumers.
- In the case of services such as hairdressing, dry cleaning, restaurants and car repairs, retailers themselves develop most of the product utilities. The services of such retailers provide aspects of *form utility* associated with the production process.

Retailers of services usually have more direct contact with consumers and more opportunity to alter the product in the marketing mix (see Chapter 13).

**TABLE 16.1 VOLUME OF UK RETAIL SALES, 1997–2002**

Index numbers of sales per week (average 1995 prices), 1995 = 100

| | | | | Predominantly non-food stores | | | | |
|---|---|---|---|---|---|---|---|---|
| | All retailers (3205) | Predominantly food stores (1441) | Total (1600) | Non-specialised stores (289) | Textile clothing & footwear (602) | Household goods (380) | Other stores (428) | Non-store retailers/ repair (165) |
| 1997 | 109 | 106 | 111 | 112 | 111 | 117 | 106 | 106 |
| 1998 | 112 | 109 | 114 | 112 | 112 | 125 | 109 | 112 |
| 1999 | 116 | 111 | 120 | 115 | 117 | 135 | 113 | 115 |
| 2000 | 121 | 114 | 128 | 122 | 125 | 149 | 117 | 116 |
| 2001 | 128 | 118 | 138 | 129 | 137 | 162 | 124 | 119 |
| 2002 | 134 | 122 | 147 | 135 | 151 | 169 | 130 | 126 |

**Note:** Figures in brackets refer to average weekly sales in 1995 (£ million).
**Sources:** 'Business Monitor SDM28 – Retail Sales', National Statistics © Crown Copyright 2003; *The European Marketing Pocket Book*, published by the World Advertising Research Center, Henley-on-Thames, 2004.

# Retail Locations

## Central Business District

**Central business district (CBD)**
The traditional hub of most cities and towns; the focus for shopping, banking and commerce, and hence the busiest part of the whole area

**Prime pitch**
The area at the centre of the shopping zone with the main shops and the highest levels of pedestrian footfall

**Customer threshold**
The number of customers required to make a profit

The traditional hub of most cities and towns is the **central business district (CBD)**, the focus for shopping, banking and commerce, and hence the busiest part of the whole area for traffic, public transport and pedestrians. Examples are London's Oxford and Regent streets, the Champs Elysées in Paris and Berlin's Kurfürstendamm.[3] The CBD is sub-divided into zones: generally, retailers are clustered together in a zone; banking and insurance companies locate together; legal offices occupy neighbouring premises; municipal offices and amenities are built on adjoining plots (town hall, library, law courts, art galleries).

Within the shopping zone certain streets at the centre of the zone will have the main shops and the highest levels of pedestrian footfall. In this area, known as the **prime pitch**, the key traders or magnets (Marks & Spencer, Boots or major department stores) will occupy prominent sites, so generating much of the footfall. Other retailers vie to be located close to these key traders so as to benefit from the customer traffic they generate. The highest rents are therefore paid for such sites. The CBD shopping centre – the city or town centre – generally offers shopping goods and some convenience items. Clothing, footwear, jewellery, cosmetics and financial services dominate the CBD. For the most part, grocers have moved out of town, along with furniture and DIY[4] stores.

Property developers build shopping malls or centres in and around the CBD. Each development has one or more magnets (big-name variety or department stores) both to attract shoppers and to encourage other retailers to locate within the development. Most city centres now have one covered shopping centre development (Eldon Square in Newcastle, the Victoria Centre in Nottingham).[5] On streets adjacent to this area of prime pitch, rents are lower but so is footfall. These secondary sites are suitable for speciality retailers or discounters, which have either lower margins or lower **customer thresholds** – the number of customers required to make a profit. Figure 16.1 shows the composition of a typical central business district (CBD).

*Figure 16.1*
*The composition of a typical central business district (CBD) Source: Lyndon Simkin and Sally Dibb*

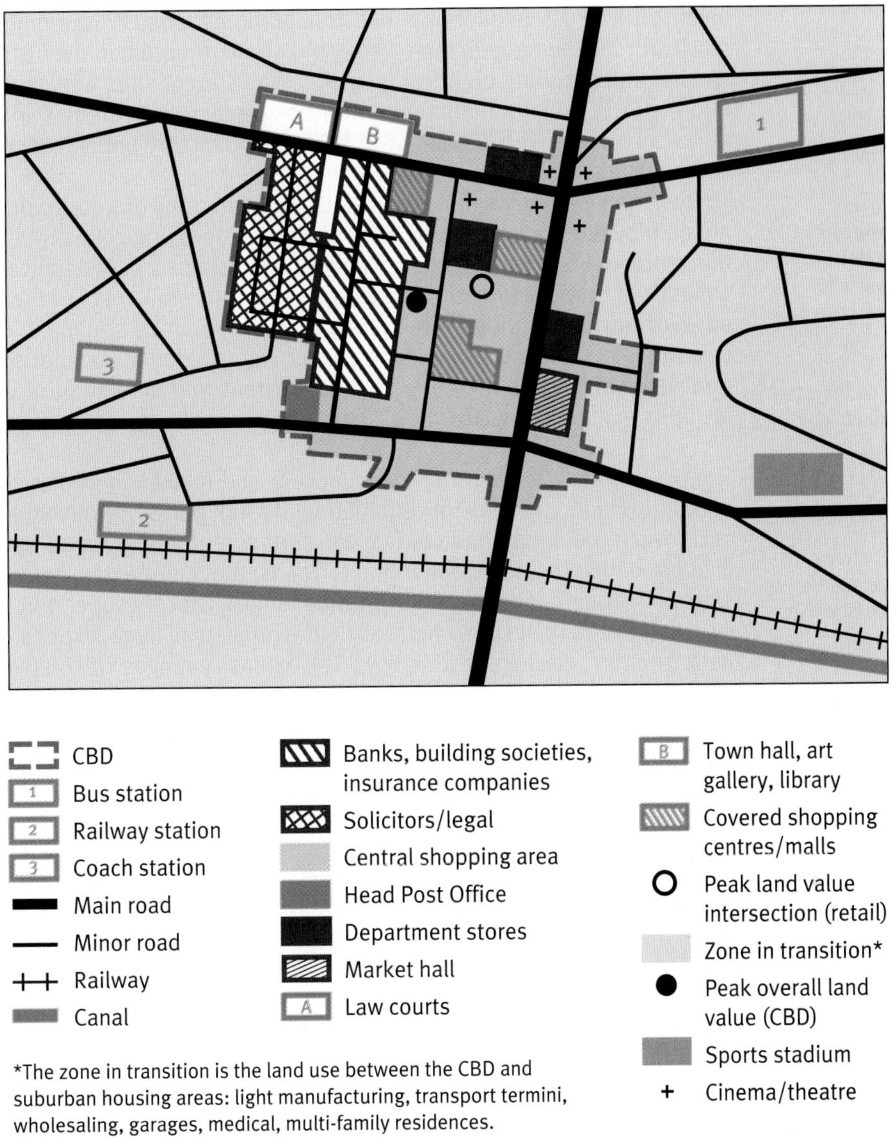

| | | |
|---|---|---|
| ⊏⊐ CBD | ▨ Banks, building societies, insurance companies | B Town hall, art gallery, library |
| 1 Bus station | ▨ Solicitors/legal | ▨ Covered shopping centres/malls |
| 2 Railway station | Central shopping area | |
| 3 Coach station | Head Post Office | ○ Peak land value intersection (retail) |
| ▬ Main road | Department stores | Zone in transition* |
| — Minor road | ▨ Market hall | ● Peak overall land value (CBD) |
| ┼┼ Railway | A Law courts | |
| ▬ Canal | | Sports stadium |
| | | + Cinema/theatre |

*The zone in transition is the land use between the CBD and suburban housing areas: light manufacturing, transport termini, wholesaling, garages, medical, multi-family residences.

## Suburban Centres

**Suburban centres**
Shopping centres created at major road junctions that cater for local shopping needs

Historically, as urban areas expanded during the early part of the twentieth century, they joined and subsequently swallowed up neighbouring towns and villages. The shopping centres of these settlements survived to become the **suburban centres** of the now larger city or town. Where the expansion of the town was planned, suburban centres were created at major road junctions to cater for local shopping needs and reduce demands and congestion in the CBD.[6] Suburban centres tend to offer convenience goods (frequently demanded cheaper items, such as groceries and drugs) and some shopping goods (clothing and footwear). Apart from a supermarket or limited-range variety store (such as Woolworth), the shops tend to be small store outlets from 150 to 250 square metres (1650 to 2750 square feet); many are privately owned – unlike those in the CBD, which tend to be owned by national retail chains.

## Edge-of-town Sites

During the 1970s, as rents in the CBD rose and sites sufficient for large, open-plan stores became harder to obtain, retailers looked to the green fields adjacent to outer ring roads for expansion. The superstore era had dawned as the major grocery, carpet and furniture, electrical and DIY retailers opened free-standing 'sheds'. Needing more space to display stock and sell their goods than they could afford or obtain in the CBD or even suburban centre, but still requiring high traffic levels, they sought sites adjacent to major road arteries into the CBD. Initially, planning authorities protected green-belt and undeveloped land, so the retailers occupied disused warehouses and factory units in once thriving industrial and commercial areas.

The planners then began to realise that stylish retail outlets could brighten up areas, create employment, attract traffic and rejuvenate decaying zones. Major retail chains such as the grocery retailers with their frequently purchased convenience goods attracted large volumes of traffic. Relocating these stores to non-retail areas of the city, and particularly to **edge-of-town sites**, helped redistribute traffic volumes and make use of the latest infrastructure. Retailers no longer had to occupy run-down warehouses; they could acquire undeveloped land on the edge of built-up areas and provide purpose-built stores, parking facilities and amenities for their customers.[7]

**Edge-of-town sites**
Retail locations on undeveloped land, providing purpose-built stores, parking facilities and amenities for their customers on the edge of a built-up area

### Retail Parks

**Retail parks**
Groupings of free-standing superstores, forming a retail village

The progression of the out-of-town concept and relaxation of planning regulations by local authorities led to the mid-1980s initiation of **retail parks**, in which free-standing superstores, each over 2500 square metres (27,500 square feet) are grouped together to form retail villages or parks. Located close to major roads, they offer extensive free parking. Most of the stores offer one-floor shopping with wide ranges. Grocery superstores locate so as to be easily accessible to their consumers, as do the retailers of large, expensive shopping goods: carpets, furniture, electrical goods, toys. The extensive ranges and displays of DIY retailers make such locations viable. Increasingly, planners are allowing clothing and footwear retailers to locate out of town. They initially feared the demise of the CBD, but forecasts now show that both CBD and out-of-town centres can survive serving the same town or city.

Most retail parks provide only superstores, but some have shopping malls of speciality and chain stores, such as Birmingham's Merry Hill or Gateshead's Metro Centre. Many shoppers now visit the CBD and retail parks for a leisure activity as much as a purchasing activity. The time when 'serious' shopping took place just once a week is long gone: many consumers shop several times each week, aided by the now commonplace Sunday opening of many retail stores. Leisure facilities are frequently incorporated to cater for a family day out: ice-skating rinks, cinemas, children's play areas, restaurants, fast-food outlets and food courts.

## Major Store Types

### Department and Variety Stores

**Department stores**
Physically large stores that occupy prominent positions in the traditional heart of the town or city, or as anchor stores in out-of-town malls

Retail stores are often classified according to width of product mix and depth of product lines. **Department stores** are physically large – around 25,000 square metres (275,000 square feet) – and occupy prominent positions in the traditional heart of the town or city, the central shopping centre. Out-of-town shopping malls, such as Manchester's Trafford Park or Kent's Bluewater, include leading department stores as 'anchors' to attract consumers and smaller retail store tenants. Department stores are characterised by wide product mixes in considerable depth for most product lines. Most towns have at least one such store; larger towns and cities have the population size to support several. The smaller town's department store is generally independently owned, whereas the larger store groups – Debenhams, House of Fraser, John Lewis or Allders in the UK; AuHPrintemps in France; El Corte Ingles in Spain; Karlstadt in Germany – have stores in many cities. Within a department store, related product lines are organised into separate departments such as cosmetics, men's and women's fashions and accessories, housewares, home furnishings, haberdashery and toys. Each department functions as a self-contained business unit, and the buyers for individual departments are fairly autonomous. Financial services, hairdressing and restaurants or coffee shops act as additional 'pulls' to attract customers into the store.

***Figure 16.2***
*Department store chain John Lewis' branch on Oxford Street in London Photo: Courtesy of John Lewis*

Quite often, concessionaires operate 'shops within shops'. Brides had its own bridal shops and agencies in secondary locations but also operated the bridal departments in many Debenhams and House of Fraser department stores. Concessionaires either pay a fixed rental per square metre of space occupied in the host department store or a percentage commission on the volume of business. In department stores, concessions or shops-within-shops are typical for fashion clothing, cosmetics and housewares.

Throughout the 1970s and 1980s, with the growth of shopping malls and covered centres, the explosion in the number of speciality shops and the move to out-of-town shopping, the demise of department stores was predicted. Yet they are still at the heart of many CBD shopping centres. With new management teams and investment, most department store groups are once again thriving and expanding, building new stores in towns where they were not previously represented and in out-of-town retail parks, as well as refurbishing existing outlets. Consumers have been educated to expect improved levels of customer service, and department store retailers are well placed to provide such service as well as a conducive shopping environment.

**Variety stores**
Slightly smaller and more specialised stores than department stores, offering a reduced range of merchandise

**Variety stores** tend to be slightly smaller and are often more specialised, offering a reduced range of merchandise. Their appeal tends to be middle market, price points are more critical and the selection of additional services is limited compared with a department store, usually to just coffee shops. C&A focuses on men's, women's and children's clothing; Marks & Spencer on clothing and food; Bhs and Littlewoods on clothing and housewares; Woolworth on housewares, CDs and DVDs, children's clothing and confectionery. Variety stores are characterised by low-cost facilities, self-service shopping, central payment points and multiple purchases; they appeal to large, heterogeneous target markets, especially price-conscious customers.

## Grocery Supermarkets, Superstores and Hypermarkets

In the 1960s, grocery retailers – led by Sainsbury's, Tesco and Fine Fare – expanded in to 1000-square-metre (11,000-square-foot) supermarkets, either in the city centre or within suburban centres. As product ranges grew, self-service requirements called for more space; and as city centre rents rose, the age of the superstore arrived. Size requirements grew further still, and there was an exodus from the city centre. In the 1980s, the average grocery superstore grew from 2500 square metres to 5500 square metres (27,500 to 61,000 square feet) and moved away from the suburban centre either to free-standing superstore sites or out-of-town retail parks with plenty of car parking.

**Supermarkets** and grocery **superstores**
Large, self-service stores that carry a complete line of food products as well as other convenience items

**Hypermarkets**
Stores that take the benefits of the superstore even further, using their greater size to give the customer a wider range and depth of products

**Supermarkets** and grocery **superstores** are large, self-service stores that carry a complete line of food products as well as other convenience items, such as cosmetics, non-prescription drugs and kitchenwares. Some, such as ASDA or Tesco, sell clothing and small electrical appliances. Grocery superstores are laid out in departments for maximum efficiency in stocking and handling products, but have central checkout facilities by the exits to the ample, free parking. Indeed, category management is now a core approach to merchandising, inventory control and display in many retailers, with similar lines from several suppliers being controlled by a category manager. Prices are considerably lower than in the independently owned supermarkets based in suburban shopping centres or in neighbourhood grocery shops. An increase in the number of price-conscious consumers demanding greater choice, improved packaging and refrigeration, as well as the advent of widespread car ownership, spurred the huge growth of major grocery superstore retailers Tesco, ASDA, Sainsbury's, Morrisons and Safeway.

Of the top retailers in Europe (see Table 16.2), many are superstore-trading grocery companies including the top five-ranked retail groups. They are at the forefront of retail technology – barcode-scanning EPoS (electronic point-of-sale) tills, shelf allocation modelling, robotised warehouse stacking, CRM systems and loyalty schemes – and of monitoring

**TABLE 16.2 EUROPE'S LARGEST RETAILERS**

| Company | Country HQ | Revenue $m |
|---|---|---|
| Carrefour | France | 64,683 |
| Ahold | Netherlands | 59,184 |
| Metro | Germany | 48,493 |
| Tesco | UK | 40,353 |
| J Sainsbury | UK | 26,939 |
| Pinault-Printemps-Redoute | France | 25,764 |
| Rallye | France | 22,287 |
| Delhaize Group | Belgium | 19,471 |
| Kingfisher | UK | 16,266 |

**Source:** *Forbes International 500*; www.forbes.com.

**Discount sheds**
Cheaply constructed, one-storey retail stores with no window displays and few add-on amenities; oriented towards car-borne shoppers

changes in customer attitudes and expectations. Increasingly, to gain an edge over the competition, they are launching more own-label products with attributes equal to, if not better than, the manufacturers' brands also on sale. In some leading supermarkets, own-label lines and non-branded fresh produce now account for 50 per cent of sales. The grocery retailers have led the transition in Europe, crossing national borders to trade in many countries. This move was initiated by the discounters, such as Aldi and Netto, plus several full-service retailers such as Holland's Ahold, France's Carrefour and, recently in eastern Europe, the UK's Tesco.

**Hypermarkets** take the benefits of the superstore even further, using their greater size – over 9000 square metres (100,000 square feet) – to give the customer a wider range and depth of products. They are common in the USA, France and Germany, but there are few genuine hypermarkets in the UK, except perhaps for Sainsbury's Savacentre.

## Discount Sheds and 'Category Killers'

**Category killers**
Large stores, tending to be superstore sized, which specialise in a narrow line of merchandise

**Warehouse clubs**
Large-scale, members-only selling operations combining cash-and-carry wholesaling with discount retailing

**Speciality shops**
Stores that offer self-service but a greater level of assistance from store personnel than department stores, and carry a narrow product mix with deep product lines

**Convenience stores**
Shops that sell essential groceries, alcoholic drinks, drugs and newspapers outside the traditional shopping hours

The move away from the city or town centre was not confined to multiple grocery retailers. Furniture, carpets and electrical appliances require large display areas, ranges with strength in depth and, if possible, one-floor shopping. The concentration of retailers in the city centre led to limited store opening opportunities – large enough sites were hard to find – and to high rents. When the electrical retailer Comet and furniture retailers Queensway and MFI sought out-of-town sites, they were initially forced by the planning authorities to occupy disused warehouses and industrial units along arteries into the city centre. As the planners reviewed their regulations, these companies, along with the major DIY and toy retailers, developed purpose-built discount 'sheds' or retail warehouses. Originally free-standing, these 2000- to 3500-square-metre (22,000- to 39,000-square-foot) stores are increasingly found in out-of-town retail parks.

**Discount sheds** are cheaply constructed, one-storey retail stores with no window displays and few add-on amenities. Oriented towards car-borne shoppers, they have large, free car parks and spacious stock facilities to enable shoppers to take delivery of their purchases immediately. Checkout points and customer services are kept to a minimum. As major retail groups have seen the cost benefits of locating out of town, more companies have opened out-of-town, free-standing or retail park superstores. Many customers would not tolerate the minimalist approach to ambience and service levels. Construction is still basic, but more resources are devoted to shopfitting expertise and customer service. US retailer Toys 'Я' Us and Sweden's IKEA typify the new generation of superstores. Most retail groups selling electrical goods, carpets, furniture, toys, groceries or DIY goods, not just the discounters, now operate superstores. Increasingly, major variety store companies, departmental store groups, and clothing and footwear retailers are developing superstores: Arcadia, Marks & Spencer and Debenhams are among them.

Often categorised separately, **category killers** are large stores, tending to be superstore sized, that specialise in a narrow line of merchandise. They are known as category killers – an 'Americanism' – because they have a huge selection within a narrow category of merchandise and 'kill off' the smaller stores retailing similar lines of merchandise. They require high footfall to be viable and tend to be located in large towns and cities on edge-of-town sites. The expansion of large DIY operators such as B&Q, Castoram and Homebase has led to the closure of many small, traditional hardware stores. Currys (electrical goods), Office World (office supplies) and the new superstores being opened by JJB Sports and Allsports (sporting goods) are examples of category killers.

## Warehouse Clubs

A rapidly growing form of mass merchandising, **warehouse clubs** are large-scale, members-only selling operations combining cash-and-carry wholesaling with discount retailing. For a nominal annual fee, small retailers can purchase products at wholesale prices for business use or for resale. Warehouse clubs also sell to ultimate consumers affiliated with credit unions, schools, hospitals and banks, but instead of paying a membership fee, individual consumers pay about 5 per cent more on each item than do business customers.

**Mall discounters** Operations that take short-term leases in unlet units in malls, selling such items as stationery, toys, confectionery and gifts at deeply discounted prices

Sometimes called 'buying clubs', warehouse clubs offer the same types of product as discount stores but in a limited range of sizes and styles. Warehouse clubs offer a broad product mix, including non-perishable foods, beverages, books, appliances, housewares, car parts, hardware and furniture. Their facilities, often located in industrial areas, have concrete floors and aisles wide enough for forklifts. Merchandise is stacked on pallets or displayed on pipe racks. All payments must be in cash, and customers must transport purchases themselves. Warehouse clubs appeal to many price-conscious consumers and small retailers unable to obtain wholesaling services from larger distributors. CostCo was the first US-style warehouse club to enter the UK.

## Speciality Shops

**Factory outlet villages** Converted rural buildings or purpose-built out-of-town retail parks for manufacturers' outlets retailing branded seconds, excess stocks and last season's lines, or trialling new lines

Most shopping centres and towns have a major department store. At the other end of the spectrum is the traditional corner shop. Few small shops these days retail a variety of product groups. In suburban areas, such shops tend to specialise in retailing one convenience product category – newsagents with cigarettes and newspapers, greengrocers, chemists, hair salons, and so on. In the town centre (CBD) few retailers of convenience goods, with their low margins, can afford the rents and business tax. Instead, the small store retailers – 250 square metres (2750 square feet) and under – in the CBD specialise in shopping or comparison items: clothing, footwear, CDs and DVDs, cosmetics, jewellery. Ownership of such retail outlets is increasingly concentrated in the hands of a few major retail groups (see Table 16.3), some of which also have retail brands that operate as department stores or out-of-town superstores. **Speciality shops** offer self-service but a greater level of assistance from store personnel than department stores, and carry a narrow product mix with deep

**TABLE 16.3 MAJOR UK RETAILING GROUPS**

| Retailer | Merchandise categories | Stores |
|---|---|---|
| Boots | Chemists, opticians, variety | 1698 |
| Arcadia<br>Burton, Dorothy Perkins, Evans, Miss Selfridge, Outfit, Topshop, Topman, Wallis | Men's clothing, ladies' clothing | 1972 |
| Dixons<br>Dixons, Currys, The Link, PC World | Electrical, telecommunications, computing | 1134 |
| Alexon<br>Bay Trading, Alexon, Minuet, Kaliko, Dash, Ann Harvey, Dolcis | Men's clothing, ladies' clothing, footwear | 1111 |
| J Sainsbury | Grocery supermarkets, hypermarkets, petrol forecourts | 715 |
| HMV<br>Waterstones, HMV | Bookshops, music stores | 340 |
| Next | Men's clothing, ladies' clothing, children's clothing, home furnishings | 337 |
| Monsoon<br>Monsoon, Accessorize | Ladies' clothing, accessories | 307 |
| Austin Reed | Men's clothing, ladies' clothing | 280 |

**Sources:** Companies' web sites, April, 2004; *The Marketing Pocketbook* 2004, World Advertising Research Center, Henley-on-Thames.

product lines. A typical 300-square-metre (3300-square-foot) footwear or clothing retail store will have window displays to entice passing pedestrians, one or two checkout points, and three or four assistants. Such stores depend on the town centre's general parking facilities and on proximity to a key trader, such as Boots or Marks & Spencer, which will generate pedestrian traffic.

## Convenience Stores

As the number of neighbourhood grocery stores declined in the 1960s and 1970s with the expansion of the superstore-based national grocery chains, a niche emerged in the market to be filled by **convenience stores**. These shops – also known as 'C-stores' – sell essential groceries, alcoholic drinks, drugs and newspapers outside the traditional 9.00 a.m. to 6.00 p.m. shopping hours. The major superstores extended their opening hours to 8.00 p.m. to facilitate after-work shopping, but no major retailers catered for 'emergency' or top-up shopping. There was a resurgence of the traditional corner shop located in suburban housing estates, offering limited ranges but extended opening hours. Consumers pay a slight price premium but receive convenience in terms of location and opening hours.

In the 1970s and 1980s, the voluntary groups (Spar, Mace, VG) and national retail groups such as Dillons, Circle K and 7-Eleven repositioned their brands into the 'open all hours' top-up or emergency shopping niche. Although they now face competition from the increasing number of 24-hour supermarkets and forecourt shops, convenience stores are on the increase. Tesco recently acquired the leading chain of C-stores in the UK, in order to broaden its grocery retailing and to cater for a wider set of customer needs.

## Mall Discounters

An emerging trend is for un-let units in malls and the CBD to be taken on very short-term leases, sometimes even weekly, by 'pile it high, sell it cheap' **mall discounters** selling items such as stationery, toys, confectionery, gifts – often 'everything under a £1!!'. Understandably, these operations invest little in shopfitting, promotion or staff training. For their landlords, such tenants may not be ideal, but they do generate rental income in what would otherwise be empty shop units. There are national chains of discounters, such as Poundstretcher or What Everyone Wants, which do invest in shopfitting and local press advertising, and which do intend long-term occupancy of sites. These operations are also no-frills, low-service, low-price trading concepts.

## Factory Outlet Villages

These retail villages initially sold seconds – imperfect new merchandise – similar to the lines stocked in many factory shops in converted mills or rural locations, in some instances with eight to ten shop units clustered together. Now developers are designing and building out-of-town **factory outlet villages**, such as Cheshire Oaks on Merseyside, for major manufacturers' and branded goods, with up to 20 mini-superstores grouped together. Increasingly, major manufacturers and retailers are using these stores to off-load last season's lines, excess stocks and branded seconds, or to trial new lines. These outlets are very popular for designer-label clothing, linens, crockery and homewares.

## Markets and Cash and carry Warehouses

**Markets**
Halls where fresh foods, clothing and housewares are sold, catering for budget-conscious shoppers who typically have a middle- and downmarket social profile

In most towns there are wholesale **markets** selling meat, greengrocery, fruit, flowers and fish from which speciality retailers make their inventory purchases. Traditional, too, is the general retail market selling to the general public, either in recently refurbished Victorian market halls or in council-provided modern halls adjacent to the town centre shopping malls. Such market halls sell fresh foods, clothing and housewares, and cater for budget-conscious shoppers who typically have a middle and downmarket social profile.

**Cash and carry warehouses**, such as Booker or Makro, retail extensive ranges of groceries, tobacco, alcohol, beverages and confectionery to newsagents, small supermarkets and convenience stores, and the catering trade (hotels, guest houses, restaurants and cafés). By purchasing from manufacturers in bulk, cash and carry companies can offer substantial price savings to their customers, who in turn can add a retail margin without alienating their customers. Many countries, particularly in Scandinavia, have hybrid outlets that combine the speciality shop, convenience store and cash and carry warehouse. Buying groups link small, often privately owned local retailers with similar shops; collectively their purchasing power is enhanced, and they increasingly operate their own wholesale warehouses and offer own-label brands.

## Catalogue Showrooms

In a **catalogue showroom** one item of each product class is on display and the remaining inventory is stored out of the buyers' reach. Using catalogues that have been mailed to their homes or which are available on counters in the store, customers order the goods at their leisure. Shop assistants usually complete the order form and then collect the merchandise from the adjoining warehouse. Catalogue showrooms, such as Argos or Index, regularly sell goods below manufacturers' list prices and often provide goods immediately. Higher product turnover, fewer losses through damage or shoplifting, and lower labour costs lead to their reduced retail prices. Jewellery, luggage, photographic equipment, toys, small appliances, housewares, sporting goods, garden furniture and power tools are the most commonly available items, listed by category and brand in the company's catalogue.

## Categories

**Cash and carry warehouses**
Outlets that retail extensive ranges of groceries, tobacco, alcohol, beverages and confectionery to newsagents, small supermarkets and convenience stores, and the catering trade

**Catalogue showroom**
Outlets in which one item of each product class is on display and the remaining inventory is stored out of the buyers' reach

Table 16.1 summarised the sales of the major categories of retailing. It is worth noting that the categories with the most stores do not necessarily top the league for highest turnover or profitability. The superstore and department store retailers have relatively few outlets, but they account for large floor areas and include many of the main retail chains. European, and UK in particular, retail statistics are notoriously poor, being based on infrequent estimates rather than regular censuses. Agencies such as Datamonitor, Euromonitor, Jordans, Mintel and Verdict produce regular reports on retail sectors and consumer expectations based on commissioned marketing research surveys. These are available by subscription or occasionally, for the newest versions, through business libraries. The British Retail Consortium and the Office of National Statistics also produce reports about retailing. These agencies tend to use categories similar to those discussed by the retail trade itself rather than the stilted, amalgamated official classification:

Food/grocery • CTN (confectionery, tobacco, news) • Off-licence beverages
Menswear/womenswear • Childrenswear • Footwear/leather goods • Accessories
Furniture/carpets/soft furnishings (household textiles)
Electrical (small appliances, brown and white goods)
Computing and software
Hardware • DIY
Drug/health/beauty
Music/video/books/greeting cards
Jewellery
Toys/hobbies
Office products
Sporting goods
Mixed retail businesses/department stores
Convenience stores/forecourts
Mail order
Restaurants/cafés/catering • Hotels
Banking/financial services

It is clear from this extensive list of retail categories just how important retailing is in the marketing channel for the bulk of consumer purchases and consumption. Producers require retailers in order to implement their marketing strategies and to satisfy targeted consumers. They must also strive to satisfy their immediate customers: the retailers. Retailers themselves require marketing strategies and programmes in order to satisfy their targeted consumers, sell their supplying producers' wares and meet financial performance targets.

**Non-store retailing** The selling of goods or services outside the confines of a retail facility

## Non-store Retailing

**Non-store retailing** is the selling of goods or services outside the confines of a retail facility. This form of retailing accounts for an increasing percentage of sales and includes personal

### Innovation and Change

#### Upmarket Clothing Retailers Opt for Multi-channels

Crew clothing is targeted at affluent singles and families, linking casual wear with outdoor activities. In addition to its principal consumer market, Crew also offers an extensive range of team and corporate clothing, with clients including Accenture, Barclays, BP, Citroën, Delloitte & Touche, Freshfields, JP Morgan, Laurent Perrier, Nokia, Microsoft, Orange, Pimm's, Saab, Tag Heuer and Veuve Clicquot. The company makes available its garments in clients' corporate colours, with their logos or marketing messages displayed wherever on the garment the client desires. Entire clothing ranges may be designed and manufactured to a corporate client's specific remit. The core target market, though, is the upscale consumer.

In order to support its brand positioning and to boost awareness of both the Crew brand and merchandise ranges, the company sponsors a variety of sporting events and teams, including the GB coxless four, a polo team, Middlesex County Cricket Club and Bath Rugby Club. These are teams that fit the upper-middle-market social groups targeted by Crew's clothing ranges. The company also displays its wares at many sporting events, such as race meetings at Cheltenham or Newbury. From small ranges of outdoor wear retailed predominantly in a few sailing resorts along the south coast of England, Crew has grown rapidly in recent years.

What makes Crew worthy of citing is how it has embraced a variety of channels to market. Its store branch network still includes sailing communities – Aldeburgh, Chichester, Cowes, Hamble, Lymington, Padstow and Salcombe – but has grown to include non-coastal tourist destinations such as Bath, Cheltenham, Chester, Oxford and Windsor, and major shopping cities including Birmingham, Bristol, Guildford and Leeds. In targeting such locations, Crew has opted to capitalise on the interest overseas visitors show in the company's ranges and to open outlets in towns offering sufficiently upscale consumer catchments. In addition to its store network, Crew has a thriving mail-order operation: orders may be placed by telephone, mail or fax. Now, a growing part of the operation is the business's on-line catalogue and purchasing provision.

While aiming its merchandise at a slightly younger age group, White Stuff also targets upscale customers with an interest in the outdoors and sporting activities. The clothing, excepting the ski wear, is similar to Crew's fashionable casual clothing. The company operates a comparable number of stores in many of the same towns as Crew. Given the similar nature of the merchandise and the target market segment, this is not too surprising. In addition to its stores, White Stuff also operates a mail-order operation and offers an e-shopping facility.

Until recently, the costs of operating such a diverse array of channels and of managing the associated volume of customer contact information, would have made such a multichannel strategy unprofitable. The growth and greater accessibility of CRM systems, database management tools and technology for interfacing with retail customers away from stores, has offered a new level of flexibility for retail marketers such as those managing Crew or White Stuff. Arguably, such niche specialist retailers now depend on the use of multiple channels to create a critical mass of customers that, overall, supports continued growth and provides adequate shareholder value: each channel by itself would not provide the cash flow to facilitate the expansion of the companies, their promotional and sponsorship activities, or their commitment to high levels of customer service. Technology has provided these marketers with the option to address their target markets through a mix of channels, in addition to the traditional retail store, notably direct marketing in the shape of mail order, tele-ordering and the web.

**Sources:** White Stuff and Crew catalogues, 2004; White Stuff and Crew stores; www.whitestuff.com; www.crewclothing.co.uk.

sales methods, such as in-home retailing and telemarketing, and non-personal sales methods, such as automatic vending and mail-order retailing (which includes catalogue retailing). A growing form of non-store retailing is the use of the Internet to promote and sell goods and services; orders can be placed using a credit card via a home-based PC. The Innovation and Change box on page 483 outlines how clothing retailers are embracing a variety of channels to market, including stores, mail order and the Internet.

Certain non-store retailing methods are in the category of **direct marketing**: the use of non-personal media, the Internet or telesales to introduce products to consumers, who then purchase the products by mail, telephone or the Internet. In the case of telephone orders, sales people may be required to complete the sales. Telemarketing, mail-order and catalogue retailing are all examples of direct marketing, as are sales generated by coupons, direct mail and Freefone 0800 numbers and the Internet.

## In-home Retailing

**Direct marketing**
The use of non-personal media, the Internet or telesales to introduce products to consumers, who then purchase the products by mail, telephone or the Internet.

**In-home retailing**
Selling via personal contacts with consumers in their own homes

**In-home retailing** is selling via personal contacts with consumers in their own homes. Companies such as Avon, Amway and Betterware send representatives to the homes of pre-selected prospects. Traditionally, in-home retailing relied on a random, door-to-door approach. Some companies now use a more efficient approach: they first identify prospects by reaching them by phone, mail or the Internet, or by intercepting them in shopping malls or at consumer trade fairs. These initial contacts are limited to a brief introduction and the setting of appointments.

Some in-home selling, however, is still undertaken without information about sales prospects. Door-to-door selling without a pre-arranged appointment represents a tiny proportion of total retail sales, less than 1 per cent. Because it has so often been associated with unscrupulous and fraudulent techniques, it is illegal in some communities. Generally, this method is regarded unfavourably because so many door-to-door sales people are under-trained and poorly supervised. A major disadvantage of door-to-door selling is the large expenditure, effort and time it demands. Sales commissions are usually 25 to 50 per cent (or more) of the retail price; as a result, consumers often pay more than a product is worth. Door-to-door selling is used most often when a product is unsought – for instance, encyclopaedias or double-glazed windows, which most consumers would not be likely to purchase in a store.

A variation of in-home retailing is the home demonstration, or party plan, which companies such as Tupperware, Ann Summers and Mary Kay Cosmetics use successfully. One consumer acts as host and invites a number of friends to view merchandise at his or her home, where a sales person is on hand to demonstrate the products. The home demonstration is more efficient for the sales representative than contacting each prospect door-to-door, and the congenial atmosphere partly overcomes consumers' suspicions and encourages them to buy. Home demonstrations also meet the buyers' needs for convenience and personal service. Commissions and selling costs make this form of retailing expensive, however. Additionally, successful party plan selling requires both a network of friends and neighbours, who have the time to attend such social gatherings, and a large number of effective sales people. With so many household members now holding full-time jobs, both prospects and sales representatives are harder to recruit. The growth of interactive telephone/computer home shopping and the growing use of the Internet may also cut into party plan sales.

## Telemarketing

More and more organisations – IBM, Merrill Lynch, Avis, Ford, Quaker Oats, Time and American Express, to name a few – are using the telephone to strengthen the effectiveness of traditional marketing methods. **Telemarketing** is the direct selling of goods and services by telephone, based on either a cold canvass of the telephone directory or a prescreened list of prospective clients. In some areas, certain telephone numbers are listed with an asterisk to indicate the people who consider sales solicitations a nuisance and do not

**Telemarketing**
The direct selling of goods and services by telephone, based on either a cold canvass of the telephone directory or a prescreened list of prospective clients

want to be bothered. Telemarketing can generate sales leads, improve customer service, speed up collection of overdue accounts, raise funds for not-for-profit groups and gather market data.[8]

In some cases, telemarketing uses advertising to encourage consumers to initiate a call or to request information about placing an order. Such advertisements will include 'a call to action' to prompt target consumers to dial an 0800 Freefone number. This type of retailing is only a small part of total retail sales, but its use is growing. Research indicates that telemarketing is most successful when combined with other marketing strategies, such as direct mail or advertising in newspapers, radio and television.

## Automatic Vending

**Automatic vending**
The use of coin- or credit card-operated self-service machines to sell small, standardised, routinely purchased products such as chewing gum, sweets, newspapers, cigarettes, soft drinks and coffee

**Automatic vending** makes use of coin- or credit card-operated self-service machines and accounts for less than 1 per cent of all retail sales. In the UK there are approximately 1.2 million vending machines, with sales in 2003 of £3.1 billion, and annual growth rates around 8 per cent.[9] Locations and the percentage of sales each generates are:[10]

- plants and factories – 38 per cent
- public locations (e.g. stores) – 26 per cent
- offices – 16 per cent
- colleges and universities – 6 per cent
- government facilities – 3 per cent
- hospitals and nursing homes – 3 per cent
- primary and secondary schools – 2 per cent
- others – 6 per cent.

The vending industry argues that the benefits of installing vending machines include flexibility and convenience, with refreshments available 24 hours per day, time saving through 'on demand' access to merchandise, hygienic storing of food with no preparation areas to clean, choice of lines, and economy, as no permanent staff need be employed to prepare snacks or serve them. The most popular vended goods are hot drinks, cans of soft drinks, confectionery and snacks, but cameras, CDs and even make-up are now available from vending machines. The Mars bar is the single biggest vend in the UK and the dominant manufacturers are Masterfoods (countline bars and sweet confectionery), McVitie's (biscuits) and KP (snacks).[11]

Video game machines provide an entertainment service, and many banks now offer machines that dispense cash or offer other services, but these uses of vending machines are not reported in total vending sales volume. Automatic vending is one of the most impersonal forms of retailing. Small, standardised, routinely purchased products (chewing gum, sweets, newspapers, cigarettes, soft drinks, coffee, condoms, teeth cleaners) can be sold in machines because consumers usually buy them at the nearest available location. Machines in areas of heavy traffic provide efficient and continuous services to consumers. Such high-volume areas may have more diverse product availability – for example, hot and cold sandwiches, and even cameras. To market its disposable cameras, Eastman Kodak is rolling out 10,000 vending machines that allow credit card transactions, are refrigerated to protect the film, and are connected to the Internet. The vending machine's Internet connection will inform Eastman Kodak about who bought each camera, where customers live, the specific location of the machine, and the machine's inventory level. The machines will be located at zoos, sports arenas, parks, hotels and resorts.[12]

The elimination of sales personnel and the small amount of space necessary for vending machines give this retailing method some advantages over stores. The advantages are partly offset by the expense of the frequent servicing and repair needed.

## Mail-order Retailing

**Mail-order retailing** involves selling by description because buyers usually do not see the actual product until it arrives in the mail. Sellers contact buyers through direct mail,

**Mail-order retailing** Selling by description because buyers usually do not see the actual product until it arrives in the mail

catalogues, television, radio, magazines and newspapers, and increasingly via the Internet. A wide assortment of products, such as compact discs, books and clothing, is sold to consumers through the mail, such as those in Figure 16.3. Placing mail orders by telephone and e-mail is increasingly common. The advantages of mail-order selling include efficiency and convenience. Mail-order houses, such as Empire (La Redoute, Daxon, Vertbaudet), Otto Versand (Freemans, Grattan, Actebis-Gruppe) or Littlewoods, can be located in remote, low-cost areas and avoid the expenses of store fixtures. Eliminating personal selling efforts and store operations may result in tremendous savings that can be passed along to consumers in the form of lower prices. On the other hand, mail-order retailing is inflexible, provides limited service and is more appropriate for speciality products than for convenience products. As shown in Table 16.4, mail order is a significant part of retail activity.

***Figure 16.3***
*A selection of popular mail order catalogues*
*Photo: Courtesy of Karen Beaulah*

**Table 16.4 Mail Order Business in the UK**

**Mail order sales value**

| **Year** | 1994 | 1995 | 1996 | 1997 | 1998 | 1999 | 2000 | 2001 | 2002 |
|---|---|---|---|---|---|---|---|---|---|
| **£ million** | 6828 | 6629 | 6828 | 7226 | 7756 | 8154 | 7491 | 8021 | 7690 |

**Mail order categories: % market shares**

| | | | |
|---|---|---|---|
| Childrenswear | 14.3 | Footwear | 5.4 |
| Menswear | 11.7 | Furniture/floor coverings | 5.3 |
| Womenswear | 10.8 | Electrical appliances | 2.8 |
| Toys/sports | 10.1 | DIY/gardening | 1.5 |
| Jewellery | 8.9 | Others | 2.5 |
| Homewares | 5.9 | | |

**Market share by retailer (%)**

| | | | |
|---|---|---|---|
| ARG Equation | 19.8 | Avon | 3.0 |
| Littlewoods | 14.3 | Findel | 3.0 |
| N Brown | 5.2 | Arcadia (Dial) | 0.8 |
| Grattan | 5.1 | M&S | 0.8 |
| Redcats UK | 4.8 | Betterware | 0.6 |
| Freemans | 4.3 | Other mail order | 26.4 |
| Next Directory | 4.3 | Other door-to-door | 7.6 |

**Sources:** Verdict Research; National Statistics; *The Marketing Pocket Book* 2004, World Advertising Research Center, Henley-on-Thames.

**Catalogue retailing**
A type of mail-order retailing in which customers receive their catalogues by mail, or pick them up if the catalogue retailer has stores

When **catalogue retailing** – a specific type of mail-order retailing – is used, customers receive their catalogues by mail, or they may pick them up if the catalogue retailer has stores, as does Littlewoods. Although in-store visits result in some catalogue orders, most are placed by mail, telephone or the Internet. In the USA, General Foods created Thomas Garroway Ltd, a mail-order service supplying gourmet pasta, cheese, coffee and similar items. Other packaged goods manufacturers involved in catalogue retailing include Hanes, Nestlé, Thomas J. Lipton, Sunkist and Whitman Chocolates. These catalogue retailers are able to reach many two-income families, who have more money and less time for speciality shopping. In the UK, manufacturers and store-focused retail groups tend not to be involved with catalogue or home shopping, but there are notable exceptions, such as Next. The specialist mail-order companies dominate this sector. Recently, though, Arcadia (with over 2000 shops) bought various mail-order brands, indicating the growing importance of this channel of distribution.

## Franchising

**Franchising**
An arrangement whereby a supplier (franchisor) grants a dealer (franchisee) the right to sell products in exchange for some type of consideration

**Franchising** is an arrangement whereby a supplier, or franchisor, grants a dealer, or franchisee, the right to sell products in exchange for some type of consideration. For example, the franchisor may receive some percentage of total sales in exchange for furnishing products, equipment, buildings, management know-how, marketing assistance and branding to the franchisee. The franchisee supplies labour and capital, operates the franchised business and agrees to abide by the provisions of the franchise agreement. This next section looks at the major types of retail franchises, the advantages and disadvantages of franchising and trends in franchising.

## Major Types of Retail Franchise

Retail franchise arrangements can ordinarily be classified as one of three general types:

1 In the first arrangement, a manufacturer authorises a number of retail stores to sell a certain brand-name item. This franchise arrangement, one of the oldest, is common in the sales of cars and trucks, farm equipment, earthmoving equipment and petroleum. The majority of all petrol is sold through franchised independent retail service stations, and franchised dealers handle virtually all sales of new cars and trucks.
2 In the second type of retail franchise, a producer licenses distributors to sell a given product to retailers. This franchising arrangement is common in the soft drinks industry. Most international manufacturers of soft drink syrups – Coca-Cola, Pepsi-Cola – franchise independent bottlers, which then service retailers.
3 In the third type of retail franchise, a franchisor supplies brand names, techniques or other services, instead of a complete product. The franchisor may provide certain production and distribution services, but its primary role in the arrangement is the careful development and control of marketing strategies. This approach to franchising, which is the most typical today, is used by many companies, including Holiday Inn, McDonald's, Avis, Hertz, KFC, Body Shop, Holland & Barrett, and Benetton.

## Advantages and Disadvantages of Franchising

Franchising offers several advantages to both the franchisee and the franchisor. It enables a franchisee to start a business with limited capital and to make use of the business experience of others. Moreover, an outlet with a nationally advertised name, such as Body Shop or Burger King, is often assured of customers as soon as it opens. If business problems arise, the franchisee can obtain guidance and advice from the franchisor at little or no cost. Franchised outlets are generally more successful than independently owned businesses: only 5 to 8 per cent of franchised retail businesses fail during the first two years of operation, whereas approximately 54 per cent of independent retail businesses fail during that period.[13] The franchisee also receives materials to use in local advertising and can take part in national promotional campaigns sponsored by the franchisor.

The franchisor gains fast and selective distribution of its products through franchise arrangements, without incurring the high cost of constructing and operating its own outlets. The franchisor, therefore, has more capital available to expand production and to use for advertising. At the same time, it can ensure, through the franchise agreement, that outlets are maintained and operated to its own standards. The franchisor also benefits from the fact that the franchisee, being a sole proprietor in most cases, is likely to be very highly motivated to succeed. The success of the franchise means more sales, which translate into higher royalties for the franchisor.

Despite their numerous advantages, franchise arrangements also have several drawbacks. The franchisor can dictate many aspects of the business: décor, the design of employees' uniforms, types of signage and numerous details of business operations. In addition, franchisees must pay to use the franchisor's name, products and assistance. Usually, there is a one-time franchise fee and continuing royalty and advertising fees, collected as a percentage of sales. In addition, franchisees must often work very hard, putting in 10- and 12-hour days, six days a week. In some cases, franchise agreements are not uniform: one franchisee may pay more than another for the same services. The franchisor also gives up a certain amount of control when entering into a franchise agreement. Consequently, individual establishments may not be operated exactly as the franchisor would operate them.

## Trends in Franchising

Franchising has been used since the early 1950s, primarily for service stations and car dealerships. However, it has grown enormously since the mid-1960s.[14] This growth has generally paralleled the expansion of the fast-food industry – the industry in which franchising is widely used. Of course, franchising is not limited to fast foods. Franchise arrangements for health clubs, pest control, hair salons and travel agencies are widespread. The estate agency industry has also experienced a rapid increase in franchising. The largest franchising sectors, ranked by sales, are: car and truck dealers (52 per cent); service stations (14 per cent); restaurants (10 per cent); non-food retailing (5 per cent).[15] Many internationally known brands, such as Burger King, McDonald's, Benetton and Body Shop, use franchising as their core means of rapid global expansion.

# Strategic Issues and Trends Facing Retail Marketers

Consumers often have vague reasons for making a retail purchase. Whereas most industrial, business-to-business purchases are based on economic planning and necessity, consumer purchases often result from social influences and psychological factors (see Chapter 6). Because consumers shop for a variety of reasons – to search for specific items, out of habit, to escape boredom or to learn about something new – retailers must do more than simply fill space with merchandise; they must make desired products available, create stimulating environments for shopping, and develop marketing strategies that increase sales and patronage. Research indicates that for many consumers, shopping is far more than the task of purchasing and collecting goods: it is a social, leisure-oriented activity. This section discusses how store location, property ownership, product assortment, category management, retail positioning, 'atmospherics', store image, scrambled merchandising, professional buying and merchandising, the wheel of retailing, the balance of retailing power, retail and technology affect these retailing objectives.[16]

## Location

**Location**
The strategic retailing issue that dictates the limited geographic trading area from which a store must draw its customers

**Location**, the least flexible of the strategic retailing issues, is one of the most important, because for store-focused retailers location dictates the limited geographic trading area from which a store must draw its customers.[17] Thus retailers consider a variety of factors when evaluating potential locations, including the location of the company's target customers within the trading area, the economic climate in the region, the kinds of product being sold, the availability of public transport, customer characteristics and competitors' locations.[18] The relative ease of movement to and from the site is important, so pedestrian and vehicular traffic, parking and transport must all be taken into account. Most retailers prefer sites with high pedestrian traffic; preliminary site investigations often include a pedestrian count to determine how many of the passers-by are truly prospective customers. Similarly, the nature of the area's vehicular traffic is analysed. Certain retailers, such as service stations and convenience stores, depend on large numbers of car-borne customers but try to avoid overly congested locations. In addition, parking space must be adequate, and transport networks – major thoroughfares and public transport – must be able to accommodate customers and delivery vehicles.

Retailers also evaluate the characteristics of the site itself: the other stores in the area, particularly the proximity of key traders or retailers whose reputation acts as magnets to shoppers; the size, shape and visibility of the plot or building under consideration; and the rental, leasing or ownership terms under which the building may be occupied. Retailers also look for compatibility with nearby retailers because stores that complement one another draw more customers for everyone. This is particularly true for clothing, footwear and jewellery retailers.[19] When making site location decisions, retailers must select from among several general types of location: free-standing structures, traditional business districts, neighbourhood/suburban shopping centres, out-of-town superstores and retail parks. In recent years, retailers have been moving away from the traditional store assessment procedure of pedestrian counts and 'eyeballing' the site's immediate location. Various agencies – notably CACI and SAMI – have detailed databases examining each shopping centre. Computer modelling, such as SLAM (Store Location Assessment Model), has become more widespread, bringing a basis of objectivity to what was previously an intuitive decision-making process based on few hard facts.[20]

## Property Ownership

Property ownership is perpetually an issue in retailing. Some companies, such as Marks & Spencer, invest heavily to own the majority of their property portfolio. This gives security of tenure, saves on rents and lease negotiations, and adds to the book value of the company. To release operating funds, companies often engage in 'sale and lease-back' deals. Property companies buy the freehold to add to their assets but immediately give a favourable lease to the retailer. In recent years, some companies that once held the freehold for most of their stores have sold off property to make available operating funds for new computer systems, store refurbishment or new store openings. Companies such as Arcadia and Next argue that they are primarily retailers and should not tie up funds in property ownership. Retailers that locate mainly in covered shopping centres and in retail parks generally have to accept lease agreements as the centre's developer maintains ownership of the property.

## Product Assortment

The product assortments that retailers develop vary considerably in breadth, depth and quality. Retail stores are often classified according to their product assortments. Conversely, a store's type affects the breadth and depth of its product offerings, as shown in Figure 16.4. Thus a speciality store has a single product line but considerable depth in that line. Tie Rack stores and Sock Shop stores, for example, carry only one line of products but many items within that line. In contrast, discount stores may have a wide product mix, such as housewares, car products, clothing and food. Department stores may have a wide product mix with different product line depths. Nevertheless, it is usually difficult to maintain both a wide and a deep product mix because of the inventories required. In addition,

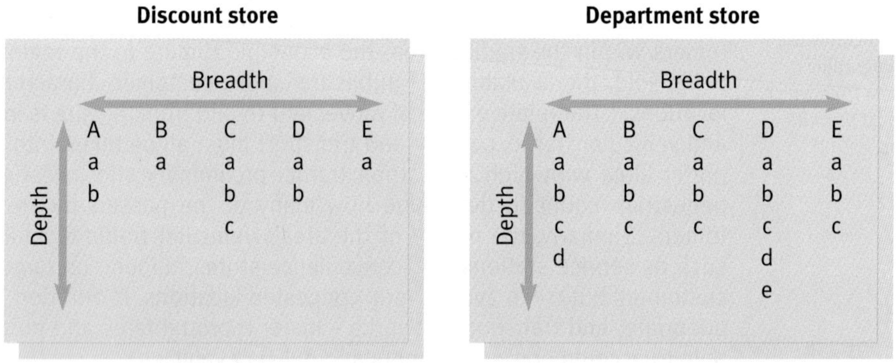


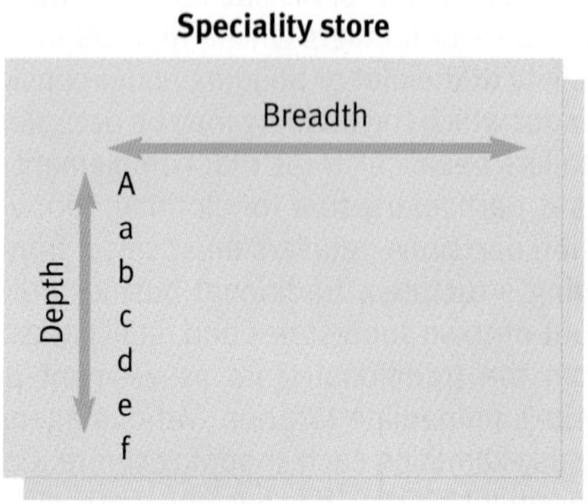


The capital letters represent the number of product lines, and the lower-case letters depict the choices in any one product line. Thus it can be seen that discount stores are wide and shallow in merchandise assortment. Speciality stores, at the other extreme, have few product lines, but much more depth in the few they carry. The typical department store falls in between, having a broad assortment with many merchandise lines and medium depth in each line.

***Figure 16.4***
*Relationships between merchandise breadth and depth for a typical discount store, department store and speciality store*
*Source: Robert F. Hartley,* Retailing: Challenge and Opportunity, *3rd edn, p. 118*
*Copyright © 1984 by Houghton Mifflin Company. Used by permission*

some producers prefer to distribute through retailers that offer less variety so that their products gain more exposure and are less affected by the presence of competing brands. Discounters such as Everything Under £1 have a wide product mix with little depth. The limited-line grocery chains, led by Netto and Aldi, have a moderate product mix with restricted depth – an approach that has brought them significant success as they target the budget-conscious shopper.[21]

Issues of product assortment are often a matter of what and how much to carry. When retailers decide what should be included in their product assortments, they consider an assortment's purpose, status and completeness:[22]

- *Purpose* relates to how well an assortment satisfies consumers and at the same time furthers the retailer's goals.
- *Status* identifies by rank the relative importance of each product in an assortment – for example, motor oil might have low status in a store that sells convenience foods.
- *Completeness* means that an assortment includes the products necessary to satisfy a store's customers; the assortment is incomplete when some products are missing.

An assortment of convenience foods must include milk to be complete because most consumers expect to be able to buy milk when purchasing other food products. New products are added to (and declining products are deleted from) an assortment when they meet (or fail to meet) the retailer's standards of purpose, status and completeness. The retailer also takes into consideration the quality of the products to be offered. The store may limit its assortments to expensive, high-quality goods for upper-income market segments; it may stock cheap, low-quality products for low-income buyers; or it may try to attract several market segments by offering a range of quality within its total product assortment.

How much to include in an assortment depends on the needs of the retailer's target market. A discount store's customers expect a wide and shallow product mix, whereas speciality store shoppers prefer narrow and deep assortments. If a retailer can increase sales by increasing product variety, the assortment may be enlarged. If a broader product mix ties up too much floor space or creates storage problems, however, the retailer may stock only the products that generate the greatest sales. Other factors that affect product assortment decisions are personnel, store image, inventory control methods and the financial risks involved.

## Category Management

**Category management**
A core approach to merchandising, inventory control and display in many retailers, with similar lines from several suppliers being controlled by a category manager and managed as a discrete unit

**Category management** involves defining the category through the consumer's eyes rather than through the producer's or retailer's eyes. For example, snacks can be a category encompassing every kind of snack from an apple to a small ready meal, to a packet of crisps, but it may not be practical in the store to physically bring them all together into one area. Instead, a retailer might set up a special fixture (for example, with sandwiches) or link them through promotions or communications materials. Managing the category means determining the most practical segmentation by consumer need and then making money from servicing the need. In retailing food, for example, this means dividing the store into departments that reflect consumer needs and wants, and then micro-managing through merchandising/display, packaging, pricing, product design and through all forms of communication. In order to attain a consumer vision of the category, marketing researchers go back to basics and ask consumers to describe their lives, eating and shopping habits, and so on. Then the marketing researcher asks them to describe how to make the store reflect this and build around a need. However, should a chicken tikka pizza be placed with Italian or Indian foods, or pizzas? A major facet of category management is often the appointment of a category 'captain' – a supplier who works as category leader in conjunction with the retailer's category manager. This supplier probably, but not necessarily, supplies the core of the category and is responsible for researching and planning the category.

## Retail Positioning

**Retail positioning**
The strategy of identifying a highly attractive market segment and serving it in a way that distinguishes the retailer from others in the minds of consumers in that segment

Because of the emergence of new types of store – for example, discount sheds, warehouse clubs, superstores, hypermarkets – and the expansion of product offerings by traditional stores, competition among retailers is intense. It is important for management to consider the retail business's market positioning.[23] **Retail positioning** involves identifying an unserved or under-served market niche, or a highly attractive market segment, and serving it through a strategy that distinguishes the retailer from others in the minds of consumers in that segment. The retailer must have a proposition, trading concept, brand image or merchandise policy that is visibly different from that of its competitors. See also Chapter 8's discussion of brand positioning.

There are several ways in which retailers position themselves.[24] A retailer may position itself as a seller of high-quality, premium-priced products providing many services. A store such as Selfridges, which specialises in expensive high-fashion clothing and jewellery, sophisticated electronics and exclusive home furnishings, might be expected to provide wrapping and delivery services, personal shopping consultants and restaurant facilities. Fortnum & Mason, for example, emphasises superlative service and even hires pianists to play in the entrance of its store. Dixons, the electrical retailer, is often referred to as 'the grown man's toy shop'. Another type of retail company, such as IKEA, may be positioned as a marketer of reasonable-quality, stylish products at value-for-money prices.

## Atmospherics

**Atmospherics**
The physical elements in a store's design that appeal to consumers' emotions and encourage them to buy

'Atmospherics' are often used to help position a retailer. **Atmospherics** are the physical elements in a store's design that appeal to consumers' emotions and encourage them to buy. Exterior and interior characteristics, layout and displays all contribute to a store's atmosphere. Department stores, restaurants, hotels, service stations and shops combine these elements in different ways to create specific atmospheres that may be perceived as warm, fresh, functional or exciting.

**Exterior Atmospherics** Exterior atmospheric elements include the appearance of the store front, the window displays, store entrances and degree of traffic congestion. They are particularly important to new customers, who tend to judge an unfamiliar store by its outside appearance and may not enter if they feel intimidated by the building or inconvenienced by the car park. Because consumers form general impressions of shopping centres and business districts, the businesses and neighbourhoods surrounding a store will affect how buyers perceive the atmosphere of a store.

**Interior Atmospherics** Interior atmospheric elements include aesthetic considerations such as lighting, wall and floor coverings, changing rooms and store fixtures. Interior sensory elements also contribute to atmosphere. Colour, for example, can attract shoppers to a retail display. Many fast-food restaurants use bright colours such as red and yellow because these have been shown to make customers feel hungrier and eat faster, thus increasing turnover. Sound is another important sensory component of atmosphere and may consist of silence, soft music or even noisiness. One study indicated that retail customers shop for longer when exposed to unfamiliar music than when exposed to familiar music.[25] Scent may be relevant as well; within a store, the odour of perfume suggests an image different from that suggested by the smell of prepared food. A store's layout – arrangement of departments, width of aisles, grouping of products and location of cashiers – is yet another determinant of atmosphere. Closely related to store layout is the element of crowding. A crowded store may restrict exploratory shopping, impede mobility and decrease shopping efficiency. An apparently empty store, however, may imply unpopularity and deter shoppers from entering.

**Displays** Once the exterior and interior characteristics and store layout have been determined, displays are added. Displays enhance the store's atmosphere and give customers information about products. When displays carry a store-wide theme – during the Christmas season, for instance – they attract customers' attention and generate sales. So do displays that present several related products in a group, or ensemble. Interior displays of products stacked or hanging neatly on racks create one kind of atmosphere; marked-down items grouped together on a bargain table produce a different kind.

**Selecting the 'Right' Atmosphere** Retailers must determine the atmosphere that the target market seeks and then adjust atmospheric variables to encourage the desired awareness and action in consumers. High-fashion boutiques generally strive for an atmosphere of luxury and novelty; discount stores must not seem too exclusive and expensive. To appeal to multiple market segments, a department store retailer may create different atmospheres for different operations within the store – for example, the discount basement, the sports department and the women's shoe department may each have a distinctive atmosphere. As discussed in Chapter 13, services marketers have extended the traditional '4Ps' of the marketing mix. For retailers, atmospherics are part of this extended marketing mix, specifically the ambience or physical characteristic element.

## Store Image

**Image**
A functional and psychological picture in the consumer's mind

To attract customers, a retail store must project an **image** – a functional and psychological picture in the consumer's mind – that is acceptable to its target market. Although heavily dependent on atmospherics and design, a store's image is also shaped by its reputation for integrity, the number of services offered, personnel, location, merchandise assortments, pricing policies, promotional activities, community involvement and the retail brand's positioning.[26]

Characteristics of the target market – social class, lifestyle, income level and past buying behaviour – also help form store image. How consumers perceive the store can be a major determinant of store patronage. Consumers from lower socio-economic groups tend to patronise small, high-margin, high-service food stores and prefer small, friendly building societies/loan companies over large, impersonal banks, even though these companies charge high interest. Affluent consumers look for exclusive, high-quality establishments that offer prestige products and labels.

Retailers should be aware of the multiple factors that contribute to store image, and recognise that perceptions of image vary. For example, one study found that in the United States consumers perceived Wal-Mart and Kmart differently, although the two sold almost the same products in stores that looked quite similar, offered the same prices and even had similar names. Researchers discovered that Wal-Mart shoppers spent more money at Wal-Mart and were more satisfied with the store than Kmart shoppers were with Kmart, in part because of differences in the retailers' images. For example, Wal-Mart employees wore waistcoats; Kmart employees did not. Wal-Mart purchases were packed in paper bags while Kmart used plastic bags. Wal-Mart had wider aisles, recessed lighting and carpeting in some departments. Even the retailers' logos affected consumers' perceptions: Wal-Mart's simple white and brown logo appeared friendly and 'less blatantly commercial', while Kmart's red and turquoise logo conveyed the impression that the stores had not changed much since the 1960s. These atmospheric elements gave consumers the impression that Wal-Mart was more 'upmarket', warmer and friendlier than Kmart.[27]

## Scrambled Merchandising

When retailers add unrelated products and product lines, particularly fast-moving items that can be sold in volume, to an existing product mix, they are practising **scrambled merchandising**. For example, a convenience store might start selling lawn fertiliser. Retailers adopting this strategy hope to accomplish one or more of the following:

1 to convert their stores into one-stop shopping centres
2 to generate more traffic

3 to realise higher profit margins
4 to increase impulse purchases.

**Scrambled merchandising** The addition of unrelated products and product lines, particularly fast-moving items that can be sold in volume, to an existing product mix

In scrambling merchandise, retailers must deal with diverse marketing channels and thus may reduce their own buying, selling and servicing expertise. The practice can also blur a store's image in consumers' minds, making it more difficult for a retailer to succeed in today's highly competitive, saturated markets. Finally, scrambled merchandising intensifies competition among traditionally distinct types of store and forces suppliers to adjust distribution systems so that new channel members can be accommodated. ASDA is predominantly a grocery retailer; however, most ASDA stores carry the George clothing ranges. The company retails small electrical appliances, DIY goods and car accessories in some stores but not in others. During the summer months, gardening supplies and equipment are sold. In the months leading up to Christmas, that floor space is given over to children's toys and gifts.

## Merchandising/Buying

A major task in retail management is the selection of which brands and products to stock, in which sizes, styles, colours, and so forth. For example, a buying executive for fresh produce in a retailer such as Tesco has significant power in terms of the budget at his/her disposal but also in managing relations with suppliers. A leading retailer can exert significant pressure on suppliers to fulfil specific product, delivery and logistical support functions. A company such as Sara Lee Courtaulds supplying clothing lines to retailers such as Marks & Spencer or C&A also has to provide packaging, labelling and even display stands. The selection of lines that sell too slowly or not at all can have dramatic implications for a retailer in terms of stock-holding and inventory management, but also in terms of the impact on the retailer's positioning and store image. Many of Marks and Spencer's performance glitches have been blamed on its fashion buyers purchasing inappropriate styles that did not fit with consumers' expectations and did not compete effectively with the ranges being offered in rival stores. The negative publicity resulting for M&S led to a tarnished image in the eyes of some customers, as well as deteriorating share prices. While retail systems, personnel, store image, atmospherics, pricing and location impact on customer satisfaction, a retailer's performance hinges significantly on the desirability of the merchandise it chooses to stock. The role of the merchandiser or buying controller is pivotal to retail success.

## The Wheel of Retailing

**Wheel of retailing** The hypothesis that new retailers often enter the marketplace with low prices, margins and status and eventually emerge at the high end of the price/cost/services scales to compete with newer discount retailers

As new types of retail businesses come into being, they strive to fill niches in the dynamic environment of retailing. One hypothesis regarding the evolution and development of new types of retail store is the **wheel of retailing**.[28] According to this theory, new retailers often enter the marketplace with low prices, margins and status. The new competitors' low prices are usually the result of innovative cost-cutting procedures, and they soon attract imitators. Gradually, as these businesses attempt to broaden their customer base and increase sales, their operations and facilities become more elaborate and more expensive. They may move to more desirable locations, begin to carry higher-quality merchandise or add customer services. Eventually, they emerge at the high end of the price/cost/services scales, competing with newer discount retailers who are following the same evolutionary process.[29] Tesco evolved from a value-led 'no frills' retailer in the 1970s to a quality-led full service market leader in the 1990s.

Figure 16.5 illustrates the wheel of retailing for department stores and discounters. Department stores such as Debenhams started out as high-volume, low-cost merchants competing with general stores and other small retailers; out-of-town discount sheds developed later, in response to the rising expenses of services in department stores. Many out-of-town discount sheds now appear to be following the wheel of retailing by offering more services, better locations, high-quality inventories and, therefore, higher prices. Some out-of-town discount sheds are almost indistinguishable from department stores. Like most hypotheses, the wheel of retailing may not fit every case. For example,

*Figure 16.4*
*The wheel of retailing, which explains the origin and evolution of new types of retail store*
*Source: adapted from Robert F. Hartley,* Retailing: Challenge and Opportunity, *3rd edn, p. 42.*
*Copyright © 1984 by Houghton Mifflin Company. Used by permission*

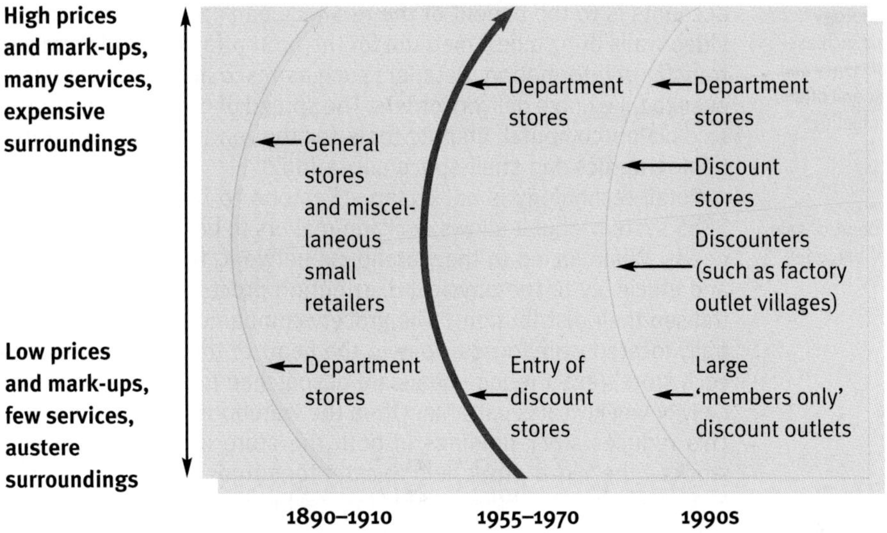


If the 'wheel' is considered to be turning slowly in the direction of the coloured arrows, then the department stores around 1900 and the discounters later can be viewed as coming on the scene at the low end of the wheel. As it turns slowly, they move with it, becoming higher-price operations, and in doing so they leave room for lower-price retailers to gain entry at the low end of the wheel.

it does not adequately explain the development of convenience stores, speciality stores and vending machine operations. Another major weakness of the theory is that it does not predict what retailing innovations will develop, or when. Still, the hypothesis works reasonably well in many industrialised, expanding economies.

## The Balance of Retailing Power

**Balance of retailing power**
The balance of negotiating and buying power between retailers and their suppliers

The **balance of retailing power** is a well-documented subject; it is the balance of negotiating and buying power between retailers and their suppliers.[30] As more retailers devote shelf space to their own-label branded goods, the major manufacturers find themselves squeezed out.[31] In the clothing market, nearly all chain retailers now give precedence to their own-label goods. Marks & Spencer takes the situation to the extreme: only Marks & Spencer's own-label goods are on sale in its stores. The company dictates quality levels, lead times, packaging and delivery conditions, and often the price it will pay to its suppliers.[32] Some years ago, retailer Sainsbury's threatened to de-stock Kellogg's cereals totally and Kellogg's then refused to supply Sainsbury's. Two giant brands were locked in a power struggle. Increasingly, compromise and negotiation are leading to deals beneficial to both sides of the equation: retailers receive preferential treatment and buying terms while manufacturers receive contracts to supply major retail chains exclusively with their own-label needs, often alongside their own manufacturer brands.[33] Certainly for most of the large retail chains, the power is in the hands of the retailers, not the manufacturers.

## Technology

Retailers are turning to **retail technology** for improved efficiency and productivity and often to create a competitive edge.[34] Barcode scanning and **EPoS** (electronic point of sale) systems enable companies to monitor exact consumer spending patterns on a store-by-store basis, to prevent stock-outs and to have detailed sales data to add weight to negotiations with suppliers. EFTPoS (electronic funds transfer at point of sale) equipment facilitates speedy payment for goods, thereby reducing checkout queues; the rapid debiting of customer

**Retail technology**
Systems that increase retailers' efficiency and productivity, and often create a competitive edge

**EPoS**
Electronic point-of-sale scanning of barcodes for inventory management

accounts is to the benefit of the retailer's bank account and cash flow. Video screens and video walls bring a new medium for the promotion of goods and services, as well as for the transfer of information. Retailers such as Tesco are using websites to promote ranges and even to take home delivery orders. The spread of computer systems has enabled consultants to develop computer graphic tools for the modelling of store location choice, customer demographics and shelf-space allocation.[35]

Retail technology is not cheap – £35,000 to bring a typical shoe shop on-line with an EPoS system – but it allows decision-makers to be fully aware of sales trends and customer needs. When linked to the warehouse network, the EPoS process brings increased speed and efficiency to the physical distribution process. Most national retail groups have centralised their distribution.[36] The grocery companies, for instance, have one or two huge, centrally located warehouses close to the heart of the motorway network. Through EPoS data, each store's exact requirements are despatched from the central warehouse to match actual daily or weekly sales patterns. Often the warehouse is automated, with robotised handling. This reduces stock-holdings in both the store itself and centrally, and minimises safety stocks – the 'extra' stock held to cater for surges in demand or supplier delays.[37]

As discussed in Chapters 4 and 19, technology is advancing the growth of direct marketing and in-home shopping. Direct retailing via mail-order catalogues, Internet selling and teleselling is increasing rapidly, bringing more choice for the consumer in terms of when, where and how to shop; greater competition to some retailers; and additional channels to manage for those retailers adding direct selling operations to their armoury.

**Retail formats**
The store type and proposition

**Micro retail marketing**
Modification by a retail chain to vary the retail marketing mix from branch to branch

In conjunction with leading IT services company Fujitsu, the authors of this book recently surveyed the leading UK retail groups to identify the 'hot topics' in terms of retail marketing strategy. These are described in the Innovation and Change box below. These developments include more rapidly evolving competitive pressures, changes to consumer lifestyles and behaviour, regulatory pressures, e-commerce and greater multi-channel retailing, more varied use of **retail formats**, branding, ethical retailing, different target marketing possibilities, the role of IT and the increasing possibilities offered by **micro retail marketing**. Retail formats are the store type and proposition, while micro retail marketing is the variation of the retail marketing mix from branch-to-branch by a retail chain.

## Innovation and Change

### Current Developments in Retail Marketing

**Company Ownership**

Many countries' governments regulate the extent of control of a particular market sector by one or only a few retailers. Traditionally, this has encouraged the largest retailers, such as Ahold or Tesco, to seek expansion in non-domestic markets. However, several major acquisitions have been permitted recently, implying a slight relaxation of the rules of monopoly ownership. For example, Morrisons' acquisition of leading supermarket Safeway, creating the UK's fourth largest chain. There have been other strategic implications of company ownership, such as a number of publicly quoted retailers choosing to 'go private', giving them increased levels of secrecy and arguably of flexibility in terms of making changes to their business strategies. New Look, Bhs and Arcadia are just some of the retailers to de-list their publicly quoted shares. Another dimension of the ownership issue has been the acquisition of large national chains by larger international players, also permitted increasingly by national regulators. For example, Wal-Mart's take-over of ASDA.

**Consumer Trends**

A recent survey of major retailers identified their awareness of a number of consumer and lifestyle trends that are impacting on their business strategies. These include 'laziness', with non-cooking consumers happy to buy city apartments with minuscule kitchens and increasing purchases of labour-saving gadgets; health values, with government concerns

## Applied Mini-Case

BAA owns and operates seven airports in the UK, including Heathrow, Gatwick and rapidly expanding Stansted. BAA's 133 million passengers account for 75 per cent of the UK's air passenger traffic. A few years ago, the then CEO John Egan instigated a policy review emphasising a commitment to quality service, on-site competition and the introduction of branded operations and concessions. All proposals followed extensive marketing research. Costa, Starbucks, Wetherspoon, Garfunkels, Burger King, McDonald's and Prêt à Manger are some of the catering businesses now operating within BAA's airports, along with retailers such as Boots, Body Shop, Accessorize, Austin Reed, Cartier, Christian Dior, Church & Co, Escada, Hamleys, HMV, Liberty, Nike, Harrod's, Ted Baker, Pink, Books Etc, and WHSmith. Only well-known retail brands are now welcome. With the EU having phased out intra-community duty-free trade, BAA sees retail operations as the way to continue BAA's impressive profits record. Already 10 per cent of terminal space – 46,000 square metres (500,000 square feet) – is devoted to retailing. BAA has taken restless passengers waiting for flights and put them into shops selling well-known brands and a variety of merchandise. Research from 120,000 interviews each year has shown that retail outlets are a high priority for passengers. The captive audience is appreciative of the changes, as are the retailers. Tie Rack's sales at Heathrow are £27,000 per square metre (£3000 per square foot) annually, 10 times the ratio achieved by the company's high-street stores.

**Sources:** BAA website, April 2004; Heathrow and Edinburgh airports.

### Question

**Why has BAA devoted so much terminal space to retailing and in particular to well-known high street-branded retail businesses? What impact has the introduction of shopping malls had on the ambience of the terminals?**

## Case Study

### Dutch Retailer Ahold's Global Ambitions

Leading Dutch retailer Royal Ahold, like many large companies in the Netherlands, has pursued a range of international expansion opportunities. The relatively small size of the Netherlands market means that companies wishing to expand their operations must often seek new business further afield. In the case of Ahold, this has involved successful expansion into central and southern Europe, the USA, Latin America and Asia.

Ahold has demonstrated a considerable interest in global expansion. Using a variety of market entry strategies, the retailer has entered a range of new markets. In 1977, Ahold arrived in the USA. This was achieved through the company's acquisition of six supermarket chains, which are grouped into four operating companies. Stop & Shop operated 200 supermarkets and superstores in the New England and New York areas. BI-LO was responsible for more than 250 outlets in North and South Carolina, Tennessee and Georgia. Giant Food Stores had around 150 stores in a variety of different locations. The 230 stores of TOPS Markets were found in the New York and Ohio regions. Ahold is now unifying these US businesses into one harmonised operation in order to gain scale economies, and is focusing on its core supermarket and hypermarket expertise rather than C-stores and discounters.

Ahold's expansion interests have not been restricted to the USA. The company's move into Portugal came in 1992 through a joint venture with local partner Jerônimo Martins, while entry into the Czech Republic was achieved through a wholly owned subsidiary in 1995. In 1996, the retailer was able to enter the Latin American market by forming a new joint venture with Bompreço, a large Brazilian retailer.

Ahold has, historically, chosen markets for two distinct sets of reasons. The US market was deemed attractive because of its size and established market structure, which reflected the traits of the domestic Benelux market. The characteristics of this well-developed, competitive environment meant that in order to survive, Ahold had to adopt a low-cost leadership strategy. By choosing an entry strategy of growth by acquisition, Ahold was able to quickly achieve the desired economies of scale. The company dealt with its unfamiliarity with the US market by giving autonomy to the different operating companies it formed. With hindsight, such autonomy failed to result in management cohesion and control. In the major wholesale food business, US Foodservice, there even emerged a significant accounting fraud, owing to the lack of centralised controls and practices.

The retailer had rather different reasons for entering its other markets. In many cases, such as in Latin America and Asia, Ahold was entering retail markets that were relatively poorly developed. Ahold clearly saw opportunities in these markets, due to a lower level of competitive activity than in mature European markets, and the prospects of high economic growth. Not surprisingly, for these markets Ahold's strategy was different from that pursued in the USA. In countries where the retail sector was under-developed, there was the opportunity to enter the market through a partnership with a local company or by developing a greenfield operation. In most cases, the preferred approach was for Ahold to enter into joint ventures with a local business. This allowed important local market knowledge to be acquired as quickly as possible. This quick entry into the market was also attractive to Ahold because it gave the company the opportunity to establish a first-mover advantage and to have early influence over the way in which the retail sector developed.

By 2003, Ahold was in serious financial difficulty owing to over-extension and the diversity of its acquisition-led and joint venture-inspired growth. Financial restructuring, the change of its US management, and disinvestment of Spanish operations and US C-stores led to an upturn in its fortunes. Ahold is still a global giant in retailing and operates around 5600 stores, including 1340 franchised outlets, employing 280,000 staff. The focus is on supermarkets, but there are also hypermarkets, discount stores, speciality stores, C-stores and even a cash and carry operation. Pundits believe the agglomeration of its various businesses into fewer formats will now bring benefits of scale and simplify management. They also welcome the objective of only operating businesses that are market leaders or very strong challengers, disinvesting from other businesses. While Ahold may have overstretched its management resources, industry observers note that the company's target territory strategy was smart: emerging markets in South America, Asia-Pacific and eastern Europe, supported by established businesses in North America and Europe.

**Sources:** Marcelo Rocha, 'The globalisation of supermarkets: a case study approach', MBA project, University of Warwick; Royal Ahold, annual reports, 1997–2004; D. Orgel, 'Ahold-ing its course: careful steering through the rough waters of acquisitions and realignments has left Ahold USA headed toward continued growth', *Supermarket News*, 48 (14), 6 April 1998; www.ahold.nl, April 2004.

## Questions for Discussion

1 Why has Ahold not simply deployed its Dutch trading concept in North and South American markets?

2 What marketing strengths may emerge from Ahold's global growth and realignment around fewer formats and only market-leading businesses?

3 Why might a national market leader such as Tesco fear a global player such as Ahold?

# Postscript

The place ingredient of the marketing mix addresses the distribution and marketing channel decisions necessary to provide the target market with convenient and ready access to a product or service. The place specification developed in the marketing mix must be beneficial to the supplier of the product or service if it is to remain in business and be commercially viable. Part IV of *Marketing: Concepts and Strategies* has examined the nature of marketing channels, wholesalers and distributors, the physical distribution of products and services, plus the nuances of retail marketing.

Before progressing, readers should be confident that they are now able to do the following.

### Explain the concept of the marketing channel

- What is the marketing channel?
- What are the functions and types of marketing channel?
- What is meant by channel integration and levels of market coverage?
- What issues determine the selection of a marketing channel and what impact is the emergence of direct marketing having?
- Why are the concepts of cooperation, relationship building, conflict and leadership important in marketing channel management?
- What legal issues concern marketers as they manage marketing channels?

### Describe the functions of wholesalers, distributors and physical distribution management

- What is meant, in its broadest sense, by wholesaling?
- What activities do wholesalers undertake and how can wholesalers be classified?
- What agencies facilitate wholesaling?
- What are the changing patterns in wholesaling?
- How are physical distribution activities integrated into marketing channels and overall marketing strategies?
- What are the objectives of physical distribution?
- What are the roles of order processing, materials handling, warehousing, inventory management and transportation in effective physical distribution?

### Outline the nature of retailing and the specialist requirements for retail marketers

- What is the function of retailing in the marketing channel?
- What are the principal retail locations and major store types?
- What are non-store retailing and franchising?
- What are the strategic issues?
- What are the current trends in retailing?

## *Strategic Case*

# FedEx
# 40 Years of Growth, Innovation and Global Expansion

In 1973, Frederick W. Smith founded the Federal Express Corporation with part of an US$8 million inheritance. At the time, the US Postal Service and United Parcel Service (UPS) provided the only means of delivering letters and packages, and they often took several days or more to get packages to their destinations. While a student at Yale in 1965, Smith wrote a paper proposing an independent, overnight delivery service. Although he received a grade C for the paper, Smith never lost sight of his vision. He believed that many businesses would be willing to pay more to get letters, documents and packages delivered overnight. He was right!

Federal Express began shipping packages overnight from Memphis, Tennessee, on 17 April 1973. On that first night of operations, the company handled six packages, one of which was a birthday present sent by Smith himself. Today, FedEx handles 3.1 million packages daily and over 500,000 calls each day. The result is a total operating income of US$1.47 billion on an astounding US$22.4 billion in total revenue. The company now employs close to 145,000 people around the world, including 42,500 couriers, serving 365 airports in 215 countries through 1200 service centres and 46 call centres. FedEx has an aircraft fleet approaching 650 and a vehicle fleet of over 43,000. Each day FedEx deals with an average of 63 million electronic transmissions between its own operations and with customers.

FedEx does not view itself as being in the package and document transport business; rather, it describes its business as delivering 'certainty' by connecting the global economy with a wide range of transportation, information and supply chain services. With close to 50 per cent market share in most key markets, customers must believe FedEx offers such 'certainty'.

## FedEx Divisions

Although most people are familiar with FedEx's overnight delivery services, the company is actually divided into seven major divisions, as listed in the table.

| | |
|---|---|
| FedEx Express | The world's largest express transportation company, serving 215 countries including every address in the USA |
| FedEx Ground | North America's second largest ground carrier for small package shipments |
| FedEx Freight | The largest US regional less-than-truckload freight company, which provides next-day and second-day delivery of heavy freight in both the US and international markets |
| FedEx Custom Critical | Provides 24/7 non-stop, door-to-door delivery of urgent shipments in the USA, Canada and Europe |
| FedEx Trade Networks | Facilitates international trade, customs brokerage and freight forwarding |
| FedEx Services | Consolidates sales, marketing, information technology and supply chain services that support all FedEx global brands |
| Kinko's | A chain of more than 1200 retail stores providing business services such as copying, publishing and shipping operations |

FedEx purchased Kinko's in 2004 to provide new business services and to expand FedEx shipping options at Kinko's 1200 retail stores – each store acts as a drop-off point for FedEx delivery services, mostly in prime-pitch retail centres or major office complexes. The purchase followed rival UPS's acquisition of 3000 Mail Boxes Etc stores. Renamed the UPS Store, the acquisition put UPS closer to small to medium-sized customers and high-profit infrequent shippers. FedEx's purchase of Kinko's, which operates 110 stores in 10 countries outside the USA, is expected to help the company reach new customers and expand in Asia and Europe.

FedEx Express and FedEx Ground provide the bulk of the company's business, offering valuable services to anyone who needs to deliver letters, documents and packages. Whether dropped off at one of 43,000 drop boxes, more than 1200 world service centres or picked up by FedEx courier, each package is taken to a local FedEx office, where it is transported to the nearest airport. The package is flown to one of the company's distribution hubs for sorting and then flown to the airport nearest its destination. The package is then taken to another FedEx office, where a courier picks it up and hand delivers it to the correct recipient. All of this takes place overnight, with many packages delivered before 8.00 a.m. the next day. FedEx confirms that roughly 99 per cent of its deliveries are made on time.

To achieve this successful delivery rate, FedEx maintains an impressive infrastructure of aircraft, vehicles, equipment and processes. FedEx operates its own weather-forecasting service, ensuring that most of its flights arrive within 15 minutes of schedule. Most packages shipped within the United States are sorted at the company's Memphis superhub, where FedEx takes over control of the Memphis International Airport at roughly 11 p.m. each night. FedEx planes land side by side on parallel runways every minute or so for well over an hour each night. After the packages are sorted, all FedEx planes take off in time to reach their destinations. Not all packages are shipped via air: whenever possible, FedEx uses ground transportation to cut costs. For international deliveries, FedEx uses a combination of direct services and independent contractors.

FedEx services are priced using a zone system where the distance a package must travel to reach its final destination determines the price. Rates vary widely by package weight and shipping zone. Saturday pick-up and delivery are also available for an additional price premium. Prices vary for larger packages and international shipments.

## Priority Service

In Europe, most FedEx users are familiar with FedEx International Priority Service, which offers:

- on-time delivery or money back
- call customer service centres throughout the world
- easy-to-use shipment paperwork
- free packaging provided by FedEx
- effective and fast customs clearance systems
- sophisticated real-time IT-enabled tracking information
- free shipping software products
- proof of delivery on every invoice.

These service benefits reflect FedEx's emphasis on customer service and ceaseless investment in IT systems.

## FedEx Maintains Leadership in IT

Despite its tremendous successes, FedEx has faced some difficult times in its efforts to grow and compete against strong rival companies. The overnight delivery market matured very rapidly as intense competition from the US Postal Service, UPS, Emery, DHL, RPS and electronic document delivery – fax machines and e-mail – forced FedEx to search for viable means of expansion.

FedEx constantly strives to improve its services by enhancing its distribution networks, transportation infrastructure, information technology and employee performance. FedEx also continues to invest heavily in IT by installing computer terminals at customers' offices and giving away its proprietary tracking software. Today, the vast majority of FedEx customers, more than 70 per cent, electronically generate their own pick-up and delivery requests. FedEx has also moved more aggressively into e-commerce with respect to order fulfilment for business-to-business and business-to-consumer merchants.

FedEx offers a wealth of electronic tools, applications and on-line interfaces for customers to integrate into their processes to shorten response time, reduce inventory costs, generate better returns and to simplify their shipping. FedEx InSight was the first web-based application to offer proactive, real-time status information on inbound, outbound and third-party shipments. It enables customers to identify issues instantly and address them before they become problems. In addition, FedEx InSight allows customers to see the progress of their shipments without requiring a tracking number, giving them convenient and unprecedented data visibility critical to effective management of their supply chain systems. FedEx technology enables customers, couriers and contract delivery personnel to access the company's information systems networks wirelessly, any time, anywhere. FedEx was the first transportation company to embrace wireless technology, more than two decades ago, and continues to be a leader in the use of innovative wireless solutions.

## The Future for FedEx

As FedEx moves ahead, the company has many strengths and capabilities on which to build. No other carrier can match FedEx's global capabilities or one-stop shopping – at least not yet. To increase its competitiveness, FedEx is focusing on increasing revenue and reducing costs through tighter integration and consolidation, improved productivity and reduced capital expenditures. Five themes frame FedEx's efforts to fully leverage the strong franchise of the FedEx brand.

1 *Vision*: It's the foundation of any successful business, and it starts with the management team. Our core strategy is clear and reinforced throughout the organization through effective communications.
2 *Service:* We must continue to streamline all our internal processes that touch the customer to deliver a flawless experience every time. We are delighted at being ranked highest in the J.D. Power and Associates 2002 Small Package Delivery Service Business Customer Satisfaction StudySM for air, ground and international delivery services, and we look forward to raising the service bar even higher.
3 *People*: Our diverse and talented employees around the world are united in their absolutely, positively, whatever-it-takes spirit. No matter which operating company they work for, their teamwork and their commitment run purple.
4 *Innovation*: We will continue to invest in new technologies such as a real-time wireless pocket PC that gives our FedEx Express couriers fast wireless access to the FedEx network.
5 *Value*: As we add more value to our customers' businesses, we believe we can also create more value for our shareowners.

## FedEx's Success

A major reason for its success is the company's enviable corporate culture and workforce. FedEx recognises that employees are critical to the company's success, so the company strives to recruit the best people and offers them the top training and pay in the industry. FedEx employees are loyal, highly efficient and – according to independent research – extremely effective in delivering good service. In fact, FedEx employees claim to have 'purple blood' to match the company's official colour. It is not surprising that FedEx has been named as one of the '100 Best Companies to Work For' for six consecutive years.

Another reason for FedEx's success is its leadership in IT and customer relationship management (CRM). The company's focus on 'delivering certainty' has allowed it to home in on opportunities that give FedEx additional capabilities in innovative information technology solutions.

A final reason for FedEx's success is outstanding marketing: FedEx is a master at recognising untapped customer needs, and building relationships. Neither is FedEx ever content to rest on its laurels as it constantly strives to improve service and offer more options to its customers. After several decades of success, there is little doubt that Fred Smith's grade-C paper has become an indispensable part of the business world.

## Questions for Discussion

1 Evaluate the methods used by FedEx to grow, both domestically and internationally.
2 For the logistics manager of a large international producer of laptops, what benefits may be provided by FedEx?
3 What has been the role of IT and CRM in the success of the FedEx Corporation?

# V Promotion (Marketing Communications) Decisions

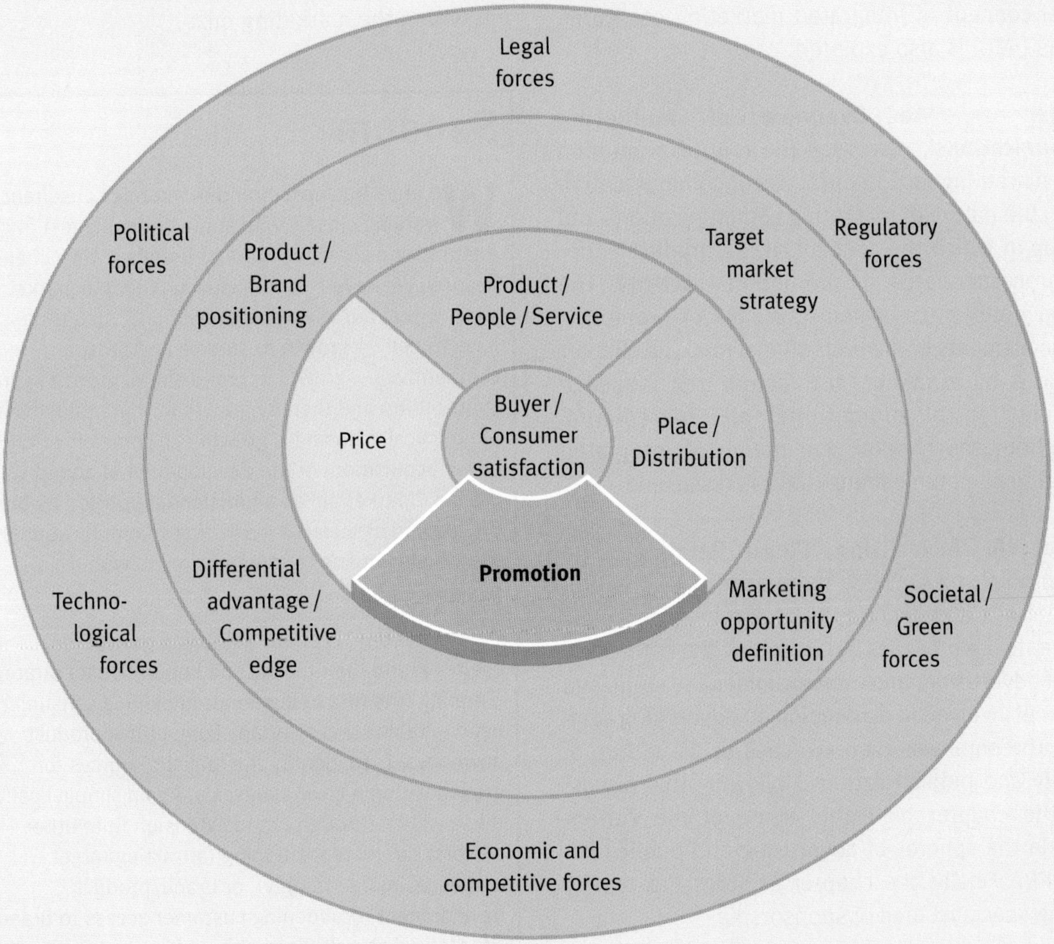


The term *promotion* encompasses all of the various tools of marketing communications. These include advertising, public relations and publicity, the growing area of sponsorship, personal selling, sales promotion, direct mail, the Internet and aspects of direct marketing. Together, these elements are generally referred to as the *promotional mix*. Many consumers believe that the promotional aspect of marketing is all that marketing encompasses. For many marketing personnel, the lay person's familiar view that 'marketing is advertising' is a tiresome but frequently encountered attitude. It must be emphasised that promotion is just another ingredient of the marketing mix, the toolkit marketers use to implement marketing strategies. Nevertheless, it is a very important ingredient, one that accounts for the vast proportion of most businesses' marketing budgets, employs millions of people in Europe alone and constitutes an essential aspect of communicating an organisation's product or service proposition and its associated brand positioning strategy.

**Part V of *Marketing: Concepts and Strategies*** presents a thorough overview of the elements of promotion – marketing communications – and how the promotional mix fits into marketing strategy. The topical concept of integrated marketing communications (IMC) is also explored.

**Chapter 17, 'An Overview of Marketing Communications',** discusses the role of promotion in the marketing mix, the process of communication per se, the nature of marketing communications and the way in which the concept of the product adoption process relates to promotional activity. The chapter goes on to explain the aims of promotion and the elements of the promotional mix. The chapter concludes by examining the factors that influence the selection of promotional mix ingredients. Throughout the chapter, the notion of integrated marketing communications (IMC) is discussed.

**Chapter 18, 'Advertising, Public Relations and Sponsorship',** takes these three aspects of the promotional mix and explores their use in more detail. The chapter commences by describing the nature and uses of advertising, and then examines the steps and personnel involved in developing an advertising campaign. The emphasis then switches to the nature of publicity and public relations; following this discussion, the chapter highlights some of the current trends in the spheres of advertising and public relations (PR). Finally, the chapter explores the rapidly evolving specialist area of sponsorship.

**Chapter 19, 'Sales Management, Sales Promotion, Direct Mail and Direct Marketing',** begins by examining the nature and major purposes of personal selling, along with the basic steps in the personal selling process. It identifies the types of salesforce personnel and goes on to explore the nature of sales management. The chapter then explains the uses of sales promotion and the wide range of related activities, and then focuses on the role of direct mail in the promotional mix. The chapter concludes with an overview of the Internet and direct marketing, and looks at the growing popularity of these promotional methods.

By the conclusion of Part V of *Marketing: Concepts and Strategies*, readers should understand the essential decisions concerning marketing communications, the nature of integrated marketing communications and the composition of the promotional mix within the marketing mix.

## Sandom

We are a business-brand-marketing consultancy, working closely with some of the biggest fmcg (fast-moving consumer goods) brands in the UK and beyond. We have a simple view on the role marketing plays within our clients' organisations. All businesses have to deliver growth to survive and prosper competitively – growth in brand share, growth in profit contribution and thereby growth in shareholder value. Simplistically, business growth can come only from either acquisition, or the development of added-value brands. 'Marketing' as a function (supported by these brands and associated marketing communications) must be an engine for organic growth within businesses.

If 'marketing' is about delivering growth for a client's brand then the second imperative for strategic planning (the first being about fulfilling a consumer need – 'table stakes' for any competitive product nowadays) is to identify the realistic sources for growth within a given timescale. Again simplistically, these will be through brand extension (into other sectors), brand repositioning (attracting target audiences more strongly), or brand/product development (broadening customer access to brands). 'Marketing' as a discipline should be the 'architect' of these plans and activity – that is, the conceptual driver and the implemented – always remembering that measurable, demonstrable results have to be delivered within a set timescale.

**John Wringe, group CEO, 'Star Chamber' (The Sandom Group)**

Sandom's 'Star Chamber'™ approach tailors individual specialists from its group companies to reveal, create, deliver, express and project growth ideas for brands and business.

# 17 An Overview of Marketing Communications

**"Marketing communication is the art of seducing a consumer on his way to your competitor."**

*Patrick De Pelsmacker, University of Antwerp*

## Objectives

- To understand the role of promotion in the marketing mix
- To examine the process of communication
- To understand the product adoption process and its implications for promotional efforts
- To understand the aims of promotion
- To explore the elements of the promotional mix
- To appreciate the nature of integrated marketing communications (IMC)
- To acquire an overview of the major methods of promotion
- To explore the factors that influence the selection of promotional mix ingredients

## Introduction

Marketers spend large sums of money and significant amounts of time developing advertising campaigns, PR programmes, sales promotions and websites, to list only some of the activities grouped under promotional activity within the marketing mix. As discussed in Chapter 1, many lay people consider there to be little more to the role of marketing than the management of a company's marketing communications. In fact, there is much more to strategic marketing – as described in Chapters 1 and 2 – but the creation, execution and control of a company's marketing communications is indeed a significant task.

Communication is a sharing of meaning through the transmission of information. Marketing communication is the transmission of persuasive information about a good, service or an idea, targeted at key stakeholders and consumers within the target market segment. Marketing communications centre on the promotional mix, which comprises advertising, public relations, personal selling, sales promotion, direct mail, sponsorship and the Internet. Until relatively recently, each of these specialist areas was handled disparately within many companies. Integrated marketing communications (IMC) has emerged to coordinate and integrate all marketing communication tools, avenues and sources within a company into a seamless programme that maximises the impact on consumers and other end users, at minimal cost.

The 'target audience' is the marketing communications practitioner's term for those within the target market segment intended as the principal recipients of the promotional message. The product adoption process is awareness, interest, evaluation, trial and adoption. Marketing communications play a key role in enticing customers to progress from awareness to adoption – consumption – of a product. In this context, there are five 'communications effects': category need, brand awareness, brand attitude, brand purchase intention and purchase facilitation. Marketers must be clear about their promotional objectives, and realistic about the likely returns.

## Opener

# End Cruelty to Children. FULL STOP.

The National Society for the Prevention of Cruelty to Children (NSPCC) exists to end cruelty to children. FULL STOP. The NSPCC wants you to join to fight to end cruelty to children. FULL STOP. Child abuse happens in many situations: in the home, at school and sports facilities and in residential care and on vacations. The NSPCC's strategy is to protect children in all areas of their lives, through action programmes such as The Child in the Family, The Child in School and Child Protection. Someone to turn to is a key part of these programmes, collectively termed the 'Full Stop' campaign. The NSPCC estimates that the first phase of this innovative campaign requires £250 million. As a charity, this requires an extensive fundraising activity. FULL STOP.

In a multimedia campaign, the NSPCC pledged to raise £300 million in just 12 months. This figure was six times more than the charity's usual target of £50 million. Through its Full Stop campaign, the NSPCC hopes to bring an end to child cruelty within a generation.

Following the trend for provocative charity advertising, the campaign began with a series of unsettling television advertisements. These depicted various toys and other children's icons, such as Action Man, Rupert Bear and the Spice Girls, covering their eyes against a soundtrack of shouting parents and crying children. At the same time, 3500 posters carrying the same message appeared, with the NSPCC website offering support (www.nspcc.org.uk). The mailing of leaflets to every UK household bearing the message, 'Together we can stop cruelty to children once and for all', followed. The intention was to capitalise on the awareness created by the advertising campaign. Through this mass targeting, the NSPCC was making clear its intention to mobilise everyone. At the centre of the campaign was a pledge document, through which the public and businesses were invited to donate funds to the charity.

The charity intended for 20 per cent of its target donations to come from businesses. There were many ways in which businesses could become involved. The NSPCC developed a special toolkit that explained some of the sponsorship opportunities and cause-related marketing possibilities. Microsoft, which sponsors NSPCC advertising and holds fundraising events for the charity, is one company that already had links with the NSPCC. The software business states it is happy to be associated with a cause that supports child welfare, particularly in view of its increasing emphasis on developing educational software for families and the young.

At the beginning of the NSPCC's campaign it was unclear whether or not the £300 million target could be met. However, the key was in the scale of the appeal and the fact that it combined a carefully constructed mix of different promotional tools and techniques. The target has not yet been met but, led by His Royal Highness the Duke of York as patron, the Full Stop campaign has so far raised a remarkable £140 million to help ease the suffering of abused children and lead the fight to end this terrible problem in society. In addition to the money raised, the Full Stop

campaign, using most aspects of marketing communications, has helped raise awareness of the problem and has inspired others to help this worthy cause. Over 140,000 have signed up to help the NSPCC's campaign.

**Sources:** 'NSPCC aims to convert abuse anger into cash', *Marketing*, 25 March 1999, pp. 37–8; Jade Garrett, 'Charities snub shock tactics for subtle approach', *Campaign*, 26 March 1999, p. 10; 'Spotlight charity', *Marketing Week*, 17 December 1998, pp. 28–9; 'Charities unite in donor appeal', *Marketing*, 14 January 1999, p. 4. Advertisement: courtesy of the National Society for the Prevention of Cruelty to Children; www.nspcc.org.uk/html/home/newsandcampaigns, July 2004.

Organisations use various promotional approaches to communicate with target markets, as the NSPCC did with its Full Stop campaign. Practitioners generally refer to the use of the promotion ingredient of the marketing mix as 'marketing communications' or 'MarComms'. It is important not to confuse the promotion ingredient of the marketing mix with either sales promotion or price offer promotions. Promotion in the marketing mix incorporates all aspects of the promotional mix, including advertising, public relations, sponsorship, direct mail, sales promotion, personal selling and the use of the Internet to communicate with an organisation's target audiences. Increasingly, these elements of the promotional mix are coordinated in the guise of integrated marketing communications (IMC).

This chapter looks at the general dimensions of promotion, defining it in the context of marketing and examining the roles it plays. Next, to understand how promotion works, the chapter analyses the meaning and process of communication, as well as promotion's role within the product adoption process. The remainder of the chapter discusses the major types of promotional method and the factors that influence an organisation's decision to use specific methods of promotion: advertising, personal selling, publicity and public relations, sales promotion, sponsorship, direct mail, the Internet and direct marketing. Chapters 18 and 19 extend this discussion of the core elements of the promotional mix. The chapter includes an explanation of integrated marketing communications.

## The Role of Promotion

People's attitudes towards promotion vary. Some hold that promotional activities, particularly advertising and personal selling, paint a distorted picture of reality because they provide the customer with only selected information.[1] Proponents of this view often suggest that promotional activities are unnecessary and wasteful, and that promotion costs are too high, resulting in higher prices. They may also argue that too much promotion has caused changes in social values, such as increased materialism. Others take a positive view. They believe that advertising messages often project wholesome values – such as affection, generosity or patriotism[2] – or that advertising, as a powerful economic force, can free countries from poverty by communicating information.[3] It has also been argued that the advertising of consumer products was a factor in the decline of communism and the move towards a free enterprise system in eastern Europe. However, none of these impressions is completely accurate.

**Promotion**
Communication with individuals, groups or organisations in order to facilitate exchanges by informing and persuading audiences to accept a company's products

The role of **promotion** in a company is to communicate with individuals, groups or organisations, with the aim of directly or indirectly facilitating exchanges by informing and persuading one or more of the audiences to accept the company's products.[4] PepsiCo, for example, recruited pop star Michael Jackson to communicate the benefits of its cola drink. Various brands currently employ David Beckham to help boost the appeal of their products. Rock Against Drugs (RAD), a not-for-profit organisation, employs popular rock musicians, such as Lou Reed, to communicate its anti-drug messages to teenagers and young adults. Like PepsiCo and RAD, marketers try to communicate with selected audiences about their company and its goods, services and ideas in order to facilitate exchanges.

Exchanges are facilitated by marketers ensuring that information is targeted at appropriate individuals and groups: potential customers, special interest groups such as environmental and consumer groups, current and potential investors and regulatory agencies. Some marketers use **cause-related marketing**, which links the purchase of their products to philanthropic efforts for a particular cause. Cause-related marketing often helps a marketer boost sales and generate goodwill through contributions to causes that members of its target markets want to support. For example, as this chapter's 'Starter' explains, the NSPCC encourages businesses such as Microsoft to become involved in joint initiatives to raise funds. Similarly, Procter & Gamble has tied promotional efforts for some of its products to contributions to the Special Olympics.

**Cause-related marketing**
Links the purchase of a product to philanthropic efforts for a particular 'good' cause

Viewed from this wider perspective, promotion can play a comprehensive communications role.[5] Some promotional activities, such as publicity and public relations, can be directed towards helping a company justify its existence and maintain positive, healthy relationships between itself and various groups in the marketing environment.

Although a company can direct a single type of communication – such as an advertisement – towards numerous audiences, marketers often design a communication precisely for a specific target market. A company frequently communicates several different messages concurrently, each to a different group. For example, McDonald's may direct one communication towards customers for its Big Mac, a second message about its salads towards health-concerned consumers, a third message towards investors about the company's stable growth, and a fourth communication towards society in general regarding the company's Ronald McDonald Houses, which provide support to families of children suffering from cancer.

To gain maximum benefit from promotional efforts, marketers must make every effort to properly plan, implement, coordinate and control communications. As is explained later, the concept of integrated marketing communications helps to harmonise and coordinate an organisation's promotional activities. Effective promotional activities are based on information from the marketing environment (see Chapter 3), often obtained from an organisation's marketing information system (see Chapter 9). How effectively marketers can use promotion to maintain positive relationships depends largely on the quantity and quality of information an organisation takes in. For example, concerns about genetically modified (GM) foods have led certain supermarkets to improve in-store labelling, so that consumers are better informed about those products affected.

The basic role of promotion is to communicate, so it is important to analyse what communication is and how the communication process works.

# The Communication Process

**Communication**
A sharing of meaning through the transmission of information

Communication can be viewed as the transmission of information.[6] For communication to take place, however, both the sender and the receiver of the information must share some common ground. They must share an understanding of the symbols used to transmit information, usually pictures or words. For instance, an individual transmitting the following message may believe he or she is communicating with readers of this book.

在工廠吾人製造化粧品，在商店吾人銷售希望。

**Marketing communication**
The transmission of persuasive information about a good, service or an idea, targeted at key stakeholders and consumers within the target market segment

However, communication has not taken place, because few readers understand the intended message.[7] Thus **communication** is defined here as a sharing of meaning.[8] Implicit in this definition is the notion of transmission of information, because sharing necessitates transmission. Communication, therefore, is a sharing of meaning through the transmission of information. **Marketing communication** is the transmission of persuasive information about a

good, service or an idea, targeted at key stakeholders and consumers within the target market segment. Marketing communications centre on the promotional mix, which comprises advertising, public relations, personal selling, sales promotion, direct mail, sponsorship and the Internet.

**Source**
A person, group or organisation that has an intended meaning it attempts to share with an audience

**Receiver**
An individual, group or organisation that decodes a coded message

**Receiving audience**
Two or more receivers who decode a message

As Figure 17.1 shows, communication begins with a source. A **source** is a person, group or organisation that has an intended meaning it attempts to share with an audience. For example, a source could be a political party wishing to recruit new members or an organisation that wants to send a message to thousands of consumers through an advertisement. Developing a strategy can enhance the effectiveness of the source's communication. For example, a strategy in which a sales person attempts to influence a customer's decision by eliminating competitive products from consideration has been found to be effective.[9] A **receiver** is the individual, group or organisation that decodes a coded message. A **receiving audience** is two or more receivers who decode a message. The intended receivers, or audience, of an advertisement for MBA courses might be junior business executives wishing to broaden their managerial skills. The source may be a European business school, such as INSEAD.

**Coding process**
The process of converting meaning into a series of signs that represent ideas or concepts; also called encoding

To transmit meaning, a source must convert that meaning into a series of signs that represent ideas or concepts. This is called the **coding process**, or encoding. When encoding meaning into a message, a source must take into account certain characteristics of the receiver or receiving audience. First, to share meaning, the source should use signs that are familiar to the receiver or receiving audience. Marketers who understand this fact realise how important it is to know their target market and to make sure that an advertisement, for example, is written in language that the target market can understand. Thus when Lever Brothers advertises its Persil washing powder, it makes no attempt to explain the chemical reactions involved when the product removes dirt and grease, because this would not be meaningful to consumers. There have been some notable problems in the language translation of advertisements. For example, Budweiser has been advertised in Spain as the 'Queen of Beers' and the Chinese have been encouraged to 'eat their fingers off' when receiving KFC's slogan 'Finger-Lickin' Good'.[10]

Second, when encoding a meaning, a source should try to use signs that the receiver or receiving audience uses for referring to the concepts the source intends. Marketers should generally avoid signs that can have several meanings for an audience. For example, an international advertiser of soft drinks should avoid using the word soda as a general term for soft drinks. Although in some places soda is taken to mean 'soft drink', in others it may connote bicarbonate of soda, an ice cream drink, or something that one mixes with Scotch whisky.

**Medium of transmission**
The tool used to carry the coded message from the source to the receiver or receiving audience

To share a coded meaning with the receiver or receiving audience, a source must select and use a medium of transmission. A **medium of transmission** carries the coded message from the source to the receiver or receiving audience. Transmission media include ink on paper, vibrations of air waves produced by vocal cords, chalk marks on a chalkboard and electronically produced communication, as in radio, television, mobile phones and the Internet.

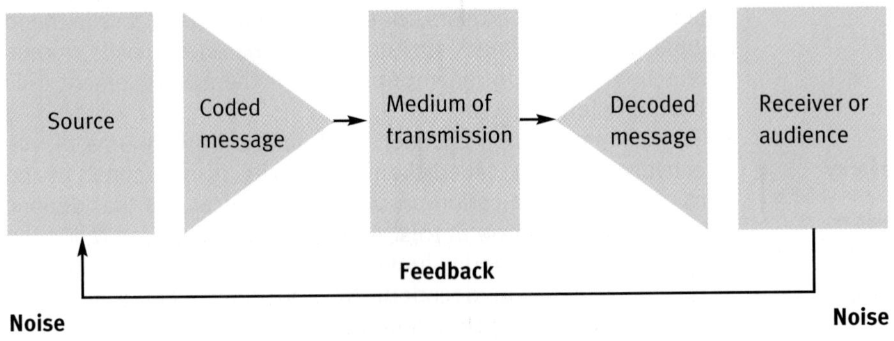


*Figure 17.1*
*The communication process*

Sometimes a source chooses an inappropriate medium of transmission. A coded message may reach some receivers, but not the right ones. For example, suppose a local theatre group spends most of its advertising budget on radio advertisements. If theatre-goers depend mainly on newspapers for information about local drama, then the theatre group will not reach its intended target audience. Coded messages may also reach intended receivers in an incomplete form because the intensity of the transmission is weak. For example, radio signals can be received effectively over a limited range that may vary depending on climatic conditions. Members of the target audience who live on the fringe of the broadcasting area may receive only a weak signal.

**Decoding process**
The process in which signs are converted into concepts and ideas

**Noise**
A condition that exists when the decoded message is different from that which was encoded

In the **decoding process**, signs are converted into concepts and ideas. Seldom does a receiver decode exactly the same meaning that a source encoded. When the result of decoding is different from what was encoded, **noise** exists. Noise has many sources and may affect any or all parts of the communication process. When a source selects a medium of transmission through which an audience does not expect to receive a message, noise is likely to occur. Noise sometimes arises within the medium of transmission itself. Radio static, faulty printing processes and laryngitis are sources of noise. Interference on viewers' television sets during an advertisement is noise and reduces the impact of the message. Noise also occurs when a source uses a sign that is unfamiliar to the receiver or that has a different meaning from the one the source intended. Noise may also originate in the receiver. As Chapter 6 discussed, a receiver may be unaware of a coded message because his or her perceptual processes block it out or because the coded message is too obscure.

**Feedback**
The receiver's response to a message

The receiver's response to a message is **feedback** to the source. The source usually expects and normally receives feedback, although it may not be immediate. During feedback, the receiver or receiving audience is the source of a message that is directed towards the original source, which then becomes a receiver. Feedback is encoded, sent through a medium of transmission – for example, a survey questionnaire – and then decoded by the receiver, the source of the original communication. It is logical to think of communication as a circular process.

During face-to-face communication, such as in personal selling or product sampling, both verbal and non-verbal feedback can be immediate. Instant feedback enables communicators to adjust their messages quickly to improve the effectiveness of their communication. For example, when a sales person realises through feedback that a customer does not understand a sales presentation, he or she adapts the presentation to make it more meaningful to the customer. This may be why face-to-fact sales presentations create higher behavioural intentions to purchase services than do telemarketing sales contacts.[11] In interpersonal communication, feedback occurs through talking, touching, smiling, nodding, eye movements, and other body movements and postures.

When mass communication such as advertising is used, feedback is often slow and difficult to recognise. If Disneyland Paris increased its advertising in order to raise the number of visitors, it might be 6 to 18 months before the theme park could recognise the effects of the expanded advertising. Although it is harder to recognise, feedback does exist for mass communication. Advertisers, for example, obtain feedback in the form of changes in sales volume or in consumers' attitudes and awareness levels, monitored through tracking research. The coupon redemption rate for the advertisement in Figure 17.2 provides an opportunity for feedback.

**Channel capacity**
The limit on the volume of information that a particular communication channel can handle effectively

Each communication channel has a limit on the volume of information it can handle effectively. This limit, called **channel capacity**, is determined by the least efficient component of the communication process. Communications that depend on vocal speech provide a good illustration of this. An individual source can talk only so fast, and there is a limit to how much an individual receiver can take in aurally. Beyond that point, additional messages cannot be decoded; thus meaning cannot be shared. Although a radio announcer can read several hundred words a minute, a one-minute advertising message

***Figure 17.2***
*This direct response advertisement provides an opportunity for feedback based on the coupon redemption rate*
*Source: Courtesy of Dr. Oetker (UK) Ltd. To find out more about Dr. Oetker (UK) Ltd, please visit www.oetker.co.uk*

should not exceed 150 words because most announcers cannot articulate the words into understandable messages at a rate beyond 150 words per minute. This figure is the limit for both source and receiver, and marketers should keep this in mind when developing radio advertisements. At times, a company creates a television advertisement that contains several types of visual material and several forms of audio message, all transmitted to viewers at the same time. Such communication may not be totally effective, because receivers cannot decode all the messages simultaneously.[12]

Now that the basic communication process has been explored, it is worth considering more specifically how promotion is used in marketing communications to influence individuals, groups or organisations to accept or adopt a company's products. Although the product adoption process was touched upon briefly in Chapter 12, it is discussed more fully in the following section in order to provide a better understanding of the conditions under which promotion occurs.

# Promotion and the Product Adoption Process

Marketers do not promote simply to inform, educate and entertain; they communicate to facilitate satisfying exchanges – products or services for money or donations. One long-run purpose of promotion is to influence and encourage buyers to accept or adopt goods, services and ideas. At times, an advertisement may be informative or entertaining, yet it may fail to entice the audience to purchase the product. For example, some advertisements seem to be weak in communicating benefits – they focus instead on getting customers to feel good about the product. The ultimate effectiveness of promotion is determined by the degree to which it affects product adoption among potential buyers or increases the frequency of current buyers' purchases.

To establish realistic expectations about what promotion can do, product adoption should not be viewed as a one-step process. Rarely can a single promotional activity cause an individual to buy a previously unfamiliar product. The acceptance of a product involves many steps. Although there are several ways to look at the **product adoption process**, it is commonly divided into five stages, as depicted in Figure 17.3 and explored in Chapter 12:

1 awareness,
2 interest,
3 evaluation,
4 trial
5 adoption.[13]

In the **awareness stage**, individuals become aware that the product exists, but they have little information about it and are not concerned about obtaining more. When Barclays launched b2 financial services, it used a provocative b2 flash teaser advertisement. Later, longer advertisements fully detailed the new portfolio of products. In Figure 17.4 JCB's teaser advertisement (left) did not reveal its innovative single-arm skid steer; later adverts did (right).

Consumers enter the **interest stage** when they are motivated to obtain information about the product's features, uses, advantages, disadvantages, price or location. During

**Product adoption process**
A series of five stages in the acceptance of a product: awareness, interest, evaluation, trial and adoption

**Awareness stage**
The beginning of the product adoption process, when individuals become aware that the product exists but have little information about it

**Interest stage**
The stage of the product adoption process when customers are motivated to obtain information about the product's features, uses, advantages, disadvantages, price or location

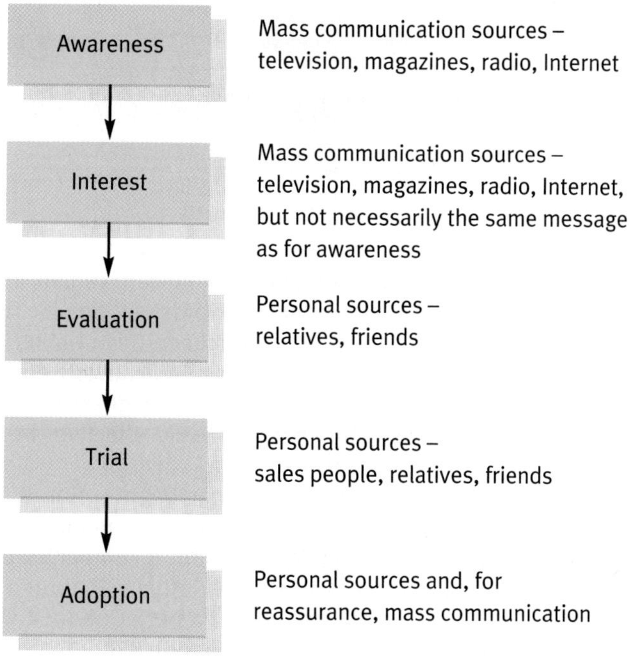

*Figure 17.3*
*Effective promotional tools for reaching consumers in various stages of the product adoption process*

Awareness — Mass communication sources – television, magazines, radio, Internet

Interest — Mass communication sources – television, magazines, radio, Internet, but not necessarily the same message as for awareness

Evaluation — Personal sources – relatives, friends

Trial — Personal sources – sales people, relatives, friends

Adoption — Personal sources and, for reassurance, mass communication

***Figure 17.4***
*Building awareness. JCB launched its skid steer initially with this teaser advertisement (above) before running the second advertisement, which revealed the actual product (opposite top).*
*Source: Courtesy of JCB Design Works*

***(figure continued over page)***

**Evaluation stage**
The stage of the product adoption process when customers decide whether the product will satisfy certain criteria that are crucial for meeting their specific needs

**Trial stage**
The stage of the product adoption process when individuals use or experience the product for the first time

the **evaluation stage**, individuals consider whether the product will satisfy certain criteria that are crucial for meeting their specific needs. In the **trial stage**, they use or experience the product for the first time, possibly by purchasing a small quantity, by taking advantage of a free sample or demonstration, or by borrowing the product from someone. Supermarkets, for example, frequently offer special promotions to encourage consumers to taste products such as cheese, cooked meats, snacks or pizza. During this stage, potential adopters determine the usefulness of the product under the specific conditions for which they need it.

Individuals move into the **adoption stage** by choosing the specific product when they need a product of that general type. It cannot be assumed, however, that because a person enters the adoption process she or he will eventually adopt the new product. Rejection may occur at any stage, including adoption. Both product adoption and product rejection can be temporary or permanent. Even if adoption occurs, as explored in Chapter 6, there is no guarantee of brand loyalty. As explained in Chapter 24's discussion of relationship marketing, marketers must work hard to ensure repeat buying and an ongoing relationship.

For the most part, people respond to different information sources at different stages of the adoption process. Figure 17.3 illustrates the most effective sources for each stage. Mass communication sources, such as television advertising or the Internet, are often effective for moving large numbers of people into the awareness stage. Producers of consumer goods commonly use massive advertising campaigns when introducing new products.

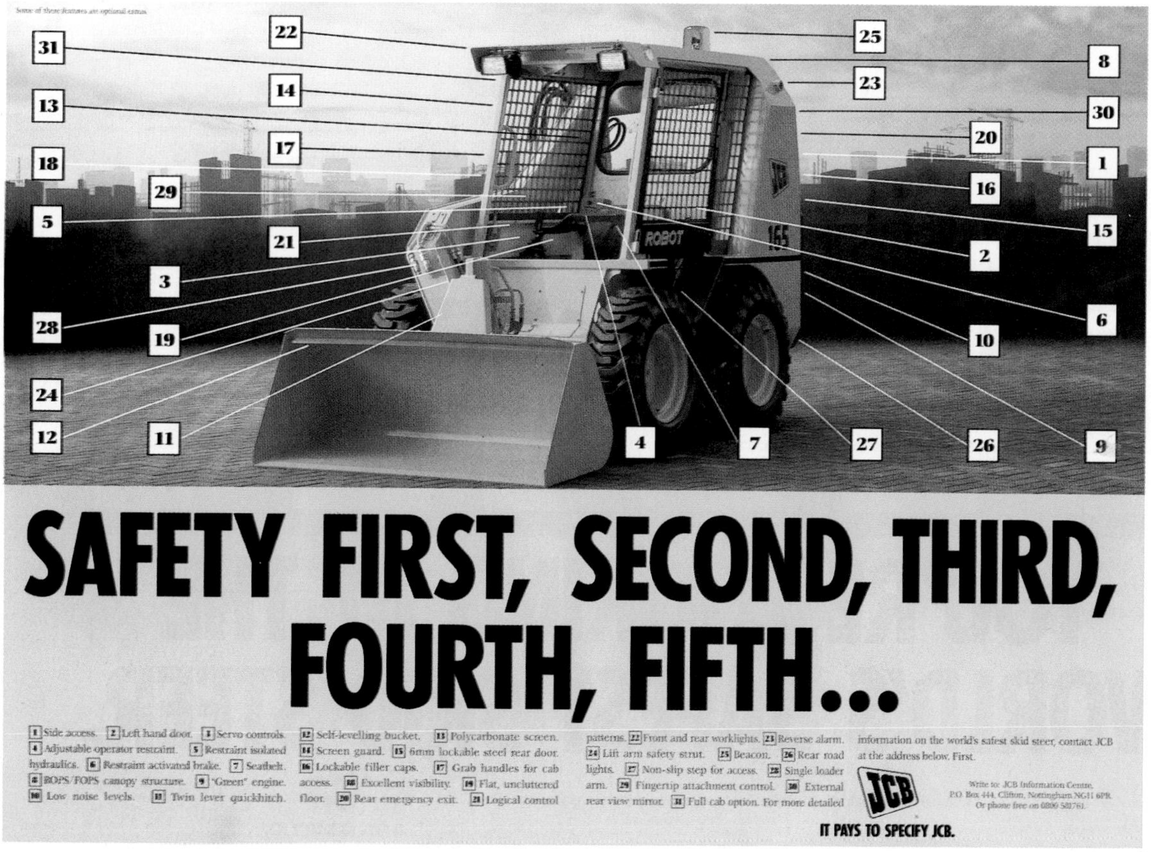


***Figure 17.4 (continued)***

**Adoption stage**
The final stage of product acceptance, when customers choose the specific product when they need a product of that type

They do so to create product awareness as quickly as possible within a large portion of the target market.

Mass communication sources may also be effective for people in the interest stage who want to learn more about a product. During the evaluation stage, individuals often seek information, opinions and reinforcement from personal sources – relatives, friends and associates. In the trial stage, individuals depend on sales people for information about how to use the product properly in order to gain the most out of it. Marketers must use advertising carefully when consumers are in the trial stage. If advertisements greatly exaggerate the benefits of a product, the consumer may be disappointed when the product does not meet expectations.[14] It is best to avoid creating expectations that cannot be satisfied, because rejection at this stage will prevent adoption. Friends and peers may also be important sources during the trial stage. By the time the adoption stage has been reached, both personal communication from sales personnel and mass communication through advertisements may be required. Even though the particular stage of the adoption process may influence the types of information source consumers use, marketers must remember that other factors – such as the product's characteristics, price and uses, as well as the characteristics of customers – also affect the types of information source that buyers desire and believe.

Because people in separate stages of the adoption process often require different types of information, marketers designing a promotional campaign must determine what stage of the adoption process a particular target audience is in before they can develop the message. Potential adopters in the interest stage will need different information from people who have already reached the trial stage. Often a campaign will include several different

advertisements and promotional mix tools in order to appeal simultaneously to different consumers who are at different stages in the product adoption process.

When a company introduces a new product, people do not all begin the adoption process at the same time and they do not move through the process at the same speed. Of those people who eventually adopt the product, some enter the adoption process rather quickly, whereas others start considerably later. For most products, too, there is a group of non-adopters who never begin the process.

## Product Adopter Categories

**Adopter categories**
Five groups into which customers can be divided according to the length of time it takes them to adopt a product: innovators, early adopters, early majority, late majority and laggards

**Innovators**
The first people to adopt a new product

**Early adopters**
People who choose new products carefully and are often consulted by people from the remaining adopter categories

**Early majority**
People who adopt products just prior to the average person

Depending on the length of time it takes them to adopt a new product, people can be divided into five major **adopter categories**: innovators, early adopters, early majority, late majority and laggards.[15] Figure 17.5 shows each adopter category and indicates the percentage of total adopters that it typically represents.

**Innovators** are the first to adopt a new product. They enjoy trying new products and tend to be venturesome. **Early adopters** choose new products carefully and are viewed as 'the people to check with' by those in the remaining adopter categories. People in the **early majority** adopt just prior to the average person; they are deliberate and cautious in trying new products. **Late majority** people, who are quite sceptical about new products, eventually adopt them because of economic necessity or social pressure. **Laggards,** the last to adopt a new product, are oriented towards the past. They are suspicious of new products or unable to afford them easily, and when they finally adopt the innovation, it may already have been replaced by a newer product. When microwave ovens first appeared, only 'technocrats' or 'food boffins' – the innovators – bought them. Then 'trend setters' – the early adopters – came into the market. After several years and prompted by many frozen food manufacturers' new product launches, many more consumers – the early majority – decided to adopt the microwave oven. Eventually, the rest of the masses – the late majority – decided that they, too, should have a microwave oven 'given that most people have one now'. There are, though, some households only now deciding to buy one – the laggards; and some – the non-adopters – never will. When developing promotional efforts, a marketer should bear in mind that people in different adopter categories often need different forms of communication and different types of information or message.

# Aims of Promotion

Product adoption is a major focus for any promotional activity. There are, though, five basic communications aims, known as the **five communication effects**. These are:[16]

1 category need
2 brand awareness
3 brand attitude
4 brand purchase intention
5 purchase facilitation.

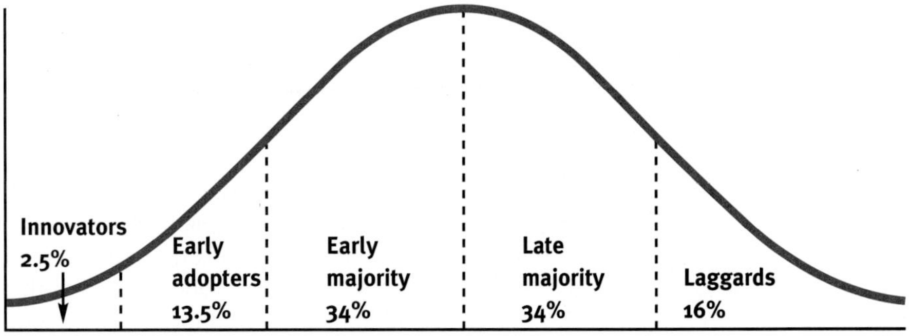


***Figure 17.5***
*Distribution of product adopter categories*
*Source: reprinted with the permission of The Free Press, a division of Simon & Schuster, Inc., from* Diffusion of Innovations, *3rd edn, by Everett M. Rogers. Copyright © 1962, 1971, 1983 by The Free Press*

**Late majority**
People who are quite sceptical about new products but eventually adopt them because of economic necessity or social pressure

**Laggards**
The last people to adopt a new product, suspicious of new products and oriented towards the past

**Five communication effects**
Communication aims that include category need, brand awareness, brand attitude, brand purchase intention and purchase facilitation

**Category need**
The consumer's perception of his or her need for a product in a certain category

**Brand awareness**
The consumer's ability to identify a manufacturer's or retailer's brand in sufficient detail to distinguish it from other brands

**Brand attitude**
A consumer's particular impression of a brand, formed by emotions and logic or cognitive beliefs

**Brand purchase intention**
The consumer's decision and efforts to purchase the particular product

**Purchase facilitation**
Circumstances that make it possible for the consumer to purchase the product: availability, location, price and familiarity of vendor

**Category Need** The consumer must realise he or she wants a particular product – particularly for innovative new category product launches – and must perceive a **category need** in order to be motivated even to consider a product. When compact disc players were launched, many consumers had perfectly adequate album and/or cassette based hi-fi systems and did not see any need to purchase a compact disc player. CD producers had to create a category need. More recently, mobile phone networks have persuaded many users of the need for built-in cameras, web browsing or music downloads – eye-catching advertising has communicated the benefits of these cellphone attributes, creating category need.

**Brand Awareness** The consumer must be able to identify – recognise or recall – a manufacturer's or retailer's brand within the category in sufficient detail to make a purchase. **Brand awareness** means that the manufacturer or retailer must make its brand stand out, initially through product attributes supported by distinctive promotional activity. Sony wants consumers to be aware of its compact disc or mp3 players rather than Aiwa or Amstrad players. In most marketing communications there is the objective of establishing brand awareness among target consumers.

**Brand Attitude** Emotions and logic or cognitive beliefs combine to give the consumer a particular impression of a product. This **brand attitude** directs consumer choice towards a particular brand. Companies need customers to have a positive view of their brands. Much promotional mix activity and the creation of the promotional message relate to developing a favourable brand attitude, but other marketing mix ingredients also impact on these perceptions, notably product design, features and performance.

**Brand Purchase Intention** Once a category need and brand awareness are established, if the consumer's brand attitude is favourable, he or she will decide to purchase the particular product and take steps to do so, showing **brand purchase intention**.

**Purchase Facilitation** Having decided to buy, the consumer requires the product to be readily available at a convenient location, at a suitable price and from a familiar dealer: **purchase facilitation**. A manufacturer must ensure that other marketing mix factors – product, people, place (distribution) and price – do not hinder the purchase. Sony customers expect wide distribution from reputable retailers, with no budget pricing. Sony produces high-quality goods, but it has several well-respected competitors and must ensure product availability and continued product improvement to prevent brand switching.

To provide a better understanding of how promotion can move people closer to the acceptance of goods, services and ideas, the next section focuses on the major promotional methods available to an organisation: the promotional mix and integrated marketing communications.

## The Promotional Mix

Several types of promotional methods can be used to communicate with individuals, groups and organisations. When an organisation combines specific ingredients to promote a particular product, that combination constitutes the promotional mix for that product. The four traditional ingredients of a **promotional mix** are advertising, personal selling, publicity/public relations and sales promotion. Increasingly, sponsorship and direct mail are elements of the promotional mix in their own right (see Figure 17.6).[17] The Internet and direct marketing are recent additions to the promotional mix, as explored in Chapter 4 and in the Innovation and Change box on page 522. For some products, businesses use all of these ingredients; for other products, two or three will suffice. This section analyses the major ingredients of a promotional mix and the chief factors that

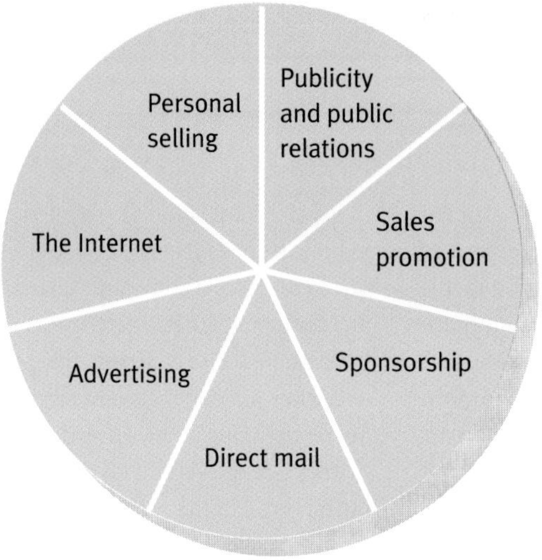


***Figure 17.6***
*Possible ingredients of an organisation's promotional mix*

influence an organisation to include specific ingredients in the promotional mix for a specific product. Chapters 18 and 19 examine the promotional mix ingredients in greater detail.

## Promotional Mix Ingredients

At this point consideration is given to some general characteristics of advertising, personal selling, publicity and public relations, sales promotion, sponsorship, direct mail, the Internet and direct marketing. The following chapters explore these tools in more detail.

**Promotional mix**
The specific combination of ingredients an organisation uses to promote a product, traditionally including four ingredients: advertising, personal selling, publicity and public relations, and sales promotion

**Advertising**
A paid form of non-personal communication about an organisation and its products that is transmitted to a target audience through a mass medium

**Advertising** **Advertising** is a paid form of non-personal communication about an organisation and its products that is transmitted to a target audience through a mass medium such as television, radio, newspapers, magazines, direct mail, public transport, outdoor displays, catalogues or the Internet. Individuals and organisations use advertising to promote goods, services, ideas, issues and people. Because it is highly flexible, advertising offers the options of reaching an extremely large target audience or focusing on a small, precisely defined segment of the population. For instance, McDonald's advertising focuses on a large audience of potential fast-food consumers, ranging from children to adults, whereas advertising for DeBeers' diamonds focuses on a much smaller and specialised target market.

Advertising offers several benefits. It can be an extremely cost-efficient promotional method because it reaches a vast number of people at a low cost per person. For example, if the cost of a four-colour, one-page advertisement in the *Sunday Telegraph* magazine is £7000, and the magazine reaches 700,000 readers, the cost of reaching 1000 subscribers is only £10 per person. Advertising also enables the user to repeat the message a number of times. Unilever advertises many of its products – cleaning products, foods, cosmetics – on television, in magazines and through outdoor advertising. Advertising repetition has been found to be especially effective for brand name extensions beyond the original product category.[18] In addition, advertising a product in a certain way can add to its value. For example, BMW cars are advertised as having more sophistication, style and technical innovation than Honda, Toyota and other Japanese companies' vehicles. The visibility that an organisation gains from advertising enhances the company's public image. There clearly is a link between a product's brand positioning and the role of marketing communications, as explained in Chapters 8 and 11.

Advertising also has several disadvantages. Even though the cost per person reached may be low, the absolute monetary outlay can be extremely high, especially for advertisements shown during popular television programmes. These high costs can limit, and sometimes

## Innovation and Change

### Web Advertising Comes of Age

During the 1990s many corporate giants avoided using banners, buttons and other early forms of Internet advertising, believing them to be inefficient and ineffective. Now most large companies embrace Internet advertising. McDonald's uses websites, banners and buttons, instant messaging, on-line games and pop-up windows to engage with consumers through interactivity. As the company's director for media explains, 'We're not going to sell burgers on-line, but we can extend the experience of the brand on-line and bring McDonald's to life on-line.' Many web experts believe few consumer or business brands can now avoid harnessing wed-based advertising, particularly if – as in the case of McDonald's – the target audience is young and made up of frequent web users.

Nike has many websites, some of which promote specific brands, linking into its sponsorship of entertainers and sports stars. Guerrilla moves, such as mentioning its websites or celebrity tie-ins in chat room messages have been hugely successful for the company in attracting hundreds of thousands of visitors to its websites for specific on-line promotions and advertising campaigns. Sports-focused video clips, mp3 downloadable tracks, musical e-postcards suitable for personalisation, and e-mail games have proved a big hit with the youth market targeted by so many Nike products. The company encourages participation and repeat visits by inviting visitors to serve as DJs, rate the videos and register to receive daily game tips via e-mail.

Pepsi is harnessing the web to advertise its wares, but also to build its brand. Daily, a quarter of a million consumers log on to enjoy Pepsi.com's ever-changing mix of entertainment, promotions, games, merchandise offers and new product information. The company ties its web activity closely to its television advertising campaigns. For example, just hours before debuting a new advertisement on television featuring Britney Spears, Pepsi.com gave a sneak preview by posting it on Yahoo! – in the next four days, an incredible one million visitors viewed the Britney advert on-line. This combined use of media has become the norm for Pepsi's advertising, with on-line clips, interviews and footage of the advertising's stars behind the scenes. Pepsi's advertising agency believes this combined attack involves Pepsi consumers much more than when Pepsi only ran TV adverts.

The web has provided advertising executives with the opportunity to interact with the specific target audience for many brands. Initially, websites were developed at arm's length from a brand's advertising, but with the growing focus on fully integrated marketing communications, web advertising is now both very popular and increasingly linked with a brand's other advertising and promotional mix activity.

**Sources:** McDonald's, Nike and Pepsi, with thanks to *Advertising Age* and *Campaign*.

prevent, the use of advertising in a promotional mix. Moreover, advertising rarely provides rapid feedback. Measuring its effect on sales is difficult, and it ordinarily has a less persuasive impact on customers than, for example, personal selling.[19] With the growth in satellite channels, the creation of ever greater numbers of consumer and trade magazines, the role of the web for advertisers and interactive television, the choice of media for advertisers is growing increasingly complex and prone to error unless handled by specialist media buyers.

**Personal selling**
The use of personal communication in an exchange situation to inform customers and persuade them to purchase products

**Telemarketing**
Direct selling over the telephone, relying heavily on personal selling

**Personal Selling** Selling that involves informing customers and persuading them to purchase products through personal communication in an exchange situation is called **personal selling**. The phrase 'to purchase products' should be interpreted broadly to encompass the acceptance of ideas and issues. **Telemarketing**, described in Chapter 13 as direct selling over the telephone, relies heavily on personal selling. The role of sales management in marketing is discussed in more detail in Chapter 19.

Personal selling has both advantages and limitations when compared with advertising. Advertising is general communication aimed at a relatively large target audience, whereas personal selling involves more specific communication aimed at one person or several people. Reaching one person through personal selling costs considerably more than doing so through advertising, but personal selling efforts often have a greater impact on customers. Personal selling also provides immediate feedback, which allows marketers to adjust their message to improve communication. It helps them determine and respond to customers' needs for information.

**Kinesic communication** Body language, including winking, head nodding, hand gestures and arm movements

**Proxemic communication** A subtle form of communication used in face-to-face interactions when either person varies the physical distance that separates the two

**Tactile communication** Interpersonal communication through touching, including shaking hands

When a sales person and customer meet face to face, they use several types of interpersonal communication. Obviously, the predominant communication form is language – both speech and writing. In addition, a sales person and customer frequently use **kinesic communication**, or body language, by moving their heads, eyes, arms, hands, legs or torsos. Winking, head nodding, hand gestures and arm motions are forms of kinesic communication. A good sales person can often evaluate a prospect's interest in a product or presentation by watching for eye contact and head nodding. **Proxemic communication**, a less obvious form of communication used in personal selling, occurs in face-to-face interactions when either person varies the physical distance that separates the two people. When a customer backs away from a sales person, for example, that individual may be indicating that he or she is not interested in the product or may be expressing dislike for the sales person. Touching, or **tactile communication**, can also be used; shaking hands is a common form of tactile communication in many countries. Management of sales people is very important in making this component of promotion effective. Sales people who are directly involved in planning sales activities develop greater trust in their company and have increased sales performance.[20]

**Publicity** Non-personal communication in news-story form about an organisation and/or its products that is transmitted through a mass medium at no charge

**Public relations** Managing and controlling the process of using publicity effectively. It is the planned and sustained effort to establish and maintain goodwill and understanding between an organisation and its target publics

**Sales promotion** An activity or material that acts as a direct inducement by offering added value to or incentive for the product to resellers, sales people or consumers

**Publicity and Public Relations** **Publicity** refers to non-personal communication in news-story form about an organisation or its products, or both, that is transmitted through a mass medium at no charge. Examples of publicity include magazine, newspaper, radio and television news stories about new retail stores, new products or personnel changes in an organisation. Although both advertising and publicity are transmitted through mass communication, the sponsor does not pay the media costs for publicity and is not identified. Nevertheless, publicity should never be viewed as free communication. There are clear costs associated with preparing news releases and encouraging media personnel to broadcast or print them. A business that uses publicity regularly must have employees to perform these activities, or obtain the services of a public relations consultancy or an advertising agency. Either way, the company bears the costs of the activities.

Publicity must be planned and implemented so that it is compatible with, and supportive of, other elements in the promotional mix.[21] However, publicity cannot always be controlled to the extent that other elements of the promotional mix can be. For example, just as Perrier's contamination problems appeared to be easing, a BBC television programme showed that the 'bottled at source' packaging was misleading because the bubbles were added during the bottling process. Sainsbury's, a major grocery retailer in the UK, refused for many months to restock Perrier until the wording on the packaging was altered, creating further adverse publicity for the mineral water company. The **public relations** mechanism manages and controls the process of using publicity effectively (see Chapter 18).[22] As explored in the Topical Insight box (see page 524), public relations is a powerful ingredient of the promotional mix. Public relations is the planned and sustained effort to establish and maintain goodwill and understanding between an organisation and its target publics.

**Sales Promotion** A **sales promotion** is an activity or material that acts as a direct inducement by offering added value to, or incentive for, the product to resellers, sales people or consumers.[23] Examples of sales promotion include coupons, on-pack deals, trade shows, bonuses and contests used to enhance the sales of a product. The term sales promotion should not be confused with promotion; sales promotion is but a part of the more comprehensive area of

## Topical Insight

### Microsoft's Image Builders: PR Deflects Regulators' Criticisms

A monopoly and a bully, a champion of free enterprise or creative, inspired genius? Microsoft, the dominant software company and instigator of Windows, engenders many different images for various people. Image is important to Microsoft, which explains why the company employs a team of over 150 experts dedicated to public relations. Microsoft uses well-honed public relations skills to maintain favourable relationships with its stakeholders and to support new product introductions.

For example, in the weeks leading up to the launch of every major update of Windows, computer users are bombarded by media coverage in newspapers, magazines, television and radio, in web bulletins, and so forth. Customers receive direct mail and e-mail pop-ups. By the time the software update is released, a real buzz has been created.

Maintaining a positive image for Microsoft is another requirement of its publicity machine and public relations programmes. Bill Gates' charitable foundation has donated huge sums to medical research, higher-education establishments and schools. Software has been donated to libraries and schools, while computing equipment sponsored by Microsoft has found its way into many educational establishments around the world. These activities enable Microsoft to visibly support education, one of its stated goals, while simultaneously building brand equity. They also provide the PR managers at Microsoft with many positive news stories.

In the USA and in Europe, Microsoft has faced regulatory and legal pressures, being accused of overly aggressive tactics, monopoly power-broking and reducing consumer choice. Violations of US anti-trust law and fights with the EU Competition Commissioner generally receive huge media coverage, rarely favourable to the organisation accused. In Microsoft's situation, while costly to defend and in fines, the regulators' attacks have rarely either dented the image of the company in the eyes of users of Microsoft products or reduced the shareholder value of the business. Microsoft's PR people have been able to maintain a positive image for the company throughout the hearings and associated press coverage.

The celebrated status of founder Bill Gates has helped the company's PR executives. During the battles with regulators, Gates talked openly about his family, promoted more Microsoft products and increased his number of school visits. This visibility enabled Gates to air his views on technology and its impact on society, deflecting public attention from the regulators' criticisms of Microsoft. The company also commissioned research examining the value of technology in the workplace and in society. These studies' findings made the headlines, thanks to the company's PR department, rather than news stories about Microsoft's market size. The interest was in the valuable impact of its software, web browsers and future developments.

While the regulators have fined Microsoft and insisted on limitations to its market muscle, few computer users have negative views of this business. Far from it: most consumers and business people working with computers now feel Microsoft and Windows to be integral to their use of computers. Many members of the public simply watch in awe, awaiting the next 'big' software development from the company.

**Source:** Bill Pride and O.C. Ferrell, *Marketing*, Boston: Houghton Mifflin, 2003, pp. 485–6.

promotion that encompasses advertising, personal selling, publicity and public relations, sponsorship, direct mail, the Internet and direct marketing. Some sales promotions, however, are closely associated with additional elements of the promotional mix, as explored in Chapter 19. Currently, marketers spend about half as much on sales promotion as they do on advertising. Sales promotion appears to be growing in use more than advertising.

Marketers frequently rely on sales promotion to improve the effectiveness of other promotional mix ingredients, especially advertising and personal selling. For example, some businesses allocate 25 per cent of their annual promotional budget to trade shows in order to introduce new products, meet key industry personnel and identify likely prospects.[24] For many business-to-business marketers, sales promotions are very important.

Marketers design sales promotion to produce immediate, short-run sales increases. For example, the major brewers, such as Heineken and Coors, use a continuous programme of sales promotion techniques to boost sales in the highly competitive beer and lager market: free drinks and prize competitions, scratch cards and trade incentives.

Generally, if a company employs advertising or personal selling, it either depends on them continuously or turns to them cyclically. However, a marketer's use of sales promotion tends to be irregular. Many products are seasonal. For example, Thomas Cook and Thomson promote summer package holidays predominantly in the winter and spring months. Qualcast pushes its lawn mowers and other gardening equipment from Easter onwards. On the whole, sales promotions are infrequent, ad hoc campaigns.

**Sponsorship**
The financial or material support of an event, activity, person, organisation or product by an unrelated organisation or donor

**Sponsorship** The financial or material support of an event, activity, person, organisation or product by an unrelated organisation or donor is called **sponsorship**. Funds are made available to the recipient of the sponsorship in return for prominent public recognition of the benefactor's generosity, and display of the sponsor's name, products and brands. Sponsorship is no longer confined to the arts or the sporting world, although many galleries, theatrical companies, sports events and teams could not survive without sponsorship. Research and development, buildings, degree courses, charitable events – all often benefit from sponsorship. The donor or sponsor gains the benefits of enhanced company, brand or individual reputation and awareness, as well as, possibly, improved morale and employee relations. Note the number of prestigious or well-known brands sponsoring the Olympics or the football World Cup.

**Direct mail**
A method of communication used to entice prospective customers or charitable donors to invest in products, services or worthy causes

**Direct Mail** The direct mail industry takes a significant slice of the promotional budgets for many companies and organisations. Few households and companies fail to receive direct mail solicitations. **Direct mail** is used to entice prospective customers or charitable donors to invest in products, services or worthy causes. Throughout Europe, direct mail is used as a pre-sell technique prior to a sales call, to generate orders, qualify prospects for a sales call, follow up a sale, announce special or localised sales, and raise funds for charities and not-for-profit organisations. Good database management is essential, and the material must be targeted carefully to overcome the growing public aversion to 'junk mail'.

**Internet**
A network of computer networks stretching across the world, linking computers of different types

**The Internet** From humble beginnings as a 'talking shop' for boffins and computer buffs, the **Internet** – a network of computer networks stretching across the world, linking computers of different types – is now firmly established in many office workers' daily routines and accessed in millions of households. As explained in Chapter 4, marketers have been quick to identify this additional medium as an opportunity for providing existing and potential customers with company, product and brand information. Most large companies now have their own websites, while the major Internet servers such as Microsoft and Yahoo! are targeting small businesses and providing e-commerce capability at affordable prices.[25] Web-based marketing is particularly important in many business-to-business markets. Use of the Internet is not uniform across all parts of society, although there is evidence to suggest that it is no longer the pastime of only the young, affluent and well educated. Scrambling of confidential information such as credit card and bank account details has enabled the recent explosion in the number of purchases made on-line.

As a promotional mix ingredient, the Internet provides a tool that can be updated or modified quickly, and that can produce material aimed at very tightly defined target groups or even individual consumers. From Interflora to Tesco to JCB, the Internet is increasingly part of the promotional mix and, for direct marketers, the actual point of the sales transaction. Many television and press advertisements for services or consumer goods now direct their target audience to associated websites for additional information. Consumers can then interact with these hosts, in many instances, via e-mail and interactive web page information request facilities. Websites must be tailored to match the target customer buying behaviour and expectations, and must be informative but not mesmerising, while reflecting the existing branding and product positioning already established by a business's marketers. They require expert design and updating, as with any ingredient in the promotional mix. Intranets – internal in-company Internet networks – have improved communications within many organisations, becoming an important facet of internal marketing, as described in Chapter 24.

**Direct Marketing** First used in the 1960s, until recently direct marketing described the most common direct marketing approaches: direct mail and mail order. Currently experiencing a surge in popularity, direct marketing now encompasses all the communications tools that enable a marketer to deal directly with targeted customers: direct mail, telemarketing, direct response television advertising, door-to-door/personal selling and the Internet. **Direct marketing** is a decision by a company's marketers to both:

**Direct marketing**
A decision by a company's marketers to select a marketing channel which avoids dependence on marketing channel intermediaries and to focus marketing communications activity on promotional mix ingredients which deal directly with targeted customers

- select a marketing channel that avoids dependence on marketing channel intermediaries
- focus marketing communications activity on promotional mix ingredients that deal directly with targeted customers.

Direct marketing is now adopted by a host of businesses ranging from fast-moving consumer goods companies, business-to-business marketers, charities and even government departments.[26] Of all elements of the promotional mix, it is reported to be the fastest growing, but this is partly a reflection of the large number of promotional mix ingredients it includes.[27]

In terms of the promotional mix, there are several key implications. Direct mail is on the increase. Telemarketing has grown and will continue to do so, with more businesses turning to the direct marketing toolkit aided by advances in automated call centres. Door-to-door selling and leaflet dropping, visible forms of direct marketing encountered by most householders, are also on the increase. Direct response advertising – containing a call for action within the advertisement either by coupon or telephone – now makes up close to a third of all advertising as marketers turn to direct marketing, and as the growth in satellite and cable television channels enables more direct response television advertising. The Internet, too, is used by direct marketers to communicate with current and prospective customers. The deployment of any direct marketing campaign must strive to reflect targeted customer behaviour, needs and perceptions; provide a plausible proposition that is clearly differentiated from competitors' propositions; and match an organisation's corporate goals and trading philosophy. Direct marketing is not a substitute for the traditional promotional mix. As described in Chapter 19, direct marketing is an increasingly popular deployment of marketing, resulting from marketers' choices regarding their preferred marketing channel and selection of promotional mix ingredients.

## Integrated Marketing Communications (IMC)

Currently popular is the concept of **integrated marketing communications (IMC)**. This is the coordination and integration of all marketing communication tools, avenues and sources within a company into a seamless programme of marketing communications activities. The intention of IMC is to maximise the impact on consumers and other target audiences, at minimal cost. IMC avoids the waste and duplication inherent in some organisations in which each element of the promotional mix is controlled by separate managers and may even be executed through different external agencies. There is nothing worse than when an advertising campaign on radio created by one agency has little resemblance to a television campaign running at the same time, and created by another advertising agency. This is often compounded by the public relations, sponsorship, packaging and sales promotions being implemented by yet more agencies in a poorly coordinated fashion. On one occasion, five different agencies were developing marketing communications for market-leading Gordon's

**Integrated marketing communications (IMC)** The coordination and integration of all marketing communication tools, avenues and sources within a company into a seamless programme that maximises the impact on consumers and other end users, at minimal cost

Gin, each using different shades of green – the brand's famous identity – and adopting various typefaces for the logo.

IMC is the integration of the whole promotional mix, but also all business-to-business, marketing channel, customer-focused and internally directed communications. IMC as a concept is focused on complete coordination and harmonised execution of various campaigns across the elements of the promotional mix. Rather than treating all aspects of the promotional mix and internal marketing (see Chapter 24) separately, often utilising many different departments and external agencies in an uncoordinated manner, the company instead opts to fully harmonise these activities. This does not have to result in only one supplying agency being commissioned: coordination ensures shared goals and common approaches to execution in a carefully scheduled manner. The benefits of IMC include greater clarity to customers, marketing channel members, employees and suppliers, as well as reduced costs, stronger impact in the marketplace and more effective branding.

Advertising, along with the rest of the promotional mix, exists to help implement a brand's target market strategy by communicating the product appeal and the brand positioning image to intended customers and other key stakeholders. Occasionally, a creative execution can be sufficiently memorable and strike a chord so well with the target audience, that a business rethinks its whole marketing mix for a brand or product. New KFC advertising agency BBH, renowned for its creativity, launched the 'Soul Food' campaign in an attempt to break away from standard fast-food chain advertising and to reflect recent menu changes at KFC. In 2003, KFC spent over £16 million on its UK advertising, depicting a soul food positioning through moody, relaxed and vivid advertisements that promoted the sharing of food. IMC built on the advertising concept to coordinate all of the brand's marketing communications activities, including website, in-store displays, sales promotions competitions, local press and radio advertising, publicity and new branch opening stunts. Now new-look interiors, using large refectory-style 'sharing' tables and atmospheric décor, are being introduced to the company's restaurants. The aim is to provide a relaxing, friendly, contemporary ambience in which to enjoy music, food and the company of family and friends. This positioning is quite different from the original no-frills, quick-meal-on-the-go imagery that the chain adopted in the past. The ground-breaking soul food advertising led to the reformulation of KFC's entire marketing mix. IMC was important in managing all of the soul food-linked marketing communications.

Now that the basic components of an organisation's promotional mix have been discussed, it is important to consider how that mix is created. The factors and conditions that affect the selection of the promotional methods a specific organisation uses in its promotional mix for a particular product need to be examined.

## Selecting Promotional Mix Ingredients

Marketers vary the composition of promotional mixes for many reasons. Although all ingredients can be included in a promotional mix, frequently a marketer chooses not to use them all. In addition, many businesses that market multiple product lines use several promotional mixes simultaneously.

An organisation's promotional mix (or mixes) is not an unchanging part of the marketing mix. Marketers can and do change the composition of their promotional mixes. The specific promotional mix ingredients employed and the intensity with which they are used depend on a variety of factors, including the organisation's promotional resources, objectives and policies; characteristics of the target market; characteristics of the product; and the cost and availability of promotional methods.

**Promotional Resources, Objectives and Policies** The quality of an organisation's promotional resources affects the number and relative intensity of promotional methods that can be included in a promotional mix. If a company's promotional budget is extremely limited, the business is likely to rely on personal selling because it is easier to measure a sales person's contribution to sales than to measure the effect of advertising. A business must have a sizeable promotional budget if it is to use regional or national advertising and sales promotion activities. Organisations with extensive promotional resources can usually include more ingredients in their promotional mixes. However, larger promotional budgets do not necessarily imply that the companies will use a greater number of promotional methods.

An organisation's promotional objectives and policies also influence the types of promotion used. If a company's objective is to create mass awareness of a new convenience good, its promotional mix is likely to lean heavily towards advertising, sales promotion and possibly publicity. If a company hopes to educate consumers about the features of durable goods, such as home electrical appliances, its promotional mix may combine a moderate amount of advertising, possibly some sales promotion efforts designed to attract customers to retail stores and a great deal of in-store personal selling, this being an excellent way to inform customers about these types of product. If a company's objective is to produce immediate sales of consumer non-durables, such as paper products and many grocery goods, the promotional mix will probably stress advertising and sales promotion efforts. Business-to-business marketers often use detailed trade advertising, personal selling through sales representatives, sales promotions – often in the guise of bulk discounts and trade show exhibits – and direct mail of brochures and price lists.

**Characteristics of the Target Market** The size, geographic distribution and socio-economic characteristics of an organisation's target market also help dictate the ingredients to be included in a product's promotional mix. To some degree, market size determines the composition of the mix. If the size is quite limited, the promotional mix will probably emphasise personal selling, which can be quite effective for reaching small numbers of people. Organisations that sell to industrial business markets, and companies that market their products through only a few wholesalers, frequently make personal selling the major component of their promotional mixes. When markets for a product consist of millions of customers, organisations use advertising and sales promotion because these methods can reach masses of people at a low cost per person. The Coca-Cola Company attempted to reach consumers through a non-traditional vehicle when it placed an advertisement for Diet Coke in the introduction to the home video version of the blockbuster *Batman*. Warner Home Video, the distributor of *Batman*, believed that it would sell more than 10 million copies of the video cassette, exposing millions of consumers to the Diet Coke message at a low cost per person.[28]

The geographic distribution of a company's customers can affect the combination of promotional methods used. Personal selling is more feasible if a company's customers are concentrated in a small area than if they are dispersed across a vast region. When the company's customers are numerous and dispersed, advertising may be more practical.

The distribution of a target market's socio-economic characteristics, such as age, income or education, may dictate the types of promotional technique that a marketer selects. For example, personal selling may be much more successful than print advertisements for communicating with poorly educated people, because it allows meaning or product attributes to be explained face to face.

**Characteristics of the Product** Generally, promotional mixes for industrial business products concentrate on personal selling. In promoting consumer goods, on the other hand, advertising plays a major role. This generalisation should be treated with caution, however. Industrial goods producers do use some advertising to promote their goods, particularly in the trade press. Advertisements for computers, road-building equipment and aircraft are not altogether uncommon, and sales promotion is deployed to promote industrial goods. Personal selling is used extensively for services and consumer durables, such as insurance, leisure and education, home appliances, cars and houses, and consumer convenience items are promoted mainly through advertising and sales promotion. Publicity appears in promotional mixes for industrial goods, consumer goods and services. Many organisations use direct mail, and more are now examining the growing use of corporate sponsorship. Most organisations are also developing websites.

Marketers of highly seasonal products are often forced to emphasise advertising, and possibly sales promotion, because off-season sales will not support an extensive year-round salesforce. Although many toy producers have salesforces to sell to resellers, a number of these companies depend to a large extent on advertising to promote their products.

The price of a product also influences the composition of the promotional mix. High-priced products call for more personal selling because consumers associate greater risk with the purchase of such products and usually want the advice of a sales person. Few consumers, for example, would be willing to purchase a refrigerator or personal computer from a self-service establishment. For low-priced convenience items, marketers use advertising rather than personal selling at the retail level. The profit margins on many of these items are too low to justify the use of sales people, and most customers do not need advice from sales personnel when buying such products.

A further consideration in creating an effective promotional mix is the stage of the product life cycle (see Chapter 10). During the introduction stage, a good deal of advertising may be necessary for business-to-business and consumer products to make potential users aware of a new product. For many products, personal selling and sales promotion are also helpful at this stage. In the case of consumer non-durables, the growth and maturity stages call for a heavy emphasis on advertising. Business products, on the other hand, often require a concentration of personal selling and some sales promotion efforts during these stages. In the decline stage, marketers usually decrease their promotional activities, especially advertising. Promotional efforts in the decline stage often centre on personal selling and sales promotion efforts.

The intensity of market coverage is yet another factor that affects the composition of the promotional mix. When a product is marketed through intensive distribution, the business depends strongly on advertising and sales promotion. A number of convenience products – such as lotions, cereals and coffee – are promoted through samples, coupons and cash refunds. Where marketers have opted for selective distribution, marketing mixes vary considerably in terms of amount and type of promotional method. Items handled through exclusive distribution frequently demand more personal selling and less advertising. Expensive watches and high-quality furniture are products that are typically promoted heavily through personal selling. Intensive, selective and exclusive distribution are discussed in Chapter 14.

A product's use also affects the combination of promotional methods. Manufacturers of highly personal products, such as non-prescription contraceptives, feminine hygiene products and haemorrhoid treatments, count on advertising for promotion because many users do not like to talk to sales personnel about such products.

**Cost and Availability of Promotional Methods** The cost of promotional methods is a major factor to analyse when developing a promotional mix. National advertising and sales promotion efforts require large expenditures. For example, some detergent brands have annual advertising budgets of £10 to £15 million. However, if the efforts are effective in reaching extremely large numbers of people, the cost per individual reached may be quite small, possibly a few pence per person. Moreover, not all forms of advertising are expensive. Many small, local businesses advertise their products through local newspapers, magazines, radio stations, outdoor signs and public transport.

Another consideration that marketers must explore when formulating a promotional mix is the availability of promotional techniques. Despite the tremendous number of media vehicles, a company may find that no available advertising medium reaches a certain market effectively. For example, a product may be banned from being advertised on television, as are cigarettes in many countries. A stockbroker may find no suitable advertising medium for investors in Manchester United Football Club – should the stockbroker use financial publications, sports magazines or general media?

The problem of media availability becomes even more pronounced when marketers try to advertise in other countries. Some media, such as television, simply may not be available to advertisers. Television advertising in Scandinavia is minimal. In the UK only seven and a half minutes of advertising are permitted per average hour of terrestrial television, with a maximum of 12 minutes in any one 'real' hour.[29] The media that are available may not be open to certain types of advertisement. For example, in Germany, advertisers are forbidden to make brand comparisons in television advertisements. Other promotional methods have limitations as well. An organisation may wish to increase the size of its salesforce but be unable to find qualified personnel. In the United States, some state laws prohibit the use of certain types of sales promotion activities, such as contests. Such prohibited techniques are thus 'unavailable' in those locations.

## Push Policy versus Pull Policy

**Push policy**
A promotional policy in which the producer promotes the product only to the next institution down the marketing channel

**Pull policy**
A promotional policy in which a business promotes directly to consumers in order to develop a strong consumer demand for its products

Another element that marketers should consider when they plan a promotional mix is whether to use a push policy or a pull policy. With a **push policy**, the producer promotes the product only to the next institution down the marketing channel. For instance, in a marketing channel with wholesalers and retailers, the producer promotes to the wholesaler, in this case the channel member just below the producer (see Figure 17.7). Each channel member in turn promotes to the next channel member. A push policy normally stresses personal selling. Sometimes sales promotion, direct mail and advertising are used in conjunction with personal selling to push the products down through the channel.

As Figure 17.7 shows, a company using a **pull policy** promotes directly to consumers with the intention of developing a strong consumer demand for the products. It does so through advertising, sales promotion, direct mail, the web, sponsorship, and packaging that helps manufacturers build and maintain market share.[30] Because consumers are persuaded to seek the products in retail stores, retailers will in turn go to wholesalers or the producer to buy the products. The policy is thus intended to 'pull' the goods down through the channel by creating demand at the consumer level.

A push policy can be combined with a pull policy. Mars, for example, has a pull policy aimed at the consumer: sponsorship of events and advertising create awareness; packaging,

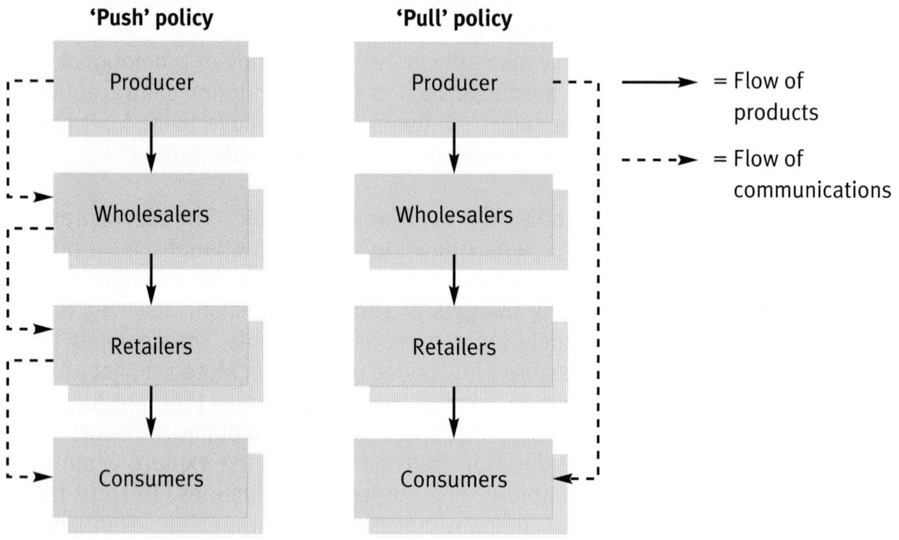


*Figure 17.7*
*Comparison of push and pull promotional policies*

sales promotions – such as competitions or discounts – and direct mail prompt product trial and adoption. Simultaneously, the company's push policy of trade advertising, sales promotions and personal selling persuades channel members to stock and retail its products.

# Summary

The primary role of *promotion* is to communicate with individuals, groups or organisations with the aim of directly or indirectly facilitating exchanges. Promotion is commonly known as marketing communications.

» *Communication* is a sharing of meaning through the transmission of information. The communication process involves several steps. Using the *coding process*, the *source* first converts the meaning into a series of signs that represent concepts. The source should employ signs that are familiar to the *receiver* or *receiving audience*, and choose signs that the receiver or receiving audience uses for referring to the concepts or ideas being promoted. The coded message is sent through a *medium of transmission* to the receiver or receiving audience. The receiver or receiving audience then uses the *decoding process* to convert the signs into concepts and usually supplies *feedback* to the source. When the decoded message differs from the encoded one, a condition called noise exists. Occasionally, *channel capacity* is reached when the volume of information can no longer be handled effectively.

» *Marketing communication* is the transmission of persuasive information about a good, service or an idea, targeted at key stakeholders and consumers within the target market segment. Marketing communications centre on the promotional mix, which comprises advertising, public relations, personal selling, sales promotion, direct mail, sponsorship and the Internet. Cause-related marketing links product purchases to a 'good' cause.

» One long-run purpose of promotion is to influence and encourage customers to accept or adopt goods, services and ideas. The ultimate effectiveness of promotion is determined by the degree to which it affects product adoption or increases the frequency of current buyers' purchases. The *product adoption process* consists of five stages: (1) in the *awareness stage*, individuals become aware of the product; (2) people move into the *interest stage* when they seek information about the product; (3) in the *evaluation stage*, individuals decide whether the product will meet certain criteria that are crucial for satisfying their specific needs; (4) during the *trial stage*, the consumer actually uses or experiences the product for the first time; (5) in the *adoption stage*, the consumer decides to use the product on a regular basis. Product rejection may occur at any stage. People can be divided into five major *adopter categories – innovators, early adopters, early majority, late majority* and *laggards* – according to how long it takes them to start using a new product.

» There are *five communication effects*. A manufacturer or retailer must establish a *category need* for a product. Consumers must have *brand awareness* and a favourable *brand attitude* towards the products. If the consumer decides to make a purchase – *brand purchase intention* – the company's overall marketing policy must guarantee distribution, suitable product quality and attributes, and set the relevant price points – *purchase facilitation*.

» The *promotional mix* for a product traditionally included the four major promotional methods – advertising, personal selling, publicity/public relations and sales promotion. Now it is usually defined as also including sponsorship, direct mail and the web. The Internet and direct marketing are currently very popular additions to companies' promotional mixes. *Advertising* is a paid form of non-personal communication about an organisation and its products that is transmitted to a target audience through a mass medium. *Personal selling* is a process of informing customers and persuading them to purchase products through personal communication in an exchange situation.

*Telemarketing* often supports personal selling. *Kinesic, proxemic* and *tactile communication* are important in personal selling. *Publicity* is non-personal communication in news-story form about an organisation or its products, or both, that is transmitted through a mass medium at no charge, and controlled by the *public relations* mechanism. *Sales promotion* is an activity or material that acts as a direct inducement by offering added value to, or incentive for, the product to resellers, sales people or consumers. *Sponsorship* involves financial or material support of an event, activity, person, organisation or product in return for prominent public recognition and display of the sponsor's name, products and brands. *Direct mail* is used to entice prospective customers or charitable donors to invest in products, services or worthy causes. The *Internet*, networked independent computers, through organisations' websites is a growing part of promotional activity. Many businesses are turning to *direct marketing*, which is a decision to avoid the use of marketing channel intermediaries and to focus marketing communications activity on promotional mix ingredients that deal directly with targeted customers, such as personal selling, direct mail, direct response advertising, telemarketing and the Internet.

Currently popular is the concept of *integrated marketing communications (IMC)*. IMC is the coordination and integration of all marketing communication tools, avenues and sources within a company into a seamless programme that maximises the impact on consumers and other end users at a minimal cost. It is integration of the whole promotional mix but also all business-to-business, marketing channel, customer-focused and internally directed communications. Rather than treating all aspects of the promotional mix and internal marketing separately, often utilising many different departments and external agencies in an uncoordinated manner, a company instead opts to fully harmonise these activities. The benefits of IMC include greater clarity, reduced costs, stronger impact in the marketplace and more effective branding.

There are several major determinants of what promotional methods to include in a promotional mix: the organisation's promotional resources, objectives and policies; the characteristics of the target market; the characteristics of the product; and the cost and availability of promotional methods. Marketers must also consider whether to use a push policy or a pull policy, or a combination of the two. With a *push policy*, the producer promotes the product only to the next institution down the marketing channel. Normally, a push policy stresses personal selling. A company that uses a *pull policy* promotes directly to consumers, with the intention of developing a strong consumer demand for the products. Once consumers are persuaded to seek the products in retail stores, retailers in turn go to wholesalers or the producer to buy the products.

## *Key Links*

This chapter overviews the role of promotion – marketing communications – within the marketing mix. It should be read in conjunction with:

- Chapter 18, on advertising, public relations and sponsorship
- Chapter 19, on sales management and personal selling, sales promotion, direct mail, the Internet and direct marketing
- Chapter 12, on the product adoption process in developing products.

## Important Terms

Promotion
Cause-related marketing
Communication
Marketing communication
Source
Receiver
Receiving audience
Coding process
Medium of transmission
Decoding process
Noise
Feedback
Channel capacity

Product adoption process
Awareness stage
Interest stage
Evaluation stage
Trial stage
Adoption stage
Adopter categories
Innovators
Early adopters
Early majority
Late majority
Laggards
Five communication effects
Category need
Brand awareness
Brand attitude
Brand purchase intention
Purchase facilitation
Promotional mix
Advertising
Personal selling
Telemarketing
Kinesic communication
Proxemic communication
Tactile communication
Publicity
Public relations
Sales promotion
Sponsorship
Direct mail
Internet
Direct marketing
Integrated marketing communications (IMC)
Push policy
Pull policy

## Discussion and Review Questions

1. What is the major task of promotion?
2. What is communication? Describe the communication process. Is it possible to communicate without using all of the elements in the communication process? If so, which ones can be omitted?
3. Identify several causes of noise. How can a source reduce noise?
4. Describe the product adoption process. In certain circumstances, is it possible for a person to omit one or more of the stages in adopting a new product? Explain your answer.
5. Describe a product that many people are in the process of adopting. Have you begun the adoption process for this product? If so, what stage have you reached?
6. What is category need? Illustrate your answer with examples.
7. Identify and briefly describe the major promotional methods that can be included in an organisation's promotional mix. How does publicity differ from advertising?
8. What forms of interpersonal communication in addition to language can be used in personal selling?
9. List the communications tools that direct marketing encompasses and explain the recent surge in popularity of this promotional tool.
10. How do target market characteristics determine which promotional methods to include in a promotional mix? Assume that a company is planning to promote a cereal to both adults and children. Along what major dimensions would these two promotional efforts have to be different?
11. How can a product's characteristics affect the composition of its promotional mix?
12. Explain the difference between a pull policy and a push policy. Under what conditions should each be used?

## Recommended Readings


- Belch, G. and Belch, M., *Advertising and Promotion: An Integrated Marketing Communications Perspective with Powerweb* (New York: McGraw-Hill, 2003).
- Fill, C., *Integrated Marketing Communications* (Oxford: Butterworth-Heinemann, 2003).
- FitzGerald, M. and Arnott, D., *Marketing Communications Classics* (London: Thomson Learning, 2000).
- Percy, L., Rossiter, J. and Elliott, R., *Strategic Advertising Management* (Oxford: Oxford University Press, 2001).
- Rapp, S. and Collins, T., *New Maximarketing* (New York: McGraw-Hill, 1999).
- Shimp, T.A., *Advertising, Promotion and Supplemental Aspects of Integrated Marketing Communications* (Cincinnati, OH: South Western, 2002).

## Internet Exercise

Most leading brands embrace a mix of promotional techniques, including advertising, sales promotions, publicity, the web and the rest of the promotional mix. Pepsi is no exception.

Pepsi's *Pepsi World* award-winning website is an important part of the company's promotional activity, integrating advertising, sales promotions activity and publicity releases with customer involvement. Brand information, TV advertisements, music links, sports, promotions and street motion – there is much on offer on Pepsi's web pages.

Log on to www.pepsi.com/home.

1 In what ways and with what messages is Pepsi engaging with customers through the pages of its website?
2 How do these approaches support the brand's positioning?
3 How do the web pages relate to the brand's television advertising?

## *Applied Mini-Case*

By now, most consumers are familiar with 'chip and pin', the e-solution to 'signing' when paying by credit or debit card. Despite regulations forcing retailers to adopt this technology, less that 10 months before the full launch of the system, under 10 per cent of retailers had made arrangements to install the required keypads and make modifications to their till systems. Leading payment processing business Barclaycard Merchant Services, whose customers include many high-street retailers, joined forces with IT vendor Fujitsu to offer a one-stop off-the-shelf solution to retailers' requirement to install chip and pin. Despite the ramifications of chip and pin, take up by retailers was slow. The very largest retail groups had their own in-house solutions, but most independents and even many large retail chains had no chip and pin provision. In cases of fraud, previously the processing banks, such as Barclaycard Merchant Services, assumed liability and reimbursed the retailer for the fraud. Under the new system, liability rests with the retailers, so it is in their interests to adopt the latest technology and prepare their staff in advance of the changeover from signature to PIN code.

### *Question*

**As marketing manager for Barclaycard Merchant Services, how would you promote the need for chip and pin installations to your retail clients? What would be the core messages and what ways could be used to communicate these messages to these retailers?**

## *Case Study*

# Häagen-Dazs: Promoting an Adult Ice Cream

Häagen-Dazs makes the best-selling super-premium ice cream in North America. Its luscious ingredients include chocolate from Belgium, vanilla from Madagascar, coffee from Brazil, strawberries from Oregon, and nuts from Hawaii. The packaging serenely asserts that it is the world's best ice cream.

London's Leicester Square shop served close to one million ice cream lovers in its first year. The success of the Victor Hugo Plaza shop in Paris, now the company's second busiest, led to the establishment of its first European factory in France. Häagen-Dazs shops have opened in Italy, Spain, Benelux and Scandinavia, among other countries. The appealing flavours can now be found not only in the company's shops but also at airports, in cafés and in carefully selected delicatessens, with rapidly growing popularity.

The product's high quality has been essential in maintaining a loyal customer following, but it was promotional work that led to the successful take-off of what was previously an unheard-of brand in Europe. Sales promotion in the guise of free tasting was a major part of the promotional mix: over 5 million free cupfuls of ice cream were given away during the company's European launch. Thousands of retailers, cafés and delis were supplied with branded freezers both to display and carefully look after the new premium ice cream. As part of its European launch, Häagen-Dazs spent £30 million on advertising, stressing the deluxe ingredients, unusual flavours and novelty of its product. Europeans currently eat 25 per cent of the 3 billion gallons of ice cream each year consumed worldwide. Häagen-Dazs plans to increase consumption by appealing to more than traditional ice cream-loving children.

The summer afternoon stroll with an ice cream cornet, the family trip to a fun park or beach, a snack during a film or concert, the sticky climax of a birthday party feast had long been the core market for Wall's and Nestlé. Ice Cream Mars changed all that by creating an ice cream bar suitable for any occasion and particularly attractive to adults. Häagen-Dazs went further. Award-winning press adverts, artistically shot, often in black and white, featured lithe, semi-nude couples entwined in exotic poses while feeding each other Häagen-Dazs ice cream. The appeal of vanilla ice cream bars hand-dipped in Belgian chocolate and rolled in roasted almonds now seems hard to resist for adults everywhere. The advertising imagery promotes an adult, upmarket, glamorous positioning for this superpremium ice cream.

The Häagen-Dazs range has grown, expanding to include frozen yoghurts, sorbets and now ice cream novelties, such as the ice cream sandwich made with cookies. Product development and quality controls are important to Häagen-Dazs' brand positioning as an upmarket, indulgent treat for adults, but so is the company's innovative promotional mix and the messages at the heart of its advertising. Industry observers suggest that despite the exceptional quality and novel flavours, without marketing communications Häagen-Dazs would not have been so successful.

**Sources:** Sainsbury's, 2004; 'Dairy produce', *Campaign*, 15 March 1996, p. 34; 'Häagen-Dazs cinema first', *Campaign*, 26 March 1995, p. 5; 'Pillsbury's global training plan', *Crossborder Monitor*, 19 April 1995, p. 9; G. Mead, 'Sex, ice and videod beer', *Financial Times*, 26 September 1992, p. 5; 'Saucy way to sell a Knicker-bocker Glory – Häagen-Dazs' new ice cream campaign', *Financial Times*, 8 August 1991, p. 8; 'Häagen-Dazs is using sex to secure an up market niche in Britain's £400m ice cream market', *Observer*, 4 August 1991, p. 25; M. Carter, 'The luxury ice cream market', *Marketing Week*, 22 May 1992, p. 30; www.haagendazs.com, July 2004.

## Questions for Discussion

1. Why did the London launch of Häagen-Dazs utilise more than just advertising?
2. Why did Häagen-Dazs target the adult market rather than families or children?
3. Was the 'adult' positioning and promotional execution risky? Why did Häagen-Dazs deploy this positioning strategy?

# 18

# Advertising, Public Relations and Sponsorship

"**The strengths and weaknesses of publicity provide a mirror image to those of advertising which, when combined, complement one another synergistically.**"

*Norman Hart*

## Objectives

- To explore the nature and uses of advertising
- To become aware of the major steps involved in developing an advertising campaign
- To find out who is responsible for developing advertising campaigns
- To gain an understanding of publicity and public relations
- To be aware of current trends in advertising and public relations
- To examine the nature and uses of sponsorship

## Introduction

Ask a lay person—someone who has not read Chapters 1 or 2 of this book!—to define marketing, and the most common polite responses are 'advertising', 'selling' or 'marketing research'. While readers of this book will by now appreciate that there is much more to marketing than these activities, it is true that advertising is a major output of the marketing process and accounts for a large proportion of marketers' budgets.

This chapter overviews the importance of advertising, and discusses its core uses and the stages required in developing an advertising campaign. It also explores public relations (PR) and a core output from a public relations programme, publicity. Sponsorship used to be limited and often was handled by those responsible for PR. While many PR consultancies do advise their clients about sponsorship, there are now also specialist sponsorship agencies, reflecting the growing role within the promotional mix of sponsorship, whether corporate or for individual brands.

## *Opener*

# BMW goes Direct

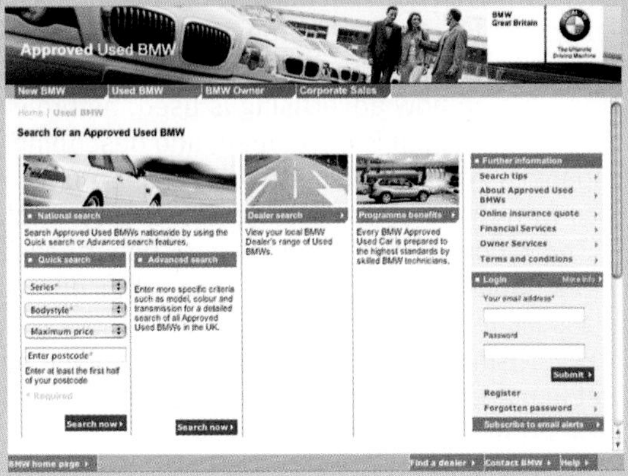


The Internet connects a rapidly growing number of homes, businesses and schools across the globe to a huge array of information and, increasingly, to the sales particulars of many companies' products and services. In its early years, the Internet was purely a vehicle for communicating information. Now, with scrambling techniques to safeguard credit card details, the Internet can be used as an interactive advertising, product information, ordering and payment tool within the marketing mix. Experts believe that, within a few years, the Internet could be taking a staggering £400 billion in orders for all types of products and services, notably banking and financial services, which are predicted to be the fastest-growing sector of the Internet for promoting and selling products, as well as for small companies with limited advertising budgets. BMW's advertising executives have fully embraced the possibilities offered by the web.

German car giant BMW has used the Internet to create a service only available on-line: the BMW Approved Used Car Directory. In this way, BMW is advertising its selection of used cars. This service is interactive, providing a search and find facility, as well as general BMW information support. Users may either specify a desired model/colour/specification/age/price combination of criteria for BMW's on-line system to search, or users may scroll through comprehensive lists of used BMWs for sale through the dealer network. All local BMW dealers are on the Internet, promoting their site through local media and press advertising. The BMW Approved Used Car Directory on-line is user-friendly and offers Quick Search, Advanced Search and Dealer Search, as well as information about the programme – 'Every BMW Approved Used Car is prepared to the highest standards by skilled BMW technicians.'

To work, a 'good' Internet site must attract target customers' attention and fulfil their expectations, just as any other product or service should. The information being offered by BMW and its dealers must be of interest to target BMW customers and relevant users of the Internet. The site should be interactive, offering users the chance to become involved. The Internet site must be interesting and of high quality. It should be promoted; otherwise users will either not track it down, or it will be swamped by the plethora of sites being set up. It must pay for itself: a good Internet site costs around £40,000 to set up. The Internet site will need to be staffed, particularly if users are likely to seek responses to very specific queries or to place an order. Above all, advertisers need to remember that the imagery and message used on the Internet must be consistent and fully integrated with the rest of their promotional mix. BMW's site appears to meet these criteria well.

Whether it is for Newcastle United Football Club, Condé Nast's *Vogue* and *Tatler* or Richard Branson's Virgin, the Internet is playing an increasingly significant role in many businesses' promotional activity and provides advertising executives with an additional outlet for their creative genius. The Internet is a growing part of the promotional mix and also of the overall marketing mix. Most TV and press advertising directs consumers to websites for additional information, particularly for those companies practising integrated marketing communications. The Internet is very much part of the advertising executive's toolkit. The recent growth of direct marketing has enhanced significantly the role of the Internet in promotional strategy.

**Sources:** www.bmw.com, 2004; *Marketing Guides: 'The Internet'*, 27 June 1996; C. Lloyd, 'On a quest to bring the Internet to the masses', *Sunday Times*, 26 November 1995; 'Innovation', *Sunday Times*, 19 and 26 November, 31 December 1995; 'Scramble to build a super showroom in cyberspace', *Independent* on Sunday, 4 February 1996, p. IB 8; 'Pay by plastic plan on Internet', *Evening Telegraph*, 3 February 1996, p. 15; www.bmw.co.uk. Screen capture: Courtesy of BMW (GB) Ltd.

This chapter explores the many dimensions of advertising, publicity, public relations, and sponsorship. It should be remembered that Chapter 17 explained how companies are increasingly benefiting from a more coordinated approach to their marketing communications through integrated marketing communications (IMC). Indeed, research suggests that higher levels of integration in marketing communications leads to enhanced performance.[1] However, this chapter examines specific ingredients of the promotional mix to aid a thorough understanding of these components – the other promotional mix ingredients are addressed in the next chapter.

The present chapter commences by focusing on how advertising is used, before examining the major steps by which an advertising campaign is developed, and describing who is responsible for developing such campaigns. After analysing publicity and public relations, and comparing their characteristics with those of advertising, the chapter explores the different forms publicity may take. The following section considers how publicity is used and what is required for an effective public relations programme. After discussing negative publicity and some problems associated with the use of publicity, the chapter examines some of the current trends in advertising and public relations, as typified by the growing use by advertisers of the Internet in marketing. The chapter concludes with a look at the increasing use of sponsorship in the promotional mix.

## The Nature of Advertising

Advertising permeates everyone's daily lives.[2] It may be perceived positively or as an annoyance, encouraging channel hopping during advertising breaks or fast-forwarding of video recordings.[3] Some advertising informs, persuades or entertains; some of it bores, even offends. For example, there were instances of consumer groups whitewashing billboards advertising tobacco products because they believed such advertisements encourage children to smoke.

**Advertising**
A paid-for form of non-personal communication that is transmitted through mass media such as television, radio, newspapers, magazines, direct mail, public transport vehicles, outdoor displays and the Internet

**Advertising** is a paid-for form of non-personal communication that is transmitted through mass media such as television, radio, newspapers, magazines, direct mail, public transport vehicles, outdoor displays and now also the Internet. As explained in the Innovation and Change box below, advertising takes on some innovative forms. An organisation can use advertising to reach a variety of audiences, ranging from small, precise groups, such as the stamp collectors of the major conurbations, to large audiences, such as all the buyers of fax machines in Sweden.

## Innovation and Change

### First Ambient and Now 'Live' Advertising

When did you last spot an advertisement in a surprising place? Perhaps it was a Volkswagen promotion on the handle of a petrol pump, an advert on a bus ticket, a large building completely draped in a Ford Mondeo banner or even the promotion of clean air in Wales on the back of a dirty van. The industry refers to the use of such media as ambient advertising. According to outdoor advertising agency Concord, which claims to have been the first to define the form, ambient advertising is 'non-traditional out-of-home advertising'. An early example, at the Atlanta Olympic games, was when sprinter Linford Christie promoted Puma by wearing contact lenses featuring the sportswear brand. Finding new and creative ways of advertising using the outdoor world represents a move away from the traditional media of television, radio, cinema, press and posters. Advocates of this approach believe that ambient advertising has huge potential.

Companies commissioning promotional work involving ambient media have been pleased to discover that considerable free press coverage can result. Ben and Jerry's, the

American ice cream business, attracted considerable publicity when it hired cows to act as mobile advertising hoardings. The animals, which were grazing alongside a major motorway, were fitted with coats sporting an ice cream advertisement. Meanwhile Beck's beer was promoted using an advertisement mown on a 30-acre field sited alongside a heavily used railway line.

In addition to identifying new surfaces as replacement billboards, ambient advertising makes use of existing objects as promotional sites. Elida Fabergé advertised its Vaseline Intensive Care deodorant by attaching fake roll-on containers to the hanging grab-straps on the London Underground. The aim was to draw attention to the product at a time when commuters might be particularly amenable to considering its benefits.

Views about the effectiveness of ambient advertising vary:

> Ambient campaigns don't always target a specific audience. The Beck's advert was successful because of the press coverage it generated but as an ad it didn't target the correct demographic spread. It targeted a whole commuter train of people, only a small number of whom like to drink Beck's.

Nevertheless, as advertisers seek novel executions and ways of attracting the attention of consumers, ambient advertising is a welcome addition to adland's armoury.

One of the latest forms of advertising, instigated in London by a leading South African agency, is so-called 'live' advertising. Cinema-goers are used to 15 minutes' preamble on the screen prior to the blockbuster feature, including trailers for forthcoming attractions and advertisements familiar from television. Early in 2004, London movie-goers were surprised by an interruption to the screened advertisements when a group of actors took to the stage and re-enacted a popular television commercial live on stage. The agency argues that this form of 'in your face' advertising is necessary when consumers are assailed by so many promotional messages every day. Certainly the London movie-goers exposed to these 'live' advertisements were distracted from shuffling in their seats, chatting and snacking! It is expected that live advertising – a variation on sales promotion stunts – will become more popular, particularly for fast-moving consumer goods but even at business conventions and trade shows for business-to-business products and services.

**Sources:** Sian Phillips, 'Space invaders', *Hotline*, Winter 1998/99, pp. 16–19; David Reed, 'Fuel injection', *Marketing Week*, 4 February 1999, pp. 37–42; John Wringe, Sandom, December 2003; BBC5 Live, April 2004.

When people are asked to name major advertisers, most immediately mention business organisations. However, many types of organisation – including governments, churches, universities, civic groups and charities – take advantage of advertising. For example, the UK government is one of the largest advertisers: 'Heroin Screws You Up', Employment Training, road safety campaigns, drink driving, the euro campaign and the Enterprise Initiative are just a few examples. So even though advertising is analysed here in the context of business organisations, it should be borne in mind that much of the discussion applies to all types of organisation. See Table 18.1 for details of advertising in Europe.

Marketers sometimes give advertising more credit than it deserves. This attitude causes them to use advertising when they should not. For example, manufacturers of basic products such as sugar, flour and salt often try to differentiate their products, with minimal success. Under certain conditions, advertising can work effectively for an organisation. The questions in Table 18.2 raise some general points that a marketer should consider when assessing the potential value of advertising as an ingredient in a product's promotional mix. The list is not all-inclusive, however; numerous factors have a bearing on whether advertising should be used at all and, if so, to what extent.

## The Uses of Advertising

Advertising can serve a variety of purposes. Individuals and organisations use it to promote products and organisations, to stimulate demand, to off-set competitors' advertising, to make sales personnel more effective, to educate a market's customers and dealers, to

**TABLE 18.1 ADVERTISING IN EUROPE**

**(a) Top European Agency Networks 2001**

| Rank | Agency network | Equity billings US$ (million) | Equity gross income US$ (million) |
|---|---|---|---|
| 1 | Y&R Advertising | 13,358.0 | 755.3 |
| 2 | McCann-Erickson Worldwide | 7,587.0 | 856.0 |
| 3 | Ogilvy & Mather Worldwide | 6,182.0 | 650.0 |
| 4 | Euro RSCG | 5,316.0 | 816.0 |
| 5 | Publicis Worldwide | 5,267.0 | 742.0 |
| 6 | BBDO Worldwide | 4,975.0 | 677.0 |
| 7 | DDB Worldwide Communications | 4,191.0 | 589.0 |
| 8 | D'Arcy Masius Benton & Bowles | 3,836.0 | 325.0 |
| 9 | TBWA Worldwide | 3,676.0 | 492.0 |
| 10 | J Walter Thompson Co. | 3,645.0 | 525.0 |
| 11 | Grey Worldwide | 3,105.0 | 522.0 |
| 12 | Leo Burnett Worldwide | 2,914.0 | 331.0 |
| 13 | Lowe & Partners Worldwide | 2,755.0 | 368.0 |
| 14 | Bates Worldwide | 2,718.9 | 306.6 |
| 15 | Saatchi & Saatchi Worldwide | 1,769.5 | 198.8 |
| 16 | Foote, Cone & Belding Worldwide | 1,360.6 | 195.3 |
| 17 | Rapp Collins Worldwide | 861.9 | 130.2 |
| 18 | Arnold Worldwide | 813.9 | 116.6 |
| 19 | Brann Worldwide | 642.6 | 122.9 |
| 20 | TMP Worldwide | 485.5 | 107.6 |

(continued)

**Sources:** Advertising Age 2002; MEC Global; *The European Marketing Pocket Book*, published by the World Advertising Research Center, Henley-on-Thames, 2004.

increase the uses of a product, to remind and reinforce customers, and to reduce sales fluctuations (see Figure 18.1).[4]

## Promoting Products and Organisations

**Institutional advertising**
The type of advertising that promotes organisational images, ideas or political issues

**Advocacy advertising**
Promotes a company's position on a public issue

**Product advertising**
The type of advertising that promotes goods and services

Advertising is used to promote goods, services, ideas, images, issues, people and indeed anything that the advertiser wants to publicise or foster. Depending on what is being promoted, advertising can be classified as institutional or product advertising. **Institutional advertising** promotes organisational images, ideas or political issues. Institutional advertisements may deal with broad image issues, such as organisational strength or the friendliness of employees. They may also aim to create a more favourable view of the company in the eyes of non-customer groups such as stakeholders, consumer advocacy groups, potential stockholders or the general public. For example, the advertising of some manufacturers of alcoholic beverages promotes the idea that drinking and driving do not mix, in order to create and develop a socially responsible image. When a company promotes its position on a public issue – for instance, a tax increase, abortion or international coalitions – institutional advertising is referred to as **advocacy advertising**. Institutional advertising may be used to promote socially approved behaviour like recycling and moderation in consuming alcohol. This type of advertising not only has societal benefits but also helps build an organisation's image.

**Product advertising** promotes goods and services. Business, government and private non-business organisations turn to it to promote the uses, features, images and benefits of

**TABLE 18.1 ADVERTISING IN EUROPE (CONTINUED)**

**(b) Advertising Expenditure by Country and Medium, 2002**

| | US$ (millions) | | | | | | |
|---|---|---|---|---|---|---|---|
| **Country** | **Total** | **Press** | **Mag.** | **TV** | **Radio** | **Cinema** | **Outdoor** |
| UK | 17,566 | 7,238 | 2,812 | 5,520 | 738 | 222 | 1,036 |
| Germany | 15,712 | 7,054 | 2,985 | 4,137 | 622 | 168 | 746 |
| France | 8,941 | 2,329 | 2,101 | 2,749 | 671 | 70 | 1,021 |
| Italy | 7,924 | 1,850 | 1,366 | 4,144 | 298 | 76 | 190 |
| Spain | 4,896 | 1,542 | 555 | 2,018 | 407 | 43 | 331 |
| Netherlands | 3,351 | 1,484 | 833 | 687 | 211 | 7 | 129 |
| Switzerland | 2,444 | 1,195 | 438 | 338 | 83 | 24 | 366 |
| Belgium | 2,031 | 572 | 290 | 814 | 196 | 22 | 137 |
| Austria | 1,843 | 794 | 371 | 412 | 133 | 9 | 124 |
| Sweden | 1,612 | 892 | 228 | 354 | 48 | 8 | 82 |
| Greece | 1,407 | 271 | 483 | 598 | 55 | – | – |
| Norway | 1,404 | 883 | 145 | 279 | 48 | 12 | 37 |
| Portugal | 1,315 | 185 | 221 | 731 | 73 | 7 | 98 |
| Ireland | 1,228 | 806 | 23 | 224 | 72 | 10 | 93 |
| Finland | 1,183 | 653 | 204 | 235 | 51 | 3 | 37 |
| Denmark | 1,094 | 644 | 158 | 212 | 28 | 9 | 43 |
| Hungary | 931 | 133 | 128 | 554 | 50 | 3 | 63 |
| Czech. Republic | 838 | 191 | 162 | 448 | 35 | 2 | – |

(continued)

**Notes:** Data are net of discounts, include agency commission and press classified advertising but exclude production costs. Countries are ranked on total adspend.
**Source:** *The European Marketing Pocket Book*, published by the World Advertising Research Center, Henley-on-Thames, 2004 (please refer to specific country sections for full details).

their products or services. When Monsanto introduced a new pesticide to help farmers clean up weeds in post-harvest stubble, it used press advertising to tout the benefits of Sting CT, including a competition – to win a trip to Italy – and a coupon to mail in for further technical details of the product. It is this type of advertising that most readers of this book, as consumers, will be familiar with, be it in the form of advertisements for Ford cars, Kellogg's cereals or Barclays' services.

## Stimulating Primary and Selective Demand

**Pioneer advertising**
The type of advertising to create category need, that informs people about a product: what it is, what it does, how it can be used and where it can be purchased

**Primary Demand** When a specific business is the first to introduce an innovation, it tries to stimulate *primary demand* – demand for a product category rather than a specific brand of the product – through pioneer advertising. This is often referred to as creating category need, as explained in Chapter 17. **Pioneer advertising** informs people about a product: what it is, what it does, how it can be used and where it can be purchased. Because pioneer advertising is used in the introductory stage of the product life cycle when there are no competitive brands, it neither emphasises the brand name nor compares brands. The first company to introduce the CD player, for instance, initially tried to stimulate primary demand – create category need – by emphasising the benefits of CD players in general rather than the benefits of its brand. Product advertising is also used sometimes to stimulate primary demand for an established product. Occasionally, an industry trade group, rather than a single company, sponsors advertisements to stimulate primary demand. For example, to stimulate demand for milk, the now defunct Milk Marketing Board sponsored advertisements that demonstrated how healthy and pleasant milk is to drink. In Figure 18.2, advertising promotes the use of Canary tomatoes.

## Table 18.1 Advertising in Europe (continued)

### (c) Advertising Expenditure in Western European Countries[1]

| | Austria | Belgium | Denmark | France | Germany | Ireland | Italy | Netherlands | Portugal | Spain | Sweden | Switzerland | UK | USA[2] |
|---|---|---|---|---|---|---|---|---|---|---|---|---|---|---|
| **Advertising expenditure, 2002** | | | | | | | | | | | | | | |
| Per capita US$ | 226 | 197 | 204 | 151 | 191 | 320 | 137 | 208 | 127 | 121 | 181 | 337 | 292 | 434 |
| Total US$ (million) | 1,842 | 2,030 | 1,094 | 8,941 | 15,712 | 1,229 | 7,923 | 3,350 | 1,315 | 4,896 | 1,612 | 2,445 | 17,566 | 127,838 |
| Per capita Euro | 240 | 209 | 217 | 160 | 203 | 287 | 130 | 221 | 135 | 129 | 192 | 358 | 311 | 459 |
| Total Euro (million) | 1,957 | 2,158 | 1,162 | 9,501 | 16,695 | 1,100 | 7,556 | 3,560 | 1,398 | 5,202 | 1,714 | 2,598 | 18,664 | 135,364 |
| Per capita local currency | 240 | 209 | 1,608 | 160 | 203 | 287 | 130 | 221 | 135 | 129 | 1,762 | 525 | 198 | 434 |
| Total local currency (million) | 1,957 | 2,158 | 8,634 | 9,501 | 16,695 | 1,100 | 7,556 | 3,560 | 1,398 | 5,202 | 15,701 | 3,811 | 11,700 | 127,838 |
| **Distribution of total advertising expenditure in US$ (million)** | | | | | | | | | | | | | | |
| Newspapers (Press) | 794 | 572 | 644 | 2,325 | 7,042 | 646 | 1,658 | 1,482 | 185 | 1,539 | 891 | 1,193 | 7,230 | 41,830 |
| Magazines | 371 | 290 | 158 | 2,098 | 2,980 | 19 | 1,224 | 831 | 221 | 554 | 227 | 437 | 2,809 | 13,913 |
| TV | 412 | 814 | 212 | 2,744 | 4,130 | 180 | 3,712 | 686 | 731 | 2,015 | 353 | 337 | 5,514 | 50,778 |
| Radio | 133 | 196 | 28 | 670 | 621 | 58 | 267 | 210 | 73 | 406 | 48 | 83 | 737 | 17,178 |
| Cinema | 9 | 22 | 9 | 70 | 168 | 8 | 68 | 7 | 7 | 43 | 8 | 24 | 221 | – |
| Outdoor | 124 | 137 | 43 | 1,019 | 745 | 75 | 170 | 129 | 98 | 330 | 82 | 368 | 1,035 | 4,140 |
| **Distribution of total advertising expenditure as a percentage of total** | | | | | | | | | | | | | | |
| Newspapers (Press) | 43.1 | 28.2 | 58.9 | 26.0 | 44.9 | 65.8 | 23.4 | 44.3 | 14.9 | 31.5 | 55.3 | 48.9 | 41.2 | 32.7 |
| Magazines | 20.1 | 14.3 | 14.4 | 23.5 | 19.0 | 1.9 | 17.2 | 24.9 | 16.8 | 11.3 | 14.1 | 17.9 | 16.0 | 10.9 |
| TV | 22.3 | 40.1 | 19.4 | 30.7 | 26.3 | 18.2 | 52.3 | 20.5 | 55.3 | 41.2 | 21.9 | 13.8 | 31.4 | 39.7 |
| Radio | 7.2 | 9.6 | 2.6 | 7.5 | 4.0 | 5.9 | 3.8 | 6.3 | 5.5 | 8.3 | 3.0 | 3.4 | 4.2 | 13.4 |
| Cinema | 0.5 | 1.1 | 0.8 | 0.8 | 1.1 | 0.8 | 1.0 | 0.2 | 0.5 | 0.9 | 0.5 | 1.0 | 1.3 | – |
| Outdoor | 6.7 | 6.8 | 3.9 | 11.4 | 4.7 | 7.6 | 2.4 | 3.8 | 7.0 | 6.8 | 5.1 | 15.0 | 5.9 | 3.2 |

**Notes:** [1]These data have been derived from national sources to produce a comparable series. They are net of discounts, include agency commission but exclude production costs.
[2]USA is shown for purposes of comparison.

**Source:** *The European Advertising & Media Forecast*, published by the World Advertising Research Center, Henley-on-Thames, 2004.

**Table 18.2 Some Issues to Consider When Deciding Whether to use Advertising**

| |
|---|
| **1 Does the product possess unique, important features?**<br>Although homogeneous products such as cigarettes, petrol and beer have been advertised successfully, they usually require considerably more effort and expense than other products. On the other hand, products that are differentiated on physical rather than psychological dimensions are much easier to advertise. Even so, 'being different' is rarely enough. The advertisability of product features is enhanced when buyers believe that those unique features are important and useful. |
| **2 Are 'hidden qualities' important to buyers?**<br>If by viewing, feeling, tasting or smelling the product buyers can learn all there is to know about the product and its benefits, advertising will have less chance of increasing demand. Conversely, if not all product benefits are apparent to consumers on inspection and use of the product, advertising has more of a story to tell, and the probability that it can be profitably used increases. The 'hidden quality' of vitamin C in oranges once helped explain why Sunkist oranges could be advertised effectively, whereas the advertising of lettuce has been a failure. |
| **3 Is the general demand trend for the product favourable?**<br>If the generic product category is experiencing a long term decline, it is less likely that advertising can be used successfully for a particular brand within the category. For example, CDs virtually extinguished the demand for turntables. |
| **4 Is the market potential for the product adequate?**<br>Advertising can be effective only when there are sufficient actual or prospective users of the brand in the target market. |
| **5 Is the competitive environment favourable?**<br>The size and marketing strength of competitors, and their brand shares and loyalty, will greatly affect the possible success of an advertising campaign. For example, a marketing effort to compete successfully against Kodak film, Heinz baked beans, or McDonald's restaurants would demand much more than simply advertising. |
| **6 Are general economic conditions favourable for marketing the product?**<br>The effects of an advertising programme and the sales of all products are influenced by the overall state of the economy and by specific business conditions. For example, it is much easier to advertise and sell luxury leisure products (hi-fi systems, sailing boats, video cameras, exotic holidays) when disposable income is high. |
| **7 Is the organisation able and willing to spend the money required to launch an advertising campaign?**<br>As a general rule, if the organisation is unable or unwilling to undertake an advertising expenditure that as a percentage of the total amount spent in the product category is at least equal to the market share it desires, advertising is not likely to be effective. |
| **8 Does the company possess sufficient marketing expertise to market the product?**<br>The successful marketing of any product involves a complex mixture of product and consumer research, product development, packaging, pricing, financial management, promotion, customer service and distribution. Weakness in any area of marketing is an obstacle to the successful use of advertising. |
| **Source:** Adapted from Charles H. Patti, 'Evaluating the role of advertising', *Journal of Advertising*, Fall 1977, pp. 32–3. Reprinted by permission of the *Journal of Advertising*. |

**Competitive advertising** The type of advertising that points out a brand's uses, features and advantages, which may not be available in competing brands

**Selective Demand** To build *selective demand*, or demand for a specific brand, an advertiser turns to competitive advertising. **Competitive advertising** points out a brand's uses, features and advantages that benefit consumers but may not be available in competing brands. For example, BMW heavily promotes the technical abilities and innovative features of its cars in its advertising.

Another form of competitive advertising is **comparative advertising**, in which two or more brands are compared on the basis of one or more product attributes. Companies

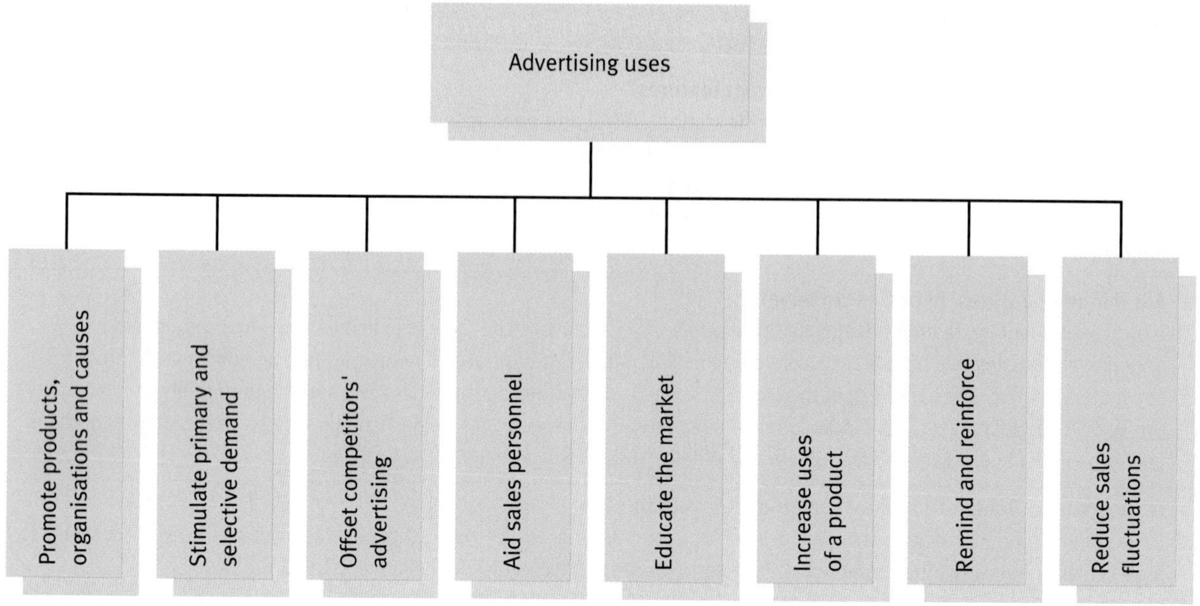


***Figure 18.1***
*Major uses of advertising*

must not, however, misrepresent the qualities or characteristics of the comparison product and, in certain countries, overt comparisons of rival products or brands are prohibited.

## Off-setting Competitors' Advertising

**Comparative advertising**
The type of advertising that compares two or more brands on the basis of one or more product attributes

When marketers advertise to off-set or lessen the effects of a competitor's promotional programme, they are using **defensive advertising**. Although defensive advertising does not necessarily increase a company's sales or market share, it may prevent a loss in these areas. For example, when McDonald's first test-marketed pizza, Pizza Hut countered with defensive advertising to protect its market share and sales. Pizza Hut advertised both on television and in newspapers in two test cities, emphasising that its product is made from scratch, whereas McDonald's was made using frozen dough.[5] Defensive advertising is used most often by companies in extremely competitive consumer product markets, such as the fast-food industry.

## Making Sales Personnel More Effective

**Defensive advertising**
The type of advertising that aims to off-set or lessen the effects of a competitor's promotional programme

Business organisations that stress personal selling often use advertising to improve the effectiveness of sales personnel. Advertising created specifically to support personal selling activities tries to pre-sell a product to buyers by informing them about its uses, features and benefits, and by encouraging them to contact local dealers or sales representatives. This form of advertising helps sales people find good sales prospects. Advertising is often designed to support personal selling efforts for business products, insurance and consumer durables, such as cars and major household appliances. For example, advertising may bring a prospective buyer to a showroom, but usually a sales person plays a key role in actually closing the sale.

## Educating the Market

A change to a business's strategy may lead to it entering new markets or introducing innovative products. This will require an orientation programme for targeted customers and the required channel intermediaries. Part of this communications task may entail advertising. Even if a company modifies its marketing mix in existing markets – new product specifications, after-sales policies or pricing, for example – it may need to educate the market, customers and dealers regarding the changes.

Sweet succulent and so versatile...
thank you, Canary Islands.
Canary Islands Tomatoes owe their sweet, succulent flavour to the glorious island sunshine and the fertile, mineral rich volcanic soil.
Look out for FREE Canary Islands Travel and Recipe booklet in each punnet. Subject to availability.
FOODS FROM SPAIN
Foods from Spain, Spanish Embassy Office for Economic and Commercial Affairs, 66 Chiltern Street, London W1U 4LS.
Canary Islands Tomatoes


***Figure 18.2***
*This advertising aims to stimulate primary demand for tomatoes but also stresses the particular merits of tomatoes from the Canary Islands*
*Source: Courtesy of Foods from Spain*

## Increasing the Uses of a Product

The absolute demand for any product is limited because people in a market will consume only so much of it. Given both this limit on demand and competitive conditions, marketers can increase sales of a specific product in a defined geographic market only to a certain point. To improve sales beyond this point, they must either enlarge the geographic market and sell to more people, or develop and promote a larger number of uses for the product. If a business's advertising convinces buyers to use its products in more ways, the sales of the products go up. For example, Shredded Wheat used advertising to inform consumers that its cereal contains no added sugar and is high in natural fibre, which is essential to a healthy and balanced diet. The aim is to position Shredded Wheat as part of a wholesome diet, as well as a popular children's cereal. When promoting new uses, an advertiser attempts to increase the demand for its own brand without driving up the demand for competing brands.

## Reminding and Reinforcing Customers

Marketers sometimes employ **reminder advertising** to let consumers know that an established brand is still around and that it has certain uses, characteristics and benefits. Procter & Gamble, for example, reminds consumers that its Crest toothpaste is still best at preventing cavities. **Reinforcement advertising**, on the other hand, tries to assure current users that they have made the right choice and tells them how to get the most satisfaction from a product.

Both reminder and reinforcement advertising aim to prevent a loss in sales or market share. Much of Ford's range-focused advertising is designed to reassure existing Ford owners that the company is forward thinking and customer oriented. The advertising for Head & Shoulders shampoo is as much concerned with reminding existing users of its virtues as it is about building awareness for potential new users.

**Reminder advertising** The type of advertising that reminds customers of the uses, characteristics and benefits of an established brand

## Reducing Sales Fluctuations

The demand for many products varies from month to month because of such factors as climate, holidays, seasons and customs. A business, however, cannot operate at peak efficiency when sales fluctuate rapidly. Changes in sales volume translate into changes in the production or inventory, personnel and financial resources it requires. To the extent that marketers can generate sales during slow periods, they can smooth out fluctuations. When advertising reduces fluctuations, a manager can use the business's resources more efficiently. Business user-oriented hotels such as Holiday Inn or Hilton promote discounted rooms for weekend leisure breaks in order to utilise otherwise unused facilities.

**Reinforcement advertising** The type of advertising that tries to assure current users that they have made the right choice and tells them how to get the most satisfaction from the product

Advertising is often designed to stimulate business during sales slumps. For example, advertisements promoting price reductions of lawncare equipment or package holidays can increase sales during the winter months. On occasion, a business advertises that customers will get better service by coming in on certain days rather than others. During peak sales periods, a marketer may refrain from advertising to prevent over-stimulating sales to the point where the company cannot handle all the demand. For example, money-off coupons for the delivery of pizza are often valid only from Monday to Thursday, not Friday to Sunday, which are the peak delivery days.

A company's use of advertising depends on its objectives and resources, as well as on external environmental forces. The degree to which advertising accomplishes the marketer's goals depends in large part on the advertising campaign.

# Developing an Advertising Campaign

**Advertising campaign** An attempt to reach a particular target market by designing a series of advertisements and placing them in various advertising media

An **advertising campaign** involves designing a series of advertisements and placing them in various advertising media to reach a particular target market. As Figure 18.3 indicates, the general steps in developing and implementing an advertising campaign are:

1 identifying and analysing the advertising target
2 defining the advertising objectives
3 creating the advertising 'platform'
4 determining the advertising budget
5 developing the media plan
6 creating the advertising message
7 executing the campaign
8 evaluating the effectiveness of the advertising.

The number of steps and the order in which they are carried out may vary according to an organisation's resources, the nature of its product, the types of target market or audience to be reached, the product's stage in its life cycle (see Chapter 10), the current sales levels and market standing of the product, the nature of competitors' promotional mix activity, and the advertising agency selected.[6] The agreed overall objectives and strategy for the marketing communications will also steer the development of the campaign, as explained in the previous chapter. However, these general guidelines for developing an advertising campaign are appropriate for all types of organisation.

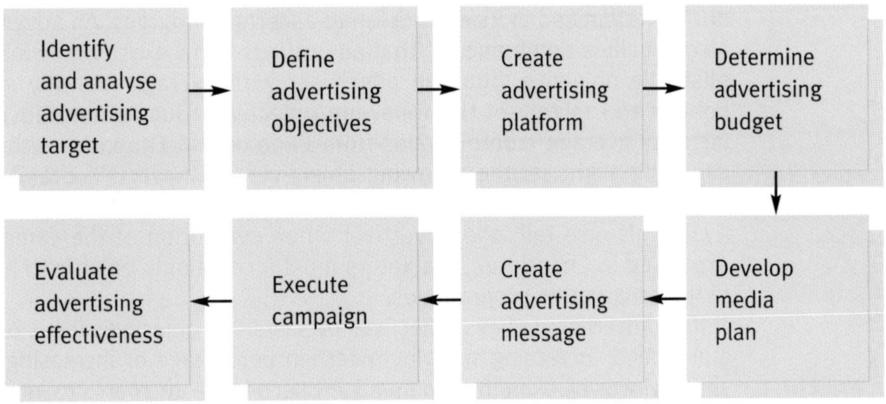


***Figure 18.3***
*General steps for developing and implementing an advertising campaign*

## Identifying and Analysing the Advertising Target

**Advertising target**
The group of people at which advertisements are aimed

The **advertising target** is the group of people at which advertisements are aimed. For example, the target audience for Special K and All-Bran cereals is health-conscious adults. Identifying and analysing the advertising target are critical processes; the information they yield helps determine the other steps in developing the campaign. The advertising target often includes everyone in a company's target market. Marketers may, however, seize some opportunities to slant a campaign at only a portion of the target market. For example, in the USA, Handspring has targeted women with advertisements in fashion and other magazines, positioning its Visor handheld computing device as a chic fashion accessory.[7]

Advertisers analyse advertising targets, or target audiences, to establish an information base for a campaign. Information commonly needed includes the location and geographic distribution of the target group; the distribution of age, income, ethnic origin, sex and education; consumer attitudes regarding the purchase and use of both the advertiser's products and competing products; the lifestyles of these consumers, their buying behaviour and their media habits. It is important to be able to profile the targeted consumers, but also to be able to understand their views – likes/dislikes, uses, anxieties about, peer expectations – of the product being advertised. It is crucial to know how consumers perceive the standing and brand positioning of the product vis-à-vis competitors' propositions. Qualitative marketing research is very important in this process, particularly the use of focus group discussions, as explored in Chapter 9.[8] The exact kinds of information that an organisation will find useful depend on the type of product being advertised, levels of brand awareness, the characteristics of the advertising target, and the type and amount of competition. Generally, the more advertisers know about the advertising target (those people intended to be influenced by the advertising), the more likely they are to develop an effective advertising campaign. When the advertising target is not precisely identified and properly analysed, the campaign may not succeed.

## Defining the Advertising Objectives

The advertiser's next step is to consider what the company hopes to accomplish with the campaign. Because advertising objectives guide campaign development, advertisers should define their objectives carefully to ensure that the campaign will achieve what they want. Advertising campaigns based on poorly defined objectives seldom succeed.

Advertising objectives should be stated clearly, precisely and in measurable terms. Precision and measurability allow advertisers to evaluate advertising success: to judge, at the campaign's end, whether the objectives have been met and, if so, how well. To provide precision and measurability, advertising objectives should contain benchmarks – the current condition or position of the business – and indicate how far and in what direction the advertiser wishes to move from these benchmarks. For example, the advertiser should state the current sales level (the benchmark) and the amount of sales increase that is sought through advertising. Brand awareness should be assessed prior to the campaign, during its run and at its conclusion to ascertain progress. An advertising objective should also specify a timeframe, so that advertisers know exactly how long they have to accomplish the objective. Thus an advertiser with average monthly sales of £450,000 (the benchmark) might set the following objective: 'Our primary advertising objective is to increase average monthly sales from £450,000 to £540,000 within 12 months.' Another company might set the following objective: 'We have 12% brand awareness in our core target market. At the end of 15 months, we wish this percentage to match that of our key rival.' This also tells the advertiser when evaluation of the campaign should begin. As explained in Chapter 24, marketers must increasingly be able to assess the performance of their marketing programmes.

If an advertiser defines objectives by sales, the objectives focus on raising absolute monetary sales, increasing sales by a certain percentage or increasing the company's market share. However, even though an advertiser's long-run goal is to increase sales, not all campaigns are designed to produce immediate sales. Some campaigns are designed to increase product or brand awareness, make consumers' attitudes more favourable or increase consumers' knowledge of a product's features. These objectives are stated in terms of communication. For example, when Apple first introduced home computers, its initial campaign did not focus on sales but on creating brand awareness and educating consumers about the features and uses of home computers. A specific communication objective might be to increase product feature awareness from 0 to 40 per cent in the target market at the end of six months. Objectives must be realistic. An advertising agency must be prepared to let a client know when its goals are not attainable. Ultimately, advertising is merely a communications tool: it cannot overcome product deficiencies or a poorly developed marketing strategy.

## Creating the Advertising Platform

**Advertising platform**
The basic issues or selling points that an advertiser wishes to include in the advertising campaign

Before launching a political campaign, party leaders develop a political platform, which states the major issues that will be the basis of the campaign. Like a political platform, an **advertising platform** consists of the basic issues or selling points that an advertiser wishes to include in the advertising campaign. A single advertisement in an advertising campaign may contain one or several issues in the platform. Although the platform sets forth the basic issues, it does not indicate how they should be presented.

A marketer's advertising platform should consist of issues that are important to consumers. One of the best ways to determine what those issues are is to survey consumers about what they consider most important in the selection and use of the product involved. For example, Procter & Gamble has developed refill packages for some of its cleaning products. These refill packages provide a unique benefit by not adding to solid waste disposal problems. Environmentally conscious consumers consider this a positive selling feature. McDonald's has added healthier eating options to its menu and advertised these, to reflect consumers' growing awareness of obesity problems. The selling features of a product must not only be important to consumers; if possible, they should also be features that competitive products do not have.

Although research is the most effective method for determining the issues of an advertising platform, it is expensive. As a result, the advertising platform is most commonly based on the opinions of personnel within the business and of individuals in the advertising agency, if an agency is used. As discussed in Chapter 9, qualitative research – typically in the form of focus groups – is often used to test the validity of these insiders' views before the campaign is produced. This trial-and-error approach generally leads to some successes and some failures.

Because the advertising platform is a base on which to build the message, marketers should analyse this step carefully. A campaign can be perfect in the selection and analysis of its advertising target, the statement of its objectives, its media strategy and the form of its message. But the campaign will still fail if the advertisements communicate information that consumers do not consider important when they select and use the product.

## Determining the Advertising Budget

**Advertising budget** The total amount of money that a marketer allocates for advertising over a period of time

**Objective and task approach** A technique for determining an advertising budget that involves determining campaign objectives and then attempting to list the tasks required to accomplish them

**Percentage of sales approach** A budgeting technique that involves multiplying a company's past sales, plus a factor for planned sales growth or decline, by a standard percentage based on both what the business traditionally spends on advertising and what the industry averages

**Competition matching approach** A budgeting technique in which marketers either match their major competitors' budgets or allocate the same percentage of sales for advertising as their competitors

**Arbitrary approach** A budgeting technique in which a high-level executive in the business states how much can be spent on advertising over a certain time period

The **advertising budget** is the total amount of money that a marketer allocates for advertising over a period of time. It is difficult to determine this amount because there is currently no way to measure the precise effects of spending a certain amount of money on advertising.

Many factors affect a business's decision about how much to spend on advertising. The geographic size of the market and the distribution of buyers within the market have a great bearing on this decision. Both the type of product being advertised and a business's sales volume relative to competitors' sales volumes play a part in determining what proportion of a business's revenue is spent on advertising. Advertising budgets for business products are usually quite small relative to the sales of the products – more is spent on personal selling, direct mail and trade shows – whereas consumer convenience items, such as soft drinks, soaps and cosmetics, generally have large budgets. In the UK in 2003, the advertising budget for McDonald's was reportedly over £50 million, whereas a market-leading business-to-business IT company had just £7 million at its disposal.

**The Objective and Task Approach** Of the many techniques used to determine the advertising budget, intuitively one of the most logical is the **objective and task approach.** Using this approach, marketers initially determine the objectives that a campaign is to achieve and then attempt to list the tasks required to accomplish them. The costs of the tasks are then calculated and added to arrive at the amount of the total budget. This approach has one main problem: marketers usually find it hard to estimate the level of effort needed to achieve certain objectives. A coffee marketer, for example, might find it extremely difficult to determine by what amount it should increase national television advertising in order to raise a brand's market share from 8 to 12 per cent. As a result of this problem, advertisers do not often use the objective and task approach.

**The Percentage of Sales Approach** In the more widely used **percentage of sales approach,** marketers simply multiply a company's past sales, plus a factor for planned sales growth or decline, by a standard percentage based on both what the business traditionally spends on advertising and what the industry averages. This approach has one major flaw: it is based on the incorrect assumption that sales create advertising, rather than the reverse. Consequently, a marketer using this approach at a time of declining sales will reduce the amount spent on advertising. But such a reduction may further diminish sales. Though illogical, this technique has gained wide acceptance because it is easy to use and less disruptive competitively; it stabilises a company's market share within an industry. However, in times of declining sales, many businesses do increase their contribution to advertising in the hope of reversing the decline.

**The Competition Matching Approach** Another way to determine the advertising budget is the **competition matching approach.** Marketers who follow this approach try either to match their major competitors' budgets or to allocate the same percentage of sales for advertising as their competitors do. Although a wise marketer should be aware of what competitors spend on advertising, this technique should not be used by itself, because a company's competitors probably have different advertising objectives and different resources available for advertising. Many companies and advertising agencies engage in quarterly competitive spending reviews, comparing competitors' expenditures in print, radio and television with their own spending levels. Competitive tracking of this nature occurs at both the national and regional levels.

**The Arbitrary Approach** At times, marketers use the **arbitrary approach**: a high-level executive in the business states how much can be spent on advertising for a certain time period. The arbitrary approach often leads to under-spending or over-spending. Although hardly a scientific budgeting technique, it is expedient.

Establishing the advertising budget is critically important. If it is set too low, the campaign cannot achieve its full potential for stimulating demand. When too much money is allocated for advertising, the over-spending that results wastes financial resources. An advertising agency being briefed must know the budget size in order to be able to plan the campaign effectively.

## Developing the Media Plan

As Table 18.3 shows, advertisers spend tremendous amounts of money on advertising media. These amounts have grown rapidly during the past two decades. To derive the maximum

**TABLE 18.3 UK ADVERTISING**

**The Top 30 Advertisers, 2002**

| Rank | Advertiser | Total £ '000s | Advertising expenditure TV % | Radio % | Press % | Other % |
|---|---|---|---|---|---|---|
| 1 | Proctor & Gamble | 161,890 | 82.3 | 3.3 | 11.1 | 3.3 |
| 2 | COI Communications | 119,765 | 47.6 | 16.4 | 23.9 | 12.1 |
| 3 | British Telecom | 96,664 | 52.1 | 9.1 | 26.7 | 12.1 |
| 4 | Ford Motor Company | 94,918 | 53.9 | 4.7 | 28.2 | 13.2 |
| 5 | L'Oréal Golden | 70,845 | 65.1 | 0.8 | 26.5 | 7.5 |
| 6 | Nestlé | 69,198 | 74.5 | 5.2 | 6.6 | 13.8 |
| 7 | Masterfoods | 66,903 | 59.9 | 3.8 | 12.0 | 24.2 |
| 8 | Renault | 66,146 | 46.7 | 5.8 | 33.0 | 14.6 |
| 9 | Toyota | 65,465 | 53.8 | 7.9 | 24.4 | 14.0 |
| 10 | Vauxhall Motors | 63,371 | 56.3 | 3.4 | 25.9 | 14.4 |
| 11 | DFS Furniture | 59,393 | 49.7 | 3.9 | 44.5 | 1.9 |
| 12 | Lever Fabergé Personal Care | 58,646 | 66.0 | 0.9 | 10.1 | 22.9 |
| 13 | Orange | 55,703 | 42.3 | 6.7 | 17.9 | 33.1 |
| 14 | Reckitt Benckiser | 53,049 | 95.2 | 0.2 | 3.8 | 0.8 |
| 15 | Sainsbury's | 48,726 | 49.1 | 17.6 | 27.7 | 5.5 |
| 16 | Boots The Chemists | 48,266 | 61.0 | 0.5 | 30.8 | 7.8 |
| 17 | Volkswagen | 45,385 | 53.2 | 5.7 | 25.7 | 15.3 |
| 18 | Lever Fabergé Home Care | 43,617 | 49.7 | 5.7 | 23.8 | 20.7 |
| 19 | Peugeot | 42,725 | 64.8 | 2.3 | 24.3 | 8.7 |
| 20 | McDonald's | 42,211 | 85.3 | 4.7 | 2.2 | 7.8 |
| 21 | Diageo | 41,906 | 71.9 | 1.4 | 2.8 | 23.9 |
| 22 | Vodafone | 41,853 | 56.6 | 7.6 | 23.3 | 12.5 |
| 23 | Unilever Bestfoods UK | 40,175 | 76.9 | 2.6 | 8.7 | 11.9 |
| 24 | Kellogg | 39,413 | 81.6 | 4.0 | 8.6 | 5.9 |
| 25 | Citroën | 39,153 | 70.2 | 1.7 | 25.1 | 3.0 |
| 26 | Glaxosmithkline | 37,963 | 83.0 | 4.0 | 9.1 | 3.8 |
| 27 | MG Rover | 37,580 | 28.0 | 10.2 | 55.6 | 6.2 |
| 28 | T-Mobile | 37,261 | 56.2 | 10.1 | 20.8 | 12.9 |
| 29 | Coca-Cola | 36,360 | 70.5 | 4.7 | 5.4 | 19.3 |
| 30 | B&Q | 33,899 | 73.8 | 1.5 | 24.0 | 0.7 |

**Source:** © Nielsen Media Research Ltd; *The Marketing Pocket Book*, published by the World Advertising Research Center, Henley-on-Thames, 2004.

**Media plan**
The process of establishing the exact media vehicles to be used for advertising, and the dates and times when the advertisements will appear

**Reach**
The percentage of consumers in the advertising target actually exposed to a particular advertisement in a stated time period

**Frequency**
The number of times targeted consumers are exposed to a particular advertisement

results from media expenditures, a marketer must develop an effective media plan. A **media plan** sets forth the exact media vehicles to be used for advertising (specific magazines, television channels, newspapers, radio programmes, movies, billboards, websites, and so forth), and the dates and times when the advertisements will appear. The effectiveness of the plan determines how many people in the advertising target will be exposed to the message. It also determines, to some degree, the effects of the message on those individuals. Media planning is a complex task that requires thorough analysis of the advertising target, as well as of any legal restrictions that might apply. For example, the EU has strict regulations pertaining to the advertising of tobacco, foods and pharmaceuticals, and to comparative advertising. More regulations are on their way too, in connection with alcohol, financial services, cars, environmental labelling and the portrayal of women.

To formulate a media plan, the planner selects the media for a campaign and draws up a time schedule for each medium. The media planner's primary goal is to reach the largest possible number of people in the advertising target for the amount of money spent on media. In addition, a secondary goal is to achieve the appropriate message reach and frequency for the target audience while staying within the budget. **Reach** refers to the percentage of consumers in the advertising target actually exposed to a particular advertisement in a stated time period. **Frequency** is the number of times these targeted consumers are exposed to the advertisement. Some experts believe that a target consumer must be exposed more than 30 times to an advertisement for a consumer durable or fast-moving consumer good before there is acceptance and full awareness of the advertising platform. However, most consumers, unless highly stimulated by the advertising, are not prepared to read, watch or hear an advertisement so many times. The platform, creativity and media choices must be smart enough to overcome this lack of interest in advertising.

Media planners begin with rather broad decisions; eventually, however, they must make very specific choices. A planner must first decide which kinds of media to use: radio, television, newspapers, magazines, direct mail, outdoor displays, ambient, public transport, the Internet,[9] or a combination of two or more of these. After making the general media decision, the planner selects specific sub-classes within each medium. Estée Lauder, for example, might advertise its Clinique cosmetic line in lifestyle magazines, as well as during daytime, prime-time and late-night television.

Media planners take many factors into account as they devise a media plan. They analyse the location and demographic characteristics of people in the advertising target because the various media appeal to particular demographic groups in particular locations. For example, there are radio stations directed mainly at teenagers, magazines for men in the 18–34 age group and television programmes aimed at adults of both sexes. Media planners should also consider the size and type of audiences that are reached by specific media. Several data services collect and, periodically, publish information about the circulations and audiences of various media. Most publishers and broadcasters offer prospective advertisers media packs, containing independently audited data about readership or viewing figures. For example, satirical magazine *Private Eye* states that each issue has the potential to be read by 700,000 people, who are carefully profiled for advertisers in terms of socio-economics. The cost of media is an important but troublesome consideration. Planners try to obtain the best coverage possible for the amount of money spent, yet there is no accurate way of comparing the cost and impact of a television advertisement with the cost and impact of a newspaper advertisement.

The content of the message sometimes affects the choice of media. Print media can be used more effectively than broadcast media to present many issues or numerous details. The makers of Tartare Light Fromage Frais produce wordy magazine advertisements, including recipes as well as product details, to boost demand and educate consumers about the product's uses. The advertisements appear in most women's and food magazines. If an advertiser wants to promote beautiful colours, patterns or textures, media that offer high-quality colour reproduction – magazines or television – should be used instead

**Table 18.4 Characteristcs, Advantages and Disadvantages of Major Advertising Media**

| Medium | Types | Unit of sale | Factors affecting rates | Cost comparison indicator | Advantages | Disadvantages |
|---|---|---|---|---|---|---|
| Newspaper | National<br>Local<br>Morning<br>Evening<br>Sunday<br>Sunday supplement<br>Weekly<br>Special<br>Local free sheets | Column cms/inches<br>Counted words<br>Printed lines<br>Agate lines | Volume and frequency discounts<br>Number of colours<br>Position charges for preferred and guaranteed positions<br>Circulation level | Milline rate = cost per agate line × 1,000,000 divided by circulation<br>Cost per column cm/inch | Many people read a newspaper; purchased to be read; selective for socio-economic groups; national geographic flexibility; short lead time; frequent publication; favourable for cooperative advertising; merchandising services | Short life; limited reproduction capabilties; large advertising volume limits exposure to any one advertisement; plethora of local free sheets annoys some householders |
| Magazine | Consumer<br>Farm<br>Business<br>Sports<br>Travel | Pages<br>Partial pages<br>Column cms/inches | Circulation level<br>Cost of publishing<br>Type of audience<br>Volume discounts<br>Frequency discounts<br>Size of advertisement<br>Position of advertisement (covers)<br>Number of colours<br>Regional issues | Cost per thousand (CPM) = cost per page × 1,000 divided by circulation | Socio-economic selectivity;- good reproduction; long life; prestige; geographic selectivity when regional issues are available; read in leisurely manner | High absolute monetary cost; long lead time; long user life |
| Direct mail | Letters<br>Catalogues<br>Price lists<br>Calendars<br>Brochures<br>Coupons<br>Circulars<br>Newsletters<br>Postcards<br>Booklets<br>Samples | Not applicable | Cost of mailing lists<br>Postage<br>Production costs | Cost per contact | Little wasted circulation; highly selective; circulation controlled by advertiser; few distractions; personal; stimulates action; use of novelty; easy to measure performance; hidden from competitors | Expensive; no editorial matter to attract readers; considered junk mail by many; criticised as invasion of privacy; increasingly regulated |

(continued)

**Table 18.4 Characteristcs, Advantages and Disadvantages of Major Advertising Media (continued)**

| Medium | Types | Unit of sale | Factors affecting rates | Cost comparison indicator | Advantages | Disadvantages |
|---|---|---|---|---|---|---|
| Radio | AM<br>FM | Programme types<br>Spots: 5, 10, 20, 30, 60 seconds | Time of day<br>Audience size<br>Length of spot or programme<br>Volume and frequency discounts | Cost per thousand (CPM) = cost per minute × 1,000 divided by audience size | Highly mobile; low cost broadcast medium; message can be quickly changed; geographic selectivity; socio-economic selectivity | Little national radio advertising; provides only audio message; has lost prestige; short life of message; listeners' attention limited because of other activities while listening |
| Television | ITV/C4/C5<br>Satellite<br>Cable | Programme types<br>Spots: 15, 20, 30, 60 seconds | Time of day<br>Length of spot<br>Volume and frequency discounts<br>Audience size | Cost per thousand (CPM) = cost per minute × 1,000 divided by audience size | Reaches large audience; low cost per exposure; uses both audio and video; highly visible; high prestige; geographic and socio-economic selectivity | High monetary costs; highly perishable message; size of audience not guaranteed; prime time limited; increasing channel hopping during commercial breaks and zapping through advertisements on video recordings |
| Inside public transport | Buses<br>Underground | Full, half and quarter showings are sold on a monthly basis | Number of passengers<br>Multiple-month discounts<br>Production costs<br>Position | Cost per thousand passengers | Low cost; 'captive' audience; geographic selectivity | Does not secure quick results |
| Outside public transport | Buses<br>Taxis | Full, half and quarter showings; space also rented on per unit basis | Number of advertisements<br>Position<br>Size | Cost per 100 exposures | Low cost; geographic selectivity; reaches broad, diverse audience | Lacks socio-economic selectivity; does not have high impact on readers |

(continued)

**Table 18.4 Characteristcs, Advantages and Disadvantages of Major Advertising Media (continued)**

| Medium | Types | Unit of sale | Factors affecting rates | Cost comparison indicator | Advantages | Disadvantages |
|---|---|---|---|---|---|---|
| Outdoor | Papered posters/ billboards<br>Painted displays<br>Spectaculars<br>Poster vans | Papered posters: sold on monthly basis in multiples<br>Painted displays and spectaculars; sold on per unit basis | Length of time purchased<br>Land rental<br>Cost of production<br>Intensity of traffic<br>Frequency and continuity discounts<br>Location | No standard indicator | Allows for repetition; low cost; message can be placed close to the point of sale; geographic selectivity; works 24 hours a day | Message must be short and simple; no socio-economic selectivity; seldom attracts readers' full attention; criticised for being traffic hazard and blight on countryside |
| Internet | Corporate web sites<br>Search engine pop-ups | Home pages<br>Menu pages on company's *own* web sites<br>Price per thousand hits for pop-ups | In-house or outsourced web site development<br>Web master's overheads<br>Host site management fees | 'Free' for media, but costs of developing web site and specific pages must be budgeted | Rapid growth in Internet use; quickly up-dated messages; interactive contact via e-mail links; ability to link to detailed editorial; multi-media messages | Skewed take-up amongst certain consumer groups; resistance by some to seeking web-based advertisements; slow access speeds and variable reproductive quality; poorly prepared material; infancy of technique; search engine pop-up blockers |

**Sources:** Some of the information in this table is from S. Watson Dunn and Arnold M. Barban, *Advertising: Its Role in Modern Marketing*, 6th edn (Hinsdale, Ill.: Dryden Press, 1986); and Anthony F. McGann and J. Thomas Russell, *Advertising Media* (Homewood, Ill.: Irwin, 1981).

of newspapers. For example, cosmetics can be far more effectively promoted in a full-colour magazine advertisement than in a black-and-white newspaper advertisement.

Table 18.1 provides data on the amounts of advertising expenditure in Europe by media. The data indicate that different countries give greater priority to certain types of advertising media. The medium selected is determined by the characteristics, advantages and disadvantages of the major media available (see Table 18.4).

**Cost comparison indicator**
A measure that allows an advertiser to compare the costs of several vehicles within a specific medium in relation to the number of people reached by each vehicle

Given the variety of vehicles within each medium, media planners must deal with a vast number of choices. The multitude of factors that affect media rates obviously adds to the complexity of media planning. A **cost comparison indicator** enables an advertiser to compare the costs of several vehicles within a specific medium – such as two newspapers – in relation to the number of people reached by each vehicle. For example, the 'milline rate' is the cost comparison indicator for newspapers; it shows the cost of exposing a million people to a space equal to one agate line (an agate line is one column wide and the height of the smallest type normally used in classified newspaper advertisements: there are 14 agate lines in one column inch).

## Creating the Advertising Message

The basic content and form of an advertising message are a function of several factors. The product's features, uses and benefits affect the content of the message. Characteristics of the people in the advertising target – their sex, age, education, ethnic origin, income, occupation, lifestyle, media habits and other attributes – influence both the content and form. When Procter & Gamble promotes its Crest toothpaste to children, the company emphasises the importance of daily brushing and decay control. When it markets Crest to adults, it discusses tartar, plaque and whiteness. To communicate effectively, an advertiser must use words, symbols and illustrations that are meaningful, familiar and attractive to the people who constitute the advertising target: the target audience.

The objectives and platform of an advertising campaign also affect the content and form of its messages. For example, if a company's advertising objectives involve large sales increases, the message demands hard-hitting, high-impact language and symbols. When campaign objectives aim at increasing brand awareness, the message may use much repetition of the brand name, and words and illustrations associated with it. Thus the advertising platform is the foundation on which campaign messages are built. Agencies strive to develop platforms with longevity in order to foster long-term brand building. For example, JWT's Andrex puppies have represented the toilet tissue in 30 years of advertising; 'ASDA price' is the long-term strapline to the supermarket chain's value-led advertising and 'the ultimate driving machine' is BMW's famous ongoing positioning.

The choice of media obviously influences the content and form of the message. Effective outdoor displays and short broadcast spot announcements require concise, simple messages. Magazine and newspaper advertisements can include more detail and long explanations. Because several different kinds of media offer geographic selectivity, a precise message can be tailored to a particular geographic section of the advertising target. Some magazine and national newspaper publishers produce **regional issues**: for a particular issue, the advertisements and editorial content of copies appearing in one geographic area differ from those appearing in other areas. A clothing manufacturer may decide to use one message in London and another in the rest of the UK. A company may also choose to advertise in only a few regions. Such geographic selectivity enables a business to use the same message in different regions at different times.

**Regional issues**
Versions of a magazine or newspaper that differ across geographic regions in their advertising and editorial content

The basic components of a print advertising message are shown in Figure 18.4. The messages for most advertisements depend on the use of copy and artwork.

**Copy**
The verbal portion of an advertisement

**Copy** The verbal portion of an advertisement is **copy**. It includes headlines, sub-headlines, body copy and the signature (see Figure 18.4). When preparing advertising copy, marketers attempt to move the target audience through a persuasive sequence called

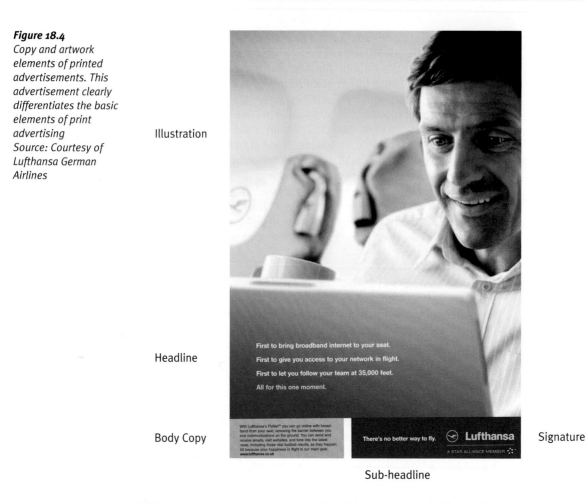

Illustration
Headline
Body Copy
Signature
Sub-headline

***Figure 18.4***
*Copy and artwork elements of printed advertisements. This advertisement clearly differentiates the basic elements of print advertising*
*Source: Courtesy of Lufthansa German Airlines*

**AIDA**
A persuasive sequence used in advertisements: attention, interest, desire and action

**AIDA**: attention, interest, desire and action. Consumers will not visit a store, trial a product or make a purchase of an unfamiliar product unless marketers first grab their attention, gain their interest and make the product appear desirable. Emotive and persuasive advertising plays a key role in this process. Not all copy needs be this extensive, however.

The headline is critical because often it is the only part of the copy that people read. It should attract readers' attention and create enough interest to make them want to read the body copy. The sub-headline, if there is one, links the headline to the body copy; sometimes it helps explain the headline.

Body copy for most advertisements consists of an introductory statement or paragraph, several explanatory paragraphs and a closing paragraph. Some copy-writers have adopted a pattern or set of guidelines to develop body copy systematically:

1 identify a specific desire or problem for consumers
2 suggest the good or service as the best way to satisfy that desire or solve that problem
3 state the advantages and benefits of the product
4 indicate why the advertised product is the best for the buyer's particular situation
5 substantiate the claims and advantages
6 prompt the buyer into action.[10]

The signature identifies the sponsor of the advertisement. It may contain several elements, including the company's trademark, logo, name and address. The signature should be designed to be attractive, legible, distinctive and easy to identify in a variety of sizes.

Because radio listeners are often not fully 'tuned in' mentally, radio copy should be informal and conversational to attract their attention and achieve greater impact. The radio message is highly perishable; thus radio copy should consist of short, familiar terms. Its length should not require a delivery rate exceeding approximately two-and-a-half words per second.

In television copy, the audio material must not overpower the visual material, and vice versa. However, a television message should make optimal use of the visual capabilities available. Copy for a television advertisement is initially written in parallel script form. The video is described in the left column and the audio in the right. When the parallel script is approved, the copywriter and the artist combine the copy with the visual material through use of a **storyboard**, which depicts a series of miniature television screens showing the sequence of major scenes in the advertisement. During the creative thinking phase, storyboards tend to be cartoon sketches. Once an idea is deemed worthy of production, a more polished storyboard is produced. Technical personnel use the storyboard as a blueprint when they produce the advertisement.

**Storyboard**
A series of miniature television screens or cartoons used to show the sequence of major scenes in an advertisement

**Artwork**
The illustration and layout of the advertisement

**Illustrations**
Photographs, drawings, graphs, charts or tables used in advertisement artwork

**Layout**
The physical arrangement of the illustration, headline, sub-headline, body copy and signature of an advertisement

**Artwork** **Artwork** consists of the illustration and layout of the advertisement (see Figure 18.4). Although **illustrations** are often photographs, they can also be drawings, graphs, charts or tables. Illustrations are used to attract attention, to encourage the audience to read or listen to the copy, to communicate an idea quickly or to communicate an idea that is difficult to put into words.[11] They are especially important because consumers tend to recall the visual portion of advertisements better than the verbal portions. Advertisers use a variety of illustration techniques, which are identified and described in Table 18.5.

The **layout** of an advertisement is the physical arrangement of the illustration, headline, sub-headline, body copy and signature. The arrangement of these parts in Figure 18.4 is only one possible layout. These same elements could be arranged in many ways. The final layout is the result of several stages of preparation. As it moves through these stages, the layout helps people involved in developing the advertising campaign exchange ideas. It also provides instructions for production personnel.

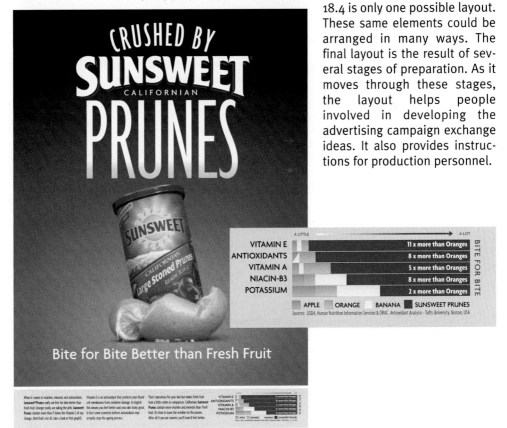

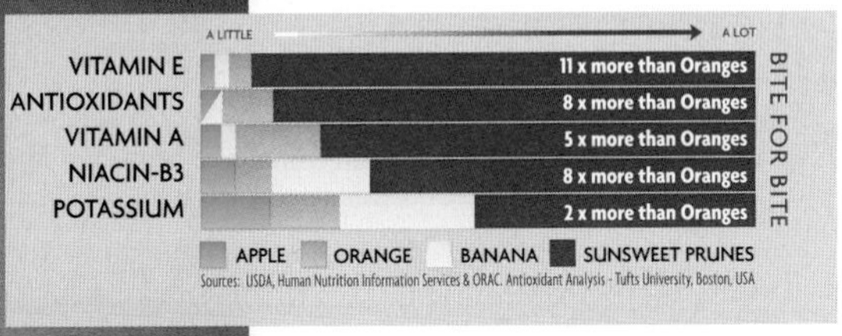


*Figure 18.5*
*While many advertisements are dominated by colourful and emotive images, many business-to-business advertisements contain extensive detail and illustrations of data. In this case, a consumer oriented advertisement includes data to support the healthy eating claims*
*Source: Courtesy of Sunsweet*

**Table 18.5 Illustration Techniques for Advertisements**

| Illustration technique | Description |
|---|---|
| Product alone | Simplest method; advantageous when appearance is important, when identification is important, when trying to keep a brand name or package in the public eye, or when selling through mail order |
| Emphasis on special features | Shows and emphasises special details or features as well as advantages; used when product is unique because of special features |
| Product in setting | Shows what can be done with product; people, surroundings or environment hint at what product can do; often used in food advertisements |
| Product in use | Puts action into the advertisement; can remind readers of benefits gained from using product; must be careful not to make visual cliché; should not include anything that will divert attention from product; used to direct readers' eyes towards product |
| Product being tested | Uses test to dramatise product's uses and benefits versus competing products |
| Results of product's use | Emphasises satisfaction from using product; can liven up dull product; useful when nothing new can be said |
| Dramatising headline | Appeal of illustration dramatises headline; can emphasise appeal but dangerous to use illustrations that do not correlate with headlines |
| Dramatising situation | Presents problem situation or shows situation in which problem has been resolved |
| Comparison | Compares product with 'something' established; the something must be positive and familiar to audience |
| Contrast | Shows difference between two products or two ideas or differences in effects between use and non-use; before and after format is a commonly used contrast technique |
| Diagrams, charts and graphs | Used to communicate complex information quickly; may make presentations more interesting |
| Phantom effects | X-ray or internal view; can see inside product; helpful to explain concealed or internal mechanism |
| Symbolic | Symbols used to represent abstract ideas that are difficult to illustrate; effective if readers understand symbol; must be a positive correlation between symbol and idea |
| Testimonials | Actually shows the testifier; should use famous person or someone to whom audience can relate |

**Sources:** Dorothy Cohen, *Advertising* (New York: Wiley, 1972), pp. 458–64; and S. Watson Dunn and Arnold M. Barban, *Advertising: Its Role in Modern Marketing*, 6th edn (Hinsdale, Ill.: Dryden Press, 1986), pp. 497–8.

## Executing the Campaign

The execution of an advertising campaign requires an extensive amount of planning and coordination. Regardless of whether or not an organisation uses an advertising agency, many people and organisations are involved in the execution of a campaign.[12] Production companies, directors, video and lighting experts, voice-over actors, research organisations, media houses, printers, photo engravers and commercial artists are just a few of the people and organisations that contribute to a campaign.

Implementation requires detailed schedules to ensure that various phases of the work are done on time. Advertising management personnel must evaluate the quality of the work and take corrective action when necessary. In some instances, changes have to be made during the campaign so that it meets campaign objectives more effectively, better satisfies the client managers or responds to consumer research feedback.

## Evaluating the Effectiveness of the Advertising

**Pre-tests**
Evaluations performed before an advertising campaign that attempt to assess the effectiveness of one or more elements of the message

**Consumer focus group**
A semi-structured discussion, led by a moderator, involving actual or potential buyers of advertised products who are asked to judge one or several dimensions of the advertisements

**Post-campaign test** or **post-test**
The evaluation of advertising effectiveness after a campaign

**Recognition test**
A test in which an actual advertisement is shown to individual respondents, who are then asked whether they recognise it

There are various ways to evaluate the effectiveness of advertising. They include measuring achievement of advertising objectives; gauging the effectiveness of copy, illustrations or layouts; and assessing certain media.

Advertising can be evaluated before, during and after the campaign. Evaluations performed before the campaign begins are called **pre-tests** and usually attempt to evaluate the effectiveness of one or more elements of the message. To pre-test advertisements, marketers sometimes use a **consumer focus group**, a semi-structured discussion, led by a moderator, involving actual or potential buyers of the advertised product. Members are asked to judge one or several dimensions of two or more advertisements. Such tests are based on the belief that consumers are more likely than advertising experts to know what will influence them.

To measure advertising effectiveness during a campaign, marketers usually take advantage of 'enquiries'. In the initial stages of a campaign, an advertiser may use several direct-response advertisements simultaneously, each containing a coupon, an 0800 contact number or a form requesting information. The advertiser records the number of coupons or calls that are returned from each type of advertisement. If an advertiser receives 78,528 coupons from advertisement A, 37,072 coupons from advertisement B and 47,932 coupons from advertisement C, then advertisement A is judged superior to advertisements B and C. For advertisements that do not demand action – coupon returning or dialling an 0800 Freefone number – enquiries are difficult to monitor.

Evaluation of advertising effectiveness after the campaign is over is called a **post-campaign test** or **post-test**. Advertising objectives often indicate what kind of post-test will be appropriate. If an advertiser sets objectives in terms of communication – product awareness, brand awareness or attitude change – then the post-test should measure changes in one or more of these dimensions. Typically, qualitative marketing research – focus groups or depth interviews – is used before, during and after a campaign to monitor shifts in consumers' perceptions. It is hoped that brand awareness will have improved following the running of a particular advertising campaign. Advertisers sometimes use consumer surveys or experiments to evaluate a campaign based on communication objectives. These methods are costly, however.

For campaign objectives that are stated in terms of sales, advertisers should determine the change in sales or market share that can be attributed to the campaign. Unfortunately, such changes brought about by advertising cannot be measured precisely[13] – many factors independent of advertisements affect a company's sales and market share. Competitive actions, government actions, and changes in economic conditions, consumer preferences and weather are only a few factors that might enhance or diminish a company's sales or market share. However, by using data about past and current sales and advertising expenditures, an advertiser can make gross estimates of the effects of a campaign on sales or market share.

Because consumer surveys and experiments are expensive, and because it is so difficult to determine the direct effects of advertising on sales, many advertisers evaluate print and television advertisements according to the degree to which consumers can remember them. The post-test methods based on memory include recognition and recall tests. Such tests are usually performed by research organisations through consumer surveys. If a **recognition test** is used, individual respondents are shown the actual advertisement and asked whether they recognise it. If they do, the interviewer asks additional questions to determine how much of the advertisement each respondent read, heard or viewed. When recall is evaluated, the respondents are not shown the actual advertisement but instead

**Unaided** or **spontaneous recall test** A test in which subjects are asked to identify advertisements that they have seen recently but are given no clues to help them remember

**Aided** or **prompted recall test** A test in which subjects are asked to identify advertisements while being shown a list of products, brands, company names or trademarks to jog their memory

are asked about what they have seen or heard recently. Recall can be measured through either unaided or aided recall methods. In an **unaided** or **spontaneous recall test**, subjects are asked to identify advertisements that they have seen recently, but are given no clues to help them remember. A similar procedure is used in an **aided** or **prompted recall test**, except that subjects are shown a list of products, brands, company names or trademarks to jog their memory. Several research organisations, such as ACNielsen, Audience Selection and Gallup, provide research services that test recognition and recall of advertisements (see Table 18.6).

The major justification for using recognition and recall methods is that people are more likely to buy a product if they can remember an advertisement about it than if they cannot. However, recalling an advertisement does not necessarily lead to buying the product or brand advertised. For example, most people can remember the zany campaigns for Tango-branded drinks, yet not everyone buys and consumes them. Research shows that the more 'likeable' an advertisement is, the more it will influence consumers. People who enjoy an advertisement are twice as likely to be persuaded that the advertised brand is best. Yet only a small percentage of those who are neutral about the advertisement feel more favourable towards the brand as a result of the advertisement. The type of television programme in which the product is advertised can also affect consumers' feelings about the advertisement

**TABLE 18.6 RESULTS OF TESTED RECALL OF ADVERTISEMENTS**

**Q: Which of the following TV commercials do you remember seeing recently?**

| | Last Week | Brand | Agency/TV Buyer | % |
|---|---|---|---|---|
| 1 | (2) | Halifax | *Delaney Lund Knox Warren/Vizeum UK* | 77 |
| 2 | (1) | Asda | *Publicis/Carat* | 75 |
| 3= | (10) | National Lottery | *Abbott Mead Vickers BBDO/OMD UK* | 74 |
| 3= | (4=) | McDonald's | *Leo Burnett/OMD UK* | 74 |
| 5 | (4=) | Specsavers | *In-house/Mediaedge:cia* | 73 |
| 6 | (7) | Churchill | *EBP/MediaCom* | 72 |
| 7= | (3) | Tesco | *Lowe/Initiative* | 70 |
| 7= | (4=) | B&Q | *J Walter Thompson/ZenithOptimedia* | 70 |
| 9 | (–) | Walkers | *Abbott Mead Vickers BBDO/OMD UK* | 68 |
| 10 | (–) | Argos | *Euro RSCG London/MindShare* | 66 |
| 11 | (12=) | Currys | *M&C Saatchi/Walker Media* | 65 |
| 12 | (–) | PC World | *M&C Saatchi/Walker Media* | 61 |
| 13= | (–) | Abbey | *TBWA\London/MindShare* | 59 |
| 13= | (–) | DFS | *Phillipson Ward Longworth Camponi/Brilliant Media* | 59 |
| 15= | (–) | 3 | *WCRS/MindShare* | 54 |
| 15= | (–) | Norwich Union | *Abbott Mead Vickers BBDO/Brand Connection* | 54 |
| 17 | (–) | Pot Noodle | *HHCL Red Cell/Initiative* | 51 |
| 18 | (–) | Quaker Oatso Simple | *Abbott Mead Vickers BBDO/OMD UK* | 50 |
| 19= | (–) | Iceland | *HHCL Red Cell/MediaCom* | 49 |
| 19= | (16) | KFC | *Bartle Bogle Hegarty/Walker Media* | 49 |

Adwatch research was conducted from 29–31 October by **NOP World** as part of a weekly telephone omnibus survey among more than 482 adults. Copies of the Adwatch data and analysis are available from Jon Crook at NOP (020 7890 9446). Advertisements were selected by **Xtreme Information** (020 7575 1800) and **Mediaedge:cia UK** (020 7803 2000).

**Source:** Reproduced from *Marketing* magazine with the permission of the copyright owner, Haymarket Business Publications Limited.

and the product it promotes. Viewers judge advertisements placed in happy programmes as more effective and recall them somewhat better.[14]

Researchers are also using a sophisticated technique called 'single source data' to help evaluate advertisements. With this technique, individuals' behaviour is tracked from television sets to the checkout counter. Monitors are placed in pre-selected homes, and microcomputers record when the television set is on and which channel is being viewed. At the supermarket checkout, the individual in the sample household presents an identification card. The cashier records the purchases by scanner, and the data are sent to the research facility. Some volunteer consumers even have bar scanners in their larders or fridges, and web cameras recording their in-home consumption patterns, cross-referenced with their media viewing habits. These techniques are offering more insight into people's buying patterns than ever before. The use of technology is discussed in more detail in Chapter 4.

## Who Develops the Advertising Campaign?

An advertising campaign may be handled by:

1 an individual or a few people within the company
2 an advertising department within the organisation, or
3 an advertising agency.

In very small businesses, one or two individuals are responsible for advertising and many other activities as well. Usually these individuals depend heavily on personnel at local newspapers and broadcasting stations for copywriting, artwork and advice about scheduling media.

In certain types of large business – especially in larger retail organisations – advertising departments create and implement advertising campaigns. Depending on the size of the advertising programme, an advertising department may consist of a few multi-skilled people or a sizeable number of specialists, such as copywriters, artists, media buyers and technical production coordinators. An advertising department sometimes obtains the services of independent research organisations and also hires freelance specialists when they are needed for a particular project.

When an organisation uses an advertising agency, such as Ogilvy & Mather or JWT, the organisation and the agency usually develop the advertising campaign jointly. How much each party participates in the campaign's total development depends on the working relationship between the client marketers and the agency. Ordinarily, a company relies on the agency for copywriting, artwork, technical production and formulation of the media plan.

An advertising agency can assist a business in several ways. An agency, especially a larger one, supplies the client company with the services of highly skilled specialists – not only copywriters, artists and production coordinators but also media experts, researchers and legal advisers. Agency personnel have often had broad experience in advertising and are usually more objective than a client's employees about the organisation's products. Figure 18.6 outlines the structure of a typical advertising agency. Most marketers using an external advertising agency cite agency creativity and media buying skills as the two main reasons for opting to use an agency rather than in-company expertise. When an agency is used it is important to carefully coordinate the activities of the various suppliers providing advertising, public relations, direct mail, sales promotion, web design, sponsorship, and so forth. All output in terms of marketing communications should reflect the desired brand positioning (see Chapter 8) and the marketing strategy. Some marketers opt, therefore, to deal with multiservice agencies that offer all aspects of promotional mix support.

Because an agency traditionally receives most of its income from a percentage commission on media purchases, marketers can obtain some agency services at a low or moderate cost. For example, if an agency contracts for £400,000 of television time for a client, it typically

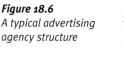

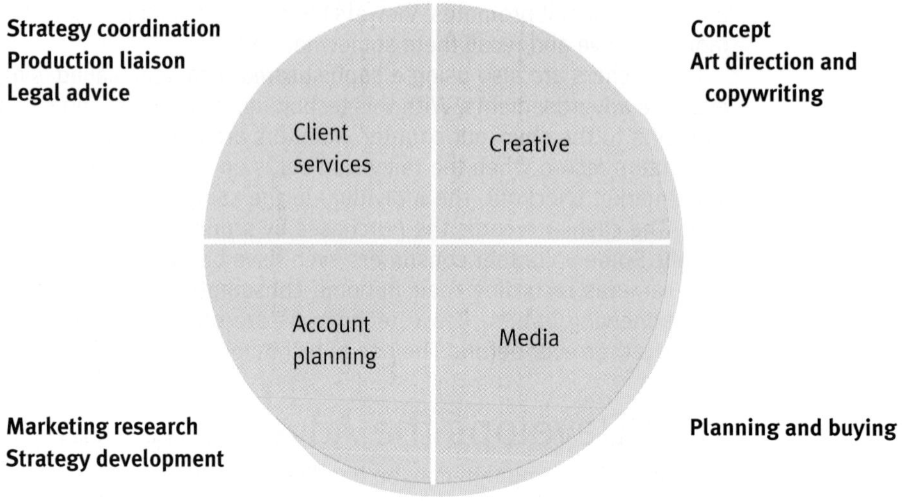


*Figure 18.6*
*A typical advertising agency structure*

receives a commission of £60,000 from the television company. Although the traditional compensation method for agencies is changing and now includes other factors, the media commission still off-sets some costs of using an agency. Some agencies have broken the mould, being paid by results. Clients pay a bonus to the agency for meeting targets or receive a payback (refund) if the advertising fails to deliver.[15] The difficulty arises when striving to agree the performance criteria and methods for assessment.

Now that advertising has been explored as a potential promotional mix ingredient, it is time to consider a related ingredient, publicity, and its controlling mechanism, public relations.

## Publicity and Public Relations

**Publicity**
Communication in news-story form about an organisation and/or its products, which is transmitted through a mass medium at no charge

**Public relations**
A planned and sustained effort to establish and maintain goodwill and mutual understanding between an organisation and its target publics

**Target publics**
An organisation's target audiences: customers, employees, the media, shareholders, trade bodies, suppliers, government officials and society in general

**Publicity** is communication in news-story form about an organisation, its products or both, that is transmitted through a mass medium at no charge – although the publicity activity will incur production and personnel costs. Publicity can be presented through a variety of vehicles, several of which are examined here.

Within an organisation, publicity is sometimes viewed as part of public relations – a larger, more comprehensive communications function. **Public relations** is a planned and sustained effort to establish and maintain goodwill and mutual understanding between an organisation and its **target publics**: customers, employees, the media, shareholders, trade bodies, suppliers, government officials and society in general.[16] Most publicity will be targeted at a single stakeholder type, whereas public relations is ongoing communication across all of an organisation's key stakeholder groups. A key foundation for effective public relations is the identification of the stakeholders or target publics, which are often diverse in nature, requiring different messages and forms of communication.

For example, core publics for Barclays Bank include customers, potential customers, staff and unions, other businesses, suppliers, shareholders, the Treasury, Bank of England and city journalists. For the Boy Scouts' Association, publics include boys (!), the younger Cubs who are destined to become Scouts, the community, business sponsors, adults as potential Scout leaders, adults as parents, adults as former members whose views will influence others, adults as teachers, plus local press journalists.

Publicity is the result of various public relations efforts. For example, when Tesco decided to make a special effort to stock environmentally safe products and packaging, its public relations department sent out press releases to various newspapers, magazines and television contacts, as well as to its suppliers. The result was publicity in the form of magazine articles, newspaper acknowledgements and television coverage. There are three broad categories of public relations (PR):

**PR event**
A public relations event concerned with a specific purpose such as an open day or VIP visit

**PR campaign**
A period of PR activity involving several events and techniques but with definite start and end dates

**PR programme**
An ongoing, lengthy-duration, awareness-building or awareness-maintaining multi-technique PR activity

1. the **PR event** – one-shot, ad hoc affairs concerned with a specific purpose such as an open day or VIP visit
2. the **PR campaign** – a period of PR activity involving several events and techniques, but with definite start and end dates
3. the **PR programme** – ongoing, lengthy-duration, awareness-building or awareness-maintaining multi-technique PR activity.

From the end of the 1980s, public relations has been the fastest growing element in the promotional mix, until the arrival of the Internet and e-marketing.[17]

There is an important distinction between *marketing public relations* and *corporate public relations*. Most large organisations have a corporate affairs function that liaises with investors, institutional analysts and the press, using the toolkit of public relations. Most marketers turn to the same toolkit in order to promote new products or market-leading developments, maintain awareness of their brands or products, and enhance their reputation with their target customers and marketing channel members. The public relations tools may be the same, but the issues and stakeholders differ between marketing public relations and corporate public relations.

## Publicity and Advertising Compared

Although publicity and advertising both depend on mass media, they differ in several respects. Advertising messages tend to be informative or persuasive, whereas publicity is primarily informative. Advertisements are sometimes designed to have an immediate impact on sales; publicity messages are more subdued. Publicity releases do not identify sponsors; advertisements do. The sponsor pays for media time or space for advertising, but not for publicity, and there is therefore no guarantee of inclusion. Communications through publicity are usually included as part of a television programme or a print story, but advertisements are normally separated from the broadcast programmes or editorial portions of print media so that the audience or readers can easily recognise – or ignore – them. Publicity may have greater credibility than advertising among consumers because as a news story it may appear more objective. Finally, an organisation can use advertising to repeat the same messages as many times as desired; publicity is generally not subject to repetition.

## Kinds of Publicity

**Press (news) release**
A publicity mechanism, usually consisting of a single page of typewritten copy

**Feature article**
A manuscript longer than a press release (up to 3000 words) that is usually prepared for a specific publication

**Captioned photograph**
A photograph with a brief description explaining its content

There are several types of publicity mechanism.[18] The most common is the **press (news) release**, which is usually a single page of typewritten copy containing up to about 300 words. A press release, sometimes called a news release, also gives the company's or agency's name, its address and phone number, and details of the contact person.[19] Car makers often use press releases to introduce new products. Figure 18.7 is an example of a press release. A **feature article** is a longer manuscript (up to 3000 words) that is usually prepared for a specific publication. A **captioned photograph** is a photograph with a brief description explaining the picture's content. Captioned photographs are especially effective for illustrating a new or improved product with highly visible features.

There are several other kinds of publicity. A **press conference** is a meeting called to announce a major news event. Media personnel are invited and are usually supplied with written materials and photographs. In addition, letters to the editor and editorials are sometimes prepared and sent to newspapers and magazines. However, newspaper editors frequently allocate space on their editorial pages to local writers and national columnists. Finally, films and tapes may be distributed to broadcasting companies in the hope that they will be aired. The broader remit of public relations also includes training personnel to meet and handle the media (journalists); arranging interviews; establishing links with VIPs and influential bodies; managing visits, seminars and meetings; and maintaining information

***Figure 18.7***
*An example of a press release, in this case for a student revision aid*

**Date as postmark**

WARWICK BUSINESS SCHOOL

**High Demand Leads to 2nd Edition** NEWS...NEWS...NEWS

In 2001, an innovative book concept was published: a revision guide that included thumbnail overviews of key concepts alongside 'how to pass' examination question tips for undergraduate, MBA and CIM exams.

This text has proved so successful that already a new edition has appeared, endorsed by the Chartered Institute of Marketing. "*Marketing Briefs: A Revision and Study Guide*" provides topical and insightful overviews of key strategic marketing concepts, supported by detailed illustrations and highly topical applied examples. In addition, there is guidance on revision and exam technique, plus recommended further readings.

Everything from buying behaviour, CRM, value-based marketing, one-to-one marketing, target marketing, portfolio analysis, marketing shareholder value analysis, competitive advantage and brand value.

"*Marketing Briefs: A Revision and Study Guide*" is authored by two of the UK's leading marketing academics, who also author many other leading texts: Sally Dibb and Lyndon Simkin of Warwick Business School.

The book is right up to date in terms of concepts, but also brings the best practice learning tools so popular in Sally and Lyndon's other market leading texts. In addition to students panicking about their exams, the book has been very popular amongst senior managers desiring a quick-learning guide to the latest strategic management tools.

ENDS

**Further information:**
Tel: Lyndon Simkin, 024 7652 2168, email lyndon.simkin@wbs.ac.uk
"*Marketing Briefs: A Revision and Study Guide*", Sally Dibb & Lyndon Simkin, Oxford: Elsevier Butterworth-Heinemann, 2nd edition July 2004, pp. 363, ISBN: 0-7506-6200-X.

Warwick Business School:
Founded in 1967, Warwick Business School is one of the most successful and highly regarded business schools in Europe. It has a turnover of £24.6 million. The current student population of 1,070 undergraduates, 170 research students and 2,824 taught masters, MPA and MBA students, come from 108 countries worldwide.

+44 (0)24 7652 4306
+44 (0)24 7652 3719
enquiries@wbs.ac.uk
www.wbs.ac.uk

THE UNIVERSITY OF WARWICK

Warwick Business School
The University of Warwick
Coventry CV4 7AL
United Kingdom

**Press conference**
A meeting called to announce a major news event

**Third-party endorsement**
A recommendation from an opinion leader or respected personality used to increase the credibility of publicity and public relations

flows within the organisation. Increasingly, PR consultants utilise the Internet to liaise with stakeholders, and they often help clients to set up their websites.

A marketer's choice of specific types of publicity depends on considerations that include the type of information being transmitted, the characteristics of the target audience, the receptivity of media personnel, the importance of the item to the public, and the amount of information that needs to be presented. Sometimes a marketer uses a single type of publicity in a promotional mix. In other cases, a marketer may use a variety of publicity mechanisms, with publicity being the primary ingredient in the promotional mix. **Third-party endorsement** – for example, from a trade body, VIP or media personality – increases the credibility of publicity and public relations. This is a recommendation – written, verbal or visual – from an opinion leader or respected personality.

## Uses of Publicity

Publicity has a number of uses. It can make people aware of a company's products, brands or activities; help a company maintain a certain level of positive public visibility; and enhance a particular image, such as innovativeness or progressiveness. Companies also try to overcome negative images through publicity. Some businesses seek publicity for a single purpose and others for several purposes. As Table 18.7 shows, publicity releases can tackle a multitude of specific issues. It must be remembered that an organisation has a number of audiences – customers, suppliers, distributors, shareholders, journalists – as well as its internal market: its employees and management. Publicity needs to target all of these publics.

**Table 18.7 Possible Topics for Publicity Releases**

**Marketing developments**
- New products
- New uses for old products
- Research developments
- Changes of marketing personnel
- Large orders received
- Successful bids
- Awards of contracts
- Special events

**Company policies**
- New guarantees
- Changes in credit terms
- Changes in distribution policies
- Changes in service policies
- Changes in prices

**News of general interest**
- Annual election of directors
- Meetings of the board of directors
- Anniversaries of the organisation
- Anniversaries of an invention
- Anniversaries of the senior directors
- Holidays that can be tied to the organisation's activities
- Annual banquets
- Conferences and special meetings
- Open house to the community
- Athletic events
- Awards of merit to employees
- Laying of cornerstone
- Opening of an exhibition

**Reports on current developments**
- Reports on experiments
- Reports on industry conditions
- Company progress reports
- Employment, production and sales statistics
- Reports on new discoveries
- Tax reports
- Speeches by principals
- Analyses of economic conditions
- Employment gains
- Financial statements
- Organisation appointments
- Opening of new markets
- Government trade awards

**Personalities – names are news**
- Visits by famous people
- Accomplishments of individuals
- Winners of company contests
- Employees' and directors' advancements
- Interviews with company officials
- Company employees serving as judges for contests
- Interviews with employees

**Slogans, symbols, endorsements**
- Company's slogan – its history and development
- A tie-in of company activities with a slogan
- Creation of a slogan
- The company's trademark
- The company's name plate
- Product endorsements

**Source:** Albert Wesley Frey, ed., *Marketing Handbook*, Second Edition (New York: Ronald Press, 1965), pp. 19–35. 

## The Requirements of a Publicity Programme

For maximum benefit, a business should create and maintain a systematic, continuous publicity programme.[20] If this is achieved, there is likely to be a sustained public relations process in place. A single individual or department – within the organisation or from its advertising agency or public relations consultancy – should be responsible for managing the programme. Relationships must be maintained with the media, particularly to facilitate crisis-management public relations. Effective public relations is impossible without well-developed ongoing contacts with newspaper, television and radio journalists. It is important to establish and maintain good working relationships with these media personnel. Often, personal contact with editors, reporters and other news personnel is essential; without their input a company may find it hard to design its publicity programme so as to facilitate the work of news people. Media personnel reject a great deal of publicity material because it is poorly written or not newsworthy. To maintain an effective publicity programme, a company must strive to avoid these flaws. Guidelines and checklists can aid in this task. Material submitted must match the particular newspaper's style – for example, in terms of length, punctuation and layout. Marketers who hire the services of a PR consultancy do so to 'buy' the consultancy's media contacts and its expertise in maintaining an ongoing flow of activity that appeals to journalists.

Finally, an organisation has to evaluate its publicity efforts.[21] Usually, the effectiveness of publicity is measured by the number of press releases actually published or broadcast. To monitor print media and determine which releases are published and how often, an organisation can hire a cuttings service – a business that cuts out, counts and sends published news releases to client companies. To measure the effectiveness of television publicity, a company can enclose a card with its publicity releases and request that the television company record its name and the dates when the news item is broadcast, but companies do not always comply. Though some television and radio tracking services do exist, they are costly.

The assessment of the effectiveness of an organisation's publicity or public relations is of growing importance (see Chapter 24). Many leading exponents of public relations believe there must be four facets to an effective PR programme:

1 *research* – into the problem opportunity
2 *action* – which includes assessment and planning
3 *communication* – of key messages to the relevant publics
4 *evaluation* – of the effects of these messages.

A public relations consultancy can be very helpful in achieving these four requirements.

## Dealing with Unfavourable Publicity

Up to this point, publicity has been discussed as a planned ingredient of the promotional mix. However, companies may have to deal with unfavourable publicity regarding an unsafe product, an accident, the actions of a dishonest employee or some other negative event. For example, when British Airways' Lord King had to apologise publicly to rival airline Virgin Atlantic and its boss, Richard Branson, for a 'dirty tricks campaign', BA's credibility was severely damaged and seat reservation numbers were reported to have declined significantly.[22] The BSE beef crisis and the uproar over GM foods forced government departments, farming bodies, meat producers, supermarket companies and consumer associations to deal with unfavourable publicity.

Such unfavourable publicity can arise quickly and dramatically. A single negative event that produces unfavourable publicity can wipe out a company's favourable image and destroy consumer attitudes that took years to build through promotional efforts. Moreover, the mass media today can disseminate information faster and to larger audiences than ever before, and bad news generally receives a great deal of attention in the media. Thus the negative publicity surrounding an unfavourable event now reaches more people. By dealing effectively with a negative situation, an organisation can minimise the damage from unfavourable publicity.

To protect an organisation's image, it is important to avoid unfavourable publicity or at least to lessen its effects. First and foremost, the organisation can directly reduce negative incidents and events through safety programmes, inspections and effective quality control procedures. However, because organisations obviously cannot eliminate all negative occurrences, they need to establish policies and procedures for the news coverage of such events. These policies and procedures should aim at reducing negative impact.

In most cases, organisations should expedite news coverage of negative events rather than try to discourage or block it. The expediting approach not only tends to diminish the fall-out from negative events but also fosters a positive relationship with media personnel. Such a relationship is essential if news personnel are to cooperate with a company and broadcast favourable news stories about it and its affairs. Facts are likely to be reported accurately, but if news coverage is discouraged, rumours and misinformation may be perpetuated. An unfavourable event can easily be blown up into a scandal or a tragedy. It can even cause public panic.

**Crisis management**
A process in which a company responds to negative events by identifying key targets (publics) for which to provide publicity, developing a well-rehearsed contingency plan, reporting facts quickly and providing access for journalists

**Crisis management** involves:

1 the identification of key target publics for which to provide material or publicity
2 the need for a well-rehearsed contingency plan and public relations exercise
3 the ability and skills of the organisation to report quickly and accurately details of the crisis itself
4 the provision of immediate access by journalists to information and personnel.

Above all, the organisation must remain in control of the situation and the material being published or broadcast. See the Case Study on page 575 for a textbook example of crisis management.

## The Limitations of Using Publicity

Free media publicity is a double-edged sword: the financial advantage comes with several drawbacks. If company messages are to be published or broadcast, media personnel must judge them newsworthy. Consequently, messages must be timely, interesting and accurate. Many communications simply do not qualify. It may take time and effort to convince media personnel of the news value of publicity releases. Even a top public relations consultancy achieves a hit rate of only one out of every four press releases being published in the press.

Although marketers usually encourage media personnel to air a press release at a certain time, they control neither the content nor the timing of the communication. Media personnel alter the length and content of publicity releases to fit publishers' or broadcasters' requirements, and may even delete the parts of the message that the business's marketers deem most important. Furthermore, media personnel use publicity releases in time slots or positions that are most convenient for them; thus the messages often appear at times or in locations that may not reach the business's target audiences. These limitations can be frustrating. Nevertheless, properly managed publicity offers an organisation substantial benefits at a relatively low cost. The commissioning of a professional public relations consultancy may come at a price, but the benefits are generally very clear as stakeholders' perceptions are managed. Compared with advertising, the costs of PR are usually trivial.

## Trends that Affect Advertising and Public Relations

The world of advertising is facing significant changes. Briefly, these include a mixture of market trends and client-induced pressures. The Innovation and Change box on page 568 describes a new media choice for advertisers of fast-moving consumer goods. For example, a growing number of agencies are having to offer pan-European capabilities as major advertisers believe they must consider pan-European campaigns. The major international agencies already have widespread office networks, but for the smaller agencies there is a need to establish links with small agencies in other countries. With the concentration of media ownership across borders, agencies and clients have to be able to negotiate package deals across countries.[23] Rupert Murdoch's media empire, which covers newspapers, magazines, radio,

## Innovation and Change

### Tesco TV

Brands turn to television advertising in order to spread their appeal to the maximum number of people within their target market segments. Recently, supermarket leader Tesco has examined the role of television in a novel context: 300 of the larger Tesco stores have received 'Tesco TV', broadcasting in-store news and product information, recipe ideas, lifestyle messages and sales bulletins. In addition to Tesco-specific advertising and publicity, innovatively Tesco TV carries tailored content and advertising from third parties.

JCDecaux – known for its poster and bus shelter sites – was asked by Tesco to sell airtime on its in-store TV channel. JCDecaux already had the contract to sell the space on Tesco's 200 six-sheet billboard sites. The outdoor media specialist is approaching leading consumer brands and their agencies, pitching the attractive nature of Tesco's customer profile and the large numbers of shoppers in-store each week.

Many media experts were wary, but Tesco had piloted the scheme in its flagship Kensington store, a Tesco Metro store in Canary Wharf, its largest UK store in Warrington, two stores in the Cambridge area and one in Surrey. Leading research agency Millward Brown found that 75 per cent of shoppers thought the service was good, but that the siting of certain screens added to the confusion and 'clutter' of store entrances.

The media experts are far from in agreement about the value of linking promotional messages to consumer decision-making at the point of purchase, or about the merits of attempting to influence purchasing in-store with advertising immediately prior to the customer's decision-making.

Tesco points out that most UK consumers see about 290 television advertisements each week and, on average, there is a 13-hour time-lag between an advertisement being viewed at home and the consumer standing in the supermarket prepared to make purchases. The Tesco proposition to prospective advertisers on its in-store TV channel is simple: if an advertiser's brand or promotional message is viewed in-store at the point of any indecision between competing brands, the Tesco TV airtime may just tip the balance at the time of purchasing. While Sainsbury's and Spar have also trialled in-store TV broadcasting, it remains to be seen how effective advertisers find Tesco TV.

**Sources:** Tesco Stores, 2004; Creg Turzynski, 'Critics' scorn won't stop Tesco's in-store television from delivering', *Marketing Week*, 18 March 2004, p. 18; Amanda Wilkinson, 'Tesco to launch TV in 300 stores', *Marketing Week*, 19 February 2004, p. 13.

and satellite and terrestrial television all the way from the Pacific Rim through North America and across Europe, is a prime illustration.

There is increasing pressure on advertising agencies and public relations consultancies to justify the value of their activities and campaigns. Simple qualitative research into the visual appeal of a particular campaign is not seen as sufficient by major advertisers. These clients have short-term sales gains as a motivation for advertising; many advertising personnel, however, believe that the role of advertising is also critical for longer-term **brand building**, as a brand's image and standing are developed with intended long-term benefits for brand awareness and brand value.[24]

**Brand building**
Developing a brand's image and standing with a view to creating long-term benefits for brand awareness and brand value

Senior advertising agency figures are also aware that the recessions of the 1990s caused many clients to downgrade their advertising budgets and to re-evaluate their promotional spend. The result has been the rationalisation of agencies, leading to mergers, even closures, and an urgency among agencies to seek a competitive edge over their rivals. There are now also far fewer medium-sized advertising agencies, the field having polarised into major international advertising agencies and numerous local or regional small agencies.[25] This trend has also affected public relations. There is now an increasing tendency for clients and agencies to develop closer and longer-term relationships, as tight budgets require a close, mutual understanding of what advertising and PR must achieve for a particular brand or product.

The sphere of public relations is also undergoing significant change. Clients are demanding pan-European and international services. Through the development of technology – such as the Internet and interactive television – plus new advertising formats – such as the growing use of mini-documentary style, lengthy 'advertorials' and infomercials – there is a move to more overt competition between public relations consultancies and advertising agencies. Advertising agencies perceive these developments to be part of their toolkit, whereas public relations consultancies have begun to include these innovations in their armoury. In addition, the public relations industry believes it is maturing and accordingly needs to become more professional, recruiting higher-calibre personnel and providing better training, while ensuring that their output is assessed in terms of client goals and expectations.[26] These enhancements require time and high budgets in an ever more competitive market. With all these changes, there is little doubt that both the marketing environment and client requirements are significantly affecting the nature of the services offered by advertising agencies and public relations consultancies.

This chapter concludes with an overview of sponsorship in marketing – an element of the promotional mix that is increasingly apparent to many consumers and a promotional tool now used by many organisations.

**Sponsorship**
The financial or material support of an event, activity, person, organisation or product by an unrelated organisation or donor

# Sponsorship

**Sponsorship** is the financial or material support of an event, activity, person, organisation or product by an unrelated organisation or donor. Generally, funds will be made available to the recipient of the sponsorship deal in return for the prominent exposure of the sponsor's name or brands.[27]

## The Increasing Popularity of Sponsorship

A decade or so ago sponsorship in the arts became an established form of funding for individual performances, tours, whole seasons or exhibitions; indeed some theatrical companies and galleries came to depend on it.[28] Many orchestras, ballet, opera or theatre companies, museums and art galleries would not have survived in the face of declining government subsidies for the arts had it not been for corporate sponsorship. Sports were soon to follow, as numerous football teams found that gate receipts and pitch advertising revenues were no longer adequate to cover wage bills and operating costs. While the larger clubs earn seven-figure revenues from shirt sponsorship by companies such as Sony, JVC and Heineken, deals for as little as £20,000 are not uncommon in the lower leagues; either way, this form of financial support is becoming essential to guarantee the survival of many clubs.

The popularity of corporate sponsorship has grown dramatically: few leading sports or arts events are without corporate sponsorship, as detailed in Table 18.8.[29] Sponsors believe there are two key benefits to the company and its products. First and foremost, media coverage is unbridled. Volvo estimates that its £2 million investment in tennis sponsorship is worth the equivalent of £15 million spent on advertising. Its banners are displayed at tournaments, as are examples of its model range. Volvo advertisements and publicity appear in the event programmes. The Volvo brand appears in advertising for the event, and usually the company's cars transport the celebrity players during the tournaments. Not only does the public see the company's advertisements, they cannot fail to see its brand name displayed extensively. In addition, the product is on hand for demonstration, while television coverage of the events takes the Volvo name into every tennis fan's home; radio and press coverage features Volvo's name prominently.

Few spectators at the Olympics or the World Cup football championships can fail to notice the identities of the leading sponsors. To many sports enthusiasts, the leading competitions become generically known as the Gillette Cup, NatWest Trophy, Prudential Series or Coca-Cola Cup. In equestrian events, the horses' names often include the name of the sponsoring company. Visitors to the Royal Shakespeare Company's performances are clearly informed of the support given by leading sponsors. Opera singer Montserrat Caballe's performance at Birmingham's prestigious Symphony Hall was made possible largely by sponsorship from the

**TABLE 18.8 UK EXPENDITURE ON SPONSORSHIP**

**Sports sponsorship: total expenditure**

| | 1996 | 1997 | 1998 | 1999 | 2000 | 2001 | 2002 |
|---|---|---|---|---|---|---|---|
| Market size, £m | 302 | 322 | 353 | 377 | 401 | 421 | 442 |
| No. of sponsorships | 977 | 995 | 969 | 1,172 | 859 | 698 | 656 |

**Corporate sponsorship of sport (Number of involvements)**

| | 2002 | | 2002 |
|---|---|---|---|
| Finance – insurance | 122 | Drinks – soft/water | 33 |
| Hotel/travel/leisure/restaurant | 49 | Professional services | 11 |
| Sports goods | 67 | Drinks – spirit/wine | 11 |
| Automotive | 55 | Dot.com | 7 |
| Electronics/computers/IT | 34 | Utilities | 11 |
| Drinks – beer | 45 | Jewellery/watches/luxury | 7 |
| Others | 29 | Health/pharmaceuticals | 6 |
| Media | 27 | Petrochemicals | 5 |
| Telecommunications | 32 | Public sector | 3 |
| Food/beverages | 32 | Tobacco | 3 |
| Manufacturing/construction | 20 | Agriculture | 2 |
| Retail | 24 | Cosmetics/toiletries | 1 |
| Household and consumer | 19 | Children's toys/games | 1 |

**Sources:** Ipsos-RSL Sponsorship, Sport and Leisure; *The Marketing Pocket Book*, published by the World Advertising Research Center, Henley-on-Thames, 2004.

Forward Trust Group, a fact made clear in all promotional material – leaflets, advertising and publicity – and in the concert's programme.

The second benefit of corporate sponsorship is internal. Many organisations believe that their sponsorship of events helps improve the morale of their workforce. On one level, high-profile, brand-building sponsorship, such as AXA Insurance's involvement with cricket, reassures the workforce and reaffirms the company's leading position in its marketplace. On a more human level, sponsorship for altruistic projects, such as worthy community causes, helps give employees a 'warm', positive feeling towards their employer. The way in which McDonald's supports Ronald McDonald Houses close to children's hospitals and its sponsorship of local school events not only helps the community but also makes its employees feel more positive towards the company.

However, sponsorship is not confined to the promotion and exposure of corporate brands. Cadbury's may be sponsors of ITV's soap drama *Coronation Street*, but each week the programme breaks feature individual Cadbury's confectionery brands. While boards of directors may like to sponsor major sporting events or the arts, increasingly many marketing managers are looking for suitable activities to sponsor for individual brands.

## Applications for Sponsorship

Sponsorship used to be a tool of public relations and the domain of public relations consultancies. Increasingly, it is a specialist area and a separate component of the promotional mix. Public relations consultancies still handle many sponsorship deals, but a growing number of specialist sponsorship advisers now introduce sponsors to appropriate recipients. It should not be thought that sponsorship is prominent only in the sports and arts worlds. It is an activity of growing importance in many fields. Universities and colleges seek sponsorship for students, technical equipment, buildings and even degree programmes. Hospitals receive and welcome the sponsorship of buildings, operating theatres and fundraising events. Engineering and scientific research, particularly in universities and 'research clubs', benefit from the sponsorship of research and development, often from organisations in completely unrelated fields of business.

No matter what the area, if a company believes its brand reputation will be enhanced and its brand awareness improved by its involvement with an organisation or event, sponsorship becomes an important element in its promotional mix. Sponsorship can be for events or competitions, equipment or buildings, ideas or research, learning or development, animals or people, commercial or charitable causes, television programmes, products or services, single activities or ongoing programmes.

## Reputable Partnerships

**Reputable partnerships** Reputable and ethical dealings between a recognised, welcome and acceptable recipient organisation and a sponsoring organisation

There are 'ground rules' to be considered by the prospective sponsor. As with any promotional activity, the sponsor must ensure that the recipient organisation, event or product is recognised by the sponsor's own target audience, that it is welcome and acceptable to its target audience, and that it is reputable and ethical in its dealings.The sponsor does not want to invest its promotional budget in activities not recognised by its own target market. **Reputable partnerships** are essential. The sponsor cannot risk becoming involved with an event or organisation that has a 'dodgy' reputation and unprofessional management; such a situation threatens the sponsor's reputation and brands. Consider the effect on a prestigious brand if an athlete sponsored by that brand failed a dope test or was found guilty of cheating. The recipient, too, needs to be wary of the donor's image and reputation.

Even with careful selection of events or sports stars to sponsor, the sponsor cannot be guaranteed value for money. During the Euro 2004 football tournament in Portugal, Pepsi's millions sponsored England's David Beckham, Italy's Francesco Totti and Spanish strikers Raul and Torres. Beckham missed two penalties as England exited at the quarter-final stage, Totti's infamous spitting incident led to him making only one tournament appearance, and the two Spanish stars failed to score a goal, with none of the players' teams achieving glory. Whether or not Pepsi felt this particular sponsorship represented value for money was not reported.

# Summary

*Advertising* is a paid-for form of non-personal communication that is transmitted to consumers through mass media, such as television, radio, newspapers, magazines, direct mail, public transport vehicles, outdoor displays, ambient advertising and now the Internet. Both non-business and business organisations use advertising. Advertising has many uses: to create awareness of products, organisations and causes; to stimulate primary and selective demand; to off-set competitors' advertising; to aid sales personnel; to educate the market; to increase uses of a product; to remind and reinforce; to reduce sales fluctuations.

» Marketers use advertising in many ways. *Institutional advertising* promotes organisational images and ideas, as well as political issues. When a company promotes its position on a public issue, institutional advertising is referred to as a*dvocacy advertising*. *Product advertising* focuses on the uses, features, images and benefits of goods and services. To make people aware of a new or innovative product's existence, uses and benefits, marketers rely on *pioneer advertising* in the introductory stage to stimulate primary demand for a general product category – often referred to as creating category need. Then they switch to *competitive advertising* to boost selective demand by promoting a particular brand's uses, features and advantages that may not be available in competing brands. *Comparative advertising* is a form of competitive advertising in which two or more brands are compared on the basis of one or more product attributes.

» Through *defensive advertising*, a company can sometimes lessen the impact of a competitor's promotional programme. A company can also make its own salesforce more effective through advertising designed to support personal selling. A business modifying its marketing mix uses advertising to educate the market regarding the changes. To increase market penetration, an advertiser sometimes focuses a campaign on promoting a greater number of uses for the product. *Reminder advertising* for an established product enables consumers to know that the product is still around and that it has certain characteristics, benefits and uses. Marketers may use *reinforcement advertising* to assure current users of a particular brand that they have selected the best brand. Marketers also use advertising to smooth out fluctuations in sales.

» Although marketers may vary in how they develop *advertising campaigns*, these should follow a general pattern. First, they must identify and analyse the *advertising target* or audience. Second, they should establish what they want the campaign to accomplish by defining the advertising objectives. The third step is creating the *advertising platform*, which contains the basic issues to be presented in the campaign. Fourth, advertisers must decide on the *advertising budget* – that is, how much money will be spent on the campaign; they arrive at this decision through the *objective and task approach*, the *percentage of sales approach*, the *competition matching approach* or the *arbitrary approach*. Fifth, they must develop the *media plan* by selecting and scheduling the media to be used in the campaign, taking into account the desired *reach* and *frequency* as well as *cost comparison indicators*. In the sixth step, advertisers use *copy*, *artwork* and *illustrations* to create the message, with the aid of *storyboards* and careful *layouts*, bearing in mind *AIDA*, the persuasive sequence of attention, interest, desire and action. *Regional issues* of magazines and newspapers allow messages to be tailored to geographic areas. In the seventh step, marketers execute their advertising campaign, after extensive planning and coordination. Finally, advertisers must devise one or more methods for evaluating the effectiveness of the advertisements, including *pre-tests*, the use of *consumer focus groups*, direct-response coupons or 0800 contact numbers, *post-campaign tests*, *recognition tests*, and *unaided (or spontaneous) recall tests or aided (or prompted) recall tests*. The single source data technique uses technology to track buying behaviour and evaluate advertisements.

» Advertising campaigns can be developed by personnel within the organisation or in conjunction with advertising agencies. When a campaign is created by the organisation's personnel, it may be developed by only a few people, or it may be the product of an advertising department within the organisation. The use of an advertising agency may be advantageous to a client company because an agency can provide highly skilled, objective specialists with broad experience in the advertising field at low to moderate costs to the client company.

» *Publicity* is communication in news-story form about an organisation, its products or both, transmitted through a mass medium at no charge. Generally, publicity is part of the larger, more comprehensive communications function of *public relations*. There are three broad categories of public relations: the *PR event*, the *PR campaign* and the *PR programme*. Publicity is mainly informative and usually more subdued than advertising. There are many types of publicity, including *press (news) releases*, *feature articles*, *captioned photographs*, *press conferences*, editorials, films and tapes. In addition, public relations encompasses training managers to handle journalists and publicity, establishing links with influential bodies and VIPs, managing visits and seminars, and providing information to employees. PR consultants utilise the Internet and help clients to set up websites. *Third-party endorsement*, in which a VIP, trade body or celebrity publicly endorses a product or a brand, is particularly effective. *Target publics* include consumers, suppliers, distributors, journalists, trade bodies, government officials and shareholders, as well as employees and managers inside the business, and society in general. Effective public relations depends on the thorough identification of target publics. To have an effective publicity programme, someone – either in the organisation or in the business's agency – must be responsible for creating and maintaining systematic and continuous publicity efforts. There is an important distinction between corporate PR and marketing PR. While the toolkit is similar, corporate PR focuses on corporate affairs, while marketing PR addresses product and brand issues. Effective PR programmes require research, action and communication of key messages to relevant publics, as well as evaluation.

An organisation should avoid negative publicity by reducing the number of negative events that result in unfavourable publicity, or at least lessen their effect. To diminish the impact of unfavourable publicity, an organisation should institute policies and procedures for implementing *crisis management* – identifying key targets, developing a contingency plan and providing access for journalists – when negative events do occur. Problems that organisations confront when seeking publicity include the reluctance of media personnel to print or broadcast releases and a lack of control over the timing and content of messages.

There are significant client-induced pressures and market trends affecting advertising agencies and public relations consultancies. These include client demands for international and pan-European service, concentration of media ownership, accountability over the effectiveness of the promotional activity, short-term goals versus longer-term *brand building*, reduced client budgets, rationalisation in terms of the number and size of agencies, the growing use of technology such as the Internet, conflict between advertising agencies and public relations consultancies over advertorials and infomercials, and the need to offer an increasingly professional service.

*Sponsorship* is the financial or material support of an event, activity, person, organisation or product by an unrelated organisation or donor in return for the prominent exposure of the sponsor's name and brands. An additional benefit can be to raise the morale of employees within the donor organisation. Once the domain of arts and sports, sponsorship applications are broadening. Universities, colleges, hospitals, and engineering and scientific research institutes also seek sponsorship. There are many corporate sponsors of events or facilities, but increasingly marketing managers are seeking relevant recipients and sponsorship partners for their individual brands. Sponsorship recipients and donors must be certain of each other's ethics, image and reputation. *Reputable partnerships* are essential.

## Key Links

The material in this chapter focuses on just some of the ingredients of the promotional mix, and should be read in conjunction with:

- Chapter 17's overview of the communications process and the requisites for effective marketing communications, including integrated marketing communications (IMC)
- Chapter 19's examination of personal selling and sales management, sales promotion, direct mail and the Internet – the remaining ingredients of the promotional mix
- Chapter 4's insights into the growing use of technology in marketing, particularly in communicating with customers and as a marketing channel
- Chapter 12's discussion of effective branding, which requires associated marketing communications.

## Important Terms

Advertising
Institutional advertising
Advocacy advertising
Product advertising
Pioneer advertising
Competitive advertising
Comparative advertising
Defensive advertising
Reminder advertising
Reinforcement advertising
Advertising campaign
Advertising target

Advertising platform
Advertising budget
Objective and task approach
Percentage of sales approach
Competition matching approach
Arbitrary approach
Media plan
Reach
Frequency
Cost comparison indicator
Regional issues
Copy
AIDA
Storyboard
Artwork
Illustrations
Layout
Pre-tests
Consumer focus group
Post-campaign test or post-test
Recognition test
Unaided or spontaneous recall test
Aided or prompted recall test
Publicity
Public relations
Target publics
PR event
PR campaign
PR programme
Press (news) release
Feature article
Captioned photograph
Press conference
Third-party endorsement
Crisis management
Brand building
Sponsorship
Reputable partnerships

## Discussion and Review Questions

1 What is the difference between institutional and product advertising?
2 When should advertising be used to stimulate primary demand? When should advertising be used to stimulate selective demand?
3 What are the major steps in creating an advertising campaign?
4 What is an advertising target? How does a marketer analyse the target audience after it has been identified?
5 Why is it necessary to define advertising objectives?
6 What is an advertising platform, and how is it used?
7 What factors affect the size of an advertising budget? What techniques are used to determine this budget?
8 Describe the steps required in developing a media plan.
9 What is the role of copy in an advertising message?
10 What role does an advertising agency play in developing an advertising campaign?
11 Discuss several ways to post-test the effectiveness of an advertisement.
12 What is publicity? How does it differ from advertising?
13 How do organisations use publicity? Give several examples of press releases that you have observed recently in local media.
14 What are target publics? Why must they be carefully identified and handled by a public relations department?
15 How should an organisation handle negative publicity? Identify a recent example of a company that received negative publicity. Did the company deal with it effectively?
16 Define public relations.
17 Explain the problems and limitations associated with using public relations. How can some of these limitations be minimised?
18 How can sponsorship enhance brand awareness for a sponsoring organisation?
19 What factors must an organisation consider before selecting a sponsor or recipient organisation?

## Recommended Readings


- Belch, G. and Belch, M., *Advertising and Promotion: an Integrated Marketing Communications Perspective* (New York: McGraw-Hill, 2003).
- Kolah, A., *Improving the Performance of Sponsorship* (Oxford: Butterworth-Heinemann, 2003).
- Moss, D. and Desanto, B., *Public Relations Case* (London: Routledge, 2001).
- Percy, L., Rossiter, J. and Elliott, R., *Strategic Advertising Management* (Oxford: Oxford University Press, 2001).
- Shimp, T.A., *Advertising, Promotion and Supplemental Aspects of Integrated Marketing Communications* (Cincinnati, OH: South Western, 2002).
- Theaker, A., *The Public Relations Handbook* (London: Routledge, 2001).

## Internet Exercise

Log on to Pepsi.com at www.pepsi.com or Nike.com at www.nike.com.
Both sites offer a selection of advertisements to view. In addition, the website pages strive to advertise the merits of these brands and the specific attributes of these products.

1 What is the advertising platform being adopted by these two brands (Pepsi and Nike)?
2 To what extent are these advertising platforms relevant to the respective target audiences?
3 In developing the advertising for Pepsi or Nike, which stage of the campaign development process will be most important? Why?

## *Applied Mini-Case*

Many well-known brands vie to sign to be leading sponsors of major sporting events such as the Olympics, European Football Championships, FIFA's World Cup or the Wimbledon Lawn Tennis Championships. While the major tournaments attract leading beer and soft drinks brands, or manufacturers of sports goods, other tournaments such as the Cricket World Cup, Rugby World Cup or Darts World Cup attract a more varied mix of sponsors.

### *Question*

**As a marketing manager tasked with identifying sponsorship opportunities for your company and its key brands, what would be the selection criteria used and why?**

## *Case Study*

### 'Textbook PR': Public Relations and the Perrier Crisis

On 10 February 1990, in North Carolina, USA, bottles of Perrier were found to be contaminated with benzene. For the best-selling brand of mineral water in the world this meant a huge crisis. 'Once a critical situation arises the most vital task is to do everything you can to reduce damage to the absolute minimum. We were fortunate that we had agreed procedures in advance and these procedures were followed absolutely,' stated Perrier spokesperson Wenche Marshall Foster. 'From the very beginning we were determined to keep everyone fully informed'.

Perrier's crisis team in the UK moved quickly; senior executives of Perrier, its PR agency at the time, Infoplan, and its then advertising agency Leo Burnett had been briefed before the contamination scare on the needs of crisis management. Within hours of the contamination announcement, Perrier had set up tests with independent consultant Hydrotechnica so as to have accurate information to give out. The crisis team knew it had to be truthful throughout. Infoplan immediately set up a telephone information service, which dealt with 1700 calls each day from distributors, retailers and consumers. Within three days of the crisis breaking, shelves worldwide had been cleared and all stocks returned to Perrier. The company achieved goodwill by moving so decisively. No press conferences were given. Instead, the five members of the crisis team individually met journalists for in-depth, head-to-head interviews to give precise and clear information and to minimise poor publicity.

Perrier risked competitors moving to take advantage of the crisis, since retailers would not leave shelves empty. Perrier, though, was the clear brand leader with the only established image worldwide. Competitors would take time to develop such strength, and their stocks were not high. Evian and others had nothing to gain from drawing further attention to Perrier's crisis, which was damaging the industry as a whole.

Perrier's PR handled the crisis in textbook fashion. With at the time 85 per cent of the American and 60 per cent of the UK market, it had a great deal to lose. The company informed its publics of its difficulties, tackled the contamination problems and relaunched the product with new packaging and bottle sizes – clearly to be seen as new stock – with a 'Welcome Back' promotional campaign. Within months, Perrier's market share was climbing back and shelf space had been regained. The company did not hide anything, it identified the various audiences to brief and it tackled its production to ensure that there were no repeat problems. Consumers, distributors, public health bodies and the media were made to feel part of Perrier's solution through the effective use of PR.

Perrier handled its crisis very efficiently, but never fully regained its domination of the bottled mineral water market – the fastest-expanding sector of the beverages market in the 1990s. Perrier's success had been noted by major beverage suppliers; the removal of its bottles from shelves and the contamination scare gave rivals the opportunity to move in. Despite repackaging, fresh designs and a new advertising agency – Publicis – Perrier struggled to rekindle its former glory days and was acquired by the mighty Swiss company, Nestlé. Today, supermarket shelves have a multitude of rival mineral water brands, many mixed with exotic fruit flavours or energy-enhancing ingredients. Nevertheless, Perrier still has very high brand awareness, market-leading share and a loyal customer base.

**Sources:** John Tylee, 'Publicis extends "eau" theme for Perrier blitz', *Campaign*, 19 May 1995, p. 7; Greg Prince, 'In hot water', *Beverage World*, March 1995, pp. 90–5; 'Perrier aims to recapture lost young drinkers', *Marketing*, 24 March 1994, p. 1; *Marketing Week*, 2 March 1990; *Personally Speaking*, 27 March 1990; *Fortune*, 23 April 1990; 'Nestlé's "world of water"', www.nestle.com, 2004.

## Questions for Discussion

1 How important is it to have an ongoing commitment to public relations in the event of a crisis?
2 Could Perrier's competitors have taken more advantage of the crisis?
3 Did the same publicity message go out to all of Perrier's publics or target audiences? Why?

# 19 Sales Management, Sales Promotion, Direct Mail, the Internet and Direct Marketing

"**If we are what we do, then we all of us, are sales people.**"

*Antonis Simintiras, The Open University*

## Objectives

- To understand the nature and major purposes of personal selling
- To learn the basic steps in the personal selling process
- To identify the types of salesforce personnel
- To gain insight into sales management decisions and activities
- To become aware of what sales promotion activities are and how they can be used
- To become familiar with specific sales promotion methods
- To understand the role of direct mail in the promotional mix
- To be aware of the growing importance of the Internet in marketing communications
- To appreciate direct marketing's use of the promotional mix

## Introduction

As indicated in Chapter 17, personal selling, sales promotion, direct mail, the Internet and direct marketing are possible ingredients in the promotional mix – along with advertising, public relations and sponsorship, which were explored in the previous chapter.

Personal selling is a very widely used ingredient of the promotional mix. Sometimes it is a company's sole promotional tool, although it is generally used in conjunction with other promotional mix ingredients. Personal selling is becoming more professional and sophisticated, with sales personnel acting more as consultants and advisers. Most organisations that have a salesforce have separate sales management staff, who are responsible for recruiting, training, allocating, motivating, rewarding and monitoring the salesforce; rarely are sales staff the direct responsibility of marketers. However, these sales personnel have to prioritise the customers identified by marketers in the target market strategy; they must communicate the agreed brand positioning and leverage any competitive advantage identified by the organisation's marketers. Sales staff also learn about customer issues and market developments, so they must be linked with marketers in a company. It is essential that the activities of the salesforce do not conflict with the marketing strategy. That is why, although it is usually a different functional area from marketing within the organisation, personal selling is still deemed to be part of the promotional mix.

Sales promotion, direct mail and the Internet are also playing an increasingly important role in marketing strategies.[1] Direct marketing, a term frequently cited by marketers these days, is also a growing tool. Although, as discussed in Chapter 16, partly an aspect of marketing channel selection – in this case opting not to utilise some of the services of channel intermediaries – there are implications for marketers' promotional strategies, as discussed in this chapter.

*Opener*

# Sampling Nappies: Huggies Competes with Pampers

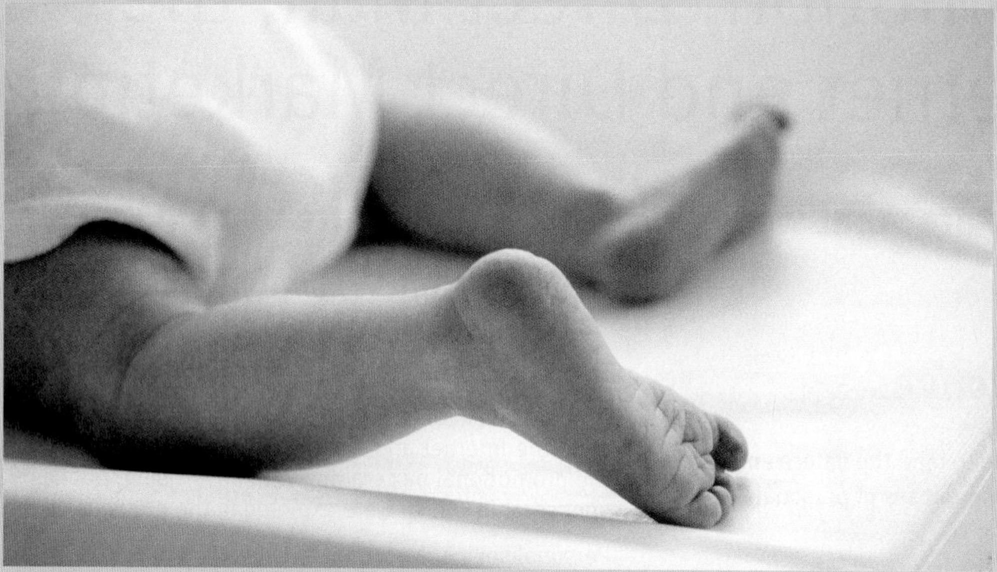

Many markets – such as fast food, colas and car rental – appear to be dominated by just a few major brands. The same is true for nappies. As soon as one brand innovates with a drier, more comfortable, easier to change or more disposable nappy, its rivals will quickly follow suit. Marketing research reveals that many parents do not switch brands, despite the enticing claims made by competing brands in television advertisements. The importance of persuading customers to actually trial a new nappy product, therefore, is particularly important.

Most new mums receive a Bounty Bag either from hospital or via a health worker. These bags contain information leaflets and trial products for nappy cream, baby wipes, nappies, baby foods and much more. Generally, only one brand of each product is included, and the major manufacturers vie to be included.

Product sampling is not confined to the Bounty Bag. Huggies recently offered parents free samples of its nappies via television advertisements. A Freefone number promised a pack of four Huggies free of charge. Kimberly-Clark, the manufacturer behind Huggies, offered parents the opportunity to trial its Super-Flex line by offering a free pack and money-off voucher to consumers who called the hotline or logged on to the huggiesforfree website. The brand's 'Look mum, no leaks' advertising strapline was amended to 'Look mum, free' in the accompanying television campaign, created by Ogilvy & Mather. In-store point-of-sale materials adopted the strapline 'Have you tried it yet?'. This was an integrated marketing communications campaign.

Rival Pampers, produced by Procter & Gamble, was included in the hospital Bounty Bags, so the television-led sampling drive was Huggies' attempt to compete in the all-important new-parent product sampling battle between the two leading brands. The £3 million advertising, radio and on-line campaign was deemed worthwhile by Huggies' marketers as more than the anticipated number of parents called the hotline for their free samples. For Huggies, this was deemed to be effective use of sales promotion as it attempted to build on a 42 per cent market share against Pampers' 48 per cent.

**Sources:** Bounty Bags; Boots; Birmingham Women's Hospital; Warwick Hospital; Kimberly-Clark; Samuel Solley, 'Huggies embarks on sampling campaign', *Marketing*, 3 June 2004, p. 9.
Photo © Royalty-Free/ CORBIS

This chapter examines the purposes of personal selling, its basic steps, the types of sales people involved in personal selling and how they are selected. It also discusses the major sales management decisions and activities, which include setting objectives for the salesforce and determining its size; recruiting, selecting, training, compensating and motivating sales people; managing sales territories; and controlling sales personnel. The discussion then goes on to explore several characteristics of sales promotion, the reasons for using sales promotion and the sales promotion methods available for use in a promotional mix, as adopted by Kimberly-Clark for its Huggies brand of nappies. Use and types of direct mail are then examined. The chapter concludes with a brief look at the role of the Internet, also examined in Chapter 4, in marketing and the growing use of direct marketing.

## The Nature of Personal Selling and Sales Management

**Personal selling**
The process of using personal communication in an exchange situation to inform customers and persuade them to purchase products

**Personal selling** is the process of informing customers and persuading them to purchase products through personal communication in an exchange situation. For example, a sales person describing the benefits of a Braun shaver to a customer in a Boots store is using personal selling. Most business-to-business transactions depend heavily on the role of personal selling, as described in Chapter 22. Personal selling gives marketers the greatest freedom to adjust a message to satisfy customers' information needs. In comparison with all other promotional methods, personal selling is the most precise, enabling marketers to focus on the most promising sales prospects. Other promotional mix ingredients are aimed at groups of people, some of whom may not be prospective customers. A major disadvantage of personal selling is its cost. Generally, it is the most expensive ingredient in the promotional mix, owing to the associated costs of salaries, cars and expenses. Personal selling costs are increasing faster than advertising costs.

Businesses spend more money on personal selling than on any other promotional mix ingredient. Millions of people earn their living through personal selling. In the UK it is estimated that 600,000 people are directly employed as sales people.[2] A selling career can offer high income, a great deal of freedom, a high level of training and a high level of job satisfaction.[3] Unfortunately, consumers often view personal selling negatively. A study of marketing students' perceptions of personal selling showed that approximately 25 per cent of the survey group associated it directly with door-to-door selling. In addition, 59 per cent of all students surveyed had a negative impression of personal selling. In the UK, the Office for Fair Trading is currently leading a drive to limit the use of door-to-door selling – a form of personal selling – because of the high numbers of complaints by householders feeling overly pressured or intimidated. Major businesses, professional sales associations and academic institutions are making an effort to change the negative stereotypes associated with sales people.[4] Ethical standards of selling practice are a major part of this enhancement, prompted by EU regulations, government and consumer groups.

Personal selling goals vary from one company to another. However, they usually involve finding prospects, persuading prospects to buy and keeping customers satisfied. Identifying potential buyers who are interested in an organisation's products is critical. Because most potential buyers seek information before they make a purchase, sales people must ascertain prospects' information needs and then provide the relevant information. To do so, sales personnel must be well trained, both in regard to their products and in regard to the selling process in general.[5]

Sales people need to be aware of their competitors. They need to monitor new products being developed, and they should be aware of all competitors' sales activities in their sales territories. They must emphasise the advantages that their products provide when their competitors' products do not offer the same advantages.[6] Sales personnel are a useful source of marketing intelligence, a fact often ignored by their marketing colleagues.

Few businesses survive solely on profits from one-sale customers. For long-run survival, most marketers depend on repeat sales. This notion is at the core of relationship marketing, as described in Chapters 1 and 24. A company has to keep its customers satisfied to obtain repeat purchases. Besides, satisfied customers help attract new ones by telling potential customers about the organisation and its products. Even though the whole organisation is responsible for providing customer satisfaction, much of the burden falls on sales people. The sales person is almost always closer to customers than anyone else in the company and often provides buyers with information and service after the sale. Such contact not only gives sales people an opportunity to generate additional sales but also offers them a good vantage point from which to evaluate the strengths and weaknesses of the company's products and other marketing mix ingredients. Their observations, if sought, are helpful in developing and maintaining a marketing mix that better satisfies both customers and the business.

A sales person may be involved in achieving one or more of the three general goals. In some organisations:

1. there are people whose sole job is to find prospects
2. this information is relayed to sales people, who then contact the prospects
3. after the sale, these same sales people may do the follow-up work, or a third group of employees may have the job of maintaining customer satisfaction.

In many smaller organisations, a single person handles all of these functions: prospect list generation, prospect calling and ongoing relationship nurturing. No matter how many personnel are involved, several major sales tasks must be performed to achieve these general goals.

The literature assisting sales management is extensive and tends to focus on the sales management process:

- the importance of preparation – understanding the products and prospective customers, predicting sales and developing systems for recording sales-related data
- the techniques for introducing the sales personnel to prospective customers, either face-to-face or via telecommunications
- the requisites for effective presentations – or pitches – and written sales proposals
- the skills required to turn a potential customer's interest into commitment
- how to negotiate
- the skills necessary to capture the order
- the ability to close the sale (win the order).

Sales personnel not only address prospective customers, they are often involved in managing ongoing client relationships, and in ensuring repeat orders are won and handled competently. There are strong links with customer relationship management (CRM) techniques, as described in Chapter 4. Personal selling involves direct customer–sales person contact, but in addition to face-to-face interaction, personal selling now often benefits from improved telecommunications and telesales. Unlike other forms of promotional activity, personal selling can customise messages for individual customer prospects and build ongoing relationships with existing customers. The per capita cost, however, is high. The Building Customer Relationships box on page 581 explains the importance of the salesforce to IBM's improved brand standing.

## Building Customer Relationships

### IBM's Salesforce Expertise in Market Sectors

Since its launch in 1914, International Business Machines (IBM) has transformed the public's perception of a sales person from shady character to knowledgeable professional. IBM sales personnel understood their customers' needs and worked with them to show how computers and IT solutions could solve their business problems. On the strength of its technology and its salesforce, IBM became an international computer powerhouse. During the 1980s, however, it began selling hardware rather than solutions, and its prominence began to fade. When GTE, one of IBM's top customers, wanted to switch from a mainframe system to a less expensive network of personal computers, IBM representatives tried to dissuade the company from changing. GTE switched not only systems but also suppliers, opting for Hewlett-Packard. After suffering a number of such staggering losses, IBM re-engineered its 35,000-strong salesforce to better meet its customers' needs.

What IBM recognised is that having talented and hard-working sales people is not enough to maintain a differential advantage. To help its sales staff win and keep customers, the company reorganised its field force by industry instead of by geography. In what industry experts call IBM's biggest restructuring in decades, the company established 14 industry areas – banking, retail, travel, insurance, and others. Instead of selling a huge and confusing array of IBM products to all customers within a geographic area, sales people specialise in specific industries, developing expertise in the businesses they serve. They know their customers better and are more familiar with the specific products that satisfy their needs. According to the company's CEO, re-engineering has transformed IBM sales personnel from order takers into business advisers.

The changes paid off. IBM's workstation sales grew by 47 per cent in one year, taking business away from market leader Sun Microsystems, Inc. Customers reported that the IBM people calling on them were more attuned to their business drivers and associated IT requirements. The world's largest IT company had been facing difficulties: by focusing on client issues and developing specialist knowledge of clients' business sectors, IBM's salesforce helped turn around the company's fortunes. Computer systems, data systems, storage and micro-electronics have been made even more customer-relevant owing to the expertise of IBM's salesforce. This upturn in the company's fortunes has resulted in IBM being named the third most valuable global brand, after Coca-Cola and Microsoft.

**Sources:** based on information from Laurie Hays, 'IBM chief unveils top-level shake-up, consolidating sales arm, software line', *Wall Street Journal*, 10 January 1995, p. B6; Craig Stedman, 'Users laud IBM reorganization – for now', *Computerworld*, 30 January 1995, p. 57; 'Reengineering: is there a doctor in the house?', *Sales & Marketing Management*. April 1995, p. S17; Chuck Paustian, 'Icons Michael Jordan, IBM journey the comeback trail', *Business Marketing*, April 1995, p. 8; James Kaczman, 'Just fix it, your sales process, that is', *Sales & Marketing Management*, September 1995, pp. 39–44; Ira Sager, 'The few, the true, the blue', *Business Week*, 30 May 1994, pp. 124–6; Interbrand, 2003; www.ibm.com, July 2004.

# Elements of the Personal Selling Process

The exact activities involved in the selling process vary from one sales person to another and differ for particular selling situations. No two sales people use exactly the same selling methods. None the less, many sales people – either consciously or unconsciously – move through a general selling process as they sell products. This process consists of seven elements, or steps, as depicted in Figure 19.1:

1 prospecting and evaluating opportunities
2 preparing to contact prospects or existing customers
3 approaching the prospect or existing customer
4 making the presentation or 'sales pitch'
5 overcoming objections and reassuring the prospect or customer
6 closing the deal or transaction
7 following up to ensure customer satisfaction and enable repeat business.

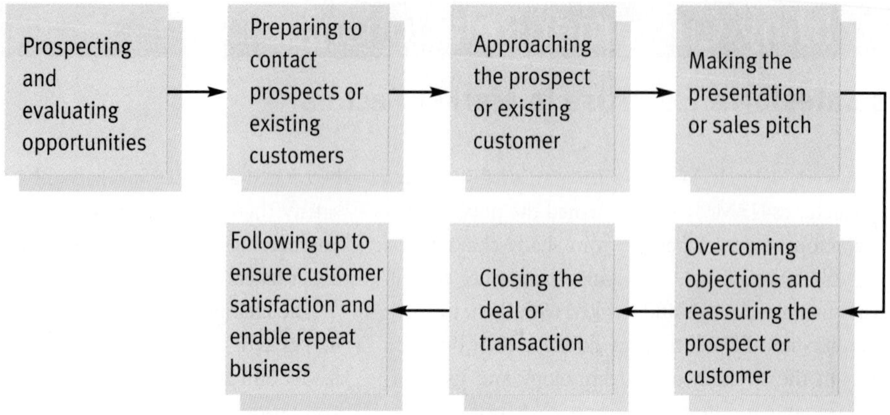


***Figure 19.1***
*Elements of personal selling*

## Prospecting and Evaluating Opportunities

**Prospecting**
Developing a list of potential customers

Developing a list of potential customers is called **prospecting**. A sales person seeks the names of prospects from the company's sales records, referrals, trade shows, press announcements (of marriages, births, deaths, and so on, or new contracts or product developments in business markets), public records, telephone directories, trade association directories, telemarketing lists,[7] on-line searches and many other sources. Sales personnel also use responses from advertisements that encourage interested people to send in an information request form. Trade shows, seminars and meetings may produce good leads. Seminars may be targeted at particular types of client, such as solicitors, accountants, the over-55s or specific business people.

Sales people sometimes prefer to use referrals – recommendations from customers – to find prospects. Obtaining referrals requires that the sales person has a good relationship with the current customer and so must have performed well before asking the customer for help. Research shows that one referral is as valuable as 12 cold calls. Also, 80 per cent of clients are willing to give referrals, but only 20 per cent are ever asked. Sales experts indicate that the advantages of using referrals are that the resulting sales leads are highly qualified, the sales rates are higher, initial transactions are larger and the sales cycle shorter.[8]

After developing the prospect list, a sales person evaluates whether each prospect is able, willing and authorised to buy the product. Certain prospects may have a better fit with the company's operating ethos, geographical coverage and product specification than others. On the basis of this evaluation, some prospects may be deleted, while others are deemed acceptable, and ranked according to their desirability or potential.

## Preparing to Contact Prospects or Existing Customers

Before contacting acceptable prospects, a sales person should find and analyse information about each prospect's specific product needs, current use of brands, feelings about available brands, and personal characteristics. The most successful sales people are thorough in their preparation. They prepare by identifying key decision-makers, reviewing account histories and reports, contacting other clients for information, assessing credit histories and problems, preparing sales presentations, identifying product needs and obtaining all relevant literature.[9] Being well informed about a prospect makes a sales person better equipped to develop a presentation that communicates precisely with the prospect.

For example, Xerox developed an automated sales process to help sales personnel prepare for complex sales situations after discovering that its sales people spent half their time on sales-inhibiting activities, such as looking for forms and gathering information. Preparing an order required between 5 and 13 forms, and a third of all orders were rejected because of mistakes on the forms. To overcome the problem, Xerox developed computer workstations to assist its salesforce in shaping proposals, prospecting and preparing, and to link sales people throughout the company without a piece of paper having to be touched.[10] Fujitsu markets a mobile office solution that enables sales personnel on the road or even delivery drivers to be fully automated and directly hooked up wirelessly to their head office IT systems.

## Approaching the Prospect or Existing Customer

**Approach**
The manner in which a sales person contacts a potential customer

The **approach** – the manner in which a sales person contacts a potential customer – is a critical step in the sales process. In more than 80 per cent of initial sales calls, the purpose is to gather information about the buyer's needs and objectives. Creating a favourable impression and building rapport with the prospective client are also important tasks in the approach, because the prospect's first impression of the sales person is usually a lasting one, with long-run consequences. During the initial visit, the sales person strives to develop a relationship rather than just push a product. The sales person may have to call on a prospect several times before the product is considered.[11]

One type of approach is based on referrals. The sales person approaches the prospect and explains that an acquaintance, an associate or a relative suggested the call. The sales person who uses the cold-canvass method calls on potential customers without their prior consent. Repeat contact is another common approach; when making the contact, the sales person mentions a prior meeting. The exact type of approach depends on the sales person's preferences, the product being sold, the business's resources and the characteristics of the prospect.

## Making the Presentation or Sales Pitch

During the sales presentation, the sales person must attract and hold the prospect's attention in order to stimulate interest and stir up a desire for the product. The sales person should have the prospect touch, hold or actually use the product. If possible, the sales person should demonstrate the product and get the prospect more involved with it to stimulate greater interest. Audio-visual materials may be used to enhance the presentation.

During the presentation, the sales person must not only talk but listen. The sales presentation gives the sales person the greatest opportunity to determine the prospect's specific needs by listening to questions and comments, and observing responses. Even though the sales person has planned the presentation in advance, she or he must be able to adjust the message to meet the prospect's information needs.

## Overcoming Objections and Reassuring the Prospect or Customer

An effective sales person usually seeks out a prospect's objections in order to address them. If they are not apparent, the sales person cannot deal with them, and they may keep the prospect from buying. One of the best ways to overcome a prospect's objections is to anticipate and counter them before the prospect has an opportunity to raise them. However, this approach can be risky because the sales person may mention some objections that the prospect would not have raised. If possible, the sales person should handle objections when they arise. They can also be dealt with at the end of the presentation.

## Closing the Deal or Transaction

**Closing**
The step in the selling process in which the sales person asks the prospect to buy the product or products

**Closing** is the step in the selling process in which the sales person asks the prospect to buy the product or products. During the presentation, the sales person may use a 'trial close' by asking questions that assume the prospect will buy the product. For example, the sales person might ask the potential customer about financial terms, desired colours or sizes, delivery arrangements or the quantity to be purchased. The reactions to such questions usually indicate how close the prospect is to buying. A trial close allows prospects to indicate indirectly that they will buy the product without having to say those sometimes difficult words, 'I'll take it.'

A sales person should try to close at several points during the presentation, because the prospect may be ready to buy. One closing strategy involves asking the potential customer to take a trial order. The sales representative should either guarantee a refund if the customer is not satisfied or make the order a free offer. Often an attempt to close the sale will result in objections. Thus closing can be an important stimulus that uncovers hidden objections, which can then be addressed.

### Following up to Ensure Customer Satisfaction and Enable Repeat Business

After a successful closing, the sales person must follow up the sale. In the follow-up stage, the sales person should determine whether the order was delivered on time and installed properly, if installation was required. He or she should contact the customer to learn what problems or questions, if any, have arisen regarding the product. The follow-up stage can also be used to determine customers' future product needs. This step provides both information and ideas that may prove helpful in selling to other likely customers, and the opportunity to cement relationships with existing customers. Many companies have specialist departments responsible for this post-sale customer service and care.

## Types of Sales People

To develop a salesforce, a company must decide which types of sales people will best sell and represent the business's products. Most companies deploy several types of sales people. Based on the functions they perform, sales people are generally classified as order getters, order takers or support personnel. Sometimes the same sales person performs all three sets of tasks. When recruiting sales personnel, marketers seldom focus on only one type of sales person: most businesses require a mix of selling skills. A product's uses, characteristics, competitive position, complexity, customer profile, selected marketing channel(s), promotional mix, price and margin influence the kinds and numbers of sales personnel recruited.

### Order Getters

**Order getters** Employees who increase a company's sales by selling to new customers and by increasing sales to existing customers

**Order getters** are tasked to increase a company's sales by selling to new customers and by increasing sales to existing customers. This entails a process of recognising buyers' needs, informing prospects and persuading them to try, then buy the product. This is often termed 'creative selling'.

There are two types of order getter: those dealing with current customer sales and those chasing new business sales.

1 *Current customer order getters* call on people who have already purchased a business's products. They seek to sell more to existing customers and to gain sales leads from these customers to contact other customers.
2 *New business order getters* are crucial for a company's longer-term survival as all businesses require additional, new customers. These sales people locate prospects and convert them into buyers.

**Order takers** Employees who ensure that repeat customers have sufficient quantities of products when and where they are needed in order to maintain and perpetuate ongoing relationships

The timeshare industry uses various promotional techniques – direct mail, competitions, road shows, free trial offers – to attract potential buyers to attend seminars or open days at the timeshare site. Once on site, it is up to the new business order getters to explain the concept of timesharing, demonstrate the facilities and close the deal. Without the involvement of sales personnel, it is unlikely that prospects would sign up for a timeshare. BMW's approved used car Internet service attracts potential buyers, but the deals are closed by sales people at the dealerships.

### Order Takers

Taking orders is a repetitive task that sales staff perform to maintain and perpetuate ongoing relationships with customers. **Order takers** seek repeat sales. A major task is to ensure that repeat customers have sufficient quantities of products when and where they are needed. This is particularly important in many business-to-business markets in which manufacturers depend on components for production of their own products. Most order takers handle repeat orders for standardised products that are purchased routinely, minimising the selling effort.[12] IT systems increasingly link suppliers with customers, enabling the relationship to be handled remotely and automatically.

There are two types of order taker: inside order takers and field order takers.

1 *Inside order takers* are located in a business's call centre or offices, and receive orders by post, fax, e-mail or telephone. They do occasionally deal face to face with customers – for example, sales assistants inside retail stores are classified as inside order takers.
2 *Field order takers* – the field force – are sales people who travel to customers. Customers often depend on these regular calls to maintain required inventories and keep abreast of any product modifications, while these field-based order takers rely on such ongoing relationships and customer loyalty to achieve their sales targets.

Neither inside nor field order takers should be thought of as entirely passive functionaries who simply record orders. In many businesses, order takers generate the bulk of sales.

## Support Personnel

**Support personnel** Employees who facilitate the selling function but do more than solely participate in selling

**Missionary sales people** Support sales people, usually employed by manufacturers to assist their customers' selling efforts

**Trade sales people** Employees who take orders as well as help trade customers promote, display and stock their products

**Technical sales people** Employees who give technical assistance to current customers

**Support personnel** facilitate the selling function but often do more than just participate in the selling process. Particularly common in industrial or business markets, support personnel locate prospects, educate customers, build goodwill and provide after-sales service. There are three main categories of support personnel:

**Missionary Sales People** **Missionary sales people** are employed by manufacturers to assist their customers' selling efforts. For example, pharmaceutical and medical product manufacturers sell to wholesalers but employ missionary sales personnel to visit retailers to promote retailers' orders being placed with wholesalers.

**Trade Sales People** **Trade sales people** undertake order taking as well as help trade customers promote, display and stock their products. The major manufacturers of alcoholic beverages deploy trade sales people to ensure prominent shelf displays of their products in off-licences and supermarkets. They restock shelves, obtain more shelf space, set up displays, provide in-store demonstrations, distribute samples and arrange joint promotions.

**Technical Sales People** **Technical sales people** give technical assistance to current customers. They advise customers on product characteristics, applications, system designs and installation, as well as health and safety issues. Agrochemicals, chemicals and heavy plant are technically advanced products requiring technical sales people to support order getters and marketers. In markets with standardised products and little product differentiation, marketers may offer superior technical support and customer service as a means of developing a differential advantage over competitors.

# Management of the Salesforce

The salesforce is directly responsible for generating a business's primary input: sales revenue. Without adequate sales revenue, a business cannot survive for long. A company's reputation is often determined by the ethical conduct of its salesforce. On the other hand, the morale and, ultimately, the success of a company's salesforce are determined in large part by adequate compensation, room for advancement, sufficient training and management support – all key areas of sales management. When these elements are not satisfactory, sales staff may leave for more satisfying jobs elsewhere. It is important to evaluate the input of sales people because effective salesforce management helps to determine a company's success.

This section explores nine general areas of sales management:

1 establishing salesforce objectives
2 determining salesforce size
3 recruiting and selecting sales personnel
4 training sales personnel

5 compensating sales personnel
6 motivating sales people
7 managing sales territories
8 controlling and evaluating salesforce performance
9 internal marketing.

## Establishing Salesforce Objectives

To manage a salesforce effectively, a sales manager must develop sales objectives. Sales objectives tell sales people what they are expected to accomplish during a specified time period. These objectives give the salesforce direction and purpose, and serve as performance standards for the evaluation and control of sales personnel. In Figure 19.2, Budweiser uses advertising to produce leads and thereby help sales people meet their sales goals. As with all types of objective, sales objectives should be stated in precise, measurable terms, and should specify the time period, customer type and geographic areas involved.

*Figure 19.2*
*Budweiser has a large sales force, highly incentivised to increase sales and gain market share Photo © Tony Arruza/ CORBIS*

Sales objectives are usually developed for both the total salesforce and each sales person. Objectives for the entire force are normally stated in terms of sales volume, market share or profit. Volume objectives refer to a quantity of money or sales units. For example, the objective for an electric drill manufacturer's salesforce might be to sell £6 million worth of drills annually or 600,000 drills annually. When sales goals are stated in terms of market share, they usually call for an increase in the proportion of the company's sales relative to the total number of products sold by all businesses in that particular industry. When sales objectives are based on profit, they are generally stated in terms of monetary amounts or in terms of return on investment. Sales objectives, or quotas, for an individual sales person are commonly stated in terms of monetary or unit sales volume. Other bases used for individual sales objectives include average order size, average number of calls per time period and the ratio of orders to calls.

## Determining Salesforce Size

Deciding how many sales people to use is important because the size of the salesforce influences the company's ability to generate sales and profits. Moreover, salesforce size affects the compensation methods used, sales people's morale and overall salesforce management. Salesforce size must be adjusted from time to time because a company's marketing plans change, as do markets and forces in the marketing environment. It is dangerous, however, to cut back the size of the salesforce to increase profits by cutting costs. The sales organisation could then lose its strength and resilience, preventing it from rebounding when growth returns or better market conditions prevail. The organisation that loses capacity through cutbacks may not have the energy to accelerate.[13] There are several analytical methods for determining the optimal size of the salesforce. Although marketing managers may use one of these methods, they normally temper their decisions with a good deal of subjective judgement.[14]

## Recruiting and Selecting Sales Personnel

**Recruiting**
A process by which the sales manager develops a list of applicants for sales positions

To create and maintain an effective salesforce, a sales manager must recruit the right type of sales people. **Recruiting** is a process by which the sales manager develops a list of applicants for sales positions. The cost of hiring, training and retaining a sales person is soaring; currently, costs in the UK can reach £60,000 or more.[15]

To ensure that the recruiting process results in a pool of qualified sales people from which to choose, a sales manager should establish a set of required qualifications before beginning to recruit. Although for years marketers have attempted to identify a set of traits that characterise effective sales people, there is currently no such set of generally accepted characteristics. Therefore, a sales manager must develop a set tailored to the sales tasks in a particular company. Two activities can help establish this set of requirements. The sales manager should prepare a job description that lists the specific tasks sales people are to perform. The manager should also analyse the characteristics of the company's successful sales people, as well as those of its ineffective sales personnel. From the job description and the analysis of traits, the sales manager should be able to develop a set of specific requirements and be aware of potential weaknesses that could lead to failure.

A sales manager generally recruits applicants from several sources: departments within the business, other companies, employment agencies, educational institutions, respondents to advertisements and individuals recommended by current employees. The specific sources a sales manager uses depend on the type of sales person required and the manager's experiences with particular sources.

The process of hiring a salesforce varies tremendously from one company to another. One technique used to determine whether potential candidates will be good sales people is an assessment centre. Assessment centres are intense training environments that place candidates in realistic problem settings in which they must assign priorities to their activities, make decisions and act on their decisions. Candidates are judged by experienced managers or trained observers. Assessment centres have proved to be valuable in helping to select good sales people.[16]

Sales management should design a selection procedure that satisfies the company's specific needs. The process should include enough steps to yield the information needed to make accurate selection decisions. However, because each step incurs a certain expense, there should be no more steps than necessary. The stages of the selection process should be sequenced so that the more expensive steps, such as physical examination, are near the end. Fewer people will then move through the higher-cost stages.

Recruitment should not be sporadic; it should be a continuous activity aimed at reaching the best applicants. The selection process should systematically and effectively match applicants' characteristics and needs with the requirements of specific selling tasks. Finally, the selection process should ensure that new sales personnel are available where and when they are needed. Recruitment and selection of sales people are not one-off decisions. The market and marketing environment change, as do an organisation's objectives, resources and marketing strategies. Maintaining the proper mix of sales people thus requires the continued attention of the company's sales management.

## Training Sales Personnel

Many businesses have formal training programmes; others depend on informal, on-the-job training. Some systematic training programmes are quite extensive; others are rather short and rudimentary. Regardless of whether the training programme is complex or simple, its developers must consider who should be trained, what should be taught and how the training should occur.

A sales training programme can concentrate on the company, on products or on selling methods. Training programmes often cover all three areas. For experienced company sales staff, training usually emphasises product information, although it also describes new selling techniques and any changes in company plans, policies and procedures.

Training programmes can be aimed at newly recruited sales people, experienced sales staff or both. Ordinarily, new sales personnel require comprehensive training, whereas experienced personnel need both refresher courses about established products and training in new product information. Training programmes can be directed at the entire salesforce or at one segment.

Sales training may be done in the field, at educational institutions, in company facilities or in several of these locations. Some businesses train new employees before assigning them to a specific sales position. Other businesses, however, put them into the field immediately and provide formal training only after they have gained a little experience. Training programmes for new personnel can be as short as several days or as long as three years. Sales training for experienced personnel is often scheduled during a period when sales activities are not too demanding. Because training experienced sales people is usually an ongoing effort, a company's sales management must determine the frequency, sequencing and duration of these activities.

Sales managers, as well as other sales people, often engage in sales training – whether daily, on the job, or periodically in sales meetings. Sales people sometimes receive training from technical specialists within their own organisations. In addition, a number of individuals and organisations sell special sales training programmes. Appropriate materials for sales training programmes range from films, texts, manuals and cases to programmed learning devices, audio and video cassettes and CDs. As for teaching methods, lectures, demonstrations, simulation exercises and on-the-job training can all be effective. The choice of methods and materials for a particular sales training programme depends on the type and number of trainees, the programme's content and complexity, its length and location, the size of the training budget, the number of teachers and the teachers' preferences.

## Compensating Sales Personnel

To develop and maintain a highly productive salesforce, a business must formulate and administer a compensation or remuneration plan that attracts, motivates and retains the most effective individuals. The plan should give sales management the desired level of control and provide sales personnel with an acceptable level of freedom, income and incentive. It should also be flexible, equitable, easy to administer and easy to understand. Good remuneration programmes facilitate and encourage the proper treatment of customers.

Even though these requirements appear to be logical and easily satisfied, it is actually quite difficult to incorporate them all into a simple programme. Some of them will be satisfied, and others will not. Studies evaluating the impact of financial incentives on sales performance indicate four general responses, as outlined below.

1. For price-sensitive individuals, an increase in incentives will usually increase their sales efforts, and a decrease in financial rewards will diminish their efforts.
2. Unresponsive sales people will sell at the same level regardless of the incentive.
3. Leisure-sensitive sales people tend to work less when the incentive system is implemented.
4. Income satisfiers normally adjust their performance to match their income goal.

Understanding potential reactions and analysing the personalities of the salesforce can help management evaluate whether an incentive programme might work.[17] Therefore, in formulating a compensation or remuneration plan, sales management must strive for a proper balance of freedom, income and incentives.

The developer of a compensation programme must determine the general level of compensation required and the most desirable method of calculating it. In analysing the required compensation level, sales management must ascertain a sales person's value to the company on the basis of the tasks and responsibilities associated with the sales position. The sales manager may consider a number of factors, including the salaries of other types of personnel in the business, competitors' compensation plans, costs of salesforce turnover and the size of non-salary selling expenses and perks.

Sales compensation programmes usually reimburse sales people for their selling expenses, provide a certain number of fringe benefits – such as health insurance, company car and pension scheme – and deliver the required compensation level. To do that, a company may use one or more of three basic compensation methods: straight salary, straight commission or a combination of salary and commission.

**Straight salary compensation/ remuneration plan** A plan according to which sales people are paid a specified amount per time period

**Straight commission compensation/ remuneration plan** A plan according to which sales people are paid solely on the basis of their sales for a given time period

**Combination compensation/ remuneration plan** A plan according to which sales people are paid a fixed salary plus a commission based on sales volume

- In a **straight salary compensation/remuneration plan**, sales people are paid a specified amount per time period. This sum remains the same until they receive a pay increase or decrease.
- In a **straight commission compensation/remuneration plan**, sales people's compensation is determined solely on the basis of their sales for a given time period. Commission may be based on a single percentage of sales or on a sliding scale involving several sales levels and percentage rates.
- In a **combination compensation/remuneration plan**, sales people are paid a fixed salary plus a commission based on sales volume. Some combination programmes require a sales person to exceed a certain sales level before earning a commission; others offer commissions for any level of sales. Car dealers pay their sales personnel small basic salaries, with sales-linked bonuses making up the bulk of earnings.

Traditionally, department stores have paid sales people straight salaries, but combination compensation plans are becoming popular. Some concessions in Debenhams department store, for example, are offering commissions – averaging 6 to 8 per cent – to a large segment of their salesforce. This practice has made the sales people more attentive to a customer's presence and needs; it has also attracted older, more experienced sales people, who tend to be in short supply.

Table 19.1 lists the major characteristics of each salesforce compensation method. Note that the combination method is most popular. When selecting a compensation method, sales management weighs the advantages and disadvantages shown in Table 19.1.

**TABLE 19.1 CHARACTERISTICS OF SALESFORCE COMPENSATION/REMUNERATION METHODS**

| Compensation/ remuneration method | Frequency of use (%)* | When especially useful | Advantages | Disadvantages |
|---|---|---|---|---|
| Straight salary | 17.4 | Compensating new sales people; company moves into new sales territories that require developmental work; sales people need to perform many non-selling activities | Gives sales person maximum amount of security; gives sales manager large amount of control over sales-force; easy to administer; yields more predictable selling expenses | Provides no incentive; necessitates closer supervision of sales-people's activities; during sales declines, selling expenses remain at same level |
| Straight commission | 6.5 | Highly aggressive selling is required; non-selling tasks are minimised; company cannot closely control salesforce activities | Provides maximum amount of incentive; by increasing commission rate, sales managers can encourage sales people to sell certain items; selling expenses relate directly to sales resources | Sales people have little financial security; sales manager has minimum control over salesforce; may cause sales people to give inadequate service to smaller accounts; selling costs less predictable |
| Combination | 76.1 | Sales territories have relatively similar sales potentials; company wishes to provide incentive but still control salesforce activities | Provides certain level of financial security; provides some incentive; selling expenses fluctuate with sales revenue | Selling expenses less predictable; may be difficult to administer |

**Notes:** *The figures are computed from 'Alternative sales compensation and incentive plans', *Sales & Marketing Management*, 17 February 1986, p. 57. The percentage for Combination includes compensation methods that involved any combination of salary, commission or bonus.

**Source:** Based on John P. Steinbrink, 'How to pay your sales force', *Harvard Business Review*, July/August 1978.

Proper administration of the salesforce compensation programme is crucial for developing high morale and productivity among sales personnel. A good sales person is highly marketable in today's workplace, and successful sales managers switch industries on a regular basis. Basic knowledge and skills related to sales management are in demand, and sometimes new insights can be gained from different work experiences. For example, one of steel company Corus's best sales managers was recruited from the grocery sector. To maintain an effective compensation programme and retain productive employees, sales management should periodically review and evaluate the plan and make necessary adjustments.

## Motivating Sales People

A sales manager should develop a systematic approach for motivating the salesforce to be productive. Motivating should not be viewed as a sporadic activity reserved for periods of sales decline. Effective salesforce motivation is achieved through an organised set of activities performed continuously by the company's sales management. For example, scheduled sales meetings can motivate sales people. Periodic sales meetings have four main functions:

1 recognising and reinforcing the performance of sales people
2 sharing sales techniques that are working
3 focusing employees' efforts on matching the corporate goals and evaluating their progress towards achieving these goals
4 teaching the sales staff about new products and services.

Although financial compensation is important, a motivational programme must also satisfy non-financial needs. Sales personnel, like other people, join organisations to satisfy personal needs and achieve personal goals. Sales managers must become aware of their sales personnel's motives and goals, and then attempt to create an organisational climate that permits their sales people to satisfy their personal needs.

A sales manager can use a variety of positive motivational incentives as well as financial compensation (see Figure 19.3). For example, enjoyable working conditions, power and authority, job security and an opportunity to excel can be effective motivators. Sales people can also be motivated by their company's efforts to make their job more productive and efficient. For example, Honeywell Information Systems developed a computerised sales support system that increased sales productivity by 31 per cent and reduced salesforce turnover by 40 per cent within a year. This system can track sales leads, and provide customer profiles and competitor data.[18]

Sales competitions and other incentive programmes can also be effective motivators. Sales contests can motivate sales people to focus on increasing sales or new accounts,

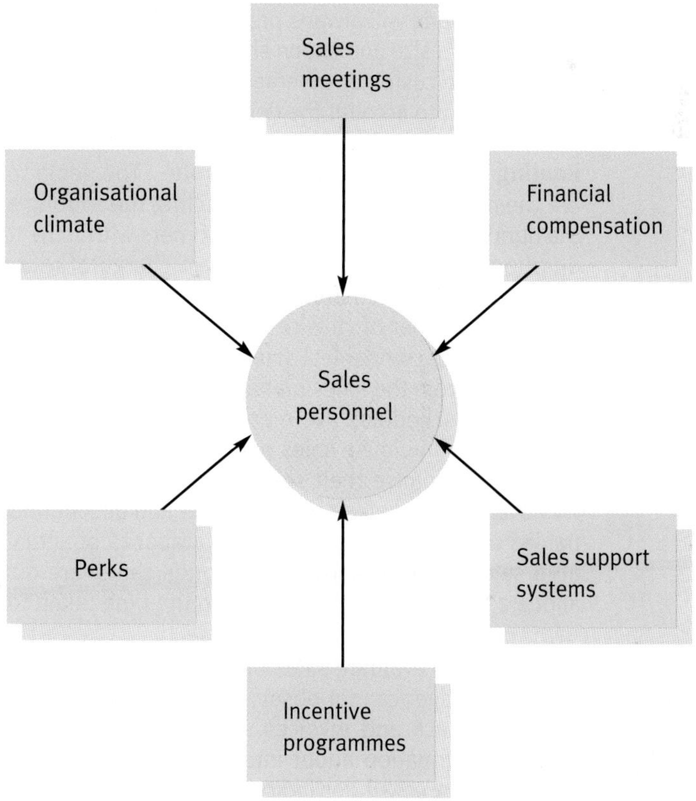


***Figure 19.3***
*Motivating salesforce performance through an organised set of activities*

promoting special items, achieving greater volume per sales call, covering territories better and increasing activity in new geographic areas.[19] Some companies have found such incentive programmes to be powerful motivating tools that marketing managers can use to achieve corporate goals. Properly designed, an incentive programme can pay for itself many times over. However, for an incentive system to succeed, the marketing objectives must be accepted by the participants and prove effective in the marketplace. Some organisations also use negative motivational measures: financial penalties, demotions, even the termination of employment.

## Managing Sales Territories

The effectiveness of a salesforce that must travel to its customers is influenced to some degree by sales management's decisions regarding sales territories. Sales managers deciding on territories must consider the size and shape of sales territories, and the routing and scheduling of sales people.

**The Size and Shape of Sales Territories** Several factors enter into the design of the size and shape of sales territories. First, sales managers must construct the territories so that sales potential can be measured. Thus sales territories often consist of several geographic units for which market data are obtainable, such as census tracts, cities, counties or regions. Sales managers usually try to create territories that have similar sales potentials or require about the same amount of work. If territories have equal sales potentials, they will almost always be unequal in geographic size. The sales people who are assigned the larger territories will have to work longer and harder to generate a certain sales volume. Conversely, if sales territories that require equal amounts of work are created, sales potential for those territories will often vary. If sales personnel are partially or fully compensated through commissions, they will have unequal income potential. Many sales managers try to balance territorial workload and earning potential by using differential commission rates. Although a sales manager seeks equity when developing and maintaining sales territories, some inequities will always prevail.

A territory's size and shape should also be designed to enable the salesforce to provide the best possible customer coverage and to minimise selling costs. Sales territory size and shape should take into account the density and distribution of customers.

**Routing and Scheduling Sales People** The geographic size and shape of a sales territory are the most important factors affecting the routing and scheduling of sales calls. Next are the number and distribution of customers within the territory, followed by the frequency and duration of sales calls. The person in charge of routing and scheduling must consider the sequence in which customers are called on, the specific roads or transport schedules to be used, the number of calls to be made in a given period and what time of day the calls will occur. In some companies, sales people plan their own routes and schedules with little or no assistance from the sales manager; in other organisations, the sales manager draws up the routes and schedules. No matter who plans the routing and scheduling, the major goals should be to minimise sales people's non-selling time – the time spent travelling and waiting – and maximise their selling time. The planners should try to achieve these goals in a way that holds a sales person's travel and accommodation costs to a minimum. Many companies use agencies to construct databases of actual and potential customers and associated sales territories. These territories can share out actual and potential customers and allocate the salesforce in relation to the time taken to service them.

## Controlling and Evaluating Salesforce Performance

To control and evaluate salesforce activities properly, sales management needs information. A sales manager cannot observe the field salesforce daily and so relies on call reports, customer feedback and invoices. Call reports identify the customers called on and present detailed information about interaction with those clients. Travelling sales personnel must often file work schedules indicating where they plan to be during specific future time periods.

The dimensions used to measure a sales person's performance are determined largely by sales objectives. These objectives are normally set by the sales manager. If an individual's sales objective is stated in terms of sales volume, then that person should be evaluated on the basis of sales volume generated. Even though a sales person may be assigned a major objective, he or she is ordinarily expected to achieve several related objectives as well. Thus sales people are often judged along several dimensions. Sales managers evaluate many performance indicators, including average number of calls per day, average sales per customer, actual sales relative to sales potential, number of new customer orders, average cost per call and average gross profit per customer.

To evaluate a sales person, a sales manager may compare one or more of these dimensions with a predetermined performance standard. However, sales management commonly compares one sales person's current performance either with the performance of other employees operating under similar selling conditions or with his or her past performance. Sometimes management judges factors that have less direct bearing on sales performance, such as personal appearance, and knowledge of the product and competitors.

After evaluating their salesforce, sales managers must take any corrective action needed, because it is their job to improve the performance of the salesforce. They may have to adjust performance standards, provide additional sales training or try other motivational methods. Corrective action may demand comprehensive changes in the salesforce.

Many industries, especially technical ones, are monitoring their salesforces and increasing productivity through the use of laptop computers and Internet links. In part, the increasing use of computers in technical sales is a response to customers' greater technical sophistication. Product information – especially information on price, specifications and availability – helps sales people to be more valuable. Companies that have provided their salesforces with the latest technology expect an increase in sales to result.

### Internal Marketing

Chapter 24 explains the importance of internal marketing: the process of ensuring that colleagues within the organisation are familiar with the marketing strategy, and appreciate their roles in implementing this strategy and the associated marketing plan. The salesforce is usually pivotal to implementing marketing programmes in order to roll out a marketing strategy, particularly in business markets. It is necessary, therefore, to have internal marketing programmes targeted at sales personnel to orientate them, explain their role, and to outline the intended marketing programmes and their expected deliverables.

## Sales Promotion

### The Nature of Sales Promotion

**Sales promotion**
An activity or material that acts as a direct inducement and offers added value to or incentive to buy the product

As defined in Chapter 17, **sales promotion** is an activity or material (or both) that acts as a direct inducement and offers added value to or incentive to buy the product to resellers, sales people or consumers.[20] The sale probably would have taken place without the sales promotion activity, but not for a while; the promotion has brought the sale forward. For example, a consumer loyal to Persil washing powder may purchase a packet every four weeks. If, however, in the third week Tesco or Carrefour has Persil on offer or with an on-pack promotion, the consumer will probably buy a week early to take advantage of the deal. Sales promotion encompasses all promotional activities and materials other than personal selling, advertising, publicity and sponsorship. In competitive markets, where products are very similar, sales promotion provides additional inducements to encourage purchase. Sales promotions are designed to generate short-term sales and goodwill towards the promoter.

Sales promotion has grown dramatically in the last 20 years, largely because of the focus of business on short-term profits and value, and the perceived need for promotional strategies to produce short-term sales boosts. Estimates in the UK suggest that consumer sales promotion is worth £2 billion annually. Include price discounting and the figure could be £4 billion higher; include trade sales promotion and the total reaches £8 billion.[21] The most significant change in promotion expenditures in recent years has been the transfer of funds usually earmarked for advertising to sales promotion. Fundamental changes in marketing, which have led to a greater emphasis on sales promotion, mean that specialist sales promotion agencies have increased and many major advertising agencies have developed sales promotion departments.

**Ratchet effect**
The stepped impact of using sales promotion and advertising together

An organisation often uses sales promotion activities in conjunction with other promotional efforts to facilitate personal selling, advertising or both.[22] Figure 19.4 depicts what is known as the **ratchet effect** – the stepped impact of using sales promotion (short-term sales brought forward) and advertising (longer-term build-up to generate sales) together. Sales promotion efforts are not always secondary to other promotional mix ingredients. Companies sometimes use advertising and personal selling to support sales promotion activities. For example, marketers frequently use advertising to promote competitions, free samples and special offers. Manufacturers' sales personnel occasionally administer sales contests for wholesale or retail sales people. The most effective sales promotion efforts are closely interrelated with other promotional activities. Decisions regarding sales promotion, therefore, often affect advertising and personal selling decisions, and vice versa.

## Sales Promotion Opportunities and Limitations

Sales promotion can increase sales by providing an extra incentive to purchase. There are many opportunities to motivate consumers, resellers and sales people to take a desired action. Some kinds of sales promotion are designed specifically to identify and attract new customers, to introduce a new product and to increase reseller inventories. Some are directed at increasing consumer demand; still others focus on both resellers and consumers. Regardless of the purpose, marketers need to ensure that the sales promotion objectives are consistent with the organisation's overall objectives, as well as with its marketing and communications objectives.[23]

Although sales promotion can support a brand image, excessive price reduction sales promotion, such as discount coupons or two-for-one pack offers, can affect it adversely. Companies must decide between short-term sales increases and the long-run need for a desired reputation and brand image.[24] Sales promotion has been catching up with advertising in total expenditure; but in the future, brand advertising may become more important relative to sales promotion. Some companies that shifted from brand advertising to sales promotion have lost market share, particularly in consumer markets where advertising is essential to maintain awareness and brand recognition. Advertising does not necessarily work better

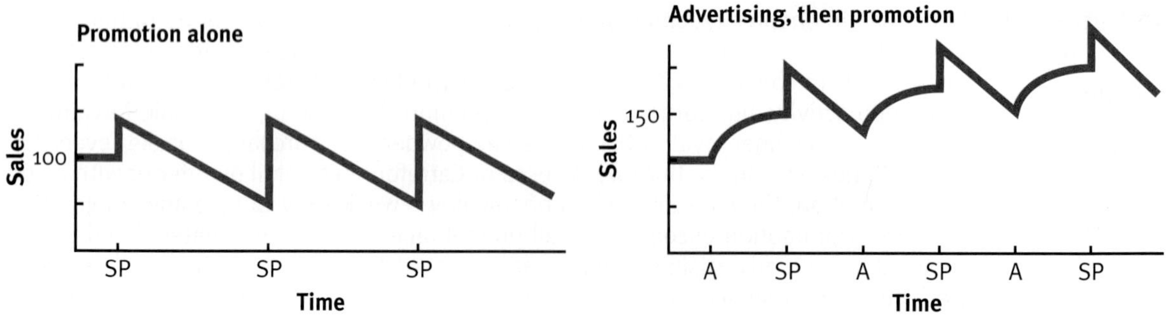


***Figure 19.4***
*The 'ratchet effect'. Sales promotion (SP) brings forward sales but has an immediate effect. An advertising campaign (A) takes time to take off and to generate sales, but can switch other brand users and non-users. The ratchet effect has been identified in most consumer and service markets*
*Source: W.T. Moran, 'Insights from pricing research', in E.B. Bailey, ed.,* Pricing Practices and Strategies *(New York: The Conference Board, 1978), pp. 7 and 13. Used by permission*

than sales promotion. There are trade-offs between these two forms of promotion, and the marketing manager must determine the right balance to achieve maximum promotional effectiveness.

## Sales Promotion Methods

**Consumer sales promotion techniques** Techniques that encourage or stimulate consumers to patronise a specific retail store or to try a particular product

**Trade sales promotion methods** Techniques that encourage wholesalers, retailers or dealers to carry and market a producer's products

Most sales promotion methods can be grouped into the categories of consumer sales promotion and trade sales promotion. **Consumer sales promotion techniques** are pitched at consumers: they encourage or stimulate consumers to patronise a specific retail store or to try a particular product. **Trade sales promotion methods** are aimed at marketing channel intermediaries: they stimulate wholesalers, retailers or dealers to carry a producer's products and to market these products aggressively. Figure 19.5 shows how all members of a marketing channel can be engaged in sales promotion activities with different target audiences and techniques.

Marketers consider a number of factors before deciding which sales promotion methods to use.[25] They must take into account both product characteristics (size, weight, costs, durability, uses, features and hazards) and target market characteristics (lifestyle, age, sex, income, location, density, usage rate and shopping patterns). How the product is distributed, and the number and types of reseller may determine the type of method used. The competitive and legal environmental forces may also influence the choice.

### Consumer Sales Promotion Techniques

**Coupons** The principal consumer sales promotion techniques include coupons, demonstrations, frequent-user incentives, point-of-sale (POS) materials, free samples, money refunds, premiums, price-off offers, and consumer competitions.

**Coupons** are used to stimulate consumers to try a new or established product, to increase sales volume quickly, to attract repeat purchasers or to introduce new package sizes or features. Coupons usually reduce the purchase price of an item. The savings may be deducted from the purchase price or offered as cash. For the best results, coupons should be easy to recognise and state the offer clearly. The nature of the product – seasonality, maturity, frequency of purchase, and so on – is the prime consideration in setting up a coupon promotion.

Several thousand manufacturers distribute coupons, which are used by approximately 80 per cent of all households. One study found that pride and satisfaction from obtaining savings through the use of coupons and price-consciousness were the most important determinants of coupon use.[26] Coupons are distributed through free-standing inserts (FSIs), print advertising, direct mail/leaflet drops and in stores. Historically, FSIs have been the dominant vehicle for coupons.[27] When deciding on the proper vehicle for their coupons, marketers

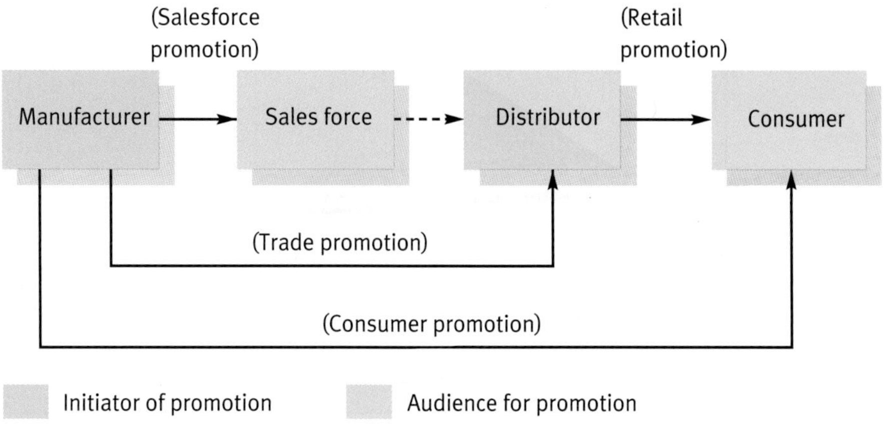


***Figure 19.5***
*Uses of sales promotion in the marketing channel. Consumer: coupons, free samples, demonstrations, competitions. Trade (aimed at wholesalers, retailers, sales people): sales competitions, free merchandise, POS displays, plus trade shows and conferences Source: John Rossiter and Larry Percy,* Advertising and Promotion Management. *Copyright © 1987 by The McGraw-Hill Companies, Inc. Reprinted with permission of the authors*

**Coupons**
A promotion method that reduces the purchase price of an item in order to stimulate consumers to try a new or established product, to increase sales volume quickly, to attract repeat purchasers or to introduce new package sizes or features

should consider strategies and objectives, redemption rates, availability, circulation and exclusivity. The whole coupon distribution and redemption business has become very competitive. To draw customers to their stores, grocers may double and sometimes even triple the value of the coupons they bring in.

There are several advantages to using coupons. Print advertisements with coupons are often more effective than non-promotional advertising in generating brand awareness. Generally, the larger the coupon's cash offer, the better the recognition generated. Another advantage is that coupons are a good way to reward present users of the product, win back former users and encourage purchases in larger quantities. Coupons also enable manufacturers to determine whether the coupons reached the intended target market because they get the coupons back. The advantages of using electronic coupons over paper coupons include lower cost per redemption, greater targeting ability, improved data-gathering capabilities and improved experimentation capabilities to determine optimal face values and expiration cycles.[28]

Coupons also have drawbacks. Fraud and misredemption are possible, and the redemption period can be quite lengthy. Table 19.2 illustrates coupon distribution and redemption rates in the UK. In addition, some experts believe that coupons are losing their value because so many manufacturers are offering them, and consumers have learned not to buy

**TABLE 19.2 UK COUPON DISTRIBUTION AND REDEMPTION**

| | 1998 | 1999 | 2000 | 2001 | 2002 |
|---|---|---|---|---|---|
| **Distribution (billions)** | **5.1** | **4.7** | **5.0** | **6.0** | **5.0** |
| **Share of coupon redemption by media (%)** | | | | | |
| Newspapers | 1.5 | 2.6 | 3.3 | 0.9 | 0.6 |
| Magazines | 6.2 | 4.9 | 4.5 | 1.9 | 1.8 |
| Door-to-door | 6.3 | 19.4 | 3.4 | 1.1 | 1.1 |
| In/on pack | 31.8 | 4.7 | 23.7 | 6.0 | 6.0 |
| In store | 22.6 | 24.6 | 24.7 | 3.9 | 4.6 |
| Direct mail | 25.6 | 37.7 | 33.3 | 80.2 | 76.7 |
| Other | 6.0 | 6.1 | 7.1 | 6.0 | 9.2 |
| **Redemptions (millions)** | **410** | **487** | **531** | **569** | **452** |
| **Average redemption rates by media (%)** | | | | | |
| Newspapers | 1.3 | 3.2 | 3.3 | 1.8 | 0.9 |
| Magazines | 1.4 | 1.5 | 1.5 | 1.4 | 1.1 |
| Door-to-door | 6.4 | 4.8 | 3.3 | 2.1 | 3.4 |
| In/on pack | 19.7 | 26.8 | 26.5 | 28.8 | 21.6 |
| In store | 5.6 | 16.8 | 16.2 | 3.1 | 6.7 |
| Direct mail | 16.7 | 20.1 | 20.9 | 10.5 | 8.2 |
| Other | – | 15.8 | 14.4 | 12.1 | 14.1 |
| **Average face value (pence)** | **50** | **57** | **46** | **53** | **99** |
| **Recommended manufacturers' handling allowance to retailers (pence per 100 coupons)** | **360** | **360** | **360** | **360** | **360** |

**Notes:** excluding retailer tailor-made promotions.
**Sources:** NCH Marketing Services Ltd; *The Marketing Pocket Book*, published by the World Advertising and Research Center, Henley-on-Thames, 2004.

without some incentive, whether it be a coupon, a rebate or a refund. There has been a general decline in brand loyalty among heavy coupon users. In addition, many consumers redeem coupons only for products they normally buy. Studies have shown that about 75 per cent of coupons are redeemed by people who already use the brand on the coupon. So, as an incentive to use a new brand or product, coupons have questionable success. Another problem with coupons is that stores often do not have enough of the coupon item in stock. This situation can generate ill-will towards both the store and the product.[29]

Although the use of coupons as a sales promotion technique is expected to grow, marketers' concerns about their effectiveness could well diminish their appeal. However, coupons will probably remain a major sales promotion component for stimulating trial of new products. Coupons will also be used to increase the frequency of purchase for established products that show sluggish sales. On the other hand, successful, established products may be reducing their profits if 75 per cent of the coupons are redeemed by brand-loyal customers.[30]

## Innovation and Change

### Tesco Moves Ahead with the Help of Clubcard

Not too long ago, Green Shield trading stamps were the most widely encountered frequent-user sales promotion. Today, it is the loyalty card. The current wave was instigated by the petrol forecourts, which offered points with petrol towards prizes or catalogue merchandise. In 1995 supermarket giant Tesco introduced its loyalty card, the Clubcard, to ridicule by competitors. Tremendously successful, the card has accordingly increased the number of Tesco shoppers, and in 1996 the company overtook arch-rival Sainsbury's as the number one grocery retailer in the UK.

Tesco's Clubcard promises 'to give you something back when shopping with Tesco'. A Clubcard point is earned for each £1 spent with Tesco. The points can be redeemed for discounted purchases or for rewards (prizes). Esso, Lifestyle Sports, mobile phone operator O2 and video rental specialist Blockbuster are now Clubcard partners and even erstwhile rival AirMiles will redeem Tesco Clubcard points for AirMiles.

Not resting on its laurels, Tesco surprised many of its rivals – including Sainsbury's, which by then had introduced their own loyalty cards – by launching Clubcard Plus. Within a year the original Clubcard had 6.5 million regular customers who used their cards to earn discounts against their spending. Clubcard Plus went further: it offered holders interest paid on their balances and could be used like any other debit card. This move into financial services is not new. Marks & Spencer has a very successful division handling its payment card, which now also sells savings schemes and pensions. Once a music business, now a hotelier and airline, Virgin sells life insurance and other financial services on the back of its highly visible and reputable brand name. The difference with Tesco is that instead of using its brand name to sell financial services, it is using its loyalty card-based financial product to sell its brand name and successful chain of supermarkets.

Tesco's Clubcard has enabled the company to overtake its rivals and has, analysts believe, increased the frequency of shopping visits to Tesco stores. Within 12 months of being launched, the Clubcard had become the most popular loyalty scheme in the UK, ahead of the more established schemes run by companies such as Esso and AirMiles. Tesco has continued to enhance its loyalty card offer, with exclusive clubs:

- Baby & Toddler Club
- Clubcard World of Wine
- Healthy Living Club.

As Tesco has expanded overseas, notably in Asia Pacific and eastern Europe, it has taken its loyalty card expertise to markets previously totally unfamiliar with the concept. The loyalty card has proved to be a major success story and not only as a sales promotion tool, particularly for Tesco.

**Sources:** David Benardy, 'Tesco plays its Clubcard right', *Marketing Week*, 3 November 1995, pp. 30–1; 'Tesco's Clubcard tops loyalty', *Marketing*, 25 May 1995, p. 4; Martin Croft, 'It's all in the cards', *Marketing Week*, 24 March 1995; Anthony Bailey, 'There's lolly in your trolley', *Independent on Sunday*, 9 June 1996, p. IB18; Tesco Annual Report, 1999; www.tesco.com, July 2004; Fujitsu, 2004.

**Demonstrations**
Occasions at which manufacturers show how a product actually works in order to encourage trial use and purchase of the product

**Demonstrations** **Demonstrations** of products at dealers, retailers or trade shows are excellent attention-getters. Manufacturers often use them to show how a product actually works in order to encourage trial use and purchase of the product. Because labour costs can be extremely high, demonstrations are not widely used. They can, however, be highly effective for promoting certain types of product, such as appliances, cosmetics and cars. Cosmetics marketers, such as those for Estée Lauder, sometimes offer potential customers 'makeovers' to demonstrate their products' benefits and proper application.

**Frequent user incentives**
Incentive programmes that reward customers who engage in repeat purchases

**Loyalty card**
A mechanism whereby regular customers who remain loyal to a particular company are rewarded with discounts or free merchandise

**Trading stamps**
Stamps, dispensed in proportion to the amount of a consumer's purchase, that can be accumulated and redeemed for goods

**Frequent User Incentives** Many companies develop **frequent user incentives** to reward customers who engage in repeat purchases. For example, most major international airlines offer a frequent-flier programme through which customers who have flown a specified number of miles are rewarded with free tickets for additional travel. AirMiles takes this concept further, extending it across many products. Supermarket loyalty cards are another popular incentive; one such is Tesco's Clubcard, as described in the Innovation and Change box below. A **loyalty card** offers discounts or free merchandise to regular customers. Thus frequent user incentives help foster customer loyalty to a specific company or group of cooperating companies that provides extra incentives for patronage. Frequent user incentives have also been used by service businesses, such as car hire companies, hotel chains and credit cards, as well as by marketers of consumer goods (see Figure 19.6).

An older frequent user incentive is trading stamps. **Trading stamps** are dispensed in proportion to the amount of a consumer's purchase, and can be accumulated and redeemed for goods. Retailers use trading stamps to attract consumers to specific stores. Stamps are attractive to consumers as long as they do not drive up the price of goods. They are effective for many types of retailer. Trading stamps were very popular in the 1960s, but their use as a sales promotion method declined dramatically in the 1970s. However, Green Shield stamps made a comeback, and petrol retailers are now offering in-house stamps redeemable for limited collections of goods.

*Figure 19.6*
*Examples of typical coupons*
*Photo: Courtesy of Karen Beaulah*

**Point-of-sale (POS) materials**
Enhancements designed to increase sales and introduce products, such as outside signs, window displays, counter pieces, display racks and self-service cartons

**Point-of-sale (POS) Materials** **Point-of-sale (POS) materials** include such items as outside signs, window displays, counter pieces, display racks and self-service cartons. Innovations in POS displays include sniff teasers, which give off a product's aroma in the store as consumers walk within a radius of four feet, in-store televisions, and computerised interactive displays, which ask a series of multiple-choice questions and then display information on a screen to help consumers make a product decision. IKEA stores offer interactive monitors on which room layouts and colour combinations may be tested prior to purchase. These items, which are often supplied by producers, attract attention, inform customers and encourage retailers to carry particular products. A retailer is likely to use point-of-sale materials if they are attractive, informative, well constructed and in harmony with the store. With two-thirds of all purchases resulting from in-store decisions, POS materials can help sustain incremental sales if a brand's essential components – brand name, positioning and visual image – are the basis of the POS display.[31]

A survey of retail store managers indicated that almost 90 per cent believed that POS materials sell products. The retailers surveyed also said that POS is essential for product introductions. Different forms of display materials are carried by different types of retailer. Convenience stores, for example, favour window banners and 'shelf talkers' (on-the-shelf displays or signs), whereas chain chemists prefer floor stands and devices that provide samples.[32]

**Free samples**
Give-aways used to stimulate trial of a product, to increase sales volume in the early stages of a product's life cycle or to obtain desirable distribution

**Free Samples** **Free samples** of merchandise are used for several reasons: to stimulate trial of a product, to increase sales volume in the early stages of a product's life cycle or to obtain desirable distribution. The sampling programme should be planned as a total event, not merely a give-away. Sampling is the most expensive of all sales promotion methods; production and distribution through such channels as mail delivery, door-to-door delivery, in-store distribution and on-package distribution entail very high costs. In designing a free sample, marketers should consider factors such as the seasonality of the product, the characteristics of the market and prior advertising. Free samples are not appropriate for mature products and products with a slow turnover.

**Money refunds**
A specific amount of money mailed to customers who submit proof of purchase

**Money Refunds** With **money refunds**, consumers submit proof of purchase and are mailed a specific amount of money. Usually, manufacturers demand multiple purchases of the product before a consumer can qualify for a refund. For example, Panasonic marketed a line of VHS tapes that featured a £1 rebate per tape for up to 12 purchases. A customer had to send in the sales receipt and a proof of purchase from inside each tape package. This method, used primarily to promote trial use of a product, is relatively inexpensive. Nevertheless, because money refunds sometimes generate a low response rate, they have limited impact on sales.

One of the problems with money refunds or rebates is that many people perceive the redemption process as too complicated. Consumers also have negative perceptions of manufacturers' reasons for offering rebates. They may believe that these are new, untested products or products that have not sold well. If these perceptions are not changed, rebate offers may degrade the image and desirability of the product being promoted. If the promotion objective in the rebate offer is to increase sales, an effort should be made to simplify the redemption process and proof of purchase requirements.[33]

**Premiums**
Items offered free or at minimum cost as a bonus for purchasing a product

**Premiums** **Premiums** are items offered free or at minimum cost as a bonus for purchasing a product. Vidal Sassoon offered a free, on-pack 50ml 'travel size' container of shampoo with its 200ml size of Salon Formula shampoo. Kellogg's offered easy art books with its Variety Packs. Premiums can attract competitors' customers, introduce different sizes of established products, add variety to other promotional efforts and stimulate loyalty. Inventiveness is necessary if an offer is to stand out and achieve a significant number of redemptions – the premium must be matched to both the target audience and the brand's image.[34] To be effective, premiums must be easily recognisable and desirable. Premiums are usually distributed through retail outlets or the mail, but they may also be placed on or in packages.

**Price-off offers**
A method of encouraging customers to buy a product by offering a certain amount off the regular price shown on the label or package

**Price-off Offers** **Price-off offers** give buyers a certain amount off the regular price shown on the label or package. Similar to coupons, this method can be a strong incentive for trying the product; it can stimulate product sales, yield short-lived sales increases and promote products out of season. It is an easy method to control and is used frequently for specific purposes. However, if used on an ongoing basis, it reduces the price to customers who would buy at the regular price anyway, and frequent use of price-off offers may cheapen a product's image. In addition, the method often requires special handling by retailers.

**Consumer contests**
Contests designed to generate traffic at the retail level in which consumers compete for prizes based on their analytical or creative skill

**Consumer Competitions** **Consumer contests** encourage individuals to compete for prizes based on their analytical or creative skills. This method generates traffic at the retail level. Marriott and Hertz co-sponsored a scratchcard contest with a golf theme to boost sales during the slow winter travel season. Contestants received game cards when they checked in at a Marriott hotel or hired a Hertz car, and scratched off spots to see if they had won prizes, such as cars, holidays or golf clubs.[35] However, marketers should exercise care in setting up such competitions. Problems or errors may anger consumers or result in legal action. Contestants are usually more involved in consumer contests than they are in sweepstakes, even though total participation may be lower. Contests may be used in conjunction with other sales promotion methods, such as coupons.

**Consumer sweepstakes**
A method of stimulating sales in which consumers submit their names for inclusion in a draw for prizes

The entrants in a **consumer sweepstake** submit their names for inclusion in a draw for prizes. Sweepstakes are used to stimulate sales and, as with contests, are sometimes teamed with other sales promotion methods. Sweepstakes are used more often than consumer contests and tend to attract a greater number of participants. The cost of a sweepstake is considerably less than the cost of a contest.[36] Successful sweepstakes or contests can generate widespread interest and short-term increases in sales or market share.

## Trade Sales Promotion Methods

Producers use sales promotion methods to encourage resellers, especially retailers and dealers, to carry their products and promote them effectively. The methods include buy-back allowances, buying allowances, counts and re-counts, free merchandise, merchandise allowances, cooperative advertising, dealer listings, premium or push money, sales contests and dealer loaders.

**Buy-back allowance**
A certain sum of money given to a purchaser for each unit bought after an initial deal is over

**Buy-back Allowance** A **buy-back allowance** is a certain sum of money given to a purchaser for each unit bought after an initial deal is over. This method is a secondary incentive in which the total amount of money that resellers can receive is proportional to their purchases during an initial trade deal, such as a coupon offer. Buy-back allowances foster cooperation during an initial sales promotion effort and stimulate repurchase afterwards. The main drawback of this method is its expense.

**Buying allowance**
A temporary price reduction given to resellers who purchase specified quantities of a product

**Buying Allowance** A **buying allowance** is a temporary price reduction to resellers for purchasing specified quantities of a product. A soap producer, for example, might give retailers £1 for each case of soap purchased. Such offers may be an incentive to handle a new product, achieve a temporary price reduction or stimulate the purchase of an item in larger than normal quantities. The buying allowance, which takes the form of money, yields profits to resellers and is simple and straightforward to use. There are no restrictions on how resellers use the money, which increases the method's effectiveness.

**Count and re-count**
A promotion method based on the payment of a specific amount of money for each product unit moved from a reseller's warehouse in a given time period

**Count and Re-count** The **count and re-count** promotion method is based on the payment of a specific amount of money for each product unit moved from a reseller's warehouse in a given time period. Units of a product are counted at the start of the promotion and again at the end to determine how many have moved from the warehouse. This method can reduce retail stock-outs by moving inventory out of warehouses, and can also clear distribution channels of obsolete products or packages and reduce warehouse inventories. The count and re-count method might benefit a producer by decreasing resellers' inventories, making resellers more likely to place new orders. However, this method is often difficult to administer and may not appeal to resellers who have small warehouses.

**Free merchandise**
Give-aways sometimes offered to resellers who purchase a stated quantity of the same or different products

**Free Merchandise** **Free merchandise** is sometimes offered to resellers who purchase a stated quantity of the same or different products. Occasionally, free merchandise is used as payment for allowances provided through other sales promotion methods. To avoid handling and bookkeeping problems, the usual method of giving away merchandise is by reducing the invoice.

**Merchandise allowance**
A manufacturer's agreement to pay resellers certain amounts of money for providing special promotional efforts, such as advertising or displays

**Merchandise Allowance** A **merchandise allowance** is a manufacturer's agreement to pay resellers certain amounts of money for providing special promotional efforts, such as advertising or displays. This method is best suited to high-volume, high-profit, easily handled products. One major problem with using merchandise allowances is that some retailers or dealers perform their activities at a minimally acceptable level simply to obtain the allowances. Before paying retailers or dealers, manufacturers usually verify their performance. Manufacturers hope that the retailers' or dealers' additional promotional efforts will yield substantial sales increases.

**Cooperative advertising**
An arrangement whereby a manufacturer agrees to pay a certain amount of a retailer's or dealer's media costs for advertising the manufacturer's products

**Cooperative Advertising** **Cooperative advertising** is an arrangement whereby a manufacturer agrees to pay a certain amount of a retailer's or dealer's media costs for advertising the manufacturer's products. The amount allowed is usually based on the quantities purchased. Before payment is made, a retailer or dealer must show proof that advertisements did appear.

These payments give retailers or dealers additional funds for advertising. They can, however, put a severe burden on the producer's advertising budget. Some retailers or dealers exploit cooperative advertising programmes by crowding too many products into one advertisement. Some retailers or dealers cannot afford to advertise; others can afford it but do not want to advertise. Still others actually put out advertising that qualifies for an allowance but are not willing to undertake the paperwork required for reimbursement from producers.[37]

**Dealer listing**
An advertisement that promotes a product and identifies the names of participating retailers or dealers who sell it

**Dealer Listing** A **dealer listing** is an advertisement that promotes a product and identifies the names of participating retailers or dealers who sell it. Dealer listings can influence retailers or dealers to carry the product, build traffic at the retail level and encourage consumers to buy the product at participating dealers.

**Premium** or **push money**
Additional compensation/remuneration provided to sales people in order to push a line of goods

**Premium or Push Money** **Premium** or **push money** is used to push a line of goods by providing additional compensation/remuneration to sales people. This promotion method is appropriate when personal selling is an important part of the marketing effort; it is not effective for promoting products that are sold through self-service. Although this method often helps a manufacturer obtain commitment from the salesforce, it can also be very expensive.

**Sales competition**
A way to motivate distributors, retailers and sales personnel by recognising and rewarding outstanding achievements

**Sales Competitions** **Sales competitions** are designed to motivate distributors, retailers and sales personnel by recognising and rewarding outstanding achievements. The Colt Car Company, importer of Japanese-made Mitsubishi cars, designed a sales contest that offered dealers an incentive trip for two to Barbados if they improved their sales figures by

10 to 12 per cent. Approximately 50 per cent of the dealers met this sales goal and won the trip.[38] To be effective, this method must be equitable for all sales personnel involved. One advantage of the method is that it can achieve participation at all levels of distribution. However, the results are temporary and prizes are usually expensive.

**Dealer loader**
A gift to a retailer or dealer who purchases a specified quantity of merchandise

**Dealer Loaders** **Dealer loaders** are gifts to a retailer or dealer, who purchases a specified quantity of merchandise. Often dealer loaders are used to obtain special display efforts from retailers by offering essential display parts as premiums. For example, a manufacturer might design a display that includes a sterling silver tray as a major component and then give the tray to the retailer. Marketers use dealer loaders to obtain new distributors and push larger quantities of goods.

# Direct Mail

**Direct mail**
Printed advertising material delivered to a prospective customer's or donor's home or work address

**Junk mail**
Unwanted mail often binned unread by uninterested recipients

**Direct mail** and telephone selling are part of the direct marketing category described in Chapter 16. Direct mail is the delivery to the target's home or work address of printed advertising material to contact prospective customers or donors. The use of direct mail to contact prospective customers and to solicit interest in products or services is not new.[39] Advertising agencies, public relations consultancies and, in particular, sales promotions houses have been using mailshots for several decades. With approximately 6 per cent of all promotional budgets in consumer goods and services, its own professional bodies and trade associations, and the growing sophistication of consumer databases, the direct mail industry believes it warrants recognition as a separate element of the promotional mix alongside advertising, sales promotion, personal selling, publicity/public relations and sponsorship.[40]

## The Uses of Direct Mail

Direct mail is not confined to consumers; it is an important promotional activity in many business-to-business markets. Direct mail delivers the promotional message – and sometimes the product – through the postal service, private delivery businesses and the expanding network of in-home fax machines. Direct mail is used to create brand awareness and stimulate product adoption.[41] There is even the growth of direct mail via e-mail addresses, but the Internet is addressed separately in this chapter. Throughout Europe, direct mail is widely used to generate orders, pre-sell prior to a sales call, qualify prospects for a sales call, screen out non-prospects, follow up a sale, announce special sales and localised selling initiatives, and raise funds for charities and non-profit organisations. In the UK, the average household receives 166 items of direct mail each year (see Table 19.3).

## Attention-seeking Flashes

**Flashes**
Headers printed on a direct mail package to gain the recipient's attention

Direct mail packages must prompt the recipient to open them, rather than treat them as **junk mail**, which is unwanted mail often binned unread by uninterested recipients. 'Prize inside', 'Your opportunity to win', 'Not a circular', 'Important documentation enclosed' are just some of the popular headers, or **flashes**, printed prominently on the address labels to gain the recipients' attention. In some markets, these are sufficient at least to persuade the recipient to open the package. With the boom in direct mail and the growing adverse reaction to junk mail, however, persuasive phrases are often not enough. Packaging design is becoming more important in enticing recipients, through attractive or unusual shapes and designs, to examine the details and contents of the direct mailshot.

## The Package

The **direct mail package** is more than just the envelope. Often it is a mix of mailing envelope, covering or explanatory letter, circular, response device and return device. The mailing envelope has to overcome the recipients' inertia, often through catchy flashes and design flair. The letter needs to be personalised and clear, to appeal to the beliefs and lifestyle of the recipients, and to elicit interest in the product or service in question. The circular contains

**Table 19.3 The Direct Mail Industry**

**a Direct mail advertising – volume and expenditure, UK**

| | Volume items (million) | | | Expenditure (£m) | | |
|---|---|---|---|---|---|---|
| | Consumer items | Business items | Total items | Production costs | Postage costs | Total costs |
| 1990 | 1544 | 728 | 2272 | 682 | 297 | 979 |
| 1991 | 1435 | 687 | 2122 | 605 | 290 | 895 |
| 1992 | 1658 | 588 | 2246 | 603 | 342 | 945 |
| 1993 | 1772 | 664 | 2436 | 555 | 352 | 907 |
| 1994 | 2015 | 715 | 2730 | 646 | 404 | 1050 |
| 1995 | 2198 | 707 | 2905 | 673 | 462 | 1135 |
| 1996 | 2436 | 737 | 3173 | 904 | 500 | 1404 |
| 1997 | 2701 | 887 | 3588 | 1039 | 596 | 1635 |
| 1998 | 3123 | 891 | 4014 | 939 | 726 | 1666 |
| 1999 | 3283 | 1062 | 4345 | 1062 | 814 | 1876 |
| 2000 | 3516 | 1148 | 4664 | 1180 | 869 | 2049 |
| 2001 | 3706 | 1233 | 4939 | 1308 | 921 | 2228 |
| 2002 | 3940 | 1293 | 5233 | 1399 | 979 | 2378 |

**Notes:** Direct mail here refers to personally addressed advertising that is delivered through the post.
**Source:** Royal Mail.

**b Senders of consumer direct mail, 2002, UK**

| | Percentage of total consumer volume | | Percentage of total consumer volume |
|---|---|---|---|
| Mail order | 14.7 | Manufacturing | 2.9 |
| Banks | 12.8 | Book clubs | 2.9 |
| Insurance | 10.1 | Building societies | 0.9 |
| Retail/store cards | 9.1 | Government | 1.4 |
| Charities | 7.4 | Education | 0.4 |
| Utilities | 5.1 | Others | 30.0 |
| Magazines/papers | 2.3 | | |

**Source:** Royal Mail.

**c Direct mail response rates, UK**

| | Base (number of campaigns) | Total response rate % | Response rate (excl. +50% campaigns) | Response rate (excl. +30% campaigns) |
|---|---|---|---|---|
| All direct mail | 3339 | 10.6 | 8.5 | 6.8 |
| Direct mail to consumers | 1857 | 11.3 | 9.1 | 7.1 |
| Direct mail to businesses | 1482 | 9.9 | 7.9 | 6.4 |
| All door drops | 354 | 6.5 | 6.5 | 5.0 |

**Source:** Direct Mail Information Service (DMIS); Response Rates Survey 2001.

**Source:** *The Marketing Pocket Book*, published by the World Advertising Research Center, Henley-on-Thames, 2004.

**Direct mail package**
A mix of mailing envelope, covering or explanatory letter, circular, response device and return device

the service or product details and specifications: colour, sizes, capabilities, prices, photographs or illustrations, and guarantees and endorsements from satisfied customers or personalities. The circular is the primary selling tool in the pack and often takes the form of a booklet, broadsheet, jumbo folder, brochure or flyer. The response device is typically an order form, which must be legally correct, must repeat the selling message and product benefits, must be simple to read and fill out, and comprehensive in the information requested. Alternatively, the response device can be an 0800 Freefone telephone number or credit card hotline. The return device is any mechanism that enables the recipient to respond with a request for information or an order or donation. It can be an information request form, order form or payment slip, and is usually accompanied by a pre-printed – and often pre-paid – return envelope.

## Mailing Lists

**Mailing lists**
Directories of suitable, relevant recipients or targets

80 per cent of direct mail is opened; 63 per cent is partially read; less still leads to an order or donation. Depending on the scale of the targeted audience, however, the costs are relatively low: that is, of design, printing, postage, and the purchase or compilation of **mailing lists** – directories of suitable, relevant recipients or targets. To be effective, appropriate targeting of direct mail is essential. Mailing lists must be as up to date as possible. There is a rule of thumb in the industry that a third of addresses on a list change each year owing to deaths and relocations. Within a year or two a list can be obsolete. Internal lists are those compiled in-house from customer addresses, account details and records of enquiries. External lists are produced by list brokers or mailing houses and are bought – or rented – at commercial rates.

The suppliers of these external lists often undertake the complete direct mail operation for clients, from identification of recipients and compilation of lists to production of printed material, postage and even receipt of response devices. External lists can either be addresses of product category customers, including those of competing businesses if available, or general lists of targets with apparently suitable demographic profiles and lifestyles. Many of the leading geodemographic databases, such as ACORN and MOSAIC, were originally developed to assist in the targeting of direct mail. Royal Mail is also a good data source (see Figure 19.7).

## Copy Writing

**Copy writing**
The creation and wording of the promotional message

Targeting does not stop with the acquisition of a mailing list. The printed and product material included in the direct mail package must be written, designed and produced to appeal to the targets. The material should be prepared by people who understand the emotions and attitudes of prospective customers. **Copy writing**, the creation and wording of the promotional message, is an important skill in the promotional mix, especially in the production of direct mail. The text has to appeal to the target audience; sell the product; reassure the reader; be informative, clear and concise; and lead to a positive response.

## The Strengths and Weaknesses of Direct Mail

There are many advantages associated with direct mail. The medium offers a wide variety of styles and formats – more than offered by a radio or press advertisement, for example. The package can be personalised and customised. Often it will be received and read alone, not in competition with other promotions from other products and services. Extensive and detailed information can be included, much more than with advertising, and product samples may be integral to the direct mail package. Marketing research and database management can lead to accurate targeting of direct mail. Sending material directly to people's homes and workplaces can hit targets otherwise inaccessible to promotional activity.

The primary disadvantage is the growing consumer view that direct mail is 'junk mail' that should be consigned to the dustbin without even being opened. If used on a large scale, direct mail can prove costly – perhaps less so than a salesforce or television advertising, but more expensive than many public relations activities and some local or trade advertising.

***Figure 19.7***
*Direct mail is familiar to most consumers and many business customers*
*Photo © Royalty-Free/CORBIS*

Direct mail packages and campaigns need to be updated to remain fresh in the fight against the junk mail image. In many countries, the paucity of up-to-date mailing lists increases the cost of direct mail, reduces response rates and adds to consumer dislike of the concept of unsolicited direct selling through the post.

For organisations as diverse as retailer Marks & Spencer, financial services group American Express, catalogue retailer Lands' End, charity Oxfam, consumer goods manufacturer Unilever, or British Airways, direct mail is an important, everyday component of the promotional mix. Whether it is on behalf of starving people in less developed countries, double glazing for windows, fast food or book clubs, direct mail is familiar to consumers in most countries. For office supplies, maintenance services, security, computing products, and raw materials and components, in business markets direct mail is another important promotional tool, often supporting trade advertising and personal selling campaigns.

## The Internet

**Internet**
A network of computer networks stretching across the world, linking computers of different types

A few years ago only computer buffs had accessed the **Internet** – a network of computer networks stretching across the world, linking computers of different types – on a regular basis and mostly for on-line discussions or searches for information. Although these are still popular activities, the information superhighway is currently a major focus of attention for marketers of consumer goods, services, charities, industrial products and most business marketing. As more and more businesses hook up to the Internet and thousands of households daily subscribe to Internet services provided by hosts such as MSN, AOL or

BT, the opportunities for interacting with prospective and current customers are immense. By the mid-1990s companies as diverse as Ford, Sony and JCB were providing product and company details on their web pages. Now, most companies and non-profit organisations – small or large – have websites and web links on their advertising, direct mail or brochures.

**Website**
A coherent document readable by a web browser, containing simple text or complex hypermedia presentations

A **website** is a coherent document readable by a web browser, containing simple text or complex hypermedia presentations. At first, these sites tended to be for information purposes rather than overtly promotional tools or selling opportunities. BMW was one of the first businesses to spot the opportunity for selling on the web, creating a directory of used cars available from its network of independent dealerships. A major hindrance to on-line sales and marketing of consumer goods and services was consumer concern about the security of making purchases on-line. Web hosts and credit card companies had to invest in technology that allowed scrambling and coding of confidential credit card or bank account information before consumers were prepared to make on-line purchases.

**E-commerce**
The use of the Internet for commercial transactions

The massive increase in **e-commerce** – the use of the Internet for commercial transactions – has led to greater use of the web by marketers, as described in Chapter 4. As more and more households connect to the Internet through increasing numbers of connections, worldwide confidence in using this medium for transactions is growing. This is not uniform across all consumers. Just as with any new product (see Chapter 17), there are innovators, early adopters and the early majority, while others are resistant to this new way of conducting business, or simply do not have the equipment, expertise or available resources to hook up. Research indicates, however, that there are signs that older consumers, the less affluent and the less educated are now accessing the web. As an ingredient in the promotional mix, there is no doubt that the Internet is of growing importance. While this is not yet true for all countries, it is a trend most observers expect to continue.

**Intranet**
Internal, in-company Internet networks for routine communications, fostering group communications, providing uniform computer applications, distributing the latest software, or informing colleagues of marketing developments and new product launches

The Internet enables frequent and customised changes of messages targeted at specific consumers. If linked to e-mail access, it also enables the consumer to have ready access to the site host, leading to an ongoing and evolving relationship between marketer and customer.[42] Internal marketing has also befriended the web, with **intranets** – in-company Internet networks – facilitating routine communications, fostering group communications, providing uniform computer applications, distributing the latest software, or informing colleagues of marketing developments and new product launches.

There is a clear process for developing a website, which includes:

1 the planning of the site's goals
2 analysis of the required content
3 examination of rival sites
4 design and build of the site
5 implementation using hypertext mark-up language (HTML)
6 ongoing development to ensure that, once up and running, the site reflects user views and is updated regularly.[43]

To be effective, a website must contain information perceived relevant and interesting by a company's targeted customers. Marketers should ensure that their particular targeted customers are in fact prepared and able to access the Internet. The pages of the site need to be stylish and eye-catching but also easy to interpret. Website branding and imagery should be consistent with the brand positioning of existing products, the product's packaging and other promotional mix executions such as advertising and sales promotion materials. The website's ethos must not contradict the work of the rest of the marketing mix or the product's heritage. The information on the website should be updated regularly and accurately, and tailored carefully to reflect the buying behaviour of the targeted customer. As with any marketing activity, the website needs to be designed to be memorable and distinctive.

Far from being a minor task, marketers have realised recently that website design is a specialised activity that requires the skills of a qualified web master and the careful design of material to reflect the characteristics of the product, the brand and of the intended consumer. The findings presented in Table 19.4 summarise a recent survey of UK consumers, revealing their likes and dislikes of a selection of well-known brands' websites. The survey revealed the overriding importance to consumers of interaction, obvious and easy navigation, topical content, relationship-building tools, search engine compliance, ease of use for the first-time user, user friendliness for experienced users, and security of use/payment. E-marketing was discussed in Chapter 4.

## Direct Marketing

So far this chapter has examined personal selling, sales promotion, direct mail and the Internet. To conclude, the chapter turns to one of the current 'in' concepts: direct marketing. This section should be read in conjunction with Chapter 4. First used in the 1960s, until its recent popularity direct marketing described the most common direct marketing approaches: direct mail and mail order. Now direct marketing encompasses all the communications tools that enable a marketer to deal directly with targeted customers: direct mail, telemarketing, direct response television advertising, door-to-door/personal selling and the Internet. Increasingly marketers are utilising the direct marketing toolkit to do more than simply generate sales, although sales generation remains the foremost task for direct marketers.

**Direct marketing**
A decision by a company's marketers to select a marketing channel that avoids dependence on marketing channel intermediaries and to focus marketing communications activity on promotional mix ingredients that deal directly with targeted customers

**Direct marketing** is a decision by a company's marketers to:

1 select a marketing channel that avoids dependence on marketing channel intermediaries
2 focus marketing communications activity on promotional mix ingredients that deal directly with targeted customers.

The American Direct Marketing Association defines direct marketing as 'an interactive system of marketing which uses one or more "advertising" media to effect a measurable

**Table 19.4 The Pros and Cons of Websites**

| Pros | Key issues | Cons |
|---|---|---|
| Clarity | Interaction | Entry page without guidance/menu |
| Non-fussy | Obvious and easy navigation | Confusing |
| Eye-catching | Topical content | Assumes product knowledge |
| Quick loading | Relationship building | Not user-led |
| Search facility | Search engine compliant | Dull |
| Cohesion with brand/MarComms | First time user/experienced user friendly | Out-of-date content |
| Motivational | Security of use/payment | Frustrating |
| The 'right' information | 3 clicks to the desired information | No language options |
| '3 clicks' from everything | | No search facility |
| Pop-up menus | | Unclear navigation |
| Animated links | | Must register to access |
| Rapid printing | | Uncertain payment security |
| No registration | | |
| Search engine compliant | | |
| Use of key words | | |

response and/or transaction at any location'. This definition raises some important aspects, as outlined below.

- Direct marketing is an interactive system. Advertising communicates via a mass medium such as television or the press. Direct marketing contacts targeted consumers directly, can tailor messages to the individual and solicits direct feedback. This interactive, one-to-one communication is essential to the definition of direct marketing.
- The American Direct Marketing Association's definition uses the term 'advertising'; this really should be *communication*[44] in its broader sense, as direct marketing utilises personal selling, direct mail, technology – telephone, fax and the Internet – plus direct response advertising containing coupon response or Freefone elements.
- Most ingredients of the promotional mix, particularly advertising and public relations, find it difficult to accurately measure responses and effectiveness. This is not the case with direct marketing: the interactive nature of the communication enables individual consumer responses to be tracked.
- Direct marketers do not utilise retail outlets, wholesale depots or industrial distributors. They do not depend on potential customers visiting their own retail outlet or depot: they can contact consumers at home or at work via direct mail, telephone or fax, and increasingly via Internet links.

Direct marketing evolved from those mail-order businesses – Littlewoods, GUS, Grattan – that developed catalogues and mailshots to customers in order to sell directly from their warehouses, negating the need for retail outlets and showrooms.[45] They were joined by a diverse mix of businesses – from factory outlets to machine tool companies to specialist food producers – that wished to sell directly to consumers. In order to achieve these aims, these businesses had to devise marketing communications tools that attracted sufficient numbers of the right types of customer who would choose to deal directly with them, rather than buying from the more traditional marketing intermediaries in the marketing channel. The agents, brokers, dealers, distributors, wholesalers and retailers were cut out of the choice of distribution channel. Although mail order sales declined in the 1980s, towards the end of that decade the major operators revitalised their fortunes and were joined by mail-order operations from major retailers such as Marks & Spencer – with its home furnishings catalogue – and the *Next Directory*. Ubiquitous telephone access has helped facilitate mail-order operations, and the recent rapid growth in home computer Internet access has provided a further growth spurt.

Direct marketing is now adopted by a host of businesses ranging from fast-moving consumer goods companies and business marketers to charities and even government departments.[46] Of all elements of the promotional mix, it is reported to be the fastest growing, but this is partly a reflection of the large number of promotional mix ingredients it includes,[47] such as direct mail, teleselling and the Internet. Various factors have contributed to this growth, as detailed in Figure 19.8. A desire by marketers to identify alternative media and promotional tools, the need to improve targeting of potential customers, improvements in marketing data and databases, advances in technology and systems permitting cost-effective direct and interactive contact with certain types of consumers – all have encouraged the growth of direct marketing.

In terms of the promotional mix, direct marketing has several key implications, as follows:

- Direct mail is on the increase: 83 per cent of the largest 1500 UK companies expect to deploy more direct mail, with the bulk focusing on prospecting for sales rather than responding to direct response advertising requests for brochures or catalogues.
- Telemarketing has grown and will continue to do so as more businesses turn to the direct marketing toolkit aided by advances in automated call centres.

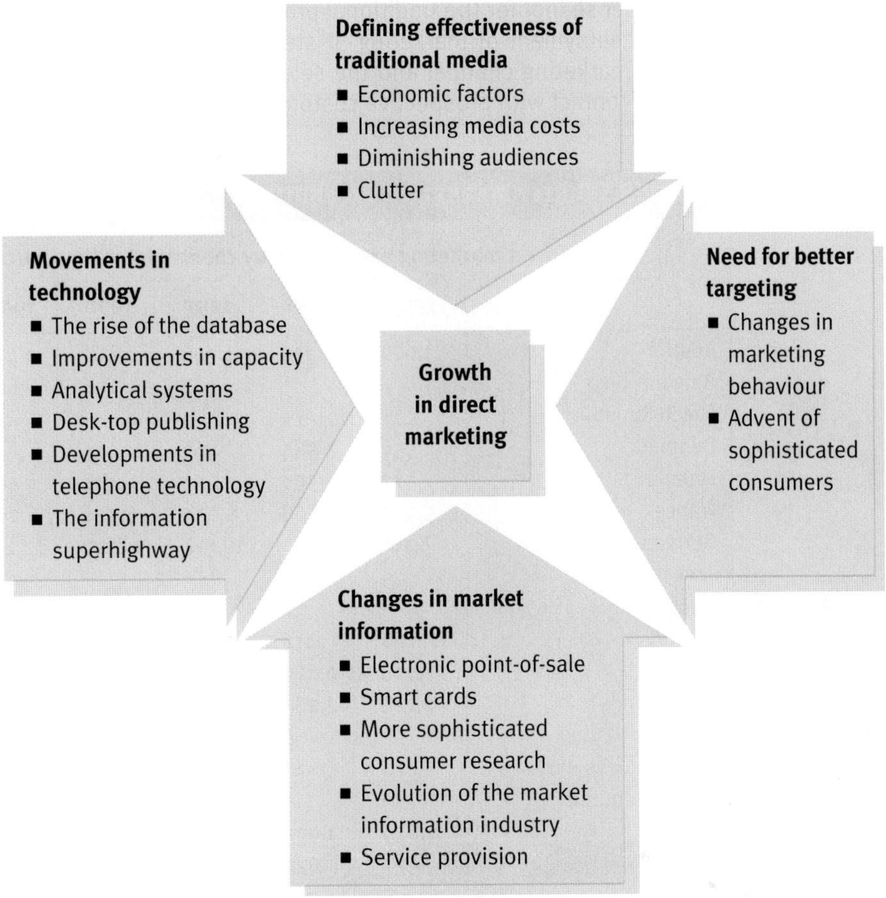


***Figure 19.8***
*Catalysts of change behind the growth of direct marketing*
*Source: Lisa O'Malley, Maurice Patterson and Martin Evans,* Exploring Direct Marketing. *Copyright © 1999, pg. 9. Reprinted with permission of Thomson Learning (EMEA) Ltd*

- Personal selling has suffered in the past from poorly identified sales targeting, but better geodemographic targeting and improved analysis of direct marketing responses are enabling more focused use of personal selling.
- Door-to-door selling and leaflet dropping are also on the increase, and are visible forms of direct marketing encountered by most householders.
- In 1989, direct response advertising – containing a call for action within the advertisement either by coupon or telephone – accounted for less than a fifth of advertising revenue. Now the figure is closer to a third as marketers increasingly jump on the direct marketing 'bandwagon', and as the growth in satellite and cable television channels enables more direct response television advertising.
- The most obvious implication is for use of the Internet to communicate with current and prospective customers. As more and more consumers hook up to the Internet either at home or at work, the opportunity is growing for marketers to communicate directly with consumers with increasingly bespoke messages.

Table 19.5 presents an indication of the growth of direct marketing promotional activity. It is important to remember, however, that – as with all marketing propositions and promotional mix executions – to be welcomed by targeted customers and effective in terms of generating sales, the deployment of any direct marketing campaign must strive to reflect targeted customer behaviour, needs and perceptions; provide a plausible proposition that is clearly differentiated from competitors' propositions; and match an organisation's corporate goals and trading philosophy. Direct marketing is not a substitute for marketing practice per se, nor for the traditional promotional mix. Direct marketing is an increasingly popular deployment of marketing. It stems from certain marketers' strategic choices in terms of marketing channel and the selection of which promotional mix tactics will best facilitate contact with prospective customers.

**TABLE 19.5 DIRECT MARKETING EXPENDITURE**

**a Direct marketing expenditure by country (€ million, current prices)**

| | 1995 | 1996 | 1997 | 1998 | 1999 | 2000 | 2001 |
|---|---|---|---|---|---|---|---|
| Austria | 1,020 | 1,175 | 1,346 | 1,409 | 1,489 | 1,580 | 1,589 |
| Belgium | – | – | 917 | 656 | 660 | 718 | 727 |
| Czech Republic | – | – | – | – | 151 | 192 | 230 |
| Denmark | 554 | 585 | 463 | 475 | 515 | 932 | 997 |
| Finland | 372 | 399 | 423 | 444 | 467 | 493 | 501 |
| France | 5,355 | 5,868 | 6,039 | 6,526 | 6,786 | 7,224 | 7,357 |
| Germany | 8,181 | 9,101 | 10,124 | 11,657 | 12,271 | 13,140 | 12,900 |
| Greece | 5 | – | – | – | – | 57 | 85 |
| Hungary | – | – | – | – | 134 | 152 | 187 |
| Ireland | 100 | 113 | 124 | 20 | 64 | 71 | 78 |
| Italy | 1,926 | 2,062 | 1,443 | 1,865 | 1,969 | 2,641 | 2,689 |
| Netherlands | 2,124 | 2,287 | 2,487 | 3,999 | 4,481 | 4,296 | 4,364 |
| Poland | – | – | – | – | – | 514 | 638 |
| Portugal | 26 | 30 | 35 | 38 | 42 | 54 | 59 |
| Slovak Republic | – | – | – | – | 10 | 14 | 47 |
| Spain | 1,844 | 1,973 | 2,151 | 2,415 | 2,825 | 3,163 | 3,196 |
| Sweden | 577 | 622 | 663 | 671 | 763 | 901 | 868 |
| Switzerland | – | – | – | – | – | 764 | 811 |
| UK | 2,847 | 3,731 | 5,509 | 5,978 | 7,145 | 7,612 | 9,007 |
| **Total** | **24,933** | **27,947** | **31,725** | **36,153** | **39,769** | **44,519** | **46,330** |

**Source:** FEDMA; *The European Marketing Pocket Book,* published by the World Advertising Research Center, Henley-on-Thames, 2004.

**b Expenditure on some direct marketing, UK (£ million)**

| | 1997 | 1998 | 1999 | 2000 | 2001 | 2002 |
|---|---|---|---|---|---|---|
| Direct mail | 1,635 | 1,666 | 1,876 | 2,049 | 2,228 | 2,378 |
| Door-to-door distribution | 353 | 403 | 523 | 523 | 609 | 677 |
| **Total** | **1,988** | **2,069** | **2,399** | **2,572** | **2,837** | **3,055** |

**Sources:** Royal Mail; Direct Marketing Association.

**Source:** *The Marketing Pocket Book,* published by the World Advertising Research Center, Henley-on-Thames, 2004.

# Summary

*Personal selling* is the process of informing customers and persuading them to purchase products through personal communication in an exchange situation. It is the most precise promotional method, but also the most expensive. The three general purposes of personal selling are finding prospects, convincing them to buy and keeping customers satisfied.

- The specialist area of sales management focuses on the importance of preparation, the techniques for introducing sales personnel to prospective customers, the requisites for effective presentations and written proposals, the skills required to turn a potential customer's interest into commitment, how to negotiate, the skills necessary to capture an order, and the ability to close the sale.

- Many sales people – either consciously or unconsciously – move through a general selling process as they sell products. In *prospecting*, the sales person develops a list of potential customers. Before contacting acceptable prospects, the sales person prepares by finding and analysing information about the prospects and their needs. The *approach* is the manner in which a sales person contacts a potential customer. During the sales presentation, the sales person must attract and hold the prospect's attention to stimulate interest and desire for the product. If possible, the sales person should handle a prospect's objections when they arise. *Closing* is the step in the selling process in which the sales person asks the prospect to buy the product or products. After a successful closing, the sales person must follow up the sale.

- In developing a salesforce, a company must decide which types of sales people will sell the company's products most effectively. The three classifications of sales people are *order getters*, *order takers* and *support personnel*. Current customer order getters deal with people who have already purchased a business's products. New business order getters locate prospects and convert them into buyers. Order takers seek repeat sales and fall into two categories: inside order takers and field order takers. Sales support personnel facilitate the selling function, but their duties usually extend beyond making sales. The three types of support personnel are *missionary*, *trade* and *technical sales people*.

- The effectiveness of salesforce management is an important determinant of a company's success because the salesforce is directly responsible for generating a business's sales revenue. The major decision areas and activities on which sales managers must focus are establishing salesforce objectives, determining salesforce size, recruiting and selecting sales personnel, training sales personnel, compensating/remunerating sales personnel, motivating sales people, managing sales territories, and controlling and evaluating salesforce performance.

- Sales objectives should be stated in precise, measurable terms, and should specify the time period, customer type and geographic areas involved. The size of the salesforce must be adjusted from time to time because a business's marketing plans change, as do markets and forces in the marketing environment.

- The task of *recruiting* and selecting sales personnel involves attracting and choosing the right type of sales people to maintain an effective salesforce. When developing a training programme, managers must consider a variety of dimensions, such as who should be trained, what should be taught and how the training should occur. Compensation of sales people involves formulating and administering a compensation/remuneration plan that attracts, motivates and holds the right types of sales people for the business. Choices include a *straight salary compensation/ remuneration plan*, a *straight commission compensation/remuneration plan* and a *combination compensation/remuneration plan*. Motivation of sales people should allow the company to attain high productivity. Managing sales territories, another aspect of salesforce management, focuses on such aspects as the size and shape of sales territories, and the routing and scheduling of sales people. To control and evaluate salesforce performance, the sales manager must use information obtained through sales personnel's call reports, customer feedback and invoices.

» *Sales promotion* is an activity or material (or both) that acts as a direct inducement and offers added value to, or incentive to, buy the product to resellers, sales people or consumers. The *ratchet effect* is the stepped impact of using sales promotion and advertising together. Marketers use sales promotion to increase sales, to identify and attract new customers, to introduce a new product and to increase reseller inventories. Sales promotion methods fall into two general categories: consumer and trade. *Consumer sales promotion techniques* encourage consumers to buy from specific retail stores or dealerships or to try a specific product. These techniques include *coupons*, *demonstrations*, *frequent user incentives* – such as *loyalty cards* or *trading stamps* – *point-of-sale (POS) materials*, *free samples*, *money refunds*, *premiums*, *price-off offers*, and *consumer contests* and *sweepstakes*. *Trade sales promotion methods* stimulate wholesalers, retailers or dealers to carry a producer's products and to market those products aggressively. These techniques include *buy-back allowances*, *buying allowances*, *counts and re-counts*, *free merchandise*, *merchandise allowances*, *cooperative advertising*, *dealer listings*, *premium* or *push money*, *sales competitions* and *dealer loaders*.

» *Direct mail* uses the postal service to contact prospective customers or donors, and to solicit interest in products or services. The main problem facing the direct mail industry is the growing adverse reaction to it as *junk mail*. Nevertheless, direct mail is widely used for consumer goods and services, and also in business marketing. Increasingly, it is also important to non-profit organisations and charitable fundraising. Direct mail must be designed carefully, with an attention-seeking *flash*, good *copy writing* and a well-constructed *direct mail package*. *Mailing lists* quickly become obsolete, and good database management is essential for the effective targeting of direct mailshots.

» The *Internet*, networked independent computers, is no longer just for computer buffs. Users are multiplying daily, including both consumers and businesses seeking to interact with prospective and current customers. Most businesses now have *websites* and recognise the potential for *e-commerce*. Scrambling and coding of credit card information has helped build consumer confidence in on-line purchase transactions. Websites are clearly flagged on much television and print advertising. In-company Internet networks – *intranets* – are enabling the rapid dissemination of routine communications, group communications, uniform computer applications, the latest software and information about product developments, and are assisting with internal marketing. Enabling frequent updating of messages, individually targeted communications and sales ordering, the Internet now features in many businesses' promotional mixes.

» To be popular with consumers, research reveals that websites must offer interaction, obvious and easy navigation, topical content, relationship-building tools, search engine compliance, ease of use for first-time users and user-friendliness to experienced users, and security of use/payment.

» *Direct marketing* is a decision to do without marketing channel intermediaries and to focus most promotional resources on activities that deal directly with targeted customers, such as personal selling, telemarketing and direct mail. Now adopted by consumer goods producers, services, business companies, charities and even government departments, direct marketing has recently enjoyed rapid growth. This is likely to continue, with more direct mail, automated call centres, personal selling, door-to-door selling and leaflet dropping, direct response television advertising and use of the Internet to contact potential customers. As with Internet sites, direct marketing must be tailored to suit the behaviour and expectations of the target audience, while reflecting existing branding and other promotional mix designs.

## Key Links

This chapter has explored various aspects of the promotional mix, but not all. It has also examined the use of the web in marketing from the perspective of marketing communications. Related chapters, therefore, include:

- Chapter 4, on technology in marketing
- Chapter 17, on the role of marketing communications and the ingredients of the promotional mix
- Chapter 18, on the use of advertising, public relations and sponsorship in the promotional mix.

## Important Terms

Personal selling
Prospecting
Approach
Closing
Order getters
Order takers
Support personnel
Missionary sales people
Trade sales people
Technical sales people
Recruiting
Straight salary compensation/remuneration plan
Straight commission compensation/remuneration plan
Combination compensation/remuneration plan
Sales promotion
Ratchet effect
Consumer sales promotion techniques
Trade sales promotion methods
Coupons
Demonstrations
Frequent user incentives
Loyalty card
Trading stamps
Point-of-sale (POS) materials
Free samples
Money refunds
Premiums
Price-off offers
Consumer contests
Consumer sweepstakes
Buy-back allowance
Buying allowance
Count and re-count
Free merchandise
Merchandise allowance
Cooperative advertising
Dealer listing
Premium or push money
Sales competition
Dealer loader
Direct mail
Junk mail
Flashes
Direct mail package
Mailing lists
Copy writing
Internet
Website
E-commerce
Intranet
Direct marketing

## Discussion and Review Questions

1 What is personal selling? How does personal selling differ from other types of promotional activity?
2 What are the primary purposes of personal selling?
3 Identify the elements of the personal selling process. Must a sales person include all of these elements when selling a product to a customer? Why or why not?
4 How does a sales person find and evaluate prospects? Do you find any of these methods ethically questionable?
5 Are order getters more aggressive or creative than order takers? Why or why not?
6 Identify several characteristics of effective sales objectives.
7 How should a sales manager establish criteria for selecting sales personnel? What are the general characteristics of a good sales person?
8 What major issues or questions should be considered when developing a salesforce training programme?
9 Explain the major advantages and disadvantages of the three basic methods of compensating sales people. In general, which method do you prefer? Why?
10 What major factors should be taken into account when designing the size and shape of a sales territory?
11 How does a sales manager – who cannot be with each sales person in the field on a daily basis – control the performance of sales personnel?
12 What is sales promotion? Why is it used?
13 Does sales promotion work well in isolation from the other promotional mix elements?
14 For each of the following, identify and describe three techniques and give several examples:
(a) consumer sales promotion techniques, and
(b) trade sales promotion methods.
15 What types of sales promotion methods have you observed recently?
16 How does direct mail gain the interest of its recipients?
17 What are the problems facing users of direct mail?
18 Marketers initially viewed the Internet primarily as a means to disseminate product and manufacturer information. What technological advances had to be

made before the Internet could be used for selling opportunities?

19 What are the essential requirements for a website likely to appeal to targeted consumers?

20 In what ways is direct marketing an 'interactive' system? Which marketing channel intermediaries are bypassed due to the nature of this system?

## Recommended Readings


- Belch, G. and Belch, M., *Advertising and Promotion: an Integrated Marketing Communications Perspective* (New York: McGraw-Hill, 2003).
- Bird, D., *Commonsense Direct Marketing* (London: Kogan Page, 2000).
- Clay, J., *Successful Selling Solutions* (London: Thorogood, 2003).
- Cummins, J. and Mullin, R., *Sales Promotion: How to Create and Implement Campaigns that Really Work* (London: Kogan Page, 1998).
- Dalrymple, D.J., Cron, W.L. and DeCarlo, T., *Sales Management* (Hokboken, NJ: Wiley, 2000).
- Honeycutt, E.D., Ford, J.B. and Simintiras, A., *Sales Management: A Global Perspective* (London: Routledge, 2003).
- Jobber, D. and Lancaster, G., *Selling and Sales Management* (Harlow: Pearson Education, 2003).
- O'Malley, L., Patterson, M. and Evans, M., *Exploring Direct Marketing* (London: Thomson Learning, 1999).
- Percy, L., Rossiter, J. and Elliott, R., *Strategic Advertising Management* (Oxford: Oxford University Press, 2001).
- Sargeant, A. and West, D.C., *Direct and Interactive Marketing* (Oxford: Butterworth Heinemann, 2001).
- Shimp, T.A., *Advertising, Promotion and Supplemental Aspects of Integrated Marketing Communications* (Cincinnati, OH: South Western, 2002).
- Thomas, B. and Housden, M., *Direct Marketing in Practice* (Oxford: Butterworth-Heinemann, 2001).


## Internet Exercise

Consider any one of your favourite brands. Log on to its website.

1 In what ways is this site finding out information about you and your product needs?

2 To what extent does the information presented help inform you of the brand's attributes and competitive advantage?

3 How would you modify this website to improve its functionality? Why?

## *Applied Mini-Case*

Many medium-sized business-to-business companies employ small salesforces, attend trade shows that present their category of products and attract relevant business customers, develop limited advertising, construct websites, direct mail their sales prospects and use publicity whenever they have anything worth publicising.

### *Question*

As a new marketing manager in such a business faced with a limited budget, how would you determine which aspects of the promotional mix should be utilised?

## *Case Study*

## Promoting Free Flights: How Hoover Came Unstuck

Whether Sainsbury's and Boots with BA, Boots and railways, Sony with Thomas Cook, or Bird's Eye Menumaster with National Express Coaches, retailers and manufacturers have frequently negotiated with carriers to offer free travel or holidays to boost sales. The depressed holiday industry has welcomed the opportunity to use excess capacity and increase demand. It was not too surprising when in 1992 consumer electronics giant Hoover joined the ranks of manufacturers offering free trips in order to stimulate demand for its white goods, first by offering free tickets to Europe with purchases of more than £100, then by extending the promotion to include free tickets to the USA. What was not predictable was the adverse publicity the scheme brought for Hoover.

The second promotion was supported by a high-profile £1 million television campaign. The offer included two free flights to either Orlando or New York for every purchase over £100, with an additional £60 towards car hire and accommodation for purchases over £300. Hoover claimed that the tickets into Europe had constituted its most successful promotion ever, putting its £130 vacuum cleaner ahead of its £100 model and making its £380 washing machine more popular than its £300 model.

In November 1992 a *Daily Record* story, 'Hoover's flight shocker', started the trouble. This story alleged that none of the airlines Hoover claimed was involved in the US deal had any knowledge of the scheme and that Hoover had yet to reserve a single airline seat. The article also stated that the sales promotion company behind the offer was £500,000 in debt. In response, Hoover launched a major damage limitation exercise, including full-page adverts assuring people that there was no mystery, that the offer was genuine and that free flights were available. Hoover's problems did not end there, however. Media attention increased, as did stories of disgruntled consumers.

From BBC consumer affairs programme *Watchdog* to the House of Commons, questions were asked about the ethics of the deal and the apparently unfair treatment of hundreds of annoyed consumers who, having purchased a Hoover product and received their vouchers, had actually attempted to claim their prizes. Many potential holidaymakers could not get first or even second choices of dates or destination. Many were refused their choices so often that Hoover's promotions company refused to permit any travel! Over 70 MPs demanded a Parliamentary investigation. Eventually, the Office of Fair Trading was brought in to investigate.

Hoover – now under different ownership – had intended neither to mislead nor to disappoint its customers, but the promotion nevertheless severely affected the company's reputation. Circumstances combined in several well-publicised cases to make a deteriorating situation even worse for the company. What began as a sales-boosting, attention-getting sales promotion rapidly turned into a damaging public relations nightmare for Hoover. Key directors were dismissed and the US parent company had to shell out millions of pounds to meet travellers' demands for their prizes. Some 12 months later, disputes had still to be settled.

US parent, Maytag Corp., had bought Britain's Hoover for US$320 million in 1989. In 1995, Maytag sold its European operation to an Italian company at a loss of US$135 million. The freeflights promotion was, as described in many newspapers, 'a fiasco', damaging not just this type of promotional activity but, more severely, the Hoover brand name and even the viability of the company. High-profile court cases pursued by disgruntled consumers only made matters worse. Over a decade later, consumers and retailers still remember this disastrous marketing communications campaign.

**Sources:** Clare Sambrook, 'Do free flights really build brands?', *Marketing*, 15 October 1992, p. 11; Mat Toor, 'Hoover retaliates over flights offer', *Marketing*, 3 December 1992, p. 3; Robert Dwek, 'Hoover extends its free flights deal', *Marketing*, 29 October 1992, p. 16; BBC and ITN television news broadcasts, March and April 1993; Chris Knight, 'Direct route', *Marketing Week*, 8 September 1995, pp. 58–9; Marcia Berss, 'Whirlpool's bloody nose', *Forbes*, 11 March 1996, pp. 90–2.

### Questions for Discussion

1. How damaging to the Hoover name and reputation was this sales promotion campaign?
2. How could Hoover have avoided these problems?
3. How, in the light of this promotional disaster, should Hoover have utilised the public relations toolkit to overcome the adverse publicity?

# Postscript

The promotion ingredient of the marketing mix addresses how a business promotes itself and its products to its target publics and target audiences. The decisions made by marketers concerning promotion – marketing communications – affect how an organisation communicates with its target markets; how consumers are made aware of its products, services and activities; and how marketers expect to explain their determined brand positioning strategies. The chapters in Part V of *Marketing: Concepts and Strategies* have explained the core aspects of the promotional mix – advertising, publicity and public relations, sponsorship, personal selling, sales promotion, direct mail and the web – and many of the key current trends and developments in the sphere of marketing communications, such as use of the Internet and direct marketing. The concept of integrated marketing communications (IMC) has also been presented.

Before progressing, readers should be confident that they are now able to do the following.

## Explain the role of promotion and communication in marketing

- What is the role of promotion in the marketing mix?
- What is the process of communication?
- What is meant by marketing communications?
- How does the product adoption process relate to promotional activity?
- What are the aims of promotion?
- What are the elements of the promotional mix?
- How do businesses select which promotional mix ingredients to use?
- What is the role of integrated marketing communications (IMC)?

## Describe the use of advertising, publicity and sponsorship

- What are the uses of advertising?
- What are the steps involved in developing an advertising campaign and whom do they involve?
- What is publicity?
- What is the nature of public relations?
- What current trends are altering the work of advertising agencies and public relations consultancies?
- What is meant by sponsorship in marketing terms?
- How is sponsorship used by marketers?

## Describe the use of personal selling, sales promotion, direct mail, the Internet and direct marketing

- What are the purposes, steps and types of personal selling?
- What are the principal tasks of sales management?
- What are the uses of sales promotion?
- What are the methods and tools of sales promotion?
- What does direct mail involve?
- What is the role of direct mail within the promotional mix?
- How are marketers using the Internet in promotional strategies?
- What is direct marketing?
- Which ingredients of the promotional mix are utilised by direct marketers?

*Strategic Case*

# Birmingham Women's Hospital
## Giving Birth: the Consumer's Choice!

The provision of maternity services is an area of healthcare that most people encounter at some point in their adult life. Despite being a significant life event, until relatively recently most women in the UK having a baby had very little control over the healthcare side of the maternity experience. The type of care on offer was largely outside a patient's control and usually determined more by locality than by patient choice. The characteristics of ante-natal care, the maternity unit where delivery took place and even the position adopted during labour, were all likely to be predetermined by others.

In recent years, much has changed. The UK government's Changing Childbirth report, compiled in 1992, indicated that women should be offered choice in their maternity provision. Regulatory changes, allowing general practitioners (doctors) more flexibility in where they are allowed to refer their patients, have helped foster a greater sense of choice. Recent government initiatives to increase patient control over these decisions have underlined this change. Social changes have led to people becoming more proactive in making decisions about issues affecting their lives. As consumers, for example, they are more likely than ever to change their bank account, shop around for insurance or buy products over the Internet. In such an environment, it is no surprise that women are increasingly likely to exert control over maternity decisions. This tendency has been supported by advances in technology that have made information about maternity services much more readily available.

Today's expectant mother and her partner now have far more control over the ante-natal and birthing process than previously. There is greater flexibility in the style of ante-natal care on offer. Perhaps the most significant issue is that women can now choose the hospital unit at which they deliver their baby. This is important because it is the characteristics of the unit, more than any other factor, that impact on the maternity care received:

> What happens to you during labour will probably depend less on what you say you want to happen than on where you choose to have your baby. The simple fact is that between two similar hospitals, you could be twice as likely to be delivered by caesarean section in one than in the other. Your postcode will often determine whether you are more likely to be induced, be assisted by forceps, or be elected for caesarean section. Your chances of benefiting from the latest antenatal scans and tests, as well as being offered a full range of pain relief also depend on which hospital you go to.
>
> *dr foster Good Birth Guide*
> (London: Vermilion, 2002, p. 10)

It is now common practice for medical staff to encourage women to write their own birth plans. Such a document describes the patient's preferences for all aspects of delivery from pain relief to monitoring and intervention. The patient's desire to exercise some form of control over this important life event is consistent with changes in how people live. Women have grown accustomed to exercising control over other aspects of their lives and careers: this expectation has been extended to the antenatal and birth experience. From the patient's viewpoint, the provision of maternity care is just like any other service.

How busy a maternity unit becomes is now partly affected by the preferences of expectant mothers. A greater level of hospital responsiveness is, therefore, needed to ensure that the needs and wants of these patients are met. Hospitals and their staff must be more aware of 'consumer' expectations, demands and information requirements. One implication is that many hospital units have been forced to devote far greater attention to the ways in which they are branded and perceived in the maternity 'marketplace', requiring improved marketing communications and more tailoring of information.

Ensuring that the services provided are acceptable to patients is a complex task. While the provision of good-quality patient care is paramount, the service on offer extends beyond the purely medical. In addition to the medical provision, units have to provide appropriate facilities with a mix of amenities to cater for patients and their visitors. The hospital environment should be amenable to the well-being of its users. Appropriate processes must be in place to control the smooth flow of patients through the unit. The mix of medical and support staff has to be managed carefully to ensure that units can cater for the peaks and troughs associated with demand for maternity services.

## The Role of Information

The decision process involved in making choices about ante-natal and delivery care is driven by the availability of information. Women making these decisions acquire this information from a variety of informal and formal sources. Some will rely on previous experiences of childbirth, either their own or those of their friends and acquaintances. Others will discuss the options with their family doctor or midwife. Some will consult the increasing array of pregnancy- and birth-related publications, or tune in to a relevant television programme or radio broadcast. Overall, an increasingly diverse array of sources is available. Pregnancy books, parenting magazines, specialist websites, midwife groups and organisations dealing with birth issues, all provide advice on how this can be achieved.

The *dr foster Good Birth Guide* is freely available on the Internet or at low cost through major bookstores. This independent guide, which is one of a range available covering health services in the UK, has been compiled under the supervision of an ethics committee of leading medical professionals. The *Good Birth Guide* contains information on all the UK's maternity units, so that comparisons can be made regarding the numbers of home births, rates of caesareans and levels of intervention during delivery. The guide also includes descriptive information capturing the characteristics of each unit.

The BirthChoiceUK website (http://www.birthchoiceuk.com) was set up to help parents make informed choices about their maternity care. The website objectives are as follows:

> For women throughout the United Kingdom there are several options for birth. This may mean choosing a particular place to give birth, such as at home, in a small maternity unit or in one of a number of hospitals. Or it could involve choosing the type of maternity care, such as care shared between a GP and a midwife, or being cared for by a team of community midwives attached to a hospital, or by an independent midwife. This website aims to bring together information to enable prospective parents to make these choices. This website does not favour one place of birth over any other, nor one type of maternity care over any other. Instead, it encourages readers to ask questions of themselves and their healthcare providers to help them make choices which will result in the birth experiences they wish for.
>
> http://www.birthchoiceuk.com/AboutWebsite.htm

The BirthChoiceUK website encourages prospective parents to visit their chosen unit and there are tips on the kinds of question to ask about facilities and services. Guidance is given on the booking-in process. The website also provides additional features designed to support those seeking further information. Further reading is offered on a variety of issues and a range of maternity-related research findings is explored. An extensive reference list of publications supporting the information provided is also available. Finally, the website provides web links to the following sources, among others:

- NCT Pregnancy and Babycare: the National Childbirth Trust (NCT) offers advice on pregnancy, birth and parenthood.
- AIMS (Association for Improvements in Maternity Services): details on maternity choices.
- *dr foster*: statistics and information on maternity units.
- Independent Midwives' Association: a register that enables patients to contact a local independent midwife.
- Association of Radical Midwives: information about birth choices.
- Home Birth Reference Site: guidance for those considering a home birth.

- MIDIRS (Midwives' Information and Resource Service): provides a series of 'Informed Choice' leaflets for patients and healthcare professionals, as well as the Informed Choice database.
- VBAC (Vaginal Birth After Caesarean): information on the birth options for mothers who have previously delivered by caesarean section.
- Sheila Kitzinger: author who campaigns for women's rights in childbirth.

## Birmingham Women's Hospital

Birmingham Women's Healthcare NHS Trust, which manages Birmingham Women's Hospital, was established in 1993. The unit provides care exclusively for women and is a teaching hospital linked to Birmingham University's Medical School. As a regional referral unit, the hospital provides maternity services for the local community in Birmingham and for more complex cases from the West Midlands as a whole. The Trust operates ante-natal clinics, offers pre-pregnancy counselling and specialises in care for patients following miscarriage or bereavement. There is also an assisted conception unit, which provides fertility treatment. In addition, the Trust runs a foetal medicine unit, which offers specialist care in relation to various foetal and maternal conditions, has a 32-cot Neonatal Intensive Care Unit to treat sick and premature babies, and provides care in the areas of genetics and gynaecology. The hospital is also home to the regional Human Milk Bank, offering a service for collecting and pasteurising donor breast milk. The donated milk is circulated to neo-natal units in the Midlands and further afield for premature and sick babies whose mothers are unable to breast feed.

Birmingham Women's Hospital is a large unit, responsible for the delivery of around 6000 babies each year. Not all women who deliver their babies at the hospital attend the unit for their ante-natal care. Some patients are completely or predominantly looked after by their local midwife and family doctor, while others may have some or all of their ante-natal care at the unit. The delivery statistics for Birmingham Women's Hospital are, to a degree, influenced by the number of complex cases referred to the unit from elsewhere. The delivery suite itself is able to cater for all kinds of births, ranging from different forms of normal delivery including water births, through to caesarean section and instrumental delivery – the use of forceps and venthouse. A full range of pain-relief options is generally available and women have the opportunity to visit and look around the unit prior to their expected due date. The patient's wishes are genuinely regarded as a key priority when determining the characteristics of care.

**Birmingham Women's Hospital Basic Features**

| Birmingham Women's Hospital basic features | |
|---|---|
| Number of beds | 98 |
| Births per midwife per year | 33 |
| Births per bed per day | 1.20 |
| Home births | 1% |
| Obstetrician available 24 hours | Yes |
| Paediatrician available 24 hours | Yes |
| Epidural pain relief 24 hours | Yes |

**Source:** adapted from *dr foster Good Birth Guide*, www.drfoster.co.uk

There is a strong focus on the provision of information for patients and visitors. Information leaflets on a wide range of topics are freely available on stands in the public areas of the hospital. There are many noticeboards displaying information on areas such as blood donation and NHS Direct (the telephone helpline members of the public can call with queries about their health). There is also a feature on the hospital's Assisted Conception Unit, together with leaflets seeking sperm donors. The provision of information in different languages helps cater for diverse ethnic catchments. For example, the 'Your Guide to the NHS' leaflet is available in many different Asian languages. Some leaflets are specific to maternity patients, who receive a welcome pack at their booking-in visit. This pack contains information about the ante-natal period, a free pregnancy magazine, and various product samples and coupons deemed appropriate for expectant mothers. A second pack containing further leaflets, product information and samples targeted at new mothers and their babies is offered to patients who deliver at the hospital. A typical pack might include leaflets on breast-feeding and the dangers of cot death, together with samples of nappy cream, detergent or fabric conditioner. There is also an option to receive a further two packs during the baby's first year.

The information theme is a particular focus in the hospital's innovative health shop. This area, which is located close to the main entrance, provides a wealth of information leaflets and posters about health-related issues and voluntary groups. The 'shop' is open to patients, the public and staff seeking information on a wide range of topics.

## Providing the Care Desired by Patients

As the emphasis on choice in maternity services increases, there is more pressure on hospitals to be responsive. Women are increasingly likely to review and compare a number of alternative care providers. Although quality of care will almost certainly remain the paramount consideration, many other aspects of the ante-natal and delivery experience are likely to influence the decisions that are made. The implications for units such as Birmingham Women's Hospital are clear. In particular, the need to understand and respond to the expectations of patients is greater than ever. The hospital has also to devote more resources to creating a brand reputation and communicating to prospective parents through an increasing array of marketing communications channels.

## Questions for Discussion

1. Given the nature of the 'buying process' for maternity care, what is the role of marketing communications?
2. What are the key pieces of information required by prospective parents? How can these best be communicated to this target audience?
3. What is the role of the Internet in patients' search for information? How must Birmingham Women's Hospital respond to the role of the web?

# VI Pricing Decisions

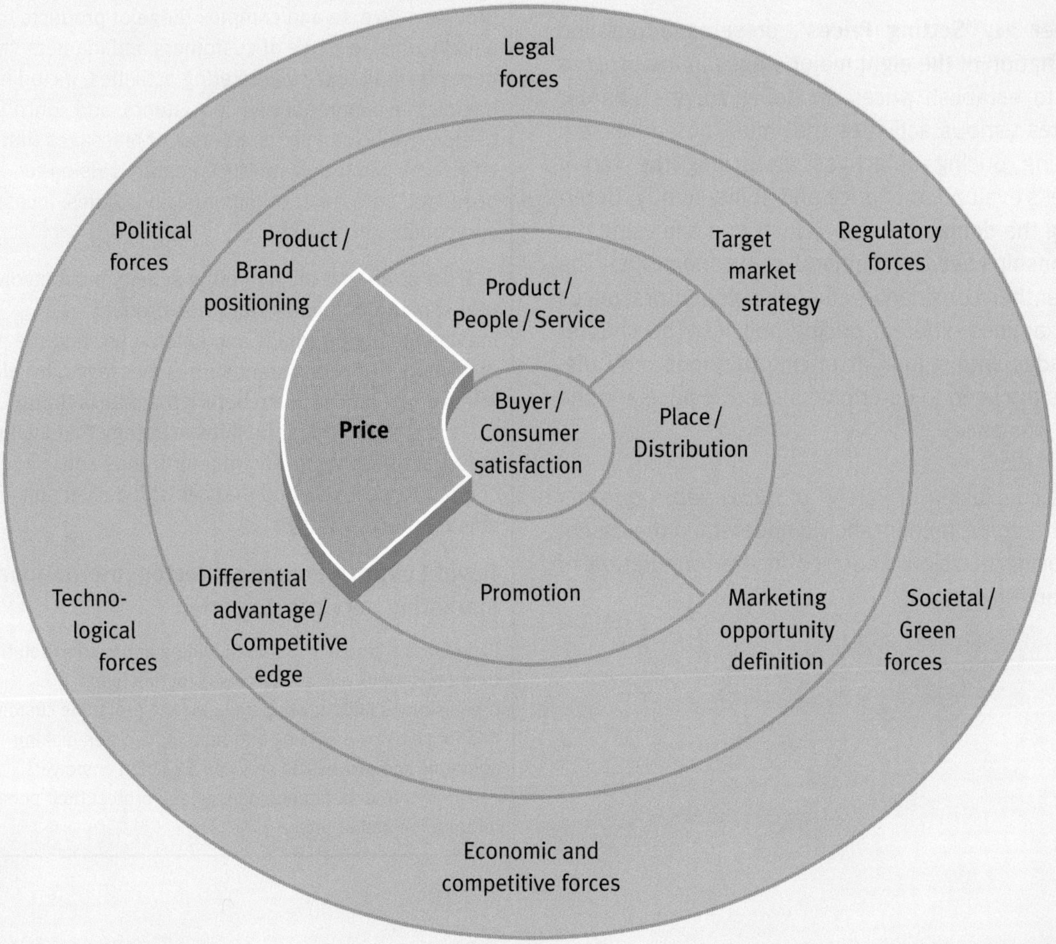


The price of a product or service will determine how consumers perceive it, reflect on its brand positioning, influence the choice of marketing channel, affect how it is promoted and have an impact on the level of customer service expected by target consumers. The price ingredient of the marketing mix will also strongly affect the viability of the supplying organisation. The pricing decisions for a business must take into account consumers' notion of value and reflect the pricing strategies of competitors' products. The concept of pricing is complex, but as a marketing mix ingredient it is of fundamental importance to the successful implementation of a marketing strategy.

**Part VI of *Marketing: Concepts and Strategies*** explains the principal concepts of pricing and the setting of prices.

**Chapter 20, 'Pricing Concepts'**, explains the characteristics and role of price in marketing, outlines the differences between price and non-price competition, examines different pricing objectives and explores key factors that affect marketers' pricing decisions.

The chapter then discusses perceived value for money before turning to the complex aspect of pricing in business markets. The chapter concludes by analysing the concept of economic value to the customer.

**Chapter 21, 'Setting Prices'**, presents a detailed examination of the eight major stages in the process used to establish prices. In doing so, the chapter explores various activities that must be addressed: selecting pricing objectives; assessing the target market's evaluation of price and ability to buy; determining the demand for a product; and analysing the relationships between demand, costs and profits. The chapter then considers evaluating competitors' prices and examines different pricing policies. The chapter concludes with a look at pricing methods, and discusses the need to determine a specific price and the 'pricing balance'.

By the conclusion of Part VI of *Marketing: Concepts and Strategies*, readers should understand the essential pricing decisions required in the formulation of the marketing mix.

## Experian

The first important thing is to have a clear vision of what you want to be – particularly when you provide a diverse and complex range of products to an equally diverse range of customers and markets. It becomes vital that *all* marketing activities, including pricing, have a predefined consistency, and contribute to an overall clear and simple set of messages that effectively communicate the company's vision to business customers, consumers, colleagues, investors and communities alike.

It's a given that all marketing activity must involve *robust* market planning, rigorous product management – internally and externally – and the development of consistent simple messages, for all relevant audiences. Even before that starts though, there has to be a clear business strategy that evaluates macro-economic and market trends and competitive activity, and that can still deliver sustainable market advantage.

**David Coupe, managing director, international marketing services, Experian**

Experian is a global leader in providing information solutions to organisations and consumers. Experian helps organisations find, develop and manage profitable customer relationships by providing information, decision-making solutions and processing services. Experian empowers consumers to understand, manage and protect their personal information and assets.

# 20 Pricing Concepts

**"The task of setting a price is one of the most important decisions in determining the marketing mix."**

*Peter Leeflang, Rijksuniversiteit Groningen*

**Price**
The value placed on what is exchanged

**Financial price**
The basis of market exchanges; the quantified value of what is exchanged

## Objectives

- To understand the characteristics and role of price
- To be aware of the differences between price and non-price competition
- To explore key factors that affect pricing decisions
- To examine different pricing objectives
- To understand perceived value for money and how it affects consumers' decisions
- To consider issues unique to the pricing of products for business markets
- To analyse the concept of economic value to the customer

## Introduction

To a buyer, **price** is the value placed on what is exchanged.[1] Something of value – usually buying power – is exchanged for satisfaction or utility. In most marketing situations, the price is very evident, and buyer and seller are aware of the amount of value each must give up to complete the exchange.[2] As described in Chapter 3, buying power depends on a buyer's income, credit and wealth. Because buyers have limited resources they must weigh up the usefulness of a product or the satisfaction derived from it against its cost to decide whether the exchange is worthwhile. **Financial price** is most usually the basis of market exchanges. This can be used to quantify almost anything of value that is exchanged, including ideas, services, rights and goods. Thus the financial value of a Paris penthouse might be 1.5 million euros. Yet price does not always have to have a financial basis. Barter, the trading of products, is the oldest form of exchange.

Price impacts strongly on how businesses fare competitively, so marketers need to give careful consideration to pricing issues. Price is critical to the marketing mix because it affects directly how much revenue is generated. As it can be changed very quickly, price is more flexible than other marketing mix elements. Businesses must avoid seeing price purely in terms of setting monetary price points. Because of the psychological impact of price on customers, price also has a symbolic value. It is therefore desirable to take a broader view of pricing, which takes into account issues such as target customers' perceptions of value for money and requirements for easy payment terms.

*Opener*

# Shoe Buying: What's Afoot?

Some people are just fanatical about shoes. Women are apparently particularly vulnerable to this passion. The recent launch of glossy magazine *Shoo*, featuring the latest in shoe designs and accessories, is testament to the depth of feeling footwear attracts. Some believe that this attraction can be traced back to the days when, as little girls, these women were fascinated with donning their mother's best stilettos and turning out the intriguing contents of their handbags. Of course, the current obsession with shoes is not new. Marie-Antoinette was said to have owned around 500 pairs of footwear, while the shoe collection of Imelda Marcos (reportedly numbering more than 1000 pairs) remains legendary.

Today's interest in footwear follows a resurgence in interest during the 1990s, with the best shoe designers achieving similar levels of acclaim to clothes designers. Pop stars and style icons have helped bring the need for perfectly attired toes to the attention of the current shoe-buying public. In the recent hit TV comedy series *Sex And The City*, the hugely popular character Carrie was almost as famous for her shoes as for her relationships. For those with particularly large shoe collections, the trend is to adhere photographs of the contents of each shoe box to the front of the container so that the required pair can be accessed readily. Among the most aspirational of brands are Manolo Blahnik, Jimmy Choo and Christian Louboutin. With prices ranging from several hundred pounds upwards, designer shoe brands are not a passion that everyone can afford.

Yet while some shoe aficionados are prepared to commit their savings and join waiting lists to acquire the latest prestigious offerings from the best designers, other women happily shop for more modest footwear in their local shopping centres. Some prefer to buy good-quality but much cheaper high-street brands. For example, styles by manufacturers like Clarkes, K Shoes and Seibel start from below £50 (€75). Other buyers spend time and effort tracking down even lower prices. As those frequenting markets around Europe can testify, bargain prices of less than £10 (€15) can readily be found. So why is it that some women are prepared to commit up to a month's pay for a pair of designer shoes that they may wear on only a handful of occasions? What is it that drives these individuals to fill every available space in their homes with the latest designs? Why, at the other extreme, are other shoes buyers apparently just as happy to adopt more price-conscious solutions to their footwear needs? And, why are many men completely disinterested in shoe buying?

**Sources:** Robina Dam, 'Head over heels', *Hildon Magazine*, Autumn/Winter 2003, pp. 20–3; John Roedder.
Photo: Courtesy of Karen Beaulah

All shoe companies, irrespective of whether their products are costly or cheap, use price, along with other elements, to distinguish their products from competitive brands. For these companies, as for most businesses, pricing is a crucial element in the marketing mix. However, as this chapter's 'Opener' clearly illustrates, a variety of factors impact upon pricing decisions. For example, perceptions about price vary for different shoe-buying consumers. This and other factors affecting pricing are considered later in this chapter.

This chapter begins by explaining what is meant by price and considers its importance to marketing practitioners. It then explores pricing objectives and the various factors affecting pricing decisions. The notion of perceived value for money is considered next. The chapter concludes by examining pricing in business markets and the concept of economic value to the customer.

# The Characteristics and Role of Price

## Terms Used to Describe Price

Price is expressed differently in different exchanges. For instance, insurance companies charge a *premium* to holidaymakers requiring protection against the cost of illness or injury. A police officer who stops a motorist for speeding writes a ticket that requires a *fine* to be paid. In London, a congestion *charge* is levied on motorists travelling in central areas. An accountant charges a *fee*, and a *fare* is charged for travelling by plane, railway or taxi. A *toll* is sometimes charged for the use of motorway bridges. *Rent* is paid for the use of equipment or for a flat. An estate agent receives a *commission* on the sale of a property. A *deposit* is made to reserve merchandise. A *tip* helps pay waitresses or waiters for their services. *Interest* is charged for loans, and *taxes* are paid for government services. The value of many products is called *price*.

Although price may be expressed in a variety of ways, it is important to remember that the purpose of this concept is to quantify and express the value of the items in a marketing exchange.

## The Importance of Price to Marketers

As pointed out in Chapter 12, developing a product may be a lengthy process. It takes time to plan promotion and to communicate benefits. Distribution usually requires a long-term commitment to dealers who will handle the product. Often price and customer service levels are the only aspects a marketer can change quickly to respond to changes in demand or to the actions of competitors. However, as customers may be alienated by significant price changes, this does not mean that price is flexible in all situations.

Price is also a key element in the marketing mix because it relates directly to the generation of total revenue.[3] The following equation is an important one for the entire organisation:

Profits = total revenues − total costs
or
Profits = (price × quantities sold) − total costs

Prices can have a dramatic impact on a company's profits. Price affects the profit equation in several ways. It directly influences the equation because it is a major component. It has an indirect impact because it can be a major determinant of the quantities sold. Even more indirectly, price influences total costs through its impact on quantities sold.[4]

Table 20.1 illustrates clearly the link between price and a company's profitability. As the table shows, for a business with a 40 per cent contribution margin and a 10 per cent net profit, even a relatively small change in the prices set can have a major impact on profit levels. Thus a 10 per cent reduction in price would cause profits to fall to zero, while a 10 per cent rise would double the level of profitability. It is also important to consider that a 10 per cent increase or decrease in volume would have a rather smaller impact on profits. Marketers need to be fully aware of these stark relationships when setting prices. In particular, this example

**TABLE 20.1 THE IMPORTANCE OF PRICE CHANGE TO PROFITABILITY**

**Income statement: Alpha Products**

| | £ million | |
|---|---|---|
| *Turnover* | | 200 |
| Discounts and allowances | 30 | |
| Materials | 30 | |
| Direct labour | 40 | |
| Other variable costs | 20 | – |
| *Profit contribution* | | 80 |
| Marketing and advertising | 10 | |
| Research and development | 10 | |
| Fixed costs | 40 | – |
| *Net profit* | | 20 |

*Sensitivity analysis*: Effect of 10% changes in price and costs on varying assumptions about volume losses.

| | Change in profits £m (+%) Volume loss | | |
|---|---|---|---|
| **Change in** | **0%** | **–10%** | **–15%** |
| Price (+10%) | 20 (100) | 10 (50)[1] | 5 (25) |
| Total overhead (–10%) | 6 (30) | –2 (–10)[2] | –6 (–30) |
| R & D (–10%) | 1 (5) | –7 (–35) | –11 (–55) |
| Marketing and advertising (–10%) | 1 (5) | –7 (–35) | –11 (–55) |
| Fixed costs (–10%) | 4 (20) | –7 (–35) | –11 (–55) |
| Volume (+10%) | 8 (40) | – | – |

**Notes:** [1]For example, if prices are increased by 10% and volume falls as a result by 10%, then profits rise by £10m (or +50%).

[2]If total overhead costs are cut by 10% (£6m) and volume falls as a result by 10%, then profits fall by £2m (–10%).

**Source:** P. Doyle, *Marketing Management and Strategy*. Copyright © 1998 Prentice-Hall Europe.

illustrates the difficulty faced by businesses attempting to build a differential advantage based on low prices.

Because price has a psychological impact on customers, marketers can use it symbolically. By raising a price, they can emphasise the quality of a product and try to increase the status associated with its ownership. The declining fortunes of Chevas Royal Scotch whisky were reversed following a substantial price rise. Lowering a price can also have a dramatic impact on demand, attracting bargain-hunting customers who are prepared to spend extra time and effort to save a small amount.

## Price and Non-price Competition

A product offering can compete on either a price or a non-price basis. The choice will affect not only pricing decisions and activities but also those associated with other marketing mix decision variables.

## Price Competition

**Price competition**
A policy whereby a marketer emphasises price as an issue, and matches or beats the prices of competitors

When **price competition** is used, a marketer emphasises price as an issue, and matches or beats competitors' prices. Budget airline easyJet engages in price competition and stresses its low prices in its advertisements. To compete effectively on a price basis, a company should be the low-cost producer of the product. If all companies producing goods in an industry charge the same, the company with the lowest costs is the most profitable. Companies that stress low price as a key element in the marketing mix tend to produce standardised products. For example, suppliers of fuel oils use price competition. Sellers using this approach may be prepared and able to change prices frequently, particularly in response to competitors altering their prices. In many parts of the world, the postal service and UPS or DHL engage in direct price competition in their pricing of overnight express-delivery services.

Price competition gives a marketer flexibility. Prices can be altered to account for changes in the company's costs or in demand for the product, or when competitors cut prices. However, a major drawback of price competition is that competitors may also have the flexibility to adjust their prices to match or beat another company's price cuts. If so, a

***Figure 20.1***
*Retailers' prominent use of 'sales' is a well known example of price competition*
*Photo: Courtesy of Karen Beaulah*

price war may result. Furthermore, if a user of price competition is forced to raise prices, competing companies may decide not to do the same. As the 1990s drew to a close, the supermarket giants were locked into a spiral of price competition. Sainsbury's was promoting low prices across hundreds of popular product lines in an attempt to claw back market share from Tesco. Tesco's response was to launch a low-price promotion of its own.[5] **EDLP**[6] (everyday low pricing) is a form of price competition, funded by reducing promotions budgets so that retail prices can be cut while retailers' margins remain static. Companies like Procter & Gamble have attempted to strengthen consumer loyalty by cutting the prices of key brands permanently. The first two categories to benefit were the core markets of washing-up liquids, such as Fairy Liquid, and disposable nappies, such as Pampers.

**EDLP**
Everyday low pricing; budget savings passed on by the manufacturer to the consumer through reduced prices

## Non-price Competition

In **non-price competition**, a seller elects not to focus on price but instead emphasises distinctive product features, service, product quality, promotion, packaging or other factors to distinguish the product from competing brands, for example Figure 20.2. As the Building Customer Relationships box shows below, price is not always the key factor for customers in deciding what to buy. Organisations that use non-price competition aim to increase unit sales in other ways. For example, Dom Perignon champagne stresses the heritage and quality of its champagnes, rather than competitive price. A company can use non-price competition to build customer loyalty towards its brand. If customers prefer a brand or store because of non-price issues, they may not easily be lured away by competing offers. Indeed, such customers

**Non-price competition**
A policy in which a seller elects not to focus on price but to emphasise other factors instead

## Building Customer Relationships

### Do Low Prices Build e-loyalty?

Throughout the Internet's short history, many e-businesses have come to believe that online customers are interested only in paying the lowest possible prices. Now this myth has been exploded by research showing that companies can more effectively strengthen e-loyalty and counteract price sensitivity by building trust and enhancing the customer's shopping experience.

When the consulting business Bain & Company studied e-loyalty, it found that online shoppers are generally more interested in convenience than in price, and tend to be loyal to sites that fulfil the promise of simplifying the buying process. Therefore, e-businesses need to build trust among new customers by projecting an image of reliability and responsiveness. In return, as customers learn to trust a site, they become willing to provide more personal information, make repeat purchases and voluntarily refer new customers. Industrial supply company Granger, for example, provides a convenient search tool and knowledgeable phone representatives to help business customers find just the right products among the one million items available on its website. Customers spend less time searching for what they want, and they can check out quickly – benefits they value more than paying a rock-bottom price for a particular product.

In another study, McKinsey & Company, a consulting company, found that few online shoppers take the time to compare prices on every product they want to buy. In fact, 89 per cent of book buyers and 84 per cent of toy buyers actually buy at the first site they visit rather than clicking from site to site seeking the lowest price. As long as they perceive a site's prices to be within a reasonable range, customers will go ahead and make the purchase. What consumers consider a reasonable price range varies from product to product. McKinsey found that although e-businesses could raise prices up to 17 per cent on brand-name beauty products without losing customers, buyers balked at a price increase of less than 1 per cent on certain financial services.

To avoid a backlash, e-businesses need to conduct ongoing research to analyse each segment's price sensitivity and to test customer reactions carefully before implementing price changes. With the right pricing, and the right mix of trust and convenience, companies can attract new customers and strengthen e-loyalty year after year to build sales and profits.

**Sources:** W. Pride and O.C. Ferrell, *Marketing: Concepts and Strategies*, 2003, Boston: Houghton Mifflin.

might become confused or irritated if price cuts are offered. Buyers of Chanel clothing, perfume or accessories enjoy the exclusivity associated with the high price. The implication is that price is not the most durable factor in terms of maintaining customer loyalty. However, when price is the primary reason that customers buy a particular brand, the competition can attract such customers through price cuts.

Non-price competition is workable under the right conditions. A company must be able to distinguish its brand through unique product features, higher quality, customer service, promotion, packaging and the like (see Figure 20.2). The brand's distinguishing features should be difficult, if not impossible, for a competitor to copy. Buyers must not only be able to perceive these distinguishing characteristics but must also view them as desirable. Finally, the organisation must promote the distinguishing characteristics of the brand extensively in order to establish its superiority and to set it apart from competitors in the minds of buyers.

***Figure 20.2***
*Although priced to be competitive with rival brands, Comfort Vaporesse promotes functional product benefits*
*Source: COMFORT and VAPORESSE are registered trade marks of Unilever*

Many European companies put less emphasis on price than do their American counterparts. They look for a competitive edge by concentrating on promotion, research and development, marketing research and marketing channel considerations. In a study of pricing strategy, many companies stated specifically that they emphasise research and development and technological superiority; competition based on price was seldom a major marketing consideration.[7]

A marketer attempting to compete on a non-price basis must still consider competitors' prices. The business must be aware of competitors' prices and will probably price its brand near, or slightly above, competing brands. As an example, Sony sells television sets in a highly competitive market and charges higher prices than other manufacturers for them. Sony can achieve this because its emphasis on high product quality distinguishes it from its competitors and allows it to set higher prices.

# Factors Affecting Pricing Decisions

Pricing decisions are affected by many factors. Often, there is considerable uncertainty about reactions to price on the part of buyers, channel members, competitors and others. Price is also an important consideration in marketing planning, market analysis and sales forecasting. It is a major issue when assessing a brand's positioning relative to competing brands. Most factors that affect pricing decisions can be grouped into one of the nine categories shown in Figure 20.3. This section explores how each of these nine groups of factors enters into price decision-making.

## Organisational and Marketing Objectives

Marketers should set prices that are consistent with the organisation's goals and mission. For example, cosmetic brands such as Chanel and Helena Rubenstein are positioned at the exclusive end of the market, and have high price tags to match. Marketers in these organisations know that discounting prices on these brands would not be in line with the overall organisational goal.

Decision-makers should also make pricing decisions that are compatible with the organisation's marketing objectives. Say, for instance, that one of a producer's marketing objectives

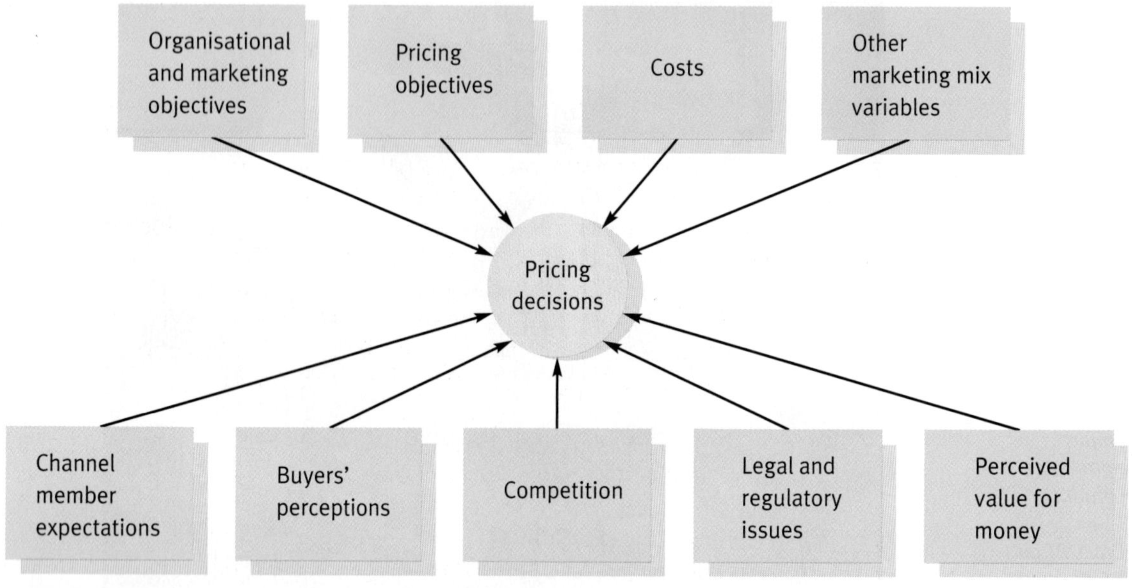


***Figure 20.3***
*Factors that affect pricing decisions*

is a 12 per cent increase in unit sales by the end of the next year. Assuming that buyers are price sensitive, increasing the price or setting a price above the average market price would not be in line with the company's sales objective. A case in point: GM (Vauxhall) has introduced high-performance, well-specified model variants to the top of each of its model ranges – for example, the £20,000 Vectra V6 GSi and the £32,000 Omega 3.0i V6 Elite. Such prices ensure that these particular models have only limited appeal. GM's stated objective, however, is to be market leader in terms of sales volume. The company, therefore, is careful to price the great majority of its cars in line with the price expectations of the bulk of the car buying public and fleet operators – far below these £20,000 Vectra and £32,000 Omega levels.

## Pricing Objectives

**Pricing objectives** Overall goals that describe what a company wants to achieve through its pricing efforts

**Pricing objectives** are overall goals that describe what a company wants to achieve through its pricing efforts. The type of pricing objective a marketer uses will have considerable bearing on the determination of prices.[8] Marketers often use multiple pricing objectives, including those that emphasise survival, profit, return on investment, market share, cash flow, status quo or product quality (see Table 20.2). Thus a market share pricing objective usually causes a company to price a product below competing brands of similar quality to attract competitors' customers to the company's brand. This type of pricing can lead to lower profits, but may be used temporarily in the hope of gaining market share. By contrast, a cash flow pricing objective may involve setting a relatively high price, which can place the product at a competitive disadvantage. Paradoxically, a cash flow pricing objective sometimes results in a low price sustained in the long term. However, this type of objective is more likely to be addressed by using temporary price reductions, such as sales, refunds and special discounts.

Because pricing objectives influence decisions in most functional areas – including finance, accounting and production – the objectives must be consistent with the company's overall mission and purpose (see Chapter 2). Banking is an area where pricing is a major concern. As competition has intensified, bank executives have realised that their products must be priced to meet both short-term profit goals and long-term strategic objectives. Changes in the pricing objectives that companies use can occur for various reasons. For example, the objective of return on investment may be used less as managers and marketers in diversified companies stress the creation of shareholder value. When shareholder value is used as a performance objective, strategies – including those involving price – are evaluated according to their impact on the value investors perceive in the company.[10]

## Costs

Obviously, costs must be an issue when establishing price. A business may temporarily sell products below cost to match the competition, to generate cash flow or even to increase market share; but in the long run it cannot survive by adopting this approach. A marketer should be careful to analyse all costs so that they can be included in the total costing for a product.

Marketers must also take into account the costs that a particular product shares with other products in the product line, particularly the costs of research and development, production and distribution. Services are especially subject to cost sharing. For example, the costs of a bank building are spread over the costs of all services the bank offers.[11] Most marketers view a product's cost as a minimum, or floor, below which the product cannot be priced. Cost analysis is discussed in more detail in the next chapter.

## Other Marketing Mix Variables

All marketing mix variables are closely interrelated. Pricing decisions can influence decisions and activities associated with product, place/distribution, promotion and customer service variables. A product's price frequently affects the demand for the item. A high price, for instance, may result in low unit sales, which in turn may lead to higher production costs per unit. Conversely, lower per-unit production costs may result from a low price. For many products, buyers associate better product quality with a high price and poorer product quality with a low price. This perceived price–quality relationship influences customers'

**Table 20.2 Different Types of Pricing Objective**

| |
|---|
| **Survival**<br>A fundamental pricing objective is survival. Most businesses will tolerate difficulties such as short-run losses and internal upheaval if they are necessary for survival. Because price is a flexible and convenient variable to adjust, it is sometimes used to increase sales volume to levels that match the company's expenses. |
| **Profit**<br>Although businesses often claim they aim to maximise profits, in practice this objective is difficult to measure. As a result, profit objectives tend to be set at satisfactory levels. Specific profit objectives may be stated in terms of actual monetary amounts or in terms of percentage change relative to previous profits. |
| **Return on investment**<br>Pricing to attain a specified rate of return on the company's investment is a profit-related pricing objective. Most pricing objectives based on return on investment (ROI) are achieved by trial and error, because not all cost and revenue data needed to project the return on investment are available when prices are set. |
| **Market share**<br>Many companies establish pricing objectives to maintain or increase a product's market share in relation to total industry sales. For example, car companies such as Volkswagen have been known to cut prices on existing models when introducing new ones, to boost share of the car market. Maintaining or increasing market share need not depend on growth in industry sales. A company can increase its market share even though sales for the total industry are decreasing. On the other hand, if the overall market is growing, a business's sales volume may actually increase as its market share decreases. |
| **Cash flow**<br>Some companies set prices to recover cash as fast as possible, especially when a short product life cycle is anticipated or the capital spent to develop products needs to be recovered quickly. However, the use of cash flow and recovery as an objective oversimplifies the value of price in contributing to profits. A disadvantage of this pricing objective could be high prices, which might allow competitors with lower prices to gain a large share of the market. |
| **Status quo**<br>In some cases, a business may be in a favourable position and may simply wish to maintain the status quo. Such objectives can focus on maintaining a certain market share, meeting (but not beating) competitors' prices, achieving price stability or maintaining a favourable public image. Such an approach can reduce a company's risks by helping to stabilise demand for its products. The use of status quo pricing objectives sometimes leads to a climate of non-price competition in an industry. |
| **Product quality**<br>A company might have the objective of product quality leadership in the industry. For example, the construction equipment manufacturer JCB aims to be ranked as one of the leading companies in its industry in terms of product quality and customer satisfaction.[9] This normally dictates a relatively high price to cover the high product quality and/or the high cost of research and development. |

overall image of products or brands. Thus consumers may be prepared to pay a high price for designer sunglasses because they believe they are a high-status item.

Pricing decisions influence the number of competing brands in a product category. When a company introduces a product, sets a relatively high price and achieves high unit sales, competitors may be attracted to this product category. If a company fixes a low price, the low profit margin may be unattractive to potential competition.

The price of a product is linked to several dimensions of its distribution. Premium-priced products are often marketed through selective or exclusive distribution; lower-priced products in the same product category may be sold through intensive distribution. For example, Montblanc pens are distributed through selective distribution and Bic pens through intensive distribution. The way in which a product is stored and transported may also be associated with its price. As Figure 20.4 shows, when deciding about a product's price, a producer must consider the profit margins of marketing channel members such as wholesalers and retailers. This way, channel members can be adequately compensated for the functions they perform.

The way a product is promoted can be affected by its price. Bargain prices are often included in advertisements, whereas premium prices are less likely to be mentioned. However, the exclusivity associated with a premium price is sometimes included in advertisements for upmarket items, such as luxury holidays or exclusive jewellery. Higher-

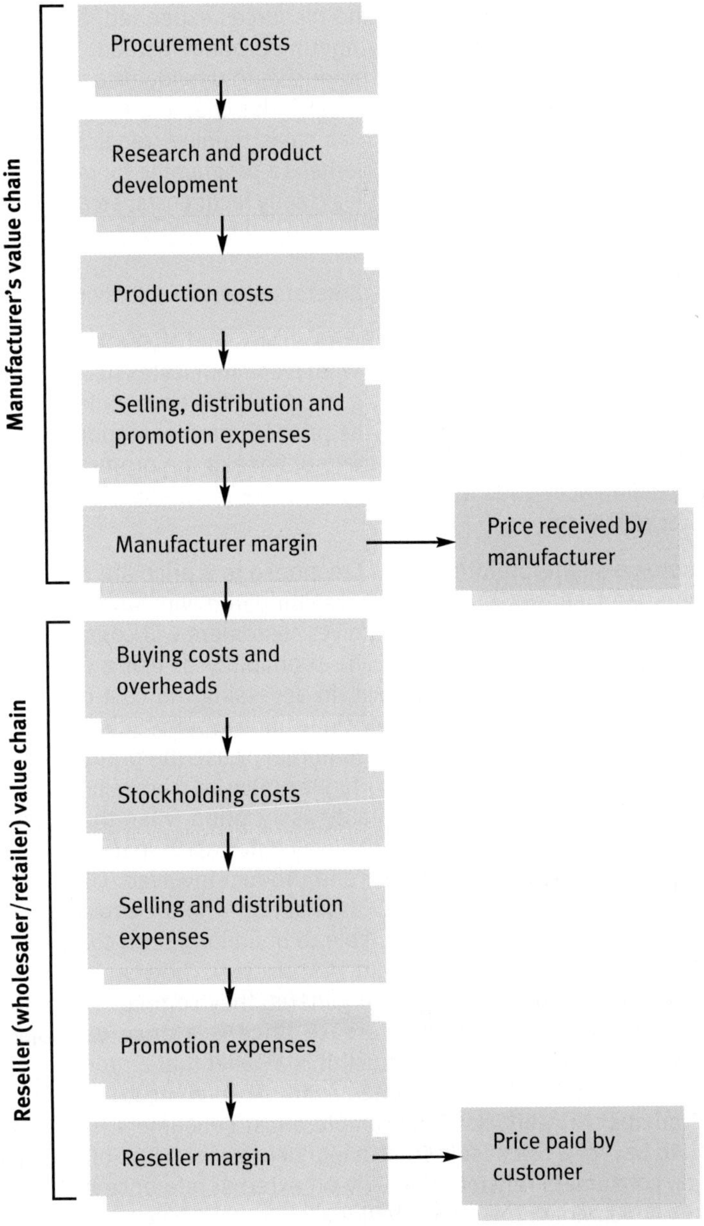


***Figure 20.4***
*Wholesaler and retailer considerations when developing price*

priced products are more likely to require personal selling efforts than lower-priced ones. Indeed, there may be an expectation that a high price is accompanied by enhanced levels of customer service. A customer may purchase an inexpensive watch in a self-service environment but hesitate to buy an expensive watch in the same store, even if it is available there.

The price structure can affect a salesperson's relationship with customers. A complex pricing structure takes longer to explain to customers, is more likely to confuse the buyer and may cause misunderstandings that result in long-term customer dissatisfaction. For example, the pricing structure used by many hotels is complex and can confuse potential guests.

## Channel Member Expectations

When making price decisions, a producer must consider what distribution channel members (such as wholesalers, retailers and dealers) expect. A channel member certainly expects to receive a profit for the functions performed. The amount of profit expected depends on the amount of time and resources expended, and on an assessment of what would be gained by handling a competing product instead.

Channel members often expect producers to provide discounts for large orders and quick payment. (Discounts are discussed later in this chapter.) At times, resellers expect producers to provide support activities, such as sales training, repair advisory services, cooperative advertising, sales promotions and perhaps a programme for returning unsold merchandise to the producer. These support activities clearly incur costs, so a producer must consider these costs when determining prices.

## Buyers' Perceptions

When making pricing decisions, marketers should be concerned with two vital questions.

1 How will customers interpret prices and respond to them? Interpretation in this context refers to what the price means or what it communicates to customers. Does the price mean 'high quality' or 'low quality', or 'great deal', 'fair price' or 'rip-off'?
2 How will customers respond to the price? Customer response refers to whether the price will move customers closer to the purchase of the product and the degree to which the price enhances their satisfaction with the purchase experience and with the product after purchase.

Customers' interpretation of and response to a price are to some degree determined by their assessment of what they receive compared with what they give up to make the purchase. In evaluating what they receive, customers will consider product attributes, benefits, advantages, disadvantages, the probability of using the product, and possibly the status associated with the product. In assessing the cost of the product, customers will consider its price, the amount of time and effort required to obtain the product, and perhaps the resources required to maintain or use the product after purchase.

At times, customers interpret a higher price as higher product quality. They are especially likely to make this price–quality association when they cannot judge the quality of the product themselves. This is not always the case: whether price is equated with quality depends on the types of customer and product involved. Obviously, marketers relying on customers making a price–quality association who are providing moderate or low-quality products at high prices, will be unable to build long-term customer relationships.

When interpreting and responding to prices, how do customers determine if the price is too high, too low or about right? In general, they compare prices with internal or external reference prices. An **internal reference price** is a price developed in the buyer's mind through experience with the product. It is a belief that a product should cost approximately a certain amount. As consumers, previous experiences provide internal reference prices for a number of products. For example, most consumers have a reasonable idea of how much to pay for a can of soft drink, a loaf of bread or a litre of milk. When there is less experience, consumers rely more heavily on external reference prices.[12] An **external reference price** is a comparison price provided by others, such as retailers or manufacturers.[13]

**Internal reference price**
A price developed in the buyer's mind through experience with the product

**External reference price**
A comparison price provided by others

Customers' perceptions of prices are also influenced by their expectations about future price increases, by what they paid for the product recently, and by what they would like to pay for the product. Other factors affecting customers' perception of whether the price is right include time or financial constraints, the costs associated with searching for lower-priced products, and expectations that products will go on sale.

Buyers' perceptions of a product relative to competing products may allow a business to set a price that differs significantly from rivals' prices. If the product is deemed superior to most of the competition, a premium price may be feasible. However, even products with superior quality can be overpriced. Strong brand loyalty sometimes provides the opportunity to charge a premium price. On the other hand, if buyers view a product less than favourably – though not extremely negatively – a lower price may generate sales.

In the context of price, buyers can be characterised according to their degree of value consciousness, price consciousness, and prestige-sensitivity. Marketers who understand these characteristics are better able to set pricing objectives and policies. **Value-conscious consumers** are concerned about both the price and the quality of a product. **Price-conscious consumers** strive to pay low prices. **Prestige-sensitive consumers** focus on purchasing products that signify prominence and status. For example, the Porsche Cayenne, one of the highest-priced sports utility vehicles ever marketed, created record sales and profits for Porsche. Only 18 per cent of Cayenne buyers had previously owned a Porsche; many of the rest were attracted to the vehicle by the prestige associated with the Porsche name. On the other hand, some consumers vary in their degree of value, price and prestige consciousness. In some segments, consumers are increasingly 'trading up' to more status-conscious products: this occurs with cars, electrical appliances, restaurants and even pet food. This trend has benefited companies such as Starbucks and BMW, which can charge premium prices for high-quality, prestige products.

**Value-conscious consumers**
Those concerned about price and quality of a product

**Price-conscious consumers**
Those striving to pay low prices

**Prestige-sensitive consumers**
Individuals drawn to products that signify prominence and status

**Perceived value for money**
The benefit consumers perceive to be inherent in a product or service, weighed against the price demanded

## Competition

A marketer needs to know competitors' prices so that a company can adjust its own prices accordingly.[14] This does not mean that a company will necessarily match competitors' prices; it may set its price above or below theirs. It is also important for marketers to assess how competitors will respond to price adjustments. Will they change their prices (some may not) and, if so, will they raise or lower them? For example, when motor insurance providers stress their keen pricing, competitors often do the same.

Chapter 3 describes several types of competitive market structure that impact upon price setting. When a company operates as a monopoly and is unregulated, it can set whatever prices the market will bear. However, the company may avoid adopting the highest possible pricing for fear of inviting government regulation or because it wants to penetrate a market by using a lower price. If the monopoly is regulated, it normally has less pricing flexibility; the regulatory body lets it set prices that generate a reasonable, but not excessive, return. A government-owned monopoly may price products below cost to make them accessible to people who could not otherwise afford them. However, government-owned monopolies sometimes charge higher prices to control demand.

In an oligopoly, only a few sellers operate, and there are high barriers to competitive entry. A business in such an industry – for example, telecommunications, drugs or steel – can raise its price, hoping that its competitors will do the same. Very little can be gained through price cuts because other companies are likely to follow suit when an organisation cuts its price to gain a competitive edge.

A market structure characterised by monopolistic competition means numerous sellers with differentiated product offerings. The products are differentiated by physical characteristics, features, quality and brand image. The distinguishing characteristics of its product may allow a company to set a different price from its competitors. However, businesses engaged in a monopolistic competitive market structure are likely to practise non-price competition, as discussed earlier in this chapter.

**Trade** or **functional discount**
A reduction off the list price given by a producer to an intermediary for performing certain functions

**Quantity discounts**
Reductions off the list price that reflect the economies of purchasing in large quantities

**Cumulative discounts**
Quantity discounts aggregated over a stated period of time

**Non-cumulative discounts**
One-off quantity discounts

Under conditions of perfect competition, there are many sellers. Buyers view all sellers' products as the same. All companies sell their products at the going market price and so there is no flexibility in setting prices.

### Legal and Regulatory Issues

At times, government action sways marketers' pricing decisions. To curb inflation, the government may invoke price controls, 'freeze' prices at certain levels or determine the rates at which prices can be increased. Following the privatisation of public utilities, the UK government set up regulatory bodies such as Ofwat for water and Oftel for telecommunications, which stressed minimum and maximum charges.

Many regulations and laws affect pricing decisions and activities. Not only must marketers refrain from fixing prices, they must also develop independent pricing policies and set prices in ways that do not involve collusion. Over the years, legislation has been established to safeguard consumers and businesses from pricing sharp practices. In the UK, the Monopolies and Mergers Commission prevents the creation of monopolistic situations. The consumer is protected by the Trade Descriptions Act, the Fair Trading Act, the Consumer Protection Act and many others. All countries have similar legislation, and the European Union legislates to protect consumers within the community.

### Perceived Value

Most discussions about pricing revolve around the actual monetary value – the price – to be charged for the good or service. However, the **perceived value for money** to consumers is also vital. This is the benefit consumers see as inherent in a product or service, weighed against the price demanded. Sometimes, particularly in consumer markets, these benefits are real and measurable, in other cases they are more psychological. For instance, interest-free credit, maintenance contracts and extended warranties are all features that may affect a consumer's perception of value for money. Consumers will not pay more than they value the benefit inherent in a product or service. Consumers balance the price demanded, typically in monetary terms, against the anticipated level of use and satisfaction to be gained from buying and using the specific product. This assessment is influenced by the consumers' previous experience of the brand and similar products, the perceived quality of the product in question, its brand image, purpose, anticipated usage, overall appeal and the nature of competing offers. These emotive issues are often difficult to quantify, but through qualitative marketing research, most businesses are able to assess their target market's views of value.

## Pricing for Business Markets

Business markets consist of individuals and businesses that purchase products for resale, for use in their own operations or for producing other products. Establishing prices for this category of business-to-business buyer sometimes differs from setting prices for consumers. Differences in the size of purchases, geographic factors and transport considerations require sellers to adjust prices. This section discusses several issues unique to the pricing of industrial products and business markets including discounts, geographic pricing, transfer pricing and price discrimination. The section concludes by considering the concept of economic value to the customer (EVC).

### Price Discounting

Producers commonly provide intermediaries with discounts from list prices. Although there are many types of discount, they usually fall into one of five categories (see Table 20.3):

1 trade
2 quantity
3 cash discounts
4 seasonal discounts
5 allowances.

**Cash discount**
A simple price reduction given to a buyer for prompt payment or payment in cash

**Table 20.3 Discounts Used For Business Markets**

| Type | Reason for use | Practical examples |
|---|---|---|
| Trade (functional) | To attract and keep resellers by compensating them for certain functions, such as transportation, warehousing, selling and providing credit | A university bookstore pays about a third less for a new textbook than the retail price paid by a student |
| Quantity | To encourage customers to buy large quantities and, in the case of cumulative discounts, to encourage customer loyalty | Large chains of tyre and exhaust outlets purchase parts at lower prices than individually owned outlets |
| Cash | To reduce expenses associated with accounts receivable by encouraging prompt payment | Companies operating in business markets often offer a discount for prompt payment |
| Seasonal | To allow resources to be used more efficiently by stimulating sales during off-peak periods | Hotels in large cities offer companies discounted accommodation for sales and other conferences during off-peak periods |
| Allowance | For trade-in allowances, the buyer is assisted in making the purchase by getting money back on used equipment; for promotional allowances, dealers are able to participate in advertising and sales support programmes | Companies such as Nabisco pay promotional allowances to supermarkets for setting up and maintaining end-of-aisle displays to push their products |

**Seasonal discount**
A price reduction given to buyers who purchase goods or services out of season

**Allowance**
A concession in price to achieve a desired goal

**Geographic pricing**
Pricing that involves reductions for transport costs or other costs associated with the physical distance between the buyer and the seller

**FOB factory price**
The price of the merchandise at the factory before it is loaded on to the carrier vehicle, which must be paid by the buyer

**Trade Discounts** A reduction off the list price given by a producer to an intermediary for performing certain functions is called a **trade** or **functional discount**. The functions for which intermediaries are compensated may include selling, transporting, storing, final processing and perhaps providing credit services. The level of discount can vary considerably from one industry to another.

**Quantity Discounts** Reductions from the list price that reflect the economies of purchasing in large quantities are called **quantity discounts**. Cost savings usually occur in four areas. Fewer but larger orders reduce per-unit selling costs; fixed costs, such as invoicing, remain the same or go down; raw materials costs are lower, because quantity discounts may be available; longer production runs mean no increases in holding costs.[15] In addition, a large purchase may shift some of the storage, finance and risk-taking functions to the buyer.

Quantity discounts can be either cumulative or non-cumulative. **Cumulative discounts** are aggregated over a stated period of time. Purchases of £10,000 (€15,000) in a three-month period, for example, might entitle the buyer to a 5 per cent, or £500 (€750), rebate. Such discounts are supposed to reflect economies in selling and encourage the buyer to purchase from one seller. **Non-cumulative discounts** are one-off reductions in prices based on the number of units purchased, the monetary value of the order or the product mix purchased.

**Cash Discounts** A **cash discount**, or simple price reduction, is given for prompt payment or payment in cash. A policy to encourage prompt payment is a popular practice in setting prices. For example, '2/10 net 30' means that a 2 per cent discount will be allowed if the account is paid within 10 days. However, if the buyer does not pay within the 10-day period, the entire balance is due within 30 days without a discount. If the account is not paid within 30 days, interest may be charged.

**FOB destination price**
A price quotation indicating that the producer absorbs the costs of shipping the merchandise

**Uniform geographic pricing**
Pricing in which the same price is charged to all customers regardless of geographic location

**Seasonal Discounts** A price reduction given to buyers who purchase goods or services out of season is a **seasonal discount**. These discounts let the seller maintain steadier production during the year. For example, hotels in holiday resorts offer seasonal discounts at times of year when the weather is poor.

**Allowances** Another type of reduction from the list price is an **allowance** – a concession in price to achieve a desired goal. Trade-in allowances are price reductions granted for handing in a used item when purchasing a new one. This type of allowance is popular in the aircraft industry. Another example is promotional allowances, which are price reductions granted to dealers for participating in advertising and sales support programmes intended to increase sales of a particular item.

## Geographic Pricing

**Zone prices**
Regional prices that take advantage of a uniform pricing system

**Base point pricing**
A geographic pricing policy that includes the price at the factory, plus freight charges from the base point nearest the buyer

**Freight absorption pricing**
A pricing policy in which the seller absorbs all or part of the actual freight costs

**Geographic pricing** involves reductions for transport costs or other costs associated with the physical distance between the buyer and the seller. Prices may be quoted as being FOB (free-on-board) factory or destination. An **FOB factory price** indicates the price of the merchandise at the factory before it is loaded on to the carrier vehicle; it thus excludes transport costs. The buyer must pay for shipping. An **FOB destination price** means the producer absorbs the costs of shipping the merchandise to customers.

To avoid the problems involved in charging different prices to each customer, **uniform geographic** pricing, sometimes called postage stamp pricing, may be used. The same price is charged to all customers regardless of geographic location, and the price is based on average shipping costs for all customers. Petrol, paper products and office equipment are often priced on a uniform basis.

**Zone prices** are regional prices that take advantage of a uniform pricing system; prices are adjusted for major geographic zones as the transport costs increase. For example, the prices of a manufacturer located in the northern French town of Lille may be higher for buyers in the south of France than for buyers in Paris.

**Base point pricing** is a geographic pricing policy that includes the price at the factory, plus freight charges from the base point nearest the buyer. This policy, which is now rarely used, can result in all buyers paying freight charges from one location, regardless of where the product was manufactured!

When the seller absorbs all or part of the actual freight costs, **freight absorption pricing** is being used. The seller might choose this method because it wishes to do business with a particular customer or to get more business; more business will cause the average cost to fall and counter-balance the extra freight cost. This strategy is used to improve market penetration and to retain a hold in an increasingly competitive market.

## Transfer Pricing

**Transfer pricing**
The type of pricing used when one unit in a company sells a product to another unit within the same company

When one unit in a company sells a product to another unit within the same company, **transfer pricing** occurs. The price is determined by one of the following methods.

- *Actual full cost* – calculated by dividing all fixed and variable expenses for a period into the number of units produced.
- *Standard full cost* – calculated on what it would cost to produce the goods at full plant capacity.
- *Cost plus investment* – calculated as full cost, plus the cost of a portion of the selling unit's assets used for internal needs.
- *Market based cost* – calculated at the market price less a small discount to reflect the lack of sales effort and other expenses.

The choice of transfer pricing method depends on the company's management strategy and the nature of the units' interaction. The company might initially choose to determine price by the actual full cost method but later move to an alternative method.[16]

## Price Discrimination

**Price discrimination**
A policy in which different prices are charged in order to give a particular group of buyers a competitive edge

A policy of **price discrimination** results in different prices being charged to give a group of buyers a competitive edge. Some forms of price discrimination are illegal. In the USA, price differentials are legal only when customers are not in competition with one another. The EU is also keen to stamp out price discrimination.

Price differentiation is a form of market segmentation that companies use to provide a marketing mix that satisfies different segments. Because different market segments perceive the value of a particular product differently, depending on the product's importance and value to the business buyer, marketers may charge different prices to different market segments. Price discrimination can also be used to modify demand patterns, support sales of other products, dispose of obsolete goods or excessive inventories, fill excess production capacity and respond to competitors' activities in particular markets.[17]

Various conditions must be satisfied for price discrimination to be feasible. It must be possible to segment the market and the costs associated with doing so must not exceed the additional revenue generated. The practice should not break the law or breed customer discontent. Finally, the segment that is charged the higher price should not be vulnerable to competitor attack.

## Economic Value to the Customer

**Economic value to the customer (EVC)**
The underlying principle that a premium price can be charged while still offering the customer better value than the competition

The relationship between price and profitability was considered briefly at the start of this chapter and will be examined in more detail in Chapter 21. It is already clear that the ability to charge a higher price can have a major impact on profitability. It is also apparent that in order to achieve higher prices, businesses must be able to offer the customer some kind of differential advantage. In business markets, this advantage must usually be measurable in economic terms because businesses are driven by the need to reduce costs and increase revenue. Thus a manufacturer of switch gears may be prepared to change to a more expensive supplier of fork-lift trucks if the products supplied have lower running costs. The concept of economic value to the customer encapsulates this notion and is a useful aid to determining prices in business markets. The underlying principle of **economic value to the customer (EVC)** is that a premium price can be charged while still offering the customer better value than the competition.

There are various reasons why a costly product may provide good economic value to the customer, including lower set-up or running costs, the provision of superior servicing or other after-sales support, or a better warranty deal. It is even possible that the life of the product may be longer or that its productivity may be greater than that of lower-priced alternatives. Whatever the reason behind the value on offer, if EVC is to be demonstrated, the initial high price of the product must be justified by an overall lower lifetime cost. The Marketing Tools and Techniques box below provides a worked example of how EVC works in practice.

## Marketing Tools and Techniques

### Business-to-business Pricing using EVC Analysis

Analysing economic value to the customer (EVC) is a useful aid to setting prices for business-to-business organisations. This example concerns the pricing of panel presses, which are supplied to the car parts business. The analysis focuses on the market leader and two other competitors.

The analysis begins by considering a reference product against which the costs of competing products are compared. In this case, the market leader is used as the reference product. In this example, a car parts company buying the panel press from the market leader would expect to pay the following costs. The purchase price of the press is £60,000. Start-up costs such as installation charges, staff training and lost production during installation are £20,000, and post-purchase costs including operating costs such as labour, servicing/maintenance and power are £130,000.

This means that, over its life cycle, the panel press will cost the car parts company a total of £210,000.

Companies competing with the market leader present the customer with a different profile of costs. Company A has, by incorporating a number of new design features, managed to cut the start-up costs for a comparable panel press to £10,000 and reduced post-purchase costs to £105,000. This means that the total costs for the press are £35,000 less than those for the market leader. The result is that Company A's press offers the customer an EVC of £210,000 less £115,000, which equals £95,000. Assuming that Company A charged a purchase price of £95,000 for the panel press, the customer would face total life-cycle costs that were equivalent to the market-leading product. If, however, Company A decided to offer the panel press at a purchase price of only £80,000, the lower life-cycle costs of the product would give the customer a considerable financial incentive to buy.

Consider the position of a second competitor, Company B, with similar start-up and post-purchase costs to the market leader. This company has, through certain technological advances, increased the rate at which the press can be operated, potentially increasing productivity and therefore revenue for the customer. As a result, the press has the potential to offer an additional £50,000 profit contribution over the presses of the market leader and Company A. The EVC associated with this is £110,000, because this is the highest price the customer may be expected to pay.

# Summary

*Price* is the value placed on what is exchanged. The buyer exchanges buying power – which depends on the buyer's income, credit and wealth – for satisfaction or utility. *Financial price* is the basis of market exchanges – the quantified value of what is exchanged. However, price does not always involve a financial exchange; barter, the trading of products, is the oldest form of exchange.

» Price is a key element in the marketing mix because it relates directly to the generation of total revenue. The profit factor can be determined mathematically by first multiplying price by quantities sold to calculate total revenues and then subtracting total costs. Price is often the only variable in the marketing mix that can be adjusted quickly and easily to respond to changes in the external environment.

» A product offering can compete on either a price or a non-price basis. *Price competition* emphasises price as the product differential. Prices fluctuate frequently, and sellers must respond to competitors changing their prices. *EDLP*, everyday low pricing, is a budget saving passed on from the manufacturer to the consumer. *Non-price competition* emphasises product differentiation through distinctive product features, services, product quality or other factors. Establishing brand loyalty by using non-price competition works best when the product can be physically differentiated and when the customer can recognise these distinguishing characteristics and views them as desirable.

» *Pricing objectives* are overall goals that describe what a company wants to achieve through its pricing efforts. The most fundamental pricing objective is the business's survival. Price can easily be adjusted to increase sales volume to levels that match the company's expenses. Profit objectives, which are usually stated in terms of actual monetary amounts or percentage change, are normally set at a satisfactory level rather than at a level designed for profit maximisation. Pricing for return on investment (ROI) sets a specified rate of return as its objective. A pricing objective to maintain or increase market share is established in relation to total industry sales. Other types of pricing objective include cash flow, status quo and product quality.

» Nine factors affect pricing decisions: (1) organisational and marketing objectives, (2) pricing objectives, (3) costs, (4) other marketing mix variables, (5) channel member expectations, (6) buyers' perceptions, (7) competition, (8) legal and regulatory issues, and (9) perceived value. Thus, pricing decisions should be consistent with the organisation's goals and mission. Pricing objectives heavily influence price-setting decisions.

» When interpreting and responding to prices, customers compare prices with internal or external reference prices. An *internal reference price* is a price developed in the buyer's mind through experience with the product. When there is less experience, consumers rely more heavily on external reference prices. An *external reference price* is a comparison price provided by others, such as retailers, manufacturers or competing products. In the context of price, buyers can be characterised according to their degree of value consciousness, price consciousness and prestige-sensitivity. Marketers who understand these characteristics are better able to set pricing objectives and policies. *Value-conscious consumers* are concerned about both the price and the quality of a product. *Price-conscious consumers* strive to pay low prices. *Prestige-sensitive consumers* focus on purchasing products that signify prominence and status.

» Most marketers view a product's cost as the floor below which a product cannot be priced. Due to the interrelationship of the marketing mix variables, price can affect product, promotion, place/distribution and service-level decisions. The revenue that channel members expect for the functions they perform must also be considered when making price decisions.

» Buyers' perceptions of price vary. Some consumer segments are sensitive to price, but others may not be; before determining the price, therefore, a marketer needs to be aware of its importance to the target market. Knowledge of the prices charged for competing brands is essential so that a company can adjust its prices relative to those of competitors. Government regulations and legislation can also influence pricing decisions through laws to enhance competition and by invoking price controls – for example, to curb inflation.

» *Perceived value for money* is an important consideration when setting prices. Consumers do not regard price purely as the monetary value being demanded in exchange for a good or a service. The quality of the item, its brand image, purpose, usage and overall appeal – along with the consumer's previous experiences and certain tangible benefits such as interest-free credit and warranties – dictate the consumer's view of value for money.

» Unlike consumers, industrial or business buyers purchase products to use in their own operations or for producing other products. When adjusting prices, business sellers take into consideration the size of the purchase, geographic factors and transport requirements. Producers commonly provide *trade* or *functional discounts* off list prices to intermediaries. The five categories of discount include (1) trade, (2) quantity, (3) cash discounts, (4) seasonal discounts, and (5) allowances. A trade discount is a price reduction for performing certain functions. If an intermediary purchases in large enough quantities, the producer gives a *quantity discount*, which can either be *cumulative* or *non-cumulative*. A *cash discount* is a price reduction for prompt payment or payment in cash. Buyers who purchase goods or services out of season may be granted a *seasonal discount*. A final type of reduction from the list price is an *allowance*, such as a trade-in allowance.

» *Geographic pricing* involves reductions for transport costs or other costs associated with the physical distance between the buyer and the seller. An *FOB factory price* means that the buyer pays for shipping from the factory; an *FOB destination price* means that the producer pays for shipping the merchandise. When the seller charges a fixed average cost for transport, the practice is known as *uniform geographic pricing*. *Zone prices* take advantage of a uniform pricing system adjusted for major geographic zones as the transport costs increase. *Base point pricing* involves prices being adjusted for shipping expenses incurred by the seller from the base point nearest the buyer. A seller who absorbs all or part of the freight costs is using *freight absorption pricing*. *Transfer pricing* occurs when one company unit sells a product to another unit within the same company.

When a *price discrimination* policy is adopted, different prices are charged in order to give a group of buyers a competitive edge. In some countries, price differentials are legal only in circumstances where competition is not damaged.

The concept of *economic value to the customer (EVC)* is sometimes used in business markets to aid price setting. The underlying principle is that a premium price can be charged while still offering better value than the competition. This is because business-to-business companies are driven by the need to reduce costs and increase revenue.

## *Key Links*

This chapter about pricing concepts should be read in conjunction with Chapter 21, which examines setting prices.

- Price impacts strongly on how businesses fare competitively. The concepts of competitive strategy and the competitive environment are explored in Chapters 2 and 3.
- Price is a key element of the marketing mix, because it directly affects how much revenue is generated. Understanding pricing concepts is critical to the development of effective marketing programmes, as discussed in Parts III–VI.
- Pricing impacts significantly on a brand's positioning, as described in Chapter 8.

## Important Terms

Price
Financial price
Price competition
EDLP
Non-price competition
Pricing objectives
Internal reference price
External reference price
Value-conscious consumers
Price-conscious consumers
Prestige-sensitive consumers
Perceived value for money
Trade or functional discount
Quantity discounts
Cumulative discounts
Non-cumulative discounts
Cash discount
Seasonal discount
Allowance
Geographic pricing
FOB factory price
FOB destination price
Uniform geographic pricing
Zone prices
Base point pricing
Freight absorption pricing
Transfer pricing
Price discrimination
Economic value to the customer (EVC)

## Discussion and Review Questions

1. Why are pricing decisions so important to a business?
2. Compare and contrast price and non-price competition. Describe the conditions under which each form works best.
3. How does a pricing objective of return on investment (ROI) differ from a pricing objective to increase market share?
4. Why is it crucial to consider both marketing objectives and pricing objectives when making pricing decisions?
5. In what ways do other marketing mix variables affect pricing decisions?
6. What types of expectation may channel members have about producers' prices, and how do these expectations affect pricing decisions?
7. How do legal and regulatory forces influence pricing decisions?
8. Why must marketers consider consumers' perceptions of value for money when setting prices?
9. What is the difference between a price discount and price discrimination?
10. Compare and contrast a trade discount and a quantity discount.
11. What is EDLP (everyday low pricing)? How does it work?
12. Why is the concept of EVC (economic value to the customer) important when setting prices in business-to-business markets?

## Recommended Readings


- E. Gijsbrechts, 'Pricing and pricing research in consumer marketing: some recent developments', *International Journal of Research in Marketing*, vol. 10, 1993, pp. 15–115.
- B.K. Monroe, *Pricing: Making Profitable Decisions*, (New York: McGraw-Hill, 2002).
- M.H. Morris, 'Separate prices as a marketing tool', *Industrial Marketing Management*, vol. 16, 1987, pp. 79–86.
- T. Nagle and R.K. Holden, *The Strategy and Tactics of Pricing* (Englewood Cliffs, NJ: Prentice-Hall, 2002).
- A. Diamantopoulos and B.P. Mathews, *Making Pricing Decisions: a Study of Managerial Practice* (London: Thomson Learning, 1995).


## Internet Exercise

Whether interested in buying a used or a new car, buying it outright, on credit terms or by leasing, www.jamjar.co.uk offers car buyers a comprehensive website. Take a look at this online retailer at:
www.jamjar.co.uk

1 Find the lowest-priced VW Golf available today and list its features.
2 If you wanted to purchase this VW, what is the lowest monthly payment you could make and what would it cost if you were to buy this model outright?
3 Compare and contrast the relative benefits of leasing and buying this car outright.

## *Applied Mini-Case*

Consumers can pay just 20 pence to write with a disposable biro, yet fancy fountain pens have become a common sight in the hands of influential businesspeople. Such pens have high price tags and are much more difficult to maintain than ballpoints, felt-tip pens or roller-ball pens. However, recent sales figures indicate that the semi-obsolete fountain pen is making a comeback as the writing instrument of choice for status-minded individuals. Of the premium-priced fountain pens, those produced by Montblanc are probably the most prestigious. Named after the highest mountain in Europe, these German-made fountain pens cost from about £100 to £5000 (for a solid-gold one). The most popular model costs about £300. Prestige pricing has worked well for Montblanc, placing the pen in the same category as Rolex watches, BMW cars and Gucci luggage.

**Sources:** Chuck Tomkovick and Kathryn Dobie, 'Apply hedonic pricing models and factorial surveys at Parker Pen to enhance new product success', *Journal of Product Innovation Management*, vol. 12, no. 4, 1995, pp. 334–5; Allen Norwood, 'Pen offers status', *Charlotte Observer*, 20 November 1988, pp. 1C–3C; Parker Pen Co. sales literature, 1996.

### *Question*

A company competing in the same sector as Montblanc has asked you to prepare a report explaining the factors that influence the pricing decisions they should make for a new range of pens. What areas should your report include?

## Case Study

# Perfume Discounting – Pricing Policies to Rattle the Leading Brands

For decades the leading perfume houses of Paris, London and New York have sought exclusive, premium-brand positioning: Joy, Chanel No. 5 and Givenchy have been marketed as high-priced, deluxe lines available only from carefully selected retailers: leading department stores, fragrance houses and only those chemists with a genuine perfumery. Even a company as reputable as Boots has failed to gain Chanel's permission to retail Chanel fragrances throughout its chain of stores. Chanel permits only certain branches of Boots to stock its brands, sometimes giving preference to an independent specialist fragrance house in a town to retail its products.

While these upmarket brands have controlled distribution, they have also prevented price discounting. The more mass-market brands, such as Revlon, Max Factor and Boots' own No. 7, have been left to take the bulk of the market on volume, pricing way below Miss Dior, Chanel No. 5 or Givenchy. In this way, these more expensive, selectively distributed brands have nurtured an exclusive, premium image to support their higher prices.

The Superdrug chain, a discounter, caught the marketplace by surprise. It brought in full in-store pharmacies to rival Boots but kept its discounting focus by reducing the prices of proprietary medicines by around 10 per cent. Superdrug also looked to the perfume market, reducing the prices of the more mass-market brands it stocked. Why, though, should Superdrug not create full perfumery sections in its larger branches and stock the more upmarket, exclusive brands? More importantly, why should Superdrug not discount the prices of these leading exclusive brands of perfume, in line with the chain's general trading philosophy as a discounter?

Shock waves were felt throughout the industry. The perfume producers had spent decades creating premium-priced, exclusive brands. Discounting by a retail chain was the antithesis of this strategy. Independent perfume retailers had been able to occupy prime pitch sites with high staffing levels and glamorous shop fittings on the basis of the higher margins offered by the slower-selling exclusive brands. The pricing and images of these brands had for decades protected them from the national retail chains and buying groups. The large department stores were less dependent on maintaining the premium pricing, but they similarly saw their sales decline as Superdrug followed through with its plans. EU and UK trading laws and anti-price fixing legislation seemed to be on Superdrug's side, too.

It was not easy going for Superdrug. Along with the other discounters, it was refused supplies from the perfume manufacturers; the company had to source from 'the grey market', mainly overseas wholesalers. The producers' PR mechanisms mobilised many industry players against the moves. Superdrug's first press advertising campaign for its discounting of fine fragrances was rejected by a string of upmarket colour supplements and publishing houses. According to the marketing press, the colour supplements of the *Independent on Sunday, The Sunday Times* and the *Observer* refused to carry the Superdrug advertisements for fear of provoking repercussions from the upmarket perfume houses, all leading advertisers in these newspapers' supplements.

Prior to Christmas, the peak selling season for all perfumes – including brands such as Joy, Chanel and Givenchy – leading department store operator House of Fraser, reduced the prices of many leading perfumes. Boots, too, retaliated against Superdrug's move. For example, in branches of Boots permitted to sell Chanel, a smaller Chanel No. 5 perfume dropped from around £28 to £21, a price still well ahead of the more mass-market brands, but the largest discount for such a brand seen in one of its core retail outlets. Boots and House of Fraser admitted they were 'reviewing daily' their pricing policies.

Years of brand building and image cultivation were in jeopardy. More to the point, the retailers were to risk reducing sales of these still lucrative brands. Superdrug wanted to enter the upper echelons of the fragrance market, but not to let discounting devalue the worth of stocking some of these brands. There were no intentions to replicate the price discounting and tit-for-tat retaliations in the DIY or grocery sectors of retailing, or in the holiday industry. The fragrance market, though, witnessed quite dramatic upheavals in a very conservative market. The entry of Superdrug, with its aggressive pricing policy and discounting, caused changes in strategies throughout the industry, by perfume producers, retailers and the media.

**Sources:** 'Superdrug finds refuge in women's magazines', *Marketing Week*, 13 November 1992, p. 6; Helen Slingsby, 'House of Fraser reviews scent pricing', *Marketing Week*, 18 December 1992, p. 5; 'Stop press', *Marketing*, 19 November 1992, p. 7; 'Eau Zone expands with new name', *Marketing Week*, 6 November 1992, p. 8; Suzanne Bidlake, 'Givenchy TV ads "plug" discounters', *Marketing*, 17 December 1992, p. 6, Suzanne Bidlake, 'Perfume firms fear wrath of retailers', *Marketing*, 29 October 1992, p. 5; Suzanne Bidlake, 'Asda apes Superdrug with discount scent', *Marketing*, 22 October 1992, p. 5.

## Questions for Discussion

1. What were the pricing objectives of perfume manufacturers such as Chanel and Givenchy? Explain.
2. What impact could a price war have on brand loyalty in this market? Why?
3. On what criteria had competition in this market previously been based? Was the new focus on price a sensible development?

# 21 Setting Prices

**"Price is the most dangerous marketing weapon a firm can use. It should be handled with great care."**

*Eric Waarts, Erasmus University, Rotterdam*

## Objectives

- To understand the eight major stages of the process used to establish prices
- To explore issues connected with selecting pricing objectives
- To grasp the importance of assessing the target market's evaluation of price and its ability to buy
- To learn about demand for a product and to analyse the relationships between demand, costs and profits
- To learn how to evaluate competitors' prices and to investigate the different dimensions on which prices can be based
- To explore the selection of a pricing strategy and to understand how to determine a specific price
- To consider the 'pricing balance'

## Introduction

Setting prices can be a complex process that must take many factors into consideration. This chapter examines the eight stages of a process that can be used when setting prices. These stages are not rigid steps that all marketers must follow but guidelines providing a logical sequence for establishing prices. Figure 21.1 illustrates these eight stages. Stage 1 is the selection of a pricing objective that is congruent with the company's overall objectives and its marketing objectives. In stage 2, both the target market's evaluation of price and the ability of these consumers to buy must be assessed. Stage 3 requires marketers to determine the nature and price elasticity of demand. Stage 4, which consists of analysing demand, cost and profit relationships, is necessary for estimating the economic feasibility of alternative prices. Evaluation of competitors' prices, which constitutes stage 5, helps determine the role of price in the marketing strategy. Stage 6 involves determining the basis for pricing. Stage 7 concerns the selection of a pricing strategy. Stage 8, the determination of the final price, depends on environmental forces, and marketers' understanding and use of a systematic approach to establishing prices.

As explained in the previous chapter, marketers need to give careful consideration to pricing issues. Price impacts strongly on how businesses fare competitively and is critical to the marketing mix because it directly affects how much revenue is generated. As price can be changed quickly, it is more flexible than other elements of the marketing mix. Businesses must avoid seeing price purely in terms of setting monetary price points. Because of the psychological impact of price on customers, it also has a symbolic value. It is therefore desirable to take a broader view of pricing, which takes into account issues such as target customers' perceptions of value for money and requirements for easy payment terms.

*Opener*

# Pricing an Experience

How do you price an experience? This is the challenge Virgin faces as it sets prices for a diverse range of 'experiences' offered via its website www.virgin.com/experience. Targeting consumers and business clients alike, those seeking a relaxing, exciting, indulgent experience for themselves, or looking for a 'different' gift for friends, family, colleagues or customers, can choose from a wide variety of options. The gifts fall into a number of different categories: Drive, Fly, Splash, Pamper, Discover, Taste, Collect, Escape and Voyage. The variety behind these titles is considerable. Perhaps your best friend has always wanted to discover scuba diving, learn circus skills or spend the day training border collies. Maybe your young sister fancies laying down a track at a recording studio, having a star named after her or just can't resist the 'I Love Chocolate Hamper'. All of these and many more activities and treats are available. The diversity of experiences on offer is clearly illustrated by the Drive category, which includes the following:

**Drive time**

- The Definitive Track Day – A day on the track in a high-powered car for experienced drivers
- Supercar Choice – The opportunity to drive a Porsche or Ferrari or take a rallying, 4x4 off-road or motor racing course
- Single Seater – The chance to drive a single-seater racing car
- Driver's Choice Plus – This voucher gives the receiver the chance to choose one of five driving experiences for themselves.

**Top gear action**

- Military Vehicle Driving – Develop your skills in driving military vehicles
- 4x4 Off-road Driving – The chance to learn to drive off-road style
- Karting – Spend some time on one of the UK's most challenging karting circuits
- Rally Driving – For those who fancy getting to grips with a rally car.

**Transport yourself**

- Harley Heaven – A journey as a passenger on a Harley-Davidson motorbike
- First Drive – The opportunity to experience a first drive in controlled conditions (no licence needed)
- Skid Control – Fun and action on the skid track
- High Speed Ride – The chance to enjoy high-speed circuit driving while someone else drives.

For customers finding it hard to make a decision, Virgin Experience Options Vouchers are available. Ranging in price from £50 (€75) to £500 (€750), these vouchers enable the holder to choose the experience they would like to get involved in. The colour of the voucher determines its value and also the experiences available to its holders. For example, the Red Virgin Experience Voucher, priced at £100 (€150), can be exchanged for a day's tuition in training border collies, the Virgin Wines Discovery Experience, a Learning to Play Golf session, an Indulgence Hamper or a range of flying, driving, cooking or other activities. In setting the price of these vouchers and deciding for which experiences they can be swapped, Virgin is making a judgement about the value that customers attach to indulging themselves or others, and spending their time in a new and interesting way.

**Sources:** www.virgin.com/experience; Virgin marketing materials.
Photo: Courtesy of Virgin Experience Days

When setting prices for its range of experiences, Virgin must take into consideration a wide range of factors. Economic conditions, fluctuations in market growth and levels of competition all affect the price that customers are prepared to pay for these innovative offerings. Careful judgement is needed to ensure that these factors are taken into consideration when setting prices, so that consumers and business customers alike regard these innovative experiences as reasonable value for money.

This chapter is structured around the eight-stage process for setting prices outlined in Figure 21.1, and its sections are devoted to each of these individual elements. The chapter concludes by considering the need for pragmatism in pricing decisions.

## Stages for Establishing Prices

When going through the stages for establishing prices, marketers must be able to grasp target customers' evaluation of price and perceived value for money, as well as understand market trends and competitors' pricing moves.[1] The 'economics' of pricing – demand curves and price elasticity, plus the relationship in the market in question between demand, costs and profits – must also be addressed. The marketer must ultimately choose from a variety of pricing approaches and specific pricing strategies. The remainder of this chapter reviews the eight stages for establishing prices in greater depth. The final section explains that, in operational situations, marketers must take a broader look at pricing concerns and exercise pragmatism in determining the price element of the marketing mix.

## Stage 1: Selection of Pricing Objectives

Chapter 20 considered the various types of pricing objective. Pricing objectives must be stated explicitly because they form the basis for decisions about other stages of pricing.[2] The statement of pricing objectives should include the time within which the objectives are to be accomplished.

Marketers must set pricing objectives that are consistent with the company's overall and marketing objectives. As the Topical Insight box on page 649 explains, retailer ASDA has a stated objective of providing customers with permanently low prices. Inconsistent objectives cause internal conflicts and confusion, and can prevent the business from achieving its overall goals. Furthermore, such inconsistency may cause marketers to make poor decisions during the other stages in the price-setting process.

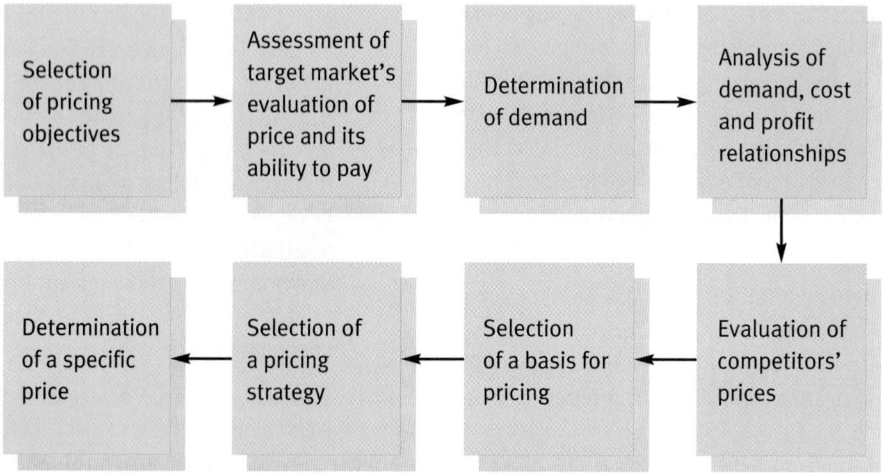


***Figure 21.1***
*Stages for establishing prices*

## Topical Insight

### ASDA's Permanently Low Prices

With a stated objective of providing customers with permanently low prices, Wal-Mart owned supermarket chain ASDA has a long-established reputation for offering shoppers value for money. This remains at the heart of the retailer's offer to customers and plays a key role in reassuring shoppers that the products they buy there are keenly priced. Initially set up by Yorkshire farmers, the ASDA Stores Ltd of today was established in 1965 when Associated Dairies and a supermarket chain called Queen's joined forces. In 1999, ASDA became part of Wal-Mart's portfolio and now boasts more than 250 stores. ASDA's value-for-money policy fits well with that of its US parent, which has a global reputation for low prices. The company's policy, which puts keen prices at the heart of its relationship with customers, is explained clearly on ASDA's website:

> We lead the way in giving UK customers the products they want at the lowest prices and continue to widen the price gap between our competitors. Underlining the difference, we have again, for the fifth successive year, been voted 'Britain's best value supermarket' by leading trade magazine, *The Grocer*.

This policy is reflected in many ways throughout ASDA's stores. For example, ASDA Smartprice is an own-label line of low-price food and basics. The fact that ASDA has been able to build on its heritage of offering value for money owes much to its relationship with its parent company. Wal-Mart's position as the world's biggest retailer and a leader in offering customer value has helped support ASDA's approach.

Building on the success of George at ASDA, the retailer's hugely successful fashion brand, the company has taken the opportunity to further grow the non-food part of its business. A particular focus has been to develop a wider range of general merchandise including electrical goods and household linen. In 2002 alone, 5000 new lines were added to the non-food business. The highly competitive prices of these products have been made possible because so many of the items are jointly sourced with Wal-Mart, taking advantages of the retailing giant's huge buying power.

Now ASDA is developing its business into a number of speciality areas, such as providing in-store opticians, pharmacies and photo centres. Once again the retailer is leveraging Wal-Mart's expertise in these areas. One of ASDA's most recent ventures has been to launch a number of good-value insurance products in conjunction with Norwich Union. Now ASDA shoppers can pick up details of motor, home and travel insurance while buying their fruit, vegetables, dishwasher tablets and new socks. Based on the notion of hassle-free, low-cost insurance, applications for the products can then be made via telephone hotlines. This is all part of the company's ongoing drive to offer permanently low prices across its growing product range. Given the importance of value for money to the retailer's customers, keeping this drive at the heart of the company's offer is critical in ensuring the ongoing loyalty of ASDA shoppers.

**Sources:** www.asda.co.uk; www.walmart.com.

Businesses normally have multiple pricing objectives, some short term and others long term. For example, the pricing objective of gaining market share is normally short term in that it often requires products to be priced lower than competitors' prices. A business should have one or more pricing objectives for each product. Different pricing objectives may be chosen for the same product aimed at different market segments. A marketer typically alters pricing objectives over time.

## Stage 2: Assessing the Target Market's Evaluation of Price and its Ability to Buy

The degree to which price is a significant issue for buyers depends on the type of product, the type of target market and the purchase situation. For example, most buyers are more sensitive to petrol prices than to the cost of a new passport. With respect to the type of target market, the price of an airline ticket is much more important to a tourist than to a business traveller. The purchase situation also has a major impact. Thus visitors to tourist attractions may be prepared to pay inflated prices for canned drinks and food, which is something they would not tolerate from their local supermarket. Assessing the target market's evaluation of price helps a marketer to judge how much emphasis to place on price.

As discussed in Chapter 8, the people who make up a market must have the ability to buy a product. This ability to buy, like buyers' evaluation of price, has direct consequences for marketers. It involves such resources as money, credit, wealth and other products that could be traded in an exchange. Understanding customers' buying power and knowing how important a product is to them in comparison with other products helps marketers correctly assess the target market's evaluation of price. As outlined in the previous chapter, it is also important to understand the consumers' view of actual price versus perceived value for money.

# Stage 3: Determining Demand

Determining the demand for a product is the responsibility of marketing managers, who are aided in this task by marketing researchers and forecasters. Marketing research and forecasting techniques yield estimates of sales potential or the quantity of a product that could be sold during a specific period. Chapter 23 describes such techniques as surveys, time series analyses, correlation methods and market tests. These estimates are helpful in establishing the relationship between a product's price and the quantity demanded.

## The Demand Curve

For most products, the quantity demanded goes up as the price goes down, and goes down as the price goes up. Thus there is an inverse relationship between price and quantity demanded. As long as the marketing environment and buyers' needs, ability (purchasing power), willingness and authority to buy remain stable, this fundamental inverse relationship will continue.

**Demand curve**
A graph of the quantity of products expected to be sold at various prices, if other factors remain constant

Figure 21.2 illustrates the effect of one variable – price – on the quantity demanded. The classic **demand curve** (D1) is a graph of the quantity of products expected to be sold at various prices, if other factors remain constant.[3] It illustrates that as price falls, the quantity demanded usually increases. Demand depends on other factors in the marketing mix, including product quality, promotion and distribution. An improvement in any of these factors may cause a shift to, say, demand curve D2. In such a case, an increased quantity (Q2) will be sold

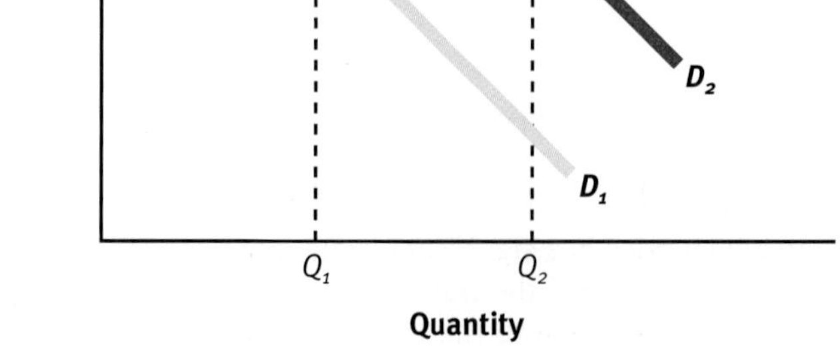

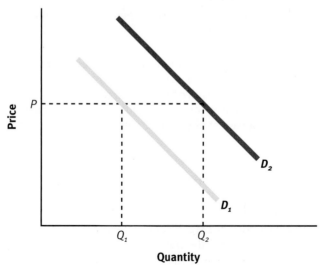

***Figure 21.2***
*Demand curve illustrating the price–quantity relationship and an increase in demand*
*Source: reprinted from* Dictionary of Marketing Terms, *Peter D. Bennett, ed., 1988, p. 54, published by the American Marketing Association. Used by permission*

at the same price (P). For example, if a manufacturer of engine oil improves the quality of its product, customers may be prepared to pay more for it because they do not need to change it as frequently.

There are many types of demand, and not all conform to the classic demand curve shown in Figure 21.2. Prestige products, such as designer jewellery, fragrances and exclusive holidays seem to sell better at high prices than at low ones. These products are desirable partly because their cost makes buyers feel superior. If their price fell drastically and many people owned them, they would lose some of their appeal.

The demand curve in Figure 21.3 shows the relationship between price and quantity for prestige products. Demand is greater, not less, at higher prices. For a certain price range – from P1 to P2 – the quantity demanded (Q1) goes up to Q2. After a point, however, raising the price backfires. If the price of a product goes too high, the quantity demanded goes down. The figure shows that if the price is raised from P2 to P3, quantity demanded goes back down from Q2 to Q1.

## Demand Fluctuations

Changes in buyers' needs, variations in the effectiveness of other marketing mix variables, the presence of substitutes and dynamic environmental factors can influence demand. Internet search engines, restaurants and utility companies experience large fluctuations in demand daily. Holiday companies, fireworks suppliers and swimming pool sellers also face demand fluctuations because of the seasonal nature of these items. The demand for laptop computers, leaded fuels and on-line banking services has changed significantly in recent years. In some cases, demand fluctuations are predictable and in others they are not. Some companies cope with unpredictable demand fluctuations by correlating demand for a specific product with demand for the total industry or with some other economic variable.

## Gauging Price Elasticity of Demand

**Price elasticity of demand**
A measure of the sensitivity of demand to changes in price

The discussion so far has considered how marketers identify the target market's evaluation of price and its ability to purchase, and how they examine whether price is related inversely or directly to quantity sold. The next stage in the process is to gauge price elasticity of demand. **Price elasticity of demand** provides a measure of the sensitivity of demand to changes in price. It is formally defined as the percentage change in quantity demanded

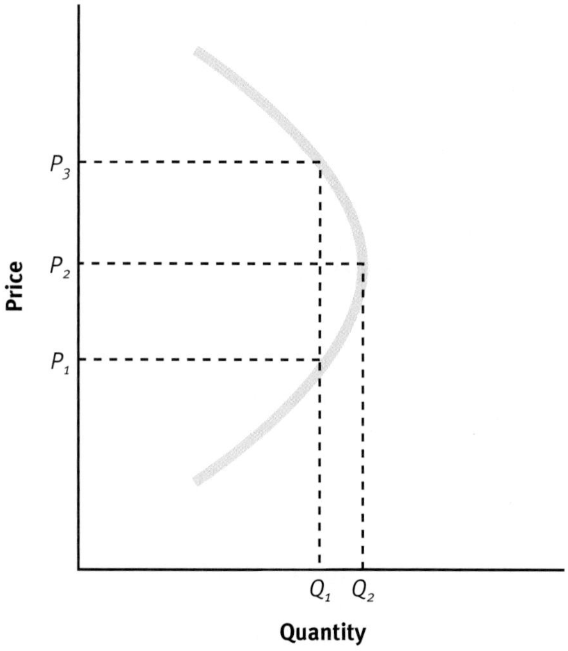


*Figure 21.3*
*Demand curve illustrating the relationship between price and quantity for prestige products*

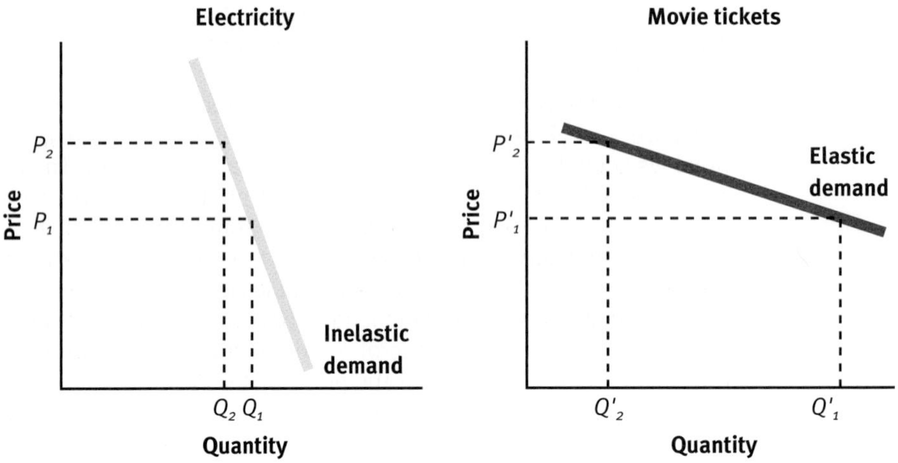


***Figure 21.4***
*Elasticity of demand*
*Source: adapted from* Dictionary of Marketing Terms, *Peter D. Bennett, ed., 1988, p. 54, published by the American Marketing Association. Used by permission*

relative to a given percentage change in price (see Figure 21.4).[4] The percentage change in quantity demanded caused by a percentage change in price is much greater for elastic demand than for inelastic demand. For products such as electricity, medicines and cigarettes, demand is relatively inelastic. When price is increased, say from P1 to P2, quantity demanded goes down only a little, from Q1 to Q2. For products such as movie tickets, demand is relatively elastic. When price rises sharply, from P1 to P2, quantity demanded goes down a great deal, from Q1 to Q2.

Understanding the price elasticity of demand makes it easier for marketers to set a price. By analysing total revenues as prices change, marketers can determine whether a product is 'price elastic'. Total revenue is price times quantity: thus 10,000 rolls of wallpaper sold in one year at a price of £10 (€15) per roll equals £100,000 (€150,000) of total revenue. If demand is *elastic*, a change in price causes an opposite change in total revenue – an increase in price will decrease total revenue, and a decrease in price will increase total revenue. An *inelastic* demand results in a change in the same direction in total revenue – an increase in price will increase total revenue, and a decrease in price will decrease total revenue. The following formula determines the price elasticity of demand:

$$\text{Price elasticity of demand} = \frac{\text{\% change in quantity demanded}}{\text{\% change in price}}$$

For example, if demand falls by 8 per cent when a seller raises the price by 2 per cent, the price elasticity of demand is $-4$ (the negative sign indicating the inverse relationship between price and demand). If demand falls by 2 per cent when price is increased by 4 per cent, then elasticity is $-\frac{1}{2}$. The less elastic the demand, the more beneficial it is for the seller to raise the price. Products for which substitutes are not readily available and for which consumers have strong needs (for example, electricity or petrol) usually have inelastic demand.

Marketers cannot base prices solely on elasticity considerations. They must also examine the costs associated with different volumes and see what happens to profits.

## Stage 4: Analysis of Demand, Cost and Profit Relationships

The previous section examined the role of demand in setting prices, and the various costs and their relationships; this section explores the relationships between demand, costs and profits. There are two approaches to understanding demand, cost and profit relationships:

1 marginal analysis
2 break-even analysis.

## Marginal Analysis

**Fixed costs**
Those costs that do not vary with changes in the number of units produced or sold

**Average fixed cost**
The fixed cost per unit produced, calculated by dividing fixed costs by the number of units produced

**Variable costs**
Those costs that vary directly with changes in the number of units produced or sold

**Average variable cost**
The variable cost per unit produced, calculated by dividing the variable costs by the number of units produced

**Total cost**
The sum of average fixed costs and average variable costs multiplied by the quantity produced

Marginal analysis considers what happens to a company's costs and revenues when production (or sales volume) is changed by one unit. Both production costs and revenues must be evaluated. To determine the costs of production, it is necessary to distinguish between several types of cost. **Fixed costs** do not vary with changes in the number of units produced or sold. The cost of renting a factory unit does not change if an extra shift is added or more rolls of wallpaper are produced. Rent may go up, but not because the factory has increased the number of shifts or raised production. **Average fixed cost**, the fixed cost per unit produced, is calculated by dividing fixed costs by the number of units produced.

**Variable costs** vary directly with changes in the number of units produced or sold. The wages for additional factory workers and the cost of the additional paper are extra. Variable costs are usually constant per unit – that is, twice as many workers and twice as much material produce twice as many rolls of wallpaper. **Average variable cost**, the variable cost per unit produced, is calculated by dividing the variable costs by the number of units produced.

**Total cost** is the sum of average fixed costs and average variable costs multiplied by the quantity produced. The **average total cost** is the sum of the average fixed cost and the average variable cost. **Marginal cost (MC)** is the extra cost a company incurs when it produces one more unit of a product. Table 21.1 illustrates various costs and their relationships. Notice that the average fixed cost declines as the output increases. The average variable cost follows a U shape, as does the average total cost. Because the average total cost continues to fall after the average variable cost begins to rise, its lowest point is at a higher level of output than that of the average variable cost. The average total cost is lowest at 5 units at a cost of £22, whereas the average variable cost is lowest at 3 units at a cost of £11.67. As shown in Figure 21.5, marginal cost equals average total cost at the latter's lowest level. In Table 21.1 this occurs between 5 and 6 units of production. Average total cost decreases as long as the marginal cost is less than the average total cost, and it increases when marginal cost rises above average total cost.

**Marginal revenue (MR)** is the change in total revenue that occurs when a company sells an additional unit of a product. Figure 21.6 depicts marginal revenue and a demand curve. Most businesses in Europe face downward-sloping demand curves for their products. In other words, they must lower their prices to sell additional units. This situation means that each additional product sold provides the business with less revenue than the previous

**Table 21.1 Costs and Their Relationships**

| 1 | 2 | 3 | 4 | 5 | 6 | 7 |
|---|---|---|---|---|---|---|
| Quantity | Fixed cost | Average fixed cost (2) ÷ (1) | Average variable cost | Average total cost (3) + (4) | Total cost (5) × (1) | Marginal cost |
| 1 | £40 | £40.00 | £20.00 | £60.00 | £60 | |
| | | | | | | £10 |
| 2 | 40 | 20.00 | 15.00 | 35.00 | 70 | |
| | | | | | | 5 |
| 3 | 40 | 13.33 | 11.67 | 25.00 | 75 | |
| | | | | | | 15 |
| 4 | 40 | 10.00 | 12.50 | 22.50 | 90 | |
| | | | | | | 20 |
| 5 | 40 | 8.00 | 14.00 | 22.00 | 110 | |
| | | | | | | 30 |
| 6 | 40 | 6.67 | 16.67 | 23.33 | 140 | |
| | | | | | | 40 |
| 7 | 40 | 5.71 | 20.00 | 25.71 | 180 | |

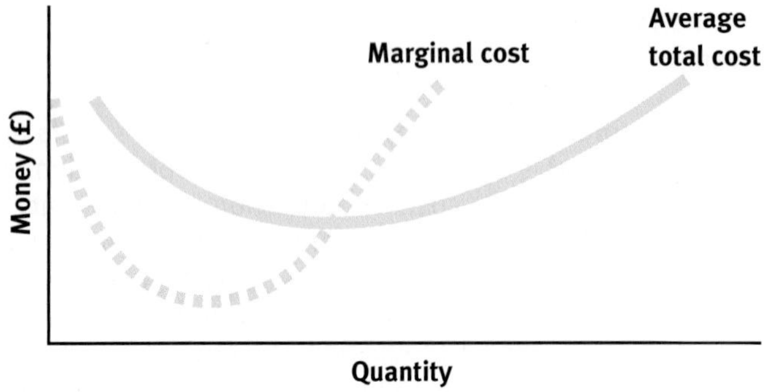


*Figure 21.5*
*Typical marginal cost and average cost relationships*

**Average total cost**
The sum of the average fixed cost and the average variable cost

**Marginal cost (MC)**
The extra cost a company incurs when it produces one more unit of a product

**Marginal revenue (MR)**
The change in total revenue that occurs when a company sells an additional unit of a product

unit sold. MR then becomes less than average revenue, as Figure 21.6 shows. Eventually, MR reaches zero, and the sale of additional units merely hurts the company.

However, before the company can determine whether a unit makes a profit, it must know its cost, as well as its revenue, because profit equals revenue minus cost. If MR is a unit's addition to revenue and MC is a unit's addition to cost, then MR minus MC tells whether the unit is profitable or not. Table 21.2 illustrates the relationships between price, quantity sold, total revenue, marginal revenue, marginal cost and total cost. It indicates where maximum profits are possible at various combinations of price and cost.

Profit is maximised where MC = MR (see Table 21.2). In this table MC = MR at 4 units. The best price, therefore, is £33.75 and the profit is £45. Up to this point, the additional revenue generated from an extra unit of sale exceeds the additional total cost. Beyond this point, the additional cost of another unit sold exceeds the additional revenue generated, and profits decrease. If the price was based on minimum average total cost – £22 (Table 21.1) – it would result in less profit: only £40 (Table 21.2) or 5 units at a price of £30 versus £45 for 4 units at a price of £33.75.

Graphically combining Figures 21.5 and 21.6 into Figure 21.7 shows that any unit for which MR exceeds MC adds to a company's profits, and any unit for which MC exceeds MR subtracts from a company's profits. The company should produce at the point where MR equals MC, because this is the most profitable level of production.

This discussion of marginal analysis may give the false impression that pricing can be highly precise. If revenue (demand) and cost (supply) remained constant, then prices could be set for maximum profits. In practice, however, cost and revenue change frequently. The competitive tactics of other companies or government action can quickly undermine a company's

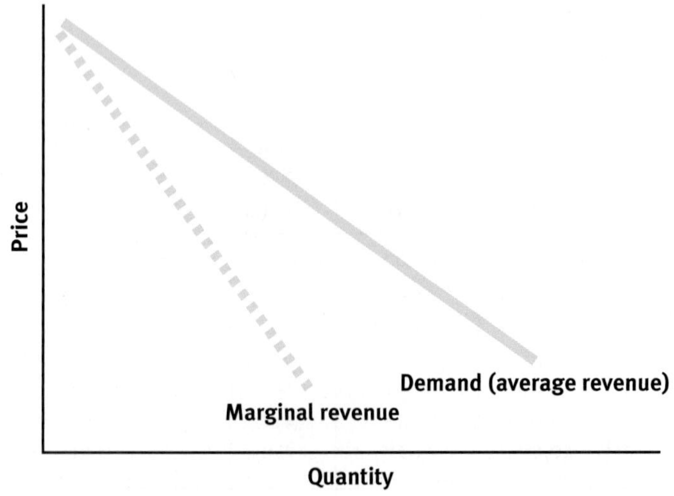


*Figure 21.6*
*Typical marginal revenue and demand (average revenue) relationships*

**Table 21.2 Marginal Analysis: Method of Obtaining Maximum Profit-Producing Price**

| 1 | 2 | 3 | 4 | 5 | 6 | 7 |
|---|---|---|---|---|---|---|
| Price | Quantity sold | Total revenue (1) × (2) | Marginal revenue | Marginal cost | Total cost | Profit (3)–(6) |
| £57.00 | 1 | £57 | £57 | £ – | £60 | £–3 |
| 55.00 | 2 | 110 | 53 | 10 | 70 | 40 |
| 40.00 | 3 | 120 | 10 | 5 | 75 | 45 |
| **33.75*** | **4** | **135** | **15** | **15** | **90** | **45** |
| 30.00 | 5 | 150 | 15 | 20 | 110 | 40 |
| 27.00 | 6 | 162 | 12 | 30 | 140 | 22 |
| 25.00 | 7 | 175 | 13 | 40 | 180 | –5 |

*Boldface indicates best price–profit combination.

expectations of revenue. Thus marginal analysis is only a model from which to work. It offers little help in pricing new products before costs and revenues are established. However, when setting the prices of existing products, most marketers can benefit by understanding the relationship between marginal cost and marginal revenue.

## Break-even Analysis

**Break-even point**
The point at which the costs of producing a product equal the revenue made from selling the product

The point at which the costs of producing a product equal the revenue made from selling the product is the **break-even point**. If a hairdressing salon has total annual costs of £150,000 and in the same year sells £150,000 worth of haircuts and treatments, then the business has broken even: no profits, no losses.

Figure 21.8 illustrates the relationships of costs, revenue, profits and losses involved in determining the break-even point. Knowing the number of units necessary to break even is important in setting the price. If a product priced at £100 per unit has an average variable cost of £60 per unit, then the contribution to fixed costs is £40. If total fixed costs are £120,000, here is the way to determine the break-even point in units:

$$\text{Break-even point} = \frac{\text{fixed costs}}{\text{per unit contribution to fixed costs}}$$

$$= \frac{\text{fixed costs}}{\text{price} - \text{variable costs}}$$

$$= \frac{£120{,}000}{£40}$$

$$= 3000 \text{ units}$$

To calculate the break-even point in terms of cash sales volume, multiply the break-even point in units by the price per unit. In the preceding example, the break-even point in terms of cash sales volume is 3000 (units) times £100, or £300,000.

To use break-even analysis effectively, a marketer should determine the break-even point for each of several alternative prices. This allows the effects on total revenue, total cost and the break-even point for each price under consideration to be assessed. Although this analysis may not tell the marketer exactly what price to charge, it will identify price alternatives that should definitely be avoided.

Break-even analysis is simple and straightforward. It does assume, however, that the quantity demanded is basically fixed (inelastic) and that the major task in setting prices is

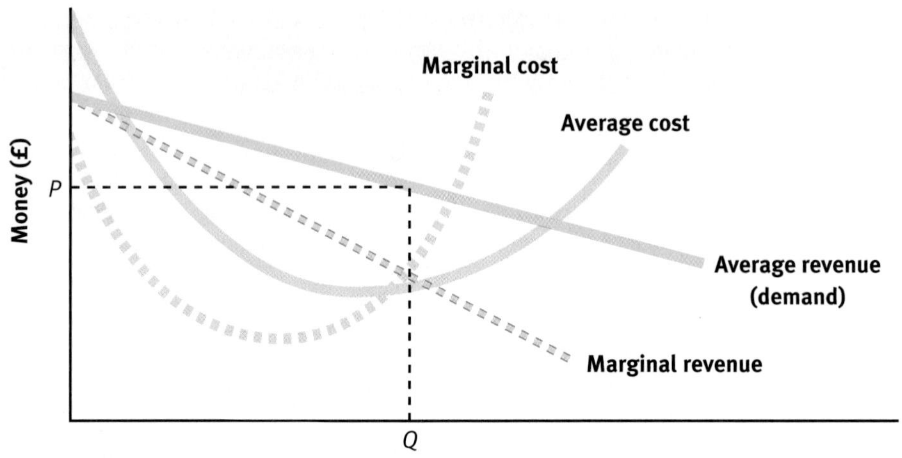


*Figure 21.7* Combining the marginal cost and marginal revenue concepts for optimal profit

to recover costs. It focuses more on how to break even than on how to achieve a pricing objective, such as percentage of market share or return on investment. None the less, marketing managers can use this concept to determine whether a product will achieve at least a break-even volume. In other words, it is easier to answer the question 'Will we sell at least the minimum volume needed to break even?' than the question 'What volume of sales can we expect?'

# Stage 5: Evaluation of Competitors' Prices

The prices marketers set will be influenced by competitors' pricing strategies. The case study at the end of this chapter explores the impact on Toys 'Я' Us of the prices charged by competing toy retailers. Marketers are better able to establish prices when they know the prices charged for competing brands. Learning competitors' prices is a regular function of marketing research. Some grocery and department stores, for example, have full-time comparative shoppers who systematically collect data on prices. Companies may also purchase price lists, sometimes weekly, from syndicated marketing research agencies.

Finding out what prices competitors are charging is not always easy, especially in producer and reseller markets. Even if a marketer has access to price lists, these may not reflect the actual prices at which competitive products are sold because those prices may be established through negotiation.

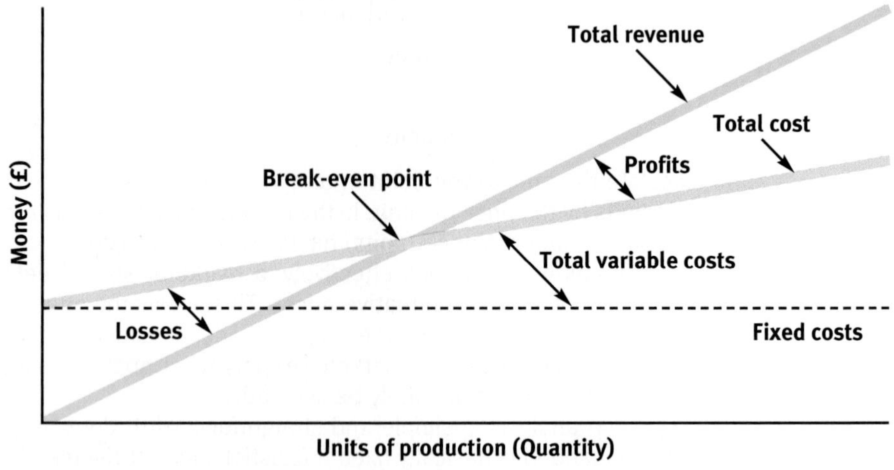


*Figure 21.8* Determining the break-even point

Marketers in an industry in which non-price competition prevails need competitive price information to ensure that their company's prices are the same as those of competitors. Sometimes a company's prices are designed to be slightly above competitors' prices to give its products an exclusive image. Alternatively, another company may use price as a competitive tool and attempt to set its prices below those of competitors. Aldi, DFS and Superdrug, for example, have all acquired market share through aggressive competitive prices.

**Basis for pricing** Structures the calculation of the actual price

**Cost-based pricing** A pricing approach whereby a monetary amount or percentage is added to the cost of a product

## Stage 6: Selecting a Basis for Pricing

After evaluating competitors' prices, a marketer must choose a **basis for pricing**. This basis structures the calculation of the actual price. The nature of a product, its sales volume or the amount of product the company carries will determine how prices are calculated. For example, a procedure for pricing the thousands of products in a supermarket must be simpler and more direct than that for calculating the price of a limited-edition ceramic figurine made by Wedgwood or Royal Doulton.

### Cost-based Pricing

In **cost-based pricing**, a monetary amount or percentage is added to the cost of a product. The method thus involves calculations of desired margins or profit margins. Cost-based pricing does not necessarily take into account the economic aspects of supply and demand, nor does it necessarily relate to a specific pricing approach or ensure the attainment of pricing objectives. It is, however, simple and easy to implement. Two common cost-based approaches are cost plus and mark-up pricing.

### Cost Plus Pricing

**Cost plus pricing** A pricing approach based on adding a specified amount or percentage to the seller's cost after that cost is determined

In **cost plus pricing**, the seller's costs are determined and the price is then set by adding a specified amount or percentage of the cost to the seller's costs. Cost plus pricing is appropriate when production costs are difficult to predict or production takes a long time. Custom-made equipment and commercial construction projects are often priced by this method. The government frequently uses pricing oriented to costs in granting defence contracts. The approach can be problematic, however, because some costs are difficult to determine. There is also a danger that the seller may increase costs to establish a larger profit base.

In periods of rapid inflation, cost plus pricing is popular, especially as the raw materials used may fluctuate in price. For industries in which cost plus pricing is common and sellers have similar costs, price competition may not be especially intense.

### Mark-up Pricing

**Mark-up pricing** A pricing approach whereby a product's price is derived by adding a predetermined percentage of the cost, called mark-up, to the cost of the product

**Demand-based pricing** A pricing approach based on the level of demand for a product, resulting in a high price when demand is strong and a low price when demand is weak

Retailers commonly use **mark-up pricing**, where a price is derived by adding a predetermined percentage of the cost, called mark-up, to the cost of the product. Although the percentage mark-up in a retail store varies for different categories (35 per cent of cost for hardware items and 100 per cent of cost for greeting cards, for example), the same percentage is often used to determine the price of items within a single product category, and similar percentage mark-ups may be standardised across an industry at the retail level. Using a rigid percentage mark-up for a specific product category reduces pricing to a routine task that can be performed quickly.

Mark-up can be stated as a percentage of the cost or as a percentage of the selling price. The following example illustrates how percentage mark-ups are determined and points out the differences between the two methods. Assume that a retailer purchases a tin of mushrooms at 45p, adds 15p to the cost, and then prices the mushrooms at 60p. Here are the figures:

$$\text{Mark-up as a percentage of cost} = \frac{\text{mark-up}}{\text{cost}} = \frac{15}{45} = 33^1/_3\%$$

$$\text{Mark-up as a percentage of selling price} = \frac{\text{mark-up}}{\text{selling price}} = \frac{15}{60} = 25\%$$

Mark-ups normally reflect expectations about operating costs, risks and stock turnovers. Wholesalers and manufacturers often suggest standard retail mark-ups that are considered profitable. An average percentage mark-up on cost may be as high as 100 per cent or more for jewellery or as low as 20 per cent for this textbook.

## Demand-based Pricing

Marketers sometimes use a pricing approach based on the level of demand for a product: **demand-based pricing**. This approach results in a high price when demand for a product is strong and a low price when demand is weak. Pricing of leisure amenities often operates on this basis, with higher prices when demand is highest at weekends and during peak holiday periods. Using this method the amounts of a product that consumers will demand at different prices needs to be estimated. The price that generates the highest total revenue is then selected. The effectiveness of demand-based pricing depends on the marketer's ability to estimate demand accurately. Compared with cost-based pricing, demand-based pricing places a company in a better position to gain higher profits.

## Competition-based Pricing

**Competition-based pricing**
A pricing approach whereby a business considers costs and revenue to be secondary to competitors' prices

In using **competition-based pricing**, an organisation considers costs and revenue as secondary to competitors' prices. This approach is important if competing products are almost homogeneous and the company is servicing markets in which price is the key variable of the marketing strategy.[5] A business that uses competition-based pricing may choose to be below competitors' prices, above competitors' prices or at the same level. The price of domestic electricity is determined using competition-oriented pricing. Competition-based pricing should help attain a pricing objective to increase sales or market share. Competition-based pricing approaches may be combined with cost approaches to arrive at price levels necessary to generate a profit.

## Marketing-oriented Pricing

**Marketing-oriented pricing**
A pricing approach whereby a company takes into account a wide range of factors including marketing strategy, competition, value to the customer, price–quality relationships, explicability, costs, product line pricing, negotiating margins, political factors and effect on distributors/retailers

More complex than cost- or competition-oriented pricing, **marketing-oriented pricing** takes account of a wide range of factors:

- marketing strategy
- competition
- value to the customer
- price–quality relationships
- explicability
- costs
- product line pricing
- negotiating margins
- political factors
- effect on distributors/retailers.

The price set must reflect the product's marketing strategy: its target market profile, brand positioning and sales targets. The price point – the actual ticket or displayed price – must also be in harmony with the other marketing mix ingredients. For example, an exclusive premium-priced restaurant will fail if located in a seedy area of town. Marketers must be aware of competing products' prices and their own product's value as perceived by the targeted customer. The customer in question has to be receptive to the determined price. This customer-focused view is also reflected in two other criteria: the price–quality relationship of the product and the explicability of the finalised prices. Just how plausible to the customer is the recommended price? If the product is part of a range, its price point will affect the other product lines on offer, and the whole range must be priced to avoid an individual product harming the achieved price and image of related lines. While a business must ensure that its costs of production, distribution and marketing are covered, it also has to recognise that its dealers and distributors must make an adequate margin on units sold and set its prices to its distribution channel partners accordingly. These channel members and the ultimate customer may expect to negotiate over price – very common in business-to-business markets – so the price must be set to permit such negotiating and discounting. Trade and government regulations may affect the flexibility a business has in establishing prices. For example, EU anti-dumping laws forbid hefty price discounting for certain markets. The intention of marketing-oriented pricing is to take account of external factors as seen by the customer and experienced by channel members, in addition to the internal cost and performance drivers for so long central to management's thinking when setting prices.

**Pricing strategy**
An approach to influencing and determining pricing decisions

## Stage 7: Selection of a Pricing Strategy

A **pricing strategy** is an approach designed to influence and determine pricing decisions. Pricing strategies help marketers to solve the practical problems of establishing prices. The most common pricing strategies are listed in Table 21.3.

### Differential Pricing

An important issue in pricing is whether to use a single price or different prices for the same product. Using a single price has several benefits. A primary advantage is simplicity. A single price is easily understood by employees and customers, and since many sales people and customers do not like having to negotiate a price, it reduces the possibilities of an adversarial relationship developing between marketer and customer. However, the use of a single price can create challenges. If it is too high, customers may be unable to afford the product. If it is too low, the organisation may lose revenue.

**Differential pricing**
A pricing strategy involving charging different prices to different buyers for the same quality and quantity of product

**Differential pricing** means charging different prices to different buyers for the same quality and quantity of a product. For example, red roses are much more expensive in the run-up to Valentine's Day than at other times of the year. Hotel accommodation is costlier during peak holiday periods. Hairdressing salons may offer reduced prices to the elderly or students. For price differentiation to work properly, it must be possible to segment a market on the basis of strength of demand and then keep the segments separate enough so that those who buy at lower prices cannot then sell to buyers in segments that are charged a higher price. Differential pricing can occur in several ways, including negotiated pricing, secondary market discounting, periodic discounting and random discounting.

**Negotiated pricing**
A pricing approach where the final price is established through bargaining

**Negotiated Pricing** **Negotiated pricing**, which is common in a number of industries, occurs when the final price is established through bargaining between seller and customer. Even when a predetermined stated price exists, manufacturers, wholesalers and retailers may still negotiate to establish the final sales price. Consumers commonly negotiate prices for houses, cars and used or second-hand equipment.

**Table 21.3 Common Pricing Strategies**

| | |
|---|---|
| **Differential Pricing** | **Psychological Pricing** |
| Negotiated Pricing | Reference Pricing |
| Secondary Market Pricing | Bundle Pricing |
| Periodic Discounting | Multiple Unit Pricing |
| Random Discounting | Everyday Low Prices |
| | Odd/even Pricing |
| **New Product Pricing** | Customary Pricing |
| Price Skimming | Prestige Pricing |
| Penetration Pricing | |
| | **Professional Pricing** |
| **Product-line Pricing** | |
| Captive Pricing | **Promotional Pricing** |
| Premium Pricing | Price Leaders |
| Bait Pricing | Special Event Pricing |
| Price Lining | Comparison Discounting |

**Secondary market pricing**
Setting one price for the primary target market and a different price for another market

**Secondary Market Pricing** **Secondary market pricing** means setting one price for the primary target market and a different one for another market. Often the price in the secondary market is lower. Examples of secondary markets include a geographically isolated domestic market, an overseas market, and a segment willing to purchase a product during off-peak times. For example, some restaurants offer 'early-bird' prices. Secondary market pricing enables companies to use excess capacity and stabilise the allocation of resources.

**Periodic discounting**
Temporary reduction of prices on a systematic basis

**Periodic Discounting** **Periodic discounting** is the temporary reduction of prices on a systematic basis. For example, many fashion retailers have annual sales in January and July. Car dealers offer discounts on current models when the next year's models are introduced. A major problem with periodic discounting is that because the discounts follow a pattern, customers know to expect them and may delay purchases until prices are lower. There is evidence that some pre-Christmas sales are being delayed, with shoppers awaiting the 'January sales'.

**Random discounting**
Temporary reduction of prices on an unsystematic basis

**Random Discounting** **Random discounting** is used to alleviate the problems of periodic discounting. This involves temporarily reducing prices on an unsystematic basis. The result is that it is difficult for customers to predict when price reductions will occur. This approach is a useful way for marketers to attract new customers. For example, Procter & Gamble may reduce the price of a floor-cleaning product to attract new buyers.

## New Product Pricing

Setting the base price for a new product is a key part of formulating a marketing strategy and a fundamental marketing mix decision. The base price is easily adjusted and can be set high to recover development costs quickly or to provide a reference point for developing discount prices to different market segments. When marketers set base prices, they also consider how quickly competitors will enter the market, the strength of their campaign and the likely effect their entry will have on primary demand. In some circumstances, a company may adopt a base price that will discourage competitive entry.[6] Two strategies used in new product pricing are price skimming and penetration pricing.

**Price skimming**
A pricing strategy whereby a company charges the highest possible price that buyers who most desire the product will pay

**Price Skimming** **Price skimming** is charging the highest possible price that buyers who most desire the product will pay. This 'pioneer approach' provides the most flexible introductory base price. Demand tends to be inelastic in the introductory stage of the product life cycle – for example, as with mobile telephones and DVD players.

Price skimming can be beneficial, especially when a product is in the introductory stage of its life cycle (see Chapter 12). A skimming approach can generate much needed initial cash flows to help off-set sizeable developmental costs. When introducing a new model of camera, Polaroid initially uses a skimming price to defray large research and development costs. Price skimming can be particularly important when a company introduces a product because its production capacity may be limited. Setting a high price helps restrict demand to the available capacity. Sometimes the use of a skimming price may attract competition into an industry because the high price makes that type of business appear lucrative.

**Penetration pricing**
A pricing strategy of setting a price below the prices of competing brands in order to penetrate a market and produce a larger unit sales volume

**Penetration Pricing** **Penetration pricing** is setting a price below the prices of competing brands in order to penetrate a market and produce a larger unit sales volume. When introducing a product, penetration pricing may be used to rapidly gain market share. As shown in Figure 21.9, penetration pricing is popular even for well-known products. This approach is less flexible than price skimming because it is more difficult to raise a penetration price than to lower or discount a skimming price. It is not unusual for a company to use a penetration price having first skimmed the market with a higher price.

Penetration pricing can be especially beneficial when marketers suspect that competitors could enter the market easily. Competitors may be discouraged from entering the market because another business has gained market share quickly. The lower per unit price – and lower per unit profit – associated with penetration may also be less attractive to competitors.

***Figure 21.9***
*Many retailers turn to price competition in order to generate footfall and cash flow*
*Photo: Courtesy of Karen Beaulah*

Penetration pricing is particularly appropriate when demand is highly elastic. Highly elastic demand means that target market members would purchase the product were it priced at the penetration level but that few would buy the item were it priced higher. A marketer should consider using penetration pricing when a lower price would result in longer production runs, increasing production significantly and reducing per unit production costs.

## Product Line Pricing

**Product line pricing**
Establishing and adjusting prices of multiple products within a product line

Rather than considering pricing for products on an item-by-time basis, some marketers use product line pricing. **Product line pricing** means establishing and adjusting the prices of multiple products within a product line. The goal is to maximise profits for an entire product line, rather than focus on the profitability of an individual product. Product line pricing can lead to flexibility in price setting.

Before setting prices for a product line, marketers evaluate the relationship among the products in the line. When the products are complementary, sales increases in one item raise demand for others. For example, desktop printers and print cartridges are complementary products. When products in a line function as substitutes for one another, buyers of one product in the line are unlikely to purchase one of the products in the same line.

In this case, marketers must be sensitive to how a price change for one of the brands may affect perceptions of and demand for other brands in the line.[7]

When marketers employ product line pricing, they have several strategies from which to choose. These include captive pricing, premium pricing, bait pricing and price lining.

**Captive pricing**
Pricing the basic product in a product line low while pricing related items at a higher level

**Captive Pricing** With **captive pricing**, the basic product in a product line is priced low, while the price of the items required to operate or enhance it may be higher. For example, a manufacturer of cameras and films, may set the price of the cameras at a low level, but set the film price relatively high.

**Premium pricing**
Pricing the highest-quality or most versatile products higher than other models in the product line

**Premium Pricing** **Premium pricing** is often used when a product line contains several versions of the same product; the highest-quality products or those with the greatest versatility are given the highest prices. Other products in the line are priced to appeal to price-sensitive shoppers or to those who seek product-specific features. Examples of product categories that commonly use this approach are small kitchen appliances, beer and ice cream.

**Bait pricing**
Pricing an item in the product line low, with the intention of selling a higher-priced item in the line

**Bait Pricing** To attract customers, marketers may put a low price on one item in the product line with the intention of selling a higher-priced item in the line. This is know as **bait pricing**. For example, a computer retailer might advertise its lowest-price model, hoping to attract customers who may then purchase a more expensive version. This strategy can facilitate sales of a line's higher-priced products.

**Price lining**
A pricing strategy whereby a business sets a limited number of prices for selected groups or lines of merchandise

**Price Lining** When a business sets a limited number of prices for selected groups or lines of merchandise, it is using **price lining**. A sports retailer may have various styles and brands of women's sweatshirts of similar quality that sell for £20 (€30). Another line of higher-quality sweatshirts may sell for £30 (€45). Price lining simplifies consumers' decision-making by holding constant one key variable in the final selection of style and brand within a line.

The basic assumption in price lining is that the demand is inelastic for various groups or sets of products. If the prices are attractive, customers will not react to slight changes in price. Thus a fashion retailer that carries dresses priced at £30 (€45), £50 (€75) and £70 (€105) may not attract many more sales if the prices are dropped by £2 or £3. The 'space' between the prices of £50 (€75) and £30 (€45), however, can stir changes in consumer response. With price lining, the demand curve looks like a series of steps, as shown in Figure 21.10.

## Psychological Pricing

**Psychological pricing**
A pricing strategy designed to encourage purchases that are based on emotional rather than rational responses

**Psychological pricing** encourages purchases that are based on emotional rather than rational responses. The aim is to influence a customer's perception of price to make a product's price seem more attractive. The following kinds of psychological pricing are considered in this section: reference pricing, bundle pricing, multiple-unit pricing, everyday low prices (EDLP), odd/even pricing, customary pricing and prestige pricing.

**Reference pricing**
Pricing a product at a moderate level and positioning it next to a more expensive model or brand

**Reference Pricing** **Reference pricing** means pricing a product at a moderate level and positioning it next to a more expensive model or brand. The hope is that customers will use the higher price as an external reference price and compare the moderately priced brand favourably. Reference pricing is based on the 'isolation effect', meaning an alternative is less attractive when viewed by itself than when compared with other alternatives.

**Bundle Pricing** **Bundle pricing** is packaging together two or more products, usually complementary ones, to be sold for a single price. The single price is usually much less than the sum of the prices of the individual items. For example, some computer manufacturers bundle together a computer, software and Internet service, making the entire package

*Figure 21.10*
*Price lining*

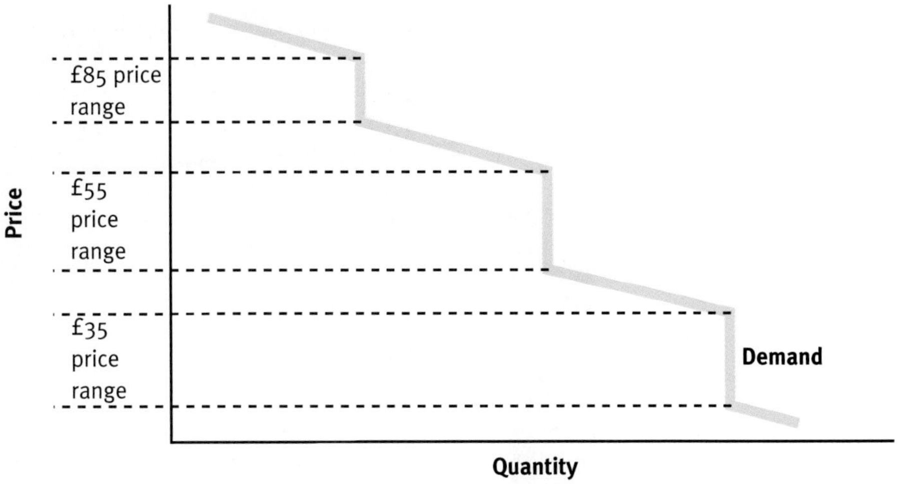


available for a single charge. Bundle pricing is commonly used in banking, travel services and car sales, but is also used for much cheaper items, such as hair products and cosmetics.

**Bundle pricing**
Pricing together two or more complementary products and selling them for a single price

**Multiple-unit pricing**
Packaging together two or more identical products and selling them for a single price

**Multiple-unit Pricing** **Multiple-unit pricing** occurs when two or more identical products are packaged together and sold for a single price, usually at a lower per-unit price. Multiple-unit pricing is commonly used for twin packs of soap, four packs of light bulbs and six packs of beer. Customers benefit from cost savings and convenience. A company may use this approach to attract new customers to its brand and, in some cases, to increase consumption. When customers buy in larger quantities, their consumption sometimes increases. For example, customers who buy multiple bags of snacks, may consume them at a faster rate than if they had only bought one. However, for some products this does not apply. For instance, greater availability at the point of consumption of light bulbs, soap and washing detergents is not likely to increase usage.

**Everyday low prices (EDLP)**
The reduction of retail prices of leading brands for a prolonged period

**Everyday Low Prices (EDLP)** To reduce or eliminate the use of frequent short-term price reductions, some organisations use **everyday low prices (EDLP)**. A low price is set for products on a consistent basis rather than setting higher prices and frequently discounting them. Everyday low prices are set far enough below competitors' prices to make customers feel confident they are receiving a fair price. Both Wal-Mart and Procter & Gamble use this approach. Benefits from EDLP include reduced losses from frequent mark-downs, greater stability in sales, and reduced promotional costs.

**Odd/even pricing**
A pricing method that tries to influence buyers' perceptions of the price or the product by ending the price with certain numbers

**Odd/Even Pricing** Through **odd/even pricing** – that is, ending the price with certain numbers – marketers try to influence buyers' perceptions of the price or the product. Odd pricing assumes that more of a product will be sold at £99.95 than at £100. The notion is that customers will think, or at least tell friends, that the product is a bargain – not £100, but £99, plus a few insignificant pence. Customers are also supposed to think that the store could have charged £100, but instead cut the price to the last penny or so. It is sometimes claimed that certain types of customer are more attracted by odd prices than by even ones. However, no substantial research findings support the notion that odd prices produce greater sales. Even prices are used to give a product an exclusive, high-quality or upmarket image. For example, a premium silk tie may retail at £50 rather than £49.95. Although even prices are less often seen than odd prices, some retailers, like Marks & Spencer, have recently decided to use even prices, perhaps because they believe that consumers are not convinced of the extra value associated with odd pricing. There is a view

***Figure 21.11***
*An example of psychological pricing: odd numbers are alleged to disguise the real cost to the customer; £3.00, £6.00, £1.00 may deter certain price-conscious shoppers*
*Photo: Courtesy of Karen Beaulah*

that customers resent being given small change, so one brewer has recently moved to charging 'round figures' for its beers.

**Customary pricing**
A pricing method whereby goods are priced primarily on the basis of tradition

**Customary Pricing** In **customary pricing**, certain goods are priced primarily on the basis of tradition. Recent economic uncertainties have caused most prices to fluctuate fairly widely, but the classic example of the customary, or traditional, price is the telephone call. Until the mid-1980s, UK public telephones were geared to the use of particular coins. For years the 2p and, later, the 10p slots were widely recognised. BT's initial response to rising prices was to alter the cost of units so that less call time was allowed for the same money. Since then, demands for greater flexibility of use have seen public call boxes altered to accept most British coins, pre-paid telephone cards and credit cards.

**Prestige pricing**
A pricing method whereby prices are set at an artificially high level to provide prestige or a quality image

**Prestige Pricing** In **prestige pricing**, prices are set at an artificially high level to provide prestige or a quality image. Businesses in Europe often associate the quality of service provided by a management consultant with price. A client of an exclusive beauty salon may be concerned if the prices of treatments are suddenly reduced, because this implies a reduction in quality. Indeed, prestige pricing is often used when buyers associate a higher price with higher quality. Typical product categories that use prestige prices include beauty products, holidays, cars, alcoholic beverages, jewellery, cameras, and electrical appliances. Dramatically lowering the prices of such products is inconsistent with their perceived images.

## Professional Pricing

**Professional pricing**
Pricing used by people who have great skill or experience in a particular field or activity

**Promotional pricing**
Pricing related to the short-term promotion of a particular product

**Professional pricing** is used by people who have great skill or experience in a particular field or activity. Some professionals who provide such products feel that their fees (prices) should not relate directly to their time and involvement in specific cases; instead charging a standard fee regardless of the problems involved in performing the job. Some estate agents' and solicitors' fees are prime examples: 2 per cent of a house sale price, plus VAT, and £600 (€900) for house conveyancing. Other professionals set prices in other ways.

The concept of professional pricing carries with it the idea that professionals have an ethical responsibility not to overcharge unknowing customers. In some situations, a seller can charge customers a high price and continue to sell many units of the product. Medicine offers several examples. If a patient with high blood pressure requires four tablets a day to survive, the individual will pay for the prescription whether it costs £5 (€7.50) or £50 (€75) per month. In fact, the patient would purchase the pills even if the price went higher. In these situations sellers could charge exorbitant fees. Drug companies claim that despite their positions of strength in this regard, they charge 'ethical' prices rather than what the market will bear.[8] However, the high cost of some anti-AIDS drugs has attracted criticism among medical professionals.

## Promotional Pricing

**Price leaders**
Products sold below the usual mark-up, near cost or below cost

Price is an ingredient in the marketing mix, and it is often coordinated with promotion. The two variables are sometimes so interrelated that the pricing approach is promotion oriented. **Promotional pricing** is a pricing approach whereby pricing is related to the short-term promotion of a particular product. Examples of promotional pricing include **price leaders**, **special event pricing** and **comparison discounting**. These types of pricing are illustrated in Table 21.4, which also explains the circumstances in which they can be used.

## Misleading Pricing

Many countries have legislation controlling the use of **misleading pricing**, which may intentionally confuse or dupe consumers. The UK Consumer Protection Act 1987, which makes it illegal to mislead customers about the price at which products or services are offered for sale,

**TABLE 21.4 TYPES OF PROMOTIONAL PRICING**

| | |
|---|---|
| **Price leaders** | Products sold below the usual mark-up near cost, or below cost; used most often in supermarkets and department stores to attract customers by giving low prices on just a few items; the intention is that while in store they will buy other, full-priced, items |
| **Special event pricing** | Advertised 'sales' or price cutting that are linked to a holiday, season or event to increase sales volume; if the pricing objective is survival, special sales events may help generate the necessary operating capital; marketers can use this pricing to generate revenue when there is a lag in sales |
| **Comparison discounting** | Setting the price at a specific level and then ensuring that it is simultaneously compared with a higher price; the higher price may be the previous price for the product, or a manufacturer's suggested retail price; customers often find comparative pricing informative, although it can be overused, leading customers to no longer believe that the higher price is the normal price[9] |

**Special event pricing** Advertised sales or price cutting that is linked to a holiday, season or event to increase sales volume

**Comparison discounting** Setting a price at a specific level and comparing it with a higher price

**Misleading pricing** Pricing policies that intentionally confuse or dupe consumers

is typical. This act contains a code of practice that, although not legally binding, encourages companies to offer explanations whenever price comparisons or reductions are made. According to the Which? handbook of consumer law, 'Unexplained reductions from a store's own prices should be used only if the goods have been on sale at the same store for 28 days in the preceding six months, and if the price quoted was the last price at which the goods were on sale.'[10]

## Stage 8: Determining a Specific Price

The basis for pricing and pricing strategies should direct and structure the selection of a final price. This means that marketers should establish pricing objectives; know something about the target market; and determine demand, price elasticity, costs and competitive factors. In addition to these economic factors, the manner in which pricing is used in the marketing mix will affect the final price.

Although a systematic approach to pricing is suggested here, in practice prices may be set by trial and error or after only limited planning. Later on, marketers determine whether the revenue minus costs yields a profit. This approach to pricing is not recommended, because unsuitable price levels are often set.

In the absence of government price controls, pricing remains a flexible and convenient way to adjust the marketing mix. In most situations, prices can be adjusted quickly – in a matter of minutes or over a few days. The other components of the marketing mix do not have this flexibility or freedom.

## The 'Pricing Balance': the Need for Pragmatism

This chapter has presented stages that a marketer must address in determining a price that will reflect customer expectations, match market developments and produce a suitable financial return. In practice, tackling these stages may be difficult. The external trading environment can change quickly and constantly: consumers are relatively fickle and revise their expectations, market developments alter the pattern of the market, and competitors continually modify their marketing mix – a price-cutting campaign, a new model launch, a high-profile advertising campaign or, perhaps, a customer service initiative. The Building Customer Relationships box opposite shows how, when economic prospects are gloomy, there is a knock-on effect across consumer sectors, particularly for luxury goods. The implication is that marketers need to monitor such trends carefully – they may sometimes happen with little warning – and respond pragmatically by modifying their own pricing basis and strategy.

In the context of the marketing mix, price can generally be altered relatively quickly, especially when compared with the time and resources required to launch a new product, modify a channel of distribution, improve customer service or create and run a new advertising campaign. Even in this context, however, the shrewd marketer should endeavour to minimise price cutting and discounting. In most cases the only short-term beneficiary of a price war is the consumer. Indeed, the business, its distributors, the brand or the long-term flexibility of the marketing mix may suffer as a consequence. The airline industry is a current example of how pricing incentives, such as discounted flights and no-frills service, can become an entrenched part of pricing. Pricing decisions should therefore be made on the basis of marketing intelligence, market trends, customer perceptions and competitor activity. Marketers must never lose sight of the 'economics' of pricing, and the fundamental relationship between demand, costs and profits: there must be a sensible trade-off, or 'pricing balance', between economic analysis and pragmatism.

## Building Customer Relationships

### Keeping in Touch with the Affluent Consumer and their Spending Power

When economic prospects are gloomy there is a knock-on effect across consumer sectors. Yet statistical evidence suggests that it is the wealthiest 5 per cent of the population that often lose the most. As the spending of these individuals drives growth in the luxury goods sector, when times are tough, the impact here is often particularly great. While consumers continue to spend on day-to-day necessities, they are less likely to splash out on luxury items. As a result, certain products and services are affected more than others. This relates to the nature of this affluent group's lifestyle: how they live and spend their time.

Recent research has investigated how these affluent consumers live and has examined their spending patterns. The results suggest that they are three times more likely to list wine tasting as a hobby and four times more likely to go sailing and skiing than non-affluent consumers. They are also much more likely to indulge in visits to health spas and to belong to a gym. These costly pastimes are apparently more accessible to those with high disposable incomes. However, the characteristics of those buying luxury goods are also changing. Some individuals who were previously classified as being non-affluent are now indulging themselves by buying high-priced luxury items. The implication is that the make-up of this affluent group may be changing.

There are obvious repercussions for companies operating in the luxury goods sector, which must be vigilant in staying in touch with changes in their customer base. Understanding who today's affluent consumers are, where they live, how they behave and spend their income, is critical to the recovery of the luxury goods sector following recent difficult times. For example, UK figures show that wealthy individuals are increasingly relocating away from London and the south-east to live in other parts of the UK. Upscale retailer Harvey Nichols responded to this change recently by expanding from its base in London to open stores in other regions of the UK. Meanwhile in Birmingham, the recently opened Mailbox shopping centre is a showcase for upscale brands targeting the affluent.

**Sources:** Caroline Parry, 'Factfile: who pays the price of luxury', *Marketing Week*, 29 January 2004, p. 38–9; 'Cadbury makes bid for premium market', *Marketing Week*, 1 April 2004, p. 9.

# Summary

The eight stages in the process of establishing prices are: (1) selecting pricing objectives; (2) assessing the target market's evaluation of price and its ability to buy; (3) determining demand; (4) analysing demand, cost and profit relationships; (5) evaluating competitors' prices; (6) selecting a basis for pricing; (7) developing a pricing strategy; and (8) determining a specific price.

- The first stage, selecting pricing objectives, is critical because pricing objectives are the foundation on which the decisions of subsequent stages are based. Businesses may use numerous short- and long-term pricing objectives.

- The second stage in establishing prices is an assessment of the target market's evaluation of price and its ability to buy. This shows how much emphasis to place on price and may help determine how far above the competition prices can be set. Understanding customers' buying power and the importance of a product to them in comparison with other products helps the target market's evaluation of price to be accurately assessed.

- In the third stage, a business must determine the demand for its product. The classic *demand curve* is a graph of the quantity of products expected to be sold at various prices, if other factors are held constant. It illustrates that, as price falls, the quantity demanded usually increases. However, for prestige products, there is a direct positive relationship between price and quantity demanded: up to a certain point demand increases as price increases. Next, *price elasticity of demand* – the percentage change in quantity demanded relative to a given percentage change in price – must be determined. If demand is elastic, a change in price causes an opposite change in total revenue. Inelastic demand results in a change in the same direction in total revenue when a product's price is changed.

» Analysis of demand, cost and profit relationships – the fourth stage of the process – can be accomplished through marginal analysis or break-even analysis. Marginal analysis is the examination of what happens to a company's costs and revenues when production (or sales volume) is changed by one unit. Marginal analysis combines the demand curve with a company's costs to develop an optimum price for maximum profit. *Fixed costs* do not vary with changes in the number of units produced or sold; *average fixed cost* is the fixed cost per unit produced. *Variable costs* vary directly with changes in the number of units produced or sold. *Average variable cost* is the variable cost per unit produced. *Total cost* is the sum of average fixed costs and average variable costs multiplied by the quantity produced. *Average total cost* is the sum of the average fixed cost and average variable cost. The optimum price is the point at which *marginal cost (MC)* equals *marginal revenue (MR)*. Marginal analysis offers little help in pricing new products before costs and revenues are established.

» Break-even analysis involves determining the number of units necessary to break even. The point at which the costs of producing a product equal the revenue made from selling the product is the *break-even point*. To use break-even analysis effectively, a marketer should determine the break-even point for each of several alternative prices, so that the effects on total revenue, total cost and the break-even point for each price can be considered. However, this approach assumes that the quantity demanded is basically fixed and that the major task is to set prices to recover costs.

» A *pricing strategy* is an approach designed to achieve pricing and marketing objectives. The most common pricing strategies are differential pricing, new-product pricing, product line pricing, psychological pricing, professional pricing and promotional pricing.

» A marketer needs to be aware of the prices charged for competing brands. This allows a company to keep its prices the same as competitors' prices when non-price competition is used. If a company uses price as a competitive tool, it can price its brand below competing brands.

» The three major dimensions on which prices can be based are cost, demand and competition. In using *cost-based pricing*, a company determines price by adding a monetary amount or percentage to the cost of the product. Two common cost-based pricing approaches are *cost plus pricing* and *mark-up pricing*. *Demand-based pricing* is based on the level of demand for a product and requires marketers to estimate the amounts of a product that buyers will demand at different prices, particularly if the company wishes to use price differentiation for a specific product. Demand-based pricing results in a high price when demand for a product is strong and a low price when demand is weak. In the case of *competition-based pricing*, costs and revenues are secondary to competitors' prices. Competition-based pricing and cost approaches may be combined to arrive at the price levels necessary to generate a profit. *Marketing-oriented pricing* involves a company taking account of a wide range of factors including marketing strategy, competition, value to the customer, price–quality relationships, explicability, costs, product line pricing, negotiating margins, political factors and the effect on distributors/retailers.

» Using *differential pricing* involves charging different prices for the same quality or quantity of product. *Negotiated pricing*, *secondary market discounting*, *periodic discounting* and *random discounting* are forms of differential pricing. Establishing the final price through bargaining between seller and customer is negotiated pricing.

Secondary market pricing involves setting one price for the primary target market and a different price for another market. Marketers employ a strategy of periodic discounting when they temporarily lower their prices on a systematic basis. Random discounting occurs on an unsystematic basis.

» Two strategies used in new product pricing are price skimming and penetration pricing. With *price skimming*, a company charges the highest price that buyers who most desire the product will pay. *Penetration pricing* sets a price below the prices of competing brands in order to penetrate the market and produce a larger unit sales volume.

» *Product line pricing* establishes and adjusts the prices of multiple products within a product line. This strategy includes: *captive pricing*, in which the marketer prices the basic product in a product line low but prices related items at a higher level; *premium pricing*, which is when prices on a higher-quality or more versatile product are set higher than those on other models in the product line; *bait pricing*, in which the marketer tries to attract customers by pricing an item in the product line low with the intention of selling a higher-priced item in the line; and *price lining*, in which the organisation sets a limited number of prices for selected groups or lines of merchandise.

» *Psychological pricing*, encourages purchases that are based on emotional rather than rational responses. In *reference pricing* marketers price a product at a moderate level and position it next to a more expensive model or brand. *Bundle pricing* is packaging together two or more complementary products that are sold for a single price. In *multiple-unit pricing*, two or more identical products are packaged together and sold for a single price. *Everyday low prices* are employed by some companies to set a low price for products on a consistent basis. When using *odd/even pricing*, marketers try to influence buyers' perceptions of the prices of the product by ending the price with certain numbers. *Customary pricing* is based on traditional prices. With *prestige pricing*, prices are set at an artificially high level to project a quality image. *Professional pricing* is used by people who have great skill or experience in a particular field. *Promotional pricing* is a pricing approach in which pricing is related to the short-term promotion of a particular product. *Price leaders, special event pricing* and *comparison discounting* are examples of promotional pricing. *Misleading pricing* – in which consumers are intentionally misled about the true cost or value of a product or service – is increasingly monitored and tackled through consumer protection legislation.

» The basis for a price and the pricing strategy should direct and structure the selection of a final price. For the most part, pricing remains a flexible and convenient way to adjust the marketing mix. Pragmatism may require the marketer to revise pricing on an ad hoc basis in response to market developments. While such reactions are to some extent inevitable, marketers must never lose sight of the longer-term implications for the brand, or the fundamental relationship between demand, costs and profits.

## » *Key Links*

This chapter, about setting prices, should be read in conjunction with Chapter 20, which examines pricing concepts.

- Understanding how to set prices is key to the development of effective marketing programmes, as discussed in Parts III–VI.
- Appropriate prices can only be set by having an understanding of what customers are able and prepared to pay. Customer buying behaviour is examined in Chapters 6 and 7.

## Important Terms

Demand curve
Price elasticity of demand
Fixed costs
Average fixed cost
Variable costs
Average variable cost
Total cost

Average total cost
Marginal cost (MC)
Marginal revenue (MR)
Break-even point
Basis for pricing
Cost-based pricing
Cost plus pricing
Mark-up pricing
Demand-based pricing
Competition-based pricing
Marketing-oriented pricing
Pricing strategy
Differential pricing
Negotiated pricing
Secondary market pricing
Periodic discounting
Random discounting
Price skimming
Penetration pricing
Product line pricing
Captive pricing
Premium pricing
Bait pricing
Price lining
Psychological pricing
Reference pricing
Bundle pricing
Multiple-unit pricing
Everyday low prices (EDLP)
Odd/even pricing
Customary pricing
Prestige pricing
Professional pricing
Promotional pricing
Price leaders
Special event pricing
Comparison discounting
Misleading pricing

## Discussion and Review Questions

1 Identify the eight stages that make up the process of establishing prices.
2 Why do most demand curves demonstrate an inverse relationship between price and quantity?
3 List the characteristics of products that have inelastic demand. Give several examples of such products.
4 Explain why optimum profits should occur when marginal cost equals marginal revenue.
5 The Chambers Company has just gathered estimates in preparation for a break-even analysis for a new product. Variable costs are £7 per unit. The additional plant will cost £48,000. The new product will be charged £18,000 a year for its share of general overheads. Advertising expenditure will be £80,000, and £55,000 will be spent on distribution. If the product sells for £12, what is the break-even point in units? What is the break-even point in sales volume?
6 Why should a marketer be aware of competitors' prices?
7 For what types of product would a pioneer price skimming approach be most appropriate? For what types of product would penetration pricing be more effective?
8 Why do consumers associate price with quality? When should prestige pricing be used?
9 What factors must be taken into consideration when adopting a marketing-oriented approach to pricing?
10 In setting prices, why must marketers take a 'balanced' view of a broad set of issues?

## Recommended Readings


- Campanelli, M., 'The price to pay', *Sales & Marketing Management*, 146 (10), 1994, pp. 96–102.
- Diamantopoulos, A. and Mathews, B.P., *Making Pricing Decisions: a Study of Managerial Practice* (London: Thomson Learning, 1995).
- Monroe, B. K., *Pricing: Making Profitable Decisions*, (New York: McGraw-Hill, 2002).
- Nagle, T. and Holden, R. K., *The Strategy and Tactics of Pricing* (Englewood Cliffs, NJ: Prentice-Hall, 2002).
- Simon, H., 'Pricing opportunities – and how to exploit them', *Sloan Management Review*, 33 (2), 1992, pp. 55–65.
- Steward, K., 'Fixing the price', in N. Hart, ed., *Effective Industrial Marketing* (London: Kogan Page, 1994).


## Internet Exercise

T-Mobile has positioned itself as a low-cost provider of mobile phones. From its website, customers can select different pricing options, and purchase phones, accessories and ringtones. For example, personal customers (as opposed to business clients) can select from:

- pay monthly – billed price plans, low call rates and inclusive minutes
- mix it – better value than pay as you go, but with no large bills
- pay as you go – no bills, pay upfront for calls.

Log on to: www.t-mobile.co.uk

1 Determine the various target markets being served by this website.
2 How do the pricing options vary across these target markets?
3 What type of pricing strategy is T-Mobile adopting for its personal customers?

## Applied Mini-Case

The fee for a UK passport can be broken down into a number of areas. For an adult, the total cost of a 10-year passport as from October 2003 was £42. The UK Passport Service breaks the fee down into the following categories:

| | | | |
|---|---|---|---|
| Application processing | £4.60 | Anti-fraud initiatives | £3.60 |
| Establishing entitlement | £6.50 | Other innovation | £3.70 |
| FCO consular protection | £9.65 | Administrative | £4.60 |
| Book production | £4.05 | Deficit recovery | £3.60 |
| Introduction of secure delivery | £1.70 | | |

**Sources:** 'Essential information about your new passport', UK Passport Service, 2004; 'Passport prices rise by 36 per cent, BBC News, www.bbc.co.uk, 18 July 2003.

### Question

**What pricing strategy is being used in setting the price of a passport? Discuss the advantages and disadvantages of using this approach in this particular case.**

## Case Study

### Buying Power Impacts on Toys 'Я' Us Pricing

Toys 'Я' Us, which leads the US toy market with its chain of over 400 warehouse-style toy supermarkets spread across the country, is expanding rapidly in Europe and the Pacific Rim. In Europe its growth is fast bringing a new style and scale of toy retailing to the UK, Germany, France, Spain and Austria. The company has long been an innovator in both its pricing policies and its supermarket-style design. Toys 'Я' Us brings customers into the store by discounting such babycare products as buggies and disposable nappies below cost. The strategy is that once parents are in the store, they will spend on toys the money they saved on the discounted baby goods.

Toys 'Я' Us stores are usually located along major arterial roads, well away from central business district (CBD) shopping malls, to keep costs down and prevent customers from being distracted by other toy merchants. Isolation from shopping malls also means that customers will load up their shopping trolleys because they do not have to lug their purchases through crowded malls.

The first Toys 'Я' Us store was opened in 1957 as the Children's Supermarket (the 'Rs' are printed backwards to encourage name recognition), offering brand name toys and baby goods below normal retail prices. Today, it still offers brand name toys at 20 to 50 per cent below retail price. Each store has a full stock of thousands of different toys and baby goods tracked by a computer system that almost eliminates stock-outs. Managers do not place orders for toys, the toys just arrive on time, thus averting the Toys 'Я' Us definition of a major disaster – not having a certain toy on display and ready to sell.

Toys 'Я' Us sets its price for a particular item based on how much it projects customers will pay for it. The company then determines the price at which it is willing to purchase the toy from the manufacturer, and negotiates fiercely with the manufacturer to get the toy at that price. The company has a definite advantage in negotiations because it buys in such large volume. Toy manufacturers also treat Toys 'Я' Us well because the company is often a testing ground for new toys. Price is so important to the Toys 'Я' Us strategy that even when demand for a toy is high and supplies are short, the company will not raise its price on the toy to make a quick profit.

Market share is the Toys 'Я' Us main pricing objective; and at present it is the number one toy store in the United States. In the UK, local independent toy shops still account for the bulk of the toy market share, but in only a few years Toys 'Я' Us has become the leading national chain. The company says it is willing to cut prices to retain its leading position. Other toy stores are scrambling to meet the competition from Toys 'Я' Us; those that do not change their strategies wind up out of the toy market altogether. Many stores, such as K-Mart, or ASDA in the UK, expand their toy lines only for the six-week pre-Christmas season and bring customers in with sales. Although Toys 'Я' Us never holds sales, it maintains its huge selection and discount prices year round. Customers who found good buys at Toys 'Я' Us at Christmas will also shop there for children's birthdays and other special days, when other retail stores have a limited selection. Even new parents who drop in to Toys 'Я' Us for discounted baby products tend to return to buy toys. The company also sells sporting goods 'toys', such as footballs and bicycles, suitable for teens, young adults and family members of almost any age.

Some competitors have adopted the Toys 'Я' Us supermarket approach and have tried to meet Toys 'Я' Us prices throughout the year. Other stores are trying non-price competition by offering educational and babysitting services. However, Toys 'Я' Us intends to rely on its non-price attributes of convenience, selection and inventory, as well as price competition, to hold its position.

Toys 'Я' Us has expanded internationally, into Europe, Canada, Japan and other parts of Asia, with close to 300 stores outside the USA. The company has plans for many more stores overseas to take advantage of the world toy market, which is nearly double that of the United States. Additionally, it opened Kids 'Я' Us in the United States, a chain of children's clothing stores similar to its toy stores.

Toys 'Я' Us has customer loyalty behind it. Customers know that they can find the toy that a child wants, at the best price, at Toys 'Я' Us. And if the child does not like the toy, the purchaser can return it for a full refund with no questions asked.

## Questions for Discussion

1 What are the major pricing objectives of Toys 'Я' Us?
2 Assess the Toys 'Я' Us practice of not raising the prices of products that are scarce and in high demand.
3 A major disadvantage of using price competition is that competitors can match prices. Or can they? Evaluate this potential threat for Toys 'Я' Us.

## Postscript

The price of a product or service is the value placed on what is exchanged by the supplying business and the consumer. There is much more to pricing, however, than the setting of a specific monetary figure. The price of a product or service will affect how it is perceived by consumers, how it is distributed and promoted, the level of customer service expected and the brand positioning strategy to be pursued. The pricing strategy developed by a business will also fundamentally relate to its performance and even to its viability. Pricing is not one of the more 'glamorous' ingredients of the marketing mix, such as product development or promotional activity, but it is very important and relatively easy to manipulate.

Before progressing, readers should be confident that they are now able to do the following.

### Outline the central concepts of pricing

- What are the characteristics and role of price in marketing?
- What are the differences between price and non-price competition?
- What factors affect marketers' pricing decisions?
- What are the different pricing objectives?
- Why is it important to consider the consumer's view of value versus price?
- What is required in setting prices in business markets?
- What is meant by the concept of economic value to the customer?

### Explain the requirements of setting prices

- What are the eight major steps of the process used to establish prices?
- What issues are faced when selecting pricing objectives?
- Why must marketers assess the target market's evaluation of price?
- How is demand for a product determined, and what are the relationships between demand, costs and profits?
- Why must marketers evaluate competitors' pricing?
- What are the different pricing strategies and methods, and how do they help to determine a specific price?
- What is the 'pricing balance'?

## *Strategic Case*

# Napster
## Napster's Creation

Napster was the brainchild of Shawn Fanning, a 17-year-old fresher at Northeastern University who left college to develop a technology to trade music over the Internet. The technology was commercialised through Napster, which allowed computer users to share high-quality digital recordings – mp3s – of music via the Internet using its proprietary MusicShare software. Napster did not actually store the recordings on its own computers, but instead provided an index of all the tracks available on the computers of members who were logged on to the service. In other words, it functioned as a sort of clearing house where members could search by artist or track title and identify mp3s of interest so that they could be downloaded from another member's hard drive. Napster quickly became one of the most popular US sites on the Internet, with 15 million users in little more than a year. Indeed so many college students were downloading tracks from Napster that many universities were forced to block the site from their systems in order to regain bandwidth.

From the beginning, Napster's service was as controversial as it was popular. Barely a year after its 1999 launch, Napster was sued by the Recording

Industry Association of America (RIAA), which represents major recording companies such as Universal Music, BMG, Sony Music, Warner Music Group and EMI. RIAA claimed that Napster's service violated copyright laws by allowing users to swap music recordings free of charge. RIAA also sought an injunction to stop the downloading of copyrighted tracks, as well as damages for lost revenue. RIAA argued that track swapping via Napster and similar companies had cost the music industry more than US$300 million in lost sales. Metallica and rap star Dr Dre filed separate lawsuits accusing Napster of copyright infringement and racketeering. Lars Ulrich, Metallica's drummer, told a Senate committee that he felt that Napster users are basically stealing from the band every time they download one of its tracks.

## The Fall of Napster

On 26 July 2000, US District Judge Marilyn Patel granted the RIAA's request for an injunction and ordered Napster to stop making copyrighted recordings available for download, which would have effectively destroyed the company by pulling the plug on its most popular feature. However, on 28 July – just nine hours before Napster would have shut down – the 9th Circuit Court of Appeals 'stayed' that order, granting Napster a last-minute reprieve until the lawsuits could be tried in court.

Despite this brief reprieve, Napster was ultimately found guilty of direct copyright infringement of the RIAA members' musical recordings and that ruling was upheld on appeal on 12 February 2001. The District Court of Appeals refuted all of Napster's defence tactics and ordered the company to stop allowing its millions of users to download and share copyrighted material without properly compensating the owners of the material.

In late September 2001, Napster agreed to pay US$26 million for past distribution of unauthorised music and made a proposal that would enable songwriters and musicians to distribute their music on Napster for a fee. This settlement would have covered as many as 700,000 tracks, but Napster still needed an agreement before the company could legally distribute the music. However, with failed attempts to reach a suitable compromise with the recording industry and litigation expenses mounting, the company entered Chapter 11 bankruptcy proceedings in June 2002 as a last-ditch effort to try and reach a deal with Bertelsmann AG, Napster's strategic partner.

The end for Napster came on 3 September 2002 when a Delaware bankruptcy judge blocked the sale of the company to Bertelsmann, ruling that negotiations with the German media company had not been made at arm's length and in good faith. Bertelsmann had agreed to pay creditors US$8 million for Napster's assets. According to the bankruptcy petition, the company had assets of US$7.9 million and debts of US$101 million as of 30 April 2002. Shortly after the judge's ruling, Napster laid off nearly all of its 42 staff and proceeded to convert its Chapter 11 reorganisation into a Chapter 7 liquidation. At the time, it seemed like the end of Napster.

## The Digital Music Revolution

Recently, the music industry has changed beyond recognition. Predictions are that sales of traditional music, mostly now in the form of CDs, will decline by between 6–9 per cent per annum, with some compensation coming in the form of DVD sales, which are forecast to increase by around 4 per cent per annum. One major reason for the decline in music sales is changing consumer preferences. Although consumers value CDs because they provide 'long-term' entertainment, surveys find that many feel that CDs cost too much. RIAA's research indicates that a significant number of consumers do not fully understand the variables that play a role in the overall pricing of a CD. Consumers say that they resent paying £7–£12 for a CD in order to own only one or two favourite tracks. Many consumers, therefore, find downloading music an appealing alternative to high CD prices.

With Napster out of the picture and the RIAA bringing lawsuits against individual downloaders of music on-line, other on-line music providers were rapidly 'getting their houses in order'. One of the first was AOL, which launched MusicNet in February 2003 with 20 music streams and 20 downloads for US$3.95 per month. Apple's iTunes, which was inaugurated in April 2003, was by far the heaviest hitter to join the foray into on-line music. Other services were available as well. Rhapsody, a division of

RealNetworks, whose RealPlayer is ubiquitous on millions of PCs, offers 400,000 tracks for download. MusicMatch, a major partner with Dell, which pre-installs MusicMatch Jukebox on all new PCs, offers 200,000 tracks for download. Amazon, too, has entered the market for music downloads.

To everyone involved with the music-downloading controversy, it is clear that on-line music distribution is here to stay. It was only a matter of time until a compromise could be reached among the recording studios, the artists and the various on-line music providers. Some thorny issues remained to be resolved, however. First, because even pay-for-download services are not immune to piracy, the recording industry wanted to develop technology that would prevent downloaders from swapping files on their own even after making a legitimate purchase. The industry also wanted to limit the number of times a track can be downloaded and copied in order to protect the artists. Suggestions included using the md5 hash – a digital fingerprint – or using software that monitors sound patterns to detect illegal copies. A second issue was the development of a revenue model. Should mp3 files be available individually, as one file in a complete album, or both? Should pricing be based on a per-download basis or on an unlimited basis for a monthly subscription fee?

## The Rise of Napster 2.0

In late 2002, Napster's name and assets were purchased by Roxio, a company well known for its CD 'burning' software. After much fanfare and excitement, Roxio revived Napster as Napster 2.0 on 29 October 2003. The new fee-based service offered 750,000 tracks for download, giving it the largest on-line catalogue currently available in the industry.

The new Napster launched in the UK in early 2004, stating:

> Napster is the legal, safe and easy way to discover and share the most music. With critically acclaimed Napster you can listen to over 750,000 songs, get advert-free radio stations or personalise your own, collect your favourite music along with new releases every Monday.

Napster offers users the opportunity to burn a CD and transfer tracks to a portable device for £1.09 per track or starting at £9.95 for an album. Subscribers save over 10 per cent – making the cost as low as 88p per track – when they buy multiple tracks at a time.

There is a second service available: Napster Light. This service permits users to search and browse 30-second clips within Napster's catalogue of 750,000 tracks free of charge. Selected full tracks are then purchased for 99p, or £9.95 for albums or Napster Custom Compilations. (Full pricing details are available on http://www.napster.co.uk/comparison.)

Napster's relaunch came with the blessing of five major record labels. Napster has also developed a number of partnerships with Microsoft, Gateway, Yahoo! and Samsung that provided advantages during its relaunch. Napster's partnership with Samsung led to the creation of the Samsung YP-910GS, a 20-gigabyte digital audio player that is fully integrated with Napster 2.0. The device allows users to transfer tracks from Napster directly to the unit via a USB connection. The player also boasts an integrated FM transmitter, which allows users to broadcast mp3 playback through their home or car stereo system. Additionally, Napster subscribers receive the industry's leading CD-creation software package, developed by parent company Roxio, as a bonus.

Although the reborn Napster currently offers the largest catalogue of tracks, it continues to face competition from a growing number of companies, particularly MusicNet and iTunes. MusicNet is marketed by AOL, the world's largest Internet service provider (ISP) with more than 35 million users. In addition to its massive potential user base, AOL's diverse business operations grant it the ability to offer music at a lower price than Napster. AOL can afford to take a volume-based approach to pricing rather than a profit-based approach. Because MusicNet is also heavily supported by advertisers and sponsors, it can offer many different promotional packages to boost sales.

Despite MusicNet's potential size advantages, Apple's iTunes is likely to pose the biggest threat to Napster. iTunes currently offers over 400,000 tracks and adds thousands more weekly. It also offers a wide selection of audio books. The popularity of Apple's iPod mp3 player also confers on Apple the distinct advantage of the iPod providing customers with a perfect vehicle to attain the music they desire.

The iTunes software application works with both Macintosh and Windows operating systems. The service is easy to use, and boasts fewer restrictions than MusicNet and other brand competitors. As a result, iTunes has developed a high customer satisfaction rating. Apple has partnered with PepsiCo to offer 1000 tracks free of charge to help bolster membership of iTunes.

Other competitors include the thousands of off-line and on-line music record stores that offer CDs and other merchandise. However, given the movement in the industry to on-line downloading of music, these competitors may soon become less of a threat. There are also still websites where music can be downloaded free of charge, albeit illegally. Some potential customers would rather chance getting caught than pay for the music. Microsoft, too, has now launched a download service of its own. Given the likelihood of future competition, it is imperative that the Napster brand becomes dominant in a short period of time. Napster's pricing strategy is fundamental to attracting sufficient customers quickly enough and creating routinised re-buying in order to combat the expected new entrants in this growing market sector.

## Questions for Discussion

1. What factors seem to have the greatest influence on Napster 2.0's pricing decisions? Explain.
2. What seem to be Napster's primary pricing objectives?
3. Assess the level of price competition in the music industry as a whole and within the on-line music distribution business specifically.
4. Assess Napster Light's pricing strategy of charging £1.09 per track. Under what circumstances should the company consider changing this strategy?

# VII Manipulating the Marketing Mix

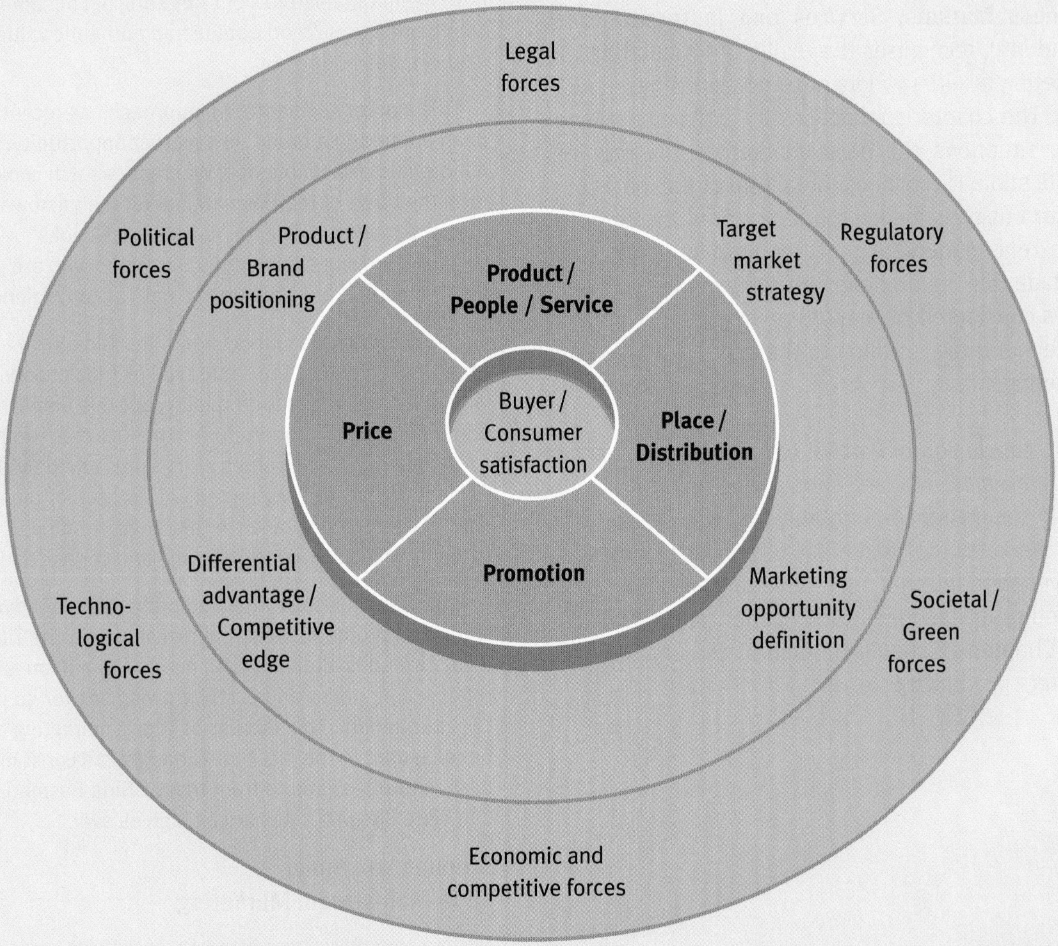


Chapter 1 of *Marketing: Concepts and Strategies* explained how marketers, after analysing marketing opportunities, must develop marketing strategies to reflect worthwhile opportunities that include target market selection. In order to implement the recommended marketing strategy, marketing programmes must be formulated based on a bespoke marketing mix for each market segment targeted. The basic ingredients of the marketing mix are product, people, place/distribution, promotion and pricing decisions. Parts III to VI of *Marketing: Concepts and Strategies* examine in detail these ingredients of the marketing mix. There are, however, situations in which market characteristics or the nature of the product require the 'standard' marketing mix to be modified. These situations occur most notably in business markets and the marketing of services, and when companies are engaged in marketing in international markets.

**Part VII of *Marketing: Concepts and Strategies*** explores the manipulation of the marketing mix to cater for business markets, the marketing of services and marketing in international markets. This material builds on the content of Chapters 5, 7 and 13, which should be read first.

**Chapter 22, 'Modifying the Marketing Mix for Business Markets, Services and in International Marketing'**, recognises the reality of formulating the marketing mix in a variety of complex business situations. The chapter commences by explaining why in many situations the basic marketing mix requires modification. It examines the nature of the marketing mix for business markets, and presents the complex and extended marketing mix required for services. To conclude, the chapter highlights the many additional issues considered by marketers involved with global markets and relates them to the development of the marketing mix.

By the conclusion of Part VII of *Marketing: Concepts and Strategies*, readers should understand why in certain circumstances – notably for business-to-business markets, the marketing of services and when involved with international marketing – the standard marketing mix requires modification and manipulation. Chapter 22 should be read in conjunction with Chapters 5, 7 and 13.

## Tilda

Over a number of years Tilda has built a brand-leading position across numerous international markets for its Pure Basmati rice brand. The success of this premium brand has been founded on the basic marketing principle of superior product quality, namely Pure Basmati, allied to tight targeting of consumers who demand real food quality and authentic values. In short, delicious food.

This market segmentation approach has recently been applied to a brand new market opportunity: two-minute microwaveable rice. Whereas 'scratch cooks' form the basis of the Basmati market the microwaveable rice market is one for 'convenience cooks', a massive and growing segment of consumers who are time-pressured but prepared to pay for convenience.

Tapping into this market trend, the Tilda Rizazz brand is targeted at the same type of Tilda consumer, who demands better food quality, but this time wants it in a convenient modern form. The Rizazz brand has all the superior food values of its sister brand, with Basmati rice as the key ingredient for each of the eight cosmopolitan recipe rices in the range, from pilau rice, through egg fried rice to Thai lime and coriander rice.

Launched in 2001 with a comprehensive TV advertising and promotional sampling campaign, the Tilda Rizazz brand is already worth nearly £10 million at retail selling prices and is still growing at over 50 per cent per annum. The success of Tilda's marketing can be measured in the fact that Tilda Rizazz's consumer base is totally separate from that of Tilda Basmati – and Tilda Basmati sales are as high as ever.

**Stephen von Speyr,**
**Tilda Mainstream Marketing**

Led by a powerfully strong brand, UK-based Tilda is now a prominent player in many international markets, including Australia and the USA. Tilda only produces rice: its marketers maintain its successful standing.

# 22

# Modifying the Marketing Mix for Business Markets, Services and in International Marketing

**"Expanding the traditional boundaries of the marketing mix is imperative for international and services contexts."**

*Constantine Katsikeas, Cardiff Business School*

## Objectives

- To recognise that in many situations the basic marketing mix requires modification
- To examine the nature of the marketing mix for business markets
- To understand the more complex and extended marketing mix required for services
- To recognise that for marketers involved with global marketing, the marketing mix requires consideration of additional issues

## Introduction

The core ingredients of the marketing mix – the marketer's tactical toolkit – are examined in detail in Parts III to VI. While the chapters in these Parts of the book have broadly covered consumer, business, service and not-for-profit markets, there has inevitably been some bias towards the marketing of consumer goods. In part this reflects the plethora of consumer brands and their coverage in the media, while in part it has been deliberate: all readers of this text, as consumers themselves, will be familiar with many of the products and services featured so far.

Marketing is marketing, and the overall approach outlined in this text and presented in Chapter 1 holds true across consumer, business, services and not-for-profit markets. It is important to acknowledge, however, that the marketing of services and business products is moderately different from the marketing of consumer goods. This chapter highlights these variations in marketing practice. Those companies involved in international marketing, trading across national borders and cultures, are also faced with additional issues that have an impact on their marketing activity.

## Opener

# Crimestoppers: Marketing the Fight Against Crime

Crimestoppers Trust was set up in 1988 with the intention of putting criminals behind bars through an anonymous Freefone number: 0800 555111. The anonymity, says the charity, is the key to the scheme's success because it provides callers with complete safety from any reprisals. Working in partnership with police, each call centre is supported by a board of volunteers drawn from the local business community and the media. The Trust believes its main function is to make sure its phones keep ringing by promoting and explaining the scheme to the public at large.

Up to 2004, Crimestoppers had received over 480,000 calls leading to over 44,800 arrests, and the recovery of property valued at £55 million and drugs at £60.5 million. Each arrest costs Crimestoppers Trust £200. There is an average of 14 arrests daily. Each week, there are 40 arrests for drug offences and one for attempted murder. Marketing Crimestoppers is a far cry from marketing soap powders or baked beans. Independent research has shown that nearly two-thirds of offenders caught through Crimestoppers were unknown to the police or not suspected of the crime in question.

If information given to Crimestoppers results in the arrest and charge of a suspect, the caller may be entitled to a cash reward, paid to them anonymously without prejudice. Only 4 per cent of callers actually ask for a reward. As the organisation's website says, 'Crimestoppers helps to empower the community and helps to harness public support in the fight against crime. It is the only UK charity helping to solve crimes.'

Crimestoppers – Call anonymously with information about crime

In 2004, the charity announced a revamped brand identity and national advertising campaign in a bid to increase the number of actionable calls received. The brief to the brand consultancy, This Way Up, was to simplify and modernise the brand, while emphasising the 0800 number, caller anonymity and the charity's independence from the police. Further activity was planned to promote the cash reward for information leading to arrests and charges. National press and poster campaigns using donated media space were prepared by agency Quiet Storm and a new website was developed by Reading Room. Capital Radio agreed to team up with Crimestoppers to promote the charity's activities across London. Such marketing activity required careful planning and professional orchestration.

**Sources:** Crimestoppers Trust; www.crimestoppers-uk.org; Emily Rogers, 'Crimestoppers to lead ads with logo overhaul', *Marketing*, 15 April 2004, p. 15.
Photo © Royalty-Free/CORBIS

There are some differences in the characteristics of the respective markets and the use of the marketing toolkit for consumer, business and service products. These are evident in the practices of business marketers, and more so in the activities of those responsible for the marketing of services. This chapter presents a summary of some of the most important, if at times subtle, variations in marketing business products and marketing services. For example, the charity Crimestoppers, as featured in the 'Opener' box, has turned to the marketing toolkit to promote its service. The chapter concludes by suggesting how international marketing requires consideration of additional issues in formulating a marketing mix. It is important that you have read Chapters 5, 7 and 13 before starting this chapter.

# Characteristics of Business Marketing Mixes

As with consumer marketers, business-to-business marketers must create a marketing mix that satisfies the customers in the target market. In many respects, the general concepts and methods involved in developing a business marketing mix are similar to those used in consumer product marketing, as outlined in Parts III to VI. In this section, the focus is on the features of business marketing mixes that differ from the marketing mixes for consumer products. Each of the main components in a business marketing mix is examined: product, place/distribution, promotion, price and people. Personnel are not particularly part of the product, but they are integral to the selling and promotional activity in all markets, and are important in developing ongoing relationships in many business markets.

## Product

After selecting a target market (see Chapter 8), the business marketer has to decide how to compete. Production-oriented managers may fail to understand the need to develop a distinct appeal for their product to give it a differential advantage. Positioning the product (discussed in Chapters 8 and 11) is necessary to serve a market successfully, whether it is consumer or business.[1]

Compared with consumer marketing mixes, the product ingredients of business marketing mixes often include a greater emphasis on services, both before and after sales. Services, including on-time delivery, quality control, custom design (see Figure 22.1) and help in specifying product requirements, a comprehensive parts distribution system and post-delivery support, may be important components of the product.

As explained in Chapter 7, in many business markets there may be only a few customers: component suppliers selling to automotive producers have only a handful of key accounts, for example. In such situations, failure to satisfy customers or to anticipate their evolving requirements is even more important than in most consumer markets, where alienation of an individual consumer is unlikely to bring a company to its knees. The ability to look after business customers is of paramount importance to business marketers. The Topical Insight box below highlights how BUPA's marketers have recognised the healthcare organisation's business customers' requirements and concerns.

Before making a sale, business marketers provide potential customers with technical advice regarding product specifications, installation and applications. Many business marketers depend heavily on long-term customer relationships that perpetuate sizeable repeat purchases.[2] Therefore, business marketers also make a considerable effort to provide services after the sale. Because business customers must have products available when needed, on-time delivery is another service included in the product component of many business marketing mixes. A business marketer unable to provide on-time delivery cannot expect the marketing mix to satisfy business customers. Availability of parts must also be included in the product mixes of many business marketers in order to prevent costly production delays. The business marketer that includes availability of parts within the product component has a competitive edge over one that fails to offer this service. Furthermore, customers whose average purchases are large often desire credit; thus some business marketers include credit

## Topical Insight

### BUPA Targets Consumers and Business Customers

BUPA now has over four million members in over 190 countries, and exists to provide reassurance and readily accessible healthcare to private policy holders and corporate members. The organisation offers insurance in the form of medical insurance, critical illness cover, life cover, income protection and travel cover. In addition to insurance policies, many customers are familiar with BUPA's healthcare services, which include hospitals – offering everything from cosmetic to major surgery – health assessments, physio and sports orthopaedic medicine, care homes, home care and fitness centres. BUPA operates 35 hospitals in the UK, 34 health screening centres and 245 care homes, employing over 40,000 people. In Spain, under the Sanitas brand, BUPA is a major provider of healthcare.

Many consumers are policy holders and visitors to BUPA clinics, but the company has a range of products targeted at business clients, as described on its website.

**Services for my business**

*Company private health cover*

If you would like to speak to someone about health cover for your business, please call 08457 66 11 15 (calls are local rate) quoting reference WO1, or you can click through for more information.

*Company cash plan*

BUPA Cash Plan is different from private medical cover because it can help to pay for the day to day health expenses your staff are almost bound to run into – such as dental bills and optical bills.

*Business International health cover*

International cover for your employees working abroad.

*Health assessments*

Our range includes new assessments specifically designed to meet key concerns voiced by organisations and employees.

*Occupational health*

We have the experience and expertise to advise you on your requirements and help you implement an occupational health programme to fit your cultural and business priorities.

*Musculo-skeletal medicine*

Our musculo-skeletal medical service supports speedy diagnosis and treatment, setting in place preventive practices and positive habits that help to boost productivity and performance.

*Dental*

Our corporate dental scheme provides extensive cover for preventative and remedial treatment, worldwide emergency treatment and oral cancer.

*Childcare services*

We offer a wide range of childcare services to companies, including help finding and arranging childcare and full on-site childcare provision.

**Find an independent financial adviser**

It is evident that BUPA has identified a range of services that employees find attractive. In addition, the company has researched employers' concerns about providing effective health cover for their employees, and how best to encourage staff to remain fit, healthy and highly productive. The products offered to BUPA's business clients reflect these diverse requirements.

**Sources:** www.bupa.co.uk/about; www.bupa.co.uk; www.bupa.co.uk/business; www.sanitas.com.

services in their product mixes. When planning and developing a business product mix, a business marketer of component parts and semi-finished products must realise that a customer may decide to make the items instead of buying them. In some cases, business marketers compete not only with one another, but also with their own potential customers.

Frequently, business products – particularly industrial products – must conform to standard technical specifications that business customers want. Thus business marketers often concentrate on functional product features rather than on marketing considerations. This has important implications for business sales people. Rather than concentrating just on selling activities, they must assume the role of consultants, seeking to solve their customers' problems and influencing the writing of specifications.[3] For example, sales people

***Figure 22.1***
*Most banks and investment houses tailor financial services to business users*
*Photo © Royalty-Free/CORBIS*

for computer hardware often act as consultants for software as well as the basic computer kit. Most customers now expect this level of service. Many suppliers have gone out of business because of their inability to offer such a service.

Because most business products are rarely sold through self-service – there are exceptions, such as office supplies – the major consideration in package design is protection. There is less emphasis on packaging as a promotional device.

Research on business customer complaints indicates that such buyers usually complain when they encounter problems with product quality or delivery time. On the other hand, consumers' complaints refer to other problems, such as customer service and pricing. This type of buyer feedback allows business marketers to gauge marketing performance. It is important that business marketers respond to valid complaints because the success of most business products depends on repeat purchases. Because buyer complaints serve a useful purpose, many companies facilitate this feedback by providing customer service departments and call centres for their business customers.[4]

If a business marketer is in a mature market, growth can come from attracting market share from another business; alternatively, a company can look at new applications or uses for its products. JCB dominates the backhoe digger market in Europe, but economic recession, which resulted in reduced construction of buildings and infrastructure, negatively impacted on its key customers. JCB looked to stimulate its sales levels by, instead, targeting products currently offered by niche rivals. The company used its existing skills and facilities to design an innovative range of very safe, single-arm skid-steer machines. These nimble, compact 'mini-diggers' are now on most building sites and are entering the hire market, proving very successful for JCB. Bringing user safety and environmental concerns to the fore, they lend themselves particularly well to buyer needs for smaller construction equipment in Germany and Scandinavia. JCB's success, managed by a well-qualified team of business marketers, stems from winning sales from its competitors, seeking new applications for its products and designing innovative products.

## Place/ Distribution

The place/distribution ingredient in business marketing mixes differs from that for consumer products with respect to the types of channel used, the kinds of intermediaries available, and the transport, storage and inventory policies. None-the-less, the primary objective of the physical distribution of business products, and particularly industrial products, is to ensure that the right products are available when and where needed. As in consumer markets, the electronic marketplace is changing the shape of distribution in some industries.[5] However, channels centred on the Internet are not always favoured by buyers. Research into the distribution of electronic components has shown that traditional channels involving distributors have prevailed, in the face of stiff competition from Internet rivals.[6]

**Direct distribution channels**
Distribution channels in which products are sold directly from producers to users

**Business distributor**
An independent business that takes title to products and carries inventories

**Types of Channel** Distribution channels tend to be shorter for business products than for consumer products. Figure 22.2 shows the four commonly used business-to-business distribution channels that were described in Chapter 14. Although **direct distribution channels**, in which products are sold directly from producers to users, are not used frequently in the distribution of most consumer products, they are the most widely used for business products. More than half of all business products are sold through direct channels (channel E in Figure 22.2). Industrial or business buyers like to communicate directly with producers, especially when expensive or technically complex products are involved. For this reason, business buyers prefer to purchase expensive and highly complex mainframe and minicomputers directly from the producers. In these circumstances, a business customer wants the technical assistance and personal assurances that only a producer can provide.

A second business distribution channel involves a business distributor to facilitate exchanges between the producer and customer (channel F in Figure 22.2). A **business distributor** is an independent business that takes title to products and carries inventories. Such distributors

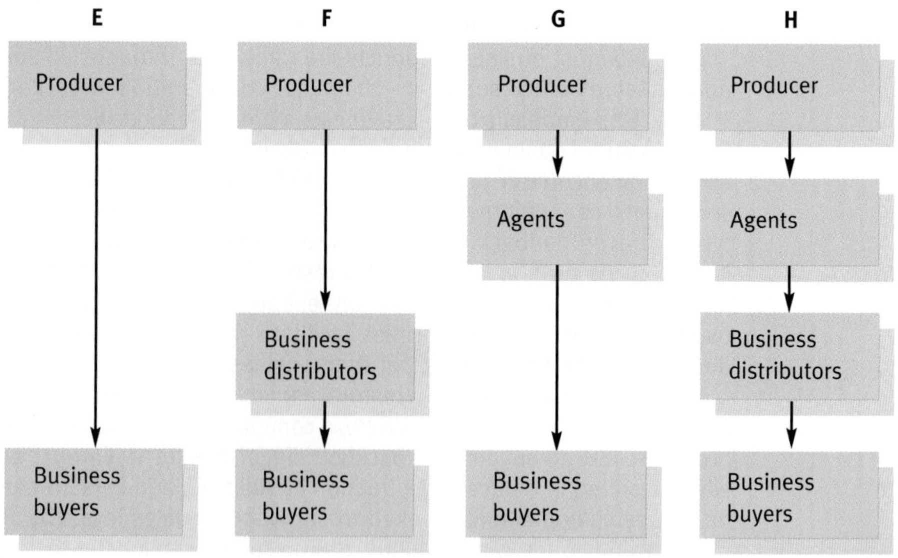


*Figure 22.2*
*Typical marketing channels for business markets*

are merchant wholesalers; they assume possession and ownership of goods, as well as the risks associated with ownership. Business distributors usually sell standardised items, such as maintenance supplies, production tools and small operating equipment. Some carry a wide variety of product lines; others specialise in one or a small number of lines. Distributors can be used most effectively when a product has broad market appeal, is easily stocked and serviced, is sold in small quantities and is needed rapidly to avoid high losses, such as a part for an assembly line machine.[7]

Business distributors or dealers offer sellers several advantages. They can perform the required selling activities in local markets at relatively low cost to a manufacturer, and they can reduce a producer's financial burden by providing their customers with credit services. Because business distributors usually maintain close relationships with their customers, they are aware of local needs and can pass on market information to producers. By holding adequate inventories in their local markets, these distributors reduce the producers' capital requirements.

There are, though, several disadvantages to using business distributors. They may be difficult to control because they are independent companies. Because they often stock competing brands, an industrial producer cannot depend on them to sell a specific brand aggressively. Furthermore, distributors maintain inventories, for which they incur numerous expenses; consequently, they are less likely to handle bulky items or items that are slow sellers relative to profit margin, need specialised facilities or require extraordinary selling efforts. In some cases, distributors lack the technical knowledge necessary to sell and service certain business items.

In the third business distribution channel (channel G in Figure 22.2), a manufacturer's agent is employed. As described in Chapter 14, a manufacturer's agent or representative is an independent business person who sells complementary products from several producers in assigned territories and is compensated through commission. Unlike a distributor, a manufacturer's agent does not acquire title to the products and usually does not take possession. Acting as a sales person on behalf of the producers, a manufacturer's agent has no latitude, or very little, in negotiating prices or sales terms.

Using manufacturers' agents can benefit a business marketer. These agents usually possess considerable technical and market information and have an established set of customers. For a business seller with highly seasonal demand, a manufacturer's agent can be an asset because the seller does not have to support a year-round salesforce. The fact that manufacturers' agents are paid on a commission basis may also make them an economical alternative for a company that has extremely limited resources and cannot afford a full-time salesforce.

Certainly, the use of manufacturers' agents is not problem-free. Even though straight commissions may be cheaper for a business seller, the seller may have little control over manufacturers' agents. Because of the compensation method, manufacturers' agents generally want to concentrate on their larger accounts. They are often reluctant to spend adequate time following up sales, to put forward special selling efforts or to provide sellers with market information when such activities reduce the amount of productive selling time. Because they rarely maintain inventories, manufacturers' agents have a limited ability to provide customers quickly with parts or repair services.

The fourth business-to-business distribution channel (channel H in Figure 22.2) has both a manufacturer's agent and a distributor between the producer and the business customer. This channel may be appropriate when the business marketer wishes to cover a large geographic area but maintains no salesforce because demand is highly seasonal or because the company cannot afford one. This type of channel can also be useful for a business marketer that wants to enter a new geographic market without expanding the company's existing salesforce.

**Choosing Appropriate Channels** So far, this discussion has implied that all channels are equally available and that a business can select the most desirable option. However, in a number of cases, only one or perhaps two channels are available for the distribution of certain types of product. In other circumstances several channels may be used simultaneously. For example, many business products that are available through traditional channels involving agents and industrial distributors can also be purchased direct via the manufacturer's website.[8] An important issue in channel selection is the manner in which particular products are normally purchased. If customers ordinarily buy certain types of product directly from producers, it is unlikely that channels with intermediaries will be effective. Other dimensions that should be considered are the product's cost and physical characteristics, the costs of using various channels, the amount of technical assistance customers need, and the size of product and parts inventory needed in local markets.

Physical distribution decisions regarding transport, storage and inventory control are especially important for business marketers. Some raw materials and other industrial products may require special handling; for example, toxic chemicals used in the manufacture of some products must be shipped, stored and disposed of properly to ensure that they do not harm people or the environment. In addition, the continuity of most business-to-business buyer–seller relationships depends on the seller having the right products available when and where the customer needs them. This requirement is so important that business marketers must sometimes make a considerable investment in order processing systems, materials handling equipment, warehousing facilities and inventory control systems. For example, without high stocks and a quickly responsive distribution system, rivals may gain an edge.

Many business purchasers are moving away from traditional marketing exchange relationships – in which the buyer purchases primarily on the basis of price from multiple suppliers – and towards more tightly knit, relational exchanges, which are long lasting, less price-driven agreements between manufacturers and suppliers.[9] Just-in-time inventory management systems are providing the rationale that underlies these new types of relationship. In order to reduce inventory costs and to eliminate waste, buyers purchase new stock just before it is needed in the manufacturing process. To make this system effective, they must share a great deal of information with their suppliers, since these relationships are collaborative.

## Promotion

The combination of promotional efforts used in business marketing mixes generally differs from those for consumer products, especially convenience goods. The differences are evident in the emphasis on various promotional mix ingredients and the activities performed in connection with each promotional mix ingredient.

**Personal selling**
The task of informing and persuading customers to purchase through personal communication

**Personal Selling** For several reasons, most business-to-business marketers rely on **personal selling** – informing and persuading customers to purchase through personal communication – to a much greater extent than do consumer product marketers (except, perhaps, marketers of consumer durables). Because a business seller often has fewer customers, personal contact with each customer is more feasible. Some business products have technical features that are too numerous or too complex to explain through non-personal forms of promotion. Moreover, business purchases are frequently high in value, and must be suited to the job and available where and when needed; thus business buyers want reinforcement and personal assurances from sales personnel. Because business marketers depend on repeat purchases, sales personnel must follow up sales to make certain that customers know how to use the purchased items effectively, as well as to ensure that the products work properly. Personal selling is often supported with advertising activity (see Figure 22.3).

Sales people need to perform the role of educators, showing buyers clearly how the product fits their needs. When the purchase of a product is critical to the future profitability of the business buyer, buying decision-makers gather extensive amounts of information about all alternative products and possible suppliers. To deal with such buyers successfully, the seller must have a highly trained salesforce that is knowledgeable not only about its own company's products but also about competitors' offerings. Besides, if sales representatives offer thorough and reliable information, they can reduce the buyer's uncertainty, as well as differentiate their company's product from the competition. Finally, the gathering of information lengthens the decision-making process. Thus it is important for sales people to be patient; to avoid pressuring their clients as they make important, new and complex decisions; and to continue providing information to their prospects throughout the entire process.[10]

As Table 22.1 illustrates, the average cost of a business sales call varies from industry to industry. Selling costs comprise salaries, commissions, bonuses, and travel and entertainment expenses. Some business sales are very large. A Boeing sales person, for instance,

***Figure 22.3***
*Personal selling is key to persuading producers of garments and home furnishings to use a supplier's fabrics.*
*Photo © Royalty-Free/ CORBIS*

closed a sale with Delta Air Lines for commercial aircraft worth $3 billion.[11] But on average, only 350 aircraft are sold each year, resulting in sales of $105 billion. Generally, aircraft sales people work hardest in the three to five years before a sale is made.

**Telemarketing** Because of the escalating costs of advertising and personal selling, telemarketing – the creative use of the telephone to enhance the sales person's function – is on the increase. Some of the activities in telemarketing include Freefone 0800 phone lines, personal sales workstations, and call centres – assisted by data terminals – that take orders, check stock and order status, and provide shipping and invoicing information.

Although not all business sales personnel perform the same sales activities, they can generally be grouped into the following categories, as described in Chapter 19: technical, missionary, and trade or inside order takers. An inside order taker could use telemarketing effectively. Regardless of how sales personnel are classified, business selling activities differ from consumer sales efforts. Because business sellers are frequently asked for technical advice about product specifications and uses, they often need technical backgrounds and are more likely to have them than consumer sales personnel. Compared with typical buyer – seller relationships in consumer product sales, the interdependence that develops between business buyers and sellers is likely to be stronger. Sellers count on buyers to purchase their particular products, and buyers rely on sellers to provide information, products and related services when and where needed. Although business sales people do market their products aggressively, they almost never use 'hard sell' tactics or behave unethically because of their role as technical consultants and the interdependence between buyers and sellers.

**TABLE 22.1 THE AVERAGE COST OF A BUSINESS-TO-BUSINESS SALES CALL BETWEEN SELECTED INDUSTRIES IN THE USA[a]**

| Industry | Number of Business-to-Business Companies Reporting | Average Daily Number of Sales Calls Per Sales Person | Average Cost of Business-to-Business Sales Call | Average Daily Sales Call Costs[b] Per Sales Person |
|---|---|---|---|---|
| Printing and publishing | 18 | 3.2 | $148.60 | $475.52 |
| Chemicals and allied products | 41 | 4.0 | $155.20 | $620.80 |
| Petroleum and coal products | 12 | 5.3 | $99.10 | $525.23 |
| Primary metal industries | 15 | 3.9 | $363.90 | $1,419.21 |
| Fabricated metal products | 113 | 3.9 | $186.10 | $725.79 |
| Machinery, except electrical | 275 | 3.5 | $257.30 | $900.55 |
| Electronic computing equipment (computer hardware) | 17 | 4.2 | $452.60 | $1,900.92 |
| Electrical and electronic equipment | 137 | 3.5 | $238.40 | $834.40 |
| Transport equipment | 41 | 2.9 | $255.90 | $742.11 |
| Instruments and related products | 73 | 3.9 | $209.50 | $817.05 |
| Wholesale trade – durable goods | 29 | 5.1 | $139.80 | $712.98 |
| Business services | 30 | 2.8 | $227.20 | $636.16 |

[a] No comparable UK/EU statistics available.
[b] This cost is determined by multiplying the average daily number of calls per salesperson by the average cost per sales call for each industry.

**Source:** Laboratory of Advertising Performance (LAP), report no. 8052.3 (date unavailable). Reprinted by permission of McGraw-Hill, Inc.

**Advertising** Advertising is emphasised less in business sales than in consumer transactions. Some of the reasons given earlier for the importance of personal selling in business promotional mixes explain why. However, advertising often supplements personal selling efforts. Because the cost of a business-to-business sales call is high and continues to rise, advertisements that allow sales personnel to perform more efficiently and effectively are worthwhile for business marketers. Advertising can make business customers aware of new products and brands; inform buyers about general product features, representatives and organisations; and isolate promising prospects by providing enquiry forms or the addresses and phone numbers of company representatives. To ensure that appropriate information is sent to a respondent, it is crucial for the enquiry to specify the type of information desired, the name of the company and respondent, the company's SIC (Standard Industrial Classification) number and the size of the organisation (see Chapter 7).

Because much of the demand for most business products is derived demand (for example, demand for construction equipment stems from consumer demand for more new houses, which in turn prompts building companies to require more plant and equipment), marketers can sometimes stimulate demand for their products by stimulating consumer demand. Thus a business marketer occasionally sponsors an advertisement promoting the products sold by the marketer's customers.

**Print Media** When selecting advertising media, business marketers primarily choose print media such as trade publications and direct mail; they seldom use broadcast media. Trade publications and direct mail reach precise groups of business customers and avoid wasted circulation. In addition, they are best suited to advertising messages that present numerous details and complex product information, which are frequently the types of message that business advertisers wish to convey.

Compared with consumer product advertisements, business – and particularly industrial – advertisements are usually less persuasive and more likely to contain a large amount of copy and detail. In contrast, marketers that advertise to reach ultimate consumers sometimes avoid extensive advertising copy because consumers are reluctant to read it. Whereas consumers desire emotional, attention-grabbing messages in advertising, business advertisers believe that purchasers with any interest in their products will search for information and read long messages.

**Sales Promotion** Sales promotion activities, too, can play a significant role in business promotional mixes. They encompass such efforts as catalogues, trade shows and trade sales promotion methods, including merchandise allowances, buy-back allowances, displays, sales contests and the other methods discussed in Chapter 19. Business marketers go to great lengths and considerable expense to provide catalogues that describe their products to customers. Customers refer to various sellers' catalogues to determine specifications, terms of sale, delivery times and other information about products. Catalogues thus help buyers decide which suppliers to contact.

**Trade Shows** Trade shows can be effective vehicles for making many customer contacts in a short time. One study found that business marketers allocate 25 per cent of their annual promotional budgets to trade shows in order to communicate with their current and potential customers, promote their corporate image, introduce new products, meet key account executives, develop mailing lists, identify sales prospects and find out what their competitors are doing. Although trade shows take second place to personal selling, they rank above print advertising in influencing business purchases, particularly as the business buyers reach the stages in the buying process of need recognition and supplier evaluation (see Chapter 7).

Many companies that participate in trade shows lack specific objectives regarding what they hope to accomplish by such participation. The companies with the most successful trade show programmes have written objectives for the tasks they wish to achieve, and they carefully select the type of show in which to take part so that those they attend match the company's target market.[12]

**Other Types of Promotion** The way in which business marketers use publicity in their promotional mixes may not be much different from the way in which marketers of consumer products use it. As described in Chapter 16, more companies are incorporating public relations automatically into their promotional mixes. There has been significant use made in recent years of the Internet by business marketers, both to promote a company's products and services, and also to help manage ongoing relationships with business customers, as described in Chapter 4. Indeed, in many markets, companies failing to develop effective websites and e-marketing capability are now at a significant competitive disadvantage.

## Price

Compared with consumer product marketers, business marketers face many more price constraints from legal and economic forces. With respect to economic forces, an individual business-to-business company's demand is often highly elastic, requiring the company to approximate competitors' prices. This condition often results in non-price competition and a considerable amount of price stability (see Chapter 20).

Today's route to sustainable competitive advantage lies in offering customers something that the competition does not offer – something that helps them increase their productivity and profitability. Most companies achieve high market share not by offering low prices but by offering their customers superior value, product quality and customer service. Many customers are willing to pay higher prices for quality products.[13] Companies such as Caterpillar, Hewlett-Packard and 3M have shown that a value-based strategy can win a commanding lead over competition. Such companies emphasise the highest quality products at slightly higher prices. Value is a trade-off between price and quality, so a value-based proposition is often not a low price proposition. Of course, some companies do focus on offering low prices and undercutting their rivals, particularly in commodity-like markets in which product differentiation is difficult to achieve. Best practice, though, would indicate that marketers should avoid emphasising low prices in their market mixes unless either the target market in question contains customers who mainly buy on the basis of low price alone, or marketers' attempts to achieve product or service differentiation have failed.

Many business-to-business companies are devoting increased resources to training, so that their personnel are better qualified and more willing to provide full customer service. Corporate image, reliability and flexibility in production and delivery, technical innovation and well-executed promotional activity also present opportunities to create a differential advantage. Price used to be the basis for differentiation in many business markets, notably in numerous industrial markets, but price can be reduced only so far if companies are to remain viable. Although cost is still important, in most markets companies have attempted to move away from a selling proposition based purely on low price. They have realised that value is not necessarily equal to a low price. Service, reliability, payment terms, image and design are just a few factors in addition to price that influence many sales. Today, value and not low price is often the deciding factor for many business customers.

Although there are various ways to determine the prices of business products, the three most common are administered pricing, bid pricing and negotiated pricing.

**Administered pricing**
A pricing method in which the seller determines the price for a product and the customer pays the specified price

**Administered Pricing** With **administered pricing**, the seller determines the price – or series of prices – for a product and the customer pays that specified price. Marketers who use this approach may employ a one-price policy in which all buyers pay the same price, or they may set a series of prices that are determined by one or more discounts. In some cases, list prices are posted on a price sheet or in a catalogue. The list price is a beginning point from which trade, quantity and cash discounts are deducted. Thus the actual (net) price a business customer pays is the list price less the discount(s). When a list price is used, the business marketer sometimes specifies the price in terms of list price times a multiplier. For example, the price of an item might be quoted as 'list price × .78', which means the buyer can purchase the product at 78 per cent of the list price. Simply changing the multiplier lets the seller revise prices without having to issue new catalogues or price sheets.

**Bid pricing**
Determination of prices through sealed or open bids submitted by the seller to the buyer

**Bid Pricing** With **bid pricing**, prices are determined through sealed or open bids. When a buyer uses sealed bids, selected sellers are notified that they are to submit their bids by a certain date. Normally, the lowest bidder is awarded the contract, as long as the buyer believes that the company is able to supply the specified products when and where needed. In an open bidding approach, several, but not all, sellers are asked to submit bids. In contrast to sealed bidding, the amounts of the bids are made public. Finally, a business purchaser sometimes uses negotiated bids. Under this arrangement, the customer seeks bids from a number of sellers and screens the bids. Then the customer negotiates the price and terms of sale with the most favourable bidders, until either a final transaction is consummated or negotiations are terminated with all sellers.

Sometimes a buyer will either be seeking component parts to be used in production for several years or custom-built equipment to be purchased currently and through future contracts. In such instances, a business seller may submit an initial, less profitable bid to win follow-on (subsequent) contracts. The seller that wins the initial contract is often substantially favoured in the competition for follow-on contracts. In such a bidding situation, a business marketer must determine how low the initial bid should be, the probability of winning a follow-on contract and what combination of bid prices on both the initial and the follow-on contract will yield an acceptable profit.[14]

**Negotiated pricing**
Determination of prices through negotiations between the seller and the buyer

**Negotiated Pricing** For certain types of business market, a seller's pricing component may have to allow for **negotiated pricing**. That is, even when there are stated list prices and discount structures, negotiations may determine the actual price a business customer pays. Negotiated pricing can benefit both seller and buyer because price negotiations frequently lead to discussions of product specifications, applications and perhaps product substitutions. Such negotiations may give the seller an opportunity to provide the customer with technical assistance and perhaps sell a product that better fits the customer's requirements; the final product choice might also be more profitable for the seller. The buyer benefits by gaining more information about the array of products and terms of sale available, and may acquire a more suitable product at a lower price.

Some business marketers sell in markets in which only one of these general pricing approaches prevails. Such marketers can simplify the price components of their marketing mixes. However, a number of business marketers sell to a wide variety of business customers and must maintain considerable flexibility in pricing.

## People

**Relationships**
Regular, ongoing contacts between businesses and their customers

This chapter has already emphasised the importance of people in the marketing of business products. The role of personal selling is especially important in many business markets, particularly those in which the purchase is deemed risky because of its size, value or complexity. For many technologically advanced products, the need to have face-to-face explanation and guidance is fundamental to the customers' perceived level of satisfaction. The development of long-term **relationships** – regular, interactive, ongoing contacts – with business customers, is increasingly a driving factor in the development of marketing mixes for businesses supplying other businesses. Where products are high value or complex, customers often expect such relationships. Even in commodity markets – for example, basic components, computer consumables or the provision of electricity – relationships are seen as a means of maintaining contact with customers, ensuring reorders and enabling a supplying business to differentiate itself through customer service rather than price alone. More attention is being given to the effective recruitment, training and motivation of personnel who are often in regular contact with a business's immediate customers, typically other businesses in the marketing channel.

## Amending the Marketing Mix for Services

The original marketing mix defined by McCarthy included the now well-known '4Ps' of product, promotion, price and place (distribution/channels). Most authors now mention an additional ingredient of the marketing mix: people. Originally suggested by services marketers who acknowledged that consumers often view the personnel providing a service as part and parcel of the service 'product' being offered, the people aspect of the marketing mix has become an accepted part of most businesses' marketing programmes, and not only for organisations marketing services. The nature of services, however, as described in Chapter 13, has led marketers to further adapt the marketing mix.[15] The intangibility of service products, inseparability of production and consumption, perishability and heterogeneity – the key characteristics of services – force the marketing mix to be amended in two ways:

1 the traditional 4Ps of product, promotion, price and place/distribution have some important extra dimensions unique to the marketing of services
2 the marketing mix is itself modified to include the additional core ingredients of process, physical evidence (ambience) and people, thereby creating the '7Ps' of what is termed the **extended marketing mix for services.**[16]

**Extended marketing mix for services**
Besides the traditional '4Ps' of product, promotion, price and place/distribution, the additional '3Ps' of people, physical evidence and process

Figure 22.4 presents this revised marketing mix for services. This section examines in more detail the amendments required when determining a marketing mix for services, commencing with the traditional 4Ps, before reviewing the additional ingredients of the extended marketing mix.[17]

### Product

Goods can be defined in terms of their physical attributes, but services, because of their **intangibility** – that is, their inability to be perceived by the senses or be stockpiled in advance of consumption – cannot. It is often difficult for consumers to understand service

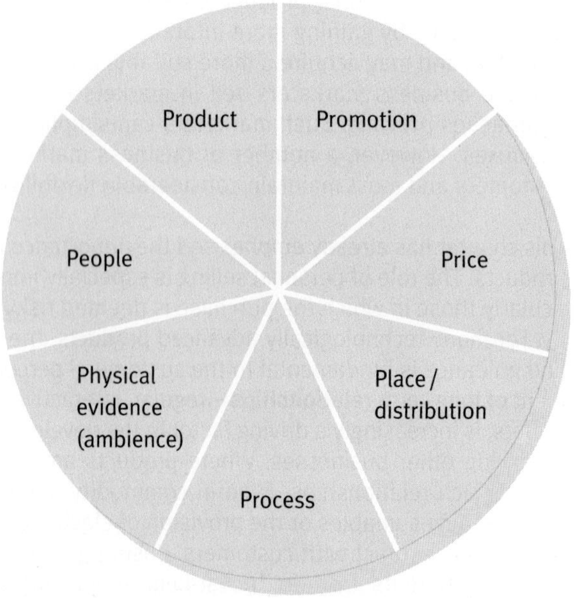


***Figure 22.4***
*The extended marketing mix for services*

**Intangibility**
A characteristic of services, which lack physical attributes and cannot be perceived by the senses

offerings and to evaluate possible service alternatives. The gas and electricity companies, for example, offer schemes to spread bill payments and to assist the financially disadvantaged, plus several methods for making payments. These services are explained in the companies' advertisements.

There may also be tangibles – such as facilities, employees or communications – associated with a service. These tangible elements help form a part of the product and are often the only aspects of a service that can be viewed prior to purchase. Consequently, marketers must pay close attention to associated tangibles and make sure that they are consistent with the selected image of the service product.[18] For example, consumers perceive public transport at night as plagued by crime and therefore hesitate to use it. Improvements in the physical appearance of tube stations and reductions in the time between trains are tangible cues that consumers can use to judge public transport services.

**Service provider**
A person who offers a service, such as a bank clerk or hair stylist

The service product is often equated with the **service provider** – for example, the bank clerk or the hair stylist becomes synonymous with the service a bank or a beauty salon provides. Because consumers tend to view services in terms of service personnel and because personnel are inconsistent in their behaviour, it is imperative that service providers are effective in selecting, training, motivating and controlling those staff members that come into contact with customers.

After testing many variables, the Strategic Planning Institute (SPI) in the USA developed an extensive database on the impact of various business strategies on profits. The institute found that 'relative perceived product *quality*' is the single most important factor in determining long-term profitability. In fact, because there are generally no objective measures to evaluate the quality of professional services (medical care, legal services, and so forth), the customer is actually purchasing confidence in the service provider.[19] The strength or weakness of the service provided often affects consumers' perceptions of **service product quality**. Of the companies in the SPI database, businesses that rate low on service lose market share at the rate of 2 per cent a year and average a 1 per cent return on sales. Companies that score highly on service gain market share at the rate of 6 per cent a year, average a 12 per cent return on sales and charge a significantly higher price.[20] These data indicate that companies having service-dominant products must score high on service quality.

**Service product quality**
The consumer's perception of the quality of service he or she receives

Because services are performances rather than tangible goods, the concept of service quality is difficult to grasp. However, price, quality and value are important considerations of consumer choice and buying behaviour for both goods and services.[21] It should be noted that it is not objective quality that matters, but the consumer's subjective perceptions. Instead of quality meaning conformity to a set of specifications – which frequently determine levels of product quality – service quality is defined by customers.[22] Moreover, quality is frequently determined through a comparison: in the case of services, by contrasting what the consumer expected of a service with his or her actual experience.[23]

Service providers and service consumers may have quite different views of what constitutes service quality. Consumers frequently enter service exchanges with a set of predetermined expectations. Whether a consumer's actual experiences exceed, match or fall below these expectations will have a great effect on future relationships between the consumer and the service provider. To improve service quality, a service provider must adjust its own behaviour to be consistent with consumers' expectations or to re-educate consumers so that their expectations will parallel the service levels that can be achieved.[24]

A study of doctor–patient relationships proposed that when professional service exceeds client expectations, a true person-to-person bonding relationship develops. However, the research also revealed that what doctors viewed as being quality service was not necessarily what patients perceived as quality service. Although interaction with the doctor was the primary determinant of the overall service evaluation, patients made judgements about the entire service experience, including factors such as the appearance and behaviour of receptionists, nurses and technicians; the décor; and even the appearance of the building.[25]

Other product concepts discussed in Chapters 10 and 11 are also relevant here. Management must make decisions regarding the product mix, positioning, branding and new product development of services. It can make better decisions if it analyses the organisation's service products in terms of **complexity** and **variability**. Complexity is determined by the number of steps required to perform a service. Variability reflects the amount of diversity allowed in each step of service provision. In a highly variable service, every step in performing the service may be unique, whereas in cases of low variability, every performance of the service is standardised.[26] For example, services provided by doctors are both complex and variable. Patient treatment may involve many steps, and the doctor has considerable discretion in shaping treatment for each individual patient. In general, to decrease costs and widen the potential market, and to better control quality, service providers seek to limit both complexity and variability.

**Complexity**
In services marketing, the number of steps required to perform a service

**Variability**
The amount of diversity allowed in each step of service provision

An examination of the complete service delivery process, including the number of steps and decisions, enables marketers to plot their service products on a complexity/variability grid, such as the one in Figure 22.5. The position of a service on the grid has implications for its positioning in the market. Furthermore, any alterations in the service delivery process that shift the position of the service on the complexity/variability grid have an impact on the positioning of the service in the marketplace. Table 22.2 details the effects of such changes. When structuring the service delivery system, marketers should consider the organisation's marketing goals and target market.

## Promotion

As intangible dominant products, services are not easily promoted. The intangible is difficult to depict in advertising, whether the medium is print or broadcast. Service advertising should thus emphasise tangible cues that will help consumers understand and evaluate the service. The cues may be the physical facilities in which the service is performed or some relevant tangible object that symbolises the service itself.[27] For example, restaurants may emphasise their physical facilities – clean, elegant, casual, and so on – to provide clues as to the quality or nature of the service. Insurance companies, such as Legal & General, use objects as symbols to help consumers understand their services. Legal & General's umbrella symbol reflects an image of paternalistic protection. HSBC's advertising explains how well the bank understands local nuances and customers' issues. Service providers may also focus their advertising on the characteristics they believe customers want from their services, such as speed of service, state-of-the-art systems or, as in the case of bank First Direct, the opportunity to talk to a person rather than deal with an automated call centre. The symbols, catch lines and imagery common to most financial organisations reflect the increasing importance of branding in services.[28] Differentiation between rival services is difficult, as is effective promotion. Branding is helping to distinguish competing services and to provide a platform for promotional activity.[29]

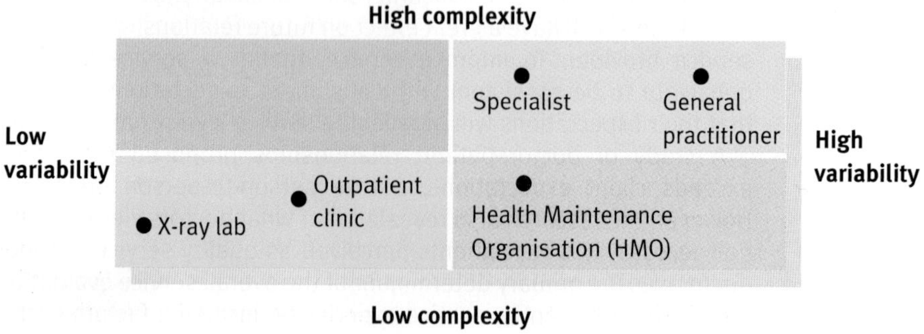


*Figure 22.5*
*Complexity/variability grid for medical services*
*Source: adapted from Lynn Shostack, 1985, American Marketing Association Faculty Consortium on Services Marketing, Texas A&M University, 7–11 July. Reprinted by permission of the American Marketing Association*

**Table 22.2 Effects of Shifting Positions on the Complexity/Variability Grid**

| Downgrading – Complexity/Variability | Upgrading – Complexity/Variability |
|---|---|
| Standardises the service<br>Requires strict operating controls<br>Generally widens potential market<br>Lowers costs<br>Indicates lower margin/higher volume strategy<br>Can alienate existing markets | Increases costs<br>Indicates higher margin/lower volume strategy<br>Personalises the service<br>Generally narrows potential market<br>Makes quality more difficult to control |

**Source:** Adapted from Lynn Shostack, 1985 American Marketing Association Faculty Consortium on Services Marketing, Texas A&M University, 7–11 July. Reprinted by permission of the American Marketing Association.

To be successful, organisations must not only maximise the difference between the value of the service to the customer and the cost of providing it; they must also design the service with employees in mind. Contact personnel are critical to the perception of quality service. They must be provided with sufficient tools and knowledge to furnish the type of service the customer desires. Because service industries are information driven, they can often substitute knowledgeable, highly trained personnel for the capital assets used in more product-oriented businesses.[30]

Thus employees in a service organisation are an important secondary audience for service advertising. Variability in service quality, which arises from the labour-intensive nature of many services, is a problem for service marketers, because consumers often associate the service with the service-providing personnel. Advertising can have a positive effect on customer-contact personnel. It can shape employees' perceptions of the company, their jobs and how management expects them to perform. It can be a tool for motivating, educating and communicating with employees.[31] For example, British Airways' famous strapline on its advertising throughout the 1980s and 1990s, 'The world's favourite airline', was designed not just to remind air travellers that more people flew with BA than with any other airline but also to develop a sense of pride among BA's flight and ground personnel.

Personal selling is potentially powerful in services because this form of promotion lets consumers and sales people interact. When consumers enter into a service transaction, they must, as a general rule, interact with the service organisation's employees. Customer contact personnel can be trained to use this opportunity to reduce customer uncertainty, give reassurance, reduce dissonance and promote the reputation of the organisation.[32] Once again, therefore, the proper management of customer-contact personnel is important.

Although consumer service organisations have the opportunity to interact with actual customers and those potential customers who contact them, they have little opportunity to go out into the field and solicit business from all potential consumers. The very large number of potential customers and the high cost per sales call rule out such efforts. On the other hand, marketers of business services, like the marketers of business goods, are dealing with a much more limited target market and may find personal selling the most effective way of reaching their customers.

Sales promotions, such as competitions, are feasible for service providers, but other types of promotion are more difficult to implement. How does an organisation display a service? How does it provide a free sample without giving away the whole service? A complimentary visit to a health club or a free skiing lesson could possibly be considered a free sample to entice a consumer into purchasing a membership or taking lessons. Although the role of publicity and the implementation of a public relations campaign do not differ significantly in the goods and service sectors, service marketers appear to rely on publicity much more than goods marketers do.[33] Customers are receptive to stories of good (and bad!) service, and public relations is highly cost effective (see Chapter 16).

Consumers tend to value word-of-mouth communications more than company-sponsored communications. This preference is probably true for all products, but especially for services, because they are experiential in nature. For this reason, service organisations should attempt to stimulate word-of-mouth communications.[34] They can do so by encouraging consumers to tell their friends about satisfactory performance. Many businesses, for instance, display prominent signs urging customers to tell their friends if they like the service and to tell the business if they do not. Some service providers, such as hairdressers, give their regular customers discounts or free services for encouraging friends to come in for a haircut. Word of mouth can be simulated through communications messages that feature a testimonial – for example, television advertisements showing consumers who vouch for the benefits of a service a particular organisation offers.

It is important to point out that the promotional activities of most professional service providers, such as doctors, lawyers and accountants, are severely limited. Until recently, all these professionals were prohibited by law from advertising. Although these restrictions have now been lifted in many countries, there are still many obstacles to be overcome. Professionals need to become familiar with developing advertising appropriate to their services, while consumers also need to adjust to seeing such service providers advertise. In many countries, lawyers are being forced to consider advertising, both because many potential clients do not know that they need legal services and because there is an oversupply of lawyers. Consumers want more information about legal services, and lawyers have a very poor public image.[35] On the other hand, doctors and dentists are more sceptical about the impact of advertising on their image and business. Despite the trend towards professional services advertising, the professions themselves exert pressure on their members to advertise or promote only in a limited way because such activities are still viewed as somewhat risqué.

## Price

Price plays both an economic and a psychological role in the service sector, just as it does with physical goods. However, the psychological role of price in respect to services is magnified; after all, consumers must rely on price as the sole indicator of service quality when other quality indicators are absent. In its economic role, price determines revenue and influences profits. Knowing the real costs of each service provided is vital to sound pricing decisions (see Chapters 20 and 21).

Services may also be bundled together and then sold for a single price. For example, Procter & Gamble tested a laundry service in various markets. The idea was that customers could choose the basic package – wash, fold and return laundry – at a single price and could also opt for additional service bundles, such as aromatherapy treatments, fragrance-free laundry or colour preservation treatments, at an extra charge.[36] Service bundling is a practical strategy, because in many types of services there is a high ratio of fixed to variable costs and high cost sharing among service offerings. Moreover, the demand for certain services is often interdependent. For example, banks offer packages of banking services – current and savings accounts and credit lines that become active when customers overdraw their other accounts. Price bundling may help service marketers cross-sell to their current customers or acquire new customers. The policy of price leaders may also be used by discounting the price of one service product when the customer purchases another service at full price.[37] Visitors to a safari park may be offered discounted entry to the adjacent fairground and amusements, or for their next visit.

Service intangibility may also complicate the setting of prices. When pricing physical goods, management can look to the cost of production as an indicator of price, but it is often difficult to determine the cost of service provision and thus identify a minimum price. Price competition is severe in many service areas characterised by standardisation.

Usually, price is not a key variable when marketing is first implemented in an organisation. Once market segmentation and specialised services are directed to specific markets, specialised prices are set. Next comes comparative pricing as the service becomes fairly standardised. Price competition is quite common in the hotel and leisure sectors, banking and insurance.

Many services, especially professional services, are situation-specific. Neither the service provider nor the consumer may know the extent of the service prior to production and consumption. As the cost is not known beforehand, price is difficult to set. Even so, many service providers attempt to use cost-plus pricing. Others set prices according to the competition or market demand.

Pricing of services can also help smooth out fluctuations in demand. Given the perishability of service products, this is an important function. A higher price may be used to deter or off-set demand during peak periods, and a lower price may be used to stimulate demand during slack periods. The railways offer cheap day returns and savers to minimise sales declines in slack periods. Airlines rely heavily on price to help smooth out demand, as do many other operations, such as pubs and entertainment clubs, cinemas, resorts and hotels.

## Place/ Distribution

In the service context, distribution is making services available to prospective users. Marketing intermediaries are the entities between the actual service provider and the consumer that make the service more available and more convenient to use.[38] The distribution of services is related very closely to product development. Indirect distribution of services may be made possible by a tangible representation or a facilitating good – for example, a bank credit card.[39]

Almost by definition, service industries are limited to direct channels of distribution. Many services are produced and consumed simultaneously; in high-contact services in particular, service providers and consumers cannot be separated. In low-contact services, however, service providers may be separated from customers by intermediaries. Dry cleaners, for example, generally maintain strategically located retail stores as drop-off centres, and these stores may be independent or company owned. Consumers go to the branch to initiate and terminate service, but the actual service may be performed at a different location. The separation is possible because the service is directed towards the consumer's physical possessions, and the consumer is not required to be present during delivery.

Other service industries are developing unique ways to distribute their services. To make it more convenient for consumers to obtain their services, airlines, car hire companies and hotels have long been using intermediaries: travel agencies. In financial services marketing, the two most important strategic concerns are the application of technology and the use of electronic product delivery channels – such as automatic cash dispensers and electronic funds transfer systems – to provide customers with financial services in a more widespread and convenient manner.[40] Consumers no longer have to go to their bank for routine transactions; they can now receive service from the nearest cash dispenser or conduct transactions via telephone, text, fax or computer. Indeed, HSBC's First Direct banking operation is managed entirely through telecommunications – phone or Internet – as there is no bank branch network. Bank credit cards have enabled banks to extend their credit services to consumers over widely dispersed geographic areas through an international network of intermediaries – namely the retailers who assist consumers in applying for and using the cards.

## Process

The acts of purchasing and consumption are important in all markets – consumer, business-to-business or service. The direct involvement of consumers in the production of most services and the perishability of these services, place greater emphasis on the process of the transaction for services. Most services, be they health, tourism, education, financial or public sector, require the client to be present when ordering and consuming the service. Compared with the consumption of consumer goods, such as a Sony Walkman or Armani suit – which may be used many times with similar results – a service experience is very transitory. Often, this sharpens the consumer's awareness of the service product and the associated service delivery experience. The manner in which the service is processed, therefore, becomes part of the customer's experience. Marketers must treat process as part of the marketing mix, and ensure that they adequately specify, control and manage the process.

Friendliness of staff and flows of information affect the customer's perception of the service product offer. Appointment or queuing systems become part of the service. Customers must comprehend how to order and then consume the service. The required process and the consumer's role should be 'transparently obvious' and readily understood. Ease or difficulty of payment can enhance or spoil the consumption of a service. The operationalisation of the service must be proficient and discernible. Diners in a TGI Friday's or Pizza Hut expect prompt service, informative menus, no waiting and no delays in paying their bills at the conclusion of their meals. These are operational issues that directly affect customer perceptions and satisfaction – they are important aspects of the marketing of services.[41]

## Physical Evidence (Ambience)

The environment in which a service is offered, and consumed, is central to the consumer's understanding of the service, and to her or his enjoyment or satisfaction. Certain services, such as weighty financial matters or health consultations, may need to be delivered in a suitably respectful setting, whereas a children's birthday treat would be better in a relaxed and informal facility designed to put children and their parents at their ease. The 'feel' of the service product is very much part of the service offer. The physical evidence, ambience or setting must be designed to reflect target customer expectations, reflect the branding and selected brand positioning (see Chapter 8), and facilitate the smooth delivery of the service.

Whether in a restaurant, hospital, sports club or bank, the appearance and ambience matter. Layout, décor, upkeep, noise and aroma, general ease of access and use – all become part of the service product. Even tyre depots have recognised this aspect of the extended marketing mix for services, providing comfortable customer waiting areas with seating, drinks machines, TV and newspapers. In services, marketers devote much attention to creating distinctive brand positionings and to delivering customer satisfaction. The physical evidence linked to a particular service can play a major role in establishing the service's branding and in delivering customer satisfaction. Inappropriate selection of the physical evidence for a service may ruin the intended experience for the targeted customers.

## People

The nature of most services requires direct interaction between the consumer and personnel representing the service provider's organisation. In many services, customers interact with one another, and the organisation's staff also interact with one another. This level of human involvement must be given maximum attention if customers are to maximise their use of the service and, ultimately, their satisfaction.[42]

Employee selection, training and motivation are central considerations. A restaurant may have a superb operation, but if the chef or waiters become demoralised and unmotivated, they will begin to deliver low-quality meals and inefficient service, possibly with a poor attitude, resulting in a poor product from the consumer's point of view. Operational staff often help 'produce' the service product, sell it and assist in its consumption. Many service businesses are totally dependent on their personnel, as Leo Burnett, founder of the international advertising agency that bears his name, summed up: 'Every evening all our assets go down the elevator' – without the agency's creative people and media experts, the business has few marketing assets.

Most well-run services businesses devote as much time and resources to managing their customer contact personnel as to creating the service product being offered to customers. Increasingly, this requires formal audits of customers' perceptions of the abilities, attitudes and appropriateness of service delivery personnel, comparative benchmarking against competitors, plus evaluations of staff attitudes towards their ability to deliver the services.

Without this attention to maintaining service delivery levels, the remainder of the marketing mix ingredients are unlikely to guarantee customer satisfaction. Marketers must devote some of their time to managing service delivery personnel.

## Strategic Adaptation of Marketing Mixes for International Markets

As explained in Chapter 5, marketing in non-domestic markets requires an understanding of the marketing environment and a specifically devised strategy. Once a company determines overseas market potential and understands the foreign environment, it develops and adapts its marketing mix(es). Creating and maintaining the marketing mix are the final steps in developing the international marketing strategy. Only if foreign marketing opportunities justify the risk will a company go to the expense of adapting the marketing mix. Of course, in some situations new products are developed for a specific country. In these cases, there is no existing marketing mix and no extra expense to consider in serving the foreign target market: new marketing programmes must be designed.

### Product and Promotion

As Figure 22.6 shows, there are five possible strategies for adapting product and promotion across national boundaries:

1 keep product and promotion the same worldwide
2 adapt promotion only
3 adapt product only
4 adapt both product and promotion
5 invent new products.[43]

**Keep Product and Promotion the Same Worldwide** This strategy attempts to use in the foreign country the product and promotion developed for the home market. This is an approach that seems desirable wherever possible because it eliminates the expenses of marketing research and product redevelopment. American companies PepsiCo and Coca-Cola use this approach in marketing their soft drinks. Although both translate promotional messages into the language of a particular country, they market the same products and promotional messages around the world. Despite certain inherent risks that stem from cultural differences in interpretation, exporting advertising copy does provide the efficiency

| Promotion \ Product | Do not change product | Adapt product | Develop new product |
|---|---|---|---|
| Do not change promotion | 1 Product and promotion same worldwide | 3 Product adaptation only | 5 Product invention |
| Change promotion | 2 Promotion adaptation only | 4 Product and promotion adaptation | |

***Figure 22.6***
*International product and promotion strategies*
*Source: adapted from Warren J. Keegan,* Global Marketing Management, *4th edn (Englewood Cliffs, NJ: Prentice-Hall, 1989), pp. 378–82. Used by permission*

of international standardisation or globalisation. As the following examples imply, however, not all brands/products are suitable for export in their existing forms:

- Zit fizzy drink (Greece)
- Bum's biscuits (Sweden)
- Krapp toilet paper (Sweden)
- Grand Dick red wine (France)
- Sor Bits mints (Denmark).[44]

Global advertising embraces the same concept as global marketing, discussed in Chapter 5. An advertiser can save hundreds of thousands of pounds by running the same advertisement worldwide.

**Adapt Promotion Only** This strategy leaves the product basically unchanged but modifies its promotion. For example, McDonald's provides similar products throughout the world but may modify the media for its advertising messages. This approach may be necessary because of language, legal or cultural differences associated with the advertising copy. When Polaroid introduced its SX-70 camera in Europe, for example, it used the same television and print advertisements featuring the same 'celebrities' it had used in the United States. However, because the personalities featured were not well known in Europe, the advertisements were not effective, and sales of the SX-70 were initially low. Only when Polaroid adapted its promotion to appeal to regional needs and tastes did the SX-70 begin to achieve success.[45] Promotional adaptation is a low-cost modification compared with the costs of redeveloping engineering and production, and physically changing products.

Generally, the strategy of adapting only promotion infuses advertising with the culture of the people who will be exposed to the promotion (see Figure 22.7). Often, promotion combines thinking globally and acting locally. At company headquarters, a basic global marketing strategy is developed, but promotion is modified to fit each market's needs, often using locally based advertising agencies.

**Adapt Product Only** The basic assumption in modifying a product without changing its promotion is that the product will serve the same function under different conditions of use. Soap and washing powder manufacturers have adapted their products to local water conditions and washing equipment without changing their promotions. Household appliances have also been altered to use different power voltages.

A product may have to be adjusted for legal reasons. Japan, for example, has some of the most stringent vehicle emissions requirements in the world. European cars that do not meet set emissions standards cannot be marketed in Japan. Sometimes, products must be adjusted to overcome social and cultural obstacles. American Jell-O introduced a powdered jelly mix that failed in Britain because consumers were used to buying jelly in cube form. Resistance to a product is frequently based on attitudes and ignorance about the nature of new technology. It is often easier to change the product than to overcome technological, social or cultural bias.

**Adapt Both Product and Promotion** When a product serves a new function or is used differently in a foreign market, then both the product and its promotion need to be altered. For example, when Procter & Gamble marketed its Cheer washing powder in Japan, it promoted the product as being effective in all temperatures. Most Japanese, however, wash clothes in cold water and, therefore, do not care about all-temperature washing. Moreover, the Japanese often add a lot of fabric softener to the wash, and Cheer did not produce many suds under such conditions. Procter & Gamble thus reformulated Cheer so that it would not be affected by the addition of fabric softener, and changed the promotion to emphasise 'superior' cleaning in cold water. Cheer then became one of Procter & Gamble's most successful

*Treauphy.*

*Bleau your own trumpet.*

*Preaupaganda.*

***Figure 22.7***
*Adapting promotion across national boundaries*
*Source: The trademark PERRIER is reproduced with the kind permission of the trademark owner, Nestlé Waters*

products in Japan. Adaptation of both product and promotion is the most expensive strategy discussed so far, but it should be considered if the foreign market appears large enough and competitively attractive.

**Invent New Products** This strategy is selected when existing products cannot meet the needs of a non-domestic market. General Motors developed an all-purpose, jeep-like motor vehicle that can be assembled in developing nations by mechanics with no special training. The vehicle is designed to operate under varied conditions; it has standardised parts and is inexpensive. Colgate-Palmolive developed an inexpensive, all-plastic, hand-powered washing machine that has the tumbling action of a modern automatic machine. The product, marketed in less developed countries, was invented for households that have no electricity. Strategies that involve the invention of products are often the most costly, but the pay-off can be great. The clockwork radio was designed as a low-cost but effective educational medium for poor regions of southern Africa. It proved a success in this context, but surprisingly also in the United States and developed economies, where it took on cult status and sold for a high price as an upmarket, trendy status symbol.

## Place/Distribution and Pricing

Decisions about the distribution system and pricing policies are important in developing an international marketing mix. Figure 22.8 illustrates different approaches to these decisions.

**Distribution** A company can sell its product to an intermediary that is willing to buy from existing marketing channels, or it can develop new international marketing channels. Obviously, some service companies, such as Citicorp or ABN AMRO, need to develop their own distribution systems to market their products. However, many products, such as toothpaste, are distributed through intermediaries and brokers. The company must consider distribution both between countries and within the foreign country. The Innovation and Change box below reveals how confectionery giant Suchard (part of Kraft Foods) seeks to acquire local companies in order to gain both ready-made production facilities and the acquired companies' distribution networks.

In determining distribution alternatives, the existence of retailers and wholesalers that can perform marketing functions between and within countries is one major factor. If a country has a segmented retail structure consisting primarily of one-person shops or street sellers, it may be difficult to develop new marketing channels for products such as packaged goods and prepared foods. Quite often in less developed countries, certain channels of distribution are characterised by ethnodomination. Ethnodomination occurs when an ethnic group occupies a majority position within a marketing channel. Indians, for example, own approximately 90 per cent of the cotton gins in Uganda; the Hausa tribe in Nigeria dominates the trade in kola nuts, cattle and housing; and Chinese merchants dominate the rice economy in Thailand. Marketers must be sensitive to ethnodomination, and must recognise that the ethnic groups operate in sub-cultures with a unique social and economic organisation.[46]

If the product being sold across national boundaries requires service and information, then control of the distribution process is desirable. Caterpillar, for example, sells more than half its construction and earthmoving equipment outside its native USA. Because it must provide services and replacement parts, Caterpillar has established its own dealers in foreign markets. Regional sales offices and technical experts are also available to support local dealers. A manufacturer of paint brushes, on the other hand, would be more concerned about agents, wholesalers or other manufacturers – for example, of paint – that would facilitate the product's exposure in a foreign market. Control over the distribution process would not be so important for that product because services and replacement parts are not needed.

Research suggests that international companies use independently owned marketing channels when they market in countries perceived to be highly dissimilar to their home

## Innovation and Change

### Pan-European Kraft Suchard Thinks Globally, Operates Locally

The chocolate confectionery business of US–Swiss Kraft Foods, part of the US Altria Group, Jacob Suchard represents 65 per cent of its SwFr11 billion turnover. Suchard had been gearing up for global markets since the late 1960s by developing global brands, such as Milka and Toblerone, and undertaking a number of strategically important acquisitions. In taking over other European confectionery companies, such as Du Lac (Italian), Pavlides (Greek), Terry's (UK), Csemege (Hungary), Kaunas (Lithuania), Olza (Poland) and Republika (Bulgaria), Suchard owner Kraft Foods has sought established distribution and retail channels in areas where it was not traditionally strong. This has helped the company to develop its own global brands alongside smaller, local products.

At the pan-European level, global brands are now assisted by the EU single market permitting the unrestricted flow of goods between EU countries. Companies with pan-European brands, including Kraft Suchard, benefit from the advertising opportunities offered by European satellites, which are less exploited by national brands. It is probable that, over several years, consumer preferences and eating habits within Europe will gradually converge as communication of this type increases. Companies such as Suchard have evolved from operating within a domestic market to being international players. As such, they must now seek additional marketing intelligence and data, rethink strategies and modify their marketing mixes. Certainly Suchard's owner, Kraft, is realigning its strategies and brand portfolios to maximise the potential of its international brands while enabling national brands to fulfil their local potential.

In the UK, Terry's of York was a major player, though relatively small next to the mighty Cadbury's and Rowntree (now owned by Nestlé). It did, however, have many well-known brands and products, good distribution coverage and modern production facilities. Acquisition by Kraft Suchard immediately increased the company's share of the UK confectionery market and improved distribution coverage for the existing range of Suchard confectionery products. The company has a 99.2 per cent stake in Romania's state confectionery maker, Poiana SA, and has promised to invest £30 million. In Lithuania, Suchard has acquired production facilities from Kaunas, rather than supplying the market with imported chocolate. Kaunas's sales have doubled since the 1993 take-over. While mainstream international brands, such as Milka, Toblerone and Suchard, are taken into these new markets, Suchard prefers to acquire locally based production and to supply existing national brands alongside those international 'best sellers' it believes have local potential. Kraft Suchard is currently focusing on eastern Europe and northern Africa.

**Sources:** www.kraft.com; Jacob Suchard archives.

**Distribution**

| Price policies | No effort to establish new marketing channels | Establish new marketing channels |
|---|---|---|
| Do not change price policies | 1 Same price policies; no control over distribution | 3 Establish new channels and use same price policies |
| Change price policies | 2 Price policies changed for international markets; no control over distribution | 4 Develop new channels and change price policies |

***Figure 22.8*** *Strategies for international distribution and pricing*

markets. However, when they market complex products, they develop vertically integrated marketing channels to gain control of distribution. To manage the distribution process from manufacturer to customer contact requires an expert salesforce that must be trained specifically to sell the company's products. Moreover, when products are unique or highly differentiated from those of current competitors, international companies also tend to design and establish vertically integrated channels.[47]

It is crucial to realise that a country's political instability can jeopardise the distribution of goods. For example, when the United States invaded Panama in late 1989, the Panama Canal was closed for several days, delaying shipments of goods through the canal. Similarly, during political unrest in China, military activity and fighting made it difficult to move goods into and out of certain areas. Instability centring on Iraq and the Persian Gulf has a similar effect. Thus it must be re-emphasised how important it is to monitor the environment when engaging in international marketing (see Chapter 5). Companies that market products in unstable regions may need to develop alternative plans to allow for sudden unrest or hostility, and to ensure that the distribution of their products is not jeopardised.

It is important to have the 'right' product or service to appeal to the target market in an international market. A significant impediment to effective international marketing, however, is distribution. It is not always easy to grasp how marketing channels operate in an alien territory. Companies setting up in Russia find the channels, bureaucracy and corruption difficult to manage. It is never easy to identify the most suitable channel members and players with which to do business, or to find those that should be permitted to sell a company's products.

**Pricing** The domestic and non-domestic prices of products are usually different. For example, the prices charged for Walt Disney videos in the UK, Germany and Spain will all vary, as well as being different from US prices. The increased costs of transport, supplies, taxes, tariffs and other expenses necessary to adjust a company's operations to international marketing can raise prices. A key decision is whether the basic pricing policy will change (as discussed in Chapters 20 and 21). If it is a company's policy not to allocate fixed costs to non-domestic sales, then lower foreign prices could result.

**Dumping**
The sale of products in non-domestic markets at lower prices than those charged in domestic markets, when all costs are not allocated or when surplus products are sold

It is common practice for EU countries to sell off foodstuffs and pharmaceuticals at knock-down prices to eastern European and African states respectively. This kind of sale of products in non-domestic markets – or vice versa – at lower prices than those charged in domestic markets (when all the costs have not been allocated or when surplus products are sold) is called **dumping**. Dumping is illegal in some countries if it damages domestic companies and workers.

A cost-plus approach to international pricing is probably the most common method used because of the compounding number of costs necessary to move products from their country of origin. Of course, as the discussion of pricing policies in Chapters 20 and 21 points out, understanding consumer demand and the competitive environment is a necessary step in selecting a price.

**Transfer pricing**
The price charged between profit centres – for example, between a manufacturing company and its foreign subsidiary

The price charged in other countries is also a function of foreign currency exchange rates. Fluctuations in the international monetary market can change the prices charged across national boundaries on a daily basis. There has been a trend towards greater fluctuation (or float) in world money markets. For example, a sudden variation in the exchange rate, which occurs when a nation devalues its currency, can have wide-ranging effects on consumer prices.

**Parallel imports**
Goods that are imported through 'non-official' channels from low-price to high-price countries

There are also pricing issues that stem from transfer pricing practices and the problems of parallel imports. **Transfer pricing** is the price charged between profit centres – for example, a manufacturing company and its foreign subsidiary. Company policies can force subsidiaries to sell products at higher prices than the local competition, even though the true costs of their manufacture may be no different. The manufacturer tries to make a profit even from its 'internal' customer, its own subsidiary.[48] **Parallel imports** – that is, goods exported from low-price to high-price countries – are an increasing problem. For example, French and Belgian beer producers export to the UK at set price levels, but consumers and small independent retailers cross by car ferry to Calais and stock up with similar brands at much lower prices than those the manufacturers 'officially' offer to UK customers. Independent operators have set up import/export businesses to take well-known beer brands into the UK to be sold at prices higher than in their native markets, but still lower than those offered by the manufacturers' official export agents. A similar trade in new cars is also now evident, undercutting UK dealers' prices.

There are also important price ramifications to consider, stemming from product or brand positioning and any differences between countries. For example, in the UK Stella Artois beer is marketed as 'reassuringly expensive', whereas in its native Belgium it is more of a commodity, mass-market brand competing against brands such as Duval or the specialist Trappist monk beers. Pricing, in any market, must reflect the brand positioning adopted.[49]

**People** As noted earlier, great importance is now attached to the people ingredient of the marketing mix. The nature of many business-to-business markets and the form of most service products often lead businesses to determine formally the role of people within their marketing mixes. In the context of international marketing, the people ingredient is also important. Chapter 5 highlighted how marketers performing across national boundaries must be aware of often striking differences, country by country or region by region, in the marketing environment. Often, cultural and social forces are the most varied – and also the most difficult for marketers based in another country and culture to understand.

Companies must deploy people with the 'right' skills to address such issues from their own ranks or from third parties in the territories under scrutiny; it is common to recruit consultants, agents or advisers to help in building up an understanding of cultural and interpersonal considerations in a non-domestic market or to hire a sales manager with local experience. Channel members are very important in supplying localised knowledge of such issues. Having personnel who understand the nuances of an international market is a fundamental requirement for effective marketing, but so too is the need for those personnel with the cultural and local knowledge to be able to implement a marketing mix, which itself may well have been modified to reflect the nuances of the relevant marketing environment.

# Summary

This chapter explains why and how the marketing mix must be manipulated differently for business markets, services marketing and international markets.

- Business marketing is a set of activities directed at facilitating and expediting exchanges involving business and industrial products and customers in business-to-business markets. Like marketers of consumer products, business marketers must develop a marketing mix that satisfies the needs of customers in the business target market. Personnel are not generally seen as integral to the product itself, but perhaps more than in consumer marketing they are central to the selling process and are a key part of promotional activity. The product component frequently emphasises services, which are often of primary interest to business customers. The marketer must also consider that the customer may elect to make the product rather than buy it. Business products must meet certain standard specifications that business users require.

- The distribution of business products differs from that of consumer products in the types of channel used, the kinds of intermediary available, and the transport, storage and inventory policies. A *direct distribution channel*, in which products are sold directly from producers to users, is common in business marketing. Also used are channels containing manufacturers' agents, *business distributors*, or both agents and distributors. Channels are chosen on the basis of several variables, including availability and the typical mode of purchase for a product.

» *Personal selling* is a primary ingredient of the promotional component in business marketing mixes. Sales personnel often act as technical advisers both before and after a sale. Advertising is sometimes used to supplement personal selling efforts, but it is not generally as emotional as in consumer marketing. Business marketers generally use print advertisements containing more information but less persuasive content than consumer advertisements. Other promotional activities include catalogues, trade shows and the web.

» The price component for business marketing mixes is influenced by legal and economic forces to a greater extent than it is for consumer marketing mixes. *Administered*, *bid* and *negotiated pricing* are additional possibilities in many business markets. Pricing may be affected by competitors' prices, as well as by the type of customer who buys the product. Increasingly, though price is still important, many companies are seeking new ways of creating a differential advantage. Value for money is important in most markets, but low price is not usually an effective competitive advantage except in the very short term. Flexibility and reliability in production and delivery can be differentiating factors, as can technical innovation, personnel and customer service, promotional activity and even payment terms. People, important in the context of personal selling, are also often required to establish ongoing long-term *relationships* with key customers.

» The basic marketing mix is augmented for services through the addition of people, physical evidence (ambience) and the process of transaction in order to produce the '7Ps' or the *extended marketing mix for services*. When developing a marketing mix for services, several aspects deserve special consideration. Regarding product, service offerings are often difficult for customers to understand and evaluate. The tangibles associated with a service may be the only visible aspect of the service, and marketers must manage these scarce tangibles with care. Because services are often viewed in terms of the *service providers*, service providers must select, train, motivate and control employees carefully, particularly to guarantee *service product quality* and service delivery. Consumers determine the quality of services subjectively, often by contrasting what was expected of a service with the actual experience. Service providers need to meet these expectations or re-educate consumers. Service marketers are selling long-term relationships as well as performance. It is important to understand the *complexity* of the service product and to seek to limit its *variability*.

» Promoting services is problematic because of their *intangibility*. Advertising may stress the tangibles associated with the service or use some relevant tangible object. Branding is used to distinguish competing services. Personnel in direct contact with customers should be considered an important secondary audience for advertising. Personal selling is very powerful in service organisations because customers must interact with personnel; some forms of sales promotion, however, such as displays and free samples, are difficult to implement. The publicity component of the promotional mix is vital to many service organisations. Because customers value word-of-mouth communications, messages should attempt to stimulate or simulate word of mouth. Many professional service providers, however, are severely restricted in their use of promotional activities.

» Price plays three major roles in the service sector. It plays a psychological role by indicating quality and an economic role by determining revenues; price is also a way to help smooth out fluctuations in demand.

» Service distribution channels are typically direct because of simultaneous production and consumption. However, innovative approaches such as drop-off points, intermediaries and electronic distribution – such as the Internet – are being developed.

International marketing requires careful planning. Marketing activities performed across national boundaries are usually significantly different from domestic marketing activities. International marketers must have a profound awareness of the foreign environment, and of social and cultural differences. The international marketing strategy is ordinarily adjusted to meet the needs and desires of markets across national boundaries.

After a country's environment has been analysed, marketers must develop a marketing mix and decide whether to adapt product or promotion. There are five possible strategies for adapting product and promotion across national boundaries: (1) keep product and promotion the same worldwide; (2) adapt promotion only; (3) adapt product only; (4) adapt both product and promotion; (5) invent new products. Foreign distribution channels are nearly always different from domestic ones. Identifying and understanding channels in foreign markets are not easy tasks. Distribution channels can become a major impediment in international marketing. The allocation of costs, transport considerations or the costs of doing business in foreign markets will affect pricing. *Transfer pricing* and *parallel imports* are important considerations, as are the regulations pertaining to *dumping*. It is also necessary to set pricing levels that reflect the nuances of a product's brand positioning in a particular market: the same brand may occupy distinctly different positionings in separate territories.

## *Key Links*

This chapter has summarised some of the ways in which marketers must modify the marketing mix in order to serve business markets, market services or reflect the requirements of international markets. Before reading this chapter, it is important to first read:

- Chapter 5, on international marketing
- Chapter 7, on business markets and business buying behaviour
- Chapter 13, on the marketing of services.

There is also related information in Chapters 20 and 21, on pricing decisions.

## Important Terms

Direct distribution channels
Business distributor
Personal selling
Administered pricing
Bid pricing
Negotiated pricing
Relationships
Extended marketing mix for services
Intangibility
Service provider
Service product quality
Complexity
Variability
Dumping
Transfer pricing
Parallel imports

## Discussion and Review Questions

1. How do business-to-business marketing mixes differ from those of consumer products?
2. What are the major advantages and disadvantages of using business distributors?
3. Why do business marketers rely on personal selling more than consumer products' marketers?
4. Why would a business marketer spend resources on advertising aimed at stimulating consumer demand?
5. Compare three methods of determining the price of business products.
6. Why must a competitive advantage be based on more than just low prices?
7. Discuss the role of promotion in services marketing.
8. What additional elements must be included in the marketing mix for services? Why?
9. Why is it difficult to create and maintain a differential advantage in many service businesses?
10. Why do the marketers of services place so much emphasis on the people ingredient of the marketing mix?
11. What are the principal choices a company can make when manipulating the marketing mix for international markets?

12 How and why can the place/distribution ingredient of the marketing mix cause problems for international marketers?
13 What additional factors determine a company's pricing policy in foreign markets?

## Recommended Readings


- Bradley, F., *International Marketing Strategy* (London: FT Prentice Hall, 2002).
- Bridgewater, S. and Egan, C., *International Marketing Relationships* (Basingstoke: Palgrave Macmillan, 2002).
- Ford, D., Gadde, L.-E., Hakansson, H. and Snehota, I., *Managing Business Relationships* (Chichester: Wiley, 2003).
- Hutt, M.D. and Speh, T.W., *Business Marketing Management: Strategic View of Industrial and Organisational Markets* (Cincinnati, OH: South Western, 2003).
- Lovelock, C.H., *Principles of Services Marketing and Management* (Englewood Cliffs, NJ: Pearson, 2001).
- Naude, P., Michel, D., Salle, R. and Valla, J.-P., *Business to Business Marketing* (Basingstoke: Palgrave Macmillan, 2003).
- Palmer, A., *Principles of Services Marketing* (Maidenhead: McGraw-Hill, 2000).
- Terpstra, V. and Sarathy, R., *International Marketing* (Cincinnati, OH: South Western, 2000).
- Zeithaml, V. and Bitner, J., *Services Marketing* (New York: McGraw-Hill, 2002).


## Internet Exercise

Log on to BUPA's website. This provider of healthcare and health insurance targets both consumers and business clients. Look at the information BUPA provides for *Individuals* (consumers) and for *Business* (corporate clients).
www.bupa.co.uk

1 What are the key BUPA service products offered to private consumers and to business clients?
2 How are BUPA's messages about its products tailored to reflect the different needs and buying behaviour of its consumers and business clients?

## *Applied Mini-Case*

Volvo Trucks is a wholly owned subsidiary of Volvo. It is the division that handles the importing, manufacturing, sales and marketing, and after-sales support for all Volvo heavy goods vehicles. The company's website states:

> Volvo is the world's second largest producer of heavy trucks. We create reliable transport solutions for clients all over the world – without ever compromising the safety and environmental care that we carefully build into each of our trucks.

For most of the major players in the European truck market, two major trends are dictating current marketing strategies. The decline in new vehicle sales is leading to an increased focus on the aftermarket. The market for replacement parts, tyres, fuels and lubricants is more stable and offers some degree of cushioning against the more extreme fluctuations in demand for new vehicles. The second trend has been a move by hauliers and large companies with their own transport fleets away from purchasing new vehicles outright. There has been a switch to leasing and contract hire, whereby the truck manufacturer ultimately retains ownership of the vehicle and has to off-load the vehicles when they are returned by the haulier.

**Source:** Volvo Trucks.

### *Question*

As sales of new trucks decline and marketers, instead, concentrate increasingly on offering financing packages and aftermarket care, what are the key skills marketers must deploy in this evolving sector?

## Case Study

# Hewlett-Packard Targets the Developing Economies

In the USA and Europe – mature markets for computers and IT – Hewlett-Packard markets its computing products and IT solutions with its own field force, advertising, direct marketing, publicity and sales promotions. Many of its products are retailed through leading computer dealers and high-street retailers. For its computers, the style of marketing emulates the approaches of leading rivals such as IBM, Apple, Toshiba and Sony. The marketing programmes – in terms of their style – could be for hi-fi or photographic equipment, or home entertainment systems.

Elsewhere in the world, HP is something of a mould-breaker. Where others may see low incomes and low-tech infrastructure, HP anticipates long term business opportunities. India, Senegal, Bangladesh and other developing countries have been targeted by the US computer and printer giant as it seeks first-mover advantage ahead of its rivals. HP has created a programme called World e-Inclusion to reach out and influence entrepreneurs and businesses in developing countries to log on to the on-line business boom. The concept aims to foster future business development while advancing a social agenda of bringing technology resources to under-served regions of the world.

World e-Inclusion has brought together public-sector, not-for-profit, government departments and local development groups to lease, buy or receive donated HP products and services. These partners, in turn, put the IT products in the hands of farmers, manufacturers and small business owners. Some will receive off-the-shelf standard HP computers while, owing to their circumstances, other users will be provided with solar-powered machines capable of wireless or satellite communication. All users will be trained and shown how to make connections with local suppliers and buyers.

To support this initiative, HP has opened research labs in India to investigate IT use and probable solutions in developing economies. These labs will create IT products that are economically and culturally sustainable as well as technically advanced. In addition, HP has boosted its service, sales and operations in these countries. The company is also working with lenders to provide loans to budding entrepreneurs. HP has joined forces with AOL to donate computers, printers, modems and Internet access to peace group volunteers in 15 countries to further encourage IT use and broaden the benefits of technology in these societies.

While there is a social mission associated with HP's World e-Inclusion programme, the company is quite clear about its commercial motives. The long-term purpose of the strategy is business development rather than charity. In the UK, France and Portugal, HP uses a more traditional set of marketing communications to support its more conventional marketing strategy. In the developing economies, such an approach is unworkable until the point is reached when the take-up of IT products is far more advanced and routinised in the business community.

**Sources:** Hewlett-Packard; Bill Pride and O.C. Ferrell.

### Questions for Discussion

1 In what ways does HP's marketing strategy in India differ from the strategy deployed in Europe?

2 What is the proposition being offered to business customers in these developing countries?

3 What are the problems and potential risks associated with operating such contrasting marketing programmes globally for a company such as Hewlett-Packard?

## Postscript

The marketing mix is the toolkit deployed by marketers to create marketing programmes designed to implement their marketing strategies, and to take their product or service offerings to their selected target markets. The basic ingredients of the marketing mix are the '5Ps' of product, people, place/distribution, promotion and price, as described in Parts III to VI of *Marketing: Concepts and Strategies*. There are, however, situations in which either market characteristics or the nature of the product requires the modification of the 'standard' marketing mix. Most notably, for business markets, the marketing of services and for international markets. Part VII of *Marketing: Concepts and Strategies* has explored how the marketing mix must be manipulated in these situations. Chapter 22 should be read in conjunction with Chapters 5, 7 and 13.

Before progressing, readers should be confident that they are now able to do the following.

### Explain why, when and how the basic marketing mix requires additional manipulation

- In what situations does the standard marketing mix require modification?
- What is the nature of the marketing mix for business markets?
- What is the extended marketing mix for services?
- Why does the marketing of services require additional ingredients in the marketing mix?
- What issues do marketers encounter in international markets?
- Why must the marketing mix be manipulated for international markets?

## *Strategic Case*

# Colgate
# Globally Known Consumer Brands

Founded in 1806 by William Colgate, New York-based Colgate-Palmolive is genuinely a multinational enterprise, deriving nearly two-thirds of its business from international sales. Having marketed its products in some regions of the world for over 75 years, the company sells its well-known brands, such as Colgate (toothpaste and toothbrushes), Palmolive (soaps and shampoos), Ajax and Axion (cleaners), Softsoap (liquid hand soap), Mennen (deodorants) and Hill's (pet products) in more than 150 countries. In the early 1990s, of particular interest was international expansion in the former East Germany, Poland and Mexico, and an ongoing association with the Operation Smile programme.

### Successful Expansion into the Former East Germany

Once the dust from the fall of the Berlin Wall had settled, and East and West Germany were united under a common currency, the shelves of retail outlets in the former East Germany were transformed virtually overnight from small and drab displays of poor-quality products into bright, western-style assortments of high-quality goods from around the world. Colgate-Palmolive was one of the first companies to have success in the new market, both because it was positioned for easy entry – it had operations in neighbouring countries – and because consumers in the former communist nation were eager to try the company's products, which they had seen on West German television, but previously had been unable to cross the border to buy. After less than three years in the region, the company was achieving 35 per cent of its total German toothpaste business on the eastern side of the crumbled Berlin Wall, even though the region accounted for only 25 per cent of the total German population.

This early success occurred even though Colgate-Palmolive had some initial problems in expanding into the newly liberated country. For example, besides the financial and political risks involved in investing in the region, recruiting a salesforce was something of a dilemma. Sales had been a non-existent and unnecessary profession under communist rule; goods were merely produced and then distributed by the all-powerful central government. To overcome this difficulty, Colgate-Palmolive initially brought in experienced West German sales people but eventually established sales training programmes in the region to teach the 'new profession' to local citizens.

## The Use of a Joint Venture Approach in Poland

By far the largest potential market in eastern Europe, with a population of 38 million prospective consumers, Poland became a primary target for Colgate-Palmolive when the country began moving to a free market economy in 1990. As soon as the Polish borders opened up to the ways of the western world, Colgate-Palmolive products were readily available at a range of retail outlets. Open-air street markets were also filled with products brought in by individuals from neighbouring countries. As with consumers in the former East Germany, Polish consumers almost overnight saw radical changes in the type and quality of products available to them.

To promote long-term growth in the Polish market, Colgate-Palmolive entered into a joint venture agreement with a local entrepreneur experienced in consumer product sales and distribution. Initially, the company planned to offer only a limited line of its top products – Colgate toothpaste, Palmolive soap and shampoo, and Ajax scouring powder – through the joint venture partner, which was entrusted with the responsibility of manufacturing and marketing the goods. For its manufacturing facilities, Colgate-Palmolive worked with its joint venture partner to buy a partially completed complex, which was then renovated into a highly modern production facility. To make this joint operating arrangement run smoothly, Colgate-Palmolive appointed a native Polish general manager for the region. The new general manager had previously served the company in a variety of senior marketing management positions in both Belgium and France.

## The Use of Video Intelligence in Mexico

To better understand Mexico's large and diverse population, particularly in terms of social and cultural differences, Colgate-Palmolive conducted what it termed a 'video anthropological study' of the country's rapidly expanding consumer market. This study had two main objectives: to find out, by observing and talking to Mexican consumers, how certain products were actually used, and to gather general information on the lifestyles of these consumers. Colgate-Palmolive was not interested in product use itself, but rather in the processes in which its products *could* be used. Five processes were studied: dish washing, house cleaning, oral care, haircare, and laundry/fabric care.

An independent team of researchers set out across the country, compiling 60 hours of videotaped discussions with consumers. The result of this exercise was a series of tapes covering each of the five main process areas. Initial analysis showed Colgate-Palmolive marketing managers that Mexican consumers' activities diverged significantly along socio-economic lines. For example, those in the higher socio-economic groups did their laundry and took care of fabrics in the same way as many middle-class Europeans, using electric appliances and even the service of maids or housekeepers. However, less affluent Mexican consumers, for whom in-home water was often a luxury, did their washing manually in tubs using washboards or in local streams using rocks, with a variety of soaps to clean their clothes.

Marketing managers at Colgate-Palmolive learned a great deal from this revolutionary use of video technology. The information directly affected new product development and the creation of advertising themes for existing products in the Mexican market. For example, marketing managers set out to develop new laundry care products that used less water and advertising messages that showed how Colgate-Palmolive products could be used in situations where little water was available. As a result of these efforts, new laundry pre-soak and spray stain removers were developed specifically for the Mexican market.

## Operation Smile

Operation Smile is a volunteer organisation of doctors, dentists and corporate sponsors that travels all over the world, performing reconstructive surgery on children who suffer from cleft palates or cleft lips (facial deformities of the mouth and nasal region). Although these disorders are fairly common and corrective surgery is not considered complicated by western medical standards, for many children in developing or less developed nations, such surgery is either unaffordable or unavailable in their immediate geographic areas. In these cases, Operation Smile goes to the patient and performs the surgery free of charge. Since its inception in 1982, Operation Smile has performed reconstructive surgery or specialised dental treatment on well over 6000 children. In addition, local doctors have been taught how to perform these corrective procedures so that they can be done on a regular basis in their particular region.

Colgate-Palmolive has joined forces with Operation Smile in several of the developing countries in which it currently operates or hopes to in the future. In Panama, for example, the company organised and funded a public relations campaign featuring a series of 'before and after' photo displays to inform parents in isolated rural regions that cleft lips or palates are in fact treatable. Then the company urged these parents to bring their children to local facilities to have the corrective work done free of charge. In addition, Colgate-Palmolive organised fundraising efforts in the local business community to off-set the cost of the services provided. In Panama, the company has been at least partly responsible for the treatment of several hundred children.

Colgate-Palmolive's affiliation with Operation Smile not only encompasses organising and funding corrective surgery, but also includes extensive oral education programmes for children in many less developed nations. For example, in Kenya the company is well known for its education programmes offered in conjunction with various community organisations in rural areas. The company also stocks the Operation Smile facilities with free toothpaste, soap and other supplies. All in all, Colgate-Palmolive's association with Operation Smile gives it a foundation for future investment and a unique opportunity to link its corporate goals with those of a well-known and well-regarded global charitable organisation.

## International Growth

Colgate-Palmolive's Operation Smile activities, and its initiatives in Mexico, Poland and the former East Germany form an integral part of its international marketing programme, which is far more extensive than just these four examples. The company's aggressive concurrent development and introduction of new products in numerous other countries around the world clearly signal its intention to maintain its international focus. As further evidence of the company's strong commitment to continuing global expansion, Colgate-Palmolive became the first western company to manufacture toothpaste in China, where a market of over four billion potential customers proved eager for the high-quality consumer products that Colgate-Palmolive could provide.

These efforts, coupled with others, such as its use of video intelligence-gathering techniques in Mexico and its association with the Operation Smile programme, ensure that Colgate-Palmolive continues to serve as a model for other companies hoping to succeed as multinational marketers in the dynamic global marketplace.

## Questions for Discussion

1. Discuss how Colgate-Palmolive has responded to changing social, economic and political forces in the former East Germany. Why should companies exercise caution when expanding into new regions?
2. What kinds of useful information did Colgate-Palmolive gain from its video anthropological study in Mexico? Why is such knowledge especially important for a company entering international markets?
3. What factors might have played a role in Colgate-Palmolive's decision to enter into a joint venture agreement in the Polish market? Discuss the possible rationale for the company's decision to initially market only a limited number of its products in Poland.

# VIII Marketing Management

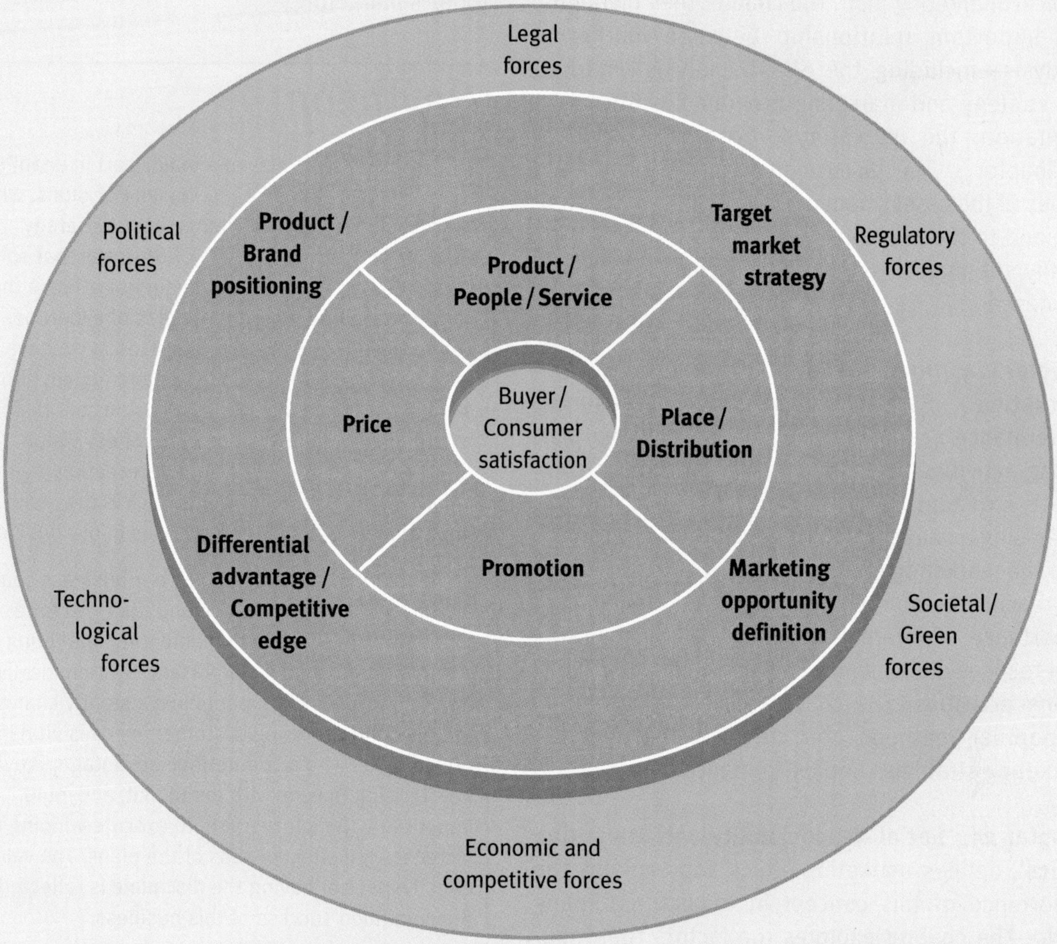


In Figure 1.5, the generic tasks of marketing strategy were identified as marketing opportunity analysis, target market strategy, marketing mix development and marketing management. Parts I to VII of *Marketing: Concepts and Strategies* examined the first three of these generic tasks. Chapter 2 discussed marketing strategy in detail, and target market selection was explored in Chapter 8. The focus of Part VIII is on the core aspects of marketing management: implementation and control of marketing strategy and marketing activity, in particular the popular and important technique of marketing planning. Of growing concern to marketers and consumers are the topics of ethics and social responsibility in marketing. These issues must be of central concern to marketers when they determine marketing strategies and then strive to implement these strategies.

**Part VIII of *Marketing: Concepts and Strategies*** explores the central issues of marketing management: marketing planning and forecasting sales potential; implementing strategies, internal marketing relationships and measuring performance; and the role of ethics and social responsibility in marketing.

**Chapter 23, 'Marketing Planning and Forecasting Sales Potential'**, examines the marketing planning process and how organisations practise marketing planning. The chapter presents an overview of a 'typical' marketing plan. The chapter then highlights the important relationship between marketing analysis—including the SWOT analysis—marketing strategy and marketing programmes for implementation: the *marketing process* as described in Chapter 1. The discussion turns to the related issues of the assessment of market and sales potential, and to the principal sales forecasting methods. Finally, the major components of a marketing audit are described.

**Chapter 24, 'Implementing Strategies, Internal Marketing Relationships and Measuring Performance'**, commences by describing how marketing activities are often organised within a company's structure, and explains the various ways of organising a marketing unit. The chapter then examines the marketing implementation process, various approaches to marketing implementation and the importance of internal marketing. The discussion next focuses on implementing and controlling marketing activities. The chapter closes with a look at popular methods and criteria for evaluating marketing strategies and performance.

**Chapter 25, 'Social Responsibility and Marketing Ethics'**, defines marketing ethics and explains the importance of this concept in today's marketing world. The chapter explores the factors that influence ethical decision-making, discussing some of the important ethical issues marketers face. Next, the chapter presents ways of improving ethical decisions in marketing. The focus of the chapter then switches to social responsibility: explaining the concept, exploring important issues and describing strategies for dealing with social dilemmas. Finally, the concepts of social responsibility and marketing ethics are compared and contrasted.

By the conclusion of Part VIII of *Marketing: Concepts and Strategies*, readers should understand more about the complexities of managing marketing strategies and marketing programmes, the role of marketing planning, forecasting sales potential, evaluating marketing performance, ways of implementing marketing strategy, and the significant influence of ethics and social responsibility in today's marketing.

## Raytheon

Marketing has played a major part in enabling our business to make fact-based decisions, which have seen a successful change in our strategy. Previously we were the type of business that spread itself 'too thinly', meaning we did not achieve the results we should in our real areas of expertise. By using tried and tested marketing tools, we have identified the attractive markets and equally those not so attractive, to enable us to focus on successfully moving towards the achievement of our vision. Currently we are achieving and forecasting major growth in turnover and profit, which is the result of implementing marketing processes in our business.

The global markets in which our business competes are increasingly competitive and the need for a marketing discipline in implementing marketing strategies is extremely important. Systematically analysing key developments in constantly changing markets and capturing customer needs is vital in providing us with a competitive advantage. Providing key decision-makers with the toolkit, and more importantly the information, to execute winning plans increases the effectiveness of the plans. The value and effectiveness of having the discipline is reflected in the continued success of this business.

**Jim Trail, chief operating officer,**
**Raytheon Systems Limited**

Power & Control Systems is a business within Raytheon Systems Limited, a wholly owned subsidiary of Raytheon Company, and was established in Glenrothes, Fife, in 1960. Core capabilities of the company are the design, development and manufacture of power products for international aerospace, industrial and defence markets.

# 23 Marketing Planning and Forecasting Sales Potential

**"The overall purpose of marketing planning and its principal focus is the identification and creation of sustainable competitive advantage."**

*Malcolm McDonald, Cranfield University School of Management*

## Objectives

- **To understand the marketing planning process**
- **To gain an overview of the marketing plan**
- **To examine the relationship between marketing analysis, marketing strategy and marketing programmes in marketing planning**
- **To examine the role of the SWOT analysis in marketing planning**
- **To become familiar with market and sales potential, and sales forecasting methods**
- **To analyse the major components of a marketing audit**

## Introduction

Manipulation of the marketing mix to match target market needs and expectations constitutes a daily activity for most marketing personnel. However, as explained in the first two chapters of this book, fundamental strategic decisions need to be made *before* the marketing mix(es) are formulated. To expedite this process and link the strategic decision-making to the development of actionable marketing programmes, many organisations – small and large – turn to formal marketing planning. This chapter examines the nature of marketing planning. Like all business activities, marketing needs to have goals; often these are sales targets and market share objectives (see Chapter 24 for a full discussion of marketing performance metrics). To set the right goals, marketers must be able to forecast future sales and market size trends.

Marketing planning is a systematic process involving the assessment of marketing opportunities and resources, the determination of marketing objectives, and the development of a plan for implementation and control. Marketing planning is often deployed by organisations, helping direct and control the activities of marketers. A sales forecast is an estimation of the amount of a service or product that an organisation expects to sell during a specific period at a specified level of marketing activity. Market potential is a prediction of industry-wide market size, everything else being equal, over a specified time period. Marketers often spend large sums on executing marketing mixes, so it is necessary to assess first whether the probable levels of sales warrant such expenditure and commitment of managerial resource. The marketing audit, where applied, is a systematic examination of the objectives, strategies, organisation and performance of a company's marketing unit. Although far from commonplace, the marketing audit has many purposes, one of which is to help develop an organisation's appreciation of its capabilities and market challenges as a prelude to marketing planning. Some companies conduct a marketing audit as a preliminary analysis to gain a realistic understanding of the organisation, its personnel and its market.

## *Opener*

# A Demon Doughnut for Healthier Snacking

In recent years, the news headlines have regularly featured alarmist stories about obesity problems in children and adults, often focusing on the unhealthy diets of many consumers. While this is, perhaps, helpful to the purveyors of healthy foods, diet products and fitness centres, for many food manufacturers and fast-food businesses, these forces of the marketing environment have been anything but good news.

McDonald's responded by reducing the size of its portions and introducing more healthy options – such as salads and fresh fruit – to its menus. Many cola brands created low-carb versions and reduced their sugar content. Leading crisp, biscuit and snack brands launched 'healthier' options. Even doughnuts responded to the threat posed by the heightened awareness of health concerns based on eating habits and product choices. To many health workers and nutritionists, few other products appeared less healthy than a dough-based product deep-fried.

After four years in development, London-based Demon Donuts launched a lower-fat doughnut, baked rather than deep-fried. The company patented a production method of oven cooking that avoided deep frying and offered consumers the same texture as a deep-fried doughnut but without the high levels of fat and saturated fat common in normal doughnuts. The result was a product with similar functionality and taste properties to the traditional doughnut but with less calories and significantly reduced levels of harmful fats. Demon claimed that its mixed berry-filled product contained 1.8 grams of saturated fat and 7.5 grams of total fat compared with 4 grams of saturated fat and 16 grams of total fat in a similar-sized traditional, deep-fried jam-filled doughnut.

Demon managed to persuade leading supermarket chains to stock its Demon Donuts, supporting the launch with trade press advertising, sales calls to retail merchandisers, point-of-sale display materials for in-store promotions, product sampling in-store and limited consumer advertising. The company is familiar with the market sector, having been formed by former employees of well-known international business Dunkin' Donuts.

The rationale for Demon Donuts has been the creation of a product acceptable to major retail chains, which reflects consumers' taste requirements and the increasing pressure to eat less harmful foods. The sector is highly competitive, with Cadbury-branded Dipping Doughnuts, Krispy Kreme and supermarket own-label doughnuts in most shapes and flavours. Demon believes its healthier eating stance offers a competitive advantage and a viable long-term future. Extensive marketing analysis, product development and marketing planning combined to bring Demon Donuts to the marketplace.

**Sources:** 'Lower fat doughnut in shops from next week', *Marketing Week*, 19 February 2004, p. 9; Demon Donuts, London; Sainsbury's. Photo: Courtesy of Demon Donuts

This chapter begins with a discussion of the marketing planning process and an overview of the marketing plan. Demon Donuts produced a marketing plan before its launch. The chapter then discusses the relationship between marketing analysis – including the SWOT analysis – marketing strategy and marketing programmes for implementation. The chapter examines market and sales potential, and forecasting techniques for predicting sales, before concluding with a discussion of the major components of a marketing audit.

# Marketing Planning

**Marketing planning**
A systematic process of assessing marketing opportunities and resources, determining marketing objectives and developing a thorough plan for implementation and control

**Marketing plan**
A document or blueprint detailing requirements for a company's marketing activity

**Marketing planning cycle**
A circular process that runs in two directions, with planning running one way and feedback the other

**Marketing planning** is a systematic process that involves assessing marketing opportunities and resources, determining marketing objectives and developing a thorough plan for implementation and control. Research shows that good-quality marketing planning can lead to a positive impact on business performance.[1] A core output of marketing planning is the **marketing plan**, a document or blueprint that details requirements for a company's marketing activity. The marketing planning process involves analysing the marketplace, modifying or updating the recommended marketing strategy accordingly and developing detailed marketing programmes designed to implement the specified marketing strategy.[2]

Figure 23.1 illustrates the **marketing planning cycle**. Note that marketing planning is a cyclical process. As the dotted feedback lines in the figure indicate, planning is not one way. Feedback is used to coordinate and synchronise all the stages of the planning cycle. Most

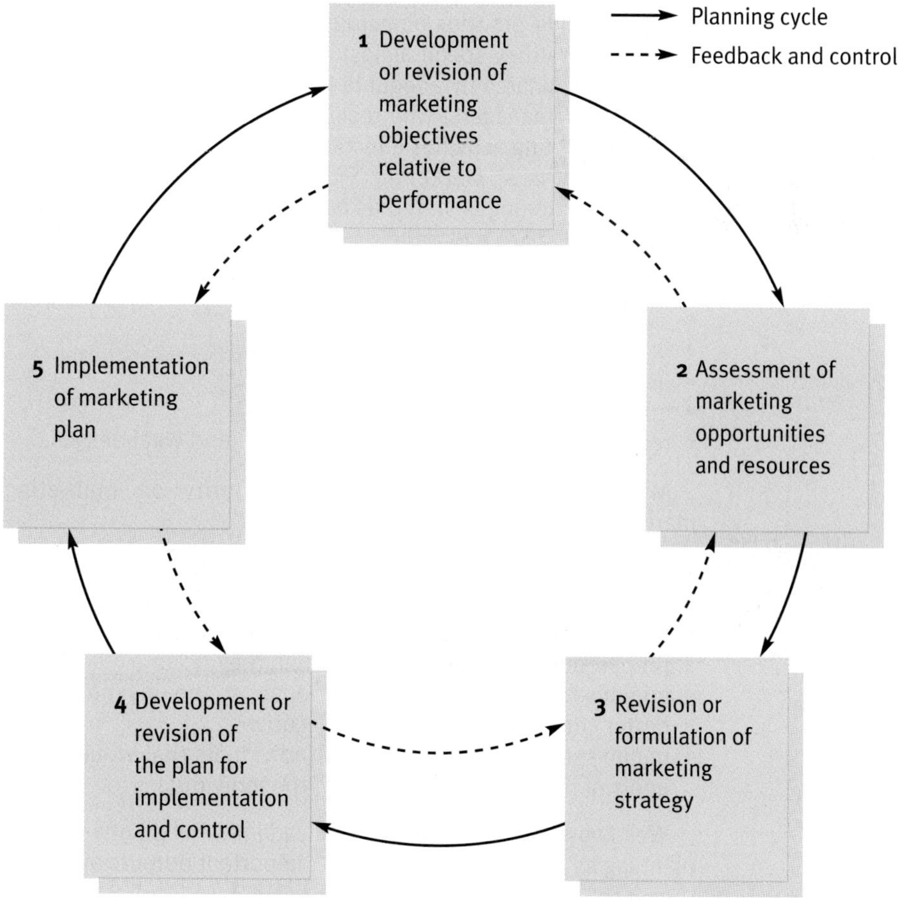


***Figure 23.1*** *The marketing planning cycle*

businesses produce marketing plans annually, typically with a three-year perspective. The immediate 12 months' marketing activity is presented in detail, with overviews provided for years two and three in the three years featured. Once up and running, this process involves revising the previous year's plan by updating the essential marketing analyses, revising the recommended strategy accordingly, before determining detailed marketing mix action plans. Once an organisation has gone through the demanding, intensive and resource-hungry process of developing a marketing plan for the first time, subsequent annual revisions are much less taxing. The resulting plan is normally presented to the board for approval before becoming a documented set of actions for sales and marketing personnel to follow.

**Short-range plans** Plans that cover a period of up to a year

**Medium-range plans** Plans that usually cover two to five years

**Long-range plans** Plans that extend beyond five years

The duration of marketing plans varies. Plans that cover a period of up to a year are called **short-range plans. Medium-range plans** are usually for two to five years. Marketing plans that extend beyond five years are generally viewed as **long-range plans.** These plans can sometimes cover a period of up to 20 years. Marketing managers may have short-, medium- and long-range plans all at the same time. Long-range plans are relatively rare. However, as the marketing environment continues to change and business decisions become more complex, profitability and survival will depend more and more on the development of long-range plans.[3] Most marketing plans are revised annually.[4] Organisations choose to update fully and revise their marketing plans, modifying their marketing programmes and changing the detail of their marketing mix(es) as a result. Strategic market plans, as described in Chapter 2, are unlikely to face annual changes of such magnitude, although strategy modifications will always be needed to respond to changes in customer needs, the marketing environment and competitors' activities.

The extent to which marketing managers develop and use plans also varies. Although marketing planning provides numerous benefits, some managers do not use formal marketing plans because they spend almost all their time dealing with daily problems, many of which would be eliminated by adequate planning. However, planning is becoming more important to marketing managers, who realise that planning is necessary to develop, coordinate and control marketing activities effectively and efficiently.[5]

In the authors' *Marketing Planning Workbook*, a practitioner text, the benefit of marketing planning is stated as being to provide the basis for an organisation:

- serving the 'best' target customers
- beating the competition
- keeping abreast of market developments
- maximising returns for the organisation
- using resources to best advantage
- minimising threats
- recognising the organisation's strengths and weaknesses.

Malcolm McDonald, a leading authority on marketing planning, argues that marketing planning facilitates:

- coordination of the activities of many individuals whose actions are interrelated over time
- identification of expected developments
- preparedness to meet changes when they occur
- minimisation of non-rational responses to the unexpected
- better communication among executives
- minimisation of conflicts among individuals that would result in a subordination of the goals of the company to those of the individual.

Well-known American marketing academic Philip Kotler summed up the role of marketing planning as follows: 'one of the most important outputs of the marketing planning process is the marketing plan'.

***Figure 23.2***
*As described in Table 23.1, planning the launch of USA Today was fundamental to the paper's success*
*Photo © John Van Hasselt/CORBIS SYGMA*

When formulating a marketing plan, a new enterprise or a company with a new product does not have current performance to evaluate or an existing plan to revise. Therefore, its marketing planning focuses on assessing opportunities and analysing capabilities. Managers can then develop a marketing strategy and marketing objectives. Many organisations recognise the need to include information systems in their plans so that they can have continuous feedback and keep their marketing activities oriented towards objectives. Research suggests that companies that increase the level of resources put into planning out-perform those that reduce their allocation to these activities. To illustrate the marketing planning process, consider the decisions that went into the planning of US national newspaper *USA Today*. Table 23.1 lists several of the more important marketing decisions. Of course, to reach the objective, a detailed course of action was communicated throughout the organisation. In short, marketing plans should do the following:

1. Execute the agreed marketing strategy by detailing appropriate marketing programmes.
2. Specify expected results so that the organisation can anticipate what its situation will be at the end of the current planning period.

3 Identify the resources needed to carry out the planned activities so that a budget can be developed.
4 Describe in sufficient detail the activities that are to take place so that responsibilities for implementation can be assigned and schedules determined.
5 Provide for the monitoring of activities and the results so that control can be exerted.[6]
6 Reflect customer needs and market developments.
7 Emphasise any differential advantages or strengths over rivals.
8 Provide clarity of purpose within an organisation.

There is a logical and relatively straightforward approach to marketing planning:

1 Analysis of markets, the marketing environment, customer expectations, competitors and trends.
2 Determination of core target markets.
3 Identification of a basis for competing and a differential advantage or competitive edge.
4 Statement of specific goals and desired product or service positioning.
5 Development of marketing mixes to create marketing programmes to implement plans.
6 Determination of required budgets.
7 Specification of schedules and the allocation of marketing tasks.
8 Monitoring of performance and evolving market conditions.

Table 23.2 illustrates these aspects of the marketing planning process in more detail. A good marketing plan addresses each of these aspects thoroughly and objectively, ensuring it is truly customer focused. To succeed, a company must have a plan that is followed closely yet is flexible enough to allow for adjustments to reflect changes in the marketing environment.[7]

Obviously, the marketing plan document needs to be written carefully in order to attain these objectives. The next section of this chapter takes a closer look at the marketing plan itself.

**TABLE 23.1 PLANNING FOR THE INTRODUCTION OF A NATIONAL NEWSPAPER: *USA TODAY***

**Objective:** Achieve 1 million in circulation by reaching an up-market segment, primarily of males who hold professional and managerial positions and who made at least one trip of 200 miles or more within the last year.

**Opportunity:** Paper tends to be a second newspaper purchase for readers. *USA Today* is not in competition directly with local papers, and it is not positioned against other national newspapers/magazines.

**Market:** Circulation within a 200 mile radius of 15 major markets, representing 54 per cent of the US population, including such cities as Chicago, Houston, New York, Los Angeles and Denver.

**Product:** Superior graphic quality; appeal to the television generation through short news items, a colour weather map and other contemporary features.

**Price:** Competitive.

**Promotion:** Pedestal-like vending machines with attention grabbing design and a higher position than competitors to differentiate the paper and bring it closer to eye level. Outdoor advertising and some print advertising promotes the paper.

**Distribution:** News stands, vending machines in busy locations, direct mail and hotel distribution.

**Implementational and Control:** Personnel with experience in the newspaper business who can assist in developing a systematic approach for implementing the marketing strategy and design, as well as an information system to monitor and control the results.

**Source:** Kevin Higgins, '*USA Today* nears million reader mark', *Marketing News*, 15 April 1983, pp. 1, 5. Reprinted by permission of the American Marketing Association.

**Table 23.2 The Core Steps of the Marketing Planning Process**

| |
|---|
| **Analysis**<br>The marketing environment and trends<br>Company's Strengths, Weaknesses, Opportunities and Threats (SWOT)<br>Customers' needs, buying behaviour and perceptions; market segmentation and brand positioning<br>Competition and competitors' strategies<br>Marketing opportunities<br>The balance of the product portfolio and ABC sales: contribution analysis |
| **Strategy**<br>Determination of core target markets; basis for competing/differential advantage; desired product/brand positioning; marketing objectives and sales targets |
| **Programmes for Implementation**<br>Specification of sales targets and expected results<br>Specification of plans for marketing mix programmes:<br>• products<br>• promotion<br>• place/distribution<br>• people (service) levels<br>• pricing<br>Specification of tasks/responsibilities; timing; costs; budgets<br>Internal marketing of the plan's goals, strategy and key programmes<br>Ongoing work<br>Monitoring progress and benchmarking performance |
| **Source:** Sally Dibb and Lyndon Simkin, *The Marketing Planning Workbook* (London: Thomson, 1996). Reprinted with permission. |

# The Marketing Plan

The marketing plan is the written document, or blueprint, governing all of a business's marketing activities, including the implementation and control of those activities.[8] A marketing plan serves a number of purposes, it:

- offers a 'road map' for implementing a company's strategies and achieving its objectives
- assists in management control and monitoring of implementation of strategy
- informs new participants in the plan of their role and function
- specifies how resources are to be allocated
- stimulates thinking and makes better use of resources
- assigns responsibilities, tasks and timing
- makes participants aware of problems, opportunities and threats
- assists in ensuring that an organisation is customer focused, aware of market and competitive movements, realistic in its expectations, and prudent in its use of resources.

A company should have a plan for each marketing opportunity it pursues. Because such plans must be changed as forces in the company and in the marketing environment change, marketing planning is a continuous process. Many companies have separate marketing managers or teams addressing different product groups or market segments. Each team would typically have its own marketing plan relevant to its marketplace. The marketing director would produce an over-arching all-inclusive marketing plan summarising the key aspects of each team's plan. Organisations use many different formats when devising marketing plans.

Plans may be written for strategic business units, product lines, individual products or brands, or specific markets.

Most plans share some common ground by including an executive summary; a statement of objectives; background to the market; market analysis and examination of realistic marketing opportunities (a description of environmental forces, customers' needs, market segments and internal capabilities); competitor activity; an outline of marketing strategy, target market priorities, differential advantage, brand and product positioning; a statement of expected sales patterns; the detail of marketing mixes required to implement the marketing plan; controls; financial requirements and budgets; and any operational considerations that arise from the marketing plan (see Table 23.3).

A leading defence conglomerate wanted to use its technological expertise in non-defence markets. Marketing planning enabled it to task its marketers to identify possible opportunities for the company to use its expertise in the oil, alarm, automotive and rail sectors. These opportunities were checked out fully, narrowed down and then addressed with appropriate marketing programmes through the marketing planning process. The resulting marketing plan was able to articulate the nature of the opportunity in non-defence markets and persuade the company's board to sanction the resources required to enter these new markets. The following sections consider the major parts of a typical marketing plan, as well as the purpose that each part serves.

## Management or Executive Summary

The management summary, or executive summary (often only one or two pages), should be a concise overview of the entire report, including key aims, overall strategies, fundamental conclusions and salient points regarding the suggested marketing mix programmes. Not many people read an entire report, tending to 'dip in' here and there, so the management summary should be comprehensive and clear.

## Marketing Objectives

**Marketing objective**
A statement of what is to be accomplished through marketing activities – the results expected from marketing efforts

Objectives are for the benefit of the reader, such as senior executives, to give perspective to the report. Aims and objectives should be stated briefly but should include reference to the organisation's mission statement and corporate goals, objectives and any fundamental desires for core product groups or brands. This section describes the objectives underlying the plan. **A marketing objective** is a statement of what is to be accomplished through marketing activities. It specifies the results expected from marketing efforts. A marketing objective should be expressed in clear, simple terms so that all marketing personnel understand exactly what they are trying to achieve. The marketing objective should be written in such a way that its accomplishment can be measured accurately. If a company has an objective of increasing its market share by 12 per cent, the company should be able to measure changes in its market share accurately. A marketing objective should also indicate the timeframe for accomplishing the objective. For example, a company that sets an objective of introducing three new products should state the time period in which this is to be done.

Objectives may be stated in terms of degree of product introduction or innovation, sales volume, profitability per unit, gains in market share, or improvements in customer satisfaction or awareness of the company's products and brands. They must also be consistent with the company's overall organisational goals.

## Product/Market Background

Product/market background is a necessary section. Not everyone reading the plan will be fully familiar with the products and their markets. Senior managers may be unfamiliar with specific aspects of the product or market. This section 'scene sets', helping the readers – for example, a chief executive or advertising manager – to understand the marketing plan.

## Marketing Analysis

The analysis section is the heart of the marketing planning exercise: if incomplete or highly subjective, the recommendations are likely to be based on an inaccurate view of the market and the company's potential. This section of the plan provides a sound foundation to the

**TABLE 23.3 PARTS OF A MARKETING PLAN**

| |
|---|
| **1 Management or executive summary** |
| **2 Marketing objectives**<br>a Company mission statement<br>b Detailed company objectives<br>c Product group goals |
| **3 Product/market background**<br>a Product range and explanation<br>b Market overview and sales summary<br>c ABC sales: contribution financial performance assessment<br>d Directional policy matrix evaluation of the product portfolio |
| **4 Marketing analyses**<br>a Marketing environment and trends<br>b Customers' needs and segments<br>c Competition and competitors' strategies<br>d Strengths, Weaknesses, Opportunities, Threats (SWOT) analysis |
| **5 Marketing strategies**<br>a Core target markets (segments)<br>b Basis for competing/differential advantage<br>c Desired product/brand positioning |
| **6 Statement of expected sales forecasts and results** |
| **7 Marketing programmes for implementation**<br>a Marketing mixes<br>b Tasks and responsibilities |
| **8 Controls and evaluation: monitoring of performance** |
| **9 Financial implications/required budgets**<br>a Delineation of costs<br>b Expected returns on investment for implementing the marketing plan |
| **10 Operational considerations**<br>a Personnel and internal marketing relationships and communications<br>b Research and development/production needs<br>c Marketing information system |
| **11 Appendices**<br>a SWOT analysis details<br>b Background data and information<br>c Marketing research findings |
| **Source:** Sally Dibb and Lyndon Simkin, *The Marketing Casebook* (London: Routledge, 1994). Reprinted with permission. |

recommendations and marketing programmes. It includes analyses of the marketing environment, market trends, customers, competitors, competitive positions and competitors' strategies, the suitability of the business's product portfolio and the financial performance of products, market segments and even certain customers. As this lengthy list of subjects implies, effective marketing planning is about much more than just being customer-focused.[9] Marketers therefore need to be careful to include all of these areas in their analyses.

The market attractiveness – business strength matrix and the ABC sales: contribution analysis detailed in Chapter 12 are popular tools employed by marketers to assess portfolio performance.

The marketing environment section of the marketing plan describes the current state of the marketing environment, including the legal, political, regulatory, technological, societal/Green, economic and competitive forces, as well as ethical considerations. It also makes predictions about future directions of those forces. For example, the retailer Safeway was among the first to respond to consumer concern about the use of artificial fertilisers and pesticides. It offered its customers a choice of either regular fruit and vegetables or organically grown produce at a higher price.

As discussed in Chapter 3, environmental forces can hamper an organisation in achieving its objectives. This section of the marketing plan also describes the possible impact of these forces on the implementation of the marketing plan. Most marketing plans include extensive analyses of competitive, technological, legal and regulatory forces, perhaps even creating separate sections for these influential forces of the marketing environment. It is important to note here that because the forces of the marketing environment are dynamic, marketing plans should be reviewed and modified periodically to adjust to change.

Marketing exists to enable an organisation to meet customers' needs properly. This is particularly true in the marketing planning process. The views, needs and expectations of current and potential customers are important as a basis for formal marketing planning. Without such an understanding and analysis of likely changes in customer requirements, it is impossible to safely target those markets of most benefit to the organisation's fortunes. It is also impossible to specify a correct marketing mix (or mixes).

The analysis of the marketing environment includes competitive forces and trends. As explained in Chapter 2, however, a meaningful marketing plan and associated programmes for implementation necessitate a prior comprehensive analysis of an organisation's competitive position in its markets and territories, together with an understanding of rival organisation's marketing strategies. The failure to understand or anticipate competitors' likely actions is a major weakness in most businesses.[10]

**SWOT analysis**
Analysis that determines a company's position by examining four factors: strengths, weaknesses, opportunities and threats

**SWOT Analysis** The **SWOT analysis** is an important foundation for any marketing plan, helping to produce realistic and meaningful recommendations. The section in the main body of the report should be kept to a concise overview, with detailed market-by-market or country-by-country SWOTs – and their full explanations – kept to the appendices. Many marketers conduct SWOT analyses (the letters SWOT stand for strengths, weaknesses, opportunities and threats). The first half of this analysis – strengths and weaknesses – examines the company's position, or that of its product, vis-à-vis customers, competitor activity, environmental trends and company resources. The second half of the SWOT takes this review further to examine the opportunities and threats identified, and to make recommendations that feed into marketing strategy and the marketing mix. The marketing environment analysis often reveals potential opportunities and threats. Understanding and then responding to these opportunities and threats enables a business to make the most of the environmental context in which it operates. Even a potential threat can be transformed into an opportunity if appropriate action is taken.[11] The result of the SWOT analysis should be a thorough understanding of the organisation's status and its standing in its markets. A SWOT analysis must be objective, with evidence provided to support the points cited. The focus should be on issues likely to concern customers. As explained in Chapter 2, which offers illustrative SWOT analyses, the checklist-style SWOT analysis is popular with marketers, particularly as part of a marketing plan.

## Marketing Strategies

Strategies should be self-evident if the analyses have been objective and thorough: the opportunities to pursue, the target markets most beneficial to the company, the basis for competing and differential advantage or competitive edge in these markets, and the desired product or brand positioning. This strategy statement must be realistic and detailed enough to act upon.

This section of the marketing plan provides a broad overview of the plan for achieving the marketing objectives and, ultimately, the organisational goals. Marketing strategy focuses on identifying opportunities to be pursued, defining a target market and developing a marketing mix to gain long-run competitive and customer advantages. There is a degree of overlap between corporate strategy and marketing strategy. Marketing strategy is unique in that it has the responsibility to assess buyer needs and the company's potential for gaining competitive advantage, both of which, ultimately, must guide the corporate mission.[12] In other words, marketing strategy guides the company's direction in relationships between customers and competitors. The bottom line is that a marketing strategy must be consistent with consumer needs, perceptions and beliefs. Thus this section should describe the company's intended target market and how product, people, promotion, place/distribution and price will be used to develop a product or brand positioning that will satisfy the needs of members of the target market.

## Expected Results

Having highlighted the strategic direction and intention, it is important to explain the expected results and sales volumes to show why the strategies should be followed. These forecasts should be quantified – typically as expected units of sales and possible market shares. This stage is important if the required marketing mix budgets are to be approved by senior managers.

## Marketing Programmes for Implementation

Marketing programme recommendations are the culmination of the various analyses and statements of strategies: exactly what needs to be done, how and why. This is the detailed presentation of the proposed marketing mixes to achieve the goals and implement the strategies. In poor marketing plans, there is a lack of analysis and strategy, with the focus falling on the tactical marketing mix recommendations. Robust planning requires the recommendation of detailed marketing mixes, but only after time has been taken to thoroughly address the core marketing analyses and determine a detailed marketing strategy.

Each market segment to be targeted may require its own, tailor-made marketing mix. This section of the marketing plan is of paramount importance, as it gives the specific details of the marketing activity required to implement the marketing plan and to achieve the organisation's strategic goals. Each element of the marketing mix should be discussed in turn, with specific recommendations explained in sufficient detail to enable managers to put them into action. Product, people (service), pricing, place/distribution and promotion (marketing communications) must all be addressed. Associated tasks should be allocated to personnel and responsibilities for action clearly identified. This is the core output of marketing planning: the detailed plan of action for the business's marketing programmes. Organisations must also be prepared to adapt their implementation plans if unexpected events arise that were not predicted by the plan. Research shows that in smaller businesses, marketing and business success are linked to how good they are at improvising if the unexpected happens.[13]

## Controls and Evaluation

It is essential that controls be established along with measures to assess the ongoing implementation of the marketing plan. This section of the plan details how the results of the plan will be measured. For example, the results of an advertising campaign designed to increase market share may be measured in terms of increases in sales volume or improved brand recognition and acceptance by consumers. Next, a schedule for comparing the results achieved with the objectives set forth in the marketing plan is developed. Finally, guidelines may be offered outlining who is responsible for monitoring the programme and taking remedial action. Financial measures such as sales volumes, profitability and market shares will be included. 'Softer' issues, such as brand awareness and customer satisfaction, should also be monitored.[14] The next chapter explains in more detail implementation controls and performance measures.

**Financial Implications/ Required Budgets** The full picture may not be known, but an indication of required resources and the financial implications must be given. The financial projections and budgets section outlines the returns expected through implementation of the plan. The costs incurred will be weighed against expected revenues. A budget must be prepared to allocate resources in order to accomplish marketing objectives. It should contain estimates of the costs of implementing the plan, including the costs of advertising, salesforce training and remuneration, development of distribution channels and marketing research.

**Operational Considerations** These strategies and marketing programmes may have ramifications for other product groups, sectors or territories, for research and development, for engineering or production, and so on. The operational implications must be highlighted, but too much detail may be inappropriate and politically sensitive within the organisation.

**Appendices** The main body of the report should be as concise as possible. The document must, though, tell the full story and include evidence and statistics that support the strategies and marketing programmes being recommended. The use of appendices – so long as they are fully cross-referenced in the main body of the report – helps to keep the report concise and well focused.

## Conducting Marketing Planning

Experienced marketers produce their own marketing plans, often with the involvement of colleagues from other functional areas within the organisation and particularly the members of the sales team, who have knowledge of market trends and customer issues. Most companies set a point in the year when each business unit is expected to submit a detailed marketing plan, with fully costed marketing programmes set against detailed sales expectations and market share targets. Most marketing teams will spend at least the month before the deadline updating their marketing analyses and strategic thinking, before detailing revised marketing mix programmes.

In organisations embarking on marketing planning for the first time, there is often a significant learning curve to address, with the first round of marketing analyses requiring a long lead time and much resourcing. The managers involved have to learn new skills and accommodate the planning tasks alongside their normal tasks.[15] By year three, the marketing planning process has generally become part of the organisation's fabric and the required analyses are being updated routinely throughout the year by marketers well versed in the planning process's requirements.[16] Initially, though, 'naive' organisations – those not experienced in the marketing planning toolkit – often seek the help of external experts and facilitators, as outlined in the Marketing Tools and Techniques box below.

## Marketing Tools and Techniques

### JCB's Adoption of Marketing Planning

Some time ago, the incumbent marketing director of construction equipment leader JCB went to study strategic marketing at INSEAD in France. On his return to the UK headquarters of JCB he introduced a formal marketing planning process to the company. Recognising the cultural diversity and complexity of a global business, the marketing director opted to focus initially on the UK. At the time the company had four core product groups, including backhoe loaders and telehandlers, plus some quickly emerging new product categories, such as skid steers and mini-excavators. Each product group had its own set of marketers, thus each team produced a marketing plan.

As the marketing planning process was new to the company, external trainers were brought in to establish a stage-by-stage sequence of activities, and to provide the company's sales and marketing staff with the required analytical toolkit. Stage one included the core marketing analyses: financial performance of the company's products and sales analysis; the marketing environment forces active in each product group's target markets; the buying behaviour characteristics and evolving customer needs; competitors' products, strengths, weaknesses and projected plans; the company's brand positioning vis-à-vis leading rivals; plus, JCB's capabilities.

These tasks proved time-consuming for already busy personnel, so some external support was commissioned in order to research customers and competitors. Small teams from within the marketing function were allocated to the different forces of the marketing environment: technological developments, regulatory pressures, economic trends, and so forth. These teams reviewed secondary sources for information, networked with JCB and dealer personnel, met with subject experts to solicit their views, and created a dialogue with industry observers. To examine competitors, the JCB marketers visited trade shows, talked with customers and dealers, analysed rivals' products and marketing programmes, reviewed financial performance and engaged with industry-watchers. Marketing research in the form of one-to-one depth interviews and focus groups gleaned customers' views of JCB, its products and customer service, changing customer needs and the customers' views of competitors. Some of these analyses were undertaken by teams of marketers working across JCB's product groups and target markets, while much research was specific to the separate marketing teams handling each product group in the company.

Within six weeks, a significant amount of marketing intelligence had been derived, updated, collated and analysed. Stage two, externally moderated by consultants, involved brainstorming workshops with sales and marketing personnel reflecting on current strategies in the light of the various marketing analyses conducted. As a result, the target market priorities were modified, new products commissioned, revised marketing communications created, modified pricing considered, dealer plans revisited and customer service improved. An important aspect of stage two was the sharing of marketing intelligence – particularly about competitors, opportunities and threats – between the separate marketing teams. The final stage of the process involved the formalisation of appropriate marketing mix programmes to operationalise the revised marketing strategy, coordination of the separate teams' proposed marketing programmes, plus the allocation of budgets, personnel, schedules and responsibilities to these emerging tasks.

In year two, when the summer marketing planning period was reached, JCB's subsidiary companies overseas were also included, producing top-line marketing plans. Managers overseas were able to learn from their UK colleagues and emulate the format of their resulting marketing plans. For the UK marketers in their second season, there was the opportunity to address outstanding marketing analysis gaps from the previous year and to focus on utilising the marketing planning toolkit rather than learning about its scope and tools.

By year three, the rest of JCB's non-UK operation had become involved, while in the UK the growing understanding of the marketplace facilitated by two years' marketing planning and marketing intelligence gathering led to the creation of new target market segments. The marketing plans by year three were segment-specific, ignoring the product groups created by JCB for operational convenience. This led to the formation of the company's Compact Division, recognising that customers of mini-excavators or mini-skid steers had different purchasing behaviour to customers buying the larger-scale versions of such products.

After three years, one manager described the marketing planning process thus:

> In the first year it was really hard – hell: learning new skills; realising we had inadequate or incomplete knowledge of market trends, competitors and even customers; adjusting to undertaking the planning work alongside our 'day jobs' ... just finding the time. The process now is routine: we never miss the opportunity to find out about customer views, examine competitors or discuss market developments with 'those in the know'. We're also much quicker in producing and delivering the marketing plan. The big difference is that now the company's strategic planning and budgeting are guided by the analyses and market understanding provided by the marketing plan. More to the point, we're selling more machines, in a larger number of segments to more satisfied customers. Even better, whether in our French subsidiary, Indian plant or American sales office, we're all addressing the market in a coordinated manner and everyone is aware of the requirements for effective marketing planning. But it has taken three years. Finding the time was hard to start with. It did 'hurt' in the first year!

Having examined marketing planning, this chapter now focuses on forecasting sales and evaluating market potential, important in marketing planning in order to justify the use of resources as recommended in the marketing plan.

## Market and Sales Potential and Sales Forecasting

Unfortunately, many organisations' sales and marketing activities are reactions to changes in the marketplace, particularly the actions of competitors, rather than planned and carefully orchestrated activities that anticipate consumer needs and expectations. In such reactive organisations, predictions of future changes in market size and potential tend to be rudimentary or non-existent. Estimations of their own likely sales are often based only on the hunches of managers or on the status quo. The forecasting of market potential and expected sales is problematic but must be undertaken thoroughly and with as much objectivity as marketing intelligence and information permit. Forecasts are integral to robust marketing planning. They are also pivotal to shrewd budgeting and the allocation of promotional mix budgets. As explored in Chapter 24, monitoring performance is an essential part of the marketing process. Without an assessment of likely sales, it is difficult to evaluate performance. This section focuses on market and sales potential, and on sales forecasting techniques.

### Market and Sales Potential

**Market potential**
The total amount of a product that customers will purchase within a specified period of time at a specific level of industry-wide marketing activity

**Market potential** is the total amount of a product that customers will purchase within a specified period of time at a specific level of industry-wide marketing activity. Market potential can be stated in terms of monetary value or units, and can refer to a total market or to a market segment. As shown in Figure 23.3, market potential depends on economic, social and other marketing environment factors. When analysing market potential, it is important to specify a timeframe and to indicate the relevant level of industry marketing activities. One airline determined that in one year 3,300,000 customers travelled to Europe on its aircraft – more customers than for any other airline. Based on this finding, its marketers were able to estimate the market potential for European travel on its flights in the following year, taking into account other environmental factors and market trends.

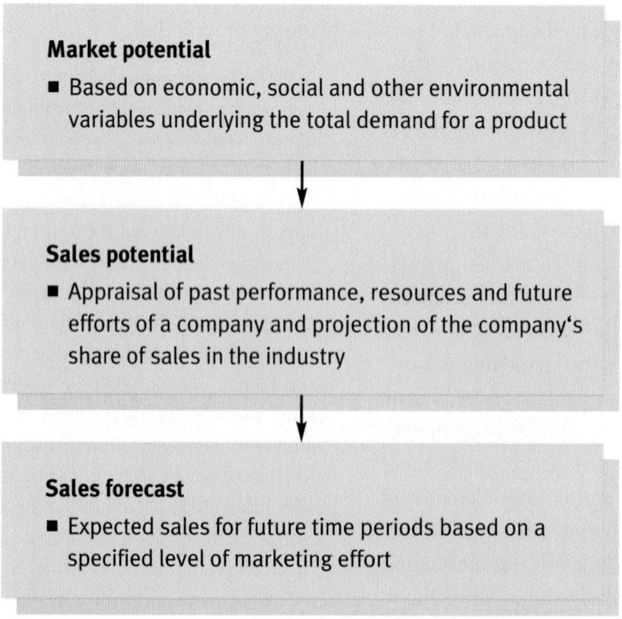

Market potential
■ Based on economic, social and other environmental variables underlying the total demand for a product
Sales potential
■ Appraisal of past performance, resources and future efforts of a company and projection of the company's share of sales in the industry
Sales forecast
■ Expected sales for future time periods based on a specified level of marketing effort


***Figure 23.3***
*The relationship between market potential, sales potential and sales forecast*
*Source: based on M.E. Porter,* Competitive Strategy: Techniques for Analysing Industries and Competitors *(New York: Free Press, 1980), from* Distance Learning MBA Notes, *Warwick Business School, 1987*

Marketers have to assume a certain general level of marketing effort in the industry when they estimate market potential. The specific level of marketing effort certainly varies from one company to another, but the sum of all companies' marketing activities equals industry marketing efforts. A marketing manager must also consider whether, and to what extent, industry marketing efforts will change. For instance, in estimating the market potential for the spreadsheet software industry, Microsoft must consider changes in marketing efforts by Lotus and other software producers. If marketing managers at Microsoft know that Lotus is planning to introduce a new version of the Lotus 1-2-3 spreadsheet product with a new advertising campaign, this fact will contribute to Microsoft's estimate of the market potential for computer software.

**Sales potential**
The maximum percentage of market potential that an individual company can obtain for a specific product or service

**Sales potential** is the maximum percentage of market potential that an individual company within an industry can expect to obtain for a specific product or service (see Figure 23.3). Several general factors influence a company's sales potential. First, the market potential places absolute limits on the size of the company's sales potential. Second, the magnitude of industry-wide marketing activities has an indirect but definite impact on the company's sales potential. Those activities have a direct bearing on the size of the market potential. When Pizza Hut advertises home-delivered pizza, for example, it indirectly promotes pizza in general; its advertisements may, in fact, also help sell competitors' home-delivered pizza. Third, the intensity and effectiveness of a company's marketing activities relative to those of its competitors affect the size of the company's sales potential. If a company is spending twice as much as any of its competitors on marketing efforts and if every unit of currency spent is more effective in generating sales, the company's sales potential will be quite high compared with that of its competitors.

**Break-down approach**
An approach that derives a company's sales potential from the general economic forecast and the estimate of market potential

There are two general approaches to measuring sales potential: break-down and build-up. In the **break-down approach**, the marketing manager first develops a general economic forecast for a specific time period. Next, market potential is estimated on the basis of this economic forecast. The company's sales potential is then derived from the general economic forecast and the estimate of market potential.

**Build-up approach**
An approach that measures the sales potential for a product by first calculating its market potential and then estimating what proportion of that potential the company can expect to obtain

In the **build-up approach**, an analyst begins by estimating how much of a product a potential buyer in a specific geographic area, such as a sales territory, will purchase in a given period. Then the analyst multiplies that amount by the total number of potential buyers in that area. The analyst performs the same calculation for each geographic area in which the company sells products, and then adds the totals for each area to calculate the market potential. To determine the sales potential, the analyst must estimate, by specific levels of marketing activities, the proportion of the total market potential that the company can obtain.

For example, the marketing manager of a regional paper company with three competitors could estimate the company's sales potential for bulk gift wrapping paper using the build-up approach. The manager may determine that each of the 66 retailer paper buyers in a single sales territory purchases an average of 10 rolls annually. For that sales territory, then, the market potential is 660 rolls annually. The analyst follows the same procedure for each of the business's other nine sales territories and then totals the market potential for each sales territory (see Table 23.4). Assuming that this total market potential is 6000 rolls of paper (the quantity expected to be sold by all four paper companies), the marketing manager would estimate the company's sales potential by ascertaining that it could sell about 33 per cent of the estimated 6000 rolls at a certain level of marketing effort (2000 rolls). The marketing manager may then develop several sales potentials, based on several levels of marketing effort.

Whether marketers use the break-down or the build-up approach, they depend heavily on sales estimates. To gain a clearer idea of how these estimates are derived, it is essential to understand sales forecasting.

**TABLE 23.4 THE MARKET POTENTIAL CALCULATIONS FOR BULK WRAPPING PAPER**

| Territory | Number of potential customers | Estimated purchases | Total |
|---|---|---|---|
| 1 | 66 | 10 rolls | 660 rolls |
| 2 | 62 | 10 | 620 |
| 3 | 55 | 5 | 275 |
| 4 | 28 | 25 | 700 |
| 5 | 119 | 5 | 595 |
| 6 | 50 | 20 | 1000 |
| 7 | 46 | 10 | 460 |
| 8 | 34 | 15 | 510 |
| 9 | 63 | 10 | 630 |
| 10 | 55 | 10 | 550 |
| | | Total market potential | 6000 rolls |

## Developing Sales Forecasts

**Sales forecast**
The amount of a product that the company actually expects to sell during a specific period of time at a specific level of marketing activity

A **sales forecast** is the amount of a product that the company actually expects to sell during a specific period of time at a specified level of marketing activity (see Figure 23.3). The sales forecast differs from the sales potential: it concentrates on what the actual sales will be at a certain level of marketing effort, whereas the sales potential assesses what sales are possible at various levels of marketing activities, based on certain environmental conditions. Companies use the sales forecast for planning, organising, implementing and controlling their activities. The success of numerous activities depends on the accuracy of this forecast. Forecasts help to estimate market attractiveness, monitor performances, allocate resources effectively and efficiently, and gear up production to meet demand. Excess stocks are wasteful and cost money; but production set too low leads to missed sales, and perhaps customer or distributor unease.[17] As described in the Topical Insight box opposite, mobile phone leader Nokia fell short of its sales expectations.

A sales forecast must be time-specific. Sales projections can be short (up to a year), medium (one to five years) or long (longer than five years). The length of time chosen for the sales forecast depends on the purpose and uses of the forecast, the stability of the market, and the company's objectives and resources.

To forecast sales, a marketer can choose from a number of forecasting methods. Some of these are arbitrary; others are more scientific, complex and time consuming. A business's choice of method or methods depends on the costs involved, the type of product, the characteristics of the market, the time span of the forecast, the purposes of the forecast, the stability of the historical sales data, the availability of required information, and the forecasters' expertise and experience.[18] The common forecasting techniques fall into five categories: executive judgement, surveys, time series analysis, correlation methods and market tests.[19]

**Executive judgement**
A way of forecasting sales based on the intuition of one or more executives

**Executive Judgement** At times, a company forecasts sales chiefly on the basis of **executive judgement**, which is the intuition of one or more executives. This approach is highly unscientific but expedient and inexpensive. Executive judgement may work reasonably well when product demand is relatively stable and the forecaster has years of market-related experience. However, because intuition is swayed most heavily by recent experience, the forecast may be overly optimistic or overly pessimistic. Another drawback to intuition is that the forecaster has only past experience as a guide when deciding where to go in the future.

## Topical Insight

### Forecasting Sales at Nokia

A short time ago, Scandinavian company Nokia was dominant in the manufacture and supply of mobile phones. Its patented operating system provided an edge that rivals struggled to emulate. In a survey, the vast majority of business users stated a preference for Nokia handsets, owing to their simplicity of use and the standardisation of functionality across models. Busy business people upgrading models could instantly use their new Nokia, as it 'behaved' in a similar manner to the redundant phone. Unlike models produced by Ericsson, Sony or the plethora of other manufacturers active in this market, Nokia models were viewed as trend setting, fashionable and intuitive to navigate.

In early 2004, US company Motorola reported record sales and a trebling of earnings in its handset business unit. According to a report in trade magazine Marketing Week, 'Nokia, the handset market leader based in Finland, is coming under increasing pressure from its rivals. Motorola's unexpectedly good results smashed its sales expectation by £1bn for the first quarter this year.'

The pressure on Nokia stems not only from North America. Samsung reported a 28 per cent increase in handset sales and a 4 per cent gain in market share. In achieving these sales and market penetration, Samsung overtook Nokia in terms of stock market value and sold a record 20 million handsets in the first quarter of the year, providing 14 per cent global market share. By contrast, Nokia issued a warning that its financial results were below expectations, leading to a 10 per cent fall in its share price.

Observers believe that Nokia once had 60 per cent share of the global market for handsets. While this figure is now down to around 35 per cent, Nokia remains a strong market leader, followed by Motorola. There is still quite a gap between first- and second-placed players in this highly competitive market. Samsung is a significant challenger, with 10 per cent market share and rising sales.

In the UK the market is estimated at £13bn per annum. It is important for marketers developing marketing strategies and judging the effectiveness of their marketing programmes to understand the size of the market, growth prospects, the shares of competing brands and likely changes. Without such awareness, it is impossible to predict sales levels or evaluate the success of a company's marketing activity. This is particularly true for Nokia's marketers as they strive to combat companies such as Sony-Ericsson, Siemens, Motorola, Samsung and many more.

At the end of 2003, Motorola introduced an extensive new range, with over 20 models designed to appeal to most types of mobile phone users and network providers. 'Clamshell' handsets – popularised by Samsung – mp3 players, cameras, colour screens and fast texting enabled the company's range to catch up and emulate the products of the market leader. Samsung, Siemens, the Sony-Ericsson partnership and other brands also launched extensive product ranges, with more fashionable designs than many Nokia lines. There is no doubt, however, that Nokia is returning fire on its enemies. In an about-face, a clamshell Nokia has appeared, and more emphasis is being placed within new product development programmes on entertainment uses for handsets, such as camera images, games, music and video clips. A market leader will inevitably be challenged by other brands. In Nokia's case, the success of leading rivals caused an unexpected drop in sales, below forecast levels in key target markets.

**Sources:** Vodafone UK; Nokia PR; Lucy Barrett, 'Nokia's rivals getting too close for comfort', *Marketing Week*, 29 April 2004, pp. 20–1; research house Strategy Analytics.

**Surveys**
A method of questioning customers, sales personnel or experts regarding their expectations about future purchases

**Surveys** A second way to forecast sales is to use **surveys,** questioning customers, sales personnel or experts regarding their expectations about future purchases.

Through a **customer forecasting survey,** marketers can ask customers what types and quantities of products they intend to buy during a specific period of time. This approach may be useful to a business that has relatively few customers. For example, a computer chip producer that markets to fewer than a hundred computer manufacturers could conduct a customer survey. PepsiCo, though, has millions of consumers and cannot feasibly use a customer survey to forecast future sales, unless its sampling is known to reflect the entire market, which is hard to verify, or it is polling the views of its main distributors.

**Customer forecasting survey**
A method of asking customers what types and quantities of products they intend to buy during a specific period of time

Customer surveys have several drawbacks. Customers must be able and willing to make accurate estimates of future product requirements. Although business-to-business buyers can sometimes estimate their anticipated purchases accurately from historical buying data and their own sales forecasts, many cannot make such estimates. In addition, for a variety of reasons, customers may not want to take part in a survey. Occasionally, a few respondents give answers that they know are incorrect, making survey results inaccurate. Moreover, customer surveys reflect buying intentions, not actual purchases. Customers' intentions may not be well formulated, and even when potential purchasers have definite buying intentions, they do not necessarily follow through with them. A common marketing research problem is probing consumers about their actual purchasing and consumption behaviour as opposed to their perceptions or anticipated behaviour. Finally, customer surveys consume much time and money.

**Salesforce forecasting survey**
A method of asking members of a company's salesforce to estimate the anticipated sales in their territories for a specified period of time

In a **salesforce forecasting survey**, members of the company's salesforce are asked to estimate the anticipated sales in their territories for a specified period of time. The forecaster combines these territorial estimates to arrive at a tentative forecast (see Figure 23.4).

A marketer may survey the sales staff for several reasons. The most important one is that the sales staff are closer to customers on a daily basis than other company personnel; therefore they should know more about customers' future product needs. Moreover, when sales representatives assist in developing the forecast, they are more likely to work towards its achievement. Another advantage of this method is that forecasts can be prepared for single territories, for divisions consisting of several territories, for regions made

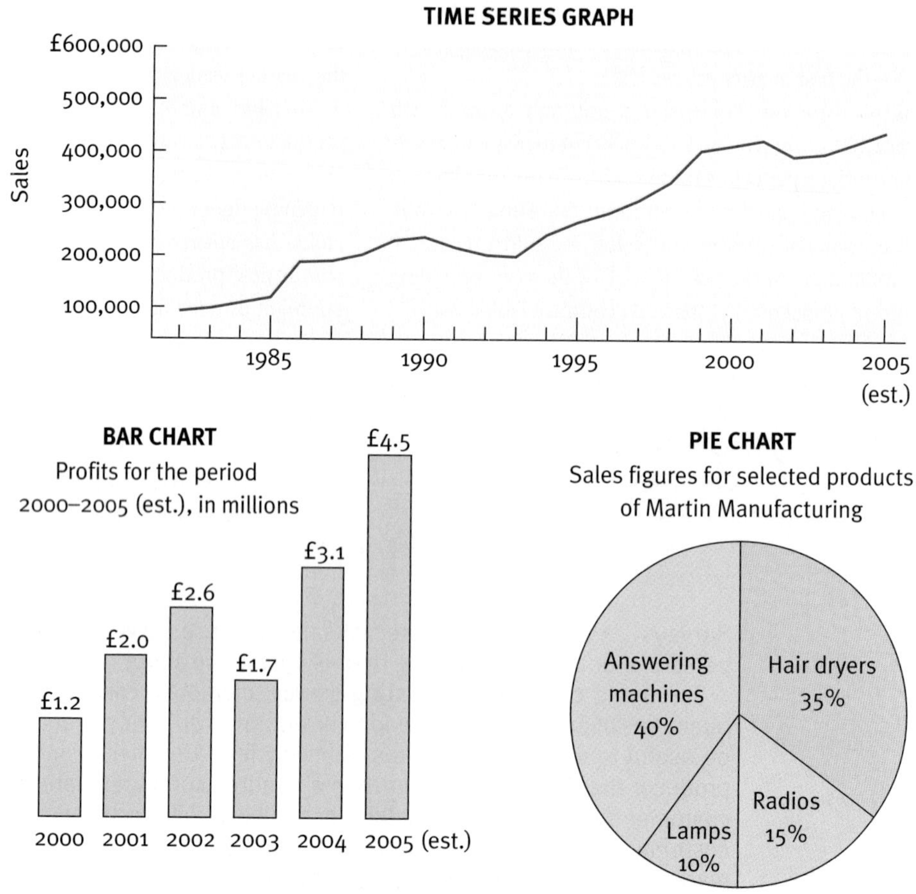


***Figure 23.4*** *Graphical presentations of forecasts and sales; visual depictions of sales and profits are popular in marketing plan documents*

up of multiple divisions and then for the total geographic market. Thus the method readily provides sales forecasts from the smallest geographic sales unit to the largest.

Despite these benefits, a salesforce survey has certain limitations. Sales people can be too optimistic or pessimistic because of recent experiences. In addition, they tend to underestimate the sales potential in their territories when they believe that their sales goals will be determined by their forecasts. They also dislike 'paperwork' because it takes up the time that could be spent selling. If the preparation of a territorial sales forecast is time consuming, the sales staff may not do the job adequately.

None-the-less, salesforce surveys can be effective under certain conditions. If, for instance, the sales people as a group are accurate – or at least consistent – estimators, the overestimates and underestimates should balance each other out. If the aggregate forecast is consistently over or under actual sales, then the marketer who develops the final forecast can make the necessary adjustments. Assuming that the survey is administered well, the salesforce can have the satisfaction of helping to establish reasonable sales goals. It can also be assured that its forecasts are not being used to set sales quotas.

The **Delphi method** is very popular: managers' and sales personnel's views are validated centrally, and the resulting forecasts are returned to those involved for further comment. Participants – such as field managers – make separate, individual forecasts. A central analyst independently aggregates and modifies their forecasts. This revised forecast is returned to the separate participants, who can then amend their forecasts in the context of the consolidated picture. The central analyst then collates the updated forecasts to produce the company's overall final forecast. The Delphi technique avoids many weighting and judgemental problems; the median of the group's overall response will tend to be more accurate; and the approach is useful for short-, medium- and long-term forecasts, as well as for new product development, for which there is no historical information on which to base a forecast.

When a company wants an **expert forecasting survey**, it hires experts to help prepare the sales forecast. These experts are usually economists, management consultants, advertising executives, academics or other people outside the company who have solid experience in a specific market. Drawing on this experience and their analyses of available information about the company and the market, the experts prepare and present their forecasts or answer questions regarding a forecast. Using experts is expedient and relatively inexpensive. However, because they work outside the company, experts may not be as motivated as company personnel to do an effective job.

**Time Series Analysis** The technique by which the forecaster, using the company's historical sales data, tries to discover a pattern or patterns in the company's sales over time is called **time series analysis**. If a pattern is found, it can be used to forecast sales. This forecasting method assumes that the past sales pattern will continue in the future. The accuracy, and thus the usefulness, of time series analysis hinges on the validity of this assumption.

In a time series analysis, a forecaster usually performs four types of analysis: trend, cycle, seasonal and random factor.[20] **Trend analysis** focuses on aggregate sales data, such as a company's annual sales figures, over a period of many years, to determine whether annual sales are generally rising, falling or staying about the same. Through **cycle analysis**, a forecaster analyses sales figures – often monthly sales data – over a period of three to five years, to ascertain whether sales fluctuate in a consistent, periodic manner. When performing **seasonal analysis**, the analyst studies daily, weekly or monthly sales figures to evaluate the degree to which seasonal factors, such as climate and holiday activities, influence the company's sales. **Random factor analysis** is an attempt to attribute erratic sales variations to random, non-recurring events, such as a regional power failure, a natural disaster or political unrest in a foreign market. After performing each of these analyses, the forecaster combines the results to develop the sales forecast.

**Delphi method**
A centralised forecasting method that takes into account the views of managers, sales personnel and individual participants; aggregates them; and modifies them

**Expert forecasting survey**
A survey prepared by outside experts such as economists, management consultants, advertising executives or academics

**Time series analysis**
A forecasting technique that uses a company's historical sales data to discover a pattern or patterns in the company's sales over time

**Trend analysis**
Analysis that focuses on aggregate sales data over a period of many years to determine whether annual sales are generally rising, falling or constant

**Cycle analysis**
A forecasting technique that analyses a company's sales figures over a period of three to five years to ascertain whether sales fluctuate in a consistent, periodic manner

**Seasonal analysis**
The study of daily, weekly or monthly sales figures to evaluate the degree to which seasonal factors influence the company's sales

**Random factor analysis**
An attempt to attribute erratic sales variations to random, non-recurring events

Time series analysis is an effective forecasting method for products with reasonably stable demand, but it is not useful for products with highly erratic demand. Seagram, the importer and producer of spirits and wines, uses several types of time series analysis for forecasting and has found them quite accurate. For example, Seagram's forecasts of industry sales volume have proved correct within ±1.5 per cent, and the company's sales forecasts have been accurate within ±2 per cent.[21] However, time series analysis is not always so dependable.

**Correlation methods**
Attempts to find a relationship between past sales and one or more variables such as population, per capita income or gross national product

**Correlation Methods** Like time series analysis, correlation methods are based on historical sales data. When using **correlation methods**,[22] the forecaster attempts to find a relationship between past sales and one or more variables, such as population, per capita income or gross national product. To determine whether a correlation exists, the forecaster analyses the statistical relationship between changes in past sales and changes in one or more variables – a technique known as regression analysis.[23] The object of regression analysis is a mathematical formula that accurately describes a relationship between the company's sales and one or more variables; however, the formula indicates only an association, not a causal relationship. Once an accurate formula has been established, the analyst plugs the necessary information into the formula to derive the sales forecast.

Correlation methods are useful when a precise relationship can be established. However, a forecaster seldom finds a perfect correlation. Furthermore, this method can be used only when the available historical sales data are extensive and reliable. Ordinarily, correlation techniques are useless for forecasting the sales of new products, or in markets where changes are frequent and extensive.

**Market test**
An experiment in which a product is made available to buyers in one or more test areas, after which purchases and consumer responses to its distribution, promotion and price are measured

**Market Tests** Conducting a **market test** involves making a product available to buyers in one or more test areas, and measuring purchases and consumer responses to distribution, promotion and price. Even though test areas are often cities with populations of 200,000 to 500,000, test sites can be larger metropolitan areas or towns with populations of 50,000 to 200,000, or ITV regions. A market test provides information about consumers' actual purchases rather than about their intended purchases. In addition, purchase volume can be evaluated in relation to the intensity of other marketing activities – advertising, in-store promotions, pricing, packaging, distribution, and so forth. On the basis of customer response in test areas, forecasters can estimate product sales for larger geographic units. For example, Cadbury's Wispa first appeared in the Tyne Tees area of north-east England. Sales showed management that the company had to build more production capacity to cope with a national roll-out of the brand and full launch.

Because it does not require historical sales data, a market test is an effective tool for forecasting the sales of new products or the sales of existing products in new geographic areas. The test gives the forecaster information about customers' real actions rather than their intended or estimated behaviour. A market test also gives a marketer an opportunity to try out various elements of the marketing mix. These tests are, however, often time consuming and expensive. In addition, a marketer cannot be certain that the consumer response during a market test represents the total market response or that such a response will continue in the future.

## Using Multiple Forecasting Methods

Although some businesses depend on a single sales forecasting method, most use several techniques. A company is sometimes forced to use several methods when it markets diverse product lines, but even for a single product line several forecasts may be needed, especially when the product is sold in different market segments. Thus a producer of car tyres may rely on one technique to forecast tyre sales for new cars and on another to forecast the sales of replacement tyres. Variation in the length of the forecasts required may call for several forecast methods. A company that employs one method for a short-range forecast may find it inappropriate for long-range forecasting. Sometimes a marketer verifies

**Table 23.5 Dimensions of a Marketing Audit**

**Part I The marketing environment audit**

***Marketing environment forces***

**A Economic**

1 What does the company expect in the way of inflation, material shortages, unemployment and credit availability in the short run, medium run and long run?

2 What effect will forecast trends in the size, age distribution and regional distribution of population have on the business?

**B Technological**

1 What major changes are occurring in product technology? In process technology?

2 What are the major generic substitutes that might replace this product?

**C Political/Legal/Regulatory**

1 What laws are being proposed that may affect marketing strategy and tactics?

2 What national and local government actions should be watched? What is happening with pollution control, equal opportunity employment, product safety, advertising, price controls and so on that is relevant to marketing planning?

**D Societal/Green**

1 What attitude is the public taking towards business and the types of products produced by the company?

2 What changes in consumer lifestyles and values have a bearing on the company's target markets and marketing methods?

3 Will the cost and availability of natural resources directly affect the company?

4 Are there public concerns about the company's role in pollution and conservation? If so, what is the company's reaction?

***Task environment***

**A Markets**

1 What is happening to market size, growth, geographic distribution and profits?

2 What are the major market segments and their expected rates of growth? Which are high opportunity and low opportunity segments?

**B Customers**

1 How do current customers and prospects judge the company and its competitors on reputation, product quality, service, salesforce and price?

2 How do different classes of customers make their buying decisions?

3 What evolving needs and satisfactions are the buyers in this market seeking?

**C Competitors**

1 Who are the major competitors? What are the objectives and strategy of each major competitor? What are their strengths and weaknesses? What are the sizes and trends in market shares?

2 What trends can be foreseen in future competition and substitutes for this product?

**D Distribution and Dealers**

1 What are the main trade channels bringing products to customers?

2 What are the efficiency levels and growth potentials of the different trade channels?

**E Suppliers**

1 What is the outlook for the availability of key resources used in production?

2 What trends are occurring among suppliers in their patterns of selling?

**F Facilitators and Marketing Organisations**

1 What is the outlook for the cost and availability of transport services?

2 What is the outlook for the cost and availability of warehousing facilities?

3 What is the outlook for the cost and availability of financial resources?

4 How effectively is the advertising agency performing? What trends are occurring in advertising agency services?

**G Publics**

1 Where are the opportunity areas or problems for the company?

2 How effectively is the company dealing with publics?

**Part II Marketing Strategy Audit**

**A Business Mission**

1 Is the business mission clearly focused with marketing terms and is it attainable?

**B Marketing Objectives and Goals**

1 Are the corporate goals clearly stated? Do they lead logically to the marketing objectives?

2 Are the marketing objectives stated clearly enough to guide marketing planning and subsequent performance measurement?

3 Are the marketing objectives appropriate, given the company's competitive position, resources and opportunities? Is the appropriate strategic

(continued)

the results of one method by using one or several other methods and comparing results.[24] No matter which technique – or mix of approaches – is deployed, it is essential that marketers produce accurate and useful sales forecasts and assessments of market potential.

## The Marketing Audit

**Marketing audit**
A systematic examination of the marketing function's objectives, strategies, programmes, organisation and performance

A **marketing audit** is a systematic examination of the marketing function's objectives, strategies, programmes, organisation and performance. Its primary purpose is to identify weaknesses in ongoing marketing operations and plan the necessary improvements to correct these weaknesses. The marketing audit does not concern itself with the company's marketing position – that is the purpose of the company's marketing plan. Rather, the marketing audit evaluates how effectively the marketing function or department performed its assigned functions.[25]

Like an accounting or financial audit, a marketing audit should be conducted regularly instead of just when performance control mechanisms show that the system is out of control. The marketing audit is not a control process to be used only during a crisis, although a business in trouble may use it to isolate problems and generate solutions. It is a useful diagnostic tool for correcting marketing activity. The marketing audit, however, is a useful precursor to undertaking marketing planning, providing an insight into the strengths of the company's marketing function and its activities.

A marketing audit may be specific and focus on one or a few marketing activities, or it may be comprehensive and encompass all of a company's marketing activities. Table 23.5 lists many possible dimensions of a marketing audit. An audit may deal with only a few of these areas, or it may include them all. Its scope depends on the costs involved, the target markets served, the structure of the marketing mix and environmental conditions. The results of the audit can be used to re-allocate marketing effort and to re-examine marketing opportunities. For example, after the rise in consumer interest in buying unleaded petrol during the 1980s, the oil companies realised that many customers were still using leaded fuel, because the engine performance of their cars was better. Launching the new 'super' unleaded brands late in the 1980s helped to counter these problems.

The marketing audit should aid evaluation by:

1. describing current activities and results in relation to sales, costs, prices, profits and other performance feedback (see Chapter 24)
2. gathering information about customers, competition and marketing environment developments that may affect the marketing strategy and the effective implementation of marketing mix programmes
3. exploring opportunities and alternatives for improving the marketing strategy
4. providing an overall database to be used in evaluating the attainment of organisational goals and marketing objectives
5. diagnosing reasons for the successes and failures experienced by a company's marketers, and their analyses, strategies and tactical marketing mix programmes.

Marketing audits can be performed internally or externally. An internal auditor may be a top-level marketing executive, a company-wide auditing committee or a manager from another office or of another function. Although it is more expensive, an audit by outside consultants is usually more effective; external auditors have more objectivity, more time for the audit and greater experience.

There is no single set of procedures for all marketing audits. However, companies should adhere to several general guidelines. Audits are often based on a series of questionnaires administered to the company's personnel. These questionnaires should be developed carefully to ensure that the audit focuses on the right issues. Auditors should develop and follow a step-by-step plan to guarantee that the audit is systematic. When interviewing

**Table 23.5 Dimensions of a Marketing Audit (continued)**

objective to build, hold, harvest, divest or terminate this business?

**C Strategy**

1 What is the core marketing strategy for achieving the objectives? Is it sound?
2 Are the resources budgeted to accomplish the marketing objectives inadequate, adequate or excessive?
3 Are the marketing resources allocated optimally to prime market segments, territories and products?
4 Are the marketing resources allocated optimally to the major elements of the marketing mix, i.e. product quality, service, salesforce, advertising, promotion and distribution?

**Part III Marketing organisation audit**

**A Formal structure**

1 Is there a high-level marketing manager with adequate authority and responsibility over those company activities that affect customer satisfaction?
2 Are the marketing responsibilities optimally structured along functional, product, end use and territorial lines?

**B Functional efficiency**

1 Are there good communications and working relations between marketing and sales?
2 Is the product management system working effectively? Are the product managers able to plan profits or only sales volume?
3 Are there any groups in marketing that need more training, motivation, supervision or evaluation?

**C Interface efficiency**

1 Are there any problems between marketing and manufacturing, research and development, purchasing, finance, accounting and legal departments that need attention?

**Part IV Marketing systems audit**

**A Marketing information system**

1 Is the marketing intelligence system producing accurate, sufficient and timely information about developments in the marketplace?
2 Is marketing research being adequately used by company decision-makers?
3 Is available marketing intelligence properly shared/accessed by managers?

**B Marketing planning system**

1 Is the marketing planning system well conceived and effective?
2 Is sales forecasting and measurement of market potential soundly carried out?
3 Are sales quotas set on a proper basis?

**C Marketing control system**

1 Are the control procedures (monthly, quarterly, etc.) adequate to ensure that the annual plan's objectives are being achieved?
2 Is provision made to analyse periodically the profitability of different products, markets, territories and channels of distribution?
3 Is provision made to examine and validate periodically various marketing costs?

**D New product development system**

1 Is the company well organised to gather, generate and screen new product ideas?
2 Does the company do adequate concept research and business analysis before investing heavily in a new idea?
3 Does the company carry out adequate product and market testing before launching a new product?

**Part V Marketing-productivity audit**

**A Profitability analysis**

1 What is the profitability of the company's different products, served markets, territories and channels of distribution?
2 Should the company enter, expand, contract or withdraw from any business segments, and what would be the short- and long- run profit consequences?

**B Cost-effective analysis**

1 Do any marketing activities seem to have excessive costs? Are these costs valid? Can cost-reducing steps be taken?

**Part VI Marketing function audits**

**A Products and service**

1 What are the product line objectives? Are these objectives sound? Is the current product line meeting these objectives?
2 Are there particular products that should be phased out?
3 Are there new products that are worth adding?
4 Are any products able to benefit from quality, feature or style improvements?

(continued)

**TABLE 23.5 DIMENSIONS OF A MARKETING AUDIT (CONTINUED)**

5 Is adequate customer service provided?
6 Is there an aftermarket support package – warranty, parts and servicing, dealer network?

**B Price**

1 What are the pricing objectives, policies, strategies and procedures? Are prices set on sound cost, demand and competitive criteria?
2 Do the customers see the company's prices as being in or out of line with the perceived value of its products?
3 Does the company use price promotions effectively?

**C Distribution**

1 What are the distribution objectives and strategies?
2 Is there adequate market coverage and service?
3 How effective are the following channel members: distributors, manufacturers' reps, brokers, agents and so on?
4 Should the company consider changing its distribution channels?

**D Promotional mix**

1 What are the organisation's advertising objectives? Are they sound?
2 Is the right amount being spent on advertising? How is the budget determined?
3 Are the ad themes and copy effective? What do customers and the public think about the advertising?
4 Are the advertising media well chosen?
5 Is the internal advertising staff adequate?
6 Is the sales promotion budget adequate? Is there effective and sufficient use of sales promotion tools, such as samples, coupons, displays and sales contests?
7 Is the publicity budget adequate? Is the public relations staff competent and creative?
8 Is use of the Internet appropriate? If so, is the web site well designed?
9 What of sponsership? Is it relevant? Are associated bodies appropriate and reputable?
10 Is direct marketing possible? Through what media and with what proposition?

**E Salesforce**

1 What are the organisation's salesforce objectives?
2 Is the salesforce large enough to accomplish the company's objectives?
3 Is the salesforce organised along the proper principle(s) of specialisation (territory, market, product)? Are there enough (or too many) sales managers to guide the field sales reps?
4 Does the sales compensation level and structure provide adequate incentive and reward?
5 Does the salesforce show high morale, ability and effort?
6 Are the procedures for setting quotas and evaluating performance adequate?
7 How does the company's salesforce compare with the salesforces of competitors?

**Source:** Adapted from Philip Kotler, *Marketing Management: Analysis, Planning, and Control*, 6th edn (Englewood Cliffs, N.J.: Prentice-Hall, 1988), pp. 748–751. Used by permission.

company personnel, the auditors should strive to talk to a diverse group of people from many parts of the company. The auditor should become familiar with the product line, meet staff from headquarters, visit field organisations, interview customers, interview competitors and analyse information for a report on the marketing environment. The audit framework and associated questionnaires should remain consistent over time, so that improvements and problems can be noted between audits.

To achieve adequate support, the auditors normally focus first on the company's top management and then move down through the organisational hierarchy. The auditor looks for different points of view within various departments of the organisation or a mismatch between the customers' and the company's perception of the product as signs of trouble in an organisation. The results of the audit should be reported in a comprehensive written document, which should include recommendations that will increase marketing productivity and determine the company's general direction. The marketing audit enables an organisation to change tactics or alter day-to-day activities as problems arise. For example, marketing auditors often wonder whether a change in budgeted sales activity is caused by general market conditions or is due to a change in the company's market share.

***Figure 23.5***
*No matter the product or the market, marketers should audit their standing and performance*
*Photo © Royalty-Free/ CORBIS*

Although the concept of auditing implies an 'official' examination of marketing activities, many organisations audit their marketing activities informally. Any attempt to verify operating results and to compare them with standards can be considered an auditing activity. Many smaller businesses probably would not use the word audit, but they do perform auditing activities. Several problems may arise in an audit of marketing activities. Marketing audits can be expensive in terms of both time and money. Selecting the auditors may be difficult because objective, qualified personnel may not be available. Marketing audits can also be extremely disruptive because employees sometimes fear comprehensive evaluations, especially by outsiders. The benefits, though, are significant. The audit reveals successes and also problem areas that need to be addressed. Many companies do not deploy a marketing audit. It is not necessary to conduct a marketing audit in order to have a marketing orientation (see Chapter 1). However, many organisations benefit significantly from routine auditing of their marketing practices, identifying good practices to replicate and share, or poor practices on which to take remedial action. As a precursor for marketing planning, a marketing audit can help rectify deficiencies and poor practices in the marketing function, so enhancing the likelihood of effective deployment of a more meaningful marketing plan.

# Summary

In order to manipulate the marketing mix to match target market needs and achieve organisational goals, a company must address fundamental strategic decisions. To expedite this process and to set appropriate goals, many companies use marketing planning.

» *Marketing planning* is a systematic process that involves assessing marketing opportunities and resources, determining marketing objectives, and developing a full plan for implementation and control. A core output of marketing planning is the *marketing plan*, a document or blueprint containing the requirements for a company's marketing activity. The marketing planning process involves (1) analysing the marketplace, (2) modifying the recommended marketing strategy accordingly, and (3) developing detailed marketing programmes designed to implement the specified marketing strategy. The *marketing planning cycle* is a cyclical process of planning and feedback that allows for revision. Most companies update their plans annually, typically with a three-year focus. However, *short-*, *medium-* and *long-range plans* are available.

» A key part of the marketing plan is the *marketing objective*, a statement of what is to be accomplished through marketing activities. Objectives should be measurable, indicate a timeframe and be consistent with a company's overall organisational goals.

» The heart of the marketing plan is the analysis section. The elements analysed include the marketing environment and market trends, customers, competitive positions and competitors' strategies, plus the company's capabilities to respond to marketing opportunities, the appropriateness of its product and brand portfolio, and an analysis of financial performance. A *SWOT analysis*, which identifies strengths, weaknesses, opportunities and threats, helps to produce realistic and meaningful marketing recommendations.

» The strategy recommendations within the marketing plan examine the opportunities to be pursued, target market priorities, the basis for competing, differential advantage, and desired brand or product positioning. Marketing strategy guides the company's direction in relationships between customers and competitors. Marketing programmes implement the recommended marketing strategy. They discuss each element of the marketing mix in detail and the allocation of schedules and tasks, personnel, budgets, responsibilities and monitoring of ongoing performance. Without such details of the operationalisation of the marketing plan, it is unlikely the plan's recommendations would be implemented.

» Marketers produce marketing plans for each business unit, product group or target market, and a synthesised overview plan for the board of the company. Usually, cross-functional teams are involved. In companies embarking on marketing planning for the first time, there is a steep learning curve and the required marketing analyses are very invasive. After three years, the planning process becomes routinised. External consultants are often brought in to support a senior management team's initial attempts to develop a marketing plan.

» Sales and marketing activities should be carefully planned activities that anticipate consumer needs and expectations. Whether using a total market or a market segmentation approach, a marketer must be able to measure the sales potential of the target market or markets. *Market potential* is the total amount of a product that customers will purchase within a specified period of time at a specific level of industry-wide marketing activity. *Sales potential* is the maximum percentage of market potential that an individual company within an industry can expect to obtain for a specific product or service. There are two general approaches to measuring sales potential: the *break-down approach* and the *build-up approach*.

A *sales forecast* is the amount of a product that the company actually expects to sell during a specific period of time and at a specified level of marketing activity. Several methods are used to forecast sales: *executive judgement, surveys* (*customer, salesforce* and *expert forecasting surveys*, including the *Delphi method*), *time series analysis* (*trend analysis, cycle analysis, seasonal analysis, random factor analysis*), *correlation methods* and *market tests*. Although some businesses may rely on a single sales forecasting method, most companies employ several different techniques. It is an essential part of the marketing process to develop objective and reliable sales forecasts and assessments of market potential.

To identify weaknesses in ongoing marketing operations and plan the necessary improvements to correct these weaknesses, it is sometimes necessary to audit marketing activities. A *marketing audit* is a systematic examination of the marketing group's objectives, strategies, programmes, organisation and performance. A marketing audit attempts to identify what a marketing unit is doing, to evaluate the effectiveness of these activities and to recommend future marketing activities. It is a useful diagnostic tool for correcting marketing activity and some companies conduct the audit as a prelude to marketing planning. Although an insightful technique, the use of the marketing audit is far from routine.

## *Key Links*

This chapter, examining marketing planning and sales forecasting, should be read in conjunction with:

- Chapter 1, on scoping out the marketing process
- Chapter 2, which deals with exploring the role of marketing planning within marketing strategy
- Chapter 24, explaining the latest views about marketing performance and managing the implementation of marketing recommendations.

## Important Terms

Marketing planning
Marketing plan
Marketing planning cycle
Short-range plans
Medium-range plans
Long-range plans
Marketing objective
SWOT analysis
Market potential
Sales potential
Break-down approach
Build-up approach
Sales forecast
Executive judgement
Surveys
Customer forecasting survey
Salesforce forecasting survey
Delphi method
Expert forecasting survey
Time series analysis
Trend analysis
Cycle analysis
Seasonal analysis
Random factor analysis
Correlation methods
Market test
Marketing audit

## Discussion and Review Questions

1. What is marketing planning? How does it help companies target their marketplaces better ?
2. In what ways do marketing environment forces affect marketing planning? Give some examples.
3. What is a SWOT analysis? How does it lead to an understanding of realistic marketing opportunities?
4. What issues *must* be analysed thoroughly during marketing planning prior to the formulation of a marketing programme?
5. Why is it important to seek a differential advantage?
6. Why does it take three years before the use of marketing planning is routinised in a company?
7. Why is a marketer concerned about sales potential when trying to find a target market?
8. What is a sales forecast, and why is it important?
9. What is the Delphi method of forecasting? Why is it a popular tool?
10. Why would a company use a marketing audit?

## Recommended Readings


- Dibb, S., Simkin, L. and Bradley, J., *The Marketing Planning Workbook: Effective Marketing for Marketing Managers* (London: Thomson Learning, 1998).
- Gilligan, C. and Wilson, R.M.S., *Strategic Marketing Planning* (Oxford: Butterworth-Heinemann, 2003).
- Jain, S.C., *Marketing Planning & Strategy* (Cincinnati, OH: South Western, 2000).
- McDonald, M.H., *Marketing Plans* (Oxford: Butterworth-Heinemann, 2002).


## Internet Exercise

A core task in developing a strong marketing plan is the analysis of competitors. There are many ways of finding information about competitors, as described in Chapters 2 and 9. One useful source of intelligence about rivals is to review their websites. Marketers look for the strengths cited by brands and for products on their websites. Additionally, by examining a range of competitors' websites, it is possible to infer their deficiencies. This is achieved by identifying themes popular on many rivals' websites but ignored on only one or two.

Take the example of food processors, mixers and blenders. Look at the websites for a selection of leading brands, such as Breville, Dualit, Kenwood, KitchenAid, Magimix, Morphy Richards, Moulinex, Philips, Solac and Waring. What are the respective apparent strengths and weaknesses of these brands and products?

## *Applied Mini-Case*

Despite various economic blips and global troubles such as those in Iraq or parts of Africa, economic indicators point to an increase in leisure time and in discretionary income. Good news for theme park operators such as Disney or Alton Towers. In the UK, Alton Towers aims to maintain its market leadership, and invests continually in new rides and facilities. It opened a £20 million holiday village next to the park – for the leisure market and the growing business conference market – and spent £10 million on the leading white-knuckle Oblivion ride. The strategy is to attract new visitors to the park, from the UK and from continental Europe, while encouraging repeat visits from current users. Key target customers are young adults aged 15 to 24, families with children, school parties and, increasingly, the corporate sector. Business clients use Alton Towers for sales incentive schemes and corporate events, such as AGMs, product launches or salesforce parties. The corporate sector was a leading reason for developing good-quality on-site hotel accommodation. Originally conceived as a day-tripper, family-oriented park, Alton Towers has monitored demographic changes and competitor activity, and has continually modified its rides, amenities and services to reflect the requirements of its evolving target market segments. The growth of corporate clients – for conferences and away-days – reflects this constant updating of the theme park's marketing strategy and associated marketing planning.

### *Question*

In producing a marketing plan for a theme park such as Alton Towers, what would be the most important elements of the marketing planning process? Explain why.

## Case Study

# Binney & Smith Plans For Crayola Crayons

While Nintendo and PlayStation games, MTV music videos, satellite TV cartoon channels and web-based interactive gaming have captured children's attention, Crayola Crayons have maintained a role in children's play and remained on store shelves. Binney & Smith, a division of Hallmark Cards, has fought the high-tech challenge with a new marketing strategy and marketing plan for the venerable crayon. The company launched a huge MTV-style campaign, targeted at children rather than parents.

Traditionally, Binney & Smith targeted Crayola Crayons at parents, using educational themes, but after recognising that children's purchasing power and influence on family purchases have increased in recent years, the company decided to change the crayon's image from that of an old-fashioned toy to an exciting way for kids and teens to express themselves. To this end, the company developed new advertisements featuring rock music, 'hip' kids and soaring colours for showing during television programmes seen by children. In-store videos provided to toy stores and retailers of children's clothing followed up the theme.

After marketing research indicated that children prefer brighter colours, the company decided to retire blue grey, green blue, lemon yellow, maize, orange red, orange yellow, raw umber and violet blue to the Crayola Hall of Fame and to replace them with the more vivid cerulean, dandelion, fuchsia, jungle green, royal purple, teal blue, vivid tangerine and wild strawberry. This decision was controversial, however. The company was inundated with phone calls, letters and petitions from people who missed the old colours. Protesters marched on the company, carrying placards with slogans like 'We hate the new 8!' and 'They call it a retirement, I call it a burial.' RUMPS, the Raw Umber and Maize Preservation Society, finally got its way. The company issued a commemorative tin containing the 64-crayon box and a special pack of the eight colours dropped a year earlier. Even though children liked the new colours, parents liked the old eight colours. The company issued a statement saying that the old colours were revived partly because the company is in the business of providing what the consumer wants.

Along with new advertisements and colours, the company introduced ColourWorks, a line of erasable crayon sticks, and retractable coloured pencils and pens. The company brought out Silver Swirls, crayons that have twirls of silver mixed in with the wax colours. Pictures coloured with Silver Swirls can be buffed to a high sheen with tissue. The new line was not only tested by children but also named by them. The company licensed its brand to Concord Cameras for a range of brightly coloured single-use cameras aimed at children under 12. Several software companies have recognised the Crayola brand appeal: Micrografx offers the *Crayola Amazing Art Adventure* and *Crayola Art Studio* – software games that encourage art and design a long way from the traditional wax crayon. IBM brought out Crayola Creation Corner to 'transform ordinary household items into toys, animals, jewellery, spaceships, greetings cards, stationery, party decorations, and all sorts of other inventions'.

A full range of PC interactive software products emerged, still focusing on drawing and creativity, but not based purely on the familiar wax crayon. The latter remains the company's core line, though it now features as part of making kits – Badge Bonanza or Crayola Jewellery – and a whole host of design sets. Clearly, the Crayola brand is still very popular with children, parents and toy stores. More and more children are discovering the Crayola name, encouraged by Binney & Smith's embracing of the Internet. The website, www.crayola.com, has a wealth of ideas to offer, with games, craft projects and products aimed at three target audiences: parents, educators and 'Crayola kids'. The company has very effectively created an on-line community around its wax crayon brand.

Despite its new focus on children, Binney & Smith has not forgotten who actually holds the purse strings. The company continues to target parents with advertisements in women's and parents' magazines, while new products or services – such as www.crayola.com – include educational and child development messages aimed at parents. However, the revised marketing strategy and accompanying marketing plan have led more children to reach for Crayola Crayons instead of the Nintendo joystick or LEGO bricks. Sales are up and shelf space in toy stores could not be better, despite stiff competition from a host of rival entertainment products and toys.

**Sources:** www.crayola.com/kids, 2004; Ellen Neuborne, 'Crayola crayons have old colors back', *USA Today*, 2 October 1991, p. 2B; Ken Riddle, 'Crayola draws brighter lines in the market', *Marketing*, 21 January 1991, p. 4; Beefeater Restaurants, 1993; Toys 'Я' Us, Leicester, 1996; Loretta Roach, 'Single use explosion', *Discount Merchandiser*, September 1995, pp. 28–30; Robyn Parets, 'Children's edutainment titles vie for shelf space', *Discount Store News*, 19 June 1995, pp. C6–C9; Binney & Smith UK, 1999; Toys 'Я' Us, 1999, 2004; www.crayola.com, 2004.

## Questions for Discussion

1 Why did Binney & Smith have to update its marketing of Crayola and change its strategy?
2 What are Crayola's target audiences? Why did the company need to approach them differently?
3 Why has the company embraced the Internet?

# 24

# Implementing Strategies, Internal Marketing Relationships and Measuring Performance

**"The real strategic problem in marketing is not strategy, it is managing implementation and change."**

*Nigel Piercy, Warwick Business School*

## Objectives

- To understand how marketing activities are organised within a company's structure
- To become familiar with ways of organising a marketing unit
- To examine the marketing implementation process
- To learn about impediments to marketing implementation and to grasp the importance of internal marketing
- To explore implementing and controlling marketing activities
- To learn how sales and marketing cost analysis can be used as methods of evaluating performance
- To describe marketing shareholder value analysis
- To discuss the popular criteria for measuring marketing performance

## Introduction

Whether an organisation creates a standalone marketing function – similar to a finance unit, human resource function or production unit – or empowers specific managers in a variety of roles to also handle the marketing process, decisions about how best to manage marketing must be made.

There is plenty of evidence to suggest that many organisations create marketing strategies and marketing plans without too many problems, but that the implementation stage is where they encounter crises. Most of these impediments to the roll-out of strategies and plans are avoidable or controllable, so long as implementation is itself planned and managed.

Marketers spend significant sums of money on specifying and executing their marketing programmes. It is necessary, therefore, to assess the expected returns for the organisation and to examine whether there are better ways of achieving the desired results.

This chapter examines some popular ways for organising marketing activity within a company, the essential 'rules' for facilitating implementation of marketing strategies and marketing plans, and the best practice approaches to evaluating marketing performance.

## Opener

# 'I'm lovin' it': McDonald's Keeps Tight Control

Mighty McDonald's, famous for its golden arches, was established in 1940 when Dick and Mac McDonald opened up in San Bernadino, California. Ray Kroc, credited with the chain's global ambitions, bought the rights to develop the brand in 1955 and created McDonald's Corporation. Every day, from Moscow to Hong Kong, McDonald's serves over 47 million people, including over a million in the UK, where the company enjoys a 70 per cent share of the hamburger market. There are 30,000 McDonald's restaurants in 119 countries. Strongest growth is currently in Europe, where the new 'I'm lovin' it' positioning and healthier eating menus have rekindled the company's fortunes. Leading branding consultancy Interbrand ranked McDonald's as the most recognised brand in the world, beating even Coca-Cola.

Whether in Lisbon, Chicago or Manchester, a McDonald's restaurant is instantly evident, with a homogeneous layout, ambience, design and ethos that are the envy of most services marketers. The menus change slightly to reflect local tastes, but for the most part there is consistency in the product the world over. Alcohol is available in Lousanne, while incredible ice cream concoctions are on offer in Porto, but everywhere the core dishes are the same – the Big Mac, Chicken McNuggets, Egg McMuffin and Filet-O-Fish – to eat in or, at many locations, available as a drive-thru take-away. Single adults snacking, business representatives lunching, children partying or teenagers dining before taking in a movie – McDonald's caters for a wide range of customers.

When McDonald's first came to Europe, it had to educate its customers to expect unbuttered rolls, no knives or forks and no table service. Despite being in Lisbon, Portugal, for years, when McDonald's opened in Porto in northern Portugal, it advertised the concept of the hamburger and explained that it could be eaten for lunch or dinner and even as a snack at any time of the day. This may seem strange to a generation that has grown up with fast-food restaurants, but it was a major marketing task. Staff, too, had to be trained and managed to perform their duties effectively. The training and orientation of staff are still central to the success of the company. Behind the scenes, internal marketing programmes ensure that staff comprehend the fundamentals of the McDonald's trading concept and ideals.

Controls are central to the trading practices of the company. Every customer ordering a Big Mac must receive a similar meal every time: cooked identically, with similar relish, wrapping, pricing and a smile. Any complaints must be handled quickly, courteously and with no damage to the well-known branding. With 70 per cent of McDonald's restaurants franchised to independently owned companies and operators, such uniformity does not occur by accident. Country managers are allowed to source locally but must conform to well-established ingredients and standards. While Burger King emphasises its food, McDonald's promotes the whole-restaurant experience and establishes performance standards to maintain a consistent customer offer. As the company continues to grow, with innovative outlets on ferries, at football grounds and even in London's Guy's Hospital, internal operational controls are just as important to its success as is the extensive promotional activity designed to keep the brand in the target audience's mind. McDonald's understands the importance of maintaining high standards and of integrating the brand, people, design, ambience, technology and food to create a winning experience. Not everyone is a McDonald's fan, but millions daily are happy to return to the trusted golden arches.

**Sources:** McDonald's stores UK, 2004; 'Progressive not McDesperate', Letters, *Marketing Week*, 22 April 1999, p. 32; 'Aroma therapy', *Marketing Week*, 8 April 1999, pp. 28–9; Ian Darby, 'Big Mac blunder hits McDonald's', *Marketing*, 7 January 1999, p. 1; Claire Murphy, 'How McDonald's conquered the UK', *Marketing*, 18 February, pp. 30–1; www.mcdonalds.com/corp, July 2004.
Photo: Courtesy of Karen Beaulah

This chapter focuses first on the marketing unit's position in the organisation and the ways the unit itself can be organised. The chapter goes on to examine several issues regarding the implementation of marketing strategies, particularly the links with relationship marketing, internal marketing – so important to the success of McDonald's – and total quality management. The most frequently encountered impediments hindering implementation are discussed. The chapter then discusses the use of cost and sales analyses to evaluate the effectiveness of marketing strategies and to measure the company's performance, the emergence of marketing shareholder value analysis (MSVA), before concluding with an examination of popular marketing performance measures.

# Organising Marketing Activities

Some companies do not have a free-standing specialist marketing function. For them, marketing's remit is allocated between managers in other functions or is the responsibility of the sales function. So long as the marketing process outlined in Chapter 1 is enacted and those involved in executing the various stages in the process – marketing analyses, marketing strategy development, the creation of marketing programmes and the execution of these programmes – are coordinated and well managed, this approach to undertaking marketing may achieve adequate results. In general, however, most companies have specialist marketing personnel, operating either together as a marketing unit or allocated to separate business units, product teams or market groups in order to manage the marketing activity required to support that specific part of the organisation's activities. These days, most medium and large companies do have a marketing function and specialist marketing personnel.

The organisation of a marketing function involves the development of an internal structure for the marketing unit, including relationships and lines of authority and responsibility that connect and coordinate individuals. Individual marketing managers, brand managers or marketing assistants must understand their roles and reporting structures. Within a business unit – typically comprising planning personnel, sales and marketing staff, managers handling operations and administrative staff – non-marketers also need to understand the remit for marketing and the specific roles of those responsible for marketing activities. It should be obvious to all concerned who is tasked with analysing customers' views, assessing competitors, monitoring the forces of the marketing environment, creating a marketing strategy, developing the brand positioning, specifying the marketing mix, creating the advertising proposition and marketing communications programme, conducting marketing research, and tracking the effectiveness of the marketing programme deployed.

This section starts by looking at the place of marketing within an organisation, and examines some of the major alternatives available for organising a marketing unit. It then goes on to show how marketing activities can be structured to fit into an organisation so as to contribute to the accomplishment of overall objectives.

## The Place of Marketing in an Organisation

Because the marketing environment is so dynamic, the importance of the marketing unit within the organisation has increased during the past 30 years. As explored in Chapter 1, companies that truly adopt the marketing concept often develop a distinct organisational culture – a culture based on a shared set of beliefs, which makes the customers' needs the pivotal point of a company's decisions about strategy and operations.[1] When this philosophy permeates the whole organisation, there is a genuine *marketing orientation* to that company's behaviour and actions. Instead of developing products in a vacuum and then trying to persuade consumers to buy them, companies using the marketing concept begin with an orientation towards their customers' needs and desires. If the marketing concept serves as a guiding philosophy, the marketing unit will be coordinated closely with other functional areas, such as production, finance and personnel. Figure 24.1 shows the organisation of a marketing unit by types of customer. This form of internal organisation works well for

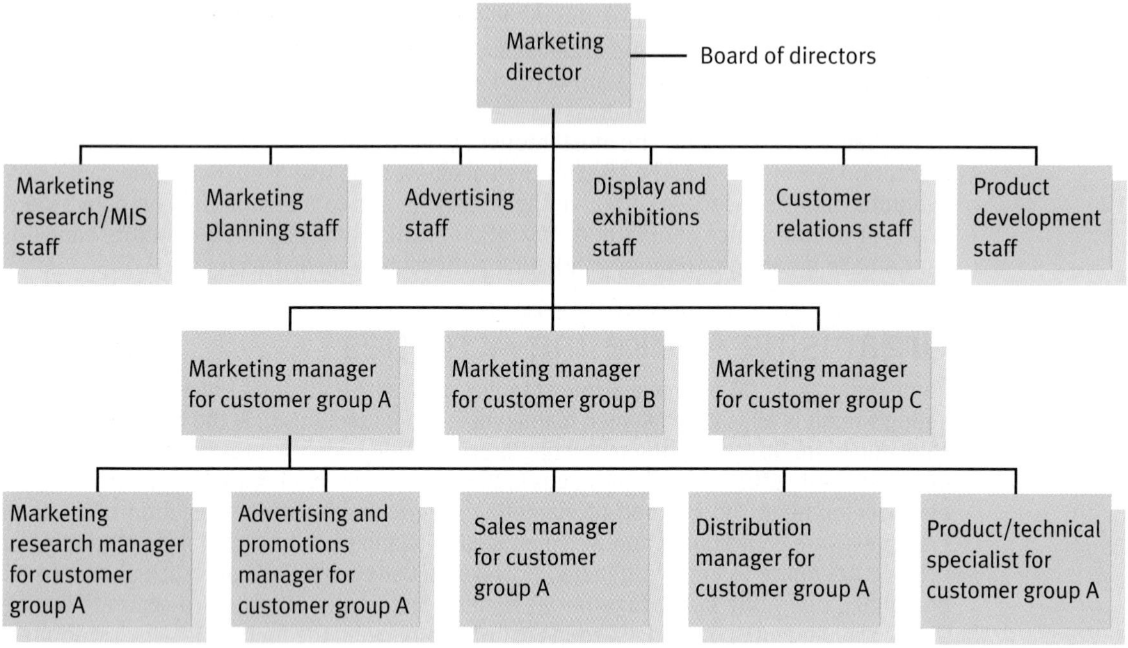


**Note:** In some organisations, each marketing manager would have responsibility for a product group rather than a customer group, and would be termed a product manager

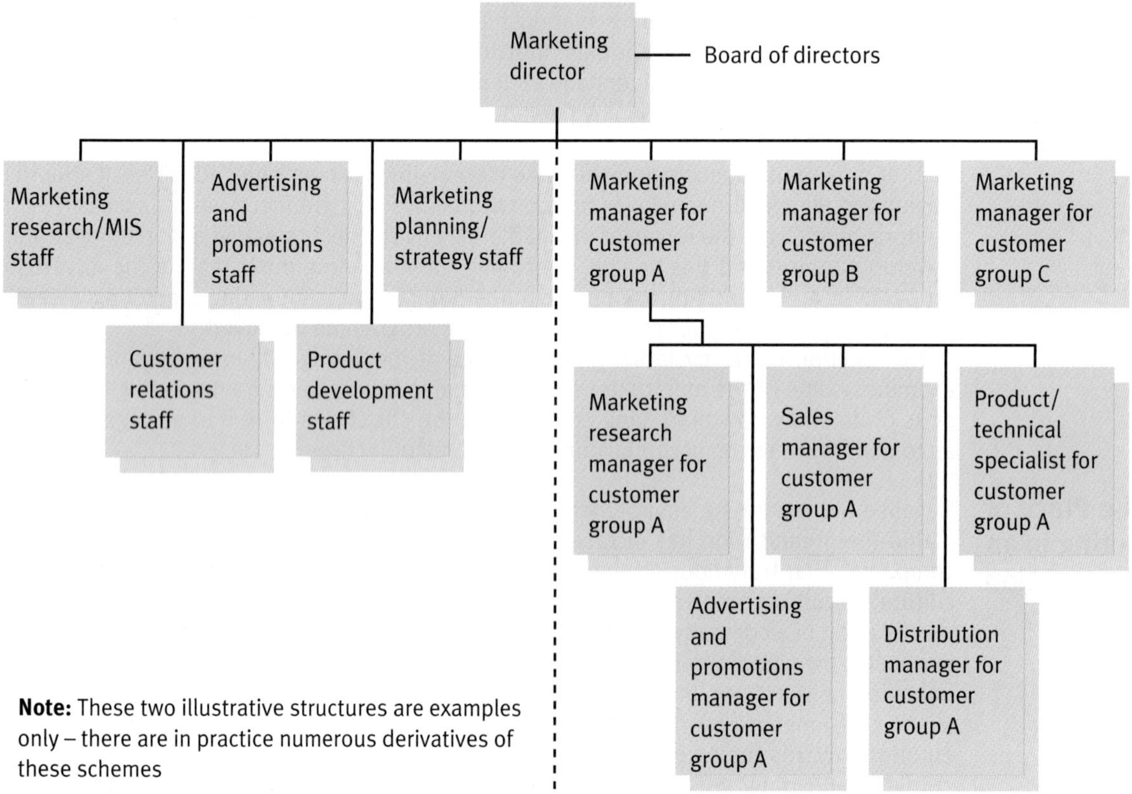


**Note:** These two illustrative structures are examples only – there are in practice numerous derivatives of these schemes

***Figure 24.1***
*Organising the marketing unit*

organisations having several groups of customers whose needs differ significantly. The version in the lower part of the figure is particularly prevalent among many business-to-business organisations, such as component suppliers serving several market sectors, an IT services company active across many markets or a firm of financial advisers specialising in more than one business sector.

Marketing must interact with other functional departments in a number of key areas. It needs to work with manufacturing in determining the volume and variety of the company's products. Those in charge of production often rely on marketers for accurate sales forecasts. Research and development departments depend heavily on information gathered by marketers about product features and benefits desired by consumers, the new products launched by competitors, the implications of marketing environment trends, as well as details of complaints concerning current products. Decisions made by the physical distribution department – logistical support – hinge on information about the urgency of delivery schedules and cost/service trade-offs.[2] In many organisations there are specialist customer service departments, whose activities must reflect the marketing strategies developed by the marketers in the company, but whose knowledge of customer issues should be fed back to the marketers tasked with developing marketing and brand strategies. Similarly, sales personnel must prioritise the key target markets selected by the marketing strategy, reflect the desired brand positioning and maximise use of any differential advantage identified by the marketers, while having links with marketing colleagues in order to share their knowledge of customer issues and market developments. Whether manufacturing, service or public sector, or consumer marketing, those tasked with managing the organisation's marketing activities must have involvement with colleagues across the organisation.

**Marketing-oriented organisation**
A company that concentrates on discovering what buyers want and providing it in a way that lets the company achieve its objectives

As discussed in Chapter 1, a **marketing-oriented organisation** concentrates on discovering what buyers want and providing it in a way that lets the company achieve its objectives. Such a company has an organisational culture that effectively and efficiently produces a sustainable differential advantage.[3] It focuses on customer analysis, competitor analysis and the integration of the business's resources to provide customer value and satisfaction, as well as long-term profits.[4]

As Figure 24.2 shows, the marketing director's position is often at the same level as those of the financial, production and personnel directors. Thus the marketing director takes part in top-level decision-making. The marketing director is also responsible for a variety of activities. Some of them – sales forecasting and supervision, and product planning – would be under the jurisdiction of other functional managers in production or sales-oriented organisations. Some organisations do not have a marketing director: the head of marketing in such companies is often at the same level as the senior managers responsible for IT, logistics, purchasing and channel management. In these cases, there is usually a director responsible for sales and marketing, to whom specialist marketing managers report.

To be successful, a company does not have to employ a marketing director. However, the core activities of marketing must be undertaken and the forward thinking enabled by the marketing process must be deployed by someone. Few other business functions are interested in external market developments, competitor moves, changing customer expectations or the likely shape of target market priorities in three years' time. Finance, production, human resources and logistics have other priorities, often – although not exclusively – focused on short-term performance improvement and the effective utilisation of corporate resources. It is the case that marketers spend much of their time rolling out marketing programmes, but when developing marketing strategies and undertaking marketing planning they do take a longer-term view of the company's fortunes and required strategy realignment. In addressing the core marketing analyses – customers, competitors, marketing environment trends, capabilities – and making marketing strategy recommendations about opportunities to pursue, target markets to prioritise, brand positioning and possible competitive advantage, marketers are well placed to warn a business about impending threats and guide their

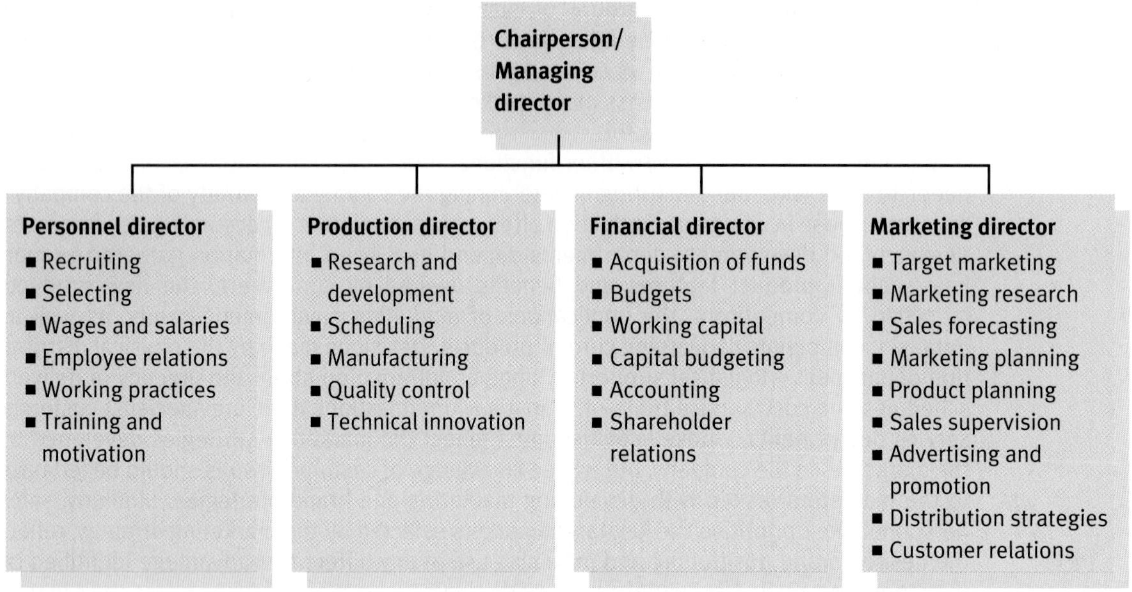


***Figure 24.2***
*Organisational chart of a marketing-oriented company*

colleagues in aligning resources to emerging opportunities. There is much to be commended in having a marketing function that is viewed by the organisation as offering a longer-term perspective on market developments and how markets will evolve, acting as the company's 'radar'.

Both the links between marketing and other functional areas – such as production, finance and human resources – and the importance of marketing to management evolve from the organisation's basic orientation. Marketing encompasses the greatest number of business functions and occupies an important position when a company is marketing oriented. Marketing has a limited impact when the company views the role of marketing as simply selling the products that it makes. For organisations – and there are many – in which senior managers view the role of marketing as simply 'creating advertisements', 'conducting customer surveys', 'dealing with customer complaints', or 'keeping dealers and distributors happy', the contribution of marketing is very limited. Such organisations are failing to benefit from the insights and direction provided from the marketing process. However, a marketing orientation is not achieved simply by redrawing the organisational chart: management must also adopt the marketing orientation as a management philosophy, using and connecting the stages of the marketing process – marketing analyses, marketing strategy formulation, marketing programme creation and implementation controls.

## Centralisation versus Decentralisation

**Centralised organisation**
A company in which top-level managers delegate very little authority to the lower levels of the organisation

The organisational structure that a company uses to connect and coordinate various activities affects its success. Basic decisions relate to how various participants in the company will work together to make important decisions, as well as to coordinate, implement and control activities. Top managers create corporate strategies and coordinate lower levels. A **centralised organisation** is one in which the top-level managers delegate very little authority to lower levels of the organisation. In a **decentralised organisation**, decision-making authority is delegated as far down the chain of command as possible. The decision to centralise or decentralise directly affects marketing in the organisation.

In a centralised organisation, major marketing decisions originate with top management and are transmitted to lower levels of management. A decentralised structure gives marketing

**Decentralised organisation**
A company in which decision-making authority is delegated as far down the chain of command as possible

managers more opportunity for making key strategic decisions. IBM has adopted a decentralised management structure so that its marketing managers have a chance to customise strategies for customers. On the other hand, Hewlett-Packard and 3M have become more centralised by consolidating functions or eliminating divisional managers.[5] Although decentralising may foster innovation and a greater responsiveness to customers, a decentralised company may be inefficient or appear to have a blurred marketing strategy when dealing with larger customers. A centralised organisation avoids confusion among the marketing staff, vagueness in marketing strategy and autonomous decision-makers who are out of control. Of course, overly centralised companies often become dependent on top management and respond too slowly to be able to solve problems or seize new opportunities. Obviously, finding the right degree of centralisation for a particular company is a difficult balancing act.

While many highly centralised organisations are quite successful, the overall trend is for companies to decentralise. This trend is partly caused by the need for organisations to remain very flexible, given the ever-changing marketing environment. For some companies, the need to adapt to changing customer needs is of critical importance. These organisations often use an extreme form of decentralisation: **empowerment**. This involves giving front-line employees the authority and responsibility to make marketing decisions without seeking the approval of their supervisors.[6] In practice, for many organisations the solution is something of a hybrid: marketing activity is decentralised within business units that are responsible for individual market segments or product groups, but the marketing personnel in the organisation also work collectively in order to manage tasks that cut across the activities of separate business units, such as brand development and communication, new product concept development, the assessment of the marketing environment forces, analysis of new territories for expansion or the creation of customer-handling programmes. For example, IT giant Fujitsu has specialist marketers supporting each of its business units, but these personnel also work together on aspects of the marketing process.

**Empowerment**
Giving front-line employees the authority and responsibility to make marketing decisions without seeking the approval of their supervisors

The concept of empowerment is increasingly important as organisations strive to become faster moving and more customer responsive. The following examples illustrate empowerment:

- A car sales person is allowed to negotiate the price or financing arrangement with a customer without speaking with the sales manager.
- A retail sales assistant decides, without seeking the approval of a manager, whether to refund customers' money on products they return.
- A receptionist at a hotel gives one night's free accommodation to a dissatisfied guest who complains about poor service.
- A retail store manager is permitted to lower prices on merchandise without asking the regional manager, in order to match a competitor.

Although employees at any level in an organisation can be empowered to make decisions, empowerment is used most often at the front line, where employees interact daily with customers. Service and retail marketers practise empowerment quite extensively because of the interactive nature of these businesses. However, empowerment can work in a manufacturing organisation as well.

One of the characteristics of empowerment is that employees can perform their jobs the way they see fit, as long as their methods and outcomes are consistent with the mission of the organisation.[7] However, the effectiveness of empowerment is tied to the organisation's culture. Empowerment works best when the corporate culture is guided by a sense of shared direction, which ensures that employees make the right decisions.[8] Obviously, creating this type of culture does not happen overnight. The corporate vision must be communicated to employees so that they understand how their job affects the vision. Employees must also be trained and persuaded to accept the corporate vision and to become part of the organisation's culture.[9]

## Major Alternatives for Organising the Marketing Unit

How effectively a company's marketing management can plan and implement marketing strategies depends on how the marketing unit is organised. Effective organisational planning can give the company a competitive edge. The organisational structure of a marketing department establishes the authority relationships between marketing personnel, and specifies who is responsible for making certain decisions and performing particular activities. This internal structure is the vehicle for directing marketing activities.

In organising a marketing unit, managers divide the work into specific activities and delegate responsibility and authority for those activities to people in various positions within the unit. These positions include, for example, the sales manager, the research manager and the advertising manager.

No single approach to organising a marketing unit works equally well in all businesses. A marketing unit can be organised according to:

- functions
- products
- regions, or
- types of customer.

The best approach or approaches depend on the number and diversity of the company's products, the characteristics and needs of the people in the target market, and many other factors.

Businesses often use some combination of organisation by functions, products, regions or customer types. Product features may dictate that the marketing unit be structured by products, whereas customers' characteristics require that it be organised by geographic region or by type of customer. Construction equipment leader JCB has organised by product type (crawler excavators, backhoe diggers, compact equipment, and so forth), but many financial institutions organise by customer type, because personal banking needs differ from commercial ones. By using more than one type of organisation, a flexible marketing unit can develop and implement marketing plans to match customers' needs precisely. To develop organisational plans that give a company a differential advantage, four issues should be considered:

1. Which jobs or levels of jobs need to be added, deleted or modified? For example, if new products are important to the success of the business, marketers with strong product development skills should be added to the organisation.
2. How should reporting relationships be structured to create a competitive edge? This question is discussed further in the following descriptions of organisational structure.
3. To whom should the primary responsibility for accomplishing work be assigned? Identifying primary responsibility explicitly is critical for effective performance appraisal and reward systems.
4. Should any committees or task forces be organised?[10]

**Organising by function**
A way of structuring a marketing department in which personnel directing marketing research, product development, distribution, sales, advertising and customer relations report to the top-level marketing executive

**Organising by Function** Some marketing departments adopt a structure known as **organising by function**, such as marketing research, product development, distribution, sales, advertising and customer relations. The personnel who direct these functions report directly to the top-level marketing executive. This structure is fairly common because it works well for some businesses with centralised marketing operations, such as Ford and General Motors. In more decentralised companies, such as some retailers or fast-moving consumer goods giants like Procter & Gamble and Unilever, functional organisation can give rise to severe coordination problems. The functional approach may, however, suit a large, centralised company, whose products and customers are neither numerous nor diverse.

**Organising by Product** A business that produces and markets diverse products may find the functional approach inadequate. The decisions and problems related to a single marketing function for one product may be quite different from those related to the same marketing function for another. As a result, businesses that produce diverse products sometimes organise their marketing units according to product groups. **Organising by product** gives a company the flexibility to develop special marketing mixes for different products.

**Organising by product**
A way of structuring a marketing department so that the company has the flexibility to develop special marketing mixes for different products

The product management system, which was introduced by Procter & Gamble, operates in about 85 per cent of companies in the consumer packaged goods industry or fast-moving consumer goods (fmcg), as they are often known. In this structure, the product manager oversees all activities related to his or her assigned product. He or she develops product plans, sees that they are implemented, monitors the results and takes corrective action as necessary. The product manager is also responsible for acting as a liaison point between the company and its marketing environment, transmitting essential information about the environment to the company.[11] The product manager may also draw on the resources of specialised staff in the company. **Category management**, currently popular in supermarkets, off-licences, CTNs and forecourt shops, takes this notion further, with marketers – 'category captains' – becoming responsible for categories of product lines, such as fresh foods, tobacco products or all alcoholic beverages in supermarkets or off-licences. Category management is explored in more detail in Chapter 16.

**Category management**
A variation of organising by product, whereby marketers are responsible for categories of product lines or categories of distributors

**Organising by Region** A large company that markets products nationally or internationally may adopt a structure for its marketing activities known as **organising by region**. Managers of marketing functions for each region report to their regional marketing manager; all the regional marketing managers report directly to the executive marketing manager. Companies often adopt this regional structure to put more senior management personnel into the field, become closer to customers, and enable the company to respond more quickly and efficiently to regional competitors. This form of organisation is especially effective for a business whose customers' characteristics and needs vary greatly from one region to another.

**Organising by region**
A way of structuring a marketing department, used by large national or international companies, that requires managers of marketing functions for each region to report to their regional marketing manager

A company with marketing managers for each separate region has a complete marketing staff at its headquarters to provide assistance and guidance to regional marketing managers. The major UK brewers had national headquarters and marketing centres, often in London, but regional brands, each with their own marketing department, in major provincial conurbations. The regional office controlled the marketing and promotion of its brand within guidelines specified by the head office. However, not all companies organised by region maintain a full marketing staff at their head offices. Businesses that try to penetrate the national market intensively sometimes divide regions into sub-regions.

**Organising by Type of Customer** Sometimes the marketing unit opts for **organising by type of customer**. This form of internal organisation works well for a business that has several groups of customers whose needs and problems differ significantly. For example, Bic may sell pens to large retail stores, wholesalers and institutions such as schools, and disposable razors to a mix of wholesaling, retail and hotel business customers. Retailers may want more rapid delivery of small shipments and more personal selling by the producer than do wholesalers or institutional buyers. Because the marketing decisions and activities required for these groups of customers differ considerably, the company may find it efficient to organise its marketing unit by type of customer.

**Organising by type of customer**
A way of structuring a marketing department, suitable for a business that has several groups of customers with very different needs and problems

In an organisation with a marketing department broken down by customer group, the marketing manager for each group reports to the top-level marketing executive and directs most marketing activities for that group. A marketing manager controls all activities needed to market products to a specific customer group.

The planning and organising functions provide purpose, direction and structure for marketing activities. However, until marketing managers implement the marketing plan, exchanges cannot occur. In fact, organisers of marketing activities can become excessively concerned with planning strategy while neglecting implementation. Before John Harvey-Jones joined ICI, some analysts believed that its management's preoccupation with procedures and plans caused the company's business to suffer. Obviously, implementation of plans is important to the success of any organisation, as described in this chapter's 'Opener'. Proper implementation of a marketing plan depends on internal marketing to employees, the motivation of personnel who perform marketing activities, effective communication within the marketing organisation and the coordination of marketing activities. In Figure 24.3, Aerospatiale promotes its teamwork philosophy in business with other countries and internally.

**Marketing implementation**
Processes and activities deployed to action the marketing strategy or roll out the marketing plan

## Marketing Implementation

**Marketing implementation** is the 'how?' of marketing strategy; it involves processes and activities directed at actioning marketing strategies or rolling out the marketing plan's recommendations. The implementation process can determine whether a marketing strategy is

***Figure 24.3***
*The development of a new car model may take six years, but its success in terms of sales volumes depends as much on the implementation of the target market strategy as on the design and features of the vehicle*
*Photo © Richard Cummins/CORBIS*

successful. Increasingly marketers are recognising the importance of managing implementation and planning for the execution of marketing programmes.[12] For example, the output of marketing planning – see Chapter 23 – used to be the specification of the marketing mix. Now, a robust marketing plan is not deemed complete until the 'how', 'by whom', 'when' and 'how much' issues are addressed: allocation of budgets, personnel, schedules and performance measures to the specific marketing mix recommendations. In providing these details, marketers identify deficiencies and inadequacies in their capabilities and resources that they must address in order to implement their marketing plans effectively. These impediments often relate to operational and managerial issues. In short, good marketing strategy combined with bad marketing implementation is a recipe for certain failure. Marketing has to be made to happen!

The exponents of marketing planning have for many years realised that internal organisational barriers are likely to impede or restrict the implementation of marketing plans and marketing strategies.[13] They propose that senior managers address the people and cultural concerns detailed in Figure 24.4 before embarking on developing marketing plans, new market segmentation schemes or marketing strategies.[14] These issues reflect the importance of addressing the internal market in effectively pursuing the implementation of marketing strategies and the deployment of recommended marketing mix programmes. Failure to control internal audiences and develop suitable control strategies will reduce the viability of the marketing function's recommended strategies and marketing plan recommendations in the external marketplace.

Already-busy managers developing marketing plans or revising market segmentation schemes need to be managed, cajoled, motivated and rewarded. Any planning process requires access to marketing intelligence; and the involvement of personnel with knowledge

**Operational considerations**
- Disruption by planning?
- Non-marketers/directors?
- Buy-in from functions?
- Accessibility of personnel/ information?
- Communication of plan?

**Level of command**
- Who?
- When?
- Involvement?
- Channels/approaches?
- Communication?

**Communications**
- Within marketing?
- Across functions?
- Through hierarchies?
- Mechanisms?
- Channels?
- Support?

**Involvement**
- Who?
- When?
- Levels?
- Functions?
- Support?

**Time frames and formats**
- How long?
- When?
- Action learning or externally supported?
- Hands-on/hands-off?
- Communications?

**Participants' expectations**
- What expectations?
- Working priorities?
- Worries/concerns?
- 'Political' cliques?
- Office politics?

**Additional resources**
- Intelligence/information?
- People?
- IT/communications?
- Time?

***Figure 24.4***
*People and culture prerequisites to effective marketing and marketing planning programmes*
*Source: adapted from: Sally Dibb, Lyndon Simkin and John Bradley,* The Marketing Planning Workbook *(London: Thomson, 1998)*

of the marketplace, customers, competitors, trends and new developments. Those directly involved must have access to their colleagues and be empowered to conduct the necessary analyses and develop appropriate strategies. 'Buy-in' from managers and colleagues, whose remit may change as a result of the planning, warrants facilitation. The necessary analytical skills and time to strategise must be provided. Senior management should be aware of the invasive nature of marketing planning or creating an updated marketing strategy, and schedule other activities accordingly. The **requisites for implementation** include process, skill, leadership, empowerment, communication, timing, information, resource and participation decisions. The learning point is straightforward: appreciation of the checklist issues outlined in Figure 24.4 *prior* to embarking on marketing planning or the creation of a new marketing strategy will significantly enhance the likelihood of a successful outcome. Unfortunately, many organisations only realise the importance of planning and facilitating the strategising activity after problems have emerged, progress has been baulked and key stakeholders within the organisation are failing to cooperate.[15]

**Requisites for implementation** Process, skill, leadership, empowerment, communication, timing, information, resource and participation decisions

**Intended strategy** The strategy on which the company decides during the planning phase

**Realised strategy** The strategy that actually takes place

An important aspect of the implementation process is understanding that marketing strategies almost always turn out differently from that expected. In essence, all organisations have two types of strategy: intended strategy and realised strategy.[16] **Intended strategy** is the strategy that the organisation decided on during the planning phase and wants to use. **Realised strategy**, on the other hand, is the strategy that actually takes place; it comes about during the process of implementing the intended strategy. The realised strategy is not necessarily any better than the intended strategy, though it is often worse.

## Problems in Implementing Marketing Activities

Why do marketing strategies sometimes turn out differently from that expected? The most common reason is that managers fail to realise that marketing implementation is just as important as marketing strategy.[17] Both strategy and implementation are important to strategic planning. The relationship between strategic planning and implementation creates a number of problems for managers when they plan implementation activities. Three of the most important problems are described below:[18]

**Marketing Strategy and Implementation are Related** Companies that experience this problem typically assume that strategic planning always comes first, followed by implementation. In reality, marketing strategies and implementation activities should be developed simultaneously. The content of the marketing strategy determines how it will be implemented. Likewise, implementation activities may require that changes be made in the marketing strategy. Thus it is important for marketing managers to understand that strategy and implementation are highly entwined, iterative processes.

**Marketing Strategy and Implementation are Constantly Evolving** This second problem refers to how strategy and implementation are both affected by the marketing environment. Since the environment is constantly changing, both marketing strategy and implementation must remain flexible enough to adapt. The relationship between strategy and implementation is never fixed; it is always evolving to accommodate changes in customer needs, government regulation or competition.

**The Responsibilities for Marketing Strategy and Implementation are Separated** This problem is often the biggest obstacle in implementing marketing strategies. Typically, marketing strategies are developed by the top managers in an organisation. However, the responsibility for implementing those strategies rests at the front line of the organisation. This separation can impair implementation in two ways (see Figure 24.5). First, because top managers are separated from the front line, where the company interacts daily with customers, they may not grasp the unique problems associated with implementing marketing activities. Second, people, not organisations, implement strategies. Front-line managers and employees are often

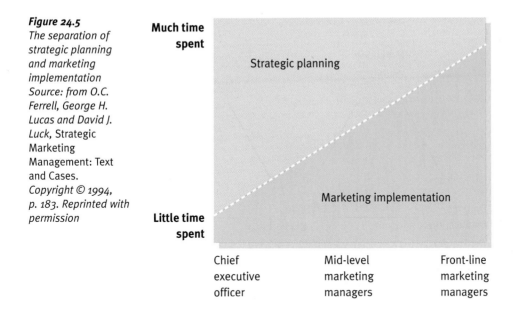

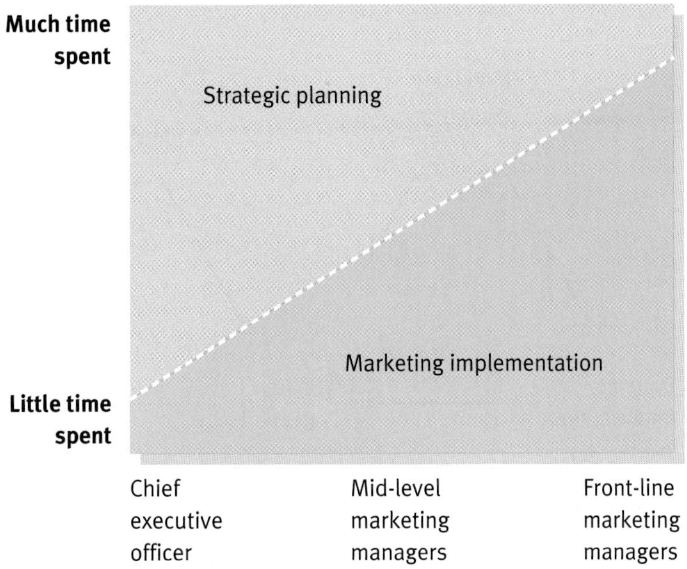


*Figure 24.5*
*The separation of strategic planning and marketing implementation*
*Source: from O.C. Ferrell, George H. Lucas and David J. Luck,* Strategic Marketing Management: Text and Cases. *Copyright © 1994, p. 183. Reprinted with permission*

responsible for implementing strategies, even though they had no voice in developing them. Consequently, these front-line employees may lack motivation and commitment.[19]

## Components of Marketing Implementation

The marketing implementation process has several components, all of which must be synchronised if the implementation is to succeed. These components are shown in Figure 24.6. The systems component refers to work processes, procedures and the way in which information is structured – elements ensuring that the organisation's day-to-day activities are carried out. Typical organisational systems include marketing information systems, strategic planning systems, marketing planning processes, budgeting and accounting systems, manufacturing and quality control systems, and performance measurement systems.

The people component in Figure 24.6 refers to the importance of employees in the implementation process. It includes such factors as the quality, diversity and skills of the workforce within the organisation, and also covers the human resources function. Issues like employee recruitment, selection and training have great bearing on the implementation of marketing activities.[20] Closely linked to the people component is leadership, or the art of managing people. It involves such issues as employee motivation, communication and reward policies.

At the centre of marketing implementation are shared goals, which draw the entire organisation together into a single, functioning unit. These goals may be simple statements of the company's objectives. On the other hand, the goals may be detailed mission statements, outlining corporate philosophy and direction. Shared goals appear in the centre of Figure 24.6 because they hold all the other components together to ensure successful marketing implementation.[21] Without shared goals, different parts of the organisation might work towards different goals or objectives, thus limiting the success of the entire organisation. These ideas have been embraced within the related concepts of *internal marketing* and *relationship marketing*, as discussed later in this chapter.

## Motivating Marketing Personnel

An important element in implementing a marketing strategy or the marketing plan is motivating marketing personnel to perform effectively. People work to satisfy physical, psychological and social needs. To motivate marketing personnel, managers must discover their employees' needs and then develop motivational methods that help them satisfy those needs. It is crucial that the plan for motivating employees be fair, ethical and well

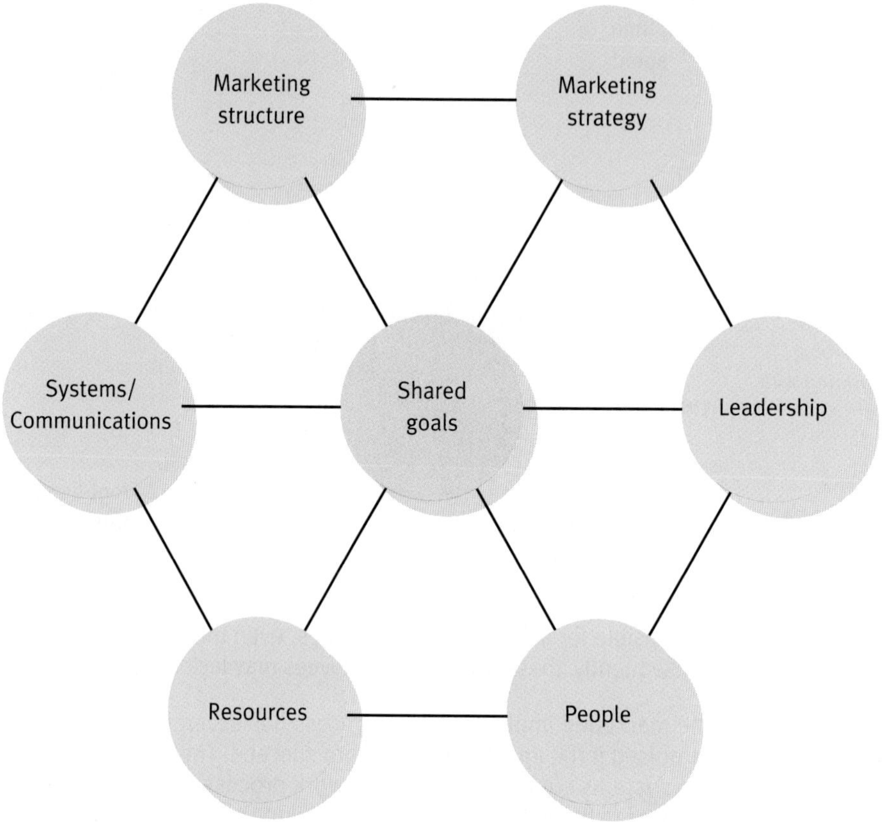


***Figure 24.6***
*Elements of marketing implementation*
*Source: Lawrence R. Jauch and William F. Glueck,* Strategic Management and Business Policy, *3rd edn. Copyright © 1988 by The McGraw-Hill Companies*

understood by them. Additionally, rewards to employees must be tied to organisational goals. In general, to improve employee motivation, companies need to find out what workers think, how they feel and what they want. Some of this information can be obtained from an employee attitude survey. A business can motivate its workers by directly linking pay with performance, by informing workers how their performance affects department and corporate results, by following through with appropriate compensation, by promoting or implementing a flexible benefits programme and by adopting a participative management approach.[22]

Consider the following example. Suppose a sales person can sell product A or B to a particular customer, but not both products. Product A sells for £200,000 and contributes £20,000 to the company's profit margin. Product B sells for £60,000 and has a contribution margin of £40,000. If the sales person receives a commission of 3 per cent of sales, he or she would obviously prefer to sell product A, even though the sale of product B contributes more to the company's profits. If the sales person's commission was based on contribution margin instead of sales, and the company's goal was to maximise profits, both the company and the sales person would benefit more from the sale of product B.[23] By tying rewards to organisational goals, the company encourages behaviour that meets organisational goals.

Besides tying rewards to organisational goals, managers must motivate individuals by using different motivational tools, based on each individual's value system. For example, some employees value recognition more than a slight pay increase. Managers can reward employees with money, plus additional fringe benefits, prestige or recognition, or even non-financial rewards such as job autonomy, skill variety, task significance and increased feedback. A survey of *Fortune* 1000 companies found that 'the majority of organisations feel that they get more for their money through non-cash awards, if given in addition to a basic compensation plan'.

## Communicating within the Marketing Unit

With good communication, marketing managers can motivate personnel and coordinate their efforts. Marketing managers must be able to communicate with the company's high-level management to ensure that marketing activities are consistent with the company's overall goals. Communication with top-level executives keeps marketing managers aware of the company's overall plans and achievements. It also guides what the marketing unit is to do and how its activities are to be integrated with those of other departments – such as finance, production or human resources – with whose management the marketing manager must also communicate in order to coordinate marketing efforts. For example, marketing personnel must work with production staff to help design products that customers want. To direct marketing activities, marketing managers must communicate with marketing personnel at the operations level, such as sales and advertising personnel, researchers, wholesalers, retailers and package designers.

To facilitate communication, marketing managers should establish an information system within the marketing unit. The marketing information system – discussed in Chapter 9 – should allow for easy communication among marketing managers, sales managers and sales personnel. Marketers need an information system to support a variety of activities, such as planning, budgeting, sales analyses, performance evaluations and the preparation of reports. An information system should also expedite communications with other departments in the organisation and minimise destructive competition between departments for organisational resources. Managers must be encouraged to communicate freely, sharing ideas, insights, marketing intelligence, strategies and tactical recommendations. Such channels of communication should be across business functions and hierarchies. Stone-walling, gatekeeping, ring-fencing and misinformation – all facets of petty 'office politics' – offer no benefits.

## Coordinating Marketing Activities

Because of job specialisation and differences related to marketing activities, marketing managers must synchronise individuals' actions to achieve marketing objectives. In addition, they must work closely with managers in research and development, production, finance and human resources to see that marketing activities mesh with other functions of the company.

## Marketing Tools and Techniques

### Practitioners' Implementation Management of Marketing Planning: The Dibb/Simkin Checklists

When a company commences marketing planning for the first time, already-busy sales and marketing personnel are going to be expected to find time to produce the marketing plan. Hardly any companies employ specialist marketing planners. The organisation must recognise the time pressures and resourcing issues associated with asking staff to become involved in marketing planning. Senior managers must be seen to be appreciative, but they must also create channels of communication between functions in the business so that marketing intelligence may be gathered, ideas generated and the resulting plan disseminated across the company. Rather than await problems of information availability, time pressure, poor internal communications, ineffective leadership, and so forth, it is better to be aware of these issues from the outset.

The Dibb/Simkin checklist below was developed for a global B2B services company that examined how to improve its annual marketing planning activity. Such a checklist should be considered by those instigating marketing planning – senior managers and the marketing function – before the launch of a marketing planning programme.

- Who to involve, what to tell them, how to control them, how to free up their time.
- Who to put in charge, their level of hands-on involvement, their liaison with other functional areas and senior managers.
- The expected timeframe for completion of the marketing plan and the timing of the planning activity given other commitments in the business.

- Resources required in terms of people, marketing information, IT and administrative support.
- Facilitation of communications within the marketing planning team, across business functions, through the hierarchies of the company.
- Coordination of the inputs from non-marketers, the buy-in to the process by managers, and the roll-out of emerging actions.
- The marketing planning process to utilise, its stages/activities and core requirements.
- The implementation of the resulting marketing plan, its launch, internal communication, external execution, required roll-out resourcing.
- A sequence of ongoing reviews to ensure effective implementation of the marketing plan occurs and any required remedial action is taken.

As explored in Chapter 23, it is also necessary to adhere to a robust marketing planning process. This should involve:

- marketing analysis – so that the business is properly informed about current market dynamics and the reality of its standing
- a period of strategy development – to ensure that the target market strategy and defined basis for competing reflect the realities of the marketplace
- the creation of marketing mix programmes – designed to execute the devised marketing strategy, and
- a process of controls and reviews – to facilitate the roll-out and execution of the marketing plan.

Once the marketing plan has been developed, it must be implemented. This partly involves ensuring that specific actions from the plan have been allocated to individual managers, with clearly defined timeframes, budgets and performance measures. The facilitation of implementation also requires reviews and monitoring of progress.

'Review days' are often utilised. These generally take one of two forms:

1 business unit teams present to senior managers and explain their progress in rolling out their part of the company's marketing plan
2 cross-functional workshops are held in order to more fully review progress, explore emerging issues and determine appropriate remedial actions.

The B2B company cited above introduces its review workshops thus:

**Review Workshop – Agenda**

- Review the current strategy.
  *Focus on the plan's product/service propositions and how effectively they are being taken to the specified target market segments.*
- Examine what is working and what is not!
  *Lessons to emulate and problems to fix.*
- Determine appropriate actions.
  *Specify tasks and responsibilities as a result of the discussion.*

Generally, such a discussion revolves around:

- the product/service propositions developed to take to market, and their fine-tuning
- the message clarity of the propositions and their communication to target markets
- marketing communications campaign development and execution
- communication across the company of the plan and its imperatives
- orientation of channel partners/members to the revised direction of the plan
- specialist skills required to help roll out the plan
- strategy for establishing/managing channel and customer relationships
- controls and incentives required to change colleagues' behaviours in order to enact the new-look marketing strategy and marketing plan.

Often, a marketing plan changes a company's thinking and direction, so a programme of change management is required in order to realign managers, budgets, the sales force, and so forth. Without the detailed planning of how best to align an organisation's resources around a marketing plan, successful implementation is unlikely.

While the sentiments above have focused on marketing planning, the same procedures and tips apply to the implementation of a marketing strategy or revised target market strategy.

**Sources:** © Dibb/Simkin. This process is adapted from and based on material from Sally Dibb, Lyndon Simkin and John Bradley, *The Marketing Planning Workbook* (London: Thomson) and Sally Dibb and Lyndon Simkin, *The Market Segmentation Workbook* (London: Thomson).

***Figure 24.7***
*The Lux message has been carefully researched and developed to appeal to the intended target market: the creative execution is part of the operationalisation of the designed marketing strategy*
*Source: LUX is a registered trade mark of Unilever*

In Figure 24.7, the Lux advertisement is the outward indication of a highly coordinated and carefully planned strategy. Marketing managers must coordinate the activities of marketing staff within the business and integrate those activities with the marketing efforts of external organisations – advertising agencies, resellers (wholesalers, retailers and dealers), researchers and shippers, among others. Marketing managers can improve coordination by using internal marketing activities to make each employee aware of how his or her job relates to others, and how his or her actions contribute to the achievement of marketing plans. The Marketing Tools and Techniques box on pages 759–760 presents one particularly well-executed process for facilitating the implementation of marketing plans.

## Concepts Related to Marketing Implementation

This section discusses three concepts that exist for their own purposes, but that also relate to marketing implementation: relationship marketing, internal marketing and total quality management. These approaches, which represent mindsets that marketing managers can adopt when organising and planning marketing activities, are not mutually exclusive. Indeed, many companies adopt a combination of these approaches when designing marketing activities.

## Relationship Marketing

**Relationship marketing**
Places emphasis on the interaction between buyers and sellers, and is concerned with winning and keeping customers by maintaining links between marketing, quality and customer service

As outlined in Chapter 1, **relationship marketing** has recently attracted considerable attention in the marketing literature.[24] It focuses on the interaction between buyers and sellers, and is concerned with winning and keeping customers by maintaining links between marketing, quality and customer service.[25] The term *relationship marketing* has been defined as attracting, maintaining and – in multi-service organisations – enhancing customer relationships.[26] The notion hinges on selling organisations taking a longer-term view of customer relationships to ensure that those customers converted are also retained. Rather than focusing on the worth of an individual transaction, the relationship marketing concept is concerned with the lifetime value of the customer relationship and in winning a larger share of a customer's spending over a prolonged period. There has been a shift from transaction-based marketing towards a relationship focus, as explained by a leading exponent: 'Transaction marketing of the 1980s placed the emphasis on the individual sale. Relationship marketing of the 1990s placed the emphasis on individual customers and seeks to establish a long term relationship between customer and company'.[27]

The fundamental message is that ongoing, longer-term relationships are essential for a business's viability and market performance. While marketers are encouraged to devote greater resources to developing such customer relationships, the relationship marketing literature explains that such long-term commitment stems not only from treating customers differently, but also from addressing other audiences. As detailed in the **five markets model of relationship marketing** in Figure 24.8, these audiences include:

**Five markets model of relationship marketing**
In addition to customer markets, the core audiences of influencers, referrals, employee recruitment, suppliers and internal markets

- referral markets, such as insurance brokers and advisers
- suppliers
- employee recruitment markets
- influencer markets, such as government bodies, EU officials and the central bank
- internal markets.

In highlighting this final 'market' or domain of the five markets model, relationship marketers are acknowledging the damage that can be done if employees do not understand their role in ensuring that marketing recommendations are adequately actioned. In order to exploit this internal market effectively, thought must be devoted to: the establishment of communication channels; leadership qualities and people skills; associated resources; information content, access and sharing; IT support systems; management controls; clear internally focused propositions and messages; as well as priorities for which employees are primary targets.

## Internal Marketing

**Internal marketing**
The application of marketing internally within the company, with programmes of communication and guidance targeted at internal audiences to develop responsiveness and a unified sense of purpose among employees

Much appears to depend on **internal marketing**, which is the application of marketing internally within the company, with programmes of communication and guidance targeted at internal audiences. For example, it has been shown that there is a relationship between satisfied employees, marketing orientation and organisational performance.[28] Internal marketing plays a vital role in developing a customer-focused organisation and helps ensure coherent relationship marketing.[29] Internal marketing is based on communication, the development of responsiveness and a unified sense of purpose among employees. It aims to develop internal and external customer awareness, and to remove functional or human barriers to organisational effectiveness. Internal marketing centres on the notion that every member of the organisation has a 'supplier' and a 'customer'. Long-term, ongoing relationships require improved customer service. High levels of service depend on individuals ensuring that their suppliers and customers are happy. The concept also requires that all members of staff work together, in tune with the organisation's mission, strategy and goals. The aim is to ensure that all staff represent the business in the best possible way in

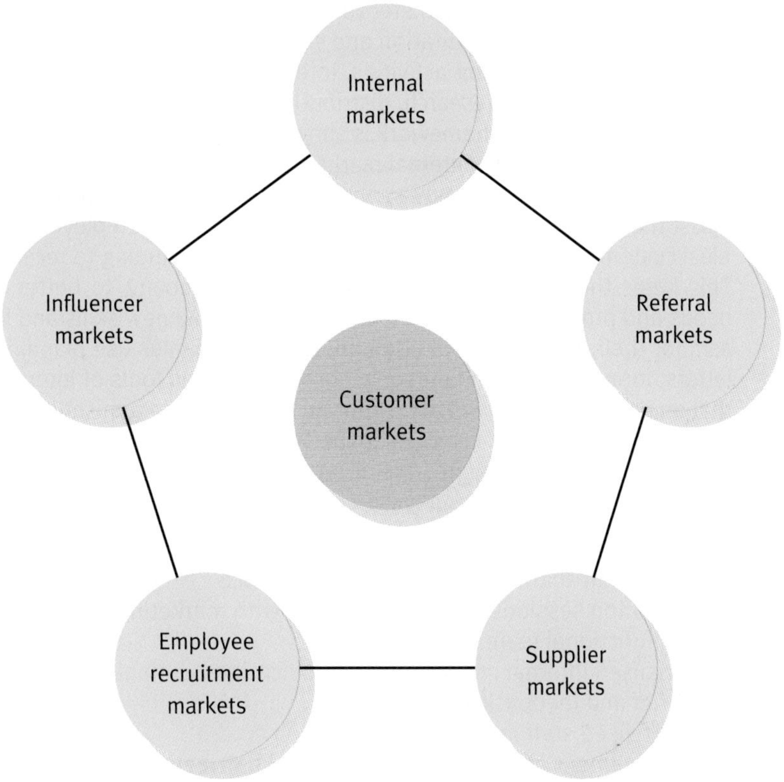


***Figure 24.8***
*The five markets model of relationship marketing*
*Source: M. Christopher, A. Payne and D. Ballantyne,* Relationship Marketing *(Oxford: Butterworth-Heinemann, 1991)*

all transactions they have with suppliers, customers and other staff. A new marketing strategy or modified marketing plan will not be implemented if personnel within the organisation do not understand the direction being recommended, fail to appreciate their role in executing the strategy or refuse to comply. Internal marketing is a philosophy for managing human resources with a marketing perspective.[30]

In order to achieve this internal cohesiveness, internal marketers propose six steps:[31]

1 the creation of internal awareness
2 identification of internal 'customers' and 'suppliers'
3 determination of internal customers' expectations
4 communication of these expectations to internal suppliers
5 internal suppliers' modifications to their activities to reflect internal customers' views
6 a measure of internal service quality and feedback to ensure a satisfactory exchange between internal customers and suppliers.

Marketing activities cannot be implemented effectively without the cooperation of employees. Employees are the essential ingredient in increasing productivity, providing customer service and beating the competition. Thus, in addition to marketing activities targeted at external customers, companies use internal marketing to attract, motivate and retain qualified internal customers (employees) by designing internal products (jobs or roles) to satisfy employees' wants and needs. Generally speaking, internal marketing refers to the managerial actions necessary to make all members of the marketing organisation understand and accept their respective roles in implementing the marketing strategy. This means that all of them, from the chairperson of the company to the hourly workers on the shop floor, must understand the role they play in carrying out their jobs and implementing the marketing strategy. Everyone must do his or her part to ensure that customers are satisfied. All personnel within the company, both marketers and those who perform other functions, should recognise the tenet of customer orientation and service that underlies the marketing concept.

Like external marketing activities, internal marketing may involve market segmentation, product development, research, distribution, and even public relations and sales promotion. The internal marketing framework is shown in Figure 24.9. As in external marketing, the marketing mix is used in the internal marketing approach to satisfy the needs of employees. For example, an organisation may sponsor sales competitions to encourage sales personnel to boost their selling efforts. Some companies encourage employees to work for their companies' customers for a period of time, often while continuing to receive their regular salaries. This helps the employees, and ultimately the company, to better understand customers' needs and problems, enables them to learn valuable new skills and heightens their enthusiasm for their regular jobs. In addition, many companies use planning sessions, workshops, letters, formal reports and personal conversations as tools of internal distribution to ensure that employees understand the corporate mission, the organisation's goals and the marketing strategy. The end result is more satisfied employees, and improved customer relations.

Internal marketing requires the acceptance of the need for improved internal communication, information sharing and liaison across business functions and managerial hierarchies.[32] The core requirements are:

- information sharing of marketing intelligence
- orientation sessions to familiarise staff with marketing strategies and marketing plans
- multifunctional team interaction
- formalised internal marketing communications campaigns
- debrief and feedback sessions
- incentivised staff motivation
- empowerment of line management to take ownership of problems
- the encouragement of 'success stories' to champion.

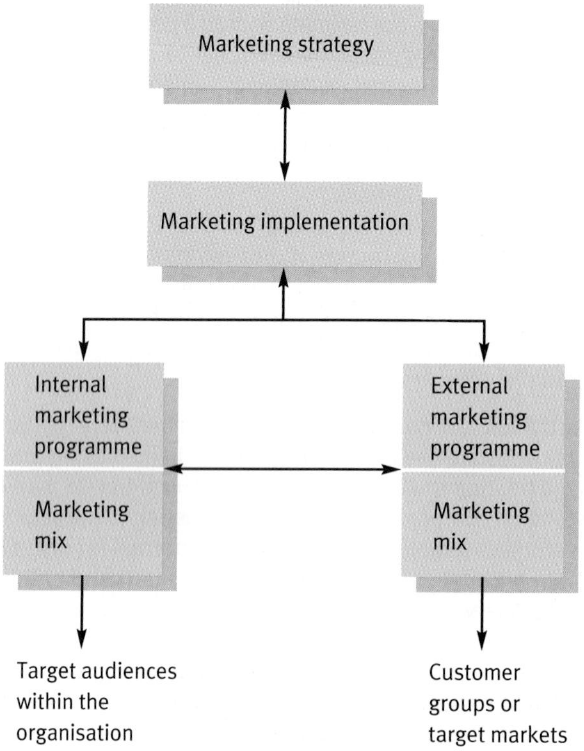


***Figure 24.9***
*The internal marketing framework*
*Source: reprinted by permission, from Nigel F. Piercy,* Market-Led Strategic Change. *Copyright © 1992*

In order to exploit the internal market effectively, thought must be devoted to establishing communication channels, leadership qualities, associated resources, information, and clear internally focused propositions and messages. All of this would routinely be undertaken for an external customer or target market, so why not within the business to ensure staff understanding and cooperation?

## Total Quality Management

**Total quality management (TQM)**
Coordinated efforts directed at improving all aspects of a business – from product and service quality to customer and employee satisfaction

A primary concern today in some organisations is total quality management. Major reasons for this concern about quality are competition, more demanding customers, and poorer profit performance due to reduced market shares and higher costs. **Total quality management (TQM)** is the coordination of efforts directed at improving all aspects of a business: enhancing customer satisfaction, increasing employee participation and empowerment, forming and strengthening supplier partnerships, and facilitating an organisational culture of continuous quality improvement. Customer satisfaction can be improved through higher-quality products and better customer service, such as reduced delivery times, faster responses to customer enquiries and treatment of customers that exhibits a caring attitude on the part of the company.

As a management philosophy, TQM relies heavily on the talents of employees to continually improve the quality of the organisation's goods and services. The TQM philosophy is founded on three basic principles: empowered employees, continuous quality improvement and quality improvement teams.[33]

**Empowered Employees** Ultimately, TQM succeeds or fails because of the efforts of the organisation's employees. Thus employee recruitment, selection and training are critical to the success of marketing implementation. Empowerment means giving employees the authority to make decisions in order to satisfy customer needs. However, empowering employees is successful only if the organisation is guided by an overall corporate vision, shared goals and a culture that supports the TQM effort.[34] Customer-contact employees often continue to maintain productivity levels (i.e. getting the tasks done) even while the quality of their work deteriorates. Providing control mechanisms that achieve desired quality standards can maintain productivity and quality.[35] Such a system cannot spring up overnight. A great deal of time, effort and patience is needed to develop and sustain a quality-oriented culture in an organisation. Three years of training workshops and evolution were required at JCB before TQM became firmly established as a managerial philosophy.

**Continuous Quality Improvement** The continuous improvement of an organisation's products and services is built around the notion that quality is free: not having high-quality goods and services can be very expensive, especially in terms of dissatisfied customers.[36] The continuous improvement of quality also means more than simple quality control, or the screening out of bad products during production. Rather, continuous improvement means building in quality from the very beginning – totally redesigning the product, if necessary. Continuous improvement is a slow, long-term process of creating small improvements in quality. Companies that adopt TQM realise that the major advancements in quality occur because of an accumulation of these small improvements over time.

**Benchmarking**
The process of comparing the quality of an organisation's goods, services or processes with those of its best-performing competitors

A primary tool of the continuous quality improvement process is **benchmarking**, or the measurement and evaluation of the quality of an organisation's goods, services or processes as compared with the best-performing companies in the industry.[37] Benchmarking enables an organisation to know where it stands competitively in its industry, thus giving it a goal to aim for over time. This goal is usually to be the best in the industry.

**Quality Improvement Teams** The idea behind the team approach is to get the best and brightest people from a wide variety of perspectives working on a quality improvement issue simultaneously. Team members are usually selected from a cross-section of jobs within the organisation, as well as from among suppliers and customers. Customers are included in the quality improvement team because they are in the best position to know what they and other customers want from the company. Suppliers, too, understand the market.

Total quality management can provide several benefits. Overall financial benefits include lower operating costs, a higher return on sales and investment, and an improved ability to use premium pricing rather than competitive pricing. Additional benefits include faster development of innovations, improved access to global markets, higher levels of customer retention and an enhanced reputation.[38] Despite these advantages, only a handful of companies use the TQM approach, although the numbers are growing. The reason is that putting the TQM philosophy into practice requires a great deal of organisational resources: time, effort, money and patience on the part of the organisation. However, companies with the resources necessary to implement TQM gain an effective means of achieving major competitive advantages in their respective industries.

Although many factors can influence the effectiveness of the internal marketing and total quality management approaches, two issues are crucial. First, top management must be totally committed to internal marketing or TQM, and must make either one or both of the approaches their top priority. Committed top managers serve as role models for other managers and employees.[39] It is naive for managers to expect employees to be committed to an approach when top managers are not. Second, management must coordinate the specific elements of these approaches to ensure that they work in harmony with each other. Overemphasising one aspect of relationship marketing, internal marketing or TQM can be detrimental to the other components, thus limiting the success of the overall programme.

## Controlling Marketing Activities

**Marketing control process**
One that establishes performance standards, evaluates actual performance and reduces the differences between desired and actual performance

To achieve marketing objectives as well as general organisational goals, marketing managers must control marketing efforts effectively. The **marketing control process** consists of establishing performance standards, evaluating actual performance by comparing it with established standards, and reducing the differences between desired and actual performance, taking corrective action if necessary. This process helped Xerox to recover ground lost to competitors. Dunkin' Donuts has developed a programme to ensure consistency throughout its franchises. Dunkin' Donuts controls the quality of operations in its franchised units by having franchisees attend Dunkin' Donuts University. Owners and managers of Dunkin' Donuts outlets are required to take a six-week training course, covering everything from customer relations and marketing to production, including a test of making 140 dozen doughnuts in eight hours. As part of the test, an instructor selects 6 of the 1680 doughnuts made at random, to ascertain that they weigh around 350 grams (12 ounces) and measure just under 20 centimetres (8 inches) when stacked. The Dunkin' Donuts University was opened to guarantee uniformity in all aspects of the company's operations throughout the 1700 franchise units.[40]

Although the control function is a fundamental management activity, it has until recently received little attention in marketing. There are both formal and informal control systems in organisations. The formal marketing control process involves performance standards, evaluation of actual performance and corrective action to remedy shortfalls (see Figure 24.10). The informal control process, however, involves self-control, social or group control, and cultural control through acceptance of a company's value system. Which type of control system dominates depends on the environmental context of the business.[41]

Most well-run organisations monitor the roll-out of their marketing strategies and marketing plans. For example, Raytheon's senior managers hold quarterly review meetings with the business unit managers tasked with implementing the annually agreed marketing plans. At each meeting, problems in effectively actioning the plan or barriers impeding progress are highlighted and appropriate steps specified to remedy the problems. This may result in senior

*Figure 24.10*
*The marketing control process*

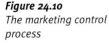

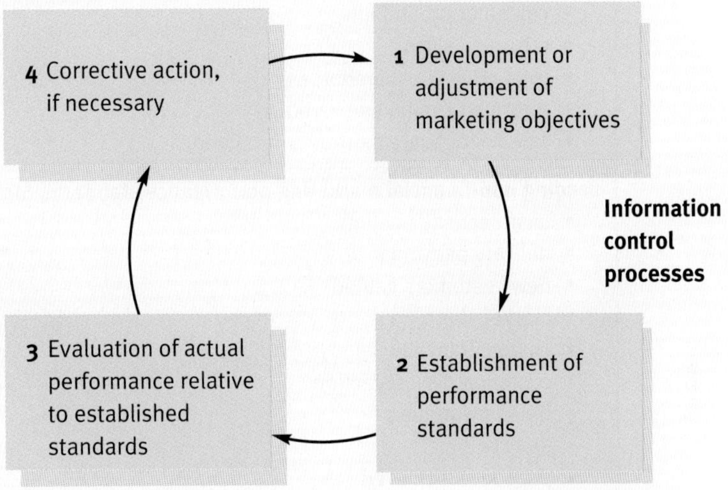


managers forcing others in the organisation to comply with the plan's recommendations or reallocating resources as required. Often, the review meeting itself is sufficient motivation for the business unit managers to increase momentum. Implicit in this approach is the need to specify deliverables from the marketing strategy, marketing plan or marketing programme that may be assessed in order to determine the extent of successful implementation and the effectiveness of the marketing activity in the marketplace.

## Establishing Performance Standards

**Performance standard**
An expected level of performance against which actual performance can be compared

Planning and controlling are closely linked because plans include statements about what is to be accomplished. For purposes of control, these statements function as performance standards. **A performance standard** is an expected level of performance against which actual performance can be compared. Examples of performance standards might be the reduction of customers' complaints by 20 per cent, a monthly sales quota of £150,000, a 10 per cent increase per month in new customer accounts or an increased measure of brand awareness. Performance standards are also given in the form of budget accounts – that is, marketers are expected to achieve a certain objective without spending more than a given amount of resources.

Performance standards can relate to product quality and should be tied to organisational goals. Table 24.1 details the most frequently used performance standards adopted among the professional members of the UK's Chartered Institute of Marketing. A more recent addition to performance standards is that of value-based marketing, utilising the concept of marketing shareholder value analysis.

**TABLE 24.1 CURRENTLY POPULAR PERFORMANCE STANDARDS**

**Key marketing financial performance standards include:**
- revenue growth
- return on investment
- product profitability
- customer profitability
- return on sales
- total return to shareholders
- return on capital employed
- sales per square metre (for retailers).

**Leading non-financial marketing performance standards include:**
- customer satisfaction
- delivery performance
- new customers gained
- market share
- customer loyalty
- customer dissatisfaction
- brand awareness
- lost customers
- price level achieved
- customer brand attitudes.

**Source:** adapted from Sally Dibb and Lyndon Simkin, *Marketing Briefs: a Revision and Study Guide* (Oxford: Elsevier, 2004); UK Chartered Institute of Marketing members' views.

## Evaluating Actual Performance

To compare actual performance with performance standards, marketing managers must know what marketers within the company are doing and must have information about the activities of external organisations that provide the business with marketing assistance. Records of actual performance are compared with performance standards to determine whether a discrepancy exists and, if so, how much of one. For example, a sales person's actual sales are compared with his or her sales quota. If there is a significant negative discrepancy, the sales manager takes corrective action. A marketing research company may be contracted to produce quarterly surveys, providing the analysed results within 10 days of each survey's completion. If the report is late and the sampling or analysis inaccurate, the marketer will probably switch to an alternative supplier.

## Taking Corrective Action

Marketing managers have several options for reducing a discrepancy between established performance standards and actual performance. They can take steps to improve actual performance, or they may review the performance standard and possibly redefine it. Changes in actual performance may require the marketing manager to use better methods of motivating marketing personnel or to find more effective techniques for coordinating marketing efforts. In order to prescribe corrective action, it is necessary to diagnose problems and investigate the challenges facing a company's marketers. The Marketing Tools and Techniques box on pages 769–771 presents the *market status audit*, as developed for a leading business-to-business company's marketing department. This is a comprehensive examination of trends in a market linked to the assessment of reasons for under-performance. Certain performance standards (see below) are included in this company's audit process, which is loosely related to the marketing audit described in Chapter 23.

## Marketing Tools and Techniques

### The Dibb/Simkin Market Status Audit – As Applied to a B2B Company

The aims of this brief questionnaire are to identify the key issues in your sector, to unearth opportunities, threats, challenges and ultimately to agree key actions. The intention is also to identify under-performance and possible reasons for this. In addition, the hope is to reveal some common themes across the sectors in our business and ensure our planned activities reflect market conditions.

Sector: ______________________________

*Currently, which are our leading clients? For what?*

For each one listed, also state how much money has been brought in during the last 12 months. Also, state how much income is anticipated in the next 12 months.

| Client | For What? | Income – Current Year | Income – Expected Next Year |
|---|---|---|---|
| | | | |

*Who are the current key target prospects for new business?*

For each one listed, say for what type of work and how much income is realistically likely. Also, say how the lead came about and why each prospect is worthwhile / relevant for XXXXXXXX.

| Prospect | Type of Work/ Relevance to Us | Likely Income/Period | How Lead Came About |
|---|---|---|---|
| | | | |

*For XXXXXXXX in this sector, what are the key market drivers?*

List the key issues, but then identify which are threats or opportunities and why.

Political:

Regulatory:

Legal:

Economic:

Social:

Technological:

*Overall, from this list which are the key threats and opportunities?*

| Leading Threats | Leading Opportunities |
|---|---|
| | |

*(continued)*

*Who are our key competitors in this sector?*
For each one listed, detail their approach/standing in the sector, their strengths and apparent weaknesses.

| Competitors | Approach in Sector/Standing | Strengths | Weaknesses |
|---|---|---|---|

*Which are the ones hurting us right now? Why?*

*Which rivals are the fast movers? On what basis?*

*In each key client, identify the main personnel with whom we have a relationship (name and job description).*

*For the clients in this sector, not XXXXXXXX, identify the key market trends and drivers of most concern to them right now.*

Political:

Regulatory:

Legal:

Economic:

Social:

Technological:

Customer:

Competitor:

Supplier:

*Of these many issues, which are the priority ones for clients right now?*

*For this sector, what are our leading capabilities?*

*Are there currently any glaring gaps and deficiencies in our capability?*

*Right now, how would clients in this sector describe XXXXXXXX?*

*How would you sum up the key challenges in this sector?*

*What is required to address these challenges?*

*(continued)*

*In which areas of our operations, marketing activity and customer delivery are we underperforming?*

*In what respect and why?*

Thank you for completing this audit.



**Note:** XXXXXXXX = the identity of the organisation conducting the Dibb/Simkin Market Status Audit. The proforma when used for real contains space for responses.

**Sources:** this audit and review process is based on material from Sally Dibb, Lyndon Simkin and John Bradley, *The Marketing Planning Workbook* (London: Thomson), and Sally Dibb and Lyndon Simkin, *The Market Segmentation Workbook* (London: Thomson).

### Requirements for an Effective Control Process

A marketing manager should consider several requirements in creating and maintaining effective marketing control processes.[42] Effective control hinges on the quantity and quality of information available to the marketing manager and the speed at which it is received. The control process should be designed so that the flow of information is rapid enough to allow the marketing manager to quickly detect differences between actual and planned levels of performance. A single control procedure is not suitable for all types of marketing activity, and internal and environmental changes affect an organisation's activities. Therefore, control procedures should be flexible enough to adjust to both varied activities and changes in the organisation's situation. For the control process to be usable, its costs must be low relative to the costs that would arise if controls were lacking. Finally, the control process should be designed so that both managers and subordinates can understand it and its requirements.

### Problems in Controlling Marketing Activities

When marketing managers attempt to control marketing activities, they frequently run into several problems. Often, the information required to control marketing activities is unavailable or available only at a high cost. Even though marketing controls should be flexible enough to allow for environmental changes, the frequency, intensity and unpredictability of such changes may hamper effective control. In addition, the time lag between marketing activities and their effects limits a marketing manager's ability to measure the effectiveness of marketing activities.

Because marketing and other business activities overlap, marketing managers cannot determine the precise cost of marketing activities. Without an accurate measure of marketing costs, it is difficult to know if the effects of marketing activities are worth their expense. Marketing control may be difficult because it is very hard to develop exact performance standards for certain marketing personnel.

## Methods of Evaluating Performance

There are specific methods for assessing and improving the effectiveness of a marketing strategy. A marketer should state in the marketing plan what a marketing strategy is supposed to accomplish. These statements should set forth performance standards, which are usually stated in terms of profits, sales, market share, brand awareness, customer satisfaction levels or the variables detailed in Table 24.1. Actual performance must be measured in similar terms so that comparisons are possible. This section describes sales analysis and marketing cost analysis, two general ways of evaluating the actual performance of marketing strategies. 'Softer' measures, such as brand awareness and customer satisfaction levels, are also important and feature in the performance standards adopted by marketing-led businesses. An emerging tool for assessing performance is also described in this section: marketing shareholder value analysis.

## Sales Analysis

**Sales analysis**
The use of sales figures to evaluate a business's current performance

**Sales analysis** uses sales figures to evaluate a company's current performance. It is probably the most common method of evaluation, because sales data partially reflect the target market's reactions to a marketing mix and are often readily available, at least in aggregate form.

Marketers use current sales data to monitor the impact of current marketing efforts. However, that information alone is not enough. To provide useful analyses, current sales data must be compared with forecast sales, industry sales, specific competitors' sales or the costs incurred to achieve the sales volume. For example, knowing that a store attained a £600,000 sales volume this year does not tell management whether its marketing strategy has been successful. However, if managers know that expected sales were £550,000, they are then in a better position to determine the effectiveness of the company's marketing efforts. In addition, if they know that the marketing costs needed to achieve the £600,000 volume were 12 per cent less than budgeted, they are in an even better position to analyse their marketing strategy precisely.

**Sales measurements**
Data regarding sales transactions that are used to analyse performance, usually in terms of cash volume or market share

**Sales Measurements** Although there are several types of **sales measurement**, the basic unit of measurement is the sales transaction. A sales transaction results in a customer order for a specified quantity of an organisation's product sold under specified terms by a particular sales person or sales group on a certain date. Many organisations record these bits of information about their transactions. With such a record, a company can analyse sales in terms of cash or sales volume, or market share.

Companies frequently use cash volume sales analysis because currency is a common denominator of sales, costs and profits. However, price increases and decreases affect total sales figures. For example, if a company increased its prices by 10 per cent this year and its sales volume is 10 per cent greater than last year, it has not experienced any increase in unit sales. A marketing manager who uses cash volume analysis should factor out the effects of price changes.

**Market share**
The company's sales of a product stated as a percentage of industry sales of that product

A company's **market share** is the company's sales of a product stated as a percentage of industry sales of that product. For example, KP, Golden Wonder and Walkers account for around 70 per cent of the UK savoury snacks market. In the carbonated drinks sector, Coca-Cola has a leading 16 per cent share by volume.[43] Market share analysis permits a company to compare its marketing strategy with competitors' strategies. The primary reason for using market share analysis is to estimate whether sales changes have resulted from the company's marketing strategy or from uncontrollable environmental forces. When a company's sales volume declines but its share of the market stays the same, the marketer can assume that industry sales declined – because of some uncontrollable factors – and that this decline was reflected in the company's sales. However, if a company experiences a decline in both sales and market share, it should consider the possibility that its marketing strategy is not effective. The *competitive positions proforma* analysis described in Chapter 2 incorporates market share analysis to infer the relative performance of the competitive set within a market segment.

Even though market share analysis can be helpful in evaluating the performance of a marketing strategy, the user must interpret results cautiously. When attributing a sales decline to uncontrollable factors, a marketer must keep in mind that such factors do not affect all companies in the industry equally. Not all companies in an industry have the same objectives, and some change their objectives from one year to the next. Changes in the objectives of one company can affect the market shares of one or all companies in that industry. For example, if a competitor increases promotional efforts significantly or drastically reduces prices to increase market share, a company could lose market share despite a well-designed marketing strategy. Within an industry, the entrance of new companies or the demise of established ones also affects a specific business's market share, and market share analysts should attempt to account for these effects. KFC, for example, probably re-evaluated its marketing strategies when McDonald's introduced its own chicken products. Most fast-food companies revised their strategies and performance expectations in the light of media attention about obesity problems and drives for healthier eating.

Whether based on sales volume or market share, sales analysis can be performed on aggregate sales figures or on disaggregated data. Aggregate sales analysis provides an overview of current sales. Although helpful, aggregate sales analysis is often insufficient, because it does not bring to light sales variations within the aggregate. It is not uncommon for a marketer to find that a large proportion of aggregate sales comes from a small number of products, geographic areas or customers. This is sometimes called the 'iceberg principle' because only a small part of an iceberg is visible above the water. To find such disparities, total sales figures are usually broken down by geographic unit, sales person, product, customer type or a combination of these categories.

In sales analysis by geographic unit, sales data can be classified by city, county, region, country or any other geographic designation for which a marketer collects sales information. Actual sales in a geographic unit can be compared with sales in a similar geographic unit, with last year's sales or with an estimated market potential for the area. For example, if a company finds that 18 per cent of its sales are coming from an area that represents only 8 per cent of the potential sales for the product, then it can be assumed that the marketing strategy is successful in that geographic unit.

Because of the cost associated with hiring and maintaining a salesforce, businesses commonly analyse sales by sales person to determine the contribution each member of the salesforce makes. Performance standards for each sales person are often set in terms of sales quotas for a given time period. Evaluation of actual performance is accomplished by comparing a sales person's current sales with a pre-established quota or some other standard, such as the previous period's sales. If actual sales meet or exceed the standard, and the sales representative has not incurred costs above those budgeted, that person's efforts are acceptable.

Sales analysis is often performed according to product group or specific product item. Marketers break down their aggregate sales figures by product to determine the proportion that each contributed to total sales. Buena Vista, for example, might break down its total sales figures by box office figures for each film produced. A company usually sets a sales volume objective – and sometimes a market share objective – for each product item or product group, and sales analysis by product is the only way to measure such objectives. A marketer can compare the breakdown of current sales by product with those of previous years. In addition, within industries for which sales data by product are available, a company's sales by product type can be compared with industry averages. To gain an accurate picture of where sales of specific products are occurring, marketers sometimes combine sales analysis by product with sales analysis by geographic area or sales person.

Analyses based on customers are usually broken down by type of customer. Customers can be classified by the way they use a company's products, their distribution level – producer, wholesaler, retailer – size, the size of orders, or other characteristics. Sales analysis by customer type enables a company to ascertain whether its marketing resources are allocated in a way that achieves the greatest productivity. For example, sales analysis by type of customer may reveal that 60 per cent of the salesforce is serving a group that accounts for only 15 per cent of total sales.

A considerable amount of information is needed for sales analyses, especially if disaggregated analyses are desired. The marketer must develop an operational system for collecting sales information; obviously, the effectiveness of the system for collecting sales information largely determines the ability of a company to develop useful sales analyses. As outlined in Chapter 19, control of a salesforce is part of effective sales management, and most organisations routinely scrutinise the performance of their salesforces.

## Marketing Cost Analysis

Although sales analysis is critical for evaluating the effectiveness of a marketing strategy, it gives only part of the picture. A marketing strategy that successfully generates sales may

**Marketing cost analysis**
The breakdown and classification of costs to determine which are associated with specific marketing activities

also be extremely costly. To obtain a complete picture, a company must know the marketing costs associated with using a given strategy to achieve a certain sales level. **Marketing cost analysis** breaks down and classifies costs to determine which are associated with specific marketing activities. By comparing the costs of previous marketing activities with results generated, a marketer can better allocate the business's marketing resources in the future. Marketing cost analysis lets a company evaluate the effectiveness of an ongoing or recent marketing strategy by comparing sales achieved and costs incurred. By pinpointing exactly where a company is experiencing high costs, this form of analysis can help isolate profitable or unprofitable customer segments, products or geographic areas.

For example, the market share of Komatsu, a Japanese construction equipment manufacturer, began to decline in the United States when prices increased because of the high yen value. Komatsu responded by developing an equal joint venture with Dresser Industries, making it the second largest company in this industry. The joint venture with Dresser allowed Komatsu to shift a large amount of its final assembly to the United States, to Dresser plants that had been running at 50 per cent capacity. By using Dresser's unused capacity and existing US plants, Komatsu avoided the start-up costs of new construction and gained an immediate manufacturing presence in the United States.[44] This cost control tactic enabled Komatsu to use price more effectively as a marketing variable to compete with industry leader Caterpillar.

In some organisations, personnel in other functional areas – such as production or accounting – perceive marketers as primarily concerned with generating sales, regardless of the costs incurred. Marketers often do commit a large proportion of resources to launching products, achieving distribution or creating promotional campaigns. By conducting cost analyses, marketers can counter this criticism and put themselves in a better position to demonstrate how marketing activities contribute to generating profits. Even though hiring a sports figure such as David Beckham is costly, in many sectors sales goals cannot be reached without large expenditures for promotion. Many advertisers believe that using celebrities helps to increase sales. Research shows that the public are good at identifying which personalities are linked to advertised brands. Ultimately, cost analysis should show if promotion costs are effective in increasing sales.

A robust marketing plan – see Chapter 23 – is not complete without a detailed budget which, when balanced with the sales forecast, marketing analyses, strategic thinking and detailed marketing mix programmes, explains the required marketing spend. In effect, a sound marketing plan should offer a cost – benefit analysis in terms of setting the anticipated costs of rolling out the proposed marketing programmes against the expected sales levels and revenue gains. Marketing cost analysis is a necessary facet for managing a well-run marketing department.

The task of determining marketing costs is often complex and difficult. Simply ascertaining the costs associated with marketing a product is rarely adequate. Marketers must usually determine the marketing costs of serving specific geographic areas, market segments or even specific customers. The ABC sales: contribution analysis outlined in Chapter 12 is a useful tool in this endeavour.

**Natural accounts**
The classification of costs based on how money was actually spent

**Marketing function accounts**
A method of indicating the function performed through the expenditure of funds

A first step in determining the costs is to examine accounting records. Most accounting systems classify costs into **natural accounts** – such as rent, salaries, office supplies and utilities – which are based on how the money was actually spent. Unfortunately, many natural accounts do not help explain what marketing functions were performed through the expenditure of those funds. It does little good, for example, to know that £80,000 is spent for rent each year. The analyst has no way of knowing whether the money is spent for the rental of production, storage or sales facilities. Therefore, marketing cost analysis usually requires some of the costs in natural accounts to be reclassified into **marketing function accounts**, which indicate the function performed through the expenditure of funds. Common marketing function accounts are transport, storage, order processing, sales, advertising, sales promotion, marketing research, consultancy and customer credit.

**Direct costs** Costs directly attributable to the performance of marketing functions

**Traceable common costs** Costs that can be allocated indirectly, using one or several criteria, to the functions they support

**Non-traceable common costs** Costs that cannot be assigned according to any logical criteria

**Full cost approach** An approach in which cost analysis includes direct costs, traceable common costs and non-traceable common costs

**Direct cost approach** An approach that includes only direct costs and traceable common costs

Natural accounts can be reclassified into marketing function accounts, as shown in the simplified example in Table 24.2. Note that a few natural accounts, such as advertising, can be reclassified easily into functional accounts because they do not have to be split across several accounts. For most of the natural accounts, however, marketers must develop criteria for assigning them to the various functional accounts. For example, the number of square metres of floor space used was the criterion for dividing the rental costs in Table 24.2 into functional accounts. In some instances, a specific marketing cost is incurred to perform several functions. A packaging cost, for example, could be considered a production function, a distribution function, a promotional function or all three. The marketing cost analyst must reclassify such costs across multiple functions.

Three broad categories are used in marketing cost analysis: direct costs, traceable common costs and non-traceable common costs. **Direct costs** are directly attributable to the performance of marketing functions. For example, salesforce salaries might be allocated to the cost of selling a specific product item, selling in a specific geographic area or selling to a particular customer. **Traceable common costs** can be allocated indirectly, using one or several criteria, to the functions that they support. For example, if the company spends £80,000 annually to rent space for production, storage and selling, the rental costs of storage could be determined on the basis of cost per square metre used for storage. **Non-traceable common costs** cannot be assigned according to any logical criteria and thus are assignable only on an arbitrary basis. Interest, taxes and the salaries of top management are non-traceable common costs.

The manner of dealing with these three categories of costs depends on whether the analyst uses a full cost or a direct cost approach. When a **full cost approach** is used, cost analysis includes direct costs, traceable common costs and non-traceable common costs. Proponents of this approach claim that if an accurate profit picture is desired, all costs must be included in the analysis. However, opponents point out that full costing does not yield actual costs, because non-traceable common costs are determined by arbitrary criteria. With different criteria, the full costing approach yields different results. A cost-conscious operating unit can be discouraged if numerous costs are assigned to it arbitrarily. To eliminate such problems, the **direct cost approach**, which includes direct costs and traceable common

**TABLE 24.2 RECLASSIFICATION OF NATURAL ACCOUNTS INTO FUNCTIONAL ACCOUNTS**

| Profit and loss statement | | Functional accounts | | | | | |
|---|---|---|---|---|---|---|---|
| | | Advertising | Personal selling | Transport | Storage | Marketing research | Non-marketing |
| **Sales** | £250,000 | | | | | | |
| **Cost of goods sold** | 45,000 | | | | | | |
| **Gross profit** | 205,000 | | | | | | |
| **Expenses (natural accounts)** | | | | | | | |
| Rent | £ 14,000 | | £ 7,000 | | £6,000 | | £ 1,000 |
| Salaries | 72,000 | £12,000 | 32,000 | £7,000 | | £1,000 | 20,000 |
| Supplies | 4,000 | 1,500 | 1,000 | | | 1,000 | 500 |
| Advertising | 16,000 | 16,000 | | | | | |
| Freight | 4,000 | | | 2,000 | | | 2,000 |
| Taxes | 2,000 | | | | 200 | | 1,800 |
| Insurance | 1,000 | | | | 600 | | 400 |
| Interest | 3,000 | | | | | | 3,000 |
| Bad debts | 6,000 | | | | | | 6,000 |
| **Total** | £ 122,000 | £29,500 | £40,000 | £9,000 | £6,800 | £2,000 | £34,700 |
| **Net profit** | £ 83,000 | | | | | | |

costs but not non-traceable common costs, is used. Opponents say that this approach is not accurate, because it omits one cost category.

Marketers can use several methods to analyse costs. The methods vary in their precision. This section examines three cost analysis methods:

1 analysis of natural accounts
2 analysis of functional accounts
3 analysis by product, geographic area or customer.

**Analysis of Natural Accounts** Marketers can sometimes determine marketing costs by performing an analysis of natural accounts. The precision of this method depends on how detailed the company's accounts are. For example, if accounting records contain separate accounts for production wages, salesforce wages and executive salaries, the analysis can be more precise than if all wages and salaries are lumped into a single account. An analysis of natural accounts is more meaningful, and thus more useful, when current cost data can be compared with those of previous periods or with average cost figures for the entire industry. Cost analysis of natural accounts frequently treats costs as percentages of sales. The periodic use of cost-to-sales ratios lets a marketer ascertain cost fluctuations quickly.

**Analysis of Functional Accounts** The analysis of natural accounts may not shed much light on the cost of marketing activities. In such cases, natural accounts must be reclassified into marketing function accounts for analysis. Whether certain natural accounts are reclassified into functional accounts and what criteria are used to reclassify them will depend to some degree on whether the analyst is using direct costing or full costing. After natural accounts have been reclassified into functional accounts, the cost of each function is determined by adding together the costs in each functional account. Once the costs of these marketing functions have been determined, the analyst is ready to compare the resulting figures with budgeted costs, sales analysis data, cost data from earlier operating periods or perhaps average industry cost figures, if these are available.

**Analysis by Product, Geographic Area or Customer** Although marketers usually obtain a more detailed picture of marketing costs by analysing functional accounts than by analysing natural accounts, some businesses need an even more precise cost analysis. The need is especially great if the businesses sell several types of product, sell in multiple geographic areas or sell to a wide variety of customers. Activities vary in marketing different products in specific geographic locations to certain customer groups. Therefore, the costs of these activities also vary. By analysing the functional costs of specific product groups, geographic areas or customer groups, a marketer can find out which of these marketing

**TABLE 24.3 FUNCTIONAL ACCOUNTS DIVIDED INTO PRODUCT GROUP COSTS**

| | | Product groups | | |
|---|---|---|---|---|
| **Functional accounts** | | **A** | **B** | **C** |
| Advertising | £29,500 | £14,000 | £ 8,000 | £ 7,500 |
| Personal selling | 40,000 | 18,000 | 10,000 | 12,000 |
| Transport | 9,000 | 5,000 | 2,000 | 2,000 |
| Storage | 6,800 | 1,800 | 2,000 | 3,000 |
| Marketing research | 2,000 | | 1,000 | 1,000 |
| Total | £87,300 | £38,800 | £23,000 | £25,500 |

entities are the most cost effective to serve. In Table 24.3, the functional costs derived in Table 24.2 are allocated to specific product categories.

A similar type of analysis could be performed for geographic areas or for specific customer groups. The criteria used to allocate the functional accounts must be developed so as to yield results that are as accurate as possible. Use of faulty criteria is likely to yield inaccurate cost estimates, which in turn lead to less effective control of marketing strategies. Marketers determine the marketing costs for various product categories, geographic areas or customer groups and then compare them with sales. This analysis allows them to evaluate the effectiveness of the company's marketing strategy or strategies.

## Marketing Shareholder Value Analysis

**Value-based marketing** The inclusion of the value of a marketing strategy and marketing activity in an organisation's financial analysis of shareholder value

**Marketing shareholder value analysis (MSVA)** Divides the estimation of the value to the organisation created by a marketing strategy into two components: (1) the present value of cash flows during the strategising and planning phases (2) the continuing value after implementation of the strategy

Building on the rationale for marketing cost analysis, the concept of value-based marketing has emerged in recent years. **Value-based marketing** is the inclusion of the value of a marketing strategy and programme in an organisation's financial analysis of shareholder value. To achieve this, **marketing shareholder value analysis (MSVA)** divides the estimation of the value to the business created by a marketing strategy into two components:

1 the present value of cash flows during the strategising and planning phases
2 the continuing value following implementation of the strategy.

MSVA provides a means of demonstrating the contribution of marketing to the organisation's financial performance. This also enables marketing assets, such as marketing knowledge, brands, customer loyalty and strategic relationships, to be included in the shareholder value analysis (SVA), as each can be shown to have quantifiable financial value to the business. MSVA enables marketers to communicate the expected results of their marketing strategies in terms comprehended by top management and investors. The analysis supports marketers' requests for budgets, notably those traditionally most at risk of cost cutting in times of reduced demand, such as advertising and marketing research.

In many organisations, the lack of a true marketing orientation has allowed the finance function to take over the notion of shareholder value analysis (SVA).[45] According to leading marketing strategist Peter Doyle, by focusing on short-term profits and ignoring intangible assets – such as brand awareness and customer satisfaction – traditional accounting practices have marginalised marketing activity. However, SVA can in fact bring the core strategic drivers of marketing to the fore in the form of MSVA. Marketing has struggled to quantify results in order to demonstrate its value. By adopting MSVA, marketers can reverse this state of affairs. MSVA can help justify marketing actions in terms of their propensity to bring financial value to the business. MSVA offers marketing a greater theoretical base and encourages profitable marketing investment. MSVA also penalises arbitrary cuts to the marketing budget, something encountered regularly by marketers when a company's fortunes decline suddenly.

Table 26.1 presents information about financial ratios useful in evaluating performance.

## Performance Measures

The evaluation of **marketing performance** – the assessment of the effectiveness of marketing programmes to implement recommended marketing strategies, fulfil corporate financial expectations and achieve the required levels of customer satisfaction – is a necessary control mechanism in the marketing process. Table 24.1 presented some popular performance measures adopted by marketers to assess overall markets, specific segments or product lines. Most UK companies are notoriously short term in their thinking, focusing on profitability as their overriding measure. Other financial measures include return on investment, return on capital employed and, for retailers, **sales per square metre** of selling space. Units produced and units sold are included as measures by most manufacturers, leading to an assessment of production capacity utilisation. Market share is a vital criterion for judging performance.

**Marketing performance**
The assessment of the effectiveness of marketing programmes to implement recommended marketing strategies, fulfil corporate financial expectations and achieve the required levels of customer satisfaction.

**Sales per square metre**
A financial measure retailers might use to assess marketing performance

**Customer satisfaction**
A qualitative measure of marketing performance that involves surveying customers over time

**Brand awareness**
A qualitative measure of marketing performance that determines whether a company's brands capture the attention of their target markets

**Clippings service**
A service that counts the frequency of mentions of a specific brand or company in selected media

While it is, unquestionably, important for businesses to be financially viable – making adequate profits to be able to fund future investments in production, people, new products, new target markets, and so forth – increasingly marketers have accepted the need to evaluate performance on additional, more customer oriented measures. Marketing aims to satisfy customers, so it is sensible to monitor customer satisfaction. A qualitative measure of marketing performance, assessing **customer satisfaction** involves surveying customers' perceptions and expectations over time in order to determine the effectiveness of the marketing programme in servicing their needs. Over time, such surveys should reveal an improvement in customer satisfaction levels, otherwise it could be argued that the marketing strategy and programme are failing to fully address target customer needs and expectations. Most hotel companies operate room card surveys of guest satisfaction in order to monitor customers' experiences and improve the performance of their staff, services and facilities. A measure of **brand awareness** is also monitored by a growing number of marketers, usually through qualitative marketing research surveys, to ensure that their marketing programmes are effectively bringing their brands and products to their target market's attention. While such tracking involves qualitative marketing research, measures of customer satisfaction and brand awareness should be integral to a business's assessment of performance, alongside the important traditional financial performance measures.

Marketing communications is a major part of marketers' activity and accounts for a significant proportion of the marketing budget. Performance in the promotional mix, however, has taxed experts for decades and there remain few proven objective solutions to determining the value of promotional spend to the business's overall fortunes. It is possible in public relations to use a **clippings service** to count the frequency of mentions of a specific brand or company in selected media, but this approach fails to assess the positive/negative mix of citations and cannot extrapolate to draw conclusions relating to sales gains resulting specifically from this PR activity. 'Hits' on a company's website are counted, but do these lead to sales or an enhanced corporate reputation? If an order is placed via the Internet a link can be shown, but if not it is difficult to demonstrate a causal relationship between the website and sales. Even if an order is placed via the Internet, it is possible that the customer was in fact responding primarily to a press or TV advertisement or to an earlier in-store demonstration. Sponsorship agencies monitor the awareness of clients' brands when linked to sporting events or the performing arts, but cannot prove that such awareness leads directly to increased sales of products, better profitability or rising market share.

Salesforce managers assess individual sales personnel in terms of the ratio of calls to orders. In addition, the salesforce is directly involved in the selling process and instantly judges its own performance. What stands for a good ratio of orders to calls is still a subjective assessment. Sales promotions are perhaps the safest to measure as they generally require customers to redeem coupons and vouchers or submit competition applications, all of which may be counted. However, subjective judgement is still used in determining what constitutes a 'good' redemption rate. Most problematic is the assessment of advertising effectiveness. This is unfortunate as advertising often accounts for the largest individual proportion of the marketing budget. It is possible, as described in Chapter 18, to monitor target audience awareness of advertising but not to prove that exposure to a specific advertisement has led to a specific sale. At the moment, there are no easy solutions to this dilemma, yet marketers must attempt to assess the performance of their activities, seeking to validate their promotional mix spending. The tools described here are far from perfect but they demonstrate a willingness to assess promotional effectiveness. Many businesses, unfortunately, fail to utilise even these simplistic tools.[46]

Ultimately, a well-managed, customer-oriented company should use a mix of financial and qualitative measures, such as those listed in Table 24.1, to judge its performance and the effectiveness of its marketing. A company should adopt a balanced set of performance measures, mixing the short-term view of profitability with the often longer-term perspective of market share gains. It often requires considerable resources to increase market share at the expense of rivals, which may reduce short-term profitability. However, market share increases are likely to bring longer-term security and rewards. In addition to the financial performance measures, marketers should insist on being assessed on dimensions such as customer retention, customer satisfaction and brand awareness. If marketing programmes are effective, these three customer-oriented criteria should all show signs of improvement. Whatever the selected criteria for assessing marketing performance, it is essential that marketers incorporate performance monitoring within their control and management processes.

# Summary

The organisation of marketing activities involves allocating responsibilities for the marketing process and the development of an internal structure for the marketing unit, including relationships and lines of authority and responsibility that connect and coordinate individuals. The internal structure is the key to directing marketing activities. In a *marketing-oriented organisation*, the focus is on finding out what buyers want and providing it in a way that enables the company to achieve its objectives. A *centralised organisation* is one in which the top-level managers delegate very little authority to lower levels of the business. In a *decentralised organisation*, decision-making authority is delegated as far down the chain of command as possible. An extreme form of decentralisation is *empowerment*, in which front-line employees are given the authority and responsibility to make marketing decisions without seeking the approval of their supervisors.

» The marketing unit can be *organised by* (1) *functions*, (2) *products*, (3) *regions* or (4) *types of customer. Category management* is an in-vogue variation of organising by products. An organisation may use only one approach or a combination.

» *Marketing implementation*, a process that involves activities to put marketing strategies into action, is an important part of the marketing management process. The *requisites for implementation* include process, skill, leadership, empowerment, communication, timing, information, resource and participation decisions. Failure to address these issues prior to embarking on marketing strategy formulation or the development of a marketing plan may result in the failure to produce recommendations that are implemented. To help ensure effective implementation, marketing managers must consider why the intended marketing strategies do not always turn out as expected. The *intended strategies* often differ from the *realised strategies* because of the three problems of implementation: marketing strategy and implementation are related; they are constantly evolving; the responsibility for them is separated. Marketing managers must also consider other vital components of implementation – resources, systems, people, leadership and shared goals – to ensure the proper implementation of marketing strategies.

» Implementation is an important part of the marketing management process. Proper implementation of a marketing plan depends on internal marketing to motivate personnel who perform marketing activities, effective communication within the marketing unit and the coordination of marketing activities. Managers can motivate personnel by linking rewards, both financial and non-financial, to organisational goals. A company's communication system must allow the marketing manager to communicate with high-level management, with managers of other functional areas in the company and with personnel involved in marketing activities both inside and outside the organisation. Finally, marketing managers must coordinate the activities of marketing personnel, and integrate these activities with those in other areas of the company and with the marketing efforts of personnel in external organisations.

» Related approaches that organisations may use to help facilitate marketing implementation include *relationship marketing*, *internal marketing* and *total quality management (TQM)*. In relationship marketing, the focus is on winning and keeping customers by maintaining links between marketing, quality and customer service. This requires a company to satisfy not only customers but also those audiences in the *five markets model of relationship marketing*: referral, supplier, employee recruitment markets, influencer and internal markets. *Internal marketing* is the application of marketing internally within the company, with programmes of communication and guidance targeted at internal audiences to develop responsiveness and a unified sense of purpose among employees. It is a philosophy for managing human resources with a marketing perspective so that all members of the marketing organisation understand and accept their respective roles in implementing the marketing strategy.

» The TQM approach relies heavily on the talents of employees to continually improve the quality of the organisation's goods and services. The three essentials of the TQM philosophy are empowered employees, continuous quality improvement and the use of quality improvement teams. One of TQM's primary tools is *benchmarking*, or measuring and evaluating the quality of an organisation's goods, services or processes in relation to the best-performing companies in the industry. Putting the TQM philosophy into practice requires a great deal of organisational resources. For relationship marketing, internal marketing or TQM to be successful, top management must be totally committed and the specific elements of these programmes must be coordinated to ensure that they work in harmony with each other.

» The *marketing control process* consists of establishing performance standards, evaluating actual performance by comparing it with established standards, and reducing the difference between desired and actual performance. *Performance standards*, which are established in the planning process, are expected levels of performance against which actual performance can be compared. In evaluating actual performance, marketing managers must know what marketers within the business are doing and must have information about the activities of external organisations that provide the company with marketing assistance. Then actual performance is compared with performance standards. Marketers must determine whether a discrepancy exists and, if so, whether it requires corrective action, such as changing the performance standards or improving actual performance.

» Effective marketing control hinges on the quantity and quality of information and the speed at which it is received. The control of marketing activities is not a simple task. Problems encountered include environmental changes, time lags between marketing activities and their effects, and difficulty in determining the costs of marketing activities. In addition to these, it may be hard to develop exact performance standards for marketing personnel.

» Control of marketing strategy can be achieved through *sales* and *marketing cost analyses*. *Sales measurements* are usually analysed in terms of either cash volume or *market share*. For a sales analysis to be effective, it must compare current sales performance with either forecast company sales, industry sales, specific competitors' sales or the costs incurred to generate the current sales volume. A sales analysis can be performed on the company's total sales, or the total sales can be disaggregated and analysed by product, geographic area, sales person or customer type.

» Marketing cost analysis involves an examination of accounting records and, frequently, a reclassification of *natural accounts* into *marketing function accounts*. Three broad categories are used in marketing cost analysis: *direct costs*, *traceable common costs* and *non-traceable common costs*. Such an analysis is often difficult, because there may be no logical, clear-cut way to allocate natural accounts into functional accounts. The analyst may choose either a *full cost approach* or *direct cost approach*. Cost analysis can focus on (1) an aggregate cost analysis of natural accounts or functional accounts, or (2) an analysis of functional accounts for products, geographic areas or customer groups.

*Value-based marketing* is the inclusion of the value of a marketing strategy and marketing activity in an organisation's financial analysis of shareholder value. *Marketing shareholder value analysis (MSVA)* enables marketing strategies and programmes to be incorporated within this financial appraisal of shareholder value. The value to the business of a marketing strategy is estimated, based on (1) the present value of the business during the strategising and planning stage, and (2) the continuing value of the business after the plans have been implemented and actioned.

Performance measures popular in evaluating *marketing performance* include assessing overall markets, specific segments or product lines in terms of financial profitability, contribution or return on investment; market share; *customer satisfaction* levels; and qualitative measures of customer *brand awareness*. Retail marketers additionally favour a measure of *sales per square metre* of store selling space. A *clippings service* can be used to count the frequency of mentions of a particular brand or company in the media.

## Key Links

The implementation of marketing strategy and programmes, controls and the assessment of performance goes hand in hand with the creation of marketing strategies and marketing plans. With this in mind, read this chapter in conjunction with:

- Chapter 1, on the evolution of marketing towards the relationship marketing era
- Chapter 2, on marketing strategy development
- Chapter 23, on marketing planning and associated processes.

## Important Terms

Marketing-oriented organisation
Centralised organisation
Decentralised organisation
Empowerment
Organising by function
Organising by product
Category management
Organising by region
Organising by type of customer
Marketing implementation
Requisites for implementation
Intended strategy
Realised strategy
Relationship marketing
Five markets model of relationship marketing
Internal marketing
Total quality management (TQM)
Benchmarking
Marketing control process
Performance standard
Sales analysis
Sales measurements
Market share
Marketing cost analysis
Natural accounts
Marketing function accounts
Direct costs
Traceable common costs
Non-traceable common costs
Full cost approach
Direct cost approach
Value-based marketing
Marketing shareholder value analysis (MSVA)
Marketing performance
Sales per square metre
Customer satisfaction
Brand awareness
Clippings service

## Discussion and Review Questions

1 What determines the place of marketing within an organisation? Which type of organisation is best suited to the marketing concept? Why?
2 What marketing activities must be undertaken by an organisation striving to establish the marketing concept at its heart?
3 What factors can be used to organise the internal aspects of a marketing unit? Discuss the benefits of each type of organisation.
4 Why might an organisation use multiple bases for organising its marketing unit?
5 What are the implementation requisites for marketing strategies and plans?
6 Why is motivation of marketing personnel important in implementing marketing plans?

7 How does communication help in implementing marketing plans?
8 What attributes distinguish relationship marketing from transaction-based marketing?
9 What is internal marketing? Why is it important in implementing marketing strategies?
10 Total quality management is a growing force in many businesses. What is TQM? How can it help to implement marketing strategies effectively?
11 What are the major steps of the marketing control process?
12 List and discuss the five requirements for an effective control process.
13 Discuss the major problems in controlling marketing activities.
14 What is a sales analysis? What makes it an effective control tool?
15 Identify and describe three cost analysis methods. Compare and contrast direct costing and full costing.
16 What is marketing shareholder value analysis? What are its strengths?
17 What performance measures are favoured by marketers?

## Recommended Readings


- Aaker, D.A., *Managing Brand Equity* (New York: Free Press, 1999).
- Aaker, D., *Strategic Marketing Management* (New York: Wiley, 2001).
- Dibb, S., Simkin, L. and Bradley, J., *The Marketing Planning Workbook* (London: International Thomson Business Press, 1998).
- Doyle, P., *Value-Based Marketing* (Chichester: Wiley, 2000).
- Jain, S.C., *Marketing Planning and Strategy* (Cincinnati OH: South Western, 2000).
- McDonald, M., *Marketing Plans* (Oxford: Butterworth-Heinemann, 2002).
- Piercy, N., *Market-led Strategic Change* (Oxford: Butterworth-Heinemann, 2001).


## Internet Exercise

If you are working, look at your organisation's website or intranet. If you are studying, look at the intranet in your academic institution.

1 What elements of internal marketing are evident in the website's sections?
2 In what ways is the content attempting to control, coordinate and share information with employees or people within the organisation?
3 How else could the organisation communicate its marketing strategy and marketing plan intentions to internal stakeholders?

## *Applied Mini-Case*

A leading IT services company had been marketing its IT outsourcing solutions to manufacturers, financial services companies, retailers, health providers, government departments and other sectors. The new head of its business unit, charged with marketing IT solutions to the manufacturing sector (automotive, pharmaceuticals, electrical components, domestic appliances, and so on) decided that, rather than market to the businesses involved with manufacturing, the company should identify the providers of facilities, such as offices and factories, purchased by these manufacturers in order to produce their products. The plan was to promote the IT business to the big construction companies so that when a new-build factory was commissioned, the IT business would already be the agreed supplier to the building contractor. There are far fewer major construction companies than manufacturers, so this novel approach to achieving sales was accepted by the IT business's board. However, the new strategy required a major change of behaviour as sales and marketing resources were moved from selling to manufacturers to building relationships with construction companies.

### *Question*

Suggest the problems likely to be encountered inside the IT company as it attempts to realign its operations around this new target market strategy. What steps would the company need to take to pre-empt such obstacles?

## Case Study

# Timex Stands the Test of Time

During the 1970s, watches took a technological leap forward, from wind-up spring mechanisms to quartz crystals, batteries and digital displays. The Timex Corporation, however, lagged behind other manufacturers in making such changes. When the Swiss-made Swatch watch invaded department stores and convinced customers that their watches were not just time-telling devices but fashion statements, Timex was not ready to offer any competition. At Timex, reliability had always been the number one priority, certainly not style and fashion. For years, Timex's sales suffered because of its drab image, especially in contrast with the colourful Swatch.

Then came the 1990s: the decade of value. As value came to take precedence over status, more price-conscious consumers were attracted by quality at moderate prices than by designer labels. Timex took advantage of this trend to revive its 41-year-old brand, the old reliable Timex watch. By blending its 'value pricing' message with some trendy new designs and diversifying its product for specific niche markets, Timex made a comeback. Now, Timex regularly features in surveys of the leading trendy fashion brands.

Consumers can still buy an unadorned Timex watch for under £10, and analysts say that these simple styles with easy-to-read faces are the company's best-sellers. To compete in a crowded market, however, Timex developed stylish special collections for separate adult divisions: dress watches, sports watches, technology watches and outdoor watches. In addition, the children's division is important to the company's sales. Timex set up studios in France and the United States to design Timex's own versions of colourful creative watches. In the adult fashion arena, Timex offers women its Images line, with neon-accented hands, floral-patterned straps, and over-sized faces, and men the Carriage III collection. For those with poor vision, Timex has created the Easy Reader, with large clear numbers. Sports watch buyers can choose from models with names like Surf, Brave Wave and Magnum, which are shock and water resistant, and offer extra features such as compasses, pedometers, chronographs and thermometers. After soliciting educators' advice, the company came up with its Gizmoz watches to help children aged from five to nine to tell the time. Colourful designs are on the band instead of the face, which displays all of the numbers, and has colour-coded hour and minute hands. For example, black-faced watches have white hour markers and hour hands but green minute markers and minute hands. There is even a Lefty Gizmoz available. To appeal to parents, whose money really buys the Gizmoz watches, Timex offers a kids' loss-protection plan that replaces a watch for only half the purchase price.

As well as clocks and watches, Timex produces healthcare products such as digital thermometers, eye wear, alarm radios, thermostats, timers and nightlights.

Timex's advertising strategy is to appeal to niche markets by reviving its traditional 'durable yet inexpensive' positioning, and revitalising its powerful brand identity. The famous Timex theme, 'It Takes a Licking and Keeps On Ticking', has taken a humorous bent in television spots where sumo wrestlers wear the watches strapped to their middles as they grapple on the mat, and rock musicians use Timex watches to strum their guitars. In a print advertising campaign, the company featured real people who, like the Timex watches they wear, have been through rough experiences but survived to tell the tale. On television talk shows, company executives introduced the Timex *Why Pay More* magazine, featuring Timex watches as part of fashion outfits selling for under £50.

With watch sales in most countries declining, most watchmakers are concerned. At Timex, however, executives are celebrating sales and market share increases. The company now controls a larger segment of the market than its four biggest competitors combined. Timex is happy to be shedding its dowdy and boring image. Rising young professional people do not have to put their wrists behind their backs to hide a Timex any more, or announce loudly to colleagues that they are only wearing a Timex while their Rolex is being repaired.

Ruthless controls and continual performance monitoring are intended to avoid a repeat of the 1980s doldrums period. Marketing executives have monitored the marketing strategy carefully in order to:

- ensure that signs of success or failure can be acted upon, and
- modify marketing programmes continually in order to enhance the impact of Timex's new approach.

Sales and financial performance are evaluated regularly; so far, they reveal a success story. Changing fashions and aggressive competitors such as Swatch caught Timex out once before. The company does not intend to be left behind again. With 7500 employees in four continents, growing sales and a successful defence against the likes of Swatch, the future looks bright for Timex.

**Sources:** Sylvesters, 2004; Cara Appelbaum, 'High time for Timex', *Adweek's Marketing Week*, 29 July 1991, p. 24; BBC/ITN news broadcasts, Spring 1993; 'Timex races for Indiglo profits', *Marketing*, 31 March 1994, p. 3; 'Briefs', *Marketing*, 6 January 1994, p. 6; 'Rzed opens shop with Timex infomercial', *Campaign*, 19 May 1995, p. 8; www.timexpo.com, July 2004.

## Questions for Discussion

1. Which environmental forces are likely to be of greatest interest to marketing managers at Timex?
2. Identify the target markets towards which Timex is aiming its products.
3. Why must Timex continually assess its performance and the impact of its marketing?

# 25 Social Responsibility and Marketing Ethics

**"Virtues such as honesty are not always self-evident when applied to complex marketing decisions."**

*O.C. Ferrell, Colorado State University*

## Objectives

- To understand the concept and dimensions of social responsibility
- To define and describe the importance of marketing ethics
- To become familiar with ways to improve ethical decisions in marketing
- To understand the role of social responsibility and ethics in improving marketing performance

## Introduction

Social responsibility and ethics can have a profound impact on the success of marketing strategies. This chapter gives an overview of how social responsibility and ethics must be considered in marketing decision-making. Most marketers operate responsibly and within the limits of the law. However, some companies engage in activities that customers, other marketers and society in general deem unacceptable. Such activities include questionable selling practices, bribery, price discrimination, deceptive advertising, misleading packaging and marketing defective products. For example, 37 per cent of the software programmes used by businesses worldwide are illegally pirated copies.[1] Practices of this kind raise questions about marketers' obligations to society. Inherent in these questions are the issues of social responsibility and marketing ethics.

## Opener

## Why the Food Industry Must Face up to its Responsibilities

Concerns about childhood obesity and its impact on future health have never been greater. A recent Health Select Committee UK government report suggested that obesity levels are up by nearly 400 per cent in 25 years, with around 75 per cent of the population now regarded as either overweight or obese. It is feared that obesity will soon overtake smoking as the major cause of premature death. The report blames a number of factors for the epidemic, but focuses particularly on the need for marketers and advertising to change the way unhealthy food is promoted. This has led to calls for the food industry to set up a self-regulatory body and to put its house in order. The implications are clear: if the industry fails to take action to market unhealthy foods in a more responsible way, legislative changes will be made. Such action might, for example, include outlawing advertisements for unhealthy food targeted at children. There has been particular criticism of campaigns for junk food, such as crisps and carbonated soft drinks, aimed at encouraging 'pester power'. The use of sporting celebrities to endorse such unhealthy snacks has also been criticised.

Key proposals from the Health Select Committee Report are as follows:

- Voluntary withdrawal of advertising of junk food aimed at children from television, within the next three years.
- A review of marketing of unhealthy foods, including product endorsement by celebrities, such as sports stars.
- The introduction of a 'traffic light' system of labelling – red for foods high in sugar and fat through to green for products low in sugar and fat.
- Guidance to be offered to schools, strongly recommending that they do not accept sponsorship from manufacturers of unhealthy foods or vending machines selling such products.
- The number of hours of sport at schools should be increased and school meals improved. Children should be encouraged to walk or cycle to school with improved cycle lanes and walkways.
- The launch of government-funded campaigns aimed at promoting healthy food options and balanced lifestyles.
- The government and the food industry to work to reduce levels of salt, sugar and fat in all products and make healthier foods more affordable.
- The government to consider introducing a 'fat tax' on food manufacturers and to monitor the progress of this in other countries.

Meanwhile the World Health Organization (WHO) has published a global strategy on diet, health and physical activity, which asks those involved in the manufacture and sale of food to introduce more healthy products and to use clear labelling that provides easy-to-understand and accurate nutritional information. The publication comes at a time when supermarkets Tesco and ASDA have recently been prosecuted by trading standards officers over the strength of their claims about fruit and vegetables preventing cancer. The WHO report encourages businesses to be responsible in how unhealthy foods are marketed to children, but also apparently supports food manufacturer initiatives that 'assist in developing and implementing physical activity programmes'. Recent examples of such initiatives include Kellogg's pedometer give-away and the Cadbury's 'Get Active' campaign.

Health experts acknowledge that the food industry is not entirely to blame for the obesity crisis, indicating that inactive lifestyles and poor parenting have also played a role. However, as the problem continues to escalate, it is clear that the food industry must be both proactive and innovative in its response if far-reaching legislative changes are to be avoided.

**Sources:** 'Key proposals' list adapted from the table 'Key proposals from the HSC report', p. 29 in Caroline Parry, 'Defusing the timebomb', *Marketing Week*, 3 June 2004, pp. 26–9; Emily Rogers, 'Pressure builds on food industry', *Marketing*, 26 May 2004, p. 4; Caroline Parry, 'Defusing the timebomb', *Marketing Week*, 3 June 2004, pp. 26–9; Emily Rogers, 'Adland takes up fat challenge', *Marketing*, 11 March 2004, p. 19; Claire Murphy, 'WHO calls for "clearer" food packaging', *Marketing*, 26 May 2004, p. 4; 'FSA to spotlight health offenders', *Marketing*, 26 May 2004, p. 4. Photo © Najlah Feanny/Corbis

As explained in Chapter 6, children play an important role in many purchases, leading manufacturers and retailers to target them in their marketing efforts. Such activities have been particularly prevalent in the marketing of so-called junk foods. However, at a time when childhood obesity is a major concern, such marketing activity has ethical and social responsibility implications. These implications are considered in more detail throughout this chapter.

This chapter begins by defining social responsibility and exploring its dimensions. Various social responsibility issues, such as the natural environment and the marketer's role as a member of the community, are then discussed. Next, the definition and role of ethics in marketing decisions are explored. Ethical issues in marketing, the ethical decision-making process and ways to improve ethical conduct in marketing are all considered. The chapter closes by exploring how social responsibility and ethics can be incorporated into marketing decisions

# Social Responsibility

## The Nature of Social Responsibility

**Social responsibility**
An organisation's obligation to maximise its positive impact and minimise its negative impact on society

In marketing, **social responsibility** refers to an organisation's obligation to maximise its positive impact and minimise its negative impact on society. Social responsibility deals with the total effect of all marketing decisions on society. Ample evidence demonstrates that ignoring society's demands for responsible marketing can destroy customers' trust and even prompt government regulations. Irresponsible actions that anger customers, employees or competitors may not only jeopardise a marketer's financial standing but could have other repercussions as well. For example, following a recent report into misleading claims on food packaging, the UK's Food Standards Agency (FSA) has instigated a campaign to 'name and shame' food manufacturers selling unhealthy products, including those with high sugar, salt or fat content.[2] In contrast, socially responsible activities can generate positive publicity and boost sales. Thus retailer Marks & Spencer has launched a programme offering 10,000 work experience places to individuals who might otherwise face problems getting a job. Unpaid placements will be offered to school children from deprived areas, the homeless and unemployed young people. In addition, paid work experience is available to students who are the first from their family to attend university.[3]

Socially responsible efforts have a positive impact on local communities; at the same time, they indirectly help the sponsoring organisation by attracting goodwill, publicity, and potential customers and employees. Thus, while social responsibility is certainly a positive concept in itself, most organisations embrace it in the expectation of indirect long-term benefits. Research suggests that an organisational culture that is conducive to social responsibility engenders greater employee commitment and improved business performance.[4]

## The Dimensions of Social Responsibility

**Marketing citizenship**
The adoption of a strategic focus for fulfilling the economic, legal, ethical and philanthropic social responsibilities expected by stakeholders

Socially responsible organisations strive for **marketing citizenship** by adopting a strategic focus for fulfilling the economic, legal, ethical and philanthropic social responsibilities that their stakeholders expect of them. **Stakeholders** include those constituents who have a 'stake', or claim, in some aspect of the company's products, operations, markets, industry and outcomes; these include customers, employees, investors and shareholders, suppliers, governments, communities, and many others. Companies that consider the diverse perspectives of stakeholders in their daily operations and strategic planning are said to have a 'stakeholder orientation', an important element of social responsibility.[5] For example, retailer B&Q secured stakeholder input on issues ranging from child labour, fair wages and equal opportunity to environmental impact. Based on consultations with store managers, employees, suppliers and government representatives, the retailer now recognises and measures its progress on all four dimensions of corporate social responsibility.[6] As Figure 25.1 shows, these dimensions can be viewed as a pyramid.[7] The economic and legal aspects have long been acknowledged, whereas philanthropic and ethical issues have gained recognition more recently.

Responsibilities
Philanthropic
Be a good corporate citizen
■ Contribute resources to the community; improve quality of life
Ethical
Be ethical
■ Obligation to do what is right, just and fair
■ Avoid harm
Legal
Obey the law
■ Law is society's codification of right and wrong
■ Play by the rules of the game
Economic
Be profitable
■ The foundation upon which all others rest

***Figure 25.1***
*The pyramid of corporate social responsibility*
*Source: Archie B. Carroll, 'The pyramid of corporate social responsibility: toward the moral management of organisational stakeholders', adaptation of Figure 3, p. 42. Reprinted from* Business Horizons, *July/Aug. 1991. Copyright © 1991 by the Foundation for the School of Business at Indiana University*

**Stakeholders**
Constituents who have a 'stake', or claim, in some aspect of a company's products, operations, markets, industry and outcomes

At the most basic level, all companies have an economic responsibility to be profitable so that they can provide a return on investment to their owners and investors, create jobs for the community, and contribute goods and services to the economy. How organisations relate to stockholders, employees, competitors, customers, the community and the natural environment affects the economy. When economic downturns or poor decisions lead companies to lay off employees, communities often suffer as they attempt to absorb the displaced employees. Customers may experience diminished levels of service as a result of fewer experienced employees. Share prices often decline when lay-offs are announced, affecting the value of stockholders' investment portfolios. Moreover, stressed-out employees facing demands to reduce expenses may make poor decisions that affect the natural environment, product quality, employee rights, and customer service. An organisation's sense of economic responsibility is especially significant for employees, raising such issues as equal job opportunities, workplace diversity, job safety, health, and employee privacy. Economic responsibilities require finding a balance between society's demand for social responsibility and investors' desire for profits.

Marketers also have an economic responsibility to compete fairly. Size frequently gives companies an advantage over rivals. Large companies can often generate economies of scale that allow them to put smaller companies out of business. Consequently, small companies and even whole communities may resist the efforts of businesses like Wal-Mart, Focus and McDonald's to open outlets in their neighbourhood, as explained in the Applied Mini-Case at the end of this chapter. These companies are able to operate at such low costs that small, local businesses cannot compete. Though consumers appreciate lower prices, the failure of small businesses creates unemployment for some members of the community. Such issues create concerns about social responsibility for organisations, communities and consumers.

Marketers are also expected to obey laws and regulations. The efforts of elected representatives and special-interest groups to promote responsible corporate behaviour have resulted in laws and regulations designed to keep European companies' actions within the range of acceptable conduct. When customers, interest groups or businesses become outraged over what they perceive as irresponsibility on the part of a marketing organisation, they may urge the government to draft new legislation to regulate the behaviour or engage in litigation. For example, following a record number of complaints about the practices of door-to-door sales people, the UK government is looking at legislative action to control this kind of selling.

**Marketing ethics**
Principles and standards that define acceptable marketing conduct as determined by various stakeholders, including the public, government regulators, private-interest groups, consumers, industry and the organisation itself

Economic and legal responsibilities are the most basic levels of social responsibility for a good reason: failure to consider them may mean that a marketer is not around long enough to engage in ethical or philanthropic activities. Beyond these dimensions is **marketing ethics**, principles and standards that define acceptable conduct in marketing as determined by various stakeholders, including the public, government regulators, private-interest groups, consumers, industry and the organisation itself. Some companies, including the Body Shop and the Co-operative Bank, have built their businesses around ethical ideas. The Marketing in Society box on page 790 illustrates ethics in action at the Co-operative Bank. The most ethical principles have been codified as laws and regulations to encourage marketers to conform to society's expectations about conduct. However, marketing ethics goes beyond legal issues. Ethical marketing decisions foster trust, which helps build long-term marketing relationships. There is a more detailed look at the ethical dimension of social responsibility later in this chapter.

**Philanthropic Responsibilities** At the top of the pyramid of corporate responsibility (see Figure 25.1) are philanthropic responsibilities. These responsibilities, which go beyond marketing ethics, are not required of a company, but they promote human welfare or goodwill, as do the economic, legal and ethical dimensions of social responsibility. That many companies have demonstrated philanthropic responsibility is evidenced by the level of corporate support attracted by events such as LiveAid and Comic Relief. Even small companies participate in philanthropy through donations and volunteer support of local good causes and national charities, such as the NSPCC, Oxfam and the Red Cross.

**Cause-related marketing**
The practice of linking products to a particular social cause on an ongoing or short-term basis

**Strategic philanthropy**
The synergistic use of organisational core competencies and resources to address key stakeholders' interests, and achieve both organisational and social benefits

More companies than ever are adopting a strategic approach to corporate philanthropy. Many businesses link their products to a particular social cause on an ongoing or short-term basis. One of the first companies to apply this practice, known as **cause-related marketing**, was American Express, which donated to the Statue of Liberty restoration fund every time a customer used his or her American Express card. The promotion was extraordinarily successful, generating new customers and dramatically increasing the use of the company's credit cards. Such cause-related programmes tend to appeal to consumers because they provide an additional reason to 'feel good' about a particular purchase. Marketers like the programmes because well-designed ones increase sales and create feelings of respect and admiration for the companies involved. Some companies are beginning to extend the concept of corporate philanthropy beyond financial contributions by adopting a **strategic philanthropy** approach, the synergistic use of organisational core competencies and resources to address key stakeholders' interests, and achieve both organisational and social benefits. Strategic philanthropy involves employees, organisational resources and expertise, and the ability to link these assets to the concerns of key stakeholders, including employees, customers, suppliers and social needs. Strategic philanthropy involves both financial and non-financial contributions to stakeholders (employee time, goods and services, and company technology and equipment, as well as facilities), but it also benefits the company.[8] For example, Marks & Spencer is one of the members of the 'One Per Cent Club', comprising businesses that pledge 1 per cent of profits to good causes.

## Social Responsibility Issues

Although social responsibility may seem to be an abstract ideal, managers make decisions related to social responsibility every day. To be successful, a business must determine what customers, government regulators and competitors, as well as society in general, want or

## Marketing in Society

### Customer Led, Ethically Guided ... the Co-operative Bank

Many companies now have a section of their annual report and website devoted to stating their involvement in the community and policies for good corporate citizenship, but the Co-operative Bank proclaims that it is 'customer led, ethically guided'. Few organisations devote as much of their website to their ethical stance and social responsibility as to promoting their products, but the Co-operative Bank proudly includes *Ethics in Action, Ethical Policy, Customers Who Care Campaigns, Community Involvement, Ecology, Have Your Say, Ethical Debate Forum* and *Partnership Report.* On its web home page, prominence is also given to *Read our Sustainability Report* and *You vote, we'll donate to charity.*

In 1990 a major research project by the bank found that, given the option, its customers would prefer their money to be invested ethically. As a result, a draft ethical policy for the bank's trading and investment activities was offered to 30,000 customers in order to gauge their response. The view was that the policy had to reflect the concerns of customers rather than management, as it was the customers' money the Co-operative Bank was investing and lending out to other customers. Only 5 per cent of customers felt that ethics and banking had no obvious relationship. This consultation exercise was repeated in 1994, 1998 and 2001, but with all of the bank's customers. The results revealed that support for the company's ethical policy had grown, with 97 per cent of customers endorsing the detail of the bank's trading practices.

The bank remains the only high-street UK retail bank to offer customers a say in how their money is used, and encourages customers to have an input in the evolution of the company's ethical policy. The policy sets out business activities that are of such concern to the bank's customers that they do not want the bank to provide services to them. The policy also contains positive statements that commit the bank to pursue business opportunities engaged in socially or environmentally beneficial activities.

The ethical policy statements cover:

- human rights
- the arms trade
- genetic modification
- social enterprise
- ecological impact
- animal welfare
- corporate responsibility and global trade.

The company will not invest in governments or businesses failing to uphold basic human rights or with links to an oppressive regime. Organisations involved with the arms trade, animal testing and genetic modification are shunned, as are organisations and individuals with a poor track record concerning ecology, global trade and social enterprise.

In order to make the policy a reality, everyday working practices and operational systems have been oriented around the recommendations of the guiding policy. An independent auditor comments on the policy's implementation and the review's findings are openly published in the bank's Partnership Report.

**Sources:** www.co-operativebank.co.uk/ethics; David Benady, 'The light fantasy', *Marketing Week*, 12 February 2004, pp. 26–9.

expect in terms of social responsibility. The success of international retailer the Body Shop has been attributed to the company's awareness of the Green movement and demonstration of social responsibility. Table 25.1 summarises three major categories of social responsibility issues: the natural environment, consumerism and community relations.

**The Natural Environment** One of the more common ways marketers demonstrate social responsibility is through programmes designed to protect and preserve the natural environment. Many companies are making contributions to environmental protection organisations, sponsoring and participating in clean-up events, promoting recycling, retooling manufacturing processes to minimise waste and pollution, and generally re-evaluating the effects of their products on the natural environment. Many supermarkets, for example, provide on-site recycling for customers and encourage their suppliers to reduce wasteful packaging. Procter

**Table 25.1 Social Responsibility Issues**

| Issue | Description | Major social concerns |
|---|---|---|
| Natural environment | Consumers insisting not only on a good quality of life but on a healthful environment so they can maintain a high standard of living during their lifetimes | Conservation<br>Water pollution<br>Air pollution<br>Land pollution |
| Consumerism | Activities undertaken by independent individuals, groups, and organisations to protect their rights as consumers | The right to safety<br>The right to be informed<br>The right to choose<br>The right to be heard |
| Community relations | Society eager to have marketers contribute to its well-being, wishing to know what marketers do to help solve social problems | Equality issues<br>Disadvantaged members of society<br>Safety and health<br>Education and general welfare |

& Gamble uses recycled materials in some of its packaging and markets refills for some products, which reduces packaging waste. Such efforts generate positive publicity and often increase sales for the companies involved.

**Green marketing**
The specific development, pricing, promotion and distribution of products that do not harm the natural environment

**Green Marketing** **Green marketing** refers to the specific development, pricing, promotion and distribution of products that do not harm the natural environment. Toyota and Honda, for example, have succeeded in marketing 'hybrid' cars that use electric motors to augment their internal-combustion engines, improving the vehicles' fuel economy without reducing their power. Ford introduced the first hybrid SUV in 2004.[9] Figure 25.2 illustrates a growth area in many supermarkets in response to some consumers' growing awareness of green issues: organic fruit and vegetables.

An independent coalition of environmentalists, scientists and marketers is one group involved in evaluating products to assess their environmental impact, determining marketers' commitment to the environment. *The Green Guide* publishes six issues a year via its website, www.thegreenguide.com, offering guidance on Green products and lifestyles. Such information sources have an important role to play during what is a confusing time for many consumers, who are increasingly faced with an array of products making a variety of environmental claims. For example, most Chiquita bananas are certified through the Rainforest Alliance's Better Banana Project as having been grown using more environmentally and labour-friendly practices.[10] Recently the confusion has been somewhat alleviated by the promotion of two standard labels throughout Europe. Both labels have government backing. Companies can voluntarily apply for an Eco-label to indicate that their products are less harmful to the environment than competing products, based on scientifically determined criteria. As Figure 25.3 illustrates, the EU also encourages labelling to reduce confusion over environmental claims.

Although demand for economic, legal and ethical solutions to environmental problems is widespread, the environmental movement in marketing includes many different groups, whose values and goals often conflict. Some environmentalists and marketers believe companies should work to protect and preserve the natural environment by implementing the following goals:

1 *Eliminate the concept of waste.* Recognising that pollution and waste usually stem from inefficiency, the question is not what to do with waste but how to make things without waste.

*Figure 25.2*
*Many consumers are increasingly aware of 'green' issues and some businesses are responding accordingly: here a retailer is offering organically produced fruit and vegetables to its shoppers*
*Photo: Courtesy of Karen Beaulah*

*Figure 25.3*
*The European Eco-label*
*Source: www.europa.eu.int/comm/environment/ecolabel; www.eco-label.com*

2 *Reinvent the concept of a product.* Products should be reduced to only three types and eventually just two. The first type is consumables, which are eaten or, when placed in the ground, turn into soil with few harmful side-effects. The second type is durable goods – such as cars, televisions, computers and refrigerators – which should be made, used and returned to the manufacturer within a closed-loop system. Such products should be designed for disassembly and recycling. The third category is unsaleables and includes such products as radioactive materials, heavy metals and toxins. These products should always belong to the original makers, who should be responsible for the products and their full life-cycle effects. Reclassifying products in this way encourages manufacturers to design products more efficiently.

3 *Make prices reflect the cost.* Every product should reflect, or at least approximate, its actual cost – not only the direct cost of its effect on production but also the cost of its effect on air, water and soil.
4 *Make environmentalism profitable.* Consumers are beginning to recognise that competition in the marketplace should not occur between companies harming the environment and those trying to save it.[11]

**Consumerism** Another significant issue in socially responsible marketing is consumerism, which is the efforts of independent individuals, groups and organisations to protect the rights of consumers. The underlying assumption is that consumers have a range of rights, including the right to safety, the right to choose, the right to be properly informed and the right to fair treatment when they complain. For example, the right to safety means that marketers are obligated not to market a product that they know could harm consumers. This right can be extended to imply that all products must be safe for their intended use, include thorough and explicit instructions for proper and safe use, and have been tested to ensure reliability and quality.

Interest groups play an important role in helping to protect consumers' rights by taking action against companies they consider irresponsible, by lobbying government officials and agencies, engaging in letter-writing campaigns and boycotts, and making public service announcements. A number of high-profile consumer activists have also crusaded for consumer rights. Consumer activism has resulted in legislation requiring various safety features in cars: seat belts, padded dashboards, stronger door catches, headrests, shatterproof windscreens and collapsible steering columns. Activists' efforts have furthered the passage of several consumer protection laws, such as the Trade Descriptions Act 1968, the Consumer Protection Act 1987, the Fair Trading Act 1973, the Food Act 1984 and the Weights and Measures Act 1985.

The power of angry consumers should not be underestimated. Indeed, research suggests that such individuals not only fail to make repeat purchases but may retaliate against the source of their dissatisfaction.[12] The consumer movement has been helped by news-format television programmes, such as the BBC's *Watchdog*. The Internet has also changed the way consumers obtain information about companies' goods, services and activities.

**Community Relations** Social responsibility also extends to marketers' roles as community members. Individual communities expect marketers to make philanthropic contributions to civic projects and institutions, and to be 'good corporate citizens'. While most charitable donations come from individuals, corporate philanthropy is on the rise, with contributions of resources (money, product, time) to community causes such as education, the arts, recreation, disadvantaged members of the community and others. British Airways' 'Change for Good' partnership with UNICEF encourages donations of foreign currency from passengers, which can then be used to fund a range of health and educational projects aimed at children around the world. McDonald's, Shell, Ogilvy & Mather and Hewlett-Packard all have programmes that contribute funds, equipment and personnel to educational reform. Similarly, Tesco has a scheme that allows shoppers to collect vouchers enabling their local schools to obtain computer equipment. From a positive perspective, a marketer can significantly improve its community's quality of life through employment opportunities, economic development, and financial contributions to educational, health, cultural and recreational causes.[13] These efforts also indirectly help the organisations in the form of goodwill, publicity and exposure to potential future customers. Thus, although social responsibility is certainly a positive concept, most organisations do not embrace it without the expectation of some indirect long-term benefit.

The manner in which organisations deal with equality is also a key social responsibility issues. Diversity in the work environment has focused attention on the need to integrate and utilise an increasingly diverse workforce. Companies that are successful in achieving this are finding increases in creativity and motivation, and reductions in staff turnover. From a marketing perspective, the more closely the workforce matches the population, the better it understands consumer needs and wants. For example, Xerox has worked hard to handle workplace diversity. Of its more than 47,000 employees, 32 per cent are women and 26 per cent are from minorities.[14]

## The Nature of Marketing Ethics

As noted earlier, marketing ethics is a dimension of social responsibility involving principles and standards that define acceptable conduct in marketing. Acceptable standards of conduct in making individual and group decisions in marketing are determined by various stakeholders and by an organisation's ethical climate.

Marketers should be aware of ethical standards for acceptable conduct from several viewpoints: company, industry, government, customers, special-interest groups and society at large. When marketing activities deviate from accepted standards, the exchange process can break down, resulting in customer dissatisfaction, lack of trust and legal action. In recent years, a number of ethical scandals have resulted in a massive loss of confidence in the integrity of businesses.[15] In fact, some research suggests that 76 per cent of consumers would boycott the products of a socially irresponsible company, and 91 per cent would consider switching to a competitor's products.[16]

For example, in the USA, after 174 deaths and more than 700 injuries resulted from traffic accidents involving Ford Explorers equipped with Firestone tyres, Bridgestone/Firestone and Ford faced numerous lawsuits and much negative publicity. Ford claimed that defective Firestone tyres were to blame for the accidents, while Bridgestone/Firestone contended that design flaws in Ford's best-selling Explorer made it more likely to roll over than other sport-utility vehicles. Many consumers, concerned more for their own safety than with the corporate blame game, lost confidence in both companies and turned to competitors' products.[17]

When managers engage in activities that deviate from accepted principles, continued marketing exchanges become difficult, if not impossible. The best time to deal with such problems is during the marketing strategy process, not after major problems have materialised.

As has already been noted, marketing ethics goes beyond legal issues. Marketing decisions based on ethical considerations foster mutual trust in marketing relationships. Although attempts are often made to draw a boundary between legal and ethical issues, the distinction between the two is frequently blurred in decision-making. Marketers operate in an environment in which overlapping legal and ethical issues often colour decisions. To separate legal and ethical decisions requires an assumption that marketing managers can instinctively differentiate legal and ethical issues. However, while the legal ramifications of some issues and problems may be obvious, others are not. Questionable decisions and actions often result in disputes that must be resolved through litigation. The legal system therefore provides a formal venue for marketers to resolve ethical disputes as well as legal ones.

Hasbro, for example, filed a lawsuit against a man who marketed a board game called Ghettopoly. Hasbro's suit accused David Chang's game of unlawfully copying the packaging and logo of Hasbro's long-selling Monopoly board game and causing 'irreparable injury' to Hasbro's reputation and goodwill. After minority-rights groups complained that Ghettopoly promoted negative stereotypes of some minorities, some retailers stopped selling the game.[18]

Indeed, most ethical disputes reported in the media involve the legal system at some level. In many cases, however, settlements are reached without requiring the decision of a judge or jury.

It is not the aim of this chapter to question individuals' ethical beliefs or personal convictions. Nor is it the purpose to examine the conduct of consumers, although some do behave unethically (engaging, for instance, in shoplifting, returning clothing after wearing it, and other abuses). Instead, the goal here is to highlight the importance of understanding and resolving ethical issues in marketing and to help readers learn about marketing ethics.

## Ethical Issues in Marketing

**Ethical issue**
An identifiable problem, situation or opportunity requiring a choice between several actions that must be evaluated as right or wrong, ethical or unethical

An **ethical issue** is an identifiable problem, situation or opportunity requiring an individual or organisation to choose between actions that must be evaluated as right or wrong, ethical or unethical. Any time an activity causes marketing managers or customers in their target market to feel manipulated or cheated, a marketing ethical issue exists, regardless of the legality of that activity. For example, organisational objectives that call for increased profits or market share may pressure marketers to knowingly bring an unsafe product to market. Such pressures represent ethical issues. Regardless of the reasons behind specific ethical issues, marketers must be able to identify these issues and decide how to resolve them. To do so requires familiarity with the many kinds of ethical issue that may arise in marketing. Some examples of ethical issues related to product, people, promotion, price and place/distribution (the marketing mix) appear in Table 25.2.

Product-related ethical issues generally arise when marketers fail to disclose the risks associated with a product, or information regarding the function, value or use of a product. Most car companies have experienced negative publicity associated with design or safety issues that resulted in a government-required recall of specific models. Pressures can build to substitute inferior materials or product components to reduce costs. Ethical issues also arise when marketers fail to inform customers about existing conditions or changes in product quality. Consider the introduction of a new size of confectionery bar, labelled with a banner touting its 'new larger size'. However, when placed in vending machines alongside older confectionery bars of the same brand, it became apparent that the product was actually slightly *smaller* than the bar it had replaced. Although this could have been a mistake, the company still has to defend and deal with the consequences of its actions.

Promotion can create ethical issues in a variety of ways, among them false or misleading advertising and manipulative or deceptive sales promotions, tactics and publicity. A major ethical issue in promotion pertains to the marketing of video games that allegedly promote violence and weapons to children. In the UK, the parents of a 14-year-old boy recently blamed their son's murderer's obsession with the video game *Manhunt*. Following the case, Dixons Group plc and the video game retailer Game removed *Manhunt*

**Table 25.2 Typical Ethical Issues Related to the Marketing Mix**

| | |
|---|---|
| **Product issue**<br>Product information | Covering up defects in products that could cause harm to a consumer; withholding critical performance information that could affect a purchase decision |
| **Place/distribution issue**<br>Counterfeiting | Counterfeit products are widespread, especially in the areas of computer software, clothing, and audio and video products; the Internet has facilitated the distribution of counterfeit products |
| **People issue**<br>Customer service | Promising or promoting aftermarket care with no intention of honouring the promise or warranty |
| **Promotion issue**<br>Advertising | Deceptive advertising or withholding important product information in a personal selling situation |
| **Pricing issue**<br>Pricing | Indicating that an advertised sale price is a reduction below the regular list price when, in fact, that is not the case |

from their shelves. The Topical Insight box below, which examines the ethics of marketing vaccines again drug addiction and smoking, shows that many other ethical issues are linked to promotion and product attributes.

## Topical Insight

### Is it Right to Market a No-smoking Vaccine?

'Children to get jabs against drug addiction' was the headline in the *Independent on Sunday* newspaper one week in 2004. The story went on to explain that UK government ministers were considering a vaccination scheme in their fight against heroin, cocaine and nicotine addiction. Under the draft plans, doctors would immunise children at risk of becoming smokers or drug users, in a similar way to the existing immunisation schemes for illnesses such as measles or rubella.

The immunisation would remove the sense of euphoria experienced by a 'nicotine fix' or use of other drugs. The idea stemmed from the Brain Science, Addiction and Drugs project, run by a group of expert scientists at the request of the UK government.

There are many good reasons for considering such a plan of action. Estimates suggest that the costs of drug addiction – from related crime and health problems – are over £12 billion per annum. The figures associated with smoking and the thousands afflicted by smoking-related cancers are even greater. In addition to the economic costs, there are the social problems caused by smoking and drug-taking, and the increasing tide of public opinion against such activities.

The fight against nicotine addiction is already big business for several leading pharmaceutical manufacturers, and anti-smoking products are lucrative for many pharmacy chains. The idea of creating pharmaceutical products to help immunise youngsters so that they 'enjoy' no benefits from smoking or drug-taking would undoubtedly be financially very rewarding for those supplying the vaccines and offering the immunisation service.

Were such a scheme ever to become a reality, it would have attractions for marketers, who would be tasked with creating awareness of the scheme, promoting its benefits and combating opposing views. If rival vaccines emerged, there would be marketing strategies and marketing programmes created by the competing brands and the spending of large sums on marketing communications.

However, while the pharmaceutical industry responsible for developing such vaccines would argue that these products are socially responsible and for the 'greater good', many consumers might feel frustrated that their recreational habits were being interfered with or stifled. While it is difficult to argue that a government is wrong to encourage products to be marketed in the fight against the taking of illegal drugs such as heroin or cocaine, the argument in favour of vaccinations against smoking, particularly of non-adults, may be more difficult to justify. While children cannot purchase cigarettes, adult consumers are currently freely entitled to choose to smoke and to select whichever brand of – legally – available cigarettes they wish. The ethics of marketing such vaccines – irrespective of the obvious health and social benefits to society – are far from clear.

**Sources:** Sophie Goodchild and Steve Bloomfield, 'Children to get jabs against drug addiction', *Independent on Sunday*, 25 July 2004, pp. 1–2; David Nutt, University of Bristol.

In pricing, common ethical issues are price fixing, predatory pricing and failure to disclose the full price of a purchase. The emotional and subjective nature of price creates many situations in which misunderstandings between the seller and buyer cause ethical problems. Marketers have the right to price their products to earn a reasonable profit, but ethical issues may crop up when a company seeks to earn high profits at the expense of its customers. Some pharmaceutical companies, for example, have been accused of pricing products at exorbitant levels and taking advantage of customers who must purchase the medicine to survive or to maintain their quality of life. Another issue relates to the quantity surcharges that occur when consumers are effectively overcharged for buying a larger package size of the same grocery product.[19]

Ethical issues in distribution involve relationships among producers and marketing middlemen. Marketing middlemen, or intermediaries (wholesalers and retailers), facilitate the flow of products from the producer to the ultimate customer. Each intermediary performs a different role and agrees to certain rights, responsibilities and rewards associated with that role. For example, producers expect wholesalers and retailers to honour agreements and keep them informed of inventory needs. Other serious ethical issues with regard to distribution include manipulating a product's availability for the purposes of exploitation and using coercion to force intermediaries to behave in a specific manner.

## The Ethical Decision-making Process

To grasp the significance of ethics in marketing decision-making, it is helpful to examine the factors that influence the ethical decision-making process. As Figure 25.4 shows, individual factors, organisational relationships and opportunity interact to determine ethical decisions in marketing.

### Individual Factors

When people need to resolve ethical conflicts in their lives, they often base their decisions on their own values and principles of right or wrong. For example, a study by the Josephson Institute of Ethics reported that seven out of ten students admitted to cheating in a test at least once in the past year, and 92 per cent admitted to lying to their parents in the past year. One out of six students confessed to showing up for class drunk in the same period.[20] People learn values and principles through socialisation by family members, social groups, religion and formal education. In the workplace, however, research has established that an organisation's values often have more influence on marketing decisions than do a person's own values.[21]

### Organisational Factors

Although people can, and do, make ethical choices relating to marketing decisions, no one operates in a vacuum.[22] Ethical choices in marketing are most often made jointly, in work groups and committees, or in conversations and discussions with co-workers. Marketing employees resolve ethical issues based not only on what they have learned from their own backgrounds but also on what they learn from others in the organisation. The outcome of this learning process depends on the strength of each individual's personal values, opportunities for unethical behaviour, and exposure to others who behave ethically or unethically. Superiors, peers and subordinates in the organisation influence the ethical decision-making process. Although people outside the organisation, such as

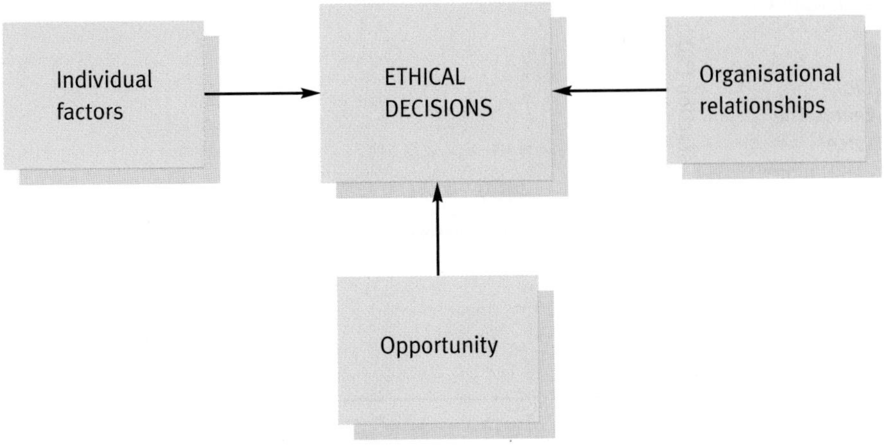


*Figure 25.4*
*Factors that influence the ethical decision-making process*

family members and friends, also influence decision-makers, organisational culture and structure operate through organisational relationships to influence ethical decisions.

**Organisational (corporate) culture**
A set of values, beliefs, goals, norms and rituals that members of an organisation share

**Organisational (corporate) culture** is a set of values, beliefs, goals, norms and rituals that members of an organisation share. These values also help shape employees' satisfaction with their employer, which may affect the quality of the service they provide to customers. Figure 25.5 indicates that at least 92 per cent of surveyed employees who see trust, respect and honesty applied frequently in their organisations express satisfaction with their employers.[23] A company's culture may be expressed formally through codes of conduct, memos, manuals, dress codes and ceremonies, but it is also conveyed informally through work habits, extracurricular activities and anecdotes. An organisation's culture gives its members meaning, and suggests rules for how to behave and deal with problems within the organisation.

Most experts agree that the chief executive, managing director or marketing director sets the ethical tone for the entire organisation. Lower-level managers take their cue from top managers, but they too impose some of their personal values on the company. This interaction between corporate culture and executive leadership helps determine the company's ethical value system.

Co-workers' influence on an individual's ethical choices depends on the person's exposure to unethical behaviour. Especially in grey areas, the more a person is exposed to unethical activity by others in the organisational environment, the more likely he or she is to behave unethically. Most marketing employees take a lead from co-workers in learning how to solve problems, including ethical problems.[24] Indeed, research suggests that marketing employees who perceive their work environment as ethical experience less role conflict and ambiguity, are more satisfied with their jobs, and are more committed to their employer.[25]

Organisational pressure plays a key role in creating ethical issues. For example, because of pressure to meet a deadline, a superior may ask a sales person to lie to a customer over the phone about a late product shipment. Similarly, pressure to meet a sales quota may result in overly aggressive sales tactics. Research in this area indicates that superiors and co-workers can generate organisational pressure, which plays a key role in creating ethical issues. In a study by the Ethics Resource Centre, 60 per cent of respondents said they had experienced pressure from superiors or co-workers to compromise ethical standards to achieve business objectives.[26] Nearly all marketers face difficult issues whose solutions are not obvious or that present conflicts between organisational objectives and personal ethics.

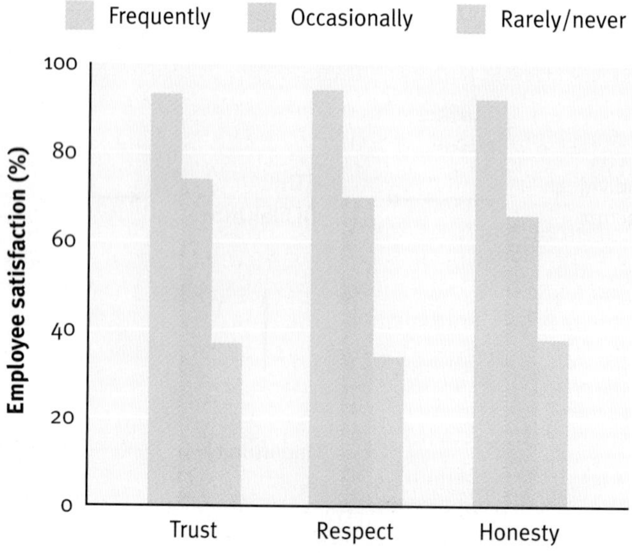


***Figure 25.5***
*The relationship of organizational values to employee satisfaction*
*Source: Ethics Resource Center,* The Ethics resource Center's 2000 National Business Ethics Survey: Howe Employees Perceive Ethics at Work *(Washington, D.C.: Ethics Resource Center, 2000), p. 85. reprinted with permission*

### Opportunity

**Opportunity**
A favourable set of conditions that limit barriers or provide rewards

Opportunity provides another pressure that may shape ethical decisions in marketing. **Opportunity** is a favourable set of conditions that limit barriers or provide rewards. A marketing employee who takes advantage of an opportunity to act unethically and is rewarded or suffers no penalty may repeat such acts as other opportunities arise. For example, a sales person who receives a bonus after using a deceptive sales presentation to increase sales is being rewarded and thus will probably continue the behaviour. Indeed, opportunity to engage in unethical conduct is often a better predictor of unethical activities than are personal values.[27] Beyond rewards and the absence of punishment, other elements in the business environment may create opportunities. Professional codes of conduct and ethics-related corporate policy also influence opportunity by prescribing what behaviours are acceptable, as will be explained later. The larger the rewards and the milder the punishment for unethical conduct, the greater the likelihood that unethical behaviour will occur.

However, just as the majority of people who go into retail stores do not try to shoplift at each opportunity, most marketers do not try to take advantage of every opportunity for unethical behaviour in their organisations. Although marketing managers often perceive many opportunities to engage in unethical conduct in their companies and industries, research suggests that most refrain from taking advantage of such opportunities. Moreover, most marketing managers do not believe unethical conduct in general results in success.[28] Individual factors as well as organisational culture may influence whether an individual becomes opportunistic and tries to take advantage of situations unethically.

## Improving Ethical Conduct in Marketing

It is possible to improve ethical conduct in an organisation by taking on ethical employees and eliminating unethical ones, and by improving the organisation's ethical standards. One way to approach improvement of an organisation's ethical standards is to use a 'bad apple/bad barrel' analogy. Some people always do things in their own self-interest, regardless of organisational goals or accepted moral standards; such people are sometimes referred to as 'bad apples'. To eliminate unethical conduct, an organisation must rid itself of bad apples through screening techniques and enforcement of the company's ethical standards. However, organisations sometimes become 'bad barrels' themselves, not because the individuals within them are unethical but because the pressures to survive and succeed create conditions (opportunities) that reward unethical behaviour. One way to resolve the problem of the bad barrel is to redesign the organisation's image and culture so that it conforms to industry and societal norms of ethical conduct.[29]

If senior management develops and enforces ethics and legal compliance programmes to encourage ethical decision-making, it becomes a force to help individuals make better decisions. The 2003 National Business Ethics Survey found that ethics programmes that include written standards of conduct, ethics training, ethics advice lines or offices, and systems for anonymous reporting increase the likelihood that employees will report misconduct observed in the workplace. The survey results also suggest that when senior managers talk about the importance of ethics, inform employees, keep promises and model ethical behaviour, employees observe significantly less unethical conduct.[30] When marketers understand the policies and requirements for ethical conduct, they can more easily resolve ethical conflicts. However, marketers can never fully abdicate their personal ethical responsibility in making decisions. Claiming to be an agent of the business ('the company told me to do it') is unacceptable as a legal excuse and is even less defensible from an ethical perspective.[31]

### Codes of Conduct

Without compliance programmes, and uniform standards and policies regarding conduct, it is hard for employees to determine what conduct is acceptable within the company. In the absence of such programmes and standards, employees will generally make decisions based on their observations of how co-workers and superiors behave. To improve ethics,

**Codes of conduct**
Formalised rules and standards that describe what the company expects of its employees

many organisations have developed **codes of conduct** (also called codes of ethics) consisting of formalised rules and standards that describe what the company expects of its employees. Most large businesses have formal codes of conduct. Codes of conduct promote ethical behaviour by reducing opportunities for unethical behaviour; employees know both what is expected of them and what kind of punishment they face if they violate the rules. Codes help marketers deal with ethical issues or dilemmas that develop in daily operations by prescribing or limiting specific activities. Codes of conduct have also made companies that subcontract manufacturing operations abroad more aware of the ethical issues associated with supporting facilities that underpay and even abuse their workforce.

Codes of conduct do not have to take every situation into account, but they should provide guidelines that enable employees to achieve organisational objectives in an ethical, acceptable manner. Table 25.3 describes the ethical commitments to which chocolate and drinks business Cadbury Schweppes is committed. These ethical guidelines cover the kinds of issue that are typical of those being included in codes of conduct.

## Ethics Officers

Organisational compliance programmes must be overseen by high-ranking members of the business, who are known to respect legal and ethical standards. Ethics officers are typically responsible for creating and distributing a code of conduct, enforcing the code, and meeting with organisational members to discuss or provide advice about ethical issues. Ethics officers may also set up telephone 'hotlines' to provide advice to employees faced with an ethical issue.

**TABLE 25.3 THE ETHICAL COMMITMENTS OF CADBURY SCHWEPPES**

**Our human rights and ethical trading policy**

As a responsible corporate citizen, Cadbury Schweppes aims to act in a socially responsible manner at all times by:

- respecting the economic, social, cultural, political and civil rights of those involved in our operations
- complying with all local human rights legislation
- implementing programmes across our world-wide operations and with our supply chain partners

**Core labour rights and dignity at work**

- preclude the use of forced labour
- respect the rights of employees to join legally recognised labour unions
- ensure that children are employed only under circumstances that protect them from physical risks and do not disrupt their education
- not tolerate any form of harassment in the workplace

**Health and safety in the workplace**

- create a healthy and safe work environment for each employee

**Fair remuneration**

- ensure that working hours and remuneration are reasonable and comparable to those offered by similar companies

**Diversity and respect for differences**

- manage diversity to promote and capitalise on cultural and individual differences to create competitive advantage through new perspectives and local market sensitivity

**Opportunity for development**

- recognise the value that employees create and reward them with opportunities for personal and career development
- provide employees with equal opportunities regardless of their gender, age, marital status, sexual orientation, disability, race, religion or national origin

**Source:** www.cadburyschweppes.com/EN/EnvironmentSociety/EthicalTrading/, accessed 10 August 2004.

### Implementing Ethics and Legal Compliance Programmes

To nurture ethical conduct in marketing, open communication and coaching on ethical issues are essential. This necessitates providing employees with ethics training, clear channels of communication and follow-up support throughout the organisation. Companies need to consistently enforce standards and impose penalties on those who violate codes of conduct. In addition, businesses must take reasonable steps in response to violations of standards and, as appropriate, revise their compliance programmes to diminish the likelihood of future misconduct.

To succeed, a compliance programme must be viewed as part of the overall marketing strategy implementation. If ethics officers and other executives are not committed to the principles and initiatives of marketing ethics and social responsibility, the programme's effectiveness will be compromised. Although the virtues of honesty, fairness and openness are often assumed to be self-evident and universally accepted, marketing strategy decisions involve complex and detailed matters in which correctness may not be so clear-cut. A high level of personal morality may not be sufficient to prevent an individual from violating the law in an organisational context in which even experienced lawyers debate the exact meaning of the law.

Because it is impossible to train all members of an organisation as lawyers, the identification of ethical issues and implementation of compliance programmes and codes of conduct that incorporate both legal and ethical concerns constitute the best approach to preventing violations and avoiding litigation. Codifying ethical standards into meaningful policies that spell out what is and is not acceptable gives marketers an opportunity to reduce the probability of behaviour that could create legal problems. Without proper ethical training and guidance, it is impossible for the average marketing manager to understand the exact boundaries of illegality in the areas of price fixing, copyright violations, fraud, export/import violations, and so on. A corporate focus on ethics helps create a buffer zone around issues that could trigger serious legal considerations for a company.

## Incorporating Social Responsibility and Ethics into Marketing Decisions

Although the concepts of marketing ethics and social responsibility are often used interchangeably, it is important to distinguish between them. *Ethics* relates to individual and group decisions: judgements about what is right or wrong in a particular decision-making situation. *Social responsibility*, on the other hand, deals with the total effect of marketing decisions on society. The two concepts are interrelated because a company that supports socially responsible decisions and adheres to a code of conduct is likely to have a positive effect on society. Figure 25.6 illustrates how GroceryAid is dedicated to working with companies in the grocery industry to channel products to charities caring for the disadvantaged. Because ethics and social responsibility programmes can be profitable as well, an increasing number of companies are incorporating them into their overall marketing ethos.

As has been emphasised throughout this chapter, ethics is just one dimension of social responsibility. Being socially responsible relates to doing what is economically sound, legal, ethical and socially conscious. One way to evaluate whether a specific activity is ethical and socially responsible is to ask other members of the organisation if they approve of it. Contact with concerned consumer groups and industry or government regulatory groups may be helpful. A check to see whether there is a specific company policy about an activity may help resolve ethical questions. If other organisation members approve of the activity and it is legal and customary within the industry, chances are the activity is acceptable from both an ethical and a social responsibility perspective. Table 25.4 provides an audit of mechanisms to help control ethics and social responsibility in marketing.

***Figure 25.6***
*The Fairtrade movement is growing, but depends on the ethical behaviour of producers and marketers in order to ensure identified products conform to the movement's standards*
*Photo © Janet Jarman/Corbis*

A rule of thumb for resolving ethical and social responsibility issues is that if an issue can withstand open discussion that results in agreement or limited debate, an acceptable solution may exist. Nevertheless, even after a final decision has been reached, different viewpoints on the issue may remain. Openness is not a neat and comprehensive solution to the ethics problem; however, it creates trust and facilitates learning relationships.[32]

## Being Socially Responsible and Ethical is Not Easy

To promote socially responsible and ethical behaviour while achieving organisational goals, marketers must monitor changes and trends in society's values. In response to the increasing popularity of low-carbohydrate diets, for example, a number of companies have developed and marketed low-carbohydrate products ranging from bread and tortillas to beer.[33] Likewise, when consumers began to demand greater transparency, or openness, from companies in the wake of a number of ethics scandals, transparency became a factor in most marketing and management decisions.[34] An organisation's senior management must assume some responsibility for employees' conduct by establishing and enforcing policies that address society's desires.

**Table 25.4 Organisational Audit of Social Responsibility and Ethics Control Mechanisms**

| Answer 'True' (T) or 'False' (F) for each statement | | |
|---|---|---|
| 1 No mechanism exists for top management to detect social responsibility and ethical issues relating to employees, customers, the community and society | T | F |
| 2 There is no formal or informal communication within the organisation about procedures and activities that are considered acceptable behaviour | T | F |
| 3 The organisation fails to communicate its ethical standards to suppliers, customers, and groups that have a relationship with the organisation | T | F |
| 4 There is an environment of deception, repression and cover-ups concerning events that could be embarrassing to the company | T | F |
| 5 Compensation systems are totally dependent on economic performance | T | F |
| 6 The only concerns about environmental impact are those that are legally required | T | F |
| 7 Concern for the ethical value systems of the community with regard to the company's activities is absent | T | F |
| 8 Products are described in a misleading manner, with no information on negative impact or limitations communicated to customers | T | F |
| *True answers indicate a lack of control mechanisms, which, if implemented, could improve ethics and social responsibility* | | |

After determining what society wants, marketers must attempt to predict the long-term effects of decisions pertaining to those wants. Specialists outside the company, such as doctors, lawyers and scientists, are often consulted, but sometimes there is a lack of agreement within a discipline as to what is an acceptable marketing decision. Some 40 years ago, for example, tobacco marketers promoted cigarettes as being good for people's health. Today, years after the discovery that cigarette smoking is linked to cancer and other medical problems, society's attitude towards smoking has changed, and marketers face new social responsibilities, such as providing smoke-free areas for customers. Most major hotel chains allocate at least some of their rooms to non-smokers, many rental car companies provide smoke-free cars, and many businesses within the food, travel and leisure sectors provide smoke-free areas.

Many of society's demands impose costs. For example, society wants a cleaner environment and the preservation of wildlife and its habitats, but it also wants low-priced products. This means that companies must carefully balance the costs of providing low-priced products against the costs of manufacturing, packaging and distributing their products in an environmentally responsible manner.

In trying to satisfy the desires of one group, marketers may dissatisfy others. Regarding the smoking debate, for example, marketers must balance non-smokers' desire for a smoke-free environment against smokers' desire, or need, to continue to smoke. Some anti-smoking campaigners call for the complete elimination of tobacco products to ensure a smoke-free world. However, this attitude fails to consider the difficulty smokers have in quitting. Thus, this issue, like most ethical and social responsibility issues, cannot be viewed in black and white terms.

Satisfying the demands of all members of society is difficult, if not impossible. Marketers must evaluate the extent to which members of society are willing to pay for what they want. For instance, customers may want more information about a product but be unwilling to pay the costs the business incurs in providing the data. Marketers who want to make socially responsible decisions may find the task a challenge because, ultimately, they must ensure their economic survival.

## Social Responsibility and Ethics Improve Marketing Performance

Increasing evidence indicates that being socially responsible and ethical pays off. Research suggests that a relationship exists between a marketing orientation and an organisational climate that supports marketing ethics and social responsibility. This relationship implies that being ethically and socially concerned is consistent with meeting the demands of customers and other stakeholders. By encouraging employees to understand their markets, companies can help them respond to stakeholders' demands.[35]

A survey of marketing managers found a direct association between corporate social responsibility and profits.[36] In a survey of consumers, nearly 90 per cent indicated that when quality, service and price are equal among competitors, they would be more likely to buy from the company with the best reputation for social responsibility. In addition, 54 per cent would pay more for a product that supports a cause they care about, 66 per cent would switch brands to support such a cause and 62 per cent would switch retailers.[37]

Recognition is therefore growing that the long-term value of conducting business in a socially responsible manner far outweighs short-term costs.[38] Companies that fail to develop strategies and programmes to incorporate ethics and social responsibility into their organisational culture may pay the price with poor marketing performance and the potential costs of legal violations, civil litigation and damaging publicity when questionable activities are made public.

Because marketing ethics and social responsibility are not always viewed as organisational performance issues, many managers do not believe they need to consider them in the strategic planning process. Individuals also have different ideas as to what is ethical or unethical, leading them to confuse the need for workplace ethics and the right to maintain their own personal values and ethics. While the concepts are undoubtedly controversial, it is possible, and desirable, to incorporate ethics and social responsibility into the planning process.

# Summary

*Social responsibility* refers to an organisation's obligation to maximise its positive impact and minimise its negative impact on society. Although social responsibility is a positive concept, most organisations embrace it in the expectation of indirect long-term benefits.

- *Marketing citizenship* involves adopting a strategic focus for fulfilling the economic, legal, ethical and philanthropic social responsibilities expected of organisations by their *stakeholders*, those constituents who have a stake, or claim, in some aspect of the company's products, operations, markets, industry and outcomes.

- At the most basic level, companies have an economic responsibility to be profitable so that they can provide a return on investment to their stockholders, create jobs for the community, and contribute goods and services to the economy. Marketers are also expected to obey laws and regulations.

- *Marketing ethics* refers to principles and standards that define acceptable conduct in marketing as determined by various stakeholders, including the public, government regulators, private-interest groups, industry and the organisation itself.

- Philanthropic responsibilities, which encompass *cause-related marketing* go beyond marketing ethics; they are not required of a company, but they promote human welfare or goodwill (this is known as *strategic philanthropy*).

- Three major categories of social responsibility issues are the natural environment, consumerism and community relations. One of the more common ways in which marketers demonstrate social responsibility is through programmes designed to protect and preserve the natural environment. *Green marketing* refers to the specific development, pricing, promotion and distribution of products that do not harm the environment. Consumerism consists of the efforts of independent individuals, groups and organisations to protect the rights of consumers.

- Whereas social responsibility is achieved by balancing the interests of all stakeholders in the organisation, ethics relates to acceptable standards of conduct in making individual and group decisions. Marketing ethics goes beyond legal issues, fostering mutual trust in marketing relationships.

- An *ethical issue* is an identifiable problem, situation or opportunity requiring an individual or organisation to choose between actions that must be evaluated as right or wrong, ethical or unethical. A number of ethical issues relate to the marketing mix (product, people, promotion, price and place/distribution).

- Individual factors, organisational relationships and opportunity interact to determine ethical decisions in marketing. Individuals often base their decisions on their own values and principles of right or wrong. However, ethical choices in marketing are often made jointly, in work groups and committees or with colleagues, and are shaped by *organisational (corporate) culture* and structure. The more someone is exposed to unethical activity in the organisational environment, the more likely he or she is to behave unethically. Organisational pressure plays a key role in creating ethical issues, as does *opportunity*, conditions that limit barriers or provide rewards.

- Improving ethical behaviour in an organisation can be achieved by developing and enforcing ethics and legal compliance programmes, establishing *codes of conduct*, formalised rules and standards that describe what the company expects of its employees, and having an ethics officer.

- To nurture ethical conduct in marketing, open communication and coaching on ethical issues are essential. This requires providing employees with ethics training, clear channels of communication and follow-up support throughout the organisation. Companies must consistently enforce standards and impose penalties on those who violate codes of conduct.

- Companies are increasingly incorporating ethics and social responsibility programmes into their marketing decisions. Increasing evidence indicates that being socially responsible and ethical results in valuable benefits: an enhanced public reputation, which can increase market share, costs savings and profits.

## Key Links

This chapter should be read in conjunction with:

- Chapter 2's explanation of developing marketing strategies
- Chapter 3's description of the forces of the marketing environment, which include the increased emphasis on ethics and social responsibility
- Chapter 24's discussion of implementing marketing strategies and marketing programmes.

## Important Terms

Social responsibility
Marketing citizenship
Stakeholders
Marketing ethics
Cause-related marketing
Strategic philanthropy
Green marketing
Ethical issue
Organisational (corporate) culture
Opportunity
Codes of conduct

## Discussion and Review Questions

1. What is social responsibility and why is it important?
2. What are stakeholders? What role do they play in strategic marketing decisions?

3 List four dimensions of social responsibility.
4 What are some major social responsibility issues? Give an example of each.
5 What is the difference between ethics and social responsibility?
6 Why are ethics an important consideration in marketing decisions?
7 How do the factors that influence ethical or unethical decisions interact?
8 What ethical conflicts could arise if a company's employees chose to fly only on certain airlines in order to accrue personal frequent-flier miles?
9 Give an example of how each component of the marketing mix can be affected by ethical issues.
10 How can ethical decisions in marketing be improved?
11 How can people with different personal values work together to make ethical decisions in organisations?
12 What evidence exists that being socially responsible and ethical is worthwhile?

## Recommended Readings


- Charter, M. and Polonsky, M.J., *Greener Marketing: A Global Perspective on Greener Marketing Practice* (Sheffield: Greenleaf, 1999).
- Ferrell, O.C., Fraedrich, J. and Ferrell, L., *Business Ethics*, 4th edn (Boston: Houghton Mifflin, 2000).
- Jones, C., ten Bos, R. and Parker, M., *Business Ethics* (London: Routledge, 2004).
- Megone, C. and Robinson, S.J., *Case Histories in Business Ethics* (London: Routledge, 2002).
- Schlegelmilch, B., *Marketing Ethics: An International Perspective* (London: International Thomson Learning, 1998).
- Smith, C.N., 'Marketing strategies for the ethics era', *Sloan Management Review*, 36, (4), 1995, pp. 85–97.


## Internet Exercise

The Institute of Business Ethics offer guidance to organisations on doing business ethically. Its website provides advice on developing codes of business ethics and presents some simple tests on ethical decisions. Visit the Institute's website at: www.ibe.org.uk

1 What role do codes of business ethics play?
2 What steps might a business take to implement a code of conduct?
3 Using the links to sample codes of conduct on the IBE website, list the kinds of area that businesses might cover in such a code.

## *Applied Mini-Case*

Is it possible for a retailer to become too large and powerful? This is a question some people have been asking about Wal-Mart, the world's largest retail company, which has 4750 stores around the globe. As it has aggressively pursued its low-price mantra, the concern is that Wal-Mart has become so big that it can do virtually anything it wants in some areas. Obviously this kind of power has enormous ethical and social implications. Suppliers suggest that Wal-Mart is able to dictate every aspect of their operations, from product design to pricing, in its efforts to maximise savings for customers. One illustration is that to meet Wal-Mart's demands for lower prices, some suppliers have been forced to lay off employees or move operations to countries where production costs are lower. Companies that hesitate risk losing their most lucrative outlet and will find their products quickly replaced by a competitor's on Wal-Mart's shelves. For the customer, seeking keen prices and great choice, there are obvious benefits to Wal-Mart's approach, but perhaps there is also a cost.

**Source:** W. Pride and O.C. Ferrell, *Marketing: Concepts and Strategies* (Boston: Houghton Mifflin, 2005).

### *Question*

What are some of the ethical and social implications of the power Wal-Mart is able to exert? What action can Wal-Mart take to manage these issues?

## Case Study

# Nestlé Faces Pressure Groups

In 1995 two university students approached Nestlé for advertising for their alternative student newspaper, the *Oxford Independent*. When the newspaper appeared in 1996, instead of a Kit-Kat advertisement, Nestlé used its copy space to oppose consumer pressure groups boycotting its products because of its marketing of infant formula in developing countries. In 1999 the Advertising Standards Authority (ASA) upheld a complaint made against this advertisement by the pressure group Baby Milk Action, which aims to halt the commercial promotion of bottle-feeding and supports breastfeeding. For Nestlé, this was simply the latest instalment in an ongoing battle against pressure groups, which began in 1977 when the US-based Infant Formula Action Coalition protested against Nestlé's role in promoting the artificial feeding of babies. Consumers were asked to boycott all Nestlé products as a protest against the company's high-profile promotion of infant formula and its policy of widely distributing free samples to medical personnel and health centres.

According to a World Health Organization (WHO) report, up to 1.5 million babies who die each year would survive if the decline in breast-feeding were reversed. The International Code of Marketing of Breast-Milk Substitutes was established in 1981, yet Nestlé did not sign up to it until 1984. The consumer boycott was suspended, only to be reinstated in 1988 when the International Baby Food Action Network (IBFAN) voiced concern over Nestlé's compliance with the code. Baby Milk Action complained about the 1996 *Oxford Independent* advertisement, supported by IBFAN.

Nestlé's advertising copy had stated that 'even before the WHO International Code of Marketing Breast-Milk Substitutes was introduced in 1981, Nestlé marketed infant formula ethically and responsibly, and has done so ever since'. The ASA provisionally ruled that Nestlé could not support this claim and that, indeed, it 'went too far'. The ASA also objected to the copy claim that Nestlé employees do not provide free samples to hospitals for use with healthy babies. The ASA ruled that the implications that such practices had ceased 'a very long time' ago were unacceptable and misleading. Nestlé had admitted to giving out free samples in South Africa until October 1992, in Thailand until July 1988, in Bangladesh until January 1993 and to hospitals in China as recently as April 1994 – only two years before the appearance of the *Oxford Independent* advertisement. ASA also ruled that Nestlé's suggestion that it had complied with the 1981 Code implied long-term and consistent agreement, which in fact could not be substantiated by Nestlé. The ASA warned Nestlé not to repeat the three claims in UK advertising.

This has been a public relations nightmare for Nestlé. The students believe Nestlé placed the advertisement as a tester of opinion and probably underestimated the ongoing hostility of consumer groups to its marketing practices for infant formula. Nestlé itself has refused to comment on its approach. In 1999, it embarked on a corporate image-boosting campaign, emphasising its high-quality, reliable products, its endorsement of the 1981 code and the company's links with developing communities. The company pointed to its 60,000 employees living in developing countries and the extensive measures in place to ensure that the business develops in harmony with changes in the local communities.

Unfortunately for Nestlé, reaction to its 'greater good' claims was far from universally positive. Greenpeace has targeted Nestlé chocolate bar Butterfinger in Germany owing to its use of GM-labelled packaging. Greenpeace believes Nestlé has an unrealistically 'bullish approach to genetic engineering ... bringing it problems worldwide'. The pressure group argues that this bullish stance is similar to that portrayed in Nestlé's handling of its baby food marketing. The charity Save The Children has endured an ongoing debate with Nestlé over its infant formula marketing drives, stating that it has 'had intermittent and unsatisfactory dealings with Nestlé' which has 'shown an unwillingness, in our view, to deal fairly with our concerns'. Save The

Children states that it takes seriously the role of corporate responsibility, particularly concerning the obligations to children in terms of feeding. As the leading producer of infant formula with 40 per cent of the market, Nestlé has an obligation, argues Save The Children, to lead the way in ethical standards and social responsibility in terms of product development and marketing campaigns.

There clearly is a need for infant formula – many mothers are unable or unwilling to provide breast milk for their children – but WHO and IBFAN concerns are with aggressive marketing campaigns persuading many mothers to turn immediately to infant formula for their babies at the expense of the nourishing and protective benefits of breast feeding. How should Nestlé have dealt with the issue? Cause Concern, Saatchi & Saatchi's cause-related marketing division, argues that Nestlé should (a) ignore it, (b) deal with it through the courts, or (c) negotiate with the pressure groups. These three options needed to be evaluated and one course of action taken. In addition, a PR offensive could have promoted Nestlé's extensive donations to charity and involvement with Kids' Clubs, for example.

To overcome the hostility, Nestlé needs to avoid undertaking any unethical marketing activity and to guarantee to comply with the 1981 code. In addition, it needs to embark on an ethical drive within the business and in terms of its communications with its various target audiences. Increasingly, consumers want a brand that satisfies them, but also they want to know in what the brand believes and for what the supplying company stands. In most markets, particularly mature ones, consumers have a choice of products from competing companies. While product attributes, supporting customer service, branding and marketing communications, undoubtedly play a significant role in consumer choice between brands, the ethical reputation of a company increasingly plays a role, too. Benetton, McDonald's, Shell and Nestlé are just some of the more high-profile companies that have faced a consumer backlash because of aspects of their trading practices. Many others will follow them as consumers become more aware of organisations' trading and business practices.

**Sources:** Amanda Wilkinson, 'Cause for concern', *Marketing Week*, 11 February 1999, pp. 28–31; David Benady and Amanda Wilkinson, 'Nestlé acts to boost its corporate image', *Marketing Week*, 13 May 1999, p. 26; Stephanie Bentley, 'Nestlé chief fights back over ethics ruling', *Marketing Week*, 18 February 1999, p. 7; Amanda Wilkinson, 'Nestlé loses ASA battle', *Marketing Week*, 4 February 1999, p. 5; Letters, *Marketing Week*, 27 May 1999, p. 33.

## Questions for Discussion

1. How should Nestlé have addressed the concerns of the pressure groups?
2. Is Save The Children right to complain about its dealings with Nestlé? Are such corporate expectations reasonable?
3. What role could a code of ethical and responsible marketing conduct play in an organisation such as Nestlé?

# Postscript

Chapter 1 explained that, in order to take advantage of any identified marketing opportunities, an organisation must first develop a marketing strategy and then create marketing programmes to help implement the recommended strategy. Parts I and II of *Marketing: Concepts and Strategies* examined marketing opportunity analysis. Chapter 2 detailed the principal aspects of a marketing strategy and Chapter 8 explored the all-important task of target market selection. Part VIII has focused on marketing management issues necessary for the operationalisation of the specified marketing strategy, namely marketing planning, implementation processes and control measures. In addition, the important issues of ethics and social responsibility in marketing management have been highlighted.

Before progressing, readers should be confident that they are now able to do the following.

## Explain the process of marketing planning and forecasting sales potential

- What is the marketing planning process?
- What constitutes a marketing plan?
- What are the purposes of the marketing plan?
- What is the relationship between marketing analysis – including the SWOT analysis – marketing strategy and marketing programmes in marketing planning?
- How are market and sales potential determined?
- What are the principal sales forecasting methods?
- What are the major components of a marketing audit?

## Understand the issues relating to implementing strategies, internal marketing relationships and measuring performance

- How are marketing activities organised within a company's structure?
- What are the ways of organising a marketing unit?
- What is the marketing implementation process?
- What are the main impediments to marketing implementation?
- What are some of the approaches to managing marketing implementation?
- Why is internal marketing important to an organisation?
- How are marketing activities implemented and controlled?
- How can sales and marketing cost analysis be used as methods of evaluating performance?
- What is marketing shareholder value analysis?
- What are the popular criteria for measuring marketing performance?

## Discuss the relevance of ethics and social responsibility in marketing

- What is meant by ethics in marketing?
- Why is it an important concept in marketing?
- What is the ethical decision-making process?
- What factors influence the ethical decision-making process?
- What are the main ethical issues facing marketers?
- How can ethical decision-making be improved?
- What is meant by social responsibility?
- What are the important social responsibility issues facing marketers?
- What strategies exist for dealing with social dilemmas?
- How are the concepts of social responsibility and marketing ethics related?

*Strategic Case*

# Mattel's Barbie
## Mattel Takes on the World

Mattel, with US$4.7 billion in annual revenues, is the world leader in the design, manufacture and marketing of children's toys. The company's major toy brands include Barbie, with more than 120 different Barbie dolls, Fisher-Price, Disney entertainment lines, Hot Wheels and Matchbox cars, Tyco Toys and Polly Pocket, plus many well-known games, including Scrabble (International), Outburst and Rebound. The company markets toys and games bearing the names of children's favourites Barney, Bear in The Big Blue House, Blue's Clues, Dora The Explorer, Sesame Street, Winnie The Pooh, Angelina Ballerina, Toy Story, Harry Potter, Rugrats and the Wild ThornBerrys.

In addition, Mattel promotes global sales by tailoring toys for specific international markets, instead of simply modifying established favourites from the company's base in the United States. The company's headquarters are in El Segundo, California, but Mattel also has offices in 36 countries. In fact, the company markets its products in more than 155 countries throughout the world.

Mattel's marketing prowess and reach have paid off. For example, in a poll conducted by the annual Power Brands study, Mattel had strong popularity among consumers: as many as four out of ten people said that if they were shopping for toys, Mattel would be the preferred brand. Retailers also singled out Mattel as the number-one performer, mentioned six out of ten times. This survey proved that both children and adults are enthusiastic about Mattel and its line of products. In 2002, the Mattel and Fisher-Price names topped a survey of consumers who were asked about their brand preferences when buying toys in discount stores or superstores, also mentioning Barbie and Hot Wheels repeatedly. Mattel owns all of the leaders in this US survey's report of top toy brands. Similar surveys in the UK, Benelux and Germany also rate the company's brands in the 'top ten' for toys.

### Customer Orientation at Mattel

Mattel's management philosophy focuses on satisfying the customer's needs and wants. For example, Mattel redesigned Barbie to more naturally reflect a 'normal' athletic woman in an attempt to meet demands for a more realistic doll. Barbie has also taken on many different professions in order to reach a wider audience. These product modifications and extensions are designed to meet consumer and social demands while still accomplishing company objectives. Likewise, some Hot Wheels cars now display the logos of famous racing teams and major championships around the world, in an attempt to meet consumer demand for more merchandise related to this popular televised sport.

Mattel's pursuit of interactive multimedia is an attempt to adapt to the shorter span of time that young girls want to spend playing with Barbie and other dolls and more traditional toys. Increasingly, children are turning to more interactive toys sooner than was the case in previous years, and Mattel's acquisition of The Learning Company was designed to meet this demand. This acquisition, however, did not prove profitable for Mattel, and the company eventually sold the division. This acquisition and disposal demonstrates the company's awareness of evolving customer trends and also a ruthless management of its portfolio against clearly laid-down performance measures.

As another indicator of its commitment to customers, Mattel employs marketing research to ensure that its strategy and tactics match customer desires. This is combined with product research and development in an effort to release new products yearly, based on these consumer needs and wants. A recent addition to the Mattel product lines includes the new construction and activity set called Ello, now receiving significant marketing communications support. The product is meant to compete with Lego AG and draws girls to building toys, which have traditionally been marketed almost exclusively to boys. Mattel research teams watched girls play with pipe cleaners, scissors, glue, paper and cardboard. The results indicated that girls wanted to make panels and tell stories about the space created. The idea behind Ello is to build a house or figures using interconnecting plastic shapes, allowing girls to build and create while engaging in social play. Mattel hopes Ello will be a globally recognised brand with a unique name that does not require translation.

## Mattel's Core Products

### Barbie

The first Barbie doll sported open-toed shoes, a ponytail, sunglasses, earrings and a zebra-striped bathing suit, with fashions and accessories also available for the doll. While buyers at the annual Toy Fair in New York City took no interest in the Barbie doll, the little girls of the time certainly did. The intense demand seen at the retail stores was insufficiently met for several years: Mattel simply could not produce Barbie dolls fast enough. Barbie is one of Mattel's major product lines, accounting for more than 50 per cent of its total sales. Around the world, Barbie-related merchandise from Mattel is worth a staggering US$3.6 billion at retail prices, making it by far the number one girl's brand globally.

March 1999 marked the 40th anniversary of Barbie. It also heralded a new Barbie campaign, called 'Be Anything', which focused on encouraging girls to become anything, from athletes to computer experts to dreamers. A Barbie doll is barely present in the Be Anything advert, and not one of Barbie's accessories appears. The whole campaign is an attempt to retain the interest of girls for another two years after the usual post-Barbie age of seven and to make Barbie more 'real' to these older girls.

However, by August 2002, Barbie's popularity had waned and she failed to make the list of the top five best-selling dolls. Mattel reacted by introducing a line of My Scene dolls, which includes a multicultural Barbie, aimed at older girls referred to as 'tweens'. The 'tween' market is comprised of girls between ages 8 and 12 who would rather watch MTV than play with dolls. A website at www.myscene.com engages girls in the lives of four friends living in the 'big city' through short 'shows' and music videos. Other efforts targeted at 'tweens' include a crime-solving crew called the Mystery Squad and the Barbie Doll as Elle Woods, which is a tribute to the blonde character in the MGM Pictures movie *Legally Blond 2: Red, White and Blonde*. These lines have given Barbie a new lease of life: recently she stood for election in the US Presidential elections, supported by a full PR campaign!

### Hot Wheels

With millions of boys aged 5–15 collecting Hot Wheels cars, this line of small die-cast vehicles is now involved with almost every racing circuit in the world, including NASCAR (the National Association for Stock Car Auto Racing), Formula One (F1), NHRA (the National Hot Rod Association), CART (Championship Auto Racing Teams), AMA (American Motorcycle Association), and many other circuits. This immense popularity has created a group of young collectors: the average boy collector owns more than 40 Hot Wheels cars.

Hot Wheels celebrated its 35th anniversary in 2003 with a massive marketing campaign called the Hot Wheels Highway 35 World Race. Mattel is creating a story-based and character-based package that includes collectible cars, racetracks, comic books, home videos, a video game, a television network special and an on-line race. The idea is to appeal to the many different age groups of collectors Mattel has acquired in more recent years.

### Fisher-Price

Acquired in 1993 as a wholly owned subsidiary, Fisher-Price is the umbrella brand for all of Mattel's infant and pre-school lines. The brand is trusted by parents all over the world and appears on everything from children's software to eyewear, and from books to bicycles. Some of the more classic products include the Rock-a-Stack and Little People play sets. New favourites include Power Wheels vehicles and Rescue Heroes, a line of fire-fighter action figures. Through licensing agreements, the brand also develops character-based toys such as *Sesame Street's* Elmo and Big Bird, plus Disney's Winnie The Pooh and Mickey Mouse.

Fisher-Price has built trust with parents by creating products that are educational, safe and useful. In recent years, the brand has earned high regard for innovative car seats and nursery monitors. While not toys, these baby and toddler products are sold to parents already familiar with the company's reputation and these are often retailed in the same stores as Mattel's toys. The company continues to innovate in its core business, too: one project includes collaboration with Microsoft to develop an activity table that teaches children from infants to pre-schoolers using 'smart technology'.

## International Sales

Under CEO Robert A. Eckert's leadership, Mattel has maintained its strategy of strong expansion overseas with a goal of raising international sales from 34 per cent in 2002 to 50 per cent of overall sales by 2010. Of the 34 per cent, almost two-thirds are in Europe and a third in Latin America, with a small amount in the Asia-Pacific region. International sales increased by 13 per cent from 2000 to 2001 and by 11 per cent from 2001 to 2002. The international segment has benefited from Mattel's strategic focus on globalisation of brands, including improved product availability, better alignment of worldwide marketing and sales plans, plus strong product launches.

Worldwide, Mattel's most recognised product continues to be Barbie. In a study conducted by Interbrand and published in *Business Week*, Barbie was the only Mattel brand that made the overall list of the '100 Best Global Brands'. However, the traditional Barbie doll is not receiving a warm welcome in some international markets. The Malaysian Consumers' Association of Penanghas tried to ban Barbie because of her non-Asian appearance and the lack of creativity needed to play with her. Government agencies in other countries, such as Iran, are carrying out similar campaigns against Barbie.

## Ethics and Responsibility at Mattel

Like most organisations, Mattel has recognised the different responsibilities it has to various stakeholders, including customers, employees, investors, suppliers and the community. These stakeholders have some claim, or stake, in Mattel's products, markets and business outcomes. Mattel demonstrates a commitment to economic, legal, ethical and philanthropic responsibilities.

Mattel's core products and business environment can present ethical issues. For example, since the company's products are designed primarily for children, the company must be sensitive to children's rights. In addition, the international environment often complicates business transactions, especially in the areas of employee rights and safety in manufacturing facilities. Different legal systems and cultural expectations about business can create ethical conflict. The use of technology may also present ethical dilemmas, especially with regard to consumer privacy. Mattel has recognised these potential issues and has taken steps to strengthen its commitment to business ethics and social responsibility. Advances in technology have created special issues for Mattel's marketing efforts. Mattel has recognised that because it markets to children, it has the responsibility to communicate with parents about its corporate marketing strategy. The company has taken special steps to inform both children and adults about its philosophy regarding Internet-based marketing tools, such as the Hot Wheels website.

At the Barbie.com website, parents are encouraged to read and follow the suggestions provided by Mattel on Internet safety. This parents' page provides tips for creating rules and regulations for their children's use of the Internet. There is also an example of an Internet Safety Promise for children and parents to complete, forming a type of 'contract' to engage in smart, safe and responsible behaviour when surfing the Internet.

As this case has shown, while the last few years of the twentieth century challenged Mattel's executive leadership and financial standing, the company also made great strides in respect to its ethical and social responsibilities. Today, Mattel faces many marketing opportunities and threats, including the rate at which children are maturing and abandoning toys, the role of technology in consumer products, purchasing power and consumer needs in global markets. Mattel has much sales growth potential, especially in the international markets. For a company that began with two friends making picture frames, Mattel has demonstrated marketing dexterity and the ability to keep abreast of market developments. The next few years will test the company's resolve and strategy within the highly competitive, yet highly lucrative, toy market.

## Questions for Discussion

1 Describe Mattel's target markets for Barbie and Hot Wheels. How does the company's marketing strategy appeal to these markets?
2 How has Mattel tried to be a socially responsible company in its world markets?
3 What environmental forces have created challenges for Mattel as its continued expansion moves it into global markets? Which markets have created opportunities?

# IX Studying and Working in Marketing

Those using *Marketing: Concepts and Strategies* have one key fact in common – they are all trying to learn more about marketing. Yet their reasons for doing so will vary. Many readers will be students; undergraduates, postgraduates or marketing practitioners working towards professional examinations. Some of these individuals will already be working in marketing, others might look for a career in the area at a later stage.

**Part IX of *Marketing: Concepts and Strategies*** explores a number of areas that may be relevant to these readers' learning experiences and aspirations: case study analysis, examination revision tips, and careers in marketing.

**Chapter 26, 'Case Study Analysis, Exam Revision Tips and Careers in Marketing'**, presents supplementary materials to aid students' understanding of marketing, and to assist in examination preparation or career selection. The first part of the chapter considers the use of case study analysis. A variety of learning tools is used in management education. Case study analysis is one of the most popular approaches for exploring how theory is applied in practice. The chapter then moves on to consider the use of case study analysis as a learning tool. This is followed by a discussion of the fundamentals of situation analysis, the process for analysing case studies and the presentation of findings. The second part of the chapter reviews examination revision tips. Emphasis is placed on how examination papers are set, coping with examination conditions and tips on preparing answers. The final section of the chapter explores careers in marketing. Here different types of marketing careers are considered and the roles of the curriculum vitae (CV) and the interview process in securing a job are considered.

By the conclusion of Part IX of *Marketing: Concepts and Strategies*, readers should be better prepared to tackle case studies, prepare for examinations and pursue a career in marketing.

## A Career in Marketing

Marketing is the most fun you can have in business, with your clothes on.

Marketing is the most fascinating aspect of business because it is about creating a profit out of studying and satisfying the needs of endlessly unpredictable customers.

You can make a million in marketing by becoming the Marketing Director of Tesco, or by starting your own consultancy, or by coming up with your own business idea and becoming an entrepreneur yourself. You can help change the world by becoming the Marketing Director of a leading charity.

Some companies have lots of marketing executives, some have very few. The company that you should try to work for does not just have a marketing department but is one where the customer is truly placed at the heart of the organisation.

**Hugh Burkitt, Chief Executive of The Marketing Society**

The Marketing Society is a professional association dedicated to raising the stature of marketing in business. It champions marketing excellence by providing the best network for senior marketers to exchange ideas and share best practice.

# 26

# Case Study Analysis, Exam Revision Tips and Careers in Marketing

## Objectives

- To introduce the role of case study analysis in learning
- To explore the areas involved in situational analysis
- To explain the process for analysing a case study
- To review how case study findings should be presented
- To present guidance on examination revision, to consider how to cope with examination conditions and how to format examination answers
- To discuss careers in marketing
- To explore the role of the curriculum vitae and how to prepare for interviews
- To describe different types of marketing career

## Introduction

Those using this book have one key factor in common: they are all trying to learn more about marketing. Yet their reasons for doing so will vary. Many readers will be students; undergraduates, postgraduates or marketing practitioners working towards professional examinations. Some of these individuals will already be working in marketing, others may look for a career in the area at a later stage. This chapter explores a number of areas that may be relevant to these readers' learning experiences and aspirations: case study analysis; examination revision tips; and careers in marketing.

The first part of the chapter considers the use of case study analysis. A variety of learning tools is used in management education. Case study analysis is one of the most popular approaches for exploring how theory is applied in practice. The popularity of case studies in marketing management education is primarily linked to the technique's ability to bridge the gap between marketing theory and practical situations, thus allowing students to apply the concepts they have learned. This section begins by considering the use of case study analysis as a learning tool. This is followed by a discussion of the fundamentals of situation analysis, the process for analysing case studies and the presentation of findings. The second part of the chapter reviews examination revision tips. Emphasis is placed on how examination papers are set, coping with examination conditions and tips on preparing answers. The final section of the chapter explores careers in marketing. Here, different types of marketing career are considered, as are the role of the curriculum vitae and the interview process in securing a job.

*Opener*

# Why You May be Reading this Book and What it Means

If you are reading this marketing textbook you are probably doing so because you want to learn more about marketing concepts. Perhaps you are studying for an undergraduate or postgraduate degree. Maybe you are a practitioner who is working towards a professional marketing qualification or who simply wants to know more about a particular marketing technique. In most cases your encounter with marketing will not end with the time spent delving into this book. If you are a student studying for an academic or professional qualification, it is likely that you will get involved in analysing case studies. Maybe you have tried to tackle some of the cases contained in this text, or perhaps your tutors have set you a longer case study to review in class. The section on case study analysis that follows this introduction is designed to give you some basic ideas about how to examine, understand and interpret this kind of material. These tips apply equally to those who are preparing a case study for a class, getting ready for an examination that includes a case study, or simply trying to understand better how marketing theory is applied in a practical context.

For many of you, your studies in marketing will culminate in an examination of some kind. Revising and getting ready for this kind of assessment can be taxing. Most people find examinations stressful, and worry about whether or not they will be properly prepared. The guidance in the second part of this chapter is designed to help with these anxieties. Obviously revision is paramount, but as you will see there are many other practical steps that you can take to ease the process of preparation. Did you know, for example, that wandering around the supermarket is a legitimate way of collecting ideas about how marketing concepts are applied in practice? Just look at all the brands on the shelves, think about how they are targeting the consumer, their brand values, and how they are packaged and displayed.

Some of you may have plans to pursue a marketing career once your studies are complete. Others may already be marketing practitioners. The final part of this chapter is aimed at those who are looking for a marketing career of some kind. If this appeals to you, it is probable that you already have some idea about the kinds of marketing jobs available. Scanning through any of the marketing news-sheets aimed at practitioners will give you a pretty clear view of the opportunities on offer. However, if you are at an early stage in this process or have yet to decide on your future career, you may find it useful to peruse the information on marketing careers towards the end of this chapter.

Photo: Courtesy of Sally Dibb and Lyndon Simkin

# The Use of Case Study Analysis[1]

At undergraduate, postgraduate and practitioner level, the case study is an accepted and widely used learning tool. The popularity of case studies in marketing education is mainly because the technique helps to bridge the gap between marketing theory and practical situations, allowing students to apply the concepts they have learned. Success in providing case study solutions, as in real life, is largely determined by the quality of the analysis carried out. Learning how to make decisions about case studies in a logical, objective and structured way is essential. Such decisions must take into consideration all relevant aspects of the marketing and competitive environment. For case studies based on particular businesses, an appreciation of the company's resources is also needed. Developing the necessary decision-making and analytical skills promotes an understanding of different corporate structures and philosophies, and provides insight into the implementation of marketing tools. The learning process also allows the risks and problems of managerial decision-making to be experienced first hand.

A popular approach to case study learning is to work in seminar or syndicate groups, which helps develop group as well as individual skills. This closely emulates actual work situations, given the extent to which managers in real business situations must work in teams and be prepared to reach consensus. The development of group skills takes time as individuals learn to cope with the differing opinions of colleagues. Although preparing cases on an individual basis may appear simpler than working in a group situation, a more limited range of alternatives may be developed. Nevertheless, tackling cases individually also builds analytical and decision-making skills.

# Situation Analysis

Conducting a situation analysis helps to identify the key issues and factors at play in any case study and provides a good starting point for those engaged in case analysis. A situation analysis refers to the activities involved in reviewing a company's internal position (structure, financial situation, marketing organisation), market analysis, external environment and competition.

## Company's Internal Position

An appreciation of the company's internal position, drawing attention to particular capabilities and resources, is vital. This analysis should take into consideration the company structure, financial situation and marketing organisation.

**Company Structure** The structure of an organisation influences operational and managerial decisions. By answering the following questions, students can develop an appropriate overview of company characteristics. This understanding should be used as a basis for assessing the extent to which the various case solutions eventually recommended are realistic.

- Is the organisational structure hierarchical or flat?
- Where does the balance of power lie?
- What is the company's mission statement?
- Does the company have particular philosophies?
- What are the key characteristics of the company?
- Is managerial activity delineated by function?
- Who are the key decision-makers for each functional area?
- How do the lines of communication operate?
- What formal and informal decision-making structures operate?

**Company Financial Situation** Various techniques can be used to assess the financial position of the company. An overview of financial health can be gleaned from the balance sheet and income statement. The website for *Marketing: Concepts and Strategies*, which can be found at www.dibbmarketing.com, presents details for marketing related financial analyses. Comparing current figures with those from earlier trading periods is especially informative because this allows changes over time to be mapped.

Financial ratios are calculated using information from the basic balance sheet and income statement (see Table 26.1). These ratios can be used to achieve greater financial insight into a company and can be compared with ratios from competing companies to allow a better understanding of each company's relative position. Sometimes a break-even analysis is also useful (see Chapter 21).

**TABLE 26.1 KEY FINANCIAL RATIOS**

**a Profitability ratios**
These ratios measure financial and operating efficiency by assessing the organisation's ability to generate profit from revenue and money invested.

| Name of ratio | Calculated |
|---|---|
| 1 Gross profit margin<br>This shows the total margin available to meet operating expenses and generate a profit. | $\frac{\text{Sales} - \text{Cost of goods sold}}{\text{Sales}}$ |
| 2 Net profit margin<br>Sometimes called return on sales, this ratio shows after-tax profit per £ (pound) spent. | $\frac{\text{Profit after taxes}}{\text{Sales}}$ |
| 3 Return on assets<br>This ratio measures the company's return on total investment. | $\frac{\text{Profit after taxes}}{\text{Total assets}}$ |
| 4 Return on net worth<br>Also referred to as return on stockholders' equity, this ratio gives a measure of the rate of return on shareholders' equity. | $\frac{\text{Profit after taxes}}{\text{Total shareholders' equity}}$ |

**b Liquidity ratios**
These ratios are used to demonstrate the company's ability to meet current liabilities and to ensure solvency.

| Name of ratio | Calculated |
|---|---|
| 1 Current ratio<br>This demonstrates the company's ability to satisfy short-term liabilities. | $\frac{\text{Current assets}}{\text{Current liabilities}}$ |
| 2 Quick ratio<br>Also referred to as the acid test ratio, this demonstrates the company's ability to meet current liabilities, in the period in which they are due, without resorting to the sale of stock. | $\frac{\text{Current assets} - \text{Inventory}}{\text{Current liabilities}}$ |
| 3 Inventory to net working capital<br>This indicates the degree to which company working capital is tied up in stock. | $\frac{\text{Inventory}}{\text{Current assets} - \text{Current liabilities}}$ |

(continued)

**TABLE 26.1 KEY FINANCIAL RATIOS (CONTINUED)**

**c Leverage ratios**
This group of ratios helps in the assessment of the company's responsiveness to debt and ability to meet repayments as scheduled.

| Name of ratio | Calculated |
|---|---|
| 1 Debt to assets ratio<br>This indicates the extent to which borrowed funds have been employed to finance the company's operations. | $\frac{\text{Total liabilities}}{\text{Total assets}}$ |
| 2 Debt to equity ratio<br>This shows the balance of equity provided by the owners, and funds provided by creditors. | $\frac{\text{Total liabilities}}{\text{Total shareholders' equity}}$ |
| 3 Long-term debt to equity ratio<br>This ratio allows the balance between owners' equity and liabilities to be viewed in context of the company's overall capital structure. | $\frac{\text{Long-term liabilities}}{\text{Total shareholders' equity}}$ |

**d Activity ratios**
These ratios can show how effectively the company generates sales and profit from assets.

| Name of ratio | Calculated |
|---|---|
| 1 Total assets turnover<br>This ratio, which signals the level of sales productivity and utilisation of total assets, can be compared with the industry average to show whether the volume of business generated justifies the level of asset investment. | $\frac{\text{Sales}}{\text{Total assets}}$ |
| 2 Fixed assets turnover<br>This measures both sales productivity and utilisation of equipment and plant. | $\frac{\text{Sales}}{\text{Fixed assets}}$ |
| 3 Inventory turnover<br>This measure of inventory turnover can be compared with the industry norm to show whether the company carries too large or small an inventory. | $\frac{\text{Sales}}{\text{Inventory}}$ |

When using financial ratios, it is important to be aware of the following points. First, ratios represent a snapshot of a company's financial state at a particular point in time. When comparing the results from more than one ratio, therefore, it is necessary to ensure that the figures applied are from the same time period and calculated according to similar accounting conventions. Second, the way in which ratios are interpreted and used is more important than the figures in isolation. To understand the significance of a particular ratio, it is essential to understand all of the internal and external factors responsible for the financial position reflected in the figures. Once the financial analysis is complete, it is necessary to pull together the different strands of the overall financial picture and identify which issues are likely to have an impact on the recommended case solutions.

**Company Marketing Organisation** Evaluating how the company handles its marketing should systematically cover all aspects of the marketing strategy and programmes: marketing research processes and marketing information systems, maintenance of the product portfolio (including new product development), pricing strategies, distribution policy (including the policing and management of distributors), all aspects of marketing communications, personnel, customer and after-sales service.

## Market Analysis

Understanding market structure and customer requirements is a fundamental stage in any case analysis. The following key questions should be addressed:

**Market Structure**

- What is the market size?
- What are the trends in market size – is it increasing or decreasing? How quickly?
- How is the market structured? What evidence is there of segments?
- Which segment(s) or customer group(s) is the company targeting?

**Customers**

- Who are the customers?
- What are the customers like?
- For what purpose do they buy the product/service? What are their needs?
- What features do they look for in the product/service?
- What is the buying process like?
- Who and what factors influence customers as they buy?
- How do they feel about the product/service?
- How do they feel about alternative suppliers?

It is necessary to assess how effectively the company is reaching its target customers and whether it is geared for expected changes in customer needs and/or market structure. This analysis will have an impact on the solution(s) selected.

## External Environment

A wide range of factors from the external marketing environment have an impact on the well-being of an organisation. These include economic, political, societal/ Green, technological, legal and regulatory issues, as discussed in Chapter 3. Changes in these factors can have a major impact on a company's business dealings. Recognising the significance of such changes early on can help companies to maximise the positive benefits and minimise the detrimental effects. Early warning of the effects of environmental factors can be achieved by assessing the potential opportunities/threats presented by changes. In case study analysis, it is often necessary to extrapolate trends and make predictions regarding the level of future change. It is helpful to remember that most potential threats can also be viewed as opportunities should an organisation have the resources and interest to pursue them.

## Competition

Understanding the competitive structure of markets helps companies put their marketing options into perspective (see Chapters 2 and 3). From the customers' viewpoint, buying decisions are based on the strengths and weaknesses of a particular player relative to other available choices. Questions to be considered in relation to the competitive situation include the following:

- Who are the key players?
- How is market share divided among competing organisations?
- What competitive positions do the players occupy; who is market leader; which companies are challengers, fast movers, followers and nichers?
- How aggressive are the competing organisations and what are the trends? Is it possible to identify fast movers?
- On what basis are key competitors competing? What are their differential advantages – are these sustainable and how are they supported with marketing programmes?
- Are there likely to be new entrants or competition from substitute solutions?

Answering these questions helps develop a fuller picture of the relative competitive strengths and weaknesses of the company, and enables an assessment of whether or not different case solutions are realistic. It may also be possible to use this information to predict how key competitors are likely to respond to different case solutions.

## The Case Study Process

### Identify and Analyse Case Problem Areas

After the situational analysis has been conducted, a clear view of the problems/key issues set out in the case study must be developed. Although any specific case questions will affect exactly where the key areas lie, the company and other analyses undertaken will usually have revealed a range of problem areas that need to be addressed. Any specific questions can be tackled once these problems have been identified. One way to assess the case material and the core issues is to carry out a marketing audit. The marketing audit involves systematically considering all aspects of the company's marketing set-up, within a predetermined structure (see Chapter 23 for a full explanation). For example, it covers the marketing environment, marketing strategy, marketing organisation, marketing systems and marketing programmes. Carrying out a marketing audit aids the case analysis by:

- describing current activities and results – sales, costs, profits, prices, etc.
- gathering data about customers, competitors and relevant environmental developments
- exploring opportunities for improving marketing strategies
- providing an overall database to be used in developing marketing strategies and programmes for implementation.

Not all cases require or have sufficient information for a formal audit. The initial situation analysis may give adequate focus and understanding. In more complex cases covering dynamic and competitive markets, the marketing audit can assist in sifting through the market and company data to identify the most pertinent issues.

When developing a list of problem areas, it is vital to distinguish between symptoms of problems and the problems themselves. Symptoms are the outward signs of an underlying problem. Symptoms may, for instance, include falling sales, declining profits and shrinking market share. The problem may be poor understanding of customers, signalling a need for closer links with customers and regular feedback from the marketplace.

The identification of symptoms and problems should start with the biggest problem(s). The associated symptoms can then be pinpointed and listed. Minor difficulties, whether or not they are related to the major problems, should be dealt with after the main problem(s) have been determined. It is helpful to signal whether the problems are affecting the company's short-, medium- or long-term position.

### Derive Alternative Solutions

Selecting a case solution is an iterative process that should start with the generation of a number of alternatives. Each potential solution must relate to the case's key problem area(s) and offer a realistic way of solving it. It is not a good idea to spend time reviewing too many similar solutions. Detailed fine-tuning can be carried out once a selection has been made. In some circumstances it is helpful to frame the generation of alternatives around the following questions.

- Where is the company now?
- How did the company get to its current position?
- Where does the company want to go/what does it want to achieve?
- How can the company achieve what it wants and move to where it wants to go?

An understanding of the organisation's current position should already have been achieved through the situation analysis, but explicitly framing the first two questions ensures that these issues from the earlier analysis are not overlooked. At this stage the more unrealistic solutions can be excluded, so that the more likely options can be analysed further.

**Analyse Alternative Solutions** The next step is a critical evaluation of the proposed solutions. This should involve a formal assessment of the advantages and disadvantages of every alternative. Each proposal should be considered within the context of the company, market, competitor and environmental analyses that have been carried out. Conducting 'What if ...?' analyses – in which attempts are made to predict the likely outcome(s) of alternative solutions – can be useful. It is also helpful to list each advantage and disadvantage, if possible, ranking the relative importance of each. This ranking should help identify the best solution.

**Recommend the 'Best' Alternative** Provided that the case analysis has been thorough, deciding on the best solution should not be too complex. Whichever option is selected, the environmental, competitor and market analyses must be double-checked to ensure that the chosen solution is consistent with prevailing market conditions. It is rarely possible to identify a course of action that is ideal in all respects, so it is helpful to consider both the acceptability and risks of the various options. Limited data availability and/or ambiguous market conditions may create problems. However, it should be remembered that managers must often make definitive decisions when only limited information is available.

Once a decision has been made, arguments should be prepared supporting the choice(s). In some circumstances, some of the recommendations may be based on the success of initial actions. Some flexibility will be needed in responding to the differing circumstances that may arise.

**Implement the Chosen Solution** Ensuring that the recommended plans and marketing programmes can be implemented is as fundamental to case study learning as the analyses and choice of the best solution. Consideration should be given to the following issues.

- At which target groups is the solution aimed?
- How will the company's offering be positioned?
- Will this provide a strong basis for competing and differential advantage?
- Exactly how will the solution be implemented?

Marketing mix considerations (product, people, price, promotion and place/distribution) include the following.

- What processes will need to be set up to ensure that implementation occurs?
- Which departments/individuals will take responsibility for the day-to-day implementation?
- When will the solution be implemented?
- What are the likely cost implications of implementing the solution?
- What are the expected benefits of implementing the solution (revenues, cash flow, competitive position, customer perceptions, etc.)?

In real situations, implementation may be affected by a range of interacting factors and unforeseen circumstances. It is helpful to have an appropriate contingency plan to be followed if the initial recommendations are unsuccessful.

## Presenting the Case Study Findings

Various formats can be used to report case study findings, among them an informal discussion, a structured formal presentation or a written report. Learning how to present case solutions, like the analysis itself, takes time. While there is a strong personal element in presentational style, the following guidelines are intended to help develop effectiveness in this area. Marketers must be able to make professional presentations and write good reports.

## Formal Presentations

Case study presentations can become turgid, clumsy and monotonous, but with care and imagination they can easily be transformed into a lively and interesting forum for debate. Following some simple rules should assist in this process. The presentation should be introduced carefully, so that its objectives are clearly set out. It is important to minimise repetition of the basic facts of the case. After all, other students will probably have read the case study, too. Presenters should endeavour to maintain eye contact with the audience. This can be achieved by not addressing the projection screen, overhead projector or whiteboard. The use of fully scripted notes should be avoided. Prompt cards inserted between overhead transparencies, or 'key word' notes made on paper copies of the transparencies can be helpful.

Visual materials should be as simple as possible. Audiences have difficulty digesting highly complex tables or slides that are covered in text or overly detailed. Clever use of colour and diagrams can make visual aids easier to follow. A lively presentational style, the use of humour and endeavouring to involve the audience can all be helpful tactics. Varying the presentation format helps to keep the audience interested.

The manner of the presentation itself must also be planned carefully. Using too much material should be avoided. Involving too many presenters can also be problematic: handover time is wasteful and boring for the audience. Rehearsal ensures that presenters are familiar with their material and have thought through in advance the key points from the presentation. Checking in advance and ensuring that you understand how all the audiovisual equipment involved works is also vital. Never be surprised by your own material. Think through in advance the points to be made at each stage of the presentation.

## Written Reports

The most appropriate structure for writing up a case analysis will be driven by the student's or tutor's objectives, as well as by individual style. Practitioners writing reports for their business may also have to fit in with company constraints regarding format. Report writing is a skill that takes practice to develop properly but offers considerable rewards when mastered. The purpose of the case study report is to present analyses and recommendations, demonstrating a thorough understanding of the situation. The emphasis should be on reasoned argument supporting the key recommendations rather than a mere reiteration of the information presented in the case.

Much has been written about report structure. Too often, reports are submitted with imperceptible structure, verbose paragraphs, and no sense of direction or clear recommendations. Although there is no standard report format that can be applied in all circumstances, the following suggested headings may help. The following basic components should be covered.

**Background to the Case Study** This should give a simple overview of the company/industry, perhaps indicating the nature of the market.

**Understanding of the Underlying Problem(s)** This involves focusing on the areas highlighted by the tutor or in the case questions. The problem should be stated briefly at this stage.

**Analysis of Case Study Material** The analysis part of the case study will involve the most extensive and detailed discussion. It is here that the student reports on the company and marketing analyses undertaken. This will probably be a lengthy section, requiring a series of sub-headings to add structure and clarity to the discussion.

**Recommendations with Justifications** The recommendations are the outcomes of the case study analysis and should emerge naturally out of the discussion section of the report. The report itself should already have *told the story*, leaving no surprises in terms of the recommended course of action.

The Marketing Tools and Techniques box below provides a simple checklist of section headings and guidance for producing the final document.

## Marketing Tools and Techniques

### Writing an Effective Report

A typical business report includes the following headings:

I Executive/management summary
II Introduction (including objectives)
III Background to the problem
IV Analysis (divided into relevant sections)
V Conclusions and recommendations
VI Bibliography/references
VII Appendices (supporting data and facts)

- The executive summary should provide a succinct, one- or two-page account of the entire report. It should explain the background to the case, discuss the key issues and themes, report on the analysis and list the recommendations.
- The report should be as user-friendly as possible, with page numbers, a table of contents, numbered sections and sub-headings. References should be sourced within the main body of the report and then listed in full in the bibliography. Diagrams and tables should also be properly labelled and referenced.
- The writing style should be as clear as possible, free of long sentences and jargon. If jargon is unavoidable, a glossary should explain any terms not in common usage.
- Arguments should be supported with appropriate sources (references, statistics, quotes, examples, comparisons, etc.) as available to add credibility to the discussion.
- Data from the case should be used with care and, if possible, interpreted; this may involve extrapolating trends or making predictions about the likely outcome of certain activities. Only relevant data should be included.
- Any relevant material that would clutter the main body of the document should be placed in appendices. Each appendix should be referred to within the main body of the report and listed in the table of contents.

# Examination Revision Tips

Each tutor, examination, educational institution and exam body will have its own requirements and ground rules. The views expressed here should be considered within this context and should not overrule any guidance given by students' own tutors and examination invigilators.

## The Examination Paper

Contrary to popular belief, tutors do not generally set examination papers in order to catch students out with trick questions or by referring questions to topics not covered in lectures or course texts. Examinations will be based on the set syllabus and on the concepts presented in any lectures and course readings. There are no substitutes for attending lectures, listening to tutors' views on key concepts and for painstaking, thorough revision. Preparation needs to start well before any examinations take place. There is usually little point in spending time trying to 'question spot' by looking at papers from previous years. The syllabus in the current year is not necessarily the same as in previous years, and many tutors do not refer to earlier papers when designing current examinations. This means that there is rarely a pattern in the topics that are chosen.

## Coping with Examination Conditions

Very few people enjoy taking examinations. Those sitting MBA or master's examinations, as well as those preparing for professional exams, will probably not have sat an examination for a long time. It is no surprise, then, that examinations are stressful. Although there are no easy ways to eliminate this problem, steps can be taken in the examination itself to make the experience less traumatic:

- Manage your time as effectively as possible. The format of the examination will specify the number of questions to be answered. There is no point in answering too many questions, as credit will not be awarded for the 'extra' answers. Failure to answer enough questions, on the other hand, will *undoubtedly* result in low marks being awarded for the paper. Poor time management is a prime reason for poor examination performance. When planning your time, leave a few minutes at the end to check back through your answers.
- Read each question properly and then answer the question actually set. Remember that the questions are there to help lead students to provide the answer that tutors are seeking. It is good practice to read each question *at least twice* to check that you are completely clear about what is required. There are two types of problem with answers that do not tackle the question that has been set.
  1. Total misunderstanding of what is required is extremely rare. Examination papers are almost always checked carefully by the staff teaching the courses, and often by an external examiner, to minimise ambiguities.
  2. Latching on to one key word or theme in a question is a much more common problem. Sometimes individuals spot a particular word or phrase in a question and then tell their tutors absolutely everything they know about that particular topic. However, in doing so they may not manage to answer the question that was set! Once again, the more carefully the question is read before starting to answer it, the less likely it is that this problem will arise.

## Format of Answers

Give some thought to how your ideas can best be presented in the examination. The following suggestions should help.

**Use Examples to Illustrate your Answers** Marketing is a practical subject, so it is important to demonstrate an understanding of how the theoretical concepts work by referring to examples. Some questions may specifically state a named example (product, brand or company), which must be referred to in the answer. With such questions, it is essential to use this named example and ensure that the relevant theoretical concepts are related to it. Some questions may ask students to illustrate their answers using examples of their own choosing. The tutors' aim here is to encourage students to demonstrate their genuine understanding of the concepts and their application.

**Prepare Some Examples in Advance of the Examination** It is much easier to think about possible examples away from the pressure of the examination itself. Doing this should save precious time. Take a break from the pain of revision and wander around the supermarket – it is surprising what can be learned there about new products and brands, and how they are marketed. Spend some time watching television advertisements or browsing through magazines for ideas. Magazines aimed at the marketing profession, such as *Marketing*, *Marketing Week* and *Campaign*, all have lively, interesting articles, and also present updates on new and existing products and marketing campaigns. Copies of these magazines are available in most libraries or on order from newsagents.

**Think About the Structure of your Answers** Make sure that each answer starts with a 'scene setting' introduction and finishes with some kind of conclusion or summary. A summary helps you to check that the question really has been addressed and reminds tutors of an answer's key points.

**Try to Avoid 'Wallpaper Syndrome'** That means pages and pages of script completely uninterrupted by new paragraphs, headings and figures. Make sure that each answer is clearly structured, that key points stand out and are easy to follow. Have an answer plan and relate sub-headings to it. Make sure your writing is easy to read!

**Be Sensible about Diagrams** Diagrams can usefully be employed to illustrate points or models in a concise and easy-to-follow manner. However, do not spend too long drawing them. A simple sketch is worth as many marks as a perfectly drawn and multicoloured piece of artwork. You will need to make sure that any diagrams are explained in the text – they cannot entirely take the place of written analysis.

Tutors involved in preparing students for examinations will know that similar concerns and anxieties prevail from one exam season to the next. The Marketing Tools and Techniques box below tackles some of the questions most commonly asked by students in the run up to sitting their examinations.

## Marketing Tools and Techniques

### Examination Techniques: Frequently Asked Questions

*How long should my answer be?*

This is impossible to answer. As might be expected, the quantity and quality of answers are not necessarily correlated. The variation in handwriting size also makes this impossible to judge. A typical essay answer, in say 45 minutes, for someone with 'average' handwriting may vary from three to six pages.

*What should I do if I run out of time?*

First of all, please do not! If, despite best efforts to manage time, this problem arises and the end of the examination is approaching fast, complete as much of the rest of the paper as possible in note form. Although this will not gain as many marks as a more considered and reasoned explanation, it will at least show the areas that would have been covered.

*I don't have time to revise all of the topics, so which ones should I leave out?*

Unfortunately, there is no easy answer to this one! It is understandable that you want to revise as efficiently as possible. However, the laws of probability dictate that the more topics you choose not to revise, the greater the risk that you will struggle to answer enough questions properly.

*Should I use essay or report format?*

Most tutors do not mind which format is adopted as long as the answer is legible, well structured and addresses the question clearly. Some examination papers may specify a required format in the opening instructions. Always read and understand an examination paper's covering instructions. You must adhere to these requirements and to your tutors' guidance. Remember that your tutors may be marking many examination scripts, so produce clear answers that are unambiguous and easy to read.

# Careers in Marketing

Although jobs in marketing are numerous and varied, not everyone will find a career in marketing satisfying. The work associated with the career that you follow should be enjoyable and stimulating. Because you will spend almost 40 per cent of your waking hours at work, you should not allow such factors as economic conditions or status to override your personal goals when choosing a career. Take the time to consider carefully how you want to spend your working life, and try to adopt a well-planned, systematic approach to finding a position that meets your personal and career objectives.

After determining your objectives, you should identify the organisations that are likely to offer desirable opportunities. Learn as much as possible about these companies before setting up employment interviews; job recruiters are impressed with applicants who have done their homework. Company websites now simplify this task.

When making initial contact with potential employers by mail, enclose a brief, clearly written letter of introduction. After an initial interview, you should send a brief letter of thanks to the interviewer. The job of getting the right job is important, and you owe it to yourself to take the process seriously.

## The Résumé or Curriculum Vitae

The résumé or curriculum vitae (CV) is key to being considered for a good job. Because it states your qualifications, experiences, education and career goals, the CV is a chance for a potential employer to assess your compatibility with the job requirements. For the employer's and individual's benefit, the CV should be accurate and current.

Effective CVs are targeted towards a specific position, as Figure 26.1 shows. This document is only one example of an acceptable CV. The job target section is specific and leads directly to the applicant's qualifications for the job. Capabilities show what the applicant can do and that the person has an understanding of the job's requirements. Skills and strengths as they relate

LORRAINE WHEELER<br>35 EAST PARK ROAD<br>REEDLEY<br>LEEDS L517 9NP<br>(0113) 482111

EDUCATION: BSc Honours, The Best University, 1984, Marketing

DATE OF BIRTH: 2/8/59

POSITION DESIRED: PRODUCT MANAGER WITH AN INTERNATIONAL FIRM PROVIDING FUTURE CAREER DEVELOPMENT AT THE EXECUTIVE LEVEL

QUALIFICATIONS:

- communicates well with individuals to achieve a common goal
- handles tasks efficiently and in a timely manner
- knowledge of advertising, sales, management, marketing research, packaging, pricing, distribution and warehousing
- co-ordinates many activities at one time
- receives and carries out assigned tasks or directives
- writes complete status or research reports

EXPERIENCE:

- Assistant Editor on student newspaper
- Treasurer of the hockey club
- Student Researcher with Dr. Steven Who, Lecturer of Marketing, The Best University
- Achieved 2.1 degree

WORK RECORD:

| | |
|---|---|
| 1989 – Present | Box Clever<br>* Account Director |
| 1984 – 1988 | Wiggins & Co.<br>* Junior Advertising Account Executive |
| 1981 – 1983 | The Place<br>* Retail sales and consumer relations |
| 1979 – 1981 | Do All Builders<br>* Labourer (part time/holidays) |

EDUCATION:

| | |
|---|---|
| 1981 – 1984 | BSc Management Science,<br>The Best University, London. 2.1 Honours awarded.<br>Dissertation topic: the marketing of charities. |
| 1978 – 1980 | Middlethorn Sixth Form College, Dullsville.<br>A levels: English (A); Economics (B); General Studies (A). |

***Figure 26.1***
*A CV targeted towards a specific position*

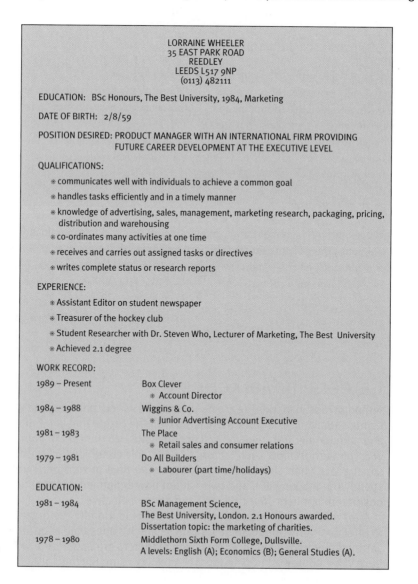

to the specific job should be highlighted. The achievement section indicates success at accomplishing tasks or goals within the job market and at school or college. The work experience section includes educational background, which adds credibility to the CV but is not the major area of focus; it is the applicant's ability to function successfully in a specific job that is vital.

Common suggestions for improving CVs include deleting useless information, improving organisation, using professional printing, listing duties (not accomplishments), maintaining grammatical perfection and avoiding an excessively elaborate or fancy format. One of the biggest problems in CVs, according to a survey of personnel experts, is distortions and lies; 36 per cent of the experts thought that this was a major problem. People lie most often about previous salaries and tasks performed in former jobs. Present career/education details in reverse order, since your most recent exploits are of most interest to potential employers.

## The Interview

Most job searches involve interviews. The Davis Company, a leading company of careers consultants, offers the following tips for candidates being interviewed:

- Work out what are your essential and desirable criteria for the new job. Do not lose sight of these during the interview.
- Prepare well. Find out about the company's products/services and the person who is interviewing you.
- Do not be late.
- Be smart, clean and presentable. Do not look glum.
- Be comfortable in your seat.
- Answer the questions asked. Do not ramble.
- If you are not sure of the question, ask for clarification.
- Keep focused on the current question. Do not be phased by interruptions.
- Ask questions. Show interest and enthusiasm for the business.
- Listen carefully.
- Maintain eye contact, but do not stare. Do not appear furtive.
- Be positive and upbeat.
- Do not discuss politics or contentious issues.
- Do not make – or appear to make – instant judgements.
- Do not strongly criticise your current employer or college.
- Ask if there are any other questions they need to ask you.
- Clarify the rest of the interview/recruitment procedure.
- Do not be afraid to ask for the job!
- Jot down the essential points of the interview afterwards – you will only remember subsequently a tiny part of what was said.
- Consider in advance of the interview how to make the employer want to recruit you!

## Types of Marketing Career

A separate volume of this book would be needed to describe fully the multitude of marketing career options. Table 26.2 presents the typical hierarchy within marketing, which commences with the junior marketing assistant, progresses to the marketing director (who may or may not have a seat on the board) and finally reaches the senior directors of the business. The choice initially relates more to the sphere of activity. An opportunity may arise in a marketing services operation such as a management consultancy, direct mail house or marketing research agency; or with a manufacturer, wholesaler, retailer or dealer; in the public sector, service sector or not-for-profit sector; or with a consumer, services or business-to-business brand.

**TABLE 26.2 A CAREER IN MARKETING**

| | Predominant Sex | Age | Education | Work Experience | Perks |
|---|---|---|---|---|---|
| **Marketing Assistant (£19,000)** | F | 25.7 | degree | less than 2 years | none |
| **Marketing Executive (£25,000)** | F | 28 | degree | 3–5 years | contributory pension |
| **Product Brand Manager (£28,000)** | F/M | 28.6 | degree | 3–5 years | company car, medical insurance, contributory pension scheme |
| **Group Product Manager (£36,000)** | M | 32.8 | degree | 6–10 years | company car, car running costs, medical insurance, contributory pension |
| **Marketing Manager (£42,000)** | M | 35 | degree | 6–15 years | company car, car running costs, medical insurance, contributory pension |
| **Marketing Director (£55,000)** | M | 30 | degree | 11+ years | company car, car running costs, medical insurance, contributory pension |
| **Proprietor (£48,000)** | M | 44.7 | degree | 21+ years | company car, car running costs |
| **Managing Director/ Deputy Managing Director (£80,000)** | M | 43 | degree | 21+ years | company car, car running costs, car telephone, medical insurance, contributory pension |
| **Chairman/Chief Executive (£120,000)** | M | 43.5 | degree | 21+ years | company car, car running costs, medical insurance, contributory pension |

**Source:** Based on 'The *Marketing* Salary Survey', *Marketing*, 17 January 1991, pp. 19–22, revised in 1996, 1999 and 2004.

Some of the wide selection of options are:

- marketing research – agency or in-house
- selling – retail, wholesale, dealer or for a manufacturer
- promotion – advertising, public relations, sales promotion, sponsorship, direct mail (creative, planning or strategy)
- telemarketing, telesales, direct marketing
- business-to-business buying
- distribution management
- product management/brand management
- retail management.

Each of these facets of marketing has been explored in *Marketing: Concepts and Strategies*. Careers consultants will be able to explain the opportunities currently available in more detail. The classified sections of the weekly trade magazines, such as *Marketing* or *Marketing Week*, provide a good indication of where there are openings and on what terms.

Good luck in your search for a career in marketing! We hope that *Marketing: Concepts and Strategies* has increased your understanding of and interest in the world of marketing.

# Summary

A variety of learning tools are used in management education. Case study analysis is one of the most popular approaches for exploring how theory is applied in practice.

- Conducting a situation analysis helps to identify the key issues and factors at play in any case study and provides a good starting point for those engaged in case analysis. A situation analysis refers to the activities involved in reviewing a company's internal position (structure, financial situation, marketing organisation), market analysis, external environment and competition.

- The case study process starts with the identification and analysis of the case problem areas. After the situational analysis has been conducted, a clear view of the problems/key issues set out in the case study must be developed. Any specific questions can be tackled once these problems have been identified. The next step is to derive alternative solutions. Each potential solution must relate to the case's key problem area(s) and offer a realistic way of solving it. After this the alternative solutions are analysed, involving a formal assessment of the advantages and disadvantages of each alternative. This allows the 'best' alternative to be selected. Implementing the chosen solution involves ensuring that the recommended plans and marketing programmes can be implemented.

- Various formats can be used to report case study findings, among them an informal discussion, a structured formal presentation or a written report. Learning how to present case solutions, like the analysis itself, takes time. Marketers must be able to make professional presentations and write good reports.

- Each tutor, examination, educational institution and exam body will have its own requirements and ground rules. In general, examinations are set to find out what students know rather than to try to trick them. Questions set will relate to topics covered in lectures and course texts. There are no substitutes for attending lectures, listening to tutors' views on key concepts and for painstaking, thorough revision. Preparation needs to start well before any examinations take place.

- Very few people enjoy taking examinations, most find this to be a stressful experience. There are ways to make the examination easier to deal with. Effective time management, reading the questions carefully and answering the questions set are all fundamental to success. Although there are no easy ways to eliminate this problem, steps can be taken in the examination itself to make the experience less traumatic.

- The format of examination answers is very important. Improving the format can be achieved by using examples to illustrate your answers, preparing some examples in advance of the examination, taking care with how the answers are structured, incorporating new paragraphs, sub-headings and diagrams, and making sure that key points stand out and are easy to follow.

- If planning a marketing career, take the time to consider carefully how you want to spend your working life, and try to adopt a well-planned, systematic approach to finding a position that meets your personal and career objectives.

- The résumé or curriculum vitae (CV) is the key to being considered for a good job. It states your qualifications, experiences, education and career goals, allowing a potential employer to assess your compatibility with the job requirements. For the employer's and individual's benefit, the CV should be accurate and current.

- Most job searches involve interviews. Tips for candidates being interviewed range from being suitably dressed and prepared for the interview to answering questions clearly, avoiding contentious issues and being positive and upbeat. Consider in advance how best to present yourself as a desirable, 'must have' prospective employee.

» There is a multitude of marketing career options. The typical hierarchy within marketing commences with the junior marketing assistant, progresses to the marketing director (who may or may not have a seat on the board) and peaks with the senior directors of the business. Such opportunities may be found in a marketing services operation such as a management consultancy, direct mail house or marketing research agency; or with a manufacturer, wholesaler, retailer or dealer; in the public sector, service sector or not-for-profit sector; or with a consumer, services or business-to-business marketer.

# Notes


**Chapter 1**

1 Ajay Kohli and Bernard J. Jaworski, 'Market orientation: the construct, research propositions and managerial potential', *Journal of Marketing*, April 1990, pp. 1–18.
2 Jim Lynch in *Effective Industrial Marketing*, Norman Hart, ed. (London: Kogan Page, 1994).
3 Sally Dibb, Lyndon Simkin and John Bradley, *The Marketing Planning Workbook* (London: International Thomson Business Publishing, 1996).
4 Hugh J. Munro, Roderick J. Brodie and Nicole E. Coviello, 'Understanding contemporary marketing: development of a classification scheme', *Journal of Marketing Management*, vol. 13, no. 6, August 1997, p. 501(22).
5 Philip Kotler, *Marketing Management: Analysis, Planning, Implementation, and Control*, 6th edn (Englewood Cliffs, N.J.: Prentice-Hall, 1988), p. 6.
6 O.C. Ferrell and George Lucas, 'An evaluation of progress in the development of a definition of marketing', *Journal of the Academy of Marketing Science*, Fall 1987.
7 Christian Gronoos, 'Defining marketing: a market-oriented approach', *European Journal of Marketing*, vol. 23, no. 1, January 1989, p. 52(9); and Rajendra K. Srivastava, Tasaddug Shervani and Liam Fahey, 'Market-based assets and shareholder value: a framework for analysis', *Journal of Marketing*, vol. 62, no. 1, January 1998, pp. 2–18.
8 Lisa M. Wood, 'Added value: marketing basics?' *Journal of Marketing Management*, vol. 12, no. 8, November 1996, p. 735(21); and Thomas Robert-son, 'New developments in marketing: a European perspective', *European Management Journal*, vol. 12, no. 4, p. 362(4).
9 Jagdish N. Sheth and Rajendras Sisodia, 'More than ever before, marketing is under fire to account for what it spends', *Marketing Management*, Fall 1995, pp. 13–14.
10 Christian Gronoos, 'From marketing mix to relationship marketing; towards a paradigm shift in marketing', *Management Decision*, 32(2), 1994, pp. 4–20; Adrian Payne, Martin Christopher, Moira Clark and Helen Peck, *Relationship Marketing for Competitive Advantage* (Oxford: Butterworth-Heinemann, 1998).
11 Gene R. Laczniak and Robert F. Lusch, 'Environment and strategy in 1995: a survey of high-level executives', *Journal of Consumer Marketing*, Spring 1986, p. 28.
12 Sally Dibb and Lyndon Simkin, *The Marketing Segmentation Workbook* (London: Thomson, 1996).

**Chapter 2**

1 B. A. Weitz and R. Wensley, *Readings in Strategic Marketing* (Chicago: Dryden, 1988).
2 P. Rajan Varadarajan, 'Strategy content and process perspectives revisited', *Journal of the Academy of Marketing Science*, vol. 27, no. 1, Winter 1999, pp. 88–100.
3 G. Homas, M. Hult, David W. Cravens and Jagdish Sheth, 'Competitive advantage in the global marketplace: a focus on marketing strategy', *Journal of Business Research*, January 2001, pp. 1–3.
4 Sally Dibb, Lyndon Simkin and John Bradley, *The Marketing Planning Workbook* (London: Thomson, 1996).
5 Derek F. Abell and John S. Hammond, *Strategic Market Planning* (Englewood Cliffs, N.J.: Prentice-Hall, 1979), p. 10.
6 P. Rajan Varadarajan, Terry Clark and William Pride, 'Determining your company's destiny', working paper, Texas A&M University, 1990.
7 J. Paul Peter and James H. Donnelly, Jr., *A Preface to Marketing Management*, 5th edn (Homewood, Ill.: Irwin, 1991), p. 9.
8 Adapted from Peter and Donnelly, *A Preface to Marketing Management*, pp. 8–12.
9 Zachary Schiller, with Russell Mitchell, Wendy Zellner, Lois Therrien, Andrea Rothman and Walecia Konrad, 'The great American health pitch', *Business Week*, 9 October 1989, p. 116.
10 Derek F. Abell, 'Strategic windows', *Journal of Marketing*, July 1978, p. 21.
11 Abell and Hammond, p. 213.
12 Liam Fahey, William K. King and Vodake K. Naraganan, 'Environmental scanning and forecasting in strategic planning – the state of the art', *Long Range Planning*, February 1981, p. 38.
13 David M. Georgaff and Robert G. Mundick, 'Managers' guide to forecasting', *Harvard Business Review*, January–February 1986, p. 120.
14 "Energy efficient house design', *House Builder Magazine*, September 1986.
15 Philip Kotler, 'Strategic planning and the marketing process', *Business*, May–June 1980, pp. 6–7.
16 Nigel Piercy, *Market-Led Strategic Change* (Oxford: Butterworth-Heinemann Ltd, 1992).
17 C. Anthony Di Benedetto, 'The relationship between strategic type and firm capabilities in Chinese firms', *International Marketing Review*, 20 (5), 2003, pp. 514–534.
18 Roger A. Kerin, Vijay Majahan and P. Rajan Varadarajan, *Contemporary Perspectives on Strategic Marketing Planning* (Boston: Allyn & Bacon, 1990).
19 Ronald Grover, 'When Columbia met Sony ... a love story', *Business Week*, 9 October 1989, pp. 44–45.

20 Graham Hooley and John Saunders, *Competitive Positioning: The Key to Market Success* (London: Prentice-Hall, 1993).
21 P. Rajan Varadarajan, 'Marketing strategy and the Internet: an organizing framework', *Journal of the Academy of Marketing Science*, Fall 2002, pp. 296–313.
22 Al Ries and Jack Trout, *Marketing Warfare* (New York: McGraw-Hill, 1986); John Saunders, 'Marketing and competitive success', in Michael Baker, ed., The *Marketing Book* (London: Heinemann, 1987).
23 Hirokazu Takada, 'Multiple time series analysis of competitive marketing behavior', *Journal of Business Research*, October 1998.
24 Peter Doyle, *Marketing Management and Strategy* (London: Prentice-Hall, 1994).
25 David A. Aaker, *Strategic Market Management*, 2nd edn (New York: Wiley, 1988), p. 35.
26 John Saunders, 'Marketing and competitive success', Michael J. Baker, ed., in *The Marketing Book* (London: Heinemann, 1987), pp. 10–28.

**Chapter 3**

1 Richard C. Becherer and John G. Maurer, 'The moderating effect of environmental variables on the entrepreneurial and marketing orientation of entrepreneur-led firms', *Entrepreneurship Theory and Practice*, vol. 22, no. 1, Fall 1997, pp. 47–58; Ravi S. Achrol, 'Changes in the theory of interorganizational relations in marketing: toward a network paradigm', *Journal of the Academy of Marketing Science*, vol. 25, no. 1, Winter 1997, pp. 56–71.
2 Philip Kotler, 'Megamarketing', *Harvard Business Review*, March–April 1986, pp. 117–124.
3 *Britain 1990: An Official Handbook* (London: Central Office of Information, 1990).
4 Joseph Plummer, 'The concept of application of life style segmentation', *Journal of Marketing*, January 1974, p. 34.
5 *The IBA Code of Advertising Standards and Practice* (London: Independent Broadcasting Authority, December 1977), p. 3. (The IBA is now the ITC.)
6 Brian Bremner, 'A new sales pitch: the environment', *Business Week*, 24 July 1989, p. 50.
7 Robin Knight, with Eleni Dimmler, 'The greening of Europe's industries', *U.S. News & World Report*, 5 June 1989, pp. 45–46.
8 Reprinted by permission from Herbert Simon, 'Technology and environment', *Management Science*, 19 (10), June 1973. Copyright 1973, The Institute of Management Sciences.
9 Wroe Alderson, *Dynamic Marketing Behavior* (Homewood, Ill.: Irwin, 1965), pp. 195–197.
10 Michael Porter, *Competitive Strategy* (New York: The Free Press, 1980).
11 P. Kotler, G. Armstrong, J. Saunders and V. Wong, *Principles of Marketing* (Hemel Hempstead: Prentice-Hall, 1999).
12 D. Abell, *Defining the Business: The Starting Point of Strategic Planning* (Englewood Cliffs, N.J.: Prentice-Hall, 1980).
13 P. Doyle, *Marketing Management and Strategy* (Hemel Hempstead: Prentice-Hall, 1998).
14 I. Ansoff and E. McDonell, *Implementing Strategic Change* (Englewood Cliffs, N.J.: Prentice-Hall, 1990).
15 D. Brownlie, 'Environmental Analysis', in M. Baker (ed), *The Marketing Book* (Oxford: Butterworth-Heinemann, 1987).
16 Sally Dibb, Lyndon Simkin and John Bradley, *The Marketing Planning Workbook* (London: Thomson, 1996).
17 J. Diffenbach, 'Corporate environmental analysis in large US corporations', *Long Range Planning*, 16 (3), 1983, pp. 107–116.

**Chapter 4**

1 Vladimir Zwass, 'Electronic commerce: structures and issues', *International Journal of Electronic Commerce*, Autumn 1996, pp. 3–23.
2 Michael J. Mandel and Robert D. Hof, 'Rethinking the Internet', *Business Week*, 26 March 2001, pp. 116–122.
3 Michael Totty, 'The researcher', *Wall Street Journal*, 16 July 2001, p. R20.
4 David W. Stewart and Qin Zhao, 'Internet marketing, business models, and public policy', *Journal of Public Policy & Marketing*, Autumn 2000, pp. 287–296.
5 Totty, 'The researcher'.
6 Jon Mark Giese, 'Place without space, identity without body: the role of cooperative narrative in community and identity formation in a text-based electronic community', unpublished dissertation, Pennsylvania State University, 1996.
7 Robert D. Hof, with Seanna Browder and Peter Elstrom, 'Internet communities', *Business Week*, 5 May 1997, pp. 64–80.
8 Kathy Rebello, with Larry Armstrong and Amy Cortese, 'Making money on the net', *Business Week*, 23 September 1996, pp. 104–118.
9 Hof, 'Internet communities'.
10 'B2B e-commerce will survive growing pains', *CyberAtlas*, 28, November 2001, cyberatlas.internet. com/markets/ b2b/article/0,,10091_930251,00.html.
11 'Company facts', Dell, www.dell.com, accessed 3 April 2002.
12 Merlin Stone and Bryan Foss, *Successful Customer Relationship Marketing: New Thinking, New Strategies, New Tools for Getting Closer to Your Customers*, London: Kogan Page, 2001.
13 Stephenie Steitzer, 'Commercial web sites cut back on collections of personal data', *Wall Street Journal*, 28 March 2002, http://online.wsj.com.
14 Peter Loftus, 'Yahoo modifies its privacy policy to allow more sharing of user data', *Wall Street Journal*, 28 March 2002, http://online.wsj.com.
15 Steitzer, 'Commercial web sites cut back on collections of personal data'.
16 'European Union Directive on Privacy', E-Centre for Business Ethics, www.e-businessethics.com/ privacy.eud.htm, accessed 3 April 2002.

17 Stephen H. Wildstrom, 'Can Microsoft stamp out piracy?' *Business Week Online*, 2 October 2000, www.businessweek.com.

18 William T. Neese and Charles R. McManis, 'Summary brief: law, ethics and the Internet: how recent federal trademark law prohibits a remedy against cyber-squatters', *Proceedings from the Society of Marketing Advances*, 4–7 November 1998.


**Chapter 5**


1 Vern Terpstra, *International Marketing*, 4th edn (Hinsdale, Ill.: Dryden Press, 1987), p. 4.

2 Dana-Nicoleta Lascu, 'International marketing planning and practice', *Journal of Global Marketing*, vol. 9, no. 3, 1996; Peter S.H. Leeflang and Charles P. de Mortanges, 'The international European market and strategic marketing planning: implications and expectations', *Journal of International Consumer Marketing*, 1993.

3 Theodore Levitt, 'The globalisation of markets', *Harvard Business Review*, May–June 1983, p. 92.

4 Ibid.

5 Subhash C. Jain, 'Standardisation of international marketing strategy: some research hypotheses', *Journal of Marketing*, January 1989, pp. 70–79.

6 'Global brands need local ad flavor', *Advertising Age*, 3 September 1984, p. 26.

7 Rajeev Batra, 'Executive insights: marketing issues and challenges in transitional economies', *Journal of International Marketing*, vol. 5, no. 4, 1997, pp. 95–114; C.C.L. Wang, 'Issues and advances in international consumer research: a review and assessment', *Journal of International Marketing and Marketing Research*, vol. 24, no. 1, February 1999, pp. 3–21.

8 Vern Terpstra, 'Critical mass and international marketing strategy', *Journal of the Academy of Marketing Science*, Summer 1983, pp. 269–282.

9 Yumiko Ono, 'Land of rising fun', *Wall Street Journal*, 2 October 1992, pp. A1, A10; Gayle Hanson, 'Japan at play', *Insight*, 27 April 1992, pp. 6–13, 34–37.

10 Douglas Bowman and Shilpa Lele-Pingle, 'Buyer behavior in business-to-business services: the case of foreign exchange', *International Journal of Research in Marketing*, vol. 14, no. 5, December 1997, pp. 499–508.

11 Brian Bremner with Edith Hill Updike, 'Made in America isn't the kiss of death anymore', *Business Week*, 13 November 1995, p. 62.

12 Nigel G. G. Campbell, John L. Graham, Alain Jolibert and Hans Gunther Meissner, 'Marketing negotiations in France, Germany, the United Kingdom, and the United States', *Journal of Marketing*, April 1988, pp. 49–62.

13 Brian Oliver, 'UK soccer advertising in trouble', *Advertising Age*, 8 July 1985, p. 36.

14 Laurel Wentz, 'Local laws keep international marketers hopping', *Advertising Age*, 11 July 1985, p. 20.

15 Lee Smith, 'Japan wants to make friends', *Fortune*, 2 September 1985, p. 84.

16 Jean-Pierre Jeannet and Hubert D. Hennessey, *Global Marketing Strategies* (Boston: Houghton Mifflin, 1995), p. 60.

17 Peter S. H. Leeflang and Charles P. de Mortanges, 'The internal European market and strategic marketing planning: implications and expectations', *Journal of International Consumer Marketing*, 1993.

18 *Europe in Figures*, 4th edn (Brussels: Eurostat, 1995).

19 Laura Mazur, 'Failing the Euro test', *Marketing*, 3 December 1998, pp. 26–27.

20 Sandra Vandermerwe and Marc-André L'Huillier, 'Euro-consumers in 1992', *Business Horizons*, January–February 1989, pp. 34–40.

21 Eric G. Friberg, '1992: moves Europeans are making', *Harvard Business Review*, May–June 1989, p. 89.

22 Warren J. Keegan, *Global Marketing Management*, (Englewood Cliffs, N.J.: Prentice-Hall, 1995), pp. 285–286.

23 Carla Rapaport, 'Why Japan keeps on winning', *Fortune*, 15 July 1991, p. 76.

24 Leslie Helm, with Laxmi Nakarmi, Jang Jung Soo, William J. Holstein and Edith Terry, 'The Koreans are Coming', *Business Week*, 25 December 1985, pp. 46–52.

25 Dori Jones Yang, with Dirk Bennett and Bill Javerski, 'The other China is starting to soar', *Business Weekly*, 6 November 1989, pp. 60–62.

26 Louis Kraar, 'Asia's rising export powers', *Fortune*, Special Pacific Rim 1989 issue, pp. 43–50.

27 Louis Kraar, 'The risks are rising in China', *Fortune*, 6 March 1995, p. 179.

28 George Paine, 'US-ASEAN dialogue in Bangkok will review economic issues', *Business America*, 21 May 1990, pp. 2–3.

29 Michael Vatiloptos, 'Sense of purpose – new challenges lead member states to examine role', *Far Eastern Economic Review*, vol. 152, no. 25, 20 June 1991, pp. 24–25; 'Trade rivalries calmed by pacific message', *Financial Times*, 2 August 1993, p. 13.

30 Jean-Pierre Jeannet and Hubert D. Hennessey, *Global Marketing Strategies* (Boston: Houghton Mifflin, 1995), p. 173.

31 Allan C. Reddy, 'The role of marketing in the economic development of eastern European countries', *Journal of Applied Business Research*, vol. 7, no. 3, Summer 1991, pp. 106–107.

32 John A. Quelch, Erich Joachimsthaler and Jose Luis Nueno, 'After the wall: marketing guidelines for eastern Europe', *Sloan Management Review*, Winter 1991, pp. 90–91.

33 www.cisstat.com, August 2004.

34 *The World Bank Atlas*, 1994, data for 1992.

35 'Rising in Russia', *Fortune*, 24 January 1996, pp. 93, 95.

36 Jean-Pierre Jeannet and Hubert D. Hennessey, *Global Marketing Strategies* (Boston: Houghton Mifflin, 1995), p. 170.

37 Peter Gumbel, 'Soviet reformers urge bold push to liberalise faltering economy', *Wall Street Journal*, 27 October 1989, p. A9.

38 Paul Meller, 'Back to the USSR', *Marketing*, 9 August 1990, pp. 22–23.
39 John Templeman, Thane Peterson, Gail E. Schares and Jonathan Kapstein, 'The shape of Europe to come', *Business Week*, 27 November 1989, pp. 60–64.
40 Richard S. Lapidus, 'Global Marketing Strategies', *Journal of Global Marketing*, 1997.
41 John A. Quelch, 'How to build a product licensing program', *Harvard Business Review*, May–June 1985, pp. 186–187.
42 Frank Bradley, *International Marketing Strategy* (London: Prentice-Hall, 1995), p. 393.
43 J. Adams and M. Mendelsohn, 'Recent developments in franchising', *Journal of Business Law*, 1986, pp. 206–219.
44 P. Stern and J. Stanworth, 'The development of franchising in Britain', *National Westminster Quarterly Review*, May 1988, pp. 38–48; D. Ayling, 'Franchising has its dark side', *Accountancy*, 99, 1987, pp. 113–117.
45 Andrew Kupfer, 'How to be a global manager', *Fortune*, 14 March 1988, pp. 52–58.
46 Kathryn R. Harrigan, 'Joint ventures and competitive advantage', *Strategic Management Journal*, May 1988, pp. 141–158.
47 A. Dunlap Smith, 'Europe's truckmakers face survival of the biggest', *Business Week*, 6 November 1989, p. 68.
48 J. Killing, 'How to make a global joint venture work', *Harvard Business Review*, vol. 60, 1982, pp. 120–127.
49 Kathryn R. Harrigan, 'Joint ventures and competitive strategy', *Strategic Management Journal*, May 1988, pp. 141–158.
50 S. C. Jain, 'Some perspectives on international strategic alliances', in *Advances in International Marketing* (New York: JAI Press, 1987), pp. 103–120.
51 "More companies prefer liaisons to marriage', *Wall Street Journal*, 12 April 1988, p. 35.
52 Thomas Gross and John Neuman, 'Strategic alliances vital in global marketing', *Marketing News*, June 1989, pp. 1–2.
53 Margaret H. Cunningham, 'Marketing's new frontier: international strategic alliances', working paper, Queens University (Ontario), 1990.

**Chapter 6**

1 James F. Engel, Roger D. Blackwell and Paul W. Miniard, *Consumer Behavior*, 7th edn (Hinsdale, Ill.: Dryden Press, 1993), p. 4.
2 John A. Howard and Jagdish N. Sheth, *The Theory of Buyer Behavior* (New York: Wiley, 1969), pp. 27–28.
3 Roy F. Baumeister and David Glen Mick, 'Yielding to temptation: self-control failure, impulsive purchasing, and consumer behavior', *Journal of Consumer Research*, March 2002, pp. 670–677.
4 G. Foxall, 'Consumer decision-making', in *The Marketing Book*, 3rd edn, M. Baker, ed. (London: Heinemann/ Chartered Institute of Marketing, 1995).
5 Kevin L. Keller and Richard Staelin, 'Effects of quality and quantity of information on decision effectiveness', *Journal of Consumer Research*, September 1987, pp. 200–213.
6 Gabriel Biehal and Dipankar Chakravarti, 'Con-sumers' use of memory and external information in choice: macro and micro perspectives', *Journal of Consumer Research*, March 1986, pp. 382–405.
7 Bobby J. Calder and Brian Sternthal, 'Television commercial wearout: an information processing view', *Journal of Marketing Research*, May 1980, pp. 173–186.
8 Michael J. Houston, Terry L. Childers and Susan E. Heckler, 'Picture-word consistency and the elaborative processing of advertisements', *Journal of Marketing Research*, November 1987, pp. 359–369.
9 Robert A. Westbrook, 'Product/consumption-based affective responses and postpurchase processes', *Journal of Marketing Research*, August 1987, pp. 258–270.
10 Roger Bougie, Rik Pieters and Marcel Zeelenberg, 'Angry customers don't come back: the experience and behavioral implications of anger and dissatisfaction in services', *Journal of the Academy of Marketing Science*, Fall 2003, 31 (4), pp. 377–394.
11 Anthony J. Capraro, Susan Broniarczyk and Rajendra K. Srivastava, 'Factors influencing the likelihood of customer defection: the role of consumer knowledge', *Journal of the Academy of Marketing Science*, March 2003, pp. 164–176.
12 Neil Denny, 'Why complaining is our new hobby', *Marketing*, 26 November 1998, p. 16.
13 Patricia Sellers, 'The ABC's of marketing to kids', *Fortune*, 8 May 1989, p. 115.
14 Judith Waldrop, 'Inside America's households', *American Demographics*, March 1989, pp. 20–27.
15 Houston, Childers and Heckler, pp. 359–369.
16 Thomas S. Robertson and Hubert Gatignon, 'Competitive effects on technology diffusion', *Journal of Marketing*, July 1986, pp. 1–12.
17 Robertson and Gatignon, pp. 1–12.
18 Al Ries and Jack Trout, *Positioning the Battle for Your Mind* (New York: McGraw-Hill Book Co., 1986).
19 James R. Bettman, *An Information Processing Theory of Consumer Choice* (Reading, Mass.: Addison-Wesley, 1979), pp. 18–24.
20 David Aaker and Douglas Stayman, 'Implementing the concept of transformational advertising', *Psychology and Marketing*, May and June 1992, pp. 237–253.
21 James H. Myers, 'Determinant buying attitudes: meaning and measurement', *Marketing Manage-ment*, Summer 1997.
22 Joseph W. Alba and J. Wesley Hutchinson, 'Dimensions of consumer expertise', *Journal of Consumer Research*, March 1987, pp. 411–454.
23 Akshay R. Rao and Kent B. Monroe, 'The moderating effect of prior knowledge on cue utilization in product evaluations', *Journal of Consumer Research*, September 1988, pp. 253–264.
24 Ibid.

25 Hans Baumgartner, 'Towards a personology of the consumer', *Journal of Consumer Research*, September 2002, pp. 286–293.

26 John L. Lastovika and Erich A. Joachimsthaler, 'Improving the detection of personality-behavior, relationships in consumer research', *Journal of Consumer Research*, March 1988, pp. 583–587.

27 Martha T. Moore, 'Spring break: brand names chase sales', *USA Today*, 17 March 1989, p. B1.

28 Angela Donkin, Yuan Huang Lee and Barbara Toson, 'Implications of changes in the UK social and occupational classifications in 2001 for vital statistics', *National Statistics*, Spring 2002, pp. 23–29.

29 Emily Rogers, 'Adland takes up fat challenge', *Marketing*, 11 March 2004, p. 19.

30 Marieke De Mooij, 'Convergence and divergence in consumer behavior: implications for global advertising', *International Journal of Advertising*, 2003, 22 (2), pp. 183–203.

31 Leonard L. Berry, 'The time-sharing consumer', *Journal of Retailing*, Winter 1979, p. 69.

32 Mona Doyle, 'The metamorphosis of the consumer', *Marketing Communications*, April 1989, pp. 18–22.

33 Randolph E. Bucklin, 'Determining segmentation in sales response across consumer purchase behaviours', *Journal of Marketing Research*, May 1998.

**Chapter 7**

1 J. Carlos Jarillo and Howard H. Stevenson, 'Co-operative strategies: the payoffs and the pitfalls', *Long Range Planning*, February 1991, pp. 64–70.

2 John I. Coppett, 'Auditing your customer service activities', *Industrial Marketing Management*, November 1988, pp. 277–284; Thomas L. Powers, 'Identify and fulfill customer service expectations', *Industrial Marketing Management*, November 1988, pp. 273–276.

3 Mary Jo Bitner, Bernard H. Booms and Mary Stanfield Tetreault, 'The service encounter: diagnosing favorable and unfavorable incidents', *Journal of Marketing*, 54, January 1990, pp. 71–84.

4 Weld F. Royal, 'Cashing in on complaints', *Sales & Marketing Management*, May 1995, pp. 88–89.

5 Moin Uddin, 'Loyalty programmes: the ultimate gift', *Dsn Retailing Today*, 5 March 2001, p. 12.

6 Jim Shaw, Joe Giglierano and Jeff Kallis, 'Marketing complex technical products: the importance of intangible attributes', *Industrial Marketing Management*, 18, 1989, pp. 45–53.

7 Frederick E. Webster and Yoram Wind, 'A general model for understanding organizational buyer behaviour', *Marketing Management*, Winter/Spring 1996, pp. 52–57.

8 E. Gummesson, 'The new marketing: developing long-term interactive relationships', *Long Range Planning*, vol. 20, issue 3, 1987, pp. 10–20.

9 H. Hakansson, *International Marketing and Purchasing of Industrial Goods* (Chichester: Wiley, 1982).

10 M. Christopher, A. Payne and D. Ballantyne, *Relationship Marketing* (Oxford: Butterworth-Heinemann, 1991).

11 David Ford, *Understanding Business Marketing and Purchasing* (London: Thomson Learning, 1982).

12 Regis McKenna, *Relationship Marketing* (Reading, Mass.: Addison-Wesley, 1991).

13 Nigel C. G. Campbell, John L. Graham, Alan Jolibert and Hans Gunthe Meissner, 'Marketing negotiations in France, Germany, the United Kingdom and the United States', *Journal of Marketing*, 52, April 1988, pp. 49–62.

14 J. Carlos Jarillo and Howard H. Stevenson, 'Co-operative strategies: the payoffs and the pitfalls', *Long Range Planning*, February 1991, pp. 64–70.

15 *Standard Industrial Classification Revision* (London: Central Statistical Office, 1979).

16 Peter Doyle and John Saunders, 'Market segmentation and positioning in specialized industrial markets', *Journal of Marketing*, Spring 1985, p. 25.

**Chapter 8**

1 P. Doyle, 'Marketing in the New Millennium', *European Journal of Marketing*, 29, 1995, pp. 23–44; N. Piercy, *Market-Led Strategic* Change (Oxford: Butterworth-Heinemann, 1997).

2 A. Weinstein, *Handbook of Market Segmentation: Strategic Targeting for Business and Technology Firms* (New York: Haworth Press, 2004).

3 David W. Stewart, 'Segmentation and positioning for strategic marketing decisions', *Journal of Marketing Research*, vol. 35, no. 1, February 1998, pp. 128–129.

4 R. Frank and Y. Wind, *Market Segmentation* (Englewood Cliffs, N.J.: Prentice-Hall, 1972); Yoram Wind, 'Issues and advances in segmentation research', *Journal of Marketing Research*, August 1978, pp. 317–327.

5 Catherine M. Schaffer and Paul E. Green, 'Cluster-based market segmentation: some further comparisons of alternative approaches', *Journal of the Market Research Society*, vol. 40, no. 2, April 1998, pp. 155–163.

6 M. Wedel and W. Kamakura, *Market Segmentation: Conceptual and Methodological Foundations* (Boston: Kluwer Academic Publications, 2000).

7 D. Peppers and M. Rogers, *The One-to-One Manager* (New York: Currency Doubleday, 1999).

8 P. Postma, *The New Marketing Era: Marketing to the Imagination of a Technology-Driven World* (New York: McGraw-Hill, 1998).

9 J. H. Sheth, R. S. Sisodia and A. Sharma, 'Customer-centric marketing', *Journal of the Academy of Marketing Science*, 28 (1), 2000, pp. 55–66.

10 D. Peppers and M. Rogers, *The One-to-One Manager* (New York: Currency Doubleday, 1999).

11 D. Chaffey, R. Mayer, K. Johnston and F. Ellis-Chadwick, *Internet Marketing* (Harlow: Pearson Education, 2000).

12 J. Saunders, 'Cluster analysis', *Journal of Marketing Management*, 10, 1994; pp. 13–28; J. Saunders, 'Cluster analysis for market segmentation', *European Journal of Marketing*, 14, 1980, pp. 422–435.

13 James U. McNeal, *Kids Marketing: Myths and Realities* (Ithaca, NY: Paramount Market Publishing, 1999).
14 Joseph G. Albonetti and Luis V. Dominguez, 'Major influences on consumer goods marketers' decision to target US Hispanics', *Journal of Advertising Re-search*, February–March 1989, pp. 9–11.
15 HMSO, *Social trends*, 1998.
16 John L. Lastovicka and Erich A. Joachimsthaler, 'Improving the detection of personality-behavior relationships in consumer research', *Journal of Consumer Research*, March 1988, pp. 583–587.
17 Joseph T. Plummer, 'The concept and application of life style segmentation', *Journal of Marketing*, January 1974, p. 33.
18 James F. Engel, Roger D. Blackwell and Paul W. Miniard, *Consumer Behavior* (Orlando, Fla.: Dryden Press, 1990), pp. 348–349.
19 Russell I. Haley, 'Benefit segmentation: a decision-oriented research tool', *Journal of Marketing*, July 1968, pp. 30–35.
20 Yoram Wind and Richard Cardoza, 'Industrial market segmentation', *Industrial Marketing Management*, vol. 3, 1974, pp. 153–166.
21 T. P. Beane and D. M. Ennis, 'Market segmentation: a review', *European Journal of Marketing*, vol. 21 (5), 1987, pp. 20–42.
22 Thomas Bonoma and B. P. Shapiro, *Segmenting the Industrial Market* (Lexington, Mass.: Lexington Books, 1983).
23 Donald F. Blumberg, 'Developing service as a line of business', *Management Review*, vol. 76, February 1987, p. 61.
24 A. Diamantopoulos and B. Schlegelmilch, *Taking the Fear out of Data Analysis* (London: Dryden Press, 1997); J. Saunders, 'Cluster analysis', *Journal of Marketing Management*, 10, 1994, pp. 13–28; J. Saunders, 'Cluster analysis for market segmentation', *European Journal of Marketing*, 14, 1980, pp. 422–435.
25 G. L. Lilien and P. Kotler, *Marketing Decision-Making: A Model Building Approach* (New York: Harper & Row, 1983); P. Naert and P. Leeflang, *Building Implementable Marketing Models* (Leiden: Martinus Nijhoff, 1978).
26 J. Maier and J. Saunders, 'The implementation of segmentation in sales management', *Journal of Personal Selling and Sales Management*, 10 (1), 1990, pp. 39–48.
27 J. Saunders, 'Cluster analysis', *Journal of Marketing Management*, 10, 1994, pp. 13–28; J. Saunders, 'Cluster analysis for market segmentation', *European Journal of Marketing*, 14, 1980, pp. 422–435.
28 A. Diamantopoulos and B. Schlegelmilch, *Taking the Fear out of Data Analysis* (London: Dryden Press, 1997); J. Saunders, 'Cluster analysis', *Journal of Marketing Management*, 10, 1994, pp. 13–28; J. Saunders, 'Cluster analysis for market segmentation', *European Journal of Marketing*, 14, 1980, pp. 422–435.
29 M. McDonald, *Marketing Plans* (Oxford: Butterworth-Heinemann, 1995).
30 S. Dibb and L. Simkin, 'Marketing and marketing planning: still barriers to overcome', *EMAC*, Warwick, May 1997.
31 Peter Doyle, John Saunders and Veronica Wong, 'A comparative study of Japanese marketing strategies in the British market', *Journal of International Business Studies*, 17 (1), 1986, pp. 27–46.
32 Y. Wind, 'Going to market: new twist for some old tricks', *Wharton Magazine*, 4, 1980.
33 T. Harrison, *A Handbook of Advertising Techniques* (London: Kogan Page, 1987), p. 7.
34 A. Ries and J. Trout, Positioning: *The Battle for Your Mind* (New York: McGraw-Hill, 1981); Jack Trout with Steve Rivkin, *The New Positioning: The Latest on the World's #1 Business Strategy* (New York: McGraw-Hill, 1996).
35 Philip Kotler, *Marketing Management: Analysis, Planning, and Control*, 6th edn (Englewood Cliffs, N.J., Prentice-Hall, 1988), p. 257.


**Chapter 9**


1 David Birks, chapter 10 in *The Marketing Book*, M. Baker, ed. (Oxford: Butterworth-Heinemann, 1994).
2 "Research" is accredited by The Market Research Society (Great Britain). Reprinted by permission.
3 'Pizza Hut studies effects of "pizza deprivation" on college and high school students', *PRNewswire*, via AmericaOnline, 30 May 2001.
4 Jerry Wind, 'Marketing research forum: state of the art in quantitative research', *Marketing Research*, Winter 1997.
5 Sally Dibb and Lyndon Simkin, *The Marketing Case-book* (London: Routledge, 1994).
6 http://www.esomar.org/print.php?a=6&p=1140.
7 'Research league tables top 65', *Marketing*, 14 July 2004, pp. 37–46.
8 Johny K. Johansson and Ikujiro Nonaha, 'Market research the Japanese way', *Harvard Business Review*, May–June 1987, pp. 16–22.
9 Donald Tull and Del Hawkins, *Marketing Research* (New York: Macmillan, 1990).
10 Vikas Mittal and Wagner A. Kamakura, 'Satisfaction, repurchase intent, and repurchase behavior: investigating the moderating effects of customer characteristics', *Journal of Marketing Research*, February 2001, pp. 131–142.
11 'Internal secondary market research', *Small Business Owner's Toolkit*, www.lycos.com/business/cch/guidebook.html?lpv=1&docNumber=P03_3020, 23 June 2001.
12 Ronald L. Vaughn, 'Demographic data banks: a new management resource', *Business Horizons*, November–December 1984, pp. 38–42. See also Chapter 5.
13 Jeffrey S. Conant, Denise T. Smart and Bruce J. Walker, 'Main survey facilitation techniques: an assessment and proposal regarding reporting practices' (working paper, Texas A&M University, 1990).
14 Riche, p. 8.
15 Stephen M. Billing, 'Go slow, be wary when considering switch to computer assisted interviewing system', *Marketing News*, 26 November 1982, secl. 2, p. 2.

16 Tull and Hawkins.
17 Yorkshire Television's *The Marketing Mix* series.
18 Hal Sokolow, 'In-depth interviews increasing in importance', *Marketing News*, 13 September 1985, p. 26.
19 Alan J. Bush and A. Parasuraman, 'Mall intercept versus telephone interviewing environment', *Journal of Advertising Research*, April–May 1985, p. 42.
20 Alan J. Bush and Joseph F. Hair, Jr, 'An assessment of the mall intercept as a data collecting method', *Journal of Marketing Research*, May 1985, p. 162.
21 Jagdip Singh, Roy D. Howell and Gary K. Rhoads, 'Adaptive designs for Likert-type data: an approach for implementing marketing surveys', *Journal of Marketing Research*, August 1990, pp. 304–321.
22 Norman Hart and John Stapleton, *Glossary of Marketing Terms* (Oxford: Butterworth-Heinemann), 1981.
23 'Closer encounters', *Marketing*, 14 July 2004, pp. 48–49.
24 Peter Jackson, Adsearch, Richmond.
25 A. Diamantopoulos and B. Schlegelmilch, *Taking the Fear out of Data Analysis* (London: Dryden Press, 1997).
26 Michael J. Olivette, 'Marketing research in the electric utility industry', *Marketing News*, 2 January 1987, p. 13.
27 Deborah Utter, 'Information-driven marketing decisions: development of strategic information systems', *Journal of the Academy of Marketing Science*, Spring 1998.
28 Laurence N. Goal, 'High technology data collection for measurement and testing', *Marketing Research*, March 1992, pp. 29–38.
29 Kathleen Cholewka, 'Tiered CRM: serving pip-squeaks to VIPS', *Sales & Marketing Management*, April 2001, pp. 25–26.
30 O. C. Ferrell and Steven J. Skinner, 'Ethical behavior and bureaucratic structure in marketing research organizations', *Journal of Marketing Research*, February 1988, pp. 103–104.
31 Michael Kavanaugh, 'Masked Brawl', *Marketing Week*, 15 October 1998, p. 65.
32 Lynn Colemar, 'It's selling disguised as research', *Marketing News*, 4 January 1988, p. 1.
33 Brandt Allen, 'Make information services pay its way', *Harvard Business Review*, January–February 1987, p. 57.

**Chapter 10**

1 Part of this definition is adapted from James D. Scott, Martin R. Warshaw and James R. Taylor, *Introduction to Marketing Management*, 5th edn (Homewood, Ill.: Irwin, 1985), p. 215.
2 Theodore Levitt, 'Marketing intangible products and product intangibles', *Harvard Business Review*, May–June 1981, pp. 94–102.
3 Robert W. Haas, *Industrial Marketing Management*, 3rd edn (Boston: Kent Publishing, 1986), pp. 15–25.
4 Peter Doyle, *Marketing Management and Strategy* (London: Prentice-Hall, 1994).
5 William P. Putsis Jr and Barry L. Bayus, 'An empirical analysis of firms' product line decisions', *Journal of Marketing Research*, February 2001, pp. 110–118.
6 M. J. Thomas, 'Product development management', in *The Marketing Book*, M. Baker, ed. (London: Heinemann/The Chartered Institute of Marketing, 1987).
7 Sonja Radas and Steven M. Shugan, 'Seasonal marketing and timing new product introductions', *Journal of Marketing Research*, vol. 35, no. 3, August 1998, pp. 296–315; Marjorie E. Adams, 'Enhancing new product development performance: an organisational learning perspective', *The Journal of Product Innovation Management*, September 1998.
8 Brian A. Lukas and O. C. Ferrell, 'The effect of market orientation on product innovation', *Journal of the Academy of Marketing Science*, February 2000, pp. 239–47.
9 Gary Lynn and Richard Reilly, 'How to build a blockbuster', *Harvard Business Review*, October 2002, vol. 80, no. 10, pp. 18–20.
10 David Benady, 'Chopping brands', *Marketing Week*, 10 June 2004, pp. 22–25.
11 Gerald Tellis and Peter Golder, 'First to market, first to fail? Real causes of enduring market leadership', *Sloan Management Review*, Winter 1996, pp. 65–75.
12 'Guinness in facelift as volume dips', *Marketing Week*, 20 May 2004, p. 8.
13 Caroline Parry, 'Cadbury axes Trebor 24-7 after poor sales', *Marketing Week*, 15 April 2004, p. 5.
14 Levitt, 'Marketing intangible products and product intangibles', p. 96.
15 Christopher W. L. Hart, 'The power of unconditional service guarantees', *Harvard Business Review*, July–August 1988, pp. 54–62.

**Chapter 11**

1 Peter D. Bennett, ed., *Dictionary of Marketing Terms* (Chicago: American Marketing Association, 1988), p. 18.
2 Peter Doyle, 'Building successful brands: the strategic options', *The Journal of Consumer Marketing*, vol. 7, no. 2, 1993, pp. 5–20.
3 James Bell, 'Brand management for the next millennium', *The Journal of Business Strategy*, vol. 19, no. 2, March/April 1998, pp. 7–10; Joseph Arthur Rooney, 'Branding: a trend for today and tomorrow', *The Journal of Product and Brand Management*, vol. 4, no. 4, 1995, pp. 48–56.
4 Henry Assael, *Consumer Behaviour and Marketing Action*, 4th edn (Boston: PWS-Kent, 1992).
5 David A. Aaker, *Managing Brand Equity: Capitalizing on the Value of a Brand Name* (New York: Free Press, 1991), pp. 16–17.
6 Chip Walker, 'What's in a name?' *American Demographics*, February 1991, pp. 54–57.
7 'British retailing: chemistry upset,' *The Economist*, 24 February 2001, p. 68.
8 Marcel Corstjens and Rajiv Lal, 'Building store loyalty through store brands', *Journal of Marketing Research*, August 2000, pp. 281–291.
9 Alan Miller, 'Gains share in dollars and units during 1990 third quarter', *Private Label*, January–February 1991, pp. 85–89.

10 Taylor Nelson, Sofres Superpanel, 1999.

11 Leonard L. Berry, Edwin E. Lefkowith and Terry Clark, 'In services, what's in a name?" *Harvard Business Review*, September–October 1988, pp. 2–4.

12 Dorothy Cohen, 'Trademark Strategy', *Journal of Marketing*, January 1986, p. 63.

13 Chiranjev Kohli and Rajheesh Suri, 'Brand names that work: a study of the effectiveness of different brand names', *Marketing Management Journal*, Fall/Winter 2000, pp. 112–120.

14 Zeynep Gurhan-Canli and Durairaj Maheswaran, 'The effects of extensions on brand name dilution and enhancement', *Journal of Marketing Research*, vol. 35, no. 4, November 1998, pp. 464–473.

15 "Trademark Stylesheet', U.S. Trademark Association, no. 1A.

16 Vicki R. Lane, 'The impact of ad repetition and ad content on consumer perceptions of incongruent extensions', *Journal of Marketing*, April 2000, pp. 80–91.

17 Graham Hurrell, 'Solpadol – a successful case of brand positioning', *Journal of the Market Research* Society, July 1997.

18 Peter Doyle, *Marketing Management and Strategy* (London: Prentice-Hall, 1994) and chapter 20 in M. Baker, ed., *The Marketing Book* (Oxford: Butterworth-Heinemann, 1995).

19 Lesley de Chernatony, 'Brand management through narrowing the gap between identity and brand reputation', *Journal of Marketing Management*, 15 (1–3), 1999, pp. 157–179.

20 Claudia Simoes and Sally Dibb, 'Rethinking the brand concept: new brand orientation', *Corporate Communications: An International Journal*, November/December 2001, pp. 217–224.

21 Samuel Solley, 'Unilever in radical identity overhaul', *Marketing*, 19 February 2004, p. 1.

22 Emily Rogers, 'Coca-Cola introduces designer glass bottles', *Marketing*, 25 March 2004, p. 19.

23 Fred W. Morgan, 'Tampered goods: legal developments and marketing guidelines', *Journal of Market-ing*, April 1988, pp. 86–96.

24 Ibid.

25 Brian Wansink, 'Can package size accelerate usage volume?', *Journal of Marketing*, vol. 60, no. 3, July 1996, pp. 1–14.

26 Thomas J. Madden, Kelly Hewett and Martin S. Roth, 'Managing images in different cultures: a cross national study of color meanings and preferences', *Journal of International Marketing*, Winter 2000, p. 90.

27 Branwell Johnson, 'Mineral water companies to launch 'purity' symbol', *Marketing Week*, 29 April 2004, p. 8.


**Chapter 12**


1 Rajesh Sethi, 'New product quality and product development', *Journal of Marketing*, April 2000, pp. 1–14.

2 Roger C. Bennet and Robert G. Cooper, 'The product life cycle trap', *Business Horizons*, September–October 1984, pp. 7–16.

3 'Product development: where planning and marketing meet', *Journal of Business Strategy*, September–October 1990, pp. 13–16.

4 Lee G. Cooper, 'Strategic marketing planning for radically new products', *Journal of Marketing*, January 2000, pp. 1–16.

5 Lisa C. Troy, David M. Szymanski and P. Rajan Varadarajan, 'Generating new product ideas: an initial investigation of the role of market information and organizational characteristics', *Journal of the Academy of Marketing Science*, January 2001, pp. 89–101.

6 Peter F. Drucker, 'The discipline of innovation', *Harvard Business Review*, May–June 1985, pp. 67–68; Wu Couchen, 'A proposed method for the design of consumer products', *Journal of International Marketing and Marketing Research*, February 1999.

7 Jonathan B. Levine, 'Keeping new ideas kicking around', *Business Week*, Innovation 1989 issue, p. 128.

8 Aric Rindfleisch and Christine Moorman, 'The acquisition and utilization of information in new product alliances: a strength-of-ties perspective', *Journal of Marketing*, April 2001, pp. 1–18.

9 Joshua Hyatt, 'Ask and you shall receive', *Inc.*, September 1989, pp. 90–101.

10 Christine Moorman and Anne S. Miner, 'The convergence of planning and execution: improvisation in new product development', *Journal of Marketing*, vol. 62, no. 3, July 1998, pp. 1–20; V. Padmanabhan, Surendra Rajiv and Kannan Srinivasan, 'New products, upgrades, and new releases: a rationale for sequential product introduction', *Journal of Marketing Research*, vol. 34, no. 4, November 1997, pp. 456–472.

11 Barry L. Bayus, Sanjay Jain and Ambar G. Rao, 'Truth or consequences: an analysis of vaporware and new product announcements', *Journal of Marketing Research*, February 2001, pp. 3–13.

12 Cyndee Miller, 'Little relief seen for new product failure rate', *Marketing News*, 21 June 1993, p. 5.

13 Chung K. Kim, Anne M. Lavack and Margo Smith, 'Consumer evaluation of vertical brand extensions and core brands', *Journal of Business Research*, March 2001, pp. 211–222.

14 Ian Grime, Adamantios Diamantopoulos and Gareth Smith, 'Consumer evaluations of extensions and their effects on the core brand: key issues and research propositions', *European Journal of Marketing*, November 2002, pp. 1415–1438.

15 Adapted from Everett M. Rogers, *Diffusion of Innovations* (New York: Macmillan, 1962), pp. 81–86.

16 Graham J. Hooley and John Saunders, *Competitive Positioning: The Key to Market Success* (Englewood Cliffs, N.J.: Prentice-Hall, 1993).

17 F. Stewart DeBruicker and Gregory L. Summe, 'Make sure your customers keep coming back', *Harvard Business Review*, January–February 1985, pp. 92–98.

18 Geoffrey L. Gordon, Roger J. Calantone and Anthony di Benedetto, 'Mature markets and revitalization strategies:

an American fable', *Business Horizons*, May–June 1991, p. 42.
19 Kim B. Clark and Takahiro Fujimoto, 'The power of product integrity', *Harvard Business Review*, November–December 1990, pp. 108–118.
20 Lynn W. Phillips, Dae R. Chang and Robert D. Buzzell, 'Product quality, cost position and business performance: a test of some key hypotheses', *Journal of Marketing*, Spring 1983, pp. 26–43.
21 Douglas M. Lambert and Jay U. Sterling, 'Identifying and eliminating weak products', *Business*, July–September 1988, pp. 3–10.
22 Joseph P. Guiltinan and Gordon W. Paul, *Marketing Management: Strategies and Programmes* (New York: McGraw-Hill, 1982), p. 31.
23 George S. Day, 'Diagnosing the Product Portfolio', *Journal of Marketing*, April 1977, pp. 30–31.
24 Sally Dibb and Lyndon Simkin, *The Market Segmentation Workbook* (London: Thomson, 1996).
25 Robert Jacobson, 'Distinguishing among competing theories of the market share effect', *Journal of Marketing*, October 1988, pp. 68–80.
26 George S. Day, *Analysis for Strategic Market Decisions* (St. Paul, Minn.: West, 1986), pp. 117–118.
27 Robert D. Buzzell and Bradley T. Gale, *The PIMS Principles: Linking Strategy to Performance* (New York: Free Press, 1987).
28 Day, *Analysis for Strategic Market Decisions*, p. 10.
29 David W. Cravens, 'Strategic marketing's new challenge', *Business Horizons*, March–April 1983, p. 19.

**Chapter 13**

1 Leonard L. Berry and A. Parasuraman, *Marketing Services: Competing Through Quality* (New York: Free Press, 1991), p. 5.
2 Glenn B. Voss, A. Parasuraman and Dhruv Grewal, 'The roles of price, performance, and expectations in determining satisfaction in service exchanges', *Journal of Marketing*, vol. 64, no. 4, October 1998, pp. 46–61; Jochen Wirtz and John E. G. Bateson, 'Consumer satisfaction with services: integrating the environment perspective in services marketing into the traditional disconfirmation paradigm', *Journal of Business Research*, vol. 44, no. 1, January 1999, pp. 55–66.
3 Donald Cowell, *The Marketing of Services* (London: Heinemann, 1984).
4 Based on K. Douglas Hoffman and John E. G. Bateson, *Essentials of Services Marketing* (Fort Worth, Texas: Dryden Press, 1997), pp. 25–28; and Valerie A. Zeithaml, A. Parasuraman and Leonard L. Berry, *Delivery Quality Service: Balancing Customer Perceptions and Expectations* (New York: Free Press, 1990).
5 John E. G. Bateson, 'Why we need service marketing', in O. C. Ferrell, S. W. Brown and C. W. Lamb, Jr, eds, *Conceptual and Theoretical Development in Marketing* (Chicago: American Marketing Associa-tion, 1979), pp. 131–146.
6 Valarie A. Zeithaml, 'How consumer evaluation processes differ between goods and services', in James H. Donnelly and William R. George, eds, *Marketing of Services* (Chicago: American Marketing Association, 1981), pp. 186–190.
7 Leonard L. Berry, Valarie A. Zeithaml and A. Parasuraman, 'Responding to demand fluctuations: key challenge for service businesses', in Russell Belk et al., eds, *AMA Educators' Proceedings* (Chicago: American Marketing Association, 1984), pp. 231–234.
8 Brian Moores, *Are They Being Served?* (Oxford: Philip Allan, 1986).
9 J. Paul Peter and James H. Donnelly, *A Preface to Marketing Management* (Burr Ridge, Illinois: McGraw-Hill/Irwin, 2000), p. 203.
10 Randi Priluck, 'Relationship marketing can mitigate product and service failures', *Journal of Services Marketing*, March 2003, pp. 37–52.
11 Dennis B. Arnett, Steve D. German and Shelby D. Hunt, 'The identity salience model of relationship marketing success: the case of nonprofit marketing', *Journal of Marketing*, April 2003, pp. 89–106.
12 James Reardon, Chip Miller, Ronald Hasty and Blaise J. Waguespack, 'A comparison of alternative theories of services marketing', *Journal of Marketing Theory and Practice*, vol. 4, no. 4, Fall 1996, pp. 61–71.
13 Christopher H. Lovelock, 'Classifying services to gain strategic marketing insights', *Journal of Marketing*, Summer 1983, p. 15.
14 Christopher H. Lovelock, *Services Marketing* (Englewood Cliffs, N.J.: Prentice-Hall, 1984), pp. 46–64.
15 Yoram Wind, 'Financial services: increasing your marketing productivity and profitability', *Journal of Services Marketing*, Fall 1987, p. 8.
16 Cathy Goodwin, 'Marketing strategies for services: globalization, client-orientation, deregulation', *International Journal of Research in Marketing*, July 1997.
17 Lovelock, *Services Marketing*, pp. 279–289.
18 Ibid.
19 Berry, Zeithaml and Parasuraman, pp. 231–234.
20 Valarie A. Zeithaml, A. Parasuraman and Leonard L. Berry, *Delivering Quality Service: Balancing Customer Perceptions and Expectations* (New York: Free Press, 1990).
21 A. Parasuraman, Leonard L. Berry and Valarie A. Zeithaml, 'An empirical examination of relationships in an extended service quality model', *Marketing Science Institute Working Paper Series*, Report no. 90–122 (Cambridge, Mass.: Marketing Science Institute, 1990), p. 29.
22 Valarie A. Zeithaml, Leonard L. Berry and A. Parasuraman, 'Communication and control pro-cesses in the delivery of service quality', *Journal of Marketing*, April 1988, pp. 35–48.
23 Valarie A. Zeithaml, Leonard L. Berry and A. Parasuraman, 'The nature and determinants of customer expectations of service', *Journal of the Academy of Marketing Science*, Winter 1993, pp. 1–12.

24 Hartline and Ferrell, 'Service quality implementation', p. 36.
25 Mary Jo Bitner, 'Evaluating service encounters: the effects of physical surroundings and employee responses', *Journal of Marketing*, April 1990, p. 70.
26 Hartline and Ferrell, 'Service quality implementation', pp. 17–19.
27 Myron Glassman and Bruce McAfee, 'Integrating the personnel and marketing functions: the challenge of the 1990s', *Business Horizons*, May–June 1992, pp. 52–59.
28 Keith J. Blois, 'Marketing for non-profit organisations', in Michael J. Baker (ed.), *The Marketing Book* (London: Heinemann, 1994), p. 405.
29 J. Whyte, 'Organisation, person and idea marketing as exchange', *Quarterly Review of Marketing*, January 1985, pp. 25–30.
30 John Garrison, 'Telethons – the positive story', *Fund Raising Management*, November 1987, pp. 48–52.
31 Philip Kotler, *Marketing for Non-profit Organisations*, 2nd edn (Englewood Cliffs, N.J.: Prentice-Hall, 1982), p. 37.
32 Ibid.
33 Meryl Davids, 'Doing well by doing good', *Public Relations Journal*, July 1987, pp. 17–21.
34 Leyland F. Pitt and Russell Abratt, 'Pricing in non-profit organisations – a framework and conceptual overview', *Quarterly Review of Marketing*, Spring–Summer 1987, pp. 13–15.
35 Kelly Walker, 'Not-for-profit profits', *Forbes*, 10 September 1984, p. 165.


**Chapter 14**


1 Erin Anderson, George S. Day and V. Kasturi Rangan, 'Strategic channel design', *Sloan Management Review*, vol. 38, no. 4, Summer 1997, p. 59.
2 Mitzi M. Montoya-Weiss, Glenn B. Ross and Dhruv Grewal, 'Determinant of online channel use and overall satisfaction with a relational, multichannel service provider', *Journal of the Academy of Marketing Science*, Fall 2003, pp. 448–459.
3 O.C. Ferrell and William M. Pride, national sample of 2,042 households.
4 Wroe Alderson, *Marketing Behavior and Executive Action* (Homewood, Ill.: Irwin, 1957), pp. 201–211.
5 Lester E. Goodman and Paul A. Dion, 'The determinants of commitment in the distributor–manufacturer relationship', *Industrial Marketing Management*, April 2001, pp. 287–300.
6 James D. Hlavacek and Tommy J. McCuistion, 'Industrial distributors: when, who, and how?' *Harvard Business Review*, March–April 1983, p. 97.
7 S. Altan Erdem and L. Jean Harrison-Walker, 'Managing channel relationships: toward an identification of effective promotional strategies in vertical marketing systems', *Journal of Marketing Theory and Practice*, vol. 5, no. 2, Spring 1997, pp. 80–87.
8 Jordan D. Lewis, 'Using alliances to build market power', *Planning Review*, September–October 1990, pp. 4–9, p. 48.
9 Leo Aspinwall, 'The marketing characteristics of goods', in *Four Marketing Theories* (Boulder: University of Colorado Press, 1961), pp. 27–32.
10 Allan J. Magrath, 'Differentiating yourself via distribution', *Sales & Marketing Management*, March 1991, pp. 50–57.
11 David W. Cravens, Thomas N. Ingram and Raymond W. LaForge, 'Evaluating multiple sales channel strategies', *Journal of Business and Industrial Marketing*, Summer–Fall 1991, pp. 3–4.
12 Bert Rosenbloom, *Marketing Channels: A Management View* (Hinsdale, Ill.: Dryden, 1987), p. 160.
13 Ibid., p. 161.
14 Donald J. Bowersox and M. Bixby Cooper, *Strategic Marketing Channel Management* (New York: McGraw-Hill, 1992), pp. 177–178.
15 Wroe Alderson, *Dynamic Marketing Behavior* (Homewood, Ill.: Irwin, 1965), p. 239.
16 Tony Seideman, 'Get with the program', *Inbound Logistics*, September 1998, p. 29.
17 Steven J. Skinner, Julie B. Gassenheimer and Scott W. Kelley, 'Cooperation in supplier-dealer relations',*Journal of Retailing, Summer* 1992, pp. 174–193; H. Hakansson, *International Marketing and Purchasing of Industrial Goods* (Chichester: Wiley, 1982).
18 J. Joseph Cronin Jr., Thomas L. Baker and Jon M. Hawes, 'An assessment of the role performance measurement of power-dependency in marketing channels', *Journal of Business Research*, vol. 30, no. 3, July 1994, pp. 201–210.
19 Nirmalya Kumar, Lisa K. Scheer and Jan-Benedict Steenkamp, 'Interdependence, punitive capability, and the reciprocation of punitive actions in channel relationships', *Journal of Marketing Research*, vol. 35, no. 2, May 1998, pp. 225–235; Robert F. Lusch, 'Interdependency, contracting, and relational behavior in marketing channels', *Journal of Marketing*, October 1996.
20 Jonathan D. Hibbard, Nirmalya Kumar and Louis W. Stern, 'Examining the impact of destructive acts in marketing channel relationships', *Journal of Marketing Research*, February 2001, pp. 45–61.
21 Adel I. El-Ansary, 'Perspectives on channel system performance', in *Contemporary Issues in Marketing Channels*, ed. Robert F. Lusch and Paul H. Zinszer (Norman: University of Oklahoma Press, 1979), p. 50.
22 Kenneth G. Hardy and Allan J. Magrath, 'Ten ways for manufacturers to improve distribution management', *Business Horizons*, November–December 1988, p. 68.
23 Ronald D. Michman and Stanley D. Sibley, *Marketing Channels and Strategies* (Columbus, Ohio: Grid Publishing, 1980), pp. 412–417.
24 Janet E. Keith, Donald W. Jackson and Lawrence A. Crosby, 'Effect of alternative types of influence strategies under different dependence structures', *Journal of Marketing*, July 1990, pp. 30–41.
25 John F. Gaski and John R. Nevin, 'The differential effects of exercised and unexercised power sources in a marketing channel', *Journal of Marketing Research*, July 1985, p. 139.

26 Rosenbloom, *Marketing Channels*, p. 98.
27 Ibid., pp. 96–97.


**Chapter 15**


1 Clarence Casson, '1988 wholesaler giants; making all the right moves', Building Supply Home Centers, September 1988, p. 56.
2 Rajesh Tyagi and Chandrasekhar Das, 'Manufacturer and warehouse selection for stable relationships in dynamic wholesaling and location problems', *International Journal of Physical Distribution and Logistics Management*, 25 (6), 1995, pp. 54–72.
3 Rebecca Rolfes, 'Wholesaling without borders', *Medical Marketing & Media*, February 1991, pp. 74–76.
4 Bert Rosenbloom, Marketing Channels: *A Management View* (Hinsdale, Ill.: Dryden Press, 1987), p. 63.
5 *US Census of Wholesale Trade*, May 1985, p. 207.
6 Rosenbloom, p. 61.
7 Ibid.
8 Ibid., p. 62.
9 Thomas V. Bonoma, 'Get more out of your trade shows', *Harvard Business Review*, January–February 1983, pp. 75–83.
10 Rosenbloom, p. 185.
11 Rosenbloom, p. 185.
12 'Why Cargo Club was off target', *Marketing*, 23 March 1995, p. 3.
13 Joseph Weber, 'Mom and Pop move out of wholesaling', *Business Week*, 9 January 1989, p. 91.
14 Carol C. Bienstock, 'Measuring physical distribution service quality', *Journal of the Academy of Marketing Science*, Winter 1997.
15 Carl M. Guelzo, *Introduction to Logistics Management* (Englewood Cliffs, N.J.: Prentice-Hall, 1986), p. 32.
16 John T. Mentzer, Roger Gomes and Robert E. Krapfel, Jr., 'Physical distribution service: a fundamental marketing concept?', *Journal of the Academy of Marketing Science*, Winter 1989, p. 59.
17 Lloyd M. Rinehart, M. Bixby Cooper and George D. Wagenheim, 'Furthering the integration of marketing and logistics through customer service in the channel', *Journal of the Academy of Marketing Sci-ence*, Winter 1989, p. 67.
18 Charles A. Taff, *Management of Physical Distri-bution and Transportation* (Homewood, Ill.: Irwin, 1984), p. 250.
19 Judith Graham, 'IKEA furnishing its US identity', *Advertising Age*, 14 September 1989, p. 79; and Jonathan Reynolds, 'IKEA: a competitive company with style', *Retail & Distribution Management* (UK), May/June 1988, pp. 32–34.
20 Rinehart, Cooper and Wagenheim, p. 67.
21 Guelzo, pp. 35–36.
22 Taff, p. 240.
23 Carol Doherty, Jens Maier and Lyndon Simkin, 'DPP modelling in retail marketing: an application', *OMEGA*, 20 (3), 1992, pp. 25–33.
24 Guelzo, p. 102.
25 Adapted from John F. Magee, *Physical Distribution Systems* (New York: McGraw-Hill, Inc., 1967). Reprinted by permission of the author.
26 The EOQ formula for the optimal order quantity is EOQ = 2DR/I, where EOQ = optimum average order size, D = total demand, R = cost of processing an order and I = cost of maintaining one unit of inventory per year. For a more complete description of EOQ methods and terminology, see Frank S. McLaughlin and Robert C. Pickardt, *Quantitative Techniques for Management Decisions* (Boston: Houghton Mifflin, 1978), pp. 104–119.
27 David N. Burt, 'Managing suppliers up to speed', *Harvard Business Review*, July–August 1989, p. 128.
28 Ibid., p. 129.
29 Peter D. Bennett, ed., *Dictionary of Marketing Terms* (Chicago: American Marketing Association, 1988), p. 204.
30 John J. Coyle, Edward Bardi and C. John Langley, Jr., *The Management of Business Logistics* (St. Paul, Minn.: West, 1988), pp. 327–329.
31 Thomas A. Foster and Joseph V. Barks, 'Here comes the best', *Distribution*, September 1984, p. 25.
32 Allen R. Wastler, 'Intermodal leaders ponder riddle of winning more freight', *Traffic World*, 19 June 1989, pp. 14–15.
33 Julie J. Gentry, 'Using logistics alliances to gain a strategic advantage in the marketplace', *Journal of Marketing Theory and Practice*, Spring 1996; Judith Schmitz Whipple, 'Logistical alliance formation motives: similarities and differences within the channel', *Journal of Marketing Theory and Practice*, Spring 1996.


**Chapter 16**


1 Roger O. Crockett, 'Chat me up ... please', *Business Week*, 19 March 2001, p. EB10.
2 www.brc.org.uk/latestdata, accessed April 2004. *Data sources: the British Retail Consortium and the Office for National Statistics.*
3 H. Carter, *The Study of Urban Geography* (London: Edward Arnold, 1972), pp. 205–247.
4 * DIY (do it yourself) merchandise includes building materials, hardware, plumbing and electrical goods, kitchen units and gardening requirements.
5 J. A. Dawson, *Shopping Centre Development* (Harlow: Longman, 1983), Chapter 2.
6 Ibid.
7 Russell Schiller, 'Out of town exodus', in *The Changing Face of British Retailing* (London: Newman Books, 1987), pp. 64–73.
8 Kenneth C. Schneider, 'Telemarketing as a promotional tool – its effects and side effects', *Journal of Consumer Marketing*, Winter 1985, pp. 29–39.
9 UK Vending Ltd, Rochester, Kent, 2004.
10 '*V/T* census of the industry issue – 1988', *Vending Times*, 1988, p. 49. Reprinted by permission.
11 UK Vending Ltd, Rochester, Kent, 2004.
12 Todd Wasserman, 'Kodak rages in favor of the machines', *Brandweek*, 26 February 2001, p. 6.

13 Al Urbanski, 'The franchise option', *Sales & Marketing Management*, February 1988, pp. 28–33.
14 Jim Forward and Christina Fulop, 'Large established firms' entry into franchising', *Retail, Distribution and Consumer Research*, 6 (1), 1996, pp. 34–52.
15 Statistical Abstract of the US, 1989, p. 760.
16 Mary Joyce, 'Retailing triumphs and blunders: victims of competition in the new age of marketing management', *Journal of the Academy of Marketing Science*, vol. 26, no. 3, Summer 1998, pp. 253–254.
17 C. H. Anderson, *Retailing* (St. Paul, Minn.: West, 1993).
18 R. L. Davies and D. S. Rogers, *Store Location and Store Assessment Research* (Chichester: Wiley, 1984).
19 R. L. Davies, *Marketing Geography* (London: Methuen, 1976).
20 L. Simkin, 'SLAM: store location assessment model – theory and practice', OMEGA, 17 (1), 1989, pp. 53–58; Lyndon Simkin, 'Tackling barriers to effective implementation of modelling in retail marketing applications', *Retail, Distribution and Consumer Research*, 6 (3), 1996, pp. 225–241.
21 Ruth Schmidt, Rupert Segal and Christy Cartwright, 'Two-stop shopping or polarisation', *International Journal of Retail and Distribution Management*, 22 (1), 1994, pp. 12–19.
22 C. Glenn Walters and Blaise J. Bergiel, *Marketing Channels*, 2nd edn (Glenview, Ill.: Scott, Foresman, 1982), p. 205.
23 George H. Lucas, Jr., and Larry G. Gresham, 'How to position for retail success', *Business*, April–June 1988, pp. 3–13.
24 G. J. Davies and J. M. Brooks, *Positioning Strategy in Retailing* (London: Paul Chapman, 1989).
25 Richard F. Yalch and Eric R. Spangenberg, 'The effects of music in a retail setting on real and perceived shopping times', *Journal of Business Research*, August 2000, pp. 139–147.
26 Terence Conran, 'The retail image', in *The Retail Report* (London: Healey & Baker, 1985).
27 Francine Schwadel, 'Little touches spur Wal-Mart's rise; shoppers react to logo, decor, employee vests', *Wall Street Journal*, 22 September 1989, p. B1.
28 Stephen Brown, 'The wheel of retailing: past and future', *Journal of Retailing*, Summer 1990, pp. 143–149.
29 Stanley C. Hollander, 'The wheel of retailing', *Journal of Marketing*, July 1960, p. 37.
30 W. S. Howe, 'UK retailer vertical power, market competition and consumer welfare', *International Journal of Retail and Distribution Management*, 18 (2), 1990, pp. 16–25.
31 Lynne Richardson, John Swan and James Hulton, 'The effects of the presence and use of channel power sources on distributor satisfaction', *Retail, Distribution and Consumer Research*, 5 (2), 1995, pp. 185–202.
32 K. K. Tse, 'Marks & Spencer: a manufacturer without factories', *International Trends in Retailing*, 6 (2), 1989, pp. 23–36.
33 R. M. Grant, 'Manufacturer-retailer relations: the shifting balance of power', in Gerry Johnson, *Busi-ness Strategy and Retailing* (Chichester: Wiley, 1987), pp. 43–58.
34 Gerry Johnson, *Business Strategy and Retailing* (Chichester: Wiley, 1987).
35 Lynd Morley, 'Mapping the future', *Retail Technology*, 2(7), 1988, pp. 40–42.
36 Tony Rudd, 'Trends in physical distribution', in *The Changing Face of British Retailing* (London: Newman Books, 1987), pp. 84–93.
37 C. Doherty, J. R. Maier and L. Simkin, 'DPP decision support in retail merchandising', *OMEGA* 21 (1), 1993, pp. 25–33.

**Chapter 17**

1 Richard W. Pollay, 'On the value of reflections on the values in "The distorted mirror"', *Journal of Marketing*, July 1987, pp. 104–109.
2 Morris B. Holbrook, 'Mirror, mirror, on the wall, what's unfair in the reflections on advertising', *Journal of Marketing*, July 1987, pp. 95–103.
3 Richard N. Farmer, 'Would you want your granddaughter to marry a Taiwanese marketing man?' *Journal of Marketing*, October 1987, pp. 111–116.
4 Colin Coulson-Thomas, *Marketing Communications* (London: Heinemann, 1986); Kusum L. Ailawadi and Scott A. Neslin, 'The effect of promotion on consumption: buying more and consuming it faster', *Journal of Marketing Research*, vol. 35, no. 3, August 1998, pp. 390–398.
5 James Engel, Martin Warshaw and Thomas Kinnear, *Promotional Strategy: Managing the Marketing Communications Process* (Boston: Irwin, 1994).
6 John Rossiter and Larry Percy, *Advertising and Promotion Management* (New York: McGraw-Hill, 1987).
7 In case you do not read Chinese, this says, 'In the factory we make cosmetics, and in the store we sell hope'. Prepared by Chih Kang Wang.
8 Terence A. Shimp and M. Wayne Delozier, *Promotion Management and Marketing Communication* (Hinsdale, Ill.: Dryden Press, 1986), pp. 25–26.
9 Judy A. Wagner, Noreen M. Klein and Janet E. Keith, 'Selling strategies: the effects of suggesting a decision structure to novice and expert buyers', *Journal of the Academy of Marketing Science*, 29 (3), 2001, pp. 289–306.
10 John S. McClenahen, 'How can you possibly say that?', *Industry Week*, 17 July 1995, pp. 17–19.
11 David M. Szymanski, 'Modality and offering effects in sales presentations for a good versus a service', *Journal of the Academy of Marketing Science*, 29 (2), 2001, pp. 179–189.
12 David Jones, 'Setting promotional goals: a communications' relationship model', *Journal of Consumer Marketing*, 11 (1), 1994, pp. 38–49.
13 Adapted from Everett M. Rogers, *Diffusion of Innovations* (New York: Free Press, 1962), pp. 81–86, 98–102.
14 Lawrence J. Marks and Michael A. Kamins, 'Product sampling and advertising sequence, belief strength, confidence and attitudes', *Journal of Marketing Research*, August 1988, pp. 266–281.
15 Rogers, pp. 247–250.

16 Rossiter and Percy.
17 J. Richard Shannon, 'The new promotions mix: a proposed paradigm, process, and application', *Journal of Marketing Theory and Practice*, Winter 1996.
18 Vicki R. Lane, 'The impact of ad repetition and ad content on consumer perceptions of incongruent extensions', *Journal of Marketing*, April 2000, pp. 80–91.
19 M. Flandin, E. Martin and L. Simkin, 'Advertising effectiveness research: a survey of agencies, clients and conflicts', *International Journal of Advertising*, 11 March 1992, pp. 203–214.
20 Scott B. MacKenzie, Philip M. Podsakoff and Gregory A. Rich, 'Transformational and transactional leadership and sales person performance', *Journal of the Academy of Marketing Science*, 29 (2), 2001, pp. 115–134.
21 Todd Hunt and James Grunig, *Public Relations Techniques* (Fort Worth: Harcourt Brace, 1994).
22 Sally Dibb, Lyndon Simkin and Adam Vancini, 'Competition, strategy, technology and people: the challenges facing PR', *International Journal of Advertising*, 15 (2), 1996, pp. 116–127.
23 This definition is adapted from John F. Luick and William L. Ziegler, *Sales Promotion and Modern Merchandising* (New York: McGraw-Hill, 1968), p. 4.
24 Roger A. Kerin and William L. Cron, 'Assessing trade show functions and performance: an exploratory study', *Journal of Marketing*, July 1987, pp. 87–94.
25 Michael Kavanagh, 'Free ISPs spur Net market growth', *Marketing Week*, 11 March 1999, pp. 30–31.
26 M.J. Evans, L. O'Malley and M. Patterson, 'Direct marketing communications in the UK: a study of growth, past, present and future', *Journal of Marketing Communications*, 2, 1996, pp. 51–65.
27 Lisa O'Malley, Maurice Patterson and Martin Evans, *Exploring Direct Marketing* (London: ITBP, 1999), p. 9.
28 Marcy Magiera, 'Holy Batvideo! Christmas already?', *Advertising Age*, 11 September 1989, p. 6.
29 *Marketing Week*, 5 July 1996, p. 13.
30 Alvin A. Achenbaum and F. Kent Mitchel, 'Pulling away from push marketing', *Harvard Business Review*, May–June 1987, p. 38.

**Chapter 18**

1 Mike Reid, 'IMC – performance relationship: further insight and evidence from the Australian marketplace', *International Journal of Advertising*, 22 (2), pp. 227–249.
2 S. Dibb, L. Simkin and R. Yuen, 'Pan-European advertising: think Europe – act local', *International Journal of Advertising*, 13 (2), 1994, pp. 125–136.
3 *Students' Briefs* (London: The Advertising Associ-ation, 1988).
4 Demetrios Vakratsas and Tim Ambler, 'How advertising works: what do we really know?', *Journal of Marketing*, vol. 63, no. 1, January 1999, pp. 26–43.
5 Scott Hume, 'Pizza Hut is frosted; new ad takes slap at McDonald's test product', *Advertising Age*, 18 September 1989, p. 4.
6 Torin Douglas, *The Complete Guide to Advertising* (London: Macmillan, 1985).
7 Tobi Elkin, 'Handspring handheld goes high fashion', *Advertising Age*, 16 March 2001, www.adage.com/.
8 Peter Jackson, Adsearch, Richmond-upon-Thames.
9 Pauline Bickerton, Matthew Bickerton and Upkor Pardesi, *Cybermarketing* (Oxford: Butterworth-Heinemann, 1996).
10 James E. Littlefield and C. A. Kirkpatrick, *Advertising Mass Communication in Marketing* (Boston: Houghton Mifflin, 1970), p. 178.
11 S. Watson Dunn and Arnold M. Barban, *Advertising: Its Role in Modern Marketing*, 6th edn (Hinsdale, Ill.: Dryden Press, 1986), p. 493.
12 Patrick Quinn, *Low Budget Advertising* (London: Heinemann, 1988).
13 M. Flandin, E. Martin and L. Simkin, 'Advertising effectiveness research: a survey of agencies, clients and conflicts', *International Journal of Advertising*, 11 (3), 1992, pp. 203–214.
14 Marvin E. Goldberg and Gerald J. Gorn, 'Happy and sad TV programmes: how they affect reactions to commercials', *Journal of Consumer Research*, December 1987, pp. 387–403.
15 *Marketing*, 24 May 1990, p. 5.
16 *Public Relations Practice – Its Role and Parameters* (London: The Institute of Public Relations, 1984).
17 The Advertising Association, London, 1990; *The Independent*, 12 August 1990; Robin Cobb, 'The art of gentle persuasion', *Marketing*, 6 September 1990, pp. 25–26; Bill Britt, 'PR leads from front as buy-up battles rage', *Marketing*, 1 February 1990, p. 13; P. J. Kitchen and T. Proctor, 'The increasing importance of public relations in fast moving consumer goods firms', *Journal of Marketing Management*, 7(4), 1991, pp. 357–370.
18 David Wragg, *Public Relations for Sales and Market-ing Management* (London: Kogan Page, 1987).
19 J. White, *How to Understand and Manage Public Relations* (London: Business Books, 1991).
20 Frank Jefkins, *Public Relations Techniques* (London: Heinemann, 1988).
21 S. Dibb, L. Simkin and A. Vancini, 'Competition, strategy, technology and people: the challenges facing PR', *International Journal of Advertising*, 15 (2), 1996, pp. 116–127.
22 BBC and ITN news broadcasts, February and March 1993.
23 Dibb, Simkin and Yuen.
24 M. Flandin, E. Martin and L. Simkin, 'Advertising effectiveness research: a survey of agencies, clients and conflicts', *International Journal of Advertising*, 11(3), 1992, pp. 203–214.
25 John Wringe, managing director of Cogent, talking to IB365 students at Warwick Business School, 1996.
26 Dibb, Simkin and Vancini.
27 S. Sleight, *Sponsorship: What It Is and How to Use It* (Maidenhead: McGraw-Hill, 1989).
28 M. G. Crowley, 'Prioritising the sponsorship audience', *European Journal of Marketing*, 25, 1991, pp. 11–21.

29 Tony Meenaghan, 'Current developments and future directions in sponsorship', *Journal of Advertising*, vol. 17, no. 1, 1998, pp. 3–28.

**Chapter 19**

1 *Marketing*, 28 June 1990, p. 13.
2 Julian Cummins, *Sales Promotion* (London: Kogan Page, 1989).
3 Myron Gable and B. J. Reed, 'The current status of women in professional selling', *Journal of Personal Selling & Sales Management*, May 1987, pp. 33–39.
4 William A. Weeks and Darrel D. Mueհing, 'Students' perceptions of personal selling', *Industrial Marketing Management*, May 1987, pp. 145–151.
5 Geoff Lancaster and David Jobber, *Selling and Sales Management* (London: Pitman, 1994).
6 'Getting ahead and staying ahead as the competition heats up', *Agency Sales Magazine*, June 1987, pp. 38–42.
7 Chris de Winter, *Telephone Selling* (London: Heinemann, 1988).
8 Sara Lorge, 'The best ways to prospect', *Sales and Marketing Management*, January 1998, p. 80.
9 Thomas W. Leigh and Patrick F. McGraw, 'Mapping the procedural knowledge of industrial sales personnel: a script-theoretic investigation', *Journal of Marketing*, January 1989, pp. 16–34.
10 Thayer C. Taylor, 'Xerox: who says you can't be big and fast?' *Sales & Marketing Management*, November 1987, pp. 62–65.
11 Leigh and McGraw, pp. 16–34.
12 William C. Moncrief, 'Five types of industrial sales jobs', *Industrial Marketing Management*, 17, 1988, p. 164.
13 A. J. Magrath, 'Are you overdoing "lean and mean"?', *Sales & Marketing Management*, January 1988, pp. 46–53.
14 Tony Adams, *Successful Sales Management* (London: Heinemann, 1988).
15 Coleman, pp. 6, 21.
16 Patrick C. Fleenor, 'Selling and sales management in action: assessment centre selection of sales representatives', *Journal of Personal Selling & Sales Management*, May 1987, pp. 57–59.
17 René Y. Darmon, 'The impact of incentive compensation on the salesperson's work habits: an economic model', *Journal of Personal Selling & Sales Management*, May 1987, pp. 21–32.
18 Dan Woog, 'Taking sales high tech', *High Tech Marketing*, May 1987, pp. 17–22.
19 Sandra Hile Hart, William C. Moncrief and A. Parasuraman, 'An empirical investigation of salespeople's performance, effort and selling method during a sales contest', *Journal of the Academy of Marketing Science*, Winter 1989, pp. 29–39.
20 John F. Luick and William L. Ziegler, *Sales Promotion and Modern Merchandising* (New York: McGraw-Hill, 1968), and Don E. Schultz and William A. Robinson, *Sales Promotion Management* (Chicago: Crain Books, 1982).
21 Cummins, p. 14.
22 P. R. Smith, *Marketing Communication: An Integrated Approach* (London: Kogan Page, 1993).
23 K. Peattie and S. Peattie, 'Sales promotion: playing to win?', *Journal of Marketing Management*, 9, 1993, pp. 225–269.
24 W. E. Phillips and Bill Robinson, 'Continued sales (price) promotion destroys brands: yes; no', *Marketing News*, 16 January 1989, pp. 4, 8.
25 Cummins, p. 14.
26 Emin Babakus, Peter Tat and William Cunningham, 'Coupon redemption: a motivational perspective', *Journal of Consumer Marketing*, Spring 1988, p. 40.
27 Donna Campanella, 'Sales promotion: couponmania', *Marketing and Media Decisions*, June 1987, pp. 118–122.
28 Arthur L. Porter, 'Direct mail's lessons for electronic couponers', *Marketing Management Journal*, Spring/Summer 2000, pp. 107–115.
29 Campanella, pp. 118–122.
30 Ibid.
31 Joe Agnew, 'P-O-P [P-O-S] displays are becoming a matter of consumer convenience', *Marketing News*, 9 October 1987, p. 16.
32 Alison Fahey, 'Study shows retailers rely on P-O-P [P-O-S]', *Advertising Age*, 27 November 1989, p. 83.
33 Peter Tat, William A. Cunningham and Emin Babakus, 'Consumer perceptions of rebates', *Journal of Advertising Research*, August–September 1988, p. 48.
34 Gerrie Anthea, 'Sales promotion putting up the premium', *Marketing*, 16 April 1987.
35 Steven W. Colford, 'Marriott sets largest promo', *Advertising Age*, 2 October 1989, p. 58.
36 Eileen Norris, 'Everyone will grab at a chance to win', *Advertising Age*, 22 August 1983, p. M10.
37 Ed Crimmins, 'A co-op myth: it is a tragedy that stores don't spend all their accruals', *Sales & Marketing Management*, 7 February 1983, pp. 72–73.
38 Gillian Upton, 'Sales promotion: getting results Barbados style', *Marketing*, 16 April 1987, pp. 37–40.
39 D. Bird, *Commonsense Direct Marketing* (London: Kogan Page, 1989).
40 Tom Duncan, 'A communication-based marketing model for managing relationships', *Journal of Marketing*, April 1998; James W. Peltier, 'The use of need-based segmentation for developing segment-specific direct marketing strategies', *Journal of Direct Marketing*, Autumn 1997.
41 B. North, 'Consumer companies take direct stance', *Marketing*, 20 May 1993, pp. 24–25.
42 Lisa O'Malley, Maurice Patterson and Martin Evans, *Exploring Direct Marketing* (London: ITBP, 1999), chapter 9.
43 J. December and N. Randall, *The World Wide Web* (New York: Unleashed Sams Publishing, 1994).
44 A. Schofield, 'The definition of direct marketing: a rejoinder to Bauer and Miglautsch', *Journal of Direct Marketing*, 9(2), 1995, pp. 37–8.
45 P. McGoldrick, *Retail Marketing* (Maidenhead: McGraw-Hill, 1997).

46 M. J. Evans, L. O'Malley and M. Patterson, 'Direct marketing communications in the UK: a study of growth, past, present and future', *Journal of Marketing Communications*, 2, 1996, pp. 51–65.
47 Lisa O'Malley, Maurice Patterson and Martin Evans, *Exploring Direct Marketing* (London: ITBP, 1999), p. 9.

**Chapter 20**

1 John Gourville and Dilip Soman, 'Pricing and the psychology of consumption', *Harvard Business Review*, September 2002, pp. 91–96.
2 Donald Lichtenstein, Nancy M. Ridgway and Richard G. Netemeyer, 'Price perceptions and consumer shopping behavior: a field study', *Journal of Marketing Research*, May 1993, pp. 234–245.
3 Ramarao Desiraju, 'Strategic service pricing and yield management', *Journal of Marketing*, January 1999.
4 Bruce L. Alford and Brian T. Engelland, 'Advertised reference price effects on consumer price estimates, value perception, and search intention', *Journal of Business Research*, May 2000, pp. 93–100.
5 Philip Buxton, 'Can marketing save falling retail giants?', *Marketing Week*, 28 January 1999, pp. 19–20.
6 Stephen J. Hoch, Xavier Dreze and Mary Park, 'EDLP – hi-lo, and margin arithmetic', *Journal of Marketing*, 58 (4), 1994, pp. 16–22; Allan Mitchell, 'Two sides of the same argument', *Marketing Week*, 16 February 1996, pp. 26–27.
7 Saeed Samier, 'Pricing in marketing strategies of U.S. and foreign based companies', *Journal of Business Research*, 1987, pp. 15–23.
8 J. Winkler, 'Pricing', M. Baker, ed., in *The Marketing Book* (London: Heinemann, 1987).
9 George S. Day and Liam Fahey, 'Valuing market strategies', *Journal of Marketing*, July 1988, pp. 45–57.
10 JCB company literature, 1992.
11 Joseph P. Guiltinan, 'The price-bundling of services: a normative framework', *Journal of Marketing*, April 1987, pp. 74–85.
12 Valerie A. Zeithaml, 'Consumer perceptions of price, quality and value: a means-end model and synthesis of evidence', *Journal of Marketing*, July 1988, pp. 2–22.
13 Eric Anderson and Duncan Simester, 'Mind your pricing cues', *Harvard Business Review*, September 2003, pp. 97–103.
14 David E. Griffith, 'The price of competitiveness in competitive pricing', *Journal of the Academy of Marketing Science*, Spring 1997; K. Sivakumar, 'Quality tier competition: how price change influences brand choice and category choice', *Journal of Marketing*, July 1997.
15 James B. Wilcox, Roy D. Howell, Paul Kuzdrall and Robert Britney, 'Price quantity discounts: some implications for buyers and sellers', *Journal of Marketing*, July 1987, pp. 60–61.
16 Robert G. Eccles, 'Control with fairness in transfer pricing', *Harvard Business Review*, November–December 1983, pp. 149–161.
17 Michael H. Morris, 'Separate prices as a marketing tool', *Industrial Marketing Management*, 16, 1987, pp. 79–86.

**Chapter 21**

1 Jack Trout, 'Prices: simple guidelines to get them right', *The Journal of Business Strategy*, vol. 19, no. 6, November/December 1998, pp. 13–16.
2 Asim Ansari, S. Siddarth and Charles B. Weinberg, 'Pricing a bundle of products or services: the case of nonprofits', *Journal of Marketing Research*, vol. 33, no. 1, February 1996, pp. 86–93.
3 Reprinted from Peter D. Bennett, ed., *Dictionary of Marketing Terms* (American Marketing Association, 1988), p. 54. Used by permission.
4 Bennett, p. 150. Reprinted by permission.
5 David E. Griffith, 'The price of competitiveness in competitive pricing', *Journal of the Academy of Marketing Science*, Spring 1997.
6 Herman Simon, 'Pricing opportunities and how to exploit them', *Sloan Management Review*, Winter 1992, pp. 55–65.
7 Kent B. Monroe, 'Effect of product line pricing characteristics on product evaluation', *Journal of Consumer Research*, March 1987, p. 518.
8 Marylin Chase, 'Burroughs-Wellcome cuts price of AZT under pressure from AIDS activists', *Wall Street Journal*, 19 September 1989, p. A3.
9 Bruce L. Alford and Brian T. Engelland, 'Advertised reference price effects on consumer price estimates, value, perception, and search intention', *Journal of Business Research*, May 2000, pp. 93–100.
10 National Federation of Consumer Groups, *A Handbook of Consumer Law, Which?* Books (London, 1989).

**Chapter 22**

1 Peter Doyle and John Saunders, 'Market segmentation and positioning in specialised industrial markets', *Journal of Marketing*, Spring 1995, p. 25.
2 Erik Jan Hultink, 'Industrial new product launch strategies and product development performance', *The Journal of Product Innovation Management*, July 1997.
3 Erin Anderson and Anne T. Coughlan, 'International market entry and expansion via independent or integrated channels of distribution', *Journal of Marketing*, January 1987, pp. 71–82.
4 Hiram C. Barksdale, Jr., Terry E. Powell and Ernestine Hargrove, 'Complaint voicing by industrial buyers', *Industrial Marketing Management*, May 1984, pp. 93–99.
5 Nicolas Bloch and Thierry Catfolis, 'The B2B e-marketplaces: how to succeed', *Business Strategy Review*, Autumn 2001, pp. 20–29.
6 Das Narayandas, Mary Caravella and John Deighton, 'The impact of Internet exchanges on business-to-business distribution', *Journal of the Academy of Marketing Science*, Fall 2002, 30 (4), pp. 500–506.
7 James D. Hlavacek and Tommy J. McCuiston, 'Industrial distributors: when, who, and how?' *Harvard Business Review*, March–April 1983, p. 97.

8 Richard Wise and David Morrison, 'Beyond the exchange: the future of B2B', *Harvard Business Review*, November/December 2000, 78 (6), pp. 86–99.
9 Gary L. Frazier, Robert E. Spekman and Charles R. O'Neal, 'Just-in-time exchange relationships in industrial markets', *Journal of Marketing*, October 1988, pp. 52–67.
10 Daniel H. McQuiston, 'Novelty, complexity and importance as casual determinants of industrial buyer behavior', *Journal of Marketing*, April 1989, pp. 66–79.
11 Steve Sulerno, 'The close of the new salesmanship', *PSA*, April 1985, p. 63.
12 Roger A. Kerin and William L. Cron. 'Assessing trade show functions and performance: an exploratory study', *Journal of Marketing*, July 1987, pp. 87–94.
13 Robert Jacobson and David A. Aaker, 'The strategic role of product quality', *Journal of Marketing*, October 1987, pp. 31–44.
14 Douglas G. Brooks, 'Bidding for the sake of follow-on contracts', *Journal of Marketing*, January 1978, p. 35.
15 Don Cowell, *The Marketing of Services* (Oxford: Butterworth-Heinemann, 1994).
16 Christopher Lovelock, *Managing Services* (Englewood Cliffs, N.J.: Prentice-Hall, 1992).
17 Walter van Waterschoot and Christophe Van den Bulte, 'The 4P classification of the marketing mix revisited', *Journal of Marketing*, October 1992.
18 G. Lynn Shostack, 'Breaking free from product marketing', *Journal of Marketing*, April 1977, pp. 73–80.
19 Sak Onkvisit and John J. Shaw, 'Service marketing: image, branding, and competition', *Business Horizons*, January–February 1989, p. 16.
20 Tom Peters, 'More expensive, but worth it', *U.S. News & World Report*, 3 February 1986, p. 54.
21 Valarie A. Zeithaml, 'Consumer perceptions of price, quality, and value: a means-end model and synthesis of evidence', *Journal of Marketing*, July 1988, pp. 2–22.
22 Leonard L. Berry, '8 keys to top service at financial institutions', *American Banker*, August 1987.
23 A. Parasuraman, Valarie A. Zeithaml and Leonard L. Berry, 'SERVQUAL: a multiple item scale for measuring consumer perceptions of service quality', *Journal of Retailing*, Spring 1988, pp. 12–40.
24 Stephen W. Brown and Teresa A. Swartz, 'A gap analysis of professional service quality', *Journal of Marketing*, April 1989, pp. 92–98.
25 Ibid.
26 G. Lynn Shostack, 'Service positioning through structural change', *Journal of Marketing*, January 1987, pp. 34–43.
27 William R. George and Leonard L. Berry, 'Guidelines for the advertising of services', *Business Horizons*, July–August 1981, pp. 52–56.
28 Sally Dibb and Lyndon Simkin, 'The strength of branding and positioning in services', *International Journal of Service Industry Management*, 4 (1), 1993, pp. 25–33.
29 Sally Dibb and Lyndon Simkin, 'Strategy and tactics: marketing leisure facilities', *The Service Industries Journal*, 13 (3), 1993, pp. 110–124; Dibb and Simkin, 'The strength of branding and positioning in services', pp. 25–35.
30 James L. Heskett, 'Lessons in the Service Sector', *Harvard Business Review*, March/April 1987, pp. 118–127.
31 George and Berry, pp. 55–70.
32 William R. George and J. Patrick Kelly, 'The promotion and selling of services', *Business*, July–September 1983, pp. 14–20.
33 John M. Rathmell, *Marketing in the Services Sector* (Cambridge, Mass.: Winthrop, 1974), p. 100.
34 George and Kelly, pp. 14–20; George and Berry, pp. 55–70.
35 Doris C. Van Doren and Louise W. Smith, 'Marketing in the restructured professional services field', *Journal of Services Marketing*, Summer 1987, pp. 69–70.
36 Jack Neff and Suzanne Bidlake, 'P&G, Unilever aim to take customers to the cleaners', *Advertising Age*, 12 February 2001, http://www.adage.com/news and features/features/20010212/article.html.
37 Joseph R. Guiltinan, 'The price bundling of services: a normative framework', *Journal of Marketing*, April 1987, p. 74.
38 James H. Donnelly, Jr., 'Marketing intermediaries in channels of distribution for services', *Journal of Marketing*, January, 1976, pp. 55–70.
39 Ibid.
40 Nigel A. L. Brooks, 'Strategic issues for financial services marketing', *Journal of Services Marketing*, Summer 1987, p. 65.
41 Dibb and Simkin, 'Strategy and tactics', pp. 110–124.
42 Adrian Payne, *The Essence of Services Marketing* (Hemel Hempstead: Prentice-Hall, 1993).
43 Warren J. Keegan, *Global Marketing Management*, 4th edn (Englewood Cliffs, N.J.: Prentice-Hall, 1989), pp. 378–382.
44 Colin Egan, De Montfort University.
45 Kamran Kashani, 'Beware the pitfalls of global marketing', *Harvard Business Review*, September–October 1989, pp. 93–94.
46 Douglass G. Norvell and Robert Morey, 'Ethnodomination in the channels of distribution of Third World nations', *Journal of the Academy of Marketing Science*, Summer 1983, pp. 204–235.
47 Erin Anderson and Anne T. Coughlan, 'International market entry and expansion via independent or integrated channels of distribution', *Journal of Marketing*, January 1987, pp. 71–82.
48 David Jobber, *Principles and Practice of Marketing* (London: McGraw-Hill, 1995).
49 Sally Dibb, Lyndon Simkin and John Bradley, *The Marketing Planning Workbook* (London: Routledge, 1996).


**Chapter 23**


1 Sue Pulendran, Richard Speed and Robert E. Widing II, 'Marketing planning, orientation and business performance', *European Journal of Marketing*, 37 (3/4), 2003, pp. 476–501.

2 Peter S.H. Leeflang, 'An empirical investigation of marketing planning', *Journal of Euro-Marketing*, 1996.

3 Ronald D. Michman, 'Linking futuristics with marketing planning, forecasting, and strategy', *Journal of Consumer Marketing, Summer* 1984, pp. 17, 23.

4 Sally Dibb, Lyndon Simkin and John Bradley, *The Marketing Planning Workbook* (London: Thomson, 1996).

5 Lyndon Simkin, 'People and processes in marketing planning: the benefits of controlling implementation in marketing planning', *Journal of Marketing Management*, vol. 12, no. 5, 1996, pp. 375–390; Lyndon Simkin, 'Delivering effective marketing planning', *Targeting, Measurement and Analysis for Marketing,* 8 (4), 2000, pp. 335–350; Lyndon Simkin, 'Barriers impeding effective implementation of marketing plans – a new research and training agenda', *Journal of Business and Industrial Marketing*, 17 (1), 2002, pp. 8–22.

6 David J. Luck, O. C. Ferrell and George Lucas, *Marketing Strategy and Plans*, 3rd edn (Englewood Cliffs, N.J.: Prentice-Hall, 1989), p. 328.

7 Hemant C. Sashittal and Avan R. Jassawalla, 'Marketing implementation in smaller organisations: definition, framework, and propositional inventory', *Journal of the Academy of Marketing Science*, Winter 2001, pp. 50–69.

8 Malcolm McDonald, *Marketing Plans: How to Prepare Them, How to Use Them* (Oxford: Butterworth Heinemann, 1989).

9 Douglas Bowman and Hubert Gatignon, 'Determinants of competitor response time to a new product introduction', *Journal of Marketing Research*, February 1995, pp. 42–53.

10 Lyndon Simkin and Anthony Chang, 'Understanding competitors' strategies', *Marketing Intelligence & Planning*, 15 (3), 1997, pp. 124–134.

11 Yoram Wind and Thomas S. Robertson, 'Marketing strategy: new directions for theory and research', *Journal of Marketing*, Spring 1983, p. 12.

12 Hemant C. Sashittal and Avan R. Jassawalla, 'Marketing implementation in smaller organisations'.

13 Lyndon Simkin, 'Addressing organisational prerequisites in marketing planning programmes', *Marketing Intelligence and Planning*, vol. 14, no. 5, 1996, pp. 39–46.

14 Lyndon Simkin, 'Barriers impeding effective implementation of marketing plans: a new research and training agenda', *Journal of Business and Industrial Marketing*, 17 (1), 2002, pp. 8–22.

15 Lyndon Simkin, 'Delivering effective marketing planning', *Targeting, Measurement and Analysis for Marketing,* 8 (4), 2000, pp. 335–350.

16 Sally Dibb and Lyndon Simkin, *The Marketing Casebook* (London: Routledge, 1994).

17 David Hurwood, Elliot S. Grossman and Earl Bailey, *Sales Forecasting* (New York: Conference Board, 1978), p. 2.

18 D. S. Tull and D. I. Hawkins, *Marketing Research* (New York: Macmillan, 1990).

19 Kenneth E. Marino, *Forecasting Sales and Planning Profits* (Chicago: Probus Publishing, 1986), p. 155.

20 Hurwood, Grossman and Bailey, p. 61.

21 G. L. Lilien and P. Kotler, *Marketing Decision-Making* (New York: Harper & Row, 1983).

22 P. Naert and P. Leeflang, *Building Implementable Marketing Models* (Leiden: Martinus Nijhoff, 1978).

23 *Accurate Business Forecasting* (Boston's *Harvard Business Review* Booklet, 1991).

24 William A. Band, 'A marketing audit provides an opportunity for improvement', *Sales & Marketing Management in Canada*, March 1984, pp. 24–26.


**Chapter 24**


1 Rohit Despande and Frederick E. Webster, Jr., 'Organisational culture and marketing: defining the research agenda', *Journal of Marketing*, January 1989, pp. 3–15.

2 Michael D. Hutt and Thomas W. Speh, 'The marketing strategy centre: diagnosing the industrial marketer's inter-disciplinary role', *Journal of Marketing*, Fall 1984, pp. 16–53.

3 Nigel F. Piercy, 'Marketing implementation: the implications of marketing paradigm weakness for the strategy execution process', *Journal of the Academy of Marketing Science*, vol. 26, no. 3, Summer 1998, pp. 222–236.

4 Ajay K. Kohli and Bernard J. Jaworski, 'Marketing orientation: the construct, research propositions, and managerial implications', *Journal of Marketing*, April 1990, pp. 1–18.

5 Larry Reibstein, 'IBM's plan to decentralise may set a trend – but imitation has a price', *Wall Street Journal*, 19 February 1988, p. 17.

6 Kenneth W. Thomas and Betty A. Velthouse, 'Cognitive elements of empowerment: an "interpretive" model of intrinsic task motivation', *Academy of Management Review*, October 1990, pp. 666–681.

7 O. C. Ferrell, George H. Lucas and David J. Luck, *Strategic Marketing Management: Text and Cases* (Cincinnati: South-Western Publishing, 1994), pp. 193–194.

8 Michael D. Hartline and O. C. Ferrell, 'Service quality implementation: the effects of organizational socialization and managerial actions on the behaviors of customer-contact employees', *Marketing Science Institute Working Paper Series*, Report no. 93–122 (Cambridge, Mass.: Marketing Science Institute, 1993), pp. 36–48.

9 Ibid., pp. 36–40.

10 Dave Ulrich, 'Strategic human resources planning: why and how?', *Human Resources Planning*, 10, no. 1, 1987, pp. 25–57.

11 Steven Lysonski, 'A boundary theory investigation of the product manager's role', *Journal of Marketing*, Winter 1985, pp. 26–40.

12 Lyndon Simkin, 'Delivering effective marketing planning', *Targeting, Measurement and Analysis for Marketing*, 8 (4), 2000, pp. 335–350.

13 M. McDonald, 'Ten barriers to marketing planning', *Journal of Business & Industrial Marketing*, vol. 7, no. 1, 1992, pp. 5–18; M. McDonald, 'Strategic marketing planning: a state-of-the-art review', *Marketing Intelligence & Planning*, vol. 10, no. 4, 1992, pp. 4–22; L. Simkin, 'People

and processes in marketing planning: the benefits of controlling implementation', *Journal of Marketing Management*, vol. 12, 1996, pp. 375–390; L. Simkin, 'Addressing organisational pre-requisites in marketing planning programmes', *Marketing Intelligence & Planning*, vol. 14, no. 5, 1996, pp. 39–46.
14 Sally Dibb and Lyndon Simkin, 'Overcoming segmentation barriers: four case studies', *Industrial Marketing Management*, 30, 2001, pp. 609–625.
15 Lyndon Simkin, 'Barriers impeding effective implementation of marketing plans – a new research and training agenda', *Journal of Business and Industrial Marketing*, 17 (1), 2002, pp. 8–22.
16 Based on Orville C. Walker, Jr. and Robert W. Ruekert, 'Marketing's role in the implementation of business strategies: a critical review and conceptual framework', *Journal of Marketing*, July 1987, pp. 15–33.
17 Nigel F. Piercy, 'Marketing implementation: the implications of marketing paradigm weakness for the strategy execution process', *Journal of the Academy of Marketing Science*, vol. 26, no. 3, Summer 1998, pp. 222–236; David Strutton, 'Marketing strategies: new approaches, new techniques', *Journal of the Academy of Marketing Science*, Summer 1997.
18 Robert Howard, 'Values make the company: an interview with Robert Haas', *Harvard Business Review*, September–October 1990, pp. 132–144.
19 Ferrell, Lucas and Luck, *Strategic Marketing Management*, pp. 190–200.
20 Myron Glassman and Bruce McAfee, 'Integrating the personnel and marketing functions: the challenge of the 1990s', *Business Horizons*, May–June 1992, pp. 52–59.
21 Ferrell, Lucas and Luck, *Strategic Marketing Management*, pp. 190–200.
22 David C. Jones, 'Motivation the catalyst in profit formula', *National Underwriter*, 13 July 1987, pp. 10, 13.
23 Jerry McAdams, 'Rewarding sales and marketing performance', *Management Review*, April 1987, p. 36.
24 P. Kotler, G. Armstrong, J. Saunders and V. Wong, *Principles of Marketing* (Hemel Hempstead: Prentice-Hall, 1998).
25 M. Christopher, A. Payne and D. Ballantyne, *Relationship Marketing* (Oxford: Butterworth-Heinemann, 1991); C. Gronroos, 'From marketing mix to relationship marketing: towards a paradigm shift in marketing', *Management Decision*, 32 (2), pp. 4–20.
26 L. L. Berry, 'Relationship marketing', in L. L. Berry, G. L. Shostack and G. Upah (eds.), *Emerging Perspectives on Services* (Chicago, Ill.: American Marketing Association, 1983), pp. 25–28.
27 A. Payne, 'Relationship marketing – making the customer count', *Managing Service Quality*, vol. 4, no. 6, 1994, pp. 29–31.
28 Lloyd C. Harris and Emmanuel Ogbonna, 'Strategic human resource management, market orientation and organizational performance', *Journal of Business Research*, February 2001, pp. 157–166.
29 W. R. George, 'Internal marketing and organisational behaviour: a partnership in developing customer-conscious employees at every level', *Journal of Business Research*, vol. 20, 1990, pp. 63–70; I. Lings and F. Brooks, 'Implementing and measuring the effectiveness of internal marketing', *Journal of Marketing Management*, vol. 14, no. 4, 1998, pp. 325–351.
30 E. Gummesson, 'Using internal marketing to develop a new culture', *Journal of Business and Industrial Marketing*, vol. 2, no. 3, 1987, pp. 23–28.
31 J. Reynoso and B. Moores, 'Internal relationships', in F. Buttle (ed.), *Relationship Marketing: Theory and Practice* (London: Chapman, 1996).
32 Sally Dibb and Lyndon Simkin, *Marketing Briefs*, Oxford: Elsevier Butterworth-Heinemann, 2004.
33 Adapted from Joseph R. Jablonski, *Implementing Total Quality Management* (Albuquerque, N. Mex.: Technical Management Consortium, 1990).
34 Hartline and Ferrell, 'Service quality implementation', pp. 36–40.
35 Jagdip Singh, 'Performance productivity and quality of frontline employees in service organizations', *Journal of Marketing*, April 2000, pp. 15–34.
36 Philip B. Crosby, *Quality is Free – The Art of Making Quality Certain* (New York: McGraw-Hill, 1979), pp. 9–10.
37 N. Piercy, *Market-Led Strategic Change* (Oxford: Butterworth-Heinemann, 1992).
38 Fred Steingraber, 'Total quality management: a new look at a basic issue', *Vital Speeches of the Day*, May 1990, pp. 415–416.
39 Hartline and Ferrell, 'Service Quality Implementation,' pp. 36–48.
40 "Higher education in doughnuts', *Ann Arbor News*, 9 March 1988, p. B7.
41 Bernard J. Jaworski, 'Toward a theory of marketing control: environmental context, control types, and consequences', *Journal of Marketing*, July 1988, pp. 23–39.
42 See Theo Haimann, William G. Scott and Patrick E. Connor, *Management*, 5th edn (Boston: Houghton Mifflin, 1985), pp. 478–492.
43 'Carbonates and concentrates', *Marketing Intelligence*, January 1990, pp. 2.10–2.17.
44 Kevin Kelly and Neil Gross, 'A weakened Komatsu tries to come back swinging', *Business Week*, 22 February 1988, p. 48.
45 Peter Doyle, *Value-Based Marketing* (Chichester: Wiley, 2000).
46 Jo-Anne Flack, 'Measure of success', *Marketing Week*, 4 March 1999, pp. 45–49.

**Chapter 25**

1 'Growth in piracy reverses trend', *Star Tribune*, 28 May 2001, p. D7.
2 'FSA to spotlight health offenders', *Marketing*, 26 May 2004, p. 4.
3 David Benady, 'The light fantastic', *Marketing Week*, 12 February 2004, pp. 26–29.

4 Isabelle Maignan and O. C. Ferrell, 'Antecedents and benefits of corporate citizenship: an investigation of French businesses', *Journal of Business Research*, 51 (1), 2001, pp. 37–51.
5 Debbie Thorne, Linda Ferrell and O. C. Ferrell, *Business and Society: A Strategic Approach to Corporate Citizenship* (Boston: Houghton Mifflin, 2003).
6 B&Q, www.diy.com/, 16 April 2001.
7 Archie Carroll, 'The pyramid of corporate social responsibility: toward the moral management of organisational stakeholders', *Business Horizons*, July/ Aug. 1991, p. 42.
8 Thorne, Ferrell and Ferrell, *Business and Society*.
9 Kathleen Kerwin with David Welch, 'Detroit is missing the boat', *Business Week*, 27 October 2003, pp. 44–46.
10 'Yes, we have no bananas: Rainforest Alliance certifies Chiquita bananas', *AgJournal*, 16 December 2003, www.agjournal.com/story.cfm?story_id=1047.
11 Paul Hawken and William McDonough, 'Seven steps to doing good business', *Inc.*, November 1993, pp. 79–90.
12 Roger Bougie, Rik Pieters and Marcel Zeelenberg, 'Angry customers don't come back, they get back: the experience and behavioral implications of anger and dissatisfaction in services', *Journal of the Academy of Marketing Science*, 31 (4), 2003, pp. 377–393.
13 Thorne, Ferrell and Ferrell, *Business and Society*.
14 Ron Trujillo, 'Good ethics pays off', *USA Today*, 23 October 1995, p. 2B.
15 Thomas L. Carson, 'Self-interest and business ethics: some lessons of the recent corporate scandals', *Journal of Business Ethics*, 43 (April) 2003, pp. 389–394.
16 '2002 Cone Corporate Citizenship Study', *Cone*, Inc., press release, 22 October 2002, www.coneinc.com/ Pages/pr_13.html.
17 'Firestone: a reputation blowout', in O. C. Ferrell, John Fraedrich and Linda Ferrell, *Business Ethics: Ethical Decision-making and Cases* (Boston: Houghton Mifflin, 2005), pp. 313–320.
18 'Hasbro: do not pass go, Ghettopoly', *USA Today*, 23 October 2003, http://www.usatoday.com.
19 David E. Sprott, Kenneth C. Manning and Anthony D. Miyazaki, 'Grocery price setting and quantity surcharges', *Journal of Marketing*, 67 (July) 2003, pp. 34–46.
20 Gisele Durham, 'Study finds lying, cheating in teens', *AOL News*, 16 October 2000.
21 Peggy H. Cunningham and O. C. Ferrell, 'The influence of role stress on unethical behavior by personnel involved in the marketing research process' (working paper, Queens University, Ont., 1998), p. 35.
22 Joseph W. Weiss, *Business Ethics: A Managerial, Stakeholder Approach* (Belmont, CA: Wadsworth, 1994), p. 13.
23 Ethics Resource Center, *The Ethics Resource Center's 2000 National Business Ethics Survey: How Employees Perceive Ethics at Work* (Washington, DC: Ethics Resource Center, 2000), p. 85.
24 O. C. Ferrell, Larry G. Gresham and John Fraedrich, 'A synthesis of ethical decision models for marketing', *Journal of Macromarketing*, Fall 1989, pp. 58–59.
25 Barry J. Babin, James S. Boles and Donald P. Robin, 'Representing the perceived ethical work climate among marketing employees', *Journal of the Academy of Marketing Science*, 28 (3), 2000, pp. 345–358.
26 Ethics Resource Center, 2000 *National Business Ethics Survey*, p. 38.
27 Ferrell, Gresham and Fraedrich, 'A synthesis of ethical decision models for marketing'.
28 Lawrence B. Chonko and Shelby D. Hunt, 'Ethics and marketing management: a retrospective and prospective commentary', *Journal of Business Research*, 50 (3), 2000, pp. 235–244.
29 Linda K. Trevino and Stuart Youngblood, 'Bad apples in bad barrels: a causal analysis of ethical decision-making behavior', *Journal of Applied Psychology*, 75 (4), 1990, pp. 378–385.
30 Margaret M. Clark, 'Corporate ethics programs make a difference, but not the only difference', *HR News*, 23 May 2003, www.shrm.org/hrnews_published/archives/ CMS_004611.asp.
31 Gene R. Laczniak and Patrick E. Murphy, *Ethical Marketing Decisions: The Higher Road* (Boston: Allyn & Bacon, 1993), p. 14.
32 Sir Adrian Cadbury, 'Ethical managers make their own rules', *Harvard Business Review*, Sept./Oct. 1987, p. 33.
33 Andrea K. Walker, 'Low-carb craze puts bread industry on defensive', *Austin American-Statesman*, 17 December 2003, www.statesman.com/.
34 Don Tapscott and David Ticoll, 'The naked corporation', *Wall Street Journal*, 14 October 2003, http://online.wsj. com/.
35 Ferrell, Fraedrich and Ferrell, *Business Ethics*, pp. 27–30.
36 Isabelle Maignan, 'Antecedents and benefits of corporate citizenship: a comparison of US and French businesses' (PhD dissertation, University of Memphis, 1997).
37 Margaret A. Stroup, Ralph L. Newbert and Jerry W. Anderson, Jr, 'Doing good, doing better: two views of social responsibility', *Business Horizons*, Mar./Apr. 1987, p. 23.


**Chapter 26**


1 This overview is an abridged version of the guidance offered in Sally Dibb and Lyndon Simkin, *The Marketing Casebook: Cases and Concepts* (London: Thomson Learning, 2001).

# Name Index

Entries in *italics* refer to publications. Page numbers in *italics* refer to figures and tables.


3M, 349

## A

ABN AMRO, 379, 381
ACORN categorisation of UK consumers, 233–6, *233–5*
Advertising Standards Authority (ASA), 807–8
Aer Lingus, 403–5
Aerospatiale, *754*
Ahold *see* Royal Ahold
Airbus, 144
Alton Towers, 742
Amazon, *104*, 109, 111, 112
American Direct Marketing Association, 608
American Marketing Association, 118
  Internet Code of Ethics, *118*
Amnesty International, 394
Anchor, *423*
Anheuser-Busch, 329
AOL, *106*, 674, 675
Apple, 674, 675–6
ASA *see* Advertising Standards Authority
ASDA, 341–2, 648–9
Ashley, Neil, 373
Aston Martin, 125
Atkins diet, 24
Avis, 154–7

## B

B&Q, 177
BA *see* British Airways
BAA, 501, *627*
BAe, 193
Barbie, 811
Barclaycard Merchant Services, 534
Barclays Bank, 356, 388
Barnardo's, 401
BCG *see* Boston Consulting Group
Beckham, David, 571
Bell, Coley Porter, 391–2
BEM research, 276
Benetton, 457
Binney & Smith, 743–4
Birmingham Women's Hospital, 617–20, *619*
BMW, 98–9, 302, 537
Bodum, *661*
Body Shop, 789
Boeing, 144, 687–8
Boots, 322, 644
Booz Allen Hamilton, 388
Boston Consulting Group (BCG), 360–1, *361*
BP, 302
Branson, Richard, 345
Bridgestone/Firestone, 794
British Airways (BA), 324, 404–5, 409, 566, 695
British Heart Foundation, 14
Budweiser, *586*
BUPA, 682
Burkitt, Hugh, 813
Burnett, Leo, 698

## C

C5 electric buggy (Sinclair), 351
CACI, 235
Cadbury Schweppes, *800*
Cadbury's, 273, 570, 734
Cadillac, 324
Calor, 407
Canary Island tomatoes, *545*
Cancer Research, 401
Carrefour, 151–2
Castlepak woodcare varnish, 333–4, *334*
Caterpillar, *224*, 702
Central Statistical Office, 75
Chanel, 644
Cheer washing powder (P&G), 700, 702
Children in Need, 392
Christian Aid, 394
Chupa Chups, 150
Clubcard (Tesco), 597
Co-Operative Bank, 789, 790
Coca-Cola
  brand licensing, 329
  clothing, 36–7, *36*
  customer satisfaction, 7
  Dasani, 307, 338
  designer bottle, 331

ERRA, 98
international marketing, 127–8
marketing communication, 528
product failure, 307

Coleman's, 373–4
Colgate-Palmolive, 328, 702, 710–12
Comfort, 343
Comfort Vaporesse, *629*
Comic Relief, 392
Compaq Computers, 207
Coupe, David, 622
Courtaulds Textiles, 296–7
Crayola Crayons, 743–4
Crew Clothing, 483
Crimestoppers Trust, 680
Cuprinol, 333–4, *334*
CyberAtlas, 109

# D

Daewoo, 63–4, 91, 447
Dalgety, *206*
Dasani, 338
Davies, George, 341–2
Debenhams, 589
DEFRA *see* Department for Environment, Food and Rural Affairs
Del Monte, 299
Dell Computers, 108, 109, 116
Demon Doughnuts, 716
Department for Environment, Food and Rural Affairs (DEFRA), 75
Design Bridge, 325
Diageo, 308
Dibb/Simkin, 55–6, 201–2, 759–60, 769–71
Doyle, Peter, 314, 325, 330
Dr. Oetker (UK) Ltd., *515*
Dun & Bradstreet, 390
Dunkin' Donuts, 766
Dutch Automobile Association, *211*

# E

Eckert, Robert A., 812
Egg (Internet banking), 113, 122
Electrolux Group, *192*
*Elle* magazine, 250
Energiser, *687*
Envirowise, *79*
ERRA (European Recovery and Recycling Association), 98
ESOMAR *see* European Society for Opinion and Marketing Research
Euro 2004, 571
European Recovery and Recycling Association (ERRA), 98
European Society for Opinion and Marketing Research (ESOMAR), 276, 282, 286
Experian, 622

# F

Fairtrade products, 80
Fanning, Shawn, 673
Federal Express, 400, 469, 503–6
First Direct Bank, 227, 254–5, 331, 356, 434–5
Fisher-Price, 811
Ford Motor Company, 125, 249–50, 325, 794
Fresh Educational Programme (Makro), 472
Fujitsu
brand value, 320–1
government sector, 194
managing customers, 115
marketing managers, 347
philosophy, 3
relationships, 751
strategic market planning, 39–40

FULL STOP campaign (NSPCC), 510–11

# G

Games Workshop, 424
Gates, Bill, 524
General Electric, 363
General Motors, 64, 702
George clothes, 341–2
Goodyear Tyres, 312
Google search engine, 101–2, *101*, *397*
GTE, 581
Guinness, 308

# H

Häagen-Dazs, 534–5
Harvey Nichols, 667
Harvey-Jones, John, 753–4
Hasbro, *794*
Heineken, 312–13
Heinz, 327, *329*
Hewlett-Packard (HP), 349, 709
Holiday Inn, 376
Honda, *170*
Honeywell Information Systems, 591
Hoover, 614–15
Hot Wheels, 811
Hovis, 302, 304
HP (Hewlett-Packard), 349, 709
Huggies, 578

# I

IBFAN *see* International Baby Food Action Network

IBM *see* International Business Machines
Identica, 373
IKEA, 33–4, 187–8
Infoplan, 575–6
Interbrand, 317, 325
International Baby Food Action Network (IBFAN), 807–8
International Business Machines (IBM), 581
iTunes, 674, 675–6

## J

JCB, 8, 9, 21–2, 51, 70–1, 91, *517–18*, 683–4, 726–7, 752
JCDecaux, 568
jkr, 378, *380*
John Lewis, 121, *425*, *477*
jra research, *263*

## K

*Kelly's*, 211
Kimberly-Clark, 578
Kinko's, 504
Kit-Kat, 308
*Kompass*, 211
Kraft, 80
Kraft Foods, 703
Kraft General Foods, 279

## L

Legal & General, 694
Lever Brothers, 343, 351
Lowndes Queensway, 42
Lufthansa German Airlines, 556
Lux, *761*

## M

M&S *see* Marks & Spencer
McDonald, Malcolm, 246, 718
McDonald's
  advertising, 522
  control, 746–7
  global marketing, 127
  health, 716
  promotion, 512
  sponsorship, 570
  test marketing, 351
  trademark protection, 326
Macleans, 229
Magnet, *39*
Makro, 471–2
Market Research Society, 282
*Marketing* magazine, 220–1
*Marketing Planning Workbook*, 718
Marks & Spencer (M&S), 190–1, 342
Marriott, 187
Mars, 212, 306, 530–1
Mars Delight, *739*
Mason, Tim 159
Mates Condoms, *5*
Mattel, 810–12
Mediaedge:cia, 255–6
Microsoft, 524
Miller, George, 3
Miller Lite, 24
Mitsubishi, 601–2
Moët & Chandon, *27*
Monsanto, 541
Montblanc, 633, 643
Multiple Sclerosis Trust/Society, 400
Murdoch, Rupert, 567–8
MusicNet, 674, 675
MyShoes, 400

## N

Napster, 673–6
National Cash Registers (NCR), 92
National Exhibition Centre (NEC), Birmingham, 450
National Health Service (NHS), 217–18
National Society for the Prevention of Cruelty to Children (NSPCC), 510–11
NatWest bank, 356, 388
NCR (National Cash Registers), 92
NEC (National Exhibition Centre), 450
Nestlé, 80, 308, 807–8
  Polo mints, 315–16, 352
Next, 341
NHS (National Health Service), 217–18
Nickelodeon, 376
Nike, 290–2, 330, 522
Nokia, 731
Nometrics process, 325
Novartis, 303
Novon, 325
NSPCC *see* National Society for the Prevention of Cruelty to Children
Nynas, 196, 203, 218–19

## O

Operation Smile, 711–12
Orange, 401

## P

P&G *see* Procter & Gamble
Palm, *128*
Pampers, 578
Pepsi, 522, 534

PepsiCo, 511
Per Una, 342
Perrier, 575–6, *701*
Peters, Michael, 373
Polaroid, 700
Polo mints, 315–16, 352
Porter, Michael, 49–50
Post Office, 178, 225, 384
*Private Eye*, 551
Procter & Gamble (P&G)
  advertising, 555
  branding, 327
  consumer loyalty, 628
  innovation, 304
  marketing mix, 700
  packaging, 335
  price, 696
  product mix, 302
  reactivity, 258–9

## Q

Quaker Oats Company, 43, 348

## R

RAD *see* Rock Against Drugs
Rainforest Alliance, 791
Raytheon Systems Limited, 714
Recording Industry Association of America (RIAA), 673–4
Reebok, 127, 290–2
Reichhold Chemicals, 300
Renault, 379
RIAA (Recording Industry Association of America), 673–4
Rivett, David, 325
Rizazz brand (Tilda), 678
Rock Against Drugs (RAD), 511
Roxio, 675
Royal Ahold, 501–2
Royal Bank of Scotland, 345
Ruys, Thony, 313
Ryanair, 383, 403–5

## S

Saab, 116
Sainsbury, 54, 325, 628, *664*
St Andrew's Group of Hospitals, 294
St Andrew's Hospital, 64–5, 217–18
Salty Dog crisps, 33
Salvation Army, 395
Sandom, 508
Sara Lee Courtaulds, 190–1, *190*
Sarah Lee, 296
Save The Children, 807–8
Scott Paper, 323
Seagram, 734
Seeds of Change, *792*
Sellotape Company, 355, 373–4
Shell, 177
Showcase, 372–3
Sinclair C5 electric buggy, 351
SKB *see* SmithKline Beecham
Sky, 182
Slimfast, 24
Smith, Frederick W., 503–4
SmithKline Beecham (SKB), 303
Snack-a-Jacks, *348*
Sony, 7, 306, 630
von Speyr, Stephen, 678
SPI *see* Strategic Planning Institute; US Strategic Planning Institute
*SpongeBob SquarePants*, 376
Stanford Research Institute, 237
Starbucks, 382–3
Stone, Merlin, 113–14
Strategic Planning Institute (SPI), 693
Suchard, 703
Sunsweet, *71*
Superdrug, 644–5
Sure, *326*
Surf, 357, *357*

## T

T-Mobile, 670
Tartare Light Fromage Frais, 551
Techsonic, 349–50
Terry's of York, 703
Tesco, 48, 54, 159, 415, 628
Tesco Clubcard, 597
Tesco TV, 568
Tetrapak, *336*
Tilda, 678
Timex, 347, 783–4
TNT, 400
Totti, Francesco, 571
Toys 'Я' Us, 671–2
Trojan condoms, 5

## U

UNICEF, 394
Unilever, 208, 209
University of Warwick, 391–2
UPS, 400
US Strategic Planning Institute (SPI), 365–6
*USA Today*, 719, *720*

## V

Vector trademark (Reebok), 291–2
Virgin, 647–8
Virgin Money, 345

VNU Inc., 261
Volkswagen (VW), 312
Volvo, 569
Volvo Trucks, 708
von Speyr, Stephen, 678
VW (Volkswagen), 312

# W

Waitrose, 367, *367*
Wal-mart, 280
Walkers, *176*
Warwick Business School, 391–2
Waterford, 328
Watkins, James, 294
Wegener DM, *267*
Wells and Gubar life cycle stages, 232
Whitbread Hotels, 187
White Stuff, 483
WHO *see* World Health Organization
Williamson, Matthew, 331
Winalot, 195, *196*
World e-Inclusion (Hewlett-Packard), 709
World Health Organization (WHO), 786, 807–8
World Society for the Protection of Animals (WSPA), 401
World Trade Organization (WTO), 141
Wringe, John, 508
WSPA (World Society for the Protection of Animals), 401
WTO (World Trade Organization), 141

# X

Xporta, *134*

# Y

Yellow Freight, 122–3

# Subject Index

Entries and page numbers in **bold** refer to key terms and the pages on which they are defined.
Page numbers in *italics* refer to figures and tables.


80/20 rule, inventory management, 460

## A

ABC sales: contribution analysis, 367–9, *368*, **368**
Ability to buy, 649–50
Abuse victims' support group, 396
**Accessibility**
  e-marketing, 106–7, **106**
  transport modes, **463**
**Accessory equipment, 300**
**Accumulation, 414**
Activities, 9–10
  importance, 14–15
  marketing mix, *10*
Activity ratios, *818*
**Actual products, 301**
Adaptations, international marketing mix, 699–704
Adapt both product and promotion strategy, 700, 702
Adapt product only strategy, 700
Adapt promotion only strategy, 700
**Addressability**, 103–5, **103**
**Administered pricing**, 690–1, **690**
Administered vertical marketing system, 420
**Adopter categories, 519**
**Adoption stage** (product adoption), 353–4, 517–18, **518**
**Advertising**, 521–2, **521**, 536–76, **538**
  agencies, *540*, 561–2, *562*, 568–9
  business markets, 212, 689
  condoms, 5
  cooperative advertising, 601
  customer expectations, 390–1
  departments, 561
  direct marketing, 608–9
  effectiveness, 559–61
  e-marketing, 109–10, *110*
  evaluation, 559–61
  illustration techniques, *558*
  integrated marketing communications, 527
  international marketing mix, 700
  media characteristics, *552–4*
  message creation, 555–8
  nature of, 538–9
  non-profit marketing, 394
  objectives, 547–8
  pricing strategies, *661*
  publicity comparison, 563
  reference groups, 179
  role, 511
  sales promotion comparison, 594–5
  services marketing mix, 695
  trends that affect, 567–9
  UK top 100, *550*
  uses, 539–46, *542–3*
**Advertising budgets**, 549–50, **549**
**Advertising campaigns, 546**
  developing, 546–61, *547*, 561–2
  execution, 558–9
**Advertising platforms, 548**
**Advertising targets**, 509, **547**, 551
**Advocacy advertising, 540**
Affluent consumers, 667
Age factors
  segmentation variables, 230
  targeting, 220–1
Agencies, advertising, *540*, 561–2, *562*, 568–9
**Agents**, 441, *442–3*, 443–6, *444*, **444**
  marketing channels, 417, *417*, 418, *418*
  *see also* Manufacturers' agents
**AIDA**, 556–7, **556**
**Aided recall tests, 560**
Air freight transportation, *461*
Airline industry, 403–5
Airport terminals, 501
**Allocation, 414**
**Allowances, 637**, 638
Alternative solutions, case study analysis, 820–1
Ambience, 698
Ambient advertising, 538–9
Analysis
  business markets, 208–12
  competitors, *51*
  demand, cost and profit relationship, 652–6
  EVC, 639–40
  input-output analysis, 210–11
  international marketing, *129*
  marketing opportunities, 21, 22
  marketing research, 278–81

*see also* Case study analysis; **Environmental analysis**; Marketing analysis; **SWOT analysis**

**Ansoff matrix, 45**, 46–7, *47*

**APEC** *see* **Asia Pacific Economic Co-operative**

Appendices
- case study reports, 823
- marketing planning, 726

**Approach, 583**

**Arbitrary approach** (advertising budgets), **549**

**Area sampling, 270**

Arts sponsorship, 569–70

**Artwork**, *556*, 557–8, **557**

**ASEAN** *see* **Association of South East Nations**

**Asia Pacific Economic Co-operative (APEC), 140**

ASP, 9
- *see also* **Marketing process**

Assessment
- competitive forces, 87–9
- technology, 81

Assets *see* **Marketing assets**

**Association of South East Nations (ASEAN)**, 139–40, **139**

**Assorting, 414, 415**

**Assortment, 414**

**Atmospherics**, 492–3, **492**

Attention-seeking flashes, 602

**Attitudes**, 177–8, **177**

Attitude scales, 177–8, **177**

Audits
- ethics/social responsibility, *803*
- non-profit organisations, 395–7
- *see also* **Marketing audits**

**Augmented products, 301**

Automated distribution systems, 457

**Automatic vending, 485**

Availability, services, 394

**Average fixed cost, 653**

**Average total cost**, 653, *654*, **654**

**Average variable cost, 653**

**Awareness stage** (product adoption), **516**

## B

B2B *see* **Business markets; Business services**

Baby food packaging, 332–3

**Bait pricing, 662**

**Balance of retailing power, 495**

Banks
- branch reopening, 388
- customer relationship management, 113, 114
- customer service, 388
- distribution channels, 697
- First Direct, 434–5
- Internet, 113, 122
- mini-case, 254–5
- personal banking, 356
- promotion, 694
- segmentation variables, 227
- service bundling, 696
- service quality, 388

Banner ads, *110*

Barcodes *see* Universal product code

**Base point pricing, 638**

Bases *see* **Segmentation variables**

**Basis for competing, 57**

**Basis for pricing**, 657–9, **657**

Behaviouristic variables, 237–8

**Benchmarking, 765**, 780

Benefits, branding, 317–19, 321

**Benefit segmentation**, 237–8, **237**

'Best' alternative solution, case study analysis, 821

**Bid pricing, 691**

Bid system, government markets, 193–4

Bitumen market, 218–19

Body copy, 556

**Bonded storage warehouse, 456**, *458*

**Brand attitude, 520**

**Brand attributes**, 320–1, **320**

**Brand awareness, 520**, 555, **778**

**Brand building, 568**

**Brand equity**, 319–20, *319*, **319**

**Brand extension branding, 328**

**Brand insistence, 319**

**Brand loyalty**, 318–19, **318**

**Brand managers, 346**

**Brand marks, 316**

**Brand names, 316**, 324

**Brand personality**, 320–1, **320**, *321*

**Brand positioning, 49**, 249–50, 705

**Brand preference**, 318–19, **318**

**Brand purchase intention, 520**

**Brand recognition, 318**

**Brands**, 3, 294, 314–31, **316**, 338–43
- benefits, 317–19, 321
- biggest brands, *328*
- business markets, 190–1, 212–13
- complaints, 746
- corporate branding, 331
- diversification, 36–7
- international marketing, 132–3
- levels, 330
- licensing, 329–30
- management, 330–1, 346
- own-label brands, 357–8
- policies, 327–9
- product decisions, 299, 313
- protection, 324–7
- retail marketing, 497
- Sellotape Company, 373–4
- types, 322–3
- United Kingdom, 313
- valuable brands, *317*

**Brand strength, 330**

**Brand values**, 320–1, **320**, *321*

Breadth and depth of merchandise, 490–1, *490*

**Break-down approach, 729**

Break-even analysis, 655–6

**Break-even point, 655**, *656*

**Brokers**, 441, *442–3*, 443–6, *444*, **444**

Bubble drawings, 174, *175*

Budgets
- marketing planning, 726
- *see also* **Advertising budgets**

**Build-up approach, 729**

**Bundle pricing**, 662–3, **663**

Bundling services, 696

**Business analysis, 350**

Business buyers
- attributes, 195
- primary concerns, 195–7

**Business buying behaviour**, 189–219, **200**
- decision process, 200–8, *205*
- dimensions of, 194–200
- influences, 207–8
- methods, 198
- tools and techniques, 201–2

**Business cycle, 82**, 85

Business demand, 199–200

**Business distributors**, 684–5, **684**

Businesses
- marketing importance, 15–16
- micro marketing environment, 89

**Business marketing**, 189, **208**

**Business markets**, 189–219, **191**, **222**
- direct mail, 602
- EVC analysis, 639–40
- marketing mix, 679, 681–92
- marketing variations, 212–14
- pricing, 636–40, *637*
- segmentation variables, 227, 238–40, *239*
- selection and analysis, 208–12
- services, 695
- telemarketing costs, *688*
- types, 191–4

**Business products**
- demand, 199–200
- product decisions, **297**, 299–301

**Business services, 301**, 377–8, **388**

Business-to-business (B2B) *see* **Business markets; Business services**

Business transactions, 194–5

Button ads, *110*

**Buy-back allowances, 600**

Buyers
- perceptions, 634–5
- *see also* Business buyers; Consumers

**Buying allowances, 600**

**Buying behaviour, 160**
- businesses, 189–219
- choosing distribution channels, 426
- consumers, 160–88

**Buying centres**, 200–3, **201**

**Buying power, 85**
- Avis, 155
- price, 623
- Toys ' я ' Us pricing, 671–2

## C

Cable television networks, 376

Call centres, 115–16

CAP *see* Common Agricultural Policy

**Capabilities**, 44–5, **44**, **463**

**Captioned photographs, 563**

**Captive pricing, 662**

Careers in marketing, 813, 815, 825–8, *828*

Car industry, 447

Car rental business, 154–7

Carrying costs, 456

Case study analysis, 814, 815, 816–23
- presenting findings, 821–3
- process, 820–1
- tools and techniques, 823
- using, 816

**Cash and carry warehouses**, 481–2, **482**

**Cash and carry wholesalers**, *442*, **444**, 469–70, 471–2

**Cash cows**, 360–2, **360**, *361*, *362*

**Cash discounts, 636**, 637

Cash flow, pricing objectives, *632*

**Catalogue retailing, 487**

**Catalogue showrooms, 482**

**Category-consistent packaging, 335**

**Category killers, 479**

**Category management, 491**, **753**

**Category need, 520**

**Causal research, 265**

**Cause-related marketing, 391**, **512**, **789**, 804

CBD *see* Central business district

**CEE** *see* **Central and Eastern Europe**

Celebrities in marketing, 290–1

**Central business district (CBD)**, **474**, *475*

**Central and Eastern Europe (CEE)**, 140–1, **140**

**Centralised organisations**, 750–1, **750**

**Channel capacity, 514**

**Channel of distribution, 410**

Channel members
- agencies relationship, 448
- pricing decisions, 633–4

**Channel power, 428**

Channels
business marketing mix, 684–6, *684*
choosing, 686
international marketing mix, 702–4
services marketing mix, 697
types, 684–5
*see also* Distribution channels

Charities, 14, 15
marketing strategy, 64–5
professionalism, 400–1

Childhood abuse victims' support group, 396

Children
demographic factors, 169
NSPCC FULL STOP campaign, 510–11
'pester power', 161–2, *161*

China, 139–40, 291

Chip and pin cards, 534

Churches, *393*, 394

**CIS** *see* **Commonwealth of Independent States**

Citizenship, 787–8, 804

Class *see* **Social classes**

Classifications
products, 297–301, 309
services, 382–4

**Client-based relationships**, *379*, **382**

**Client publics, 393**

**Clippings services, 778**

Clockwork radios, 702

**Closing, 583**
deals, 583–4
transactions, 583–4

Clothing market, 36–7, *36*

Code of Ethics, Internet marketing, *118*

**Codes of conduct**, 799–800, **800**, 805

**Coding process, 513**

**Cognitive dissonance, 168**

Collection of data *see* Data

Colours
international marketing, 130–2, *131*
packaging, 333

**Combination compensation, 589**, *590*

**Commercialisation, 352**, 353

Commercial organisations, 14–16

Commission compensation, *589*, *590*

**Commission merchants, 445–6**

Common Agricultural Policy (CAP), 67

**Commonwealth of Independent States (CIS), 140**

**Communication, 512**
marketing implementation, 759
process, 512–15, *513*
service quality, 390–1
*see also* **Marketing communications**

**Community, 105**
relations, 793–4

Compact disc players, 355

Companies
demographics, 239
financial situation, 817–18
internal position, 816–19
marketing organisation, 818–19
ownership, 496
structure, 816

**Comparative advertising**, 543–4, **544**

**Comparison discounting**, *665*, **666**

Compensation, sales personnel, 588–90

**Competition**, 8, **87**
airline industry, 403–5
brands, 323
business markets, 213
case study analysis, 819–20
micro marketing environment, 91
personal selling, 579–80
pricing concepts, 626–30, 635–6
product adoption process, 354
service pricing, 696–7
target market segments, 246
test marketing, 351–2

**Competition-based pricing, 658**

**Competition Commission, 73**

**Competition matching approach, 549**

Competitions, promotion, 600, 601–2

**Competitive advantage**, 49–50, **49**, *50*
international marketing, 156–7
sustainable, 715–44

**Competitive advertising**, 543–4, **543**
off-setting, 544

Competitive edge *see* Differential advantage

**Competitive forces**, 82–9, **82**
assessment, 87–9

**Competitive positions**, 51–4, **53**
categories, 53
differential advantage, 50–8

**Competitive positions proforma**, 54–6, **54**

**Competitive set, 50**

**Competitive structures**
characteristics, *87*
types, 87–8

Competitive tools, 88

**Competitor monitoring, 89**

**Competitors, 49**
analysis, *51*, 225
intelligence, 55–6
market segmentation, 225
price evaluation, 656–7

**Competitor scanning, 54**

Complaints
branding, 746
business markets, 683
consumer buying decisions, *168*

Completeness, product assortment, 491
**Complexity**, *694–5*, **694**
Compliance programmes, 801
**Component parts, 300**
**Comprehensive spending patterns, 86**
**Computer-assisted telephone interviewing, 272**
**Concentration strategy**, **242**, *243*, 244
**Concentric diversification**, 47–8, **48**
**Concept testing, 350**
Concessionaries, department stores, 477
Condom advertisements, 5
Conflict, channel members, 427–8
**Conglomerate diversification, 48**
**Consumable supplies**, 300–1, **300**
Consumer awareness, 16
**Consumer buying behaviour**, 160–88, **160**
  types, 162–4
**Consumer buying decision process**, 164–8, **164**
  personal factors, 168–71
  possible influences, *164*
  psychological factors, 171–8
  social factors, 178–83
**Consumer contests, 600**
Consumer demand, 85–7
**Consumer focus groups, 559**
Consumerism, 793
**Consumer markets, 222**
  BUPA, 682
  Colgate-Palmolive, 710–12
  positioning, *248*
  segmentation variables, 226–7, *228*, 229–38
  services marketing mix, 693–4, 695–6
**Consumer movement, 78**
**Consumer products**
  business markets, 190–1
  marketing channels, 416–18, *417*
  product decisions, 297–9, **297**
Consumer protection legislation, 74–5
**Consumer purchase diaries**, 271–2, **272**
Consumers
  affluence, 667
  *see also* Customer...
**Consumer sales promotion techniques**, 595–600, *595*, **595**
**Consumers' Association**, 74–5, **74**, 78
Consumer satisfaction, 293, *293*
Consumer services, 377–8, **388**
**Consumer spending patterns**, 86–7, **86**
**Consumer sweepstakes, 600**
Consumer trends, retail marketing, 496–7
**Containerisation, 455**
Contests, sales promotions, 600
Continuous quality improvement, 765
**Contract manufacturing, 142**
Contracts
  business buying methods, 198
  government markets, 193
Contractual vertical marketing system, 420–1
**Control, 105**
  corrective action, 768–71
  e-marketing, 105–6
  international distribution, 702
  market activities, 766–71, 780
  marketing control process, 766–7, *767*
  marketing management, 28
  marketing planning, 725–6
  marketing process, 13, 14
  non-profit marketing, 395–7, *396*
  performance standards, 767–8, *768*
  problems encountered, 771
  requirements, 771
  salesforce performance, 592–3
  tools and techniques, 769–71
  trading practices, 746
Controversy, non-profit organisations, 392
**Convenience products, 298**
**Convenience stores**, 209, **479**, 481
**Cookies**, **104**, 117
Cooperation/relation building, marketing channel members, 427
**Cooperative advertising, 601**
Coordinating marketing activities, 759
**Copy**, 555–7, **555**, *556*
**Copy writing, 604**
**Core products, 301**
**Corporate branding, 331**
**Corporate culture**, **798**, 805
**Corporate identity, 331**
**Corporate image, 331**
Corporate sponsorship, 569–70
**Corporate strategy**, 42–3, **42**
Corporate vertical marketing system, 420
Corrective action, 768–71
**Correlation methods, 734**
**Cost analysis**, 773–7, **774**, 780–1
**Cost-based pricing, 657**
**Cost comparison indicators, 555**
Cost leadership, 49–50
**Cost plus pricing, 657**
**Costs**, 16
  business telemarketing, *688*
  demand and profit relationship, 652–6
  packaging, 332
  personal selling, 579

pricing decisions, 631
profit impact on marketing strategy, 367
promotional mix, 529–30
relationships, *653*
transportation, **462**

**Cost trade-offs, 454**

Counterfeiting, 327

**Count and re-count**, 600–1, **600**

Countries' marketing, 14–15

County Council regulations, 76

**Coupons**, 595–7, *596*, **596**, *598*

**Credence qualities, 378**

Credit
impulse buying, 163
services, 309
spending behaviour, 85

**Crisis management, 567**, 575–6

Crisps market, 33, 176

**CRM** *see* **Customer relationship management**

Cross-cultural comparisons, 132–3

Cross-docking, 437

Cross-selling opportunity, 114

**Culture, 181**
consumer buying decision process, 181–3
international marketing, 130–4, *131*

**Cumulative discounts, 635**, 637

Current customer order getters, 584

Curriculum vitae (CV), 826–7, *826*

**Customary pricing, 664**

Customer analysis, market segmentation, 225

Customer-based assets, 44

**Customer contact**, 382–3, **382**, *383*, 582–3

Customer evaluation, services, 387

Customer expectations, services, 389–91

**Customer forecasting surveys**, 731–2, **732**

Customer loyalty, 628–9
*see also* loyalty

**Customer relationship management (CRM)**, 101, 102, 110–16, **110**
customer satisfaction, 116
Daewoo, 447
Games Workshop, 424
international marketing, 132–3
Stone's requirements, 113–14
systems, 114
technology, 111–12, 114–16

Customers
analysis by type, 776–7
approaching, 583
case study analysis, 819
identifying potential, 208–12
international marketing, 153, 154
micro marketing environment, 91
objections, 583
organising by type, 753–4, **753**
pricing perceptions, 634–5
targeting, 158–292
types, 753–4, **753**, 776–7
understanding, 158–292
*see also* Consumer...

**Customer satisfaction**, 7–8, **11**, 17, *20*, **778**
customer relationship management, 116
follow-ups, 584
implementing marketing concept, 19
marketing mix, 293, *293*
services marketing mix, 698

**Customer service**, 452–3, **452**
banks, 388
cash and carry wholesalers, 469–70
FedEx Custom Critical, 469
marketing channels, 416

**Customer's zone of tolerance**, 389–90, **390**

**Customer threshold, 474**

Customisation, 145–7

CV *see* Curriculum vitae

**Cycle analysis, 733**


# D


Data
collection, 129–30, 265–78, *265*, *266*
international marketing, 129–30
mining, 286
types, 265–6

**Databases, 105**, 111, 114, 280–1

**Dealer listings, 601**

**Dealer loaders, 602**

Deals, closing, 583–4

**Decentralised organisations**, 750–1, **750**

Decision-making
case study analysis, 816
consumer buying behaviour, 162–4
marketing mix, *10*, 58–9
marketing research role, 261–2
pricing, 621–76, *621*
products, 293, 295–313

Decision process
business buying behaviour, 200–8, *205*
consumer buying behaviour, 164–83

**Decline stage**
marketing strategies, 358
product life cycles, 305–7, **306**, 358

**Decoding process, 514**

**Defensive advertising, 544**

**Defensive warfare**, 53–4, **53**

Deletion, products, 358–9, *359*

Delivery
business buyer concerns, 197
business marketing mix, 681

**Delphi method, 733**

Demand
cost and profit relationship, 652–6
determining, 650–2
fluctuations, 651, 697
marginal revenue relationship, *654*
supply and demand strategy, 384–5
*see also* Business demand

**Demand-based pricing, 657**, 658

**Demand curve**, 650–1, *650*, **650**, *651*

Demographic analysis, 269

**Demographic factors, 169**
consumer buying decision process, 168–9
market segmentation, 229–32, 239
media plans, 551

**Demonstrations, 598**

**Department stores**, 476–7, **476**
merchandise breadth and depth, *490*
wheel of retailing, *495*

**Dependent variables, 277**

**Depression, 82**

**Depth interviews, 273**

**Depth of product mix, 302**

Deregulation, 76–7

**Derived demand, 199**

Description of products, 198

**Descriptive research**, 264–5, **264**

**Descriptors**, 241–2, **241**

Design, packaging, 342–3

Desk jobber *see* Drop shipper

Developing countries
Hewlett-Packard, 709
Operation Smile, 712

Developing products, 344–74

Diagrams, examinations, 825

**Diary tests, 278**

Dibb/Simkin
buying proforma, 201–2
checklists, 759–60, 769–71
competitive positions proforma, 55–6

**Differential advantage**, 56–8, **56**
competitive positions, 50–8
services, *385*, **385**

**Differential pricing**, 659–60, *659*, **659**

**Differentiated strategy**, *243*, **245**

Differentiation, 49–50

**Digitalisation, 107**

Digital music, 674–5

**Direct cost approach**, 775–6, **775**, 780

**Direct costs, 775**

**Direct distribution channels, 684**, 697

**Directional policy matrix (DPM)**, 363–5, **363**, *365*

**Direct mail, 525**, 602–5, **602**
advertising, 552
charity marketing, 401
industry, *603*, 609
non-profit marketing, 394
strengths and weaknesses, 604–5
uses, 602

**Direct mail packages**, 602, **604**

**Direct marketing, 484, 526**, 607–10, **608**, *609–10*

Directors of marketing, 749–50

Direct response advertising, 609

Discounts, 635–6
business markets, 636–8, *637*
comparison discounting, *665*, 666
negotiated pricing, 660
perfume market, 644–5

**Discount sheds, 479**

Discount stores
merchandise breadth and depth, *490*
wheel of retailing, *495*

Discrepancies, marketing channels, 413–14

**Discretionary income, 85**

Displays, store design, 492–3

**Disposable income, 85**, 163

Distinctive competencies, 44

**Distribution**
business marketing mix, 684–6
definition, 408
electronic marketing, 109
international marketing mix, 702–4, *703*
services marketing mix, 697
*see also* Physical distribution; Place/distribution

Distribution-based assets, 44

**Distribution centre, 456**, *458*

Distribution channels
choosing, 686
pricing decisions, 633–4
strategic windows, 92
types, 684–5

**Distribution variable**, 10, 12, **26**

**Distributors**, 436–70, **441**

District Council regulations, 76

Diversification
brands, 36–7
marketing opportunities, 21

**Diversified growth**, 47–8, **47**

Doctor-patient relationships, 693–4

**Dogs**, 360–2, **360**, *361*, *362*

**Domestic marketing**, 126–7, **126**
international marketing mix, 704
levels of involvement, *126*

Door-to-door selling, 609

Dotcoms, 103

Downgrading, effects, *695*

Downloading music, 673–6

DPM *see* Directional policy matrix

**Drop shippers**, *442–3*, **444**

**Dual distribution, 419**

**Dumping, 141, 704**
Dynamic marketing environment, 11, 12

# E

**Early adopters, 519**
**Early majority, 519**
Eastern Europe, 140–1
East Germany, 710–11
E-banking, 356
E-booking, British Airways, 409
Eco-labels, 791, *792*
**E-commerce** *see* **Electronic commerce**
**Economic forces**, 82–9, **82**
  international marketing, 135
  target market segments, 246
**Economic order quantity (EOQ), 459**, *460*
**Economic value to the customer (EVC)**, 639–40, **639**
the Economy, marketing importance, 15
**Edge-of-town sites**, 475–6, **476**
EDI *see* Electronic data interchange
**EDLP (everyday low pricing), 628, 663**
Educating markets, advertising, 544
Effectiveness
  advertising, 559–61
  marketing management, 28
  market segmentation, 240–1
  resource allocation, 225
  sales personnel, 544
Efficiency
  marketing management, 28
  *see also* Exchange efficiencies
EFTPoS (electronic funds transfer at point of sale), 495
Elasticity of demand, prices, 651–2, *652*
**Electronic commerce (e-commerce)**, 100, **102**, **417**, **606**
  case study, 122–3
  grocery shopping, 415
  travel booking, 409
**Electronic data interchange (EDI)**, 122, **455**
Electronic funds transfer at point of sale (EFTPoS), 495
**Electronic marketing (e-marketing)**, 100, 102–7, **102**
  characteristics, 103–7
  customer relationship management, 111–12
  ethical issues, 117–19
  legal issues, 117–19
  strategies, 107–10
Electronic point of sale (EPoS), 495–6, **496**
E-loyalty, price competition, 628
**E-marketing** *see* **Electronic marketing**
Employees
  non-profit organisations, 395
  performance, 390
  service quality, 390
  *see also* Personnel
**Empowerment, 751**, 765
Endorsements, publicity types, 564–5
Enduring involvement, consumers, 170–1
Entry strategies, international marketing, 141–5
**Environmental analysis, 69**
**Environmental factors, 207**, 790–3
  case study analysis, 819
  choosing distribution channels, 426
  international marketing, 130–7
  packaging, 342–3
  *see also* **Marketing environment**
**Environmental scanning, 44, 69**
EOQ *see* Economic order quantity
**EPoS** (electronic point of sale), 495–6, **496**
Equity, brands, 319–20
**Ethical issues**, 795–7, *795*, **795**, 805
  consumer buying decision process, 177, 183
  e-marketing, 117–19
  international marketing, 137
  management strategies, 713, 714
  marketing research, 281–2
  *see also* **Marketing ethics**
Ethics officers, 800
Ethnic diversity
  consumer buying decisions, 182–3
  market segmentation, 231, 255–6
Ethnodomination, 702
Ethnographic research, 275
**European Union (EU)**, 138–9, **138**
  advertising, *540–2*
  cultural forces, *131*
  economic performance, *83–4*
  government markets, 193
  international marketing mix, 703, 704
  Internet access and growth, *108*
  legal forces, 74
  market density, 233
  population statistics, *230–1*
  regulatory influence, 67–8
  single market, 67–8, *67*
  top 100 companies by revenue, *146*
Evaluating performance, 768, 771–9
  marketing cost analysis, 773–7
  marketing shareholder value analysis, 747, 777, 781
  performance measures, 777–9
  sales analysis, 772–3
  salesforce, 592–3

Evaluation
advertising, 559–61
alternatives, 167
competitors' prices, 656–7
consumer buying decision process, 167
customers, 387
employees, 390
marketing planning, 725–6
markets, 251
opportunities, 582
physical distribution systems, 464
post-purchase, 167–8
pricing by target markets, 649–50
**Evaluation stage** (product adoption), **517**
**EVC** *see* **Economic value to the customer**
**Everyday low pricing (EDLP), 628, 663**
**Evoked set, 167**
Examination papers, 823
Examinations, 815, 823–5
coping with conditions, 823–4
format of answers, 824–5
techniques, 825
Exceptional service quality, 387–91
**Exchange**, 10–11, *11*, **11**
business buying behaviour, 203, *204*
efficiencies in marketing channels, 412–13, *413*
relationships, 11, 203–4
Exchange rates, 704
**Exclusive dealing, 430**
**Exclusive distribution, 355, 422**
**Executive judgements, 730**
Executive summaries, 722
Existing customers
approaching, 583
contacting, 582–3
Expectations
Aer Lingus, 404
customers, 389–91
**Experience qualities, 378**
'Experiences', pricing, 647–8
**Experimentation**, 277–8, **277**
**Expert forecasting surveys, 733**
**Exploratory research, 264**
**Exporting**, 141–2, **141**
**Export marketing**, 126–7, *126*, **126**
Express carriers, 400
**Extended marketing mix for services**, *386*, **386**, *692*, **692**
**Extensive decision-making**, 162, 163–4, **164**
Exterior atmospherics, stores, 492
External environment, case studies, 819
**External reference price, 634**
**External search, 166**
External sources, data, *268*

## F

Fabric fragrances, 296–7
Fabrics market, 190–1
Face-to-face communications, 514
Face-to-face fundraising, 400–1
**Facilitating agencies, 448**
**Factory outlet villages, 480**, 481
Failure, products, 307, 310
**Family packaging, 333**
Family roles, 178–9
**Fast movers, 53**
**FDI** *see* **Foreign direct investment**
**Feature articles, 563**
**Feedback, 514**
Field order takers, 585
**Field public warehouse, 456**, *458*
**Field settings, 278**
**Finance companies, 449**
Financial factors
companies, 817–18
resources, 21–2
target market segments, 246
**Financial price, 395, 623**
Financial ratios, *817–18*
Financial Services Act (1986), 73
Financial shocks, 93
Fish and birds test, *171*
**Five-category classification** (services), **382**, *383*
**Five communication effects**, 519–20, **520**
**Five competitive forces**, *52*, **52**
**Five markets model, 762**, *763*, 780
**Fixed costs, 653**, 655
**Flashes, 602**
Fluctuating demand, 200, 651, 697
Fluctuating sales, 546
**FOB destination prices, 638**
**FOB factory prices, 637**, 638
Focus, 50
*see also* Strategic focus
**Focus group interviews, 273**, 287–8
**Focus groups, 173**, 559
Follow-up stage, sales, 584
**Food brokers, 446**
Food products, 24
Football sponsorship, 571
**Forecasting sales potential**, 251, 714, 728, 730–6, **730**, *732*, 740–1, 809
Forecourt sales, 209
**Foreign direct investment (FDI), 145**
Formal presentations, case studies, 822
Format, consumer information search, 166–7
Form utility, retailing, 473
Fragrant Fabrics, 296–7

Framing alternatives, consumers, 167

**Franchising, 142, 487**
 advantages and disadvantages, 488
 trends, 488–9
 types, 488

Free flights, Hoover, 614–15

**Free merchandise, 601**

**Free samples, 599**

**Freight absorption pricing, 638**

**Freight forwarders, 463**

**Frequency, 551**

**Frequent user incentives, 598**

Fresh produce, Makro, 472

**Full cost approach, 775**, 780

**Full service wholesalers**, *441*, **441**, *442–3*

Function, organising by, **752**

Functional accounts, 774, 775, 776, 780

**Functional discounts, 635**, 637

**Functional middlemen, 410**, *413*, 441–2, **444**

**Functional modifications, 357**

Fund management, 396

Fundraising, charities, 400–1

Furnishings market, 187–8

## G

Garments market, 190–1

**GATT** *see* **General Agreement on Tariffs and Trade**

**GDP** *see* **Gross domestic product**

Gender variable, 230–1

**General Agreement on Tariffs and Trade (GATT), 141**

General economic conditions, 82–5

**General merchandise wholesalers, 441**, *442*

**General publics, 393**

**Generic brands, 323**, 326

**Generic routes to competitive advantage**, 49–50, *50*, **50**

**Geodemographic segmentation, 233**, 236

**Geographic pricing, 637**, 638

Geographic variables, 232–3

Germany, 710–11

**Globalisation**, 145–7, **147**

**Globalised marketing**, 127–8, **127**

**Global marketing**, *126*, 127–8, **127**

Global markets
 Airbus versus Boeing, 144
 Aston Martin, 125
 Avis, 154–7
 Colgate-Palmolive, 710–12
 FedEx, 503–6
 local operations, 703
 Royal Ahold, 501–2

Goals, 41–3, *383*, 384

**Goods, 12, 297**

Go-to-market strategy, 3

**Government markets**, 193–4, **193**

Government regulations, 75–7

**Green forces**, 77–8, **77**

**Green marketing**, 791–3, **791**, 805

**Green movement, 78**

**Gross domestic product (GDP), 135**

Growth
 services, 377–8
 strategic objectives, 47–8

Growth-share matrix, 361, *361*

**Growth stage** (product life cycles), 305–6, **306**, 354–5

**Guarantees, 309**

## H

Handling issues, 336–7

Harvesting, market attractiveness-business position model, 363

Health issues, 716, 785–6

Health Select Committee, 785–6

**Heterogeneity** (services), *379*, 380–2, **380**

**Heterogeneous markets, 223**

Higher-quality products, 366

High-street shops, 410

Hip-hop celebrities, 290–1

**Home placements, 278**

**Horizontal channel integration, 421**

**Horizontal diversification, 47**

Hospitals, 617–20

Human rights, 401, 796

**Hypermarkets**, 151–2, **478**, 479

**Hypotheses, 264**

## I

Ice cream market, 534–5

**Idea generation**, 349–50, **349**

**Ideas, 12**
 Internet marketing, 108
 product decisions, **297**

**Illustrations, 557**, *558*

Image, stores, 493

**IMC** *see* **Integrated marketing communications**

**Immediate drop**, *359*, **359**

Implementation
 case study solutions, 821
 marketing concept, 18–19
 marketing management, 28
 marketing process, 13, 14
 marketing strategy, 59
 programmes, 725
 strategies, 713, 714, 809
 *see also* **Marketing implementation**

Imports, 704–5

**Impulse buying**, 162–3, **162**

Incentive programmes *see* Motivating personnel

**Income, 85**, 163
**Independent variables, 277**
**In-depth interviews, 173**
India, *131*
Individual activities, 10
**Individual branding, 327**
**Individual factors, 208**
**Industrial distributor**, *418*, **418**
**Industrial marketing** *see* **Business markets**
**Industrial products**
  marketing channels, 418–19, *418*
  product decisions, **297**, 299–301
**Industrial services, 301**
**Inelastic demand, 199**
Information
  consumer buying decisions, 166–7
  entitlement, *282*
  gathering technology, 279–81
  marketing research, 281, *282*
  maternity services, 618–20
  retail marketing, 497
  services, 281
**Information inputs**, 171–3, **171**
Information technology (IT)
  branding, 320–1
  FedEx, 505
  *see also* **Internet; Technology**
**In-home interviews**, 273, **274**
**In-home retailing, 484**
Inland waterway transportation, *461*
Innovation, 3, 335
**Innovators, 519**
Input-output analysis, 210–11
**Input-output data, 210**
Inputs
  consumer buying decisions, 171–3
  marketing environment, 68
**Inseparability**, services, *379*, **379**
Inside order takers, 585
Inspecting products, business buying, 198
**Institutional advertising, 540**
**Institutional markets, 194**
**Intangibility, 378, 693**
  non-profit marketing, 394
  product characteristics, 307
  services, 375, 377–9, *377*, *379*, *385*, 387, 394, 692–3, 696
**Integrated growth, 48**
**Integrated marketing communications (IMC)**, 509, 511, 526–7, **527**
Intellectual property, 117–18
Intelligence
  international marketing, 129–30
  *see also* **Marketing intelligence**
**Intended strategy, 756**
**Intense growth, 47**
**Intensive distribution, 355, 422**
**Interactivity**, 104–5, **104**
Interest groups, 793, 807–8
**Interest stage** (product adoption), **516**
Interior atmospherics, stores, 492
Intermediaries
  micro marketing environment, 90–1
  reseller markets, 191–3
  *see also* **Marketing intermediaries**
**Inter-modal transport, 463**
**Internal marketing**, 593, 745, 747, 757, 762–4, **762**, *764*, 780, 809
  assets, 44
  relationships, 713, 714
Internal organisational factors, 21–3
Internal position of company, 816–19
**Internal reference price, 634**
**Internal search, 166**
Internal sources, data, 266, *267*, 268
Internationalisation effects, 567–9
**International marketing**, 124–57, **127**
  analysis, *129*
  definition, 127
  entry strategies, 141–5
  environmental forces, 130–7
  intelligence, 129–30
  involvement in, 126–8
  levels of involvement, 126–7, *126*
  marketing mix, 679, 699–704
  strategies, 141–7, 151–2
**Internet**, 100–22, **525**, 606–7, **606**
  advertising, 109–10, 522, 537, *554*
  banking, 356
  business marketing mix, 690
  charity marketing, 401
  Code of Ethics, *118*
  direct marketing, 609
  European access and growth, *108*
  impact, 81
  marketing, 102–3, *118*
  marketing research, 281
  Napster, 673–6
  price competition, 628
  promotional mix, 525–6
  retailing *see* **Electronic commerce**
  websites, 394, *397*
**Interpersonal factors**, 207–8, **207**
Interpretation, information inputs, 172
Interviews
  careers in marketing, 827
  consumer motives, 173
  survey methods, 272–4
**Intranets, 606**
**Introduction stage** (product life cycles), 305–6, **305**
Intuition, **261**, *262*
Invent new products strategy, 702

**Inventory management**, 437, **456–60**
business buyer concerns, 197
cash and carry wholesalers, 469–70
systems, 686

Investment, profit impact, 367

**Involvement, 166**
consumer buying decisions, 166, 169–71
international marketing, 126–8

Ireland, 15, 403–5

IT *see* Information technology

## J

Japan, 139–40
adaptation strategies, 700
cultural forces, *131*, 133
social forces, 135

**Joint demand, 200**

**Joint ventures, 143**
Colgate-Palmolive, 711
international marketing, 142–3

**Junk mail, 602**, 604–5

Just-in-time inventory management, 459–60, 686

## K

'Keep product/promotion the same worldwide' strategy, 699–700

Keyword ads, *110*

**Kinesic communication, 523**

**Knowledge, 176**

## L

**Labelling**, 314–15, 337–43, **337**

**Laboratory settings**, 277–8, **277**

Labour intensiveness, services, 383, *383*

**Laggards**, 519, **520**

**Late majority**, 519, **520**

Latin America, *131*

Laws
interpretation, 75
strategic windows, 93
*see also* Legal issues

**Layout** (advertisements), **557**

Leadership, marketing channels, 428–9, *428*

**Learning**, 174–7, **174**

Legal compliance programmes, 801

Legal issues
e-marketing, 117–19
international marketing, 135–7
labelling, 338
marketing environment, 73–5
pricing concepts, 636

Legislation *see* Laws

**Level of involvement, 170**
consumer buying decisions, 169–71
international marketing, 126–7, *126*

**Levels of brands, 330**

Leverage ratios, *818*

Libraries, 194

**Licensing, 142**, 329–30

Life cycle stages, 231–2

Lifestyle segmentation, 236–7, *237*

Likert scale questions, 275

**Limited decision-making, 162**, 163–4

**Limited line wholesalers, 441**, *442*

**Limited service wholesalers**, *441*, **441**, *442–3*

**Line extensions, 352**

**Line family branding, 328**

Liquidity ratios, *817*

List prices, 690–1

'Live' advertising, 539

Living standards, 77–8, 80–1

Local governments
business markets, 193–4
regulations, 76

Local operations, global markets, 703

**Location, 489**

**Long-range plans, 718**

Long-term goals, 42

Low consumer involvement, 171

Low cost airlines, 403–5

Loyalty, 318–19
*see also* Customer loyalty

**Loyalty cards**, 597, **598**

## M

**Maastricht Treaty, 138**

**Macro marketing environment**, 66, **89**
forces, 68, *90*
practitioners' assessment, 69–70

Magazine advertising, *552*, 555

**Mailing lists, 604**

Mail marketing, 394, 401
*see also* **Direct mail**

Mail-order businesses, 608

**Mail-order retailing**, 485–6, *486*, **486**, *487*

**Mail order wholesalers**, *443*, **444**

**Mail panels**, 271–2, **271**

**Mail surveys**, 270–1, **270**

**Maintenance, repair, operating (MRO) items, 301**

**Major equipment, 300**

**Mall discounters, 480**, 481

Management
brands, 330–1
product management, 346–7
product portfolios, 360–74
sales personnel, 585–93
sales territories, 592

summaries, 722
*see also* **Customer relationship management; Marketing management**; Sales management
**Manufacturer brands**, 322–3, **322**
Manufacturer-dealer relationships *see* Marketing channels
Manufacturers *see* **Producer markets**
**Manufacturers' agents**, 444–5, **445**, *684*, 685
Marginal analysis, 653–5, *655*
**Marginal cost (MC)**, 653, **654**
average cost relationship, *654*
marginal revenue combination, *656*
**Marginal revenue (MR)**, 653–4, **654**
demand relationship, *654*
marginal cost combination, *656*
Market analysis, 819
Market attractiveness, *247*, 361–5, *363*
**Market challengers**, 53–4, **53**
**Market density, 233**
**Market development, 47**
Market entry strategies, 141–5
**Market followers, 53**
Market information, 197
**Marketing, 7**
definition, *1*, 7–12
importance, 14–16
myths, *16*
technology in, 100–22
Marketing analysis, 9, 12–14, 19–20, 722–4
**Marketing assets**, 44–5, **44**
**Marketing audits**, 395–6, *396*, *735*, 736–9, **736**, *737–8*, 741
case study analysis, 820
Marketing channels, 394, 408–35
activities, *411*
choosing, 423, 425–6
coverage, 422
functions, 412–16
integration, 419–21
legal issues, 429–30
member behaviour, 426–9
nature, 410–12
summary, 430–2
types, 416–19
*see also* Channel of distribution
**Marketing citizenship**, 787–8, **787**, 804
**Marketing communications**, 507, 509–35, **512**
*see also* **Promotion**
**Marketing concept**, 16–19, **17**
**Marketing control process**, 766–7, **766**, *767*
**Marketing decision support systems (MDSS), 281**
Marketing directors, 749–50
**Marketing environment, 8**, *20*, 66–99, **68**
case study analysis, 819
competitive set, 51
examining, 68–72
forces, 23–4
responding, 71–2
strategic opportunities, 92–4
tools and techniques, 69–70
variables, 41
*see also* **Environmental factors**
**Marketing era, 18**
**Marketing ethics**, 785–6, **789**, 794–805, *797*, *803*, 809, 812
**Marketing function accounts, 774**, *775*, 776, 780
**Marketing implementation**, 745, 754–66, **754**, *757*, *758*, **762**, 779
communication, 759
components, 757
coordinating activities, 759
internal marketing, 745, 747, 757, 762–4, *764*, 780
motivating personnel, 757–8
problems encountered, 756–7
relationship marketing, 757, 762, *763*
tools and techniques, 759–60
total quality management, 765–6, 780
**Marketing information systems (MIS)**, 279–80, **279**, *280*
**Marketing intelligence, 259**
**Marketing intermediaries**, 90–1, **410**, *413*
**Marketing management**, *22*, **28**
implementing marketing concept, 19
marketing environment, 71–2
marketing programmes, 26
marketing strategies, 22–3
**Marketing managers**, 346–7, **346**
**Marketing mix**, 20–1, **20**
adaptations, 699–704
amendments, 692–9
business markets, 679, 681–92
customer satisfaction, 293, *293*
decisions, 58–9
development, *22*, 25–6
differential advantage, 56–7
international markets, 679, 699–704
manipulating, 677–712, *677*
modifications, 679–81
non-profit marketing, 393–5
'pricing balance', 666
pricing concepts, 623, 631–4
programmes, 8
promotion element, 511
services, 386, 393–5, 679, 692–9
strategic adaptations, 699–704
variables, *10*, 631–4
**Marketing objectives**, 58, 630–1, **722**
**Marketing opportunities, 21**, 43–4, **43**
Marketing opportunity analysis, 21, *22*, 45
**Marketing orientation**, 4, 6–7, **6**, 35

**Marketing-oriented pricing,** 658–9, **658**
**Marketing performance,** *777–9,* **778**
*see also* Evaluating performance; Performance
**Marketing planning,** 713, 714, 715–44, **717,** 809
appendices, 726
application, 742
budgets, 726
controls, 725–6
core steps, *721*
developing a plan, 719–21, *720–1*
evaluation, 725–6
executive summaries, 722
expected results, 725
implementation, *755,* 759–60
internal procedures, 726
Internet exercise, 742
marketing analysis, 722–4
marketing objectives, 722
marketing plans, **717,** 721–6, *723,* 740
marketing strategies, 724–5
product/market background, 722
programmes for implementation, 725
SWOT analysis, 721, 724, 740
tools and techniques, 726–7
**Marketing planning cycles,** *717,* **717,** 740
**Marketing plans,** 38–9, **38, 717,** 721–6, *723,* 740
**Marketing process,** 9, 12–14, **12,** *13*
**Marketing programmes,** 9, 12–14, 25–8, 40–1, **40**
**Marketing research,** 257–92, **257**
analysis of findings, 278
ethical issues, 281–2
five steps, *262*
importance, 259–62
information entitlement, 282
interpretation of findings, 278
process, 262–*79*
reporting findings, 279
technology, 279–81
types, 264–5
UK budgets, *271*
**Marketing shareholder value analysis (MSVA),** 747, **777,** 781
**Marketing strategies,** 9, 12–14, 20–5, **20,** 35–65, **37,** 724–5
components, *38*
definition, 37–41
electronic marketing, 107–10
implementation, 59
international marketing, 141–7, 151–2
non-profit organisations, 393–5
organisational factors, 41–6
packaging, 335–7
product life cycle management, 354–8
services, 384–6, *385,* 393–5
tools and techniques, 45–6, 55–6
Marketing unit
communication, 759
organising, 747–54, *748*
**Market leader,** 53–4, **53**
**Market nichers, 53**
**Market-orientated organisations,** 749–50, **749,** *750*
**Market penetration, 47**
Market position, profit impact, 366
**Market potential,** 728–9, **728,** *730,* 740
Market redefinition, 92
**Market requirements, 44,** 222
**Markets, 222, 481**
characteristics, 425–6
evaluation, 251
services classification, 382–3
types, 222, 382–3
**Market segmentation,** 48–9, 220–56
approach, *223*
basic elements, *226*
business markets, 211–12
definition, **223**
effectiveness, 240–1
international marketing, 156
reasons to use, 224–5
tools and techniques, 249–50
**Market segments, 223,** 241–2
**Market share,** 772–3, **772,** 780
pricing objectives, *632*
Toys ' я ' Us, 672
Market status audits, 769–71
Market structure, 819
**Market tests, 734**
**Mark-up pricing,** 657–8, **657**
Mass communication
feedback, 514
product adoption process, 518
**Materials handling,** 436–7, **455**
Maternity services, 617–20
**Maturity stage** (product life cycles), 305–6, **306,** 355–8
**MC** *see* **Marginal cost**
**MDSS** *see* **Marketing decision support systems**
**Measuring performance,** 713, 714, 745, 809
**Mechanical observation devices, 277**
**Media plans,** 550–5, **551**
Medical services, 693–4, *694*
**Medium-range plans, 718**
**Medium of transmission, 513,** 514
**Megacarriers, 463–4**
**Memory, 105**
Merchandise
breadth and depth, 490–1, *490*
categories, *480*
strategic retailing, 494
**Merchandise allowances, 601**
**Merchants, 410**
**Merchant wholesalers, 440,** *441*
Message creation, advertising, 555–8

Mexico, 711

**Micro marketing environment**, 66, 68, 89–92, **89**, *90*

**Micro retail marketing, 496**, 497

Middle East, *131*

**MIS** *see* **Marketing information systems**

**Misleading pricing**, 665–6, **666**

**Mission**, 41–3, **41**

**Missionary sales people, 585**

Mobile phones, 401

Moderator guides, 287

Modification, products, 295, 355–7

**Modified rebuy purchase, 198**

**Money refunds, 599**

Monitoring
- competition, 89
- performance, 59

**Monopolies**, 87–8, **87**, 635

**Monopolistic competition**, 88, 635

Motivating personnel, 590–2, *591*, 757–8

**Motives**, 173–4, **173**

Motor vehicle transportation, *461*

**MR** *see* **Marginal revenue**

**MRO (maintenance, repair, operating) items, 301**

**MSVA** *see* **Marketing shareholder value analysis**

Multi-channel clothing retailers, 483

**Multinational companies, 127**

**Multinational enterprises, 145**

**Multinational marketing**, *126*, **127**

Multiple forecasting methods, 734–6

Multiple marketing channels, 419

**Multiple packaging, 336**

**Multiple sourcing**, 206–7, **206**

**Multiple-unit pricing, 663**

Multiplex cinemas, 372–3

**Multivariable segmentation, 227**, *228*

Music industry
- marketing channels, 434
- Napster, 673–6

Mustard, Coleman's, 373–4

Mystery shopper research programmes, 276

Myths of marketing, *16*

## N

**NAFTA** *see* **North American Free Trade Agreement**

Nappies, samples, 578

Nationalism, 403–5

National Statistics SEC socio-economic classification, *181*

**Natural accounts**, 774–7, **774**, *775*, 780

Natural environment, 790–3

Negotiated contracts
- business buying methods, 198
- government markets, 193

**Negotiated pricing, 659, 691**

**Negotiation**
- business buying, 194–5, 198
- non-profit marketing, **391**

Netherlands, 501–2

'Netiquette', 118–19

New business order getters, 584

New market strategic windows, 92

**New product development**, 347–52, *348*, **348**, *349*

New products
- international marketing mix, 702
- pricing, *659*, 660–1

Newspaper advertising, *552*, 555

News releases *see* **Press (news) releases**

**New task purchase, 198**, 201

Nichers *see* **Market nichers**

Nicotine replacement therapy (NRT), 303

**Noise, 514**

Nometrics process, brand names, 325

**Non-cumulative discounts, 635**, 637

Non-governmental regulations, 76

**Non-price competition**, 626, 628–9, **628**, 657

**Non-profit marketing**, 391–7
- control aspects, 395–7, *396*
- differing approaches, 391–2
- objectives, 392, *393*
- services, 391–7, **391**
- strategies, 393–5

**Non-store retailing**, 483–4, **483**

Non-tariff barriers, 135–6, *136*

**Non-traceable common costs, 775**, 780

**North American Free Trade Agreement (NAFTA)**, 137–8, **138**

Not-for-profit organisations, 14, 15

NRT *see* Nicotine replacement therapy

## O

**Objective of physical distribution, 452**

Objectives
- distribution channels, 423, 425
- pricing decisions, 630–1
- promotional resources, 527–8
- salesforce, 586–7
- *see also* **Marketing objectives; Pricing objectives; Strategic objectives**

**Objective and task approach, 549**

**Observation methods**, 275–7, **275**

Occupation variable, 232

**Odd/even pricing**, 663–4, **663**
**Offensive warfare, 54**
**Office of Fair Trading, 73**
Off-setting competitive advertising, 544
**Oligopolies, 88**, 635
**One-to-one marketing, 110**, 114, **227**
On-line information services, 281
**On-line surveys, 272**
**On-site computer interviewing, 274**
On-time delivery
  business buyer concerns, 197
  business marketing mix, 681
Open bid pricing, 691
Operating variables, segmentation, 239
**Opinion leaders, 179**
**Opportunities, 799**
  evaluation, 582
  sales promotion, 594–5
  *see also* **Marketing opportunities**; Strategic opportunities
**Opportunity cost, 395**
**Order getters, 584**
**Order lead time, 458**
**Order processing**, 436, 454–5, **454**
**Order takers**, 584–5, **584**
Organisation
  alternative strategies, 752–4
  of this book, 29–30
  centralisation versus decentralisation, 750–1
  culture of marketing, 747–50
  market activities, 747–54, *748*
  marketing management, 28
Organisational audits, *803*
**Organisational (corporate) culture, 798**, 805
**Organisational factors**, 10, 21–3, **207**
  marketing strategy, 41–6
  pricing decisions, 630–1
  situation analysis, 818–19
**Organisational marketing** *see* **Business markets**
Organisations, advertising, 540–1
**Organising by customer type**, 753–4, **753**
**Organising by function, 752**
**Organising by product**, 752–3, **753**
**Organising by region, 753**
Outdoor advertising, *554*
Outputs, marketing environment, 68
**Outsourcing, 464**
Over-50s, targeting, 220–1
**Overall family branding**, 327–8, **327**, *329*
**Own-label brands, 323**, 357–8

# P

Pacific Rim nations, 139–40
**Packaging**, 294, 314–16, 331–7, **332**, 338–43
  criticisms, 337
  functions, 332
  handling, 336–7
  innovative packaging, 335
  major considerations, 332–4
  marketing strategies, 335–7
**Packaging development**, 334–5, **334**
Panama, 712
Pan-European level markets, 703
**Parallel imports**, 704–5, **704**
Parents' buying behaviour, 161–2
Partnerships
  international marketing, 142–3
  sponsorship, 571
Passport service, 671
**Patronage motives, 173**
**Pavement intercept interviews**, 273–4, **274**
**Penetration pricing**, 660–1, **660**
Pens market, 643
People
  business marketing mix, 691–2
  international marketing mix, 705
  services marketing mix, 698–9
**People variable**, 10, 12, 27–8, **27**
**Perceived value for money, 635**, 636
**Percentage of sales approach, 549**
**Perceptions, 171**
  consumer buying decisions, 171–3
  pricing decisions, 634–5
**Perceptual mapping**, 248–9, **248**
**Perfect competition, 88**, 636
Performance
  businesses, 16
  ethics/social responsibility, 804
  evaluation, 592–3, 768, 771–9
  measuring, 713, 714, 745, 777–9, 809
  monitoring, 59
  salesforce, 592–3
**Performance standards**, 767–8, **767**, *768*, 780
Perfume market, 644–5
**Periodic discounting, 660**
**Perishability** (services), *379*, **380**
Permanently low prices, ASDA, 648–9
Personal banking, 356
Personal factors
  business buyers, 195
  consumer buying decisions, 168–71
  segmentation variables, *239*, 240
**Personal influencing factors, 168**
**Personal interview surveys, 272**
**Personality, 178**, 236

**Personal selling**, 522–3, **522**, 577, **579**, 609, **686**
business marketing mix, 686–8, 691
elements, 581–4, *582*
nature of, 579–80
process, 581–4
services marketing mix, 695

Personnel
empowerment, 765
ethics, *798*, 799
motivating, 757–8
*see also* Employees; People; Sales personnel; Service personnel

**Persuasion, 391**

**PEST analysis**, 93–4, **93**

'Pester power', 161–2, *161*

Petrol industry, 410

**Phase out**, *359*, **359**

Philanthropic responsibilities, 789, 804, 807–8

Physical characteristics, products, 308, 310

**Physical distribution**, 436–70, **451**
cash and carry wholesalers, 469–70
FedEx Custom Critical, 469
importance, 451–4
inventory management, 456–60
materials handling, 455
objectives, 452
order processing, 454–5
strategic issues, 464
transportation, 460–4
warehousing, 455–6

Physical evidence, services marketing, 698

PIMS *see* Profit impact on marketing strategy

**Pioneer advertising, 541**

Pipeline transportation, *462*

Place/distribution
business marketing mix, 684–6
decisions, 406–506
international marketing mix, 702–5
services marketing mix, 697

**Place/distribution variable**, 10, **26**

Place utility, retailing, 473

Planning
marketing management, 28
*see also* **Marketing planning**

**Point-of-sale (POS) materials, 599**

Poland, 711

Policies
branding, 327–9
promotional resources, 527–8

Political forces
international marketing, 135–7, 704
marketing environment, 72–3, 93

**Populations, 269**

Population statistics, EU, *230–1*

Pop-under ads, *110*

Pop-up ads, *110*

**Portals, 106**

Portfolio management, 360–74

**POS** *see* **Point-of-sale materials**

**Positioning**, 8, 247–51, **247**
brands, 249–50
determining, 247–51
market segmentation, 220–56
plans, 249–51
products, 226
*see also* **Brand positioning; Competitive positions**

**Positioning statements, 251**

Possession utility, 473

**Post-campaign tests, 559**

Post-purchase evaluation, 167–8

**Post-tests** *see* **Post-campaign tests**

Potential customers
identifying, 208–12
locating, 211–12

Power, non-economic sources, 428–9, *428*

**PR** *see* **Public relations**

**PR campaigns, 563**

**Premium pricing, 662**

**Premiums**, 599–600, **599**, **601**

Presentations, 583, 821–3

**Press conferences**, 563, **564**

**Press (news) releases, 563**, *564*

Pressure groups, 793, 807–8

**Prestige pricing**, 664–5, **664**

**Prestige-sensitive consumers, 635**

**Pre-tests** (advertising), **559**

**PR events, 563**

**Price, 623**
business marketing mix, 690–1
characteristics, 625–6
competitors, 656–7
determining specific prices, 666
discounts, 635–8
importance to marketers, 625–6
role, 625–6
services marketing mix, 696–7
setting, 646–76
stages for establishing, 648–66, *648*
terminology, 625

**Price competition**, 626–30, **627**, 696–7

**Price-conscious consumers, 635**

**Price discrimination, 639**

**Price elasticity of demand**, 651–2, **651**, *652*

**Price leaders**, *665*, **665**

**Price lining, 662**, *663*

**Price-off offers, 600**

**Price skimming, 660**

**Price variable**, 10, 12, 26–7, **26**

Pricing
basis for pricing, 657–9
business buyer concerns, 197
business markets, 636–40

concepts, 623–45
consumer buying decisions, 187–8
decisions, 621–76, *621*
electronic marketing, 110
'experiences', 647–8
factors affecting, 630–6, *630*
fluctuating demand, 200
international marketing mix, *703*, 704–5

'Pricing balance', 666

**Pricing objectives, 631**
selection, 648–9
types, *632*

**Pricing strategies, 659**
advertising, *661*
Aer Lingus, 405
non-profit marketing, 394–5
product life cycle management, 358
selection, 659–66

**Primary data**, 265–6, **265**
collection methods, 269–78
international marketing, 130

Primary demand, 541, *545*

**Prime pitch, 474**

Print media
advertising, 551, *552*, 555
business advertising, 689
*see also* Magazine advertising; Newspaper advertising

Priority service, FedEx, 505

Privacy issues, 117, 118

**Private warehouse, 455**, *458*

**Probability sampling, 269**

**Problem children**, 360–2, **360**, *361*, *362*

**Problem definition**, 263–4, **263**, 820

Problem recognition
business buying decisions, 204
consumer buying decisions, 165

Problem-solving approach, 134

Process, services marketing mix, 697–8

**Process materials, 300**

**Procompetitive legislation**, 73–4, **73**

**Producer markets, 191**

Producer services, 438–9

**Product adoption process**, 509–10, **516**
adopter categories, 519
product development, 353–4, **353**
promotion, 516–19, *516*

**Product advertising**, 540–1, **540**

Product assortment, 490–1

**Product deletion**, 358–9, **358**, *359*

**Product development, 47**, 294, 344–74, **351**
adoption process, 353–4
life cycle management, 344, 354–9
management organisation, 346–54
portfolio management, 360–74

**Production era, 17**

Production orientation, 6, 16–17

**Product items, 302**, 310

**Product life cycles**, 304–7, **304**, 310

**Product-line pricing**, *659*, 661–2, 661

**Product lines, 302**, 304

**Product managers**, 346–7, **346**

**Product mix, 302**, 304

**Product modification**, 355–7, **355**

**Product portfolio analysis**, 360–74, **360**

Product portfolios
brand management, 330
product decisions, 294

**Products, 12, 297**
adaptations, 700–2
advertising, 543, 545
analysis by, 776–7
business buying, 198, 204–7
business demand, 199–200
business marketing mix, 681–4
decisions, 293, 295–313
definitions, 295
distribution channels, 426
electronic marketing, 107–9
failure/success, 307, 310
increasing usage, 545
intangibility, 307–9, 692–3
international marketing, 133–4, 699–702, *699*
'keep the same worldwide' strategy, 699–700
levels, 301–2, *301*, 310
market background, 722
market segmentation, 238
modification, 295
organising by, 752–3, **753**
positioning, 226
pricing objectives, *632*
promotional mix, 528–9
quality, *632*
reseller markets, 193
sampling, 578
services marketing mix, 692–4
tangible characteristics, 307–9
types, 360–2

**Product-specific spending patterns**, 86–7, **86**

**Product variable**, 10, **26**

Professionalism, charities, 400–1

**Professional pricing**, *659*, **665**

Professional services, 696, 697

**Profiling, 241**
ACORN categorisation, 235–6
market segments, 241–2

Profit, demand and cost relationship, 652–6

Profitability
price impact, 625–6, *626*
pricing objectives, *632*
pricing relationship, 639
ratios, *817*

**Profit impact on marketing strategy (PIMS)**, 365–7, *366*, **366**

Programmes for implementation, 725
*see also* **Marketing programmes**
**Projective techniques**, 173–4, **173**, *175*
**Project teams, 347**
**Promotion**, 507, **511**
adaptations, 700–2
aims, 519–20
business marketing mix, 686–90
electronic marketing, 109–10
international marketing mix, 699–702, *699*
'keep the same worldwide' strategy, 699–700
non-profit marketing, 394
product adoption process, 516–19
resources, 527–8
role, 511–12
services marketing mix, 694–6
*see also* **Advertising; Marketing communications; Sales promotion**
**Promotional mix**, 507, 513, 520–31, *521*, **521**
availability of methods, 529–30
cost, 529–30
direct marketing, 609–10
ingredients, 521–6, 527–30
selecting ingredients, 527–30
*see also* **Personal selling**
**Promotional pricing**, *659*, **665**
**Promotion variable**, 10, 12, **26**
**Prompted recall tests, 560**
Property ownership, 490
**Prospecting, 582**
Prospects
approaching, 583
contacting, 582–3
objections, 583
**Prosperity, 82**
Protection, brands, 324–7
**Proxemic communication, 523**
**PR programmes, 563**, 566
PSAs *see* Public service announcements
Psychographic variables, 236–7
**Psychological factors**, 171–8, **171**
**Psychological pricing**, *659*, 662–5
Public health, 716, 785–6
**Publicity, 523**, 562–9, **562**
advertising comparison, 563
limitations, 567
programmes, 566
releases, *565*
services marketing mix, 695–6
types, 563–5
unfavourable, 566–7
uses, 565
**Public relations (PR), 523**, 524, 562–9, **562**
case study, 575–6
sponsorship applications, 570
trends that affect, 567–9
Publics
micro marketing environment, 91–2
publicity, 562
**Public-sector markets**, 193–4, **193**
Public service announcements (PSAs), 394
Public transport advertising, *553*
**Public warehouses, 448, 456,** *458*
**Pull policies**, 530–1, **530**
**Purchase facilitation, 520**
Purchases
business buying, 194–5, 198–9
consumer buying, 167
Purchasing approach, *239*, 240
Purity symbol, mineral water, 338
Purpose, product assortment, 491
**Push money, 601**
**Push policies**, 530–1, **530**

# Q

**Quali-depth interviews, 273**
**Qualitative research, 259**, 260–1
**Quality**
brands, 319
improvement teams, 765–6
product decisions, **308**, 310
profit impact, 366
services, 386–91, *398*, 693
Quality of life, 77–8, 80–1
**Quality modifications**, 356–7, **356**
**Quantitative research, 259**, 260
**Quantity discounts, 635**, 637
**Questionnaires**, 270–1, 274–5, **274**
**Quotas, 135**
**Quota sampling, 270**

# R

**Rack jobbers**, *443*, **443**
Radio advertising, *553*, 557
Rail transportation, *461*
**Random discounting, 660**
**Random factor analysis, 733**
**Random sampling, 269**
**Ratchet effect**, *594*, **594**
**Raw materials, 300**
**Reach, 551**
Reactivity, 258
**Realised strategy, 756**
Recall tests, 559–61, *560*
**Receivers, 513**
**Receiving audience, 513**
**Recession, 82**
**Reciprocity, 195**
**Recognition tests**, 559–61, **559**
Recommendations, case studies, 822–3
**Recovery, 85**

**Recruiting**, 587–8, **587**
Recycling, 77, 98–9, 334, 342–3
**Reference groups, 179**
**Reference pricing, 662**
Referrals, 582
Refunds, 599
**Refusal to deal, 430**
Refuse disposal, 77
Region
  analysis by, 776–7
  organising by, **753**
**Regional issues, 555**
Regional trade alliances, 137–41
Registration, brand names, 324–7
Regulations, 75–7
  EU single market, 67–8
  international marketing, 135–7
  pricing concepts, 636
  public relations, 524
  strategic windows, 93
  target market segments, 246
**Reinforcement advertising, 546**
**Relationship management**, 203–4, **203**
  *see also* **Customer relationship management**
**Relationship marketing**, 110, 203–4, **203**, 757, **762**, *763*
**Relationship marketing era, 18**
**Relationships, 691**
  business marketing mix, 691–2
  client-based relationships, *379*, 382
Relative market share, 360–2
**Reliability, 265, 462–3**
**Reminder advertising**, 545–6, **546**
**Remuneration plans, 589**, *590*
**Reorder point, 457**
Repeat business
  follow-ups, 584
  personal selling, 580
Repetition, consumer buying, 166
Replacement parts, 309
Replenishment costs, 456
Reports
  case study analysis, 821–3
  research findings, 279
  retailing, 482
**Reputable partnerships, 571**
**Requisites for implementation, 756**
Research *see* **Marketing research**
**Research design**, 264–5, **264**
**Research objectives, 264**
**Reseller markets**, 191–3, **191**, 333
Resources, 43–6
  allocation effectiveness, 225
  distribution channels, 423, 425
Responsibility *see* **Social responsibility**
**Restricted sales territories, 429–30**
Restrictive Trade Practices Act (1976), 73–4
Résumés, 826–7
**Retailers**, 192–3, **192, 473**
  electronic marketing, 109
  Europe's largest, *478*
  impulse buying, 163
  international distribution, 702
  marketing channels, 417, *417*, 420, *421*
  pricing decisions, *633*
  services, 440
  UK major groups, *480*
**Retail formats, 496**, 497
**Retailing**, 471–506, **473**
  BAA, 501
  categories, *480*, 482
  economic importance, 473
  FedEx, 503–6
  franchising, 487–9
  locations, 474–6
  mail-order, 485–6, *486*, **486**, *487*
  major store types, 476–83
  Makro, 471–2
  nature, 473
  non-store, 483
  Royal Ahold, 501–2
  sales volumes, *474*
  strategic issues/trends, 489–97
**Retail parks, 476**
**Retail positioning, 492**
**Retail technology, 496**
Return on investment (ROI), *632*
Revenue, European retailers, *478*
Review systems, products, 359
Revision tips, 815, 823–5
Rewards
  employees, 390
  *see also* Compensation
ROI *see* Return on investment
**Roles** (consumers), 178–9, **178**
Roll-outs, 354
**Routine response behaviour, 162**
Routing sales personnel, 592
**Run out**, *359*, **359**
Russia, 140

# S

**Safety stock**, 458, *459*, **459**
Salary compensation, 589, *590*
Sales
  advertising budgets, 549
  advertising objectives, 548
  fluctuations, 546
  forecasting, 251
  management, 577–620
  objectives, 586–7
  personnel effectiveness, 544
  territories, 592
**Sales analysis**, 772–3, **772**
**Sales branches, 446**
**Sales competitions**, 601–2, **601**
**Sales era**, 17–18, **17**

Salesforce
management, 585–93
objectives, 586–7
performance evaluation, 592–3
size determination, 587
*see also* Sales personnel
**Salesforce forecasting surveys**, 732–3, **732**
**Sales forecasting**, 728, 730–6, **730**, *732*, 740–1
Sales-led organisations, 6
**Sales measurements, 772**
**Sales offices, 448**
Sales personnel
business marketing mix, 682–3, 686–8
compensation, 588–90
IBM, 581
motivation, 590–2, *591*
personal selling, 579–84
recruiting, 587–8
routing and scheduling, 592
selection procedure, 587–8
telemarketing, 688
training, 588
types, 584–5
*see also* Salesforce
**Sales per square metre**, 777–8, **778**
Sales pitch, 583
**Sales potential**, 714, 728–9, **729**, 809
forecasting, 728, 730–6, **730**, *732*, 740–1
**Sales promotion**, 523–5, **523**, 593–5, **593**
business marketing mix, 689
Hoover, 614–15
limitations, 594–5
methods, 595–602, *595*
opportunities, 594–5
services marketing mix, 695
**Salience, 167**
**Samples, 269**, 578, 599
**Sampling**, 198, 269–70, **269**
**SBUs** *see* **Strategic business units**
Scheduling sales personnel, 592
**Scientific decision-making, 261**, *262*
Scoring, directional policy matrix, 364
**Scrambled merchandising**, 493–4, **494**
**Screening ideas, 350**
Sealed bid pricing, 691
**Search qualities**, services, **378**
**Seasonal analysis, 733**
**Seasonal discounts, 637**, 638
**Secondary data**, 265–6, **265**
international marketing, 130
sources, 266–9, *267*
**Secondary market pricing, 660**
**Secondary use packaging, 335**
**Security, 463**
Segmentation, 225
analysis, 240–1, *241*
business markets, 211–12
marketing strategies, 355
*see also* **Market segmentation**
**Segmentation variables**, 226–40, **226**
business markets, 238–40, *239*
consumer markets, 226–7, *228*, 229–38
selection, 227–8
Selection of sales personnel, 587–8
Selective demand, 543–4
**Selective distortion, 172**
**Selective distribution, 355, 422**
**Selective exposure, 172**
**Selective retention, 172**
**Self-concept, 173**
Self-regulatory programmes, 76
**Selling agents, 445**
Sentence completion tests, 174, *175*
**Service expectations, 387**
Service personnel, 695, 697–9
**Service product quality, 693**
**Service providers**, 324, **693**
**Service quality**, 197, 386–91, **386**, *398*
**Service quality factors**, 388–9, **389**
**Services, 12, 297**, 375–405
bundling, 696
business marketing mix, 681–2
characteristics, 378–82
classifications, 382–4
growth, 377–8
industrial/business services, 301
marketing, 294, 375–405, *379*
marketing mix, 679, 692–9
market strategies, 384–6, *385*
nature/importance, 377–82
non-profit marketing, 391–7
product-related services, 309
Setting prices, 646–76
Shareholder value analysis (SVA), 747, 777, 781
Share-of-customer perspective, 112
Shocks, 93
Shoe markets, 624–5
**Shopping mall/pavement intercept interviews**, 273–4, **274**
**Shopping products, 298**
'Shops within shops', 477
Short-haul air routes, 405
**Short-range plans, 718**
Short-term goals, 42
Short-termism, 246
**SIC** *see* **Standard Industrial Classification System**
Signatures, 556
Simulated test marketing, 352
Single market (EU), 67–8
**Single-source data, 280**, 561

**Single variable segmentation, 227**
**Situational factors, 169**, 171, *239*, 240
Situation analysis, 816–20
Skills, service providers, *383*, 384
Smoking, 303
**Social classes**, 180–1, **180**
**Social factors**, 178–83, **178**
**Social responsibility**, 785–94, **787**, 801–5, *803*, 809, 812
  management strategies, 713, 714
**Societal forces**, 77–8, **77**
  international marketing, 134–5
  recycling, 98–9
  technology impact, 80–1
Socio-economic classifications, *180–1*
Socio-economic variables, 232
Socio-political factors, 246
**Sole sourcing, 206**
Solutions, case study analysis, 820–1
**Sorting activities**, *414*, **414**
**Sorting out, 414**
**Sources, 513**, 514–15
Sourcing suppliers, 206–7
South Korea, 139–40
Soviet Union (former), 140–1
**Spam, 117**
**Special event pricing**, *665*, **666**
**Speciality line wholesalers**, *442*, **443**
**Speciality products**, 298–9, **298**
**Speciality shops, 479**, 480–1, *490*
Specifications
  business buying, 195–6, 204–7
  service quality, 390
Spending behaviour, 85–7
  affluent consumers, 667
**Sponsorship, 525**, 569–71, **569**, 575
  ads, *110*
  applications, 570–1
  increasing popularity, 569–70
  UK expenditure, *570*
**Spontaneous recall tests, 560**
Sports celebrities, 290–1
Sports sponsorship, 569–70, 571, 575
Sports wear, 296
**Stakeholders**, 787–8, **788**, 804
**Standard Industrial Classification (SIC) System**, 208–11, **209**, *210*
Standardisation
  international markets, 699–700
  marketing channel transactions, 416
  services, 696–7
Standard of living *see* Living standards
Standard marketing mix, services, 386
**Stars**, 360–2, **360**, *361*, *362*
**Statistical interpretation, 278**
Status, product assortment, 491
Status quo, pricing objectives, *632*
**Stock-outs**, 456, **456**
**Storyboards, 557**
**Straight commission compensation, 589**, *590*
**Straight rebuy purchase**, 198–9, **199**, 201
**Straight salary compensation, 589**, 590
Strategic adaptations, international marketing, 699–704
**Strategic alliances, 143**
Strategic Business Planning Grid, 363
**Strategic business units (SBUs)**, 37–8, **37**, 360, 363, 366
**Strategic channel alliance, 419**
Strategic focus, 46–8
**Strategic market plan, 37**
**Strategic market planning**, *37–41*, **38**
  components, *40*
  market segmentation, 225
**Strategic objectives**, 46–8, **46**
Strategic opportunities, 92–4
**Strategic philanthropy, 789**, 804, 808
**Strategic windows, 43, 92**
  importance, 93–4
  marketing environment, 92–4
Strategies
  electronic marketing, 107–10
  implementation *see* **Marketing implementation**
  international marketing, 141–7, 151–2, *703*
  targeting, 242–6, *245*
  target market, 22
  value-based strategies, 690
  *see also* **Marketing strategies**
**Stratified sampling, 269**
Students, targeting, 220–1
Studying marketing, 813–30
**Style modifications, 357**
**Sub-cultures, 183**
Subsidiaries, 145
**Suburban centres, 475**
Success, products, 307, 310
**Successful brands**, 330–1, **330**
**Supermarkets, 478**
**Superstores, 478**
**Supplier analysis**, 205–6, **205**
Suppliers
  business buying decisions, 204, 206–7
  micro marketing environment, 90
  sourcing, 206–7
**Supply chain management, 411, 438**
Supply and demand strategy, 384–5

**Support personnel, 585**
**Survey methods**, 270–4, **270**
**Surveys**, 731–6, **731**
Survival objective, *632*
Sustainable competitive advantage, 715–44
SVA *see* Shareholder value analysis
Sweepstakes, 600
**SWOT analysis**, 45–6, **45**, 57, 721, **724**, 740
Symbolic value of price, 623, 626, 646
Symptoms, case study analysis, 820
**Syndicated data services**, 268–9, **268**

## T

**Tactile communication, 523**
Taiwan, 132–3, 139–40
Tamper-resistant packaging, 332–3
Tangibles
  product characteristics, 307, 316
  services, *377*, *377*, 387, *389*
Target audience *see* **Advertising targets**
**Targeting, 242**
  ACORN categorisation, 235–6
  customers, 158–292
  market attractiveness, *247*
  market segmentation, 220–56
  strategies, 226, 242–6, *243*, *245*
**Target markets**, **25**, 153
  electronic marketing, 107
  non-profit marketing, 393
  price evaluation, 649–50
  promotional mix ingredients, 528
  selection, 25
**Target market strategy**, *22*, 48–9, **49**, 213
  *see also* **Targeting**
**Target publics, 393, 562**
**Tariffs, 135**, 141
**Technical sales people, 585**
Technological forces, 78–81
**Technology**, 78–9, **78**, 100–22
  adoption and use, 81
  advertising agencies, 568–9
  customer relationship management, 111–12, 114–16
  impact, 80–1
  marketing research, 279–81
  retail marketing, 497
  segmentation variables, 227
  strategic retailing, 495–6
  strategic windows, 92
  target market segments, 246
**Technology assessment, 81**
Telecommunications technology, 100, 103
**Telemarketing**, 484–5, **485**, **522**, 609, 688
**Telephone surveys, 272**
Telethons, 392
Television (TV)
  advertising, 568
  banking, 356
  characteristics, *553*
  copy, 557
  e-marketing comparison, 105
  promotional mix ingredients, 530
**Test marketing**, 351–2, **351**
**Third-party endorsements, 564**, 565
Three-dimensional packaging, 342–3
**Time series analysis**, 733–4, **733**
Time utility, retailing, 473
Tomato advertising, *545*
**Total cost, 653**
**Total cost analysis**, *453*, **453**
**Total market approach** *see* **Undifferentiated approach**
**Total quality management (TQM)**, 765–6, **765**, 780
**Traceability, 463**
**Traceable common costs, 775**, 780
Trade association regulations, 76
Trade barriers, 135–7, *136*
**Trade discounts, 635**, 637
**Trade markets, 450**
**Trademarks, 317**, 325–6, 329
**Trade names, 317**
**Trade sales people, 585**
**Trade sales promotion methods**, *595*, **595**, 600–2
**Trade shows, 450**, 689–90
**Trading companies**, 143, **145**
Trading practice controls, 746
**Trading stamps, 598**
Training
  employee performance, 390
  sales personnel, 588
Transactions
  closing, 583–4
  marketing channels, 416
  standardising, 416
  *see also* Business transactions
Transatlantic air routes, 404–5
**Transfer pricing, 638, 704**
**Transit time, 462**
**Transportation**, 437, 460–4, **460**
**Transport companies, 449–50**
**Transport modes, 460**, *461–2*
**Trend analysis, 733**
Trends, advertising effects, 567–9
**Trial stage** (product adoption), **517**
Truck jobbers *see* **Truck wholesalers**
Truck market, 708

**Truck wholesalers**, *442*, **444**
TV *see* Television
**Tying contract, 430**

## U

UCE *see* Unsolicited commercial e-mail
UK *see* United Kingdom
**Unaided recall tests, 560**
**Undifferentiated approach**
market segmentation, **223**
targeting strategy, 242, *243*
**Uniform geographic pricing, 638**
**Uniform resource locators (URLs)**, 106–7, **106**
United Kingdom (UK)
ACORN consumer categories, 233–6, *233–5*
advertising top 100, *550*
branding, 132–3
coupon distribution, *596*
research budgets, *271*
sponsorship expenditure, *570*
United States of America (USA)
Internet marketing, *118*
legal forces, 74
NAFTA, 137–8
**Unit loading, 455**
**Universal product code (UPC), 337**
Universities, 391–2, 396
Unsolicited commercial e-mail (UCE), 117
**Unsought products, 299**
UPC *see* Universal product code
Upgrading, effects, *695*
Urban markets, Reebok, 290–2
**URLs** *see* **Uniform resource locators**
USA *see* United States of America
**Usage rate, 458**
Users, buying centre, 201
Utility
marketing channels, 412
retailing, 473

## V

**Validity, 265**
VALS *see* Value and Lifestyle Programme
**Value analysis**, 204–5, **204**
**Value-based marketing**, 690, **777**, 781
**Value-conscious consumers, 635**
Value and Lifestyle Programme (VALS), 237
Value for money *see* **Perceived value for money**
Value pricing, 783
Values, brands, 320–1
**Variability**, *694–5*, **694**
**Variable costs, 653**
Variables *see* **Segmentation variables**
**Variety stores, 478**
Vending machines, 485
**Venture teams, 347**
**Vertical channel integration**, 420–1, **420**
**Vertical marketing system (VMS)**, **420**, *421*
Video intelligence, Mexico, 711
Viewing facilities, focus group interviews, *273*
Visual aids, presentations, 822
**VMS** *see* **Vertical marketing system**

## W

'Wallpaper syndrome', examinations, 824–5
**Warehouse clubs**, 479–80, **479**
**Warehousing**, 437, *437*, **455–6**, *458*
Warfare analogies, 53–4
Warranty back-ups, 197
**Wealth, 86**
**Websites**, 606–7, **606**, *607*
advertising, 522
non-profit marketing, 394, *397*
*see also* **Internet**
**Wheel of retailing**, 494–5, **494**, *495*
**Wholesalers, 192**, 436–70, **438**
classification, 440–8
facilitating agencies, 448–50
marketing channels, 417, *417*, 420, *421*
new types, 451
power consolidation, 451
pricing decisions, *633*
services provided, *445*
**Wholesaling, 438**
activities, 438–40, *439*
changing patterns, 450–1
nature and importance, 438
**Width of product mix, 302**, 304
**Willingness to spend, 86**
Word association tests, 174, *175*
Word-of-mouth communications, 696
Working in marketing, 813–30
Written reports, 822–3

## Z

**Zone prices, 638**